DATE DUE

			PRINTED IN U.S.A.

Literature Criticism from 1400 to 1800

Guide to Gale Literary Criticism Series

For criticism on	Consult these Gale series
Authors now living or who died after December 31, 1959	*CONTEMPORARY LITERARY CRITICISM (CLC)*
Authors who died between 1900 and 1959	*TWENTIETH-CENTURY LITERARY CRITICISM (TCLC)*
Authors who died between 1800 and 1899	*NINETEENTH-CENTURY LITERATURE CRITICISM (NCLC)*
Authors who died between 1400 and 1799	*LITERATURE CRITICISM FROM 1400 TO 1800 (LC)* *SHAKESPEAREAN CRITICISM (SC)*
Authors who died before 1400	*CLASSICAL AND MEDIEVAL LITERATURE CRITICISM (CMLC)*
Black writers of the past two hundred years	*BLACK LITERATURE CRITICISM (BLC)*
Authors of books for children and young adults	*CHILDREN'S LITERATURE REVIEW (CLR)*
Dramatists	*DRAMA CRITICISM (DC)*
Hispanic writers of the late nineteenth and twentieth centuries	*HISPANIC LITERATURE CRITICISM (HLC)*
Poets	*POETRY CRITICISM (PC)*
Short story writers	*SHORT STORY CRITICISM (SSC)*
Major authors from the Renaissance to the present	*WORLD LITERATURE CRITICISM, 1500 TO THE PRESENT (WLC)*

ISSN 0740-2880

Volume 26

Literature Criticism from 1400 to 1800

Excerpts from Criticism of the Works
of Fifteenth, Sixteenth, Seventeenth, and
Eighteenth-Century Novelists, Poets, Playwrights,
Philosophers, and Other Creative Writers, from
the First Published Critical Appraisals
to Current Evaluations

James E. Person, Jr., Editor

Jelena O. Krstovic´
Michael Magoulias
Zoran Minderovic´
Anna J. Sheets
Associate Editors

Gale Research Inc.

An International Thomson Publishing Company

NEW YORK • LONDON • BONN • BOSTON • DETROIT • MADRID
MELBOURNE • MEXICO CITY • PARIS • SINGAPORE • TOKYO
TORONTO • WASHINGTON • ALBANY NY • BELMONT CA • CINCINNATI OH

STAFF

James E. Person, Jr., *Editor*

Jelena O. Krstović, Michael Magoulias, Zoran Minderović, Anna J. Sheets, *Associate Editors*

Deron Albright, Thomas Carson, Paul Sassalos, Debra A. Wells, *Assistant Editors*

Marlene H. Lasky, *Permissions Manager*
Margaret A. Chamberlain, Linda M. Pugliese, *Permissions Specialists*
Susan Brohman, Diane Cooper, Maria Franklin, Pamela A. Hayes, Arlene Johnson, Josephine M. Keene,
Michele Lonoconus, Maureen Puhl, Shalice Shah, Kimberly F. Smilay, Barbara A. Wallace,
Permissions Associates
Brandy C. Merritt, Tyra Y. Phillips, *Permissions Assistants*

Victoria B. Cariappa, *Research Manager*
Mary Beth McElmeel, Tracie A. Richardson, *Research Associates*
Maria E. Bryson, Eva M. Felts, Michele McRobert, Michele P. Pica, Amy T. Roy,
Laurel D. Sprague, Amy Beth Wieczorek, *Research Assistants*

Mary Beth Trimper, *Production Director*
Catherine Kemp, *Production Assistant*

Cynthia Baldwin, *Product Design Manager*
Sherrell Hobbs, *Desktop Publisher*
Willie Mathis, *Camera Operator*

This book is printed on acid-free paper that meets the minimum requirements of American National Standard for Information Sciences—Permanence Paper for Printed Library Materials, ANSI Z39.48-1984.

Library of Congress Catalog Card Number 94-29718
ISBN 0-8103-8464-7
ISSN 0732-1864
Printed in the United States of America
Published simultaneously in the United Kingdom
by Gale Research International Limited
(An affiliated company of Gale Research Inc.)

 Gale Research Inc., an International Thomson Publishing Company.
ITP logo is a trademark under license.

10 9 8 7 6 5 4 3 2 1

Contents

Preface   vii

Acknowledgments   xi

Preface

*L*iterature Criticism from 1400 to 1800 (LC) presents criticism of world authors of the fifteenth through eighteenth centuries. The literature of this period reflects a turbulent time of radical change that saw the rise of drama equal in stature to that of classical Greece, the birth of the novel and personal essay forms, the emergence of newspapers and periodicals, and major achievements in poetry and philosophy. Much of modern literature reflects the influence of these centuries. Thus the literature treated in *LC* provides insight into the universal nature of human experience, as well as into the life and thought of the past.

Scope of the Series

LC is designed to serve as an introduction to authors of the fifteenth through eighteenth centuries and to the most significant interpretations of these authors' works. The great poets, dramatists, novelists, essayists, and philosophers of this period are considered classics in every secondary school and college or university curriculum. Because criticism of this literature spans nearly six hundred years, an overwhelming amount of critical material confronts the student. *LC* therefore organizes and reprints the most noteworthy published criticism of authors of these centuries. Readers should note that there is a separate Gale reference series devoted to Shakespearean studies. For though belonging properly to the period covered in *LC*, William Shakespeare has inspired such a tremendous and ever-growing corpus of secondary material that the editors have deemed it best to give his works extensive coverage in a separate series, *Shakespearean Criticism*.

Each author entry in *LC* attempts to present a historical survey of critical response to the author's works. Early criticism is offered to indicate initial responses, later selections document any rise or decline in literary reputations, and retrospective analyses provide students with modern views. The size of each author entry is intended to reflect the author's critical reception in English or foreign criticism in translation. Articles and books that have not been translated into English are therefore excluded. Every attempt has been made to identify and include the seminal essays on each author's work and to include recent commentary providing modern perspectives.

The need for *LC* among students and teachers of literature was suggested by the proven usefulness of Gale's *Contemporary Literary Criticism (CLC)*, *Twentieth-Century Literary Criticism (TCLC)*, and *Nineteenth-Century Literature Criticism (NCLC)*, which excerpt criticism of works by nineteenth- and twentieth-century authors. Because of the different time periods covered, there is no duplication of authors or critical material in any of these literary criticism series. An author may appear more than once in the series because of the great quantity of critical material available and because of the aesthetic demands of the series's *thematic organization*.

Thematic Approach

Beginning with Volume 12, all the authors in each volume of *LC* are organized in a thematic scheme. Such themes include literary movements, literary reaction to political and historical events, significant eras in literary history, and the literature of cultures often overlooked by English-speaking readers.

Organization of the Book

Each entry consists of the following elements: author or thematic heading, introduction, list of principal works (in author entries only), annotated works of criticism (each followed by a bibliographical citation), and a bibliography o further reading. Also, most author entries contain author portraits and others illustrations.

- The **Author Heading** consists of the author's full name, followed by birth and death dates. If an author wrote consistently under a pseudonym, the pseudonym is used in the author heading, with the real name given in parentheses on the first line of the biographical and critical introduction. Also located here are any name variations under which an author wrote, including transliterated forms for authors whose native languages use nonroman alphabets. Uncertain birth or death dates are indicated by question marks. The **Thematic Heading** simply states the subject of the entry.

- The **Biographical and Critical Introduction** contains background information designed to introduce the reader to an author and to critical discussion of his or her work. Parenthetical material following many of the introductions provides references to biographical and critical reference series published by Gale in which additional material about the author may be found. The **Thematic Introduction** briefly defines the subject of the entry and provides social and historical background important to understanding the criticism.

- Most *LC* author entries include **Portraits** of the author. Many entries also contain illustrations of materials pertinent to an author's career, including author holographs, title pages, letters, or representations of important people, places, and events in an author's life.

- The **List of Principal Works** is chronological by date of first book publication and identifies the genre of each work. In the case of foreign authors whose works have been translated in to English, the title and date of the first English-language edition are given in brackets beneath the foreign-language listing. Unless otherwise indicated, drama are dated by first performance, not first publication.

- **Criticism** is arranged chronologically in each author entry to provide a useful perspective on changes in critical evaluation over the years. For the purpose of easy identification, the critic's name and the composition or publication date or the critical work are given at the beginning of each piece of criticism. Unsigned criticism is preceded by the title of the source in which it appeared. All titles by the author featured in the critical entry are printed in boldface type. Publication information (such as publisher names and book prices) and parenthetical numerical references (such as footnotes or page and line references to specific editions of works) have been deleted at the editors' discretion to provide smoother reading of the text.

- Critical essays are prefaced by **Annotations** as an additional aid to students using *LC*. These explanatory notes may provide several types of useful information, including: the reputation of a critic, the importance of a work of criticism, the commentator's individual approach to literary criticism, the intent of the criticism, and the growth of critical controversy or changes in critical trends regarding an author's work. In some cases, these notes cross-reference the work of critics within the entry who agree or disagree with each other.

- A complete **Bibliographical Citation** of the original essay or book follows each piece of criticism.

- An annotated bibliography of **Further Reading** appears at the end of each entry and suggests resources for additional study of authors and themes. It also includes essays for which the editors could not obtain reprint rights.

Cumulative Indexes

Each volume of *LC* includes a cumulative **Author Index** listing all the authors that have appeared in *Contemporary Literary Criticism, Twentieth-Century Literary Criticism, Nineteenth-Century Literature Criticism, Literature Criticism from 1400 to 1800, and Classical and Medieval Literature Criticism,* along with cross-references to the Gale series *Short Story Criticism, Poetry Criticism, Children's Literature Review, Authors in the News, Contemporary Authors, Contemporary Authors Autobiography Series, Contemporary Authors Bibliographical Series, Dictionary of Literary Biography, Concise Dictionary of Literary Biography, Something about the Author, Something about the Author Autobiography Series, and Yesterday's Authors of Books for Children.* Readers will welcome this cumulative author index as a useful tool for locating an author within the various series. The index, which includes authors' birth and death dates, is particularly valuable for those authors who are identified with a certain period but whose death dates cause them to be placed in another, or for those authors whose careers span two periods. For example, F. Scott Fitzgerald is found in *TCLC,* yet a writer often associated with him, Ernest Hemingway, is found in *CLC.*

Beginning with Volume 12, *LC* includes a cumulative **Topic Index** that lists all literary themes and topics treated in *LC, NCLC* Topics volumes, *TCLC* Topics volumes, and the *CLC* Yearbook. Each volume of *LC* also includes a cumulative **Nationality Index** in which authors' names are arranged alphabetically under their respective nationalities and followed by the numbers of the volumes in which they appear.

Each volume of *LC* also includes a cumulative **Title Index,** an alphabetical listing of the literary works discussed in the series since its inception. Each title listing includes the corresponding volume and page numbers where criticism may be located. Foreign-language titles that have been translated followed by the tiles of the translation—for example, *El ingenioso hidalgo Don Quixote de la Mancha (Don Quixote).* Page numbers following these translated titles refers to all pages on which any form of the titles, either foreign-language or translated, appear. Title of novels, dramas, nonfiction books, and poetry, short story, or essays collections are printed in italics, while individual poems, short stories, and essays are printed in roman type within quotation marks.

A Note to the Reader

When writing papers, students who quote directly from any volume in the Literary Criticism Series may use the following general forms to footnote reprinted criticism. The first example pertains to material drawn from periodicals, the second to material reprinted from books.

T. S. Eliot, "John Donne," *The Nation and the Athenaeum,* 33 (9 June 1923), 321-32; excerpted and reprinted in *Literature Criticism from 1400 to 1800,* Vol. 10, ed. James E. Person, Jr. (Detroit: Gale Research, 1989), pp. 28-9.

Clara G. Stillman, *Samuel Butler: A Mid-Victorian Modern* (Viking Press, 1932); excerpted and reprinted in *Twentieth-Century Literary Criticism,* Vol. 33, ed. Paula Kepos (Detroit: Gale Research, 1989), pp. 43-5.

Suggestions Are Welcome

In response to various suggestions features have been added to *LC* since the series began, including a nationality index, a Literary Criticism Series topic index, thematic entries, a descriptive table of contents, and more extensive illustrations.

Readers who wish to suggest new features, themes or authors to appear in future volumes, or who have other suggestions, are cordially invited to write to the editor.

Acknowledgments

The editors wish to thank the copyright holders of the excerpted criticism included in this volume, the permissions managers of many book and magazine publishing companies for assisting us in securing reprint rights, and Anthony Bogucki for assistance with copyright research. We are also grateful to the staffs of the Detroit Public Library, the Library of Congress, the University of Detroit Mercy Library, Wayne State University Purdy/Kresge Library Complex, and the University of Michigan Libraries for making their resources available to us. Following is a list of the copyright holders who have granted us permission to reprint material in this volume of *LC*. Every effort has been made to trace copyright, but if omissions have been made, please let us know.

COPYRIGHTED EXCERPTS IN *LC*, VOLUME *26*, WERE REPRINTED FROM THE FOLLOWING PERIODICALS:

French Studies, v. XVIII, October, 1964.—*Journal of the History of Ideas,* v. XL, January-March, 1979. Copyright 1979, Journal of the History of Ideas, Inc. Reprinted by permission of the publisher.—*The New York Review of Books,* v. XX, March 22, 1973; v. XL, March 4, 1993. Copyright © 1973, 1993 Nyrev, Inc. Both reprinted with permission from *The New York Review of Books.*—*Studies on Voltaire and the Eighteenth Century,* v. LX, 1968. © Theodore Besterman. Reprinted by permission of the publisher./ v. 264, 1989. © 1989 University of Oxford. Reprinted by permission of the publisher.—*The Times Literary Supplement,* n. 3490, January 16, 1969. © The Times Supplements Limited 1969. Reproduced from *The Times Literary Supplement* by permission.

COPYRIGHTED EXCERPTS IN *LC*, VOLUME *26*, WERE REPRINTED FROM THE FOLLOWING BOOKS:

Aarsleff, Hans. From *From Locke to Saussure: Essays on the Study of Language and Intellectual History.* University of Minnesota Press, 1982. Copyright © 1982 by the University of Minnesota. All rights reserved. Reprinted by permission of the publisher.—Barzun, Jacques. From "Why Diderot?" in *Varieties of Literary Experience: Eighteen Essays in World Literature.* Edited by Stanley Burnshaw. New York University Press, 1962. © 1962 by New York University. Renewed 1990 by Stanley Burnshaw. Reprinted by permission of the publisher.—Bréhier, Émile. From *The History of Philosophy, Vol. 5: The Eighteenth Century.* Translated by Wade Baskin. The University of Chicago Press, 1967. © 1967 by The University of Chicago. All rights reserved. Reprinted by permission of the publisher.—Brewer, Daniel. From "Ordering Knowledge" in *A New History of French Literature.* Edited by Denis Hollier. Cambridge, Mass.: Harvard University Press, 1989. Copyright © 1989 by the President and Fellows of Harvard College. All rights reserved. Excerpted by permission of the publishers and the author.—Cassirer, Ernst. From *The Philosophy of the Enlightenment.* Translated by Fritz C. A. Koelln and James P. Pettegrove. Princeton University Press, 1951. Copyright 1951 by Princeton University Press. Renewed 1979 by James P. Pettegrove and Fritz C. A. Koelln. Reprinted by permission of the publisher.—Cranston, Maurice. From *Philosophers and Pamphleteers: Political Theorists of the Enlightenment.* Oxford University Press, Oxford, 1986. © Maurice Cranston 1986. All rights reserved. Reprinted by permission of Oxford University Press.—Crocker, Lester G. From *Diderot's Chaotic Order: Approach to Synthesis.* Princeton University Press, 1974. Copyright © 1974 by Princeton University Press. All rights reserved. Reprinted by permission of the publisher.—Darnton, Robert. From *The Business of Enlightenment: A Publishing History of the "Encyclopédie", 1775-1800.* Cambridge, Mass.: The Belknap Press of Harvard University Press, 1979. Copyright © 1979 by the President and Fellows of Harvard College. All rights reserved. Excerpted by permission of the publishers and the author.—Deane, Seamus. From *The French Revolution and Enlightenment in England, 1789-1832.* Cambridge, Mass.: Harvard University Press, 1988. Copyright © 1988 by the President and Fellows of Harvard College. All rights reserved. Excerpted by permission of the publishers and the author.—Dock, Terry Smiley. From *Woman in*

Étienne Bonnot de Condillac

1714-1780

French philosopher.

INTRODUCTION

Condillac was an influential philosopher of the French Enlightenment who is noted primarily for his theories on the nature of knowledge, language, and scientific methodology. Inspired by the empiricism formulated by the English thinker John Locke, he promoted a philosophical system founded upon well-established facts and observable natural phenomena. This mode of thinking represented a profound break with the tradition of rationalism begun in the seventeenth century by French philosopher René Descartes, who sought to create a unified system of natural science based on universal principles and abstract or hypothetical ideas. Condillac believed that all human understanding was an outgrowth of experience, and he traced such faculties as language and reason, considered by Cartesians to be innate, to specific sensory elements. His theories found wide support during his lifetime among the Philosophes—a group of Enlightenment thinkers that included Jean Jacques Rousseau, Denis Diderot, and Jacques Turgot—and after his death influenced a short-lived philosophic movement known as *Idéologie*.

Biographical Information

Condillac was born in Grenoble into a family of the petty nobility. As a child, he suffered from sickness and poor eyesight which made formal education difficult, and his family came to regard him as simple-minded. Rousseau, who for a time tutored Condillac's nephews, describes the young Condillac in his *Confessions* (1781) as troublesome: "He understood nothing, never made an answer, and was never affected by anything. His obstinacy was immovable, and he never enjoyed anything more than the triumph of putting me in a rage." By the 1730s, however, Condillac was studying theology at the Sainte-Sulpice seminary and, later, at the Sorbonne under the direction of his older brother, the Abbé de Mably, a prominent Socialist. A devout Catholic, Condillac was ordained in 1740. Instead of taking up the duties of priesthood he elected to follow his elder brother to the Parisian salons, acquiring there an interest in philosophy. Publication of the *Essai sur l'origine des connaissances humaines*, the *Traité des systèms*, and the *Traité des sensations* established Condillac's reputation among the Philosophes and other influential members of the salon, and these connections secured him an invitation to tutor the Prince of Parma in 1758. The lessons on grammar, style, scientific methods, and history prepared by Condillac during his stay in Italy were later published as the *Cours d'étude*. He returned to France in 1767 and was elected to the Académie français the following year. Condillac spent his later life away from Paris, residing at his estate of Flux, near Beaugency. Here he worked on *La Logique*, a textbook on elementary logic commissioned by the Polish government, as well as *La Langue des calculs*, which remained in manuscript form upon his death in 1780.

Major Works

The primary intellectual influences on Condillac were such English empiricists and natural philosophers as Locke, Francis Bacon, George Berkeley, and Isaac Newton. His first work, the *Essai sur l'origine des connaissances humaines*, intended as a supplement to Locke's *Essay on the Human Understanding*, argues that reflective thought is fundamentally sense perception. Tracing the origin of language to primitive sensations, Condillac concluded that it was the development of linguistic signs, not an inherent ability to reason, which first allowed man to shape and control his mental processes. The *Traité des systèmes*, Condillac's second work, represents his strongest critique of the speculative metaphysics and deductive reasoning that characterizes the philosophic and scientific thought of the seventeenth century. Rejecting as futile the attempts by Descartes, Baruch Spinoza, and Gottfried Wilhelm von

Leibnitz to explain the nature of the universe with vast, abstract systems, he advocated instead a less ambitious, empirical methodology based on observation, experimentation, and analysis. In the *Traité des sensations*, Condillac returned to the argument of the *Essai*, providing a more detailed analysis of the relationship between sensations and human consciousness. The work contains the well-known image of an inanimate statue which, after it is endowed one by one with the basic senses, gradually develops the capacity for rational thinking. Published posthumously, *La Langue des calculs* attempts to formulate a grammar of algebra. Although not a mathematician, Condillac admired algebra's clarity and logic, and intended to apply its analytical structure to language, which he felt should be free from any ambiguity or misinterpretation. This philosophy is reflected in his own writing style, which is noted for its simplicity and precision.

Critical Reception

Condillac's ideas were highly regarded and elicited little controversy during his lifetime. Most of his contemporaries in French intellectual circles shared both his admiration of Newton and Locke and his hostility toward seventeenth-century metaphysical systems. As Isabel F. Knight has noted, "His position was one of popularity rather than influence, suggesting his books had more of the familiarity that confirms than the impact that converts." After his death, the appeal of Condillac's philosophy remained widespread. His thesis that sensations form the basis of the human intellect was appropriated by a group of philosophers known as the Ideologues, who took as their course of study the analysis of the human mind. In the nineteenth century, Condillac's critical reputation began to diminish. Growing awareness of the complexity of human psychology led many philosophers and scientists to dismiss his doctrine of sensationism as an oversimplification. Recent commentators, however, have come to regard Condillac as an important disciple of Locke, and renewed interest in linguistic philosophy also has drawn attention to his elaborate discussion of semiotics and language. Wrote Ellen McNiven Hine, "Not only is Condillac important as a representative figure of his time but he is also significant for the originality of his contribution as a logician, as a grammarian and as a psychologist to the history of ideas. In all three capacities, contemporary scholars have pointed to rich veins of gold, which were for a long time overlooked."

PRINCIPAL WORKS

Essai sur l'origine des connaissances humaines [*Essay on the Origin of Human Understanding*]. 2 vols. (essay) 1746
Traité des systèms [*Treatise on Systems*] (essay) 1749
Traité des sensations [*Treatise on Sensations*]. 2 vols. (essay) 1754
Traité des animaux [*Treatise on Animals*] (essay) 1755
Cours d'étude pour l'instruction du Prince de Parme

[*Course of Study for the Instruction of the Prince of Parma*]. 16 vols. (essays) 1776
La Logique [*Logic*] (essay) 1780
La Langue des calculs [*The Language of Calculus*] (essay) 1798
Oeuvres de Condillac [*Condillac's Works*]. 23 vols. (essays) 1798
Oeuvres philosophiques de Condillac [*Condillac's Philosophical Works*]. 3 vols. (essays) 1947-51

CRITICISM

Etienne Bonnot de Condillac   (essay date 1746)

SOURCE: An introduction to his *Essay on the Origin of Human Knowledge,* translated by Thomas Nugent, 1756. Reprint by Scholars' Facsimiles & Reprints, 1971, pp. 1-12.

[*In the following introduction to his* Essay on the Origin of Human Knowledge, *first published in 1746, Condillac asserts that the primary aim of philosophers is to inquire into the origin of ideas through observation and experimentation.*]

Of all sciences that which contributes most to open, as well as to fix and enlarge the understanding, and which, consequently, ought to prepare it for the study of every other branch of knowledge is metaphysics. But this science is so greatly neglected at present, that the above assertion will doubtless to a great many of my readers appear no less than a paradox. I confess there was a time, when I should have formed the same judgment of it myself. Of all philosophers the metaphysicians appeared to me the most superficial; so far was I from receiving any instruction from their writings, that I met with nothing but airy speculations, so that I began to charge the science with those extravagances which should have been imputed only to its professors. But endeavouring afterwards to remove this illusion, and to discover the cause of so many errors, I found those who are widest from the truth, to be of the greatest service to me. I had scarce discovered the unsafe paths they had trod, when I thought I had hit upon the only and sure way of arriving at the truth. It seemed to me that we might reason in metaphysics and in morals with as great exactness as in geometry; that we might frame as accurate ideas as the geometricians; that we might determine, as well as they, the meaning of words in a precise and invariable manner; in short that we might prescribe, perhaps better than they have done, a plain and easy order for the attainment of demonstration.

We must distinguish two sorts of metaphysics. The one, vain and ambitious, wants to search into every mystery; into the nature and essence of beings, and the most hidden causes; all these she promises to discover to her admirers, who are pleased with the flattering idea. The other more reserved, proportions her researches to the weakness of the human understanding; and not concerning herself about what is above her sphere, but eager to know whatever is within her reach, she wisely keeps within the bounds prescribed by nature. The first makes all nature a kind of magic incantation, which vanishes like herself; the second, desirous only of seeing things as they really are, is as simple as truth itself. The former is the source of innumerable errors, as it fills the mind with vague and indeterminate notions, and with words that have no meaning: the latter conveys indeed no great store of knowledge, but it helps the understanding to avoid falling into mistakes, to reason exactly, and to frame clear ideas.

Philosophers have applied themselves more to the study of the former, and have considered the latter only as an accessory part which scarcely deserves the name of metaphysics. Mr. Locke is the only one, I think, that ought to be excepted: he has confined himself to the study of the human understanding, and has succeeded in the pursuit. Descartes was acquainted neither with the origin nor the formation of our ideas. To this we must attribute the insufficiency of his method: for we shall never discover a sure way of conducting our thoughts, so long as we are strangers to the manner in which they are formed. Of all the Cartesians Malebranche is he who saw most into the causes of our errors; and yet this philosopher sometimes draws his comparisons from matter to explain the faculties of the soul: at other times he is lost in the *intellectual world,* where he imagines he has discovered the source of our ideas. Others create and annihilate beings, which they superadd to or take from the soul according to their fancy, vainly thinking by this means to account for the different operations of the mind, and of the manner in which it acquires or loses its knowledge. In fine, the Leibnitzians make a far completer being of this substance: it is, according to them, a microcosm, a living mirror of the universe; and by the power they give it of representing every thing that exists, they imagine they are able to explain its essence, its nature, and properties. Thus it is that each is biassed by his own system. We see only what surrounds us, and we think we see every thing: we are like children who imagine that when they come to the end of a plain, they shall be able to touch the sky with their hand.

I would not have it inferred from hence that the writings of philosophers are of no manner of use: all that I mean, is, that whoever flatters himself to succeed better than so many celebrated genius's, must study them at least with a view of improving by their mistakes. It is an essential point to every person that is desirous of making any progress by himself in the search after truth, to know the mistakes of those who first undertook to shew him the way. The experience of a philosopher, like that of a pilot, consists in being acquainted with the rocks on which others have split; and without this knowledge no compass can direct them.

It would not be sufficient to discover the errors of philosophers, unless we searched into the causes of them: we should even ascend from one cause to another, till we reached the first. For there must be one and the same to all those who have gone astray; and this is the very point, as it were, at which the several roads begin that lead to error. Then perhaps, and close to this point, we should

perceive another, where begins the only path that conducts to the knowledge of truth.

Our first aim, which we ought never to lose sight of, is the study of the human understanding; not to discover its nature, but to know its operations; to observe with what art they are combined, and how we ought to conduct them, in order to acquire all the knowledge of which we are capable. We must ascend to the origin of our ideas, we must unfold their formation, and trace them to the limits which nature has prescribed, to the end that we may fix the extent and boundaries of our knowledge, and new model as it were the whole frame of the human understanding.

This inquiry cannot be carried on with success but by the way of observation; and our only aim should be to discover a fundamental experiment which no one can question, and will be sufficient to explain all the rest. It ought sensibly to point out to the source of our ideas, to the materials of which they are formed, the principle which sets them in motion, the instruments employed about them, and the manner in which we should apply them. I think I have found the solution of all these problems in the connection of ideas, either with signs, or with one another: whether I am right the reader will judge in proportion as he advances in the perusal of this work.

My purpose therefore is to reduce to a single principle whatever relates to the human understanding, and this principle shall neither be a vague proposition, nor an abstract maxim, nor a groundless supposition, but a constant experience, all the consequences of which shall be confirmed by new observations.

The ideas are connected with the signs, and it is only by this means, as I shall prove, they are connected with each other. Hence it is that after touching upon the materials of our knowledge, the distinction of the soul and body, and the different sensations, I have been obliged, in order more fully to explain my principle, not only to follow the workings of the mind through all their gradations, but likewise to inquire in what manner we have contracted the habit of signs of every kind, and what use we ought to make of them.

In order to execute this undertaking, I have traced things as high as possible. On the one hand, I have ascended to perception, because it is the first operation we observe in the mind; and I have shewn how, and in what order it produces every other operation of which we can acquire the act and habit. On the other hand, I have begun with the language of action: here the reader will see how it has produced every art proper to express our thoughts; such as gesture, dancing, speech, declamation, arbitrary marks for words or things, pantomimes, music, poetry, eloquence, writing, and the different characters of language. This history of language will disclose the circumstances in which the signs were invented, will shew the true meaning of them, will help to prevent the abuse they may be turned to, and, in my opinion, will remove all doubt concerning the origin of our ideas.

At length after laying open the progression of mental operations, as well as that of language, I have attempted to point out the means by which we may avoid falling into error, and to shew the order we ought to follow, either in endeavouring to make discoveries, or instructing others concerning those we have already made. Such is the general plan of this essay.

It often happens that a philosopher declares himself on the side of truth, without knowing it. He sees an opinion hitherto abandoned, and he adopts it, not because it appears the best grounded, but with the expectation of becoming the founder of a new sect. And, indeed, the novelty of most systems has generally secured their success.

This perhaps was the motive which induced the Peripatetics to assume as a principle, that all our knowledge is derived from the senses. So far were they from having any certainty of this truth, that not one of them could ever explain it, and after a long succession of ages, the discovery was not yet made.

My lord Bacon is perhaps the first who perceived this truth: it is the foundation of a work, in which he lays down excellent rules for the advancement of knowledge. The Cartesians rejected this principle with contempt, because they judged of it only from the writings of the Peripatetics. At length Mr. Locke seized upon it, and has the honour of being the first to demonstrate it.

And yet this philosopher does not seem to have made it the principal object of the *essay,* which he has left *on the human understanding.* He fell upon it occasionally, and so continued to do as opportunities offered. And though he was sensible that a work written after that manner must disgust the judicious, yet he had not, as he says himself, either courage or leisure to model it a-new. To this we may attribute the tediousness, the repetitions, and confusion which prevail throughout the work. Locke was very capable of amending these defects, and this is what perhaps renders him more inexcusable. He saw, for instance, that the consideration of words, and of our manner of using them, might give some light into the principle of our ideas: but because he perceived it too late, he handled this subject in his third book, which ought to have been discussed in the second. If he could have prevailed upon himself to recommence the subject, there is reason to presume, he would have given a far better explication of the springs of the human understanding. But through neglect of this, so far is he from searching deeply into the origin of human knowledge, that he touches the subject but very slightly. He supposes, for instance, that when once the understanding is stored with ideas by means of the senses, it has the power to repeat, compare, and unite them, even to an almost infinite variety, and so can make at pleasure new complex ideas. But it is beyond all doubt that in our infancy we have had sensations, long before we could derive any ideas from them. Thus, the soul not having had immediately and from the first instant the exercise of all its operations, it was a point of the utmost consequence, for the better unfolding the origin of knowledge, to shew in what manner she acquires this exercise, and what progress she makes in it. Locke does not seem to have even thought of this, nor does it appear that any one ever charged him with the omission, or endeavoured to supply this part of his work. Nay, perhaps the design of explaining the origin of the operations of the mind, by deriving them from a simple perception, will appear so new, that the reader will have a difficulty to comprehend, in what manner I shall execute it.

Locke in the first book of his essay examines into the opinion concerning innate ideas. Perhaps he has dwelt too long on the refutation of this error; the following work will explode it indirectly. In some parts of the second book, he treats but in a superficial manner, of the operations of the mind. In the third he inquires into words, and he seems to be the first that ever handled the subject like a philosopher. And yet I have thought proper to make this fame subject a considerable part of the following work, as well because it may be viewed in a new and more extensive light, as because I am convinced that the use of signs is the principle which unfolds all our ideas as they lye in the bud. But among many excellent things which Locke says in his second book, concerning the formation of several sorts of ideas, such as space, duration, &c. and in his fourth book entitled *Of Knowledge,* there are several articles which I am very far from approving; but as they belong more particularly to the extension of our ideas, they do not come under my plan, and therefore it is needless for me to dwell long upon them.

The New Englander   (essay date 1876)

SOURCE: "Condillac and the Principle of Identity," *The New Englander,* Vol. XXXV, July 1876, pp. 440-65.

[*In the following excerpt, the critic provides an overview of Condillac's philosophy.*]

Etienne Bonnot de Condillac, Abbé de Mureaux, was born at Grenoble in 1715, and died on his estate at Bangenci where he passed much of his life in 1780. This made him the contemporary of Hume, a somewhat older man (1711-1776), and of Kant who was somewhat younger (1724-1804). He is usually described as the thinker who imported the doctrines of Locke into France and gave them the French stamp and continental circulation. Mr. Mill speaks of him with considerable scorn as a shallow person who had no room for the profundities of the system he was bringing over the channel, and Dugald Stewart accuses him specifically of misapprehending and misrepresenting the fundamental thing in it. Locke derived all ideas from experience, but then he split experience into Reflection and Sensation. In Stewart's opinion this division while referring all ideas to experience withdrew the mind itself, the faculties of the mind, and the operations of the faculties, from sensation, so that the real doctrine of Locke is to be looked for in the amendment of Leibnitz rather than in the supposed version of Condillac. Sir Wm. Hamilton has replied to this with an equally elaborate argument going to show that Locke was perfectly understood by Condillac and suffered no other injury than the development of his own theory according to his own principles, for his Reflection, or Self-consciousness which seems to open a new source of ideas is in fact only reflex-sensation, the water of the other fountain at second-hand. So far as Locke is concerned the dispute is an interesting illustration of the ambiguity which underlies the apparent plain speaking of the *Essay* and which perhaps it is too late now for anybody to clear up. So far as Condillac is concerned it quite forgets that he is to be interpreted not only as the disciple of Locke but as a successor of Leibnitz and therefore as a thinker likely to have a position of his own somewhere between the two. Locke, says Condillac after a hearty eulogy of his merits, "missed a number of truths which it seems that he ought to have seized; and at times he becomes obscure and even inexact. So his analysis of the human understanding is imperfect. It did not occur to him to look for the generation of the operations of the mind; he did not see that they too come from sensation as well as our ideas, and that they are all only sensation transformed; he did not observe that evidence consists wholly in identity; and he did not know that the true principle of the art of thinking is the intimate association of ideas (la plus grande liaison des idées). He touched upon nearly all these discoveries; and he might have made them if he had treated his subject more methodically." Condillac, therefore, neither misrepresented Locke as Stewart says, nor was he merely a faithful follower as Hamilton says. Starting from the principal doctrine of the *Essay* and from the retort of Leibnitz, he declared: I. that all our ideas, and all the faculties which receive, or form them, equally come from experience, which is nothing but sensation, or transformed sensation; II. that these identities of all the contents of consciousness yield the one principle of all evidence, which is Identity; and III. that the art of thinking consists in an association of ideas close enough to make this identity clear. These three discoveries are claimed by Condillac as his own, and we believe belong to him. If they do, his rank in philosophy is much more important than the one assigned to him by his English critics or even by his own school in France. Where would Mr. Spencer, or any of the Sensationalists be without the analysis of the faculties? or either of the Mills, without the *liaison des idées?* or Mr. Lewes, without the principle of identity? It was Condillac and not Locke who cleared the continent of the Cartesian cosmologies; and it was Condillac who furnished the original draft of the final form of the Empirical Philosophy.

Condillac's first treatise is the ***Essai sur l'Origine des Connoissances Humaines,*** exactly described in the title as an "ouvrage ou l'on réduit à un seul principe tout ce qui concerne l'entendement humain." It is the work of a very young man and as might be expected tells rather more of the influences under which he was trained than of the original position he was about to assume. The most curious thing about it is the abundant evidence it furnishes of the fact which everybody seems to have forgotten, although it might have been taken for granted that Condillac was a Cartesian long before he knew anything of Locke. Not only does he define the soul as a single, indecomposable, indestructible substance distinct from the body which is a mere temporary agglomeration of substances, but he fully accepts the old Cartesian consequence of non-intercourse and occasional causes. What was the state of things before the fall we do not of course know except as an article of faith; but in this life as a consequence of Original Sin the soul is yoked like a galley-slave to the body, the penal union being so intimate, and the dependence so abject, that the changes in the body which are only occasional must be taken as if they were truly physical causes of the changes in the soul. What the real efficient causes

at work in this semblance of intercourse may be, Condillac declines to say, for the very sufficient reason that he did not in the least pretend to know. Here is his exact point of departure from the Cartesians and of approach to Sensationalism. The gap filled up by Malebranche with the energies of the deity is left a blank, and the ideas supposed to be their products are replaced by the sensations which arise in the soul nobody knows how, or flow into it nobody knows whence, on occasion of changes taking place in the body. These sensations are the constituents of consciousness, the problem of psychology being nothing but the processes of their composition, —how they fuse into faculties, how they refine into ideas. They are a countless host, of whose real nature we can only say that we feel them, that we are aware of their presence; while consciousness or perception is the earliest operation of the understanding, and the fruitful germ of all the others. Of the whole number, by far the larger portion vanish as they come leaving no trace behind; but often it happens to us to have a more vivid perception of some of them than of the others, an emphatic accentuation of one or two overpowering our consciousness of the remainder. This usurpation of consciousness is the earliest form of the faculty of Attention, and is a momentous event, for when such conspicuous and impressive sensations repeat themselves they are directly recognized as having arisen before and as belonging to the same self they belonged to then. Thus the unity of consciousness and the identity of the Ego are disclosed while the primal faculty of Perception is differentiated into the faculties of Attention, Reminiscence, Contemplation, Imagination. So far, however, we have only automatic action and the elements of animal psychology. Sensations have poured into the receptacle of the soul, have vanished at once or tarried behind, and tarrying have fallen apart or fallen together according to their own affinities, the *liaison des idées* working without interference of any kind from within. It is clear that what is needed to lift the soul out of mere brute sentiency is some improved sort of association of ideas which will give it mastery over its sensations, enable it to put some of them aside, to summon others into its presence, and to muster and manoeuvre them at will. This improvement is provided by the wonderful artifice of Language. Sensations themselves in their native diffuse state have a sluggish affinity for one another, a perception or reminiscence or imagination lying nearly inert in the presence of its most closely related associates. But a word holds an immense quantity of crude sensation in a condensed and portable form; you can take it anywhere and fire long trains of other sensations with it. It signifies so much itself and suggests so much more than it signifies that you can make it do anything if you only know how. Condillac was so pleased with this conception that after the manner of young men he rather ran it into the ground, twothirds of his exposition of the origin of human knowledge being devoted to a history of language, all going to show that the natural and artificial signs by which we express our states of mind, first to one another and finally to ourselves, are the supreme development of the principle of association of ideas, and the factor to which we owe all our superiority to the speechless and irrational brutes. It is language which has given us Memory (as distinguished from mere Reminiscence), Reflection (as distinguished from Attention), Comparison, Judgment, Reasoning; the conclusion of the whole matter being that the Human Understanding is the sum total of all our faculties and all their operations; its source the abundant fountain of sensations; its single principle of unity the association of ideas.

The success of this striking little essay was so great that three years after Condillac assumed the offensive more openly in his *Traité des Systèmes,* a detailed criticism of the *premiers principes* or innate ideas of the Cartesians. It is of no great value except as accentuating the contrast between the rational and empirical procedures, for Condillac was evidently puzzled by the mysticism of Malebranche and the monadology of Leibnitz while he makes the capital mistake of supposing that the "ideas" of Descartes are abstract universals from which the system of particulars is to be reached by deduction; and he is totally unaware that the pantheism of Spinoza is a form of the Identical Philosophy which would have fitted his discovery later on, of the principle of certitude far better than the system he finally adopted. Having delivered this parting blow at the Cartesians he returned to the English Sensationalists who now had a great surprise in store for him. While Locke was busy with the *Essay,* Molyneaux sent him the following question: whether a man born blind who had learned to distinguish by touch between a cube and a sphere of the same metal and bigness could on recovery of his sight tell without touching which was the globe and which the cube. To this the "learned and judicious proposer answered: Not," and Locke agreed with him, neither gentleman seeming to be aware that they had effected a revolution in philosophy, that their innocent query into the modus operandi of vision cut the single thread which held the objective world to Sensationalism and gave the push which toppled it over into the Idealism of Berkeley and the Nihilism of Hume. In the *Essay on the Origin of Knowledge* Condillac had strenuously contested this conclusion. Although holding the old doctrine of non-intercourse he yet insisted that the sensations of the soul contain trustworthy intuitions of the external world. "The slightest attention, he says, ought to make us know that when we perceive light, colors, solidity, these and the like sensations are more than enough to give us all the ideas we commonly have of bodies. In effect what one of them is not included in these first perceptions? Are not the ideas of extension and so on all found there?" which of of course they are, the only question being whether they have any business there and being there what they mean; a question concerning no man so much as Condillac. It was the *New Theory of Vision* undoubtedly which opened his eyes to the insufficiency of his analysis and the temerity of his assumption by showing him that he had made as uncritical and extravagant a use of sensations as any Cartesian of innate ideas; that the constituents of feeling into which he had decomposed the Understanding are themselves highly complex judgment whose affirmations of external realities can be verified, if at all, only by farther decomposition into their ultimate elements. So there was nothing left for it but to recast his whole system, to dig down to the very first beginnings of sensation and to show how these are built up into a consciousness of self and a perception of the external world. The result was the best known of Condillac's works, the *Traité des Sensations,* published in 1754, as

beautiful an essay in psychology as can be found anywhere. He supposes a perfectly organized but inanimate statue which is gifted with one sense at a time—smell, hearing, taste, vision—and then with combinations of these, out of whose operations he builds up a perfect interior consciousness, but a consciousness without the faintest 'hint or suspicion in it anywhere of realities beyond itself. The tremendous revelation of these breaks in with the prophetic sense of Touch. Until its appearance experience is wholly idealistic, sense and self are one and the same thing, the passive Ego is what its feelings are. But with the first touch there comes obstruction. resistance, reaction—the announcement of a something that is not self, the dim disclosure through the clouds of subjective feeling of the outer world. The whole consciousness reorganizes itself around this *sentiment fondamental;* all the other sensations forsake the interior self to which they have clung and follow this one of touch to fasten themselves upon the new world which bursts upon the astounded statue with its wonders of odor, sound, motion, heat, light, color; an obtrusive materialism overpowering the idealism of primitive sensation.

But Condillac was far too intelligent and conscientious a thinker to suppose that all this ingenuity had taken him to the bottom of the matter. He was sure to reflect sooner or later, that the sense of touch however adequate to explain the generation of our perceptions is not for that a better guarantee of the truth of our beliefs. We do not verify the conclusion by merely discovering the original; to trace the multitude of our ideas back to their roots in one *sentiment fondamental* is to concentrate there the whole distributed burden of the proof. My perceptions of the outer world through the eye or the ear are not direct and intuitive as they seem to be but an unconscious inference from my perceptions of it through the fingers; but then what is *this* perception? derivative too? or if underived then any the more certainly true for that? We are as much in need of a certificate of character as ever; more so for having taken all the other senses *in flagrante delictu;* this one of touch comes into court with a presumption against it. It makes that same stupendous assertion of an external world directly perceived which they have been caught falsely making and we want to know what its claims to exceptional credit are. That is, we want a Principle of Certitude; all the more urgently for having just read the *Traité des Sensations.*

Condillac was now a very distinguished man; an eminence confirmed within a few years by an appointment to the vacant post of instructor to the young Prince of Parma, grandson of His Most Catholic Majesty Louis Fifteenth. Perhaps nothing could have indicated more distinctly the complete change in the temper of Europe since the 17th century; and the result was one of the most curious experiments in education since Seneca was made tutor to Nero, or Aristotle to Alexander. Its interest in philosophy is no less considerable for it forced upon Condillac's attention the necessity of providing the principle of certitude lacking in the *Origine des Connoissances* and the *Traité des Sensations.* At the head of a staff of instructors and under the very eye of the Papal court he undertook to bring up his pupil in all humane and princely virtues by bestowing upon him the whole encyclopedia of knowledge. Nothing, he observed to the young gentleman with tutorial candor, is worse for a prince who is one day to be a ruler of men than undue conceit of himself. The best corrective for the foul air of the court is the large atmosphere of the universe; to escape the adulation of the snobs about you it is needful for you to know what you really are yourself, what other men are and have been, what nature is. . . . But clearly in order to be able to teach all this, even to a small boy who can't contradict you it is quite essential to have not only systematized learning but certitude, not only to know but to know that you know; and not only to know that you know yourself but to show the learner that he knows too; there must be a criterion of truth capable of communication from teacher to scholar and clear enough to satisfy both. This criterion, says Condillac, which we have all been hunting for since two thousand years I have the honor to introduce to you, Monseigneur, as the Principle of Identity. Whether Monseigneur who had at this time reached the anxious age of ten years, was relieved by the discovery does not appear, but there can be no doubt that Condillac himself very considerably was, for it enabled him at once to save and to complete his philosophy by turning what had been a mere psychological hypothesis into cosmological theory. This is the proposal of the **Art de Raisonner** and the **Art de Penser,** the 3d and 4th volumes of the **Cours d'Étude.** I distinguish, he says, three sorts of evidence: the evidence of *sentiment* (the consciousness that I have a certain sensation); the evidence of *fact* (the perception of an external object); and the evidence of *reason* (which is the intuition of identity). This most suspicious classification is a broad hint that Condillac is after all likely to shirk the fundamental problem of our cognition of the external world, for to co-ordinate our consciousness of a sensation and our perception of an objective reality as two intuitions of equal validity is to beg the whole question. On reaching the point, however, he explains, although in the most slipshod fashion, that the evidence of fact is ranked with the evidence of sentiment by virtue of the evidence of reason. Our sensations are effects of causes—an identical proposition: some we cause ourselves, the rest must have causes outside; these outside causes are what we call bodies: anything perceived in a body is what we call a fact; and so the evidence of fact is quite as good as the evidence of sentiment. In this off-hand manner he promotes a perception to the rank of an intuition and smuggles the whole material universe into consciousness under cover of an identical proposition; all with an air of honest importation which probably took in not only the innocent Prince of Parma but Condillac himself.

Knowledge, then, in its elementary intuitive form is simply the consciousness we have of our own sensations. It is developed into a rational knowledge of ourselves and of the world about us by applying the principle of identity. This application is always through the process of analysis. Since sensations as they stand in consciousness do not disclose their identity of themselves we must take them to pieces and then put them together again in our own way; we must first decompose and then recompose, and when the differences which precede decomposition make way for the unity which follows recomposition, when the kalei-

doscope of sensations is turned into the mosaic of rational knowledge, our work is complete.

Zora Schaupp (essay date 1926)

SOURCE: *The Naturalism of Condillac,* University of Nebraska Press, 1926, 123 p.

[*In the following essay, Schaupp surveys Condillac's life, philosophy, and critical reception. She notes that "he steered a careful course between two hostile factions [the Encyclopedists and the government], not by compromising, but by avoiding any suggestion that there were issues to be compromised."*]

When Descartes published his *Meditations* in 1641, he was obliged to answer some very pertinent objections urged against the principles he had there tried to establish. Among his adversaries was Hobbes; and Descartes became thoroughly exasperated with the persistent questions of this matter-of-fact Englishman whom he found it so difficult to meet on common terms. The objections detracted little from the success of the work to which they were appended. Cartesianism triumphed in France, and the followers of Hobbes were confined, for the most part, to his own countrymen. But the philosophical spirit in France during the next century followed almost imperceptibly the stages of development marked in England by Hobbes, Locke, and Berkeley. It became increasingly empirical and naturalistic; and when, in 1733, Voltaire called the attention of the French to English thought and institutions, the seeds of the new philosophy fell upon fertile soil. It was not in Hobbes, however, that Voltaire found a herald of the new philosophy, but in the more romantic person of Bacon, who was more of an empiricist, and less of a materialist than his successor. "The father of experimental philosophy" he calls him, and sees in him the pioneer of the great naturalistic reaction against rationalism. "The Lord Bacon," he says, "was not yet acquainted with Nature, but then he knew, and pointed out the several Paths that lead to it. He had despised in his younger Years the thing called Philosophy in the Universities; and did all that lay in his Power to prevent those Societies of Men, instituted to improve human Reason, from depraving it by their Quiddities, their Horrors of the Vacuum, their substantial Forms, and all those impertinent Terms which not only ignorance had rendered venerable, but which had been made sacred, by their being ridiculously blended with religion."

France was ready for a new philosophy; but she could not appropriate a foreign system, even when it had such an enthusiastic interpreter as Voltaire. It was necessary for the ideas of Bacon and Locke to be recast, to acquire different emphasis, before they could become an integral part of French thought. Condillac was the man who effected this transformation of English empiricism into French sensationalism. Perhaps it would be fairer to say that the same movement which culminated in empiricism in England gave birth to sensationalism in France; for it is difficult to determine just how far Condillac was actually dependent upon his English predecessor, or what the outcome of the naturalistic movement in France would have been without the importation of Locke's philosophy. Casual critics are content to remark that Condillac simply adopted the teachings of Locke and pushed them to their extreme consequences. He did both more and less than this. He was not an original genius; but there is much in him that is not contained in Locke, and the extreme consequences, whether in the direction of materialism or idealism, were left for his successors to draw. "If Locke had never written the Essay on the Human Understanding," remarked Voltaire, "Condillac would have written it, and, praise God, he would have made it shorter."

Few details of Condillac's private life are known. This is rather surprising for the eighteenth century, when men of letters excited so much public interest and were so much talked about among themselves. A few references to him may be found in the writings of Rousseau, Diderot, and D'Alembert; but so far as his private activities are concerned, he seems to have been quite outside the interest of his contemporaries. Moreover, he had a position in the church to maintain, and, in France, the less that could be said about a churchman, either of good or of evil, the safer for him. When, in his later years, the political and the moral order seemed to be going to pieces and there were rumors that his philosophy was proving the basis of a new materialism, he left Paris, and in the security of the country, devoted himself to the most peaceful of enterprises—agriculture.

Condillac was born at Grenoble on the thirtieth day of September, in 1714. He was thus two years younger than Diderot, four years younger than Hume, and twenty years younger than Voltaire. His family was originally from Briançon. Gabriel Bonnot, the father of Condillac, lived in Grenoble from 1680 until 1720, when he bought the estates of Condillac and Banier, near Romans. He held various positions under the government, being first a tax collector, then successively a squire, counselor to the king, secretary of the chancellery, and eventually Viscount of Mably. He died in 1727, leaving five children: Jean Bonnot de Mably, Gabriel, known later as the Abbé de Mably, Etienne, who took the name of Condillac, François, (Bonnot de Saint-Marcellin), and Anne. Jean, the eldest, became counselor to the king and provost general, and it was in his household that Jean Jacques Rousseau spent the year of 1740 as tutor.

Etienne was sickly in his youth and reached the age of twelve without having learned to read. His eyes were very weak, and this rendered intense application to study impossible. When he finally began his studies under the instruction of the village Curé, he made rapid progress; and upon the sudden death of his father he was sent to his elder brother at Lyon and there continued his study. He was very quiet and meditative, and was considered by his relatives to be rather dull. It is recorded that in his youth "he appeared almost stupid, dawdling and obstinate as a mule, and unable to learn anything." This was evidently the general opinion which persisted until his full maturity, for Rousseau says of him: "I myself have seen a man, no longer a mere youth, who honored me with his friendship, who was regarded by his family and his friends as lacking in intelligence; but this was a superior mind maturing in

silence. All at once he showed himself a philosopher; and I doubt not that posterity will assign him a distinguished place among the best reasoners and the most profound metaphysicians of his age."

Rousseau was a young man of twenty-eight when he held the position of tutor in the same household of which Condillac was a member. He had been highly recommended by a woman of Grenoble, whose husband was associated with M. de Mably; but the situation was a trying one, and Rousseau, according to his own account, acquitted himself very badly. His pupils were difficult to manage; and Rousseau, with his violent and capricious temperament, was not the man to train them in the ways of industry and self-control. At the end of the year he left, dissatisfied with this mode of life, and convinced that teaching was a profession for which Nature never intended him. He departed on good terms with the family, and Condillac, for one, always maintained very friendly relations with him and defended him even when practically all the literary men of France had become his enemies.

After some years spent in doubt and uncertainty as to his future, Condillac was taken to Paris by his brother—the Abbé de Mably—and placed in a Jesuit seminary there. At the completion of his studies he was ordained to the priesthood; but it is related that he said only one mass in the entire course of his life. He continued to read and meditate, although he was somewhat handicapped in his study by his inability to read English. His knowledge of English philosophy and science was confined, therefore, to that which had been written in Latin, or translated into Latin or into his native French. He became acquainted with Locke through Coste's translation and the brief exposition of his philosophy in Voltaire's *Letters sur les Anglais.* Some of Berkeley's writings were also known to him in translation.

During these first years of independent study he met Diderot and again came under the influence of Rousseau. Indeed, it was through Rousseau that Diderot and Condillac were first brought together if we may believe his account in the *Confessions.*

> I was also connected with the Abbé de Condillac, who had acquired no more literary fame than myself, but in whom there was every appearance of his becoming what he is today. I was perhaps the first who discovered the extent of his abilities, and esteemed them as they deserved. He on his part seemed satisfied with me, and whilst shut up in my chamber in the Rue Jean Saint Denis, near the opera-house, I composed my act of Hesiod, he sometimes came to dine with me tête-à-tête. We sent for our dinner, and paid share and share alike. He was at that time employed on his **Essay on the Origin of Human Knowledge,** which was his first work. When this was finished, the difficulty was to find a publisher who would take it. The publishers of Paris are very shy of new authors, and metaphysics, not being then in vogue, was not a very inviting subject. I spoke to Diderot of Condillac and his work and I afterward made them acquainted with each other. They were worthy of each other's esteem and were presently on the most

friendly terms. Diderot persuaded the publisher, Durand, to take the manuscript from the Abbè, and so this great metaphysician received for his first work, and almost as a favor, a hundred crowns, which perhaps he would not have obtained without my assistance. As we lived in quarters of the town **very** distant from each other, we all assembled once a week at the Palais Royal, and went to dine at the Hôtel du Panier Fleuri.

The interchange of ideas between Condillac and Diderot is somewhat more apparent than that between Condillac and Rousseau, although some critics profess to find an affinity between the economic theories of the latter two. It is hard to say how far Diderot's *Lettre sur les aveugles* may have influenced Condillac, and equally impossible to known just how far Condillac's conversations and his interest in Locke may have stimulated Diderot's psychological speculation. The *Lettre* is an inquiry into the part played by sensation in human intelligence, and the possible alteration of our ideas with changed capacities of sensation. This kind of speculation is exactly in harmony with Condillac's chief interest at this time, when the plan and project of the *Traité des sensations* were forming themselves in his mind, but it would be quite impossible to determine definitely the nature or the extent of their respective obligations. It was rumored that Condillac had borrowed his statue analogy from Diderot, and he takes considerable pains to refute the charge, although Diderot himself, it is said, never accused him. Indeed, it is hard to imagine Diderot, as prodigal of his ideas as of his money and his time, resenting even a much more serious plagiarism than this reputed one of Condillac's. There seems to be no really strong evidence, however, that there was conscious imitation in this case. The two men were contemporaries and friends; they were interested in the same type of problems; speculation by analogies and hypothetical cases was the mode of the time; and the inevitable consequence is that there are strong similarities between them.

Contempt for the learning of the past had been a popular pose since the time of Descartes. Unlike most of his contemporaries, however, Condillac firmly believed in the value of a study of classical and mediaeval thought as part of the equipment of every scholar who wished to advance beyond it. It must not be inferred, however, that his attitude toward the subject was modern in the sense of demanding either profundity or objectivity in researches into the past. Convinced that the method introduced by Bacon—though not consistently followed by him—was to revolutionize philosophy, he saw in Locke the gifted disciple of this prophet of science, and the *Essay on the Human Understanding* became his guide and inspiration. In 1746, at the age of thirty-one, he published the result of this book's influence upon him in the *Essai sur l'origine des connaissances humaines.* He has been frequently criticized for not having made in this work more explicit acknowledgment of his debt to Locke. The many references to Locke scattered throughout the book, and the warm praises of his genius, bear stronger testimony, however, to the extent of his influence, than any single statement of indebtedness could have done. Condillac was only following the mode when he paid elaborate thanks to a woman for

her share in the *Traitè des sensations,* and failed to acknowledge the real inspiration of his philosophy.

After the publication of the *Essai,* three years elapsed, spent chiefly in the study of the philosophical systems of Descartes, Malebranche, Leibnitz, and Spinoza. Condillac had earlier reached the conclusion that the greatest evil of philosophy is rationalistic system-building with its *a priori* reasoning and its unverifiable principles. The *Traitè des systèmes,* published at the expiration of this period, is an elaboration of this idea and a more definite formulation of the counts against rationalism, illustrated from the systems of these four philosophers. Condillac, in the meantime, had been accepted by the literary circle of Paris; and, with the publication of this volume of criticism, his popularity increased. He even enjoyed considerable popularity in the salons of the day and numbered many well known ladies among his friends. Through Diderot he had met Duclos, Cassini, d'Holbach, Morellet, Helvetius, Grimm, and Voltaire. His philosophical views were generally adopted by his contemporaries, and were incorporated into the *Discours Prèliminaire* of the *Encyclopédie;* while the articles on *Divination* and *Systèmes* are taken verbatim from the *Traitè des systèmes.* While he enjoyed the friendship of the encyclopedists, he was out of sympathy with them in their attacks upon religion. In the salon of Mme. de Tencin, however, religion was a sacred subject, and here the free thinkers and scoffers were obliged to declare a truce out of respect for the feelings of the hostess. Here Condillac could indulge his love of society and intellectual companionship without compromising his ecclesiastical position, but this rare privilege was lost to him in 1749, with the death of Mme. de Tencin.

In 1752 he was elected to the academy of Berlin, and two years later he published the famous *Traitè des sensations,* the first of his works to appear under his own name. He left France in 1758, having been chosen by Queen Marie Leczinska—wife of Louis XV—as the tutor of her grandson, the young duke Ferdinand of Parma. For this post he was recommended by Nivernois, the former ambassador to Rome, and by Duclos, historiographer of France. Louise Elizabeth, the mother of the Duke, took a keen interest in her son's education and had high hopes of Condillac's tutelage; but she died soon after his appointment, leaving a weak and irresolute husband to oversee the training of their child. Ferdinand himself fell ill with smallpox during Condillac's residence in the family, and many biographers report the tender solicitude with which the tutor cared for his charge. In fact he caught the disease from him in such a severe form that for some days his life was despaired of. In December of 1764 Voltaire announced to Damilaville that Condillac had died of natural smallpox. "Doubtless you know that we have lost the Abbè of Condillac, dead of natural smallpox and the physicians of Italy, while the Esculapeus of Geneva assured the life of the Prince of Parma by inoculation. Thus we lose a good philosopher, a good enemy of superstition: the Abbè of Condillac dies, and Omer is alive!" To Argental he wrote on the following day: "You know that the Abbè of Condillac, one of our brothers, is dead of natural smallpox. . . . He would have returned to France with a pension of ten thousand pounds and the assurance of a large abbey; he was about to enjoy leisure and a large fortune; he dies, and Omer is alive! I know an ungodly fellow who finds Providence defective on this occasion." Another letter, written in February of the following year by Deleyre to J. J. Rousseau relates in more detail the seriousness of Condillac's illness, and the philosophical resignation with which he bore it, with more respect for facts than is displayed in Voltaire's report. The latter was set right by D'Alembert and cheerfully corrected the report he had circulated. He wrote to Bordes on January fourth: "You know now, my dear sir, that the Abbè of Condillac is resuscitated, and what resuscitated him is that he was not dead . . . . Thank God, there is a philosopher whom nature saved. It is good to have one more Lockist in the world when there are so many asinists, and Jansenists, etc."

As a tutor, Condillac justified the trust put in him and proved himself a worthy member of the long line of philosopher pedagogues. He took his responsibilities very seriously and composed a six volume course of study for his pupil, trying hard to instill, along with the more conventional learning, a proper sense of the virtues befitting a monarch. He sought to impress upon the Duke that sovereigns are made by and for the people, that conquests only increase the power of nations without increasing their happiness, and that the well-being of the subject lies in peace, and the safety of princes in moderation and justice. Although the results of Condillac's years of instruction are not altogether flattering, the mental calibre of the pupil rather than defective teaching was to blame. Don Ferdinand was lazy and weak like his father. The latter was grateful to Condillac for his faithful services, and at the end of his tutorship asked from his father-in-law, Louis XV, an abbey in France for him. Accordingly Condillac was granted the abbey of Mureau in the diocese of Toul.

Soon after his return to France he was elected to the French Academy in the place left vacant by the death of the Abbè d'Olivet. His speech of acceptance did not make a very favorable impression—perhaps, as Théry suggests, because it contained too much philosophy and too few fine phrases, or perhaps because Condillac seemed too radical a successor to the traditionalist Olivet to suit the conservative taste of the Academy. His address would hardly strike anyone today as revolutionary, nor as being too philosophical. It presented in broad outline the development of the human mind from barbarian times, through the classical period, the Middle Ages, the Crusades, and the Renaissance. After his initial appearance Condillac never attended the meetings of the Academy or took much interest in its proceedings. He was chiefly occupied at this time with the publication of the *Cours d'études* which he had prepared for the instruction of the Duke of Parma. This series contained *L'Art de penser, L'Art de raisonner, L'Art d'écrire, Grammaire,* and the *Histoire générale des hommes et des empires.* History was considered by Condillac to be the most important study in the education of a prince, and the other subjects on which he wrote were treated as preliminary to it. The year following the appearance of these works, 1776, he published *Du commerce et du gouvernement considérés relativement l'un á l'autre.*

Condillac was asked to supervise the education of the three sons of the dauphin but he declined. In 1777 the council appointed for the superintending of education in Poland invited him to contribute an elementary work on logic for use in the Palatinal schools. (This occurred at about the same time that the Polish government asked of Rousseau and the Abbè de Mably assistance in drawing up a constitution.) In response to this invitation Condillac wrote his *Logique* which was published only a few months after his death. His last work, the *Langue des calculs,* was [also] published posthumously.

The last years of his life were spent with his niece on the estate of Flux which he had bought for her in 1773. He continued to spend a short part of each year in Paris; but the growing spirit of immorality and discontent was very distasteful to him, and soon drove him back to the peace of the country. He disapproved particularly of Voltaire with his satire and scorn of all things holy, with his attack upon the laws and customs, as well as upon the faith of France. In the spring of 1780 Condillac made his last journey to Paris. Feeling an attack of illness coming on, he returned as quickly as possible to Flux, arriving there on July twentyfirst. He died on the second of August, 1780. In accordance with his wish, he was buried in the village cemetery without a monument or inscription; and, as the cemetery has been moved since that time, all trace of his grave has been lost.

Théry states that Condillac, at the time of his death, was intending to correct all of his writings and to enlarge several of them; but he is of the opinion that had he done so there would have been no important change in his doctrine. Laromiguière, however, believes that many of his theories would have been modified had he lived to revise his works; and Bérenger supports this opinion. Neither of the two offers very substantial proof of his position, remarking only that Condillac had always shown himself willing to retract if he were shown to be in error. A careful comparison of his earlier works with those written later does not indicate, however, that his philosophical position had altered essentially. True, there are minor differences, particularly between the *Essai sur l'origine des connaissances humaines* and the *Traité des sensations;* but the *Art de penser,* written much later, goes back to the earlier *Essai,* and takes whole pages from it, almost word for word. There are small inconsistencies to be sure, and shifts in emphasis; but on the whole, and considering the amount of time they cover, the various works of Condillac present a remarkably homogeneous body of doctrine.

The *Langue des calculs* is often pointed to as representative of a shifting of interest and point of view between his earlier and later works. It is true that on the face of it there seems to be an inconsistency between the desire to create a symbolic logic, a method of demonstration, mathematical in its exactness, for all sciences, and the ideal of empirical philosophy. For him, however, the two projects existed side by side from the beginning and were not found to be incompatible. His pragmatic sympathies never condoned loose thinking and vague expression. All obtained knowledge he believed to be capable of precise formulation, and in order that it may be reasoned on with any degree of profit, such formulation is absolutely essential. All that the later work contains, is to be found in germ in the first book he produced.

It is a singular circumstance that at a period when the slightest departure from orthodoxy in philosophy, politics, or religion led to official censure, Condillac escaped the opposition of both state and clergy. This can hardly be explained as a failure to attract sufficient attention. His works were read and his opinions respected, not only by the intellectual leaders of the day, but also by the dilettantes in learning. The encyclopedic circle held him to be the philosopher of France, and they regarded his opinions as those of an authority. This popularity should, one might think, have aroused the antagonism of the government officials or brought him into disrepute with the church; but his life passed without conflict with either. That he was a clergyman in good standing, always respecting the outward forms of his profession, might account for the tolerance of the ecclesiastical powers. On the other hand, his scrupulous avoidance of social and moral problems kept him from conflict with the political reformers and from persecution by the government. Nor could the savants of the Sorbonne find in his writings any statement which they could condemn as atheistic or materialistic. He steered a careful course between two hostile factions, not by compromising, but by avoiding any suggestion that there were issues to be compromised. The only reforms advocated by him were reforms of philosophical method, changes which could not seriously upset society.

Among critics of philosophy there are always some who try to trace the cause of social and political upheavals to philosophical theories, assuming, doubtless, that the criticism of abstract theory is not justified unless it can be shown how it touches practical affairs. Thus there are some who pretend to see in the sensationalism of Condillac the beginnings of the Revolution, as if a definite change of theory must, by the very nature of things, precede all human activity, whether of a public or a private nature. One may easily imagine how certain aspects of Condillac's philosophy may have suggested materialistic inferences, and how these may have been popularized and their practical applications to the problems of life developed, until what was originally an abstract philosophy had descended to personalities, so to speak, and ended in a revolution. To charge Condillac with all this, however, would be to distort his thought and to read into his theories a significance which is foreign to the author's intention. Perhaps the germ of materialism contained in Condillac's system and developed by Helvetius, and certain atheistic implications worked out by d'Holbach were in some degree contributing causes of the Revolution; but these developments of his thought were never sanctioned by Condillac himself nor does it aid in the better understanding of him to insist upon this particular connection.

It was doubtless because Condillac expressed so well the philosophical spirit of his time, without striking the particularly radical note which brought official condemnation upon others, that his life was serene and unharassed. He became known without those publicity-aids so common in his day. Not one treatise was condemned by the University; not a book was burned; not a manuscript confiscated;

and no publisher ever came to grief for publishing a work of his. Fame came during his life-time and lasted for a period of fifty years after his death. During the Revolution and the Empire his philosophy was taught in the schools of France, not as a phase in the history of thought, but as the authoritative doctrine. By the encyclopedists he was announced to the world of science and letters; and through the colleges, then under ecclesiastical control, he gained the following of the younger generation. His work was regarded as the standard psychology by those who had charge of the reorganization of education after the Revolution; and only with the ascendance of Cousin's eclecticism in the early part of the nineteenth century did his influence come to an end. Recently, however, the philosophical pendulum has swung and the works of Condillac again appear on the list of subjects for university degrees.

Estimates of Condillac's genius vary from the terse criticism of Joseph de Maistre, "Condillac est un sot," to the fervid eulogies of Théry or Bérenger. The latter says of him: "All of Condillac's works are profound and easy to read, and this virtue no philosopher before him had attained. . . . In few philosophers does one find more truth and less error. Few have followed a better method or have loved and pursued truth with more sincerity." A similar or even greater extravagance comes from Destutt de Tracy: "Before Condillac we have scarcely any observations on the human mind except very sparse and faulty ones. He was the first to make a body of doctrine, a science of ideology." Such passages as these are significant only as examples of the uncritical way in which Condillac's disciples took over his doctrine. Some of the judgments passed upon his work by contemporaries have less of this obituary style and give somewhat more specific reasons for approval or disapproval. One critic, writing in December of 1754, says of French philosophy in general, and of Condillac in particular:

> For a long time metaphysics has been in its last extremities among us; the dryness of this science, the slowness of its progress, the uncertainty of its principles, the lack of utility that can be discovered in it, all this has destroyed the taste for it; but, in my opinion, what has given metaphysics its death blow is the despotic reign of geometry which has tyrannized over everything else, and has been thought to be applicable to everything. We cannot better describe our poverty in metaphysicians than by saying that we can count no more than four: Buffon, Diderot, Maupertuis, and the Abbé de Condillac. . . . The Abbé de Condillac has had more success, but I do not think that he has restored the taste for metaphysics. His first work is an ***Essay upon Human Understanding,*** where he has done little more than expound Locke, and when he avoids this he goes wrong. His ***Treatise on Systems*** is, in my opinion, more agreeable and more estimable. Here we find analyses developed with method and clarity. These two works have had a great reputation. . . . It is not that M. de Condillac lacks metaphysical knowledge, clearness of imagination, precision and naturalness in style;

but it is the deficiency of his ideas. . . . His style
is clear, but dry.

Another critic, writing in the same year, comments appreciatively upon the "beautiful quotation from Cicero" which heads the *Traité des sensations,* as one of "those little things of taste" which play so large a part in determining our judgment of an author. After an enthusiastic but superficial estimate of the *Traité* he adds:

> You will not find in this treatise those marks of genius, that sublime and brilliant imagination, admirable even in its errors, those gleams which make you see from afar a light that you will never attain, and finally that boldness which characterizes the metaphysics of our Buffon and our Diderot; but you will find in him great acuteness and precision, a rare clarity and accuracy, much discretion and many very ingenious observations.

The reaction against the philosophy of Condillac was begun by Maine de Biran but by far its most vigorous opponent is [victor] Cousin. He writes:

> Condillac follows Locke but goes beyond and denatures him. Locke's diffusiveness, contradictions, and indecision have disappeared, but also his good sense, his spirit of observation, his taste for truth, his ingenious and profound remarks. The charm which makes Locke's works popular has given way to stiffness, dryness, and affectation of logical rigor. . . . He [Condillac] lacks a sense of the real. He does not know men, life, or society, nor is he constrained by common sense. He is a victim of an excessive love of simplicity, and sacrifices everything to the pleasure of deriving all from a single principle. He has no power of observation and feels more at ease in combining words and figures than in a faithful description of facts. His style is dry and precise, good but without inspiration. It is the style of Aristotle, the Scholastic peripatetics, Thomas Aquinas, Occam, and Hobbes, not that of Locke, Descartes, or Malebranche. His style has erroneously come to be taken as the true philosophical one, but it rather belongs only to a very particular school.

There is a grain of truth in Cousin's criticisms; but his entire point of view is too radically different from Condillac's to permit fair and sympathetic evaluation. It might well enough be questioned whether the rather doubtful "charm" of Locke has disappeared in Condillac, or whether the proper philosophical style is that of Descartes and Malebranche rather than the "dry and precise" manner of Condillac. These are matters of taste; but anyone who has read Condillac carefully cannot deny him a spirit of observation or common sense; and as for a knowledge of men, he shows himself quite as expert in this field as Locke, or as the average philosopher of that time. On several of the other counts, Condillac cannot be so easily defended; but in accusing him one prefers charges against all the thinkers of his time. They were all afflicted with an "excessive love of simplicity," and this trait, perhaps more than any one other, characterized the thought, scientific, sociological, and philosophical, of the eighteenth century. Again, an "ease in combining words and figures" is not peculiar to Condillac. It was one of the accomplishments of the day; and a writer who did not show himself familiar with the use of figures and hypothetical fancies had little chance of attracting the attention of the literary public, —a public that liked a neat quotation from Cicero, a sentimental dedication that showed "un auteur qui a le bonheur de connaître le prix de l'amitié," and, instead of a "triste exactitude de raisonnement," the "feu d'une imagination philosophique."

Cousin remarks further, that in reading the excellent chapter on hypotheses, one would hardly imagine its author to be the inventor of the famous hypothesis of the statute, or that one who could expose with such force the danger of abstract systems should one day end in the most abstract dogmatism by the substitution of algebraic analysis for observation, that the author of the *Traité des systèmes* should be the author of the *Logique* and the *Langue des calculs.* "He pretends to observe," says Cousin, "and he supposes; to analyze, and he deduces; to experiment, and he invents. . . . Guessing is what his vaunted method of analysis turns out to be." All of these charges must be met by the same, perhaps too simple, answer. It is true that Condillac's theory of method is far ahead of his practice, and that he is by no means free from the very faults which he condemns. But it is grossly unfair to accuse him of failing to observe and experiment according to modern scientific requirements, when the very meanings of these terms have grown so enormously since his time. With new discoveries in physical science, new instruments and means of measurement, new methods of interpreting and evaluating results, 'experimentation' and 'observation' have grown far beyond their connotations of a hundred and seventy-five years ago. In order that we may observe to some purpose we must have some idea of what we are looking for, as Condillac himself rightly remarked, but neither he nor his contemporaries had a very clear idea of the kind of facts which would throw light upon the problems of philosophy. And if the invention of a new terminology for philosophy, projected in his *Logique* and *Langue des calculs,* seems out of harmony with an empirical ideal, as implying a permanent and unchanging body of truth, it was thoroughly consistent with that passionate insistence upon definiteness and precision in language as a means to clear and valid thinking, which figured so conspicuously in all of his writings.

It is natural that estimates of Condillac's contributions to philosophy should vary with succeeding generations, and that what some would regard as his strongest theories should be condemned by others as the weakest points in his philosophy. Thus we find Théry, Mulhaupt, and others lamenting Condillac's failure to emphasize the activity of the soul. Up to the point at which his philosophy passes beyond Locke, his interpreters are willing to follow him, but beyond that they refuse to follow, or they distort his teachings to make them harmonize with their own convictions. A bone of contention for many years was the question whether Condillac's doctrines were materialistic or spiritualistic in their implications. It is always soothing to be able to brand a philosopher with a name and dispose of his system in a word, but to classify Condillac as either a materialist or a spiritualist is misleading and unfair.

When materialism carried a stigma, his opponents were eager to find materialistic implications in his teachings. These they professed to find in his sensationalism, maintaining that his failure to provide a special inner activity of soul, and his admission of a physical basis for sensation, led directly to a mechanistic psychology. His adherents, in an effort to vindicate his moral and philosophical reputation, overstressed his idealistic tendencies. He himself was not interested in maintaining a consistent spiritualism or materialism. Again and again he repeats that he is trying to observe facts, unbiased by any principles which he might be trying to defend. His aim is to investigate facts and let the consequences be what they may; thus he fails in perfect consistency and gives his critics grounds for a variety of interpretations.

George Boas (essay date 1957)

SOURCE: "Knowledge as a Complex of Sensations," in his *Dominant Themes of Modern Philosophy: A History,* The Ronald Press Company, 1957, pp. 414-37.

[*In the following essay, Boas outlines Condillac's theory of sensations.*]

Though Rousseau did not deny that much of our knowledge was perceptual in origin, he insisted that the most important knowledge came from within. Importance to his way of thinking was to be measured in moral terms, and he followed what he believed to be the Socratic lead in assessing what was of moral value and what not. Condillac (1715-80) on the other hand made an attempt to compose all knowledge whatsoever out of sensory materials, following, as he erroneously thought, the teachings of Locke. His attempt which was expounded in his *Traité des Sensations* (1754) started a train of philosophizing in France that is one of the few cases of a logical development of an idea to the point where its exponents throw up their hands in despair and admit their failure to account for one of the most ordinary of human experiences. I refer to that short-lived philosophical tradition known as Ideology. The debates between the Ideologists and their opponents, the disciples of Rousseau and the Traditionalists, constituted the philosophical atmosphere of the last half of the eighteenth century in France.

Condillac began his epistemological studies with his *Essay on the Origin of Human Knowledge,* 1746 (*Essai sur l'Origine des Connaissances Humaines*). In this work he started from the premises of John Locke, for Locke, he maintained, was the sole philosopher who had tried to discover the origin of our ideas instead of accepting them ready-made and seeking to divine their nature. The great error of Descartes, Malebranche, and Leibnitz, whose systems he criticized in a book published three years later, was to assume the possibility of knowing natures rather than operations. Condillac never rejected the distinction between these two possible subjects; like David Hume he admitted its legitimacy but maintained that natures were impenetrable to the human mind. Inner natures were going to turn into things-in-themselves in the first Critique of Kant. It was not until post-Kantian philosophy and

positivism had gained the upper hand that the existence of unknowables was flatly rejected by philosophers.

Neither in his volume on the origin of knowledge nor in his better known *Traité des Sensations* (1754) does Condillac deny the existence of a soul. The soul is needed in both works to perform the operations which constitute knowing. It is the agent which receives sensations from without and puts them together to form ideas. In Locke's fourth book of the *Essay* it is the mind, the knowing subject, which compares, contrasts, remembers; that is, the Ego, if one will; or the grammatical subject of judgments. Therefore Condillac never decomposed the soul or subject into a complex of sensations, nor did he, like Hume, deny that the term had any meaning. This is worth remembering, for his psychophysical dualism entailed, he thought, the explanation for those personal errors of judgments which were peculiar to the human race. The contents of the mind for him were not images of the external world. Knowledge was, above all, judgments, and to his way of thinking judgments were formed through the use of signs. The very opening sentence of his *Essay* asserts in no wavering terms that we can know only our own thoughts; we can never emerge from ourselves. If I insist upon this it is because one of the influences of Condillac was on French literature. When Stendhal boasts of being an Ideologist, he also is asserting that psychological analysis is the one task worthy of a writer and, if the long tradition of psychological analysis in French literature obtained the hold which it has had upon the French imagination, it is perhaps owing to the extraordinary precision of such investigators as Condillac, Destutt de Tracy, and their followers. One could not, of course, say that before 1750 men and women were not interested in what was happening in their inner life. Neither Ovid when he wrote the *Tristia* nor for that matter St. Augustine when he wrote his *Confessions* had to read a treatise on the analysis of sensations before sitting down to write. But the narrative of action could be said to have been the rule before the nineteenth century, whereas the narrative of psychological analysis became the rule afterwards. Rules are nothing more than generalizations which admit of exceptions, and it is in that sense of the term that I speak of the influence of psychological analysis on literature.

In the *Essay* Condillac gives what he believes to be a proof of the existence of a soul distinct from the body; in the *Treatise* he takes it for granted. His proof is interesting. If the soul were material, it would be a composite of several individual substances, an "assemblage or collection." When material particles are assembled or collected together, they are not united into a whole but are simply closer together than they were previously. Their multiplicity is not lost and, if such a collection were to be the subject of thought, there would have to be a thought for each particle to possess. But thought is actually a unit, as its subject is a unit. If each particle were to have its own thoughts, then when, for instance, comparisons are made, who is to make them? Particle A could not compare thought X with thought Y if it possesses only thought X. It is therefore necessary to posit "a meeting point," a substance which would be at the same time the simple and indivisible subject of various perceptions, distinct from the body, *une âme, en un mot.*

This existence of a thinking subject once having been demonstrated, its cognitive possessions may be analyzed. These possessions are primarily sensations, but sensations not merely as sensory qualities, such as red, blue, green, loud, soft, sweet, sour; every sensation is seen to have three distinguishable traits: (1) the perception itself, that is, the perceptual quality; (2) its relation to something external to ourselves, a relation made by us, that the color is the color of an external object; (3) the judgment that this relation is veridical. Thus Condillac, when he analyzes our ideas into their primary sensations, is talking of elements which in themselves have several properties. A sensation as he uses the term would be expressed by a sentence such as the following: "I am seeing a real red apple." Sensations are assertive. They are not the sense data of the modern New Realists. He does not deny the existence of such sense data, but he does not consider them the elements of knowledge. Knowledge, in short, cannot be reduced to anything more elementary than simple judgments and judgments have to be made by someone. In the *Treatise* sensations are handled somewhat differently. There each sensation is said to have four separable properties: the sensible quality itself; its affective character, that is, its pleasantness or unpleasantness; its duration; and its likeness or unlikeness to other sensations. But here, too, it is the soul's awareness of these properties which determines its judgments, and judgments are still the elements of cognition.

If judgment always involves relating what is immediately before the soul to something else, whether the operation be that of simply relating a color to an external object or of comparing two colors or of pronouncing on the reality or unreality of what is before one, then some instrument for binding ideas together or for distinguishing between them must be provided. In the *Essay* this instrument is signs. Signs, he says may be of three sorts: (1) accidental signs, or objects which by chance happen to be associated with certain of our ideas and which when experienced arouse the ideas associated with them; (2) natural signs, "or the sounds which nature has established for the feelings of joy, fear, griefs, etc.," in other words, emotional ejaculations; (3) conventional signs, which we have instituted ourselves and whose relation to ideas is arbitrary. Signs of these three sorts, in varying degrees, explain the operations of memory, imagination, and reflection, each of which utilizes signs to replace that of which they are the signs. Signification then is the secret of thinking, and it is because we can substitute signs for what they signify that our minds can operate in the absence of the external world. The invention of signs alone can explain, he maintains, such sciences as arithmetic, for we can form no clear idea of large numbers but do have names for them, which names are defined by means of signs for clear ideas of, for instance, a unit and for relations which constitute a progressive series. The idea of 1000, to take his example, acquires meaning simply because we have invented names for the unit, for the operation of addition, and for the serial order which that operation entails. Even a person who did not wish to communicate his ideas would have to invent a system of signs for himself if he were to do any calcula-

tion. Condillac is careful to point out that he is not talking here about the order of the genesis of our ideas at all; he realizes that we have the idea of 1000 without knowing how we acquire it. But when we wish to define it, we do so inevitably by analyzing the meaning of the sign by which it is named. Genetically we often learn the name before knowing anything about that which it names. Analysis enters when we wish to discover the meaning of these names. This would seem to imply that knowledge is the satisfaction of curiosity, the exploration of significance. But one should be wary of reading more into Condillac than he attempted to put there. He does, however, say explicitly that we have more words in our memory than we have ideas. "This must be," he adds, "naturally so; either because reflection, since it comes only after memory, has not always gone over carefully enough the ideas to which it has given signs; or because we see that there is a long interval between the time at which we begin to cultivate the memory of a child by inscribing on it many words of which the child is not yet able to note the ideas, and the time at which he begins to be able to analyze his notions so as to become aware of them." We use words as we acquire them without being too sure of their precise meaning. If only teachers would begin by talking to their charges exclusively of those things fitting to their age and needs, if only they would use precise words for definite things, even when playing with them, children would grow up without mental confusion. But this scarcely ever occurs.

Having started his epistemological studies in this way, Condillac enlarged them with his better known *Treatise on the Sensations.* There is no need to begin a discussion with Condillac's fiction of a statue endowed with the sense of smell and continuing with each of the senses. The fiction is known to everyone who has ever read a bit of philosophy and it served merely as a device, like that of man in a state of nature, to show how the contents and faculties of the mind could be constructed out of a human being who had none of the possessions of experience. It is more important for our purposes first to set down in an orderly fashion Condillac's principal assumptions. They are (1) the soul is a spiritual substance without character; (2) the analytical theorem: all wholes can be broken up into elementary parts; (3) these parts are externally related to one another. The first assumption means that the notion of a substance without attributes is retained by Condillac and that the contents of knowledge, and the psychic faculties as well, do not constitute the substance being discussed but are properties of it. In other words, it is meaningful to speak of a soul that has no consciousness whatsoever, no powers of remembering, attending, wishing, thinking, comparing, and the like. Consequently Condillac's problem is not merely to construct the contents of knowledge, both simple and complex, out of elementary sensations, but also the operations of the mind. The analytical theorem involves the belief that the elements can move into and out of composition without changing their nature. The soul-substance provides simply an agent which acquires functions through experience, manipulates the contents of that experience but does not modify them. The great problem which has to be faced by this sort of analysis is what is an element. Elements are normally determined by the processes used in analysis. Thus psychological inspection can find nothing composite in a color. such as violet or orange; they are *sui generis.* But if one is thinking in terms of pigments, then each is a compound and we know that, if one looks at a patch of violet or orange paint with a microscope, one will see little grains of blue and red pigment or of yellow and red as the case may be. One cannot see these in the perceptual violet and orange, but one can see them in the material violet and orange. But the red, blue, and yellow pigments are themselves chemically composite and other processes of analysis are needed to decompose them. It then turns out that a certain yellow (cadmium) is a sulfide (CdS), and a certain red (red lead) is Pb3O4. Are we then to say that when we are looking at a patch of red we are "really" seeing a compound of lead and oxygen? No one would be so extreme, for, if he were, he too could be pushed back to the point of breaking up the molecules into atoms, the atoms into subatomic parts. Condillac is content with going as far as the sensations, by which he means the sensory qualities, but how he reaches them he does not tell us. Nor does he seem to feel the need of justifying his belief in the permanence of the sensation once it is discovered. Yet even the perceptual quality of a sensory datum will vary in accordance with neighboring sensory data, which every painter and every musician knows. So every word in a sentence may vary in meaning with the context in which it appears. The work of the Gestalt psychologists has shown us that the elements reached by introspective analysis are far from being elements of the *Gestalt* in the sense that psychologically—whatever may be the case of the physical things perceived—they are elemental. Just as middle C on the piano may be the tonic of the major triad of C major, or the mediant of A minor or any one of a host of other things, so we often have to perceive a whole as a whole and then determine what its parts are by a quite different type of perceptual operation. It is the operation which determines what will be elemental and not the elements which determine the operation. This is specially important nowadays when the meanings of whole sentences are said to be found as complexes of the meanings of their so-called elements. The meaning of the sentence, "This apple is red but that one is green," depends as much on the conjunction "but" as on the two elemental clauses.

According to Condillac, every sensation will have the following four properties: its sensible character, its affective character, its duration, and its similarity to other sensible qualities. These will or may be all perceived by the soul as soon as it has more than one sensation. To put it somewhat differently, all sensibles have specificity; that is, are red, or green, or sweet, or sour, or hard, or soft, and so on; are agreeable or disagreeable; appear and disappear and thus have a temporal dimension; are like and unlike others. As a result of these four properties, the soul will develop operations which are functions of them. From specificity, there will arise no idea of matter whatsoever, but simple awareness of what is before one. From the affective coefficient will arise desire or aversion. From the duration of a sensation will arise memory, and from its repetition, habit. From similarity and dissimilarity will arise comparison and judgment. If sensations did not have these four properties, but, let us say, only specificity, the

soul would be identified with each sensation as it appeared and presumably if we had before our eyes only redness for an indefinite period, we should have neither desire, nor attention, nor memory, nor any other faculty.

Habit became, for Condillac, the basis of attention, recall, comparison, judgment, imagination, and recognition. It was all-important to him, as it was to be to Maine de Biran, Ravaisson, and in some respects to Bergson. Condillac knew—as Hume apparently did too—that habit was not simple repetition. Habits may be "only a facility of repeating what we have already done," but repetition brings increased facility. This facility is strengthened by frequent repetition, so that habitual processes never retain their original character. Furthermore, Condillac recognized what is called nowadays the compulsive force of habit, when he says that a desire when it has become habitual is what is called a passion, "that is to say, a desire which drives out all others, or at least becomes dominant," If by "facility" he includes the idea of the process being shortened in the amount of time it takes to perform it, then he also recognizes the telescoping of the temporal dimension in habitual action. Moreover, habit establishes for us certain truths about the world which we do not question; it is what is called by other philosophers common sense. Thus in discussing the sense of touch, Condillac argues that touch would make us familiar with groups of properties being constantly conjoined but would never give us ideas such as those of being, substance, essence, nature, etc. And he adds, "From its habit of judging that each body is a collection of many qualities it will seem to it quite natural that they can exist united, and it will not trouble itself about any underlying connection or support. Habit often takes the place of reason in ourselves, and we must agree that sometimes it is worth more than the reasoning of philosophers." Habit here actually gives rise to a new notion which replaces that of substance or rather makes any idea of substance unnecessary. The habit of perceiving—in this place through touch—a group of qualities constantly connected makes, so to speak, a thing out of the collection. The same objection that has been made to Hume, who explained our idea of causation as arising out of the habit of seeing constant regularities, would be made to Condillac. But, unless I am reading too much into them, they are both giving a psychological explanation of why we believe in something and not a logical definition of that which is believed in. By a logical definition, I mean a definition in terms of logical primitives. No one could deny that the meaning of the word "thing" as usually found is not equivalent to the meaning of the words "a collection of qualities." But that is not an objection against the psychological explanation of our belief in things or of the psychological origin of our idea of a thing unless habit does not actually have the power which Condillac and Hume give to it: that of changing the nature of what is habitually done or perceived. Similarly one cannot deduce from "I am habituated to smoking twenty cigarettes a day", the sentence "I ought to smoke twenty cigarettes a day"; but on the other hand the habit of smoking twenty cigarettes a day will produce in a person the compulsion to smoke that many. That Condillac had seriously considered the nature of habit is obvious throughout his ***Treatise,*** but the most compendious evidence is in a paragraph which concludes his section on the sense of touch. He is talking about instinct and calls it "the habit of directing oneself by ideas for which one does not know how to account. This habit, once contracted, guides one surely, without one's having the need to recall the judgments which made one contract the habit." It may very well be true that Condillac has not succeeded in explaining through habit all that he wishes to explain through it; but he should not be criticized for what he was not attempting to do.

There is an interesting sentence or two which indicate that for Condillac judgments become transmuted into sensations. Having pointed out that one learns the origin of sounds in tangible objects through the habit of touching sonorous things as one hears them, he says that we judge that the sounds come from the objects; we do not hear them coming from them or obviously feel them coming from them. This judgment which is repeated on several occasions induces us to confuse judgments with sensations. "And when a judgment has been confused through habit with a sensation, it will be confused with all sensations of the same kind." This important sentence is an attempt to explain what is traditionally called immediate knowledge. Immediate knowledge appears when we have some experience or other of a very simple kind and say "I hear the bell," or "I see a red rose." Such judgments are not strictly true, since one cannot hear a bell; one can hear only a sound. Similarly one cannot see a rose; one can see only a color. The attribution of the sensory data to objects is made by repeated associations, and since anything repeated may become habitual and, if habitual, very rapid and compulsive, the judgment is immediately made. Condillac does not doubt its truth, for its truth is not in question. But he gives us a reason for thinking such judgments immediate, when they are in fact learned, and for believing in them so strongly. "If one had never heard the same sound except upon touching the same shape had always heard the same sound, one would think that shapes carried in them the sounds, and that sounds had in them the ideas of shapes, and one would not be able to assign to touch and to hearing the ideas which belong to each of these senses. In the same way, if each sound had continually been associated with a certain color, and each odor with a certain sound, it would not be possible for one to distinguish the ideas which one owes to smell from those which one owes to hearing." These very rapid and habitual judgments which give us our knowledge of objects, of externality, of duration, of complex things with several sensory properties existing at various distances from us, he calls "practical judgments."

Condillac had insisted that no sensory quality in itself is evidence of an external world of independent objects. They are all "modifications" of the soul. In that he was in agreement with Berkeley and with the Cartesian tradition in France. But both Berkeley and Descartes felt the need of demonstrating the existence of an external world; the latter, through the impossibility of God's deceiving us; the former, through the appearance of ideas of which we cannot be the cause. Condillac attempts a new demonstration through the sense of touch. Dr. Johnson had made a

similar demonstration against Berkeley's immaterialism. But the verb "touch" was used more subtly by Condillac.

The imaginary man whose soul is void of sensations, the famous statue, was given one sensation at a time. All sensations, it will be recalled, have an affective aspect, they are either pleasant or unpleasant. If a man be given the power of movement, it may be expected that as long as his sensations are pleasant he will enjoy them in repose. But as soon as he experiences an unpleasant sensation he will shrink away from it. This withdrawal does not have to be learned the first time—Nature will take care of it; one's muscles will automatically contract at the experience of pain. The change from an agreeable sensation to a disagreeable one will be the source of movement, and the utility of the movements resides in their helping a man to avoid the harmful—that is, the painful—and to enjoy the pleasurable. These movements will help a man discover that he has a body, for his hands will move over his body and discover its difference from his soul. It then discovers that bodies are impenetrable. "We do not, strictly speaking, feel that bodies are impenetrable: we judge that they are. This judgment is a consequence of the sensations that they produce in us." It is made from the sensation of solidity, for we perceive that when two objects that we feel as solid collide, they resist each other and do not interfuse. But touch has a property which the other sensations do not have. If we were limited to sight, hearing, smell, and taste, we should never have any idea of external objects, for such sensations are purely subjective. But the perception of solidity is immediately attached to solid objects, first to one's own body and later to objects in space that can be perceived as not part of our souls. First, we perceive that parts of our body are different from our hands, which in turn are different from whatever part of the body they are touching. If we press a hand against our chest, we are bound to feel the difference between the hand and the chest, especially if one is cold and the other warm. But though one then has the perception of two bodies, one does not as yet realize that all the different parts of one's body which the hands touch form one single body. To get this perception, one must run the hand over an area of one's body continuously; and, since a person is identical with each sensation which he is experiencing, until he has formed an idea of himself as distinct from his sensations, our imaginary man will have to experience a continuity of tactile sensations in his body to be able to judge it as one and as his own. As long as we confine our tactile sensations to our own body, we will have no idea of external objects; but, the moment we touch a foreign body, we feel a sensation in our hand but not in the foreign body. We thus awake to the fact of the separateness between ourselves and other things.

This argument is interesting in that it does not involve interferences either from causation or from God's veracity. It is based entirely on the primitive sensation of touch and the ability to move. That is, touch itself reveals the externality of material objects, reveals it through the perceptual differences experienced. Condillac does not deny that these sensations are equally subjective, but does assert that they inevitably produce different judgments. He also grants that the status would not be able to have practical knowledge on this shaky basis. Until it has acquired language, it will be unable to form general ideas. Its knowledge is purely "instinctive." All it knows is that external objects are not part of its body. . . .

Robert McRae (essay date 1961)

SOURCE: "Condillac: The Abridgement of All Knowledge in 'The Same Is the Same'," in his *The Problem of the Unity of the Sciences: Bacon to Kant,* University of Toronto Press, 1961, pp. 89-106.

[*In the following essay, McRae discusses Condillac's theory of the unity of knowledge and the sciences, focusing on his unique blending of the ideas of Locke, Descartes, and Malebranche.*]

Like other philosophers of the French Enlightenment, Condillac set himself against the philosophy of Descartes and turned with admiration to Locke and Newton. To Locke he acknowledged his greatest debt, but not without criticism. Among other things Locke lacked "order." Condillac's own thought is characterized by an extreme concern with the systematization and unity of knowledge. His attitude towards systematization was, nevertheless, in his own time the subject of misunderstanding. Though he himself did not misunderstand Condillac, d'Alembert was to remark that "the taste for systems . . . is today banished almost completely," and to Condillac he gave the credit for having delivered the final blows to "*l'esprit de système.*" As the author of the *Traité des systèmes* (1749) Condillac was ironically destined to bear the reputation of being the principal enemy of *system* as such. On this undeserved reputation he commented sadly:

> . . . a good *system* is only a well developed principle. I know that many people take this word in bad part, thinking that every *system* is a gratuitous hypothesis, or something worse like the dreams of the metaphysicias. . . . If I am told that I have written against *systems,* I beg people to read my work right to the end, although it is humiliating for a writer to recognize that he is not read to the end. If at least they were to read the beginning carefully, they would see that I do not reject all *systems.*

It was one of Condillac's reiterated maxims that "a well treated science is a well made system." Systematization he took to be an essential and inescapable feature of all thinking. It is not merely philosophers who systematize; everyone does, progressing naturally from prejudice to prejudice, from opinion to opinion, and from error to error. Nature compels us to make systems and for Condillac nature is the ultimate authority on method in the sciences.

The *Traité des systèmes* presents an exhaustive classification of the possible types of system. There are only three, and of these the third is the true or legitimate one. The difference between the three systems does not consist in the way in which their parts are connected, but in what they take for their principles or starting point, for in any system there are only two things—principles and consequences. The first kind of system starts with definitions and axioms and proceeds by the method of synthesis. These abstract principles even when they happen to be true and well-formed—though in metaphysics, ethics, and theology they are generally vague and badly formed—are improperly called principles for the simple reason that they are not what we know first. Merely to refer to them as abstract is to acknowledge that other things are known before them. They are useless for the making of discoveries since they are no more than abbreviated expressions for knowledge already acquired, and as such the most that they can do is to carry us back again to that knowledge. "In short," says Condillac, "they are maxims containing only what we know, and just as the people have their proverbs, these so-called principles are the proverbs of the philosophers, and that is all they are."

The second is the hypothetical system, which adopts for principles certain suppositions which are designed to explain known phenomena. The suppositions are said to be *proved* by their felicity in *explaining*. Metaphysicians in particular have been extremely inventive in this kind of principle, and indeed there is no longer anything which remains mysterious for metaphysics, which they describe as "the science of first truths, or of the first principles of things." Condillac does not deny that hypotheses can perform a legitimate rôle in scientific inquiry. Inquiry begins with provisional observations which give rise to suspicions or conjectures suggesting further observations to be made. But such conjectures cannot provide the logical foundations of a science.

> Since suppositions are only suspicions, they are not established facts. Therefore they cannot be the principle or beginning of a system, otherwise the whole system would reduce itself to a suspicion.
>
> But if they are not the principle or beginning of the system, they are the principle or beginning of our means for discovery of the system. Now, it is just because they are the principle of these means that they have also been taken to be the principle of the system. Thus two quite different things have been confused with one another.

There is, nevertheless, one circumstance in which it is possible for a supposition to function, not merely as a means to the discovery of a first principle, but as itself an actual first principle. This occurs only when there is some way of establishing the truth of the supposition. For this two things are required. First, we must be able to exhaust all possible suppositions bearing on a question, and, secondly, we must be in possession of some means for determining our choice among them and of eliminating those which are false. In mathematics this is possible; in physics it is not. It was the taste for this second kind of system, resting on conjectures, which d'Alembert was to identify with *l'esprit de système*. No more than Condillac did he condemn all system, but he distinguished between what he called *le véritable esprit systématique* and *l'esprit de système* and warned that we must be careful not to take the one for the other.

The third and only valid system is that which takes experience for its starting point and proceeds by analysis. This analysis forms the subject of a major part of Condillac's philosophical writings, for it is common to every science and to every inquiry he himself undertakes for the instruction of his royal pupil in his *Cours d'études* (1775): ". . . this method is the only one, and . . . it must be absolutely the same in all our investigations, for to study the different sciences is not to change the method, but to apply the same method to different objects." Its unswerving uniformity is asserted with tireless repetition.

Condillac's conception of analysis plainly owes much, either directly or indirectly, to Descartes, but in one important respect he goes beyond Descartes. This marked feature of originality is to be found in the rôle which he assigns to language. Analysis is possible only by means of language. Condillac may have opposed himself to Descartes' apriorism of innate ideas and asserted with Locke that all ideas have their origin in sensation, but he substituted for Descartes' apriorism another of his own, that of an innate language. This language is an essential condition of the possibility of there being any beginning for human knowledge. "It is necessary that the elements of some language or other, prepared in advance, should precede our ideas; for without signs of some kind it would be impossible for us to analyse our thoughts in such a way as to have any distinct awareness of what we think." The innate language consists of those bodily gestures and attitudes which are the natural expressions of feeling. Condillac calls it "the language of action." Since its nature is determined by the conformation of our bodily organs, members of the same species, sharing similar organs, will express their feelings in the same way and will consequently be able to understand one another whereas members of different species will not.

Today it would seem to be generally acknowledged that all attempts to find the origins of language in the natural expression of feeling have been failures, and that there is an impassable gulf separating these symptoms of feeling from the artificial symbols for our conceptions of things, the cry of pain or joy from propositional discourse about matters of fact. While Condillac suggests in his opening description of the nature of language that discourse originates in these overt bodily symptoms, it is not long before he attributes more to the primitive language of action than a mere giving vent to feeling. Thus he writes, "In him who is not yet acquainted with the natural signs determined by the conformation of the organs, the action makes a very composite picture; for it indicates the object which affects him, and at the same time it expresses both the judgment he makes and the feelings he experiences." This implies that besides symptoms of feeling, the most primitive type of expression contains both the symbolization of objects and the formulation of judgments.

But though analysis, or making our ideas clear to ourselves and others, is the function of a deliberately developed language, it is not the function of language considered in its origin. Language begins to become analytic only when men feel the necessity of communicating with one another. Nor do they form any intention of making themselves understood by others until after they have observed that they are in fact understood by them. Primitive expression is extremely confused because it expresses everything

that is thought and felt simultaneously. It is only by decomposing the expressive movements of others, distinguishing one after the other the constituent elements of complex actions, that men come to understand each other's different feelings and thoughts.

> Each will notice then sooner or later that he never understands others better than when he has decomposed their actions, and as a result he will come to see that if he is to make himself understood by others he will have to decompose his own actions. Then little by little he will form the habit of repeating successively the movements which nature would cause him to perform all at once, and the language of action will become naturally for him an analytic method. . . .

> In decomposing his action he decomposes his thought for himself as well as for others; he analyses it and makes himself understood because he understands himself.

> Just as the total action is a picture of his whole thought, so equally the partial actions are pictures of the ideas which make up the parts of his thought. Thus, if again, he decomposes his partial actions, he will at the same time be decomposing the partial ideas of which his actions are the signs, and he will continually be forming new distinct ideas.

The signs belonging to primitive language are not deliberately chosen by us, but are determined for us by nature. At the same time, nature has set us on the road to imagining and therefore to choosing signs for ourselves. It is in this way that the use of artificial signs arises. But even if these deliberately chosen signs are artificial, they are not arbitrary, for they are always formed by analogy with the original natural signs. Just as soon as men begin to decompose their thoughts, the language of action begins to become an artificial language. "It becomes every day more artificial, because the more they analyse, the more they feel the need to analyse. To facilitate these analyses they will imagine new signs analogous to the natural signs."

When in *La Langue des calculs* (published posthumously in 1798) Condillac considered the most perfect language, algebra, he attached extreme importance to analogy as the clue to development of a language.

> Since algebra is a language made by analogy, analogy which makes language makes methods, or rather the method of discovery is only analogy itself.

> It is to analogy that the whole art of reasoning reduces, as also the whole art of speaking, and in this single word, analogy, we see how it is possible to instruct ourselves in the discoveries of others as well as how to make them for ourselves.

Condillac worked out this thesis in a detailed examination of the development of mathematics, beginning with its origin as a language of action, that is to say, as a calculatio with the fingers. When, later, numbers and then letters are substituted, analogy with the original operations by the fingers is carefully retained. Condillac's insistence on the development of language by analogy arises from two main concerns. The one is to prevent any rupture between artifice and nature, for nature is our original mentor in matters of method. The language of science may be artificial, but it is not arbitrary, nor merely conventional. Analogy is also important to him as providing support for his theory that the steps of a demonstration are merely successive linguistic transformations of the same proposition. The retention of the identity of the propositions throughout these transformations is the work of analogy.

In algebra Condillac saw "a striking proof that the progress of the sciences depends uniquely on the progress of languages, and that well-constructed languages alone can give analysis the degree of simplicity and precision of which it is susceptible." The success of a scientific genius is insuperably conditioned by the degree of development in the language of the age to which he belongs. Newton's immense achievement was made possible by the devices of language and the consequent methods of calculation made available to him by his predecessors. Where words are lacking a science will encounter the same obstacles as geometry did before the invention of algebra, and Newton's work would have suffered similar limitations if he had been born in an earlier age.

Different sciences are not by the nature of their subject-matters susceptible to different degrees of precision. There are only different degrees of success in the construction of their languages—"all would have the same precision if they were always spoken with well-made languages. . . . All sciences would be exact if we knew how to speak the language of each." It was Condillac's unachieved ambition, as expressed to his friends, to construct the languages for metaphysics and the moral sciences, and to rescue them from the chaos into which the abuses of language had plunged them. His editors of 1798 wrote "The unintelligible jargons which they too often speak would have been converted into as many beautiful languages, which everyone would easily have learned since everyone would have understood them; and in these languages the ideas which appeared to be the most inaccessible to the human mind would have been seen issuing of themselves and effortlessly from the commonest notions."

Although Condillac conceived of one universal method for all the sciences, he did not propose, like Leibnitz, a single language for them all. Each science has its own language. Algebra is but one of these languages, that one which is appropriate to the subject-matter of mathematics. Other subjects would have their equally appropriate languages. While the symbolization employed in mathematics represents for Condillac a wonderful simplification of the language of words, he never suggests, as Leibnitz did, that metaphysics or the moral sciences would be able to find a corresponding kind of simplification, or that they would ever depart from calculation with words. There is one method for the sciences, but a plurality of languages, and through their differences of language the sciences remain distinct from one another.

Condillac extends unity of method not only to all the sciences, but also to all arts employing language, whether the language involved consists of bodily movement or of sounds. Thus the arts of the dance, the theatre, music, oratory, poetry, and every branch of literature, are all produced by this one method. *"To invent,* it is said, *is to find something new by the force of one's imagination.* This definition is thoroughly bad." Invention is not the product of imagination, nor is genius the product of inspiration.

> A geometer will tell you that Newton must have had as much imagination as Corneille, since he had as much genius, but he fails to see that Corneille himself had genius only because he analysed as well as Newton. Analysis makes poets just as it makes mathematicians, and although it causes them to speak different languages, it is always the same method. In short, given the subject of a drama, to find the plan, the characters, their speech, means just so many problems to be solved, and every problem is solved by analysis.

The artist, then, is not a creator. His activity consists in finding something which is already there to be found. There is nothing in artistic invention to correspond to the divine creation *ex nihilo.* The artist's invention is only an analysis through the device of language of something given to him. By means of expression in language he becomes the first to see what we as the result of his work are then also able to see.

A proposition taken by itself is an analysis—the analysis of a complex idea. Such an idea will remain vague and confused until a proposition is used to articulate its components. Consequently, a true proposition asserts only an identity. Since it states what is contained in the complex idea, "it is limited to saying that the same is the same." All true propositions are either self-evident or provable. Those are self-evident in which the identity of the terms is immediately seen. But one proposition is said to be the consequence of another when, by a comparison of their terms, they are seen to assert the same thing. Hence a proof is only a succession of propositions all asserting the same thing.

> To demonstrate is then to translate an evident proposition, to make it take different forms until it becomes the proposition we wish to prove. It is to change the terms of the proposition, and to arrive, by a succession of identical propositions, at a conclusion identical with the proposition from which it is immediately drawn. It is necessary that the identity which is not perceived as we pass over the intermediary propositions should be evident by the mere inspection of terms, as we go directly from one proposition to another.

It is this theory of the proposition which determines that there can be only one method for all the sciences, and Condillac undertakes to show how this method is exactly the same whether we are solving a problem in algebra or in metaphysics.

He first proposes an elementary mathematical problem. We are to suppose that I have a number of tokens in my hands, and that if I transfer one of these from the right hand to the left, I shall have an equal number in each hand, while if I transfer one from the left to the right, I shall have twice as many in the right as in the left. How many tokens have I in each hand? The solution to the problem involves two operations of reasoning. The first consists in what Condillac calls "reasoning on the conditions of the problem"; the second, in the actual finding of the solution. Both operations consist in a series of translations.

In the first operation the initial statement of the problem is transformed through a series of successively simpler expressions until it finally attains its simplest possible expression. For the case under consideration this simplest expression in its verbal form would be

The right, minus one, is equal to the left plus one;

The right, plus one, is equal to two lefts minus two.

A further simplification of expression can be introduced, however, by the substitution of symbols for words, x and y being made to stand for the unknown quantities in the right and left hands respectively, $+$ being made to stand for "plus," $-$ for "minus," and $=$ for "is equal to." We then get the two equations

$$x - 1 = y + 1$$
$$x + 1 = 2y - 2$$

In this operation we have begun with a statement of the conditions of the problem, which contains within it both the known and the unknown factors. It is an absolute requirement that this statement should contain within it *all* the known factors necessary to the solution of the problem; otherwise the problem will be insoluble. The initial mode of stating the conditions does not, however, prepare us for the solution of the problem. Preparation consists in the reduction of the question to its simplest possible expression through a succession of translations. This reduction performs two important functions. In the first place, it clearly determines whether all the knowns necessary for the solution are actually contained in the statement of the conditions. And in the second place, it gives to the statement of the conditions the explicit form of a statement of identity, i. e., formulates it as an equation—or, as in the example provided where there are two unknowns, the reduction results in two equations. This concludes the reasoning on the conditions and the problem is now ready for solution.

The second operation of reasoning, like its predecessor, consists in a series of translations in which we go from identical proposition to identical proposition, or from equation to equation, until we have the unknowns equated with the knowns,

$$x = 7; y = 5.$$

The problem is now solved, and we know that I had seven tokens in the right hand, and five in the left.

Mathematics reasons with equations, but so do all the sciences, for all propositions are equations, and consequently there is no difference in the way in which we reason in the different sciences. In mathematics, however, the statement of a problem usually formulates explicitly the conditions of the problem, whereas in the other sciences this is unusual. If, for example, we ask the metaphysical question,

What is the origin and generation of the faculties of the human understanding? the conditions of the question have still to be found.

As we have seen, in every question capable of being answered the conditions must be present in the statement of the question, and the knowns necessary for finding the unknowns must be included in those conditions. In a question capable of solution, if the conditions are not explicitly stated, then they must at least be implicitly contained in the form of the question, otherwise we should never be able to find them. It is true that they are not always equally recognizable in the original form in which questions are asked. To discover them means to translate the initial statement into its simplest terms and, when this is done, the conditions which were contained implicitly in the question will be rendered explicit.

"What is the origin and generation of the faculties of the human understanding?" To get the conditions of the problem, this should be translated into the question, "What is the origin and generation of the faculties by which man, capable of sensations, conceives things by forming ideas of them?" We then see that attention, comparison, judgment, reflection, imagination, and reason are, along with sensation, the known factors in the problem, while the *origin* and the *generation* are the two unknowns. The conditions are now clearly apparent. The first part of the problem is to determine which of the knowns is the origin, i. e., the principle or beginning, of all the other knowns. Very little observation tells one that it is the faculty of sensation which is involved in all the other faculties. Sensation, therefore, is the *origin*. What still remains to be done is to show how sensation becomes successively attention, comparison, judgment, etc. We shall then know their *generation*. And this is what Condillac claims to have done in the first part of his ***Logique*** (1780).

> . . . just as the equations $x - 1 = y + 1$ and $x + 1 = 2y - 2$ undergo different transformations to become $y = 5$ and $x = 7$, so sensation in the same way undergoes different transformations to become the understanding.

> The device of reasoning is therefore the same in all the sciences. Just as in mathematics the question is established by translating it into algebra, so in the other sciences it . . . is established by translating it into the simplest expression; and when the question is established, the reasoning which solves it is itself still only a series of translations in which a proposition translating the one preceding it is in turn translated by the one which follows it. In this way evidence passes with identity from the statement of the question to the conclusion of the reasoning.

Since, from this account, method appears to operate wholly within the realm of language, something should be said about the rôle which Condillac assigns to experience. To begin with, experience supplies the materials on which we reason. But the clear and distinct perception of any matter of fact is a judgment and therefore it is an analysis. Analysis is, however, possible only by means of language. Hence the perception of a matter of fact is identical with the linguistic affirmation of that fact. Thereafter, any reasoning from what is perceived will consist only in the linguistic transformation of the original proposition in which the perception is expressed. But Condillac also maintains that in an empirical science like physics "the evidence of reason" (i. e., the perception of the identity of two verbally different propositions) and "the evidence of fact" (i. e., observation) should always go together. When we draw the logical consequences of an observation, the evidence of reason needs to be confirmed by new observations; in other words, our transformations of the original proposition expressing an observation should be verified by new observations. Thus, in its second rôle, observation functions as a test of the correctness of our translations.

Since the sequence of propositions in a science is only a sequence of translations of an original assertion of an identity, Condillac raises the question whether the sciences are not then simply collections of frivolous propositions. He replies that if there were any thinking being who was not under the necessity of acquiring his knowledge but knew everything already, he would never formulate anything in a proposition. God alone is such a being. For him every truth has the same immediate evidence of identity that 2 + 2 = 4 has for us. God sees all truths in a single truth, and doubtless all the sciences of which we are so proud frivolous to him.

But although every true proposition is identical, it will not necessarily seem to be so when we first consider it. If we were to see the identity immediately, then, of course, it would be frivolous. But if the identity requires to be established, then it can be instructive, and that for two reasons. In the first place, the human mind is capable only of acquiring successively the partial ideas which go to make up a complex idea, and, secondly, our minds are unable to embrace simultaneously in a distinct manner all the partial ideas contained in a complex idea. From the nature of a proposition and of the relations of propositions to one another in a demonstration it follows that any science considered as a logical system is simply the articulation of a single complex idea. "A complete system can only be one and the same idea." Thus, for example, in metaphysics, we see how sensation becomes in turn each of the faculties, and each of the kinds of ideas. It contains a series of propositions which are instructive when taken in relation to us, but which when taken in themselves are identical. The whole science of the origin of human knowledge can be abridged in the proposition *sensations are sensations.* "If in all sciences we were equally able to follow the generation of ideas . . . we should see one truth giving birth to all the rest, and we should find the abridged expression of all our knowledge in this identical proposition, *the same is the same.*"

A detailed working out of this conception of the nature of a science as a system is provided for his royal pupil in several examples. After considering some taken from geometry he points out that he has begun with the definition of the word "to measure," and that this definition is found in all the following propositions, the only thing which changes being the terms in which it is expressed. Indeed all mathematical truths are but different expressions of this first definition. "Thus mathematics is an immense science contained in the idea of a single word."

At the conclusion of his examination of "Newton's system," he points out that a little reflection on the balance, the lever, the wheel, pulleys, the inclined plane, and the pendulum shows that these machines and others more complicated are reducible to a single one, the balance or lever. Their identity is evident. They take different forms for producing different effects, but in principle all are the same machine. The universe is only a great balance.

> Now as all machines, from the simplest to the most complicated, are only one and the same machine which assumes different forms in order to produce different effects, in the same way the properties we discover in a series of machines, each more complicated than the previous, reduce to one first property which in being transformed is at once one and multiple. For if there is in the end only one machine, there is in the end only one property. To be convinced you need only to consider that we have ascended from knowledge to knowledge only because we have passed from identical propositions to identical propositions. Now, if we were able to discover all possible truths and to be assured of them in an evident manner, we should produce a succession of identical propositions equivalent to the succession of truths, and as a result we should see all truths reduced to a single one.

Condillac has no doubt that there is one single principle which would explain all observable phenomena, although this principle has not yet been discovered. He combats the claim of the bolder Newtonians that attraction is that principle. Attraction is a phenomenon which explains many others, but it is far from explaining all. It is a principle which presupposes, or appears to presuppose, a principle even more general than itself, and Condillac sees no reason for supposing that with Newton we have reached the limits of knowledge in physics.

Although he knew Leibnitz's metaphysical theory of the monad and was one of its severest critics, Condillac probably had little, if any, acquaintance with his logical theory. It is, therefore, of passing interest to note how he shares with Leibnitz the same view of the nature of the proposition and of the nature of proof. For both of them every true proposition is either a self-evidently identical proposition or reducible to one. Condillac differs, however, in maintaining that the whole of a science is reducible to a single self-evidently identical proposition. This conception of what makes a science one has no counterpart in Leibnitz.

Not only is the individual science a system, but there is a system of all the sciences taken together. It is impossible, however, that the second system should be the same sort of thing as the first, for if it were it would require that we should be able to reach that one truth which includes within it all truths. Condillac believes there is such a truth but that it is known by God alone and its possession is equivalent to omniscience. Thus, although Condillac suggested that the one fundamental truth of physics might in due course be attained by us, he never entertained the possibility of our attaining the fundamental truth which would embrace the truths of all the different sciences. Moreover, as we have seen, a single science consists in the construction of a single language, but there is no proposal such as we find in Leibnitz that we might construct the single language of a universal science, containing within it all the particular sciences. The languages of mathematics and metaphysics, for example, remain irreducibly different for Condillac.

It is, then, in a quite different way that Condillac conceives of all the sciences as forming a unified whole or system. His model for this conception is the living organism, with its integrated system of needs and its means of satisfying them. Although Condillac purported to be a follower of Locke's sensationalist theory of knowledge, he retained certain fundamental features of Descartes' and Malebranche's conceptions of sense knowledge. According to Descartes and Malebranche scientific knowledge, which is knowledge of things as they are in themselves, is possible through the intellect alone, even if, as in the case of mathematics and physics, but not metaphysics, the intellect can be aided by the imagination and the senses. In contrast to the scientific knowledge of things as they are in themselves, there is for them both a type of knowledge which is essential for the conduct and self-maintenance of man as a composite being, who is made up of a mind and a body, and who interacts with a physical environment. The foundation of this practical knowledge resides in the senses, whose function is not to inform us of the nature of things as they are in themselves, but of their existence and how they affect us. Through intellect alone we know the essential nature of things; through the senses we know things in relation to us and to our needs.

Condillac's departure from Descartes and Malebranche lies in his assertion that there is no knowledge of things as they are in themselves, that all knowledge is through the senses, and that, therefore, knowledge has for its objects only things in so far as they are related to us and our needs. Thus all knowledge is practical in nature. There is no science of the kind envisioned by Descartes and Malebranche. Science is based on sensation and therefore its function is to direct the action towards self-maintenance of an organism situated in an environment.

Our faculties have been bestowed on us to show us how to avoid the harmful and to seek what can be useful to us. For this there is no need for us to have knowledge of the essences of things.

> The author of our nature does not require it . . . he wills only that we judge of the relations which things have to us and to one another, when the knowledge of these relations can be of some use.
>
> We have a means of judging of these relations, and it is unique; it is to observe the sensations which objects produce in us. Just so far as our sensations can be extended, the sphere of our knowledge can be extended; beyond that all discovery is forbidden us.

It is this intrinsic relativity of all knowledge to our nature which gives to the sciences a systematic unity. Condillac conceives of the human organism and its environment as interacting with a perfect, divinely-contrived coordination. Human needs and the means of their satisfaction are a function of this relation, and it is experience, or nature, through pleasures and pains, which very promptly instructs us as to what is necessary for our self-maintenance. Our needs, like the different organs to which they are related, comprise an integrated system, and so also do the teachings of nature. The one system will correspond exactly to the other. "I see in the sphere of my cognitions a system corresponding to that which the author of my nature has followed in making me; and that is not surprising; for, given my needs and my faculties, my inquiries and my cognitions will be given also. Everything is connected in the two systems in the same way." In pursuing scientific inquiry it is important to study this system of needs and faculties, for since all our knowledge is concerned, not with things as they are in themselves, but only as they are in relation to us, it must form a system corresponding to the organization of our nature. Answering to each need there will be the idea of the thing appropriate to its satisfaction, and the analysis of this idea will in turn give rise to a whole chain of ideas, or what is the same thing, a succession of formulations in language of that one idea. Accordingly the total system of knowledge will consist in a series of fundamental ideas, answering to fundamental needs and interrelated in the same way as these needs, and then, issuing from each of these fundamental ideas, there will be the series of their constituent ideas as elicited by analysis. These constituent ideas, however, will not form isolated series but will be interwoven with one another as they ramify, "for the same objects and the same ideas are often related to different needs." Since any individual science is for Condillac the analysis or progressive articulation of a fundamental idea, there will be a plurality of sciences as there is a plurality of needs, but like the needs they will be co-ordinated in an organic whole. Although Condillac describes the sciences as logically interrelated in this system, the description is incompatible with his definition of a logical system, for the way in which the differentiated functions of the parts of an organism are united in the common service of the well-being or preservation of the organism is quite distinct from the way in which the different terms of a proposition are united in an equation. It is the latter kind of union alone which is the basis of a logical system.

In spite of the fact that no philosopher has ever presented a theory providing a simpler and easier basis for identifying a science than did Condillac—all that was required of him was to name the fundamental idea of which any given science is the analysis—yet so concerned was he for the unity of knowledge that he expressed the strongest disapproval of any attempt to classify or define the different sciences. He despised theory about their divisions as characteristic of scholasticism, and he found the eighteenth century, in spite of the great scientific advances it had made, still dominated by this scholastic passion for distinctions and the separation of intellectual disciplines. "We are more scholastic than we think." His royal pupil is reminded that in Greece a scholar cultivated all the arts and sciences together and his mind was thereby strengthened by all the helps which they mutually supply to one another. The superiority of the Greeks to the Romans was owing to this universality in their approach to knowledge. "Nature shows us by a thousand examples that there are things which must not be studied separately. Indeed, a grammarian will never be anything but medicore or bad if he is only a grammarian. It is the same with a rhetorician, a logician, etc. We shall ourselves, therefore, be badly instructed in these arts if we study them separately." To study them in this way is to separate things which by their nature are intended to throw light on one another. But, one might ask, if the sciences are not pursued separately, will they not all end by becoming confused? Condillac agrees that ultimately, when our intellectual possessions become too many to be embraced together, specialization is necessary. Nevertheless, in their beginnings the different branches of knowledge must be taken together, as they were by the Greeks. Unfortunately, instead of trying to find out how the Greeks arrived at their knowledge, we have concerned ourselves only with the results of their inquiries. Instead of trying to recover a course of education in which all our studies are blended, we have slavishly followed the order and divisions of the scholastics, and in the end have succeeded in producing even more divisions than they, ontol-

ogies, psychologies, cosmologies, and so one. Despite his admiration for Bacon, Condillac considered him particularly guilty of this excessive multiplication of divisions in the sciences.

In conclusion it may be remarked that on its logical side Condillac's theory of unity of method fractures knowledge into a set of sciences each of which is reducible to a single member of a set of logically discrete and independent identical propositions. But on its utilitarian side, in which inquiry is directed to the means of satisfying human needs, his method integrates all knowledge into one whole of mutually interrelated parts.

Etienne Gilson and Thomas Langan   (essay date 1963)

SOURCE: "Condillac," in their *Modern Philosophy: Descartes to Kant,* Random House, 1963, pp. 274-88.

[*In the following essay, Gilson and Langan present an overview of Condillac's critique of methodolgical systems and of his theory of sensations as developed in the* Essay on the Origin of Human Knowledges.]

The first sentence ever published by Condillac was in praise of metaphysics. No science, he says, has done as much as metaphysics to give the human mind clarity, precision, and amplitude. It seems, therefore, that this science should be used in order to train the mind for the study of other sciences; yet "today metaphysics is so neglected in France that this remark will no doubt sound paradoxical to many readers." This opening sentence of the ***Essay on the Origin of Human Knowledges*** suggests a philosophical climate very different from that of the seventeenth century.

Two main influences had contributed to bring about that striking change on the Continent. Newton had not only substituted for the cosmology imagined by Descartes a solidly demonstrated one, he also had laid down the precepts of the only method capable of achieving solidly demonstrated knowledge in astronomy and physics. On this point the doctrine of Newton was as explicit as it was clear. In his *Mathematical Principles of Natural Philosophy* (1687) Newton had announced his decision "not to feign hypotheses"—*hypotheses non fingo*—for indeed "whatever is not deduced from phenomena, must be called a hypothesis, and whether they be metaphysical or physical, of occult qualities or mechanical, hypotheses have no place in experimental philosophy."

The second influence at work in France around 1740 was that of John Locke. The *Essay [Concerning Human Understanding]* had been translated into French and the book had been widely read. Its "plain historical method" had created a favorable impression. As Voltaire was to say, after so many reasoners had told the romance of the soul, "a wise man came who told us its history." In eighteenth-century French, *le sage Locke* was as hackneyed a formula as, in scholastic Latin, *Philosophus* had once been to designate Aristotle. And those who used it, mentally contrasted the "wise Locke" with the less wise Descartes. In all this, Condillac was a child of the century, but he was not giving up metaphysics as a lost cause. On the contrary, convinced

---

An excerpt from the *Treatise on Sensations:*

As soon as there is twofold attention, there is comparison, because to attend to two ideas or to compare them is the same. However, one cannot compare them without seeing some difference or some resemblance between them; to see such relations is to judge. The acts of comparing and of judging are, thus, nothing but attention itself: it is in this way that sensation becomes successively attention, comparison, judgment.

The objects which we compare possess numerous relations, whether because the impressions they make upon us are themselves wholly different, or because these impressions differ solely in degree, or because the impressions, though similar themselves, yet combine differently in each object. In such cases, the attention that we give the objects starts by enveloping all the sensations which they occasion. But this attention being so much divided, our comparisons are vague, the relations that alone we grasp are confused, our judgments are imperfect or unsure. Hence we are compelled to shift our attention from one object to another, regarding their qualities separately. After, for example, judging their color, we judge their shape, and after that their size; and by running through in this way all the sensations that the objects make upon us, we discover, by means of a succession of comparisons and judgments, the relations that obtain between the objects, and the result of these judgments is the idea which we form of each object. The attention thus directed is like a beam of light which is reflected from one body to another to illuminate them both, and this I call reflection. Thus sensation, after becoming attention, comparison, judgment, ends by becoming reflection too.

Étienne Bonnot de Condillac, in his Treatise on Sensations, *1784.*

---

that Locke had given the proof that a sound metaphysics was possible, he only wanted to improve it.

A period of intense metaphysical productivity is usually followed by one of critical examination and judgment. After Platonism and the flowering of Greek systems came the skepticism of the New Academy; at the end of its golden age scholasticism had heard the objections of Ockham, Montaigne, and Sanchez to overconfidence in the demonstrating power of reason; Condillac comes to play a similar role at the end of the seventeenth-century metaphysical flowering. Still he himself is in no way a skeptic; the proof of this can be found in the fact that, having decided to criticize systems, he undertakes in a positive spirit to find the cause of their errors.

Condillac does not say "the causes," for he thinks that a true philosopher should be able to detect the cause of causes that lies at the origin of all such errors. His criticism of systems is part of his general design, which is the study of the human power of knowing (*l'esprit humain*) not in order to know its nature (an impossible undertaking indeed) but in order to know the way it operates. This can be done, and it is a helpful knowledge to acquire because it can found an art of directing these operations so as to acquire all the knowledge of which man is capable. Avoiding error is part of the problem of knowing truth.

Systems are not to be condemned as such, but there are good and bad ones. It is important to remember that there is a good way to systematize, for the whole doctrine of Condillac will aim at realizing this ideal, in which regard at least it will differ from the plain historical method of Locke. Good systems, the only ones that should lay claim to the title, are identical with science: they start from observed facts. The wrong systems are of two sorts. First, there are the "abstract systems." Instead of starting from ascertained facts, these begin by laying down abstract principles. Others start from some supposition. This second kind of system can be called "hypothetical": their principle being a supposition, they themselves are mere suppositions. "In all true system, there is a prime fact, a fact that is its beginning and which, for this very reason, should be called *principle,* for *principle* and *beginning* are two words that primarily mean the same thing. Suppositions are but suspicions, and if we need to make some, we are doomed to grope our way. Since suppositions are but suspicions, they are not observed facts; so they cannot be the principle or the beginning of a system, for then the whole system would reduce itself to a suspicion."

Suspicions, or suppositions, cannot become principles of any true system, but they have their part to play in the quest for truth, for they are the principle, or beginning, of the means at our disposal to find the beginning, or principle, of the system.

A similar remark accounts for the multiplication of "abstract systems." Abstraction is indeed a necessary operation of the mind. Rightly used, it enables us to gather particular facts into classes, and since these classes themselves can be ordered according to their respective degrees of generality, we find there an abridged way to take stock of our cognitions; the more general the abstraction, the more

abridged the summary. For instance, *being* is a short way to signify all that which is. But here again a common mistake must be avoided: One should not mistake the principles of the representation of acquired knowledge for the principles of the acquisition of knowledge; they are two different things.

Abstract systems rest upon the belief that God, in creating our minds, endowed them with certain principles, and that the whole of human knowledge can be deduced from them. In fact, nothing can be deduced from such principles. Suppose we start from a principle like *all that which is, is;* or from *it is impossible for a thing to be and not to be at the same time;* where do we go from there? No knowledge has ever been acquired from such beginnings. In order to give such principles some appearance of usefulness, one often starts from a proposition true in some cases and to which one ascribes universal validity. For instance, it is often true that "one can affirm of a thing what is included in the idea we have of the thing"; so the Cartesians lay it down as a principle; still, this is not always true, for most of our ideas are only partial ideas, and what is "true" of such ideas may turn out to have no validity at all. The Cartesians made great use of this principle, and it led them to costly mistakes.

All abstract systems have in common one terrible defect: their uselessness. If a man is lost in a labyrinth, will he lay down general principles concerning what to do in such cases if he wants out? Such is precisely our human lot.

> We are born in the middle of a labyrinth wherein a thousand turns and returns are indicated only to lead us to error; if there is a way to truth, it does not show first; it often least looks like the one to be trusted. We could not be too cautious. Let us go slowly. Let us carefully examine all our steps, and know them so well that we always be able to retrace them. It is more important for us to find ourselves back where we were at first than too lightly to imagine ourselves out of the labyrinth.

The Cartesian precept that one always is better off anywhere else than in the middle of a forest meets here with rebuke. Condillac knows something worse than merely to be in the middle of a forest; it is believing oneself out of it when still there.

Judged on the strength of these principles, the great systems of the seventeenth century became for Condillac an easy target. Their main errors followed from the common prejudice that there are innate ideas. This notion is particularly harmful because it makes it so easy to justify any so-called principle of human knowledge; for example, the erroneous Cartesian principle already mentioned, that *all that which is included in the clear and distinct idea of a thing can be truthfully affirmed of it;* for example again, Malebranche's peculiar way of distinguishing understanding and will by resorting to the abstract principle that *ideas and inclinations are to the soul as figures and motion are to matter.*

Generally speaking, there are two perils to avoid in a system: the one is to assume the phenomena one intends to explain; the other is to explain them by means of principles that are not clearer than the phenomena themselves. If Descartes made the first mistake, Leibnitz has made the second. Such is clearly the case when he accounted for extended substance by describing it as composed of inextended substances, without clearly saying what an inextended substance actually is. Leibnitz does clearly say what his "monads" are not, but he fails to say what they are. They are not extended, that is clear; but when he adds they are "forces," this is not clear. He does not clearly say what such forces are, nor why they should have perceptions, nor what such perceptions should be, nor why there should be in each monad an infinity of perceptions representing the universe.

If one wants to give a tangible example of the way abstract systems are made and of the errors to which they lead, "no work is better calculated for it than that of Spinoza." The title of his *Ethics* announces that the work is "geometrically demonstrated." Two conditions are required for that kind of demonstration, clarity of the ideas and precision in the meaning of the words. Not one of Spinoza's definitions meets these requirements. What is it, for a thing, to be *causa sui?* No thing can be cause of itself, for the reason that, in order to cause, a cause has to be distinct from its effect. Since Spinoza intends to prove that there is only one single substance, it would seem important to define exactly the meaning of the word, but that is something neither Spinoza nor any other philosopher will ever be able to do. Let them try. "Substance" is *that which* is in itself; or *that which* subsists by itself (as the scholastics would say); or *that which* can be conceived independently from any other thing (this would be Descartes); or again, *that which* preserves essential determinations and essential attributes while its modes vary and succeed one another (this is in Wolff's style); in all these definitions, do not the words *that which* point out some unknown and indeterminate subject? Whoever heard a geometer say: A circle is *that which* is this and that? They say at least this much, that a circle *is a figure* which is such, or which has such and such properties. In defining substance as he does, Spinoza merely acknowledges that he does not know what is the subject of the properties he attributes to it.

Condillac has well observed that the famous words of Newton, *hypotheses non fingo,* cannot be taken absolutely. In seeking after truth, the mind cannot avoid making suppositions, but suppositions should be of such nature that their verification be possible, and in no case should any of them be used as a principle until it is verified. On this problem, Chapter XII of Condillac's *Essay,* "On Hypotheses," and the following one, "On the Genius of Those who in Order to Reach up to the Nature of Things, Make Abstract Systems or Gratuitous Hypotheses," are a condemnation of the arbitrariness of Cartesian physics as contrasted with the solidity of the science of Newton; in common with the whole French eighteenth century, Condillac sides with Newton against Descartes.

To conclude, let it be recalled that Condillac is not condemning systems as such. On the contrary, his point is that "abstract systems" (i. e., systems whose principles are mere abstractions) do not properly deserve the title of systems. The essential requirement for constructing systems is sufficient observation to grasp the way phenomena condition one another. In no case can we hope to start from absolutely unconditioned conditions; in the last analysis, "the best principles one can have in physics, are phenomena that explain other phenomena, but which themselves hang on causes unknown."

Condillac's own ambition was to achieve a system of metaphysics whose object would be "to go to the origin of our ideas, to observe the way they combine and how we should conduct them in order to acquire all the intelligence of which we are capable." So the "nature" of understanding is not at stake. On the other hand, and in the this Condillac shows himself a disciple of Descartes more than of his beloved Locke, his "design is *to reduce to one single principle all that concerns human understanding.*" That principle will be neither a vague proposition nor an abstract maxim, but rather a duly ascertained experience, of which all the consequences will be confirmed by new experiences.

That initial fact (beginning; i.e., principle) is sensation. This is of course no new discovery. Aristotle had said that all knowledge comes through the senses, but then he immediately proceeded to describe an entirely different source of knowledge which he called intellect. In modern times, Bacon had seen the importance of the principle; the Cartesians scorned it because they could see in it only the use the Peripatetics had made of it; at last Locke grasped it and, says Condillac, was the first to *demonstrate* it. For Condillac this statement has a very precise meaning. It signifies that, to his perpetual honor, Locke has been the first philosopher to demonstrate that *there are no such things as innate ideas*. The point was of capital importance, for to prove that there are no innate ideas is, by the same token, to prove that all knowledge indeed comes from sense.

The *Essay* of Locke nevertheless suffers from serious defects. It is the intention of Condillac to remedy the most serious of all. In his own **Essay on the Origin of Human Knowledges,** Condillac points out, from the very title, the point neglected by Locke and which he himself intends to clear up: How do all our cognitions arise from sense knowledge?

In saying that all knowledge comes from sense, Locke meant to say that there was nothing in understanding that had not first been in sense, yet he never doubted the distinction between sense and understanding. This is so true that he emphasizes that these constitute *two sources of* human knowledge. This belief in the initial duality of our knowing powers is what made it impossible for Locke to achieve a really unified "system" of human knowledge; the aim and scope of Condillac's own philosophy will be to remove that duality. When Locke said that all comes to intellect from sense, Leibnitz answered yes, except intellect itself. In the light of his own principles, Locke really could offer no reply. The doctrine of Condillac will avoid this pitfall, for he intends to prove that intellect itself comes from sense; for what comes from sense is sensation, and intellect is nothing but *transformed sensation.* In other words, in showing that "the origin of human knowledge" is sensation, and sensation *alone,* Condillac was to wipe out intellect as a distinct power of the soul; his aim was to bring to completion the task Locke had left incomplete.

Condillac has often stressed the difference between his method and that of Descartes. The two doctrines, he says, diverge from their very beginnings. Descartes begins by the methodical doubt; that is to say, by deliberately holding for uncertain or false all his previous cognitions, but he does not really ask himself of what they are made up. The result is that, at the end of his doubt, his ideas themselves have been left uncriticized. For instance, Descartes doubts that two and two are four or that man is a rational animal, but though he doubts those propositions, he does not question the ideas they correlate: two, four, man, animal, and rational. Since error mostly arises from badly formed ideas, the method of Descartes does not permit us to redress them. On the contrary, Condillac's method makes it possible to decompose ideas into their elements. These elements are sensations, so, instead of saying with Descartes that he will reduce our knowledge to the ideas that are the simplest, he contents himself with starting from the simplest ideas *transmitted to us by sense.* These are no abstract notions; each sensation is a particular fact. They are, so to speak, the materials out of which human knowledge is made.

Since they are facts, sensations should be taken at their face value. Judgments about sensations may be erroneous. I may err in saying that a tower is round, while it simply appears to be round; but these errors of attribution can be corrected. In themselves, sensations are sound material for the building up of knowledge. In themselves, and despite what Cartesians say to the contrary, sensations are clear and distinct; our ideas of extension, lines, angles, figures—in short, all those that constitute the object of geometry—contain nothing deceptive; in themselves, they deserve to be trusted. They likewise deserve to be trusted as witnesses to the existence of a world distinct from us. Condillac posits the existence of the external world as an immediate datum of sense perception.

What is sensation? Condillac seems to use the words "sensation" and "perception" indiscriminately. Both words mean to him that which is immediately grasped by sense. Some perceptions are stronger, others less strong, and a large number of them are so weak that they are immediately forgotten, but none of them is unconscious. Condillac will have nothing to do with Leibnitz' *petites perceptions.* The notion of an unperceived perception is a contradiction in terms.

Starting from any such sensation or perception, the genealogy of the operations of the mind can be reconstructed.

At the beginning there is in the soul one single perception which is but an impression received from the presence of some object. Considered as warning the soul of its presence, this sensation is called *consciousness.* Perception and consciousness are one and the same operation called by two names. Sensations are more or less intense; if my perception of one of them is such that it seems to be the only one of which I am conscious at the moment, *attention* comes into action. Such strong impressions usually reappear later on in the soul; a thus-reappearing sensation is

called *reminiscence.* "Consciousness so to speak says to the soul: here is a perception; attention says, here is a perception which is the only one you have; reminiscence says: here is a perception you have already had."

The first effect of attention is to cause perceptions to subsist in the mind even in the absence of the objects which caused them. Sensations are usually preserved in the same order in which they have been perceived. Hence a sort of bond (later called "association") between perceptions, and this bond becomes the origin of other operations.

These later operations are three: The first is *imagination,* which takes place when, by the force alone of the bond established between a perception and its object, this perception reappears at the sight of its object. In other cases, the perception itself does not reappear whole, but only its name and the abstract notion that it refers to a perceived object seen somewhere, say a "flower"; such an operation is *memory.* A third operation follows from the bond established by attention between our ideas; it consists in uninterruptedly keeping present to the mind the perception, or the name, or the circumstances of a sensation whose object has just disappeared. This is called *contemplation.* It is related either to imagination, if it preserves perception itself; or to memory, if it preserves the name or the circumstances only.

Having reached this point, Condillac finds himself confronted with his hardest problem. So far, all the operations of the soul have been accounted for by a kind of mental atomism consisting in the spontaneous associations of simple elements, the sensations. No active power, or faculty of the soul, has been brought into play. One might feel tempted to say that Condillac conceives the operations that take place in the soul, if not as resulting from a downright passivity, which would sound absurd, at least as manifesting a non-reflexive spontaneity. From sensation to contemplation, everything follows its natural course without requiring the slightest collaboration on the part of the knowing subject. Since he acknowledged the existence of a soul endowed with active powers of its own, Locke could easily proceed beyond this point. For Condillac, the problem was to account for the possibility of reasoning, searching for more knowledge, forming new conclusions and demonstrating them, without resorting, beyond self-transforming sensation itself, to any other principle of explanation.

He found an answer to the difficulty in a personal theory of signs and of the part they play in the life of the mind.

There are three kinds of signs: (1) accidental signs; that is, any object accidentally tied up with one of our ideas and apt to revive it (the sight of a man reminds me of a place where I chanced upon him); (2) natural signs established by nature to signify some feelings (groans, tears, laughter, etc.); (3) arbitrary signs, or institutional signs; that is, those which were freely chosen and have no natural relationship with the ideas which they signify.

When arbitrary signs were first attached to different ideas in order to signify them, this was a progress of decisive importance. In the first place, it liberated the mind from the necessary relations between ideas created by chance or by nature. Condillac considers as one of the more essential elements in the quest for truth "the operation whereby we give signs to our ideas," but, he says, it is among the least recognized. One might wonder how that operation is possible. In a doctrine where all so-called faculties of the soul are but transformed sensations, how can arbitrary signs "choose" themselves in order to attach themselves to certain classes of objects?

One looks in vain to the *Essay* for an answer to the question. On second thought, one should not expect it to be there. The *Essay* is built along different lines. Condillac is bringing the work of Locke to completion. He *knows* that it is possible to reduce the operations of the human mind into a system by decomposing them into their simplest elements and then recomposing them from there. The only thing one can expect from the philosopher is a truthful description of what, in fact, is happening in the human mind. All the operations of the mind *cannot be* anything else than sensation variously transformed; consequently, the question of the possibility of such transformations does not arise; they simply have to be observed. This is what Condillac undertakes to do.

Before the institution of arbitrarily chosen signs, he tells us, the exercise of "contemplation" (i.e., dwelling on a certain idea) is impossible to him, but

> . . . as soon as a man begins to attach ideas to signs he himself has chosen, memory develops in him. He then begins to dispose by himself of his imagination and to give it a new exercise; for, by means of the signs which he can recall at will, he revives, or at least he *can* revive, the ideas that are bound to them. Later on, he acquires more power over his imagination as he invents more signs, hence a larger number of means of exercising this imagination.

Here is where one begins to discern the superiority of our soul over that of the beasts. Their body does not prevent them from speaking; in fact, some of them actually do pronounce some of our own words. So the cause for their inability to think must rest with their souls: these are unable to attach their ideas to conventional signs. In beasts, therefore, sensation cannot transform itself by reflection.

By "reflection," Condillac understands the aptitude of the soul to recall whatever ideas it chooses and, dismissing the others, to associate or to dissociate them at will.

> That way ourselves to apply our attention, by turns, to diverse objects or to diverse parts of one and the same object, is what is called *to reflect.* This shows so to speak tangibly, how reflection is born of imagination and memory.

After all this, one shares in the feeling of relief experienced by Condillac when he says: "We have at last developed what was hardest to discern in the progress of the operations of the soul." And indeed, once endowed with the ability to apply reflection to a system of institutional signs which it can combine at will, there is no "human knowledge" of which a mind is not capable. Still, if one remembers that Condillac himself does not hesitate to speak of the degrees of "effort" required from attention according to the different classes of objects with which it deals, can-

not one help wondering of what kind of effort purely passive sensations are capable? Obviously, Condillac's "sensations" belong to a soul, and the "soul" belongs to a man—all notions this clever analyst seems to take for granted. One cannot help wondering whether, while he professed to follow the method of Locke against that of Descartes, it was not the spirit of system so powerful in Descartes that was carrying Condillac beyond Locke. Let us recall the way Condillac himself had defined the aim and scope of this philosophical inquiry: "to explain the generation of the operations of the soul by deriving them from one simple perception." He knew full well that this was an entirely new design, and he admitted it. He also knew, and said, "Locke does not seem to have thought of it." He might perhaps have added that the "long chains of reasons" so dear to Descartes, and so mistrusted by Locke, still exercised on his mind their power of seduction.

Condillac was never to go back on the positions developed in his *Essay on the Origin of Human Knowledges.* Far from it, and one might rather wonder at the remarkable unity and continuity of his thought. One reason for it was his extraordinary aptitude not even to see problems when he could not do them justice without going out of his way. One cannot read the opening chapters of his *Essay,* where he deals with the essential veracity of senses, without wondering why he should bother about their objects. This is particularly striking in the passage of Chapter I, 1, 2, where he calmly declares that there is neither error nor obscurity, nor confusion in our way to relate sensations to something outside us. How could one justify such a certitude *on the strength of sensations alone?* For a philosopher writing in 1746, this shows a callous disregard of the warning Berkeley had issued many years before.

The problem was placed under the eyes of Condillac by Denis Diderot in his *Letter on Blindmen for the Use of Those Who See* (1749). Diderot defined the *idealists* as those philosophers who, having awareness of nothing else beyond their own existence and their sensations, refuse to recognize anything else. An extravagant system indeed, and one which, to the greater shame of the human mind, is both the most absurd and the hardest of all to refute. Then he added that Condillac's idealism should be pointed out to its author; it would be no doubt most interesting to watch him try to refute it on the strength of his own principles, "for these are precisely the same as those of Berkeley." Does not the author of the *Essay on the Origin of Human Knowledges* expressly declare that, wherever we may go, "we never get out of ourselves, and it is only our own thought that we apprehend: now this is the result of the first Dialogue of Berkeley and the foundation of his whole system"?

This was to Condillac a challenge to vindicate himself of the charge of teaching principles from which an idealism such as that of Berkeley necessarily followed. He did so in his *Treatise of Sensations* (1754). Written with faultless elegance, this work begins by restating the doctrine already taught in the *Essay.* "Immediately after Aristotle came Locke, for one must not take into account the others who wrote on the same subject." Still faithful to Locke, he remains firm in his design to go beyond him:

> Locke distinguishes two sources of our ideas, senses and reflection. It would be more exact to acknowledge only one, either because, in its principle, reflection is but sensation itself, or because it is less the source of ideas than the channel through which ideas flow from senses.

As could be expected, there were many improvements in the new presentation of the doctrine, and in the Second Part of the *Treatise* the dangerous question asked by Diderot was faced and received an answer.

Condillac was clearly aware of the nature of the problem: On the one hand, all our cognitions come from sense; on the other hand, our sensations are but our own modes of being. How, then, can we see objects outside us? "Indeed, it seems that we only should see our soul differently modified." In the Second Part of the *Treatise,* the title of Chapter IV bluntly defined the question: "How we pass from our sensations to the knowledge of bodies." Now, since one can make extension out of extension only, and bodies out of bodies only, "it is evident that we shall pass from our sensations to the knowledge of bodies, only to the extent that our sensations will produce the phenomenon of extension. . . ." A carefully guarded statement indeed, since Condillac does not say: "to the extent that they will produce *extension*" but, simply, *"the phenomenon* of extension." But his very prudence was making it impossible for him to refute Berkeley on the strength of his own sensism: however hard we may try, the sensed phenomenon of extension will never be more than one particular modification of our mind.

His answer to the problem is none the less interesting to follow. Condillac first shows that the perception of a continuum answering all the conditions of space is possible by means of touch only. Next, well aware that all our senses seem likewise to perceive external objects, he proceeds to show that touch "teaches the other senses to judge of external objects." The conclusion of this demonstration, then, is that the sense which perceives extension is touch, all the other senses perceiving it indirectly by reason of their association with it.

The successive redactions of Condillac's *Treatise* prove that the problem is exceedingly hard to solve, be it only to his own satisfaction. "Questions well asked are questions already answered," Condillac once said on the occasion of this difficulty. To which he added that the remark was particularly true in metaphysics, where it is hard to speak with simplicity. From this point of view, the Second Part of the *Treatise* does great honor to Condillac. Imagine a statue coming to life gradually, he challenges us. Its senses open successively. So long as it only has sensations of smelling, hearing, tasting, and seeing colors, the statue cannot take cognizance of external objects. Even with the sense of touch, it would remain in the same ignorance, if it *remained immobile.* Unless it moves, the statue can only perceive the sensations produced in it by the air around it; it can feel cold or warm, and it can experience pleasure or pain, but in such a case it perceives itself only.

In order to make a man judge that there are bodies, three conditions must be fulfilled: 1) His limbs must be determined to move themselves; 2) his hand, the main organ of tact, must touch him as well as what is around him; 3) among the sensations he experiences, there must be one that necessarily represents bodies.

This latter requirement is of decisive importance. Extension is a continuum constituted by the contiguity of other bodies, and, generally speaking, all continuum is formed by the contiguity of other continuums. Consequently, even touch will give us no knowledge of bodies "unless, among the sensations it gives us, there be one that we shall not perceive as a mode of our own being (*une manière d'être de nous-mêmes*) but, rather, as a mode of being of a continuum formed by the contiguity of other continuums. It is necessary that we be forced to judge this sensation itself to be extended."

In other words, our knowledge of an external world can be accounted for only by a certain type of sensation, and that sensation must be such that it necessitates our mind to affirm the existence of its object. I am perceiving extension as an actually existing non-ego. To come back to our supposed statue, we should not imagine that it would pass from itself to bodies by means of some reasoning. In a statement of decisive importance, Condillac observes that "there is no reasoning that could make it to effect that passage." With exemplary constancy in his views, Condillac insists that the judgment "bodies exist" should be given in a sensation.

But how could this be? At the moment the statue of Condillac receives the sense of touch, it has not yet begun to reason. Yes, Condillac replies, "but nature has reasoned for the statue; nature has organized it so that it would be moved, that it would touch and that it would have, in touching, a sensation that causes it to judge that there is, outside of its feeling being, continuums formed by the contiguity of other continuums, that is to say extension and bodies." The demonstration of this thesis fills up the Second Part of the *Treatise of Sensations.*

A simple sketch of what is central in the philosophy of Condillac does not do him justice. As a philosopher, Condillac is at his best in the detail of his subtle demonstrations. Moreover, his effort to solve metaphysical problems by the lone resources of psychological introspection, with occasional appeals to recently made medical observations, has been rewarded, if not in the field of metaphysics, at least in that of psychology. Artificial as it may be, his method of mental reconstruction of the operations of the mind has at least helped impart precision to problems in which vagueness was prevailing.

It may be that the ideal of scientific knowledge entertained by Condillac did not fit him for the kinds of problems he wanted to handle. A passionate love for clarity and lineal order cannot hope to find much satisfaction in the analysis of the human mind such as we now know it. Condillac hated obscurity, confusion, and disorder in all domains. An *Art of Writing,* followed by an *Art of Reasoning,* then by an *Art of Thinking* and by a *Logic,* of which he himself declared that it was unlike any logic ever written, are as many titles witnessing to what was uppermost in his mind. To him, logic was one with analysis; analysis itself was a method taught to man by nature and served by an art of reasoning which Condillac promised to "bring down to a well made language." This philosophy of *homo loquens* had its limitations; nature refused to display the simplicity Condillac had hoped to find there; the results of his philosophy failed to be convincing, but an extraordinary number of other philosophers felt tempted to take up after him the task he had not successfully achieved. Condillac had a large posterity, which naturally blended with that of Locke, in Italy as well as in France. Associationism, which Bergson will still have to oppose in the philosophy of Taine, found its origin in Condillac's *Treatise of Sensations.*

Isabel F. Knight   (essay date 1968)

SOURCE: *The Geometric Spirit: The Abbé de Condillac and the French Enlightenment,* Yale University Press, 1968, 321 p.

[*In the following essay, Knight discusses Condillac's ideas on the origin and nature of language.*]

Condillac's interest in the methodology of science and philosophy led to a lifelong concern with the problem of language and with related aspects of human expression. The desirability of a genetic and structural analysis of all forms of expression follows from the conviction that the value of any inquiry depends on the approximation of its method to that of mathematical analysis, and that mathematics is essentially a language. In order to show how language could be made precise, Condillac had first to show how it had become careless, which led him to explore its origin and development. The resulting theory that both the language and the art forms of primitive times sprang from the same impulses and at first were not distinguishable from one another elicited an aesthetic theory of some originality in an age still dominated by the classical conception of art as imitation of *la belle nature.* Finally, as the crown of his linguistic speculations, he tried to work out a system of logic, based on mathematics, which would be a perfect form of expression. The sections on language, method, and art in the *Essais ur l'origine des connaissances humaines,* several volumes of the *Cours d'études* (the *Grammaire,* the *Art de penser,* the *Art d'écrire,* with the *Dissertation sur l'harmonie du style* subjoined to it, and the *Art de raisonner*), the *Logique,* the *Dictionnaire des synonymes,* and the unfinished and posthumously published *Langue des calculs* all testify to the extent and persistence of Condillac's interest in the subject.

Speculation about language was one of the many new, or at least young, subjects to arouse the curiosity of the Enlightenment. The debased coinage of scholastic and conventional language—Bacon's Idols of the Market-Place—had provoked a number of seventeenth-century writers, many of them scientists, into considering the problem of communication. In England, Cave Beck, John Wilkins, and Seth Ward, as well as Newton and Boyle, expressed interest in the possibility of a brand new mintage, of stable value and universal currency. Newton, Wilkins, and Beck

drew up extensive plans for a universal philosophical language (and were satirized for their pains in *Gulliver's Travels*), and on the Continent Descartes and Leibnitz devoted some effort toward the same end. Behind this new interest, of course, lay the needs and philosophy of the New Science. Medieval Latin, the only universally understood language available, was inadequate to the task of expressing scientific concepts with the desired precision. It not only lacked the proper vocabulary, but it was mired deep in the scholastic tradition and breathed a spirit which seventeenth-century scientists found sterile.

The changing character of philosophy also played a role in stimulating interest in language. As we have seen, the Enlightenment was the beneficiary of a shift in seventeenth-century philosophy from speculation about the objects of thought to speculation about the mechanics of thought. This change is apparent in the many works devoted to exploring the functioning of the senses, the analysis of mental operations, and the formation and constitution of ideas. The epistemological problem, with its ramifications, was a key factor behind the fundamental subjectivism of such speculation, but even more specifically, the interest in language reflects the inherent nominalism of the empirical philosophy. What the realist had believed to be things, the nominalist thought were only names. Consequently, the nominalist tended to limit himself to the study of names rather than pursue the things, which he felt would always turn out to be mirages.

For various reasons, then, practical and philosophical, critical and constructive, problems of language and meaning had become living issues by the end of the seventeenth century. The eighteenth century continued to discuss these issues and added another of its own—language as a natural phenomenon. Speculation about the historical origin of language was scarcely possible until two traditions had been discarded or modified. The scriptural tradition and the rationalist tradition both precluded, or at least inhibited, such speculation. According to the Bible, man was directly and supernaturally endowed with language (specifically Hebrew, traditionally believed to be the oldest form of speech) at the moment of his creation. Not only did Adam have the prerogative of naming the animals that shared his paradise, but he was provided with a companion and helpmate, and as Bishop Warburton disarmingly pointed out, without language there would have been no means of enjoying such companionship. Moreover, God gave Adam religious knowledge, which would have been beyond his understanding had he lacked words in which to express it. To consider the natural origin of language, then, required a willingness to abandon the biblical account, and this disposition was rare before 1700, at least in public. Indeed, even in mid-century many writers, including Condillac, felt constrained to use the story in Genesis as a screen behind which to put forth their own naturalistic theories, while remaining immune from censure.

The rationalist tradition also inhibited discussion of the origin of language, not because it presented an explicit and dogmatic theory of its own, but because of its general understanding of the nature of human reason. Man's possession of innate ideas, his ability to make varied sounds, and his impulse toward social intercourse, all produced, naturally, self-consciously, and rapidly, a spoken language. Language, in this view, is itself an innate capacity, the inevitable expression of man's innate reason. So directly does language correspond to rationality that for Descartes the fact that animals do not have language was sufficient proof that they have no reason whatever. Bossuet and Buffon concurred. It was not necessary, then, to re-create the circumstances in which language first occurred or to suppose a long period of gradual development. Man came, man thought, man spoke. The only problem language posed for the rationalist was the problem of clarity and exact definition. As a phenomenon, it is given in the nature of man.

If Condillac's interest in the origin of language reflects the empiricist side of his philosophy, his method of inquiry reflects his rationalism. He was convinced that man becomes man only through experience. Man is what he has acquired. He has acquired reason and language, and therefore the origins of both are appropriate objects of inquiry. Language is the gradual, sporadic, undetermined outgrowth of experience. Art, another product of experience, originated as the most primitive forms of spoken and written language, from which ordinary prose and phonetic script were more sophisticated offshoots. Even logic is rooted in experience, because the way to a valid logic is to "observe what nature teaches us." "What nature teaches us"—in this innocent phrase we have left the concrete world of empirical data behind and are on the high road to rationalism. Experience is equivalent to nature, and nature for Condillac is regular, mechanical, mathematical, and to be understood by applying to it the method of reductive analysis—a method which, in Condillac's hands, always turns out to have a remarkable kinship to rational intuition. One need not read much of Condillac's linguistic speculation before discovering that, as always, he may profess empiricism in his theories but has smuggled rationalism into his methodology—the hiding place of more than one man's unacknowledged metaphysics.

Eighteenth-century speculation on the origin of language deserves a more exhaustive treatment than has yet been given it or than can be given it here. Its novelty as a field of inquiry in the Enlightenment would alone justify such a study, but beyond that it affords an unusually fruitful entry into the nature of eighteenth-century thought, touching as it does upon a whole catalogue of characteristic intellectual problems: the search for the primitive, the priority of reason or the passions in human nature, the supposed universality of human nature, the meaning and value of human society, the role of convention in man's development, and so on. Moreover, the conditions of such speculation in the eighteenth century—i. e. its purpose and method—are especially helpful in tracing particular theories of language to the philosophical background from which they sprang. In most cases, especially before 1760, speculation about language was entered into not for its own sake but incidentally to some larger question. Furthermore, the method employed was nearly always exclusively a priori. In attempting to reconstruct what must have happened on the basis of certain assumptions about the nature of man, Enlightenment thinkers tell us much

more about their assumptions than about the origin of language.

Few writers before Condillac had any notion that man originated language by natural means, and fewer still tried to imagine how he did it. There were perhaps half a dozen between Lucretius and Leibnitz who said something about the natural origin of language, but only two before Condillac who speculated seriously about it: William Warburton, the latitudinarian Bishop of Gloucester, and Bernard de Mandeville, the cynical author of the *Fable of the Bees.* Condillac acknowledged his debt to Warburton. Indeed, a substantial part of his discussion was taken from him directly, sometimes with quotation marks and sometimes without. And he could easily have come across the work of Mandeville, whose ideas closely resemble Condillac's.

After the appearance in 1746 of Condillac's ***Essai sur l'origine des connaissances humaines,*** which contains the bulk of his speculation on the origin of language, the literature began to multiply. In 1751 Diderot published his *Lettre sur les sourds ét muets,* in which he discussed the foundation of language and the relationship of speech and gesture. The *Encyclopédie* contained several articles on the subject: Jaucourt's "Langage," Cahuzac's "Geste" and "Chant," d'Alembert's "Caractère," and Turgot's "Etymologie." In 1754 came Rousseau's *Discours sur l'origine de l'inégalité parmi les hommes.* Rousseau, avowedly influenced by Condillac although differing from him, considered the problem of the relationship between the beginnings of knowledge and the beginnings of language as part of his attempt to show the obstacles placed by nature in the way of civilization.

By 1760 interest in the subject was clearly becoming intense, and the list of books written about the genesis of language, either exclusively or as part of the study of primitive culture, grew longer with each decade, until nineteenth-century positivism made suspect all speculation on questions beyond the reach of observation. During its period of respectability, however, the subject elicited such works as these: Maupertuis, *Réflexions philosophiques sur l'origine des langues et la signification des mots;* Antoine-Yves Goguet, *De L'Origine des lois, des arts, et des sciences et leurs progrès chez les anciens peuples* (1758); Nicholas Sylvestre Bergier, *Les Eléments primitifs des langues* (1764); Charles de Brosses, *Traité de la formation mécanique des langues et des principes physiques de l'étymologie* (1765); Nicholas Boulanger, *L'Anti-quité dévoilée* (1766); Claude François de Radonvilliers, De La *Manière d'apprendre les langues* (1768); Herder, *Abhandlung über den Ursprung der Sprache* (1770); Court de Gébelin, *Le Monde primitif, analysé et comparé avec le monde moderne, considéré dans son génie allégorique, et dans les allégories auxquelles conduisit ce génie* (9 vols., 1773-84); l'Abbé Copineau, *Essai synthétique sur l'origine et la formation des langues* (1774). Voltaire also discussed the origin of language, without committing himself to any particular theory, in the articles "Alphabet" and "Langues" in his *Dictionnaire philosophique* of 1764.

The genetic analysis of the human mind, so well typified by Condillac in the 1740s, became by the 1760s a sort of quasianthropology. It was an inevitable development. The eighteenth-century conviction that the key to anything—reason, human nature, society, religion—lies in its origins, was bound to arouse interest in man's primitive history, an interest reinforced by travelers' tales of savage peoples, noble or ignoble, in the Americas and the several Indies. Still, even in the 1760s, interest in primitive culture was rarely for its own sake, nor was it pursued in the light of a genuinely evolutionary understanding of history, such as emerged in the next century. Rather, the search for the primitive was undertaken, for the most part, in order to shed light on some aspect of man's present condition and often to suggest ways of improving it.

Condillac's concern with the origin of language, however, reflects an earlier stage. The section on language in the *Essai sur l'origine* was not anthropological. He did not consider the origin or structure of early society; he was not interested in the realities of primitive culture. He was, however, engaged in a search for the primitive. But this did not mean to him what it meant to Rousseau, for example. Condillac was not seeking the underlying nature of man. He did not wish to assess the value of civilization. He was not a social critic. He had a problem—or, rather, three problems—to solve in his psychology of knowledge, and he sought the answers to those problems in the origin, nature, function, and development of language. First, he had to show how man, beginning as the passive object of changing sensations, could take control of his mental processes and become master of his understanding, Condillac claimed that man accomplished this by the invention of language. When he had words to stand for things, he could manipulate chains of associated ideas at his pleasure, and this capacity opened the door to fully developed reason. However, this answer raised another question. How did man invent language? Does language not suggest an innate rationality or at least some kind of mental attribute preceding experience? It was in an attempt to answer this question, which challenged his whole philosophy, that Condillac really became involved with the genesis of language. He had to show that language, too, could be explained as the product of experience. Finally, since he tended to define error as a function of careless or vague language, and since he also always asserted that nature teaches us valid ideas and good language, it became necessary for him to explain how error had arisen in the first place. This, also, led him into his investigation of the formation of language.

Condillac again took up the origin of language in the *Grammaire,* the first volume of the *Cours d'études* for the Prince of Parma (in which he shows, incidentally, that he was keeping up with current primitive studies by citing Goguet, De Brosses, and Rousseau). In the *Grammaire* he had another purpose in considering the origin of language: a quest for a model of the way in which language ought to be constructed. In the Essai his search for the primitive had been explanatory, the use of genetic analysis as the key to understanding a set of phenomena. In the *Grammaire* the normative use of the primitive prevails. The primitive, the original, the natural—this was the ideal, and it implied not barbarism or crudeness but rationality, symmetry, truth. Condillac's concept of the primitive was not based on empirical investigation. It had little to do with

a concrete primitive, with the way real individual men actually conducted their lives and learned to think and communicate. It was a primitive akin to the statue-man, abstracted from experience, reduced to a formula, freed from extraneous details that would tend to obscure its precise outlines. Or, to revert to an image used earlier, it was the potentially symmetrical gem hidden beneath the "unnatural" rough and uncut diamond of actuality.

This concept of the primitive as simple, rational, and universal accounts, in part, for the way Condillac went about establishing the origin of language. It is not that he did not try to be empirical. He used concrete examples from time to time, but usually in that most unprimitive language, French. Still, if human nature is at all times and everywhere the same, and if the natural products of human reason and experience must be uniform, one language will in fact do as well as another to illustrate the principles of language formation. Besides, Condillac had no more idea than any of his contemporaries of the real antiquity of man. He accepted the biblical tradition that Hebrew was man's original language. Indeed, no one in the eighteenth century, however unscriptural his outlook, was prepared to challenge the assumption that Hebrew was at least one of the original languages. By the chronology then used, Greek was a very early language, second only to Hebrew in antiquity, and followed in turn by Latin. This led to two assumptions about the formation of language: first, that its development from primitive cries of joy and warning to a large vocabulary and a complex grammar was extremely rapid, and second, that the structure of modern languages is really very little different from that of the most primitive languages. Therefore, since it could be assumed that the structure of modern language corresponds to and reveals the way in which language was originally formed, it is not at all surprising that Condillac should expect to find the genesis of language by analyzing French and Latin (he does not seem to have known Greek or Hebrew).

Condillac's method, however, depended much less on the empirical data he thought to find in French and Latin than it did on a priori reasoning from the fundamental principles of his philosophy. He began with a supposition reminiscent of the statue-man and of his "observation" of animals. He postulated two children after the deluge, separated from society before they had learned to speak, and he reconstructed, on the basis of his sensationalist psychology, the manner in which they would have formed a language. From that point it was only a matter of showing how, on his principles, the present and historically known states of language and the arts could have been attained. This method Condillac admitted to be conjectural. We cannot, he said, really know how it happened, but it must have come about in a manner similar to the one he described.

Language originated, according to Condillac, in man's natural, instinctive, and physical capacity for expression. In its most primitive beginnings language was individual, not social; expressive, not communicative. For the first language consisted of those natural and spontaneous cries and movements of the body with which man, like animals, responds to certain situations and expresses certain feelings—fear, joy, pain, hunger, contentment. They are not intended, at the beginning, to communicate these feelings. Indeed, these cries and gestures are so instinctive to the race that they can scarcely be described as intended at all. They are the individual's undeliberated self-expression, but they are not peculiar to the individual. The uniformity of physical conformation of the members of the same species means that each individual will instinctively express the same feeling or respond to the same situation with the same cry or action. Natural language, then, is a universal and instinctive expression of feeling through cries and gestures.

In order to become a language in the usual sense of the word, this instinctive expression must become communicative and deliberate. It must convey ideas from one person to another and it must be intentionally used for that purpose. It is necessary, therefore, to explain how man became conscious of the utilitarian possibilities of his expressive actions and how he developed them beyond the limited store provide by nature. The key to man's transition from spontaneous, noncommunicative language to deliberate, communicative language lies in three characteristics of the species: universality, sympathy, and the association of ideas. The first step was the instinctive sympathetic response of one man to the expressions of emotion of another just like himself.

> For example, the one who was suffering because he was deprived of an object his needs made necessary to him would not confine himself to uttering cries. He would make efforts to obtain it, moving his head, his arms, and all parts of his body. The other, moved by this spectacle, would fix his eyes on the same object, and feeling in his soul emotions which he could not yet explain, he would suffer on seeing his unhappy companion suffer. From that moment he would feel himself inclined to help him, and he would obey this feeling as far as he could. Thus by instinct alone men asked for help and gave it to one another.

By accident and instinct, then, expression had become unintentionally communicative. Gradually, through the familiar mechanism of association, natural cries and gestures became linked with the objects or situations that gave rise to them—the need for certain things, fear of particular places, animals, kinds of food, and so on: "For example, one of them, on seeing a place where he had been frightened, would imitate the cries and movements that were signs of fear in order to warn the other not to expose himself to the same danger."

Now these growing habitual associations both extended the range of natural communication and opened the way to consciousness of it. Man, reflecting upon his feelings and actions, became aware, albeit vaguely and inarticulately, of the association of signs with things and began the deliberate invention of arbitrary or conventional signs by analogy with the natural signs he had acquired by instinct. The final step had been taken in transforming unconscious natural expression into real language.

The nature of primitive language as it limped and stuttered its slow progress was concrete and crude. Man could not form abstractions. Since his experience was with individual material objects, his vocabulary was limited to names of objects, invented in the order of experience and need. The first words were names like "tree," "water," "fire." As man came to extend the range of thought and meaning to include abstractions or descriptions of mental phenomena, he did not know how to extend his vocabulary except by analogy with the material things he knew. Hence the first abstract words were figurative, depending upon an extended or quasi-poetic meaning given to concrete words. Modern languages still reveal this phenomenon: "Having always perceived motion and rest in matter, having noticed the tendency or inclination of bodies, having seen that the air is agitated, overcast, or made light, that plants develop, grow strong and then weaken, men talk of the 'motion,' 'rest,' 'inclination,' and 'tendency' of the soul, they say that the mind is 'agitated,' 'overcast,' 'enlightened,' 'develops,' 'grows strong' and 'grows weak.' "

Primitive language was poetic because of its inventors' limited vocabulary and brief experience with language. Primitive man would have been unable to hear the small differences in accent or subtle variations of pitch which characterize modern speech. His speech, therefore, was akin to music, although lacking a sustained melody. He spoke with marked rhythmic stresses and pronounced differences in pitch in order to make himself understood. The poetic and musical quality of primitive speech was reinforced by the continued influence of the original language of cries and gestures. Natural language had been emphatic, crude, concrete, and its early spoken offshoot inevitably preserved its characteristic imitativeness, imagery, and rough-hewn expressiveness. Moreover, in a society without writing, memory was vital in the preservation of solidarity and continuity, in handling down law and religion from generation to generation. Poetry and music, gesture and dance not only lent dignity to solemn occasions in the community but provided natural mnemonic devices to ensure that the legends, laws, myths, and lore of the society not be forgotten.

It was not long, however, before man invented a written language to convey to absent persons the thoughts that he had already learned to communicate by articulate sounds. The invention of writing, unlike the invention of speech, was in no sense accidental or instinctive. It was a deliberate creative act of man's intelligence. But man still had to work within a framework of experience governed by the influence of the language of action, and his first written signs were attempts to reproduce "the same images which they had already expressed by actions and words, and which had from the very beginning made language figurative and metaphorical." Inevitably, then, the first attempt at writing was the drawing of a simple picture. Although Condillac discussed—or, rather, borrowed Warburton's discussion of—the evolution of picture-writing into hieroglyphics, he was extremely vague on the still more significant development of the alphabet. He talked as if hieroglyphics naturally evolved into the running phonetic script we are familiar with today. But although the transition from the natural representation of picture-writing to the conventional symbolism of hieroglyphics was important and certainly required a creative intelligence, it is based on quite a different principle from that of the still more important phonetic script. The jump from conventional signs representing whole words to conventional signs representing sounds must have been an enormous step in the history of communication and indeed in the progress of civilization. Apparently, however, neither Condillac nor Warburton gave it much thought.

Condillac's theory of the origin and development of language was in so many ways a new departure (Mandeville's discussion being too brief and Warburton's too specialized to count as more than hints of what was to come) that it might be profitable to examine it in relation to the theories of his contemporaries.

The break with rationalism not only permitted but demanded the formation of theories of the origin and growth of language. Condillac and his fellows did not believe that language originated as an expression of reason, since man does not possess reason except as he acquires it, or at least realizes it, through experience. So while the traditional rationalists had a ready-made explanation for the impulse to language, the sensationalist had to find an alternative in man's experience. Condillac's philosophy did not permit him to take the evolution of language for granted as given in the nature of man. The imperatives of sensationalism and genetic analysis required him to explain just how, as a result of experience working on man's natural needs and capacities, language could have evolved as a rational tool. This meant that Condillac and the sensationalists, unlike the rationalists, were interested in the nature and history of primitive language.

The methodological character of Condillac's search for the primitive was, as we have pointed out, a rationalist's ideal—an abstract model. The substantive content of his primitive, however, was anything but rational, as the nature of the impulse to language illustrates. As we have just seen, in Condillac's theory man's earliest language of cry and gesture did not originate in a desire to communicate an idea, or even a feeling, to his fellows. He was instinctively, spontaneously, and quite unself-consciously expressing his own momentary moods and passions. Since there was no intent to communicate, the presence or absence of another person was a matter of indifference. Alone or in company, when primitive man was in pain, he cried out; when he was afraid, he cowered; when he desired something, he reached for it; when he felt joy, he laughed. The form his expressions of emotion took reflected no rational appropriateness but the physiological necessities of his own body. It would seem, then, that the passions, not reason, are basic to man, that the emotions of the soul and the needs of the body, not the logic of the mind, are the given elements of humanity which ultimately dictate behavior. Reason, along with deliberate communication, must be learned.

It would be difficult to imagine two thinkers more different in temperament and philosophy than Condillac and Rousseau, and yet Rousseau's intellectual debt to Condillac was great. From Condillac he learned that reason is not innate and that language originates in feeling, not in thinking. These were critical ideas, part of the philosophical foundations of Rousseau's decisive break with the ra-

tionalist assumptions of the Enlightenment. The idea of the emotive origin of language took on a radical significance for Rousseau, impressed as he was by the uniqueness and irreducible diversity of things, which it could not have had for Condillac, still persuaded of their uniformity. Condillac believed that he was giving full value to the concreteness of experience when he argued that man's first words must have been the names of sensible objects— words meaning "tree," "river," "animal." But Rousseau maintained that "tree" is already an abstraction at least once removed from experience. Man's first words, he argued, must have meant "this tree," "that tree," "this river," "that river." Moreover, there would have been no etymological connection between the words signifying "this" tree and "that" tree, because primitive man would not have known how to recognize and classify them according to their similarities. He would name them as unique experiences.

Rousseau, in his theory of the origin and development of speech, could not bridge the gap between the fundamentally atomistic character of experience and the highly abstract character of conventional language. He ended with an unresolved dilemma. If language was necessarily anterior to thought, so much the more was thought necessarily anterior to language. If the world presents itself to man's senses in discrete and unclassifiable units, and if man's reason is not innate and prior to experience, then there is nothing in the nature of things experienced to bring forth the abstracting and classifying processes which underlie rational thought. Yet we have rational thought and we have language. The point of Rousseau's paradox was to draw the lines between nature and civilization, to show that reason and language are the products of civilization and not of nature, indeed that nature puts such obstacles in the way of the development of these attributes of civilized man that it cannot be imagined how he overcame them. However the trick was accomplished, it was clear to Rousseau that it was done contrary to nature.

Condillac's insights into the origin and nature of primitive language, which impressed Rousseau even while he criticized them, and which are still current in twentieth-century speculation, were all antirational in character. The impulse to speech and gesture was expressive, not communicative, emotive, not logical. As a result, primitive language was rhythmic and highly metaphorical, chanted poetry rather than spoken prose. Moreover, when language became utilitarian, it did so under the pressure of need, not as a free act of autonomous reason. Survival value determined the direction of early language development. Practical reason, shaped by the experience of pain, the knowledge of deprivation, hunger, danger, and death, governed the order of word formation. The mechanism behind the growth of language was not logic but the involuntary, almost accidental association of ideas. Indeed, there seems little room, in this picture, for the pure light of reason.

If we give Condillac's theory another turn and look at it from a slightly different angle, we shall find reason once again. For even though Condillac denied the innate or pure rationality of man, he left that of nature intact. Nature, full of laws and purposes, makes use of man's passions to teach him reason. The haphazard irrational struggle to seek pleasure and avoid pain, which Condillac described as the dynamic force behind man's mental development, takes on a systematic, purposive, and rational character when seen in the light of cosmic planning. Man is moved to cry out by needs and passions which lie below the level of rationality, but the universality of those passions, the single human nature shared by all men, gives his blind inarticulate cries meaning to other men. Moreover, this common human nature, provoking each man to recognize himself in all other men, is the spring of identification and sympathy, the spontaneous emotional response that is the condition for making rational communication out of mere instinctive expression. Finally, the association of ideas, mechanical, habitual, and often arbitrary, provides the logical structure for emergent speech. Now the law by which the association of ideas operates is a mechanical and contingent law. It carries no guarantee of rationality. If x and y occur together, x and y will be associated in the mind of the observer, but nothing in this law provides that x and y will have an intrinsic relationship that makes their association objectively rational. It might be supposed, then, that a language developed on the principle of the association of ideas would also not be objectively rational but would be haphazard and arbitrary. However, Condillac's faith in the natural order came to the rescue. His universe of cause and effect, regularity and symmetry—still the rationalist's Great Watch—is sufficient guarantee that those things which man associates together in his mind are also associated in the nature of things. The humble and suspicious origins of man's reason—the animal, the passionate, and the mechanical in him—do not negate his reason, for all the cosmos has conspired to make it good.

It is not, then, surprising to find that Condillac's analysis of grammar and the evolution of language beyond the primitive was simply another version of the conventional rationalist theory. Man's acquisition of language precisely paralleled his acquisition of reason. Both reflect his experience and his reflection upon his experience, but his developing reason holds a certain priority over his developing language. Language, in Condillac's view, developed and took on grammatical structure as an analytic method—that is, as a form—*the* form, according to Condillac, of reason. Language, in other words, once out of swaddling clothes, is nothing other than the vocal expression of reason, just as it had been from its very inception for the traditional rationalist. Experience provides the content of language, the names of objects and actions, and the circumstances in which growth occurs; but reason—that is, analysis, analogy, and the association of ideas—provides the form.

The form of language means, of course, its grammar. Condillac, in his capacity of tutor at Parma, used his theory of language in studying French grammar. Grammatical science was in its infancy in the eighteenth century. There was much confusion about its aims, its techniques and method, and its philosophical presuppositions. The principles of comparative grammar had not yet been formulated. In keeping, however, with eighteenth-century interest

in language in general, there was a great deal of lively, although often incidental, discussion of grammar, in which nearly all the philosophes engaged at some time or other. The background of this discussion was the famed *Grammaire de Port-Royal,* whose principles served as the point of departure for virtually all philosophic discussion of grammar in the eighteenth century.

The *Port-Royal Grammar* supplanted two alternative approaches to the subject. Medieval grammar had been prescriptive in nature, laying out rules of correct usage which ought to be followed in composition. It was governed by two major assumptions: first, that Latin is the model language whose structure should be copied by all languages, and second, that the study of grammar, the first subject in the *Trivium,* is not an end in itself, because grammar shares with logic the role of a tool in the service of rhetoric, which in turn serves theology as the technique of disputation. There was also a postmedieval grammatical method that had arisen from man's growing awareness, in the sixteenth and seventeenth centuries, of the varieties of human life, thought, and behavior. The tendency toward cultural relativism that cosmopolitan experience fostered affected approaches to the study of language and gave rise to a new school of grammarians. Vaugelas' *Remarques sur la langue française,* which appeared in 1647, was the representative work in France. Vaugelas made the important and new assumption that languages are an expression of convention, not of nature, and that therefore there is no "right" order which a language ought to follow. A language must be taken as it is and studied empirically. The grammarian should not prescribe laws; his business is with facts—to observe, to describe, to verify, and to report them. "They are greatly deceived," Vaugelas observed, "and sin against the first principles of language who want to reason about ours, and who condemn many generally accepted usages because they are contrary to reason. For reason is not a factor here; there is only usage and analogy."

Against both these approaches to language stands the *Grammar* of Port-Royal, first published in 1660. The Port-Royal grammarians, Lancelot and Arnauld, shared to a certain extent the pedagogical intent of the medieval grammarians, but for them the teaching of correct usage did not imply either the belief that the study of grammar is a means to an end, the mere acquisition of a technical skill, or the limitation of the grammarian's function to the collecting of rules which are given in the tradition. The *Port-Royal Grammar's* primary purpose was neither to prescribe rules nor to report facts but to explain the structure of language, to account for French grammar on rational principles. The assumption behind this aim was the purest Cartesianism—that language is a reflection of an innate human reason. The laws of grammar express, point for point, the laws of thought. The most important consequence of this assumption for grammatical study was a doctrine which the philosophes accepted without question—that there is a general and universal grammar common to all languages, and that the peculiarities of each individual language are merely incidental and unimportant variations that do not obscure their basic and wholly rational underlying structure.

Condillac, as a grammarian, was well within the Port-Royal tradition, to which he paid deserved tribute in his *Grammaire.* Like the Port-Royal grammarians, he believed that the structure of grammar corresponded to the structure of human reason. However, having a different notion of the nature of reason, Condillac did not simply repeat the *Port-Royal Grammar,* which assumed an innate reason expressing itself immediately in a fully developed grammar, whose parts parallel the elements of logic. Condillac assumed an acquired reason. The development of reason was accompanied, step by step, by the growth of language, whose structure reflects the order of the acquisition of ideas. For Port-Royal the laws of thought must first be grasped in order to learn grammar, while for Condillac grammar should be used as a means to the understanding and mastery of the laws of thought. Grammar is "the first part of the art of thinking," because a language is nothing but an "analytic method."

To understand what Condillac meant by defining language as an analytic method we must return to his theory of the origin and development of language, as he does himself in the **Grammaire.** The language of action expresses ideas just as we have them—in clusters, several at a time. That is to say, the ideas which the language of words would render as a logical sequence—e. g. "I see a wolf; wolves are dangerous; wolves cannot climb trees; we must climb that tree immediately"—are in fact experienced not as a sequence but simultaneously. Moreover, when expressed with spontaneous gestures and natural cries, they are expressed simultaneously, or very nearly so. It is only when he has the use of an artificial and symbolic language that man can analyze such a cluster of ideas into its constituent parts. Thus the progress of analysis and the progress of language were interdependent developments in human thought, and grammar reflects not the given and static categories of reason but the steps in the evolution of the analytic method.

Approaching the study of grammar from this point of view, Condillac devoted nearly half his book to what he called the "analysis of discourse"—the examination of the symbols that languages give us for analyzing thought, or, in more conventional language, the "general grammar" that will reveal the universal elements and rules common to all languages. He undertook to subject language to a genetic analysis which would lay bare its fundamental structure. His starting point was the language of action. By showing how the language of action could itself be transformed into an analytic method once the symbolic principle was introduced to replace its primitive natural expressiveness, Condillac demonstrated the use of the three keys of language formation: analysis, analogy, and the association of ideas. In this connection he was much interested in the sign language of the deaf and dumb, which of course is as artificial and analytic as any spoken language.

The process of converting spontaneous expression into an analytic language appears simple enough where the names of sensible objects are concerned, but the process men followed to analyze their own thoughts in order to name their inner experiences seems more difficult to reconstruct. Condillac found the key to the problem in the figurative character of the names of the operations of the understanding: they were named by analogy with the operations of the senses. Here is his reconstruction of the development of the verb "to be," which, it should be noted, he defined as meaning "to have sensations."

> As I have supposed that the word "attention" was given to the action of the organs when we are attentive by sight, hearing, or touch, so I suppose that the words "to be" were chosen to express the condition in which each organ is found when, without action on its part, it receives the impressions that objects make on it. On this supposition, it is evident that "to be" joined to "eye" will mean to see; and joined to "ear" it will mean "to hear." This word will then become a name common to all impressions, and, at the same time that it expresses what seems to happen in the organs, it will also express what happens in fact in the mind. When an abstraction is made from the organs, "to be," spoken alone, becomes synonymous with what we call "to have sensations," "to feel," "to exist." Now that is precisely what the verb "to be" means. Reflect on yourself, Monseigneur, and you will see that it is thus that you came to grasp the meaning of this verb.

Condillac then went on to perform the same sort of analysis of the formation of combinations of words, such as the inflected form "I am," and to show how sentences are made up.

Having prepared the way by considering how the elements of all language came to be, Condillac turned to French grammar itself—the parts of speech, the conjugation of verbs, the use of dependent clauses, and so on. In this he was not at all original, and his work calls for no extended discussion. Acknowledging his eclecticism, he cited several of the standard works of grammar and linguistics as the basis of his own. Besides the *Port-Royal Grammar,* he referred to Du Marsais' *Des Tropes* (1730) and *Principes de grammaire* (1769), Duclos' commentary on the *Port-Royal Grammar* (1754), De Brosses' *Traité de la formation mécanique des langues* (1765), and Beauzée's *Grammaire générale* (1767). Condillac's only personal contribution was to eliminate technical jargon in an attempt to explain grammatical usage in simple and everyday language.

A corollary to the eighteenth-century faith in a universal grammar was the equally rationalist notion of a "perfect" language. Such a notion implied that once the state of perfection had been achieved, language should and could remain fixed and unchanging, for change could only mean corruption and decline. This idea was quite in keeping with the failure of the philosophes to recognize both the haphazardness in the history of language and the inevitability of continued change in a living language. Seeing language as the natural expression of universal reason, whether immediately formed or historically developed, they felt that a perfect conjunction of language and reason was possible, and that man, dominated by his reason, would then have no further need or impulse to change his language. In spite of the fact that some of the philosophes—Condillac among them—often asserted that language was more the product of convention than of nature, in their hearts they were convinced of the contrary. Since nature, in their image of it, implied a state of perfection, the conclusion was perhaps inevitable.

For Voltaire the state of perfection in language had already been reached in the classical French of the *Grand Siècle*. Indeed, it has been pointed out that all of Voltaire's observations on the subject of language and grammar were dictated by his concern to preserve seventeenth-century French unchanged. For conformation to reason and *le bon sens*, for clarity, purity, and resonance in all genres, the French of the century of Louis XIV, according to Voltaire, could not be surpassed and would remain forever fixed. D'Alembert likewise felt that French had been perfected in the preceding century as a literary instrument, but he advocated the revival of Latin as the international language of science and philosophy. Diderot had a similar bias in favor of French, but not necessarily the French of the past century. Although he felt that the vital components of a *langue perfectionnée*—namely, the analytic tools of a fully developed grammar and the aesthetic qualities of syllabic and periodic harmony—had already entered the language, its real perfection depended upon the achievement of universal knowledge that was still to come. When man had perfected his knowledge, there was no question but that he would communicate it in French: "French was made to instruct, enlighten, and convince; Greek, Latin, Italian, and English to persuade, move, and deceive. Speak Greek, Latin, or Italian to the people, but speak French to the wise." When knowledge has become perfect and cosmopolitan, universal grammarians and lexicographers will be needed to systematize French, to stop change and decay so that no knowledge will be lost. To that end Diderot suggested a rigid system of analytic definitions given in dead languages, preferably using quotations, so that corruption would not enter by the back door, through changes in the meaning of the words that make up the definition. Moreover, he recommended orthographic reform in the direction of phonetic spelling, a uniform, fixed, and logically based grammar, and a reactionary aesthetics that would prescribe a fixed and general vocabulary for all poetry.

Although Diderot placed the development of a perfect and universal French in the future, he did not really call for much change in the language. Both he and Voltaire were quite well satisfied with the French they knew. Condillac, however, was not. Condillac approached language primarily as a logician, which meant that the literary values that counted heavily with Voltaire and Diderot carried little weight with him. He was not impressed by the grace and sophistication of classical French, nor was he convinced of its clarity and precision.

As far as Condillac was concerned, all modern languages were only degraded remainders of the dead languages that had preceded them. Far from exhibiting improvement or progress after crude beginnings, they have lost the primitive virtues taught by nature. Condillac summed up these virtues in the word "analogy." Primitive language was made up of words formed not arbitrarily but by the strictest analogy with the ideas they stand for. Every word invented by primitive man had some kind of intrinsic correspondence to the idea it represented. Most frequently it was an imitative correspondence, as in naming an animal with an imitation of its characteristic cry, or an expressive correspondence, such as the naming of a human emotion with a word which seemed to express it by its tone or accent. At a more sophisticated level, words were formed by logical correspondence—that is, the extension of the meaning of an already existing word to a new but parallel idea. For example, if the language already contained a word meaning "to look," the phrase "to look with the ears" could be invented to mean "to listen," because both operations are characterized by an attentive disposition of the appropriate sense-organ. Another example might be the extension of a word with a concrete sensory meaning to a metaphorical usage that seems analogous, such as "a heavy heart."

On this basis primitive language allowed nearly perfect communication. Every word stood for either a simple idea known to all, because it was a direct and common sensation or perception, or a complex idea whose constituent simple ideas were clearly indicated by the word itself. Thus a high degree of accuracy was possible, for everyone knew what he was talking about in the most literal sense. Had languages continued to grow naturally, every language would contain within itself the whole history of culture, clearly recognizable. Etymology would be equivalent to an entire course of science, philosophy, and the arts. There would be no disjunction between words and knowledge. Every scientific or philosophical term would be totally self-explanatory.

Unfortunately, however, languages did not develop according to nature. Man became careless as culture advanced beyond mere necessity and subsistence. Nature's great aids in enforcing her commandments, the sanctions of pleasure and pain, no longer operated with such direct effectiveness, because men had the leisure to concern themselves with things irrelevant to their survival or even to their physical comfort. In these new areas of human concern pain would not be the immediate consequence of error, and so errors grew and multiplied, piling one upon the other, until not even pain could point the way back to truth and accuracy. Men became, and remain, content to say almost what they mean and to understand almost what others are trying to tell them. Language has degenerated into jargon, in which spurious metaphysical questions, which would never have arisen if language had retained its purity, are disputed. Language, in short, has become completely detached from both logic and reality.

There is, however, one significant exception to this bleak picture. Algebra, which Condillac regarded as nothing more nor less than a language, is still pure, exact, and analytic—the very model of what a language ought to be. This claim can be best understood in the light of three other assertions which Condillac often made about language—namely, that the art of reasoning is a well-made language, that a language is nothing but an analytic method, and that grammar is the first part of the art of thinking. In other words, language is identified with analytic logic, and there is no more perfect example of analytic logic than algebra. The solution of an algebraic equation is to be found in a series of analytic propositions in which the unknowns are extracted from the givens. For Condillac this is the only legitimate from of reasoning. From this point of view the parallel between the vocabulary of algebra—i. e. numbers—and the vocabulary of his ideal language becomes clear. Any number implies all possible relationships contained within it, and these relationships are extracted by analysis. Thus twelve equals six plus six, equals seven plus five, equals two times six, equals three times four, equals ten plus two, and so on. This series of identical or analytic propositions is simply the process of making explicit the ideas already implicit in the number twelve. Now if every word stood for an idea whose parts were as clearly grasped as are the parts of the number twelve, then all propositions would be identical or analytic propositions, and would be as absolutely reliable as algebraic equations.

Condillac illustrated his meaning by reminding the reader of his explanation of the understanding. He claimed that this was an analytic demonstration in the strictest logical sense, because, since all the faculties of the understanding are fundamentally identical with the faculty of sensation, his demonstration did no more than make explicit that which was already implicit in the idea of sensation. Ignoring the blatant *petitio principii* involved, Condillac even went so far as to cast it in the form of a simultaneous equation.

> Now to ask what is the origin and generation of the faculties of the human understanding is to ask what is the origin and generation of the faculties by which man, capable of sensations, conceives things by forming ideas about them. It is immediately seen that attention, comparison, judgment, reflection, imagination, and reasoning are, with the sensations, the known elements of the problem to be solved, and that the origin and generation are the unknown elements. These are the data in which what is known is mixed with what is unknown.
>
> But how can we separate the origin and generation, which are the unknown elements, from the others? Nothing is simpler. By origin we mean the known factor which is the principle or the beginning of all the others; and by generation we mean the manner in which all the known factors come from a first known factor. This first element, which is known to me as a faculty, is not yet known to me as the first. It is therefore properly the unknown element which is mixed with all the known elements, and which we must separate. Now the most casual observation shows me that the faculty of sensation is mixed with all the others. Sensation is therefore the unknown quantity that we have to separate in order to discover how it becomes successively attention, comparison, judgment, etc. This is what we have done, and we have seen that as the equations x-1=y+1 and x+1=2y-2 pass through different transformations to become y=5 and x=7, sensation likewise passes through different transformations to become the understanding.

The relevant implication of this exercise is that reasoning equals calculation, and words, like numbers, are, or at least should be, signs of exact ideas to be manipulated in various relationships. To show how this can be done, Condillac began the *Langue des calculs*.

The purpose of this unfinished work was to examine the "grammar" of algebra so that it might be appropriated by all language. Or, to put it more precisely, Condillac set out to formulate for the first time the grammar of algebra. He was, as he pointed out, approaching algebra as a metaphysician rather that as a mathematician, for the mathematicians do not realize that algebra is a language and therefore it has as yet no grammar. Only metaphysics can provide it with one.

Condillac based his analysis of the grammar of algebra on what he presumed to be the origin of all mathematical calculation—namely, counting with fingers. By showing how the fundamental arithmetical operations—addition, subtraction, multiplication, and division—can be done with fingers, he tried to get at the principle of analogy on which the language of calculation is based. Numbers, he argued, are the signs of ideas that man expressed with fingers in the prelinguistic stage of his development. If the names of numbers are to be truly useful, they should be invented by analogy with finger-counting. For the most part, the names of numbers do express this analogy: our number system is based on a unit of ten because we have ten fingers. Unfortunately, however, the system is made imperfect by the existence of anomalies like "eleven" and "twelve," which Condillac would rename "ten plus one" and "ten plus two." This is an abuse or corruption which has crept only into our decayed modern languages. More primitive languages, like Latin, still preserve the ancient analogy. Nevertheless, in general, even in modern languages numbers are models of the principle of analogy, which should be used as the basis for all language.

Condillac asserted that if modern languages could be remodeled according to the principles of algebra, they would lose the character of arbitrariness and capriciousness which presently disfigures them. This would be an improvement in taste as well as in communication, for he felt that what are considered to be beauties of style are only beauties by convention and should be supplanted with a more rational and natural set of criteria. In order to achieve this goal, he suggested that men should take lessons from ignorant and primitive people, who, because they are still disciples of nature, have not yet made an art of false reasoning and capricious language. Their words are as perfectly formed as numbers. They are genuinely signs or tokens of experience.

Perhaps the most surprising of Condillac's recommendations is his rejection of the idea, so dear to the hearts of his contemporaries, of a single universal language of science. The result of such a universal language, he felt, would be that while everyone could understand it equally, no one could understand it very well. For once, we see Condillac's rationalism tempered by a real concern for concrete experience. Arguing that even numbers evolve out of experience and are named by analogy with it, he asserted that all language must equally evolve from experience, and the analogy must be preserved for the sake of understanding. Since each people has a unique history and formulates its language as a reflection of its history, words from an alien culture cannot be adequate signs of ideas and cannot serve the fundamental purpose of communication. Condillac excoriated modern languages for their habit of borrowing words from one another—words which can have no analogy with the experience of the borrower. He drew a picture of the French pillaging from other languages like barbarians. "Our languages seem to be only what remains after ravages and devastations. They resemble our empires: everything turns out badly if it was badly begun."

Condillac did not share the dream of a single perfect language because his criteria of perfection were both rational and empirical, both universal and particular. All languages ought to approximate the language of algebra, and insofar as they succeed, they will resemble one another in the perfection of their clarity. But each language must also reflect the unique experience of the people that has evolved it, and insofar as it meets this criterion, it will be different from all other languages in the perfection of its force and integrity. Instead of one perfect language, then, there would be many in Condillac's ideal world—the difficulties of international communication being compensated for by the perfect understanding within each community.

Charles Frankel   (essay date 1969)

SOURCE: "The Experimental Physics of the Soul" in his *The Faith of Reason: The Idea of Progress in the French Enlightenment,* 1948. Reprint by Octagon Books, 1969, pp. 39-56.

[*In the following essay, Frankel critiques Condillac's empiricism, noting that "the consequences of the separation of [his] rationalism from his empiricism, of reason from experience, are exhibited most precisely in his theory of language."*]

Among the philosophers who adapted Locke's empiricism to the French situation the most important in developing Locke technically was the Abbé de Condillac. Condillac was regarded as having provided the semi-official formulation of the Encyclopedic program as it bore upon technical philosophic issues. Although Condillac did not devote specific attention to the question of progress, his "empiricist" theory of the origin and development of reason has an obvious bearing upon the idea of progress, and it provided the most immediately influential philosophic context controlling reflection on progress during the Enlightenment. A fairly lengthy consideration of Condillac's technical "empiricism" is necessary here in order to understand the interpretation of science which was fundamental in ideas of progress during the Enlightenment, and in order to see how the Cartesian idea of science, as translated into the language of "empiricism," continued to provide distinguishing features of the *philosophes'* ideas of progress.

The rebellion against Cartesian rationalism, and the adoption of "empiricism" in the tradition of Newton and Locke was often expressed in France as a rejection of the *"esprit de système"* of the seventeenth century, and the substitution of an *"esprit systématique."* The *philosophes* were op-

posed to systems based upon universal, abstract principles, like those of Descartes, Spinoza and Leibnitz. In place of this rationalism they proposed that systems be founded not upon general principles but upon what Condillac called "well-established facts." D'Alembert's statement of the issue was representative: "The art of reducing, as far as possible, a great number of phenomena to a single one which can be regarded as the principle of them . . . constitutes the true *esprit systématique,* which one must be careful not to take for the *esprit de système* with which it does not always coincide."

Condillac's **Traité des systèmes** was the most systematic technical exposition by any of the *philosophes* of their characteristic attitude towards systems. In this work Condillac expressed the empiricist ideal: "In every system there is a first fact, a fact which is the beginning of it, and which, for this reason, is called a *principle:* because *principle* and *beginning* are two words which originally signify the same thing." In contrast with "hypothetical" systems there is a type of system in which sets of "facts" are so organized that they support and "explain" each other. The ideal system is one in which one fact will explain all the rest. "Well-established facts can alone be the true principles of the sciences." Abstract or hypothetical systems are permissible under certain very limited conditions but they are not permissible in physics, where such conditions cannot be approximated. "Everything . . . in physics consists in explaining facts by facts."

This shift from "rationalism" to "empiricism," from "abstract" principles to particular "facts," also involved the surrender of the Cartesian dream of attaining an absolutely certain or complete system of natural science. "It is to expect too much of the progress of physics to imagine that enough observations will ever be possessed to make a complete system. . . . There will always remain phenomena to discover. . . ."

Nevertheless, despite the real vigor and the apparent plainness of this opposition to Cartesian rationalism, there is a question as to how fundamental the envisaged shift to empiricism was. Descartes conveyed to the French Enlightenment the habit of wholesale doubt, and most eighteenth-century thinkers were indisposed to begin *in medias res.* Such perimetal figures as Buffon and Rousseau begin their works by adopting the methodological device of Descartes (and of Locke as well): they try to make sure that they are divesting the mind of all its prejudices by initially divesting it of all the ideas imposed upon it by its environment. The *philosophes* took it for granted that inquiry must be based upon an absolute and infallible beginning, one free from special interest or even selective bias, and they consequently perpetuated in their empiricism problems similar to those of Cartesian rationalism.

What the empiricist *philosophes* attempted to do was to substitute unmistakable sensations for indubitable ideas as first principles of inquiry. But this did not release them from the problems we find in Descartes. The Cartesian transcendental doubt persisted in Condillac. For example, Condillac criticized Descartes for failing to distinguish the psychological sense in which ideas may be clear and distinct from the logical sense, and asserted that his own first principles were psychological. Nevertheless, inquiry still began properly with the indubitable, the clear and distinct: and, fortunately, what was psychologically first was also a logical way to begin. "It is very certain that nothing is more clear and distinct than our perception when we experience sensations." This produced for Condillac, as it did for Locke, the well-known epistemological problem of the existence of the external world. In stripping the mind of all its ideas Locke had been required to account for the initial occurrence of ideas in the empty mind, and to do so he had invoked the prior supposition of an external world of physical bodies in motion. Unfortunately, however, the ideas in our mind, of which all knowledge is composed, provided no empiricist evidence (i. e. no "idea") of the existence of a material something outside our minds. The empiricist was in the position, therefore, of presupposing an external world, but finding that his conclusions and his empirical criteria left him with no basis for believing in such a world. In this situation, Condillac chose to demonstrate the existence of the external world *a priori.* He was of course not alone in doing so, but, as Hume demonstrated, the *a priori* proof of a matter of fact involved the surrender of a consistent empiricist position.

This problem is mentioned briefly simply to show that the shift from "rationalism" to "empiricism" did not succeed in avoiding the epistemological difficulties of Cartesianism. But what is more directly relevant to our present interest is that the attempt to get back to an infallible beginning gave a peculiar cast to Condillac's theory concerning the development and reform of human inquiry. For example:

> Because, in our childhood, we think in imitation of others, we adopt all their prejudices: and, when we arrive at the age where we believe we are thinking for ourselves, . . . we only think in accordance with the prejudices that they have given us. Thus, the more the mind appears to make progress, the more it goes astray, and errors accumulate from generation to generation. When things have come to this point, there is only one means for putting order back into thought: that is to forget everything we have learned, to take our ideas back to their origin, to follow the generation of them, and to remake, as Bacon says, the human understanding.

Condillac, like Descartes, thought that progress must begin with a sweeping rejection of received modes of thought, by a return to the valid ingredients of knowledge, available to any man at any time. That these basic elements were simple sensations rather than self-evident principles does not make Condillac's position seem less paradoxical than Descartes'. If a valid idea is one composed exclusively of simple sensations, and if all ideas begin with simple sensations, how does it happen that there are any invalid ideas? To say that improper association of these original elements is the cause of invalid ideas is no answer, because association is a passive response to the environment, and also because analysis—which eliminates invalid associations—is what we are always doing. "To analyze . . . is what nature makes us do at every turn. Analysis, which is believed to be known only by the philosophers, is therefore known to everybody, and I have

taught the reader nothing; I have only made him notice what he does continually." If we pick up our bad ideas from other people, where do these other people originally get their ideas? How do we get off to a bad start if only a good start is possible? These questions naturally arise because Condillac's theory of the origin and development of human ideas appears to permit ideas to begin only in valid simple sensations, and accounted for their valid compounding by means of a method we cannot help but employ. In other words, he appeared to guarantee the validity of any idea.

In fact, of course, there was a not wholly explicit distinction between the natural, and the actual, history of the human understanding, and it was a distinction of critical importance in understanding Enlightenment theories of progress. Condillac was proposing that we remake the human understanding by returning to a different beginning from the one which we actually took historically. The peculiar problem which confronted him through all his philosophy was to give an empiricist interpretation of norms. Past inquiry had clearly been in error; inquiry could be redirected on sound foundations only if the appropriate norms were employed. But in order to support these norms Condillac felt impelled to show not only that they originate in experience but, like Descartes, to demonstrate that they are always available to the mind of any man any place. In other words, Condillac afflicted his empiricism with the burden of a rationalist ideal of science, and made his normative simple sensations the unchangeable and universal ingredients of any idea. Consequently, just as Descartes found difficulty in squaring the existence of God with the occurrence of vague and unclear ideas, Condillac had the difficult problem of explaining the occurrence of error.

A great deal of the confusion in Condillac's position is eliminated only when we distinguish between two accounts of human inquiry, both of which are present in his analysis. The one is normative and "natural," and lays down the conditions for the development of true ideas; the other is a descriptive account of the growth of error. The first rests on universal principles and does not refer to any specific event; the second describes what has happened and appeals to principles which are not included in the psychology that guarantees that valid ideas will be achieved by the compounding of the simple sensations that come before the mind. Condillac explained why we make errors in terms of one theory. He then proposed that we cure ourselves by reminding ourselves of the other set of principles: we ought to go back and notice what "Nature" teaches us.

Condillac's history of human error leaned heavily in its details on Fontenelle's *Histoire des oracles.* But there was more straining after system in Condillac. To explain the origin of error he appealed to a principle of human nature and to the historical situation in which reflection first began. Men have made errors because they begin to think under the pressure of necessity, where they have to depend on guesses and partial observations. These errors persist after the original pressure is gone. Systems of hypotheses develop because men continue to use the same kind of method that governed man in the earliest stages of inquiry. The existence of hypothetical systems was thus the product of a confusion between the *true* principles or beginnings of a system, and the *actual* principles—the historical beginnings—out of which the system has been developed.

On the other hand, Condillac argued that systems of true ideas are developed by proceeding with sensations as the basis. He criticized hypothetical systems because they did not square with the rule that "all our knowledge comes from the senses," which can only present particular facts. In other words, when Condillac rejected the hypothetical type of system for the fundamental reason that it did not conform to the true order and generation of ideas, he was criticizing this historically derived type of system in the light of another type of system explicitly disengaged from the actual history of inquiry as he saw it. Condillac's criticism of the *esprit de système,* for all his "empiricism," was like Descartes' criticism of scholasticism: he employed criteria which had not been developed historically, but which were "rational," and superior to history, because they were eternally present in all minds.

This dual explanation of the origin of ideas persisted in the Enlightenment and produced a peculiar paradox in theories of progress. Turgot, for example, was aware of the paradox in his maintaining, on the one hand, a belief in progress on the basis of the principle that knowledge grows steadily more adequate as experience accumulates, while, on the other hand, he saw that the history of human opinion was largely the history of error. The paradox was sometimes extremely effective. Voltaire, Holbach, Diderot, and Jeremy Bentham turned to political use what Condillac had developed in a more restricted and specialized context, tracing contemporary institutions back to their origins in custom and usage, and so satisfying themselves that these institutions had no warrant at all. For in the light of their rationalist canons, the fact that something was customary, and had begun merely in history, provided *prima facie* evidence that it was unreasonable. The human understanding was to be remade by following a different path from the one that had been followed historically. Condillac's position was similar. His empiricism served a critical function, his rationalism a constructive one, but these two ingredients of his thought did not interact upon one another. His empiricism was not an instrument of discovery, and his rational principles remained uncriticized. The Cartesian dualism of *res cogitans* and *res extensa* persisted in the shape of the division between experience and reason.

At most crucial points, indeed, Condillac subordinated his empiricism to his rationalism. In his treatment of moral standards, for example, the paradox so characteristic of Enlightenment thought emerges clearly. As in connection with inquiry, the problem was the status of norms claimed to have the universal validity of rational standards at the same time that they are said to originate in particular experiences. Condillac argued that ideas of morality were traceable to specific sensations—namely, to the perceived conformity of our actions to laws. These laws are empirically "conventions that men have made." Nevertheless,

they may be justified by an appeal to Nature rather than to convention.

> The laws that determine the morality of our actions are not arbitrary. They are our work, because they are conventions that we have made: however we have not made them alone; nature made them with us, it dictated them to us, and it was not in our power to make others. The needs and faculties of man being given, the laws were also given; and, although we made them, God, who has created us with such needs and such faculties, is, in truth, our only legislator.

This could be interpreted as an argument in favor of accepting any existing law as the inevitable product of human needs and faculties. Being what we are, we can have no real choice about what happens. This was of course not Condillac's intention. Nevertheless, the fact that such an interpretation is possible points to the paradox at the core of Condillac's empiricist criticism of rationalism. Condillac retained the rationalist ideal, and consequently persisted in the separation of history from philosophy, and in formulating moral laws which satisfied the rationalist demand for the universal, the eternal, and the necessary. And similar consequences attended the theory of the progress of human intelligence. The development of inquiry was evaluated in terms of standards that were themselves sanctioned by Nature, which was beyond alteration. The standards invoked to measure progress were thus held to be apart from developing human inquiry, and supplied and supported by a higher authority.

As a natural result of the attempt of the Enlightenment to disengage itself from the supernatural and to lay down a program for human control of human history, there was a marked growth of interest during the eighteenth century in a theory of language. Language is a basic human tool whose presence is perhaps the most pervasive characteristic distinguishing man's social life from other natural events. In a theory of human progress, and especially in a theory that would explain progress as a human achievement, the theory of language held a place not entirely dissimilar from that which the theory of grace held in traditional theology. Among Scottish philosophers language became a subject of major concern; and in France Condillac developed a theory of language that made the study of the progress of the human mind primarily a study of the progress of language. Turgot made much of this approach in his reflections upon progress; we find extensive considerations of language in Rousseau's *Discourse on Inequality;* and Condorcet appends a long discussion of language to the conclusion of his *Progress of the Human Mind.*

Condillac both reflected and reinforced this trend in Enlightenment thought, giving language a place of central importance in the development of the human understanding. Locke's reflections on language seem almost like an afterthought; Condillac, on the other hand, made his own theory of language the distinctive feature of his improvement on Locke. Comparing his work to Locke's at the end of the **Essai sur l'origine des connaissances humaines,** Condillac remarked:

> I have tried to do what this philosopher forgot

to do; I have gone back to the first operation of the soul, and I have, it seems to me, not only given a complete analysis of the understanding, but I have also discovered the absolute necessity of signs and the principle of the association of ideas.

Condillac considered Locke's contribution to have been the introduction of Newtonian method into the study of man. Condillac attempted to carry Locke's attempt further and to find in the realm of the mind the same kind of pervasive single principle that he saw as the basis of Newton's physics. The sub-title of Condillac's *Essai* is revealing: *ouvrage où l'on réduit à un seul principe tout ce quÌ concerne l'entendement.* Newton had brought both celestial and terrestrial phenomena together in terms of the principle of universal gravitation. The whole of physics seemed to rest on a "well-established fact." Condillac proposed to carry Locke's suggestions to the same kind of consummation.

The crucial problem for both Locke and Condillac was to explain the emergence of reflective thought. Dissatisfied with Locke's resolution of the problem, which seemed to him to have departed from a consistent empiricist appeal to observed facts, Condillac had to account for the development of abstract thought (in which the mind is capable of going beyond the present sensation) while retaining the notion of a passive mind. His solution lay in the fact of language. In Condillac's account of the mind language holds the role which the principle of gravitation holds in Newtonian physics. The use of signs is the source of the capacity to recall past sensations at will instead of having to depend on the chance occurrence of sensations. Language allows man to control the contents of his mind. "By the help of signs he can recall at will, he revives, or at least he can often revive, the ideas that are attached to them." Reflection stems from this capacity.

Condillac's theory of language was of critical importance to his philosophy. He believed that it permitted him to account for the development of reflective thought consistently with his empiricist attempt to trace all ideas back to simple sensations in a passive mind. Condillac took great pains to show that language is not the product of a previously existing power of reflection, but that reflective powers are the products of language. He argued that systems of signs are constructed mechanically in the elementary operations of imagination and sensation—that is, originally from sensation. According to Condillac, language began in the instinctive cries and gestures evoked spontaneously by felt needs. These cries, in evoking in other persons sentiments of an analogous kind, were natural signs. When attention was paid to this automatic process of association, the sounds became words, used intentionally to evoke in others the ideas with which they were associated. Language was thus developed without the intercession of any mysterious power of thought inaccessible to observation.

> Through instinct alone men asked and gave help to one another. I say, "By instinct alone," because reflection could not yet play any part in it. The one did not say, "It is necessary for me to act in such and such a manner in order to make

known what I need, and in order to get him to help me," nor the other, "I see by his movements that he wants such and such a thing, I am going to give him possession of it," but both acted in consequence of the need which urged them on.

Once language had been evolved in this way, reflection was possible because words enable us "to consider our ideas separately." In his later works Condillac pursued the suggestion of his *Essai* and argued that "the art of reasoning, reduced to its greatest simplicity, can only be a well-made language." The analytic method of decomposing ideas into the simple sensations of which they consist results in exhibiting the fact that the progress of the understanding is reducible to the progress of language. "True analysis . . . is that which, beginning at the beginning, shows the formation of language in analogy, and in the formation of language the progress of the sciences."

Condillac's account, however rudimentary, and however speculative theories of the origin of language tend to be, is an illustration of his determination to be consistently empiricist, to employ no concept that does not stem from a sensation, and to eliminate occult and unobservable qualities or powers even (and especially) when studying the human mind. To make language the point of departure for a theory of reflective thought has the advantage of placing logical principles in a concretely specifiable context rather than in some super-sensible realm. Nevertheless, Condillac's empiricist account of language retained Cartesian elements that vitiated much of the advantage gained.

Condillac shared with Descartes the belief that the subject-matter of knowledge is such as to lend itself peculiarly and exclusively to analysis of a mathematical kind. This belief governs his theory of the progress of language. In his *Essai sur l'origine des connaissances humaines* Condillac declared himself a Cartesian in the specific sense that he too began with the simplest things. Reflection is a matter of breaking complex ideas down to simple ones, and then rebuilding. "In the art of reasoning, as in the art of calculating, all is reduced to compositions and decompositions." Condillac thus carried over into the field of "experience" the conception made fashionable by physics that the alphabet of nature is mathematics alone. In the light of this mathematical ideal he regarded the goal of progress in language as the development of an abstract system of signs, in which calculation would be facilitated as it came to deal increasingly with simple rather than complex notions. He envisaged giving "to all the sciences that exactness which is believed to be the exclusive portion of mathematics." The progress of science thus moves towards the elaboration of a *language des calculs*. "A more perfect method . . . is only a more simple language, substituted for a more complicated language."

The concept of analogy played a basic part in Condillac's system. Since a well-established fact is in itself singular and particular, it cannot function as a general principle except through the operation of analogy. For example, Newton observes that terrestrial movements may be described in terms of the observed "phenomenon" of gravitation. He then goes on to assert that the same "phenomenon" is the basis of celestial motions. In the case of terrestrial motions, however, he can observe gravitation, according to Condillac, while in the case of celestial movements he can only observe effects similar to those produced by gravitation. In this situation, he reasons by "analogy": since his experience of terrestrial events displays gravitation he infers analogously that the same principle explains celestial events. Analogy thus plays a crucial role in Newton's method, allowing him to establish a system in physics that meets the ideal condition of resting on a single well-established fact. In the last analysis, the formation of language, and consequently the development and progress of the human mind, rests on this operation of analogy. "Analogy: that is what the whole art of reasoning, the whole art of speaking, reduces itself to."

Condillac's notion of analogy was patterned after Newton's *Rules of Reasoning in Philosophy,* and the emphasis he gave to it was anything but unusual. Hume's is a representative statement of what the philosophers of the Enlightenment held to be Newton's basic methodological principle: "It is entirely agreeable to the rules of philosophy, and even of common reason; where any principle has been found to have a great force and energy in one instance, to ascribe to it a like energy in all similar instances. This indeed is Newton's chief rule of philosophizing." By "analogy" Condillac referred to the process by which one reasons from a present sensation to one that is absent on the basis of the principle of uniformity.

In short, analogy was "a relation of resemblance," based on the postulate of the uniformity of nature. And since reasoning in the last analysis reduces itself to analogy, this conception has a most important consequence with respect to a theory of language and the progress of understanding. All reasoning is ultimately analytic, and the progress of language is formal and dialectical rather than experimental. The progress of science is the explication of what is contained from the beginning in the simplest kind of calculation with the fingers.

> It is analogy that leads us from one language to another, and it leads us only because the new one that we adopt says fundamentally the same thing as the old one for which we substitute it. In the same way it only conducts us from method to method because each is present in the one that precedes it, and because all are present in calculation with the fingers. Therefore in order to discover the new we have only to observe what we have already found.
>
> So the beginning of all the knowledge that we can acquire is in the most common notions.

This view of the progress of science from "the most common notions" thus resembles Descartes' picture of the development of science out of clear and distinct ideas. Condillac's analytic method was concerned to display basic principles (or sensations) which were universally valid, that is, the ultimate ingredients of any possible experience. The meaning of these principles was established retrospectively, by leading them back to their origins in experience. "Insofar as we distinguish different sensations we distinguish kinds of ideas; and these ideas are either actual sensations, or they are only a memory of the sensations that we have had." Consequently, as Condillac argued in *La Langue des calculs* on the basis of his interpretation of "analogy," to invent is only an act of analysis. The analytic method does not lead to new ideas; all new ideas are reducible to those already known—"the most common notions." Condillac developed a picture of a completely formal science developing within the fixed frame of reference set by primitive sensations, identically repeated.

Condillac's empiricism can certainly not be accused of being blind to the fact that formal and analytic reasoning plays a large part in scientific inquiry. But Condillac misconstrued the role it does play, by interpreting it in terms of his prior psychological theory that all ideas are composed of particular sensations supplied to the blank and passive mind by the external world. Consequently, he failed to show the part played by formal reasoning in directing and organizing inquiry into matters of fact as yet unknown. The attendant consequence was of great importance: progress to genuinely new ideas became a matter of chance. The consequences of the separation of Condillac's rationalism from his empiricism, of reason from experience, are exhibited most precisely in his theory of language. On the one hand, progress in the sciences is wholly deductive. On the other hand, discovery—the emergence of genuinely new ideas, not entirely composed of elements previously experienced—must depend on the chance occurrence of new sensations. The conditions for having a genuinely new experience are uncontrollable. Condillac's account of the progress of language and inquiry emphasized the importance of experience, but it was an experience which could not be controlled purposively. Progress towards new ideas depended almost literally upon a "break," upon an intruding and fortunate novelty in the circle of repeating sensations.

L. Rosenfeld   (essay date 1972)

SOURCE: "Condillac's Influence on French Scientific Thought," in *The Triumph of Culture: 18th Century Perspectives,* edited by Paul Fritz and David Williams, A. M. Hakkert Ltd., 1972, pp. 157-68.

[In the following essay, Rosenfeld analyzes the influence of Condillac's ideas on French scientific thought.]

There is a widespread tendency among historians of science to look down upon the eighteenth century as a period of stagnation in scientific development, contrasting with the triumphant achievements of the great creative period which preceded it. Newton's towering personality is indeed such as to overshadow investigators of nature, who would otherwise have ranked as the foremost of their time and on a par with their great followers of the nineteenth century and of our own time. The main achievement of Newton, if we look at it in a wider historical perspective, is not what impressed so much the popularizers of his own time—his formulation of the law of universal gravitation, his experimental discoveries in optics, his vindication of a theological conception of the laws of nature. Above all, he initiated a new approach to nature, a new method of investigation of natural phenomena. This inductive method, starting from the direct observation of phenomena by painstaking, accurate experiments, and leading to a rational account of them, has since demonstrated its unfailing efficiency and power. It is the only method in human endeavour that leads to an unending accumulation of ever improved, ever expanding knowledge, which never suffers any set-back. This is not to say, of course, that it is the only way in which we establish relationships of lasting value with nature, but it is unique in this cumulative character, and the resulting certainty, of its acquisitions. For Newton, the source of such certainty was not in doubt: brought up in the Puritan ideology, with its deeply religious mode of expression, he naturally regarded the concept of a personal creator of the world as inherent in his natural philosophy, and saw in the divine origin of human reason the ultimate justification of the uncompromising rationalism that characterizes his whole approach.

From this point of view, one may say that the time of Newton, and above all Newton's own contribution, marks the birth of modern science, of science as we understand it, as the rational description of our experience of nature. No doubt Newton had a precursor in Galilei, who had a clear vision of the meaning of experiment as the source of our knowledge of natural phenomena, and of the power of human reason to discover the laws of these phenomena; but Galilei was still groping for the right way of experimenting, his mathematics had not the needed sophistication, and on both counts Newton was truly the innovator. As to Descartes' influence on Newton, deep as it was, it was more in the nature of an inspiration and a challenge than of a direct guidance. If any philosopher may be called a rationalist, it is certainly Descartes, but he lacked balance in his judgment: he tended to give rational thinking too large a part in the elaboration of a coherent view of the world, and to neglect the role of information derived from observation. As a result, his theoretical constructions about natural phenomena soon proved complete failures; the real point at issue, however, between Newton and the Cartesians was not, despite appearances, the contrast between their conceptions of the laws of nature, but above all the question of the method leading to the discovery and formulation of these laws.

With regard to the fundamental physical principle underlying the description of the world, there was no opposition between Newton and the followers of Descartes: all accepted the view that the material universe was a huge mechanism, a system of various kinds of particles moving in various ways and interacting only by direct contact. This mechanistic conception remained in fact unchallenged throughout the eighteenth and the nineteenth century, until it finally foundered against the problem of the nature of light, which was already puzzling Newton. About the necessarily hypothetical modalities of the mechanical world-picture there was much arbitrariness, and consequently much quarrelling: Newton dodged such fruitless speculations by his insistence on proceeding inductively to the stage which observation would lead to, and provisionally renouncing complete mechanical explanation rather than indulging in unverifiable hypotheses. It is on this methodical issue that Newton took his stand against the Cartesian advocacy of a purely rational con-

struction of the mechanism underlying the phenomena. The paramount importance of this issue was keenly felt by Newton's contemporaries and those that upheld the Newtonian tradition in the eighteenth century. The latter were no mere epigones: their boundless admiration for Newton was perfectly genuine; it was prompted by a clear recognition of the superiority of his scientific method.

As to Newton's opponents, Cartesians in the broad sense of the word, special mention should be made of Leibnitz, whose mathematical conceptions, quite independently of the philosophy underlying them, proved even more successful than Newton's. The notorious clash between the two giants about the discovery of the calculus should not be judged on the basis of the superficial course that it took; if this conflict arose and took such proportions, it must have been more deeply motivated than by a mere quarrel of priority. Indeed, we again see that it did not really concern the facts of the case: the contestants and their supporters knew perfectly well that the two methods, the Newtonian method the Newtonian method of fluxions and the Leibnitzian differential calculus, were essentially the same—otherwise, there would have been no question of possible plagiary. The real cause of the conflict is not difficult to establish, not by conjecture, but on the basis of actual documents, some of them only recently published: it was the opposition of two powerful temperaments, both of them imbued by the belief in rational thinking as the instrument of scientific inquiry, but disagreeing about the way in which this instrument should be handled in order to achieve a quantitative description of the phenomena. Newton was of the intuitive type: his whole conception of fluxion was derived from a visual picture of the motion of a particle on its trajectory, whereas Leibnitz was of the abstract logical type, laying the emphasis on the practical advantage of a neat formal representation of the various aspects of the phenomena by carefully chosen symbols, subject to precise mathematical and logical rules. The next generation, having assimilated these apparently conflicting approaches, was quite happy to use both of them and nobody would have dreamt of arguing which of the two was more fruitful or more powerful. But for the great pioneers, the issue was one aspect of the deep-lying questions of method, concerning which they held irreconcilably opposite views.

Thus was the scene set, at the beginning of the second quarter of the eighteenth century, for an exploration of nature stimulated by the impulse that Newton and Leibnitz had given to the development of adequate methods of investigation. The history of the following period may conveniently be divided into two stages. The second quarter of the century was a time of consolidation, so to speak, during which the natural philosophers learned to handle the new mathematical tools and refined them, while the experimental method opened up the new domains of electricity and "pneumatic" chemistry (the discovery of various kinds of gases, paving the way to a quantitative study of chemical reactions). Then, in the second half of the century, we see a new generation at work, fully trained in the use of the new methods, both as regards their technical aspects and their philosophical implications. There was no lack among them of powerful and original thinkers: the greatest perhaps was Euler, who came from the Leibnitzian school, but carried further, and systematized Newton's ideas: of comparable eminence were the French "geometers" who professed to be Newton's disciples—Clairaut and Alembert, followed by the latter's brilliant pupils Lagrange and Laplace—and the French chemists under Lavoisier's leadership. To get the measure of their achievements, one has only to compare Newton's *Principia* with the *Mécanique céleste* of Laplace, or the chemical ideas of Stahl with those of Lavoisier: the progress accomplished in those fifty or sixty years is quite comparable in importance and scope with the progress we have witnessed in the first half of our own century.

Against this background, Condillac is indeed a natural choice, for he is quite representative of the evolution of ideas about scientific method during the two stages that have been distinguished—the period of consolidation and the period of expansion and progress. Condillac is not a scientist in the modern sense of the term; he did not make any contribution to the scientific activity he was witnessing; but he did observe this activity with deep understanding, and managed in a masterly way to analyse and formulate the general methodical principles which guided his philosophical friends in their scientific endeavours.

The conceptions of Newton entered France rather late, because they had to overcome the formidable obstacle of the Cartesian tradition, whose influence was still so strong by the middle of the century that Voltaire himself, that knight errant of progressive ideas, had to champion the Newtonian philosophy in full armour. He was of course not alone in this fight, nor indeed the most influential. His role as a clever propagandist should not be underestimated, but cannot be compared with Clairaut's much weightier intervention: not only had Clairaut a hand in the French translation of the *Principia,* but he was the first to make a significant contribution to a problem discussed in the *Principia*—the problem of the shape of the earth—which went further than Newton's own treatment.

The Cartesians had one supporter of tremendous vitality, Fontenelle, who, as late as 1752, published a theory of the solar system based on an improved version of the Cartesian "tourbillions." Much more important, however, was the influence of Malebranche—I am not concerned here with Malebranche's theology, but with his scientific views, which are often under-rated: he saw clearly the insufficiency of Descartes' physics and did his best to improve it, without abandoning its fundamental principles. Now, the Oratorian order, to which Malebranche belonged, introduced this better brand of Cartesianism into their schools, in which more place was given to the teaching of science than in most Jesuit colleges: this circumstance accounts for the prolonged hold of Cartesianism on French thought. Indeed, even such a staunch Newtonian as Alembert betrays in his philosophical attitude a greater influence of his Oratorian schooling than he would have liked to acknowledge: in the preface to his *Traité de Dynamique,* for instance, one perceives a distinct undercurrent of Cartesian rationalism.

The interest of the French "philosophes" in Newton was not purely scientific; of course, they were able to appreci-

ate his scientific achievements, but (as clearly appears from Voltaire's *Lettres philosophiques*) they, above all, regarded his natural philosophy as a part of a wider intellectual and political movement that they had good reasons to contrast with the oppressive régime they were subjected to; hence their keenness in promoting Newtonian studies and Newton's natural philosophy. In the turbulent company of the "philosophes," Condillac, modest and retiring, stands out as a sharpsighted and acute thinker, grasping the essential points and expounding them with unequalled lucidity. His role in the philosophical debate was to discuss the epistemological issues raised by the Newtonian view of science. In England, this role had been fulfilled by Locke, whose *Treatise on Human Understanding* offered a systematic exposition of a theory of knowledge in harmony with Newton's conceptions. Condillac's first contribution, the **Exposition des origines des connaissances humaines,** had no other pretension than to introduce Locke to the French public—though it achieved much more. It was soon supplemented by a **Traité des systèmes,** which exposed the weaknesses of the metaphysical attitude common to Descartes and Leibnitz, and contrasted them with the firm guidance afforded by Newton's inductive method.

These two slender treatises, written with sharp precision and luminous simplicity, won him immediate recognition as the spokesman of the "philosophes" in matters of epistemology and psychology; but these qualities did not by far exhaust their significance. Locke had traced the origin of our knowledge of the laws of nature to sensations and abstract ideas, but he had left undecided the question of the nature of the latter; Condillac took this last step and showed that our abstract ideas could themselves be referred to sensations. This was a bold step indeed, which carried epistemology from what I called the stage of consolidation to that of innovation, implying as it did a definitive break with the idea of the divine origin of rational thinking, a possibility that Locke had still left open. Yet Condillac's thesis did not at first appeal to the materialists among the "philosophes": Diderot pointed out the danger implicit in it of bringing support to Berkeley's idealistic opposition to Newton. If, he argued, our ideas come from our sensations, they are somehow elaborated in our brain, and in this process become separated from the sensations and belong to our internal world; hence our rational thinking is a purely internal activity, without direct contact with the external world, as Berkeley asserted. It was this paradoxical conclusion that prompted Diderot to denounce idealism as the scandal of philosophy, because it was so difficult to prove its absurdity.

Condillac took up the challenge, and his answer to Diderot's query was the **Traité des sensations,** his masterpiece and a landmark in the history of epistemology. The argument he developed in this book is extremely remarkable, both by its logical subtlety and by the deep insight it reveals in an essential feature of the perceptive process. In a boldly dialectical way, he started by carrying Berkeley's thesis to the extreme, by means of his famous artifice—we would now say "Gedanken-experiment"—of the statue endowed with sensibility: beginning with the sensation of smell, and proceeding successively to the other senses, he showed that the statue could very well develop a kind of rational thinking, without being aware of any relation of this thinking to an external world. There is one exception, however: the sense of touch—we would speak of haptic sensations. The preceding argument holds only so long as the statue does not move, remains passive: this is its essential difference from a living being. As soon as we add the possibility of touching objects, which implies an active exploration of the environment, the spell of solipsism is broken: the thinking subject realizes that he is acting upon an external world. This tremendous intellectual achievement is all the more impressive when it is brought into relation with the modern development of genetic psychology: one of the fundamental features brought out by Piaget's studies of the mental development of children is precisely the inseparable union of the passive reception of a sensation and of the motor reaction it leads to, the building up of a sensory-motor scheme, which is the true unit with which our thinking, both concrete and abstract, operates.

The next work of Condillac was a direct continuation of the trend of argument by which he had established that there is nothing in our rational thinking that does not come from a purely material interaction with the external world. Buffon at the time **had** developed speculations about the evolution of the **animal** world, which seemed to suggest a separation of principle between animals and man, the animals being deprived of the power of building up abstract ideas. In his ***Traité des animaux,*** Condillac examines this question, and concludes, against Buffon, that there is no recognizable discontinuity between the behaviour of higher animals and that of man: it is in animals that the beginnings of consciousness and of our mental properties can be perceived. This was a contribution of great importance to the development of the materialistic view of the world, which Diderot and his friends were attempting, but from which Condillac himself kept aloof. In fact, Diderot's materialism remained rather ambiguous, since he was forced, as a result of Condillac's analysis, to extend the fundamental property of "sensibility" to all the constitutive elements of his material world.

In order to appreciate the scientific value of Condillac's psychology from the point of view of his own time, it is interesting to compare it with the views of one of the most powerful contemporary thinkers, Euler. As a mathematician and a theoretical physicist (as we would now call him), he dominates the eighteenth century in the same way as Newton dominated the second half of the seventeenth: the mathematical tools and the concepts of classical mechanics found in our textbooks and taught to students from generation to generation have the form that was given them by Euler. It is, therefore, important to know what opinions a man like Euler would have about the origin of the ideas he was so instrumental in shaping. We are fortunate in having from him a popular exposition of his view of the world, which he wrote in the form of letters, addressed to a German princess whose preceptor he was. Now, the psychology developed in these letters is very interesting, and certainly does not deserve the contempt which Alembert expresses about it. In fact, Euler goes even further than Condillac in trying to put psychology on a biological basis, by discussing the physiological processes underlying our thinking. Of course, such a discussion must remain very rudimentary and speculative, but at any rate he puts the question of the relation between our ideas and our nervous system. He fully accepts the thesis that our ideas have their origin in sensations which are located somewhere in the brain; he mentions the *corpus callosum* as the likely seat of sensations, the organ where they are collected and from which signals from motor reactions go out—thus he elaborates a physiology perhaps a bit primitive, but essentially correct (we might rather speak of the cerebellum, but this does not change the general picture). When he comes to the concept of *idea,* however, he is very embarrassed, because as a mathematician, he feels the need for a sharp definition; and since he has no basis for identifying any part of the nervous system with what we call *idea,* he introduces the abstract concept of "esprit" as an immaterial, individual element, whose role is to elaborate ideas and combine them according to the rules of thought. With mathematical rigour, he specified the properties which differentiate these "esprits" from matter—foremost among them being the impossibility of localizing them in space and time.

The dark point in this system was of course the problem of how the connection between "esprit" and sensations comes about. Euler plainly declares that the establishment of such a connection is a "miracle": this was the statement that aroused Alembert's wrath. What it amounts to, however, is just a confession of ignorance; unable to imagine any material way in which sensations could be related to ideas, Euler introduces "esprit" as a conceptual (not to say fictitious) representative of this necessary, but unknown link. What has Condillac to say about this problem, which he had also to face (even though he does not explicitly inquire about the processes going on in the brain)? He seems to dismiss it by the remark that talking about the "mind" is just confused thinking. This means, actually, that he felt as keenly as Euler the need for some clear conception of the relationship between sensations and ideas, and, like the latter, was at a loss as to what picture to imagine. Unlike Euler, he was reluctant to operate with such elusive concepts as "esprit" or "âme," which do not provide any picture at all. This difference of attitude illustrates once more the fundamental opposition between the Cartesian procedure which Euler followed when he introduced the purely ideal, but sharply defined, concept of "esprit," and the Newtonian method which Condillac favoured. At any rate, the comparison shows that the French philosopher was not unequal to the leading scientist of the time.

In the last quarter of the century, the intellectual movement inspired by the "philosophes" was on the wane, but a brilliant constellation of young scientists had taken over the tradition they had initiated, and was carrying on the exploration of nature with undiminished vigour. The impact of Condillac's theory of knowledge upon this new generation was profound, although it is not easy to document. They had little occasion to quote him (with one exception soon to be mentioned); but his influence is noticeable in their whole manner of thinking. In the field of psychology, in which he was a pioneer, Condillac had direct followers in the "idéologues" of the period of the Directoire and the Empire, but there was then hardly anything to add to his work. In fact, it is only in our own time that his views can be fruitfully taken up again in the light of increased knowledge of psychical phenomena derived from experimental investigation. Incomparably more significant, however, was the influence of Condillac's didactic writings—the course of instruction he wrote up for his pupil the duke of Parma. These volumes, in which he develops his epistemological considerations with the same wonderful simplicity, straightforwardness and clarity as in his original treatises, were the source from which the French scientists, all through the years of the Revolution, the Empire and the Restoration, received guidance and inspiration.

The most explicit evidence we have of an immediate application of Condillac's ideas to a scientific problem concerns Lavoisier's elaboration of a rational chemical nomenclature. This was a major advance in the development of chemistry, and was much more important than the analogy with Linne's system of classification of the three "reigns" of nature might suggest: for Linne's nomenclature was purely conventional, while Lavoisier's embodied his fundamental ideas—the precise definition of a chemical element and the theory of the acidifying principle, which mark the beginning of modern chemistry. It was quite natural for Lavoisier, faced with a chaotic mass of arbitrary denominations, to feel the need for a more orderly designation of the substances whose composition he was able to determine. Nevertheless, the emphasis he laid on the significance of this task, and the methodical way in which he accomplished it, are directly inspired by Condillac's teaching. Both in the preface to the *Méthode de Nomenclature chimique* and in the introduction to the *Traité de chimie,* Lavoisier invokes the theory of the function of language, presented in Condillac's **Logique,** for a deeper justification of the characteristic features of the nomenclature he proposes. In the framework of Condillac's psychology, language occupies a prominent position. Emanating somehow from the sensations, the ideas and the relations between ideas have in turn to be represented by material signals: these constitute the language, which therefore provides us not only with a means of communication of our perceptions, but with an exquisitely flexible tool for the logical combination of ideas. Hence, it is a true analytical method, by means of which we proceed from the known to the unknown, just as mathematicians do. A language, describing a certain order of phenomena can even attain, ideally, the same precision as mathematics: it then becomes what we denote as the "science" of these phenomena—"a science is a well-contrived language." Mathematics itself is a language—"la langue des calculs," as Condillac calls it. When one realizes that his conception of language, with all its implications, was vividly present in Lavoisier's mind, one understands the full import of his concern with nomenclature, and his insistence on the active part it could play in the investigation of chemical processes.

There is in Lavoisier's considerations on the role of language a remark of striking modernity: the scientist, he says, is like a child. The child has also to learn the language, and how to use it. In this learning process, he makes mistakes, which he corrects by experience—let the scientist take a lesson from the child, and do the same. We know more, thanks to Piaget's studies, about the acquisition of language by the child, than Condillac and Lavoisier could imagine, and this more precise knowledge only goes to support Condillac's conception of the nature and function of language, and to strengthen the comparison of the scientist with the child. The learning of the language proceeds in two steps: in the first stage, the child has to learn the correspondence between the words and the sensory-motor schemes they symbolize; but the great discovery the child makes, in a second stage occurring at the average age of eleven, is that the word-symbols can be detached, so to speak, from the concrete representations of the sensory-motor schemes, and used by themselves in an infinity of logical combinations. This abstract mode of thinking pays for its tremendous increase in speed and scope with the danger of losing in the process the necessary contact with the sensory-motor experience—a danger to which children and scientists are indeed equally exposed. Lavoisier has a lapidary formula to summarize the profound insight into our thinking which he owed to Condillac and had made his own: "faits, idées, mots sont comme trois empreintes d'un même cachet." Facts, ideas, words—three imprints of the same seal: is this not the wisest legacy of the enlightenment?

James H. Stam   (essay date 1980)

SOURCE: "Condillac's Epistemolinguistic Question," in *Psychology of Language and Thought: Essays on the Theory and History of Psycholinguistics,* edited by R. W. Rieber, Plenum Press, 1980, pp. 77-90.

[*In the following essay, Stam discusses Condillac's theories on the origin of linguistic signs and their role in the formation of ideas.*]

It is arguable, but it makes good sense nonetheless, to say that Etienne Bonnot de Condillac [1715-1780] was the first thinker to give systematic consideration to "the psycholinguistic question," as that term is characteristically understood today. Perhaps "epistemolinguistic question" would be the more accurate designation. The question entailed is that of the influence or relationship between language (in particular or in general) and an individual's mental development. It is a significantly different issue from that posed by so many students of universal or rational grammar in the previous century: the relationship between language, "fully grammatical," and mind, "fully rational"—a formulation of the problem which focused the genesis neither of language nor of rationality. Nor is Condillac's epistemolinguistic question entirely the same as the problem of the origin of language *per se,* one of the most popular topics of late eighteenth-and early nineteenth-century speculation. Again, it is different from the examination of **lóga** as both reason and speech among the Stoics and earlier Greek philosophers. The epistemolinguistic issue was, to be sure, adumbrated in context by sundry empiricist philosophers: Hobbes and Locke, for example, assigned an appropriate place to language in the sequence of mental faculties and operations. With the possible exception of David Hartley, however—whose *Observations on Man, his Duty, his Frame, and his Expectations* appeared after Condillac's *Essai* in any case—none had previously tried to work out the full range of consequences entailed in the correlation of linguistic and mental development.

Condillac was born Etienne Bonnot in Grenoble in 1714. Sickly, of poor vision, and slow to learn, his youth was unpromising, but he pursued theological studies nonetheless at Saint-Sulpice and the Sorbonne, only to abandon any active priesthood immediately upon his ordination. His formal education was spotty, and the man whose theoretical interests in language endured throughout his life never learned any languages other than Latin and his native French. Nor was his reading impressively extensive, but his personal contacts were of the first rank: the Abbé Gabriel Bonnot de Mably, the socialist *philosophe,* was his brother; d'Alembert was his cousin; Rousseau was tutor to Condillac's nephews—and their personal friendship lasted well into Rousseau's years of madness; and by frequenting the Parisian salons he had contact with most of the luminaries of the French Enlightenment.

Condillac's first book, *Essai sur l'origine des connaissances humaines* (1746) expounded and revised the empiricist epistemology of John Locke, already popular with French thinkers. His secure position in Enlightenment circles was fully established with his second book, in 1749, the *Traité des systèmes,* an attack on metaphysical dogmatism and the accepted rationalism and in general on the *"esprit de système."* The *Traité des sensations* (1754) elaborated the image now most often cited in the textbooks—an inanimate, insensate statue, endowed one by one with the basic senses and higher faculties (but not including language)—an image designed to give illustrative demonstration of the theory that all human cognition can be reduced to elements of sense. A *Dissertation sur la liberté* was published as an appendix to the *Treatise on the Sensations.* In the following year, 1755, a *Traité des animaux* was published together with a *Dissertation sur l'existence de Dieu,* anti-materialist defenses of the uniqueness of man, directed against the mechanistic interpretations of beasts as automata in Descartes and Buffon. Condillac was tutor to the Prince of Parma from 1758 until 1767, and while there, he composed a variety of works on grammar, logic and history for his student's instruction. These works were finally published, a few years before Condillac's death, and after numerous complications and some resistance to their appearance, as the *Cours d'études.* After his return to France from Parma, Condillac was elected to the Académie française, in which he was inactive, and later to the Société royale d'agriculture d'Orléans. In 1776, he published *Le Commerce et le gouvernment considérés relativement l'un à l'autre,* a treatise in the newly fashionable area of political economy. At the request of the Polish government, which wanted to use Condillac's work in public instruction, he composed his most systematic exposition of the "method of analysis," *La Logique,* which appeared in 1780, the year of his death. Finally, *La Langue des calculs,* which was published posthumously as a fragment, explained algebra and mathematics as exemplars of methodically analytic language. These very titles betray the persistence of Condillac's interests in language and mind.

Condillac's philosophical preferences inclined toward the English, particularly Newton and Locke, all of whom he read in French summary or translation. The subtitle of the *Essay on the Origin of Human Knowledge* modestly advertised it as a *"Supplement to Mr. Locke's Essay on the Human Understanding."* Locke was, to a great extent, "The Philosopher" for the *philosophes,* but the other British empiricists, too, were embraced and appropriated by the French enlighteners. Voltaire's *Philosophical Letters,* which first appeared in English translation as *Letters Concerning the English Nation,* popularized the school for Frenchmen, and Condillac's *Essai* systematized the master as well. A whole line of British empiricists—Bacon, Hobbes, Locke, Berkeley, Hume, many minor figures and earlier ones—had argued in varying degrees of generality that all knowledge, all contents of the mind, could be traced back to experience of some kind. Locke had argued in his own *Essay* that the full array of human knowledge was derivable from two primary sources, sensation and reflection. The former involved data acquired through any of the five senses, whereas the latter was described by Locke as an "internal sense," or the mind's awareness of its own operations. Thus Locke was a consistent empiricist—all contents of the mind are derivable from experience of some sort; but he was not a strict sensationalist—not all experience is of a sensuous kind. He considered sensation a *sine qua non* for reflection and necessarily prior to it, since the mind cannot be aware of its own operations until they are actually in operation; but Locke stoutly maintained that reflection is nonetheless autonomous, because its contents cannot be reduced to more primitive data of sense. Out of the building blocks provided by these two independent and primary sources, Locke sought to assemble all the most elevated and complex functions of human understanding and affection.

Condillac not only popularized and systematized Locke, he also revised him. Condillac objected that Locke's doctrine of autonomous reflection was an unnecessary concession, an inconsistency which weakened the entire edifice. It implied that there was something innate in the mind, incited perhaps by circumstance, but not explicable as a response to the stimulative phenomena of the world perceived by sense. Condillac tried to show, particularly in the *Essay* and in the *Treatise on the Sensations,* that all supposedly independent reflections are derivable as compositions from sensory data, since ideas are formed by a prereflective process of association requiring the use of signs. "The ideas are connected with the signs, and it is only by this means . . . they are connected with each other."

Condillac's emendation of the Lockean explanation of reflection helped bring problems of language and its genesis into the stage center of epistemology. Locke himself had devoted an entire book of his *Essay* to the subject "Of Words." Locke, however, was concerned almost exclusively with the classificatory and communicative functions of language, hence with its utility in scientific taxonomy and social intercourse. In neither context did Locke emphasize any role of language in the cognitive development of the psyche. Language served the goal of scientific precision in properly distinguishing genera and species *after* the mind had fully evolved the capacity to make such distinctions; and, on the other hand, language was assumed as something already given when Locke treated it as a means of communication or as a parent's assistance to the child's developing mind in the formation of general concepts. Locke sometimes spoke as though little babies not only sensed, for example, a cube of sugar, but as though they recognized it *as* cubical, white, and sweet, and as though the attachment of names were simply the conventional designations for such recognitions. It is in these regards that Condillac's approach differed from Locke's by much more than a point or so of epistemological schematism. For Condillac, the seeds of language, if not its full flower, were present and well rooted prior to reflection. Indeed, the whole mental development up to and beyond reflection would have been quite impossible in the absence of a linguistic factor—*signs*.

Signs were of such critical importance because it was in terms of the "connexion of ideas" (*la liaison des idées*) that Condillac explained the development from sensation to reflection and the higher faculties. The impressions made by sense upon the mind are not neutral or even in their force. Instead they are regulated, patterned, and brought into relief by the progressive operations of *perception* (the mind's reception of the sense datum), *consciousness* (the mere awareness of perceptions), *attention* (concentration on certain perceptions over others), *reminiscence* (recognition that some of the perceptions so heeded have occurred before)—and beyond these, *imagination* (the ability to revive some perceptions as recollected images in the mind), *contemplation* (the power to preserve "the perception, the name or the circumstances of an object which is vanished out of sight"), and *memory* (which retains only the name or circumstances of perceptions, because it is impossible to revive the image itself). The last group of these—imagination, contemplation, and memory—come into operation on account of the connection or association of ideas. But the mechanism of *liaison*, the "real cause of the progress of the imagination, contemplation, and memory" is the use of signs, which reinforce and preserve the associations.

The critical role of signs for Condillac led him to criticize Locke on still another point. Locke did not recognize the deeper epistemological relevance of signs, or of language generally for that matter, because he saw the main purpose of language in the communication of already formed ideas and overlooked its role in the very process whereby such ideas are formed. According to Condillac, the function of signs is so basic that deaf-mutes or isolated children would, in order to reason, have to contrive some system of internal signs. He distinguished three types of signs: *accidental* (when the circumstances or part of an experience evokes association with the whole), *natural* (cries or gestures expressive of passionate response), and *instituted* (conventional words or other arbitrary means of signification). In imagination and contemplation all three kinds may be operative, and for memory all three are necessary. Thus, the brutes, who have no instituted signs, cannot advance beyond reminiscence or, at most, imagination. The use of signs puts the mind in command of itself and raises it to a human level, so that it is no longer a merely passive

receiver. Instead, it can recall ideas at will, compound and decompound them, distinguish and abstract and compare, affirm and deny, and ultimately reason. On the other hand, the necessity for signs stems, in part, from the limitations of human understanding: signs assist the finite mind when ideas involve such a manifold of qualities that it is impossible to grasp them all at once. Condillac even remarked that an infinite being would have no need of any language or sign system. It is only through the use of signs that mere consciousness can pass over into meaningful reflection, and that the mind can become aware of its true strengths as well as its limits.

The role assigned to linguistic signs in Condillac's epistemological system tended to force the question of language origin. If the recourse to signs is already required at the earliest stages of the evolution of the human mind, then how did the use of signs itself develop? The *Essay* was published during a decade and early in a period somewhat longer than a century when speculations about the first beginnings of language were rife. Vico, La Mettrie, Rousseau, Herder, Hamann, Fichte, the Schlegels, British romanticists, French conservatives, numerous comparative linguists, and pioneering evolutionists—to mention only the most prominent—placed critical emphasis on the interpretation of linguistic origins. The entire second half of Condillac's *Essai* was devoted to language and method, beginning with a lengthy section, "Of the Origin and Progress of Language." Here again Condillac departed from Locke, to whom this whole area of interest was foreign. Locke virtually took for granted a language which had somehow or other fully developed, and his real concern in the *Essay* was not with the origin of language but with "the original of all our notions and knowledge."

In approaching the problem, Condillac made use of a device occasionally employed by eighteenth-century explicators of primitive obscurities. He affirmed—perhaps sincerely, but in any case conveniently—that the gift of speech was bestowed upon Adam and Eve supernaturally by the Deity; but he quickly went on to suppose how two children, alone and astray after the Deluge, might have gone about the creation of signs without such divine intervention. (A similar device had been used by Bishop William Warburton, whom Condillac acknowledges, in his *The Divine Legation of Moses* IV, 4; and, though direct influence cannot be substantiated, Bernard de Mandeville took a parallel approach in his *Fable of the Bees*.) Such a supposition would allow investigation of the way in which language *might have been* invented by man. The remainder of the Second Part, of course, was an elaboration of the supposition with no regard to the initial affirmation of miraculous origin. Condillac's epistemology already postulated the necessity of "inward language," the use of signs for the advancement of thought; but the device of an isolated boy and girl allowed him to sketch a conjectural account of the way in which external language, language for interaction and communication, might come about.

Like other living creatures, the isolated children would have expressed their states of pleasure or pain, fear or satisfaction, with natural cries, facial expressions, and emotive gestures. Because human beings are innately compassionate, according to Condillac (as later for Rousseau), such gesticulations would gradually become the basis for mutual understanding. The first of the hypothetical children might have moved his arms and hands in a certain way in pressing need or danger. The second child would have responded with automatic sympathy and assistance. This combination of pressing need and instinctive compassion would transform some of the cries and gestures into functional signs.

> Thus by instinct alone they asked and gave each other assistance. I say by instinct alone; for as yet there was no room for reflexion. One of them did not say to himself, I must make such particular motions to render him sensible to my want, and to induce him to relieve me; nor the other, I see by his motions that he wants such a thing, and I will let him have it; but they both acted in consequence of the want which pressed them most.

It took some time before fully articulate language developed. First, some of the manual gestures and bodily movements must have come to be associated with particular causes of concern, sources of contentment, or objects of the world. Condillac lingered long on the theme of chironomic and pantomimic media of expression—a theme which became important for aesthetic theories of the day, was taken up by Diderot in his *Letter on the Deaf and Dumb for the Use of Those Who Hear and Speak* (1751), and was given practical application in the sign language devised for the instruction of deaf-mutes. Once reflection was activated by the use of signs, the hypothetical children (or the actual children of the human race) would have become aware that vocal sounds can serve as easily as conventional gestures to convey meaning. Language then became a mixture of articulated voice with the "language of action." Gradually, articulate speech came to predominate and nearly replace gesture and mimicry, because it was economical and convenient—all of which the mind would not have recognized in its prereflective state. In primitive understanding and communication, linguistic signs were already created, and without them the mind would never have progressed.

Since the role of signs was so important for him, Condillac was not only led to a concern with linguistic beginnings, but also to a much different understanding of the very function of language from that which had been implied by Locke. Bishop Berkeley, in several works, had anticipated the objection to Locke's narrow view of language as an instrument for the expression of already formed ideas: Berkeley had suggested that all sensation is akin to a form of language and he spoke especially of "visual language." It is difficult to ascertain, however, whether Berkeley's criticisms were known to Condillac—Berkeley was still untranslated—since Condillac read no English and seems to have relied heavily on comments by Voltaire. Regardless, the basic point common to Berkeley and Condillac was that the importance of language extended beyond the communication of thoughts arrived at independently of language and prior to it. Rather, they saw language as a necessary component in the very formation of ideas and particularly in the advancement of the "higher faculties."

It would become one of the commonplaces of German theories of language from Herder on that language cannot adequately be understood as a tool or instrument.

Language and its origin was of more than psychological interest: for Condillac, psychogenesis was a near perfect recapitulation of phylogensis. The progression of mental powers could be temporally projected as a tableau of the historical advancement of the human mind. Genetic epistemology in the style of Locke—the derivation of more complex from the more simple mental operations—was seized as the key which might unlock riddles of the forward movement of humanity. The progression from the sensate to the rational in the individual mind had its correlative in the progress from a primitive poetry of vague but concrete images to a modern science of abstract but precise formulas. Primitive language was metaphorical and sensuous, like the primal operations of the psyche. Early speech featured the visual and active along with the articulate; highly figurative and rhythmic, it was a medium well suited to poetry. Verbs, the most active elements, probably came first, then nouns representing undifferentiated wholes, and so on. The evolution of writing followed similar course: first picture writing, then hieroglyphics in which a partial image represented a complete idea, and finally the more abstract and entirely conventional use of alphabets. With the growing domination of abstract rationality, language became characteristically prosaic. Poetry was lost, but knowledge gained. As the art of reasoning is inseparable from that of speaking, so every language is itself a kind of method. Improvements in language and the advancement of science move in parallel progression, for, as Condillac commented in **La Langue des calculs** "it is the method that does the inventing, just as telescopes do the discovering."

The history of language, as Condillac perceived it, provided the irrefutable documentation of progressive illumination. It was a picture drawn in more exact detail by Turgot and Condorcet. And it implied an outline of world history lifted out of the enlighteners by a majority of continental and English romanticists and their precursors, thought these generally transvalued the terms involved and—to exaggerate and simplify their tendencies crudely—despaired of "cold" modern abstraction while they pined for the "warmth" of ancient poetic metaphor. This "historicization" of epistemology and psychology corresponded to the widely recognized "temporalizing of the great chain of being," whereby the ontological scale of classical metaphysics was reinterpreted in terms of cosmic origins, biological evolution, and human change. Later authors would fill in details of system and adjustments of value, but Condillac's picture of man's development of language is clearly intended as a miniature of the progress of human rationality.

Condillac's documentation for this historicolinguistic sketch was, to be sure, rather meager. He lifted a few examples from Hebrew out of his reading of Warburton; otherwise all his evidence for "primitive language" was taken from classical Latin, the only foreign language he knew. And he assumed without question that Hebrew, Greek, and Latin were the most original forms of human speech. But he was modest and acknowledged the speculative character of his endeavors. He took the motto for the entire *Essai* from Cicero's *Tusculan Disputations:*

> As far as I am able, I will explain; however, like Pythian Apollo, as though the things which I will say are certain and fixed; but simply as a limited man, following probable conjectures.

Condillac did not claim to deal with necessary truths, but with reasonable possibilities. And although a stiff dogmatism would eventually develop out of sensationalist epistemology, Condillac himself was cautious.

In his *Letter on the Blind for the Use of Those Who See* (1749), Denis Diderot, though generally full of praise for Condillac, intimated that in the end his principles were "the same as those of Berkeley," since we are left with no way of getting beyond our own ideas and our own signs for them. In response to this and other critiques, Condillac began to revise somewhat his views on language. In a letter to Maupertuis of June 25, 1752, he conceded that he had perhaps "given too much to signs." Of all Condillac's works, the *Treatise on the Sensations* shows the shift most obviously. The statue which the Pygmalion-philosopher brings gradually to sensate life never does acquire language or even need it, and Condillac makes hardly a reference to the function of signs. Instead, the animated statue is led to general ideas simply through the repeated experience of particular ones, unaided even by especial powers of association. The statue, to be sure, never becomes a significantly social being; but that is beside the point, since Condillac had argued earlier that even for the isolated child the use of signs would be a necessary prerequisite of mental development. In the *Treatise on the Animals* Condillac also downplayed somewhat the role of language, even though one of his objectives in that work the differentiation of animal and human natures, a logical context in which to introduce some of the points made so emphatically in the *Essai.* Since, however, Descartes had made his own differentiation to hang upon the human capacity for language, perhaps Condillac was reluctant to take his fire from the enemy.

In later works, however, particularly in the *Grammaire, La Logique,* and *La Langue des calculs,* Condillac renewed his emphasis on language, now with particular reference to the correlation between language and method and his interest in the construction of a logically perfected language. The correlation was already implied in the Second Part of the *Essai,* "Of Language and Method." Condillac refers to the method he proposes as "analysis," a procedure which would come to have dogmatic status among the *idéologues* of the French Revolution. A synthetic method, according to Condillac, proceeds from ideas already compounded—but if there is any fallacy in the composition, that fallacy will be preserved in the deductions from it; whereas an analytic method begins from the simple idea, where that is accessible, or else reduces the compound to its simpler constituents. Analysis then recomposes these simples only as clarity and distinctness dictate and allow—and the similarity of these methodological principles to the Cartesian ones has often enough been noted.

Unlike Descartes, however, who rejected the notion that any certain knowledge could derive from history, Condillac tied his explication of method to his own conjectures about linguistic history. Whatever may have been his faith in doctrinaire Enlightenment teachings about progress, Condillac sought instruction in the primitive as well. It was in the primordial and "natural" sequence of things that Condillac thought to find a corrective against future error. Mankind had advanced in many ways, but metaphysics and some other sciences had gone far astray because they did not adhere to the natural order of development. The mind progresses through the association of ideas, but such compounding turns to disadvantage whenever men lose the power to decompose their ideas. All too easily they become attached to words, abstractions, and composite figments, as though these were the very substance of life itself. The mind moves forward through processes of synthesis, but once error has occurred or has come to prevail, it is a method of analysis that is required. By decomposing composite ideas into their original components and individual elements, analysis brings the mind "back to its senses," reawakening awareness of the sensory elements with which mental processes began. In this way the obfuscations of pseudo-metaphysics and false science can be dispelled once and for all. Reductions of this kind will reveal that properly all languages are analytic methods and that "the art of reasoning amounts to a well-constructed language." The abuse of language and consequent promulgation of error derive from the lazy tendency to take synthetic ideas and words as though they themselves were the foundations on which to build. The future of science—both "natural" and "social," as we should say today—is fully dependent on analytic method, for linguistic precision is as important to every scientist as is the telescope to the astronomer and the microscope to the biologist. In dealing with political economy in *Le Commerce et le gouvernement* it was this kind of a linguistic-analytic method that Condillac tried to apply. Anarchical fallacies, as Bentham would later call them, could be avoided if political slogans and ideals were reduced to their original elements as a test of their substance. On the other hand, in the posthumous *Langue des calculs,* Condillac explicated algebra as a clarified language with its own grammar and vocabulary. Although more limited in some ways than those human languages more spontaneously developed, algebra and other mathematical systems and notations stood unassailably as models of *langue bien faite.* Unlike Condorcet and other proponents of universal characteristics, Condillac doubted the possibility that mankind would ever arrive at a single perfected idiom, but he nonetheless firmly believed that the clarification of language could lead to a more general and popular enlightenment. Thus, the search for the elementary and original in language was, for Condillac, inseparable from the preparation for a more perfect human future.

We asserted at the outset that Condillac was the first major thinker specifically to pose the psycholinguistic or epistemolinguistic question. Others before him had been led to conclusions about language and knowledge, language and reason, language and mind; but he was the first to make a genetic epistemology hinge upon the development of language and the use of signs. Despite its unassuming title, Condillac's *Essai,* and the whole of his philosophy, was more than a supplement of addenda to Locke; it entailed a fundamental shift of orientation in which considerations of language were decisive. Condillac anticipated the insight of Kant that there is in Locke's empiricism an unacknowledged but subtle form of *innatism.* The different faculties are really not so many potentialities given by the nature of the mind, which must inevitably actualize themselves at the proper point in the normal course of development. Rather the mind must come upon these powers and each individual must first learn to use them; and it is the utilization of signs, according to Condillac, which enables us to do this. Questions of the genesis of intellect led to the problem of linguistic origins on the one hand, and to the proposal of an analytic method on the other. And elaboration of these themes, in turn, led Condillac to more general considerations of history and of the hopes and means of future improvement. In this way the problem of language became critical for epistemology and psychology and for inquiries into history and society as well.

Hans Aarsleff   (essay date 1972)

SOURCE: "Condillac's Speechless Statue," in his *From Locke to Saussure: Essays on the Study of Language and Intellectual History,* University of Minnesota Press, 1982, pp. 210-24.

[In the following essay, Aarsleff discusses the figure of the statue presented in the Treatise on Sensations, *then examines some commonly held misconceptions about Condillac's philosophy.]*

It is widely recognized that Condillac occupies a commanding position in the intellectual life of Europe during the latter half of the eighteenth century. Between 1746 and the year of his death in 1780, at the age of sixty-five, he published a number of works that caused excitement and influence not only in France, but also in Germany, England, and Italy. In France his importance and influence is acknowledged by Diderot, d'Alembert, Rousseau, Turgot, and de Brosses (to mention only the best-known names among his French contemporaries), and the French *Encyclopédie* is heavily indebted to him. As early as 1748, his philosophy was introduced in Germany by Maupertuis, who had recently become president of the Berlin Academy; he raised a Condillacian discussion of language, man, and knowledge that laster over the next twenty-five years, culminating in Herder's *Abhandlung über den Ursprung der Sprache.* In England Condillac gave the impulse to several works, of which Lord Monboddo's great work *Of the Origin and Progress of Language* is the best known. Given this wide influence on figures who were themselves significant and influential, it is clearly a matter of importance to know and understand Condillac well. Since the nineteenth century, his place in intellectual history has in fact not been well understood, and it is for this reason that I wish to examine the crucial question in Condillac's philosophy: the role that language plays in his understanding of the nature of man. This problem can be approached in several ways, but perhaps the most revealing avenue is to ask why Condillac's statue doesn't speak. The first part of

my essay will deal with this problem. In the second part I shall try to indicate the kinds of misunderstanding Condillac has suffered and explore some of the reasons for it.

That the statue neither speaks nor is in a position to learn to speak is evident enough, but why is that so? Since the nineteenth century, commentators and historians have either not seen the problem or have offered interpretations that carry the implication that the statue speaks or is so placed that it could if it should choose to do so, in other words that the full gift of language is within its reach, thus being able to rise to "the richest intellectual and emotional experiences of man," to cite a recent statement that is representative of the conventional understanding of Condillac. You may recall that the statue occurs in the *Traité des sensations* first published in 1754, but written during the years immediately following 1749. This work is commonly seen as the most important expression of Condillac's philosophy, even as a thoroughgoing revision or rejection of the arguments and principles presented in the *Essai sur l'origine des connoissances humaines* (1746). You may recall that the statue is gradually brought to life as Condillac endows it with the five senses one by one, first smell, then taste, hearing, and vision in that order, none of which alone or together give the statue any assurance of the existence of anything outside itself. But being finally endowed with the sense of touch and with motion, it gains enduring awareness and conviction that there is indeed a world outside itself. This conclusion was the aim of Condillac's entire argument, for it was his answer to Diderot who in his *Lettre sur les aveugles* (1749) had suggested that Condillac was a Berkeleian idealist on the basis of the emphatic opening of Part One of the *Essai:* "Whether we raise ourselves, to speak metaphorically, to the heavens or descend into the abyss, we never step outside ourselves and we never perceive anything but our own private thoughts."

Bound within its sparse mode of being, the statue develops a certain measure of mental life and even a certain crucial success, in spite of the fact that the statue throughout remains "un homme isolé," a point repeatedly stressed by Condillac. It is successful because it learns enough to ensure its own preservation. This accomplishment it shares with man, or with human beings, for when the ideas we owe to the five senses are joined together, "they give us all the knowledge that is necessary for our preservation." This capacity for preservation is acquired by experience, that is by interaction with nature, because the statue naturally seeks the attainment of pleasure and the avoidance of pain. It learns to recognize its basic needs, "ses besoins," which Condillac calls "the knowledge of a good that it finds it is necessary for itself to have . . . it is in this fashion that pleasure and pain will always determine the exercise of its faculties." Thus, "the order of its studies is determined by its needs." The statue's needs are limited to those natural ones that relate to its preservation: "To eat, to protect itself against any adversity or to defend itself against it, and to satisfy its curiosity: those are all the natural needs of the statue."

In order to meet the needs that secure its preservation, the statue is capable of learning from experience. It develops certain rudimentary mental capacities, guided by its innate, natural tendency to avoid pain and gain its opposite, pleasure: it can remember sensations it has had in the past; these sensations, Condillac calls "idées intellectuelles" which are distinguished from the mere "sensations actuelles" it happens to have at any particular moment in the present. Memory makes it possible for the statue to compare past sensations with actual and present sensations. By this means it can, for instance, compare and judge regarding differences in size. It learns from nature and it learns naturally owing to those faculties that are part of its nature. It also has the power of imagination which is a heightened from of memory: "Imagination is memory itself, brought to the full vivacity of which it is capable."

When we note that the statue cannot merely have sensations, but also remember, imagine, and judge, we may feel that Condillac has already moved a good distance away from the mechanical sensualism, let alone materialism, that is generally attributed to him. For whereas actual sensation is passive, the other powers are active, and this activity is in the "mind" of the statue—Condillac never tires of insisting on the activity of the mind. In all his works this activity is crucial to his argument: yet practically all interpretations make it their chief point to assert that man and his mind are entirely passive according to Condillac, a fact that shows how profoundly he has been misunderstood since the nineteenth century. Thus though his argument is certainly directed against innate ideas as commonly understood, it still retains mentalism—it may be recalled that Du Marsais, with whom Condillac was personally acquainted, also forcefully rejected innate ideas. To say, therefore, as has often been said (indeed along with passivity it is one of the commonplaces of the interpretation of Condillac), that he reduced Locke's reflection to mere sensation, thus allowing only a single source of ideas and knowledge, is a mere play on words that quite fails to produce any conviction. It is true that a few phrases may seem to support that interpretation, but only if—and that is a very great if—they are read out of context without regard for his argument. Condillac often insists that his entire method is guided by observation of the operations that are open to our inspection. He maintains the temporal priority of sensation, just as Locke had also argued that reflection cannot go into action and reveal itself until sensation has furnished the mind with materials to work on.

So far I have dealt with the statue's abilities, and it is evident that they do not at all suffice to make it a human being. I shall now deal with the limitations. But before proceeding it must be mentioned that there are two versions of the *Traité des sensations,* the original 1754 version, which I have used so far, and the later version that was presented in the *Oeuvres complètes* published in 1798. The second version contains the entire text of the 1754 version, but adds a number of new passages. Thus the second version does not present a new argument, but strengthens and clarifies the original argument. The new passages underscore Condillac's commitment to the argument of the *Essai* in 1746, a commitment that is also indicated by some of his later works. This fidelity to his first work is important since it has most often been either ignored or denied with serious consequences for the understanding of Condillac's position and influence in the intellectual history of the latter half of the eighteenth century.

Let me now turn to two passages that are new in the second version. The first occurs in Section II at the end of the long Chapter viii entitled "Of the ideas that a human being can acquire when limited to the sense of touch." Here the description of the final paragraph has been changed from "Conclusion de ce chapitre" to "Its knowledge is only practical; and the light that guides it is merely instinct." He has then added a passage on the severe limitations imposed on the statue owing to its lack of language: "Its method in the acquisition of ideas is to observe in succession, one after the other, the qualities it attributes to objects: It analyzes naturally, but it has no language. But an analysis that is made without signs can only give very limited knowledge . . . and since it has not been possible to put them in order, the collection must be very confused. Thus when I treat the ideas that the statue acquires, I do not mean to say that it has knowledge of which it can render an exact account to itself: It has only practical knowledge. All the light it has is properly speaking instinctive, that is to say, a habit of conducting itself according to ideas of which it does not know how to render account to itself, a habit which when acquired guides it safely, without any need for it to recall the judgments that made it assume that habit. But as soon as its ideas have taught it how to conduct itself, it no longer thinks of it and it acts by habit. To acquire knowledge, it is necessary to have a language: for the ideas must be classified and determined, which presupposes signs employed according to method. See the first part of my grammar of my logic." The second passage enforces the same point: "If you recall that I have demonstrated how much signs are necessary in order to produce distinct ideas of any kind, you will tend to believe that I attribute more knowledge to the statue than it can acquire. But we must make a distinction . . . between knowledge of theory and practical knowledge. To have those of the first kind we need a language."

Thus the answer to the question why the statue does not speak is simple: because it cannot. It is in a profound sense speechless. And it is speechless because it exists all by itself, in total isolation. The progress of knowledge, which must include "les connoissances de théorie," depends on the development of man's innate capacity for reflection, and this development can occur only with the aid of man's greatest artificial accomplishment, speech and language, that is by means of voluntarily created arbitrary signs which record experience, give structure to reality, make communication and thus also tradition possible, make past knowledge retrievable, and allow the combination of ideas according to any deliberate plan. Thus language, knowledge beyond what is needed for mere preservation (in the form of unreflective habit turned into instinct), and the progress of mind are all functions of society. This was also the argument of the *Essai,* which is not superseded or subverted by the *Traité des sensations.* Though the statue served to answer Diderot's observation about Condillac's seeming commitment to Berkeleian idealism, the statue remains on the mental level of the animals.

A brief consideration of Condillac's next work will show

what I mean. The aim of the *Traité des animaux* (1755) is well known; it was to show that the animals are not, as the Cartesians held, mere automatons. They think in certain rudimentary ways exactly like the statue: they acquire ideas, learn from experience, judge, compare and discover, meet the needs of preservation, develop habits, act by instinct, and have no language. Again like the statue, they gain some practical but no theoretical knowledge. But the *Traité des animaux* is not merely about animals, it is also about man. In a chapter "De l'instinct et de la raison," we encounter these passages: "There are somehow two selves in each human being: the self of habit and the self of reflection. . . . The measure of reflection we have beyond our habits is what constitutes our reason. . . . The instinct of animals has only practical knowledge for its object: it does not lead to theory; for theory presupposes a method, that is, convenient signs for the determination of ideas, for arranging them in order and for gathering the results. Ours embraces both theory and practice: it is the effect of a method that has become second nature. But every human being endowed with language has a means of determining its ideas, to arrange them and to appropriate the results: it has a method more or less perfect." Thus we can make this chart:

Statue, animals	*Man*
moi d'habitude	moi de réflexion
instinct	raison, réflexion
connoissances pratiques	connoissances de théorie
animals: cris naturels but no language	voluntary, arbitrary signs, language
satisfaction only of needs of preservation	satisfaction of needs beyond preservation

The contrast between the statue and the animals on the one hand and man on the other is a contrast between Nature and Art.

If some animals are known to live in groups or societies, we may ask why they do not have language. Condillac's answer is: "It is not surprising that only man, who is as superior in regard to organic being as by the nature of the spirit that animates him, has the gift of speech." Here again Condillac is repeating doctrine that he had already advanced in the *Essai* in 1746. Here he said: "From all the operations we have described results one that, so to speak, crowns the understanding: it is reason . . . [which] is nothing but the knowledge of the manner in which we are obliged to rule the operations of mind." Later in the same chapter, he says in summing up: "We are capable of more reflection in proportion as we have more reason. Consequently, this last faculty produces reflection." Thus Condillac emphatically says that reason is fundamental in the nature of man. It places him in a realm of being and potentiality that is altogether different from that of the animals. Reason is the *sine qua non* of language.

In this light the common belief that Condillac is a sensualist or a materialist appears very odd indeed. In 1937 Georges le Roy said: "In fact, the *Treatise on the sensations* does not have the exclusive character it has often been given. It does not deny the role of language in the development of the mental faculties, and consequently it

does not constitute a refutation of the *Essai.* It deals solely with the operations of mind that precede the acquisition of languages, and it limits itself to the analysis of those operations." Condillac's statue does not have the means of rising "to the richest intellectual and emotional experiences of man." The statue and the argument in which it moves underscore the central and crucial importance Condillac assigned to speech and language in his philosophy of the nature of man. Almost blinded by an altogether different mode of looking at language, the nineteenth century missed Condillac's point and turned him into their own image of the superficial philosopher, sensualist, materialist, or whatever he was called. For the nineteenth century that may be understandable, but it is distressing to find these views repeated today in books that lay claims to understanding, and scholarship. And if, as may well be argued, Condillac is the most important and influential philosopher of the French enlightenment, not least as seen in the *Encyclopédie,* then this error is more than odd; it gets in the way of intellectual history.

Let me now indicate briefly some of the ways in which this stubborn misunderstanding and ignorance of Condillac have arisen. I think there are four main factors, and I shall consider each in turn.

The first is this: in the tradition of intellectual history dating from the early decades of the nineteenth century, Condillac's philosophy of language has been found most fully and typically represented by his last, unfinished, and posthumous work *La langue des calculs,* which was first published in the *Oeuvres complètes* (1798). This view makes two serious errors. Condillac's *Langue des calculs* presents only a particular aspect of his philosophy of language, and it is not, for obvious reasons, the work by which he gained such enormous influence during the latter half of the eighteenth century. Inspired by Garat and occurring during the years of the Directoire, the publication of the *Oeuvres* in 1798 was designed to serve the purposes of a new philosophy of signs, man, and the progress of knowledge; this philosophy was made the foundation of the radical educational program promoted by the Directoire. (The same intention had guided the first publication of the *Oeuvres* of Du Marsais in 1797.) The best known exponent of these views is Destutt de Tracy; during 1796 and February of 1798, he read five papers to the Institut national which in August of 1798 (a few months after the appearance of Condillac's *Oeuvres*) were published in the *Mémoires* under the title "Mémoire sur la faculté de penser." A few years later began the publication of Destutt de Tracy's *Élémens d'idéologie.* His main text was the *Traité des sensations,* and the *Langue des calculs* came to be seen as a "Programmschrift" for a radical doctrine of man and education. The *Essai sur l'origine des connoissances humaines* received attention only in so far as it satisfied these needs.

The consequences have been overwhelming, for as soon as the reaction set in, Condillac became chiefly known and understood in the version of his thought that had been presented by Destutt de Tracy and the *idéologues.* Condillac and the *idéologues* became the victims of the violent reaction that from the early decades of the nineteenth century was directed against eighteenth-century thought and the Revolution. This distorted, even contemptuous view of Condillac was presented to vast audiences in the lectures and writings of Victor Cousin who gained astonishing influence both in France and England. For similar reasons, Cousin also gave a very peculiar account of Locke which had a powerful effect in England—it is the sort of version of Locke's philosophy Professor Chomsky has recently taken to be a "commonplace," something that is true and obvious. In the history of the study of language, one example will serve to show the effect. Both in the first and second edition (1955 and 1969) of his great commentated anthology *Sprachwissenschaft,* Hans Arens bases his account of Condillac on the *Langue des calculs.* Summing up, he says about Condillac's philosophy that it is characterized by "intellectual impatience and intolerance toward life that can only be mastered mathematically when it is conceived as pure mechanism." For the philosophy of language we are told that the consequence is the following: "Language is not at all seen as the mode and expression of life, but throughout as a mere logical system of signs for concepts and the statement of propositions." Clearly, such ignorance precludes historical understanding. It also removes the possibility that German interest in the problem of the origin of language, as in Herder for instance, might be heavily indebted to Condillac.

The second source of confusion about Condillac springs from the simple matter of chronology. After the publication of the *Essai* in 1746, writings on the philosophy and especially the origin of language followed in close succession so that it is important to follow the sequence of publication before deciding on questions of priority and influence. In fact, most major figures, not merely in France, explicitly state their indebtedness to Condillac, but even these statements have often been ignored. The most serious, indeed fateful error is the tacit assumption that Condillac said nothing about language until the publication of his *Cours d'études* in 1775, the work that includes his *Grammaire, L'art d'écrire, L'art de raisonner,* and *L'art de penser,* or the publication of his *Logique* in 1780. The *Cours d'études* was written between 1758 and the end of 1766, and its basic linguistic doctrines are already in the *Essai;* thus Condillac expressly says that the greater part of the *L'art de penser* is drawn from the *Essai,* a fact that must be obvious to any reader even without such assurance. A few examples drawn from the recent secondary literature will show the consequences of failing to pay attention to the chronology. An article from 1938, says that Diderot in 1751 in the *Lettre sur les sourds et muets* found the origin of language in gestures and inarticulate cries and then goes on to observe, with reference to the *Cours d'études,* that this doctrine was later taken up, as the article says, by "Condillac himself." Now, this doctrine forms a fundamental part of the argument of Condillac's *Essai,* from which Diderot took it with explicit acknowledgement to Condillac. Many other similar examples could be cited. Jean Starobinski, for instance, finds that the principle of the linearity of speech is first found in Rousseau, though it also is crucial in the philosophy of the *Essai.* Both Diderot and Rousseau have often been credited with doctrines which they themselves credited to Condillac—

which shows that even Diderot and Rousseau are not always being read with much care.

A third cause of confusion lies in the nineteenth century's immersion in a strict historical view, combined with positivism, that altogether blocked understanding of the conjectural and theoretical mode of eighteenth-century thought. This mode did not aim at establishing historical fact and did not claim to have done so. A typical instance of this failure of understanding is found in Renan's *De l'origine du language.* Renan says of Condillac and his contemporaries, with disapproval of course: "They addressed themselves to theoretical questions before they had dedicated themselves to the patient study of precise details. . . . Eighteenth-century philosophy had a strong penchant for artificial explanations in everything that pertains to the origins of the human mind." The nineteenth century failed to see the import of the eighteenth century's distinction between nature and art, and without that distinction Condillac becomes incomprehensible.

Finally, there is a fourth factor that has caused endless confusion: the tendency, prompted one suspects by desire, to see a sharp division between the philosophies of language in France and Germany, as if they fall in altogether separate compartments. There is even a word for it: Herder is said to belong to the "Deutsche Bewegung." In his *Sprachwissenschaft* Arens makes it a principle that whereas the French busied themselves with universal grammar, the special linguistic province of the Germans was the question of the origin of language: "Related to the orientation of the time toward general problems about mankind and especially to 'universal grammar,' is also the problem of its origin, in France treated more peripherally, in Germany, where philosophical grammar only appears much later, for a long time a current topic." As already mentioned, it can easily be demonstrated that the philosophy of Condillac's *Essai* and especially its long section on the origin of language were debated in the Berlin Academy, deliberately chosen and introduced by Maupertuis. It was this debate that caused the formulation of the two prize-topics that were answered by Johann David Michaëlis and Herder. It was not a problem which in that form had a German origin. A book that offers perhaps the most detailed discussion we have of Herder's *Abhandlung* and its philosophy of language shows the confidence with which Condillac's *Essai* is ignored. The author of this book shows no knowledge of the *Essai,* but—and that is fantastic—takes the *Abhandlung* as a reliable secondary source. Ignorant of the *Essai,* he then assures the reader that in his book, "the subject is throughout the origin-of-language theory of the *Essai,* and . . . never of the far more important one in the *Langue des calculs."* In this work, the author says, "is shown how an articulate language gradually emerges from an original language of gestures (langue d'action), a language, it is expressly said, that does not merely serve the needs of communication and outward understanding, but above all comprehension. . . . Here the talk is no longer about the animalistic origin of language, of the 'noises' and 'cries of emotion'." The implication is clearly that if Herder had known the doctrine of the *Langue des calculs,* then the story would have been altogether different. The problem is indeed bothersome, for the brief passage on the origin of language and the language of action in the latter work merely recapitulates what Condillac had presented and argued at much greater length in the *Essai.* This total misunderstanding becomes especially curious when we consider that there has for at least seventy years been published proof that Herder as early as 1764 had read Part Two of Condillac's *Essai,* that is the very part which, under the title "Du langage et de la méthode," contains the long section entitled "De l'origine et des progrès du langage," which takes up a full third of the entire *Essai.* One feels tempted to see a conspiracy of silence to keep the "Deutsche Bewegung" free of French influence.

I am of course suggesting that Herder, along with the other participants in the debate in the Berlin Academy, was directly and profoundly influenced by Condillac's *Essai.* Remembering that human speech and language (with its voluntary, arbitrary signs) is exclusively a product of "réflexion," is it possible to read this often-quoted statement from Herder's *Abhandlung,* always cited as his basic and original doctrine, without immediately thinking of the *Essai:* "Endowed with the capacity for thought that is peculiar to him and this capacity for thought (reflexion) for the first time being given free exercise, man has invented language." Or we may consider the following doctrines that are taken to be so typical of Herder: "Everything confirms that each language expresses the character of the people who speak it." Or the doctrine that, "Of all the writers, it is with the poets that the genius of language gains the most lively expression." Or this: "For anyone who understandings them well, languages would be a painting of the character and genius of each people. He would see how the imagination has combined ideas according to the given outlook and the passions." Or the related and equally celebrated doctrine that the first speech occurred in situations of strong emotion and reactions to nature. These doctrines are all fully stated and argued in the *Essai,* from which the quotations are taken. I may add this: It is often dogmatically asserted that Wilhelm von Humboldt continued the study of language in the tradition of Herder and Hamann; this claim is taken to be so safe that no one seems to have bothered to substantiate it. Though I think I have an extensive knowledge of Wilhelm von Humboldt's writings and of his often very revealing correspondence, I have never found any evidence that this claim can be substantiated and much that casts it seriously into doubt. It is, however, evident and universally admitted that Humboldt's interest in anthropology, already strong during the 1790s, did not find its locus in the study of language until the years in Paris and immediately following, during the journeys to the Basque Provinces and Spain. His orientation may be Kantian, though there is much uncertainly about precisely how, but his early linguistic writings clearly show the influence of the philosophy he encountered in Paris, where he moved much in the circles of the idéologues and where he read all of Condillac's major works as soon as they came out in the late spring of 1798. He may have said that he didn't agree with them, have contrasted their philosophy with Kant's, and much else. But it remains significant that his orientation towards language occurs precisely at this time and within the spirit of the thought of Condillac and the idéologues.

The reputed similarity of the linguistic thought of Herder and von Humboldt (and of course others) may be a common but separate indebtedness to similar sources rather than a tradition that links Herder and Humboldt sequentially. But this, so far as I know, is a possibility that has never been considered, yet it is in large measure demonstrable and much more plausible than the unsubstantiated (sometimes even fabricated) claims that are assumed to take care of the matter.

Without trying to summarize, let me briefly conclude in this fashion. The speechless statue of the *Traité des sensations* shows the supreme role that Condillac assigned to language in the nature of man, mind, and knowledge; in this respect the *Traité* merely follows the argument of the *Essai,* which separately considered would have served equally well for our purposes. Wide ignorance of the *Essai,* misunderstanding of the *Traité,* and unquestioning faith in a number of curious historical errors have obscured the intellectual history of the latter half of the eighteenth century. If we pay attention to the texts and to the context of intellectual cross-influence of that period, we may be able to see things in a better and more interesting light.

Berlin on Condillac's central theoretical flaw:

Condillac attempts to improve on Locke's inadequate account of "ideas of reflection" by explaining them as the results of "attention," which is, for him, merely another sensation. His theory cannot be regarded as successful, as anyone who troubles to read relevant discussions in the works of Kant or of Maine de Biran can see for himself. Attention, comparison, belief, knowledge, cannot be identified with "pure sensation" which is, presumably, pure receptivity, incapable of rounding on itself and choosing, weighing, rejecting, and building theories out of the undifferentiated "raw material" which, *ex hypothesi,* is all that it itself is. A succession of sensations cannot be turned into a sensation of succession. Similar difficulties have been encountered by all those who identify knowledge with sensation, or belief with the succession of atomic data, from Condillac to Carnap. But Condillac's careful analysis of actual sensations, which constitute more of our experience than had hitherto been allowed, and his emphasis on the central importance of attention, are still interesting.

Isaiah Berlin, in his The Age of Enlightenment, *Houghton Mifflin Co., 1956.*

Suzanne Gearhart   (essay date 1984)

SOURCE: "The Limits and Conditions of Empirical Knowledge or the Theaters of Perception," in her *The Open Boundary of History and Fiction: A Critical Approach to the French Enlightenment,* Princeton University Press, 1984, 161-99.

[In the following excerpt, Gearhart addresses logical flaws

in Condillac's assertion that sensations are the origin of all knowledge.]

Condillac begins his ***Essai sur l'origine des connaissances humaines*** with the assertion that "whatever our knowledge, if we want to go back to its origin, we will ultimately arrive at a first, simple idea." All mental life thus has a simple origin for Condillac. Experience can be reduced to a series of mental operations with sensation, the simplest, at the beginning of the chain, so that the "first" sensation that comes to "a man at the first moment of his existence" is the origin of all ensuing knowledge. Sensation is the simple foundation on which Condillac hopes to build in the following chapter dealing with perception, consciousness, attention, and reminiscence.

Condillac writes in his ***Traité des sensations*** that he is dissatisfied with his earlier ***Essai*** for having "given too much importance to signs," that is, for having placed too heavy an emphasis on the role of language in developing "the germ of all our ideas," to the detriment of his thesis that all mental life stems from sensation. But a close reading of the ***Essai*** belies Condillac's own subsequent interpretation of it, for Condillac himself begins to undercut sensation as the unique origin of mental processes in the chapter immediately following the one on sensation, and thus well before the issue of the sign has been raised "for the first time." The chapter on perception, consciousness, attention, and reminiscence runs counter to the affirmations of the chapter on sensation, for it shows that sensation in and of itself is not and cannot be the simple origin of all knowledge. Sensation itself can only take place when it is accompanied (or supplemented) by these "secondary" mental operations. This is clear in Condillac's discussion of each of the concepts dealt with in the chapter in question, but most explicitly in his discussion of reminiscence:

> Once objects attract our attention, the perceptions they occasion in us link themselves with the sense of our being and with everything that has some relation to it. . . . Consciousness, considered in relation to these new effects, is a new operation which serves us at every instant and which is the basis of experience. Without it each moment of life seems to be the first in our existence, and our knowledge would never extend beyond a first perception: I will call this [operation or faculty] *reminiscence*.

Contrary to his opening argument that sensation is the basis of all experience, here reminiscence plays that role. Without reminiscence, the perceiving or sensing substance would have no way of distinguishing successive sense impressions one from another. Experience would consist of one uninterrupted perception or sensation which, because the subject would have nothing to compare it to, could not be identified in even the most rudimentary way as a sensation. For Condillac, reminiscence permits the subject to link and at the same time to distinguish between different impressions, and, thereby, makes sensation itself possible.

In Condillac's view, reminiscence is to be distinguished from memory. The latter faculty is "higher" in the hierarchy or chain linking the various faculties to each other, and thus is held by Condillac to be more active, more general, and less concrete than reminiscence. But reminiscence itself prevents sensation from being a purely passive faculty, inasmuch as the subject must recall a past sensation in order to experience a present one. Reminiscence also prevents sensation from being purely specific and concrete, inasmuch as it links the attention we bestow on an object to "the sensation of our being" and to "everything that might have a relationship" to the sensation of our being. Thus the sensation of a "concrete" object is always abstracted from a complex of relationships that are the condition of the sensation of the object. Moreover, the concept of reminiscence implies that sensation takes place where a relationship, however rudimentary, is established between the object and its background or between the object and the perceptual system itself, and this distinction could not exist were the system purely passive. Finally, reminiscence not only implies a relative degree of activity and abstraction in sensation itself, it also implies that sensation is to a degree like memory in that neither takes place in the full presence of the object. For the necessity that reminiscence already be at work in order for the *first* sensation to take place means that no object is fully present in its integrity to the perceiving system; instead, sensation takes place only when *more than one* object competes for the attention of the sensory apparatus. Memory, then, can be said to grow out of reminiscence, but, for that very reason, the distinction between memory and sensation cannot be hard and fast. Reminiscence is a protomemory—it is memory *as* sensation.

Simple sensation, then, cannot be the origin of mental life, since sensation itself implies difference and complexity. Indeed, there could be no such thing as sensation if there were only *one* sensation or perception. There are three other faculties—consciousness, perception, and attention—that, like reminiscence, must be operative in sensation itself if there is to be any such thing as sensation. These faculties all imply each other, and thus Condillac's descriptions of them overlap significantly. Each bears the same relationship to memory as does reminiscence; each implies that memory is already at work in sensation; and each, like reminiscence, can be considered a form of sensation *as* memory.

In his analysis of perception, Condillac emphasizes a point already implicit in his definition of reminiscence. In sensation, there must be differentiation, not only between various sensations, but also between sensation and the perceptual apparatus itself: "Objects would act to no avail on the senses, and the soul would never have knowledge of them, if it did not perceive them. Thus the first and least degree of knowledge is to perceive." Perception is a redoubling or consciousness of sensation, and without it, there would be no sensation. Furthermore, because perception implies an awareness or consciousness for Condillac, it also implies (as does the notion of reminiscence) that there must be *more than one* sensation in order for *even one* sensation to be recorded: perception takes both the perceiving system itself and the sensation as its objects, and it is produced by the difference between the two. Condillac's definition of perception clearly implies a third operation or faculty—consciousness—that functions as a resistance to sensation, for it does not allow the perceiving subject to be totally invaded by sensation, and thus it maintains his sense of his existence independent of his sensations.

Condillac's discussion of reminiscence, perception, and consciousness not only undercuts sensation as the simple origin of all mental processes, it also serves to introduce a crucial problem and set the stage for that problem's solution. For, Condillac acknowledges, consciousness is not full, consistent, and neutral, but partial and inconsistent, full . . . of gaps. Condillac's description of sensation and the secondary faculties is intended to explain how the subject remembers and perceives, but it does not yet explain why and how the subject forgets. Condillac's task, then, is to interpret reminiscence, perception, and consciousness in such a way that they can explain the partial nature of consciousness and, ultimately, the incomplete nature of memory. It is at this point in his argument that the unity of the perceiving subject is most seriously threatened. The ability of consciousness to resist external impressions and, ultimately, to forget seems to be leading the philosopher to produce a concept of an unconscious, where the impressions that are put into the background by reminiscence and ultimately lost to consciousness altogether would be stored in some way. But, intent on preserving the unity of his model of the mind, Condillac explicitly rejects the notion of an unconscious when he denies the possibility of perceptions of which the subject might not be aware. For Condillac, the notion of unconscious perception is ruled out because it involves a logical inconsistency:

> At this point one could hold two views different from mine. . . . The second view would be that there is no impression upon the senses that does not communicate itself to the brain. . . . But one would have to add that it [the impression] is without consciousness, or that the soul does not become conscious of it. Here I declare myself to be with Locke; for I cannot conceive of such a perception: I would just as willingly have it said that I perceive without perceiving.

According to Condillac, then, there is no such thing as an unperceived perception.

Having rejected the notion of an unconscious, however, it still remains for Condillac to explain how, if all perception is *conscious,* the subject does not retain all of his perceptions, and how what was present in or to consciousness can be lost. According to the logic by which Condillac distinguishes sensation and perception or consciousness, there must be some analogous mechanism that resists perception and thus is responsible for the distinction between perception and memory. Having rejected the notion of an unconscious, it remains for Condillac to explain the workings of memory in relation to perception without violating the unity of the perceiving subject. The concept to which Condillac turns to resolve his difficulty is that of attention, but the metaphor he uses to "illustrate" this concept will only cause the same difficulty to be resuscitated in another form.

According to Condillac, the perceptions that attract our attention make the greatest impression on us and are thus remembered. Others are perceived but without our being attentive to them, and as a result they are immediately for-

gotten. Attention is thus responsible for endowing the different sense impressions with the different value or quantity of force without which there could be no memory (and no forgetting), and thus, no perception. Condillac "illustrates" the concept of attention by citing the experience of a spectator in a theater. It should be stressed that this use of the theater as a model for perception occurs several chapters before Condillac explicitly discusses the whole question of the sociohistorical origins of the theater in connection with the development of language. And this recourse to the theater as an example is neither innocent nor neutral, no more so than is perception itself. While the example used to "illustrate" a philosophical argument is, in principle, replaceable and inessential, the common denominator of all the examples Condillac uses to explain his concept of attention is that they imply society. In this respect, at least, the metaphor of the theater appears to be irreplaceable and essential for Condillac. Just as it is necessary to supplement sensation and perception by memory and attention, so it is necessary to supplement the individual mind, *before it is even fully constituted as such,* by a "sociality" even more fundamental than the society to which the fully constituted subject gains access through perception.

Memory is both possible *and* partial because, according to Condillac, the more our consciousness of certain impressions increases, the more our ability to remember contiguous impressions decreases:

> The illusion that is created in the theater is proof of this. There are moments when consciousness does not appear to divide itself between the actions taking place on stage and the rest of the spectacle. It would seem at first that the illusion ought to be all the more vivid when there are fewer objects capable of distracting from it. However, everyone has had occasion to remark that one is never more apt to believe oneself the only witness of an interesting scene, than when the theater is filled to capacity. This is perhaps because the number, the variety, and the magnificence of the objects stir the senses, heat up and lift up the imagination, and thereby make us more susceptible to the impressions the poet wants to arouse. Perhaps too the spectators mutually prompt each other, through the examples they give each other, to fix their gaze on the stage.

Condillac's metaphor is intended to explain how it is that attention bestows not only greater value on the object of our attention but also a lesser value on related perceptions that are not objects of attention and that, as a result, "disappear" from memory and consciousness. But the logic of this passage undermines his argument, for, as he himself notes, it is precisely when the theater is packed, that is, when there are the most "objects" present to distract the spectator from the spectacle, that it fixes his attention most firmly. Our attention for the stage may even be a result of our emulation of the other, attentive spectators. If this is so, then in an "attentive" audience, all the spectators in fact must be at once attentive to and forgetful of the other spectators. Condillac has rejected the notion of an unperceived perception only to create the nortion of an inattentive attention.

According to the theatrical model proposed in his discussion of attention, perception is possible not because the perceiving system is originally simple and passive, but because it is originally differentiated and active. For the model for attention is not the individual spectator in the theater, but rather the theater itself, including the individual spectator, the other spectators, and the stage. If the stage represents the object of attention, and if the individual spectator represents the perceiving consciousness, it still remains to be seen what the other spectators represent *within* the perceiving subject. For they are neither the perceiving subject nor the perceived sensation; they are an essential background *within* the subject, a condition of consciousness without being an object of consciousness. If Condillac refuses to see the division between the individual consciousness and the other spectators as constituting an "unconscious," his use of the theatrical metaphor nonetheless threatens the fundamental postulate of the unity of the perceiving system conceived as a conscious subject.

Condillac's use of the image of the theater reveals a paradox at the heart of the concept of attention. But lest it be thought that this paradox is introduced into Condillac's explanation of the workings of the mind accidentally, by a metaphor that is only casually invoked, it should be noted that the theatrical model can serve to illustrate not only attention but also the other mental operations that "precede" it. The stage, by creating or implying a frame that sets it off from the audience, makes it possible to differentiate and thus to perceive both the stage itself and the audience, just as consciousness differentiates itself from its object. The theatrical model also underscores the active nature of perception and memory, for our attentiveness to the events on the stage is in direct proportion to our resistance to those impressions coming from the direction of the audience. We cannot perceive anything without at the same time resisting other sensations or perceptions. Finally, the theater is a reminiscence of "life" or "reality" in the same way that a perception is more or less a replica of an "earlier" perception with which it must be compared to be perceived. But the theater, as a "representation" or "figure" of reality, must be present *from the beginning* in order that "life" or "reality" may define themselves in opposition to the stage, just as a "second" perception must be present at the origin for the "first" perception to be registered. The differentiation and, ultimately, the alienation characterizing the theatrical situation are present at every level of perception—reminiscence, consciousness, and attention—and this means that the social and theatrical situation that illustrates attention is implicit in perception itself. Before I can perceive the theater as an object, or any object, a structure of differentiation that implies an apparatus analogous in form to the theater has already become the necessary condition of my being able to perceive at all. Before I can see others as objects or even as constituting a society, others are the necessary structural condition of perception. Moreover, it should not be forgotten that the metaphor of the theater is called forth by the problem of the selective nature of memory. "The theater" is Condil-

lac's answer to the question, What apparatus can account for *both* memory and perception? It accounts for both by showing, as Condillac implies in his earlier discussion of reminiscence, that memory is already at work in the "first" sensation.

At this point, one could expect that Condillac might seriously revise his postulate of the unity of the perceiving subject and of the simple nature of perception in a manner consistent with the complexity and differentiation implied by these "secondary" processes. Instead, he returns to a simple model for sensation in the chapter on imagination, contemplation, and memory. There, sensation serves as the guarantee of the distinction, judged by Condillac to be capital, between imagination and memory: "It is important to distinguish clearly the point that separates imagination from memory. . . . Until now what philosophers have said on this subject is so confused that one can often apply to memory what they say about imagination, and to imagination what they say about memory." The distinction between imagination and memory is based, for Condillac, on their different relation to sensation. Imagination, he asserts, is a retracting of perception "as if one . . . had before one's eyes" the object that caused the original perception. Memory is more "abstract" than imagination. It does not produce a reexperiencing of the perception, but a (partial) representation of it, such as a name, a set of circumstances, and a general notion of the nature of the sensation (an odor, a color, etc.). The distinction between imagination and memory is threatened, however, by the fact that it rests on a question of degree. As Condillac himself remarks, there is nothing *in principle* to distinguish imagination from sensation itself. The inability to distinguish the two is characteristic of certain forms of madness, he writes, and, moreover, it is an experience accessible to the "normal" subject in sleep: "Sometimes, even, our ideas retrace themselves without our participation, and present themselves with such liveliness that we are duped, and we believe that we have the objects before our eyes. This is what happens to madmen and to all men, when they dream."

At the other end of the spectrum from this vivid form of imagination indistinguishable from sensation is an imagination without force that functions much as memory does. We can imagine a triangle, says Condillac, because of its simplicity and regularity. We cannot imagine forms with one thousand or with nine hundred and ninety-nine sides. Such complex figures can only be grasped through language and thus, through memory. But at what precise point do figures become unimaginable and only memorable? How many sides does the most complex figure we can still imagine have? Condillac's definitions of imagination and memory are ultimately based on their *degree* of proximity to an original sensation. But the difficulty of determining the exact degree reflects the underlying complexity of sensation itself. The problems raised by sleep and by imagination are not "new" in Condillac's exploration of the chain of mental faculties: rather they are inherent in the discussion of sensation itself. For though, in the chapter on memory and imagination, sensation is the state of having the object "before one's eyes"—a state that imagination and memory can only approximate in their ways—

the earlier chapters reveal that sensation does not take place in the full presence of *an* object and that it already requires the participation of memory in order that the "first" sensation might take place. The difficulty of distinguishing between imagination and memory, then, is already implicit in sensation itself.

Many readers of Condillac have argued that his ***Traité des sensations*** and his ***Logique*** differ significantly from the early ***Essai.*** Nonetheless, all of Condillac's work does in a sense return to these early chapters and to the conflict in them between memory and sensation. In the ***Traité des sensations,*** the complexity of sensation is evident in Condillac's assertion that *interest* is an essential component of all sensation. He argues that the perceiving subject registers sensations because they are all either pleasurable or painful: a sensation that would be neither does not exist or, what is the same thing, would not be registered by the perceiving subject. Sensation occurs, then, because it is in the interest of the subject to seek pleasurable sensations and avoid painful ones and because the subject discriminates sensation according to the pain or pleasure it causes. Pleasure and pain, however, are not themselves inherent in objects. According to Condillac, they are only qualities of sensation and as such have no meaning except in opposition to each other. But if all sensation must have a quality in order to register, and if, at the same time, the quality of one sensation is always relative to the quality of another, then this is further confirmation of the argument that there must be more than one sensation for even one sensation to occur. In the ***Traité,*** as in the ***Essai,*** sensation implies memory.

The ***Logique*** too confronts anew the problem of the relationship between memory and sensation when Condillac criticizes those who have conceived of the brain as a "substance molle" for not having recognized the difficulty of reconciling these two faculties: "Others say that the brain is a soft substance, in which animal spirits make traces. These traces are conserved; the animal spirits pass through the traces again and again; the animal is thus endowed with sense and memory. They don't take note of the fact that if the substance of the brain is soft enough to receive traces, it will not have enough consistency to conserve them." In the ***Logique.*** Condillac proposes a new model to resolve and account for the conflict between memory and sensation—the harpsichord:

> The brain, like all the other sensory organs, has the capacity to affect itself according to its habitual determinations. We experience sensations more or less the way a harpsichord makes sounds. The exterior organs of the human body are like keys, the objects that strike them are like the fingers on the keyboard, the interior organs are like the body of the harpsichordist, sensations and ideas are like sounds; and memory takes place when ideas that have been produced by the effect of objects on the senses are reproduced by motions that have become habitual to the brain.

In sensation, it is the harpsichordist who acts as the agent of sensation, and the harpsichord as the sensory apparatus. But it is less clear how the harpsichord model illus-

trates memory. What is it that touches the keys of the harpsichord and produces memory or sound if it is not the harpsichordist or the "external" cause of sensation? Is it the harpsichord itself? How does a harpsichord play itself? If it is the harpsichord, how can it know when it is being played and when it is playing itself? If it is not the harpsichord, if it is, once again, the harpsichordist doing the playing, how can the harpsichord distinguish between memory and sensation? When raised in terms of this model, such questions are unanswerable. The unity assumed to be the foundation necessary to provide definitive answers to such questions has been complicated to such a degree in this and the other models used by Condillac that they no longer illustrate that unity but instead put it into question.

The fact that the boundary between sensation, imagination, and memory is never conclusively drawn and is even actively questioned by Condillac, in his later works as well as in the ***Essai,*** has far-reaching implications when one considers the role of perception in the theory of knowledge. Just as, in Condillac's ***Essai,*** perception is at times invoked as the criteria by which each ought to be defined, so rationalism and empiricism define literature and history according to their proximity to a science considered to be more directly rooted in perception. But if memory and imagination are both potentially active in all perception, then the distinction between science, history, and fiction, like the distinction between perception, memory, and imagination is at most one of degree and not of kind. As Condillac notes in his ***Essai,*** the most vivid observation is at times indistinguishable from a fiction or dream, and Condillac himself provides no test by which to ascertain whether the subject is awake or asleep at any given moment. Ultimately, the complex model of perception that emerges from the ***Essai*** shows that memory is the condition of all perception or sensation, and thus in an important sense all acts of observation are historical in character. The historicity of perception is not simple however; rather, it is complicated by the relationship of memory to imagination. Indeed, the logic that implicates memory in all acts of perception also implicates imagination in all acts of remembering. Just as perception is complicated, historicized by memory, so memory is complicated and historicized, that is, fictionalized, by imagination.

John C. O'Neal   (essay date 1987)

SOURCE: "Condillac's Contribution to Eighteenth-Century French Aesthetics," in *Studies on Voltaire and the Eighteenth Century,* Vol. 264, 1989, pp. 1064-66.

[In the following essay, O'Neal draws parallels between the aesthetic implicit in Condillac's example of the statue-man in the Treatise on Sensations *and that in eighteenth-century French literature.]*

In their search for an aesthetic for the Enlightenment, scholars have paid little attention to Condillac's ***Traité des sensations*** in which a theory of the mind can be seen as a theory of literature. In his ***Traité des sensations,*** Condillac provides indirectly a kind of handbook of literary aesthetics for many in his century. As this work unfolds the theory of sensationalism, it also richly suggests useful ways in which novelists might develop particularly their characters, plots, and narratives as well as shape the attitudes of their readers.

In the *Traité des sensations,* the statue-man may serve as a metaphorical figure for a literary character. Like the countless protagonists of eighteenth-century fiction, it personifies sensitivity, if not sensibility, itself. It reacts to the slightest change in environment and initially knows no indifferent states, which will come later only when it has itself undergone the greatest pleasures and pains and has attained the ability to compare them with weaker sensations. Its sense of self develops slowly across time as the statue first confuses its very existence with the presented object and sensation, namely, the odour of a rose. Such a confusion necessarily gives rise to a certain egocentricity, which can be seen in many of the century's characters whose knowledge of themselves, their world, and their own sexuality develops along parallel lines.

As characters, the statue and many of the protagonists in eighteenth-century literature, not surprisingly, have the same gender. Numerous authors chose female protagonists to portray the world of sensibility and the way in which one acquires knowledge, for they serve as ideal characters to reflect the arduousness involved in everyone's acquisition of human knowledge. Curiosity, vulnerability, and dependence on the immediate environment characterise the statue's activities as well as those of many eighteenth-century heroes and heroines.

As for the plots of much eighteenth-century literature, these can be found in the statue's activities, which like its curiosity, necessitate movement. After an adequate notion of self has been attained, movement becomes the outward sign of an internal desire: 'our statue cannot desire a sensation without at the same instant moving in order to seek the object that can procure the sensation for it'. It is suspended only when the statue delivers itself entirely to a new pleasurable feeling, when *jouissance* is at once enjoyment and fetishistic orgasm as the statue wishes 'to touch with all the parts of its body the object that occasions [the new feeling]'. Only such a passage as the preceding one from the *Traité des sensations* evidences the sheer driving force behind desire that literally propels many French Enlightenment characters at a frenetic pace of uninterrupted action and leaves them often with the same sense of utter astonishment experienced by the statue.

If living consists in enjoying oneself and 'life is longer for whomever can maximise the objects of his or her enjoyment', as Condillac states in his *Traité des sensations*, then there are seemingly no limits to libertine behaviour. The novel of seduction springs from just such a rationale. Although the statue's activities suggest its significant preoccupation with pleasures, there are, however, major checks such as fear and repentance to its hedonism so that it can ultimately represent progress of a positive kind. Condillac sees his entire treatise as a contribution to the progress of the art of reasoning. The plots of many literary works in the period advance, as does the statue, towards reason. Indeed an entire subgenre, the *Bildungsroman,* accentuates a process of growth and maturation through

which one refines one's sensibilities and taste, acquires greater experience, and loses the intolerance for cultural relativism that sometimes circumscribes one's world view.

In addition to the movement and the progressive nature characteristic of eighteenth-century literary plots and the statue's activities, one discerns a marked tendency towards repetition. The statue's very learning process is based on repetition; experience comes from incessant experiments of a similar nature. One can link, as Freud did, the desire for repetition, which has as its object the simple reproduction of a pleasurable sensation, to instinct and the forms of life associated with it. For the Enlightenment, however, the desire for repetition illuminates man's dual nature, his lower and his higher natures. It does not merely reflect an instinctive, mechanical, and circular search for knowledge in which the mind's active qualities receive, as they did with astonishment, positive recognition. Like the statue, the characters of the period's literature must repeat many of the same or similar operations before they can learn.

For the narratives of eighteenth-century literature, the statue provides a model through the sequentiality and succession of its activities. It proceeds one step, indeed often, one sensation, at a time, freezing time, as it were, allowing for an adequate representation of the complexity of each new sensation presented alternately. Increased knowledge by differentiation comes from the separation or succession of the presented sensations. Quite paradoxically, clarity of thinking results from an order that is discontinuous.

Because of its sequential nature, eighteenth-century narrative emphasises, as does sensationalistic psychology, not the general undifferentiated mass of events and voices but the particular ones, which retain their distinctiveness precisely because they are presented successively. The discrete units of the age's narratives, which often took the form of epistolary novels because of their separate and successive presentation of letters, also have a kind of cumulative effect on the reader who ultimately feels overwhelmed by the evidence presented throughout the work.

As for the reader, his or her task is the same as one of the principal goals of the statue—literally to 'unmix' (*démêler*) or decode the confusing perceptual world. When Condillac uses the expression 'démêler', as he does, not infrequently, he does so to indicate the separation of sensations necessary to progress in one's knowledge. As the statue evolves, pleasure results from separation from, rather than its initial symbiotic and primary narcissistic attachment to itself. In the process, it moves as does the ideal reader from self to other, from a finite world to one with limitless possibilities, from naïveté to enlightened experience.

Condillac's *Traité des sensations* thus furnishes a kind of sensationalistic aesthetics for the period that precedes its publication and that which follows it. In it, Condillac demonstrated his singular ability not only to formulate the philosophical ideas that had currency at the time but also to generate a richly suggestive piece of writing for aesthetics. Through descriptions of the statue-man, the enumeration of its activities, and the way in which they took place, he gives us insight into the characters, plots, and narratives of the literature of the eighteenth century, showing who and what might best represent the contemporary world and how they would do so. The readers profit from an author's judicious use of character, plot, and narrative, growing wiser from their literary experience. This exercise, albeit one that remains at one step's remove from the actual world, will presumably prove useful to them in their own lives in the future by imparting to them an enhanced awareness of the ways in which human beings encode and decode knowledge.

FURTHER READING

Aarsleff, Hans. "The Tradition of Condillac: The Problem of the Origin of Language in the Eighteenth Century and the Debate in the Berlin Academy before Herder." In *Studies in the History of Linguistics: Traditions and Paradigms*, edited by Dell Hymes, pp. 93-156. Bloomington: Indiana University Press, 1974.

Discusses Condillac's *Essay on the Origin of Human Understanding* and its influence on linguistics.

Beal, M. W. "Condillac as Precursor of Kant." In *Studies on Voltaire and the Eighteenth Century*, Vol. CII, edited by Theodore Besterman, pp. 193-229. Banbury, Oxfordshire: The Voltaire Foundation, 1973.

Examines Kant's philosophical debt to Condillac's later work.

Derrida, Jacques. *The Archeology of the Frivolous: Reading Condillac*, translated by John P. Leavey, Jr. Pittsburgh: Duquesne University Press, 1980, 143 p.

Focuses on Condillac's theories of the development of semiotic systems from sensations. This work was originally published in French in 1973.

Hine, Ellen McNiven. *A Critical Study of Condillac's* "Traité des systèmes." The Hague: Martinus Nijhoff Publishers, 1979, 226 p.

Comprehensive study of Condillac's *Treatise on Systems*.

O'Meara, Maureen F. "The Language of History and the Place of Power: Male and Female Versions of Condillac's *Histoire Ancienne et Moderne*." In *Discours et Pouvoir*, edited by Ross Chambers, pp. 177-204. Ann Arbor: Michigan Romance Studies, 1982.

Compares two editions of Condillac's *Histoire ancienne et moderne*, one written for the Prince of Parma as part of the *Cours d'étude*, the other adapted for a female audience.

Simone, Raffaele. "Language as *Méthodes Analytiques* in Condillac." In *Speculative Grammar, Universal Grammar and Philosophical Analysis of Language*, edited by Dino Buzzetti and Maurizio Ferriani, pp. 65-73. Amsterdam: John Benjamins Publishing Co., 1987.

Examines Condillac's theories on the analytic character of language.

Wells, G. A. "Condillac, Rousseau, and Herder on the Origin of Language." In *Studies on Voltaire and the Eighteenth Century*, No. 230, pp. 233-46. Oxford: The Voltaire Foundation, 1985.

Discusses Condillac's theory of linguistic genesis.

Denis Diderot

1713-1784

French philosopher, encyclopedist, satirist, novelist, literary and art critic, and dramatist.

INTRODUCTION

Described by Paul Hazard as the "heart and mind of the eighteenth century," Diderot is credited with the most original and powerful intellect of all the philosophes. His beliefs and concerns found expression in virtually every major genre of the period, encompassing dialogue, encyclopedia articles, philosophical treatises, scientific discourses, dramas, literary and art criticism, and essays. The sheer number and variety of his ideas defy synthesis and systematic classification; nevertheless, scholars have discerned in Diderot's oeuvre the project of linking the scientific philosophies of sensationalism, materialism, and empiricism with the search for the ethical life and the Enlightenment preoccupation with happiness. Diderot was additionally concerned with defining the role of the creative individual within society and with the reputation of the artist over time. Scholars believe that he witheld his greatest works from publication out of the fear of censorship, as well as from the conviction that they could only be understood by posterity. It is thus only in the twentieth century that Diderot's achievement has come to be fully appreciated. Arthur M. Wilson has written that Diderot's mature writings have "an elusive but unmistakable quality of seeming to see far and deep into the mysteries of life, . . . perhaps further and deeper than any other man of his century save Goethe."

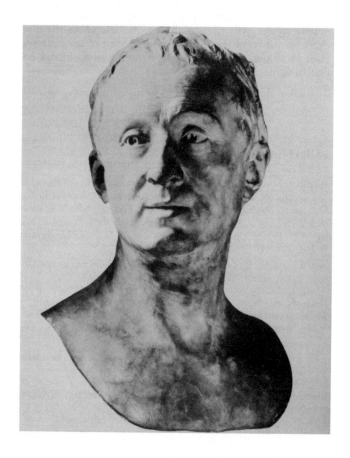

Biographical Information

Diderot was born in Langres, in northeastern France, the son of a respected master artisan who instilled in him the lasting admiration for technical skills and craftmanship that made the *Encyclopédie* (1750-65) such a revolutionary document. Denis was an exceptional student at the Jesuit college in Langres, where he received a solid grounding in Greek and Latin, far surpassing that achieved by the other philosophes. After a period of considering a career in the church, Diderot pursued his further education, receiving the Master of Arts degree from the University of Paris in 1732. Throughout the next decade he vacillated between careers, and was employed variously as a tutor and freelance translator. In 1743 he secretly married Antoine Champion, a poor and uneducated woman whose fiery temper was to make Diderot's domestic life a constant trial. Following his translation into French of Robert James's *Medicinal Dictionary* in the years 1746-48, Diderot and the mathematician Jean d'Alembert were appointed co-editors of a French adaptation of Ephraim Chambers's *Cyclopaedia, or Universal Dictionary of the Arts and Sciences* (1728). Diderot thereby acquired for the first time

financial and professional security; however, he suffered imprisonment in 1749 as a result of his controversial work *Lettre sur les aveugles* (1749; *Letter on the Blind*), which cast doubt on the ideas of a good God and an ordered universe. In the 1750s Diderot focused his literary energies on the *Encyclopédie*, while concurrently writing such works as *Lettre sur les sourds et muets* (1751; *Letter on the Deaf and Dumb*), *Pensées sur l'interprétation de la nature* (1753; *Thoughts on the Interpretation of Nature*), and the dramas *Le fils naturel* (1757; *The Natural Son*) and *Le Père de famille* (1758; *A Father and His Family*). Diderot fell in love in 1755 with the forty-year old, unmarried Sophie Volland, and his letters to her constitute some of his best writing and are considered among the greatest love letters ever written. At the close of the decade he began writing reviews of the biennial exhibitions of the Academy of Painting and Sculpture in the Grand Salon of the Louvre. These were published in a privately circulated newsletter, the *Correspondance littéraire*, and represent the beginnings of modern art criticism. In the 1760s Diderot began work on some of his most celebrated writings, including *La Religieuse* (1760-82; *The Nun*); *Le Neveu de Rameau* (1765-85, *Rameau's Nephew*); *Jacques le fataliste* (1765-84; *Jacques the Fatalist*); and *Le Rêve de d'Alembert*

(1769; *D'Alembert's Dream*). After publishing the last volume of text for the enormously successful *Encyclopédie*, Diderot attracted the notice of Empress Catherine II of Russia, who bought the philosophe's library, with the understanding that it would be sent to St. Petersburg only after his death. In 1773 he journeyed outside France for the first time, travelling to Holland and then to St. Petersburg, where he held regular conversations the Empress. His writings from this period reveal a preoccupation with political issues, most significantly expressed in his anonymous contributions to the abbé Raynal's *Histoire des deux Indes*, a radical work that denounced European colonialism. In the final years of his life Diderot concluded work on such writings as *Paradoxe sur le comédien* (1769-78; *Paradox on Acting*); *Réfutation d'Helvétius* (1773; *Refutation of Helvetius*); and his most successful play, *Est-il bon? Est-il méchant?* (1781; *Is He Good? Is He Wicked?*). After several months of illness, he died in Paris in 1784.

Major Works

Within Diderot's extensive corpus of writings, the works for which the philosophe is best known include his contributions to the *Encyclopédie*, the novels *Jacques the Fatalist* and *The Nun*, and the dialogues *Rameau's Nephew* and *D'Alembert's Dream*. Diderot's encyclopedia articles have been acclaimed for their descriptions of technological processes and traditional crafts—hitherto deemed beneath the attention of belles-lettres—and for their deft handling of the history of philosophy. For example, in one of his most notable philosophical entries, "Beau," Diderot summarizes the aesthetic theories of previous thinkers, expresses his own concept of beauty, and elucidates the variety of distinctions which typically surround this concept. *Rameau's Nephew* takes the form of a dialogue between Diderot and Jean-François Rameau, the nephew of the eminent composer Jean-Philippe Rameau. Despite its random and extemporaneous appearance, the dialogue is carefully structured around such problems as the role of the artist in society, the extent to which genius is subject to popular morality, and the appropriate system of education for a corrupt society. *D'Alembert's Dream*, a series of three dialogues, is viewed as the culmination of Diderot's scientific philosophy. This work elaborates a highly original conception of the nature of life in which Diderot asserts that the universe is composed entirely of sensitive matter, and that life, far from being the result of divine fiat, represents a minor transition from one form of matter to another. The dialogue further explores this concept through intensely poetic imagery and concludes with a radical discussion of the practical and moral applications of the theory. Diderot's first mature novel, *The Nun*, is an epistolary narrative that relates the tribulations endured by a young woman who is forced to join a convent. To emphasize the deceptive and illusory portrayal of reality in prose fiction, Diderot employs sophisticated literary devices, including dramatic dialogues, *tableau vivants*, and gesture. More experimental in form, *Jacques the Fatalist* presents the journeys of the servant Jacques and his anonymous master as a means of parodying the traditional concerns and style of the novel. This work was inspired by Laurence Sterne's *Tristram Shandy* and is similarly punctuated by frequent anecdotes and digressions that subvert the reader's expectations, leading some commmentators to praise *Jacques the Fatalist* as the first anti-novel.

Critical Reception

Despite living constantly under the threat of censorship, and occasionally falling foul of the authorities, Diderot was widely esteemed in his own lifetime for his fertile imagination, mental energy, and conversational prowess. Yet in the years following his death, his reputation suffered a decline in France, being eclipsed by that of his former friend, Jean-Jacques Rousseau. In Germany, however, Diderot exerted a powerful influence on the writers of the Sturm und Drang movement, particularly Johann Wolfgang von Goethe and Friedrich Schiller. In fact, the existence of *Rameau's Nephew* first became known in Goethe's translation of the work, which appeared in Leipzig in 1805. In England, Thomas Carlyle published an essay in 1833 which, while praising Diderot on certain points, presented an overwhelmingly negative assessment of the man as an intellectually undisciplined atheist. A critical step in the rehabilitation of of Diderot's reputation was taken by the pioneering French critic C. A. Sainte-Beuve who in essays written between 1831 and 1851 praised the philosophe as the first great writer of modern democratic society. The eminent Victorian commentator on French Enlightenment thought, John Morley, echoed Sainte-Beuve's appraisal in the two-volume study *Diderot and the Encyclopaedists* (1878). The twentieth century has witnessed a massive resurgence of critical interest in Diderot. Following the example of Sigmund Freud, whose conception of the Oedipus complex was inspired by a passage in *Rameau's Nephew*, many modern scholars and writers have focused on the prophetic quality of Diderot's writings. Diderot has been credited with prefiguring theories of psychology and evolution, as well as the invention of braille, the typewriter, and the cinema. While some critics maintain that his prodigious intellect did not result in any single, indisputable masterpiece, he is by general consent regarded as one of the great geniuses of eighteenth-century letters.

PRINCIPAL WORKS

Pensées philosophiques [*Philosophical Thoughts*] (philosophy) 1746
Les Bijoux indiscrets [*The Indiscreet Jewels*] (novel) 1748
Lettre sur les aveugles [*Letter on the Blind*] (philosophy) 1749
Encyclopédie. 11 vols. (encyclopedia) 1750-65
Lettre sur les sourds et muets [*Letter on the Deaf and Dumb*] (philosophy) 1751
Pensées sur l'interprétation de la nature [*Thoughts on the Interpretation of Nature*] (philosophy) 1753
Le Fils naturel [*The Natural Son*] (drama) 1757
Le Père de famille [*A Father and His Family*] (drama) 1758

Discours sur la poésie dramatique [*Discourse on Dramatic Poetry*] (criticism) 1758
Salon de 1759 (art criticism) 1759
Eloge de Richardson [*Elogy of Richardson*] (criticism) 1761
Salon de 1761 (art criticism) 1761
Le Neveu de Rameau [*Rameau's Nephew*] (dialogue) 1761-83?
Salon de 1763 (art criticism) 1763
Jacques le fataliste [*Jacques the Fatalist*] (novel) 1765-84
Salon de 1765 (art criticism) 1765
Essais sur la peinture [*Essays on Painting*] (art criticism) 1766
Salon de 1767 (art criticism) 1767-68
Le Rêve de d'Alembert [*D'Alembert's Dream*] (dialogue) 1769
Salon de 1769 (art criticism) 1769
Paradoxe sur le comédien [*Paradox on Acting*] (dialogue) 1769-78
Les Deux amis de Bourbonne [*The Two Friends from Bourbonne*] (novella) 1770
Salon de 1771 (art criticism) 1771
Supplément au Voyage de Bougainville [*Supplement to Bougainville's Voyage*] (dialogue) 1772
Réfutation d'Helvétius [*Refutation of Helvetius*] (philosophy) 1773
Salon de 1775 (art criticism) 1775
Est-il bon? Est-il méchant? [*Is He Good? Is He Wicked?*] (drama) 1781
Salon de 1781 (art criticism) 1781
La Religieuse [*The Nun*] (novel) 1782
Essais sur le règnes de Claude et de Néron [*Essay on the Reigns Claudius and Nero*] (essay) 1782
Oeuvres complètes. 20 vols. (dramas and prose) 1875-77
Salons. 4 vols. (art criticism) 1957-67

CRITICISM

Thomas Carlyle (essay date 1833)

SOURCE: "Diderot," in *Critical and Miscellaneous Essays: Collected and Republished,* Vol. III, Brown and Taggard, 1860, pp. 257-329.

[*A Scottish-born essayist, historian, critic, and social commentator, Carlyle was a central figure of the Victorian era who vigorously attacked the materialism and religious indifference of his age, stressing the importance of work, order, piety, and spiritual fulfillment. His historical and political writings, especially* The French Revolution *(1837), are dominated by the idea that "great men," or heroic figures, determine the course of history. In the following excerpt from an essay that originally appeared in the* Foreign Quarterly Review *in 1833, Carlyle castigates Diderot's character and works, maintaining that "he did the work of many men; yet nothing, or little, which many could not have done."*]

Two things . . . are celebrated of Diderot. First, that he had the most encyclopedical head ever seen in this world: second, that he talked as never man talked; —properly, as never man his admirers had heard, or as no man living in Paris then. That is to say, his was at once the widest, fertilest, and readiest of minds.

With regard to the Encyclopedical Head, suppose it to mean that he was of such vivacity as to admit, and look upon with interest, almost all things which the circle of Existence could offer him; in which sense, this exaggerated laudation, of Encyclopedism, is not without its fraction of meaning. Of extraordinary openness and compass we must grant the mind of Diderot to be; of a susceptibility, quick activity; even naturally of a depth, and in its practical realised shape, of a universality, which bring it into kindred with the highest order of minds. On all forms of this wondrous Creation he can look with loving wonder; whatsoever thing stands there, has some brotherhood with him, some beauty and meaning for him. Neither is the faculty to see and interpret wanting; as, indeed, this faculty to *see* is inseparable from that other faculty to *look,* from that true wish to look; moreover (under another figure), intellect is not a *tool,* but a *hand* that can handle any tool. Nay, in Diderot we may discern a far deeper universality than that shown, or showable, in Lebreton's *Encyclopédie;* namely, a poetical; for, in slight gleams, this too manifests itself. A universality less of the head than of the character; such, we say, is traceable in this man, at lowest the power to have acquired such. Your true Encyclopedical is the Homer, the Shakespeare; every genuine Poet is a living embodied, real Encyclopedia, —in more or fewer volumes; were his experience, his insight of details, never so limited, the whole world lies imaged as a whole within him; whosoever has not seized the whole cannot yet speak truly (much less can he speak *musically,* which is harmoniously, *concordantly*) of any part, but will perpetually need new guidance, rectification. The fit use of such a man is as hodman; not feeling the plan of the edifice, let him carry stones to it; if he *build* the smallest stone, it is likeliest to be wrong, and cannot continue there.

But the truth is, as regards Diderot, this saying of the encyclopedical head comes mainly from his having edited a Bookseller's Encyclopedia, and can afford us little direction. Looking into the man, and omitting his trade, we find him by nature gifted in a high degree with openness and versatility, yet nowise in the highest degree; alas, in quite another degree than that. Nay, if it be meant farther that in practice, as a writer and thinker, he has taken-in the Appearances of Life and the World, and images them back with such freedom, clearness, fidelity, as we have not many times witnessed elsewhere, as we have not various times seen infinitely surpassed elsewhere, —this same encyclopedical praise must altogether be denied him. Diderot's habitual world, we must, on the contrary, say, is a half-world, distorted into looking like a whole; it is properly, a poor, fractional, insignificant world; partial, inaccurate, perverted from end to end. Alas, it was the destiny of the man to live as a Polemic; to be born also in the morning-tide and first splendour of the Mechanical Era; not to know, with the smallest assurance or continuance, that in the Universe other than a mechanical meaning could exist; which force of destiny acting on him through his whole course, we have obtained what now stands before us: no Seer, but only possibilities of a Seer, transient irradiations of a Seer, looking through the organs of a Philosophe.

These two considerations, which indeed are properly but one (for a thinker, especially of French birth, in the Mechanical Era, could not be other than a Polemic), must never for a moment be left out of view in judging the works of Diderot. It is a great truth, one side of a great truth, that the Man makes the Circumstances, and spiritually as well as economically is the artificer of his own fortune. But there is another side of the same truth, that the man's circumstances are the element he is appointed to live and work in; that he by necessity takes his complexion, vesture, embodiment, from these, and is, in all practical manifestations, modified by them almost without limit; so that in another no less genuine sense, it can be said Circumstances make the Man. Now, if it continually behooves us to insist on the former truth towards ourselves, it equally behooves us to bear in mind the latter when we judge of other men. The most gifted soul, appearing in France in the Eighteenth Century, can as little embody himself in the intellectual vesture of an Athenian Plato, as in the grammatical one; his thoughts can no more be Greek, than his language can. He thinks of the things belonging to the French eighteenth century, and in the dialect he has learned there; in the light, and under the conditions prescribed there. Thus, as the most original, resolute and self-directing of all the Moderns has written: 'Let a 'man be but born ten years sooner, or ten years later, his 'whole aspect and performance shall be different.' Grant, doubtless, that a certain perennial Spirit, true for all times and all countries, can and must look through the thinking of certain men, be it in what dialect soever: understand meanwhile that strictly this holds only of the highest order of men, and cannot be exacted of inferior orders; among whom, if the most sedulous, loving inspection disclose any even secondary symptoms of such a Spirit, it ought to seem enough. Let us remember well that the high-gifted, high-striving Diderot was born in the point of Time and of Space, when of all uses he could turn himself to, of all dialects speak in, this of Polemical Philosophism, and no other, seemed the most promising and fittest. Let us remember too, that no earnest Man, in any Time, ever spoke what was wholly meaningless; that, in all human convictions, much more in all human practices, there was a true side, a fraction of truth; which fraction is precisely the thing we want to extract from them, if we want anything at all to do with them.

Such palliative considerations (which, for the rest, concern not Diderot, now departed, and indifferent to them, but only ourselves who could wish to see him, and not to mis-see him) are essential, we say, through our whole survey of his Opinions and Proceedings, generally so alien to our own; but most of all in reference to his head Opinion, properly the source of all the rest, and more shocking, even horrible, to us than all the rest: we mean his Atheism.

David Hume, dining once in company where Diderot was, remarked that he did not think there were any Atheists. "Count us," said a certain Monsieur————: they were eighteen. "Well," said the Monsieur————, "it is pretty fair if you have fished-out fifteen at the first cast; and three others who know not what to think of it." In fact, the case was common: your Philosophe of the first water had grown to reckon Atheism a necessary accomplishment. . . .

Diderot was an Atheist, then; stranger still, a proselytising Atheist, who esteemed the creed worth earnest reiterated preaching, and enforcement with all vigour! The unhappy man had 'sailed through the Universe of Worlds and found 'no Maker thereof; had descended to the abysses where 'Being no longer casts its shadow, and felt only the rain-drops 'trickle down; and seen only the gleaming rainbow of 'Creation, which originated from no Sun; and heard only 'the everlasting storm which no one governs; and looked 'upwards for the DIVINE EYE, and beheld only the black, 'bottomless, glaring DEATH'S EYE-SOCKET:' such, with all his wide voyagings, was the philosophic fortune he had realised.

Sad enough, horrible enough: yet instead of shrieking over it, or howling and Ernulphus' cursing over it, let us, as the more profitable method, keep our composure, and inquire a little, What possibly it may mean? The whole phenomenon, as seems to us, will explain itself from the fact above insisted on, that Diderot was a Polemic of decided character, in the Mechanical Age. With great expenditure of words and froth, in arguments as waste, wild-weltering, delirious-dismal as the chaos they would demonstrate; which arguments one now knows not whether to laugh at or to weep at, and almost does both, —have Diderot and his sect perhaps made this apparent to all who examine it: That in the French System of Thought (called also the Scotch, and still familiar enough everywhere, which for want of a better title we have named the Mechanical), there is no room for a Divinity; that to him, for whom *intellect,* or the power of knowing and believing, is still synonymous with *logic,* or the mere power of arranging and communicating, there is absolutely no proof discoverable of a Divinity; and such a man has nothing for it but either, if he be of half spirit as is the frequent case, to trim despicably all his days between two opinions; or else, if he be of whole spirit, to anchor himself on the rock or quagmire of Atheism, —and farther, should he see fit, proclaim to others that there is good riding there. So much may Diderot have demonstrated: a conclusion at which we nowise turn pale. Was it much to know that Metaphysical Speculation, by nature, whirls round in endless Mahlstroms, both 'creating and swallowing—itself ?' For so wonderful a self-swallowing product of the Spirit of the Time, could any result to arrive at be fitter than this of the ETERNAL NO? We thank Heaven that the result *is* finally arrived at; and so now we can look out for something other and farther. But above all things, *proof* of a God? A *probable* God! The smallest of Finites struggling to *prove* to itself, that is to say if we will consider it, to picture-out and arrange as diagram, and *include* within itself, the Highest Infinite; in *which,* by hypothesis, *it* lives, and moves, and has its being! This, we conjecture, will one day seem a much more miraculous miracle than that negative result it has arrived at, —or any other result a still absurder chance might have led it to. He who, in some singular Time of the World's History, were reduced to wander about, in stooping posture, with painfully constructed sulphur-match and farthing rushlight . . . or smoky tarlink (as Denis Diderot), searching for the Sun, and did not find it; were *he* wonderful and his failure; or the singular Time, and its having put him on that search?

Two small consequences, then, we fancy, may have followed, or be following, from poor Diderot's Atheism. First, that all speculations of the sort we call Natural Theology, endeavouring to prove the beginning of all Belief by some Belief earlier than the beginning, are barren, ineffectual, impossible; and may, so soon as otherwise it is profitable, be abandoned. Of final causes, man, by the nature of the case, can *prove* nothing; knows them, if he know anything of them, not by glimmering flint-sparks of Logic, but by an infinitely higher light of intuition; never long, by Heaven's mercy, wholly eclipsed in the human soul; and (under the name of Faith, as regards this matter) familiar to us now, historically or in conscious possession, for upwards of four thousand years. To all open men it will indeed always be a favourite contemplation, that of watching the ways of Being, how animate adjusts itself to inanimate, rational to irrational, and this that we name Nature is not a desolate phantasm of a chaos, but a wondrous existence and reality. If, moreover, in those same 'marks of design,' as he has called them, the contemplative man find new evidence of a designing Maker, be it well for him: meanwhile, surely one would think, the still clearer evidence lay nearer home, —in the contemplative man's own head that *seeks* after such! In which point of view our extant Natural Theologies, as our innumerable Evidences of the Christian Religion, and such like, may, in reference to the strange season they appear in, have a certain value, and be worth printing and reprinting; only let us understand for whom, and how, they are valuable; and be nowise wroth with the poor Atheist, whom they have not convinced, and could not, and should not convince.

The second consequence seems to be, that this whole current hypothesis of the Universe being 'a Machine,' and then of an Architect, who constructed it, sitting as it were apart, and guiding it, and *seeing* it go, —may turn out an inanity and nonentity; not much longer tenable: with which result likewise we shall, in the quietest manner, reconcile ourselves. 'Think ye,' says Goethe, 'that God made the Universe, and 'then let it run round his finger (*am Finger laufen liesse*)?' On the whole, that Metaphysical hurly-burly, of our poor jarring, self-listening Time, ought at length to compose itself: that seeking for a God *there,* and not *here;* everywhere outwardly in physical Nature, and not inwardly in our own Soul, where alone He is to be found by us, —begins to get wearisome. Above all, that 'faint possible Theism,' which now forms our common English creed, cannot be too soon swept out of the world. What is the nature of that individual, who with hysterical violence theoretically asserts a God, perhaps a revealed Symbol and Worship of God; and for the rest, in thought, word and conduct, meet with him where you will, is found living as if his theory were some polite figure of speech,

and his theoretical God a mere distant Simulacrum, with whom he, for his part, had nothing farther to do? Fool! The ETERNAL is no Simulacrum; God is not only There, but Here or nowhere, in that life-breath of thine, in that act and thought of thine, —and thou wert wise to look to it. If there is no God, as the fool hath said in his heart, then live on with thy decencies, and lip-homages, and inward greed, and falsehood, and all the hollow cunningly-devised halfness that recommends thee to the Mammon of this world: if there *is* a God, we say, look to it! But in either case, what art thou? The Atheist is false; yet is there, as we see, a fraction of truth in him; he is true compared with thee; thou, unhappy mortal, livest wholly in a lie, art wholly a lie.

So that Diderot's Atheism comes, if not to much, yet to something: we learn this from it, and from what it stands connected with, and may represent for us, That the Mechanical System of Thought is, in its essence, Atheistic; that whosoever will admit no organ of truth but logic, and nothing to exist but what can be argued of, must even content himself with this sad result, as the only solid one he can arrive at; and so with the best grace he can, 'of the aether 'make a gas, of God a force, of the second world a coffin;' of man an aimless nondescript, 'little better than a kind of vermin.' If Diderot, by bringing matters to this parting of the roads, have enabled or helped us to strike into the truer and better road, let him have our thanks for it. As to what remains, be pity our only feeling; was not his creed miserable enough; nay, moreover, did not he bear its miserableness, so to speak, in our stead, so that it need now be no longer borne by any one?

In this same for him unavoidable circumstance, of the age he lived in, and the system of thought universal then, will be found the key to Diderot's whole spiritual character and procedure; the excuse for much in him that to us is false and perverted. Beyond the meagre 'rushlight of closet-logic,' Diderot recognised no guidance. That 'the Highest cannot be spoken of in words,' was a truth he had not dreamt of. Whatsoever thing he cannot debate of, we might almost say measure and weigh, and carry off with him to be eaten and enjoyed, is simply not there for him. He dwelt all his days in the 'thin rind of the Conscious;' the deep fathomless domain of the Unconscious, whereon the other rests, and has its meaning, was not, under any shape, surmised by him. Thus must the Sanctuary of Man's Soul stand perennially shut against this man; where his hand ceased to grope, the World ended: within such strait conditions had he to live and labour. And naturally to distort and dislocate, more or less, all things he laboured on: for whosoever, in one way or another, recognises not that 'Divine Idea of the World, which lies at the bottom of Appearances,' can rightly interpret no Appearance; and whatsoever spiritual thing he does, must do it partially, do it falsely.

Mournful enough, accordingly, is the account which Diderot has given himself of Man's Existence; on the duties, relations, possessions whereof he had been a sedulous thinker. In every conclusion we have this fact of his Mechanical culture. Coupled too with another fact honourable to him: that he stuck not at half measures; but resolutely drove-on to the result, and held by it. So that we cannot call him a Sceptic; he has merited the more decisive name of Denier. He may be said to have denied that there was any the smallest Sacredness in Man, or in the Universe; and to have both speculated and lived on this singular footing. We behold in him the notable extreme of a man guiding himself with the least spiritual Belief that thinking man perhaps ever had. Religion, in all recognisable shapes and senses, he has done what man can do to clear-out of him. He believes that pleasure is pleasant; that a lie is unbelievable; and there his *credo* terminates; nay there, what perhaps makes his case almost unique, his very fancy seems to fall silent.

For a consequent man, all possible spiritual perversions are included under that grossest one of 'proselytising Atheism;' the rest, of what kind and degree soever, cannot any longer astonish us. Diderot has them of all kinds and degrees: indeed, we might say, the French Philosophe (take him at his word, for inwardly much that was foreign adhered to him, do what he could) has emitted a Scheme of the World, to which all that Oriental Mullah, Bonze or Talapoin have done in that kind is poor and feeble. Omitting his whole unparalleled Cosmogonies and Physiologies; coming to his much milder Tables of the Moral Law, we shall glance here but at one minor external item, the relation between man and man; and at only one branch of this, and with all slightness, the relation of covenants; for example, the most important of these, Marriage.

Diderot has convinced himself, and indeed, as above became plain enough, acts on the conviction, that Marriage, contract it, solemnise it in what way you will, involves a solecism which reduces the amount of it to simple zero. It is a suicidal covenant; annuls itself in the very forming. 'Thou makest a vow,' says he, twice or thrice, as if the argument were a clincher, 'thou makest a vow of eternal con-'stancy under a rock, which is even then crumbling away.' True, O Denis! the rock crumbles away: all things are changing; man changes faster than most of them. That, in the mean while, an Unchangeable lies under all this, and looks forth, solemn and benign, through the whole destiny and workings of man, is another truth; which no Mechanical Philosophe, in the dust of his logic-mill, can be expected to grind-out for himself. Man changes, and will change: the question then arises, Is it wise in him to tumble forth, in headlong obedience to this love of change; is it so much as possible for him? Among the dualisms of man's wholly dualistic nature, this we might fancy was an observable one: that along with his unceasing tendency to change, there is a no less ineradicable tendency to persevere. Were man only here to change, let him, far from marrying, cease even to hedge-in fields, and plough them; before the autumn season, he may have lost the whim of reaping them. Let him return to the nomadic state, and set his house on wheels; nay there too a certain restraint must curb his love of change, or his cattle will perish by incessant driving, without grazing in the intervals. O Denis, what things thou babblest, in thy sleep! How, in this world of perpetual flux, shall man secure himself the smallest foundation, except hereby alone: that he take preassurance of his Fate; that in this and the other high act of his life, his Will, with all solemnity, *abdicate*

its right to change; voluntarily, become involuntary, and say once for all, Be there then no farther dubitation on it! Nay, the poor unheroic craftsman; that very stocking-weaver, on whose loom thou now as amateur weavest: must not even he do as much, —when he signed his apprentice-indentures? The fool! who had such a relish in himself for all things, for kingship and emperorship; yet made a vow (under a penalty of death by hunger) of eternal constancy to stocking-weaving. Yet otherwise, were no thriving craftsmen possible; only botchers, bunglers, transitory nondescripts; unfed, mostly gallows-feeding. But, on the whole, what feeling it was in the ancient devout deep soul, which of Marriage made *a Sacrament*: this, of all things in the world, is what Denis will think of for aeons, without discovering. Unless, perhaps, it were to increase the vestry-fees?

Indeed, it must be granted, nothing yet seen or dreamt of can surpass the liberality of friend Denis as *magister morum;* nay, often our poor Philosophe feels called on, in an age of such Spartan rigour, to step forth into the public Stews, and emit his inspiriting *Macte virtute!* there. Whither let the curious in such matters follow him: we, having work elsewhere, wish him 'good journey,' —or rather 'safe return.' Of Diderot's indelicacy and indecency there is for us but little to say. Diderot is not what we call indelicate and indecent; he is utterly unclean, scandalous, shameless, sansculottic-samoeidic. To declare with lyric fury that this is wrong; or with historic calmness, that a pig of sensibility would go distracted did you accuse him of it, may, especially countries where 'indecent exposure' is cognisable at police-offices, be considered superfluous. The only question is one in Natural History: Whence comes it? What may a man, not otherwise without elevation of mind, of kindly character, of immense professed philanthropy, and doubtless of extraordinary insight, mean thereby? To us it is but another illustration of the fearless, all-for-logic, thoroughly consistent, Mechanical Thinker. It coheres well enough with Diderot's theory of man; that there is nothing of sacred either in man or around man; and that chimeras are chimerical. How shall he for whom nothing, that cannot be jargoned of in debating-clubs, exists, have any faintest forecast of the depth, significance, divineness of SILENCE; of the sacredness of 'Secrets known to all?'

Nevertheless, Nature is great; and Denis was among her nobler productions. To a soul of his sort something like what we call Conscience could nowise be wanting: the feeling of Moral Relation; of the Infinite character thereof, as the essence and soul of all else that can be felt or known, must needs assert itself in him. Yet how assert itself? An Infinitude to one, in whose whole Synopsis of the Universe no Infinite stands marked? Wonderful enough is Diderot's method; and yet not wonderful, for we see it, and have always seen it, daily. Since there is nothing sacred in the Universe, whence this sacredness of what you call Virtue? Whence or how comes it that you, Denis Diderot, *must* not do a wrong thing; could not, without some qualm, speak, for example, one Lie, to gain Mahomet's Paradise with all its houries? There is no resource for it, but to get into that interminable ravelment of Reward and Approval, virtue being its own reward; and assert louder and louder, —contrary to the stern experience of all men, from the Divine Man, expiring with agony of bloody sweat on the accursed tree, down to us two, O reader (if we have ever done one Duty), —that Virtue is synonymous with Pleasure. Alas! was Paul, an Apostle of the Gentiles, virtuous; and was virtue its own reward, when *his* approving conscience told him that he was 'the chief of sinners,' and if bounded to this life alone, 'of all men the most miserable?' Or has that same so sublime Virtue, at bottom, little to do with Pleasure, if with far other things? Are Eudoxia, and Eusebeia, and Euthanasia, and all the rest of them, of small account to Eubosia, and Eupepsia; and the pains of any moderately-paced Career of Vice, Denis himself being judge, as a drop in the bucket to the 'Career of Indigestions?' This is what Denis never in this world will grant.

But what then will he do? One of two things: admit, with Grimm, that there are 'two justices,' —which may be called by many handsome names, but properly are nothing but the pleasant justice, and the unpleasant; whereof only the former is binding! Herein, however, Nature has been unkind to Denis; he is not a literary court-toadeater; but a free, genial, even poetic creature. There remains, therefore, nothing but the second expedient: to 'assert louder and louder;' in other words, to become a Philosophe Sentimentalist. Most wearisome, accordingly, is the perpetual clatter kept up here about *vertu, honnêteté, grandeur, sensibilité, âmes-nobles;* how unspeakably good it is to be virtuous, how pleasant, how sublime: —In the Devil and his grandmother's name, *be* virtuous; and let us have an end of it! In such sort (we will nevertheless joyfully recognise) does great Nature in spite of all contradictions, declare her royalty, her divineness; and, for the poor Mechanical Philosophe, has prepared, since the substance is hidden from him, a shadow wherewith he can be cheered.

In fine, to our ill-starred Mechanical Philosophe-Sentimentalist, with his loud preaching and rather poor performing, shall we not, in various respects, 'thankfully stretch out the hand?' In all ways 'it was necessary that the logical side of things should likewise be made available.' On the whole, wondrous higher developments of much, of Morality among the rest, are visible in the course of the world's doings, at this day. A plausible prediction were that the Ascetic System is not to regain its exclusive dominancy. Ever, indeed, must Self-denial, *'Annihilation of Self,'* be the beginning of all moral action: meanwhile, he that looks well, may discern filaments of a nobler System, wherein this lies included as one harmonious element. Who knows, for example, what new unfoldings and complex adjustments await us, before the true relation of moral Greatness to moral Correctness, and their proportional value, can be established? How, again, is perfect tolerance for the Wrong to co-exist with ever-present conviction that Right stands related to it, as a God does to a Devil, —an Infinite to an opposite Infinite? How, in a word, through what tumultuous vicissitudes, after how many false partial efforts, deepening the confusion, shall it at length be made manifest, and kept continually manifest, to the hearts of men, that the Good is not properly the highest, but the Beautiful; that the true Beautiful (differing from the false, as Heaven does from Vauxhall) comprehends in it the Good? —In some future century, it may

be found that Denis Diderot, acting and professing, in wholeness and with full conviction, what the immense multitude act in halfness and without conviction, has, though by strange inverse methods, forwarded the result. It was long ago written, the Omnipotent 'maketh the wrath of the wicked,' the folly of the foolish, 'to praise Him.' In any case, Diderot acted it, and not we; Diderot bears it, and not we: peace be with Diderot!

The other branch of his renown is excellence as a Talker. Or, in wider view, think his admirers, his philosophy was not more surpassing than his delivery thereof. What his philosophy amounts to, we have been examining: but now, that in this other conversational province he was eminent, is easily believed. A frank, ever-hoping, social character; a mind full of knowledge, full of fervour; of great compass, of great depth, ever on the alert: such a man could not have other than a 'mouth of gold.' It is still plain, whatsoever thing imaged itself before him was imaged in the most lucent clearness; was rendered back, with light labour, in corresponding clearness. Whether, at the same time, Diderot's conversion, relatively so superior, deserved the intrinsic character of supreme, may admit of question. The worth of words spoken depends, after all, on the wisdom that resides in them; and in Diderot's words there was often too little of this. Vivacity, far-darting brilliancy, keenness of theoretic vision, paradoxical ingenuity, gaiety, even touches of humour; all this must have been here: whosoever had preferred sincerity, earnestness, depth of practical rather than theoretic insight, with not less of impetuosity, of clearness and sureness, with humour, emphasis, or such other melody or rhythm as that utterance demanded, —must have come over to London; and, with forbearant submissiveness, listened to our Johnson. Had we the stronger man, then? Be it rather, as in that duel of Coeur-de-Lion with the light, nimble, yet also invincible Saladin, that each nation had the strength which most befitted it.

Closely connected with this power of conversation is Diderot's facility of composition. A talent much celebrated; numerous really surprising proofs whereof are on record: how he wrote long works within the week; sometimes within almost the four-and-twenty hours. Unhappily, enough still remains to make such feats credible. Most of Diderot's Works bear the clearest traces of extemporaneousness; *stans pede in uno!* They are much liker printed talk, than the concentrated well-considered utterance which, from a man of that weight, we expect to see set in types. It is said, 'he wrote good pages, but could not write a good book.' Substitute *did not* for *could not;* and there is truth in the saying. Clearness, as has been observed, comprehensibility at a glance, is the character of whatever Diderot wrote: a clearness which, in visual objects, rises into the region of the Artistic, and resembles that of Richardson or Defoe. Yet, grant that he makes his meaning clear, what is the nature of that meaning itself? Alas, for most part, only a hasty, flimsy, superficial meaning, with gleams of a deeper vision peering through. More or less of disorder reigns in all Works that Diderot wrote; not order, but the plausible appearance of such: the true heart of the matter is not found; 'he skips deftly along the radii, and skips over the centre, and misses it.'

Thus may Diderot's admired Universality and admired Facility have both turned to disadvantage for him. We speak not of his reception by the world: this indeed is the 'age of specialties;' yet, owing to other causes, Diderot the Encyclopedist had success enough. But, what is of far more importance, his inward growth was marred: the strong tree shot not up in any one noble stem, bearing boughs, and fruit, and shade all round; but spread out horizontally, after a very moderate height, into innumerable branches, not useless, yet of quite secondary use. Diderot could have been an Artist; and he was little better than an Encyclopedic Artisan. No smatterer, indeed; a faithful artisan; of really universal equipment, in his sort: he did the work of many men; yet nothing, or little, which many could not have done.

Accordingly, his Literary Works, now lying finished some fifty years, have already, to the most surprising degree, shrunk in importance. Perhaps no man so much talked of is so little known; to the great majority he is no longer a Reality, but a Hearsay. Such, indeed, partly is the natural fate of Works Polemical, which almost all Diderot's are. The Polemic annihilates his opponent; but in so doing annihilates himself too, and both are swept away to make room for something other and farther. Add to this, the slight-textured transitory character of Diderot's style; and the fact is well enough explained. Meanwhile, let him to whom it applies consider it; him among whose gifts it was to rise into the Perennial, and who dwelt rather low down in the Ephemeral, and ephemerally fought and scrambled there! Diderot the great has contracted into Diderot the easily-measurable: so must it be with others of the like.

In how many sentences can the net-product of all that tumultuous Atheism, printed over many volumes, be comprised! Nay, the whole ***Encyclopédie,*** that world's wonder of the eighteenth century, the Belus' Tower of an age of refined Illumination, what has it become? Alas, no stone-tower, that will stand there as our strength and defence through all times; but, at best, a wooden *Helepolis* (City-taker), wherein stationed, the Philosophus Policaster has burnt and battered-down many an old ruinous Sorbonne; and which now, when that work is pretty well over, may, in turn, be taken asunder, and used as firewood. The famed Encyclopedical Tree itself has proved an artificial one, and borne no fruit. We mean that, in its nature, it is mechanical only; one of those attempts to parcel-out the invisible mystical Soul of Man, with its *infinitude* of phases and character, into shop-lists of what are called 'faculties,' 'motives,' and such like; which attempts may indeed be made with all degrees of insight, from that of a Doctor Spurzheim to that of Denis Diderot or Jeremy Bentham; and prove useful for a day, but for a day only.

Nevertheless it were false to regard Diderot as a Mechanist and nothing more; as one working and grinding blindly in the mill of mechanical Logic, joyful with his lot there, and unconscious of any other. Call him one rather who contributed to deliver us therefrom: both by his manful whole spirit as a Mechanist, which drove all things to their ultimatum and crisis; and even by a dim-struggling faculty, which virtually aimed beyond this. Diderot, we said, was gifted by Nature for an Artist: strangely flashing

through his mechanical encumbrances, are rays of thought, which belong to the Poet, to the Prophet; which, in other environment, could have revealed the deepest to us. Not to seek far, consider this one little sentence, which he makes the last of the dying Sanderson: '*Le temps, la matière et l'espace ne sont peut-être qu'un point* (Time, Matter and Space are perhaps but a *point*)!'

So too, in Art, both as a speaker and a doer, he is to be reckoned as one of those who pressed forward irresistibly out of the artificial barren sphere of that time, into a truer genial one. His Dramas, the ***Fils Naturel,*** the ***Père de Famille,*** have indeed ceased to live; yet is the attempt towards great things visible in them; the attempt remains to us, and seeks otherwise, and has found, and is finding, fulfillment. Not less in his ***Salons*** (judgments of art-exhibitions), written hastily for Grimm, and by ill chance on artists of quite secondary character, do we find the freest recognition of whatever excellence there is; nay an impetuous endeavour, not critically, but even creatively, towards something more excellent. Indeed, what with their unrivalled clearness, painting the picture over again for us, so that we too *see* it, and can judge it; what with their sunny fervour, inventiveness, real artistic genius, which wants nothing but a *hand,* they are, with some few exceptions in the German tongue, the only Pictorial Criticisms we know of worth reading. Here too, as by his own practice in the Dramatic branch of art, Diderot stands forth as the main originator, almost the sole one in his own country, of that many-sided struggle towards what is called Nature, and copying of Nature, and faithfulness to Nature: a deep indispensable truth, subversive of the old error; yet under that figure, only a half-truth, for Art too is Art, as surely as Nature is Nature; which struggle, meanwhile, either as half-truth or working itself into a whole truth, may be seen, in countries that have any Art, still forming the tendency of all artistic endeavour. In which sense, Diderot's ***Essay on Painting*** has been judged worth translation by the greatest modern Judge of Art, and greatest modern Artist, in the highest kind of Art; and may be read anew, with argumentative commentary and exposition, in *Goethe's Works.*

Nay, let us grant, with pleasure, that for Diderot himself the realms of Art were not wholly unvisited; that he too, so heavily imprisoned, stole Promethean fire. Among these multitudinous, most miscellaneous Writings of his, in great part a manufactured farrago of Philosophism no longer saleable, and now looking melancholy enough, —are two that we can almost call Poems; that have something perennially poetic in them: ***Jacques; le Fataliste*** in a still higher degree, the ***Neveu de Rameau.*** The occasional *blueness* of both; even that darkest indigo in some parts of the former, shall not altogether affright us. As it were, a loose straggling sunbeam flies here over Man's Existence in France, now nigh a century behind us: 'from the height of luxurious elegance to the depths of shamelessness,' all is here. Slack, careless seems the combination of the picture; wriggling, disjointed, like a bundle of flails; yet strangely united in the painter's inward unconscious feeling. Wearisomely crackling wit gets silent; a grim, taciturn, dare-devil, almost Hogarthian humour, rises in the back ground. Like this there is nothing that we know of in the whole range of French Literature: La Fontaine is shallow in comparison; the La Bruyère wit-species not to be named. It resembles *Don Quixote,* rather; of somewhat similar stature; yet of complexion altogether different; through the one looks a sunny Elysium, through the other a sulphurous Erebus: both hold of the Infinite. This *Jacques,* perhaps, was not quite so hastily put together: yet there too haste is manifest: the Author finishes it off, not by working-out the figures and movements, but by dashing his brush against the canvas; a manoeuvre which in this case has not succeeded. The *Rameau's Nephew,* which is the shorter, is also the better; may pass for decidedly the best of all Diderot's compositions. It looks like a Sibylline utterance from a heart all in fusion; no ephemeral thing (for it was written as a Satire on Palissot) was ever more perennially treated. Strangely enough too, it lay some fifty years in German and Russian Libraries; came out first in the masterly version of Goethe, in 1805: and only (after a deceptive *re*-translation by M. Saur, a courageous mystifier otherwise) reached the Paris public in 1821, —when perhaps *all,* for whom and against whom it was written were no more! —It is a farce-tragedy; and its fate has corresponded to its purport. One day it must also be translated into English; but will require to be done by *head;* the common steam-machinery will not properly suffice for it.

Diderot on death (1762):

You ask me why, the more our life is filled up and busy, the less are we attached to it? If that is true, it is because a busy life is for the most part an innocent life. We think less about Death, and so we fear it less. Without perceiving it, we resign ourselves to the common lot of all the beings that we watch around us, dying and being born again in an incessant, ever renewing circle. After having for a season fulfilled the tasks that nature year by year imposes on us, we grow weary of them, and release ourselves. Energies fade, we become feebler, we crave the close of life, as after working hard we crave the close of the day. Living in harmony with nature, we learn not to rebel against the orders that we see in necessary and universal execution. . . . There is nobody among us who, having worn himself out in toil, has not seen the hour of rest approach with supreme delight. Life for some of us is only one long day of weariness, and death a long slumber, and the coffin a bed of rest, and the earth only a pillow where it is sweet, when all is done, to lay one's head, never to raise it again. I confess to you that, when looked at in this way, and after the long endless crosses that I have had, death is the most agreeable of prospects. I am bent on teaching myself more and more to see it so.

Denis Diderot in a letter to Sophie Volland, quoted by John Morley, in his Diderot and the Encyclopedists *Vol. II, 1888.*

C. A. Sainte-Beuve (essay date 1831-51)

SOURCE: "Denis Diderot (1713-1784)," in *Portraits of*

the Eighteenth Century: Historic and Literary, Part II by C. A. Sainte-Beuve, translated by Katharine P. Wormeley, G. P. Putnam's Sons, 1905, pp. 89-128.

[*Sainte-Beuve is considered the foremost French literary critic of the nineteenth century. Asserting that the critic cannot separate a work of literature from the artist and the artist's historical milieu, Sainte-Beuve regarded an author's life and character as integral to the composition of his work. In the following excerpt, taken from essays originally written over a period of several decades, Sainte-Beuve provides an overview of Diderot's career, describing the philosopher as "the first great writer in point of time who definitely belongs to modern democratic society."*]

Every man endowed with great talents, if he has come into the world at a time when they can make themselves known, owes to his epoch and to mankind a work suited to the general needs of that epoch, a work which will assist the march of progress. Whatever his private inclinations, his caprices, his slothful humour, or his fancy for incidental writings, he owes to society a public monument, on pain of disregarding his mission and squandering his destiny. Montesquieu by the *Esprit des Lois,* Rousseau by *Émile* and the *Contrat Social,* Buffon by the *Histoire Naturelle,* Voltaire by the grand total of his labours, bore witness to this sanctified law of genius, by virtue whereof it devotes itself to the advancement of mankind; nor did Diderot, whatever may once have been said too thoughtlessly, fail to do his part.

His great work, his own special work, so to speak, was the *Encyclopédie.* As soon as the booksellers who first conceived the idea of it had laid their hands on him, they were confident that they had their man; the idea instantly expanded, took on body and life. Diderot seized upon it so eagerly and presented it in such an attractive light that he succeeded in winning the approbation of the pious Chancellor d'Aguesseau, and in inducing him to give his assent, his patronage, to the undertaking; d'Aguesseau was its earliest patron.

It was originally intended to be nothing more than a translation, revised and augmented, of Chalmers's English Dictionary—a bookseller's speculation. Diderot fertilised the original idea and boldly conceived the scheme of a universal compendium of human knowledge in his day. He took twenty-five years (1748-1772) to carry it out. He was the living corner-stone within of this collective structure, and also the target of all the persecution, of all the threats from without. D'Alembert, who had joined him mainly from self-interest, and whose ingenious Preface assumed far too much, for the benefit of those who read only prefaces, of the surpassing glory of the whole undertaking, deserted when it was half executed, leaving Diderot to contend against the frenzy of the pietists, the cowardice of the booksellers, and to struggle beneath an enormous increase of editorial labour. The history of philosophy, which he treats at second hand, it is true; the description of the mechanic arts, in which perhaps he displays more originality; three or four thousand plates which he caused to be drawn under his own eye; in a word, the responsibility and superintendence of the whole affair were never able to engross him or to quench the sparkle of his energy. Thanks to his prodigious activity, to the universality of his knowledge, to the manifold adaptability which he acquired at an early age, in poverty, —thanks above all to his moral power to rally his associates about him, to inspire and arouse them, he completed that daring edifice, threatening in its massiveness, yet built according to rule. If we seek the name of the architect, his is the name that we must read upon it.

Diderot knew better than any one else the defects in his work; he even exaggerated them to himself, considering the time spent upon it; and believing that he was born for the arts, for geometry, for the stage, he deplored over and over again that he had wasted his life over a matter the profit of which was so paltry and the glory so promiscuous. That he was admirably constituted for geometry and the arts, I do not deny; but surely, things being as they then were, a great revolution, as he himself observed [in his *Interprétation de la Nature*], being under way in the sciences, which were descending from the higher geometry and from metaphysical contemplation, to include in their scope morality, belles-lettres natural history, experimental physics, and trade; furthermore, art in the eighteenth century being falsely turned aside from its more elevated aim, and debased to serve as a philosophical speaking-trumpet, or as a weapon in the conflict; —amid such general conditions, it was difficult for Diderot to employ his powerful talents more profitably, more worthily, and more memorably than by devoting them to the *Encyclopédie.* He aided and hastened, by that civilising work, the revolution that he had noted in the sciences.

Diderot, in his first *Pensées Philosophiques,* seems especially indignant at the tyrannical and waywardly savage aspect which the doctrine of Nicole, Arnauld, and Pascal gave to the Christian God; and it is in the name of misjudged humanity and of a saintly commiseration for his fellow-men that he begins the daring criticism in which his impetuous fervour will not allow him to stop. So it is with the majority of unbelieving innovators: at the starting-point the same protestation of a noble purpose makes them one.

The *Encyclopédie,* then, was not a peace-bringing monument, a silent cloistral tower, with scholars and thinkers of every variety distributed among the different floors. It was not a pyramid of granite with an immovable base; it had no feature of those pure and harmonious structures of art which ascend slowly during centuries of fervent devotion toward an adored and blessed God. It has been compared to the impious Babel; I see in it rather one of those towers of war, one of those siege-machines, enormous, gigantic, wonderful to behold, such as Polybius describes, such as Tasso imagines. There are ruinous portions, and unsymmetrical, much plaster, and firmly cemented and indestructible fragments. The foundations do not extend into the ground; the structure wavers, it is tottering, it will fall; but what does it matter? To apply here an eloquent observation of Diderot himself: "The statue of the architect will remain standing amid the ruins, and the stone that is detached from the mountain will not shatter it, because its feet are not of clay."

Diderot's atheism, although he flaunts it at intervals with a deplorable flourish of trumpets, and although his adversaries have too pitilessly taken him at his word, can generally be reduced to the denial of an unkind and vindictive God. In truth, it often seems that all that he lacks is a ray of light to illuminate everything; and one might well say of Diderot's atheism, as he himself said of those two landscapes of Vernet, in which everything is darkened and obscured by the coming of night: "Let us wait till to-morrow when the sun will have risen."

If the *Encyclopédie* was Diderot's great social work and his principal work, his principal glory in our eyes to-day is the having been the creator of earnest, impassioned, eloquent criticism; it is by his work in this direction that he survives and that he must be ever dear to us all, journalists and extemporaneous writers on all subjects. Let us salute in him our father and the earliest model of the race of critics.

Before Diderot, criticism in France had been exact, inquisitive, and shrewd with Bayle, refined and exquisite with Fénelon, straightforward and useful with Rollin; I omit in modesty the Frérons and Des Fontaines. But nowhere had it been lively, fruitful, searching, —if I may so express it, it had not found its soul. Diderot was the first who gave it a soul. Naturally inclined to overlook defects and to take fire at good qualities,

> "I am more affected," he said, "by the attractions of virtue than by the deformities of vice; I turn gently away from the wicked and I fly to meet the good. If there is in a literary work, in a character, in a picture, in a statue, a beautiful spot, that is where my eyes rest; I see only that, I remember only that, all the rest is well-nigh forgotten. What becomes of me when the whole work is beautiful!"

This propensity to extend a cordial welcome, to universal condescension and to enthusiasm, doubtless had its risks. It has been said of him that he was singularly fortunate in two respects, "in that he had never fallen in with a bad man or a poor book." For if the book were poor, he made it over and unconsciously attributed to the author some of his, Diderot's, own inventions. Like the alchemist, he found gold in the crucible because he had put it there. However, it is to him that is due the honour of having first introduced among us the fruitful criticism of *beauties,* which he substituted for the criticism of *faults;* and in this respect Chateaubriand himself, in that part of the *Génie du Christianisme* where he eloquently discusses literary criticism, simply follows the path blazed out by Diderot.

Abbé Arnaud said to him: "You have the reverse of dramatic talent: it should transform itself into all the characters, and you transform them all into yourself." But if it be true that Diderot was nothing less than a dramatic poet, that he was in no wise competent for that species of sovereign creation and of transformation altogether impersonal, he had by way of compensation, and in the very highest degree, that power of *semi*-metamorphosis which is the game and the triumph of criticism, and which consists in putting oneself in the author's place and at the point of view of the subject that one is examining, in reading every written work *according to the mind that dictated it.* He excelled in taking to himself for a time, and at his pleasure, the mind of another person; in gathering inspiration from it, often to better effect than that other himself had done; in arousing the enthusiasm not only of his own brain, but of his heart; and at such times he was the great modern journalist, the Homer of the profession, intelligent, ardent, effusive, eloquent, never at home, always abroad; or if it happened that he received others at his home and amid his own ideas, then he was the most openhearted, the most hospitable of mortals, the most friendly to all men and to everything, and gave to all his circle, readers no less than authors or artists, not a lesson but a fête.

Such an one does he appear in his admirable *Salons de Peinture.* One day Grimm, who supplied several sovereigns of the North with the latest news of literature and the fine arts, asked Diderot to write for him a report on the Salon of 1761. Diderot had theretofore turned his attention to many subjects, but never to the fine arts in particular. At his friend's request he undertook to observe and scrutinise for the first time what he had never up to that time done more than casually glance at; and the result of his observations and reflections gave birth to those pages of admirable *causerie* which really created criticism of the fine arts in France.

I am aware of one objection which is commonly made to such noble discourses upon art, and to which Diderot's *Salons* are peculiarly obnoxious. It is that they are *beside* the subject, that they discuss it from the literary, the dramatic standpoint, which is the standpoint dear to the French. Madame Necker wrote to Diderot: "I continue to be infinitely entertained by reading your *Salon; I do not care for painting except in poetry;* and that is how you have had the skill to interpret all the works, even the most commonplace, of our modern painters." That is praise indeed, and, according to some people of intelligence, it is the severest kind of criticism.

> "It is a fact," they say, "that it is a peculiarity of the French to judge everything with the mind, even forms and colours. It is true, that, as there is no language to express the delicate refinements of form or the various effects of colour, whenever one undertakes to discuss them, one is forced, for lack of power to express what one feels, to describe other sensations which can be understood by everybody."

Diderot is more open than others to this reproach, and the pictures which he sees are generally simply a pretext and a motive for those which he makes of them, and which he imagines. His articles almost invariably consist of two parts: in the first, he describes the picture that he has before his eyes; in the second, he suggests his own. Such talkative writers, however, when they are, as he was, saturated with their subject, imbued with a lively appreciation of art and of the things which they are discussing, are at the same time useful and interesting: they guide you, they make you pay attention; and while you follow them, while you listen to them, while you go along with them or take another road, the sense of form and colour, if you have such a sense, awakens, takes shape, and becomes sharpened; unconsciously you become in your turn a good

judge, a connoisseur, for mysterious reasons which you cannot describe and which there are no words to express.

To how great a degree Diderot is a *littérateur* in his way of criticising pictures, we may discover at the very outset. A painter has represented "Telemachus on Calypso's Island": the scene shows **them** at table, where the young hero is narrating his adventures, and Calypso offers him a peach. Diderot considers that this offering a by Calypso is an *absurdity,* and that Telemachus has much more sense than the nymph or the painter, for he continues the tale of his adventures without accepting the proffered fruit. But if the peach were gracefully offered, if the light fell upon it in a certain way, if the nymph's expression were consistent with her act, if, in a word, the picture were a Titian or a Veronese, that peach might have been a chef-d'oeuvre, despite the *absurdity* which the mind thinks that it detects therein; for in a picture, the narrative of adventures, which we do not hear, and which the offer of the peach runs the risk of interrupting, is only secondary; we have no use for our ears, we are all eyes.

In a great number of instances, however, Diderot has some just observations, strikingly true, which he offers less as a critic than as a painter. For example, addressing M. Vien, who has painted a Psyche holding her lamp in her hand and surprising Cupid in his sleep, he says:

> Oh! how little sense our painters have! how little they know nature! Psyche's head should be bent over Cupid, the rest of her body thrown back, as it is when we creep toward a place we are afraid to enter and from which we are all ready to fly; one foot resting on the ground, the other barely touching it. And that lamp—ought she to let the light fall on Cupid's eyes? Should she not rather bold it away and interpose her hand so as to shield the light? Besides, that would be an excuse for arranging the light in the picture in a very fetching way. These fellows do not know that the eyelids are transparent in some sort; they have never seen a mother come at night to look at her child in the cradle, with a lamp in her hand, and afraid of waking him.

In all this Diderot is a great critic, and in that kind of general criticism which no art can possibly escape on the pretext of technique.

> "It seems to me," he says, "that when one takes up the brush, one should have some powerful, ingenious, delicate, or interesting idea, and should have in mind some definite effect, some impression to be produced. . . . There are very few artists who have ideas, and there is hardly a single one who can dispense with them. . . . There is no middle way—either interesting ideas, an original subject, or wonderful workmanship."

This wonderful workmanship, which is, after all, the condition without which the idea itself cannot live; this exceptional and superior execution which is the hall-mark of every great artist—when Diderot detects it in one of them, he is the first to feel it and to interpret it for us by words no less wonderful, —unusual words from a wholly new vocabulary of which he is, as it were, the inventor. And, in general, all the powers of improvisation, of picturesque and quick imagination, with which he was endowed; all his stores of bold, profound, and ingenious conceptions; the love of nature, of the country, and of family; even his sensuality, his decided tendency to touch and describe forms; the sentiment of colour, *the sentiment of the flesh,* of blood and of life, "which **is** the despair of colourists" and which came to him as his pen flew—all these priceless qualities of Diderot found employment in those *feuilles volantes* which are still his surest title to the admiration of posterity.

He surpasses himself whenever he speaks of Vernet and of Greuze. As an artist, Greuze is Diderot's ideal; he is a sincere, sympathetic painter, a painter of the family and the drama, affecting and straightforward, slightly sensual, yet moral at the same time. And so, when Diderot falls in with him, he makes fast to him, translates him, interprets him, explains him, adds to his meaning, and never again releases his hold of him. "I am a trifle long, perhaps," he says, "but if you knew how I am enjoying myself while boring you! I am like all the other bores in the world." The analyses, or rather the *paintings,* which Diderot has given us of the "Village Bride," the "Girl Weeping for her Dead Bird," the "Beloved Mother," and the rest, are masterpieces, little poems appropriate to the pictures and printed on the opposite page as it were. Diderot frequently says of a painter, "He paints freely (*large*), he draws freely." The same may be said of himself as a critic; he spreads his colours freely; his criticism is effusive. Even when describing to us with keen delight some family idyl of Greuze, he finds a way to mingle some tones of his own. In his analysis of the "Girl Weeping," he does more, he introduces a complete elegy of his own invention. That child, who seems to be weeping for her bird, has her secret, she is weeping for something very different.

> "Oh! what a lovely hand," cries the intoxicated critic as he gazes at her; "what a lovely hand! what lovely arms! Observe the accuracy of the detail of those fingers, and those dimples, and that soft flesh, and the reddish tint of the finger tips caused by the pressure of the head, and the fascination of it all. One would draw near to that hand to kiss it, were it not that one respects the child and her grief."

And, even while enjoining upon himself respect for the child's grief, he does draw near; he begins to speak to her, to raise, as gently as he can, the veil of mystery:

> "Why, my dear, your grief is very great, very profound. What means this dreamy, melancholy expression? What! all for a bird? You are not weeping, you are in deep affliction; and your affliction is accompanied by thought. Come, my dear, open your heart to me; tell me the truth: is it really this bird's death that has withdrawn you so entirely and so sadly into yourself?"

And so he goes on and transfixes the idyl with his elegy. Thus the picture is, with him, simply a pretext for reverie, for poetic thoughts.

Diderot is the king and the god of those half-poets who become and appear whole poets in criticism; all that they

need is an external fulcrum and a stimulus. Observe that, in analysing this picture, and others of Greuze's works as well, Diderot delights in noting therein, or in introducing, a faint vein of sensuality amid the moral meaning—a vein which is really there, perhaps, but which at all events he loves to trace out, to point his finger at, and which he is tempted to magnify and exaggerate rather than pass over. The curves of the breast, the fulness of contour, even in the family pictures, even in wives and mothers, he recurs to again and again, he delights to let his glance and his pen rest upon them, not as a critic or an artist, not as a fastidious libertine either (Diderot is not depraved), but as a natural, materialistic man, and sometimes a little indelicate. That is a weak side in him, a vulgar and even rather ignoble side. This excellent man, sincere, exalted, warmhearted, this critic so animated, so ingenious, so keen, who has above all else a mania for preaching *morality,* is utterly unable, in presence of an object of art, to content himself with elevating and determining our idea of the beautiful, or even with satisfying our sensitiveness to impressions; he does more, he disturbs our senses a little. And so when you see at times on his brow a reflection of the Platonic ray, do not trust to it; look closely, there is always a satyr's foot.

We have divers fugitive writings of Diderot, brief narratives, tales, skits, which it is the fashion to call chefs-d'oeuvre. A chef-d'oeuvre! there is always more or less courtesy in the use of this word with respect to Diderot. The chef-d'oeuvre properly so-called, the finished, definitive, complete work, in which good taste sets the measure of the movement and sentiment, is not his forte: the superior quality, always scattered about in his work, is nowhere concentrated, nowhere set in a frame and glowing with a steady radiance. He is, as we have seen, much more truly *the man of the sketch.*

In the short pieces written for a purpose, such as the ***Éloge de Richardson*** or the ***Régrets sur ma Vieille Robe de Chambre,*** he has much grace of expression, happy thoughts, original conceits; but the emphatic manner recurs and manifests itself in spots, the apostrophe spoils the naturalness for me. There are gusts of emphasis here and there. In this direction he lays himself open to caricature to some extent, and that fact has been made use of without compunction in the portraits, generally overcharged, which have been drawn of him. Diderot is altogether successful, and without art too, when he makes no preparation, and has no particular object in view, when his thoughts escape him, when the printer is at his elbow, waiting for him and hurrying him; or when it is time for the postman to come, and he writes in haste, on a tavern table, a letter to his friend. It is in his ***Correspondance*** with that friend, Mademoiselle Voland, and in his ***Salons,*** written for Grimm, that we find his most delightful pages, the outspoken, rapid sketches in which he lives again just as he was.

Diderot set forth his views on the substance, the cause, and the origin of things in the ***Interprétation de la Nature,*** under the shelter of Baumann, who was no other than Maupertuis; and even more explicitly in the ***Entretien avec d'Alembert*** and the strange ***Rêve (Dream)*** which he attributes to that philosopher. It is sufficient for our purpose to say that his materialism is no dry geometrical mechanism, but a confused vitalism, fruitful and potent, a spontaneous, unceasing, evolutionary fermentation, wherein, even in the least atom, delicacy of feeling, latent or patent, is always present. His opinions were those of Bordeu and the physiologists, the same that Cabanis afterward expressed so eloquently. From the way in which Diderot appreciated external nature, *natural* nature so to speak, which the experiments of scientists had not as yet distorted and falsified—the woods, the streams, the charm of the fields, the harmonious beauty of the sky, and the impression that they make on the heart—he must have been profoundly religious by nature, for no man was ever more sympathetic and more accessible to universal life. But this life of nature and of created beings he purposely left undefined, vague, and in some sort diffused about him, hidden in the heart of the seeds, circulating in the air-currents, fluttering over the tree-tops, breathing in the puffs of wind; he did not gather it about a central point, he did not idealise it in the radiant example of a watchful, guiding Providence. However, in a work which he wrote in his old age, a few years before his death, the ***Essai sur la Vie de Sénèque,*** he gratified himself by translating the following passage from a letter to Lucilius, which filled him with admiration:

> If there is before your eyes a vast forest, peopled by ancient trees, whose tops ascend to the clouds and whose interlacing branches conceal the heavens from you, that immeasurable height, that profound silence, those masses of shadow which the distance makes more dense and unbroken, — do not all these signs *hint* to you the presence of a God?

It was Diderot who underlined the word *hint* (*intimer*).

I am delighted to find in the same work a criticism of La Mettrie which indicates in Diderot some slight forgetfulness perhaps of his own cynical and philosophical extravagances, but also a bitter distaste for and a formal disavowal of immoral and corrupting materialism. I like to have him reprove La Mettrie for not having *the first idea of the true fundamentals of morality,* "of that enormous tree whose head touches the heavens and whose roots reach down to hell, in which everything is bound together, in which modesty, reserve, courtesy, the most trivial virtues, if such there be, are attached as the leaf is to the twig, which one dishonours by stripping it."

This reminds me of a dispute concerning virtue that he had one day with Helvetius and Saurin; he writes to Mademoiselle Voland a charming description of it, which is a picture in a few words of the inconsequence of the age. Those gentlemen denied the innate moral sense, the essential and unselfish motive of virtue, for which Diderot argued.

> "The amusing part of it," he adds, "is that the discussion was hardly at an end before those excellent folk began unconsciously to use the strongest arguments in favour of the sentiment they had been combating, and to furnish the refutation of their own opinions. But Socrates, in my place, would have extorted it from them."

He says in one place, referring to Grimm: "The severity of our friend's principles is thrown away; he distinguishes two sorts of morality, one for the use of sovereigns." All these excellent ideas concerning virtue, morality, and nature recurred to his mind with greater force than ever, doubtless, in the meditative seclusion, the solitude which he tried to arrange for himself during the painful years of his old age. Several of his friends were dead; he often felt the loss of Mademoiselle Voland and Grimm. To conversation, which had become fatiguing, he preferred his dressing-gown and his library on the fifth floor, under the eaves, at the corner of Rue Taranne and Rue de Saint-Benoît; he read constantly, meditated much, and took the keenest pleasure in superintending his daughter's education.

In his old age Diderot wondered whether he had made a good use of his life, —whether he had not squandered it. Reading Seneca's treatise *De Brevitate Vitace,* especially the third chapter, where the reader is appealed to so earnestly: "Come, review your days and your years, call them to account! Tell us how much time you have allowed to be stolen from you by a creditor, by a mistress, by a patron, by a client. How many people have pillaged your life, when you did not even dream what you were losing!" Diderot, thus reminded to search his conscience, wrote as his only comment: "I have never read this chapter without blushing; *it is my history.*" Many years earlier he had said to himself: "I am not conscious of having as yet made use of half of my powers; up to this time I have only fiddle-faddled." He might have said the same thing when he died. But, as an antidote, an alleviation of these ill-concealed regrets of the writer and the artist, the philosopher and the moralist in him rejoined: "My life is not stolen from me, I give it voluntarily; and what better could I do than bestow a portion of it upon him who esteems me enough to solicit that gift?" It was in precisely the same frame of mind that he wrote somewhere or other these kindly and admirable words:

> A pleasure which is for myself alone touches me but little and lasts but a short time. It is for myself and my friends that I read, that I reflect, that I write, that I meditate, that I listen, that I observe, that I feel. In their absence my devotion refers everything to them I think unceasingly of their happiness. If a beautiful line impresses me, they know it at once. If I have fallen in with a fine drawing, I promise myself to tell them about it. If I have before my eyes some entrancing spectacle, I unconsciously think how I shall describe it to them. I have consecrated to them the use of all my senses and all my faculties, and that perhaps is the reason that everything is exaggerated, everything is glorified a little in my imagination and in my language; sometimes they reprove me for it, the ingrates!

We, who are of his friends, of those of whom he thought vaguely at a distance, and for whom he wrote, we will not be ungrateful. While regretting that we find too often in his writings that touch of exaggeration which he himself admits, a lack of discretion and sobriety, some laxity of morals and of language, and some sins against good taste, we do homage to his kindness of heart, his sympathetic nature, his generous intellect, his shrewdness and breadth of view and of treatment, his freedom and delicacy of touch, and the admirable vigour, the secret of which he never lost throughout his incessant toil. To all of us Diderot is a man whom it is encouraging to observe and to study. He is the first great writer in point of time who definitely belongs to modern democratic society. He points out to us the road and the example to follow: to be or not to be of the *Académie,* but to write for the public, to address the whole people, to be always in haste, to go straight to the reality, to the fact, even when one has a mania for reverie, to give, give, give, with no purpose ever to take back; *to wear oneself out rather than rest,* is his motto. And that is what he did to the very end, with energy, with devotion, with a sometimes painful consciousness of this constant loss of substance. And yet, through it all, and without a too manifest effort to that end, he succeeded in saving, of all these scattered fragments, some enduring ones, and he teaches us how one may make his way to the future and to posterity, and arrive there, though it be only as débris from the shipwreck of each day.

Diderot's beneficent-life, replete with good counsels and good works, must have been a source of the greatest inward consolation to him; and yet, perhaps, at certain times, there came to his lips this saying of his old father: "My son, my son, an excellent pillow is that of reason; but I find that my head rests even more softly on that of religion and the laws."

Diderot in a letter to Sophie Volland:

Ah, what a fine comedy this world would be, if only one had not to play a part in it; if one existed, for instance, in some point of space, in that interval of the celestial orbs where the gods of Epicurus slumber, far, far away, whence one could see this globe, on which we strut so big, about the size of a pumpkin, and whence one could watch all the airs and tricks of that two-footed mite who calls itself man. I would fain only look at the scenes of life in reduced size, so that those which are stamped with atrocity may be brought down to an inch in space, and to actors half a line high. But how bizarre that our sense of revolt against injustice is in the ratio of the space and the mass. I am furious if a large animal unjustly attacks another. I feel nothing at all if it is two atoms that tear and rend. How our senses affect our morality. There is a fine text for philosophizing!

Denis Diderot in his Correspondance, *quoted in* Diderot and the Encyclopedists, *Vol. I, by John Morley, 1878.*

John Morley (essay date 1878)

SOURCE: "The Encyclopaedia," in *Diderot and the Encyclopaedists* Vol. I, Chapman and Hall, 1878, pp. 113-241.

[*Morley was a noted Victorian politician and critic who wrote extensively on French eighteenth-century thought. In the following excerpt from his* Diderot and the Encyclopedists (1878), *he analyzes Diderot's guiding role in the publication of the* Encyclopedie, *as well as his individual contributions on philosophical subjects.*]

Diderot's articles [for the ***Encyclopédie***] fill more than four of the large volumes of his collected works.

The confusion is immense. The spirit is sometimes historical, sometimes controversial; now critical, now dogmatic. In one place Diderot speaks in his own proper person, in another as the neutral scribe writing to the dictation of an unseen authority. There is no rigorous measure and ordered proportion. We constantly pass from a serious treatise to a sally, from an elaborate history to a caprice. There are not a few pages where we know that Diderot is saying what he does not think. Some of the articles seem only to have found a place because Diderot happened to have taken an interest in their subjects at the moment. After reading Voltaire's concise account of Imagination, we are amazed to find Diderot devoting a larger space than Voltaire had needed for the subject at large, to so subordinate and remote a branch of the matter as the Power of the Imagination in Pregnant Women upon the Unborn Young. The article on Theosophs would hardly have been so disproportionately long as it is, merely for the sake of Paracelsus and Van Helmont and Poiret and the Rosicrucians, unless Diderot had happened to be curiously and half sympathetically brooding over the mixture of inspiration and madness, of charlatanry and generous aim, of which these semi-mystic, semi-scientific characters were composed.

Many of Diderot's articles, again, have no rightful place in an Encyclopaedia. *Genius,* for instance, is dealt with in what is neither more nor less than a literary essay, vigorous, suggestive, diffuse; and containing, by the way, the curious assertion that, although there are few errors in Locke and too few truths in Shaftesbury, yet Locke is only an acute and comprehensive intelligence, while Shaftesbury is a genius of the first order.

Under the word *Laborious,* we have only a dozen lines of angry reproach against the despotism that makes men idle by making property uncertain. Under such words as *Frivolous, Gallantry, Perfection, Importance, Politeness, Melancholy, Glorieux,* the reader is amused and edified by miniature essays on manners and character, seldom ending without some pithy sentence and pointed moral. Sometimes (e. g., *Grandeur*) we have a charming piece after the manner of La Bruyère. Under the verb *Naître,* which is placed in the department of grammar, we find a passage so far removed from grammar as the following: —

> The terms of life and death have nothing absolute; they only designate the successive states of one and the same being; for him who has been strongly nourished in this philosophy, the urn that contains the ashes of a father, a mother, a husband, a mistress, is truly a touching object; there still remains in it life and warmth; these ashes may perhaps even yet feel our tears and give them response; who knows if the movement

that our tears stir, as they water those ashes, is wholly without sensibility?

This little burst of grotesque sentimentalism is one of the pieces that justify the description of Diderot as the most German of all the French. Equally characteristic and more sensible is the writer's outbreak against Formalists. 'The formalist knows exactly the proper interval between receiving and returning a visit; he expects you on the exact day at the exact time; if you fail, he thinks himself neglected and takes offence. A single man of this stamp is enough to chill and embarrass a whole company. There is nothing so repugnant to simple and upright souls as formalities; as such people have within themselves the consciousness of the good-will they bear to everybody, they neither plague themselves to be constantly displaying a sentiment that is habitual, nor to be constantly on the watch for it in others.' This is analogous to his contempt for the pedants who object to the use of a hybrid word: —'If it happens that a composite of a Greek word and a Latin word renders the idea as well, and is easier to pronounce or pleasanter to the ear than a compound of two Greek words and two Latin words, why prefer the latter?' (*Hibrides*). Some articles are simply diatribes against the enemy. *Pardon,* for instance: —'It needs much attention, much modesty, much skill to wring from others pardon for our superiority. The men who have executed a foolish work, have never been able to pardon us for projecting a better. We could have got from them pardon for a crime, but never for a good action.' And so forth, with much magnanimous acrimony. *Prostitution* is only introduced for the pleasure of applying the unsavoury word to certain critics 'of whom we have so many in these days, and of whom we say that they prostitute their pens to money, to favour, to lying, and to all the vices most unworthy of an honourable man.'

We are constantly being puzzled and diverted by Diderot's ingenuity in wandering away from the topic nominally in hand, to insinuate some of those doctrines of tolerance, of suspended judgment, or of liberty, which lay so much nearer to his heart than any point of mere erudition. There is a little article on Aius-Locutius, the Announcing Speaker, one of the minor Roman gods. Diderot begins by a few lines describing the rise of the deity into repute. He then quotes Cicero's pleasantry on the friendly divinity, that when nobody in the world had ever heard of him, he delivered a salutary oracle, but after people had built him a fine temple, then the god of speech fell dumb. This suggests to Diderot to wonder with edifying innocence how so religious a people as the Romans endured these irreverent jests in their philosophers. By an easy step we pass to the conditions on which modern philosophers should be allowed by authority to publish their speculations. Diderot throws out the curious hint that it would be best to forbid any writing against government and religion in the vulgar tongue, and to allow those who write in a learned tongue to publish what they please. And so we bid farewell to Aius-Locutius. In passing, we ask ourselves whether Diderot's suggestion is not available in the discussion of certain questions, where freedom of speech in the vernacular tongue is scarcely compatible with the *reverentia quce debetur pueris?*

Diderot is never prevented by any mistaken sense of the

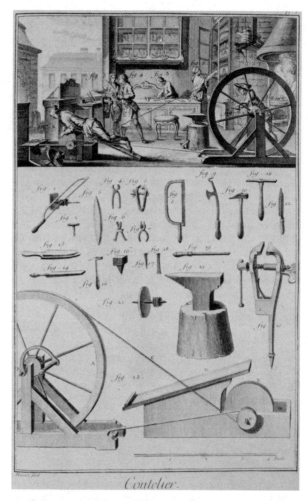

Engraving for the Encyclopédie *entry "Coutelier," which had been written by Diderot.*

dignity of his enterprise from interspersing his disquisitions on science and philosophy with such practical thoughts on the common matters of daily life as come into his ingenious head. He suggests, for instance, by way of preventing the frauds of cab-drivers on their masters and on the public, that all payments of fares should be made to appointed officers at the various cab-stations, and that no driver should take up a fare except at one of these stations. In writing about lackeys, after a word on their insolence and on the wretched case in which most of them end their days, he points out that the multitude of them is causing the depopulation of the fields. They are countrymen who have thronged to Paris to avoid military service. Peasants turned lackeys to escape the conscription, just as in our own days they turn priests. Then, says Diderot, this evil ought to be checked by a tax upon liveries; but such a tax is far too sensible ever to be imposed.

Yet, notwithstanding the practical and fervid temper of his understanding, Diderot is not above literary trifling when the humour seizes him. If he can write an exhaustive article on Encyclopaedia, or Spinosa, or Academies, or Weaving, he can also stoop to Anagrams, and can tell us that the letters of Frère Jacques Clément, the assassin of

Henry III., make up the sinister words, *C'est l'enfer qui m'a créé.* He can write a couple of amusing pages on Onomatomancy, or divination of a man's fortune from his name; and can record with neutral gravity how frequently great empires have been destroyed under princes bearing the same name as their first founders; how, again, certain names are unlucky for princes, as Caius among the Romans, John in France, England, and Scotland, and Henry in France.

We have now and then an anecdote that is worth reading and worth preserving. Thus, under Machiavellist: —'I have heard that a philosopher, being asked by a great prince about a refutation of Machiavellism, which the latter had just published, replied, "Sire, I fancy that the first lesson that Machiavelli would have given to his disciple, would have been to refute his work." Whether Voltaire ever did say this to the great Frederick is very questionable, but it would not have been ill said. Again, after the reader has been taken through a short course of Arabian philosophy, he is enlivened by a selection of poetic sayings about human life from the Rosegarden of Sadi, and the whole article winds up with an eastern fable, of no particular relevancy, of three men finding a treasure, and of one of them poisoning the food for which the other two had sent him; on his return they suddenly fell on him and slew him, and then ate the poisoned food, and so the treasure fell to none of them.

We have spoken in the previous section of the contempt expressed by D'Alembert for mere literary antiquarianism—a very different thing, let us remember, from scientific inquiry into the origin and classification of institutions and social organs. Diderot's article on the Germans is an excellent illustration of this wholesome predominance of the scientific spirit over the superficialities of barren erudition. The word 'Allemand,' says Diderot, 'has a great many etymologies, but they are so forced, that it is almost as well to know none of them as to know them all. As for the origin of this famous stock, all that has been said on that matter, between Tacitus and Clovis, is simply a tissue of guesses without foundation.' Of course in this, some persons will see a shameful levity; others will regard it as showing very good sense, and a right estimate of what is knowable and worth knowing, and what is neither one nor the other. In the article on Celibacy we notice the same temper. A few sentences are enough for the antiquarianism of the subject, what the Egyptians, Greeks, and Romans thought and ordained about celibacy. The substance of the article is a reproduction of the Abbé Saint Pierre's discussion of the advantages that would be gained for France, with her declining population, if her forty thousand curés were allowed to marry, and to bring into the world eighty thousand children. We may believe that Diderot smiled as he transcribed the Abbé's cunning suggestion that a dispensing power to relieve from the obligation of celibacy should be recognised in the Pope, and that the Roman court should receive a sum of money for every dispensation so granted.

Although, however, Diderot despised mere bookishness, his article on Libraries is one of the longest and most painstaking, furnishing a tolerably complete list of the

most famous collections, from the beginning of books down to the latest additions to the King's Library in the Rue Vivienne. In the course of this article he quotes with seeming approval the quaint words in which old Richard of Bury, author of the *Philobiblon* (1340), praised books as the best of masters, much as the immortal defender of the poet Archias had praised them: —'Hi sunt magistri qui nos instruunt sine virgis et ferulis, sine cholera, sine pecuniâ; si accedis non dormiunt; si inquiris non se abscondunt; non obmurmurant si oberres; cachinnos nesciunt si ignores.'

In literature proper, as in philosophy, Diderot loses no opportunity of insisting on the need of being content with suspended judgment. For instance, he blames historians of opinion for the readiness with which they attribute notions found in one or two rabbis to the whole of the Jews, or because two or three Fathers say something, boldly set this down as the sentiments of a whole century, although perhaps we have nothing else save these two or three Fathers left of the century, and although we do not know whether their writings were applauded, or were even widely known. 'It were to be wished that people should speak less affirmatively, especially on particular points and remote consequences, and that they should only attribute them directly to those in whose writings they are actually to be found. I confess that the history of the sentiments of antiquity would not seem so complete, and that it would be necessary to speak in terms of doubt much more often than is common; but by acting otherwise we expose ourselves to the danger of taking false and uncertain conjectures for ascertained and unquestionable truths. The ordinary man of letters does not readily put up with suspensive expressions, any more than common people do so.' All this is an odd digression to be found under the head of Hylopathianism, but it must always remain wholesome doctrine.

We cannot wonder at Diderot's admiration for Montaigne and for Bayle, who with Hume would make the great trinity of scepticism. 'The work of Montaigne,' said Diderot, 'is the touchstone of a good intelligence; you may be sure that any one whom the reading of Montaigne displeases, has some vice either of heart or understanding. As for Bayle, he has had few equals in the art of reasoning, and perhaps no superior; and though he piles doubt upon doubt, he always proceeds with order; an article of his is a living polypus, which divides itself into a number of polypuses, all living, engendered one from the other.' Yet Diderot had a feeling of the necessity of advancing beyond the attitude of Bayle and Montaigne. Intellectual suspense and doubt were made difficult to him by his vehement and positive demand for emotional certainties.

Diderot is always ready to fling away his proper subject in a brust of moralising. The article on *Man,* as a branch of natural history, contains a correct if a rather superficial account of that curious animal; at length the writer comes to a table showing the probable duration of life at certain ages. 'You will observe,' he says, '1st, that the age of seven is that at which you may hope a longer life; 2nd, that at twelve or thirteen you have lived a quarter of your life; at twenty-eight or twenty-nine you have lived half; at fifty more than three quarters.' And then he suddenly winds up the whole performance by the exclamation: —'O. ye who have laboured up to fifty, who are in the enjoyment of comfort, and who still have left to you health and strength, what then are you waiting for before you take rest? How long will you go on saying *To-morrow, to-morrow.'*

There are many casual brilliancies in the way of analogy and parallel, many aptnesses of thought and phrase. The Stoics are called the Jansenists of Paganism. 'For a single blade of grass to grow, it is necessary that the whole of nature should co-operate.' 'A man comes to Pyrrhonism by one of two opposite ways; either because he does not know enough, or because he knows too much; the latter is not the most common way.' And so forth.

If we turn to the group of articles dealing with theology, it is difficult for us to know exactly where we are. Sometimes Diderot writes of popular superstitions with the gravity proper to a dictionary of mythology. Sometimes he sews on to the sober grey of his scepticism a purple patch of theistic declamation. The article on Jesus Christ is obviously a mere piece of common form, and more than one passage in his article on *Christianisme* are undoubtedly insincere. When we come to his more careful article, *Providence,* we find it impossible to extract from it a body of coherent propositions, of which we could confidently say that they represented his own creed or the creed that he desired his readers to bear away in their minds.

It is hardly worth while to measure the more or the less of his adherence to Christianity, or even to Deism, as inferred from the *Encyclopaedia.* We need only turn to his private letters to find that he is in no degree nor kind an adherent, but the most hardy, contemptuous, and thoroughgoing of opponents. At the risk of shocking devout persons, I am bound to reproduce a passage from one of his letters, in which there can be no doubt that we have Diderot's true mind, as distinguished from what it was convenient to print. 'The Christian religion,' he says, 'is to my mind the most absurd and atrocious in its dogmas; the most unintelligible, the most metaphysical, the most intertwisted and obscure, and consequently the most subject to divisions, sects, schisms, heresies; the most mischievous for the public tranquillity, the most dangerous to sovereigns by its hierarchic order, its persecutions, its discipline; the most flat, the most dreary, the most Gothic, and the most gloomy in its ceremonies; the most puerile and unsociable in its morality, considered not in what is common to it with universal morality, but in what is peculiarly its own, and constitutes it evangelical, apostolical, and Christian morality, which is the most intolerant of all. Lutheranism, freed from some absurdities, is preferable to Catholicism; Protestantism to Lutheranism, Socinianism to Protestantism, Deism, with temples and ceremonies, to Socinianism. Since it is necessary that man, being superstitious by nature, should have a fetish, the simplest and most harmless will be the best fetish.' We need not discuss nor extend the quotation; enough has been said to relieve us from the duty of analysing or criticising articles in which Christianity is treated with all the formal respect that the secular authority insisted upon.

This formal respect is not incompatible with many veiled and secret sarcasms, which were as well understood as they were sharply enjoyed by those who read between the lines. It is not surprising that these sarcasms were constantly unjust and shallow. Even those of us who repudiate theology and all its works for ourselves, may feel a shock at the coarseness and impurity of innuendo which now and then disfigures Diderot's treatment of theological as of some other subjects. For this the attitude of the Church itself was much to blame; coarse, virulent, unspiritual as it was in France in those days. Voltaire, Diderot, Holbach, would have written in a very different spirit, even while maintaining and publishing the same attacks on theological opinion, if the Church of France had possessed such a school of teachers as the Church of England found in the Latitudinarians in the seventeenth century, or such as she finds now in the nineteenth century in those who have imported, partly from the poetry of Wordsworth, partly from the historic references of the Oxford Tracts, an equity, a breadth, an elevation, a pensive grace, that effectually forbid the use of those more brutal weapons of controversy which were the only weapons possible in France a century ago.

We have already said so much of the great and important group of articles on arts and trades, that it is unnecessary to add anything further as to Diderot's particular share in them. He visited all the workshops in Paris; he sent for information and specifications to the most important seats of manufacture in the kingdom; he sometimes summoned workmen from the provinces to describe to him the paper works of Montargis, and the silk works and velvet works of Lyons. Much of Diderot's work, even on great practical subjects, was, no doubt, the reproduction of mere book-knowledge acquired at second-hand. Take, for instance, Agriculture, which was undoubtedly the most important of all subjects for France at that date, as indeed at every other date. There are a dozen pages of practical precepts, for which Diderot was probably indebted to one of the farmers at Grandval. After this he fills up the article with about twenty pages in which he gives an account of the new system of husbandry, which our English Jethro Tull described to an unbelieving public between 1731 and 1751. Tull's volume was translated into French by Duhamel, with notes and the record of experiments of his own; from this volume Diderot drew the pith of his article. Diderot's only merit in the matter—and it is hardly an inconsiderable one in a world of routine—is that he should have been at the pains to seek the newest lights, and above all that he should have urged the value of fresh experiments in agriculture. Tull was not the safest authority in the world, but it is to be remembered that the shrewd-witted Cobbett thought his ideas on husbandry worth reproducing seventy years after Diderot had thought them worth compiling into an article.

It was not merely in the details of the practical arts that Diderot wrote from material acquired at secondhand. The article on the Zend-Avesta is taken from the Annual Register for 1762. The long series of articles on the history of philosophy is in effect a reproduction of what he found in Bayle, in Deslandes, and in Brucker. There are one or two considerable exceptions. Perhaps the most important is under the heading of Spinosa, to which we shall return presently. The article on *Hobbisme* contains an analysis, evidently made by the writer's own hand, of the bulk of Hobbes's propositions; it is scarcely, however, illuminated by a word of criticism. If we turn to the article on *Société,* it is true, we find Hobbes's view of the relations between the civil and temporal powers tolerably effectively combated, but even here Diderot hardly does more than arm himself with the weapons of Locke.

Of course, he honestly refers his readers to these sources of wider information. All that we can say of the articles on the history of philosophy is that the series is very complete; that Diderot used his matter with intelligence and the spirit of criticism, and that he often throws in luminous remarks and far-reaching suggestions of his own. This was all that the purpose of his book required. To imitate the laborious literary search of Bayle or of Brucker, and to attempt to compile an independent history of philosophy, would have been to sacrifice the Encyclopaedia as a whole to the superfluous perfection of a minor part. There is only one imperative condition in such a case, namely, that the writer should pass the accepted material through his own mind before reproducing it. With this condition it was impossible for a man of Diderot's indefatigable energy of spirit not, as a rule, to comply.

But this rule too had exceptions. There were cases in which he reproduced, as any mere bookmaker might have done, the thought of his authority without an attempt to make it his own. Of the confusion and inequalities in which Diderot was landed by this method of mingling the thoughts of other people with his own, there is a curious example in the two articles on Philosopher and Philosophy. In the first we have an essentially social and practical description of what the philosopher should be; in the second we have a definition of philosopher which takes us into the regions most remote from what is social and practical. We soar to the airiest heights of verbal analysis and pure formalism. Nothing can be better, so far as it goes, than the picture of the philosopher. Diderot begins by contrasting him with the crowd of people, and clever people, who insist on passing judgments all day long. 'They ignore the scope and limits of the human mind; they think it capable of knowing everything; hence they think it a disgrace not to pronounce judgment, and imagine that intelligence consists in that and nothing else. The philosopher believes that it consists in judging rightly. He is better pleased with himself when he has suspended his faculty of coming to a conclusion, than if he had come to a conclusion without the proper grounds. He prefers to brilliancy the pains of rightly distinguishing his ideas, of finding their true extent and exact connection. He is never so attached to a system as not to feel all the force of the objections to it. Most men are so strongly given over to their opinions, that they do not take any trouble to make out those of others. The philosopher, on the other hand, understands what he rejects, with the same breadth and the same accuracy as he understands what he adopts.' Then Diderot turns characteristically from the intellectual to the social side. 'Our philosopher does not count himself an exile in the world; he does not suppose himself in an enemy's country; he would fain find pleasure with others,

and to find it he must give it; he is a worthy man who wishes to please and to make himself useful. The ordinary philosophers who meditate too much, or rather who meditate to wrong purpose, are as surly and arrogant to all the world as great people are to those whom they do not think their equals; they flee men, and men avoid them. But our philosopher who knows how to divide himself between retreat and the commerce of men is full of humanity. *Civil society is, so to say, a divinity for him on the earth;* he honours it by his probity, by an exact attention to his duties, and by a sincere desire not to be a useless or an embarrassing member of it. The sage has the leaven of order and rule; he is full of the ideas connected with the good of civil society. What experience shows us every day is that the more reason and light people have, the better fitted they are and the more to be relied on for the common intercourse of life.'

The transition is startling from this conception of Philosopher as a very high kind of man of the world to the definition of Philosophy as 'the science of possibles quâ possibles.' Diderot's own reflection comes back to us, *Combien cette maudite métaphysique fait des fous!* We are abruptly plunged from a Baconian into a Leibnitzian atmosphere. We should naturally have expected some such account of Philosophy as that it begins with a limitation of the questions to which men can hope for an answer, and ends in an ordered arrangement of the principles of knowledge, with ultimate reference to the conditions of morals and the structure of civil societies. We should naturally have expected to find, what indeed we do find, that the characteristic of the philosopher is to 'admit nothing without proof, never to acquiesce in illusory notions; to draw rigorously the dividing lines of the certain, the probable, the doubtful; above all things never to pay himself with mere words.' But then these wholesome prescriptions come in an article whose definitions and distribution of philosophy are simply a reproduction from Christian Wolff, and the methods and dialect of Wolff are as essentially alien from the positive spirit of the Encyclopaedia as they were from the mystic spirit of Jacobi.

Wolff's place in the philosophical succession of German speculation (1679–1754) is between Leibnitz and Kant, and until Kant came his system was dominant in the country of metaphysics. It is from Wolff that Diderot borrows and throws unassimilated into the pages of the Encyclopaedia propositions so fundamentally incongruous as this, that 'among all possibles there must of necessity be a Being subsisting by himself; otherwise there would be possible things, of the possibility of which no account could be given, an assertion that could never be made.' It is a curious thing, and it illustrates again the strangely miscellaneous quality of Diderot's compilation, that the very article which begins by this incorporation of the author of a philosophical system expounded in a score of quartos, ends by a vigorous denunciation of the introduction of the systematic spirit into philosophy.

I shall venture to quote a hardy passage from another article (*Pyrrhonienne*) which some will think a measure of Diderot's philosophical incompetency, and others will think a measure of his good sense. 'We will conclude,' he says, 'for our part that as all in nature is bound together, there is nothing, properly speaking, of which man has perfect, absolute, and complete knowledge, because for that he would need knowledge of all. Now as all is bound together, it inevitably happens that, from discussion to discussion, he must come to something unknown: then in starting again from this unknown point, we shall be justified in pleading against him the ignorance or the obscurity or the uncertainty of the point preceding, and of that preceding this, and so forth, up to the most evident principle. So we must admit a sort of sobriety in the use of reason. When step by step I have brought a man to some evident proposition, I shall cease to dispute. I will listen no longer to anybody who goes on to deny the existence of bodies, the rules of logic, the testimony of the senses, the difference between good and evil, true and false, etc., etc. I will turn my back on everybody who tries to lead me away from a simple question, to embark me in discussion as to the nature of matter, of the understanding, of thought, and other subjects shoreless and bottomless.' Whatever else may be said of this, we have to recognise that it is exactly characteristic of the author. But then why have written on metaphysics at all?

We have mentioned the article on Spinosa. It is characteristic both of the good and the bad sides of Diderot's work. Half of it is merely a reproduction of Bayle's criticisms on Spinosa and his system. The other half consists of original objections propounded by Diderot with marked vigour of thrust against Spinosa, but there is no evidence that he had gone deeper into Spinosa than the first book of the *Ethics.* There is no certain sign that he had read anything else, or that he had more of that before him than the extracts that were furnished by Bayle. Such treatment of a serious subject hardly conforms to the modern requirements of the literary conscience, for in truth the literary conscience has now turned specialist and shrinks from the encyclopaedic. Diderot's objections are, as we have said, pushed with marked energy of speech. 'However short a way,' he says, 'you penetrate into the thick darkness in which Spinosa has wrapped himself up, you discover a succession of abysses into which this audacious reasoner has precipitated himself, of propositions either evidently false or evidently doubtful, of arbitrary principles substituted for natural principles and sensible truths; an abuse of terms taken for the most part in a wrong sense, a mass of deceptive equivocations, a cloud of palpable contradictions.' The system is monstrous, it is absurd, and ridiculous. It is Spinosa's plausible method that has deceived people; they supposed that one who employed geometry, and proceeded by way of axioms and definitions, must be on the track of truth. They did not see that these axioms were nothing better than very vague and very uncertain propositions; that the definitions were inexact, defective, and bizarre.

We have no space to follow the reasoning by which Diderot supports this scornful estimate of the famous thinker, of whom it can never be settled whether he be pantheist, atheist, akosmist, or God-intoxicated man. He returns to the charge again and again, as if he felt a certain secret uneasiness lest for scorn so loudly expressed he had not brought forward adequate justification. And the reader feels that Diderot has scarcely hit the true line of cleavage that would have enabled him—from his own point of view—to shatter the Spinosist system. He tries various bouts of logic with Spinosa in connection with detached propositions. Thus he deals with Spinosa's third proposition, that, *in the case of things that have nothing in common with one another, one cannot be the cause of the other.* This proposition, Diderot contends, is false in all moral and occasional causes. The sound of the name of God has nothing in common with the idea of the Creator which that name produces in my mind. A misfortune that overtakes my friend has nothing in common with the grief that I feel in consequence. When I move my arm by an act of will, the movement has nothing in common in its nature with the act of my will; they are very different. I am not a triangle, yet I form the idea of one and I examine its properties. So with the fifth proposition, that *there cannot be in the universe two or more substances of the same nature or the same attributes.* If Spinosa is only talking of the essence of things or of their definition, what he says is naught; for it can only mean that there cannot be in the universe two different essences having the same essence. Who doubts it? But if Spinosa means that there cannot be an essence which is found in various single objects, in the same way as the essence of triangle is found in the triangle A and the triangle B, then he says what is manifestly untrue. It is not, however, until the last two or three pages that Diderot sets forth his dissent in its widest form. 'To refute Spinosa,' he says at last, 'all that is necessary is to stop him at the first step, without taking the trouble to follow him into a mass of consequences; all that we need do is to substitute for the obscure principle which he makes the base of his system, the following: namely, that *there are several substances*—a principle that in its own way is clear to the last degree. And, in fact, what proposition can be clearer, more striking, more close to the understanding and consciousness of man? I here seek no other judge than the most just impression of the common sense that is spread among the human race. . . . Now, since common sense revolts against each of Spinosa's propositions, no less than against the first, of which they are the pretended proofs, instead of stopping to reason on each of these proofs where common sense is lost, we should be right to say to him: —Your principle is contrary to common sense; from a principle in which common sense is lost, nothing can issue in which common sense is to be found again.'

The passage sounds unpleasantly like an appeal to the crowd in a matter of science, which is as the sin against the Holy Ghost in these high concerns. What Diderot meant, probably, was to charge Spinosa with inventing a conception of substance which has no relation to objective experience; and further with giving fantastic answers to questions that were in themselves never worth asking, because the answers must always involve a violent wrench of the terms of experience into the sphere transcending experience, and because, moreover, they can never be verified. Whether he meant this or something else, and whether he would have been right or wrong in such an intention, we may admit that it would have been more satisfactory if in dealing with such a master-type of the metaphysical method as Spinosa, so acute a positive critic as Diderot had taken more pains to give to his objections the utmost breadth of which they were capable.

The article on Leibnitz has less original matter in it than that on Spinosa. The various speculations of that great and energetic intellect in metaphysic, logic, natural theology, natural law, are merely drawn out in a long table of succinct propositions, while the account of the life and character of Leibnitz is simply taken from the excellent éloge which had been published upon him by Fontenelle in 1716. Fontenelle's narrative is reproduced in a generous spirit of admiration and respect for a genius that was like Diderot's own in encyclopaedic variety of interest, while it was so far superior to Diderot's in concentration, in subtlety, in precision, in power of construction. If there could exist over our heads, says Diderot, a species of beings who could observe our works as we watch those of creatures at our feet, with what surprise would such beings have seen those four marvellous insects, Bayle, Descartes, Leibnitz, and Newton. And he then draws up a little calendar of the famous men, out of whom we must choose the name to be placed at the very head of the human race. The list contains, besides Julian the Apostate—who was inserted, we may presume, merely by way of playful insult to the ecclesiastical enemy—Socrates, Marcus Aurelius, Trajan, Bacon, and the four great names that have just been cited. Germany derives as much honour from Leibnitz alone, he concludes with unconsidered enthusiasm, as Greece from Plato, Aristotle, and Archimedes, all put together. As we have said, however, there is no criticism, nor any other sign that Diderot had done more than survey the façade of the great Leibnitzian structure admiringly from without.

The article on Liberty would be extremely remarkable, appearing where it does, and coming from a thinker of Diderot's general capacity, if only we could be sure that Diderot was sincere. As it happens, there is good reason to suppose that he was wholly insincere. It is quite as shallow, from the point of view of philosophy, as his article on the Jews or on the Bible is from the point of view of erudition. One reason for this might not be far to seek. We have repeatedly observed how paramount the social aim and the social test are in Diderot's mind over all other considerations. But this reference of all subjects of discussion to the good of society, and this measurement of conclusions by their presumed effect on society, is a method that has its own dangers. The aversion of ecclesiastics to unfettered discussion, lest it should damage institutions and beliefs deemed useful to mankind, is the great leading example of this peril. Diderot, it might be said by those who should contend that he wrote what he thought, did not escape exactly the same predicament, as soon as ever he forgot that of all the things that are good for society, Truth is the best. Now, who will believe that it is Diderot, the persecuted editor of the ***Encyclopaedia,*** and the author of the manly article on Intolerance, who introduces such a passage as the following into the discussion of the everlasting controversy of Free Will and Necessity: —'Take away Liberty, and you leave no more vice nor virtue nor merit in the world; rewards are ridiculous, and punishments unjust. The ruin of Liberty overthrows all order and all police, confounds vice and virtue, authorises every monstrous in-

famy, extinguishes the last spark of shame and remorse, degrades and disfigures beyond recovery the whole human race. *A doctrine of such enormity as this ought not to be examined in the schools; it ought to be punished by the magistrates.'* Of course, this was exactly what the Jesuits said about a belief in God, about revelation, and about the institutions of the church. To take away these, they said, is to throw down the bulwarks of order, and an attempt to take them away, as by encyclopaedists or others, ought to be punished by the magistrates. Diderot had for the moment clearly lost himself.

We need hardly be surprised if an article conceived in this spirit contains no serious contribution to the difficult question with which it deals. Diderot had persuaded himself that, without Free Will, all those emotional moralities in the way of sympathy and benevolence and justice which he adored, would be lowered to the level of mere mechanism. 'If men are not free in what they do of good and evil, then,' he cries, in what is surely a paroxysm of unreason, 'good is no longer good, and evil no longer evil.' As if the outward quality and effects of good and evil were not independent of the mental operations which precede human action. Murder would not cease to be an evil, simply because it had been proved that the murderer's will to do a bad deed was the result of antecedents. Acts have marks and consequences of their own, good or bad, whatever may be the state of mind of those who do them. But Diderot does not seem to divine the true issue; he writes as if Necessarians or Determinists denied the existence of volitions, and as if the question were whether volitions do exist. Nobody denies that they exist; the real question is of the conditions under which they exist. Are they determined by antecedents, or are they selfdetermined, spontaneous, and unconnected? Is Will independent of cause?

Diderot's argumentation is, in fact, merely a protest that man is conscious of a Will. And just as in other parts of his article Diderot by Liberty means only the existence of Will, so by Liberty he means only the healthy condition of the soul, and not its independence of causation. We need not waste words on so dire a confusion, nor on the theory that Will is sometimes dependent on cerebral antecedents and sometimes not. The curious thing is that the writer should not have perceived that he was himself in this preposterous theory propounding the very principle which he denounced as destructive to virtue, ruinous to society, and worthy of punishment by the government. For it seems that, after all, the Will of those whose 'dispositions are not moderate' is not free; and we may surely say that those whose dispositions are least moderate, are exactly the most violent malefactors against the common weal. One more passage is worth quoting to show how little the writer had seized the true meaning of the debate. 'According to you,' he says to Bayle, 'it is not clear that it is at the pure choice of my will to move my arm or not to move it: if that be so, it is then necessarily determined that within a quarter of an hour from now I shall lift my hand three times together, or that I shall not. Now, if you seriously pretend that I am not free, you cannot refuse an offer that I make you; I will wager a thousand pistoles to one that I will do, in the matter of moving my hand, exactly the opposite to what you back; and you may take your choice. If you do not think the wager fair, it can only be because of your necessary and invincible judgment that I am free.' As if the will to move or not to move the arm would be uncaused and unaffected by antecedents, when you have just provided so strong an antecedent as the desire to save a thousand pistoles. It was, perhaps, well enough for Voltaire to content himself with vague poetical material for his poetical discourse on Liberty, but from Diderot, whether as editor or as writer, something better might have been expected than a clumsy reproduction of the reasoning by which men like Turretini had turned philosophy into the corrupted handmaid of theology.

The most extraordinary thing about this extraordinary article still remains to be told. It was written, we may suppose, between 1757 and 1762, or about that time. In June, 1756, Diderot wrote to a certain Landois, a fellow-worker on the *Encyclopaedia,* a letter containing the most emphatic possible repudiation of the whole doctrine of Liberty. 'Liberty is a word void of sense; there are not and there never can have been free beings; we are only what fits in with the general order, with organization, with education, and with the chain of events. We can no more conceive a being acting without a motive, than we can conceive one of the arms of a balance acting without a weight; and the motive is always exterior and foreign to us, attached either by nature or by some cause or other that is not ourselves. *There is only one sort of causes, properly speaking, and those are physical causes.'* And so forth in the vein of hard and remorseless necessarianism, which we shall find presently in the pages of the System of Nature.

There is only one explanation of this flagrant contradiction. Diderot must have written on Liberty just as he wrote on Jesus Christ or the Bible. He cannot have said what he thought, but only what the persons in authority required him to pretend to think. We may be sure that a letter to an intimate would be more likely to contain his real opinion than an article published in the *Encyclopaedia.* That such mystifications are odious, are shameful, are almost too degrading a price to pay for the gains of such a work, we may all readily enough admit. All that we can do is to note so flagrant a case, as a striking example of the common artifices of the time. One other point we may note. The fervour and dexterity with which Diderot made what he knew to be the worse appear the better cause, make a still more striking example of his astonishing dramatic power of throwing himself, as dialectician, casuist, sophist, into a false and illusive part.

Turning from the philosophical to the political or social group of articles, we find little to add to what has been said in the previous section. One of the most excellent essays in this group is that on Luxury. Diderot opens ingeniously with a list of the propositions that state the supposed evils of luxury, and under each proposition he places the most striking case that he can find in history of its falseness. He goes through the same process with the propositions asserting the gains of luxury to a society. Having thus effectually disposed of any wholesale way of dealing with the subject, he proceeds to make a number of observations on the gains and drawbacks of luxury; these are full of sense and freedom from commonplace. Such articles as *Pouvoir,*

Souverain, Autorité, do little more than tell over again the old unhistoric story about a society surrendering a portion of its sovereign power to some individual or dynasty to hold in trust. It is worth remarking how little democratic were Diderot and his school in any Jacobinical, or anarchic, or even more respectable modern sense. There is in Diderot's contributions many a firm and manly plea for the self-respect of the common people, but not more than once or twice is there a syllable of the disorder which smoulders under the pages of Rousseau. Thus: —'When the dwellers among the fields are well treated, the number of proprietors insensibly grows greater, the extreme distance and the vile dependence of poor on rich grow less; hence the people have courage, force of soul, and strength of body; they love their country, they respect the magistrates, they are attached to a prince, to an order, and to laws to which they owe their peace and wellbeing. And you will no longer see the son of the honourable tiller of the soil so ready to quit the noble calling of his forefathers, nor so ready to go and sully himself with the liveries and with the contempt of the man of wealth.'

No one can find fault with democratic sentiment of this kind, nor with the generous commonplaces of the moralist, about virtue being the only claim to honour, and vice the only true source of shame and inferiority. But neither Diderot nor Voltaire ever allowed himself to flatter the crowd for qualities which the crowd can scarcely possess. The little article on Multitude seems merely inserted for the sake of buffeting unwarranted pretensions. 'Distrust the judgment of the multitude in all matters of reasoning and philosophy; there its voice is the voice of malice, folly, inhumanity, irrationality, and prejudice. Distrust it again in things that suppose much knowledge or a fine taste. The multitude is ignorant and dulled. Distrust it in morality; it is not capable of strong and generous actions; it rather wonders at such actions than approves them; heroism is almost madness in its eyes. Distrust it in the things of sentiment; is delicacy of sentiment so common a thing that you can accord it to the multitude? In what then is the multitude right? In everything, but only at the end of a very long time, because then it has become an echo, repeating the judgement of a small number of sensible men who shape the judgment of posterity for it beforehand. If you have on your side the testimony of your conscience, and against you that of the multitude, take comfort and be assured that time does justice.' It is far from being a universal gift among men of letters and others to unite this fastidious estimation of the incapacity of the crowd in the higher provinces of the intellectual judgment, with a fervid desire that the life of the crowd should be made worthy of self-respecting men.

The same hand that wrote the defiance of the populace that has just been quoted, wrote also this short article on Misery: —'There are few souls so firm that misery does not in the long run cast them down and degrade them. The poor common people are incredibly stupid. I know not what false dazzling prestige closes their eyes to their present wretchedness, and to the still deeper wretchedness that awaits the years of old age. Misery is the mother of great crimes. It is the sovereigns who make the miserable, and it is they who shall answer in this world and the other for the crimes that misery has committed.'

So far as the mechanism of government is concerned, Diderot writes much as Montesquieu had done. Under the head of *Représentants* he proclaims the advantages, not exactly of government by a representative assembly, but of assisting and advising the royal government by means of such an assembly. There is no thought of universal suffrage. *'It is property that makes the citizen;* every man who has possessions in the state is interested in the state, and whatever be the rank that particular conventions may assign to him, it is always as a proprietor; it is by reason of his possessions that he ought to speak, and that he acquires the right of having himself represented.' Yet this very definite statement does not save him from the standing difficulty of a democratic philosophy of politics. Nor can it be reconciled in point of logic with other propositions to which Diderot commits himself in the same article. For instance, he says that 'no order of citizens is capable of stipulating for all; if one order had the right, it would very soon come to stipulate only for itself; each class ought to be represented by men who know its condition and its needs; *these needs are only well-known to those who actually feel them.'* But then, in that case, the poorest classes are those who have most need of direct representation; they are the most numerous, their needs are sharpest, they are the classes to which war, consumption of national capital and way of expending national income, equal laws, judicial administration, and the other concerns of a legislative assembly, come most close. The problem is to reconcile the sore interests of the multitude with the ignorance and the temper imputed in Diderot's own description of them.

An interesting study might be made, if the limits of our subject permitted such a digression, on the new political ideas which a century's experience in England, France, Germany, the American Union, has added to the publicist's stock. Diderot's article on the Legislator is a curious mixture of views which political thinkers have left behind, with views which the most enlightened statesmen have taken up. There is much talk after the fashion of Jean Jacques Rousseau about the admirable legislation of Lycurgus at Sparta, the philosophical government of the great empire of China, and the fine spirit of the institutions of Peru. We perceive that the same influences which made Rousseau's political sentimentalism so popular, also brought even strong heads like Diderot to believe in the unbounded power of a government to mould men at its will, and to impose institutions at discretion. The idea that it is the main function of a government to make its people virtuous, is generally as strong in Diderot as it was in Rousseau, and as it became in Robespierre. He admires the emperors of China, because their edicts are as the exhortation of a father to his children. All edicts, he says, ought to instruct and to exhort as much as they command. Yet two years after the *Encyclopaedia* was finished (1774), when Turgot prefaced his reforming edicts by elaborate and reasoned statements of the grounds for them, it was found that his prefaces caused greater provocation than the very laws that they introduced.

Apart from the common form of enthusiasm for the 'sublime legislation' of countries which the writer really knew nothing about, the article on the Legislator has some points worth noticing. We have seen how Diderot made the possession of property the true note of citizenship, and of a claim to share in the government. But he did not pay property this compliment for nothing. It is, he says, the business of the legislator to do his best to make up to mankind for the loss of that equality, which was one of the comforts that men surrendered when they gave up the state of nature. Hence the legislator ought to take care that no one shall reach a position of extreme opulence otherwise than by an industry that enriches the state. 'He must take care that the charges of society shall fall upon the rich, who enjoy the advantages of society.' Even those who agree with Diderot, and are ready to vote for a graduated income-tax, will admit that he comes to his conclusion without knowing or reflecting about either the serious arguments for it, or the serious objections against it.

What is really interesting in this long article is its anticipation of those ideas which in England we associate with the name of Cobden. 'All the men of all lands have become necessary to one another for the exchange of the fruits of industry and the products of the soil. Commerce is a new bond among men. Every nation has an interest in these days in the preservation by every other nation of its wealth, its industry, its banks, its luxury, its agriculture. The ruin of Leipzig, of Lisbon, and of Lima has led to bankruptcies on all the exchanges of Europe, and has affected the fortunes of many millions of persons.' In the same spirit he foresees the decline of patriotism in its older and narrower sense, and the predominance of the international over the national sentiment. 'All nations now have sufficiently just ideas of their neighbours, and consequently, they have less enthusiasm for their country than in the old days of ignorance. There is little enthusiasm where there is much light; enthusiasm is nearly always the emotion of a soul that is more passionate than it is instructed. By comparing among all nations laws with laws, talents with talents, and manners with manners, nations will find so little reason to prefer themselves to others, that if they preserve for their own country that love which is the fruit of personal interest, at least they will lose that enthusiasm which is the fruit of an exclusive self-esteem.'

Yet Diderot had the perspicacity to discern the drawbacks to such a revolution in the conditions of social climate. 'Commerce, like enlightenment, lessens ferocity but also, just as enlightenment, lessens ferocity but also, just as enlightenment takes away the enthusiasm of self-esteem, so perhaps commerce takes away the enthusiasm of virtue. It gradually extinguishes the spirit of magnanimous disinterestedness, and replaces it by that of hard justice. By turning men's minds rather to use than beauty, to prudence rather than to greatness, it may be that it injures the strength, the generosity, the nobleness of manners.'

All this, whether it come to much or little, is at least more true than Diderot's assurance that henceforth for any nation in Europe to make conquests must be a moral impossibility. Napoleon Bonaparte was then a child in arms.

Whether his career was on the whole a fulfilment or a contradiction of Diderot's proposition, may be disputed.

And so our sketch of the great book must at length end. Let us make one concluding remark. Is it not surprising that a man of Diderot's speculative boldness and power should have failed to rise from the mechanical arrangement of thought and knowledge, up to some higher and more commanding conception of the relation between himself in the eighteenth century, or ourselves in the nineteenth, and all those great systems of thought, method, and belief, which in various epochs and over different spaces of the globe have given men working answers to the questions that their leading spirits were moved to put to themselves and to the iron universe around them? We constantly feel how near Diderot is to the point of view that would have brought light. We feel how very nearly ready he was to see the mental experiences of the race in east and west, not as superstition, degradation, grovelling error, but as aspects of intellectual effort and aspiration richly worthy of human interest and scientific consideration, and in their aim as well as in their substance all of one piece with the newest science and the last voices of religious or anti-religious development. Diderot was the one member of the party of Philosophers who was capable of grasping such a thought. If this guiding idea of the unity of the intellectual history of man, and the organic integrity of thought, had happily come into Diderot's mind, we should have had an Encyclopaedia indeed; a survey and representation of all the questions and answers of the world, such as would in itself have suggested what questions are best worth putting, and at the same time have furnished its own answers.

For this the moment was not yet. An urgent social task lay before France and before Europe; it could not be postponed until the thinkers had worked out a scheme of philosophic completeness. The thinkers did not seriously make any effort after this completeness. The encyclopaedia was the most serious attempt, and it did not wholly fail. As I replace in my shelves this mountain of volumes, 'dusky and huge, enlarging on the sight,' I have a presentiment that their pages will seldom again be disturbed by me or by others. They served a great purpose a hundred years ago. They are now a monumental ruin, clothed with all the profuse associations of history. It is no Ozymandias of Egypt, king of kings, whose wrecked shape of stone and sterile memories we contemplate. We think rather of the grey and crumbling walls of an ancient stronghold, reared by the endeavour of stout hands and faithful, whence in its own day and generation a band once went forth against barbarous hordes to strike a blow for humanity and truth.

Ernst Cassirer   (essay date 1932)

SOURCE: "Nature and Natural Science," in *The Philosophy of the Enlightenment,* translated by Fritz C. A. Koelln and James P. Pettegrove, Princeton University Press, 1951, pp. 37-92.

[*Cassirer was a German neo-Kantian philosopher best known for his lucid and comprehensive interpretation of modern culture, which places particular emphasis on sym-*

bolic systems such as language and myth. In addition, his Die Philosophie der Aufklarung *(1932; The Philosophy of the Enlightenment, 1951) is considered a seminal work. In the following excerpt from that text, Cassirer examines the revolutionary quality of Diderot's materialist philosophy.*]

Materialism as it appears in the eighteenth century, as it is justified and defended, is no mere scientific or metaphysical dogma; it is rather an imperative. It not only aims to establish a thesis concerning the nature of things but also to command and to forbid. This feature is especially evident in Holbach's *System of Nature.* Viewed superficially Holbach's doctrine looks like a system of the strictest and most consistent determinism. No aspect of nature is to be introduced into the philosophy of nature which is explicable only in terms of man and his appetites and desires. In nature nothing is just or unjust, good or bad; here all beings and all happenings are equal in value and in validity. All phenomena are necessary; and in view of its given qualities and of the specific circumstances of its existence, no being can act otherwise than it actually does. Hence there is no evil, no guilt, no disorder in nature: "All is in order in a nature, no part of which can ever deviate from the certain and necessary rules which issue from the essence it has received" [La Mettrie in his *L'homme machine*]. If man believes himself free, he is merely exhibiting a dangerous delusion and an intellectual weakness. It is the structure of the atoms that forms him, and their motion that propels him forward; conditions not dependent on him determine his nature and direct his fate. But with this content of the materialistic thesis, its presentation becomes involved in a curious antagonism. For it by no means follows Spinoza's motto: "not to laugh at, not to lament, nor to detest, but to understand." Superficially considered Holbach's philosophy of nature is only intended as an introduction to a more comprehensive whole. His *System of Nature* merely forms the basis for his *Social System* and for his *Universal Morality,* and the real tendency which dominates his thought clearly appears only in these last two books. Man must free himself from all idols, from all illusions concerning the original cause of things, for only by so doing can he succeed in ordering and establishing the world according to his own ideas. Hitherto theological spiritualism has prevented any truly autonomous regulation of the politico-social system. It is the dragon of the sciences, obstructing their development at every stage. "As the born enemy of experience, theology, the science of the supernatural, has been an insuperable obstacle to the progress of the natural sciences. Physics, natural history, and anatomy were not allowed to see anything except through the malevolent eyes of superstition" [Système de la nature]. But this rule of superstition becomes even more dangerous if it is permitted to shape the moral order. For here it not only annuls human knowledge but robs human happiness of its real foundation. It frightens man with a thousand phantoms and deprives him of every uninhibited joy of existence. Only a resolute and radical break with all spiritualism can cure this situation. The notions of God, freedom and immortality are to be uprooted once and for all, so that the rational order of nature shall not be threatened and overthrown by constant intervention from the supernatural world which these notions seem to construct. The same line of reasoning is to be found in Lamettrie's

Man a Machine. The world will never be happy so long as it does not decide to become atheistic. When the belief in God vanishes, all theological disputes and religious wars will cease too: "nature, hitherto infected with a sacred poison, would resume its rights and purity." The *System of Nature* itself encounters a difficult dilemma when it appears thus as challenger and accuser, and when it is not content with theoretical conclusions but rather sets up a norm for human thought and faith. The doctrine of the absolute necessity of the events of nature gets caught in the net of its own reasoning. For on the basis of this doctrine what right have we to speak of norms at all, what right to demand and evaluate? Does not this doctrine see in every "ought" a mere delusion which it transforms into a "must"? And is there any alternative but to yield to this "must"? Can we guide it and prescribe its course? Even eighteenth century criticism of the *System of Nature* bared this fundamental weakness of its argument. Frederick the Great's reply to the book calls attention emphatically to this point. "After the author has exhausted all evidence," this reply objects, "to show that men are guided by a fatalistic necessity in all their actions, he had to draw the conclusion that we are only a sort of machine, only marionettes moved by the hand of a blind power. And yet he flies into a passion against priests, governments, and against our whole educational system; he believes indeed that the men who exercise these functions are free, even while he proves to them that they are slaves. What foolishness and what nonsense! If everything is moved by necessary causes, then all counsel, all instruction, all rewards and punishments are as superfluous as inexplicable; for one might just as well preach to an oak and try to persuade it to turn into an orange tree." A more subtle and elastic dialectic than Holbach's could of course endeavor to overcome this objection and weave it skillfully into its own argument. Diderot saw and expressed clearly all the antinomies into which the system of fatalism finally leads; but he utilizes these antinomies as the motivating force, as the vehicle, for his own thoroughly dialectic thought. He admits a vicious circle but he transforms this situation into a grand jest. A most ingenious and original book took this impulse as its inspiration. The novel ***Jack the Fatalist*** endeavors to show that the concept of fate is the alpha and omega of all human thinking; but it also shows how thought time and again comes into conflict with this concept, how it is forced implicitly to deny and revoke the concept even while affirming it. There is no alternative but to recognize this situation as inevitable, and to extend our very idea of necessity so as to include that inconsistency with respect to this idea of which we are guilty in all our thoughts and judgments, in all our affirmations and negations. According to Diderot it is this oscillation between the two poles of freedom and necessity which brings the circle of our thought and existence to completion. By such oscillation, not by a simple assertion or denial, we can discover the all-inclusive concept of nature, that concept which in the last analysis is just as much beyond agreement and contradiction and beyond truth and falsehood as it is beyond good and evil because it includes both extremes without differentiation.

The eighteenth century as a whole remained aloof from this whirlpool of Diderot's dialectic which carries him along from atheism to pantheism, from materialism to dynamic panpsychism, and back again by turns. The *System of Nature* played a relatively unimportant part in the general development of Diderot's thought. Even the thinkers closest to Holbach's circle not only rejected the radical conclusions of his work but denied his very premises. Voltaire's sure judgment appeared when he at once attacked Holbach's book at its weakest point. With ruthless clarity he pointed to the contradiction in the fact that Holbach, who dedicated his banner to the fight against dogmatism and intolerance, in turn set up his own thesis as dogma and defended it with fanatical zeal. Voltaire refused to permit his viewpoint as a free thinker to be based on such arguments, and he was unwilling to receive from the hands of Holbach and his followers the "patent of an atheist" (*le brevet d'athée*). And Voltaire was even more critical of Holbach's presentation of his views and of the literary value of the book. He classified the work [in his poem "Les Cabales"] as belonging to the only literary genre he could not tolerate, namely, the "boring genre" (*genre ennuyeux*). In fact Holbach's style, apart from its prolixity and digressiveness, is peculiarly harsh and dry. Its objective is to eliminate from the philosophy of nature not only all religious, but all aesthetic elements as well, and to neutralize all the forces of feeling and phantasy. It is silly to adore and worship a nature which operates absolutely blindly and mechanically. "Let us consider that we are the sensitive parts of a whole which is entirely devoid of feeling, of a whole all of whose forms and combinations will perish after they have arisen and endured for a longer or shorter period. Let us regard nature as a huge workshop which contains everything required to produce all those formations we see before us, and let us not attribute nature's works to an imaginary cause which exists only in our own brain." Words like these were no doubt in Goethe's mind when he says that he and his youthful friends in Strasbourg, when they heard of the Encyclopaedists, felt as if they were walking among countless moving spools and looms in a great factory where the bewilderment produced by the machinery, the incomprehensibility of the complicated interlocking process, and the consideration of all that goes into the production of a piece of cloth, caused them to grow disgusted with the very coats they had on. Of the *System of Nature* Goethe relates that he and his friends could not understand how such a book could be dangerous: "It seemed to us so grey, so Cimmerian, so deathlike that we could hardly stand its presence, and we shuddered at it as if it were a ghost." The reaction against Holbach's work, which began soon after its appearance, is owing to the fact that it drew the fire not only of all the religious but of all the most vital artistic forces of the epoch. These were the forces which were not only urging a reformation of systematic aesthetics but which were also active in the formation of the philosophy of nature of the eighteenth century. From them arose a movement destined to exercise an epoch-making influence on the growth of modern science.

. . . . .

In his essay ***On the Interpretation of Nature*** (1754) Diderot, who among the thinkers of the eighteenth century probably possessed the keenest sense for all intellectual movements and transitions of that epoch, remarks that the century seems to have reached a decisive turning-point. A great revolution in the field of science is now in the offing. "I dare almost assert that in less than a century we shall not have three great geometers left in Europe. This science will very soon come to a standstill where Bernoullis, Eulers, Maupertuis, Clairants, Fontaines, d'Alemberts, and La Granges will have left it. They will have erected the columns of Hercules. We shall not go beyond that point." We know how far this prophecy came from fulfillment so far as the history of pure mathematics is concerned. Diderot's hundred years had not yet elapsed before the death of Gauss—who had revolutionized mathematics and extended its frontiers both in content and method in a manner the eighteenth century could not foresee. Yet there was, nonetheless, a genuine sentiment behind Diderot's prediction. For the point he wishes to emphasize is that among the various natural sciences mathematics will not be able to maintain its sole mastery much longer. A rival is appearing on the horizon which mathematics will not be able to suppress entirely. However perfect mathematics may be within its own province and to whatever precision it may evolve its concepts, yet this perfection will necessarily remain its immanent limitation. For it cannot reach out beyond its own self-made concepts; it has no immediate access to empirical concrete reality. This reality becomes accessible to us only through experiment, through faithful exact observations. But if the experimental method is to be completely effective, we must grant it full autonomy and free it from all tutelage. It is therefore necessary in the field of natural science to combat the systematizing spirit in mathematics as well as in metaphysics. As soon as the mathematician develops not merely his own conceptual world, but is convinced that he can catch reality in the meshes of his concepts, he has himself become a metaphysician. "When geometers have decried metaphysicians, they were far from thinking that all their science was simply metaphysics." With this observation the ideal of mathematical natural science, which dominated all eighteenth century physics, begins to fade; and in its place a new ideal arises, the demand for a purely descriptive science of nature. Diderot had grasped and described this ideal in its general outlines long before it was realized in detail. Why, he asks, do we possess so little really reliable knowledge of nature despite all the striking progress of mathematical science? Have geniuses been lacking, or has there been a dearth of thought and study? By no means. The reason lies rather in a systematic neglect of the relation between conceptual and factual knowledge. "The abstract sciences have occupied the best minds for too long. Words have been multiplied endlessly, but factual knowledge has lagged behind. . . . Yet the true wealth of philosophy consists in facts, of whatever kind they may be. But it is a prejudice of rational philosophy that he who cannot count his crowns is scarcely richer than somebody who only possesses one crown. Unfortunately, rational philosophy is much more concerned with comparing and combining facts already known than with collecting new ones." In these words [from *De l'Interprétation de la Nature*] Diderot formulates a new slogan which announces a new mode of thinking. The counting, systematizing, and calculating spirit of the seventeenth century is now challenged by a new tendency, a tendency to subdue the sheer profusion of reality by attacking it without reservations as to whether it can be described in clear and distinct concepts or reduced to measurement and number. Even though such systems may still be constructed, the delusion of their relation to reality vanishes. "Fortunate the systematic philosopher whom, like Epicurus and Lucretius or like Aristotle and Plato of old, nature has endowed with a lively imagination, great eloquence, and the art of expressing his ideas in striking and sublime pictures. The building he has erected may some day tumble down, but his statue will remain upright even beneath the ruins." The system thus possesses more individual than universal, more aesthetic than objectively logical meaning. As a tool of knowledge it is indispensable, but one must beware of becoming the slave of a mere tool. One should possess a system without being possessed by it: "May you have Lais, provided Lais does not have you." A new scientific trend, a new temper in research, now emerges which demands recognition and justification for itself as such and for its method.

This justification can begin with a consideration which had already been employed in mathematical physics. The followers and pupils of Newton in their controversy with Descartes' "rational" physics had emphasized again and again that the demand for an explanation of nature was to be superseded by the demand for a full description of nature's processes. Instead of definition, as known in pure mathematics, there will have to be description. For the physicist, of course, exact description of an event is the same thing as its measurement; only that which can be determined in purely numerical values and expressed in terms of such values can be described with real precision. As we go from physics to biology the postulate of pure description takes on a different meaning. It is no longer a question of transforming directly observed reality into an aggregate of quantities, into a network of numbers and measures; it is now rather a matter of retaining the specific form of empirical reality. It is this specific form which is supposed to lie before us in all the wealth and variety of its being as well as in the profusion of becoming. The logical structure of those concepts of classes and species, by virtue of which we usually seek insight into nature, are directly opposed to the actual profusion of nature. These concepts must necessarily limit direct observation; instead of leading to complete understanding of its content, they lead to impoverishment. This impoverishment is to be counteracted by seeking a method of forming concepts which permits us to come into direct contact with the specific welter of phenomena and individual instances of the forms of nature, and to focus our attention here while our concepts remain as flexible as the phenomena themselves. Diderot offered a model for such a formation of concepts in his formulation of botanical science. "If I dared," he writes here, "I should like to make the paradoxical statement that under certain circumstances there is nothing more laborious and wasteful than method. Method is a guide to truth which one cannot afford to dispense with, for as soon as one loses sight of it one must necessarily go astray. If one were to undertake to teach a child to speak by starting with the words that begin with A, then by proceeding to those that begin with B, etc., half a lifetime could go by before the child would finish the alphabet. Method is excellent in the realm of reasoning, but in my estimation it is detrimental in the case of natural history in general and in botany in particular." This does not mean that these sciences can dispense with system and method; it means rather that their form of system must not be borrowed from that of the rational disciplines, but that it must be derived from, and adapted to, the specific subject matter of these sciences.

Paul Hazard   (essay date 1946)

SOURCE: "Diderot," in *European Thought in the Eighteenth Century: From Montesquieu to Lessing,* translated by J. Lewis May, 1963. Reprint by Peter Smith, 1973, pp. 378-90.

[*Hazard was a leading French historian of ideas in the first half of the twentieth century. In the following excerpt from his* La Pensee Europeene au XVIIIeme Siecle: De Montesquieu a Lessing *(1946;* European Thought in the Eighteenth Century From Montesquieu to Lessing, *1963), Hazard provides a general account of Diderot's character and ideas, viewing him as both a herald of Enlightenment and precursor of Romanticism.*]

"When we essay to delineate Rousseau by contrasting him with the philosophers of his time, there is one of them who provides us with something of a problem, and that is Diderot, Diderot the Nature-worshipper, the sensation-monger, the well-spring of enthusiasm. Roughly speaking, we should say that he was a sort of understudy to Rousseau, playing his part, and often indistinguishable from him" [quoted from Gustave Lanson, *Histoire de la littérature française*]. However, the fact is that if we attempt a rigid classification and put things as it were into separate water-tight compartments, Reason in this one, Sentiment in that, and so on, Diderot is undoubtedly something of a puzzle. Nevertheless, to anyone setting out to trace the course of intellectual and spiritual evolution, Diderot is useful, indeed he is indispensable, for he typifies the precarious and temporary coalition of two forces which were soon to part company, and pursue their separate ways.

What an excellent companion he was! What a picturesque figure, swathed in the ample folds of his grey plush frock-coat, its pockets crammed with books; or in that ancient dressing-gown which still lives on for posterity in his description of it! So frank, so free, without a trace of pose or affectation. You never felt that you were not wanted, still less like someone trying to pump him against his will. Pump him! You just had to sit back in your chair and listen; listen as he unburdened himself of all that was in his mind, the whole day long. On one occasion Garat went to see him and could not manage to get a word in edgeways. Diderot started by laying down what the legislature ought to do, what laws they ought to pass, then he ran through five or six plots that he thought would make good plays, then he said what he thought about Tacitus and translations, acted a scene from Terence, sang a song he had made up impromptu at some supper-party or other and finally, having recited a comedy, told the youthful Garat that he was an admirable conversationalist and bade him a cordial farewell. Bubbling over with energy, his head was full of all sorts of ideas, plans, projects, dreams. Writing one day to Mme d'Épinay, Rousseau, who knew his Diderot, said, "I am undone if he arranges to come and see me. He'll plan to come over and over again, yet not once shall I see him. He's the kind of man you have to go and dig out by force if you want to make him do what he wants to do." On another occasion he says, "For my part, what I think about it is that the ante-meridian Diderot will always be wanting to go and see you, and that the post-meridian Diderot will never see you. You know how rheumatism gets hold of him sometimes; and when he's not soaring on his two great wings as high as the sun, he's to be found doubled-up on the ground, unable to budge an inch." Diderot of the morning, Diderot of the night; Diderot up in the skies, Diderot on all fours—yes, that is Diderot, that is the man right enough. And what a generous fellow he was, too! How prodigal with his belongings, his money, his time, his energies and even his writings. He was one of those rare men of letters who are not so desperately attached to their writings. He did not mind putting them on one side, leaving them in manuscript, letting his friends have them, or abandoning them to their fate, like apples fallen from a tree which had hundreds more to send after them. A little unpolished, a little plebeian, he would sample at a supper party bottle after bottle of champagne red or sparkling, of Canary sack, to say nothing of several kinds of liqueur, and after dinner he was not above letting go a button or two for comfort. And he was headstrong and no mistake, forever butting in and meddling with things that did not concern him. He was hail fellow well met with everyone and very free with his friendly embraces and slaps on the back; a little overpowering, but never mean, or petty or hypocritical, never envious, and even his faults had something half-attractive about them. So teeming was his brain, so prodigal was he of information and ideas, that, though you might come across profounder geniuses, you would never meet a richer one.

His riches were various and sharply contrasted, yet they got on peaceably enough together; he gave them house room without feeling the least uneasy because of their diversity. And why should he have felt uneasy? He was but too glad to behold this spate of incongruities flowing in upon him, only, in due time, to flow forth from him again.

Here is an epigraph, "My parents left behind them a son called 'Denis the Philosopher'; I am that son."

He is Denis the Philosopher. He is one of the brethren; he knows them all, for he has grouped them all around him, and with some of them he is on intimate terms, Grimm, Helvetius, d'Alembert, Condillac, the Baron d'Holbach; he admires Montesquieu, to whom he has solemnly rendered homage. He does not care much for Voltaire, their characters are too unlike, but Voltaire esteems him, because he considers him one of the leading members of the philosophic confraternity. For this reason he wanted to get him into the Academy. If the Atlas who bore the Encyclopaedia on his shoulders were to make one of the Forty, that body would be considerably strengthened. In Diderot's view, there could be no limit to what the philosopher might aspire to; the magistrate dispenses justice; the philosopher teachers him to distinguish justice from injustice.

The soldier fights for his country; the philosopher makes him understand what his country really is. The priest calls on the people to pay honour to the gods; the philosopher explains to the priest what the gods are. The sovereign rules over all; the philosopher instructs him as to the origin and limitations of his power. If he had the management of things, he would adorn the brows of the philosopher with the civic crown, *ob servatos cives*.

He was responsible for the metaphor, to which we have already alluded, about knowledge being destined to dispel the tracts of darkness that still obscured the surface of the earth. To him, too, we owe that picture of Experiment in the guise of a giant, bringing down the pillars of the Temple of Error. He followed every successive step in the evolution of science, proceeding from, geometry to mathematical physics, and from mathematical physics to natural history; he took a passionate interest in anatomy and physiology; he studied fibres and tissues, nerves, bones and the various organs; he had seen flesh palpitate and the blood circulate, he had taken away from the metaphysician the right to talk authoritatively about man, and conferred it on the doctor.

Examining his ideas about morality is more or less like retracing the dogmas and the tentative theories of the philosophers: the taste for examining moral problems; moral science; rational morality; morality which connects the interests of the individual with the interests of the race. On the other hand, there was the disappointment at the failure to arrive at any definite moral code; the feeling that morality is a relative matter; the uncomfortable suspicion that the morality which was suitable to the scholar, the intellectual, was not equally adapted to the multitude; and, above all, that growing determinism which denied that there was, or could be, any such thing as morality at all. Jacques the Fatalist's master would have been only too pleased to regard himself as a free agent; but the arguments that Jacques the Fatalist threw into the scales tipped the balance towards the negative; we are what the general order of things and our own particular organization compel us to be. We are powerless to alter the laws which condition our lives; therefore, if freedom is a word devoid of meaning, as philosophically speaking it is, nothing that we do is deserving either of praise or blame, there is no such thing as vice or virtue, and nothing which calls for reward or punishment.

And that is the same Diderot who raised his voice in denunciation of tyrants; who declared that man possessed an indisputable right to political freedom; that the members of the State voluntarily dispossessed themselves of a portion of their liberty in order to entrust it to a power which exercised its authority solely by delegation; a power safeguarding security and property; the same Diderot who, in the matter of the training of the young, was all for taking education out of the hands of the regular clergy and making it a government responsibility, at once obligatory and non-clerical; a system in which Latin should give place to modern languages; in which teachers should pay careful attention to the stages in the development of the child's understanding, beginning with what was quite simple, and proceeding by degrees to the more complex; the kind of education which should aim at producing men of science, agriculturists, economists, in a word the sort of men who would be capable of rendering useful service to the State; a system of education in which the useful arts, its special care, should occupy the place of honour. It was that same Diderot, eager to know everything, who, like everyone else, had sought to discover the basic principle of the fine arts. He had read Plato and St. Augustine, Shaftesbury and Hutcheson, the Abbé Le Batteux and Père André, Wolff and Hagedorn, everyone in fact that was readable and a good few that were not. After learning so many conflicting ideas, he found himself in some perplexity. Finally he decided to define Beauty in the following terms. "I apply the term beautiful in respect of the external world to whatever contains within itself something that awakens in my understanding the idea of relationship, of association; and, in respect of myself, anything which awakens that idea"; association being "an operation of the understanding which considers either a being or a quality in so far as it implies the existence of another being or another quality." "Regard Beauty as a matter concerning the perception of relations, and you will have the history of its progress from the birth of the world down to the present day."

That Diderot did not make anti-clericalism the dominant business of his life; all the same, he was one of Christ's most violent accusers in the great trial. To begin with he professed Deism, but he soon got beyond that. If you don't

Bust of Diderot by Jean-Baptiste Pigalle, 1777.

believe in the gods, why banish them to the intermundane spaces? Better deny them outright. And that is what he did. He turned atheist. He believed, as did Naigeon, who followed him as a dog follows its master, that all would be peace and happiness on earth if only the idea of God could be obliterated. Towards God he was filled with wrath, bitterness and rage; witness his story about the misanthropist who hid himself in a cave and meditated long and deeply as to how he should take vengeance on the human race. At length he came out of his cave shouting loudly, God! God! "His voice resounded from pole to pole, and behold, men fell to quarrelling, hating and cutting one another's throats. And they've been doing the same thing ever since that abominable name was pronounced, and they will go on doing it till the process of the ages is accomplished." Materialist as he was, he believed in the atoms of Epicurus and Lucretius, assigning to them, however, the sort of dim sensibility and intelligence with which Maupertuis had invested them; and he treated himself to the pleasure of looking on at the birth and destruction of worlds.

If we were to stop short at this aspect of his character, he would somehow contrive to protest, even from the depths of the realm of shadows. When Van Loo painted his portrait, he was not pleased with it. Van Loo had only brought out one physiognomy, one kind of expression, whereas, said Diderot, "I had a hundred different ones a day, according to the mood that was on me. I was serene, sad, dreamy, tender, violent, passionate, eager. The outward signs of my many and varying states of mind chased one another so rapidly across my face that the painter's eye caught a different one from moment to moment, and never got me aright." So, too, with his mind; he was Pantophilus, the universal lover. What he liked best for himself was the impromptu effusion, and, next to that, dialogue, where one voice affirms and the other denies; Himself and The Other. Not to put too fine a point on it, let us say that there was always something of Himself in the Other and something of the Other in Himself. It was always a case of the **Neveu de Rameau** and his Interlocutor. Not that he was hesitant, or undecided, or like that personage Manzoni was later on to describe, the man who was always against everything, whatever it was. In point of fact he took up a very definite stand, but so all-embracing was his intellectual outlook that he always kept a soft spot in his heart for things his reason had told him to abandon. It was well said that into the plain solid truth which so many of his contemporaries looked upon as fixed and stable he imported the mobility of life and so made truth something that was mobile too. His mind, acting on the various data that came before it, deprived them of their stability so that he was like some magical Master of the Ceremonies making his company continually assume whatever forms he might for the moment desire. That is the key to all the various Diderots that inhabited a single body. But now let us turn from the man who by means of the Encyclopaedia heralded in the age of enlightenment and contemplate him who by the influence he undoubtedly exerted over the pioneers of the *Sturm und Drang,* proved to be himself one of the pioneers of romanticism in Europe.

Here is another epigraph: "If Nature ever made a sensitive soul, that soul, and you know it, is mine."

And first of all the soul imaginative. A ceaseless outpouring of rough sketches, themes, expansions, alluring digressions, a host of works in one. A full-blooded, vital force that looked on reality as a poorish thing compared with what that force itself could produce. Comfortably installed in a corner of his habitation, the imaginative man piled up dream upon dream. No need for him to travel in order to make discoveries; why come down from the garret to the cellar, and mount up again from the cellar to the garret, when you can dream so well sitting in the same armchair? If it so happens that he does accept an invitation to the country, he goes with a romantic outfit in which some subtle *nuances* are already packed. From his window at Le Grandval he descries the little wood which weather-fends the dwelling against the northern blast, the little brook that flows by brambles and reeds, by mossy banks and pebbly beaches, and the view strikes him as "picturesque and wild". Of a night he loves to lie in his bed and listen to the billowing wind, to the rain lashing the eaves, to the storm that makes the branches loud, and to the ceaseless undertone that sounds like a neverending diapason through it all. Save for Langres and Bourbonne, that was about the limit of his wanderings, until, as an old man and despite his vows, he went to Russia. All the same he contributed, and that mightily, to bringing the beauties of Nature into the stock of human acquisitions. Take pictures: he will describe so vividly the landscapes he has seen at the Salons, rocks, precipices, ruins, sunsets, moonlight, and, in particular, shipwrecks, that the privileged few who read him are in the end quite carried away by his magic. Who was it that gave these pieces of advice to the artist? "Don't leave your studio, unless it be to consult Nature. Live with her in the open fields. Go and gaze at the sunrise and the sunset, see the sky as it adorns itself with coloured clouds. Go and walk in the meadows among the flocks and herds. See the blades of grass all glistening with drops of dew." It was Diderot [in his **Salon de 1765**]. Who was it told poetry the way it should go, saying, "Poetry requires something of the vast, the uncouth, the untamed"? That, too, was Diderot [in his **De la poésie dramatique**]. His heart is in a ferment. He is thrilled he knows not why; nor wherefore he is sad, nor wherefore he rejoices. His whole being is stirred, and tears betray the intensity of his emotion. Diderot gives his daughter in marriage, and then sheds tears of grief at losing her; he sees that she is happy, and behold he weeps for love of her; his thoughts turn to the death of his parents and he weeps tears of hopeless grief. Diderot will fly into such a rage that he will tear his hair, and strike his head against the wall—"The worst of it is I can never put myself into such a rage as to quiet my entrails even for a few days on end." Diderot never continues in the peaceful state that comes of a contented mind; his temperature is always above normal; he burns with feverish sensibility.

So far from being ashamed of itself, that sensibility glories in its transports—if there is someone that does not share them, that "someone" is greatly to be pitied. It keeps bursting out into "O my friend!" "O my Sophie!" for the living; for the dead, "O Seneca!" It scolds, it hustles, it frets. It strikes attitudes, it piles on the pathetic, it surveys itself in the glass, and listens to itself approvingly. It is quite individual, unique; and it is fatal. It overdoes the dramatic, and becomes—just melodrama.

Such faculties as those, given free play, differentiate him from his friends; he is as different from d'Alembert, for example, as fire is from ice. They inspire him, atheist though he be, with words of praise for the Catholic religion. Who, he asks, witnessing the Good Friday devotions, or looking on at a Corpus Christi procession, seeing the majesty of it, listening to the chanting of the priests and the responses of the crowd, impressed by the sombre magnificence and solemnity which always accompany religious ceremonial, who could help protesting at those "absurd rigorists" who remain unmoved? Thus it happened that the enemy of Christianity associated himself, for the nonce, with those apologists who seek to show that religion is true because it is touching. A materialist, he firmly believed in the supremacy of the mind, the spirit; a determinist, he would not admit, when he dwelt on his love for Sophie Volland, that it had any origin other than his own personal and independent choice; he was furious when Naigeon ascribed it to the influence of a passing comet, and he chafed angrily against a philosophy which his heart could not but force him to deny. He was a tyrant-hater, but he had a tremendous enthusiasm for Catherine of Russia. Professing a moral code based on self-interest, the code he practised was wholly one of sentiment; he made much of a maxim already regrettably illustrated by the Abbé Prévost, the motto that said everything is permitted to a man provided he has a kind heart. A professed aesthete, he made Beauty something to be accounted for by the reason; yet in spite of all his pet theories about government, utility, morality, philosophy, the ideal and many another besides, he finished up as the champion of sincerity as opposed to artifice, upholding the "inward spirit" of the artist against the bondage of convention, and proclaiming the emotional value of the arts. "Be moved", he said when others said, "Be sensible". At the same time, he extolled the emotional value of the stage. O unfeeling onlooker, why did you come to the theatre, if not to weep? And he revelled in tears; he wept as he read about the woes of Pamela and Clarissa, and, across the sundering distance, he embraced Richardson, all bathed in tears.

Everything yields to analysis; or would do if our psychological life were not animated by tiny dim perceptions so minute that they elude the analyst. Everything we do should be guided by method; if, that is to say, method were not a cold and clumsy process, infinitely inferior to the spirit of invention which lives and moves and stirs in a manner all its own; compared with genius, method was like the call of the cuckoo compared with the song of the nightingale. And how delightful to go and launch out on a boundless sea of hypotheses, of majestic systems which, may be, were not sound, but were at all events seductive. With that sensibility of his, he endowed the infinitely small, the indivisible particles of matter; he sent it heavenward as far as to the stars. By means of it he counted on setting death itself at defiance. The marble tomb which had inurned the bodies of two lovers, would crumble into dust and mingle with the soil around it; the soil would feed

the cells of the plants, and the plants the cells of living beings, and two of these might one day remember and recognize each other again. His philosophic speculations took a lyrical tone:

> The first vows exchanged by two beings of flesh and blood were made at the foot of a rock which was crumbling into dust. To bear witness to their constancy, they called aloud to a heaven whose aspect was ceaselessly changing; all was evanescent, all was changing, within them and around them, and they deemed that their hearts were immune from vicissitude. [*Jacques le Fataliste*]

The only thing which that poetic effusion lacks is metre, and with that Alfred de Musset supplies it in his *Souvenir:*

> Oui, les premiers baisers, oui les premiers serments
> Que deux êtres mortels échangèrent sur terre,
> Ce fut au pied d'un arbre effeuillé par les vents,
>   Et sur un roc en poussière.
> Ils prirent à témoin de leur joie éphémère
> Un ciel toujours voilé qui change à tout moment,
> Et des astres sans nom que leur propre lumière
>   Dévore incessamment. . . .

> (Yes the first time two mortals exchanged kisses and vows on earth was at the foot of a tree despoiled of its leaves by the winds and on a rock crumbling into dust.)

> (They called to bear witness to their transient joy a heaven for ever veiled and changing every moment and nameless stars which their own light was ceaselessly devouring.)

If we were trying to collect together the various meanings we have seen gathering round the word Nature, we should find a good many, if not all, in Diderot.

For him, according to the moment, the day, the mood, the caprice, the train of thought, the theory, the system, whatever happened to be uppermost at the particular time, Nature was the aggregate of all the phenomena external to ourselves; and our understanding is the little square upon which the image of it comes to be depicted. It is all that is created; men ought to erect a mighty temple to Nature, in which specimens of all the animals and all the plants in existence should be shown. Nature is benevolent and full of kindnesses; sometimes she is pleased to plant a sensitive soul and a tender heart in a man of the humblest station. Nature is an artist; she made the sky blue, and of her green she wove the earth's Spring mantle; in our art we imitate the cunning with which she has dissembled the scheme of her effects. Nature knows her business; she never produces anything that has not some part to play, no evil without its remedy, and in particular no form of government in which some limits are not set to the sufferings of the people. Nature is artful; of set purpose she made love and hate terrible, because her aim is the reproduction and conservation of the species; the force of the human passions is always proportioned to that end. Nature busies herself with the minutest details; she prepares the cellular tissue, she fabricates membranes, aided in that, it is true, by sickness and chance. Nature is just and punishes offences against society; you live a life of debauchery, you will have the dropsy.

Nature is indifferent; provided the race goes on, she is satisfied; she cares nothing for good or evil. And Nature is capricious; the race is made up of individuals, but of individuals she recks nothing. Nature works by fits and starts; sometimes she will remain for an age in a sort of torpor, as though exhausted; sometimes she bestirs herself to make great men. Nature is capable of strange blunders and does not always give good counsel in time of danger. Nature is treacherous; beware of always yielding to her lure. She is cruel, and exterminates those whose organism accords ill with the laws of the universe. She is the unrelenting foe of man and pursues him from the day of his birth. Man, if he would survive, must fight against her in company with other men, his brothers. She is immoral; she is always trying to benefit herself at the expense of others. She is incoherent; and she is blind. She does not *will* anything; she simply *is*. And is that strictly true? A multiplicity and concatenation of various contingencies, she has no intrinsic *raison d'être*. Can our senses take cognizance of her? Some of the causes of sensible phenomena are outside the range of our senses. . . .

However, among all these different meanings, and we do not claim to have exhausted the list, there is one that seems to preponderate in his mind—Nature is the hidden instinct which inspires the individual, and gives him his great and privileged position. Were it not for this instinct, there would be no strong characters, no original types, no geniuses. Without it we should just be borne along, with everything else that is, on the great ever-flowing stream. For we go our way, never getting any clear idea of the place we occupy, or the limits of time assigned to us; we flit past like so many May-flies; the world is a composite whole perpetually tending to its own destruction, a swift succession of beings that follow closely one upon another, press hard on one another's heels, and disappear; but for all that, the individual obtains, by the intensity of his powers, what time denies him. Save for this instinct we should be, each one of us, but a slave in a drove of slaves. It is open to the individual to create a compromise between the spontaneous and the studied, between the untutored and the corrupt; he may quite well decide to build himself a dwelling mid-way between the cot and the castle; but just as he begins to think about contenting himself with this compromise, he gives a shout and scuttles away:

> L'enfant de la nature abhorre l'esclavage;
> Implacable ennemi de toute autorité,
> Il s'indigne du joug; la contrainte l'outrage;
> Liberté c'est son Voeu; son cri, c'est Liberté.
> Au mépris des liens de la société,
> Il réclame en secret son antique apanage.
> Des mœurs ou grimaces d'usage
> Ont beau servir de voile à sa férocité;
> Une hypocrite urbanité,
> Les souplesses d'un tigre enchaîné dans sa cage,
> Ne trompent point l'oeil du sage;
> Et dans les murs de la cité,
> Il reconnaît l'homme sauvage
> S'agitant dans les fers dont il est garrotté [*Les Elevthéromahes*].

(The child of Nature abhors slavery; implacable foe of all authority, he rages at the yoke, constraint infuriates him. Liberty is his longing, Liberty his cry. Scorning the bonds of society he secretly lays claim to his ancient appanage. The manners and make customary make-believe faces are powerless to hide his ferocity; a sham urbanity, the graceful movements of a tiger shut up in its cage do not deceive the wise man's eye; and in the city walls he recognizes the man of the wilds chafing at the fetters by which he is bound.)

Thus does the eleutheromaniac, the fanatic of freedom, behold himself beneath the guise of the citizen. He is thrilled as he reads the account that Bougainville gives of his sojourn in the happy isle where his vessels came to anchor; he feels a stirring in that residue of the wild, the untamed, that lingers far down in the depths of his soul. He would fain be as that Tahitian who delights in all the joys of primitive existence. But he realizes that that is impossible, and so he finds himself in conflict, not only with society, but with himself, the combat which rends the romantic's heart asunder. "Would you like to hear an epitome of almost all our troubles? Well, this is it. There once existed a natural man, child of nature. Into this natural man was introduced an artificial man; and there started within the cave a civil war which went on for life. Sometimes the natural man gets the better, sometimes he is floored by the moral and artificial man; in either case the unhappy monster is pulled about, pinioned, tortured, broken on the wheel. Forever moaning, forever woebegone, whether because some hollow expectation of glory transports and intoxicates him, or because some false idea of shame hampers him, and casts him down." [quoted from Diderot's ***Supplément au voyage de Bougainville***].

When Rousseau came to visit Diderot, while he was a prisoner in the castle of Vincennes, he told him about the subject set for competition by the Dijon Academy, *Has progress in the sciences and the arts contributed to the corruption or to the purification of morals?* Did Diderot, inventive man, advise him to run counter to received opinion and thus start him on the career which was in due time to lead him to upset the whole psychology of Europe? Of course

---

Friedrich Melchior Grimm [1763]:

Profound and vigorous in his writing, but even more astonishing in conversation, he delivers oracles on every subject imaginable. Of all men he is the least inclined to know in advance what he will do or say: whatever he says, he is always original, always surprising. His imagination is so strong, so impetuous, that it might be alarming at times, were those qualities not tempered by his irresistible bonhomie.

Friedrich Melchior Grimm in his Correspondance Littérraire *[October 1763]. Translated by Francis Steegmuller in his* A Woman, A Man, and Two Kingdoms, *1991.*

we shall never know exactly what took place that day, but some such intervention on his part is within the range of possibility. From that moment it was all over with me, said Jean Jacques. From that moment a new attitude towards life came into being.

Jacques Barzun (essay date 1958)

SOURCE: "Why Diderot?" in *Varieties of Literary Experience: Eighteen Essays in World Literature,* edited by Stanley Burnshaw, New York University Press, 1962, pp. 31-44.

[*Barzun is a French-born American man of letters whose wide range of learning has produced distinguished works in several fields, including history, culture, musicology, literary criticism, and biography. In the following essay, originally written in 1958, Barzun offers a favorable appraisal of Diderot's literary and philosophical achievement, describing him as one of the great* uncompleting *men—"finders and initiators, not concluders and finishers."*]

I

Whenever I am looking for enjoyment from literature and the arts, and also when, in the modern manner, I "study" them for clues to intellectual or social history, I find myself most drawn to the geniuses whose fame is unsettled. Of the ancients I prefer Euripides and Lucian; in recent times, William James, Walter Bagehot, and Samuel Butler; before them, Berlioz and Diderot. Their works and characters pull me back again and again to speculate and admire.

This preference may be temperamental in part, just as their incomplete or grudging recognition is in part accidental. But my choice is also rational, like the state of their reputations, and both are possibly instructive. Of course, if the situation is to tell us something new, we must be sure that we have got hold of a truly great mind, and not merely an approximation of one. Nor should we confuse what I call unsettled fame with obscurity. The group of geniuses I have in mind are figures known, at least by name, to all who discuss ideas and their history. Nor has praise been withheld from my chosen men. Their distinction lies in the perennial disquiet they inspire. Their praise is mixed with doubts. Most significant, perhaps, the reasons for valuing their work are many and conflicting. In a word, the men and their achievements resist classification.

The effect of this lack of pliability upon the ordinary critic is extraordinary. Thus in the excellent *Oxford Companion to French Literature* one reads that Diderot "had not the patience and method to produce any single great work." This comes after the statement that the direction of the *Encyclopédie* was "the most notable of his contributions to the advancement of knowledge, and a vast burden of which, with great courage and perseverance, he bore the main share." Apparently perseverance is not patience and the *Encyclopédie* is not a work of method. What is more, this estimate of Diderot's character tells us that he was "affable, generous, a faithful friend . . . bubbling over with ideas, enthusiasm and coarse gaiety; at the same time violent and unbalanced."

I attach great importance to such summaries in reputable handbooks, for they reflect in their bland confusion the general uncertainty I speak of; and they naturally spread it farther, to the newcomers for whom such books are intended. In these same pages Diderot's great works—and particularly that masterpiece, *Rameau's Nephew*—are listed as "minor philosophical works," while the doctrine to which they contribute in this minor way is said to be philosophical determinism. Diderot was "an experimental materialist" who anticipated "in some respects later evolutionary ideas." He was in addition an "ardent moralist" and "the founder of art criticism in France," though "his underlying principles are full of fallacies." I am reminded by these wondrous judgments of the "authoritative" literature on Berlioz thirty years ago, when I began wading through its naive incoherence and factual inaccuracy.

For this state of affairs, which recurs and will recur in the history of civilization, I discern two causes: profound originality and transcendent imperfection. I say transcendent to suggest a superior quality, that of work produced at a time when perfection along established ways is no longer of any value. For example, after the tales of Voltaire—after *Candide* especially—and after Rousseau's *Confessions,* no possibility is left of insinuating philosophy, morality, and psychology agreeably, through narratives couched in a diction limpid and calm. Nothing less than the scabrous irregularities of *D'Alembert's Dream* and the vulgar language and detail of *Rameau's Nephew* satisfy the need to re-establish contact with common life.

Men such as Diderot, then, are *uncompleting* men because they are finders and initiators, not concluders and finishers. That is why they puzzle the tidy minds of the academy, whose valuable role is to affix labels and put away in glass cases. Diderot, they rightly say, cannot be "associated with a stabilized genre" (this failure sounds ominous) "much less with a single recognized masterpiece." Here one might demur. If *Rameau's Nephew* is not a masterpiece, then the term had best be abandoned. "Recognized" is again a matter of opinion. If Goethe and Freud recognized in Diderot a master of reality, he can wait for the professors of literature. Meantime we grant them that Diderot is not of those who, to the sound of public acclaim, drive the last nail into the edifice their predecessors have built. Rather, they destroy and build anew, groping and stumbling at times, seeming paradoxically full of old ideas as well as of new, and unable to point to unmistakable followers because posterity altogether, in all its diversity and warfare, follows in their steps.

Their very career, in a worldly sense, is untoward. Here is Diderot, a great figure in his own day, courted by the crowned heads of states and of intellect, a hero in the struggle for liberty of thought, a voluminous, indefatigable writer not one of whose productions is without originality or importance, yet whose ultimate greatness depends on three or four works, written relatively late in life, nearly lost, and published half a century after his death. In life, his friends might dub him *"le philosophe"* and Voltaire liken him to Plato, but the high performance justifying these epithets was hidden from those who spoke them.

II

Under "Diderot" in Flaubert's *Dictionary of Accepted Ideas* we read: "Always followed by d'Alembert"; and under "Encyclopédie," which the joining of the names evokes, we find: "Quaint and old-fashioned; but even so, thunder against." To get at Diderot, to read him, understand him, one must push to one side the gigantic and successful enterprise to which he devoted thirty years of his life. Not that the twenty-eight folio volumes of the encyclopedia, packed with knowledge and doctrine, wit and good prose, are a negligible achievement. They testify to Diderot's enormous intelligence, just as the story of the vicissitudes endured by the solitary editor defines his heroic character. But on the scale of the eighteenth century the work was but a mass medium for spreading culture. Diderot himself described it in terms we recognize as good advertising copy: "a complete library"—"lavishly illustrated"—"no one who wants to be up to date can afford, etc. . . ." But strange as it may seem after the consequences, good and evil, that have been ascribed to the **Encyclopédie,** Diderot's superhuman labors to produce it were but his tribute to the spirit of the day. One proof of this is that the work was a great commercial success. Many of the "best people" were encyclopedists. To write the text Diderot found a hundred contributors. To write his late masterpieces or to read them aright he found only himself, and we are still "discovering" him 175 years after his death.

There is even a subtle contradiction between the bearing of the **Encyclopédie** and Diderot's innermost convictions. The idea of knowledge codified and portable, of enlightenment by system, went against Diderot's earliest and deepest perception. If ever the editor wondered why he was striving so hard to put that loaded alphabet in order, he may have told himself that he was doing it only to clear the public mind for receiving his own fluid speculations. He did not, of course, reason in this way, so far as I know; I only make up this internal dialogue to render the contrast I see between the plain business of the **Encyclopédie** and the evocative meaning of the final great works. Yet my fancy is not wholly without warrant. In his **Letter on the Blind,** just before Diderot enters the long tunnel of editorial work, he gives as it were a last look at reality and exclaims: "I cannot conceive why people do not grow bored reading so much and learning nothing."

For his own part, Diderot had been reading a great deal since early youth, when he was a very fair student of the arts and sciences, particularly mathematics. He had made his bohemian way in Paris by tutoring in that science, by translating from English and Italian, which he had mastered alone, and by other hack-work. But none of this was meant to foster a respectable career as man of letters. Diderot was a hot, passionate, rebellious youth. He quarrelled with his well-loved father over marrying, and was even sent to prison on that account. And for his earliest *Pensées* (1746) Diderot used Shaftesbury's name to cover his own, so that he might express his faith in "enthusiasm," in rash deviation from eighteenth-century taste.

What is more, this fledgling philosopher spoke in a new voice. His prose was rapid, trenchant, sinewy. One might suppose that these adjectives apply as much to Voltaire,

but the two styles are worlds apart: Diderot's tone becomes less and less "polite" as he becomes more and more himself. He relies increasingly on colloquialism—and hence on dialogue—to achieve what he seeks, which we should today call "realism." He is dissatisfied with anything less than the exactitude of intimacy and concreteness, and he says so:

> In general any language is poor in words adequate to the uses of writers with a lively imagination. They are as badly off as intelligent foreigners—the situations they invent, the delicate nuances of character they perceive, the naturalness [*naïveté*] of the depictions they want to give, make them continually depart from ordinary modes of speech and make them use turns of phrase that are always admirable provided they are neither precious nor obscure. . . . The license taken with the common tongue is overlooked, the truth of the rendering alone strikes us.

This is the creed of a literary Romantic, dated 1749, the year of Goethe's birth. Nor is it with Diderot an isolated intention, a vagary. His "psychology" (as we say today to mean his view of man), his artistic tastes, his morality, his science, his metaphysics, and his ultimate philosophy are in tune with this new *impatience*. Diderot wants to cut through the resilient web of conventional words and tested generalities so as to reach and grip the reality that flashes and beckons to him from between the joints of the neoclassic. And the first particle of that new truth shows him that Descartes' founding universal reason on the thinking self is an illusion. Men are diverse, each is unique, individualism and pluralism follow: "Since I am someone who acts thus and so, anyone who could act otherwise could not be me."

In the relativism of that sentence and in others about "matter capable of thought," critics have found Diderot's materialism and determinism. The propriety of using these terms can be plausibly argued, but then their definition has to be made so singular that they cease to have the common meaning in order to denote a position peculiar to Diderot. It would seem simpler to begin by saying what Diderot meant. Whatever he was, he cannot be classed with those who take comfort in the explanation that matter-in-motion alone exists, giving rise to human consciousness as an "epiphenomenon" which chemistry will one day explain. Diderot believes the opposite:

> Man is the sole starting point and end to which everything must finally be related. It would be absurd to put a cold, insensitive, speechless being in place of man, for if you banish man . . . from the face of the earth, this sublime and moving spectacle of nature will be but a sad and lifeless scene—the universe will be hushed, silence and darkness will regain sway . . . why should we not indeed make man the center of all that is?

Deciding to do so does not, it is true, account for the mystery of life, but that is a mystery which it is permissible to fail to solve. When Diderot supposes "thinking matter," he is but trying to get rid of the dualism of soul and body, like Goethe, Coleridge, the elder Darwin, and other vitalists half a century later. It was Diderot's "lively imagination" that enabled him to seize by direct intuition the primacy of life and the likelihood of organic evolution. These notions present difficulties, like all philosophic beliefs, and it is not my concern to prove them right or wrong in whole or in part. They show the direction of Diderot's thought and his intellectual temper and it is these I am concerned with. They announce a tendency which takes its rise in the late eighteenth century and dominates the early nineteenth; it lacks an historically ratified name; but supposing the thing and the name each properly understood, it could be called pragmatism.

Certainly William James, had he studied Diderot, would not have disowned him as a forerunner. They have in common the sense, rare in philosophers and undeveloped in the ordinary man, of the native and irremediable variety, the autonomous confusion of things. Hegel had this sense only to clamp down a waffle iron over the plastic mass. Other philosophers assure themselves that the disorder is but Appearance. Very few are sufficiently radical empiricists to adopt stubborn rules in the philosophical task of making order out of chaos, saying to themselves: "Remember! Concreteness, direct contact with the given, first and last!"

It is very likely that this rule is no more reliable than any other. The algebraist, for example, does pretty well when he leaves concreteness behind and leaps across the void of abstraction—as Diderot the mathematician was fully aware. But I am describing a philosophical complexion, and one must admit that the empirical pluralist, whose obsession is to find out first what the experience feels like, tastes and smells and thinks like, and only afterwards connects it, in patches, to create local order—such a philosopher avoids many errors and makes many discoveries. His temper is in fact the generator of novelty. Since I have paired Diderot and William James, it is apposite to give an example of Diderot's concreteness in psychological method, which is also a specimen of his originality in self-knowledge. The passage is from his *Letter on the Deaf and Dumb for the Use of Those Who Can Hear and Speak:*

> Sensation does not follow the successive unfolding of speech. If it could dictate to twenty mouths, each mouth uttering its word, all the preceding ideas would be expressed together. That is indeed what sensation would wonderfully perform on an ocular keyboard.

III

On this "ocular keyboard," I presume, the world played with Diderot's unconscious a duet to which he listened in order to transcribe it. His views on art and on morality reflect his determination not to tamper with his own naive, uncorrected impression. If he interprets it, he must do so without distorting the given; if he explains, he amplifies merely, and does not explain away. It is characteristic that in the great dialogue called *D'Alembert's Dream,* the true philosopher is man *dreaming.* Only in that state can he at once perceive and convey the nature of life. Waking, he suffers from too many constraints; the presence and the expectations of an interlocutor and a woman would spoil

the deliverance. When Diderot wants to push farther the exploration of the self and examine the coercion of wild impulse by society, he makes use of *Rameau's Nephew* to render plausible the inner dialogue of a double self, id and ego, each embodying a Reason the other cannot assimilate or defeat. It is the nephew, a Panurge-like character speaking in the accents of a modern novelist—Joyce or Céline—who points out to the philosophic "I" that the aim of being a good man by fulfilling one's duty to society is self-contradictory.

The repression that society exerts on appetite, that is, on the creature's urge to survive, master its environment, and enhance its share of life, is fitful but inescapable. The upshot of the struggle is what fills the prisons and the pages of history—pain, violence, and disgrace, the warping of character and the tragic downfall of ambitious talents. But that same erratic force is also the cause of the world's false standards. Diderot is not resigned to the hypocrisy which the good must put up with, and sometimes imitate, in order to live. As he says in *Rameau's Nephew,* in the whole kingdom everybody must dance his little cowardly dance of social flattery. Only one man walks—the King—and even he goes through contortions if he is ruled by a mistress.

Such is the price of civilization, which makes Diderot long for the primitive simplicity of Tahiti, or—what comes to the same thing—makes him understand the calculating selfishness of the disabused, typified by the wastrel Rameau. Yet Diderot is not a cynic and he cannot return to a primitive existence. He knows as well as Rousseau that there is no "going back to nature." In this predicament he solaces himself with the anodyne of his age: sentimentality. When warmth of feeling and cold egoism press equal claims upon the philosopher, the only escape is into a storybook tenderness contrasting the two and making virtue triumph. Hence the absurd stories inserted in Diderot's most lifelike dialogues, the maudlin passages in his art criticism, and the bad plays which were his contribution to the new bourgeois drama.

That this weakness was cultural rather than individual need hardly be demonstrated. Sentimentality afflicted all the great writers of the century, from the puritanical Richardson (whom Diderot worshipped as a psychologist) to Richardson's opposite, Fielding; and from the worldly wits, Voltaire, Sterne, and Beaumarchais, to the grave young lyricist Goethe. Goethe purged himself of the fault by writing *Werther,* but it has continued to plague other oppressed spirits down to our day, when it occurs in its inverted form of contrived brutality.

In Diderot we must take this blemish as accidental and dwell on the vision which his sentimentality seems to contradict. For it was from passion, not enlightenment, that the whole bent of his genius was naturalistic. He loved the actual. When he first undertook the Encyclopedia as a translator of the English work by Chambers, he noticed that his author relied on books for his information about crafts and trades, and that the books were wrong. Diderot decided to visit the craftsmen's shops and set things straight. Before the end of his eleven volumes of plates, he had five assistants doing nothing else but verify processes and draw tools and machines from life.

The originality of this outlook is shown by the discrepancy between it and what d'Alembert propounds in his Preface to the same work. The mathematician has little use for trade and technology. Only science interests him—science, the glory of the modern age, because it is universal and abstract and certain. Feeling, which is not subject to scientific inquiry, appears to d'Alembert as an inconvenience, like the imperfections in the glass of a telescope. And the practical arts, less "difficult" than science, always empirical and ridden with imperfection, form but the crude foundations of the cultural edifice.

Against this prevailing view, Diderot's origins and upbringing spoke consistently with his judgment and his tastes. The son of a cutler, he knew the value of technology in the making of civilization. Again like Rousseau, he had made his way upward from a social class well below that of the comfortable bourgeoisie, and he saw society as much more chaotic than "polite." Once at the top he kept his impressions and some of the manners of his beginnings: in all Europe only Diderot conversing with Catherine the Great could have seized her knee to make her listen to an argument. This naturalness was of a piece with his complaint to his family about the portrait that was painted of his father: "What you have done, you and the painter, is altogether worthless. I asked you for my everyday father and you have sent me nothing but my Sunday one."

It would be rash to make of Diderot a democrat, even by anticipation. The significance of his naturalism is not primarily political. It lies in the realm of what is now called culture. By being himself *à outrance,* he supplied a fresh model of human consciousness. To know this new man we must recognize intuitively how it is that an appreciation of the work of craftsmen and inventors goes with a respect for strong feeling and a skepticism about the social order. It is a very modern combination. Diderot was in fact developing a new sensibility. Diderot is *artiste* in a way in which Voltaire, for all his poetry, is not. And the new sensibility, as the coming age of Romanticism was to prove, was that of the artist in the comprehensive sense of the man whose perceptions and judgments are first and last esthetic, regardless of subject matter.

IV

That sensibility, Diderot did not, of course, achieve completely—or perhaps he lost part of it when young, under the pressure of circumstance. In middle life he thought back with regret to the days when he looked *"vif, ardent, et fou."* But the fire thus freely shown did not die. Of all the men of his generation Diderot is the only one in whom I see the signs of a Faustian spirit and a Faustian quest. Like Faust, he abandoned a dry and mechanical interpretation of life and grew into an awareness that nature is alive.

Similarly, Diderot passes in his lifetime from the conception of art as a judicious sort of manufacture, subject to rules and graced with *je ne sais quoi,* to the conception that art is an unconscious study of nature—"foreknown by imagination or genius and rendered in cold blood." His

own practice was increasingly that of the romanticist observer who quarries nature and himself for the materials of his art. Whether it is the description of female homosexuality in *La Religieuse* or the battle of wits in *Rameau's Nephew,* the author is making fiction and morality out of autobiography and the lives and deeds of his contemporaries. His art is historical and documentary in the manner consecrated only after Diderot's death, by the nineteenth century.

As a critic, Diderot frames as propositions what he believes in as a creator. This in itself is a departure from the neo-classic order of events, in which the canons of taste pre-exist and determine production. In his youth Diderot had studied music; in his old age he calls for what amounts to music drama. In this he was not alone; the emancipation of music was one of the first signs, in the eighteenth century, of the approaching artistic revolution. But in the criticism of painting Diderot was a solitary pioneer. His *Salons* were the first journalistic reports upon the fine arts, and despite all subsequent cavils they have not been equaled for liveliness, judgment, and critical audacity. They stand in the history of reviewing with Lessing's *Hamburgische Dramaturgie,* with the critical journalism of Berlioz, Baudelaire, and Shaw.

Here again Diderot's touchstone is the reality he sees, but used with superior judgment. Take, for example, his words on Boucher in 1761:

> What color! What variety! What a wealth of forms and ideas! The man has everything except Truth. No part of his compositions would please if separated from the rest. But the whole will captivate you. You will ask yourself, "Where in the world has anybody seen shepherds dressed with such rich elegance? What occasion has ever brought together in the open country, under the arches of a bridge and far from any house, so many men, women, and children, cattle, sheep, dogs, bottles of straw, water, fire, a lantern, braziers, cauldrons, and pitchers? . . . What a racket of miscellaneous objects!" You feel the absurdity of it and yet you cannot leave the picture. It will not let you go. You come back to it. The vice is so agreeable, the extravagance so inimitable and so rare.

To a love of external reality akin to the desire for an "everyday father," a love which is in large measure accessible to all once the spell of convention and abstraction is broken, Diderot added the less common love of emotional truthfulness. Long cultivated, this power is what enabled him to throw out in his dialogues so many remarkable hints of later systems, such as the famous argument by which Diderot tries to convince Rameau of the necessity of moral education: "If your little savage were left to himself and to his native blindness, he would in time join the infant's reasoning to the grown man's passions—he would strangle his father and sleep with his mother."

We have a glimpse of Diderot's method—if method it was—in the frequent asides that interrupt his dialogues. For example, after a wonderful pantomime by Rameau in behalf of expressiveness in music, Diderot asks himself: "Did I admire? Yes, I did admire. Was I moved to pity?

I was moved. But a streak of derision was interwoven with these feelings and denatured them." It is reasonable to suppose that the dialogue form became his chosen medium because of its adaptability to this sort of interruption and introspection. The novel in the eighteenth century was too rigid and monotone to permit the nuance-seeking which became Diderot's chief concern as thinker and writer. The dialogue form is not dramatic but dialectical; it is not narrative but anecdotal. Its advantages are precisely those which the artist-philosopher requires, permitting him to render the dramatic and narrative quality to be found in ideas, without having to delay the movement or distort the shape of the regular play or novel form.

This latitude does not mean that the writer of dialogues can let his pen run on as statement and rejoinder occur to him, nor again that his work is but the parceling out of arguments and objections among lay figures. One has only to compare with Diderot's the dialogues of Hume "Concerning Natural Religion" to see the difference between a philosopher *tout court* and one who is also an artist. Diderot's figures are vivid creatures, even when asleep, as is d'Alembert in the famous **Dream.** In **Rameau's Nephew,** as Goethe pointed out, the aimlessness is a superficial appearance. The work has the tightest weave imaginable and is cut to a perfect model. In fact, since Plato and Lucian, literature affords but few examples of mastery in this difficult though oft-attempted genre. In the last two hundred years, unless one takes Peacock's novels as dialogues (which is legitimate), Diderot stands alone: Wilde and Landor and Santayana, admirable as they are, lack both his originality and his power.

His originality could, of course, be illustrated much more fully than I have done. His remarkable views on sexuality, on pragmatic religion, on the emancipation of women, and on innumerable issues of esthetics and social philosophy would make a long list. And it would justify the claim that he belongs among the half-dozen geniuses that stand out among the great galaxy of eighteenth-century minds. This small company of the incomparable are: Lessing and Kant, Goethe and Burke, Rousseau and Diderot.

Jean Seznec   (lecture date 1963)

SOURCE: "Diderot and Historical Painting," in *Aspects of the Eighteenth Century,* edited by Earl R. Wasserman, The Johns Hopkins Press, 1965, pp. 129-42.

[*Seznec is a prominent French literary critic and the editor of Diderot's* Salons. *In the following lecture, originally delivered in 1963, he examines Diderot's views on the genre of historical painting.*]

In 1767 Diderot had been a professional art critic for eight years for the *Correspondance littéraire* of his friend Grimm, an association that was to continue for another fourteen years. It was in this capacity that he reviewed the exhibition of painting and sculpture in the **Salon of 1767,** which was one in a series of biennial exhibitions held at the Louvre since the seventeenth century.

. . . . To hang and to present such a number of exhibits was no mean task. The man in charge of these arrange-

ments was called *le tapissier.* For most of the exhibitions attended by Diderot, the *tapissier* was Chardin.

The catalogue, or *livret,* which was sold at the door to the visitors, makes it clear that the Salon was a very official affair. Only the fellows of the Academy were allowed to exhibit; and the whole show was placed under the high supervision of a Minister, the Director General of Fine Arts—namely, during those years, Marigny, the brother of Madame de Pompadour. It is also to be noticed that the artists in the catalogue are not listed in alphabetical order but in order of dignity, according to their titles and offices. First came the *Premier peintre du Roi,* then the *Rector,* then the *Assistant Rector;* after them came the *Professors,* the *Academicians,* and the *Agréés.* In his reviews of the Salons Diderot follows that order; but he does not accept the hierarchy; far from it: he is apt to upbraid a *Rector,* or a *Premier peintre,* as fiercely as a mere *Agréé.*

. . . [The paintings were arranged hierarchically] along the walls. On the very top are the great canvases depicting historical subjects. They have been placed up there because, being huge, they can be seen from a distance; however, they are not on top in the physical, literal sense only. Their towering position is symbolic: they dominate all the other types of painting—portraits, landscapes, still lifes, etc. —because they are held to be the first in importance. According to the academic doctrine, there is a hierarchy among works of art: the supreme rank belongs to historical painting; everything else is considered more or less inferior. The doctrine had been formulated in the seventeenth century by Félibien in a lecture delivered in 1667 to the Academy itself. Félibien reminds his listeners that painting is an intellectual pursuit. To draw lines and mix colors does not qualify one as an artist, but as a simple craftsman; it is a purely mechanical activity—whereas painting concerns the mind. Félibien goes on to unfold the consequences of this principle. Inasmuch, he says, as artists concern themselves with more difficult and more noble objects, they emerge from the lower regions of their art and rise to a more dignified status. For instance, a painter who deals with landscapes is above another who paints only fruits, flowers, or shells; again, a painter who represents living animals deserves more esteem than the one who represents only lifeless things; and since the human figure is God's most perfect work on earth, the painter who imitates God by depicting human figures is far superior to anyone else.

Now, just as there is a hierarchy of subjects based on their nature, there is another hierarchy based on the importance of the scene represented when it includes human figures. A portrait painter, for instance, although he does represent the human figure, has not yet reached the summit of painting; nor can he claim the honor due only to the most excellent. The most excellent are the artists who know how to represent a group of figures borrowed either from history or from mythology. To be truly superior, one must depict either great actions, like the historians, or pleasing scenes, like the poets. Such is the doctrine; and such are the ascending steps of painting.

Diderot, who does not accept the official hierarchy of ranks among the artists, does accept the hierarchy of the categories of paintings—which means, in fact, the hierarchy of subjects. He has the highest regard for historical paintings, for what he calls "les grandes machines" and what his friend Galiani called "le machine da stupire." For him they are *the* important part of an exhibition—so much so that he rates the quality and the interest of a Salon according to the number of historical paintings. For example, he starts the review of the Salon of 1769 with the following complaint: "What a poor Salon we had this year! Almost no historical painting—no great composition at all."

This attitude may come as a surprise to us, but this is simply because our perspective and our values are different. When we think of eighteenth-century French painting today, the pictures which are likely to come first to our mind are images such as Fragonard's *L'Escarpolette* ("The Swing"): to us it looks like an epitome not only of Fragonard's spirit but of the mood of a frivolous age. Let us realize, however, that for Diderot *L'Escarpolette* was a very minor production indeed: his praise and admiration went to a different Fragonard, the serious, tragic, melodramatic one, the Fragonard who painted *The Great Priest Corésus Sacrificing Himself In Order To Save Callirhoé*. Correspondingly, in the eyes of their contemporaries the great eighteenth-century painters were not, or at least were not always, the ones whom we consider great: they were Pierre, Vien, Lagrenée, Taraval, Doyen, Hallé, and Durameau. Most of them are forgotten today; but let us remember that in their own day they were big men.

Historical painting derives its subjects from three main sources: Scripture and the lives of Saints, ancient history, and pagan mythology. Painters drew alternately from these sources, a practice, as Diderot observes, which produces some awkward results; for while they shift constantly from the Bible to the Fable, and vice versa, painters end up in representing Ulysses as a St. Joseph, the child Jesus as a Cupid, or in placing an apostle's head on the shoulders of a Roman senator. . . .

The picture [*St. Denis Preaching the Christian Faith in Gaul* by Vien.] was painted for St. Roch, and it is still there today, facing another picture exhibited at the same Salon of 1767, *The Miracle of the Plague-Stricken* by Doyen. . . . The public, according to Diderot, was divided between these two canvases, and certainly, he says, they are both great compositions: "ce sont deux grandes machines." Their merits, however, are very different. The *St. Denis* is widely painted in a free, broad style; the figures are correctly drawn; the drapery is nobly arranged; the expressions are simple and natural; there is no agitation, and everything is beautifully peaceful.

The contrast of Doyen's picture with Vien's is striking. Vien was quiet, effortless, harmonious. He reminded one of Le Sueur, while Doyen reminds one of Rubens. As you turn to Doyen, says Diderot, everything becomes vigorous and fiery, and Vien appears lifeless and cold by comparison. There is however a particular element which attracts Diderot, besides the verve—namely horror. The picture is full of gruesome details—corpses, dying people, sick people covered with sores; there are even two feet sticking out

from a sewer. Now, Diderot feasts his eyes on all these details.

> These two big naked feet are a wonderful invention; so is this frantic man rushing out of the hospital, and this other moribund man who scratches and lacerates his own flesh; and again this dead man whose naked arms and hair are hanging from the terrace.

> I know that some pusillanimous visitors have recoiled from this canvas, and refused to look at it; but what do I care? I am not pusillanimous; I am not one of those fainthearted people, who have a timid, overrefined taste. Furthermore, where should I expect to find horrible scenes, terrifying sights, if I don't find them in a plague, a famine, an epidemic?

In fact, this kind of sight can be found somewhere else, namely, in the annals of the Christian religion. Christianity, being a creed of fanatics, is rich in episodes of terror and cruelty; from this point of view, it is far superior to paganism, because (as Diderot explains) it is far more favorable to the fine arts.

> Those who think otherwise have no idea of the proud attitude of Christians facing the praetorian tribunal; they are unaware of the cold ferocity of the priests; they have not seen those men, possessed with the demon of fanaticism, interrupting a sacrifice, overthrowing an altar, tearing down the idol of a pagan god, insulting a pontiff, defying a magistrate, and undergoing martyrdom.

Here lies a mine of great tragedies and of frightening pictures. Such as *St. Andrew Refusing to Sacrifice to the Gods* by Deshays; or *St. Cyr and Ste Julitte Delivered unto the Hands of the Executioners* by Durameau. . . .

Diderot incidentally does not distinguish between the victims and the torturers. The important thing is that there should be bloodshed. Christians cause blood to be shed. Therefore, Christianity is a storehouse of ghastly subjects for historical painters. This is Diderot's version of *Le Génie du Christianisme*.

Let us now turn to ancient history. At the Salon of 1765, a big canvas by Carle Van Loo was exhibited; it represented *Augustus Ordering the Doors of the Temple of Janus To Be Closed,* which means proclaiming the return of peace. This painting and two others had been commissioned for the king; the choice of the subjects was inspired by political circumstances and philosophical intentions. Peace had just been signed in 1763, after the Seven Year's War—and not a victorious peace. Cochin, secretary to the Academy, had been invited by Marigny to submit a program of decoration for Choisy, one of the royal residences. This is what he suggested:

> For too long have painters celebrated warlike deeds, which result only in the destruction of mankind; would it not be sensible, for once, to illustrate some of those generous, beneficent acts through which good monarchs of the past have achieved the happiness of their peoples? I therefore beg to submit to you some of the deeds per-

formed by the Emperors Augustus, Trajan, and Marcus Aurelius.

Nothing, for instance, could be more in keeping with the peaceloving disposition of our own monarch than a picture of *Augustus Closing the Doors of the Temple of War.* Another episode, quite worthy of the king's kindness, would be *Trajan, on His Way to a Military Expedition, Stops and Dismounts from His Horse In Order To Grant Justice to a Poor Woman.* A third episode would be: *Marcus Aurelius Relieving the Sufferings of His People at a Time of Famine and Pestilence.*

Cochin, a friend of the *philosophes,* was very pleased with this humanitarian program celebrating enlightened despots, the ultimate purpose of which was to flatter the king; but the king was neither pleased nor flattered. Louis XV did not care for serious, moralizing pictures; he preferred nymphs. He had the paintings removed from Choisy.

They were not lost forever, though. Two of them, *Marcus Aurelius* and *Augustus,* are in the Museum of Amiens today. A peace between England and France was signed at Amiens in 1802; and since Bonaparte wanted appropriate pictures to decorate the room where the treaty was to be signed, he was glad to use those which had been rejected by Louis XV.

Diderot of course approved of the program and the subjects; but he was far from satisfied with the way they had been dealt with.

M. Van Loo, your Augustus is miserable. Haven't you in your studio a pupil who had the courage to tell you that he is stiff, short, ignoble? Do you call *that* an Emperor? With this long palm leaf which is stuck against his shoulder, he looks like a member of the brotherhood of Jerusalem—coming back from the procession.

And that priest, behind him, what does he mean with his casket and his awkward gesture? and that senator, all hampered and entangled by his cloak and his paper? And what is the meaning of the whole, anyway? Where is the interest of the scene? Where is the subject? To close the doors of the Temple of Janus means announcing peace throughout the Empire; it is a public rejoicing: it is a festival. I look in vain in the canvas for the slightest trace of joy. Everything is cold, insipid, silent, mournful: it is the funeral of a vestal.

So much for Van Loo. Now for Hallé.

M. Hallé, your Trajan is flat; he lacks nobility, expression, character. He seems to be saying to this woman: My good woman, you do look tired; I would gladly lend you my horse—unfortunately, it is as skittish as the devil.

The officers in the Emperor's escort are just as ignoble as himself.

Vien does not fare any better.

The face of your Marcus Aurelius is without expression—and indeed expression is absent from all the characters in your picture.

This long, lean, thin young man resembles the child Jesus preaching in the Temple; and why did you make these senators look like apostles?

This expiring young girl is cold; what shall I say of this colossal woman, spread all over the steps of the terrace? Is she asleep? Is she dead? I don't know. And that baby? Is this the way a baby should behave over the corpse of his mother? I am looking for some trace of famine and pestilence, for some of the horrible incidents which characterize such calamities. I am looking in vain. There are none. Everything is stiff, dry and cold. What a picture for a sensitive man!

Diderot, then, is severe upon all three pictures, and essentially for the same reasons. What he blames in each case is the *conception* of the subject. In each case the artist had a great subject, but to begin with he failed to realize its dramatic or pathetic possibilities. Also, none of the three artists has been able to rise to the dignity of Roman history; none of them has been able to *imagine* an emperor. Do you call *those* emperors? he exclaims again. They are puny, stingy, wretched little fellows, incapable of anything great. A poor, flat imagination which can conceive only insipid physiognomies and mean, petty personalities—this to Diderot is the curse of historical painters.

From this point of view, those who deal with mythological subjects are just as bad as those who deal with ancient history. Take La Grenée, for instance; his *Ceres and Triptolemus* or his *Bacchus and Ariadne.* Again, the great sin of the painter is the lack of style.

What shocks me in this kind of subject is the childish type of the figures. I would rather have peasants with all their rusticity than this bastard race that does not belong to any condition, any time, or any country.

This goddess, for instance, instead of showing me that inexpressible quality of greatness, of vigor, that denotes the divine, is just a suburban wet nurse with a lot of fine linen and no bust. This half-god, who should look passionate, noble and proud is nothing but an effeminate boy of eighteen.

As for the Bacchus, he looked like a vapid St. John.

Diderot feels that historical painting, like tragedy and epic, calls for "a great module" and large-scale characters; saints, emperors, and gods require superhuman proportions. These are petty and diminutive. Worse still, they are cold.

Now Boucher certainly lacked majesty. His goddesses and his nymphs looked like so many young ladies of easy virtue; at best, they looked like some marquise *en déshabillé;* but Boucher, at least, had a compensating grace: his nudes were voluptuous. La Grenée is pale, dull, and anemic by comparison. True, but Boucher is at the very end of his career. Voluptuousness is no longer the fashion. The eighteenth century, alas, is becoming virtuous.

As early as 1750, Rousseau, in his famous *Discours,* declaimed against sensuous pictures.

Our gardens, he wrote, are full of statues; our

galleries are full of paintings. What do you suppose these paintings, these statues represent? You might think that these masterpieces, exhibited in public places, celebrate the defenders of the fatherland, or perhaps, those even greater men whose virtues added to the glory of the nation. Not at all. What you see are pictures of every perverted passion, carefully borrowed from ancient mythology; these are the scenes that are offered to the curiosity of our children, so that they have under their eyes, even before they can read, examples of vicious actions!

Amorous mythology was going out of fashion. "Avoid nudities; exhibit decent pictures"; such is now the official motto. On the eve of the opening of the Salon of 1775, Marigny's successor as Superintendent of the Arts, d'Angiviller, wrote to the committee in charge of the selection of pictures that they must banish from the Salon any lascivious subject; no picture should be admitted to the Exhibition which could imperil morality. D'Angiviller added that such was the wish of the King himself, and the King is no longer Louis XV, but the dull, honest Louis XVI. Anyway, the change in taste was the general tendency of the century. Following the lead of Jean-Jacques, *philosophes,* critics, men of letters were clamoring for moral subjects: they firmly believed that from now on historical painting should be a school for virtue.

Let us now consider *La Vertueuse Athénienne* by Vien. Ever since 1763 Diderot had been writing ecstatically about these Greek girls offering sacrifices on tripods borrowed from Herculaneum; he had praised their artlessness and their innocence. Ten years later, in 1773, to decorate her pavilion at Louveciennes, Madame du Barry herself preferred Vien's anemic virgins to those delightful figures by Fragonard which are today one of the glories of the Frick Gallery. In her eyes, Fragonard panels were old-fashioned, first, because they were not *à la grecque,* but also because they illustrated the progress of love with too much liveliness.

The Piety of Fabius Dorso . . . by Lépicié, exhibited at the Salon of 1781, is even more edifying. The subject is explained in the catalogue. During the siege of the Capital by the Gauls, Fabius Dorso, in order to perform a sacrifice instituted by his family, came out of that fortress, taking with him all the paraphernalia needed for the ceremony. He walked through the enemy camp, went up the Quirinal Hill, there performed the sacrifice, and then returned to the Capitol, having inspired respect and admiration from both the Romans and the Gauls. The picture shows him returning to the Capitol. Here is Diderot's comment:

> They say that the main figure is well put together; that its clothing is well draped; that the head is handsome and noble. As for myself I don't even know whether it is a man or a woman; it is a broomstick, a beanpole. There is nothing to characterize the action: Fabius carries his gods as if he were taking them from one apartment to another. No shadow of expression appears on any of the other faces; the soldiers see Fabius get out, and go back, as if this was of no concern to them.

Once more Diderot is blaming not the subject but the deficiency of the artist, who has neither the sense of the sacred nor the gift of dramatic imagination.

Now this kind of subject was not exceptional. In 1777 d'Angiviller had selected the following scenes for a set of Gobelins tapestries:

> 1. An example of religious piety among the Greeks: Cleobis and Biton, sons of a priestess, being afraid that their mother would be late for a sacrifice because the oxen which were to drive her chariot to the temple had been delayed, decide to place themselves under the yoke and to drag the chariot.
>
> 2. An example of religious piety among the Romans: Lucius Albinus, having met Vestals who were on foot while carrying the sacred vases, orders his own wife and children to get off his carriage, and invites the Vestals to get aboard in their place.

In his ***Salon of 1767,*** Diderot tells us, not without a certain pride, that painters sometimes come to him to ask for a subject. This he is only too pleased to give; he likes to think of himself as a provider of subjects for the artists. For instance, he says an artist comes and asks me: "Give me a historical subject"; and I answer: "You should paint the *Death of Turenne.* " This answer is surprising at first. How is it that Diderot, fond as he is of Antiquity, now recommends a modern subject taken from national history? National history, in fact, is in the process of invading painting, just as it is invading literature (remember Voltaire's tragedies).

At the same Salon of 1767, Cochin exhibited some drawings destined for the illustration of President Hénault's *Abrégé chronologique de l'histoire de France.* There was, among them, *King Louis VII Leaving for the Crusade.* . . .

> The fiery Saint Bernard is dragging his monarch to the Crusade, in spite of the wise Suger. The king has drawn his sword; Bernard seizes him by that hand which holds the sword. Suger seizes the other hand: he speaks, he argues, he prays, he urges earnestly—all in vain. The monk is very imperious; the Abbé, very sad.

Diderot however does not approve of the allegorical trappings of the picture; this mixing of real characters with imaginary beings, this *galimatias* as he calls it, is both confusing and shocking. Apart from this defect, he is pleased with Cochin's undertaking; he acclaims this illustration of scenes from our history. This new source will provide painters with an inspiration just as fruitful as that of ancient history.

Take for instance *William the Conqueror Landing in England* by Lépicié. "What a wonderful subject for a painter!" Diderot exclaims, provided of course the painter is not Lépicié; for alas, Lépicié depicting William the Conqueror shows no more intelligence, no more genius than his colleagues when they try to represent Augustus or Caesar.

> One sees in this picture a few idle, dumb, mo-

tionless soldiers; then all by himself a big short man, his arms extended, screaming. (I asked him a hundred times what was the matter with him—but I still don't know.) Then comes William, in the center, on horseback, the man and the horse equally monstrous. The whole army is on the march in the background. No noise, no tumult, no military enthusiasm. It is a thousand times duller than the march of a regiment passing along the walls of a provincial town, on the way to its garrison.

Such is Diderot's indignation at seeing the subject wasted, that he recomposes the whole picture, according to his own conception.

Rousseau deplored the fact that painting did not represent "the defenders of the fatherland, nor those even greater men whose virtues added to the glory of the nation." This is precisely what painters are now set to do: they celebrate, more and more often, the great men of France. First the good kings, of course, beginning with Henri IV, the king of toleration and of chicken in every pot, already celebrated in epic verse and on the stage, but also virtuous heroes, magnanimous and humane soldiers. Diderot suggested Turenne; Duguesclin and Bayard are now among the pet subjects of historical painters. A good example of this type of painting is *Bayard, Having Made a Girl Prisoner, Returns Her to Her Mother, and Provides Money for Her Dowry . . . ,* which is an episode that is treated several times. A similar story is told about Scipio; and indeed *La Continence de Scipion* is also represented toward the end of the century (by Vien, for instance, in 1779), but chastity for chastity, Bayard's continency now has the preference. If the function of historical painting is truly to transmit to posterity great examples of honor and morality, some of these examples at least are being provided by France.

Yet, Antiquity remains the main repertory of subjects; but it is an increasingly graver, more grandiose Antiquity, and also a more and more rigid one, stiffened as it is by the influence of British painters such as Benjamin West and Gavin Hamilton. To begin with, the frivolous is now decidedly superseded by the grand, and the erotic by the epic. Ovid has been unthroned by Homer, and for good. Scenes borrowed from the *Iliad* become more and more numerous; this is just what Diderot wants, for the triumph of Homer over Ovid means the triumph of *le grand goût* over *le petit goût.* The trouble is that, once more, artists are not up to their subjects, incapable as they are to conceive Homeric majesty and poetic terror.

For instance, *Juno and Vulcan Coming to the Rescue of Achilles* by Deshays are again mean, puny figures. "Vulcan looks like a young boy. Where is the vigorous, the formidable god of the foundries, of the blazing caverns? This is not the way the old poet pictures him." There lies, of course, the root of the misunderstanding. Diderot's mind, the mind of a humanist, is filled with imposing images: the poor painter, sometimes illiterate, cannot see through the eyes of Homer. In the same way, *The Battle between the Greeks and the Trojans around Patroclus's Body* by Brenet (1781) fails to convey the Homeric grandeur: it is too mannered, too affected. Achilles, who comes to the rescue on tiptoes like a dancer, is ridiculous.

If we now turn to Roman history, we shall find a stiff, severe Antiquity, the paragon of civic virtues. At the Salon of 1771 Beaufort exhibited *Brutus and Collatinus Swearing To Avenge Lucretia's Death, and To Expel the Tarquins from Rome.* Another great and proud subject, says Diderot; but

the painter should have transported his imagination at Collatie; he should have visualized the stabbed Lucretia—and from that moment he should have become a Roman himself, burning with rage against the Tarquins. Instead, what do I see in Beaufort's picture? The forced and stilted figures of a painter who strives vainly to whip himself into a frenzy. As for Lucretia, O the ugly girl—much better to kill than to rape, if you ask me.

Yet with all its shortcomings this canvas is of great interest, for it points out the way to David (who indeed painted the same subject); and David is the very type of painter whom Diderot has in mind, the type of painter he is forever calling out for. Another composition points the same way: *The Fight between the Romans and the Sabines Interrupted by the Sabine Women* by Vincent. It prefigures the famous picture by David of the same subject.

But at the Salon of 1781, where this canvas was exhibited, David himself appeared for the first time. Diderot, who reviews the Salon for the last time, experiences at last the joy of finding a historical painter who fulfills his dearest wishes. Let us realize, however, that this advent, this arrival of David on the scene is also a resurrection: the resurrection of Poussin.

For Diderot, the absolute masterpiece of historical painting was *The Will of Eudamidas.* Eudamidas, a citizen of Corinth, was very poor, but he had two rich friends. When he died, he dictated his will: of one of his friends, he requested that he maintain his wife; of the other, he asked that he provide a dowry and a husband to his daughter. In Diderot's eyes, this is the supreme achievement of historical painting, because it combines a morally sublime subject with a sober, austere, style—the style of a bas-relief. Poussin is the master par excellence to whom French painters should return. Incidentally, Diderot here agrees with Napoleon. During his campaign in Egypt, Bonaparte had taken with him an engraving of that very same painting, and he once said to Denon: "After one has seen this austere composition, one cannot forget it; Denon, our school of painting has grown stale; we must bring it back into the ways of Poussin."

This will be David's task; and he had already started. At the Salon of 1781, Diderot stops in front of David's *Belisarius . . . ,* in which Justinian's old general, now blind and destitute and reduced to begging his bread, is recognized by one of his old soldiers. At last, there is a young painter with a sense of nobility and restraint and a gift for the grand manner. *Il a de l'âme;* David feels the greatness, the gravity of his subject, and he knows how to express it, for he knows how to pose an attitude and arrange a piece of clothing in a way which is both natural and dignified. He has recaptured the moral austerity of the seventeenth century; at the same time, he has replaced the cheap or ridiculous travesties of his predecessors with a sculptural style which restores the heroes of Greece and Rome to their majestic stature. One should paint as they spoke in Sparta (*Peindre comme on parlait à Sparte*); this was Diderot's wish, and David carried it out.

Are we, then, going to make Diderot a champion of neo-classical painting? This would be to oversimplify his role and to restrict his taste. Let us remember that the same Diderot takes delight in violent and tumultuous scenes, in the horrors of plague and torture. This is the sign of another demand, of another tendency. Remember Doyen's canvas at St. Roch. Its gruesome, passionate features no longer forecast David; rather they forecast Gros, Géricault, and Delacroix. One can already discern the scattered elements of those great romantic melodramas, the *Massacre at Chios,* the *Plague-Stricken of Jaffa,* and *The Raft of the Medusa.*

Diderot's attitude in front of the historical pictures of his day is significant in other respects. Until his very last Salon, he seems to retain his admiration for that type of painting and his belief in its supremacy. When discussing pictures of another kind, a landscape, a domestic scene, or even a portrait, he is apt to deplore the absence of the dramatic element; he feels, for instance, that Loutherbourg's shepherds and animals, that Lépicié's family groups, or even Hubert Robert's ruins fail to interest the spectator because the artist has not been able to devise an anecdote, a story which would have animated the scene; and in each case Diderot remarks that only historical painters know how to invent such incidents.

But what about Greuze? He certainly knows how to tell a story; you can make a drama, or even a novel, out of his pictures; and indeed Diderot seems almost ready to confer upon Greuze, in spite of his rustic or bourgeois subjects, the supreme title of *peintre d'histoire.* I protest, he says, that to me the *Ungrateful Son* or the *Village Bride* are truly historical paintings because they offer me all sorts of dramatic incidents. Greuze in fact thought that he could easily raise himself to the highest rank simply by selecting, for once, an antique subject where all his dramatic qualities would be displayed to the full. He decided to represent *Septimius Severus Reproaching His Son Caracalla for Having Tried to Assassinate Him;* and he submitted that picture to the Academy in 1769, precisely to support his application for the official title of *peintre d'histoire.* Alas, Greuze brought upon himself, on that occasion, the worst humiliation of his career. He was granted only the inferior rank of *peintre de genre:* the Academy decided that his picture was too mediocre to qualify him as historical painter.

The verdict of the Academy may seem unduly severe. After all, Greuze's *Septimius Severus* is no worse than Vien's *Marcus Aurelius* or Hallé's *Trajan.* Yet Diderot in this case agrees with the Academy. Greuze, he says, has proved himself unable to rise to that kind of exaggeration which is required by historical painting. His Septimius is ignoble; Caracalla is ignobler still. He would do very well in a rustic or domestic scene; for instance, he would make a *Bad Brother,* or an *Ungrateful Son.* In a word, Greuze has remained incurably, inevitably bourgeois. This would suggest that Diderot accepts the aristocratic character of historical painting. It is an exclusive club; any painter of common, ordinary scenes who tries to force the entrance to the club does so at his own risk.

Yet Diderot's faith in the dogma of academic hierarchy is not unshaken. One artist did oblige him to reconsider that dogma and to wonder about the whole question of subject in painting. There is obviously no story, no heroic episode, no dramatic interest in some pieces of crockery, two biscuits, a jar full of olives, two glasses of wine; and yet Diderot stops in front of such a still life and exclaims: "There is a painter for you! Chardin is not a historical painter, *but* he is a great man." Chardin indeed upsets the whole system of academic values and starts Diderot thinking. Historical painters, he says, look down on these humble artists and their humble subjects. They consider them as narrow minds devoid of lofty ideas and poetic genius, crawling miserably on the ground, never daring to lose sight of nature. To the historical painter such people are just copyists—at best, craftsmen, and nothing else. But for his part, the man who represents nature scrupulously sees historical painting as a fictitious and extravagant performance; he finds no truth in it, nor even any semblance of truth: everything is arbitrary, inflated, and hollow.

In short, it is the quarrel between prose and poetry. Diderot perceives the merits of prose, its integrity, its honest

---

Diderot on a painting by Joseph Vien:

Psyche approaching with her lamp to surprise Love in his sleep. —The two figures are of flesh and blood, but they have neither the elegance, nor the grace, nor the delicacy that the subject required. Love seems to me to be making a grimace. Psyche is not like a woman who comes trembling on tiptoe. I do not see on her face that which ought all to be there. It is not enough to show in Psyche a curiosity to see Love; I must also perceive in her the fear of awakening him. She ought to have her mouth half open, and to be afraid of drawing her breath.' Tis her lover that she sees—that she sees for the first time, at the risk of losing him for ever. What joy to look upon him, and to find him so fair! Oh, what little intelligence in our painters, how little they understand nature! The head of Psyche ought to be inclined towards Love; the rest of her body drawn back, as it is when you advance towards a spot where you fear to enter, and from which you are ready to flee back; one foot planted on the ground and the other barely touching it. And the lamp; ought she to let the light fall on the eyes of Love? Ought she not to hold it apart, and to shield it with her hand to deaden its brightness? Moreover, that would have lighted the picture in a striking way. These good people do not know that the eyelids have a kind of transparency; they have never seen a mother coming in the night to look at her child in the cradle, with a lamp in her hand, and fearful of awakening it.

Denis Diderot in his Salon de 1761, *quoted by John Morley in his* Diderot and the Encyclopedists *Vol. II, 1888.*

beauty, just as he perceives the weaknesses and the perils of poetry; and he realizes the flimsy character of historical painting. The fault of course rests first with the artists, but the genre itself carries with it the danger of unreality. How could one give back some substance to those vast compositions? Perhaps by injecting into them a dose of *vérité commune*. Ah, says Diderot, "if only a sacrifice, a battle, a triumph, a public scene could be rendered with the same truth in all its details as a domestic scene by Greuze or Chardin!" And Diderot dreams of the ways of bringing some prosaic solidity into poetic artifice. This is of course what he himself has been trying to achieve with his *drame bourgeois:* to stuff the empty nobility of classical tragedy with the substantial simplicity of everyday life. There we detect one of the many links which connect his art criticism with his attempts at renovating literary forms.

I feel that the problem of Diderot and historical painting, limited as it may appear, is, therefore, a central one: its aesthetic implications extend beyond the history of taste, and even beyond the field of fine arts. But I also feel that in this case one has to begin at the beginning: no generalization can be valid until one has *seen* the actual pictures which first provoked Diderot's reactions, and stimulated his thought.

Peter Gay   (essay date 1969)

SOURCE: "The Emancipation of Art: A Groping for Modernity," in his *The Enlightenment: An Interpretation, Volume II: The Science of Freedom,* Alfred A. Knopf, 1969, pp. 249-318.

[*A German-born American, Gay is a social historian who has written numerous books and essays on Enlightenment thought, nineteenth-century middle-class culture, and the arts and politics of Imperial and Weimar Germany. In the following excerpt from the second volume of his highly influential study* The Enlightenment: An Interpretation *(1969), Gay explores the originality of Diderot's dramas, dramatic theory, and art criticism.*]

Diderot and lessing have often been treated as kindred spirits. The pairing is apt; in aesthetics even more than in other matters, they confronted similar problems and offered similar solutions, in a similar spirit. And their affinity went deeper than a certain convergence of concern and temperament: they directly influenced one another. Diderot, impressed by Lessing's bourgeois tragedy, *Miss Sara Sampson,* thought of having it translated; Lessing translated Diderot's first two plays and his discourses on the drama, reflected upon—and reflected—Diderot's aesthetics, and advertised him to German readers in lyrical language, all the more striking for Lessing's notorious aversion to hyperbole: "After Aristotle," he wrote in 1760 [in *Das Theater des Herrn Diderot*] "no more philosophical spirit has concerned himself with the drama than he." Other Germans thought as Lessing did: they found Diderot's atheism shocking, but they were receptive to his novels, his dramatic theories, and his bourgeois plays; *Aufklärer* and *Stürmer und Dränger* alike prized him as a fascinating and fertile thinker, and drew courage as well as

ideas from his rebelliousness. But when Lessing said, near the end of his life, "Diderot appears to have had far greater influence on the German theatre than on the theatre of his own nation," he was speaking about himself even more than others.

The affinity between Lessing and Diderot is very close and highly instructive. Both were intent upon independence and dignity for the estate of letters, both were contentious and inquisitive, both were learned and cultivated critics of Christianity and modern lovers of antiquity. "Let us go to school to the ancients," Lessing wrote to Moses Mendelssohn in 1756. "What better teachers, after nature, could we choose?" And in the following year, Diderot exclaimed [in his ***Entretiens sur le Fils naturel***] "I shall not get weary of shouting at Frenchmen: Truth! Nature! The Ancients! Sophocles! Philoctetes!" Here were two revolutionaries who never lost their respect for tradition.

No one bore the burdens of the past more heavily, and suffered them more publicly, than Diderot. He exacted admiration for antiquity and, at the same time, freedom of action for himself, and combated with equal eloquence the anticomaniacs who adored the old for the sake of its age, and the modern barbarians who did not know, or affected to despise, the classics. Diderot himself understood the classics—both Homer and Racine—too thoroughly to imitate them blindly, and he loved them too well—at this point he parted company with Falconet—to be easy about the overthrow of artistic canons that had made them possible.

While Diderot for many years experienced these two attitudes as an unresolvable tension, and paid for his irresolution with a certain vacillation, an unsureness of touch, Voltaire's persistent lucidity proves that there was nothing inherently inconsistent about loving the classics and independence at the same time. As Voltaire saw it—and the contrast with Diderot, who admired Voltaire's work, is instructive—the proper task of the eighteenth century was to rescue neoclassicism from deadly academicism, to preserve in it what was valuable and discard what could be spared. The product of the age of Louis XIV, and its most distinguished spokesman in the Enlightenment, Voltaire consistently advocated decorum, clarity, obedience to rules. Yet, nourished by his wide reading, his linguistic facility, and a passionate if selective alertness to literary excellence, he also permitted his taste to modify and modernize his doctrine: if he found Addison's *Cato* correct and elegant, he was constrained to admit that it was frigid and dull; if he condemned Shakespeare's irregularities, vulgarity, and mixture of styles, he was haunted by the force and sublimity of his genius; if Racine's *Athalie* was filled with the kind of "fanaticism" Voltaire most abhorred, its poetry compelled him to call it a masterpiece. And in his own plays he subjugated his principles to dramatic necessities: he introduced action that closely skirted the edges of pathos and melodrama, though he hoped, without overwhelming traditional decorum: "One must be novel," he wrote [in *Candide*, 1759] "without being bizarre, often sublime, and always natural." But in defiance of his own injunction, Voltaire resorted to stage business that startled his audiences; he brought ghosts onto the stage, cannon shots and howling mobs, ideas in tragic combat, exotic personages and remote ages—Chinese, Muslims, medieval Frenchmen. And as his plays explored territory unknown or unpleasant to his seventeenth-century predecessors, his philosophical tales, which he professed to take lightly and passed over in his correspondence with almost complete silence, were, in their own unobtrusive way, innovations. Voltaire, the self-proclaimed conservative, began an aesthetic revolution that others, younger than he, would carry further.

In comparison, Diderot long was unadventurous, content to leave most of the neoclassical structure untouched. He explicitly defended, and in his first two plays strictly observed, the unities of time, place, and action, accepting them as "difficult" but "sensible" He accepted, if a little uneasily, the hierarchy of subject matter in painting. He drew on classical doctrines for his early ideals of art as imitation and art as moral. And he justified his experiments in the bourgeois drama by insisting that they owed less to the modern Lillo than to the ancient Terence. It was not until the 1760s—always remaining himself, or, rather, becoming himself more and more—that he discarded inherited ideas and began to grope for a modern aesthetic.

It was a groping, no more, a series of fitful thought not fruitless raids. As he was aware, his ideas on the arts were anything but systematic: in 1767 [*Salon de 1767*], he compared himself to an undisciplined hunting dog who chases whatever wild game rises before him—not without justice: his preoccupation with aesthetic questions was as unorganized as it was persistent. He began to theorize early and ended late. He moved, with his characteristic ease, from a response to a particular painting to a general inquiry into beauty. He wasted some of his most interesting ideas in private letters, hid others in unpublished dialogues, and never wrote the treatise that he sometimes thought he should write.

Yet his explorations ended with the victory of independence over memory; the sum of his writings stamps him as one of the fathers of modern aesthetics. For his very failings—his early dependence, his uncontrolled profusion, his irreducible inconsistencies—were only the shadow side of his infatuation with experience. Diderot's empiricism is all of a piece: he was committed to experience on principle and by temperament, through the philosophical style he shared with the other philosophes and in the aesthetic ideas he developed on his own. His best plays, novels, and dialogues—I am thinking especially of *Est-il bon? Est-il méchant?* and *Jacques le fataliste* and *Le neveu de Rameau,* all dating from the sixties and later—are conscious experiments. The mobility of his moods and ideas, his alertness, his restlessness, his powerful sensuality—all of which he cultivated so energetically that his ease sometimes seems forced and his spontaneity strenuous—kept him from bookishness and rigidity. That is why his later pronouncements are almost invariably superior to his earlier pronouncements: as he saw, and read, and listened, and wrote, the pressure of experience enlarged his perspective, deepened his taste, and clarified his ideas.

There was nothing passive about Diderot's encounter with life and art. Just as he had prepared himself—or announced [in his "prospectus" for the *Encyclopédie*] that he had prepared himself—for his *Encyclopédie* by consulting "the ablest craftsmen of Paris and the kingdom," visiting "their workshops, interrogating them, taking down their dictation, developing their thoughts," so he prepared himself for his vocation as critic and theorist by going to school to the artists themselves. He shared Falconet's contempt for contemporary art critics—for the venal reviewers, timid and superficial, who compiled lists and lavished praise, and for arrogant and capricious connoisseurs, who underscored their preferences with purchases: a "cursed race." Artists needed protection from both, but they also needed, for their own sake as much as the public's, informed criticism. When in 1747 La Font de Saint Yenne had dared to claim the right to exercise his taste on the paintings of the day, his little book, cautious though it was, had called forth outrageous slanders and a painters' strike; the artists behaved like guildsmen invaded by unlicensed outsiders. This far Diderot was not prepared to go—had he not laid it down that everything is subject to criticism? Fortunately, Falconet had admitted that while the best judge of art is an artist, there were a few—a very few—experienced, sensitive men whose aesthetic judgment had some merit, and he graciously included Diderot among these *"vrais connoisseurs."* And Diderot did his best to deserve Falconet's good opinion; he at least would judge works of art drawing on reliable technical knowledge. He frequented painters' studios to watch them at work, sat for his portrait asking a stream of questions, and walked through the Salons with discriminating painters like Chardin—"perhaps no one," he said [in his *Salon de 1761*], "talks about painting better than he does"—and with the opinionated, articulate Falconet. He studied the language of the studio, borrowing, as he put it, the painters' "very eyes." And all this made him magnificently independent after a time, and thoroughly professional: "If I happen to wound the artist," he wrote in 1765, "it is often with the weapon he himself has sharpened; I have questioned him."

As he practiced he preached. Again and again he would justify his views by an appeal to his experience—to paintings or plays he had seen. He often regretted that he had not seen more; it would have helped him make pertinent comparisons, detect plagiarisms, and further improve his taste. And he commended his own education to others: "Do you want to make reliable progress in your knowledge of the techniques of art, which is so difficult? Stroll through a gallery with an artist, have him explain to you, and show you on the canvas, the meaning of technical words. Without this you will never have anything but confused notions." Later, in the *Paradoxe sur le comédien,* he extended this principle to actors. Nature only laid down the foundation on which experience must build: "It is up to nature to supply the qualities of the person—face, voice, judgment, sensitivity. But the study of great models, knowledge of the human heart, exposure to the world, assiduous labor, experience, and the habit of the theater will perfect the gift of nature." The artist and his judge alike must forget theories and plunge instead into experience—to look, to listen, to act, and it was experience itself that had taught Diderot this lesson.

In his first pronouncements on the arts, his first plays and *Salons,* his experience—largely of books and some great examples—committed Diderot to an almost unrelieved moral naturalism: only perfect imitation can produce the proper aesthetic effect on the public; [as he wrote in *Les bijoux indiscrets*] "only the true pleases and moves."

The idea was antique, commonplace, and in this simple formulation, ambiguous. Aristotle had held that the work of art is a work of imitation, although to him this had meant rational selection, the elimination of the fortuitous and the particular, in a word, the idealization of the actual as it could or should be. But from the Renaissance on, a number of Aristotle's interpreters had read his dicta as injunctions to literalism: the artist is the ape of nature; the better the artist, the more complete the realism; the greatest painter is the one who can induce birds to peck at his grapes in a still life. Yet literalism never wholly displaced idealization: the celebrated story of Zeuxis, who captured Helen's incomparable beauty by choosing the most beautiful single features of several lovely virgins, argued for a kind of selective, intelligent naturalism—and educated men in the age of the Enlightenment, including Diderot, were fond of this anecdote.

Yet, with the choice of several versions of mimesis open to him, Diderot selected the crudest. Doubtless it never occurred to him—it would have embarrassed him greatly if it had—that in those years his criterion for judging the merit of a play was in perfect agreement with the uninformed judgment of the most uneducated playgoer. "The perfection of a play," he wrote, "consists in the imitation of an action so accurate that the spectator, continuously deceived, imagines himself to be present at the action itself." Dramatic speech should reproduce the authentic accents of passion, the hesitations, exclamations, incomplete sentences characteristic of real speech. And, transferring this reasoning to his first essays in art criticism, Diderot reserved his highest praise for painters who could evoke nature itself.

In his own dramas, Diderot took his own advice, and searched for ways to insure verisimilitude. His first play, *Fils naturel,* published though not performed in 1757, is an experiment in *trompe l'oeil,* and the *Entretiens sur le Fils naturel,* published with it, is its apology: the *Fils naturel,* Diderot insists, is "not a fiction but a fact," a report designed "to preserve the memory of an event" and to "represent it as it took place." Criticism of improbabilities in the action or the speeches of individual personages is therefore beside the point. If Dorval, the hero, drinks a cup of tea on stage, why not? He has traveled, and adopted the habit of drinking tea from the Dutch. "But on stage?" The question is irrelevant: "My work must be judged in the salon." In fact, Diderot makes Dorval into the chief spokesman of his *Entretiens,* a device that in no way anticipates the metaphysical mystifications of Pirandello: it permits Diderot to advertise not the ambiguities haunting reality but the truthfulness of his "report."

It is this concern with journalistic verisimilitude that moved Diderot boldly to place the action of his drama in the present and in a realistic setting. More: he exacted realistic acting (less declamation, more pantomime), pre-scribed realistic settings, and wrote realistic speeches, or, rather, speeches he thought were realistic. Far from mastering experience, Diderot in this phase of his career became its servant, confounding art and life, to the detriment of art.

Diderot's next play, *Le père de famille,* of 1758, and the *Discours sur la poésie dramatique* that accompanied it show no deepening of aesthetic perception. Diderot drew the action, with almost embarrassing fidelity, from his own life, and loaded down the stage business with sentimental tableaux. Precisely like its predecessor, *Le père de famille* strives for realism in every possible way: it contains pointed references to contemporary events and social problems, its dialogue is naturalistic rather than elevated, and its stage directions prescribe settings and movements drawn from nature. And Diderot pressed the point that his efforts at naturalism constituted a deliberate program: "My good friend," he wrote [on 27 November 1758] to Madame Riccoboni, actress and novelist, "I believe that you have not read me well. My first and second play from a system of theatrical action; one should not quibble about a point here or there, but accept or reject it in its entirety."

Diderot had no doubt that the highest, ultimate purpose of his "system" was ethical. One of his characters in *Fils naturel*—clearly a spokesman—comments favorably on the prevalence of moral books and moral plays: "These are the lessons with which our stage resounds, and cannot resound too often." What, he asks, is the object of a dramatic composition? and replies, "It is, I think, to inspire men with love of virtue and horror of vice." His simplistic view that art directly imitates reality was matched by his expectation that the spectator directly applies in his own life the lesson he has learned from the play.

Nothing could have been more conservative. The idea that art has a didactic purpose is almost as ancient as the idea that it consists of imitation. It goes back to two much-quoted passages from Horace's *Ars poetica* asserting that art must be useful as well as delightful, and it had been continually reiterated since the Renaissance. The claim that art was useful was useful to the artist; it justified his existence. By the seventeenth century, it had been firmly embedded in neoclassical theory; allowing artists wide latitude in practice, it underlay familiar demands that in drama, as in poetry, and as much as possible in painting, the good be rewarded and the bad punished, and that artists choose elevated actions and avoid repellent ones. Decorum demanded, as Horace had said long ago, that Medea kill her sons offstage.

Late in the seventeenth century, Boileau once again insisted on the moral purpose of art in his influential *Art poétique,* and so did La Bruyère and many others. The most vicious Restoration playwrights piously proclaimed that it was their purpose to hold up mirrors to corrupt society; their pretensions were ironic, cynical, or self-protective, but they suggest that the old doctrine had lost none of its power. In the eighteenth century neoclassicists bravely said it again: in art, virtue should attract and vice disgust, rewards and punishments be properly distributed in accord with merit, degraded persons or actions not be shown. But gradually it became clear, even to neoclassicists, that this was doubtful philosophy, and they appealed, in Samuel Johnson's words, "from criticism to nature." Johnson himself conceded that an artist might properly portray reality even if it violated poetic justice. Nicolai, with his pedestrian good sense, introduced these doubts into Germany: a poet, he reasoned, could be a lawgiver only among barbarians, while in civilized modern Europe he had a different function; the very idea, in fact, that the stage is a school of morals is a "fad" refuted "daily" by experience. And in the latter part of the century, Sir Joshua Reynolds [in his *Portraits*] bluntly broke with the whole system: "The business of art is rationally to amuse us and not send us to school. If it is, we should go unwilling to school. We must be recreated with variety." In his thirteenth Discourse, Reynolds laid it down quite formally: "The end of art," he told his listeners, is "to produce a pleasing effect on the mind"—not a word about instruction.

This was a welcome relaxation of the old strenuousness, opening new vistas on art, but the philosophes, who visibly longed to join the radicals, could not easily bring themselves to yield up their cherished schoolmasterly role. "Forget your rules," Diderot exclaimed in 1758, "put technique aside: it's the death of genius." It was a heartfelt cry, but there was simply too much work to be done—too many injustices to be righted, superstitions to be exposed, tastes to be improved, to permit the philosophes to abandon their poses as modern Socrateses, or modern Catos; with their humorless didacticism they continued to find the old doctrine appealing and even offered some new rationalizations for it. Most of what they wrote, after all, whether it was history, fiction, or art criticism, was designed to improve the reader as it persuaded him, and they saw no reason why art should be left out of the great venture of changing the general way of thinking. What was surprising about Diderot's moralizing was its naïveté, the triviality of its lessons—what *are*, when one thinks of it, the lessons imparted by Greuze? —and its singleminded neglect of aesthetic considerations.

It is only this highly saturated atmosphere that could have produced Rousseau's famous *Lettre à d'Alembert sur les spectacles,* written and published in 1758, the year of Diderot's *Père de famille.* It is Rousseau at his most Platonic, most Genevan, and most paradoxical: he argues, in essence, that Horace is right in principle—art should inculcate virtue and discourage vice—but since this has become impossible in corrupt modern civilization, there should be no theater, at least in Geneva. Rousseau's *Lettre à d'Alembert* is, to be sure, more than an attack on the theater and a criticism of d'Alembert; it is part of Rousseau's break with his old associates and a veiled attack on Voltaire. But it explicitly insists on the intimate relation of art and morality: the modern theater is essentially French, that is to say, Parisian, and to import the theater into Geneva would be to poison a simple manly society with effeminate spectacles. Rousseau offers the *Misanthrope* as a significant example: in this famous play, Molière encourages vice by ridiculing virtue, for he portrays Alceste, an "upright, sincere, estimable, truly good man," as an absurd creature whose courageous, independent conduct the spectator is induced to despise. If Geneva wants spectacles, let it conduct public festivals, carefully supervised balls, and edifying gymnastic shows, where young people can meet openly, where the aged are respected, and honest marriages encouraged.

The *Lettre à d'Alembert* tempted the philosophes into cheap jokes about an unsuccessful playwright who has turned against the theater in which he has failed, and it infuriated Diderot, but not because Rousseau had mistaken social for aesthetic criticism, misread Molière, and connected action on the stage with action in life—Diderot had after all done much of this himself. The issue was not Rousseau's principle, but his prescription.

Indeed, three years after Rousseau's *Lettre à d'Alembert,* late in 1761, Diderot restated his doctrine, in his **Éloge de Richardson:** "Richardson is no more. What a loss for letters and for humanity!" —a significant conjunction. If pressing need should ever compel him to sell his library, Diderot exclaimed, "You would be left to me, you would be left on the same shelf with Moses, Homer, Euripides, and Sophocles." And Richardson deserved to be in this distinguished company because he was the subtle psychologist who had "carried the torch into the bottom of the cavern," an eloquent rhetorician who had known "how to make the passions speak," and above all because he was a moralist, a writer who had taught Diderot to love his fellow men and his duties better than before, who had taught him pity for villains and new sympathy for the unhappy, greater veneration for good men, contempt for life, and love of virtue. To read Richardson, it seems, was less a literary experience than an ethical one: "All that Montaigne, Charron, La Rochefoucauld, and Nicole have put into maxims, Richardson put into action." Historians falsify; Richardson has made his readers spectators to hundreds of real situations: "O painter of nature, you never lie!"

None of this was new; much of it, reactionary. But Diderot drew one radical conclusion from the naïve neoclassicism of these years, a conclusion that links him directly to Lessing. "I like to see the sphere of our pleasures enlarged," he wrote in 1757 [in **Entretiens sur le Fils naturel**], and what he had in mind, quite specifically, was a reform of the theater that would permit dramatists to treat the lives of ordinary people as seriously as neoclassical tragedy had treated kings and aristocrats. The last century, he suggested, had left the eighteenth century much work to do, notably a need for reform in acting, staging, and the dance, but, most urgently, the need to create "the domestic and bourgeois tragedy."

Diderot held up his own two plays as moral dramas belonging to this new genrè, the *genre sérieux,* and as moving with ease from it to tragedy and comedy. This relaxation, Diderot thought, would permit the modern dramatist to expand traditional notions of *vraisemblance* and raise the bourgeoisie to dramatic acceptability. Genres, after all, he argued, are not the product of nature but of a single genius whose invention is then repeated, hardened into rules by imitators and imprisoned in habit. But times change and forms must change with them: "Nothing prevails against the truth." And the truth of Diderot's time was patently larger, wider, deeper than could be comprehended in the neoclassical genres. Certainly the initial pressure on Diderot to loosen his rigid theory of imitation came from his experience, which was teaching him that there was more to be worthily imitated than Poussin or Racine had imagined.

It must be admitted that there was more bourgeois ideology in his writings on the drama than in the dramas themselves; Diderot was more radical in his program than in his practice. The central figures in his first two plays are highly placed, wealthy, and probably noble as well, and the morality they preach, or represent, is a decency, a family loyalty, a sentimentality that was as available to aristocrats as it was to commoners. The ambiguity that shadows the status of some of Diderot's characters testifies to the novelty of his social ideal and his uncertainty, and reflects the persistence of aristocratic tastes, and aristocratic audiences, in the theater of Diderot's time. . . .

. . . . .

The 1760s were as decisive for Diderot as they were for Lessing, though for different reasons. They were years of education through adversity. Diderot was visibly depressed by the failure of his *Père de famille* in 1761, harassed even beyond his endurance by his editorship of the *Encyclopédie,* disappointed by the desertion of d'Alembert and shaken by his estrangement from Rousseau. He thought he was getting old: he was nearing fifty, with little to show for his pains but some fugitive successes and an uncertain fame. But his resiliency served him well. Late in 1762 [writing in a letter to Sophie Volland dated 7 October 1762] he discovered *Tristram Shandy,* by "Mr. Stern," the "English Rabelais," and he permitted the novel to work in him, unconsciously. In the deepest privacy he began to write *Le neveu de Rameau.* Perhaps most beneficial of all, he discovered art criticism.

In 1759, Diderot's friend Grimm, who had been reviewing the biennial Salons in his *Correspondance littéraire* since 1751, had asked Diderot to relieve him of this burden. It proved to be a piece of luck that Diderot's talents deserved; his *Salons,* probably even more than Laurence Sterne, became the agents of his aesthetic liberation. As early as 1751, in his *Lettre sur les sourds et muets,* Diderot had dismissed Batteux's attempt to reduce all aesthetics to an imitation of *la belle nature,* but his own aesthetic ideas had been in some respects as simplistic as Batteux's, in others, more confused. Now, in the course of testing his ideas in a new field, he revised them in all fields.

His first three *Salons,* it is true, were still under the sign of his uncompromising moral realism. But as he moved from 1759 to 1761, and from 1761 to 1763, his reports swelled in volume, grew in brilliance, and displayed more and more touches of his passionate and problematic individuality. In 1759, he was still in search of veracious imitation; he singled out Chardin—not for the last time—for embodying "nature and truth": one is tempted to "take his bottles by the neck"; his "peaches and raisins awake the appetite and invite the hand." And he praised a head of the sculptor Le Moyne by his pupil Pajou for the same reason: "What a beautiful bust! It lives, it thinks, it looks, it sees, it hears, it is about to speak." In contrast, Carle Van Loo's *Medea* is a bad painting because it is theatrical and

false: "This painter neither thinks nor feels." Yet in this very first *Salon;* his sensibility contended with his principles. Boucher, whom he despised as corrupt, courtly, and lascivious, in a word, immoral, exhibited a nativity scene that Diderot found offensive in many respects: its color is wrong, its brilliance is out of place—and yet, how gratifying to the senses: "The Virgin is so beautiful, so loving and so touching." And he confessed, "I would not be displeased to have this picture. Every time you came to see me, you would criticize it, but you would look at it." Diderot the critic was trying to be honest with himself.

In the *Salons* of 1761 and 1763, Chardin remains Diderot's favorite for his extraordinary realism: "O Chardin! It is not white, red, black you grind on your palette: it is the very substance of objects, it is air and light which you put on the tip of your brush and attach to your canvas." Chardin paints nothing less than "nature itself"; his subjects are "of a veracity that deceives the eye"—as though successful *trompe l'oeil* were the highest form of art. Vien, too, is admirable because his pictures are truthful, free from exaggeration; while Le Bel's *Soleil couchant* arrests the attention for its skillful imitation of the atmosphere. And Diderot's contrast between Greuze and Boucher remains on the ground of morality: Boucher is wasting his valuable time and ruining his remarkable talent with his lasciviousness: "What colors! What variety! What wealth of objects and ideas! That man has everything, except the truth." Greuze, on the other hand, whom Diderot compliments with detailed descriptions, is magnificent because he is moral. His *Paralytique* is a *tableau de moeurs;* his celebrated *Accordée de village* is a wholly successful scene, full of pathos, crowded without being disorderly, and touching: "His choice of subjects is a mark of sensibility and good morals."

But this is not all. As Diderot's perceptions sharpen, his praise and his criticisms reach for new subtlety. Boucher is repellent in part because his realism is too explicit: "When one writes, must one write everything? When one paints, must one paint everything? Please, let my imagination supply something"—a real advance over the literalism of his early plays. Yet Greuze, the moralist, is appealing in part because he is erotic: the young girl in the *Accordée de village,* though decently dressed, displays—or rather, lets the onlooker suspect—a lovely bosom. Besides, Diderot is beginning to introduce criteria other than verisimilitude and morality. He finds Deshays's painting of *Saint Victor* impressive because it is at once simple and grand; Amédée Van Loo's *Deux Familles de satyres* gives him pleasure because it has "poetry, passion, naked flesh, character." Visibly, Diderot was introducing new complications into his judgments.

Complication did not mean conversion; Diderot's continued admiration of Greuze and detestation of Boucher alone suggest the persistence of his tastes. Greuze's sly eroticism masquerading as didactic morality never wholly lost its power over him: "Here is your painter and mine," Diderot exclaimed in 1765, repeating an exclamation of 1763, "the first among us who dared to give morals to art." In fact, Diderot failed to see in 1765 what he had seen in 1761: that Greuze's plump young mother surrounded by her adoring children, and his nubile young girl mourning her dead bird, are "charming" and "delicious" largely because they display their abundant physical charms in sentimental poses. And, as Greuze remained the beneficiary, Boucher remained the victim of Diderot's sentimentality: in 1765, he decisively disposed of Boucher, candidly and severely, as a whoremaster, a depraved courtier whose vices, the counterparts of his gifts, are on a grand scale. "I don't know what to say about that man. The degradation of taste, color, composition, characters, expression, design, have followed the depravation of morals step by step. What do you want this artist to throw on the canvas? What he has in his imagination. And what can a man have in his imagination who spends his life with prostitutes of the lowest possible birth?" —a daring rhetorical question, since the *prostituées du plus bas étage* Diderot had in mind were not merely Boucher's models but Louis XV's mistresses—"I venture to say that that man does not really know what grace is; I venture to say that he has never known the truth; I venture to say that the ideas of delicacy, decency, innocence, simplicity, have practically become strangers to him," the man is mincing, affected, unacquainted with "severe art." Nor are his faults only moral: his colors are wrong and his compositions confused and busy: "He is the most mortal enemy of silence I know." He is not even a successful sensualist: "That man takes brush in hand only to show me tits and bottoms. I am delighted to see them, but I don't want them to be shown to me." In a word, Boucher is "a false good painter."

While Diderot's cast of heroes and villains remained substantially unchanged, the *Salons,* like his other writings of the sixties, reach beyond the easy simplicities of melodrama to the problematic ambiguities of true drama. Had he ceased to write about art in 1763, he would be remembered mainly as a lively, often perceptive though rather unoriginal neoclassicist who had strained to force even his novel ideas into traditional patterns. But, to everyone's benefit, he went on writing.

He knew that his work was better than ever. In November 1765, after two exhausting weeks of writing the great *Salon* of that year, he reported to Sophie Volland that Grimm was stupefied, convinced that "no man under heaven ever had made, or would make, a work like it." Engagingly, Diderot confessed that he was secretly vain enough to agree with him. Certainly, he told his mistress, "this is the best thing I've done since I began to cultivate literature." He admitted that at times he was torn apart by contradictory ideas, and assailed by guilt for his severity, but on the whole he was proud of his essay.

He had every right to be. The *Salon of 1765,* like its successor of 1767 and, to a lesser degree, that of 1769, eloquently testifies to the evolution of Diderot's sensibility. He continued to moralize, but with more wit, more discrimination, and more control than before. Thus, in 1767, he lectured Baudouin for his *Coucher de la mariée,* a painting of a young bride being urged to enter the marriage bed. Her husband is imploring her on his knees, and a maid whispers to her—one can imagine what. The bride is *en déshabille,* crying; the bed, a looming affair with an enormous canopy, is open, and several other maids busy themselves about the room, unpacking, extinguishing candles. The whole picture, as Diderot instantly recognizes, breathes lubricity. "Monsieur Baudouin," he writes, "kindly tell me where in the world this scene took place. Certainly not in France. Here you have never seen a wellborn, well-brought up young lady half nude, one knee on the bed, being solicited by her husband in the presence of her women who tug at her." Even "without the base, low, and dishonest faces the painter has given them, the role of these servants would be of an intolerable indecency." This is not a conjugal bedroom; it is a house of assignation: "All that's missing is an old crone." Diderot insists that he is not a bigot or a religious man, and that he has little taste for censorship: "I know that the man who suppresses a bad book, or destroys a voluptuous statue, resembles an idiot who is afraid to piss in a river for fear he might drown someone." Yet Baudouin's painting, with its improbability, its ill-chosen moment, its suggestiveness, unwittingly proves that morality and taste are inseparable. "Artists, if you are anxious for your work to last, I advise you to stick to decent subjects. Everything that urges men toward depravity was made to be destroyed; and destroyed all the more surely the more perfect the work." This, like most of Diderot's art criticism, concentrates on the subject matter, the message of the painting, at the expense of purely aesthetic considerations, but Diderot is at last ready to present morality as a problem, with a lighter hand than before.

Diderot now offers better reasons for his continuing enthusiasm for Chardin. "Chardin is not a history painter," he writes in 1769, "but he is a great man"—and what could be higher praise from a critic who still respected the old hierarchies? He continues to call Chardin truthful, but his truth—Diderot sees this now—is the truth of the creative artist: he achieves it through the energy and precision with which he lays on his colors, the sure taste with which he disposes of his masses. Chardin's is the harmony only an "old magician" can produce—and it is notorious that magicians achieve their effects not by slavishly copying but by persuasively suggesting an illusion of reality.

That Diderot could admire Chardin, painter of humble domestic scenes and even humbler still lifes, had suggested from the outset the possibility that Diderot's taste might be superior to his principles. In the mid-1760s, his principles rose to meet his taste, and in the introductory pages to his *Salon of 1767,* a minor masterpiece of autobiographical musings, aesthetic theorizing, and invective against amateurs, Diderot at last seriously confronted the question of just where the artist is to find his model. A portrait, no matter how lovely, does not depict general beauty; by imitating the individual, it is only a copy of a copy. "Your line will not be the true line, the line of beauty, the ideal line, but a line somehow altered, deformed, portrait-like, individual." (This, parenthetically, is why a history painter is likely to be a poor portraitist.) Where, then, the painter asks, is my true model? It is not in nature: "This model is purely ideal, and is not directly borrowed from any individual image in Nature." That, the painter objects, is embarrassing, it is metaphysics. Well, replies Diderot, anxious to share his newly found clarity: "You blockhead—

grosse bête—doesn't your art have its metaphysics?"
—and the most sublime metaphysics at that? In rebuttal,
the painter offers Zeuxis' example: if I want to make a statue of a lovely woman, I shall have a large number of girls
undressed and then choose the most beautiful parts of
each. But Diderot rejects even this compromise: "And
how will you recognize beauty?" By conforming to the ancients. Once again, Diderot, in full flight, refuses to accept
what he would have taken for granted in earlier years.
"And if there were no antiquity, what would you do? You
don't answer. Then listen, for I'll try to explain to you how
the Ancients, who had no ancients, proceeded." Aware
that every individual they could choose was somehow imperfect, in some way remote from the ideal, the ancients
advanced through "long observation, consummate experience, with exquisite tact, with a taste, an instinct, a sort
of inspiration given to a few geniuses," gradually, slowly,
laboriously erasing false lines, rising above the individuality of the portrait to find the true line of beauty. We moderns can follow them, not by correcting our view of nature
by looking at the ancients, for that would be to reverse
their procedure, but by looking at nature as the ancients
did.

In these fiery and inconclusive pages, Diderot attempts to
define the "ideal model" at which he had only hinted earlier. Grimm, to whom they were addressed, was puzzled by
them: his epithet for Diderot, "our modern Plato," is half-
ironic, half-admiring—and half-mistaken. For Diderot
did not merely correct his misreading of Aristotle by appealing to Plato; his ideal model was beyond nature only
in the sense that no individual, no matter how beautiful,
wholly embodied it, and that no collection of individuals
could, by a simple process of combination, produce it. The
ideal model was the product of the artist's creative, inspired imagination, but it was, far from being laid up in
heaven, the fruit of labor and experience. In 1769, Diderot
summed up his new empirical Idealism with epigrammatic
economy: "In your place," he pointedly told Baudouin,
"I'd rather be a poor little eccentric—*original*—than a
great copyist." He could not have written that sentence
ten years before.

While Lessing was breaking the grip of French neoclassicism in *Laocoön* and the *Hamburgische Dramaturgie*, Diderot was writing stories and dialogues in which he translated his private experience into fictions that could appeal
to a circle wider than his intimates, a public that knew
nothing of him. He was transforming biography into art.
He was also returning, with new confidence and finer perceptions, to his first interest, the theater, and his writings
of these years often read like answers to the *Entretiens* and
the *Discours* of the 1750s. If his last *Salons* lack the fire
and inventiveness of his masterly, profuse productions of
the mid-sixties, this was not (as he put it, with excessive
self-denigration) because he was burned out. Rather, he
was turning his attention to a supremely difficult problem,
central to his own aesthetics, as it was to the Enlightenment as a whole: the management of man's most magnificent and most dangerous endowment—the passions.

Diderot, as we know, praised the passions more freely and
more frequently than his fellow philosophes. He celebrat-

ed them in his first philosophical essay, in his early writings on the theater, in his letters to Sophie Volland. He
dared to prize enthusiasm—a mental state that all philosophes, including Diderot, viewed with deep suspicion as
a source of religious fanaticism—as a quality essential for
the creation of sublime works of poetry, painting, eloquence, and music. And as late as 1765 [in his *Salon de
1765*] he could praise man's irrational, amoral powers regardless of their consequences: "I hate all those sordid little things that reveal only an abject soul; but I do not hate
great crimes: first, because one makes beautiful paintings
and fine tragedies of them; and besides, because great and
sublime actions and great crimes have the same quality:
energy."

Diderot never made a secret of the sexual roots nourishing
his enthusiasm for enthusiasm. In his early *Entretiens* he
had portrayed Dorval carried away by nature as though
he were experiencing orgasm: "Enthusiasm is born of an
object in nature." If the poet's spirit "has seen it in striking
and diverse phases, it is absorbed, agitated, tormented.
The imagination heats up; passion is stirred." It is in turn
"amazed, moved, shocked, irritated." The moment of enthusiasm, which arrives after the poet has meditated, announces itself to him "by a shudder that starts from his
chest and moves, deliciously and rapidly, to the extremi-
ties of his body. Soon it is no longer a shudder; it is a
strong and enduring heat that inflames him, makes him
pant, consumes him, kills him, but which gives spirit, life,
to everything he touches. If this heat were to increase further, phantoms would multiply before him. His passion
would rouse itself almost to madness. He would know relief only by pouring out a torrent of ideas which crowd,
jostle, and chase one another." Reason plays no part in artistic creation, and so, Diderot quite consistently concludes, "Poets, actors, musicians, painters, first-rate singers, great dancers, tender lovers, truly religious men—all
that enthusiastic and passionate troop feels vividly and reflects little."

This outburst was simply another instance of Diderot's
early confusion of life and art. But his experience with
both taught him the inadequacy of this facile equation. He
retreated neither from his affection for spontaneity and
imagination nor from his admiration for the genius who
is sublimely indifferent to rules, but came to see that feelings must be subjected to the control of reason, and acquired new respect for the technical mastery of the craftsman. Sensibility alone, he now argues, is not enough; in
fact, sensibility alone is likely to be unproductive and even
dangerous. The creative artist cursed with extreme sensibility, he wrote, evidently and painfully using himself as
an example, must make a real effort to dominate that sensibility and master his impulses. The unitarian priest of
sensibility had become the trinitarian priest of sensibility,
work, and intelligence.

Diderot long hesitated before his new, cooler aesthetic
doctrine and felt visibly uncomfortable with it. As late as
1767 [in his *Salon de 1767*], when he analyzed La Tour,
one of his favorite painters, he uneasily mingled praise and
criticism in almost undefinable quantities. "There is no
poetry here; there is only painting. I have seen La Tour

paint; he is calm and cold; he does not torture himself; he does not suffer; he does not pant." La Tour is simply a genius in technique, a "marvelous mechanic—*machiniste merveilleux.*"

Whatever Diderot's residual uneasiness, the theoretical gain of all this is considerable. In conceding that in art inspiration must be controlled by skill and sensibility by judgment, Diderot finally abandoned his simplistic view of art as a sheer outpouring of feeling, the direct translation of enthusiasm into tangible forms, and recognized that if the academic rationalism of his day had induced a deadly monotony, the naked emotionalism to which he had long been committed must induce an art as chaotic and private as it was self-indulgent. Diderot saw deeper and farther than this. He saw that the collaboration of reason and passion, or craftsmanship and enthusiasm, was at best uneasy and produced unending tensions, unstable compromises, and unresolvable ambiguities.

Diderot's **Paradoxe sur le comédien,** which he began to write in 1769, the very year he started on his **Rêve de d'Alembert** and began to lose interest in the **Salons,** is therefore an instructive document. It is, as is usual with Diderot's writings, autobiographical. Diderot portrays himself burdened by his sensibility, and makes himself into the victim of some self-lacerating anecdotes in which reflective intelligence wins out over the kind of uncontrollable spontaneity that he, with obvious regret, finds typical of himself. The anecdotes do not quite make the point they are intended to make: in the very telling, Diderot shows himself superior to the self-caricature he has drawn. But they relate, once again, Diderot's experience to his philosophy. And the **Paradoxe** is autobiographical in still another way: just as it had been his study of painters that helped him to refine his art criticism, it was his study of actors that helped him to refine his drama criticism: Garrick did for the **Paradoxe** what Chardin had done for the **Salons.**

But it is the objective rather than the biographical meaning that gives the **Paradoxe** its importance. With great dialectical skill, Diderot confronts his doctrine of experience with his doctrine of artfulness, in language familiar to, and often drawn directly from, his **Salons.** The great actor, like the great painter, performs with his ideal model in his mind's eye, a model he has purified, step by step, in long practice. Chardin had proved that great genre painting is possible only to old men or men who are born old; similarly, only an actor who "has trod the boards for long years" is likely to do justice to a part calling for the first youth.

This argument, though important, is only a preface to the central problem of Diderot's dialogue: the successful actor, who must convincingly portray emotions, must himself be cool. Diderot wants the actor to have "much good judgment," and to be a "cold and tranquil spectator." He must have "penetration and no sensibility, the art of imitating everything or, which comes to the same thing, an equal aptitude for all sorts of characters and roles." No sensibility—essentially the **Paradoxe** is a debate rehearsing variations on this single point. The actor who feels the passions he portrays can never give the same performance two days running: even if he feels them at the premiere, routine must take over: everything must be "measured,

combined, learned, ordered in his head." It is the task of "*sang-froid* to temper the delirium of enthusiasm." This is why the good actor leaves the tragedy tired, while the spectator leaves it sad. This is why the actor who portrays himself—the miser playing a miser, the voluptuary playing a voluptuary—must miss the essence of his role, and descend to satire: "Satire is about a tartuffe, and the play is about Tartuffe." This is why the actor finds sensibility a liability rather than an asset. "Sensibility is scarcely the quality of a great genius"; inborn or cultivated, sensibility is, after all, nothing more than a "disposition that accompanies the weakness of the organs, a consequence of the mobility of the diaphragm, the vivacity of the imagination, the delicacy of the nerves, which inclines a person to sympathize, shiver, wonder, fear, become agitated, weep, faint, help, flee, shout, lose his reason, exaggerate, despise, disdain, have no precise idea of the true, the good, and the beautiful, be unjust, be mad." Such a quality can only lead to bad acting. "The tears of the actor descend from his head; those of the sensible man rise from his heart." A good actor has listened to himself, and "his whole talent consists not of feeling, as you suppose, but of rendering as scrupulously as possible the external signs of sentiment." His "cries of pain are noted down in his ear." In a word, "great poets, the great actors, and perhaps all the great imitators of nature in general, whoever they are, endowed as they are with a fine imagination, excellent judgment, fine tact, absolutely sure taste, have less sensibility than anyone. They are equally well equipped for too many things; they are too busy looking, recognizing, and imitating, to be vividly affected within themselves. I see them ceaselessly with their portfolios on their knees and their pencil in their hand." Sir Joshua Reynolds, who, like Diderot, had learned much of what he knew about acting from Garrick, said the same thing in his own way: he rejected "the vulgar opinion" that the artist, whatever his art, is "possessed himself with the passion which he wished to excite." This was certainly true of the great actor. "Garrick's trade was to represent passion, not to feel it." Clearly, "Garrick left nothing to chance. Every gesture, every expression of countenance and variation of voice, was settled in his closet before he set his foot upon the stage." The English and the French Enlightenments discarded the naïve theory of imitation at about the same time.

Some years before he wrote the **Paradoxe,** Diderot had told a young friend, the actress Mlle. Jodin, dogmatically enough: "An actor who has only good sense and judgment is cold; the one who has only verve and sensibility is mad." But the **Paradoxe** itself is free from this paradox. It is, rather, a forceful claim in behalf of intelligence in artistic creation and the autonomy of art. This is Diderot's great insight of the 1760s: the truth the actor obeys is the ideal model that he acquires—wrests, as it were, from experience—through patient practice and long refinement, fully aware that even when he seems to be imitating nature he is really obeying art, for art and nature are not the same. The actor who dies must die dramatically, following certain rules, just as the ancient gladiator did. "How could nature form a great actor without art, since nothing happens on stage precisely as it does in nature, and since dramatic works are all composed on a certain system of principles? And how could a role be acted in the same manner by two different actors, since in the clearest, the most precise, the most energetic writer the words are only, and can only be, signs approached by a thought, a sentiment, an idea?" With this rhetorical question, Diderot has wholly overcome naturalism.

There is one respect in which acting reaches down to the deepest ambiguities of creativity. The actor is the accomplished craftsman, but he enters, at the same time, into his character; that great actress, Mlle. Clairon, whom Diderot and Voltaire so much admired, remains, yet transcends, herself: "In that moment, she is double: the little Clairon and the great Agrippina." Diderot had observed this inner split before, in his own person; in 1758, he had told Madame Riccoboni that he was not a wit but a deeply sensitive being, ready to smile, weep, admire freely, and at the same time, capable of stepping outside himself. *"Je sais aussi m'aliéner."*

As Diderot's aesthetics grew more rigorous, more disciplined, this capacity for detachment, which gave him inner distance and permitted him to analyze and to check passion without freezing it to death, came to occupy an ever more prominent part of his thinking. In the early 1770s it even invaded a strategic stronghold—Diderot's view of genius.

The most conservative neoclassical theorists had made room for the untrammeled originality of the genius. Even a rationalist like Boileau acknowledged the elemental force of genius, and Pope spoke [in his *Essay on Criticism*], in measured tones but with full approval, of "a grace beyond the reach of art." For these writers, as for reformers like Dubos, genius was the highest form of talent, it was originality, great power of invention and execution, a happy natural endowment for finding aesthetic forms and making aesthetic impressions that differed from ordinary craftsmanship merely in degree. This was the view of Reynolds as it was the view of Voltaire. "Fundamentally," Voltaire rhetorically asked in the early 1770s [in his *Questions sur l'Encyclopédie*], "is genius anything else but talent?" Genius is great talent, intelligently recognized and assiduously cultivated.

Diderot found this prevalent view dry and rationalistic; it gave too little play to individuality. As a good disciple of Shaftesbury, as an advocate of the passions and of enthusiasm, the young Diderot strictly differentiated the talented craftsman from that unusual, highly individualistic creature, the genius: he is nature's gift to art; others are laborious, he is quick; far from imitating, he finds imitators—he is original in the best sense of this word. Diderot never gave up his admiration for such an extraordinary being, and he pursued this train of thought into the 1770s. When he wrote his refutation of Helvétius's posthumous *De l'Homme* in 1773 he insisted that Helvétius had spoken of genius in the way "a blind man speaks of colors": the "tyrannical impulsion of genius is alien to him."

At the same time, in full accord with his later emphasis on reason and control, Diderot refused to drive his irrationalism to the length it was being driven by the *Stürmer und Dränger,* and would be driven by the Romantics. In a fragment, probably of 1772, Diderot defined genius as

a mysterious but not wholly inexplicable quality in which alertness and detachment were as important as sheer inner irrational potency: Men of genius, he writes, poets, philosophers, painters, musicians, have a certain secret, indefinable quality of mind without which nothing great or beautiful can be produced. What is this quality? It is not imagination, or judgment, or wit, or warmth, or sensibility, or good taste. Diderot is willing to accept the common view that it consists of a certain "conformity of head and viscera," but he insists that nobody knows the precise character of that conformity, and insists, in addition, on adding another quality to it, the *esprit observateur,* a gift for effortless seeing and self-instruction, a rare form of judgment which is a kind of prophetic spirit. It does not guarantee success, but the failures of the genius are never contemptible: "The man of genius knows what he stakes, and he knows it without having weighed the chances for and against; that calculation was all made in his head."

The fragment is short and incomplete, as elusive as the quality it seeks to define. But its attempt to combine rationalism with irrationalism, its insistence that the quality of genius, though rare, mysterious, and nonrational, is still human, amenable to analysis, and allied to reason, is typical of the later Diderot. It makes Diderot's last works—the long defense of the Stoic Seneca and, even more important, his last play, *Est-il bon? Est-il méchant?* —wholly comprehensible.

Est-il bon? Est-il méchant?, Diderot's best play—it has been badly neglected—was written out of Diderot's capacity for detachment and analysis; its protagonist, Hardouin, conducts a public examination of his innermost motives. It has all the characteristics of a late work; it is an autumnal comedy, light and yet curiously grave, and its tone perfectly matches the time of its composition: Diderot began to write it in the early 1770s, revised it several times and completed it around 1783, when he was seventy. It was precisely in these years—1776 to 1779—that Lessing worked out the final version of his *Nathan der Weise;* the two most striking representatives of Enlightenment theater, one psychological, the other didactic, belong to its last period.

Est-il bon? Est-il méchant? is a kind of belated criticism of *Le Fils naturel* and *Le pére de famille;* it demonstrates that these earlier plays had to fail because they had not been, for all their supposed realism, realistic enough: they had put on stage caricatures rather than characters and offered, with their prosaic speeches and naturalistic stage settings, the mere surface of reality. *Est-il bon? Est-il méchant?* is, in its own way, a realistic play; it draws most of its characters, and most of its incidents, from life. Yet it leaves the realm of anecdote to explore the mysteries of character and of moral action. An air of resignation hangs over it: *Est-il bon?* reads like the last word of a pagan sage who expects little from the world and, indeed, from himself.

Le Fils naturel and *Le pére de famille* were nothing if not obvious; *Est-il bon? Est-il méchant?* is a puzzle, almost a mystification. Diderot forces an unconventional action into a conventional setting: the play is like a French provincial room hung with abstract paintings. Hardouin acts on the surface like a stock figure of comedy. With unbelievable ease, and within an unbelievably short time, he solves the problems of his friends and of strangers who happen to come his way. He persuades a temperamental mother to let her daughter marry the man she loves. He obtains a pension for the beautiful young widow of a captain drowned in the line of duty. He settles a lawsuit to everyone's satisfaction. But he employs unconventional, shabby, even vicious means to accomplish his purposes: he intimates that the young widow—whom he has only seen once—is his mistress and her son his bastard; he wins the mother's consent by claiming—falsely—that her daughter is pregnant. While all ends well and everyone forgives Hardouin, his beneficiaries are often angry at him and not likely to be grateful.

The action of the play is slight, but Hardouin—that is, Diderot—is thoroughly modern in his complexity. He is daemonic, almost diabolical, but he is no Mephistopheles: it is not that he wills the evil and does good; he wishes to do good, but with evil—or at least with his own—means. Hardouin is puzzled, gravely troubled, by himself; he knows his capacity for making mischief and regrets the pleasure he takes in playing games with the lives of others: "I, a good man, as people say? I'm nothing of the kind. I was born essentially hard, bad, perverse. I'm practically moved to tears by the tenderness of that mother for her child, her sensibility, her gratitude; I might even develop a taste for her; and despite myself I persist in the project that may make her miserable . . . Hardouin, you amuse yourself with everything; nothing is sacred to you; you're a regular monster . . . That's bad, very bad . . . You must absolutely get rid of this bad inclination . . . and renounce the prank I've planned? . . . Oh, no . . . But after this one, no more, no more. It will be the last one of my life."

The play is a psychological drama, an unsparing self-exploration, partly serene in its acceptance of life, partly heavy with world-weariness. But it is also a morality tale about the meaning of freedom. Hardouin is tired of the world, "very tired," largely, it seems, because he is not his own master. A dramatist well supplied with friends, but poor and unrecognized, he has spent his life working too hard, depending on others, and making compromises that disgusted him. His restlessness is a critique of his passivity. "I was born, I think, to do nothing that pleases me, to do everything that others demand, and to satisfy nobody—no, nobody—not even myself." In his disappointment with himself and his persistent desire for autonomy, Hardouin feels compelled to resist what he really wishes to do, and to refuse to do—or at least do in his strange and solitary way—what he thinks he really should do. The question, Is he good, is he bad?, baldly asked in the title, is asked again in the last scene, and answered with commonplaces that solve nothing:

> "Is he good? Is he bad?" "One after the other."
> "Like you, like me, like everybody."

Diderot has deepened the meaning of realism while, indeed precisely because, the mystery of the play remains intact. And he has connected both the realism and the mystery to the overriding question of the eighteenth century:

how to find the proper sphere and justified boundaries of freedom. The modernity of Diderot's aesthetics lies here.

Robert Niklaus   (essay date 1970)

SOURCE: "Diderot," in *A Literary History of France: The Eighteenth Century 1715-1789,* Ernest Benn Limited, 1970, pp. 211-33.

[*In the following excerpt, Niklaus surveys Diderot's life and career, describing him as "perhaps the greatest genius of a century of brilliant men," and concluding that "he fulfilled his total promise within his own lifetime, but it is only in our time that he has been understoood."*]

Denis Diderot straddles the eighteenth century like a colossus. He was a powerful genius; philosopher, thinker, critic, scientist, and artist; and an ardent, impetuous man, with a great gift for friendship and a personality so exuberant and so overwhelming that he made his mark not only upon the circles he frequented, but upon the century into which he was born, and subsequent centuries to the present day.

He was a Champenois, born at Langres on 5 October 1713, the son of a master cutler who was widely respected in his own milieu, and by his son as soon as he grew old enough to recognise his father's worth. The boy was educated by the Jesuits at Langres from the age of nine, since his father destined him for the Church. He was tonsured at the age of thirteen, by which time his extraordinary brilliance, his intellectual quality, and his bold and daring spirit had manifested themselves, together with athletic prowess equally remarkable. He did not in fact enter the Church. From 1729 to 1732 he studied in Paris at the Jansenist Collège d'Harcourt, or at the Jesuit Lycèe Louis-le-Grand, or most probably at both these institutions, receiving the degree of Master of Arts at the University of Paris in 1732, after three years of progress and development that startled and sometimes dismayed his teachers, because of the precocity and audacity of his questing mind, and the tempestuous ardour of his personality.

He spent the following two years studying law as an articled clerk in the office of Maître Clément de Ris, during which time he brought all his scholar's enthusiasm to bear upon an increasing interest in languages, in literature and philosophy, and above all in mathematics, in all of which he showed exceptional ability. As Naigeon has stated, Diderot was drawn towards geometry and the abstract sciences all his life, because of their independence and generality.

It was by this time clear that he was not sufficiently interested in law to make it his career; and for the next ten years (1734-44), to the dismay of his father, he led a precarious existence earning his living by whatever means came to hand: as a tutor, and one who would spend the whole day on a brilliant pupil, and never return at all for a second brief session with a dull one; one who accepted payment in kind—food, furniture, linen—and in cash, or went without it if it pleased him; he worked also as a publisher's hack, and wrote sermons for missionaries at fifty *écus* each. He was a great frequenter of cafés, where the discussion of ideas and attitudes stimulated and excited him, and in which he played his full part, a well-known figure in the Régence, the Laurent, and most of all in the Procope, where he met Jean-Jacques Rousseau in 1741, establishing a friendship with him that lasted for fifteen years. There is evidence that Diderot planned to enter the Church in that same year; but none that he did in fact ever enter the seminary of Saint-Sulpice, perhaps because it was at this time that he met Antoinette, daughter of Mme Champion, a linen-draper, and fell in love with her. He had no career, no prospects; and his father, who had already suffered so much from watching his brilliant son apparently frittering his life away, thoroughly disapproved of the match. They were, however, secretly married in 1743, when Diderot was thirty, and had not yet published anything at all.

In spite of his estrangement from his father, he was strongly attached to his family, and it was possibly this attachment that had made him consider entering the Church in 1741, since he knew it to be the pious hope of his parents. Throughout his subsequent career, he showed an excellent grasp of religious principles and modes of thought, as well as considerable familiarity with the writings of the Fathers of the Church and of lesser divines, and with religious controversies through the centuries. There is no doubt also that his latent idealism and positive emotionalism prolonged his religious phase.

It was his marriage that first impelled him to undertake literary work, since now he had a wife to support. He became an experienced translator, rendering into French Temple Stanyan's *History of Greece* in 1743, the *Inquiry Concerning Virtue* or Merit of the third earl of Shaftesbury in 1745, and Robert James's *Medicinal Dictionary* in 1746-48.

His marriage, begun so romantically, showed itself almost immediately to be an unhappy failure, the union of two people who, once the first rapture had disappeared, proved to have nothing in common. Only one of their four children survived, a daughter Angélique, born in 1753, to whom Diderot was devoted all his life, attending personally to her education, both moral and academic, and in 1772 arranging a successful marriage for her with Caroillon de Vandeul. Madame de Vandeul later wrote extremely interesting and appreciative *Mémoires* of her father.

In 1745 the publisher André Le Breton approached Diderot with a view to bringing out an encyclopaedia. It was originally intended to be a translation in French of Ephraim Chambers's *Cyclopaedia,* drawing upon the *Dictionnaire de Trévoux,* and had been entrusted in 1743 to John Mills and Gottfried Sellius. Diderot soon changed the nature of the project, which in his hands became an important method of radical and revolutionary opinion. He seized upon every opportunity of broadening the scope of the encyclopaedia, gathering together a team of energetic and devoted workers, literary men, philosophers, scientists, and priests, some already well established, others just at the beginning of their careers, and all united in a common purpose—to extend the boundaries of knowledge, and by so doing to strike a resounding blow against reactionary forces in the Church and in the state.

As the responsibilities of a married man had impelled Diderot to launch himself as a translator, so the inadequacies of that marriage indirectly impelled him into the publication of his own works. Lacking any form of intellectual understanding from his wife, he turned to a certain Mme de Puisieux, who appeared to be an intelligent and witty woman. As soon as she became his mistress, however, she revealed herself as a harpy, and her demands for money were so incessant that Diderot could only meet them by publishing such works as *Les Bijoux indiscrets* (1748), a novel in the fashionable mode, held to be indecent, but with serious undertones of a philosophical and critical nature which have only recently been studied.

Les Pensées philosophiques, his earliest original work, already shows a strong current of anti-Christian thought, the first public expression of his growing religious perplexity that had held him back from entering the Church in 1741. It was an opuscule of some sixty pages, crammed with new and explosive ideas written down in a vivid and virile prose. There were some who went so far as to attribute it to Voltaire; an attribution which may have contributed in some measure to its sensational success, and its condemnation to burning. Diderot's revolt from orthodoxy sprang as much from his temperament as from his philosophical convictions, and from his protean character which caused comparisons to be drawn with Socrates on the one hand and the powerful, tempestuous, and full-blooded men born of the Renaissance on the other.

It is very probable that he led a modestly dissipated life in his twenties, and this, coupled with the moral laxity of the times, freed him from conventional ethics and left him to discover moral codes suited to his mind and his strong and fearless character. He was able throughout his life to distinguish prevailing modes of thought and behaviour from the intellectual speculation that marks his original thought; so managing to combine intellectual freedom with a relatively conventional life, led according to the shibboleths of the bourgeois society of his day. His knowledge of normal family life, the pattern of his relationship with his parents, and his lifelong contacts with Langres, the place of his birth, his roots among ordinary people, even his unsatisfactory marriage to a woman who, though without malice, could not begin to share or even to understand his major preoccupations in life, but who yet gave him his adored daughter; all these factors enriched his human experience in a way unknown to his great contemporaries, and provided him with practical criteria of normal behaviour, to serve as a check and a corrective to uninhibited speculation.

In addition to his work on the *Encyclopédie,* and on his translations, Diderot followed the *Pensées philosophiques* with the *Promenade du sceptique* in 1747 (pub. 1830), which took his argument several steps further, and with the *Lettre sur les aveugles* in 1749, the most audacious of the three, in which he expounded the doctrine of materialist atheism, and which stressed human dependence on sense impressions. The *Lettre* is remarkable for its proposal to teach the blind to read through the sense of touch, preparing the way for Louis Braille in the following centu-

Portrait of Diderot by Michel Van Loo, 1767.

ry; and for the presentation of the first step in his evolutionary theory of survival by superior adaptation.

Diderot was arrested for the irreligion and audacity of his work—and also because it gave offence to Mme Dupré de Saint-Maur, an intimate friend of d'Argenson, then Minister of Police—and imprisoned in Vincennes for three months. While there he began to question the extra-curricular activities of Mme de Puisieux, who was still dunning him for money; he climbed over the prison walls to follow her after a visit she made to him, so beautifully dressed that he grew suspicious, watched her with the lover who was consoling her in his absence, returned to prison, and severed all connections with her.

His imprisonment, his lost mistress, his diverse literary activities, his family and social life in no way interfered with the great work of his life. In 1750 he published his *Prospectus* of the projected *Encyclopédie,* which d'Alembert, his co-editor, expanded into a brilliant *Discours préliminaire* in 1751.

The *Encyclopédie* is the magnificent testament of the Age of Enlightenment, and one of the three or four great intellectual landmarks of the eighteenth century; and it is equally important both in its conception and in its realisation. Diderot was perhaps the only man in his century with the quality of mind and spirit, and the intellectual power to carry the weight of an undertaking that was intended to present knowledge as an organised whole, as a vast genealogical tree stressing the interconnections between the sciences. Its secondary purpose was to serve as a *dictionnaire* **raisonné,** to propound the essential principles and applications of every art and science known at that time. Its underlying philosophy, given the co-editors Diderot and d'Alembert, was rationalist, and based on faith in the progress of the human mind.

Eighteenth-century philosophy examined, following in the foot-steps of Locke rather than of Descartes, some of the great questions of the age and of the modern society then evolving. Montesquieu, Voltaire, Rousseau, d'Alembert, Condillac, and d'Holbach all brought their encyclopaedic knowledge and their unparalleled range of interests to bear upon these problems; but of all these exceptionally brilliant men, Diderot alone had the breadth of mind and type of genius that made him able to interpret and synthesise the data at his disposal, to evolve the new methodology required for the intensive study of nature, and to foreshadow some of the major scientific discoveries of the following century. 'C'était', wrote Grimm, 'la tête la plus naturellement encyclopédique qui ait existé'; and even Voltaire, not easily given to praise of rival philosophers, said of him: 'Tout est dans la sphère d'activité de son génie.'

Diderot never oversimplified the issues with which he was dealing, whether they were concerned with the universe, life, man and human destiny, religion, the origin and government of the world, society, ethics, or aesthetics. His mind was wide, and powerful enough to allow him to accept the diversity of facts; his extraordinary talent for synthesis impelled him to try to account for this diversity; and with great intellectual integrity he never forced the facts to fit in with his theories, but instead enlarged and changed his theories to explain the facts. His approach, in all his writings, was undogmatic, empirical, and dialectical, and this was of particular value in his work, which lasted nearly thirty years, on the *Encyclopédie:* it also brought about many difficulties for him, and some of the real or apparent contradictions in his thought.

'Tout se tient dans la nature' . . . he wrote, and again, 'Tout ce qui est ne peut être ni contre nature ni hors de nature'. . . . He was deeply and constantly aware of the 'grande chaîne qui lie toutes choses', which is defined in the *Encyclopédie* as 'l'enchaînement des connaissances'. If the natural forces are all one, this will be reflected in the microcosm of man as well as in the macrocosm of the universe. 'Je suis porté à croire que tout ce que nous avons vu, connu, aperçu, entendu', he wrote later in the *Eléments de physiologie,* 'jusqu'aux arbres d'une longue forêt . . . tous les concerts que nous avons entendus, tout cela existe en nous à notre insu'. . . . He concluded that the link between man and the world was very close. For Diderot, who believed in the objective reality of nature, there was a necessary parallel between the laws of the universe, and those that govern the working of the mind—'Le type de nos raisonnments les plus étendus, leur liaison, leur conséquence, est nécessaire dans notre entendement comme l'enchaînement, la liaison des effects, des causes, des objets, des qualités des objets l'est dans. . . . This is reasoning by analogy and it leads to an awareness of the link between the spiritual and the physical worlds and of the validity of thought whenever it is based upon fact.

It is the awareness of this link, allied with a refusal to accept the premise that the determinism of the physical world could be translated without modification into the world of the spirit, which made him draw back from the mechanical materialism of La Mettrie, as expressed in such works as *L'Homme-machine* and *L'Homme-plante*.

Diderot undertook to write articles on history, philosophy, and the mechanical arts for the *Encyclopédie,* as well as to edit, with d'Alembert, all the work of their collaborators; and an examination of his total output of work serves to show that this vast labour, over so many years, did not even begin to exhaust his vast mental and physical strength. But it was with this herculean task that he came most truly into his own, since each of his many aptitudes and talents—his naturally encyclopaedic mind, his protean knowledge of science and of the methodology of his time, his powers of intuition that enabled him to extend his already great store of learning with unusual speed and clarity—was called upon. To these factors must be added the power and rhythm of his writing—an inexhaustible fount of ideas—and an intellectual fertility and energy that has scarcely been equalled. There was no branch of human knowledge unknown to him - mechanics, geometry, mathematics, philosophy, theology, moral law, linguistics, the arts, music, drama, the sciences, metaphysics, philology, and politics.

Here clearly was the comprehensive genius, more than adequate in his physical and mental prowess, to bring so vast a conception as the *Encyclopédie* to full fruition. In his hands, and those of his co-editor d'Alembert, it became much more than a compendium of past and present knowledge. It became the mirror of advanced thought, embodying necessary social and political reforms, and pointing the way to a scientific and technological revolution. Diderot's passionate concern for mankind, projected into the *Encyclopédie,* was essentially revolutionary and philosophic, hostile to the *ancien régime* and to the inadequacies of the aristocracy in their exceptionally privileged position. The *Encyclopédie* contained a rehabilitation of honest labour and industry, until then mocked and despised. By making every effort to elevate, from their secular degradation, the backbone of the race, the vast mass of the middle and working classes, upon whom society does in fact depend, Diderot offered a calculated deathblow to the parasites within the aristocracy and the Church.

The publication of the *Encyclopédie,* with its seventeen volumes of text, and eleven volumes of plates, prepared over the period 1751-72, was the greatest publishing venture of the century. It provided Diderot with his chief occupation and source of income during those years. His work first as co-editor, and then as sole editor, suffered many vicissitudes. His enemies manoeuvred against him, and some of his friends deserted him. Publication was suspended in 1752, resumed in 1753, and suspended again in 1759, before it was brought to its splendid conclusion in 1772. There was a critical moment in 1758 when d'Alembert, alarmed at the way in which the *Encyclopédie* attracted trouble, resigned from his post as co-editor after the publication of the seventh volume, which brought Rousseau's attack on d'Alembert's 'Genève' article. There was to be an even more shattering experience in 1764, when Diderot discovered that Le Breton had se-

cretly deleted compromising or dangerous material from the corrected proofs of some ten folio volumes. He was throughout bedevilled by both friends and enemies, forced to fight the increasing and splenetic opposition of Church and *parlement,* and to deal with the vacillations of government policy and censorship. Yet in spite of minor and major irritations and frustrations, he continued to be an energetic and conscientious general editor, revising all articles submitted, and giving his closest attention and detailed technical knowledge to the choice and presentation of the illustrations for 3,000 to 4,000 plates, of exceptional practical and historical interest. He also contributed innumerable articles in his own name, dealing mainly with the history of philosophy ('Eclectisme', a full-length study of the subject), with social theory ('Droit naturel'), with general aesthetics ('Beau'), and with the mechanical arts.

Diderot's rejection of Christianity, and the deepening of his materialist philosophy, provide the key to all his writing, and led him into the expression of some of his most interesting ideas. For his exhaustive work on the *Encyclopédie* miraculously left him with time, thought, and energy to spare for other writings. Yet his best work belongs to later years.

Those ideas he had first presented in the *Lettre sur les aveugles* (1749), adumbrating an evolutionary theory of survival by superior adaptation, challenging the existence of an intelligent God, and stating that the order we see in the universe is simply the human apprehension of the laws of motion in matter, were developed still further in the *Pensées sur l'interprétation de la nature* (1754), generally recognised as the *discours de la méthode* of the eighteenth century. Here emphasis was laid upon empiricism, and the inductive form of reasoning generally associated with the name of Francis Bacon; and Diderot offered examples of the sort of scientific results obtainable through scientific investigation and conjectures supported by evidence. His emphasis on the new experimental approach to science points to the failure of Cartesianism to explain reality, and his recourse to hypotheses demonstrates the inadequacy of contemporary scientific knowledge. As his evolutionary doctrine expanded, he took up his position beyond Democritus, Epicurus, and Lucretius, and close to that of Lamarck and Darwin.

Diderot published few other works in his lifetime, though he never ceased to write. Special mention should be made of his *Lettre sur les sourds et muets* (1751), which deals with the function of language and the question of aesthetics. His manuscripts were known only to his intimates, among whom they were circulated, and to the privileged subscribers to Grimm's *Correspondance littéraire,* to which he contributed articles, following a friendship established between them in 1750.

Among his most noteworthy philosophical works, in which his monistic materialism was most brilliantly expressed, were *L'Entretien entre d'Alembert et Diderot* and the *Rêve de d'Alembert,* both written in 1769, but not published until 1830, and the *Eléments de physiologie* (1774-80). Diderot towers above the contemporary philosophers of his age, even above Voltaire, not only through his power and grasp of principles, and his direct and unremitting attack upon Church and state, on which they all were engaged; but also because he alone among them, having completed the negative and destructive aspects of attack, sought to discover and express the positive principle of a new philosophy. Before him, no one had attempted this major constructive effort: and Diderot was immediately suspect, dubbed leader of the new materialist movement, and subject to prolonged attack throughout the second half of the century.

In the works quoted above, Diderot not only developed his materialist philosophy, and foreshadowed the evolutionary doctrine, but also evolved the first modern theory of the cellular structure of matter. He started from sensationalist premises, to give positive content to Leibnitz's idealistic monad, following in the steps of Maupertuis, and tried to demonstrate that the passage from the inorganic to the organic may be achieved stage by stage. He saw matter as an entity lending itself to many forms and invariably endowed with *sensibilité,* active or kinetic. His molecular theory of the universe hinged on his non-Cartesian conception of motion inherent in matter: 'Le mouvement est également et dans le corps transféré et dans le corps immobile. Le repos est un concept abstrait qui n'existe point en nature.' . . . Time is the factor underlying all changes, and an essential part of the evolutionary processes. As his thought progressed, he discarded the theory of preformation, leading to a mechanical and static conception of the universe, and replaced it by epigenesis, which explained organic formation in terms of juxtaposition and contiguity. He found himself in disagreement with Buffon and Needham, who had discovered infusoria, on the question of spontaneous generation, since such a hypothesis left unresolved the problem of the special sensitivity of living organisms. His knowledge of medicine led him to give a place of increasing importance to *organisation.*

In 1759, while his wife was away visiting his family, he had met and taken as mistress Sophie Volland, an attachment that lasted more than twenty years. For the first time in his life, as far as records show, and at the age of forty-six, he met a woman equal to being his companion. It was a liaison founded on common interests, natural sympathy, and a deepening friendship. She never disturbed his marriage or made claims on him, as Mme de Puisieux had done. With her he found the companionship lacking in his marriage with Antoinette, who could not appreciate his intellectual struggles and triumphs. His witty Sophie, with her alert, questing mind and wide culture, filled that vacuum in his life.

It was in a letter to her, dated October 1759, that he attempted to clarify the problem of the organisation of matter as he saw it—molecular combinations possessing specialised functions, with the autonomous working of the brain seen as a kingpin of neural mechanism, a kind of sixth sense of extraordinary power.

His speculations in these areas of science are of particular interest, but it is the dialectical brilliance of their presentation that is exceptional. Diderot successfully took over the method already used by Bernard de Fontenelle, but was himself more concerned with deepening and developing his thought for its own sake, and giving rein to his aston-

ishing imagination, which allowed him to penetrate to the heart of mysteries as yet unsolved, than with popularising his views for the sake of the general reader. He often expressed his ideas in paradox, and unvariably in dialogue form; they stem from a sense of reality, and a rare understanding of the complexities and contradictions inherent in human nature, the result of a prolonged examination upon which the whole of his exceptionally well-stocked and original mind was brought to bear.

Diderot's ideas on embryology were well in advance of his time, and in line with modern discoveries. While his contemporaries were still refusing to accept bi-parental heredity, he propounded his own theory to account for birth factors and inherited characteristics, foreshadowing the future scientific data concerning genes and chromosomes, explaining the phenomena occasioned by recessive genes, and stressing the fundamental role of chromosomes; incredibly enough, in view of the state of research into these matters at that time, he linked the production of monstrous or abnormal children to the unpairing of one or other of the pairs of chromosome 'threads' at the moment of generation. He was handicapped in his exposition by the lack of a vocabulary fitted to his new theories, and had to anticipate scientific verification, in view of inadequate laboratory facilities; and there is some confusion in his mind between cellular organisation and the nervous system. His hypotheses were confirmed, together with the soundness of his methodology, by the discovery of organic cells and the principle of cell division. His analysis of the old problem of which came first, the chicken or the egg, is masterly: 'Si la question de la priorité de l'oeuf ou de la poule vous embarrasse, c'est que vous supposez que les animaux ont été originairement ce qu'ils sont à présent' . . . this leads him into the proposition that the problem is false, and one that is solved by the continuity and evolvement of the evolutionary pattern; this discussion is followed by some of his most remarkable pages on embryology.

In his attempts at breaking down the previously existing barrier between inorganic and organic nature, Diderot arrived astonishingly close to the modern molecular theory, and if, in view of his necessarily restricted vocabulary, the modern cell be substituted for his 'living molecule', and the atom for his 'dead molecule', then it will be seen that he expounded the complete chain, from the molecule to the universe, which is as all-embracing as that of any modern materialist philosophy. 'Le prodige, c'est la vie, c'est la sensibilité; et ce prodige n'en est plus un. . . . Lorsque j'ai vu la matière inerte passer à l'état sensible, rien ne doit plus m'étonner.' . . . He adumbrates the theories of Lamarck in his own century, and Darwin in the next, concerning the principles governing heredity and natural selection, and the necessary link between organs, functions, and needs, or, as he expresses it with great concision in the *Eléments de physiologie,* 'L'organisation détermine les fonctions et les besions'. . . .

Diderot made it clear that, as a living part of a living world, man could only be understood in his cosmological context. His genetic theory is particularly impressive, and takes him far beyond the sensationalist doctrine of Locke,

Condillac, and Helvétius. In the *Suite de l'entretien*, a postscript to the *Rêve de d'Alembert*, he approaches the question of abnormality with the same insight and intuition he had shown in earlier aspects of his research. Starting from the premise 'Tout ce qui est ne peut être ni contre nature ni hors de nature', he denies that anything called monstrous or perverted is in fact outside the scope of nature. The large number of abortive species thrown up by nature argues against divine design, and may more properly be explained by genetics, or by a peculiar reaction to any given environment.

Diderot's main concern in the *Rêve de d'Alembert* is with physiology, with particular reference to monstrosity, deviation, and hybrids. As he had previously done in the *Lettre sur les aveugles*, he stresses the close connection between physiology and psychology, and the inter-reaction of responses. From this point he developed his theory of dreams, which was destined later to impress Sigmund Freud. In his later works, he gave increasing importance, within the framework of his monistic and energetistic materialism, to the power of the brain in the determination of life and events.

It is remarkable that Diderot was able, in the absence of scientific proof, to advance such accurate theories. This was partly due to the fact that he kept himself well informed concerning all recent scientific writings and discoveries. The reading list he drew up in preparation for the *Eléments de physiologie* proves this. He had read and annotated Haller's major work on physiology, the writings of Charles Bonnet, Bordeu, Robert Whytt, a and of Buffon; and he knew of Malpighi's experiments, and of those of Needham. In the ordinary course of his extraordinary life he came into frequent and sustained personal contact with scientists and doctors. It was also due to his exceptional powers of logic, deduction, and synthesis, and to the power of his imaginative vision of the universe. He was moreover, a man with an intellect capable of encompassing and organising all the known knowledge of his time.

Accepting the evidence offered by men of science and of medicine, he had recourse to hypotheses only where necessary to account for the facts presented, bearing in mind the preservation of the essential unity of matter. 'La sensibilité, propriété générale de la matiére'. . . was one of such hypotheses, and by probing further he came to understand that this was a latent *sensibilité*, and significant only in living matter. This in turn led him to examine the organisation of matter, with sensitivity concentrated in specific organs, and so to establish a hierarchy between the brain and nerve centres, so that a full and simple explanation of the universe was made to include the mental processes of man.

Unlike Bonnet and Robinet, who believed that the fundamental unity of nature finds expression in forms determined by God, and is therefore fixed and lasting, Diderot envisaged an ever-changing world without God, in which forms are born of chance, and are then indefinitely and necessarily subject to change. We are therefore limited in our apprehension of nature, which must remain ultimately unknowable. As he had already written in 1753: 'Si l'état des êtres est dans une vicissitude perpétuelle; si la nature est encore à l'ouvrage, malgré la chaîne qui lie les phéno-

ménes, il n'y a point de philosophie. Toute notre science naturelle devient aussi transitoire que les mots. . . . Diderot certainly had the power to select significant data, synthesise known facts, and interpret them. He used carefully chosen analogies, inductive as well as deductive reasoning, and his mind was able to seize upon hidden connections and correspondences. He also made use of his faculty of intuition, or *esprit d'observation*, which Spinoza called *scientia intuitiva*, the whole illumined by his creative and imaginative drive. Step by step he unfolded his new and majestic vision of life, building up a grandiose picture which he expressed with natural eloquence, sometimes bordering on lyrical ecstasy. In the *Rêve de d'Alembert*, there are mature passages which echo the new cosmic revelation of the blind Saunderson, where Diderot conveys a deep, almost mystical, communion with the very processes of nature. The excitement of gradual discovery is conveyed through the ebb and flow of discussion. He maintained that thought as well as life has its organic complexity, and becomes creative when, without ever denying the authenticity of facts, it goes beyond them, to reach a cosmic understanding of the universe. In the age of destructive criticism, Diderot's ability to synthesise appears extraordinary. He knew that experimental philosophy was destined to take the place of rational speculation, and that the question 'how?', and not the question 'why?', was the key to intellectual progress; and, since the one who knows and the knowable facts are of the same substance, conjectures that are well founded have validity.

The question whether the *Rêve de d'Alembert* in particular should be considered as a speculative essay, or as a reflection of Diderot's definitive opinion, has exercised many critics, but it focuses attention on the wrong point. On 2 September 1769, Diderot wrote to Mlle Volland, referring to the *Rêve:* 'Il n'est pas possible d'être plus profond et plus fou'. . . . And again: 'Cela est de la plus haute extravagance, et tout à la fois de la philosophie la plus profonde'. . . . No one could improve upon this final comment by Diderot. It is certain that he was particularly attached to this work, whose peculiar quality lies not only in the merit of the scientific theory or the new and viable philosophy propounded, but in the author's ability to convey his satisfaction at having fulfilled an intellectual need, and his conviction that the literary form adopted matched the quality of the thought. He realised that, following in the footsteps of Fontenelle, he had enlarged even further the realm of literature, since the dialogue on scientific facts is presented as a real dialogue between known people, and this dialectical method coupled with Diderot's fine prose style combined the acquisition of scientific knowledge with literary entertainment. Diderot's humour and subtlety, as well as incongruous schoolboyish sense of mischief, were put to good use in the text, where real names and transferred names, real and fictional people, rub shoulders in a comedy much enjoyed by the contemporary élite of close friends and acquaintances, the 'in-people' who would have caught every *nuance*, understood every transference, and enjoyed full awareness of the reasons for which Mlle de Lespinasse asked Diderot to suppress the work.

In several particulars the *Eléments de physiologie* takes

Diderot's theories further than the ***Rêve de d'Alembert,*** but it does not enjoy the same literary interest or vitality, nor is it as convincing. But whether wholly successful or not, Diderot always has an active concern for literary values, concentrating on discovering the form of expression ideally suited for his thought. So philosophy and science become the subject of stylised dialogues, scenes from plays with an element of *marivaudage.* He broke down the idea of narrow genres, and evolved new and broader literary forms; so that his drama includes moral sermons, and his novels disquisitions on ethics and aesthetics.

The determinist materialism which he had evolved had grave bearing on the moral issues which were never far from his mind. If it is true that 'les êtres ne sont jamais ni dans leur génération, ni dans leur conformation, ni dans leur usage que ce que les résistances, les lois du mouvement et l'ordre universel les déterminent à être,' there can be no liberty, virtue must spring from a felicitous natural disposition, and *bienfaisance* and *malfaisance* must take the place of good and evil. At the time he wrote the ***Lettre sur les aveugles,*** he saw the world as one in which morality was almost entirely dependent on the senses, yet he was inwardly convinced of the need for morality, and in the absence of God he was unable to find a basis for virtue. Starting from Shaftesbury's standpoint in the ***Essai sur le mérite et la vertu,*** which he freely translated 'Point de vertu sans croire en Dieu, point de bonheur sans vertu' he vacillates, trapped, along with most contemporary thinkers, into the self-deception of believing, because he wanted to, that virtue necessarily produces happiness.

This is a point of view that is consistently expressed in his work for the theatre, and particularly stressed in his two major plays, ***Le Fils naturel*** (1757) and ***Le Père de famille*** (1758). Diderot, as might be expected from someone of his dramatic temperament, gift of dialogue, and didactic frame of mind, was from the beginning deeply interested in the theatre, and managed to find time for several plays, articles, and treatises on drama; yet he never brought off a resounding success in the theatre itself. The delightful ***Est-il bon? Est-il méchant?*** (1781) is a small masterpiece, but it was never given a public performance before the twentieth century, and even his major plays met with no success when they were staged.

The belief that virtue necessarily produces happiness lies behind his theory of *le drame.* 'On distingue dans tout objet moral unmilieu et deux extrêmes: il semble donc que, toute action dramatique étant un objet moral, il devait y avoir un genre moyen et deux genres extrêmes', he wrote. Since comedy and tragedy offered the two extremes, Diderot concentrated, in theory and in practice, upon the genre half-way between them: the serious, bourgeois, real-life drama, written and presented for the moral welfare of its participants and spectators. It was deliberately didactic, with the intention of delivering moral sermons that would have wider appeal and greater emotional value than those delivered from the pulpits.

Diderot's theories on drama, to be found in the ***Entretiens sur Le Fils naturel*** (1757) and his ***De la poésie dramatique*** (1758), are important landmarks in the history of the theatre. Beginning with *comédie larmoyante,* a genre for which he had great admiration, he stressed the need for greater realism on the stage, and insisted that characters should be presented in their milieu, should belong to specific professions, and establish recognisable relationships, the better to add force to the moral and social implications of the play, which were, for him, of primary importance. He urged changes in stagecraft and décor, and showed a weakness for *tableaux vivants,* which he was convinced would profoundly affect audiences.

His theories exercised paramount influence over Lessing, whose *Hamburgische Dramaturgie* appeared in 1767-68; but it was not until the nineteenth century, with Emile Augier and Dumas *fils,* that certain of his suggestions were adopted. In his best-known writing on the theatre, the ***Paradoxe sur le comédien*** (1773-78, published 1830), presented in dialogue form, Diderot argues that great actors, like great poets, are insensitive, for sensibility would impede interpretation, and confuse the necessary judgement and penetration they must bring to bear upon it. His definition of the actor is of particular interest: 'un pantin merveilleux dont le poéte tient la ficelle et auquel il indique la véritable forme qu'il doit prendre'—and offers scope for argument on the nature of acting.

Diderot's *drames* were in effect social theses expressed in dramatic form, and of remarkable moral power and eloquence. So also were his novels, bringing equal innovation to the current literary form.

In the preface to ***Le Pére de famille,*** and in other writings on the theatre, Diderot argued that education holds the key to moral progress. From the standpoint of philosophic propaganda, this principle reinforced the cause of the Encyclopaedic movement, but it was more for the unthinking crowd than for the honest thinker. Diderot soon came to believe that the only thing to do with the *méchant,* that is the man born bad, whom nothing can modify, was to destroy him, a view he expressed as late as in the ***Neveu de Rameau,*** where, however, his admiration for genius as such leads him to wonder whether genius, which must take its course, does not carry its own justification. He now thought increasingly in terms of the individual, and not solely of society. It is 'Moi' (i. e. Diderot) and not 'Lui' (i. e. Le Neveu de Rameau) who is thankful for the genius of Racine, and is ready to endure his alleged wickedness because of it. His consideration of genius, of the nature of man in his social context, and his dissatisfaction with common, bourgeois, prejudiced morality prompts him to say: 'Il n'y a point de lois pour le sage' . . . and to proclaim: 'Il est une doctrine spéculative qui n'est ni pour la multitude, ni pour la pratique et que si sans être fat on n'écrit pas tout ce qu'on fait, sans être inconséquent on ne fait pas tout ce qu'on écrit.' This being so, it is difficult to see how the problem of the *doctrine spéculative*—the establishment of moral law in an immoral society—may be achieved. Diderot's inner conflict was clearly shown in the ***Neveu de Rameau*** (written between 1761 and 1774, translated by Goethe in 1805, retranslated into French in 1823, first authentic text in 1891). The dialogue between Diderot and Rameau's nephew is spontaneous and witty, and the comments are pungent, bitter, and ironic. In essence, the work, which may properly be called a satire, challenges the cant of contemporary society and the hypocrisy of conventional morality. It offers, in the nephew, a vigorous and dramatic sketch of a parasite and an eccentric, a musician who is gifted yet unable to make his mark through insufficient talent, and who is shamelessly selfish and amoral. He is challenged up to a point by Diderot, and each antagonist scores in turn, each, however, remaining basically faithful to his views and to himself; and the debate is in the end inconclusive. This brilliantly conceived, highly original, and entertaining *divertissement* cuts deep. It has authenticity, and reveals the full complexity of Diderot's nature, and of his philosophical ideas. He argues that man may be devoid of meaning outside the context of society, since he must necessarily subordinate himself to the society of which he is an integral part. Yet man is unique, whether he be a genius or a *génie manqué*—great creative artist or an interpretative artist with some small element of creative power—thereby transcending the whole concept of man as predetermined. But perhaps the nephew, in his freedom from social convention, and from unquestioned belief in absolutes, may well owe his disposition to the *maudite fibre paternelle,* as he himself alleges, and to a natural reaction, given his nature, to the corrupt society in which he must fight for survival. From the philosophical standpoint, the work may be reconciled with determinism; it is the ethics that are ambivalent.

This inner conflict reached crisis point by 1773. Only a new work of fiction, superimposing on reality an imaginary story closely connected with, but not determined by reality, could crystallise his new attitude. His novel, *Jacques le fataliste* (1773, published 1796), which owes something to Laurence Sterne, and which has been considered as a kind of 'anti-*Candide*', is in the tradition of the picaresque novel and of the *conte philosophique*. L. G. Crocker has seen in *Jacques le fataliste* a moral experiment leading to no final or decisive result, and in a sense this is true. All Diderot's important late literary works may be seen as investigations of the psycho-physiological condition of man, his moral behaviour and his relative independence, with a view to confirming or modifying his materialist philosophy. Jacques, who believes in Fate, is involved in an endless argument with his master, who does not. As they journey along together, they retell the story of their lives and loves and listen to those of others whom they chance to meet. H. Bénac and others believe that Jacques and his master incarnate two aspects of Diderot. Yet Jacques' popular fatalism has little in common with Diderot's scientific determinism; and his sardonic interest in others differs greatly from Diderot's normal attitude of profound interest in the value of other people as individuals. It is possible that Diderot underwent a kind of catharsis in writing this novel, for although he does not reject determinism, he perceives that it cannot be made to apply indiscriminately to every action in life, as Jacques so ridiculously asserts that it can. The moral world is not wholly and obviously dependent on the physical, as Jacques believes, since man in his actions is incalculable. But the master's championship of free-will is equally foolish. Diderot demonstrates the limitations of man's understanding, leaving him able to discover only partial truth, for the limitations of Jacques and his master are common to all mankind, and make it difficult to establish philosophical

and ethical codes. Here it is the philosophical standpoint that is ambivalent, as was the ethical one in *Le Neveu de Rameau.*

In *La Religieuse* (1760, published 1798), a profoundly moving novel of the horrific experiences of a young girl without vocation immured as a nun, Diderot did not directly attack the Church, but opposed a man-made system running counter to nature, and vividly demonstrated some of the dangers of celibacy and of sexual repression. In the *Supplément au Voyage de Bougainville* (1772, published 1796), Diderot unfolded his dream of a free society based on tolerance and on sexual liberty in far-off Tahiti, without, however, indulging in Rousseau's form of primitivism, nor wishing to bring Tahiti to Paris. But in *Jacques,* as in many of his *contes* (*Les Deux Amis de Bourbonne,* 1773, *Ceci n'est pas unconte,* 1772, and *Mme de La Carlière,* 1773), he examined individual cases without assuming absolute moral standards. Jacques and his master are posturing mimes, just like the nephew, and remain pasteboard parodies of man. Their stories, with the countless but always significant digressions, nevertheless seem real to us; but they never illustrate the views of either the master or Jacques. The examination of one very long and constantly interrupted episode in the book—that of Mme de La Pommeraye—is enough to show the curious juxtaposition of psychological truth based on the facts of life, and of the ratiocination of would-be philosophers. Madame de La Pommeraye can scarcely be held to have been biologically determined either for good or evil, since her feelings can change from love to hate and revenge in a trice. Her transformation, like the change of heart of the prostitute d'Aisnon, is not predetermined but is presented as being possible in the circumstances. Side by side with such surprising transformations, the childish disputation of Jacques and his master forms a strange and seemingly irrelevant counterpoint. The conclusion reached is that there is no strict moral code even for ordinary people, and that man forced into a code of virtue is not necessarily happier. Punishment does not necessarily discourage wrongdoing: and it becomes clear that the easy morality Diderot had stressed so emotionally in the *drames* was founded upon unrealistic precepts. Each individual case has its *raison d'être,* for 'chacun apprécie l'injure et le bienfait à sa manière'. All mankind, like the characters in the book, protects itself with an artistic distortion of the truth, a simplification based on selection, which is part of the human creative force. When Jacques caused his master's saddle-strap to break and his master fell as a result, he thought he was proving the effects of cause and effect at the expense of free-will, whilst in fact he was simply demonstrating his own power. J. R. Loy [*in his Diderot's Determined Fatalist,* 1950] sees in this a demonstration of moral freedom, as opposed to unmotivated or pure free-will. It can, and should, however, be argued, that Diderot at no point invalidates his scientific determinism, nor closes the door on psychological determinism, since, unlike Condillac, he believes that the brain acts as a sixth sense and, unlike Helvétius, that heredity is stronger than environment in determining aptitudes and shaping a destiny. He also, unlike modern behaviourists, believed in the inheritance of acquired characteristics. In the *Réfutation de l'ouvrage d'Helvétius intitulé L'Homme* (published in

1875) and in the *Essai sur les régnes de Claude et de Néron* (1778), known as *Essai sur Sénèque* (which may be regarded as a late apologia), he revealed his new philosophical preoccupations, dissociating himself from the simpler theories held by his contemporaries, and modifying his own in the light of experience. At the personal level, he accepts a stoicism in which virtue is its own reward. At the philosophical level, it is the behaviour of man in his unpredictable creative life, whether it be ultimately determined or not, that fascinates him. His moral attitude, a *recherche du bonheur,* is founded on his monistic conception of the universe; so that society is seen as the union of mankind, and the solitary man remains condemned, as he was in the *Essai sur le mérite et la vertu,* as well as in the *Entretiens sur Le Fils naturel.*

Yet Diderot, whose life and works show constantly a deepseated desire to belong, is aware of being an outsider; this serves to explain his interest in the genius, who is an exceptional creature striving to live among ordinary men, and in individual man who also, after his fashion, partakes of genius. Faced with an apparently insoluble philosophical problem, and one which he does not intend to try to solve in a novel in which he himself as author determines the limited terms of reference, he manages to avoid opting for one answer or jettisoning one of two opposing philosophies. He now finds solutions of no practical consequence from the humanist standpoint, which he has discovered to be the only one truly based on an observation of reality, and from this discovery stems the humorous and ironic tone of his writing. Neither science nor philosophy can provide the total explanation of man, who in some measure shares the creative power commonly attributed to God, and who alone in the universe can seemingly make time itself stand still, as happens in moments of ecstasy and emotional stress. The apparent waywardness of Diderot's thought, if not of his reasoning, serves to prove the complexity of the exterior world it mirrors, and his method is not now simply the one he favoured in his *Pensées sur l'interprétation de la nature,* nor one that can be applied indiscriminately. It is the development of a personal form of apprehension and expression of reality. The dialogue form, which he made his own, can serve, as in the *Rêve de d'Alembert,* for the linear exposition of a thought, allowing pauses, for purposes of clarification, or as a springboard for a further development; it can also, as in *Jacques le fataliste,* prove even more exciting when a large number of characters, and we must include the author and the reader among them, bring out in lively conversation the strange complexity of human nature, the *pantomime des gueux,* which is the substance of the novel and summary of mankind.

Diderot, who had all the makings of a dramatist, and who sought to establish himself triumphantly in the theatre, achieved his ambition only by indirect means. For those of his plays that were presented brought no real success; and the most charming, *Est-il bon? Est-il méchant?,* is so closely related to Diderot's personality, experience, and situation in his own day that it has become esoteric, and has proved to be not wholly intelligible today. His best plays were those not specifically written in that form, nor for the theatre. In 1963, Pierre Fresnay and Jacques Ber-

theau proved superbly on the stage of the Michodière that *Le Neveu de Rameau* was outstandingly good theatre.

Some of his finest dramatic scenes are to be found in *Jacques le fataliste,* worthy of similar dramatic treatment to that accorded to *Le Neveu de Rameau,* in his *Correspondance* with Sophie Volland and also in his *Salons.*

His correspondence with Sophie, covering most of their long association, goes from May 1759 to September 1774, and forms one of the most fascinating revelations of a buoyant personality, an active mind incessantly reaching out towards new discoveries. To read that correspondence is to know intimately what manner of man Diderot was, in all his many parts—philosopher, artist, thinker, scientist, poet, dramatist, and wit; and to enjoy his ebullience, the anecdotes that pour from his ready pen, the hilarious juxtaposition of scabrous tales and moral dissertations, of joyous obscenities and prim judgements, of an incredible dialogue concerning the Grand Lama and a commentary on the arts. The personality emerging is gargantuan, admirable, and sympathetic: and the revelation so unaffected and so total that it leads to a more intimate understanding of his whole work. Apparent inconsistencies and contradictions disappear in the ample unfolding of his thought in all its diversity and all its unity.

Considerable light is also shed upon the milieu he frequented, and upon his social connections: Mme d'Epinay and her circle; his close friend the baron F.- M. Grimm; the baron d'Holbach; Abbé Ferdinando Galiani; and many other prominent people in his day. The letters are written in a vivid colloquial style, which is to be found in his essays, among them *Regrets sur ma vieille robe de chambre* (1792) and *Entretien d'un père avec ses enfants* (1773). These are the work of an exuberant conversationalist, an enthusiast, a gifted narrator, and an emotional warm-hearted lover: as indeed he was a warm-hearted friend, who must have suffered when his fifteen-year-long friendship with Rousseau came to an end in 1758, over an involved entanglement concerning J. P. F. de Saint-Lambert, Mme d'Houdetot, and Rousseau, and his newly formed friendship with Grimm.

In 1759, Diderot turned his attention to new problems and became an art critic, largely to help Grimm, to whose *Correspondance littérair* he had already made notable contributions. Grimm had asked Diderot to cover for him the [biennial] . . . exhibition of paintings at the Louvre, and was at first dismayed, and then amazed and delighted, to receive a book instead of the article he had envisaged. For the . . . years 1765-67 in particular he covered most successfully the salon, and in so doing developed an insight into the minds and techniques of painters, and into the growth of his own taste. It is recorded that, in . . . those years, he spent every night for a fortnight in assembling his ideas and writing his reports. These, now known as the *Salons* (1759-81), have set a standard for all subsequent art criticism, and although his approach is a literary one— it is the subject of the canvas, its meaning and message, that are of primary importance so far as he is concerned— he does frequently transcend the contemporary to grapple with the fundamentals of art. His vast enthusiasm for beauty and perfection, and his infallible instinct, led him to sound judgement far in advance of limited aesthetic considerations, and enabled him to arouse the delight he himself experienced in those who read his critical reviews; and to guide the public to look upon Chardin, Fragonard, Falconet, Vernet, Houdon, and above all, Greuze, with new eyes.

The aesthetic principle implied in his comments is sometimes at variance with his theories. Association with painters and artists, and his own observation, made him realise the inadequacy of the current theory of *le beau idéal*. He admired Greuze for his well-balanced pathos and bourgeois values; but he was equally appreciative of the realism and gift for colour of Chardin, and the subtle technique of Vernet. He condemned the artificial in style, and the rococo associated with Boucher. The catholicity of his taste, and his instinctive understanding of technical matters, remarkable in one with no practical experience of painting, prompted him to write commentaries so illuminating that they affected the later schools of painting, the Impressionists, and even the Surrealists.

Diderot's aesthetic theories and his criticism are closely linked with his ethics. They are to be found in a number of works, in particular in the *Encyclopédie* article 'Beau' (1751), in his *Salons,* and in the *Essai sur la peinture.* His article 'Beau', based as it is on a careful perusal of the works of French and English writers on the subject, develops a theory of beauty defined as the perception of relationships, in accordance with sensationalist philosophy and the relativity of all things. The great artist is defined as the man who seizes on significant relationships and analogies. He needs to be fired with enthusiasm and to be able to communicate his vision through sounds, colours, lines, or words. Diderot had already stressed the importance of gesture and expression in communication in *Lettre sur les sourds et muets* (1751), which deals with words as signs and symbols, abstractions not to be confused with reality; and also at some length with the problem of language especially inversion. The need for the close association of word and gesture, of sound and rhythm in the case of the poet, he stressed in the *Paradoxe sur le comédien.* Beauty springs from an awareness of harmonies of sound, colour, sense, rhythm, and structure, innumerable *correspondences,* to borrow Baudelaire's term, between sense impressions; and the quality of a work must depend upon the adequacy of the artist's power of expression. Art mirrors life, but cannot be equated with life: it is rather like the *clavecin oculaire* of Père Castel, . . . which Diderot found so fascinating. This clavichord had coloured ribbons, so that when it was played a 'symphony' of colour resulted.

The completion of the *Encyclopédie* had left Diderot without a regular source of income. To relieve him of financial worry, Catherine the Great first bought his library for a substantial sum, through an agent in Paris, with a request that he retain the books in Paris until she required them; she then appointed him librarian of them, with a yearly salary for the duration of his life. Diderot went to St Petersburg in 1773 to thank her, and was received with great honour and warmth. He wrote for her the *Plan d'une université pour le gouvernement de Russie* (first published

in an abridged form 1813-14), but his political ideas were too radical for the empress. After his death, his books and copies of all his manuscripts were dispatched to Catherine the Great by his daughter, Mme de Vandeul. The set of manuscripts which the latter retained, with a view to their ultimate publication, and was allowed to moulder for many years, was preserved and is now deposited in the Bibliothèque Nationale. It is only recently, through the availability of these and other texts, and the research that they have promoted, that a more exact impression of his thought has been achieved. In particular, it can now be shown that Diderot, in his later years, held more radical political views than was believed. The *Encyclopédie* was a major instrument in the war on existing social and political institutions: articles such as 'autorité politique', which stated that sovereignty rested with the people, and that on 'droit naturel', are of equal importance with those specifically aimed at abuses from which the people suffered, and in which he developed economic theories, discussing luxury, taxation, and population problems, as well as the principle of equality. Diderot stressed the need to divorce the powers of the state and Church and refused to subordinate political institutions to religious sanction. In *Observations sur les instructions de Catherine II à ses députés,* he went even further, in identifying sovereignty with the nation, which was invested with legislative power; and in voicing criticism of a benevolent despotism, as well as of tyranny. But although Diderot's political theories after 1765 are particularly interesting, it is the earlier ones that exercised some influence in shaping political opinion before 1789. These were not as conservative as has sometimes been stated: his suggested curbs on absolute power may appear Utopian, but they suggest a more democratic ideal than Rousseau's politics. They include natural law, and the inalienable civil liberty of the individual in society; the right to free speech transcending any reason of public security; and individual fulfilment in an open society. He has, however, little to say on structures of government or fundamental constitutional law. His theories are not always consistent, and vacillate between the idea that social controls are necessary, and the idea of anarchy. His politics spring from his ethics, and his philosophical determinism impedes his political thought, with which it appears to be at variance, though it is important to point out, as L. G. Crocker has done [in his *Nature and Culture,* 1963] that belief in determinism does not logically exclude belief in political freedom, in individual rights, or in the action of will and reason in history. The weakness of his political thought lies rather in his failure to relate the self-centred, anarchical man to the moral and political structure of society.

. . . The death of Sophie Volland in 1784 was a great grief to him, and he survived her by only five months, dying of coronary thrombosis on 30 July 1784, in the house in the Rue de Richelieu which Catherine the Great had put at his disposal.

It was through the intervention of his son-in-law that he was buried in consecrated ground at St Roch. Apocryphally his last words were: 'Le premier pas vers la philosophie, c'est l'incrédulité', a ghostly reiteration of a statement made in the early *Pensées philosophiques.* His open-minded scepticism, always present, is also always provisional: scepticism is simply an avenue to truth, and should never lead to mere negativism. He thus stands with Montaigne and takes up a position of great consequence within the tradition of humanism. A new definition of the philosopher emerges from Diderot's deceptively simple statement: 'Si l'on voit la chose comme elle est en naturem on est philosophe.'

Diderot was essentially of his age, and he transcended that age; 'Nous sommes l'universe entier,' Diderot once wrote [in his **Correspondance**] . . . and he might have been writing his own epitaph; he elaborated his original philosophical ideas in the light of this intuitive truth, within the terms of reference of his own age. The great bulk of his literary production was written mainly for his friends and circulated among them, and yet it may also be said that he wrote for the hypothetical intelligent future reader, who somehow managed to be present as a character, and a confidant, in so much of his work.

Perhaps the greatest genius of a century of brilliant men, he fulfilled his total promise within his own lifetime, but it is only in our time that he has been understood.

Arthur M. Wilson   (essay date 1972)

SOURCE: *Diderot,* Oxford University Press, 1972, 917 p.

[*In the following excerpt from his monumental biography* Diderot *(1972), Wilson analyzes the evolution of Diderot's aesthetic thought.*]

'We approach the moment of the Salon,' wrote Diderot to Falconet. 'Who will replace you at my side? Who will point out to me the good parts, the weak places?' Nevertheless, Diderot managed, and managed triumphantly. The Salon opened on 25 August 1767, and Diderot's letters to Sophie show that he visited the exhibition not less than twelve times.

Diderot approached this Salon with a vast panorama of ideas about the appreciation of beauty and the philosophy of art. His self-education in art had been proceeding for a long, long time. Between 1747 and 1751 he was doing extensive reading in treatises on painting, as the register of books borrowed from the Royal Library shows. Leonardo da Vinci's *Trattato della pittura* especially influenced him, as did the seventeenth-century French painter Le Brun's *Méthode pour apprendre á deviner les passions* (1702). Le Brun's treatise described and illustrated the gestures and expressions accompanying emotional states. Diderot shows not only in his art criticism but also in his dramas and novels an intense fascination with the physical manifestations of the emotions. His study of gestures, pantomime, and tableaux, and his interest in physiognomy—the relation between character and physical appearance—either originated in or was reinforced by his readings in Le Brun.

Diderot also kept abreast of contemporary writings on art. His widely known article 'Beau' in the **Encyclopédie,** as well as his later writings, show that he was familiar with the standard treatises though he often disagreed with them. Thus he summarized and commented upon Francis

Hutcheson's *Inquiry into the Origin of our Ideas of Beauty and Virtue* (1725), the *Traité du beau* (1715) of Jean-Pierre de Crousaz, the *Essai sur le beau* (1741) by Pére Yves-Marie André, *Les Beaux-Arts réduits á un même principe* (1746) by Abbé Charles Batteux, and Daniel Webb's *An Inquiry into the Beauties of Painting* (1760). Also influential, though Diderot mentioned it explicitly only once, was Abbé Jean-Baptiste Du Bos's *Réflexions critiques sur la poésie et sur la peinture* which had appeared in 1719. It furnishes many parallels to Diderot's ideas on allegory in painting and on the differences between poetry and painting, if indeed it is not the source. In the appreciation of art Du Bos was the schoolmaster of an age, a man whose influence in the long run was that of softening the rigidity of the rules of classicism. Du Bos was an empiricist much more than he was a traditionalist. His influence upon Diderot was considerable, so pervasive that perhaps it did not occur to Diderot that it required explicit acknowledgment. Diderot was also greatly influenced by the seventeenth-century painter and writer on painting, Roger de Piles. Familiarity with such standard works grounded his training more solidly in understanding the principles of art.

Through the years Diderot also educated his taste by studying whatever works of the Old Masters were available to him. Though his opportunities were restricted in comparison with those of the most casual tourist today, the collection of the Duke of Orléans at the Palais Royal and those of a few wealthy amateurs were accessible. He supplemented his knowledge by studying engravings; 'But what is a print,' he asked, 'in comparison with a painting?' All of this gave him standards of comparison, however, and as one leafs through his **Salons** one finds his pages peppered with references to Annibale Carracci, Claude Lorrain, Correggio, Domenichino, Guido Reni, Le Brun, Le Sueur, Michelangelo, Poussin, Raphael, Rembrandt, Rubens, Teniers, Titian, Van Dyck, Veronese, Watteau, Wouwermans, and many others. Diderot was always hungry to see pictures. And when he did, his comparisons were quick. In this very year 1767 he wrote to Falconet, 'I never thoroughly realized how great is the decline in painting until the acquisitions Prince Galitzin has made for the Empress caused my eyes to rest upon [these Old Masters]. . . . The skill of Rubens, Rembrandt, Poelenburg, Teniers and Wouwermans is lost. What a beautiful collection you are about to receive.'

Of all the painters of the past it was perhaps Poussin whom Diderot most admired. The references to Poussin, some forty of them scattered in Diderot's writings, show him seeking a model by which to inform his judgment and refine his taste. He mentions especially 'The Testament of Eudamidas.' This, he said, is 'the summit of painting.' What distinguishes this and all other Poussin paintings is great skill in grouping and composition, and deep concern for mood, gesture, and drapery. There is a classicism and formalism in Poussin's genius that make his art austere and it is significant that Diderot constantly holds him up as an example and unceasingly tries to plumb the secrets of his art. That Diderot, once the prophet of uncritical emotional response, could come to admire Poussin's genius shows how forcefully having to write the *Salons* was changing Diderot's ideas about discipline and control.

Although the exhibition of 1767 did not have the intrinsic interest of that of 1765—as Diderot himself wrote, 'There is nothing by Pierre nor Boucher nor La Tour nor Bachelier nor Greuze'—it is memorable to all students of Diderot for containing the Louis-Michel Van Loo portrait of him. The artist subsequently gave this magnificent portrait to Diderot. It now hangs in the Louvre. Diderot's comments regarding it are almost as revelatory as the portrait itself. He thought it a good likeness, 'But what will my grandchildren say when they come to compare my sorry works with this laughing, cute, effeminate, old male coquette? My children, I assure you that this is not me. In any one day I had a hundred different physiognomies, according to what was affecting me. . . . I have a mask that eludes an artist, whether there are too many things blended in it or because, the impressions of my soul painting themselves on my face in very rapid succession, . . . his [the painter's] task becomes much more difficult than he thought it was.'

More necessary than ever in writing the *Salon de 1767,* because it was the longest yet, was the inventiveness required to avoid monotony and keep the reader turning the page. Diderot displays 'the most incredible literary virtuosity in the art of incessantly varying the method of expression, tone and style.' His inveterate tendency to be divigatious, like an ill-trained hunting dog (as he described himself) that indiscriminately pursues anything that jumps up, here stood him in good stead. His tendency toward free association became an asset by awakening and keeping a reader's interest. In addition, he always strove to be concrete, and if he had to be abstract, at least not abstruse. Thus we see him criticizing a picture that he admires of a hen, but pointing out nevertheless that a broody hen has her feathers fluffed out. He interpolates a 'Satire against Luxury, in the Manner of Persius,' posing numerous political and social questions as well as aesthetic ones. When he comes to the seascapes of Joseph Vernet, he pretends that he is on a trip to the seaside, where he describes seven sites. This 'promenade de Vernet,' some fifty pages long and ranging over such subjects as the nature of dreams and what is virtue and the impossibility of free will, is a famous show piece, regarded as a model of Diderot's type of criticism. He keeps his readers on the alert, too, so as not to miss any of the erotic patches. 'You see, my friend, that I am becoming dirty, like all old men.'

Not least among the autobiographical bits that enlivened the *Salon de 1767* was Diderot's account of his misadventures in assisting a Polish-Prussian woman portraitist who was admitted to the Royal Academy of Painting in 1767 and who exhibited in the Salon of that year. This painter, Anna-Dorothea Therbusch, did not prosper in Paris at first and was in real necessity when Galitzin befriended her and put her up in the house he had rented from Falconet, on the Rue d'Anjou. Mme Therbouche (as she spelled her name in France) painted a portrait of Diderot that he and his daughter thought was superior to the one by Van Loo. This portrait depicted Diderot with only some loose covering thrown over one shoulder and in fact

on his own initiative he had sat for this portrait in the nude. 'She painted me and we chatted together with a simplicity and an innocence worthy of the earliest times.' Nevertheless, Diderot confessed in the *Salon de 1767* that he had been apprehensively aware of the fact that 'Since the time of Adam's sin one cannot command all the parts of one's body as one does one's arm; and that there are parts which want to when the son of Adam does not, and which do not want to when the son of Adam would very much like to.'

Diderot—in retrospect he called himself 'the poor *philosophe*'—entered with his usual zest into the campaign of helping Mme Therbouche. 'The poor *philosophe,* who is sensitive to destitution because he has experienced it himself . . . put himself out for nine months peddling the work of the Prussienne,' so much so that people promptly concluded that she must be his mistress. 'The poor *philosophe* put both great and small, friends and strangers, under contribution and caused the spendthrift artist to earn five or six hundred louis, of which not a penny remained at the end of six months.' Eventually the lady left Paris, laden with debts.

> What had not the poor *philosophe* done for her? And what reward did he get?
>
> Why, the satisfaction of having done good.
>
> No doubt, but nothing more than that except the marks of the blackest ingratitude. . . . The unworthy Prussienne ignores her creditors, who constantly come clamoring to my door. The unworthy Prussienne has already collected here her fees on pictures which she will not finish. The unworthy Prussienne insults her benefactors. . . . The unworthy Prussienne has given the poor *philosophe* a good lesson from which he will not profit; for he will remain goodhearted and foolish the way God made him.

Sometimes even Diderot knew that he was an easy mark.

With the *Salon de 1767,* Diderot had reported on five of the biennial exhibitions over a period of eight years. Taking each by itself, it might readily be supposed that Diderot's criticism was merely and simply impressionistic. But taking them as a whole, it begins to be seen that Diderot was consistently applying to them certain criteria and principles common to them all. In the first place, though he had many ways of looking at pictures and looked for many things in them, there was one method of seeing them that he tells us in 1751 he always employed. He looked at pictures as a deaf man (who already knows the topic of conversation) would observe the expressions and gestures of a group in conversation. This method, he claimed in his *Letter on the Deaf and Dumb,* allowed him to detect what was fumbling and ambiguous in a picture, what was really false in it. And long after 1751, his abiding interest in gesture and expression suggests that through the years this continued to be one of his criteria.

Diderot also trained himself to look for what he called 'the line of liaison.' In every composition, he claimed, there is a line that can be traced from the summit of one mass or group to another, traversing planes, sometimes receding into the depth of the picture, sometimes advancing towards the foreground. If this line is too tortuous and labyrinthine, the painting will be obscure. If the line comes to a full stop, then there will be a 'hole' in the picture. 'A well-composed picture will never have more than one true, unique line of liaison. Here we see the basis of Diderot's consistent emphasis on the importance of composition.

With equal consistency Diderot combated the persistent notion that a picture is just like a poem. This was what Horace had written in his *Ars poetica,* line 361—'Ut pictura poesis'—or at least this was the conventional way in which the Renaissance and its successors had interpreted the verse. Diderot was fond of pointing out that the attempt to follow 'Ut pictura poesis' involved artists in trying to paint ideas that were more verbal than pictorial. 'What goes well in painting will always go well in poetry, but this is not reciprocal'; and Diderot, whose *Letter on the Deaf and Dumb* had emphasized the difference between painting and poetry, returned to the same point in his *Salon de 1767.*

The distinction between painting and poetry was made even more emphatically by Lessing, whose *Laocoön* was published in 1766. Lessing had admiringly reviewed Diderot's *Letter on the Deaf and Dumb* in 1751. In all probability, therefore, his views as expressed in the *Laocoön* were influenced by Diderot. It is hard to say how much.

One of the essential differences between painting and poetry, according to Diderot (and here he followed the Abbé Du Bos more than he chose to admit), is that poetry readily calls up to the imagination a whole series of successive moments. Painting, on the other hand, is limited to just one (or at least it was until twentieth-century artists began working out the implications of Marcel Duchamp's 'Nude Descending a Staircase'). Diderot demonstrated his contention by analyzing in the *Salon de 1767* some lines from Lucretius. This limitation of painting brings Diderot back to a point that he had made earlier: Whether inspired by poetry or his own imagination, it becomes very important for the painter to choose for depiction the most precisely appropriate moment. Thus Diderot scolds Le Prince: 'You have chosen the ambiguous moment and the insipid one.' He prided himself that he could plan a picture and designate the moment of greatest interest and greatest pictorial potential. 'Chardin, La Grenée, Greuze and others have assured me (and artists do not flatter literary men) that I am almost the only one among men of letters whose ideas can pass on to the canvas almost as they are arranged in my head.'

Numerous are the other consistencies one may detect in Diderot's *Salons* through the years. He could always be counted on, again following the Abbé Du Bos, to dislike allegories in pictures; he always deplored the fussiness and non-functionalism of modern dress, comparing it unfavorably to the dress of the Ancients; he consistently valued 'historical' painting over genre painting or still lifes or portraits; and he consistently asserted that technique alone, though he progressively valued it more and more highly, can never be an end in itself and can never be a complete substitute for the quality of the imagination of the artist. 'Painting,' he wrote in the *Salon de 1765,* 'is the art of

reaching the soul through the eyes. If the effect stops at the eyes, the painter has gone only half way.'

The *Salon de 1767* does not repudiate any of the critical insights Diderot had exhibited in the previous *Salons,* but it adds to them some striking new ones. Most significant of all is his new awareness of the sublime as a component in the impact made by art. Why is this a fact, he asks, and what constitutes the sublime? In asking these questions Diderot is clearly showing the influence of Edmund Burke, whose *Philosophical Inquiry into the Origin of our Ideas of the Sublime and Beautiful* had been published in 1757. Diderot's answer is like Burke's. 'Whatever strikes the soul with wonder, whatever imparts a feeling of terror, leads to the sublime.' Obscurity, dimness, shadows add to the sense of wonder and awe. 'Great noises heard from afar, waterfalls that one hears but does not see, silence, solitude, deserts, ruins, caverns, the sound of muffled drums . . . there is in all these things an undefinable something of the terrible, the grand, and the obscure.'

Diderot, in pondering over what seems sublime, found that the consciousness of solitariness, of being alive when all about us has decayed or perished, the feeling of melancholy and nostalgia, are components of perceived sublimity. This led him to lay ever greater emphasis on the depiction of ruins, so that he has a great deal to say about the paintings of Hubert Robert, a young artist just back from Rome in 1767 and exhibiting in the Salon for the first time. 'The effect of these compositions, good or bad, is to let you sink into a gentle melancholy. . . . Majestic are the ideas awakened in me by ruins. All things come to nothing, everything perishes, all things pass away. Only the earth remains. Only time lasts. How old the world is! I walk between two eternities. Wherever I cast my eyes, the objects round about me announce their end and reconcile me to my own.' This, thought Diderot, was one of the ways in which Poussin was 'sublime': in a smiling, idyllic scene of shepherds in Arcadia, 'he lets my eyes fall on a tomb, where I read "Et in Arcadia ego."'

Another artistic interest of Diderot's accented more strongly in the *Salon de 1767* than in his previous ones was his speculation about sketches and their relation to the finished work of art. Why is it, Diderot asks himself, that sketches are so fascinating? The answer is Janus-faced: it concerns both the artist and the beholder. For each it signifies the overwhelming importance of the imagination. For the artist, the distinction between sketch and finished picture helps to define the relationship between genius and technique. 'A poor sketch will never give birth to anything but an inferior picture; a good sketch will not always give birth to a fine one. A good sketch can be the production of a young man full of verve and fire, whom nothing confines and who abandons himself to his impetuosity. A good picture can never be other than the work of a master who has deeply reflected, meditated, toiled. Genius it is that makes the good sketch, and genius cannot be had for the asking.' With that fascination Diderot would have turned to that serendipity of the disastrous flood of 1967, the uncovered synopias on Florentine walls.

Similarly, for the beholder a sketch powerfully stimulates the imagination, not infrequently satisfying it to a greater degree than does the finished work of art. 'Movement, action, even the passions are indicated by a few characteristic strokes; and my imagination does the rest. I am inspired by the divine afflatus of the artist. . . . One stroke only, one main feature: leave the rest to my imagination.' Diderot was here trying to analyze the secret of the elusive but indispensable communication between artist and viewer. It is not surprising that a man with an imagination as active and powerful as his would emphasize the role of the imagination not only in the creation of art but also in the appreciation of it.

Even before he began the series of the *Salons,* Diderot had declared that art—in this case he was discussing poetry—'demands a certain something of the enormous, the barbarous and the wild.' This conviction deepened because of his admiration of the poetic quality of the manners and customs of primitive peoples. Often he spoke of the Ancients in this regard, and the Ossianic poems, as we have already seen, were a revelation to him. In the *Salon de 1767* he continued to mention Ossian appreciatively, though the poem he paraphrased is in fact Thomas Gray's *The Bard.* 'The imitative arts,' wrote Diderot, 'need something savage, raw, striking, and enormous,' a conviction which had evidently been reinforced by Burke's ideas on the sublime. Naturally such conceptions carried Diderot far from an admiration of the rococo and probably explain his dislike of Watteau. 'By the late 1760's the creative impulse behind rococo art was virtually spent,' writes a British critic, 'and there are many signs in this *Salon [de 1765]* that Diderot is writing in the early stages of a period of transition.'

Diderot's trajectory as a critic of art proceeded from the general to the specific and then, much enriched by the empiricism of the concrete, back to the general again. In his early career, as exemplified by his article *'Beau,'* his analysis of beauty was abstract and rather rigid and circumscribed. But with the reporting of the Salons, Diderot's observations, focused on a continuing succession of actual paintings of all genres, became specific. Some years of this reporting made Diderot a humbler man. He became much more aware of the artist's point of view, of the way in which a painter or a sculptor perceives, and of the tremendous technique that a proficient artist must acquire. Had Diderot in the long run been satisfied only to comment on art picture by picture he would no doubt have ended up with a very impressionistic and disjunctive theory of aesthetics. Fortunately, as the years went by, his mind continued to work inductively on these problems, so that we see him trying to formulate general maxims as well as to express apt critiques on individual pictures. Such attempts at induction, at trying to state what might almost be called a 'field theory' of art, are visible in his *Essais sur la peinture,* completed in July 1766.

He had announced his intention to write a small treatise on painting in the concluding paragraph of the *Salon de 1765:* 'After having described and judged four to five hundred pictures, let us finish by presenting our credentials.' These credentials consisted of chapters whimsically entitled 'My Bizarre Thoughts on Draughtsmanship,' 'My Little Ideas on Color,' 'All that I have Ever Understood about Chiaroscuro,' 'What Everyone Knows about Expression, and Something that Everyone Does not Know,' 'Paragraph on Composition, in which I Hope that I Shall Speak of It.' This self-deprecatory way of presenting his credentials in fact raised some great issues. Diderot called for the scrupulous imitation of nature, the true imitation of nature, which of course he knew perfectly well was more difficult technically and philosophically than people commonly suppose. Incidentally, when Diderot used the word 'imitation,' as he did very frequently in his aesthetic writings, it was in the sense more readily conveyed to twentieth-century students by the word 'expression.' The scrupulous imitation of nature that he called for is accomplished by expressing her. In the *Essais sur la peinture* Diderot deplored the mannerism that comes from studying models one step removed from observation of nature itself. 'Mannerism comes from the drawing master, the academy, the school, even from the antique.' He recommended students' studying carefully the changes brought about in the human body and countenance by the way people earn their livings, by their station in life, by the subtle and pervasive effects on their appearance of any crippling or maiming they may have sustained. As for the use of color, he said sententiously, 'It is draughtsmanship that gives form to beings, it is color that gives them life.' And in regard to chiaroscuro he showed how minute and acute his own observations had been by mentioning the effect of gradations in light and 'the infinite reflections of bodies and shadows.' No wonder, then, that posterity has credited him with anticipating Monet and the impressionists, or, when he asks his reader to imagine a painting in which 'the depth of the canvas is cut up into an infinity of infinitely small planes,' with foreshadowing cubism. The *Essais sur la peinture* also raised (but did not settle) the exceedingly controversial problem of the relationship of art to morality.

The *Essais sur la peinture* is a transitional work, more experimental than satisfying. It shows Diderot asking the big, universal questions, but not as yet articulating replies as satisfactory as, with further thought, his answers were later to become. Nevertheless, the *Essais sur la peinture* greatly stimulated Schiller and Goethe, and Goethe published in 1798 a translation and an extensive commentary upon it.

In a letter to Grimm prefatory to the *Salon de 1767,* written perhaps a year later than the *Essais sur la peinture,* Diderot shows himself trying to find that eternal, immutable rule for the beautiful. And he has a name for it, 'the ideal model of beauty, the true line.' To many people it seems strange that Diderot the empiricist, the skeptical Diderot, the nominalist Diderot, should be seen groping for what appears to be a universalist, Platonic solution to his question. But this is to misunderstand Diderot's method. He was still the experimentalist, the man looking for inductions. He was trying to apply to the understanding of art a kind of Baconianism, and when he assumes that it is possible for an artist to achieve the ideal model of beauty, he is talking as a Newtonian might do when seeking to descry a law of nature.

Finding the ideal model of beauty is in Diderot's mind

very much like finding the good or searching for truth. To find them, he trusts the method that permeates his thinking and his writings, the dialectical method. In so unlikely a place as the *Essais sur la peinture* the presentation is essentially like a dialogue even though the second person is not present. The method of seeking truth through the tension of opposites is as conspicuous a characteristic of Diderot in his aesthetic as it is in his scientific or ethical thought.

In the quest for the ideal model of beauty, Diderot no sooner assumes that the Ancients can reveal it to us than he acknowledges that the study of nature, on the contrary, must never be disregarded. Here is Diderot's habit of dialectical thought at work. What are the relative merits of the two positions, he asks himself. How far may they be combined? No sooner does he say to the artist 'Copy nature,' than he realizes that the imitation of nature is something very different from nature itself. No sooner does he say that we must find truth in nature than he admits to himself that perhaps we find the truth of nature paradoxically in illusion. No sooner does he declare that no man can be a genius without giving himself up to the onslaught of the emotions than he begins to explore the proposition that great artistic creation requires the exercise of perfect self-command and self-control. This confrontation of opposing arguments, instead of rendering Diderot irresolute and inert, energizes and fructifies his thought.

By winnowing, it is possible to come to quite a firm conception of his aesthetics. But his method of articulating conflicting propositions makes it possible, indeed even unavoidable, to find numerous contradictory statements in his works. Perhaps the greatest virtue of this way of seeking truth is that it presupposes a tentative and nondogmatic approach. There is little, if indeed there is any, of the *a priori* in Diderot's thought. Yet the forcefulness of his style often misleads a reader into supposing that his views are more dogmatic than they really are. And confusing and contradictory statements do abound, greatly comforting his critics and leaving his adherents not altogether undismayed. He himself put it best:

> Look, my friend, if you consider the matter carefully, you will find that in everything our true opinion is not that from which we have never wavered, but that to which we have the most habitually returned.

Just how, according to Diderot, is the 'true ideal model of beauty' to be found? Certainly not by any reliance upon innate ideas of beauty. By this time John Locke's theories of psychology, set forth in his *Essay Concerning Human Understanding* (1687), had pervaded the western world. Based on a principle as old as Aristotle and one that had been perfectly acceptable to the medieval schoolmen, *nihil est in intellectu quod non fuerit in sensu*, Locke taught that the mind at birth is a blank slate on which the evidence of the five senses begins to write. Considering the venerability of this doctrine, the impact with which Locke's restatement and expansion of it struck the learned world is surprising. But it was a world getting used to the scientific method, a world digesting the discoveries of a Galileo, a Harvey, a Torricelli, and, latterly, a Newton, and adjust-

ing itself to the speculations of an empiricist like Lord Bacon. Locke's demolition of the doctrine of innate ideas had proved to be a powerful solvent of orthodox and traditionalist notions about religion and morality: the uproar in the eighteenth century over 'natural religion' and 'rational religion' testifies to that. But a doctrine corrosive to absolutist ideas in religion and ethics was equally so to absolutist ideas in art. God has not already placed inside us the criteria for judging art. What we know about the ideal model of beauty we have to learn.

This view of aesthetics fitted very comfortably into Diderot's accustomed patterns of thought. Even so, he still had the obligation of explaining who discovers 'the ideal model of beauty,' and how it is done. The discoverer, according to Diderot, is the genius. This is one of his functions, in fact his most important one. He is the one capable of new insights and fresh departures, and lesser men learn from him, distorting or attenuating his insights as they do so. 'The true line, ideal model of beauty, does not exist except in the head of the . . . Raphaels, the Poussins . . . the Pigalles, the Falconets.' The genius is rare. He is perhaps the most precious thing on earth, and, incidentally, so valuable to mankind that it can be argued that in a sense he is above good and evil. Much of *Le Neveu de Rameau* had argued this point. Was it not more important for Racine to be a great genius than a good man, even at the cost of his remaining 'deceitful, disloyal, ambitious, envious, and mean . . . ? A thousand years from now he will be drawing tears, be admired all over the earth. . . .' In contrast, most other men are 'mediocre'—damning word—content to be 'servile and almost stupid imitators of those who have preceded them.'

How does genius make the supreme discovery of the ideal model of beauty? One of Diderot's answers to this question is the common sense one that genius intuits the ideal model as a result of experience. Diderot was fond of telling how Michelangelo, seeking the most beautiful curve possible for the dome of Saint Peter's, hit upon exactly the one, as the calculations of the French geometrician Philippe de La Hire showed over a century later, that was the curve of greatest resistance. This is functionalism with a vengeance. It is not surprising that Diderot, with his constant solicitude that things should have utility, should find functionalism aesthetically satisfying.

Where does genius go to get the experience requisite for discovering the ideal model of beauty? Obviously genius goes to nature. This is indispensable, says Diderot, though he makes some qualifications in regard to the study of nature and nothing but the study of nature. For, in addition, genius must learn from the Ancients.

Diderot's conclusions about the interplay between the study of nature and the study of the Ancients is an example of his dialectical thinking at what is perhaps its subtlest, its most ambivalent and confusing, and its best. On the one hand, he wanted it understood that he was not a slavish and undiscriminating admirer of the Ancients: 'I do not have anticomania,' he insisted to Falconet. Had he lived in the 1680's when the Quarrel between the Ancients and the Moderns was taking place, Diderot would of course have sided with Fontenelle in defense of the Moderns. This was a position from which Diderot never wavered; but at the same time he was convinced that 'It may be generally observed that one rarely becomes a great writer, a great man of letters, a man of great taste, without being intimately familiar with the Ancients.' Falconet could insinuate that Diderot's knowledge of the Ancients was too much confined to their literature, and of course it is true that anyone in the eighteenth century trying to reach the spirit of ancient times had to rely in great part on literary remains. But Diderot not only attained a profound penetration of the Greek language, but was also well informed about Greek and Roman antiquities. In fact, Diderot was quite severe about the deficiencies of others in this department of learning, leaving one to infer that he was quite confident of his own competency. As he contemptuously said of the author of a book on the discoveries at Herculaneum, '. . . you have written a pretty bad book; and how could you have done better, having no taste for the fine arts and no profound knowledge of antiquity?' It is essential, if one is to understand Diderot the modern, to know also Diderot the Classicist.

Diderot's knowledge of Greek sculpture was of necessity based on the Hellenistic and Roman period, rather than the classic Hellenic models. Even Johann Joachim Winckelmann, in his famous and influential *Geschichte der Kunst des Altertums* (1764) was 'restricted entirely to late Greek works and copies of them.' And although Diderot poked fun at Winckelmann, saying that he was a fanatic who demanded that everyone acknowledge the superiority of the charms of his particular Dulcinea, it is nevertheless quite plain that Winckelmann's dwelling on the theme of ideal beauty had its influence upon Diderot's conception of the ideal model.

The success of the Ancients, according to Diderot, came from their having closely studied all the differences and alterations and deformities of the human body, and in this they showed themselves as possessing infinite patience and the most prodigious skill in observing nature. But this was the lesser part of their accomplishment. Using this knowledge, and 'with an astonishing discrimination, constantly eliminating the alterations and deformities of a defective Nature . . . [they were able] to raise themselves to the true model of beauty, to the true line. . . .' Diderot thought of this as the secret of the Ancient's tremendous achievement.

But the very success of the Ancients was a pitfall to their successors. A modern artist must learn from the Ancients, but he must do more than copy them. Merely to do so is no better than to copy a copy. The Modern artist must have the instinct, as they had had, of going to nature.

At this point it might be argued that Diderot's high-minded musings on how to attain the ideal model of beauty land with a bump in bathos. To follow nature is a truism. All of the exponents of the theory that art is the imitation of nature have for centuries been pressing the point home. It is very important to realize that Diderot was not content with the ordinary banalities about imitating nature. According to his quite surprising view, nature herself may be defective. Diderot even thought that 'the rigorous imitation of nature will render art poor, small-scale,

petty,' though he admitted that such imitation would never make art false or mannered.

The ideal model of beauty, then, is not found merely by imitating the Ancients nor even by imitating what Diderot calls 'subsistent nature,' the nature that subsists about us. The artist, while calling upon his knowledge of subsistent nature, must attain something that is more than *imitatio naturae*. He does this by the creative act. Thus is achieved the true line, the ideal model.

This theory of art may seem to many to be too Platonic—Diderot refers to Plato in the letter introducing the *Salon de 1767*. The merit of the theory, however, lies in the importance it allots to the artist. Implicit is a very exalted conception of his role. He is more than an imitator; he is a creator. Since the time of Plato and Aristotle the principle that art is an imitation of nature had been almost sacrosanct, and even in the eighteenth century the writings of Du Bos, Batteux, and even Burke and Hume had fitted in with it. Diderot carries forward what is essentially a new aesthetic, formulated earlier in the century by Shaftesbury and involving revolutionary new conceptions of what the artist does.

The novelty of Diderot's aesthetic lies in its analysis of the part played in the creative process by the imagination. His ideal model of beauty is an interior model. It is related to outside reality and is shaped and formed by a knowledge of the realness of objective facts, but nevertheless it is something which exists in the mind of the artist and exists nowhere else. It is to be discovered by an act of the imagination, disciplined by observation of nature and by a knowledge of technique. 'Confess, then, that this model is purely ideal and that it is not borrowed directly from any individual image in nature.' Diderot believed this so deeply that he declared that Phidias 'had in his imagination something beyond nature.' This conviction was reinforced by the advice Garrick had given to a French amateur as to how to improve his acting: 'There is an imaginary being whom you must take for a model.' There is no sort of poet, cried Diderot—our idiom would say 'creative person'—to whom Garrick's lesson is not appropriate. Diderot of course recognized that less gifted persons, sensitive to nature and content with simply copying her, could also practise the arts, but such artists, he agreed with Garrick, will be mediocre. The pace is set by the genius, whose knowledge of the ideal model is vouchsafed to him by the quality of his imagination.

Diderot's early conviction, a quite uncomplicated one, was that genius was little more than quickness of sensitive reaction added to copiousness of emotional response. Little by little he came to add to this formula the counterbalancing elements of self-discipline and self-control. Accordingly his aesthetic theory underwent a slow but extremely significant evolution which most of the nineteenth-century critics quite overlooked, deeming him simply an exponent of *sensibilité*. Today this evolution is being more thoroughly explored. Probably because Diderot was becoming familiar with the professional hazards and difficulties of artists, he inclined more and more to the view that the great artist, though his imagination must be stimulated and fructified by emotional response, must not allow it to overwhelm him and make him incoherent or, in Diderot's word, 'mediocre.' His theory, fully enunciated a few years later in his *Paradoxe sur le comédien,* is strikingly similar to the Wordsworthean formula of emotion recollected in tranquillity.

Diderot's theory of aesthetics was comprehensive enough to include not only the artist but also the auditor and the viewer. Their paths cross at the point on the aesthetic map marked 'Taste'. Like so many of his generation, like Hume in his important essay 'Of the Standard of Taste,' Diderot tried hard to answer satisfactorily the question, What is taste? The eighteenth century wrestled mightily with this problem—which is one of the reasons why the very word 'aesthetics' was invented at that time.

The new Lockean epistemology and psychology, by undermining the doctrine that ideas of beauty are innate, inevitably raised the whole question of how, then, does an artist or a public know when a thing is beautiful. The very word 'taste' connotes standards and values against which a specific work of art can be measured. Therefore the concept of taste bulks large in the consideration of any critic who is concerned, as Diderot was, lest the artist become too exclusively subjective, too oblivious either of objective reality or of artistic traditions. Correlatively, a critic such as Diderot is also concerned with discovering the criteria by which the public can be educated, and educate itself, in the appreciation of beauty.

Writing in 1776, Diderot defined taste. His was a definition, it is to be noticed, that includes both the artist and the public. Taste is acquired through experience and study, both on the part of the one who creates and of the one who appreciates.

> [It is] a facility, acquired by repeated experimentation, of seizing hold of the true or the good, with the attendant circumstances that make it beautiful, and of being promptly and vividly touched by it.

In the desire to understand the mystery of how an artist communicates with the person who views his art—and probably in the desire to assist in this process—Diderot became as fascinated with communication theory in the domain of plastic art as he was in the area of linguistics. He believed, as one aesthetician has recently remarked, that works of art require an active participation on the part of the beholder. And the artist, he further believed, should communicate not only with his contemporaries but also with succeeding generations. By doing so the artist helps to shape both the present and the future. This is the artist's supreme function, this is his glory. And it is this conception, reached after a rather fumbling start, that explains why Diderot's letters to Falconet about posterity finally reach such a high plane.

Surveying the artist's function from a height as lofty as this, Diderot is evidently thinking of a public—a posterity—that expands, rather than of one so specialized that it narrows to the point of vanishing. To Diderot art is socially important, so that in much of his art criticism he sounds like a sociologist quite as much as an aesthetician. He has in mind an art that speaks to a whole nation. Patently Di-

derot thought that art was too important to be left just to the patrons and collectors and 'amateurs,' a race that he emphatically cursed. Probably he thought, though he never made such a claim explicitly, that people like himself performed the very important function of educating people's taste.

Part of Diderot's problem, which he never solved satisfactorily, was to discover how to popularize art without vulgarizing it. It was highly characteristic of the Enlightenment to seek greater participation for an increasing number of human beings—participation in rational inquiry, in the benefits of technological improvement, in a broader range of decision making: the logic of the whole orientation of the *philosophes* impelled them towards a greater democratization. Yet, with the exception of Rousseau, they were often hesitant and ambiguous about believing that *le peuple* was capable of making decisions without caprice. A comparable problem arose for Diderot in the realm of art. He was not satisfied to accept a greater democratization of art appreciation if its quality was threatened by the process. 'But what,' he had asked agonizingly, 'do all these principles signify, if taste is a matter of caprice, and if there is no eternal, immutable rule for the beautiful?'

Diderot had identified an enormously important question. His difficulty lay in trying to define the term 'taste' in a way that anybody could readily follow and practise. How does one help a public to know what are the canons of good and bad taste? An insoluble problem perhaps. Diderot tried to be basic; he tried to trace aesthetic experience to its psychological fundamentals and to find in the nature of man the specifications for recognizing beauty. But his definition of taste becomes slippery and unsatisfactory because he links the abstract idea of beauty with those other abstract terms, the true and the good. Such a definition of taste, as Cassirer pointed out [Ernst Cassirer in his *The Philosophy of the Enlightenment,* 1951], though it tries to avoid dogmatism and preserve an empirical approach, despairs of defining beauty in itself and begins to speak of art in terms of ethics.

The pitfall of making art a handmaiden of morals is an obvious one, but not easy to avoid when one entertains, as Diderot did, the very highest opinion of the function of art in a culture. Had he thought of art as being a subordinate or insignificant aspect of culture, it would have been possible for him to adopt a top-lofty attitude of art-for-art's sake, thus escaping the confusions and ambiguities of the moral meaning of art. But this he did not do. Probably it was from Shaftesbury that he first derived the conviction that in some profound and unsentimental way art must serve a moral purpose.

Some of Diderot's comments in the *Salons* are surprisingly puritanical. Speaking of lascivious works of art, he asked, 'What can strike the balance between a picture, a statue, no matter how perfect, and the corruption of an innocent heart?' He admired Boucher's technique but thought that his subjects corrupted morals, and he was even harsher about Boucher's son-in-law, Pierre-Antoine Baudouin, whose subjects did rather tend towards the suggestive. In the *Essais sur la peinture* Diderot wrote:

I am not over-strict. I read my Petronius sometimes. Horace's satire, *Ambubaiarum,* pleases
me as much as it does the next man. The infamous little madrigals of Catullus, why, I know
three-fourths of them by heart. . . . I pardon
the poet, the painter, sculptor, even the philosopher, an instant of good spirits and folly. But I
do not want a painter to dip his brush there all
the time, and thus pervert the aim of the arts.

And a few years later he wrote,

I am not a Franciscan; nevertheless I confess
that I would willingly sacrifice the pleasure of
seeing beautiful nudes if I could hasten the moment when painting and sculpture become more
decent and moral, would think of co-operating
with the other fine arts in inspiring virtue and
purifying *moeurs.*

Diderot is here expressing the effect of the gradual disappearance of one style, the rococo, and the emergence of a
new one, neo-classicism. He was in the spirit of the age,
and he probably contributed considerably to its spread
himself by his discussions of art with artists and connoisseurs, though of course his written *Salons* could have little
direct effect on the substitution of the new style for the old.
The frivolity as well as the grace of the rococo, so admirably suited to the tastes of a leisured and aristocratic society, was giving way to a somewhat sterner art, more concerned with heroes, with Roman virtue, with grandness in
simplicity, and with the family virtues that Diderot himself highly esteemed. What, then, did Diderot think
should be the aim of the arts?

To make virtue attractive, vice odious, and ridicule hard-hitting, such is the intention of every
honest man who picks up the pen, the brush, or
the chisel.

This statement excellently portrays Diderot's moral seriousness in relation to the arts, though it has often been
criticized as laying too heavy a burden on them.

Diderot's fondness for the paintings of Greuze has greatly
contributed to the accusations that his taste was often
'dreadfully sentimental.' Greuze nowadays is enjoying a
revival of esteem, but it is for his portraits more than for
the genre scenes that Diderot and his contemporaries admired him so much. Diderot was usually disdainful of por-
traiture, his reason being that the better the portrait as to
likeness, the further it was from the ideal model of beauty.
Although he admitted that 'there is no great painter who
has not known how to do portraits' (he mentioned Raph-
el, Rubens, Le Sueur, and Van Dyck), what he found most
to admire in Greuze were canvases like 'The Village
Bride,' 'The Paralytic, or The Fruits of a Good Education,' 'Filial Piety,' and 'The Ungrateful Son.' 'This
Greuze, truly he's my man. The genre pleases me; it is
moral painting.' And of a picture entitled 'The Well-
Loved Mother,' showing a large family of children romp-
ing with their mother—Mme Geoffrin called this picture
'une fricassée d'enfants'—Diderot wrote, 'It is excellent,
both in respect to talent and to morals. It preaches population. . . .'

Had Diderot confined himself to admiring Greuze's genre

pictures, he would have saved himself from anything
worse than seeming now to be slightly ridiculous. But he
was also exceedingly fond of Greuze's sentimental pictures of young girls, canvases such as 'The Broken Pitch-
er,' 'The Little Laundress,' 'The Girl with a Broken Mirror,' and 'The Girl Weeping for her Dead Bird.' Of this
last, hung in the Salon of 1765, Diderot wrote, 'Soon one
surprises oneself conversing with this child and consoling
her. This is what I remember having said to her on different occasions'; and there follow several pages of over-
heated apostrophe. It is dismaying to realize that Diderot
mistook these feelings of his to be appreciation of art. The
plain fact is that when he looked at these pictures he felt
the way middle-aged men are likely to feel when they see
a provocative young starlet in a movie. 'Such, alas, is the
effect produced upon him,' Jean Seznec writes [in his "Diderot and the Pictures in Edinburgh," *Scottish Art Review*
VIII, No. 4 (1962)], 'by the false innocence of Greuze's
girls, those little hypocrites who have always broken their
pitchers, cracked their mirrors, or lost their pets.'

Having reached the nadir of Diderot's art criticism, it is
well to remind ourselves of his apogee. This is to be found
in his admiration of Chardin. Of the some 120 contemporary artists with whose works he was familiar, Chardin is
the one Diderot consistently praised the highest. This he
did even though he thought Chardin's subjects, his still-
lifes and domestic scenes, belonged to a subordinate and
somewhat inferior category of art. To explain why Chardin's paintings were nevertheless so excellent, Diderot repeatedly referred to Chardin's 'magic' and spoke of him
as being 'the greatest magician that we have.' Diderot
sometimes wrote as though hard put to explain Chardin's
greatness precisely. 'One pauses before a Chardin instinctively, just as a traveler, fatigued by the road, sits down
almost without noticing in the spot that offers him a grassy
seat, silence, flowing water, coolness and shade.'

More specifically, Diderot speaks of the 'sublimity' of
Chardin's technique, of the simplicity and lifelikeness of
his pictures, of the 'largeness' of his execution. Largeness,
he thought, is 'independent of the extent of the canvas and
the size of the objects. Reduce a Holy Family by Raphael
as much as you like, you will not destroy its largeness of
execution,' a statement which shows Diderot thinking in
terms of pictorial concepts. Diderot spoke repeatedly of
Chardin's being a consummate colorist, and also appreciated his skill in reproducing reflections. 'This is the man
who understands the harmony of colors and reflections. . . . He it is who observes how the light and its reflections flow over the surface of objects, who inexpress-
ibly seizes and reproduces them in their inconceivable
confusion.' In short, 'Nature,' wrote Diderot, speaking
both of Buffon the naturalist and Chardin the painter, 'has
admitted them into her confidence.'

As the author of the *Salons,* Diderot has usually been favorably received by posterity, the precedent being set by
Sainte-Beuve's influential essay 'Diderot' (1851) and continuing on to a recent judgment [by F. J. B. Watson
(1958)] in the *Connoisseur* that the *Salons* are 'the best
journalistic art-criticism that has ever been written. . . .'
Now and again a vociferous minority report has been filed,

as in the fulgurous essay by Ferdinand Brunetière (1880), complaining that Diderot was too subject-bound and too literary in his judgments: 'There is nothing for us, or almost nothing, to take from the **Salons** of Diderot. It is even to be regretted that our century has taken as much as it has.' And a twentieth-century Brunetière *redivivus* [Virgil W. Topazio in "Art Criticism in the Enlightenment," *Studies on Voltaire and the Eighteenth Century* XXVII (1963)] complains of Diderot's approach to art as being 'highly subjective, dogmatic, moralistic, and subject-oriented.' The preponderance of critical opinion, however, is consonant with the recent judgment [of Georges de Traz in his *De Diderot à Valery: Les écrivains et les arts visuels,* 1960] that it is 'his inimitable style, so living, so colorful, that makes the reading of him, even when one does not agree with him, an enchantment.' The numerous reviews of Jean Seznec's definitive edition of the **Salons** testify by their consensus to the appeal of Diderot's criticism and to the impact that it has had.

As one surveys Diderot's aesthetic theory as a whole, including his criticism in the **Salons,** it is well to concede that his touch was surer in the discovery of unexplored relationships than it was in the neat and thoroughgoing disposition of them. This is because Diderot was, as has been well said, an uncompleting man, a finder and initiator, not a concluder and a finisher. This is characteristic of almost everything he thought about, his views on science as well as on art, his theories of the origin of the universe and of life as well as his search for proper guidelines in ethics and in politics. But this characteristic, rather than being a reproach to him, is the reason for his importance in the life of his century and the source of his being so deeply interesting to ours.

Jean Starobinski   (essay date 1973)

SOURCE: "The Man Who Told Secrets," in *The New York Review of Books,* Vol. XX, No. 4, March 22, 1973, pp. 18-21.

[*Starobinski is a Swiss scholar who is considered one of the outstanding critics of the latter part of the twentieth century and who is best known for studies of Rousseau, Montaigne, and Diderot. In the following excerpt, he focuses on Diderot's goal of laying bare "everything which is so painstakingly concealed by ignorance, hypocrisy, and falsehood."*]

Diderot indeed occupies a central place in the Enlightenment. Stubborn courage enabled him to bring the great ark of the **Encyclopedia** safe to harbor in 1772 after twenty-five years of untiring labor. The **Encyclopedia** has been seen, and rightly so, as a symbol of the triumph of the bourgeois spirit; it aimed at bringing together knowledge of all kinds and harnessing it to the rational exploitation of natural resources for the common good. To use Bernard Groethuysen's expression, it gave its readers a proprietor's view of the world. Similarly, Diderot made a decisive contribution to almost every field he touched on. He launched aesthetics and art criticism on a new career, he was instrumental in changing the face of the theater, he invented the first experimental novels. He had an impressive insight into the tasks and methods of the new biology.

He was master enough of the learning of his age to be able to claim without exaggeration that nothing human was foreign to him; mathematics, technology, music, painting, sculpture, medicine, economics, education, and politics, all of these, in almost equal measure, were his concern as a *man of letters.* This expression possessed in his day a breadth of meaning which it has gradually been losing ever since. In his role as a European, too. Diderot is a central figure; he is among those who introduced, assimilated, and popularized in France Bacon, Shaftesbury, Richardson, and Sterne—and in his turn he was to influence Lessing and Goethe and leave his imprint on Hegel and his progeny. . . .

One of the dominant tendencies of Diderot's mind is his urge to discover secrets, to bring them to light, to expose them to the general gaze; his aim is to lay bare everything which is so painstakingly concealed by ignorance, hypocrisy, and falsehood. Such is the lesson which his early work **The Indiscreet Jewels** (1748) inculcates in its libertine and rococo fashion. The starting point of this youthful "novel" is the merry hypothesis of a magic ring which enables bystanders to hear the words spoken by a part of the female body that is not normally endowed with speech; a potentially endless succession of short narratives interspersed with commentaries lets the amused reader into secrets which decency would have kept hidden. It is the lifting of a taboo. And what we discover by way of this near-pornography is what Lockean philosophy had already taught us in more modest terms: that man falls prey to *uneasiness* if he does not constantly renew the sensations which give him the feeling of his own existence, that boredom lies in wait for him if he does not maintain a rapid sequence of pleasures, surprises, and occupations of every possible kind.

This is why modes of behavior and works of art inspired by Lockean psychology place so much stress on variety, unexpectedness, and inconstancy, and time comes to be experienced as a string of discontinuous moments, this being reflected in literature by occasional verse, brief tales, miscellanies, and collections of anecdotes and letters where the serious and pleasurable are mixed in an unforeseeable combination. Voltaire was a master of this technique; Diderot did no more than experiment with it. He was not the sort of man to make frequent use of the frivolous literary devices which had served his purpose in **The Indiscreet Jewels.** It was easy for him to do without allegory, satirical fairy tales, and fairground exoticism, but he never lost his curiosity about the life of the body, about desire and sexuality, or his taste for pulling aside the draperies and revealing the truth for all to see.

There is no denying that the reason why many of Diderot's works are so attractive (and so provocative) is that they are largely made up of the revelation and complete exposure of an inside story. What makes **The Nun** (1760) such a scandalous novel? Essentially it is the sudden light which it casts on what goes on behind convent walls, the unwilling vocations, the secret illegitimate births, the disastrous physiological effects of forced chastity. It is on the body, deep down in the organism, that convent life finally leaves its mark. In his nun's confessional tale Diderot's penetrating medical insight shows us how illness, sexual perversion, and madness are the ultimate consequences of a refusal to obey what he calls "nature." The reader not only sees into the cells of the convent, he gains access to the secret mechanisms of female existence (as it was understood by the medical science of the eighteenth century).

It is just the same with *Rameau's Nephew* (begun in 1761); the satire here consists largely of the way Diderot uses his uninhibited bohemian hero to expose to the public gaze the secret way of the world. Driven from the rich man's house where he has been living the life of a parasite, the nephew reveals the intrigues and hidden vices of the world of high finance; expelled, because of his impertinence, from the circles where an anti-*philosophe* plot is being hatched, he reveals all their most secret absurdities and crimes; he knows everything and hides nothing, and above all he flaunts his own immorality, which is so perfectly adapted to the immorality of his society.

In all these examples Diderot reveals the truth by proxy: the "jewels" confessing their own misdemeanors, the nun Suzanne Simonin telling the tale of her torments, the unruly nephew lifting the veil which hides the dinner table and boudoir of a financier living with a mediocre actress. What of the times when Diderot speaks in his own name? This is Diderot the editor of the *Encyclopedia,* and here again he strives to reveal and divulge secrets to the general public. To undertake a task of this size it is not enough to be spurred on by a deep hate for irrational systems of belief, not enough even to be convinced of the need for a complete inventory of the arts and sciences. It needs too a certain instinctive urge, which enables one to find pleasure in exposing what is concealed. To uncover Nature's secrets, to capture the secrets of technology and share them with the whole world, to reinforce the written word with visual representation: these were some of Diderot's most cherished aims.

Arthur M. Wilson [in his *Diderot,* 1972] gives us an illuminating quotation from a text on *The History and Secret of Painting in Wax* (1775) in which Diderot proclaims quite openly his passion for bringing things into the light of day and defends it in the noblest moral terms. Of course it is quite possible to accept these humanitarian arguments. But at the same time it is hard not to give equal weight to a less rational sort of motive. This is how Diderot puts it:

> Nothing is more contrary to the progress of knowledge than mystery. . . . If it happens that an invention favorable to the progress of the arts and sciences comes to my knowledge, I burn to divulge it; that is my mania. Born communicative as much as it is possible for a man to be, it is too bad that I was not born more inventive; I would have told my ideas to the first comer. Had I but one secret for all my stock in trade, it seems to me that if the general good should require the publication of it, I should prefer to die honestly on a street corner, my back against a post, than let my fellow men suffer.

This is his constant refrain. Elsewhere we read:

> We must make public both the results of our research and the means by which we have achieved them. Mere publication is not enough; it must be complete and unequivocal. Let us hasten to make philosophy more accessible. Is not nature already hidden enough without our adding a veil of mystery; is experimental science not difficult enough as it is?

In his aesthetic theory, Diderot shows the same taste for bringing everything completely into the open, the same desire to have inner life totally accessible to the eye. This is why he always gives expressiveness pride of place in his art criticism. Among painters, even though he appreciates the "magical" colors of a Chardin, he gives the highest praise to artists who can catch on canvas the high point of an emotional drama, and he is full of admiration for painters who can make every attitude, every face, and every gesture both expressive and immediately comprehensible. He always demands the fullest possible manifestation of emotion in a code or language which is that of the body itself. It is the same with the theater, which he expects to convey in full both the characters' social position and their moral dilemmas. His social realism goes hand in hand with emotional expressionism. In the theater of his dreams the most intense moments are *tableaux* where gesture, originally the servant of the spoken word, finally supersedes language in the name of a more immediate, more "hieroglyphic" rendering of emotion.

These feelings which the heroes of Diderot's "serious comedies" are all too ready to display hardly seem to correspond to the real secrets of our inner lives; in them we recognize, somewhat despondently, the old repertoire of mime laid down by the most conventional theories concerning the physical expression of the passions. Perhaps Diderot felt embarrassed when the laws of the theater obliged him to give his characters a fixed and stable identity. Conversely, he is extraordinarily successful in laying bare the "inside story" of natural forces beneath the apparent stability of individual existence. He is at his masterful best when he abandons himself to the pleasure of debunking the illusion of personal autonomy and imagines, beyond the diversity of living beings, the still more amazing diversity of atoms, all endowed with their own life and combining and recombining *ad infinitum* in the flux of space and time.

The ocean of matter so enthusiastically evoked in Diderot's dialogue *D'Alembert's Dream* (1769) is made up of an unimaginable number of particles, each one unique, each one possessing an elementary kind of life and impelled by a basic erotic energy which must eventually give rise to every conceivable combination of matter. What Diderot loves above all else is to reveal by an act of imaginative insight the universal force of generation which haphazardly gives birth to ephemeral and monstrous forms of life, to species capable of survival, and to strange hybrids; it is this force, aided by time and chance, that eventually produces thinking beings, men of genius, and the achievements of science.

Diderot's evolutionism, which does not rule out the possibility of periodic returns to chaos, is bound up with a dynamic and somewhat anthropomorphic image of matter as an obstinate *arriviste*. He uses all his lyrical powers to sing the praises of the material world; nothing excites him more than images of the production and reproduction of life. We should remember that he was writing at a time when one of men's greatest fears was the depopulation of the globe. This is why questions of morality and immorality give way to the claims of public utility. **D'Alembert's Dream** ends on the daring and entertaining hypothesis of a hybrid race produced by cross-breeding men with goats; why condemn bestiality if it can give us a vigorous new subproletariat to do our dirty work for us? The utility principle comes first.

This image of the hybrid is a significant one. The inspiration to which Diderot owes it is itself a hybrid of intellectual insight and erotic curiosity. The continuing appeal of **D'Alembert's Dream** is due to a cross-fertilization of scientific thought and cosmic lyricism. It soon becomes clear that in every field, including that of literary style, Diderot was a propagator and creator of hybrids. Of the traditional genres the only one he retained and renewed was satire. Why was this? Because satire is by definition the genre which invites and welcomes heterogeneity. Diderot excels in confusing every kind of hierarchy and blurring every kind of boundary; he is a creator of half-breeds.

Rameau's nephew, the most typical of them all, is a rare blend of villainy and intelligence; he has surprising sensitivity and artistic ability, yet he is incapable of creating anything—he is a hybrid of talent and impotence. Jacques in **Jacques the Fatalist** is a mixture of intellectual superiority and social inferiority. The work named after him is a hybrid of dialogue and narration. The middle-class drama which Diderot advocated is in reality the bastard child of comedy (which was thought a "low" genre) and tragedy (which until then had been considered the only theatrical genre capable of attaining the "sublime"). It is no accident that Diderot's first stage hero is a "natural son." Nor should we forget that Diderot's nun is an illegitimate daughter and that by having her write her life story in the first person Diderot is attempting the curious experiment of identifying himself with the tormented existence of a woman's mind and body. The principle of hybridization leads to literary androgyny.

To think of man as an aggregate of living molecules; to admit the possibility of each organ having its own separate existence; to reduce the diversity between living beings simply to differences of physical organization: is not this tantamount to propounding a doctrine of implacable determinism? In this scheme of things man becomes the plaything of the various elements which make up his body—and of the chance which brought them together. If we read it to the bitter end, doesn't his "inside story" lead us to an "outside story" where everything depends on the laws of matter?

Arthur M. Wilson's book is very illuminating on the subject of Diderot's atheism; in particular he shows with the utmost clarity how this deterministic atheism raised more problems than it solved. If Diderot was tempted by a hedonist ethic which removes all moral barriers and encourages man to make himself happy by satisfying all his supposedly "natural" instincts, he never abandoned the sto-

ical tradition which advocates discipline and self—mastery. In the most elaborate account he has left us of his thinking on biological subjects, he anticipates the ideas of modern neurology about the unifying control exercised over the "peripheral" functions by the cerebral "centers." However indulgent his moral thinking may be to the satisfaction of the senses, he always endeavors to go beyond the kind of pleasure which is limited to isolated impulses. Man, even if he is matter through and through, can and should exert his will, controlling his sensibility (thought of as peripheral and located in the diaphragm) and performing deeds of outgoing generosity which will win him admiration and gratitude from generations yet unborn.

Self-control and detachment are the qualities which the **Paradox of the Actor** (1773) ascribes to the great actor, and which Diderot elsewhere attributes to "great men" in general. Resistance to despotism, which Diderot preached more and more fervently in the final years of his life, presupposes a rebellious individual capable of preferring death to slavery. Political freedom is thus made dependent on a power of self-determination which can only spring from the individual will. So Diderot's determinism leads not to fatalism but to voluntarism, a voluntarism conscious of the conditions which limit the exercise of the will. Willed action may depend on the bodily make-up of the individual and the chain of cause and effect in the physical world, but this does not prevent man from being a creature who can be modified and can modify himself. Diderot particularly likes to cast himself in the role of the master-mind who manipulates others for their own good and enlightens them for their greater happiness. The concluding pages of Arthur M. Wilson's book show very well how for Diderot the hope for posthumous fame in this world replaces the promised immortality which theology had located in the next.

In this way Diderot maintains a belief in the autonomy of the individual. He preserves a constant balance between the forces that work for the unity of the whole and the centrifugal tendency of the parts, the molecular elements, to live their own separate lives. This results in a vitalist mythology in which the synthesizing efforts of the active faculties are pitted against the happy passivity of dissolution into elementary living particles. Diderot's way of choosing active self-determination while still recognizing the pleasure that comes from spontaneity is not without its resemblance to Freudian metapsychology and could be considered its equal as a poetic-scientific account of reality. Diderot favors the victory of the whole over the separatism of the parts. But ultimately this victory cannot be a complete one; some sort of compromise is inevitable. We may desire the unity of the individual, but we must accept that death, sleep, inconsistency, and internal contradiction are inseparable from the human condition.

Diderot was preoccupied then by the opposition between continuity and discontinuity. This problem faced him equally in the field of scientific knowledge. As first envisaged by its authors, the **Encyclopedia** was to provide a complete exposition of the system of human knowledge. Their desire for coherence and systematic order is shown, among other things, by their use of cross references to compensate for the arbitrary discontinuity of the alphabet. But Diderot himself was the first to admit that these cross references were less successful than had been hoped in making the *Encyclopedia* a systematic whole. Each separate article is an entity in itself, a mini-treatise followed by another mini-treatise—and so on. Instead of a vast unified map of the sciences and arts, all linked together and mutually interdependent, we are given a succession of rapid images, each one relatively independent of the rest. Dispersion has won the battle against systematic organization.

This love of Diderot's for what is immediately and manifestly present shows itself similarly in his willingness to give expression to flashes of thought, sudden bursts of feeling, and unforeseen objections. His flow of speech is always being deflected and interrupted; unexpected questions, digressions, and breaks of continuity are the ever-recurring signs of the sudden and disruptive incursion of the living present into the pre-established order of logical thought. In his work we find a permanent tug of war between the stability which a rationalist representation of the world strives after and the instability of present time as it forces itself irresistibly upon a mind perpetually in motion.

Diderot never wanted to leave anything out. His last project was a book on the *Elements of Physiology,* which would have been a systematic treatise laying out the main lines of a vitalist anthropology; all that survives of this work is a mass of fragments. For Diderot never closes his ears to his own internal contradictions and unforeseen trains of thought; his reaction is to embody them in an interlocutor. When he hears in himself the presence of a new thought, he immediately transforms it into an imaginary being with whom he can exchange ideas. In him the dialectic of contradiction and the dialectic of discussion are one and the same thing.

Thus is born the dialogue, a succession of moments in the present, where the author's thought is distributed among several voices whose very opposition gives rise to a superior harmony. Dialogue is in Diderot the manifestation of superabundant presence which needs to be divided among a number of actors, each of them giving vivid expression to a feeling, a reflection, or a silence at the very moment when it emerges into existence. Even when his works are most skillfully constructed, Diderot makes them read like improvisations. It is as if he were continually letting himself be guided by the replies and gestures of an interlocutor, anticipating his questions, asking them on his behalf, and answering them in advance.

Small wonder then that physical absence favors this victory of the present in his writing. Fortunately for us the long absences from Paris of his mistress Sophie Volland forced Diderot to take up the pen, imagine her presence, and speak to her on paper. In these letters . . . we find what is perhaps the quintessence of Diderot: a voice stimulated by the imagined presence of a listener, a joyful freedom kept within bounds by respect for someone else's freedom, and a frankness which never conceals the slightest variation of mood or thought.

In these letters to Sophie Volland we only hear the voice

of Diderot; the dialogue has reached us in a truncated form. The masterpiece of dialogue is *Jacques the Fatalist.* Here the author converses with the reader over the heads of his heroes, while they in their turn converse as they ride along, telling one another stories, and listening to the talk in inns where new dialogues are born in a virtually infinite succession. But in this work, which Arthur M. Wilson rightly considers the most modern of all Diderot's writings, the author, as he apostrophizes his reader and declares himself free to say whatever he wants, to make his characters say whatever he wants, and to leave whatever he wants unsaid, is in fact giving us an example of that freedom to which the Romantics later gave the name of irony. He is the master of ceremonies, the indispensable voice, at once responsible and irresponsible, without which all the others would be condemned to silence. In this way the truly modern discovery of the problems of determinism combines in Diderot with another modern discovery, that of the arbitrary powers of the writer.

John Morley on Diderot's employment in the years 1739 to 1744:

Once he had the good hap to be appointed tutor to the sons of a man of wealth. He performed his duties zealously, he was well housed and well fed, and he gave the fullest satisfaction to his employer. At the end of three months the mechanical toil had grown unbearable to him. The father of his pupils offered him any terms if he would remain. 'Look at me, sir,' replied the tutor; 'my face is as yellow as a lemon. I am making men of your children, but each day I am becoming a child with them. I am a thousand times too rich and too comfortable in your house; leave it I must; what I want is not to live better, but to avoid dying.'

John Morley in his Diderot and the Encyclopedists, *1878.*

Lester G. Crocker   (essay date 1974)

SOURCE: *Diderot's Chaotic Order: Approach to Synthesis,* Princeton University Press, 1974, 183 p.

[*Crocker is an American scholar who has written extensively on eighteenth-century literature and philosophy. In the following excerpt, he examines the role of order and chaos in Diderot's thought, concluding that these concepts unify the philosopher's view of life and guide his thinking on the subjects of metaphysics, natural philosophy, morality, politics, and aesthetics.*]

Diderot's attempt to fathom the ultimate reality of the cosmos led him to a view of universal process and law. The categories of the human mind obliged him to inquire whether the world is a rational harmony, a rational structure, a logical necessity, a coherent system. Rational causes are those that are understandable to the human reason, in terms of the structures of thought and its modes of operation. He knew that these are limited and do not correspond to the fullness of reality. Thus determinism was necessary to his world-system; but human life reveals another dimension of existence, evolves on its own level of law.

In other ways, too, what he found was both enigmatic and disturbing to the reason. In one sense the universal law of cause and effect, of structuring and disintegration, is coherent and logically understandable. In another sense, the process itself, even when an order results, is disorderly, unstable, without plan, purpose or meaning, profoundly irrational to the human understanding. Important consequences follow. Religion and the deity are eliminated. The scientific enterprise is seen to fabricate an order of its own, not false but incomplete and ephemeral, by the abstraction of phenomena amenable to its methods. But nature itself, if we go beyond, far from being a perfect machine or a rational system, remains a savage, mysterious chaos.

Some natural phenomena are manifestly rational, especially mechanics. This explains the hold of mechanics on Diderot, and his tendency to explain biological phenomena, as far as possible, in terms of such mechanical causes as heat and movement. But many essential phenomena, especially organism and life itself, could not be so explained. He knew that the conceptions he elaborates went beyond rational or empirical justification, and he offers them only as conjectures. But he assumes there are justifications unknown to us. An explanation of phenomena in rational terms, such as celestial mechanics, substantiates a universe of orderly process. On the other hand, the introduction of time and becoming, of process and change, injects disorderly elements—the evolution of worlds, the production of animals and monsters, leading to the central conclusion of an order of disorder.

We have in the twentieth century come closer to an understanding of phenomenal realities, but only by surpassing the limits of rational conceptualizations, by a new awareness that reality cannot be comprehended in conventionally rational images. Relativity allows and embraces rational contradiction. It posits a universe both finite and unbounded, having a beginning without having begun, filled with energy without the need of a creator to account for it. On the microscopic scale, it is no longer thought possible to know whether what is observed is in matter or in the structures of our thought.

Diderot intuited some of these limits. He knew that to reduce reality to the rational is to reduce it to the human. It follows that the questions of order and disorder, so intrinsic to human rationality, cannot be answered in completely objective terms, since their very essence and definition is what the mind conceives of as rational and irrational.

Still, the conception of process Diderot gradually achieves does provide a workable, if incomplete, understanding of natural events, and especially of the most baffling of these, life itself. It delineates the basic problems of the moral life, by establishing [in the words of S. Kabelac, "Irony as Metaphysics in *Le Neveu de Rameau*," *Diderot Studies* XIV (1971)] "a metaphysical flux which would imply a correlative ethical flux." The metaphysical ground of

moral values had long rested on the divinely ordered Christian cosmos. Now it was sheared off. The essential problem is thus posed: Can we establish valid, efficacious ethics without a metaphysical ground, on a natural and social foundation?

Once put on this basis, the moral problem retains its negative relation with the metaphysical, but becomes inextricably involved with the political. The social "order" is false and productive of moral disorder. Two instances that concern Diderot particularly are the conventual system and marriage, but he sees social institutions in general, insofar as they stimulate the natural human drives for power and importance at the expense of others—the fount of aggressiveness—as engendering moral disorder. The temptation of anarchism is that of the dissolution of false orders and the liberation of the instinctual. Its contrary begins with the admission that evil is a necessary part of the world system, a subjective evaluation or one made by society, but indifferent in itself. From this viewpoint the validity of the distinction between right and wrong becomes trivial. However, a society, like any other structure, responds to the universal effort to resist disintegration. If anything may be called "right," or "a right," these words are attributable to the social structure at least as much as to individuals. The struggle against the evildoers becomes "une af-

Statue of Diderot by L.-A.-J. Le Cointe, which disappeared during World War II.

faire de police," a social tyranny, an enforcement of decent human relations, of morality (which from this viewpoint is not denied), on grounds that are not themselves moral, but purely natural—precisely the grounds of the immoralist's refusal to subject himself to them.

Morals are thus absorbed into politics. Although Diderot does not conceive the reply to the immoralist in the strictly and profoundly political terms of Rousseau's refutation [in the second chapter of the first draft of his *Contrat social*] of [Diderot's *Encyclopédie* article] "Droit naturel," he emphasizes the dependency of morals on law and government. But morals are also indissociable from the aesthetic experiences. Not only because of the "holy trinity," "le bon, le vrai et le beau," but because Diderot is less interested in theory than in the concrete case or individual, which allows him to carry on his imaginary "moral experiments" as he observes, fascinated by his own creations, the spectacle of the play of forces.

The weakness of Diderot as moralist is his inability to extricate himself from the bog of the nature-culture antithesis and to find footing on firmer ground. Even within the narrow circle of the natural, the relative status of the individual and the species remains unclarified, the latter implying similarity or order, the former a claim against uniformities.

> Every being tends toward its happiness; and the happiness of one being cannot be the happiness of another. Morals, then, are enclosed within the circumference of the species. What is a species? A multitude of individuals organized in the same way. What! Organization the basis of morals! I do believe so. [*Salon de 1767*]

When we consider virtue as the synonym of order, and vice or evil as that of disorder, we are, Diderot knows, taking the anthropocentric point of view that confers value on acts according to their effects on others, and on social life in general. Men are both the object or victims of evil and the agents or causes of it. It is quite clear that for Diderot virtue is by definition a surpassing of the disorder created by the egoistic vitalities, for by themselves they can produce only disorder. Despite the fatal confusion of morals and happiness in Diderot's thinking—which at times leads him to the equation, "what is just is what makes me happy"—he praises altruism and self-sacrifice and attempts to justify them as the true path to happiness. At other times, he denies the very same claim as theoretical and empirical fallacies or illusions.

A further complication arises. His insistence on individual uniqueness in regard to happiness corresponds to his general idea of the emergence of individuality at the human level of cosmic evolution. At the same time, the primacy of the social implied by the idea of virtue is also justified by the universal ordering process and the tendency to seek stability in a viable structure. The inertia of stability is contrary to the dynamic law of things and to human nature itself, even as it coexists with it: "Together with a more or less considerable fund of inertia, Nature, who watches over our preservation, has given us a portion of energy that prods us constantly to movement and action." These are conditions of existence, and they enfold man.

On the other hand, man has no choice but to live in his own realm of moral judgment and valuation: "What is a man? An animal? Without doubt. But a dog is an animal, too; the wolf is an animal, too; but man is neither a wolf nor a dog."

Thus Diderot takes two contrary viewpoints at different times, and they faithfully reflect the human dilemma. Seen one way, morality is a necessary, justifiable, human order, a structure imposed on the disorderly energy of natural impulse. Seen another way, it is a disordering of the natural order. The respect of certain engagements, such as conjugal fidelity, substitutes for the natural order (such as it is) the disorder of repressed temptations, suffering, jealousy, unhappiness. Only a prior commitment to a moral order can make virtue a higher value than the satisfactions it denies. Even then, no moral code can go too far in contravening nature, or it will be ineffective and compound natural disorder with its own consequences, frustrating its very purposes.

Unlike Rousseau, Diderot conceives of no clear or rigorous solution to the dilemmas he propounds. He enounces no system of ethics. Man is compelled to live in a tenuous equilibrium, one that is really a state of flux, between two legitimate demands. Both the moralist and the politician must use their reason, skills, and practical insights to work out the best possible arrangements, theoretical and practical, for society and for the individuals who compose it, who are in the ambiguous position of being both its beneficiaries and its antagonists.

Just as Diderot's cosmic speculations have as their starting point the question, Is the world a rational harmony?, so his political speculations center on the unspoken question, Can society be a rational harmony? Just as the ethical inquiry involves all other manifestations of the universal processes of order and disorder, so the search for polity cannot be separated from ethics and even, at an ultimate reach, from metaphysics. Politics is another approach to the same disorder or lack of harmony inherent in the conflict between nature and culture, between the rights of the individual, fully emerged in his own determined structure, and those of the "higher" structure that requires his subordination. In his political writings, Diderot is constantly asking questions such as these: What are the causes of disorder in our societies? Can order be brought about? What institutions would be most favorable to it, and especially to a just order?

In the political inquiry, the ethical conclusions, especially the view of man's nature and potentialities, are determining in shaping the kind of response, and ultimately, the institutions to effectuate it. The moral and the political problems both involve the mutual rights and duties of a multiplicity of "others" and their relation to the larger whole. In both spheres the efforts to construct and maintain an order are countered by the same disruptive forces of self-assertion. Virtue is rational behavior, defined as that which is favorable to the best possible order of general happiness; paradoxically, individual happiness may consist of disorderly (irrational) behavior. In the governance of men, the order of violence is denounced as a false and irrational order. The order of law (the rational order), however, is never attained, and society depends on violence to maintain itself.

The struggle to control political power and the acts of aggression and exploitation form the substance of a labyrinthine riddle that Diderot finds as baffling as the moral riddle. The best form of government allies the greatest stability with the greatest latitude of individual self-expression. Although Diderot sees the individual as a disruptive force, he does not, like Rousseau, consider political or civil liberty in itself to be a disorder in the social body. He does not accept Rousseau's definition, with its totalitarian implications, of a society as a true organism, like the human body. A society, like the universe itself, is a system of interacting forces, not an organic whole dependent for its survival on a harmony and a unity into which the parts are completely subsumed. As a humanist, Diderot is willing to sacrifice the dream of complete order and stability to the higher value of individual self-realization. For Rousseau, on the other hand, happiness and justice are contingent on the complete and unreserved socialization of the individual components.

It may be said that in both his moral and political philosophy, and especially in the political, Diderot flounders and vacillates. Nonetheless, he has the merit, many would claim, of seeing all sides, of not diminishing real complexities, of not embracing easy and rigid panaceas.

Diderot's shape of mind was hostile to the fanaticism and optimism of utopianism, and rejected its essentially static conceptualizations. Although he had no philosophy of history—Vernière [Paul Verniere in his edition of Diderot's **Oeuvres politiques** (1963)] affirms that he was "hostile à l'histoire"—he does have an attitude toward history, considering it as one manifestation of his general concept of change as the law of being, of energy operating through combination, disintegration and reconstruction, in endless cycles. The state of the human species, he notes in the **Encyclopédie,** in the article "Hobbisme," is one of "vicissitude perpétuelle." In 1778 he made this plea to the American insurgents: "May they postpone, at least for several centuries, the decree issued against all the things of this world; a decree that has condemned them to have their birth, their period of flourishing, their decline and their end!" Moreover, the events of history are like all others in their obedience to the law of causality. "A further secret contradiction is detected," remarks Ronald Mortier [in "Diderot anti-colonialiste," *Revue belge de philologie et d'histoire* XLIX (1971)]; "the belief in a kind of internal necessity in history, formulated in almost fatalistic terms." The contradiction, however, is not one peculiar to history. It joins history to the universal laws of all being, as Diderot has conceived them in his cosmic, biological, moral, and political philosophy. All process is chaotic, at least to the human eye and understanding, but, in an objective sense, necessary. The life of nations follows the same course of disorder-order-disorder that constitutes the universal "order" of things. It may well be that Diderot's avoidance of the problem of history and a philosophy of history reflects his awareness that history is not understandable in terms of a rational science. It is more perplexing even than the natural processes, which continue to operate in history, but are perturbed by a multiplicity of factors peculiar to the human level of motivation and conscious will.

Aesthetics, finally, is inextricably intertwined, in Diderot's thinking, with cosmic realities and with ethics. With the former, because the aesthetic harmony created by art must deal with disorder; with the latter, because that disorder is to a considerable extent moral, and because art's highest function is to help us understand disorder in human affairs and the value of moral order. In fiction and the theater, no art is possible that is not involved with these problems of life. The same tensions we have discussed are art's substance. "Between the ideal zone of virtue and that of sensual pleasures," writes Mauzi [R. Mauzi in "Diderot et le bonheur," *Diderot Studies* III (1961)], "lies the immense field of the imaginary." Or, as M. T. Cartwright puts it the artist "imposes and justifies himself by aiming, through the expressive character of his work, at a definition of man and of his place in the world."

Diderot's fiction is deeply concerned with the problem of finding new and better aesthetic processes to express the experience of human and cosmic disorder. He breaks out of the classical aesthetic imitation, which is "an expertly modeled representation of what *might* be a natural order," into forms that themselves have some kinship with anarchy, and that befit "an attitude toward the world which finds in experience no underlying reason but only a series of circumstances" [S. Kabelac]. Although Diderot's theory usually expresses the classical aesthetics of "la belle nature," his own practice is quite different, and relies instead on fragmentation and dissonance. "To understand the genesis of Diderot's most living works," writes Yves Benot cleverly [in his *Diderot, de l'atheisme à l'anticolonialisme,* 1970], "it is essential to estimate to what extent he wrote them *against* the dominant taste of his period, and against his own." . . .

[*Jacques le Fataliste* is a] remarkable and innovative aesthetic expression of metaphysical and human order and disorder, as Diderot conceived them. It is as if he were saying that form itself structures meaning; that the function of aesthetic creation is to organize its constructs so that they convey meaning; and that, since experience itself is disorganized, art must reflect that reality if it is to be a true interpretation of it. Thus, movement and rupture in *Jacques le Fataliste* are essential. The course of the action is literally and figuratively ambulatory, rambling, meandering, and jumbled. Circularity overlays the submerged linear movement of the main thread of Jacques' journey and love affair. The episodes need not occur in the order in which they do occur, but depend on the creator's arbitrary will, a metaphor for contingency and chance. Each is meaningful in itself, a different mirror of the same reality. Movement is anti-movement; meaning conveys the ultimate lack of meaning. We have the aesthetic paradox of complex structure, embodying and illustrating the principles of disorder and instability.

Diderot's aesthetic theory is centered on the idea of relationships, on the creator's accomplishment of a structure that is intrinsically satisfying to the receptor, one that must also, to achieve full value, be satisfying in its communication of meaning and emotion. Art is the conscious process of seeking viable form, precisely as the cosmos is such an unconscious process. However, the meaning of form is quite different, not only because of self-conscious purpose, but because aesthetic form contains value—and a plurality of values. Art's unique attribute, which does not exist in any other aspect of known processes in the cosmos, is that in it human control makes possible an order eminently satisfactory to the mind.

Art may thus be considered as man's effort to conquer and overcome the universal law of transient forms, of construction and destruction. Here again it is unique. In nature and in all other spheres of human action, there is no escape from that law. Aesthetic structure, however, unlike others, does not disintegrate. Although it is subject to the vagaries of taste and appreciation, in art alone man can defy the dissolution of form and win immortality within a limited yet vast cycle of time, despite the dissolution of his own structure. The necessary fictions of art are man's assertions against increasing entropy, against a blind and valueless "mechanical" universe, against the contingency and alienation of his cosmic status. But all this can only be within the microcosmic level of the species, which is one little configuration of the solar system (Diderot knew nothing of galaxies), which itself is one tiny fold in the seas of time. Pascal, on thinking of this, would have experienced a cosmic shudder. Diderot experienced no *frisson* of cosmic alienation, but he had a clear-sighted, luminous intellectual perception of it. Trilling [Lionel Trilling in his *Sincerity* and *Authenticity* (1973)] goes too far: "For Diderot, the silence of the infinite spaces is not frightening; it is not even heard. For Diderot society is all in all the root and ground of alienation." Society, though it is for Diderot the ground of alienation, is also the ground of accomplishment, and our only ground. He did not rebel against the human condition, but accepted it as the one within which we have to work and live. At least there were the joys of sex and social life, of doing good to others, of speculation and the aesthetic experience: "le bon, le vrai, et le beau."

Can we summarize what, in Diderot's mind, "the human condition" is? It will be useful for us to recognize his overall view, for he did have one clearly in mind, even though he never set it down in systematic form.

The human existential situation begins with the fact of a world beyond rational control and beyond rational explanation. The struggle for order against the contrary forces of disorder is universal. But if men are a part of that universal law of process, their self-awareness and consequent moral dimensionality make them accomplices in disorder, and fomenters of it. Utopian dreams are excluded: "Let us then accept things as they are," Moi suggests in *Le Neveu de Rameau.* However, this attitude is not equivalent to apathy. Diderot is a man of the Enlightenment, a meliorist, and a reformer within the limits of the possible, limits that are both intrinsic to reality and a function of the antithetical forces at play.

Let us review the major limiting factors. First, the actions of others are beyond our control. They are frequently irrational and unpredictable. His protagonists undergo changes of fortune beyond their power to command, heedless of their consent. Our judgments of their actions and motives are wrong. The cruel judge in *Les Deux Amis de Bourbonne,* Gardeil, Mme. Reymer, Mme. de la Pommeraye—to cite a few instances—are really not understandable. Of the last, the master says, "Elle est incompréhensible." She is a force, like a powerful wind or an earthquake, that nothing can halt.

Second, we frequently cannot exercise rational control over our own impulses and actions, and we do not control our destiny. "But in heaven's name, Author, you say to me, where were they going? But in heaven's name, Reader, I shall answer you, do we know where we are going? And you, where are you going?" Diderot cannot control his thoughts—his "whores." Lui has impulses he cannot predict or explain. Jacques' "why's," like Zadig's [in Voltaire's *conte Zadig*], have no answer. Gardeil cannot explain his own actions, and Diderot concludes his tale by moralizing: "one has neither the power of halting a passion that is enkindled, nor of prolonging one that is dying." "Let us leave," Mlle. de la Chaux says with final resignation; "let us leave quickly; I cannot answer for what I would do or what I would say." And this is Diderot's own comment:

> Let us pity men greatly, and blame them temperately. Let us look on the years gone by as so many moments in which we have escaped the wickedness that pursues us. And let us never think without shuddering of the violence of certain natural attractions. . . . The spark that chances to fall on a barrel of powder does not produce a more frightening effect. The finger that is ready to shake that fatal spark on you or on me is perhaps already raised.

The image of the finger is not dissimilar from Jacques' capricious, "It was written up there."

Third, the natural law of self-interest, and its peculiarly human forms of satisfaction—superiority and domination over others—are the human reaction to existential contingency and the intuition of human disorder. If Diderot does not use these words, the ideas and feelings are omnipresent. Rousseau had said, "The wicked man orders everything in relation to himself." The same idea is illustrated by Lui and many of Diderot's fictional characters. However, for him this is not always or necessarily the act of wickedness. Our natural impulse is to put order into our lives, to protect ourselves against the similar enterprise of others who wish to impose their own "order." The result is a general disorder. We recall the conclusion of the *Eléments de physiologie:* "The world is the house of the strong." Diderot never lets us forget it. "Let us look on the years gone by as so many moments in which we have escaped the wickedness that pursues us."

Diderot's view of the human comedy, or drama, is evidenced by his constant return to the master-slave theme. It winds its way throughout *La Religieuse, Ceci n'est pas un conte, Le Neveu de Rameau,* and not least *Jacques le Fataliste.* Between Jacques and his master there is a constant ambiguity and versatility of roles. Their unending joust forms a context for other patterns of mastery and servitude. Mme. de la Pommeraye had been her lover's slave: "she had submitted to all his fantasies, all his tastes; to please him, she had upset the plan of her life." To secure her revenge, she will enslave two other women, use them as her instruments: "But above all, submissiveness, absolute, unlimited submissiveness to my will." The result is intended to be a godlike, or rather a satanic, control over the destiny of her lover, Des Arcis. The Chevalier, an evil exploiter like the moral anarchist in "Droit naturel," warns Jacques: "Do you want to be the master or the slave, and the most abused of slaves?" The tale of Father Hudson is the counterpart of that of Mme. de la Pommeraye. Even Mme. de la Carlière cannot help thinking in the same categories: "the fresh memory of the suffering she had endured under a first husband's tyranny." And she goes on to tell her suitor: "I am going to become the mistress of your happiness or unhappiness; you, the master of mine."

This is the intrinsic nature of human relationships, of our interdependency. It is twice generalized in *Jacques le Fataliste.* The first time by the narrator: "But who was the master of Jacques' master? —Come, do we lack masters in this world? Jacques' master had a hundred for one, like you." And a second time by Jacques himself, in the more telling image of the dogs, which is only another rendition of Lui's "pantomime des gueux," or the figures of the "positions de Noverre."

There is obviously a direct relation between Diderot's conceptualization of human drives and relationships and his picture of our world as one of disorder, largely of our own making. The problem of a rational moral life appears in ever darker hues and more insolvable riddles. In some cases—Mme. de la Pommeraye, Mme. de la Carlière—both master and slave are destroyed. Only Jacques and his master approach a solution, or more exactly, a *modus vivendi.* They transcend the master-slave relationship by recognizing it. They work out, through a rational dialogue between reasonable men, a combination of interdependence and freedom, one of mutual support in life's aimless and unpredictable journey. They go through a process of negotiation: "Let us stipulate." Jacques will remain subservient, but the Master will tolerate his insolence. They will allow each other what will inevitably happen anyway.

Such a solution seems rare enough, though in life it is undoubtedly more common than Diderot makes it appear. Similarly, he recognizes our potentiality for altruistic acts, in *Jacques le Fataliste* and *Les Deux Amis de Bourbonne,* but too often questions or denies their value. They are vain gestures, reflecting our longing for a world of moral order, destined to be engulfed in the more general disorder. Diderot's last play, *Est-il bon? Est-il méchant?* (1781) tells us that there may be no way of translating ideals into action except by means that contradict them. As we experience life, it is not an orderly pattern of cause and effect, but a chance concatenation of events that defies our notions of logic and necessity. It is never really intelligible—except in terms of Diderot's calculated aesthetic plan. If this is a logical and ordered world, one that "makes sense," then these qualities are hidden from our sight. *Jacques le Fatal-iste* begins and ends with an emphasis on "le hasard." This is our experience, and perhaps all we can know.

If domination on an interpersonal level is destructive, it is still more so in the government of men. The freedom, dialogue, and contentious give-and-take exemplified by Jacques and his master are even more valuable in the realm of political life.

The movement of ideas we call the Enlightenment conceived its task as the release of men from error and prejudice—forms of disorder—and as the achievement of truth and human welfare—forms of order. With intellectual courage and clear-sightedness, Diderot saw such efforts in a universal or cosmic context. Subject to the laws he understood to govern all being and all activity, they could not escape a fate common to all. The basic paradox of the universe as an anarchic order is the paradigm of all else. He understood, as Jean-Paul Sartre was to put it [in *Les Mots,* 1963], that "the ordered world hid intolerable disorders," and that the world of explanations and reasons is not the world of existence.

Throughout the universe, a meaningless game is being played. Convolutions of matter are blindly seeking stable structure. This *conatus* to persist in viability, and the eventual, inevitable dissolution, are parts of a deeper, more baffling cosmic process, the tendency to evolve ever more complex structures and "higher" levels of being. Life, species, and finally the self-conscious individual—these are the significant gradations of being.

If one looks beyond varying states of particular configurations to the all-encompassing whole, the universe is at any time in a state of equilibrium. Some structures are being formed, others broken down; but the overall situation remains the same. The same truth applies to man. He is engaged in a continuing struggle, but always (except in art) a losing one—as an individual and eventually as a species. He is enmeshed in the unique forms of intercourse that create the fabric of culture, which in turn struggles endlessly to establish moral and political structures capable of surviving the insolvable stresses between it and nature.

Diderot is often called a contradictory genius. We have seen, however, that contradiction is the essence of reality. Order and disorder are the complementary qualities of the same reality. This truth he has understood, explored, and applied. In this regard there is fundamental consistency in his attitude and his approach to the operations of the world and of man. His philosophy is humanistic, man-centered. It suffers technically from the lack of a radical critique of his postulates and suppositions, such as we find in Hume. But he has properly apprehended man's place in the order of things, entirely a part of nature, yet unique in his way of being. Each level of structure brings into existence new kinds of law or process; but the lower levels are not abolished thereby. Man stands by himself, on the summit of the entire structure, with triumphs and problems that are his alone. He, too, is the creator of orders and the fomenter of disorders, but in his own way. The work of his reason is to create viable forms, to impose a novel order of culture upon the order of nature, and to suffer, as he alone can suffer, from his failures and frustrations. For him alone, "there are tears for things and mortal woes touch the mind."

John Hope Mason   (essay date 1982)

SOURCE: *The Irresistible Diderot,* Quartet Books, 1982, 403 p.

[*In the following excerpt, Mason places Diderot's writings in the context of eighteenth-century intellectual trends and describes the preoccupations and characteristics of his works, maintaining that "the heart of Diderot's achievement lies . . . in a quality of openmindedness, a persistent desire to do justice to whatever makes the individual detail what it is, to catch the living moment in all its mobility, and a wonderful ability to show how the life of the mind interweaves with the complex texture of our whole experience."*]

I

The eighteenth century is not what it was. Admired for its lucidity and envied for its calm, it once had the character of a picturesque bay, sheltered from the dense forests of the sixteenth and seventeenth centuries and the turbulent seas of the nineteenth and twentieth centuries. It was seen as a time of order, an age of reason, when 'the wealthy and educated of Europe must have enjoyed almost the nearest approach to earthly felicity known to man'. A century when tours were grand, gardens were landscaped and music was Mozart; when the intellect had broken free from centuries of serving the Church but had not yet grown heady with Hegelian, Marxist or Nietzschean excess. Not everyone admired these qualities; to some the century was 'the natural era of compromises and half-convictions', a period which displayed 'an incapacity of producing deep or strong feelings', a 'winter of the imagination'. It lacked the exuberant splendour of the Renaissance, the vivid extravagance of Romanticism, the restless invention of modern times. But the century such critics looked down on was the same as that which others admired—a century of clarity, rationality and comparative calm.

All that has gone. For the clarity cast deep shadows, the calm was illusory. 'A level of disorder existed in eighteenth-century England,' a leading historian wrote recently, 'which if it occurred today would certainly result in the declaration of martial law.' [Lawrence stone in *New York Review of Books* (29 May 1980)] Through the clear surface strange and unexpected life-forms have been seen; behind the glittering couplets of Alexander Pope, no less than behind the sonorous judgements of Dr Johnson, there was an agitated uneasy mind. What was once regarded as melancholy or sardonic humour has assumed the dimensions of metaphysical panic. Voltaire's work is no longer dismissed as 'a chaos of clear ideas' but seen as a sombre struggle against the spectre of a world without meaning; he has been called 'a great poet of anxiety'. Rousseau's writings were not an exhibition of facile paradoxes and paranoid ravings but the sustained development of profound insights into man's place in society and the world. The eighteenth century, in fact, was as aware of fundamental problems, contradictions and tensions as our own bewildered century. And it was equally ready to face such problems and make what sense it could of them. That sense was not achieved through simple rationality but by means of a rationality that existed alongside, and within, more complex patterns of mind.

In this new perspective the writings of Diderot have come to occupy a central place. Diderot's importance, his status as a major figure in the eighteenth century, has never been in doubt. His immense achievement—editing almost singlehandedly the **Encyclopédie,** the twenty-eight folio volumes which seemed to embody the Enlightenment's ambition and achievement—was sufficient to ensure that; quite apart from the other works which in their different ways won the admiration of Goethe, Stendhal, Hegel, Comte, Carlyle, Sainte-Beuve and so on. But Diderot's writings taken as a whole seemed to raise so many problems, his contradictions seemed so pervasive, his inconsistencies so habitual, that it was difficult to see how they could all emerge from one mind and remain valid. For one person to hold apparently irreconcilable opinions may not be uncommon, but prominent writers and thinkers owe their prominence precisely to the fact that their ideas are coherent. Diderot seemed a case of being all exceptions and no rule.

But now that we are more aware of the complexities of his time we can appreciate better the particular merits of his work. We can see how large a part of its value lies in the attempt to go beyond common assumptions and accepted categories. In his most searching works Diderot operated on and over the borders of rationality; he valued clarity but he was conscious of how it could fall short of a comprehensive grasp of living reality and he valued that comprehension more. A preoccupation that underlay much of his work, though never explicitly formulated, was that his writing should convey the whole experience of the living moment; that it should be both precise enough and flexible enough to describe the world as it is, in all its richness, density and variety. Hence the extraordinary openness, mobility and directness of his best work. At the same time, however, much of his thought remained rooted in the general assumptions of the period; although individual insights may have called these into question, Diderot never outgrew them or discarded them. The result is the strange and idiosyncratic nature of his work, in which the conventional and the audacious, the commonplace and the original, exist not only side by side but in a curiously symbiotic relationship.

Once this is realized Diderot's writings can be seen for the achievement they are, displaying the individuality, versatility and brilliance which those who knew him well say he possessed in person. To read him now is to recapture some of the excitement which his friends felt in his presence. 'This astonishing, universal, perhaps unique genius', wrote Rousseau; a man, according to Grimm, who 'seemed inspired, stirred up by the demon of enlightenment and truth . . . [who] encompasses everything he comes near.' 'When I remember Diderot,' wrote Meister, 'the immense variety of his ideas, the astonishing range of his knowledge, the rapidity and warmth and impetuous tumult of his imagination, all the charm and disorder of his conversation, I am tempted to compare his mind to nature as he saw it himself, rich, fertile, abounding in seeds of every kind, gentle and wild, simple and grand, good and sublime.'

II

The generation who reached maturity around the middle years of the eighteenth century in France came into a rich intellectual inheritance. In the preceding 150 years several powerful intellectual systems had either been built or sketched out by Bacon, Descartes, Spinoza, Newton, Locke and Leibniz. Despite the specifically Renaissance flavour of Bacon's writings, and the sense of human limitations stressed by Locke, despite the errors soon revealed in Descartes' physics and the unsolved problem arising from Newton's key notion of attraction, despite the obscurity or unavailability of much of Spinoza and Leibniz, these thinkers handed on to those who came after a striking confidence in the ability of the human mind to understand the world. They had stepped forward out of the brilliant confusion of the Renaissance into a world which we can recognize as modern; a world, that is, which regarded truth as a matter of evidence and examination, the result of human thought, rather than a matter of belief, tradition or supernatural revelation. A hundred years before Kant's celebrated summary of the Enlightenment—*Sapere aude,* Dare to know—Fontenelle had written: 'You must be daring in every activity.'

Such daring needs freedom to explore and toleration to survive. Although all the above thinkers did in their different ways believe in God, many of their ideas were anathema to the Churches. Since in France one of the monarchy's claims to legitimacy, the divine right of kings, rested on a religious foundation, there were additional restrictions to freedom. The expulsion of the Protestants, by the Revocation of the Edict of Nantes in 1685, and the stricter operation of government censorship in subsequent years, meant that much intellectual activity had to be conducted abroad, as was the case with Bayle, or was driven underground, as was the case with the large number of writings which, in the early part of the century circulated clandestinely, usually in manuscript. Some critical works were published openly, notably Montesquieu's *Lettres persanes* (1721) and Voltaire's *Lettres philosophiques* (1734), but these were exceptions. The more searching works remained unpublished. These developed bold lines of thought about such forbidden questions as the existence of God, the immortality of the soul and the nature of the world. A few, of which those by Jean Meslier became best known later in the century, went a stage further in questioning the existence of privilege, the (apparent) eternity of oppression and the nature of society. This marked a significant change of emphasis, a change made consciously in a short work, first published anonymously in Amsterdam in 1743, entitled *Le Philosophe.*

Le Philosophe was, in effect, the first of a number of manifestos around the middle of the century which proclaimed the importance of free enquiry not merely in metaphysics or ethics, for the good of the soul, but in matters specifically concerned with the good of society. (Most of the essay later appeared as the article 'Philosophe' in Volume Twelve of the **Encyclopédie.**) The role of the philosopher

was being redefined; he was becoming what we would call an intellectual. Instead of conducting his thought in isolation, shut away from the world, he was now among his fellow men and like-minded thinkers, *la république des lettres.* Le Philosophe attacked religion for its concern with the next world rather than this world, and it attacked the asceticism of the Stoics. For the *philosophe* 'civil society is, so to speak, the only divinity he recognizes on earth'; he 'does not believe himself to be an exile in this world', he wants 'to please and make himself useful'. His activity can change the way things are: 'This love of society, so vital to the *philosophe,* makes plain the truth of the comment by the Emperor Antoninus—"How happy the people will be when kings are *philosophes* or when *philosophes* are kings!" '

This conception of their place at the centre of their society was shared by all Diderot's fellow *philosophes.* He himself, in his last published work, gave a striking example of their ambition:

> The magistrate executes justice; the *philosophe* teaches the magistrate what the just and unjust are. The soldier defends his homeland; the *philosophe* teaches the soldier what a homeland is. The priest advises the people to love and respect the gods; the *philosophe* teaches the priest what the gods are. The sovereign commands everyone; the *philosophe* teaches the sovereign about the origin and limit of his authority. Every man has duties to fulfil in his family and in society; the *philosophe* teaches each person what his duties are . . . I love to see the wise man on display, like the athlete in the arena; a man only recognizes his strength when he has opportunities to show it.

In short, as he wrote elsewhere [in **Éléments de physiologie**], 'Man is born for action.'

This active practical spirit animated all Diderot's public writing. The publication of the **Encyclopédie** was undertaken, carried out and sustained against innumerable obstacles and discouragements precisely in order 'to change the general way of thinking'. . . . Ideas must be communicated. 'The priest tight-fisted with his money and the *philosophe* tight-fisted with his discoveries, are both stealing from the poor. What is more, I think discoveries are only valuable and secure when they circulate among the general mass of people; I am impatient to take them there.'

Foremost among these ideas were the beliefs held in common by Montesquieu, Voltaire and the author of *Le Philosophe* (probably Dumarsais), and the younger generation responsible for the important works which began to appear around the middle years of the century: Condillac in his *Essai sur l'origine des connaissances humaines* (1746), Buffon in the first volumes of his *Histoire naturelle* (1749), Turgot in his *Tableau philosophique des progrès* (1750), and the work that is often seen as a summation of all these, D'Alembert's *Discours prèliminaire* to Volume One of the **Encyclopédie** (1751). These ideas were that man has no innate knowledge, learning about the world empirically, through his senses; that however the world may have been created it now obeys laws which we can discover through observing facts and exercising our reason; that human beings are naturally sociable and reasonable, and from these capacities have developed common ideas of justice and morality; that human nature is not fallen or sinful, the emotional and passionate aspects of our personality being as valuable and essential to us as our minds, brains or souls; that intellectual freedom is a necessary prerequisite for the discovery of the truth-which makes it, wrote Diderot, 'the finest prerogative of mankind'—and toleration must follow as an obvious corollary.

All these works conveyed a remarkable sense of confidence, a firm belief in human potential. There was a sense that change was at hand and that these works were helping to bring about that change. However, it is wrong to suppose that this was synonymous with a faith in progress. Turgot, it is true, did state that 'the overall mass of the human race is continually moving, though slowly, by good and evil, calm and unrest in turn, towards greater perfection. But this was not the attitude of Diderot or D'Alembert. For them improvement and advance were possible and in the short term very probable, but they were not inevitable and would never be continual. 'The fate which rules the world wants everything to pass away. The most fortunate condition of a man or a State has its limit. Everything carries within it a secret seed of destruction.' There were always upheavals and there were always limits to the spread of enlightenment: 'the bulk of a nation will always remain ignorant, afraid and consequently superstitious'. This should not surprise us; there were few reasons for them to suppose otherwise. It was quite different for those who succeeded them and were able to see the transformations that were beginning to occur later in the century.

The fact remains that, judged in the light of their own time, the men of this generation displayed great self-assurance and an invigorating belief in human nature. 'I love the philosophy that exalts humanity,' wrote Diderot. Human beings belong in the world and in the final analysis it is their existence alone that gives this world meaning. 'If man . . . was banished from the earth's surface the sublime and moving spectacle of nature would become no more than a silent, desolate scene. The universe would be dumb; night and silence would take hold of it. Everything would be transformed into an immense solitude where unobserved phenomena would occur dimly and unheard.'

The practical spirit was not confined to such general attitudes. It extended to almost all human activities: 'The spectacle of human industry is in itself great and satisfying.' There was a constant emphasis on experience, facts, things: 'to speak informatively about bakery you have got to have put your hands in the dough.' Diderot's short work on scientific method, *Pensées sur l'interprétation de la nature* (published in 1754) was remarkable for its awareness of the place of intuition and inspired conjecture in scientific discovery; but he gave equal weight to the need for experiments and the factual confirmation which alone could validate such discoveries. One of his principal concerns in the *Encyclopédie* was to change people's attitudes to what were termed 'the mechanical arts'. He himself wrote in detail and with great care about such subjects

as the manufacture of stockings and steel, activities which were not only useful but could be beautiful as well. The main reason for collecting the huge variety of plates which filled the final eleven volumes of the work was to supplement such descriptions and show as clearly as possible how things were made, what processes, skills and techniques were involved. It is those who work in such activities who make us not 'think we are happy' but make us actually 'happy in fact.' Manufacturing, he wrote elsewhere, is 'the state which sets you free', because it does not depend on seasonal fluctuations, like agriculture. (Which is not to say that manufacture, which at this date meant mostly small-scale industry, was being in any way promoted at the expense of agriculture; the latter was still the basis of every economy and recognized as such.) This belief in the value of technology was the most original feature of Diderot's contribution to the *Encyclopédie* and of obvious historical importance.

Besides the awareness of practical benefit there was a strong humanitarian impulse. 'It is good to know how the different contributions each person makes relate to the general benefit of society. Diderot always had a keen sense of the effects of poverty; he had himself spent a number of precarious years in Paris before the editorship of the *Encyclopédie* brought him a regular income, and he argued vehemently against Helvétius when the latter suggested that the labouring poor enjoyed a happier existence than the bored rich. This humanitarian concern was evident in many articles in the *Encyclopédie.* It was one manifestation of the moral impulse that was an integral part of the practical spirit. To spread ideas, to change people's attitudes, to call attention to poverty and injustice was necessary in order to make people not only happier or more comfortable, but to make them better.

Indeed, for Diderot and his generation the concept of happiness was essentially linked to the idea of goodness. Given two of their premises—the empirical basis of knowledge (if everything is learnt through the senses moral ideas must develop through pleasure and pain), and man's natural sociability—this association was no surprise. Moreover, ethical naturalism of this kind—the belief that man's moral character owes nothing to divine guidance or any innate ideas—had been a feature of the seventeenth-century revival of interest in the ideas of Epicurus, particularly associated with Gassendi and evident in many clandestine manuscripts. The promotion of Locke's ideas in the first part of the eighteenth century had provided additional support for this point of view; (even though Locke's own treatment of the subject was ambivalent, since despite his empirical premises he did refer [in his *Essay on Human Understanding*] to man's moral awareness as 'a candle of the Lord'). But these ideas took on a new practical emphasis in the mid-century. Diderot said of himself that he was 'a man who loves to moralize', everyone has his 'tic . . . mine is to moralize'. A moral impulse informed all his public writings. When he turned his attention to writing plays it was not simply through the desire to succeed in a prestigious literary activity, or to reform the dramatic conventions of the time, though both these motives did apply; it was also because of a belief that the theatre when used in the right way could be morally beneficial. This was not a new idea, to be sure, but Diderot's persistent advocacy of the theatre as a means of moral instruction, in his ***Entretiens sur le Fils naturel*** (1757) and the ***Discours sur la poésie dramatique*** (1758), was influential. His faith in the idea survived, despite setbacks and evidence to the contrary, because he believed that 'there is a trinity against which the gates of hell will never prevail: the true which brings forth the good, and emerging from both of these the beautiful'.

The self-assurance of the 1750s did not last. Major disagreements arose among the *philosophes,* and despite all that they did achieve—and were conscious of having achieved, as Diderot showed in 1769—their analyses and remedies did not match up to the serious problems that were developing. France's defeat in the Seven Years War, with the loss of most of her colonies, aggravated an already bad economic position. An archaic and grossly unjust tax structure, which exempted the rich, the aristocracy and the clergy, from paying taxes, was reinforced by an archaic and inflexible political structure, which allowed little scope for reforming initiatives and no expression for general grievances. The monarchy and the privileged were locked into an increasingly bitter conflict which would eventually destroy them both.

For a number of reasons Diderot had neither an aptitude nor an inclination for political thought. But the growing seriousness of the crisis in France (first perceived as a crisis with Maupeou's so-called coup in 1771, when the Parlement of Paris was exiled and the judiciary replaced by hand-picked men), and his journey to Russia in 1773-4 to meet his benefactress Catherine II, made him turn his attention more fully to political matters. Most of his political writing was not published till long after his death but one important work did appear in his lifetime, Raynal's *Histoire des Deux Indes* which appeared in three editions in 1770, 1774 and 1780, and to which Diderot made a large number of contributions.

These contributions were anonymous and it was only thirty years ago, with the discovery of the collection of Diderot manuscripts known as the Fonds Vandeul, that it became possible to identify what exactly they were; only in the last few years has this knowledge become generally available. The result has been a reappraisal of Diderot's political ideas and a widespread belief that at the end of his life he was a radical, if not a revolutionary. However, this view is not supported by a rigorous examination of the evidence. There are many striking and forceful passages among Diderot's writings for the *Histoire;* there is a sense of outrage and indignation, we read impassioned protests at injustice, eloquent affirmations of liberty. But there is no vision of a new order, no call for or belief in popular or particular revolt in any European context, not even a properly developed political theory. Nor do the occasional references to the possible need for extreme measures show evidence of a revolutionary temperament; they relate to a different matter, the old and well-established tradition that justifies tyrannicide.

Diderot's outrage and indignation were sincere, and they were more acute in so far as they clashed with no less strongly held convictions about the cyclical patterns of history and about the basic contradictions in human nature—he saw man as a 'bizarre combination of sublime qualities and shameful weaknesses', both 'a truthteller and a liar, cheerful and sad, wise and mad, good and bad', not as intrinsically wicked as Hobbes might have suggested, but neither as intrinsically innocent as Rousseau might have suggested. . . . And Diderot did not complain about this. On several occasions he asserted that the good qualities people displayed were essentially linked to the bad, and he also said that in society generally speaking 'everything balances out (*tout se compense*)'. Moreover, his attitude to how human nature was formed, more the result of heredity than environment or social conditioning, provided him with no alternative to accepting these contradictions; it precluded him from envisaging any transition to a new order. Above all, his imagination was not of the kind that is fired by general concepts or visionary schemes. Diderot's contributions to Raynal's *Histoire* were important; in several respects they amount to the culmination of the work that had occupied the later years of his life. But they do not reveal a new ability in handling political problems. This should neither surprise us nor disappoint us. For Diderot's limitations as a political thinker were essentially linked to his brilliance in other areas. A thorough consideration of the reasons why he was not a revolutionary brings us face to face with the characteristics that constitute his true originality. This was evident less in any of the works published in his lifetime, than in those that were only published after his death.

III

Diderot's writings took two forms, a public form and a more confined, intimate and private form. To understand his work it is necessary not only to know this but also to realize that neither form was for him more 'true' or more 'real'. Both forms had their value and Diderot was equally committed to them both, even when they displayed contradictory impulses.

Although he complained at times of the burden of editing the ***Encyclopédie*** and although his output in the years following the publication of the last volumes of text in 1765 was prodigious, he was willing nevertheless in 1774 to undertake another *Encyclopédie* for Catherine II, and he made no particular effort to publish those more private works which he had written in the meanwhile. We may be pleased that he did not devote the rest of his life to another *Encyclopédie* and that he was able to give time to completing, improving or writing the other works which we now value more. But it is vital to understand that Diderot himself thought otherwise, because the published works were the public structure within which he lived, which provided the necessary conditions without which the more private works could never have been written. This was not merely the social fact of identity, definition, occupying a place in the world; it was also a mental fact, a peculiarity of his own temperament and intellectual character.

The beliefs Diderot shared with his fellow *philosophes* did not form a precisely worked-out system; they were a body of ideas which to some extent owed their force to what they opposed. The process of enlightenment had obvious imperatives and the confidence of the 1750s was in part due to the shared sense of such imperatives being fulfilled. But what exactly was visible when the dark was cleared away? At this point disagreement set in, problems were admitted, difficulties became plain. The rich inheritance of the previous century was no longer sufficient to explain many aspects of the world that were then coming into focus. Many ideas retained their efficacy, but others were found wanting. It was in this confused and fluid context—the second half of the eighteenth century as it is now understood—that Diderot's most interesting work was done. In his unpublished works he explored the new problems and difficulties.

On one major issue Diderot made up his mind early: there was no God or spiritual being, either transcendent (like the Christian God or the God of the deists) or immanent (like the God of Spinoza or any of the occult, mystical or pantheist thinkers). He was assisted in coming to this decision by a crucial change of emphasis in scientific thinking which was taking place in the middle years of the century; this was a move away from a mechanistic view of nature, based on astronomy, physics and mathematics, towards a dynamic view based on biology, physiology and chemistry. The universe of Descartes and Newton was one in which matter was moved by forces external to it in accordance with certain fixed laws; the world that biological discoveries began to reveal was one in which living forms were animated by internal forces in a far less regular way. The former model would be grasped as a single entity, beautiful in its unity and simplicity; the latter seemed to manifest a prolific diversity, strikingly varied yet also bewilderingly elusive. These two models were not seen as being incompatible. The belief that there was an underlying unity, a basic natural order, and the Cartesian criterion that what was true could be formulated in clear distinct notions—these remained valid. But the new view of nature being in some way self-creating and continually changing was a growing challenge to all the arguments and beliefs based on the previous attitude.

Foremost among these were the arguments for the existence of God. The universe described by both Descartes and Newton contained matter which by itself was inert and therefore needed a God to set it in motion (and maybe keep it in motion as well). The laws of the universe discovered by Newton revealed an intelligence, design and sense of order which also seemed to need a God to explain them. But what if matter could somehow animate itself? And what if the order we see is only a temporary phenomenon, a momentary pattern, even perhaps only a projection of our minds? The evidence of biology and other life-sciences gave these questions overwhelming force and led Diderot to become an atheist.

However, it would be wrong to see this development as a purely intellectual matter. Diderot had ineradicably religious inclinations; that is to say, he always felt a sense of awe when he faced the ultimate questions of existence, and although he denied any essential purpose or finality to the universe he did believe that life was more than the mere play of chance. Rational arguments alone would not have converted him to atheism; emotional reasons were also necessary, and in his case they were central. There was a profound affinity between his temperament, his instinctive manner of being, and the view, then coming to prominence, of a nature that was neither stable, uniform nor simple. It is this affinity which more than anything else explains both the difficulty and fascination of his writing.

The first characteristic that strikes any reader of Diderot is the bewildering disorder and lack of focus that most of his writings display. Both the subject-matter and the viewpoint are continually shifting, there are endless interruptions and digressions, and the last page or a later work often seems to contradict or call into question what has gone before. Many critics have concluded that his remark about his fellow townsmen having 'the inconsistency of weathercocks . . . never fixed in any one direction', must be seen as a fair comment on Diderot himself. He would not have disagreed with them completely—after this remark about his fellow townsmen he went on to admit that he had much in common with them—but he would not have regarded this entirely as a failing. What one of the characters in his last play called his *héracliterie*—meaning his changeableness, his personal demonstration of Heraclitus' conception of reality as a state of constant flux—was not a quality which set him apart from the world but, on the contrary, showed how close was his response to it and his contact with it. 'Happy the person who has received from nature a sensitive and mobile soul!' The most frequent criticism Diderot makes of other writers is that they impose an order or arrangement or symmetry on their material which that material does not itself have. They lack the 'apparent negligence', 'the disordered manner' which he admired in Horace or Montaigne . . . , not purely out of aesthetic preference but because it was closer to the truth as he saw it. He liked a writer who 'does not compose [but] pours out his mind and soul onto the paper; [who] does not wear himself out giving his phrase a [good] cadence . . . , [but] sounds the depth of his heart'. He looked for a similar quality in painting—'the effect of art should be a beautiful disorder'—for truth emerges in a disorderly way. It would be a mistake to suppose that Diderot did not take care over his writing, because he did. But it explains the apparent shapelessness of much of his work, and why he could say that a book could be 'a great obstacle to truth'.

Nature is in a state of endless flux: 'the general order of nature changes unceasingly', 'the whole [universe] alters continually'. Since man is part of nature he too is in 'a state of continual vicissitude', not only were no two men alike but no person was the same in any two consecutive moments, 'the condition of man varies unceasingly'. Being so aware of this was both Diderot's delight and his torment. He was caught between the exhilaration of feeling in touch with the living moment and the despair of the intellectual relativism which this attitude could entail. This was why he valued a sense of immediacy and personal involvement so highly in his written work, and this is also why that work so often approached a form of conversation, as dialogue or letter or marginalia. What was spoken, or written down as speech, retained the ebb and flow of present time.

A remarkable aspect of this combined sense of immediacy and transitoriness was that it was not accompanied by any feelings of impatience or panic. Faced with the mutability of life Diderot did not exclaim, like so many writers before him or since, *Carpe diem,* Seize the day. He disliked the thought of extinction or the idea that he might be forgotten but the pleasure of the moment did not turn sour at the prospect of its passing. There are several reasons for this. One was that his quasi-religious sense of wonder at the mystery of existence survived his rejection of any belief in God; he could go so far on occasion as to imagine some form of life after the fact of physical death. Another was his belief in a basic natural order; there was 'a natural interconnection, the law of unity', everything was 'bound together, interconnected', which gave it a kind of sense. Most important of all was the fact that his imagination was animated not by images of decay but by ideas of creation, generation and growth. Sexuality and reproduction were to him not only opportunities for pleasure but occasions for wonder and reverence at the renewal of life. Connected with all of these was Diderot's fascination with the uniqueness of the individual, his attention to the *petits phenomènes,* his capacity to grasp the particular detail. He could capture the moment and transmit its immediacy and sensuality as though he was somehow immersed in the body of nature itself. (Sexual metaphors are entirely appropriate here: Diderot himself sometimes referred to his thought in sexual terms.) And this was how he characterized genius: 'there is no intermediary between nature and genius'.

Man and nature are one substance. When Buffon wrote, in his soul which in his *Histoire naturelle,* 'It is . . . the way we are constituted, our life, our soul which in effect makes our existence. From this point of view matter is [only] an extraneous envelope', Diderot objected strongly: 'It is constant fact that this despicable cocoon . . . has a prodigious influence on the sequence of thoughts which forms our being.' The soul 'is nothing without the body. I defy anyone to explain anything without the body.' Anything that might be described as spiritual, such as a sense of virtue or a state of inspiration, had a physical explanation of some kind. Although this belief can be correctly described as materialist, and Diderot himself would have agreed with such a description, the word suggests something too narrow (and probably also too positivist) to be entirely accurate. This point was made shortly after his death by Meister: 'Although he was a passionate defender of materialism you could say that as far as his manner of feeling and living were concerned he was no less the most decided idealist; he was like that in spite of himself, as a result of the unconquerable aspiration of his character and imagination.'

The material basis of all reality, the existence of only a single substance—these were unaltered features of Diderot's mature thought. The problems that arose from them were his constant preoccupations and form the subject-matter of some of his major works. How does life arise? How does inert matter become living matter? What forms our physical character? How do physical sensations develop into complex ideas? What is the difference between thinking and dreaming? These are the questions that produced the

three dialogues known as *Le Rêve de d' Alembert.* In his answers to them Diderot threw out remarkable insights into evolution and the structure of matter but it is not the ideas alone that make this work a masterpiece; it is the extraordinary way in which Diderot presents them. What gives his ideas their force and conviction—for the evidence to support them had not yet been found—is the way they emerge from a living situation, the way the characters in the dialogues search for explanations, and lead us forward with them. We share both the excitement of discovery and Diderot's intense delight in relating all human experience to the natural world of which it is a part.

However, the conviction that we are part of nature, combined with what was for Diderot an equally fundamental belief that everything in nature is necessary . . . , faced him with an acute problem, that of human freedom. If our ideas are determined by our physical state, then how can we be said to be free? And if we have no freedom, how can there be any morality? In *Le Rêve de d'Alembert* he denied that notions of virtue and vice could have any meaning. In subsequent writings, the three extended works of marginalia—the *Éléments de physiologie,* the *Réfutation d'Helvétius,* the *Commentaire sur Hemsterhuis*—and in his last novel *Jacques le fataliste* he turned over this question obsessively.

One reason why this issue troubled him so much was that he experienced it personally as a problem. He often felt he was the passive plaything of external forces. He saw himself at times in the same terms as the sultan Mangogul in his first novel *Les Bijoux indiscrets:* 'Isn't it true that we are only puppets?' In a letter of 1769, in which he complained of being 'tangled up in a devil of a philosophy which my mind cannot resist confirming and my heart denying', he wrote: 'It is hard to abandon oneself blindly to the universal torrent, [but] it is impossible to resist it.' This 'universal torrent' was experienced by Diderot in many forms; it could be the climate, the countryside, financial pressures, sexual impulses. In his last play *Est-il bon? Est-il méchant?* he depicted himself as someone constantly put upon by friends or acquaintances, 'I think I was born to do nothing of what suits me [but] everything that others demand', and many contemporaries testify to this characteristic, though they saw it more as his willing generosity than as reluctant self-denial.

His intellectual character displayed similar features. Diderot was not alone in needing the stimulus of other writers to develop his own ideas, but he was unusual in the way his own writing so often borrowed, took over, or assumed characteristics of those who stimulated him. The tone of each of the three works of marginalia mentioned above differs according to the author and subject-matter in question. His exclamation in the *Réfutation d'Helvétius* 'I contradict you: therefore I exist' reveals how central this dual function of stimulation and dependence was. A similar conclusion can be drawn from the amount of plagiarism in his writing. The number of authors who, frequently unacknowledged, provided him with ideas was legion; Diderot must be included among the great plagiarists of all time. Yet there is a certain innocence about his pillaging, a lack of either self-awareness or self-promotion. It was as though his attitude was like his attitude to property (derived from Locke); by his own labour he made the ideas his own. He very often did put other authors' ideas to work in a new way and endow them with new perspective, vitality, a personal flavour. But he needed those other authors to build on in the first place.

The problem of human freedom also occupied a central place in Diderot's work because it arose at the point of intersection between the natural realm and the human realm. Being convinced that man and nature existed in a continuum, and not in conflict, Diderot then had to explain how and why men differed from the rest of nature, and how it was possible for them to have 'natural' impulses that were incompatible. This problem had also concerned Rousseau and his solution, first indicated in the *Discours sur l'inégalité* (1755), constituted one of the major intellectual achievements of the eighteenth century. However, Diderot neither adopted Rousseau's solution, nor was able to provide a solution of his own. Nature and culture, nature and society always existed for him within the same conceptual framework: 'All that is can neither be outside nature nor opposed to nature.'

How is it then that human society has come to be in opposition to many of our needs or desires? Diderot could not answer this question. He stared at it again and again. In his fiction and his plays he depicted the problem in graphic detail, in dialogues like the *Entretien d'un père avec ses enfants* and the important *Supplément au Voyage de Bougainville* he tried to think his way through it; in one of his contributions to the *Histoire des Deux Indes* he made a final attempt to provide an answer. . . . But instead of insights we find only anecdotes; the analysis degenerates into a mere episodic sequence of events.

The fact is that Diderot had an aversion to abstraction (apart from mathematics) and no special gift for conceptual thinking. 'The act of generalization tends to strip concepts of everything tangible (*sensible*) that they possess'; 'I [am] a physician [or] a chemist . . . who grasps the body in its material substance and not in my head.' He believed that 'the wing of a butterfly, well described, would bring me closer to divinity than a volume of metaphysics'. Abstract sciences, such as mathematics, could be like 'the fable of Daedalus. Men made the labyrinth and then got lost in it.' Given this aversion he was not inclined to develop ideas in a logical, conceptual manner. But even when he was so inclined it must be admitted that he was out of his element. He never freed himself from mental patterns set down early in his life; this is why audacious insights that may logically alter the whole basis of an argument can be followed by the reiteration of an earlier position as if no such insights had been made, why his insights can be vivid but his theories pallid.

In one sense this aspect of Diderot's work is obviously a weakness, but in another sense that weakness is beside the point. For much of his writing is a complex and fascinating argument between his routine conceptual equipment and his spontaneous instinctive responses. Given the uncertainty of the latter and the weakness of the former he often lacked confidence in his own achievements; (this is one reason why so much of his best work was written for a small select audience or a circle of friends: 'O how vital my friends are to me! Without them my heart and my mind would be dumb'). Given this lack of confidence he often fell back into either fixed ways of thought or into the scepticism that always hovered around the edge of his mind. But faced with a particular image, individual or event that fired his imagination Diderot could display remarkable brilliance.

Nothing illustrates this better than his art criticism, the *Salons.* Asked to write an account of the biennial exhibitions in the Grand Salon of the Louvre, he provided at first a workmanlike description of the paintings. He then became more interested and with each successive *Salon* his comments became longer and more penetrating. Painters are praised, castigated, asked for their advice or their intentions; pictures are taken apart, reassembled, or used as examples in a continuous discussion about the nature of art. Ideas are thrown up, asserted, offered to the reader: 'When one writes must one write everything? When one paints must one paint everything? Please, leave something for my imagination to provide.' What Diderot demands of a painting he in turn exemplifies in his writing. He engages us in a conversation into which we are immediately drawn and which is resumed whenever we return to these pages. Furthermore, in giving free rein to his imagination he broke out of the restrictions within which his conceptual thinking usually operated. In the *Salon de 1767,* as in the *Paradoxe sur le comédien* (dealing with how actors operate), Diderot saw a clear distinction between nature and culture, he described an area of specifically human creation. These speculations about the nature of art, fragmentary though they are, occupy an important position in the development of romantic and modern ideas of what exactly art is.

There is a similar sense of freedom and a similar fascination with the individual detail in his last novel *Jacques le fataliste et son maître.* This is an extraordinary ragbag of a book which operates at three levels. Jacques and his master are travelling, and as they do so they discuss the problems of human freedom (Jacques being a *fataliste,* denying freedom exists); they also tell and are told stories; but both their journey and their stories are subject to endless interruptions from the author calling attention to the basic problem of fiction—is this story true? —and showing how arbitrary the events of the novel are. The achievement of the book is uneven but it is written with great verve and at its centre is a problem which Diderot experienced intensely; the relationship between our concepts, values and mental attitudes, and the actual dynamic and texture of our lives.

This problem is also at the heart of his best-known work, *Le Neveu de Rameau.* In this dialogue Diderot *in propria persona* meets an eccentric but brilliant character, the nephew of the composer Rameau, who confronts him with a manifest and, it seems, overwhelming denial of almost every value he upholds. As in *Le Rêve de d'Alembert* it is not the ideas as such that make this work a masterpiece, striking though those ideas are. It is rather the way they arise out of a particular situation, the two men meeting and arguing, the collision of their attitudes, the elemental force of the nephew's attack on Diderot, his unpredictability, brilliance and pathos. We do not know why, nor precisely when, Diderot wrote this dialogue; although it is now his best-known work there is not a single reference to it in any of his other writings nor those of any contemporary. Nor have critics been able to agree on the outcome of the work, on which of the two men gets the better of the argument, whether they are both vindicated or both shown to be wrong. All readers have agreed, however, about the vivid force of the dialogue and the disturbing cogency of the questions it raises. In other words, the fact that the conclusion remains in doubt does not affect the value of the work as a whole.

In this respect *Le Neveu de Rameau* could be taken as the epitome of Diderot's achievements as a writer. We do not read him for the clear articulation of particular problems, even less for conclusive answers. 'Who knows where the interconnection of ideas will lead me? *Ma foi!* not me.' The person who writes good dialogue, he wrote, is the one who lets himself be carried away by his characters. 'The spirit of invention is agitated, moved, and active in a disordered way; it seeks. The spirit of method arranges, orders and assumes that everything is found.' Diderot was an inventive spirit who went in search and we read him most of all for the risks and delight he took in that search. We read him for the pleasure of being with such a lively, engaging, unpredictable person, a pleasure that brings the realization that where we arrive is less important than how we travel. This is not to say that there are no fixed points, or that sudden revelations cannot be caught, retained and then sent home on a postcard. Much of the excitement in reading Diderot comes from the fact that not only do these exist but that many of them are so modern: his ideas about materialism, the mind-body relationship, and what makes us specifically human; about scientific discovery, artistic creation, the value of poetry, the nature of fiction; most modern of all, his intimations that the ultimate nature of reality cannot be disentangled or defined apart from our own perception of reality.

But to be adequate to Diderot as he attempted himself to be adequate to reality we must try to see him whole. 'There is a poetic embroidery which is so closely bound up with its material that it is impossible to separate it without tearing the fabric.' In his own time Diderot was criticized for his 'continual digressions', and for the fact that his works seemed to be 'never finished'. In our own time he has been acclaimed as a precursor of every conceivable intellectual fashion; particular insights have been bundled up into modern conceptual schemes and presented as the essence of his thought. Both these emphases seem to me misplaced. His writings do digress continually and his works are full of insights we can call modern, but they cannot be contained within either of these aspects or attitudes. The heart of Diderot's achievement lies rather in a quality of openmindedness, a persistent desire to do justice to whatever makes the individual detail what it is, to catch the living moment in all its mobility, and a wonderful ability to show how the life of the mind interweaves with the complex texture of our whole experience. He wrote at a time when a new world was beginning to emerge, when people were beginning to have new confidence in their powers and to be apprehensive with new fears. It was a time rich with a sense of potential and opaque with a sense of confusion. Diderot lived that potential and that confusion, openly, honestly and zestfully. His writings were true to his experience. That is why they remain so vivid today.

Peter France   (essay date 1983)

SOURCE: *Diderot,* Oxford University Press, Oxford, 1983, 116 p.

[*In the following excerpt, France analyzes Diderot's attempt to formulate a rational system of explanation of the physical world, focusing on such issues as dualism, materialism, and determinism.*]

The history of thought in eighteenth-century France is often presented in terms of a conflict between rationalism and empiricism. On the one hand are those whose aim is to work out reasoned systems of philosophy, great edifices of conceptual thought which explain the totality of things. Opposed to them are the enemies of systems: believing, with Locke, that all our ideas originate in sense impressions (already a sizeable hypothesis), they devote themselves to observable facts, and are suspicious of the great constructions of such philosophers as Descartes, Leibniz or Spinoza—let alone Plato. In reality, of course, few thinkers fit neatly into either camp.

. . . [There is a] disruptive, questioning element in Diderot's writing, but this is not the whole picture. Perhaps because he was temperamentally inclined to free exploration, more a nightingale than a cuckoo, he also felt very strongly the desire for order. Chaos excited him, alarmed him and made him want to master it. The disruptive, questioning approach . . . is usually the first step towards the discovery or creation of a new, more satisfying order. The history of his thinking can be seen as a series of attempts to formulate rational systems of explanation—of the physical world, of moral, social and political behaviour, of aesthetics. . . . [He] was too perceptive (and too good a writer) not to admit objections to the orders he proposes, but that does not prevent him from aiming at a global understanding of the natural world and man's place within it.

The belief that everything that exists forms one great, connected system is one that has inspired philosophers and scientists for centuries. In Diderot's time it took the classic form of the Great Chain of Being, in which all the phenomena of nature could be assigned their rightful place. Such a notion is quite explicitly stated at several points in the work that is sometimes regarded as its author's 'discourse on method', the *Thoughts on the Interpretation of Nature.* For instance, discussing a theory put forward by the philosopher Maupertuis, Diderot asks rhetorically:

> I ask him . . . whether the universe or the general collection of all thinking and feeling molecules forms a whole or not. If he replies that it does not form a whole, he will be undermining with a single word the existence of God by introducing disorder into the universe, and he will be destroying the basis of philosophy by breaking the chain that links all beings. . . .

Here the postulate of unity is linked with God; although Diderot will try to explain the universe without recourse to God, in his philosophy he is seeking a substitute for the satisfying universe of his fathers. Nature will replace God.

This prophetic work looks far ahead, to a time when, thanks to a proper combination of deductive reasoning, hypothesis, empirical observation and experiment, the dark places of ignorance will be conquered by the light of scientific knowledge (such is the rhetoric of the Encyclopedist). Diderot is conscious of the limited achievements of the science of his day, but confident that a real beginning has been made on the enterprise which Francis Bacon had advocated 150 years earlier, the advancement of learning. Bacon's influence is visible throughout the *Thoughts on the Interpretation of Nature,* and he was indeed one of the chosen ancestors of the *Encyclopedia.*

Order is of the essence of encyclopedias. In a stock-taking article which is actually entitled 'Encyclopedia', Diderot declares that 'the aim of an encyclopedia is to gather together the knowledge which is scattered over the surface of the earth, and to expose the general system of knowledge to those with whom we live'. . . . The words 'general system' imply an underlying coherence, and it was one of his objectives in the *Encyclopedia* to lay out his material so that these inter-relationships were evident. It was not possible to achieve the God's-eye view of which d'Alembert had spoken in his Preliminary Discourse to the work, a vantage point from which 'the whole universe would be simply a single fact, one great truth.' But one might hope to place the reader on an eminence from which 'it would not be a tortuous labyrinth in which you lose yourself and can see no further than the place where you are standing, but a vast avenue stretching into the distance . . .'. . . . This was to be achieved by a *plan,* laying out the different fields of knowledge—or alternatively the diagram of the tree of knowledge—and by the constant use of cross-references to link one article with all related ones. Like-wise Diderot was conscious of the need for order within each article. In particular he set great store by the description of technological processes, which was so important a feature of the work and its greatest claim to usefulness. These descriptions were to be clear and exhaustive, following the same general order and attempting to introduce a more uniform terminology into activities which had grown up in a haphazard way. The beautiful plates which make up such a huge part of the complete work also contribute to an attractive image of rational human labour exploiting the natural world in an orderly and productive manner.

Such was the ideal of the *Encyclopedia.* In fact the finished product was considerably more chaotic than all this suggests; it hardly puts the reader in the position of clear-sighted mastery which Diderot envisaged. Nor indeed could the *Encyclopedia,* written as it was by many hands (and in many voices), expound a single system of thought. It is true that one can detect in numerous articles a common belief in the primacy of sense experience, together with an insistence on the value of experiment, and there are others which point cryptically towards a new way of thinking, but Diderot was not really able to use this great public compilation as a vehicle for his own theories about the nature of the universe and man's place within it. These are to be found rather in the *Letter on the Blind,* the *Thoughts on the Interpretation of Nature* and, above all, *D'Alembert's Dream.*

The last of these works consists of a sequence of three dialogues, written in the summer of 1769. It is the culmination of a long period of thought in which Diderot tried to work out a completely materialist theory of existence. The deism which we find in the *Philosophical Thoughts*—though by no means unchallenged—proclaims a complex but unchanging world order, designed and sustained by God, a supremely good and rational being. Such an order is compatible with the cosmology of Newton, as it had been with that of Descartes. It usually implies, though this is not spelt out in the *Philosophical Thoughts,* a distinction between two substances, *matter,* which is characterised by the property of 'extension' (i. e. it occupies a given place in space), and *spirit,* which is characterised by thought. In this way God is distinguished from the physical world and the human soul from the human body. It is this distinction, or *dualism,* which provides the initial problem in *D'Alembert's Dream:*

> I admit [says Diderot's interlocutor, d'Alembert] that a being which exists somewhere and which does not correspond to any point in space; a being which has no extension, and which occupies extended space and is present beneath every part of this space; which differs in essence from matter and is united to it: which moves it and is moved by it without moving; which acts upon it and is influenced by all its modifications; a being of which I have not the least idea—I admit that such a being is hard to accept. . . .

This challenge to the matter-spirit dualism (and indeed to the idea of God) highlights some of the difficulties encountered by the followers of Descartes. How, for instance, if the mind is immaterial, can one explain the way in which I decide (mentally) to raise my hand, and my muscles contract (physically) in the necessary way for my hand to be raised? Is there, as Descartes suggested, a sort of middle ground, located in a part of the brain called the pineal gland, where the two substances somehow interact? Or is there, as Leibnitz argued, a 'preestablished harmony' which makes thought coincide miraculously with action? Such notions seemed absurd to many thinkers of the eighteenth century, but as d'Alembert goes on to point out at the beginning of the dialogue, 'other obscurities await those who reject [them]'. If one was to avoid dualism, it was necessary to eliminate one of the two substances, declaring either that there is nothing but spirit, or that there is nothing but matter. The former position, idealism, is defended by the British philosopher Berkeley, who argued that as thinking beings we can only have knowledge of ideas; if we say that there is a tree in front of us, this means merely that we have formed certain ideas to which we give this name, but we have no way of knowing that there is a material substance in the world that corresponds to these ideas.

Diderot knew Berkeley's idealism, calling it an 'extravagant system . . . which to the shame of the human mind and of philosophy is the most difficult of all to refute, even though it is the most absurd of all systems'. . . . He himself, from the time of the *Letter on the Blind,* looked rather to materialism, which corresponded better with his fundamentally non-religious cast of thought, and which offered a more fruitful basis for the scientific study of human life.

Materialism was very much a minority view in eighteenth-century France—indeed it was a scandalous view. It had nevertheless a distinguished ancestry. Diderot himself was influenced not only by contemporaries such as La Mettrie, author of *Man a Machine (L'Homme-machine),* but by the ancient Epicurean doctrine expounded for instance in the *De Rerum Natura* of the Latin poet Lucretius. A view of this kind is advanced by the spokesman for atheism in the *Philosophical Thoughts;* assuming that matter is eternal, and that movement is essential to it, as it changes its position over infinite time and space it must, according to the laws of probability, eventually arrange itself in the relatively durable and (to us) satisfactory order which we are tempted to attribute to an act of intelligent creation: 'Thus the mind should be more surprised by the hypothetical duration of chaos than by the actual birth of the universe' . . .

Such a speculative theory of matter in movement allows Diderot to suggest an alternative to the idea of creation. It does not, however, take him very far towards an explanation of how matter is made up and how it behaves. And it tells one very little about the nature and behaviour of living beings—and above all of human beings. It was these questions which increasingly attracted Diderot as he turned his attention from mathematics and physics (still very important in the *Letter on the Blind*) to the rapidly developing sciences of biology, chemistry and medicine. In the two decades after 1750 he studied these subjects enthusiastically if spasmodically, keeping abreast of recent developments, so that by the time he came to write *D'Alembert's Dream* (yet another work of private exploration) he was able to put forward hypotheses for a materialist explanation not only of animal life, but also of human feeling and thought.

His fundamental idea is that all matter possesses 'sensibility', the ability to feel. This may remain latent, but it is made active when a 'dead' molecule is assimilated to others which are 'living'. The prime example of this is eating:

> When you eat, what do you do? You remove the obstacles which prevented the sensibility of the food from becoming active. You assimilate it to yourself, you make flesh of it, you animalise it, you make it capable of feeling. . . .

Thus he throws a bridge between the animate and the inanimate. It is a shaky bridge, as he realises ('If I cannot solve the problem you set me, at least I come very near to doing so'). He finds support for the theory of universal sensibility in the recent experiments of Needham and Buffon, who had claimed (mistakenly) to have observed the process of spontaneous generation. Further corroboration came from studies of the development of the embryo; there is an eloquent passage on the egg:

> Do you see this egg? It is with this that we can overturn all the schools of theology and all the temples on earth. What is the egg? An insensible mass until the germ is introduced into it. And what is it after the germ has been introduced? Still an insensible mass, for the germ itself is only a crude and inert fluid. And how will this mass acquire a different sort of organisation, sensibility and life? By heat. And what will produce the heat? Movement. . . .

Of course there are great unanswered questions here. Diderot addresses himself in particular to the question of the unity of the sentient being. How can all the different molecules which make up a chicken or a philosopher act as one being? How does contiguity become continuity? The difficulty of such problems is indicated by the fact that Diderot's answers consist partly of analogies—with a swarm of bees, a monastery or quicksilver. As he himself says, quoting an older saying, 'comparison is not reason', and the reader is probably left with a feeling that he has not been taken very far towards a real understanding of such matters.

There are bound to be weaknesses in what is essentially an attempt to solve the problem of the origin of life, but it is important to see that the notion of universal sensibility, vague as it is, clears the way for an exploration of human behaviour and thought which does without the mysterious notion of soul or spirit. In the second dialogue of *D'Alembert's Dream,* Diderot introduces a doctor, Bordeu (a famous doctor in real life), who goes a lot further in the detailed explanation of the way the human body and mind work. He talks about the interrelation of the different parts of the body, the functioning of the nervous system, the role of the brain, the physical causes of various forms of pathological behaviour, the operation of memory and many other matters. The essential point to emerge is that for Bordeu (and he convinces his interlocutor, Mademoiselle de Lespinasse) each individual's personality is above all the result of his or her biological make-up. For Diderot, as for Locke, all our ideas do indeed originate in the senses, but our mental operations, our intelligence or dullness, sensitivity or insensitivity, depend primarily on the state of what he calls our 'fibres', which may broadly be equated with the nervous system.

It is noteworthy that Diderot (through Bordeu) seeks to demonstrate this thesis quite largely by way of exceptional cases, what the period called 'monsters'. . . . [The] upset a belief in a comfortably ordered universe; here we observe that the exception can also serve to reveal the real physical laws that govern us. In *The Nun* the strange behaviour of women in a convent is meant to show something about the natural reaction of human beings to different environments; so here the stories of Siamese twins and the like bring out more clearly the dependence of mental states on bodily conditions.

All well and good, but what use are these ancient speculations to a present-day reader? The basic philosophical question of the nature of mind remains an open one, of course, but I doubt if there is much to interest a modern biologist or doctor in *D'Alembert's Dream.* The historian of scientific ideas will obviously find more in it; Diderot was not an isolated pioneer, but he was in the forefront of new thinking about man's place in the natural order. However, what most modern readers can derive from these dialogues is above all the feeling of expansive excitement as Diderot pursues all kinds of ideas, throwing out wild suggestions and analogies and miming in the form of his work his dynamic vision of the universe. It is not only a set of dialogues, it also contains a dream. In the sequences of the second dialogue which record d'Alembert's supposed dream, Diderot pushes his ideas to the limit, expanding his materialist account of man and the animals to a great vision of cosmic change. It is here above all that we see how far he has moved from the reassuring and majestic harmony of the Newtonian world system. Like Saunderson in the *Letter on the Blind,* the sleeping d'Alembert envisages Nature in a state of constant flux, where there is no longer any fixity of species:

> Who knows what species of animals preceded us? And who knows what species of animals will follow ours? Everything changes, everything passes, only the All remains. . . .
>
> The miracle is life and sensibility, and this miracle is no longer a miracle . . . When once I have seen inert matter pass into a sensitive state, nothing can astonish me. . . .

Nothing is surprising, all is possible. And indeed this section of the work is full of heady speculations about the origin and development of species. Diderot is a long way removed from Darwin's teleological notion of natural selection, but there are moments when he seems to hint at the scheme of evolution which was later developed by Lamarck. Take for instance the remark thrown out by Bordeu: 'Our organs produce our needs, and conversely our needs produce our organs'. . . . This is a strikingly bold statement in an age when most people believed—and were expected to believe—that the different parts of creation always had been, and would always remain, what they are now.

Through the dreaming d'Alembert, whose words are explicated by the sober Bordeu, Diderot thus paints a vivid picture of a cosmos of matter in constant movement, a vision of universal flux which is both stimulating and frightening. It must be stressed, however, that this is still an ordered world. It is subject to physical laws and to the overriding law of cause and effect. Nowhere in Diderot do we find anything like his contemporary Hume's critique of causality. On the contrary, he declares that we live in and are part of a material world whose laws govern all our actions and all our thoughts. Like Freud over a century later, he combines a view of man which is profoundly disturbing to habitual ways of thinking with the scientist's insistence that all the phenomena he is describing have the regularity (and thus, if we knew enough, the predictability) of the laws of matter.

Determinism is therefore a recurrent theme in his thinking. As early as 1756, in a celebrated letter to the playwright Landois, Diderot explains his views in these terms:

> The word *freedom* has no meaning; there are and there can be no free beings; we are simply the product of the general order of things, our

physical organisation, our education and the chain of events. These things exert an irresistible influence over us. One can no more conceive of a being behaving without a motive than of one arm of a scales moving up or down without the action of a weight. . . .

This was not necessarily a comfortable view for a man with a warm attachment to the idea of virtue, since as he says in the letter to Landois and again in *D'Alembert's Dream,* vice and virtue are also empty words (in that they imply an idea of personal responsibility) and should be replaced in a philosophical vocabulary by the terms 'beneficence' and 'maleficence'. Men and women cannot be rationally punished or rewarded for a free exercise of will, but they can be 'modified' by praise, blame, laws, examples, rewards and punishments (and presumably brain surgery and the like). Of course in his turn the 'modifier' is no more free than the person modified. Diderot is facing here the issue raised in Marx's third thesis on Feuerbach: 'The materialist doctrine concerning the changing of circumstances and education forgets that the circumstances must be changed by people, and that the educator must himself be educated.' In fact, in his later writing, Diderot puts forward a more complex idea of determinism than that proposed in the letter to Landois, and suggests that the well-organised person, the *philosophe* for instance, may be capable of self-modification. He also makes fun of the whole intractable question in his novel *Jacques the Fatalist.* Here the hero repeats parrot-like his former master's lessons of fatalism, but still manages to act resourcefully and (for those about him) unpredictably. Determinism, though it may seem at odds with our normal perceptions, provides a comfortable and unconstraining framework for ordinary life.

At all events, the postulate of physical determinism was essential to Diderot's philosophical and scientific vision. As I have said, he envisaged a natural world (including man) in a state of constant though law-governed change, which scientists will gradually come to understand more fully. But what is the relation between this complex and dynamic order of nature and the ordered systems which men and women create in the fields of morals, politics or aesthetics.? If we rule out the possibility that there are God-given laws which can govern our behaviour, can we hope to find a solid foundation for our laws in nature? What reason have we to think that nature is on our side? These are questions which taxed Diderot in his mature years, unanswerable questions it may be said, and questions which remain unanswered, yet difficult to ignore.

At one extreme there is the awareness that 'vice and virtue, everything is equally in nature,' . . . or, in Dostoevsky's words, 'if God does not exist, everything is permitted.' Diderot approached this position at times but, as with his contemporaries, his dearest wish was to root his own moral and aesthetic values securely in a natural order. From first to last nature was one of his key words. It figures in two of his titles, *Thoughts on the Interpretation of Nature,* where it stands for the natural world, and *The Natural Son,* where it draws our attention both to the artificiality of French marriage laws and to the 'natural' virtues in which all the characters are finally and happily united. What then does Diderot mean by natural morality?

An article entitled 'Natural Law', which appeared in the *Encyclopedia* in 1755, spells out more clearly the idea of a law of nature which can underpin a satisfactory social code. Diderot takes up the traditional debate against pessimistic thinkers such as Hobbes. The challenge which he has to answer is that of the violent man (an ancestor of the marquis de Sade), who speaks in the following terms:

> I realise that I am carrying terror and disorder into the midst of the human species; but either I must be unhappy or I must cause unhappiness for others, and no one is dearer to me than I am to myself. Let no one blame me for this hateful predilection; I am not free to be otherwise. The voice of nature never expresses itself more strongly within me than when it speaks in favour of myself. . . .

Diderot's answer to this lies in an appeal to a 'general will' which is 'always good'. This is not Rousseau's political 'general will' which is confined to one particular community; this article expresses a belief in the general agreement of all human beings on a universally valid moral code:

> It is your conformity with all other men and their conformity with you which will indicate to you when you are parting company with your species and when you are remaining within it. Never lose sight of it therefore, or you will see the notions of goodness, justice, humanity and virtue begin to crumble in your mind. Say to yourself frequently: 'I am a man, and I have no other truly inalienable rights than those of humanity.' . . .

'I am a man' seems to refer to the famous dictum of Terence: 'I am a man and I do not regard anything human as foreign to me.' This universalism never left Diderot; he shared it with many of his contemporaries, though not with Rousseau, whose political ideal of citizenship was at odds with the cosmopolitanism of many of his former friends. It may seem to contradict the evolutionary vision of *D'Alembert's Dream,* but Diderot explains in 'Natural Law' that 'even if one were to suppose the notion of species in a state of constant flux, the nature of *natural law* would not change because it will always be relative to the general will and the common wishes of the whole species'. . . . At any time, therefore, one might hope to draw up a natural code based on the general consent of all peoples, a set of laws which are always found to lead to the greater happiness of the individual and the species.

For of course the ultimate criterion of this code of nature is happiness. Diderot does not propose the sort of calculation of relative sums of happiness which we find in utilitarian moral thought, but he certainly sees no other justification for virtuous behaviour than that it will increase happiness. This will even be true when the individual sacrifices his or her selfish interests, since nature has conveniently installed in us all a moral sense which will make us unhappy if we ignore it (what Diderot's Scottish contemporary Adam Smith called the 'impartial spectator'). This is how the heroine Constance preaches to the hero Dorval in *The Natural Son:*

> The effect of virtue on our souls is no less necessary and no less powerful than that of beauty on our senses . . . in the heart of man there is a taste for order which is older than any process of reflective thought . . . it is this taste which makes us susceptible to shame, and it is shame which makes us fear contempt more even than death. . . .

In this way nature acts as a moral policeman. Just as excessive drinking or debauchery brings illness, so anti-social behaviour will bring us the unhappiness that comes from knowing that we seem despicable to others. It is this natural moral order which gives us the strength to act virtuously in the face of ridicule and apparent unhappiness. Quite late in life, in the *Refutation of Helvétius,* Diderot declared yet again, as he had at various stages throughout his career:

> Even in a society as badly ordered as ours, when successful vice is often applauded and unsuccessful virtue almost always ridiculed, I am convinced that in the last analysis our best way to happiness is to act virtuously. . . .

In a 'badly ordered' society this is an act of faith. It would be better of course if society could be ordered more in accordance with the laws of nature. In the *Supplement to Bougainville's Voyage* and elsewhere, Diderot puts forward the idea of the 'three codes', the code of nature, the civil code and the religious code. These are almost always at odds in society. Inevitably, therefore, people are torn between different duties, whereas ideally we should either dispense with the two man-made codes or bring them into line with the code of nature.

But what is this elusive set of rules? It is all very well to use words like goodness, justice or humanity—we are all in favour of virtue. But can such words be given any positive content? Very often it seems, as the previous chapter suggested, that the idea of nature is an essentially *critical* one. The vague notion of natural goodness serves to throw into sharper relief the follies of existing society. Thus in Diderot's novels *Jacques the Fatalist* and *The Nun,* in such stories as **"This is not a Story"** or **"Madame de la Carlière"** and in the *Conversation of a Father with his Children* various misfortunes are seen as the result of the clash between natural morality and the laws or customs of society. The *Conversation,* for instance, raises the question: is a wise man justified in breaking an unjust law? The discussion turns on a series of anecdotes. Of these the most striking concerns the finding of an old will which seems to deprive the rightful and poverty-stricken inheritors of a small fortune in favour of a rich and apparently undeserving man. Should the person who finds the will burn it? Diderot, who appears as a character in this conversation piece, has no doubt that he should, because 'the reason of the human species is far more sacred than the reason of a legislator.' On the other hand, the philosopher's firm statement is equally firmly rejected by his father, and we cannot take the character 'Myself' as speaking unequivocally for the author. But in any case it is evident that bad laws cause unhappiness.

It is interesting to note that a work entitled the *Code of Nature* by Morelly was attributed by contemporaries to

Diderot and even figured in the first collected edition of his works. It puts forward an alarmingly regimented utopian social organisation. It is odd that this should have been thought of as his work, since, with its deathly rigidity, it seems precisely the sort of work he could not have written. Nor is there anything in his writings like Rousseau's *Émile,* which outlines stage by stage an upbringing supposedly in accordance with the laws of nature. However, in certain of his later writings, Diderot does paint some rapid sketches of a better social order. Writing for Catherine of Russia, for instance, he speaks of the need for a nation to have a written code, a 'uniform and general law'. . . . He also suggests the sort of reforms which in any country would bring about greater general happiness: reduction of the power and wealth of the church, greater fairness in the distribution of the tax burden, removal of unjustified privileges, rewards for merit and virtue, reform of the penal code and so on. Likewise, in his contributions to Raynal's *History of the Two Indies* we can see the expression of a more rational approach to legislation and social organisation. There is nothing very remarkable about all this; Diderot shares the liberal reformist position of many of his contemporaries, appealing like them to a universal (and therefore natural) standard of reason, though tempering it to suit the situation of particular countries.

The order of nature is most directly invoked in Diderot's most utopian work, the *Supplement to Bougainville's Voyage.* As we have seen, this is by no means a straightforward work, and the utopian element in it is framed by conversations that show it to be a dream rather than a blueprint for reform. The main thrust of the dialogue is satirical, but the satire rests on a vision of a more 'natural' organisation of sexual, family and social life. Diderot's Tahiti is a society with a minimum of laws, not a society without laws. For instance, because nature invites men and women to mate so as to perpetuate the species, there are in this earthly paradise no rules enjoining marital fidelity, and children are regarded as the common wealth of the whole community. There are however rules against unproductive sexual practices—dissolute women who continue to receive men after they have passed the age of childbearing are exiled to another part of the island. None of this is very ferocious perhaps, but it shows that nature can provide a sanction for repression—and incidentally that the laws of Diderot's nature are aligned with the concern for increasing the birth-rate which was common among the *philosophes,* and which has persisted in France to the present day.

The final conversation of the *Supplement* makes it clear that the establishment of a natural code of sexuality is no easy matter for members of an advanced society. The speaker 'B', who seems most to represent Diderot, says, 'I should be inclined to think that the most savage people on earth, the Tahitians, who have kept scrupulously to the law of nature, are nearer to a good system of laws than any civilised people'. . . . Similar remarks are to be found in his writings for Raynal. The editor of the *Encyclopedia,* like several of his friends and acquaintances, had a considerable streak of primitivism, and this became stronger as he grew older. Committed though he was to technical and scientific progress and to the cause of rational thought, he also looked nostalgically to the simpler, nobler and happier world of the savage, the Ancients and even—at times—the peasant. One of his stories, *The Two Friends of Bourbonne (Les Deux Amis de Bourbonne),* shows the sublime friendship of two simple country people and contrasts it favourably with the civilised inhumanity and folly of judges, landowners and priests. Such notions remained pretty theoretical of course, but they kept alive the faith that a better moral and social order might be found.

The theme of the 'noble savage' is only one aspect of the search for universally valid systems with which this chapter has been concerned. I have concentrated on scientific and moral questions, but we may rapidly note the same universalising urge at work in two other fields, aesthetics and language.

In the speech from *The Natural Son* quoted above, the moral sense is compared to the sense of beauty that is shared by all men and women. In thinking about beauty Diderot was torn between a relativist awareness of the difference of tastes ('there is no disputing about tastes') and the familiar desire to find what David Hume called the 'standard of taste', some generally applicable criterion of beauty. In his *Discourse on Dramatic Poetry* he wrote:

> It is certain that there will be no end to our disputes as long as each person takes himself as model and judge. There will be as many standards as there are individuals, and for each individual there will be as many different standards as there are different periods in his life.
>
> That is enough, I think, to show the necessity of seeking for a standard which is not peculiar to me. Until this is done most of my judgements will be wrong and all of them will be insecure. . . .

Between his translation of Shaftesbury of 1745 and his last art criticism of the 1770s, he puzzled over this problem, seeking always to overcome the chaos of mere subjectivism. Corresponding to the *Encyclopedia* article 'Natural Law' there is the article entitled 'Beauty' (Beau). This contains an attempt to found the idea of beauty on the abstract notion of 'relationships'. The notion is so general as to be virtually meaningless, but only through this degree of generality can Diderot preserve the idea of a beauty which does not depend on particular perceptions. Thus he is able to reach the reassuring if hollow conclusion that 'Whatever may be the causes of the diversity of our judgements, this is not a reason for believing that real beauty, the beauty that consists in the perception of relationships, is merely a figment of the imagination'. . . .

The *Encyclopedia* article is hardly satisfactory. It is likely to reveal to the modern reader simply an excessive faith in the power of reason to account for beauty. In this faith Diderot was a man of his time; indeed, in some respects he holds to ideas about art which were derived from the French classical period, if not earlier. In later years, as he acquired a much greater practical knowledge of many of the arts, he did not abandon the belief that beauty exists in reality and not just in the eye of the beholder. Now, however, he was more inclined to situate it in the 'imitation of nature'. But of course the word 'nature' once again raises all kinds of problems: above all, is the nature to be imitated an ideal nature or the nature of **D'Alembert's Dream?**. . . .

Diderot's thinking about language exhibits the same uncertain belief in a universally valid order. The eighteenth century was the golden age of 'general grammar'. Philosophical grammarians tried to describe the fundamental structure which underpinned the variety of actual languages, a structure which was supposed to correspond to the processes of human thought, since these were everywhere the same. At one point in his **Letter on the Deaf and Dumb** (which includes some of his most interesting remarks on language and art) Diderot declares that Cicero, before speaking his sentences in their Latin order must have thought them in their logical French order (subject - verb - predicate). It is not surprising therefore that he, like Leibniz or Condillac, toyed with the dream of a universal language which would represent the natural world as it impinges on the mind of human beings:

> Once such a language was accepted and established, our ideas would become permanent, distant times and places would come together, links would be set up between every inhabited point in space and time and all living and thinking beings would be able to communicate. . . .

But again this universal order is a dream rather than an attainable reality. Diderot speaks elsewhere of his 'well-founded habit of suspecting all general laws concerning language'. . . . In observing language, as in observing life, he was too conscious of multiplicity to be an untroubled apostle of universal order. He wanted order and laws, and up to a point he found them or created them, but he also saw variety and exceptions.

John Morley on Diderot's relationship with Catherine the Great:

On most days he was in her society from three in the afternoon until five or six. Etiquette was banished. Diderot's simplicity and vehemence were as conspicuous and as unrestrained at Tsarskoe-selo as at Grandval or the Rue Taranne. If for a moment the torrent of his improvisation was checked by the thought that he was talking to a great lady, Catherine encouraged him to go on. *"Allons,"* she cried, *"entre hommes tout est permis."* The philosopher in the heat of exposition brought his hands down upon the imperial knees with such force and iteration, that Catherine complained that he made them black and blue. She was sometimes glad to seek shelter from such zealous enforcement of truth, behind a strong table.

John Morley in his Diderot and the Encyclopedists, *1888.*

Maurice Cranston   **(lecture date 1984)**

SOURCE: "Diderot," in *Philosophers and Pamphleteers:*

Political Theorists of the Enlightenment, Oxford University Press, Oxford, 1986, pp. 98-120.

[*In the following lecture, originally delivered in 1984, Cranston examines Diderot's political ideas, dividing these into four successive groups: a materialist theory of politics during his friendship with Rousseau; a scientific theory of absolutism during his editorship of the* Encyclopedie; *a critique of despotism that had much in common with the ideas of Montesquieu; and a final position that castigated European colonialism and shared many of the features of Rousseau's political philosophy.*]

Diderot is almost always spoken of as the most attractive philosopher of the French Enlightenment. All his contemporaries—except Rousseau after he had quarrelled with him—thought well of him. He is also the most elusive of the *philosophes.* In the first half of his career, Diderot published almost everything he wrote; later, he put his manuscripts away in a drawer, and it was only after his death that his best books were published. It is hard to say what prompted him to withhold them from the Press. It was certainly not lack of courage, for Diderot was the most fearless writer of his time.

The **Encyclopédie,** which he edited, is the great monument of the Enlightenment, and it was the product of a bold and unremitting struggle, which Diderot had often to undertake alone. He was a victim of censorship, persecution, and imprisonment; he was betrayed by his publisher and deserted by his collaborators, but he battled on doggedly for what he always thought of as a *cause.* He understood philosophy not simply as the enlargement of knowledge, or even the enlargement of useful knowledge, or even the enlargement of useful knowledge plus the improvement of men's conduct; besides all this it was a fight against traditional beliefs and the institutions which upheld them.

Like Rousseau, Diderot had a hard life. They were born within a few months of each other and they arrived in Paris at about the same time, two ambitious young men from the provinces seeking fame and fortune in the republic of letters. It is often said that a generation separated Diderot and Rousseau from Montesquieu and Voltaire. But it was something more than age. Montesquieu and Voltaire were grandees; in their different ways they both became famous writers before they were 30, whereas Diderot and Rousseau had a long wait for recognition. Moreover, Diderot and Rousseau never ceased to be short of money; they contemplated life from garrets, while Montesquieu and Voltaire looked out on the world from the windows of their stately châteaux. Naturally their perspectives were different, especially in matters of economics and politics.

Diderot is every bit as paradoxical a philosopher as is Rousseau; perhaps even more so. His political writings do not add up to a system in the sense that Rousseau's do. Diderot will have to be called a 'dialectical' thinker, in that he has a way of pushing a thesis to its limits and then stepping back to argue against it. Professor Wade [in his *The Structure and Form of the French Enlightenment*] suggests that 'whereas Voltaire debates with the public, Diderot debates with himself'. It may be denied that Voltaire even debated with the public, since he talked without listening; but Diderot did undoubtedly debate with himself, and to that extent he is a philosopher in the style of Socrates. He is also a very intense and creative thinker, pouring out ideas like flames from a volcano, in all directions at once.

One consequence of this is that commentaries on Diderot are as often as not attempts to impose on Diderot's thinking a systematic order which he failed to arrange himself, and this is particularly true of his political ideas. He has been depicted as an exponent of liberal pluralism, of constitutional monarchy, of enlightened despotism, of socialism, even of communism, and passages in his writings can be invoked to support any of these interpretations, some more plausibly than others. He is a great favourite with Marxists, and he has come to be highly honoured in the Soviet Union. There is more than one reason for this: Diderot's papers, acquired by Catherine the Great, are in Leningrad, and with the Russian flair for turning every fragment of its *patrimoine* to the service of national self-esteem, Diderot had only to be shown to be ideologically acceptable in order for him to be revered as a forerunner of Lenin.

Since Diderot attacked metaphysics and religion, wrote ungracious words about the rich, and was an early critic of colonial policies which Lenin later denounced as 'imperialism', it cannot have been difficult to make him sound like a hero of the Soviet Union. It was only necessary to ignore his doubts about materialism, his belief in economic freedom, his passion for individual liberty, and his arguments in favour of checks and balances against monolithic government.

Like many other philosophers Diderot had different views at different times of his life, and while he cannot be said to have given unreserved assent to any doctrine at any period, there are certain discernible phases in the unfolding of his political thought. The first corresponds to the period of his collaboration and friendship with Rousseau, when he tried to work out a materialist theory of politics which was an alternative both to Hobbes's materialist theory and to Rousseau's non-materialist theory. The second coincides with Diderot's activity as editor of the *Encyclopédie,* when he attempted to set forth a scientific theory of absolutism which was an improvement on Voltaire's. The third originates in his association with Catherine the Great, when personal experience of a despotic regime impelled him to work out a political theory which had much in common with that of Montesquieu. In the final phase, when he became increasingly critical of the colonial expansion of European monarchies, he returned to a position which is closer to that of Rousseau.

Although Diderot never followed the example of Montesquieu and Voltaire in visiting England, he read English, and owed much to English philosophers, especially Bacon, Shaftesbury, and Hobbes. He had learned English less from scholarly curiosity than in order to find work as a translator, for Diderot had to earn his living solely as a writer—and was one of the first men in France to do so. He refused to follow his father's advice and become either a priest or a lawyer; and he had no private means. His fa-

ther was a master cutler in Langres, where Diderot was born in October 1713. He had thus much the same kind of bourgeois origins as Rousseau, born in 1712 the son of a watchmaker of Geneva—the most notable difference between them being that while Rousseau was largely an autodidact, Diderot received a superior Jesuit education, which left him with a highly sophisticated mind and an unwavering hostility to Christianity in general and to priests in particular.

It is not easy to say what Diderot owed to Rousseau and Rousseau to Diderot in the course of their many conversations together. Rousseau, undoubtedly, had the genius, Diderot the culture; Rousseau the temperament of a Plato, Diderot that of an Aristotle; Rousseau the insight into unseen things; Diderot the eye for the visible, with no less imagination, and perhaps rather more admirable qualities of character. Rousseau complains in the *Confessions* that Diderot tried to dominate him, and even to insert some of his black thoughts into the *Discourse on Inequality;* but if Diderot did try to impose his ideas on Rousseau, Rousseau for his part succeeded in making Diderot apply his mind to certain subjects and to think about them in certain ways.

On several crucial points of social theory they seem always to have disagreed. Whereas Rousseau argued that man was solitary by nature and social only by convention, Diderot insisted that man was naturally social. Diderot may well have arrived at this belief as a result of reading (and translating) Shaftesbury; at any rate, the natural sociability of man was a key element in the theory of civil society which he attempted to construct on the basis of a naturalistic conception of the universe.

Like Rousseau, Diderot was an evolutionist, but he told a different story of man's evolution. He argued that man was originally a social animal in the way that flocks or herds of beasts are social, having altruistic sentiments which united neighbours together on peaceable and friendly terms. In time, differences of natural strength led to certain members of these human societies dominating others, so that the flocks or herds came to be transformed into packs, that is, groups controlled by masterful and aggressive leaders. At a further stage of evolution, Diderot suggested, these packs based on violence were transformed into civil societies based on contract; force was thus changed into right, and the ferocious chiefs became civilized as anointed kings.

From this account of the origin of political societies Diderot drew more than one set of conclusions. The first was an idealized primitivism: the argument that man was designed by nature to live in amicable communitarian association with others, without being intimidated by bullies or having to tame those bullies by introducing systems of positive law. Here we have a much more 'Utopian' image of man than that suggested by Rousseau, for whom man, if originally innocent, was also utterly solitary. Diderot's original man, social by nature, is the real 'noble savage', so often mistakenly thought to have been an invention of Rousseau.

We meet Diderot's noble savage again in a book which

dates from his later years, his ***Supplément au voyage de Bougainville.*** [The critic adds in a footnote that this work was written in 1772, immediately after the publication of Bougainville's *Voyage autour du monde.* Diderot circulated copies of his text, but the book was not published until 1796.] This is written in Diderot's favourite dialogue form, which prevents us from being sure which voice is that of Diderot himself. The participants in the conversation discuss Bougainville's reports of the societies he encountered in Tahiti and other islands of the South Seas. They understand him to have found people who live happily and wholly according to natural impulse, a people with no institutions of private property or of marriage. These people engage without inhibitions in sexual congress; the word 'incest' does not exist in their language. The very idea of crime is unknown to them. They are content to live frugal, healthy lives; or rather they were content before Bougainville arrived, and the lives of the Tahitians were ruined by the modern Christian culture that the French mariners took to their islands, a culture which introduced the concepts of sin, guilt, greed, chastity, and jealousy, together with diseases hitherto unknown.

One has the impression, reading the ***Supplément au voyage de Bougainville,*** that Diderot himself is using the experience of Tahiti as an argument for anarchistic communism, but in a letter to a friend we find him writing:

> Shall I tell you a fine paradox? It is true that I am convinced that the only real happiness for the human race lies in a social state in which there would be no king, no magistrate, no priest, no laws, no 'mine' and 'thine', no movable property, no landed property, no vices, no virtues. And this social state is damnably *ideal.*

Indeed in later sections of the ***Supplément*** itself, Diderot seems to dismantle the romantic image of Tahiti and to suggest that behind the façade the Tahitians are neither happy nor innocent. He points out the flaws of primitivism; he warns us not to be deceived by an all too beautiful fantasy. The ***Supplément*** is 'Utopian' only in the very exact sense that it belongs to the same genre as Sir Thomas More's *Utopia,* a dialogue in which the author's own attitude is veiled, and which every reader must interpret for himself.

The second set of conclusions which Diderot drew from his doctrine of the natural sociability of man was that the history of human societies was a felicitous development from the rule of force to the rule of law; so that side by side with his doctrine of original innocence, which had much in common with that of Rousseau, Diderot developed a doctrine of progress which was at odds with Rousseau's thinking, although he came in the end to question progress as he questioned most things.

It was the doctrine of progress which led Diderot to advocate for a time that policy of authoritarian government and social engineering which prompted nineteenth-century historians to speak of 'enlightened despotism' and to ascribe it to Diderot and the other philosophers of the French Enlightenment as a shared political creed. In fact, only very minor *philosophes* advocated enlightened despotism. What Diderot favoured at a certain period was a kind of absolutism, along the lines of Voltaire's 'enlightened royalism', the rule of the philosopher-king. Even Diderot's attachment to this doctrine was characterized by reservations, and in his later years he rejected it entirely. He was drawn to it in the first place by the teaching of Francis Bacon, who was also the inspiration of the ***Encyclopédie,*** of which Diderot was appointed editor at the age of 33.

Originally the idea had been for Diderot to translate into French *Chambers's Encyclopaedia,* a routine job of the kind to which he had reconciled himself in the course of earning his living as a free-lance writer; but he succeeded in transforming the enterprise into the fulfilment of a grand design envisaged by Francis Bacon nearly a century and a half earlier: the assembly of all available knowledge, and especially scientific and technical knowledge, in a systematic compendium. This was intended to be no mere scholarly edifice, but an instrument of progress; a guide to salvation through science. For Diderot, as for Bacon himself, science was less a theoretical activity designed to furnish knowledge of nature than a practical activity designed to give man mastery over nature, a mastery to be used, in Bacon's words [in his preface to *The Great Instauration*], 'for the benefit and use of life'.

Bacon's programme for salvation through science called for a number of innovations: no more wasting time on traditional metaphysics or Classical texts, but the institution of laboratories, colleges, research stations, and academies for scientific activity, and, what is more, a strong centralized government unhindered by medieval obstruction from parliament and law courts to ensure that the policy was put into effect. Diderot, enthralled by Bacon's vision, resolved to produce, instead of a mere translation of *Chambers,* a comprehensive survey of the kind Bacon had proposed; a record of scientific achievement which would also be a work of propaganda for the new Baconian faith. In a letter to Voltaire, Diderot wrote:

> This shall be our device: no quarter for the superstitious, for the fanatical, for the ignorant, or for fools, malefactors, or tyrants. I would like to see our brethren united in zeal for truth, goodness, and beauty—a rather more valuable trinity than the other one. It is not enough for us to know more than the Christians; we must show that we are better, and that science has done more for mankind than divine or sufficient grace.

The ***Encyclopédie*** was advertised in 1750 as a work to be in ten volumes of text, with two volumes of plates. It grew to be a work of seventeen volumes of text and eleven volumes of plates. It ran to twenty million words and absorbed twenty-five years of Diderot's life. He considered the plates to be as important as the text, because they illustrated not just the forms of nature, but the instruments and techniques of work. Industry, or what he called 'manufacturing', Diderot regarded as even more important than agriculture as an instrument of progress; for 'manufacturing', as he put it, 'is the activity which sets men free'. He took it upon himself as editor of the ***Encyclopédie*** to visit all the workshops of artisans and all the little factories he could find in Paris to make sure that the illustrators he employed made accurate drawings of the most up-to-date machines and processes.

One thing Diderot was not qualified to do was to supervise the strictly scientific articles; and here he had, at any rate for the first few years, a co-editor in d'Alembert. Jean le Rond d'Alembert, who had started life as a foundling on the steps of the Church of Saint-Jean le Rond, was four years younger than Diderot, but he had risen at an early age to fame as a scientist in the fields of geometry and physics, and was already well established in Paris at a time when Diderot was an unknown literary journalist. D'Alembert provided for the *Encyclopédie* the scientific expertise that Diderot lacked. If less hostile to religion, he shared Diderot's belief in the doctrine of salvation through science; but he did not have the same willingness to suffer for that belief.

Diderot's own courage was remarkable. When interrogated by the police, he denied having written things he had written, but he would not desist from his activities. He was put in prison at Vincennes, just as Voltaire had been put in the Bastille; but he did not think of quitting Paris when he was released, as Voltaire had done, and as Voltaire urged him to do. Diderot continued to publish the *Encyclopédie* in France, courting further persecution, when Voltaire begged him to remove it to safety in Holland or Switzerland. When further trouble threatened—in 1758— his co-editor d'Alembert resigned and several of his most eminent contributors, including Charles Duclos and Marmontel, dissociated themselves from the *Encyclopédie.* But Diderot carried on defiantly; and in the end his courage was rewarded. The *Encyclopédie* proved to be a prodigious success.

Almost all the writers connected with it became fashionable. The *parlements* and the Church remained hostile, but the government at Versailles, which was constantly at odds with the *parlements* and which had no great love of the Church, ceased to make serious efforts to suppress the *philosophes*. Diderot's friends took over all the leading cultural institutions of the kingdom, and after the death of Louis XV an *encyclopédiste,* Turgot, actually became for a time the first minister of the government. Diderot himself, however, accepted no honours. He was too jealous of his freedom, and did not feel the need that Voltaire felt to build up a fortune to protect his independence. He preserved his liberty by living frugally.

I have referred to Diderot's disagreement with Rousseau on the subject of human sociability. He disagreed with him also on the subject of determinism. On this question it was Diderot, rather than Rousseau, who took the side of Hobbes. Partly as a result of reading Hobbes, Diderot was persuaded that the whole universe was a vast machine and that human beings were simply small machines within the larger system, operating according to the same laws of cause and effect as everything else in nature. Such a system appeared to Diderot to exclude free will altogether, and he regarded philosophers who tried to be at the same time determinists and libertarians as illogical and unscientific. In a letter he wrote in 1756, Diderot declared:

> The word 'freedom' has no meaning: there are and there can be no free beings; we are simply the product of the general order of things, our physical organization, our education, and the chain of events. These things exert an irresistible influence over us. One can no more conceive of a being behaving without a motive, than one can conceive of one arm of a balance moving up or down without a weight.

If there was no free will, could there be any morality? Diderot was ready to admit that there could be no morality as traditionally understood, and that public policy could not be based on the assumption of free will. It would be necessary to establish the enforcement of justice and the suppression of crime on deterministic principles. Diderot suggested that actions traditionally seen as crimes could be considered as falling into two categories: those which injured society and those which contravened the rules of the Church. The latter Diderot proposed to eliminate from the class of crimes altogether. When there was no injury to persons—as in sodomy, incest, blasphemy, and so forth—he said there was no crime. Where there was an injury to persons—as in murder, theft, assault, and so on—he suggested that it was a case not so much of wrongdoing as of aberration or mental sickness. On the basis of his theory that all men were by nature social, he argued that any antisocial behaviour must be unnatural; and hence that the individual who acted in an antisocial manner—that is, the criminal—must be acting against his own nature as well as against nature in general. He needed corrective treatment, not punishment.

On these grounds Diderot put forward a radical theory of penology according to which judges and prisons would be replaced by doctors and mental hospitals (here he undoubtedly foreshadows the penology of the Soviet Union as well as the jurisprudence of Jeremy Bentham). He was not soft-hearted in all this. Indeed he accused other progressive penologists, such as Beccaria and Voltaire, of being humanitarian in a sentimental way, of seeking to soften punishments instead of eliminating punishment altogether and replacing it with scientific remedies— remedies which might well have to be unpleasant because they would have to act as deterrents as well as cures. Diderot said he hoped that all aberrant persons could be 'modified' by reeducation as therapy; if not, as he expressed it bluntly, society would have to 'destroy the malefactor on the public square'.

Social surgery did not stop short of the death penalty; and if Diderot in general favoured prolonged imprisonment rather than death, it was because he believed that fear of the 'torture' of a whole life behind bars would be more effective in keeping potential malefactors in order than fear of a quick death on the scaffold.

Few philosophers have explored the practical implications of determinism so boldly as Diderot, and yet, Diderot being Diderot, we soon find him expressing doubts about it all. It occurred to him that determinism might lead to fatalism, for if every single thing that happens is the result of a preceding cause, then there would seem to be no point in wishing that things were different from what they are. If, for example, all the political institutions, the laws, the morals, and manners of France were determined by sociological and other factors, it would be futile to criticize them and suggest that they might be different—unless, of course, one could see oneself as determined by the causal process itself to act an initiating role in the sequence of events.

Diderot, however, was most unwilling to see himself as determined by anything. If he denied free will, he had a passionate belief in human freedom in other senses of the word 'freedom'. One such sense was the autonomy of a man who was master of his own life. Diderot was resolved that he would never be anyone's servant or employé. Since he had no private means, it was not easy for him to stick to this design. It became even harder after he married his working-class mistress (which is something Rousseau firmly refused to do), for Madame Diderot was demanding, complaining, and always berating her husband for the hardships she had to endure in a Bohemian existence with an ill-paid *homme de lettres.* But for Diderot himself the freedom of the free lance was infinitely precious. He despised those writers and scholars who took jobs as clergymen or functionaries, or sold themselves to rich patrons or ministers or kings in order to live comfortably. He even felt guilty himself when late in life he accepted the patronage of Catherine the Great. In doing so, he compared himself to Seneca entering the service of Nero. One of the very last things Diderot wrote was a defence of Seneca which was really a defence of himself against the accusations of his own conscience.

Diderot's conception of human freedom was not simply one of the individual's autonomy; he also developed something very like John Stuart Mill's notion of freedom as 'self-realization'. In spite of the belief that men were little machines, with two 'main springs', the brain and the diaphragm, Diderot argued that each individual machine was unique. He asserted this theory most forcefully in his *Réfutation* of Helvétius. This celebrated *philosophe* (who was not a contributor to the *Encyclopédie*) had argued that all human beings were virtually identical in construction and further that by means of the right training and motivation anyone could be made to do anything that anyone else could do. Diderot rejected this somewhat extreme form of behaviourism. The variety of human achievements, he claimed, not only showed that men had different upbringings and lived in different environments, but that they possessed different innate aptitudes.

Diderot went beyond the mere observation of such differences. He attached great value to them. Like John Stuart Mill, he had the highest admiration for people who cultivated their own originality. He said it was from the ranks of *les originaux* that men of genius sprang. He was even attracted by wicked men, and evidently enjoyed writing about them in the occasional works of fiction he found time to write—in *La Réligieuse,* for example, and *Jacques le fataliste*—which illustrate the great variety of human characters in the world.

One of the reasons why Diderot admired 'originals' was that they achieved that freedom which is 'self-realization', the unimpeded expression of a man's own individuality. This form of human freedom seemed to him to be even less widely enjoyed than freedom as 'independence', so there was no question of Diderot ascribing it to everyone, as

champions of free will ascribed that to everyone. He simply thought that people who achieved such freedom were the best people, and he had a low opinion of those who gave it up for the sake of a comfortable life:

I hate all those sordid little things that reveal only an abject soul: but I do not hate great crimes; first because beautiful paintings and great tragedies are made out of them; and secondly because noble and sublime deeds share with great crimes the same quality of *energy.* [*Salons,* Vol. II]

When Diderot writes like this, we seem to be far from the rationalism of the eighteenth century and closer to the spirit of romanticism or existentialism; and indeed Diderot, no less than Rousseau, presages much that was to be said by philosophers who rejected the Enlightenment. Already, in Diderot's own thinking, there is a conflict between his love of freedom and his attachment to the ideology of progress.

Diderot remained, however, a materialist in his attitude to religion, becoming if anything increasingly an atheist. His conception of the universe as a vast machine was much the same as Voltaire's, but he ceased to accept the argument that the watch-like nature of the system proved the existence of a divine watchmaker, who deserved men's adoration. One explanation of this development is that Diderot's materialism was not based, as was Voltaire's, on the seventeenth-century physical sciences as practised by Newton. Diderot was influenced rather by the biological sciences of his own time, where nature was studied in its animate forms and not in the lifeless geometrical categories of astronomy. Nature for Diderot was a living machine, an organism. And having life in it already, it did not need an external spirit to breathe life into it—it did not need, as the Newtonian universe seemed to need, God. And if God was unnecessary, why introduce him?

Voltaire had said that God must be introduced because his existence was needed to make people act morally. Voltaire had a low opinion of men's characters; but Diderot did not need to accept this argument, precisely because he thought that men were social—that is to say, good—by nature. He claimed that there existed in all men what he called the 'general will of the human race', a will which impelled every individual to act in the interest of the whole species although each had also a 'private will' directed to his own interest. Diderot's *volonté générale* is obviously not to be confused with Rousseau's concept of the same name. Rousseau's 'general will' is a political concept, based on the reflection that if a number of essentially individualistic men are to live together as a civil society, every one must will the conservation and general good of that group. However, the human race as a whole is clearly *not* a civil society, united by covenant or agreement for any common end. In the jargon of sociology, the human race is a *series*—a large number of persons existing at the same time. What is distinctive about Diderot is that he saw the human race as something more than a *series;* he saw it as a natural group, a whole held together by the *volonté générale* which nature had implanted in each member of the race. Moreover Diderot regarded the human race as something which was worthy of much the same kind of veneration which the Christians addressed to God.

'Man', he wrote in the *Encyclopédie,*

> is, and must be, the centre of all things. If we
> banish man, the whole noble spectacle of nature
> becomes no more than an inert and woeful
> scene . . . it is the existence of man alone which
> makes the existence of everything else signifi-
> cant.

In passages such as these there are echoes of the philosophers of Greek Antiquity. Indeed, although Diderot wanted to follow the advice of Bacon and forget Greek philosophy in order to concentrate on modern science for the sake
of serving the interests of humanity, he found himself, in
asking what were the interests of humanity, thrown back
to the Greek philosophers. And there we meet him alternating between the Epicureans and the Stoics [in the *Encyclopédie*]: 'You can make yourself a Stoic; you are born
an Epicurean.'

Diderot's sympathy for the Epicurean philosophy did not
impel him to become, with Voltaire, an apologist of luxury: and his economic theory put him at odds with other
encyclopédistes besides Voltaire. Diderot agreed with the
champions of luxury that the production of high-quality
artifacts was advantageous to the nation as a whole—to
the rich, in providing them with ornaments of life; to the
poor, in providing opportunities for skilled artisan work.
But Diderot favoured the production only of useful
goods—not 'luxury' goods in the sense of ostentatious and
wasteful finery with which the rich could indulge themselves while the poor were starved of necessities. 'The
rich', he wrote, 'eat too much and suffer from indigestion,
while the poor eat too little and suffer from malnutrition.
It would be good to put each on the diet of the other.'

Diderot was a man with a social conscience. He was troubled by the wretched conditions which prevailed where
men were forced—by hunger—to work in dangerous
trades like mining, smelting, and lumbering; and he would
never accept, as Voltaire did, Mandeville's suggestion that
very low wages were a necessary means to keep workers
from idling. As for the argument of Helvétius that the
poorest classes in society were the happiest, Diderot protested that Helvétius being immensely rich, had no experience whatsoever of what it meant to be poor. Helvétius
knew *about* reality; but he did not *know* reality. Diderot's
own impoverished condition was not such as to blind him
to the miseries of the working classes, and when they complained, he upheld their right to do so.

Sympathy for the poor prompted Diderot to reject the arguments of Turgot and Morellet and the other physiocrats
in favour of free trade, a policy based on the theory that
unrestricted commerce advanced the wealth of all. The
physiocrats were Diderot's friends and contributors to the
Encyclopédie, but he opposed their economic theory when
he saw that it did not stand up to the test of concrete experience. In the early 1760s, when the French government
acted on the proposals of the physiocrats and abolished restrictions on the grain trade, a series of bad harvests led
to shortages, excessive charges, hoarding, monopolies,
and the exploitation of hunger on the part of merchants
unrestrained by law. Diderot judged that an economic policy which produced so much suffering and so much profi-

teering was a bad policy, and he rallied to the side of the
leading opponent of free trade among contemporary economists, the Abbé Fernando Galiani, author of *Dialogues
sur le commerce des blés.*

Diderot entered the controversy with a pamphlet entitled
Apologie de l'Abbé Galiani, in which he attacked the
physiocrats on two grounds: first, for thinking that one
could solve practical problems in the light of abstract principles, and secondly, for hardening the hearts of the comfortably off against the sufferings of the poor. 'Is the sentiment of humanity not more sacred than the right to property?' he demanded. Diderot had never shared Voltaire's
attachment to the doctrine of a natural right to property.
He recognized a right to property, but only on grounds of
utility, which would set limits to it; not on grounds of natural law.

In the language of our own times, Diderot was to the left
of both Rousseau and Voltaire. If, as he undoubtedly did
in his years with the *Encyclopédie,* he leaned towards absolutist government, it was neither towards the republicanism of Rousseau nor the royalism of Voltaire. There
was in Voltaire a nostalgia for the past, for *le grand siècle,*
a hint that he would enjoy playing the part of a secular
Richelieu to a monarch with total power; in Rousseau
there was a nostalgia for Sparta as well as for Calvin's Geneva. Diderot's absolutism looked to the future, and it was
of a kind to eliminate politics altogether. Teams of experts
would plan; the monarch would authorize; and profes-
sionals would execute the plan. Diderot's rule of science
would have introduced government by social scientists; in
effect, the kind of people who wrote for the *Encyclopédie,*
neither very grand people nor very humble ones, but men
from the educated bourgeoisie with a vocation for public
service. The contributors to the *Encyclopédie* were sometimes spoken of as clergy who had lost their faith; but they
can also be seen as bureaucrats who had not yet found
their mission.

For a time Diderot was prompted by one of his physiocratic friends, Mercier de la Rivière, to advocate an absolutism
of an all-pervasive kind, the total rule of experts. One can
see how he arrived at this position. Society, as Diderot saw
it, was composed of individuals impelled by *la volonté
générale* to maximize the happiness of all, but ignorant,
for the most part, of the means of achieving that end. The
great majority should therefore agree to allow the minority of experts who did know what methods and policies
would maximize happiness to take the decisions. All so-
called political problems were thus seen as practical problems, to be solved in the light of what Mercier de la Rivière
called 'l'évidence'—a word which Diderot adopted, with
enthusiasm. 'Evidence' he declared, 'is the key to reform:
we do not need to listen to opinions; what we must do is
collect the facts.'

However, Diderot the dialectician, having thus pushed the
Baconian gospel of salvation through science to these positivist extremes, proceeded to dismantle the edifice. He
began by calling into question the empiricist methodology
on which it all rested. He put forward objections to empiricism which have been advanced in our time by such critics as karl Popper and Arthur Koestler. Diderot suggested

that science was not primarily an exercise of observation and induction, but largely a matter of imagination and conjecture.

The element of imagination in science Diderot spoke of [in his *Pensées sur l'interprétation de la nature*] as 'l'esprit de divination', the capacity to 'smell out' hidden connections by pursuing vague ideas, suspicions, hints, and even fantasies 'which the mind, when excited, easily takes for accurate pictures'. The true scientist for Diderot was not essentially different from the artist; both required 'a delicate awareness derived from a sustained observation of nature' and both required intuition. In an eloquent passage in his *Pensées sur l'interprétation de la nature* he wrote:

> Nature is like a woman, who likes to disguise herself and whose different disguises, revealing now one part of her, now another, permit those who follow her assiduously to hope that one day they will know the whole of her person.

Once he had abandoned Baconian induction in science, Diderot could hardly be expected to cling to the Baconian absolution in politics which went with it; he would no longer have any good reason for sacrificing freedom for the sake of efficiency. Here we are introduced to the political theory of Diderot's later years, which mark a return, in several respects, to the liberalism of Montesquieu, for whom, all his life, Diderot had kept a deep personal esteem; he was the only *philosophe* who walked in the procession at Montesquieu's funeral.

Ironically Diderot worked out this later theory just at a time in his life when it looked as if he might be given the opportunity of realizing the Baconian dream of directing the policy of an all-powerful monarch. Catherine the Great, who held despotic sway over the vast territories of the Russian Empire, was captivated by the ideas of the French Enlightenment, and took a particular interest in the work and the person of Diderot. In 1765, she had learned, among other things, that he was more than usually worried about money because of the impending marriage of his daughter. The Empress thereupon offered to buy his library. Her terms were extremely generous; she undertook to pay at once, but would not expect delivery of the books until after Diderot's death; moreover she would appoint him for life as salaried custodian of the library while it remained under his roof.

Voltaire was excited when he heard the news: 'I embrace you', he wrote to his friend, 'and I embrace also the Empress of All the Russias. Would one have suspected fifty years ago that the Tartars would so nobly reward in Paris the virtue, the science, and the philosophy that are so ill used by our own people?'

Diderot soon discovered that the Empress was as interested in the political ideas as in the philosophy of the Enlightenment, and showed every sign of willingness to learn. Already as a result of reading Montesquieu and Beccaria she had decided after four years on the throne to convene an assembly of the Russian Empire to meet in the summer of 1767 to draw up a new code of laws which would have as its purpose the promotion of the greatest happiness of the greatest number of her subjects.

Diderot, who had never been taken in by the pretensions of Frederick II of Prussia to be a philosopher-king, saw in the Empress Catherine the living embodiment of the sage he had described in his *Le Réve de d'Alembert,* a great soul who understood that in order to make her people happy she needed to consult them about their wishes. He imagined her addressing her people in these words: 'We are all made to live under laws. Laws are only laid down in order to render us happier. No one, my children, knows better than you yourselves the conditions under which you can be happy. Come therefore and teach me. Come and express your thoughts to me.'

It seems that Diderot, when he wrote those words, had not yet read the *Nakaz,* or *Instructions,* which Catherine had drawn up for the imperial assembly she had convoked. It was a document which leaned heavily on the jurisprudence of Beccaria, banishing torture, restricting the use of the death penalty, and generally proposing to promote the reform of criminals rather than retribution. Nor did Diderot at first realize that the Empress intended to consult her imperial assembly only for the purpose of reforming the laws, and then to dissolve it for good. He imagined her addressing the assembly in the words of Henri IV of France: 'Je vous ai fait assembler pour recevoir vos conseils, pour les croire, pour les suivre: en un mot pour me mettre en tutelle entre vos mains.'

Diderot did not immediately accept Catherine's invitation to visit her in St. Petersburg. Rather surprisingly—if anything Diderot did can be surprising—he sent instead Mercier de la Rivière, the exponent of an extreme form of absolutism which he called 'le déspotisme légal'. In the event, Mercier's sojourn in St. Petersburg was disastrous for several reasons, and in the summer of 1773 Diderot decided that there was nothing for it but to yield to the imperial will and go to St. Petersburg himself. He was now nearly sixty, and had no experience of foreign travel; but he was fortified by Catherine's confidence in him and the assurance that he would be able to expound to her in private conversation his ideas on government and politics. Those ideas had no longer much in common with the theories of Bacon or Mercier de la Rivière.

An essay entitled *Sur la Russie,* written some months before Diderot went to St. Petersburg, expresses grave doubts about the wisdom of the Empress in inviting to her capital 'men of genius from foreign countries'. Diderot suggests here that she ought really to have modernized the economic and industrial base of her country before calling in philosophers to tell her how to govern it. He notes that Russia is not France or England; it has no educated middle class from which an enlightened bureaucracy or corps of experts could be recruited; it has no skilled mechanics or engineers; and no factories. Russia, in short, is simply not ready for the Enlightenment.

In another document [a contribution to the *Correspondance littéraire* (1772)], Diderot proposed that reform in Russia should start at the bottom, 'by invigorating the mechanical arts and the lower occupations'. He adds: 'Learn how to cultivate the land, to treat skins, manufacture wool, make shoes, and in time . . . people will then be painting pictures and making statues.' This quotation comes from his *Mémoires pour Catherine II,* which seems to have been written after his return from Russia, and which needs to be read together with his *Observations sur le Nakaz* for an indication of Diderot's political thought at this period.

He begins the *Mémoires* with some reflections on French history: 'The first fault, the original sin of the French people', he writes, 'was to have handed over all public power to the king.' He suggests that in the original pact of submission, the French people ought to have set up an institution to act as 'a barrier to defend the people against the arbitrary power of a wicked or stupid sovereign'. The *parlement* of Paris had never enacted this role because its members served their own interest and not the national interest. Even so, Diderot considered the king's suppression of the *parlement* in 1771 a great misfortune, since it transformed France 'from a monarchical state to a completely despotic state'.

It is clear from all this that the closer Diderot came to absolutism, the more keenly he disapproved it. In his *Observations sur le Nakaz* he wrote:

> There is no true sovereign except the nation; there can be no true legislator except the people.
>
> The first act of a well-made constitutional code should bind the monarch to obey the law. Any monarch who refused to take such an oath would declare himself in advance to be a despot and a tyrant.

In another paragraph Diderot specifies the kind of institution an assembly of deputies must be if it is to represent the will of a free people, and he suggests that it would be wise 'to fix the rights of these intermediate powers and fix them in such a way that they cannot be revoked even by the legislator himself or by his successors'. With the example of England in mind, he writes, 'Good government is that in which the freedom of individuals is least restricted, and the freedom of sovereigns as much restricted as it is possible to be.'

Elsewhere in the same treatise, Diderot considers whether political institutions should be fortified by religious ones, only to reject the idea: 'Religion is a support which always ends by toppling the house. The distance between the altar and the throne can never be too great.'

Although Diderot remained on good terms with the Empress throughout his stay in St. Petersburg, he soon realized that he was not going to persuade her of the wisdom of a parliamentary constitution. The imperial assembly she had convoked had failed to reach any conclusions after 203 sessions, and was adjourned indefinitely in December 1768. She had never any intention of setting up a permanent parliamentary body which could block or hinder her use of power in any way. She had wanted only a short-term legislative assembly to draw up a code which would make her personal rule more efficient, more enlightened, more legitimate; and once the code was approved, the assembly was to be dissolved.

Diderot used to meet Catherine almost daily to discuss matters which he was authorized to introduce as subjects for conversation, and the French Ambassador reported in December 1773: 'the conferences with Catherine continue without interruption and get longer from day to day'. Her pleasure in his company did not, however, signify assent to his ideas. She is reported to have said to him once, 'You forget, Monsieur Diderot, in your plans for reform, the difference between our two positions: you work on paper, which puts up with everything. I, poor Empress, work on human skin, which is altogether more sensitive, ticklish, and resistant' [quoted in the *Mémoires* of Louis-Philippe Segur].

She told the Comte de Ségur some time later:

> I frequently had long conversations with Monsieur Diderot, but with more curiosity than profit. Had I placed faith in him, every institution in my empire would have been overturned; legislation, administration, politics, and finances would all have been changed for the purpose of substituting some impracticable theories.

Diderot left Russia in many ways a disappointed man, and a few months spent in Holland on his way home reinforced his belief that free government was more valuable than good government. There is an eloquent paragraph in his so-called *Fragments échappés* which seems to date from this period:

> It is sometimes said that the most felicitous government would be that of a just and enlightened despot; but this is a very bold assertion. It could easily happen that the will of this absolute master was at odds with that of his subjects. Then, in spite of his justice and his enlightenment, he would be wrong to strip them of their rights even for their own good . . . it is never permissible for a man, whoever he is, to treat his fellow men as a herd of cattle. If they say 'We like it this way and we want to stay as we are' then one should try to educate them, to undeceive them, to lead them to more sensible views by means of persuasion, but never by means of force.

The theme of liberty is a dominant one in all Diderot's political writings in the last years of his life (and he was to live for ten more years after his return from Russia). Soon after the rebellion of the American colonists against the British Crown in 1775, Diderot produced the book which has contributed much to his reputation as a revolutionary: *La Révolution de l'Amérique anglaise.* This is a fairly wide-ranging defence of the American action, with summaries of the Declaration of Independence and of Thomas Paine's *Common Sense* and various other pamphlets which Diderot had read in English. It also sets forth a general doctrine of revolution which invokes at the same time a utilitarian and a natural rights argument:

> If people are happy under the form of their government they will keep it. If they are unhappy, it will not be your opinions or mine, but the impossibility for them to endure that government any longer which will determine them to change it—a salutary moment which the oppressor will call 'revolt', but which is nothing other than the legitimate exercise of an inalienable and natural right of men who are oppressed, and indeed of those who are not oppressed.

La Révolution de l'Amérique anglaise is the least original and perhaps also the least interesting of Diderot's writings on politics, and has to be seen as part of a flood of pamphleteering that came out in France in the late 1770s in support of the American rebellion. The Versailles government, seeking revenge for the French defeat by the British in Canada, sponsored the American rebels not only with military and naval aid, but by the dissemination of revolutionary propaganda. It is often said that the Enlightenment provided ideological impetus for the French Revolution; it could equally be argued that Louis XVI, by encouraging the Americans to rebel against their king, put his own head on the block, since every argument set forth to justify the American action against George III could be—and was—used by discontented elements against his own regime. But since the intervention in America had cost French taxpayers a great deal of money at a time when the French treasury was low, the American cause had to be made popular in France.

Diderot's contribution to this exercise differed from others in that he, characteristically, went beyond the defence of the American rebels to call into the question the right of these rebels to be in America in the first place. Much of this later argument he did not publish under his own name, but in the form of contributions, only recently identified as his, to *L'Histoire des deux Indes,* published under the name of Diderot's friend the Abbé Guillaume Raynal. Here new questions are introduced. Who are the American colonists? They are Europeans, not true Americans. Many of them are religious enthusiasts; they have sailed to the New World, elbowed out the native redskins, and developed the land with the aid of African slaves.

Diderot, like every other philosopher of the French Enlightenment, disapproved passionately of slavery; what is more, he joined Rousseau in considering the redskins to be in many ways superior to Europeans. And so we meet the dialectical Diderot once more. He can justify the American colonists' rebellion against the British Crown, but only with arguments which undermine their right to be colonists. One of the reasons given for the claim that Diderot was a forerunner of Lenin is that he was an early critic of imperialism. However, Diderot did not use the word, and he did not attack what Lenin attacked as 'imperialism'—'the last phase of capitalism'. What Diderot criticized was something with an older history, the endeavour of more advanced peoples to take over the territories of more primitive peoples. In his *Supplément au voyage de Bougainville* he had indicted the visiting Europeans for corrupting the innocent; in the *Histoire des deux Indes* he attacks the increasingly aggressive endeavours of the European rulers to build empires and colonies overseas. 'A new kind of fanaticism has developed,' he wrote, 'the search for continents to invade, islands to plunder, peoples to despoil, subjugate, and massacre.'

The *deux Indes* of this book's title are the 'Indies' of the West, that is the whole of the New World, north and south, and the 'Indies' of the East—India and beyond. A few, very few such places were 'empty'; most were not. Diderot wrote: 'Reason and equity allow colonies to be established only in a country where no other people is already living. For thus one can earn the right to it by work. A country that is wholly deserted and uninhabited is the only one that can be legitimately appropriated.'

Diderot's history of the Spanish conquest of South America is as hostile as are most such histories written by French, English, or Dutch authors, but unlike those historians, Diderot does not suggest that the Spanish imperial enterprise was uniquely cruel. He sees injustice in all empire-building, using arguments which would hardly be expected of an *encyclopédiste*. For empire-building was favoured by progressive opinion in the eighteenth century as it was in the nineteenth, because it was seen as a means of diffusing the advantages of modern science, technology, medicine, and so forth in undeveloped areas of the globe. If Diderot as much as Rousseau stood against the current of opinion, it was because, for all his devotion to the Baconian *ethos,* he shared many of Rousseau's doubts about the advantages of modern progress and had an even greater belief in the nobility of the savage. Precisely because he believed that man was naturally social, Diderot could count on the possibility of finding simple uncorrupted societies in the modern world.

In his *Discourse on Inequality* Rousseau describes the experience of a Hottentot in South Africa who is brought up by a Dutch benefactor, but finally refuses to be 'civilized' in the European fashion; Rousseau praises his determination to return to his origins. Diderot goes further. He urges the Hottentots to get out their bows and poisoned arrows and kill the Dutch settlers before those so-called benefactors can destroy their native culture with their gifts of beads and Bibles.

Such is the voice of the radical Diderot. But at the same time and in the same book another voice can be discerned—not the Abbé Raynal's, but Diderot's other voice—the conservative-liberal voice of the follower of Montesquieu warning Louis XVI against the dangers of too rapid reforms: 'All innovations should be gradual. .. To create or destroy suddenly is to corrupt the good and make the evil worse.'

It is no good listening to one of Diderot's voices, and pretending that it is Diderot's definitive word. There are as many Diderots as their protagonists in his dialogues. He is the least Cartesian, the least 'French', of the *philosophes* of the Enlightenment; and at the same time the closest to the thoughts and the problems of later generations, for whom he may be supposed to have intended the writings which he concealed from his own contemporaries. He believed in a better future, and he wrote for his posterity.

P. N. Furbank   (essay date 1992)

SOURCE: *Diderot: A Critical Biography,* Alfred A. Knopf, 1992, 524 p.

[*In the following excerpt, Furbank examines Diderot's novel* La Religieuse (The Nun) *as an example of the "novel as deception," a work that never formally severs its ties with real life and that always leaves open the possibility that it may turn out to be a genuine document.*]

With hindsight, one is inclined to view the early history

of the European novel from the point of view of the direction that the form eventually took.

The potentialities of the novel-form would have seemed somewhat different at the time. If I put the point in terms of the English novel, this will not take us too far from Diderot, for his chief inspirations as a novelist were Richardson and Sterne.

To a contemporary of Defoe, Sterne and Richardson a basic choice would have seemed to be offered: the choice between, on the one hand, a conception of the novel as *deception,* as falsehood dressed up as truth and leaving a margin of possibility that it might in fact turn out to be truth; and on the other hand a conception of the novel as *illusion*—or, as one may express it, illusion unambiguously acknowledged as such.

Plainly, any novel (one, say, like *Tom Jones*) that has an elaborately contrived plot is bound to belong in the second category, the novel of "accepted illusion". It is a genre which entails a certain fundamental contract with the reader, according to which the novelist should, as it were, be continually nursing the reader and looking after his or her comfort. Over the years the genre would develop a whole conventional narrative rhythm, with dramas and lulls, suspenses and aftermaths, pauses for reminiscence and endings that are like deathbeds. What is developed is a form of mimicry of time, according to which reflections, character-descriptions, exposition, pauses and reintroductions of characters have an understood relation to the pace of events and help in depicting that pace. By a natural turn of logic, moreover, one way in which such a novel—that is to say an object so remote from common experience as an elaborately plotted tale—will aspire to be praised is for its "lifelikeness". It was, and still is, a very fruitful genre, and over the years and through the genius of Jane Austen, Dickens and George Eliot and kindred writers it came to seem to be the only genre and to constitute "the novel" itself.

This, of course, was an error, and what I have called the *novel as deception* offered equally rich possibilities. The "novel as deception" works by never formally and finally severing its ties with real life, including the real life of the reader. The possibility is always left open that the work may turn out to be a genuine document, written by a real Pamela or Moll Flanders or Cavalier, or perhaps a piece of "secret history". It may indeed, make such lavish use of genuine documents that readers do not suspect it of being a novel; but then this is to defeat its own artistic end. For in this genre the point is continually to exploit the reader's uncertainty. Novels of this school will develop quite different conventions from those of the "accepted illusion" kind. In the nature of things, they will have to simulate artlessness and eschew the more familiar devices of the professional story-teller. Further, since the author has absconded, passing on the responsibility for the narrative to "real life", a quite different, more demanding and bewildering, role is imposed upon the reader. In this kind of fiction the author can be expected to be hiding his or her intentions much more effectively than in the novel of accepted illusion; and then there exists, for the reader, always the possibility that there is no "author" anyway. Faced with

this double difficulty, the reader may grow uneasy—may hedge himself around with caution as in a difficult real-life situation. Or he may simply flounder, as, for instance, readers have so often floundered about Defoe's *Roxana.* (Shall they regard it as a very moral, or as a very immoral, tale?) But more valuably, in the case of a scrupulous reader, he or she may be placed in a tender and vulnerable position, which it will be open to the *novelist of deception* to practise upon in all sorts of ethical and philosophical ways.

Nor is this the only form that the *novel as deception* may take. Richardson discovered another very potent form when he had the idea of writing what is simultaneously a novel and a behaviour-manual. This, again, entails a double or ambivalent relationship with the reader. The reader's interest in a behaviour-manual is, *in theory,* educational, a matter of learning how to behave in such-and-such circumstances. It is, that is to say, a practical and real-life activity on the reader's part, a direct invitation to apply the story to his or her actual life. Richardson is inviting him, and quite sincerely, to study Pamela's letters and Grandison's conduct as a model and guide, and the fiction is *in theory* subordinate to this end. The novelist is thus able to play upon the reader in a false-dealing manner, as it were, appealing under this exemplary front to the reader's credulity, emotionality and, perhaps, even prurience. It produces a very different kind or novel, evolving quite different conventions, from one of the "accepted illusion" kind.

But then a further and even wider consideration arises; for it would seem that the novel-as-deception lies close to the novel-of-undeception. The writer who conceives of the novel as falsehood is liable also to be the writer who is tempted to blow the gaff: to frustrate the reader's desire for a "romance" and remind the reader that a "narrator" may be a real-life author—perhaps a teasing, bored or angry one. One can perceive a logical affinity between this Sternian kind of novel and the Richardsonian or Defoean kind. The writer who can throw his or her genius into "practising" on the reader may equally be tempted to triumph over the reader by showing the whole business to be a fraud and a confidence-trick. The three cases, the pretended document, the pretended behaviour-manual and the novel that blows the gaff, share the same underlying decision, that of never finally severing the link with the outside world.

These two great genres, the novel-of-accepted-illusion and the novel-as-deception (and undeception) seemed at first, and perhaps were, equally rich in artistic potential. However, as I have said, it was the former genre—the novel of Fielding, Jane Austen, George Eliot and Dickens—which triumphed, and this has a distorting effect on one's picture of the past. It has meant that the idea of pretending that your novel may be a real-life document, "true confession" or "secret history", now tends to look naive or primitive, as if belonging to the pre-history of the novel, while the novel-as-undeception, the novel which disrupts narrator-reader relations, has, on being rediscovered in the twentieth century, come to be seen as *avant-garde*.

Diderot, as novelist, belongs entirely to the novel-as-deception school. In his novels, as in his philosophic fantasies (like his *Letter on the Blind, D'Alembert's Dream* and *Supplement to Bougainville's "Voyage"*), the "fiction" always remains embedded, to very subtle effect, in its real-life matrix. This is, indeed, just what one would expect, given his bent towards the "supposititious" and towards "mystifications". (He entitles one of his short stories **"Mystification"**, and another **"This Is Not a Story".**) What is striking, moreover, is that he produced a masterpiece in each of two separate veins of the novel-as-deception. *The Nun* is a masterpiece of the fraudulent "true confession" type, and *Jacques the Fatalist* is a masterpiece of narrator—reader disruption (asking—in emulation of Jacques with his own master—"who shall be master, novelist or reader?"). But indeed *The Nun,* with its final blowing-of-the-gaff, is a masterpiece in both genres: the novel-as-deception and the novel-as-undeception.

What one discovers in this first novel of Diderot's, possibly with a shock of surprise, is that it exhibits hardly a trace of sentimentality. This, indeed, proves true of all his novels and stories. The art of fiction evokes in him a salutary and impressive coldness, a detachment in the manner of Stendhal, and with it various other very un-Richardsonian qualities, like swiftness, incisiveness and economy. The note is struck very early in the novel, in the incident of the heroine's nosebleed. Having successfully staged a refusal to take her vows, she is returning home with her implacable mother. They face each other in silence in the carriage, and then, writes Suzanne:

> I do not know what was going on inside me, but suddenly I threw myself at her feet and laid my head in her lap. I could not speak but sobbed and choked. She repelled me harshly. I did not get up. My nose began to bleed. I seized one of her hands, against her will, and bathing it with my tears and the blood streaming from me, I pressed it to my mouth and kissed it, saying: "You are still my mother, I am still your child!" She replied, pushing me away more roughly and pulling back her hand: "Get up, wretched child, get up!" I obeyed and sat down, hiding my face in my coif. There was so much firmness and authority in her voice that I felt I needed to hide from her. My tears and the blood from my nose mingled together, running down my arms, till, without my realising, I was covered in them. From something my mother said, I gathered they had dirtied her dress and that she was displeased.

The verisimilitude of that nosebleed belongs to nineteenth-century and not to eighteenth-century fiction.

It is this coldness which upset the critic Barbey d'Aurevilly, who, in his *Goethe and Diderot* (1880), was eager to depict Diderot as a man of warmth and "fire", as against the "reptilian" frigidity of Goethe. *The Nun,* wrote the royalist and Catholic d'Aurevilly, was a novel no one now would read, "were it not for its ignobly libertine details which, for corrupted minds, give a spice of cantharides to this cold book, which the hatred, always faintly simmering in Diderot's pusillanimous soul, was unable to warm." It is a reaction worth pondering, and for one thing

because Barbey d'Aurevilly reacted to Diderot with passion—in this he was rather rare among critics—and drew a portrait of him on heroic lines.

It is a point of significance that, until quite recently, *The Nun,* like *Indiscreet Jewels,* was regarded as a pornographic novel. (It was actually banned in 1824, and again in 1826, no doubt partly for that reason - and as late as 1968 Mme de Gaulle forced the Ministry of Information to ban the film of it by Jacques Rivette.) One was simply not supposed to depict lesbianism, as Diderot does in the later pages of *The Nun;* and a cold and objective treatment of it was liable to appear to readers as an especially unpleasant kind of liberatinism, and evidently did so to d'Aurevilly. Anyway, leaving aside the matter of lesbianism, there was quite a school of titillating fiction about convent life, with titles like *Venus in the Cloister; or, a Nun in her Shift,* and this is a fact very relevant to Diderot's complex purposes in *The Nun.* But furthermore *Indiscreet Jewels* really is a cold novel, rather jarringly so. Thus it is not too hard to see how *The Nun* could have been misread and not seen for the heartfelt and impassioned work that it is, one that is made all the more poignant by its refusal of sentimentality.

This matter of "coldness" touches on something central to Diderot's intellectual life. He was, as we have seen, very ready to proclaim himself a sentimentalist and believed that virtue tended to be of the party of the sentimentalists. On the other hand—the thought could not be suppressed—sentimentality seemed to go hand-in-hand with mediocrity and to be, as it were, the antithesis of "genius". The issue was summed up in an anecdote [recounted in *Paradoxe sur le comédien*] about an encounter he had with the playwright Michel-Jean Sedaine. He believed Sedaine to be a disciple of his, with all the right ideas about the drama, and was greatly excited by a successful performance of Sedaine's *A Philosopher Without Knowing It.* He rushed half across Paris to congratulate the author, arriving, according to Sedaine's account, "all out of breath, sweating, and exclaiming, with tears in his eyes, 'Victory, my friend, victory!' "—to which Sedaine's only reply was, "M. Diderot, how beautiful you look!" In this, Diderot said, one saw all the difference between the sentimentalist and the "observer and man of genius". It was a favourite story with him and helped to inspire one of his most influential writings, his *Paradox of the Actor,* where he argues that the actor of genius portrays emotions so powerfully precisely because he feels none of them.

When writing fiction, Diderot seems instinctively to have fallen into a "genius" tone. This must not be misunderstood. He was emphatically *not* the actor who feels nothing; indeed he could become, towards his own fiction, the same enthusiastic, naively credulous reader as Richardson created for himself. He later told a story [recounted in Grimm's "Preface—Annex de *La Religieuse*"] of how, at the time of writing *The Nun,* a friend of his called on him and found him in floods of tears. "What on earth is the matter?" exclaimed his friend. "What a state you are in!" "I will tell you what is the matter," replied Diderot. "I am breaking my heart over a story I am telling to myself." For all this, though, the actual tone of *The Nun* shows that very marked "coldness" that separates his fiction, in a striking manner, from most of the rest of his work. It is at bottom the same unmistakable but somehow unclassifiable quality—not "bleak", not "savage", not "amoral"—which has disconcerted readers of *Rameau's Nephew*. Diderot, both by experience and by instinct, was a self-censorer. He was a compunctious man and saw a good deal of virtue, as well as necessity, in self-censorship and respect for certain common prejudices. In writing fiction, however, it seems to come naturally to him to forget all such compunction.

The Nun falls into four broad sections. First we read of the young Suzanne Simonin's family unhappiness, her entry into her first convent (the Sainte Marie), her realisation that she has no religious vocation and her bold public refusal to take vows. Next comes the callous and punitive treatment she receives on her return home, her discovery of her bastardy, her more or less forcible despatch to the convent of Longchamps and her long sequence of vicissitudes there: her friendship with the saintly Mother de Moni, her unwilling taking of vows, her ferocious victimisation at the hands of Mother de Moni's successor, and her decision to take legal steps to cancel her vows, bringing on her an even more appalling series of persecutions. The third section concerns her removal to the convent of Sainte-Eutrope outside Paris, her exposure to a new form of persecution there, at the hands of its lesbian Prioress, and her eventual escape from the convent with a rascally Benedictine monk. Finally (I am describing the novel in the shape it took in the *Correspondance littéraire* in 1780-82) a "Preface to the Preceding Work", revealing the hoax or "horrible conspiracy" out of which the novel has sprung and giving the text of the letters exchanged between the imaginary "Suzanne" and the real-life Marquis de Croismare.

When, now an old man, Diderot came to offer [in a letter dated 27 September 1780], *The Nun* to Henri Meister, Grimm's successor on the *Correspondance littéraire,* he wrote: "I do not believe anyone has ever written a more terrifying satire on convents." The word "satire" will need some glossing, but plainly the work is a polemic. It is not, however, a polemic against religion as such, nor is it much concerned with the Jesuit-versus-Jansenist controversy. It is not even, initially, a wholesale attack on the conventual system, though it certainly becomes one. The focus of his actual plot is very precise, it is the crime and outrage to the human soul of forcing the religious life on someone with no vocation for it; and neither Diderot nor his protagonist Suzanne (a tenacious and inflexible character) ever loses hold of this issue. To "crime" and "outrage", though, the reader is asked to add "danger". For the paradox, very clearly understood by Suzanne herself, is that whereas she lacks all vocation for the religious life, she has a definite natural talent for it; and altogether she is a formidable and disruptive personage.

For this, among other reasons, the Mother de Moni episode, and its placement, are crucial to the novel's strategy. For the humane, far-seeing and truly spiritual Mother de Moni represents the very best that the conventual system can offer, and her relationship with Suzanne underlines a

tragic irony: that, in the convent system, such superior virtues may be as dangerous as, or even more dangerous than, the common vices—worldliness, intolerance, herd-instinct and lust for cruelty—of the monastic life. Suzanne herself comes to realise that her contact with the noble and inspiring Mother de Moni was "fatal". "I cannot say enough good of her," she writes to the Marquis. "But it is her goodness that was my undoing." It is her feeling for Mother de Moni that, against not just instinct but the certain knowledge that she is doing wrong, persuades her to take religious vows. Again, of course, it is jealousy of Mother de Moni and irritation at Suzanne's cult of her memory, that provoke such hostility in her ferocious successor. This "fatality" is not an innocent accident, for their relationship, and Mother de Moni's relationship with all her chosen flock, is (it is Suzanne's own word) a "seduction". For some of the novices, to receive consolation from Mother de Moni becomes a craze and a morbid addiction. "She did not intend to seduce; but certainly that is what she did. One came from her presence with a heart on fire and joy and ecstasy painted on one's face. One wept such sweet tears!" "Seduction" is a strong word. It is one that the reader is expected to remember; and later Diderot, by a number of cunning touches, suggests the parallel between this spiritual seduction and the physical seduction attempted by the Prioress of Sainte-Eutrope.

We remember, too, that it is through her friendship with Mother de Moni that Suzanne finds that the herself has a "genius" for the spiritual life. Suzanne is made to reflect what dire use she could have made of this rare gift, what a gift it would have been in the hands of a hypocrite or a fanatic. The wise Mother de Moni makes a chilling remark, which Suzanne often has cause to remember: "Among all these creatures you see around me—so docile, so innocent, so sweet—well, my child, there is hardly one, no, not one, whom I could not turn into a wild beast." Her words prove all too true, and under the influence of her successor the inhabitants of Longchamps in fact become "wild beasts", pursuing the hapless Suzanne with insane vindictiveness. The whole place, indeed, for a time goes mad.

Nor is the "fatality" only on one side. Innocent victim though she is, neither now nor later can Suzanne be said to be harmless to her fellows. If Mother de Moni is "fatal" to Suzanne, Suzanne is fatal to Mother de Moni, dispossessing her of her "genius" and hastening her end.

All these ironies, so subtly drawn out by Diderot, are directed towards a single conclusion: that the root of the trouble is not "fate" or original sin but a profoundly, an irremediably, vicious human institution. Its vices can be detected at work even in so mild and enlightened a régime as that of Mother de Moni; thus the horrors that are to come, so runs the logic of the narrative, need not take us by suprise.

These horrors and persecutions fall into two separate sequences. The *donnée* of the novel, as we know, is the real-life nun Marguerite Delamarre and specifically her effort to repudiate her vows; and the moment when the same idea occurs to Suzanne is a turning-point in the novel. Up to this moment she has been a doomed figure. In her rebellion against Mother de Moni's successor she succeeds in destroying her own character, making herself hard, horrible and legalistic; and the rebellion, anyway, is bound to be hopeless. The only real possibilities for her in the long run are an unsustainable hypocrisy, madness or suicide. Indeed the only reason for not committing suicide, she reflects with a last flicker of obstinacy, is that everyone seems to *want* her to commit it.

As soon as she thinks of repudiating her vows, however, her strength of character returns; it helps to give force to all that follows—that crescendo of hardly conceivable malignities (though, in fact, they can all be paralleled in contemporary records)—in that they fall on no passive victim but on a most courageous, resourceful, obstinate and even "violent" woman (so at least she describes herself).

On the day of her arrival at the rich and worldly convent of Longchamps Suzanne is persuaded to perform at the clavichord, and ("without irony", she tells the Marquis) she finds herself singing Telaire's great air from Rameau's *Castor and Pollux* bidding farewell to the sun, "Sad attire, pale torch-flames, day more terrible than night itself." It is a telling stroke. Diderot himself, in recommending his novel to Meister, said that it would be a gift to painters. Indeed, indirectly, it would inspire Delacroix; for his sensational "L'Amende Honorable" illustrates a scene from Maturin's *Melmoth the Wanderer*—the victimised monk Moncada being dragged from his cell into the presence of the Bishop—which Maturin had filched directly from Diderot.

The nocturnal *tableaux* which follow—the nuns being ordered to step on the prostrate Suzanne's body, their dressing her in a shroud and laying her out on a bier, their leading her to a mock-execution, and so on—make an extraordinary sequence. One especially is most moving. The Archdeacon is completing his public inquisition, during which Suzanne has answered every question about her sufferings firmly but laconically. He asks her if she wants to accuse anyone in particular. She replies "No," and he dismisses her to her cell. On a sudden instinct, though, she turns back, falls down before him, and, displaying her bruised head, her bloodstained feet, her fleshless arms and filthy clothes, says simply: "You see!"

Many strands in the novel come together here. Such a charge of emotion and indignation has built up in us that Diderot can risk enlarging his book into a universal statement.

We need to stand back for a moment and form a clear idea of Diderot's strategy. A passage in his ***Essays on Painting,*** where he discusses painterly composition, is helpful here.

> A man is giving a friend an interesting reading. Without conscious thought on either's part, the reader disposes himself in the manner he finds most appropriate, and the listener does the same. If it is Robbé reading, he will have the air of a fanatic: he will not look at his text but will be gazing into the air. If I am the listener, I will have a serious look; my right hand will move to my chin, to prop my drooping head, and my left hand will reach for my right elbow, to support

the weight of both head and arm. This is not how I would listen to Voltaire.

> Add a third character to the scene, and he will submit to the law of the two former: it is a combined system of three interests.

A "combined system of three interests" is precisely what we find in Suzanne's narration, working, implicitly, at three different levels: she has been telling the story of her wrongs for its own sake, she has been telling it for the special benefit of the Marquis, and she (or Diderot) is telling it, over the Marquis's head, to the world at large. Now Diderot dares to make all this explicit. He causes Suzanne to raise, to the Marquis, the very issue of credibility that will have troubled the reader—could one person have suffered the whole imaginable repertory of evils in the conventual system? Is this not more like some insane fantasy? —and her answer is a good one. Given our sense of something unique and challenging in Suzanne's personality, a sort of lightning-conductor quality, we find ourselves happy to accept it.

> The more I reflect, the more I persuade myself that what is happening to me has never happened up till now and will perhaps never happen again. Just once (and pray God that it be the first and last time) it has pleased Providence, whose ways are not to be fathomed, to assemble upon one unfortunate creature all the mass of cruelties otherwise distributed—in its unsearchable decrees—among the infinite multitude of wretches who have preceded her in the cloister and who are to come after.

The Suzanne who was stoical and laconic to her clerical inquisitor now unlooses her tongue and makes unashamed and imperious appeal to the Marquis's feelings. "Monsieur le Marquis, beware lest a fatal moment come when you wear your eyes out weeping over my fate. You might then be wrung with remorse, but this would not help me return from the abyss where I had fallen; it would have closed for ever over a castaway." And finally, gathering strength from the story of her own defeat (for it is at this point that she learns that her legal suit has failed) she is made to deliver what the reader is now most willing to hear, a searing and magnificent tirade against the whole convent system. The structure of feeling that has been built up almost requires that Diderot's voice should now mingle with Suzanne's.

> What need has the Bridegroom of so many foolish virgins? Or the human species of so many victims? Shall we never feel the need to close up those gulfs where future races fall to their destruction? All the formal prayers made there, are they worth one farthing given in fellow-feeling to the poor? Does God, who created Man for society, approve of his being immured? Can God, who created him so inconstant and so frail, encourage him in such a reckless thing as vows? . . . etc.

When, unexpectedly, Suzanne is at last released from her sufferings at Longchamps and is transferred to a new convent, that of Sainte-Eutrope, she finds that Providence has played a fresh trick on her, plunging her into a quite new dilemma. In this Sainte-Eutrope episode, in weight and extent a balance to the Longchamps section, there is not only a shift to a new evil of the cloister, a sexual one, but also a shift in our sympathies. For the real victim in the new episode is not Suzanne but the Prioress, a figure only driven to tragedy by the convent system.

There was a principle which would loom large for Diderot as an art-theorist and amateur physiologist. It was that there was a "system" in deformity, so that an expert need only see a pair of feet to say that they belonged to a hunchback, or a woman's throat and shoulders to say that she had lost her eyesight in childhood. From an aesthetic point of view the implication was that an artist ought to forget academic rules of "correctness", for "Nature does nothing that is incorrect," and should study, rather, the "secret liaison" and "necessary concatenation" of natural phenomena. "Every form, beautiful or ugly, has its cause, and of all creatures that exist there is not one which is not as it has to be." One is reminded of this theory when it comes to Diderot's moving portrait of the lesbian Prioress. "Her head is never still on her shoulders," writes Suzanne; ". . . there is always something astray in her dress; her face is attractive on the whole; her eyes, of which one, the right one, is higher and larger than the other, are *distraits* and full of fire . . . The unsymmetry of her features expresses all the disconnectedness of her character." When, later, Suzanne gives the charming picture of the Prioress's *levée,* she notes that her tender, shining black eyes "are always only half-open", a neat symbolic suggestion that she does not want to see what she is doing. Diderot is evidently treating the Prioress, very compassionately but "scientifically", as a "system of deformity", with a "skew" running visibly right through her moral as through her physical makeup.

In this new episode, Diderot's novel, so full of surprises, has a further and even bolder surprise in store. For the reader finds that a trick, of a most disturbing kind, has been played on himself or herself. Throughout this new episode the possibility looms for the reader that the book is a titillating or pornographic convent-romance, a steamier variation on the story of a nun breaking her vows because she has a lover. (Indeed Suzanne is eventually rescued by a "lover".) Suzanne's way of reporting her superior's sexual advances is erotic in itself. She is caught up in her own innocent amazement and describes it excitedly and excitingly.

> After this, as soon as a nun had committed any fault, I interceded for her, and I was sure to obtain her pardon in exchange for some innocent favour; it was always a kiss on the forehead or on the neck or on the eyes or on the cheeks or on the mouth or on the hands or on the bosom or on the arms but most often on the mouth . . . She declared I had sweet breath, white teeth and fresh and rosy lips.

Though Suzanne now much less often addresses herself directly to the Marquis, the reader is soon speculating on the effect of all this on that ardent and impressionable man; and of course all the more so when it comes to the heated if semi-comic scene of the Prioress's first successful seduction of Suzanne (if "seduction" is the word; in any event,

The church of Saint-Roch, Paris, where Diderot was buried on 1 August 1784.

when she first achieves an orgasm in Suzanne's arms). Evidently it is to Suzanne's advantage to involve the Marquis's feelings, by any means almost; indeed in a "postscript" to her narration Suzanne frankly admits she may half-consciously have been manipulating him. "Is it because we believe men less sensitive to the painting of our distress than to the image of our charms, and that we promise ourselves it will be easier to seduce them than to stir their pity?"

The obliquities and calculation in Suzanne's narration to the Marquis are a most important element in the novel; nevertheless they are only, in a sense, an adjunct to something even more essential: the obliquities in Diderot's relationship with the reader. For, from the beginning, what the Prioress of Sainte-Eutrope finds sexually exciting in Suzanne is not just her beauty but her past sufferings. The great erotic thrill that she promises herself is to hear Suzanne tell her story; and eventually she stage-manages this event in the most voluptuous style, entwining her whole body with the story-teller's. It is to be, as she says herself, a supreme indulgence: the two of them will weep delicious tears, and "perhaps we shall be happy in the middle of the story of your sufferings. Who knows where tender compassion may lead us . . . ?" Suzanne begins, and the reader is treated to a *louche* parody of his own emotions—you might say, the emotions of any person of good will—in reading of the same events earlier.

So I began my story more or less as I have been writing it for your eye. I cannot tell you the effect it had on her, the sighs she breathed, the tears she shed, the indignation she voiced against my cruel parents, against the terrible girls at Sainte-Marie and the ones at Longchamps. I would be very sorry if they suffered the tiniest portion of the evils that she wished them; I would not myself want to pull a single hair from the head of my most cruel enemy. From time to time she interrupted me and got up and walked about and then returned to her place. At another time she raised her hands and her eyes to heaven, then she buried her head between my knees. When I spoke of the scene in the dungeon, of my exorcism, of my *amende honorable,* she practically cried out. When I reached the end of my story I fell silent, and for some minutes she lay with her body stretched out on her bed, her face hidden in the coverlet and her arms across her head. I said: "Dear Mother, I beg your pardon for causing you such pain; I warned you, but you would persist . . . ," but her only reply was: "The wicked creatures! The horrible creatures! Only in convents could people be so lost to human feeling . . . But how could that frail health have borne so many torments? How were those little limbs not all broken? How was that delicate machine not wrecked? How were those bright eyes not dimmed for ever by tears? The cruel creatures! To bind those arms with cords! . . . ," and she took my arms and kissed them. "To have drowned those eyes with tears . . . !", and she kissed them . . .

The Prioress's reactions grow more and more orgiastic, and, for a second time, she has an orgasm while in the uncomprehending Suzanne's arms.

This ambush for the reader is a marvellously audacious stroke on Diderot's part, and there is a natural progression, an advance into scepticism, from this episode onwards to the final blowing-of-the-gaff about the de Croismare hoax in the "Preface to the Preceding Work." The novel is revealed as what Stanley Fish calls a "self-consuming artifact" and raises doubts about "innocence" of all kinds, but especially the innocence of those who tell stories and those who listen to them.

We seem to be at the heart of Diderot's way of looking at the world, both as philosopher and as artist. His scepticism is certainly very profound, but it would be a mistake to think of it as pure negativity (expressing "the nothingness of all things"), or for that matter as pessimism, in a La Rochefoucauldian vein; it does not feel like pessimism, let alone cynicism. Suzanne's sufferings, after all, remain a harrowing and all-too-believable possibility that an enlightened society might do something to prevent. Nor is the reader of such horrors being asked to give up generous emotion and indignation; he or she is merely being asked to look more deeply into the lengths to which he can push his questioning and the bottomlessness of the abyss in ourselves into which he asks us to peer.

Stuart Hampshire   (essay date 1993)

SOURCE: "The Last Charmer," in *The New York Review of Books,* Vol. XL, No. 5, March 4, 1993, pp. 15-19.

[*Hampshire is an eminent English-born philosopher and critic. In the following excerpt, he provides a brief account of Diderot's major works and themes, emphasizing his evocation of the "ambiguities, the uncertainties, and incoherences which the contrast of virtue and vice, and any conventional ethics always entails."*]

Of the great triumvirate of the century in France—Voltaire, Rousseau, Diderot—only Voltaire can possibly be represented as exalting rationality in morals and politics, and even he appealed more often to common sense and to the observation of nature. Rousseau and Diderot made natural sentiments and emotions the center of their moralities and left logic and reasoning, in any strict sense, on the periphery. For conservative pamphleteers, now as in the last century, it has been easier to lump them all together to form a single target and to denounce a false notion of philosophical rationality as responsible for the September massacres during the French Revolution, and even for the later excesses of totalitarian planning.

Like so many arguments drawn from the history of ideas, this one is superficially plausible only in so far as it is kept vague and remote from specific texts. As joint editor with D'Alembert of the **Encyclopedia,** the great monument of advanced thinking in the eighteenth century, Diderot gets caught up in this controversy because several contributors to the **Encyclopedia,** who were also his friends, were indeed utilitarians and rational optimists in philosophy, and some of them also believed in scientific determinism and in the dawn of a new age of harmony and peace: Condorcet, Helvétius, Condillac, Holbach, La Mettrie, did believe, with different emphases and for different reasons, that their new theories of knowledge would enable humanity to be remodeled for the benefit of all in a splendid future.

Diderot certainly had no such confidence. He argued that the human sciences were still in their infancy and that we still know almost nothing about the workings either of the mind or of the brain or of their relation to each other. He often wrote and spoke of the vast range of different possibilities open to men and women and of new forms of happiness that would unpredictably arise. Famously he evoked in his dialogue *Le Neveu de Rameau* the ambiguities, the uncertainties, and incoherences which the contrast of virtue and vice, and any conventional ethics, always entails.

Diderot neither sought nor achieved purity of soul either in his life or in theory. He was amused by his own inconsistencies and weaknesses, as we know from his letters to Sophie Volland, at one time his mistress: letters still wonderful to read, comparable with the letters of Keats or Byron. When in prison, as he was on two occasions, or later threatened with prison for subversion, he did not try to be a hero. He was ready for every compromise and concession. He did not believe in perfectibility or acknowledge the idea of the good. In *Le Neveu de Rameau* he dramatizes the destructive element, the play-acting and the role reversals, which are no less natural in men and women than honesty and good feeling. Sincerity, in his view, could not be a cardinal virtue, because creativity is closely linked to mixed intentions and to confusions of identity.

Denis Diderot was born in 1713 in the still beautiful, and very provincial, town of Langres, the son of a cutler, whom he deeply loved and admired and who was able to send him to study in Paris in 1729. He often returned there and died there in 1784. Diderot from the beginning rejected the Church and despised intolerance and piety, and he rejected chastity as an ideal. He began his literary career with a rather feeble and mildly pornographic story, *Indiscreet Jewels,* which he published after his translation of Shaftesbury's *Inquiry Concerning Merit and Virtue* and his own immature *Pensées Philosophiques.* In the mid-1740s he began work on a vast and glorious project, glorious in its own time and still of interest now, the *Encyclopedia.* Diderot was always preoccupied with glory, fame, and immortality, debating their value with himself and in his letters to friends. Why should one care so much about posthumous fame and glory? Does not happiness consist principally in the admiration of one's family and friends? The *Encyclopedia* was intended to bring glory to him and to France.

The *Encyclopedia of the Arts and Sciences* was to take the place of a French translation of the *Cyclopaedia, or Universal Dictionary of the Arts and Sciences* published by Ephraim Chambers, a Scotsman, in 1728. Chambers had produced a mere work of reference, an inert catalog of names and facts without theme or inspiration. Diderot's *Encyclopedia* was to make a statement about the expanding domain of human knowledge, its present frontiers and future possibilities. The great empire of the new sciences and applied arts called for a charter and a written constitution, and this was the time, the 1740s, for a many-volumed manifesto summarizing its numerous conquests and their mutual dependencies.

Diderot's fellow editor was his close friend, the internationally celebrated mathematician D'Alembert, a forthright atheist and free-thinking wit, who dominated the salons of Madame du Deffand and Madame Geoffrin, and later was the lover of Julie de l'Espinasse, whose house became the house of friendship for the free-thinkers of Paris. Unlike D'Alembert, Diderot throughout his life was capable of some pliancy in the face of the authorities, and his prospectus for the Encyclopedia made a successful patriotic appeal to the chancellor, the licensing authority. Explicit mockery of the Church and of Christian theology was never to be prominent in Diderot's own contributions, even though the whole enterprise was unavoidably radical and subversive. Its editors were always liable to be imprisoned or otherwise punished.

For two decades Diderot walked a tightrope as chief editor, restraining himself and his contributors from any blatant attacks on the Church or the monarchy. He even printed some grave discussions of Christian thought. But he did fall off his tightrope early in his life on a famous occasion. His first serious philosophical work, *Pensées Philosophiques,* was burned by the public hangman, a common procedure at the time, because it was obviously the work of a dangerous freethinker. In 1749 he published *Lettre sur les aveugles,* an empiricist's essay, and he was immediately arrested and imprisoned in the Castle of Vincennes, where his wife joined him and Rousseau visited him, and he continued to read voraciously, as he always did, wherever he might be.

But he was a man who could not bear the stillness and repose of prison life, with its uniformity and predictability. He always needed movement, impulsive starts and stops, contrasts and contradictions in conversation and argument, constant talk and social variety. There were fears that he would go mad in confinement, and, once interrogated, he humbly confessed his guilt, abjured his evil opinions, and revealed the names of his printers.

Thereafter he was released and wrote *Lettre sur les sourds et les muets (Letter on the Deaf and the Mute),* his second clever essay on the theory of knowledge. Exaggerating the empiricism of John Locke, who had denied that there could be innate ideas independent of experience and perception, Condillac in his *Traité des sensations* had traced all knowledge back to its alleged foundation in the association of ideas, which had their origin in the separate senses of sight, touch, and hearing. But how are the data of the separate senses coordinated to form some stable and coherent picture of the external world? Is there not an assumption of a unitary self which coordinates? Against Condillac and the pure empiricists, the so-called "sensualist philosophy," Diderot was always to insist that it is of the nature of mind to be active in its interaction with the external world, and that it is bad philosophy to represent our minds as just passive and receptive in perception—as empty buckets. This, he held, could not be true of any organism in the natural order.

Mr. Furbank [in his *Diderot: A Critical Biography,* 1992] stresses the innovations of form in his philosophical writing which are to be explained by the tentative, wholly speculative, and undogmatic positions which he took up. He habitually used the dialogue form, which enabled him to evade stating any final conclusions of his own. The topic had been opened and thereafter the talk should continue—that was the design. In the course of his dialogues he attributed views to friends and contemporaries (Condillac, D'Alembert, a famous doctor Théophile Bordeu, Mlle. de l'Espinasse, Rameau's nephew) which were not his, but they were arguable and were among the principal strands in modern thought. He did not mind contradicting himself between one work and another. Apart from any changes and development in his philosophy, the different contexts of argument were meant to explain why he rejected free will in one place and why in another place he rejected determinism applied to human actions and beliefs.

Determinism was one of the many issues on which he followed Spinoza. The multiplicity of causes in the common order of nature, he argued, is inexhaustibly complex and, for all human purposes, determinism is therefore irrelevant to our lives and to our morals. Successes and failures, particularly in the arts, present themselves to us as matters of chance as much as of skill. On the other hand if belief in free will is the belief that persons are originating causes, it is an illusion and a harmful illusion. You can dissolve the apparent contradiction between free will and determinism if, and only if, you always remember that human knowledge, and particularly self-knowledge, is pathetically limited, and that it always will be.

For Diderot writing was an extension of talking. Sometimes the talk was a monologue rather than a conversation, as in the early philosophical treatises *Philosophic Thoughts,* and *On the Interpretation of Nature.* Even there the sentences drift forward in the loose and informal manner of a lecturer or popular journalist, not in the magisterial manner of Leibniz or Voltaire. Diderot intends his readers to "picture the movements and march of his mind," and not only to picture but to participate in the movement. That is what he meant when he said that he was the most "communicative" of men. It was part of his theory of knowledge, repudiating the mighty authority of Descartes, that truth emerges in the flash and friction of conversation, typically around a dinner table, rather than in the detached soul of a solitary thinker sitting by a stove and interrogating his own mind. At least in the realm of natural philosophy and metaphysics, truth is a social construction. His image of intelligence is not Rodin's heavy and immobile *Penseur,* but rather the fluid and variegated outlines of the figures in Raphael's *School of Athens.*

The reason for this anti-Cartesian conception of thought is to be found in Diderot's philosophy of nature. For Descartes, still a Christian philosopher, the individual human soul or mind stands outside, and above, the natural order, to which it is attached only by its association with a body. Hence the splendor and majesty of the declaration *Cogito, ergo sum:* my unique existence as a thinking creature is known, but known not through any of the fallible channels of natural knowledge. When we are thinking, and thinking methodically, Descartes and you and I are transcendent beings, not caught up in the accidents and complexities of the natural order, which we liftily observe and inquire into.

Diderot reversed this metaphysics consistently and Spinozistically in all his writings, including in his fiction and in his moral speculations. His deepest conviction, the clue to his own way of life as well as to his art and thought, was that human beings are inextricably parts of nature (which he called *le tout*) and, physically and mentally, are subject to all its unpredictable contingencies. This is the kernel of what was later called his materialism, and it was this so-called his materialism that made him one of the saints in the old Marxist calendar. But it was a materialism with a difference, not the reductive, rather lumpish materialism of his contemporaries La Mettrie, Baron Holbach, and others, which survived throughout the nineteenth century and which flourishes among the computers in Australia and in the US even today.

The second aspect of Diderot's materialism was his passionate interest in the applied arts and in technology and in all forms of craftsmanship. He loved to explain how elementary machines worked, for example, in the printing trade and to find good illustrations of their workings. This passion, as much as philosophy, was the inspiration of the *Encyclopedia:* an interest in concrete causes in place of

spiritual mysteries was characteristic of the French Enlightenment, so different from the German, and the *Encyclopedia* was the instrument of this new light.

There were to be seventeen volumes of the *Encyclopedia* and Diderot needed twenty-one years (1751-1772) to complete his editorial labor, sometimes working ten hours a day. He himself contributed a great variety of articles, about twenty on philosophical subjects, and even more on applied arts and crafts. The whole was a campaign of demystification with a clear Baconian aim: disseminated knowledge would be disseminated power, and modern minds would be opened up to the real resources of the modern world, after the long sleep in the darkness of ecclesiastical ignorance. Material improvement came before spiritual gains. A consequence of Diderot's materialism was that the beauty and wisdom in a craftsman's work is not to be ranked lower, as a natural achievement, than abstract speculation, as Plato had required, or as mathematicians, including D'Alembert, still insisted. Mr. Furbank quotes Diderot:

> In what physical or metaphysical system do we find more intelligence, discernment, and consistency than in the machines for drawing gold or making stockings, and in the frames of the braid-makers, the gauze-makers, the drapers, or the silk workers? What mathematical demonstration is more complex than the mechanism of certain clocks or the different operations to which we submit the fibre of hemp or the chrysalis of the silkworm before obtaining a thread with which we can weave?

This is pure Diderot in its love of the concrete and the mundane. In its perception of the beauty of instruments, the passage is typical of the new sensibility of his century, the sensibility of the amateur experimentalist, illustrated in England by Wright of Derby. Diderot celebrated the glory of productive processes and of the mastery of pre-industrial skills, with the clock-maker coming nearer to God's work than the metaphysician. He loved the variety and the jagged intricacy of instruments. He had wanted to be an inventor himself and he had plans for a kind of typewriter, a new instrument on which a person could compose, even a design for an encoding machine.

But his co-editor, D'Alembert, wrote the preliminary discourses, subsequently famous, which set forth the proper scheme of the sciences, glorifying mathematics as the pinnacle, while Diderot wrote a prospectus for subscribers which based distinct disciplines on three distinct faculties of the mind—memory, reason, and imagination. Although they began as very close friends, and although Flaubert was later to remark irritably that one seemed never to be mentioned without the other, the two editors in fact had largely different philosophies, and different plans for the future of humanity. D'Alembert was a rationalist in every sense of the word, and thought of Nature as submitting to our understanding under natural laws mathematically expressed: physics was for him the basic science. Mr. Furbank quotes a typical D'Alembert doctrine: "Obscurity invades our ideas of an object in proportion as we study more of its sensible properties." Again: the Universe, for someone who was able to take it in as a whole from a single standpoint, would appear, if one may so put it, as a unitary fact and a single great truth—an anticipation of Laplace.

In *Of the Interpretation of Nature* Diderot launched an attack on the dominance of mathematics in the natural science of his time.

> We are just coming to a great revolution in the sciences. In the inclination that intellects [*les esprits*] have toward ethics, literature, natural history, and experimental physics, I would be bold enough to guarantee that in less than a century one will not count three great geometers in Europe.

In a famous letter to Voltaire in 1758 he wrote: "The reign of mathematics is no more. Taste has changed. It is now the hour of natural history and *belles-letters*," and he insisted that D'Alembert's thought was mired in the past. Biology, and the study of organic processes, was to be the dominant science.

Diderot had the flair and the fluency of a born journalist, shamelessly plagiarizing secondary authorities rather than leaving a gap unfilled, and aiming always at readability, sometimes by introducing names of persons to make technical issues more memorable and more dramatic. What was later to be known as the higher journalism has one of its origins in the *Encyclopedia,* although its select subscribers did not compare in numbers with Hazlitt's public or with that of *The Quarterly Review*. The subscribers were a tiny group of princes and aristocrats. The unique genius of Diderot was to combine, on the same level of seriousness, the metaphysics of Spinozism with a technical analysis of handloom weaving. Having dethroned mathematics from its position as the paradigm of all knowledge, Diderot lost interest in the Cartesian boundary that had been supposed to divide, cleanly and clearly, the works of the intellect from the works of the imagination. Parts of nature ourselves, we can reconstruct natural processes of development, and come to understand them in several different ways, sometimes through artistic constructions, and through formal experiments in the arts, no less than through the observations and generalizations of physiology and of physics.

In his famous *Salon,* a periodical review of recent paintings exhibited in the Louvre, Diderot introduced discriminations between true and false, authentic and inauthentic, in the art of painting. In his *On the Interpretation of Nature,* or in his treatise on physiology, he distinguished between authentic and inauthentic science. In both cases one must first rid one's mind of the idea of truth as essentially a matching of thought to external reality. The greatness of Chardin's paintings resides in the invented naturalness of the forms, which are not a triumph of piecemeal copying, but rather show a genius in tracing a whole pictorial structure that has suggested itself to the artist, he knows not how, as natural and fitting for this particular subject. Through true artistic invention, in art and in fiction, we may come to participate in the processes and forms of nature through an affinity and a sympathy that can never be further explained. In the art of painting we first invent, and thereby discover, an analogy for the mixed moods of

the sea and for the relations between colors, shapes, and surfaces.

Diderot throughout his life was preoccupied with the notion of genius, not only in his classic treatment of its destructiveness in *Le Neveu de Rameau,* but in application to his own insights. Mr. Furbank quotes him as suffering "from a violent desire to discover, to invent. . . ." For fifty years he had waited in vain for "the happy chance" that would entitle him to call himself a genius. His genius, it finally emerged, was in the immense variety and range of his thought as short-story writer, novelist, art critic, philosopher, scientist, dramatist, moral philosopher.

When one thinks of Diderot and of his philosophy, it is always appropriate to think first of conversation and of discussions among friends. In composing the *Salon,* no less than in his correspondence with friends, he remains informal and discursive and delightedly chases after irrelevancies if they are intellectually amusing. One never knows when a speculation may turn out to be suggestive and productive. He liked his work to be a series of sketches, dashed off at different times, and not marmoreally composed. His life also was not composed and was not all of a piece. His writing was to be an expressive part of his life, showing the natural movement of his mind: a fluent and multidirectional movement, not chopped up into hard and well-marked fragments like Voltaire's. He was before all things an inspired talker, both by nature and on principle. In *Le Rêve de D'Alembert,* the doctor Bordeu and Julie de l'Espinasse each exhibit their own perspective and their foibles and sensitivities: the formality of assertion and counter-assertion is softened and dissolved.

Socrates was for Diderot the supreme and immortal hero of thought, but the gossipy, free-for-all, intellectually uncertain quality of Diderot's two great dialogues is a long way from Socrates' measured speech in his dialogues: they are in a particular eighteenth-century style, neither neoclassical nor academic. Mr. Furbank quotes Taine on Diderot:

> Forgetting himself, carried away by his own story, listening to inward voices, taken by surprise by reports which come to him unawares, he has said everything on Nature, Art, ethics in two little works [*Le Rêve de D'Alembert* and *Le Neveu de Rameau*] of which twenty successive readings will not lessen the charm or exhaust the significance. . . . There lies the advantage of these geniuses who do not have empire over themselves.

Diderot cultivated his spontaneity and the inspiration of the moment. He wanted to be the exemplary dilettante of genius, experimenting with his own identity, an example that Stendhal was to follow when he addressed himself in his Journals by different names. Diderot was happiest in a group of free-thinking disputants—typically, in Baron d'Holbach's country house—when he and his friends, "felt free to utter whatever came into their minds." In his brilliant dialogue *Le paradoxe sur le Comédien* (*The Paradox of the Actor*), one character is the man of feeling who loses his head and only recovers it at the bottom of the stairs (*l'esprit d'escalier*). But the other character is the calm and detached actor who stands apart from the emotion which he carefully enacts.

Like Lichtenberg writing about Garrick, Diderot sees in acting an exaggeration of the duality of the self and of multiple personalities, which he takes to be the normal conditions of human wholeness. It is natural to enter into dialogues and disputes with others because it is natural first to enter into disputes with oneself. The mind works by contradiction. That is why in *Le Neveu de Rameau* there are the characters Moi and Lui. In a person's inner life actors move on a crowded stage where contrary passions come and go, masked and in disguise.

Scientific theory and fiction were equally interpretations of Nature for Diderot. *La Religieuse* (*The Nun*), posthumously published, is the greatest of his pure fictions. It was written to deceive a friend who, in a cruel and unpleasant hoax, was meant to take the story as a true story and to try to rescue the heroine. He was in fact deceived. . . .

Diderot continued to work at intervals on the novel, which developed into a vivid and subtle study of passion uncontrolled, a lesbian passion in which maturity and innocence are brought into conflict. As a philosophical materialist, always at war with Descartes's mind-body dualism, sexuality and physical passion are for Diderot the central knot of personality, where self-awareness and sensuality are intertwined. Society's efforts to confine sexuality within general rules and conventions will, he wrote, often end in disaster. This moral is elaborated in the dialogue *Supplément au voyage de Bougainville,* which compares the generous and philoprogenitive sexuality of the Tahitians, who are free from all possessiveness, with the jealous and stifled impulses of a visiting Christian gentleman. On the whole the Tahitians in their arcadia come out better than the damp and inward-looking Christians, who admittedly have an advantage in learning, but have lost their feeling for natural happiness.

But Diderot was not committed to a naive dichotomy between natural impulse and the thoughtful artificialities of high culture, which is sometimes implied in Rousseau's *Discourse on Inequality.* Human beings for Diderot are by nature comedians, poseurs, prone to art and to artificiality, and their impulses are not simple and uncorrupted by circumstance. Any return to nature is also a return to conflicts and to contradiction. The power of reflection and thought is part of the nature of organisms which are as complex in structure as human beings and which are also pliable and adaptable, each in a singular way. We shall therefore encounter possessive and imprisoning passions, like that of the Mother Superior in *The Nun,* as naturally as the passions that are associated with liberation and with escape from repression. The opposition between good and bad is not between Nature and Civilization, two universals, but always between happy and unhappy adaptations of individuals to their particular surrounding conditions. When individual natures are in harmony with the particular conditions to which they are responding, then happiness supervenes: as Diderot himself was happy when plotting his publications with Grimm in Madame d'Epinay's garden, or arguing with Abbé Galiani at dinner with the Baron D'Holbach, or making a philosophical point in a letter to his lover Sophie Volland, or at home with his daughter Angélique, or in his conversation at any hour of day or night with the Empress Catherine in St. Petersburg.

In the spirit of Montaigne, Diderot took it to be evident that the soul, or self, was in constant flux, transforming itself just as the cells of the body are constantly changing within a constant structure. His favorite image of identity, and particularly of personal identity, was a swarm of bees, which holds together and preserves its identity in the way that a human personality, with its myriad thoughts and sensations, still holds together. We can distinguish within the swarm of any individual's memories and passions the contrary desires and conflicting beliefs that keep the swarm alive and in motion. Diderot's moral and aesthetic attitudes, and even the direction of his own life, depended upon this doctrine of the insubstantial self as well as on his materialism. The integrity of a person was like the integrity of the swarm, and not that of a block of marble, a material that he particularly disliked. "Marble does not laugh."

According to Spinoza's materialism, human beings perceive and interpret nature, including human nature, in two distinct ways: teleologically, in terms of desires, beliefs, and the self-conscious pursuit of ends; mechanically, in terms of laws of motion. Nature ("the whole") is inexhaustible and forever exceeds our knowledge and understanding. The duality of the two orders resides in us as embodied observers. Observing the plucking of the strings of a musical instrument, I may attend to the physical motions occurring or I may attend to the tune: the same event in the natural order, but different interests.

This is Diderot's example. As a theorist of portrait painting and of dramatic art and of sculpture, and a theorist also of sexuality, Diderot recognized that human bodies, unlike machines, are visibly animated by changing thoughts and passions: he was always thinking, as a novelist, dramatist, art critic, and physiologist, of the changing expressions in a person's eye, the tone of a voice, the harmony of colors of fruit and glass on a table in a Chardin, the thought that entered into the sculptor Falconet's carving and molding. Blind and deaf persons are compelled to think more abstractly. For purposes of explanation, as physicists and physiologists, we also need to think more abstractly, looking for laws and generalities. But we talk with whole persons, irreducibly singular, and we find friendship, and therefore happiness, in noticing and dwelling on particularities—particularities of place and of the countryside as well as of persons.

Diderot took his place in the line that passes from Democritus through Lucretius to Spinoza, and that Marx sometimes, and in spite of his Hegelian obfuscations, claimed to continue. Philosophy was for all of them demystification; they were the metaphysicians of fearlessness, who refused to be haunted by anything that could not be felt or seen, or that could not be heard as natural sound or as man-made music: no ghosts and no mysteries, except the mystery of human genius. The melody is waiting in the strings of the instrument, and even the inspiration of a poet exists also as an excited physical state, from which the poet's words and rhythms emerge.

For Diderot, as for Spinoza, Nature is a seamless whole ("*le tout*"), one all-inclusive system of systems of systems . . . ad infinitum: nothing super-natural and transcendent can conceivably exist, and we must restore in our own consciousness a sense of acting within the undivided universe, and by this means restore also a sense of personal, mind-body wholeness. Our morality comes from our passions, and not from any authority, and therefore its prescriptions are not in their nature absolute: they need to be modified and adapted to circumstance. . . .

When in the last two centuries the French Enlightenment has been discussed, it has often been accused of reducing all human interest to two basic instincts—the pursuit of pleasure and the avoidance of pain. In the **Refutation of Helvétius** Diderot argues that Helvétius's reductions are an elementary confusion of preconditions with causes. Characteristically he imagines the "heroic vanity" of those who think of their posthumous fame, and who tremble with joy at "the sweet melody of this distant concert of voices occupied in celebrating them." Susceptibility to physical sensations is the biological precondition of this heartfelt feeling, but its cause is human thought and reflection, a specifically human cause. We should not look for universal causes in human life: chance and diverse contingent needs determine our lives. "Who should know this better then?" wrote Diderot. "That is the reason why I have spent about thirty years on end, contrary to my taste, on the **Encyclopaedia** and have only written two plays."

FURTHER READING

Alter Robert. "Diderot's *Jacques*: This Is and Is Not a Story." In his *Partial Magic: The Novel as a Self-Conscious Genre*, pp. 57-83. Berkeley and Los Angeles: University of California Press, 1975.
    Analysis of *Jacques the Fatalist*, focusing in particular on Diderot's extensive use of Laurence Sterne's novel *Tristram Shandy*.

Barthes, Roland. "Diderot, Brecht, Eisenstein." In his *Images, Music, Text*, translated by Stephen Heath, pp. 69-78. New York: Hill and Wang, 1977.
    Discusses Diderot as a precursor of the modern drama and film.

Blum, Carol. *Diderot: The Virtue of a Philosopher*. New York: The Viking Press, 1974, 182 p.
    Examines the central importance of morality in Diderot's thought.

Fellows, Otis. *Diderot*. Boston: Twayne Publishers, 1977, 193 p.
    Overview of Diderot's life and career.

France, Peter. "Diderot: The Order of Dialogue." In his *Rhetoric and Truth in France*, pp. 191-234. Oxford: Clarendon Press, 1972.
    Analysis of Diderot's use of rhetoric in his dialogues, paying particular attention to the philosopher's notion of order.

Green, Frederick C. *Literary Ideas in 18th Century France and England: A Critical Survey*. New York: Frederick Ungar Publishing Co., 1966, 489 p.
    Classic study of eighteenth-century literature, containing numerous references to Diderot's works.

Laski, Harold J. "Diderot." In his *Studies in Law and Politics*, pp. 48-65. 1932. Reprint. Freeport, N.J.: Books for Libraries Press, 1968.
    Favorable assessment of the philosopher, maintaining that "Diderot is one of the few seminal figures in the history of thought who never gave birth to a masterpiece and was incapable of building a system."

Loy, J. Robert. *Diderot's Determined Fatalist: A Critical Appreciation of "Jacques le fataliste."* New York: King's Crown Press, 1950, 234 p.
    Seminal study of *Jacques the Fatalist*, arguing that the novel focuses on three major themes: the artistic problem of realism in the novel; the philosophical issue of fatalism; and the moral difficulty of assessing virtue and vice.

May, Gita. "Diderot and Burke: A Study in Aesthetic Affinity." *PMLA* LXXV, No. 5 (December 1960): 527-39.
    Examines the presence of Edmund Burke's *A Philosophical Enquiry into the Origin of our Ideas of the Sublime and Beautiful* (1757) in Diderot's *Salon de 1767*.

Mylne, V. G. "Diderot: Theory and Practice." In his *The Eighteenth-Century French Novel: Techniques of Illusion*, pp. 192-220. Cambridge: Cambridge University Press, 1981.
    Analysis of Diderot's creation of the illusion of reality in his novels, focusing on *The Nun* and *Jacques the Fatalist*.

O'Gorman, Donal. *Diderot the Satirist*. Toronto: University of Toronto Press, 1971, 265 p.
    Important, controversial study of Diderot's satirical works that pays particular attention to *Rameau's Nephew*.

Read, Herbert. "The Disciples of Diderot." In his *Poetry and Experience*, pp. 71-87. New York: Horizon Press, 1967.
    Discussion of Diderot as a precursor of modern drama.

Saintsbury, George. "Diderot's 'Salons'." In his *A Last Vintage*, pp. 217-22. London: Methuen & Co., 1950.
    Praises Diderot's achievement as the inventor of art criticism.

Spitzer, Leo. "The Style of Diderot." In his *Linguistics and Literary History: Essays in Stylistics*, pp. 135-91. New York: Russell & Russell, 1962.
    Imaginative discussion of Diderot's literary styles, which the critic characterizes as "a self-accentuating rhythm, suggesting that the 'speaker' is swept away by a wave of passion which tends to flood all limits."

Steegmuller, Francis. *A Woman, A Man, and Two Kingdoms: The Story of Madame d'Epinay and the Abbé Galiani*. Princeton: Princeton University Press, 1991, 280 p.
    Engrossing account of Diderot's social and intellectual milieu, focusing on the relationship of two of his closest friends, Louise d'Epinay and Ferdinando Galiani.

Undank, Jack. "On Being 'Human': Diderot's *Satire Première*." *Eighteenth-Century Studies* 20, No. 1 (Fall 1986): 1-16.
    Discussion of the major theme of Diderot's *Satire Pre-*

miè, which the critic defines as "the way we perceive (or misperceive), speak, write, and fall short of being human."

Vartanian, Aram. "From Deist to Atheist: Diderot's Philosophical Orientation 1746-1749." *Diderot Studies* I (1949): 46-63.
   Examination of the complexities present in Diderot's early deism and scepticism, which eventually culminated in the atheism of the *Letter on the Blind*.

Waldauer, Joseph L. "Society and the Freedom of the Creative Man in Diderot's Thought." *Diderot Studies* V (1964): 13-156.
   Monograph that explores Diderot's views on the place of the artist and the genius in society.

The Encyclopedists

INTRODUCTION

Having developed from a projected translation of Ephraim Chambers's *Cyclopedia* (1728) to an original reference work of gigantic proportions, the *Encyclopédie* was composed by some 150 contributors, among whom only a handful are widely known as the Encyclopedists. Since traditional criticism and commentary have tended to ignore the lesser contributors, the Encyclopedists most frequently discussed by scholars are those who helped editor Denis Diderot to realize his encyclopedic dream, including such figures as Claude-Adrien Helvétius, Etienne Bonnot de Condillac, Francois Quesnay, Anne-Robert-Jacques, baron de Turgot, Francois Marie Arouet Voltaire, Charles Louis de Secondat, baron de Montesquieu, Paul Henry Thiry, baron d'Holbach, Jean-Jacques Rousseau, Jean Le Rond d'Alembert, and Julien Offray de La Mettrie. A literary monument to the French Enlightenment, the *Encyclopédie* was dominated by the contributions of Enlightenment figures; yet, it may be said that work on the *Encyclopédie* was a marginal activity for the philosophes who contributed, with the obvious exception of Diderot. For example, Montesquieu submitted an unfinished entry on "Taste," Voltaire contributed very little, and Rousseau seemed quite distant from the project. Furthermore, despite their common belief in the sacrosanct power of reason alone, the Encyclopedists did not constitute a philosophical group, presenting an characteristic philosophic and scientific world view, as did Holbach's atheistic coterie. For example, their views on religion ranged from the traditional Catholicism of Condillac to La Mettrie's dogmatic atheism; in fact, their views ran the gamut of typical eighteenth-century religious views, including Deism, the belief in an impersonal God the Creator. In the area of political economics, some Encyclopedists—for example, Turgot—showed genuine interest in the welfare of the people, while others, eloquently represented by Voltaire, espoused an individualistic elitism. Further, the Encyclopedists individually held varied philosophical views, exemplified by the beliefs of Condillac and La Mettrie. On the one hand, the Jesuit-educated Condillac strove to balance the pervasive sensationalism—the belief that knowledge can be attained only through the senses—of eighteenth-century French thought with the Cartesian dualism of body and soul. La Mettrie, on the other hand, who was raised in the Jansenist tradition, which subscribed to a rigidly deterministic conception of Divine Grace, formulated, in his *L'Homme machine* (1747; *Man a Machine*), the fundamental statement of absolute atheism and dogmatic materialism, completely relinquishing Cartesian dualism, which was still quite prominent in the intellectual landscape of the Enlightenment. Under scrutiny, even the Encyclopedists' treatment of the arts and music reveals profound ambiguities and contradictions. Despite these divergences, the *Encyclopédie* did not lack a logical general methodology. However, the systematic method was not provided by the Encyclopedists' collective effort, but by one man, d'Alembert, scientist and mathematician, whose *Discours preliminaire* (1751) reflected his personal view that the *Encyclopédie* should provide a clear, intelligible, organically structured exposition of theoretical and practical knowledge. Similarly, just as it reflects the scientific mind of d'Alembert, the *Encyclopédie* also mirrors the extraordinary literary versatility and intellectual curiosity of Diderot, who, in addition to editing, wrote articles on a wide variety of subjects, applying his rich descriptive talent to truly revolutionary depictions of industrial and artisanal production.

Among critical scholars, the Romantic view of the Encyclopedists is crystallized in Johann Wolfgang von Goethe's autobiographical *Dichtung und Wahrheit* (1822; *Poetry and Truth*), in which he describes a feeling of visceral repulsion and alienation provoked by detailed descriptions of manufacture in the *Encyclopédie*. Notable among nineteenth-century views is Thomas Carlyle's criticism of the Encyclopedists. Largely inspired by Goethe, Carlyle regarded the Encyclopedists as the antithesis to an active, energetic, optimistic conception of life. As Ernst Cassirer wrote in his *The Myth of State* (1946), "Man will always form his image of nature after his own image. If he fails to see in himself an original and creative power, nature too becomes to him mere passive things—a dead mechanism. According to Carlyle this was the fate of the French Encyclopedists and the 'philosophers' of the eighteenth century. Their theory of nature was the exact counterpart of their theory of man. Holbach's *Systeme de la nature* and La Mettrie's *L'Homme machine* are closely akin. The express the same skeptical, destructive, negative spirit." In a different vein, Michel Foucault praised the Encyclopedists for their intellectual originality, particularly in their creating a multidisciplinary discourse. Foucault cited the progressive economist Turgot, author of such articles as "Existence" and "Etymologie," in which he demonstrated the significant connection between words and money. Twentieth-century scholars have also noted the multidisciplinary thought of Quesnay, the physician turned economist, who wrote seminal articles on farming. Other recent critics have contributed to an anthropology of the Encyclopedists by studying their cultural and biological prejudices, particularly those exhibited in their attitudes toward women.

REPRESENTATIVE WORKS

Alembert, Jean Le Rond d'
  Discours preliminaire de l'Encyclopedie 1751
Condillac, Etienne Bonot de
  Traite des sensations 1754
  [*Condillac's Treatise on the Sensations*, 1930]

Helvetius, Claude Adrien
   De l'esprit 1758
    [*De l'esprit; or, Essays on the Mind and Its Several Faculties,* 1759]
Holbach, Paul Henry Thiry, baron d'
   Le systeme de la nature 1770
    [*The System of Nature; or, The Laws of the Moral and Physical World,* 1797]
La Mettrie, Julien Offray de
   L'homme machine 1747
    [*Man a Machine,* 1750]
Montesquieu, Charles Louis de Secondat, baron de
   L'esprit des lois 1748
    [*The Spirit of Laws,* 1750]
Quesnay, Francois
   Le tableau economique 1758
Rousseau, Jean-Jacques
   Du contrat social ou Prinicipes du droit politique 1762
    [*The Social Contract; or, The Principles of Political Rights,* 1893]
Turgot, Anne-Robert-Jacques, baron de
   Reflexions sur la formation et la distribution des richesses 1766
    [*Reflections on the Formation and Distribution of Wealth,* 1793]
Voltaire, Francois Marie Arouet
   Candide, ou l'optimisme 1759
    [*Candide; or, The Optimist,* 1792]

OVERVIEWS

John Viscount Morley

SOURCE: "The Encyclopaedia," in *Diderot and the Encyclopaedists,* Vol. I, Macmillan and Co., Limited, 1923, pp. 115-222.

[*Morley was an English writer and politician whose works include* Studies in Literature *(1981),* Critical Miscellanies *(1908), and* Recollections *(1917). In the following excerpt from a book originally published in 1879, he provides a richly documented history and evaluation of the* Encyclopedia.]

The history of the encyclopaedic conception of human knowledge is a much more interesting and important object of inquiry than a list of the various encyclopaedic enterprises to be found in the annals of literature. Yet it is proper here to mention some of the attempts in this direction which preceded our memorable book of the eighteenth century. It is to Aristotle, no doubt, that we must look for the first glimpse of the idea that human knowledge is a totality, whose parts are all closely and organically connected with one another. But the idea that only dawned in that gigantic understanding was lost for many centuries. The compilations of Pliny are not in a right sense encyclopaedic, being presided over by no definite idea of informing order. It was not until the later Middle Age that any attempt was made to present knowledge as a whole. Albertus Magnus, "the ape of Aristotle" (1193-

1280), left for a space the three great questions of the existence of universals, of the modes of the existence of species and genus, and of their place in or out of the bosom of the individuals, and executed a compilation of such physical facts as had been then discovered. A more distinctly encyclopaedic work was the book of Vincent de Beauvais (d. 1264), called *Speculum naturale, morale, doctrinale, et historiale,* —a compilation from Aquinas in some parts, and from Aristotle in others. [In his *Introduction to the Literature of Europe in the 15th, 16th and 17th Centuries,* Henry] Hallam mentions three other compilations of the thirteenth and fourteenth centuries, and observes that their laborious authors did not much improve the materials which they had amassed in their studies, though they sometimes arranged them conveniently. In the mediaeval period, as he remarks, the want of capacity to discern probable truths was a very great drawback from the value of their compilations.

Far the most striking production of the thirteenth century in this kind was the *Opus Majus* of Roger Bacon (1267), of which it has been said that it is at once the Encyclopaedia and the *Novum Organum* of that age; at once a summary of knowledge and the suggestion of a truer method. This however was merely the introductory sketch to a vaster encyclopaedic work, the *Compendium Philosophice,* which was not perfected. "In common with minds of great and comprehensive grasp, his vivid perception of the intimate relationship of the different parts of philosophy, and his desire to raise himself from the dead level of every individual science, induced Bacon to grasp at and embrace the whole" [J. S. Brewer]. In truth, the encyclopaedic spirit was in the air throughout the thirteenth century. It was the century of books bearing the significant titles of *Summa* or *Universitas* or *Speculum.*

The same spirit revived towards the middle of the sixteenth century. In 1541 a book was published at Basel by one Ringelberg, which first took the name of Cyclopaedia, that has since then become so familiar a word in western Europe. This was followed within sixty years by several other works of the same kind. The movement reached its height in a book that remained the best in its order for a century. A German, one J. H. Alsted (1588-1638), published in 1620 an *Encyclopaedia scientiarum omnium.* A hundred years later the illustrious Leibnitz pronounced it a worthy task to perfect and amend Alsted's book. What was wanting to the excellent man, he said, was neither labour nor judgment, but material and the good fortune of such days as ours. And Leibnitz wrote a paper of suggestions for its extension and improvement. Alsted's Encyclopaedia is of course written in Latin, and he prefixes to it by way of motto the celebrated lines in which Lucretius declares that nothing is sweeter than to dwell apart in the serene temples of the wise. Though he informs us in the preface that his object was to trace the outlines of the great "latifundium regni philosophici" in a single syntagma, yet he really does no more than arrange a number of separate treatises or manuals, and even dictionaries, within the limits of a couple of folios. As is natural to the spirit of the age in which he wrote, great predominance is given to the verbal sciences of grammar, rhetoric, and formal logic, and a verbal or logical division regulates the distribution of the matter, rather than a scientific regard for its objective relations.

For the true parentage, however, of the Encyclopaedia of Diderot and D'Alembert it is unnecessary to prolong this list. It was Francis Bacon's idea of the systematic classification of knowledge that inspired Diderot, and guided his hand throughout. "If we emerge from this vast operation," he wrote in the Prospectus, "our principal debt will be to the chancellor Bacon, who sketched the plan of a universal dictionary of sciences and arts at a time when there were not, so to say, either arts or sciences." This sense of profound and devoted obligation was shared by D'Alembert, and was expressed a hundred times in the course of the work. No more striking panegyric has ever been passed upon our immortal countryman than is to be found in the Preliminary Discourse. The French Encyclopaedia was the direct fruit of Bacon's magnificent conceptions. And if the efficient origin of the Encyclopaedia was English, so did the occasion rise in England also.

In 1727 Ephraim Chambers, a Westmoreland Quaker, published in London two folios, entitled *Cyclopaedia or an Universal Dictionary of the Arts and Sciences*. The idea of it was broad and excellent. "Our view," says Chambers, "was to consider the several matters not only in themselves, but relatively, or as they respect each other; both to treat them as so many wholes, and as so many parts of some greater whole." The compiler lacked the grasp necessary to realise this laudable purpose. The book has, however, the merit of conciseness, and is a singular monument of literary industry, for it was entirely compiled by Chambers himself. It had a great success, and though its price was high (four guineas), it ran through five editions in eighteen years. On the whole, however, it is meagre, and more like a dictionary than an encyclopaedia such as Alsted's for instance.

Some fifteen years after the publication of Chambers's Cyclopaedia, an Englishman (Mills) and a German (Sellius) went to Le Breton with a project for its translation into French. The bookseller obtained the requisite privilege from the government, but he obtained it for himself, and not for the projectors. This trick led to a quarrel, and before it was settled the German died and the Englishman returned to his own country. They left the translation behind them duly executed. Le Breton then carried the undertaking to a certain abbé, Gua de Malves. Gua de Malves (b. 1712) seems to have been a man of a busy and ingenious mind. He was the translator of Berkeley's *Hylas and Philonous*, of Anson's *Voyages*, and of various English tracts on currency and political economy. It is said that he first suggested the idea of a cyclopaedia on a fuller plan, but we have no evidence of this. In any case, the project made no advance in his hands. The embarrassed bookseller next applied to Diderot, who was then much in need of work that should bring him bread. His fertile and energetic intelligence transformed the scheme. By an admirable intuition he divined the opportunity that would be given by the encyclopaedic form, of gathering up into a whole all the new thought and modern knowledge existing as yet in unsystematic and uninterpreted fragments. His enthusiasm fired Le Breton. It was resolved to make Chambers's

work a mere starting-point for a new enterprise of far wider scope.

"The old and learned D'Aguesseau," says Michelet [in *Louis XV*],

> notwithstanding the pitiable, the wretched sides of his character, had two lofty sides, his reform of the laws, and a personal passion, the taste and urgent need of universality, a certain encyclopaedic sense. A young man came to him one day, a man of letters living by his pen, and somewhat under a cloud for one or two hazardous books that lack of bread had driven him to write. Yet this stranger of dubious repute wrought a miracle. With bewilderment the old sage listened to him unrolling the gigantic scheme of a book that should be all books. On his lips, sciences were light and life. It was more than speech, it was creation. One would have said that he had made these sciences, and was still at work, adding, extending, fertilising, ever engendering. The effect was incredible. D'Aguesseau, a moment above himself, received the infection of genius, and became great with the greatness of the other. He had faith in the young man, and protected the Encyclopaedia.

A fresh privilege was procured (Jan. 21, 1746), and as Le Breton's capital was insufficient for a project of this magnitude, he invited three other booksellers to join him, retaining a half-share for himself, and allotting the other moiety to them. As Le Breton was not strong enough to bear the material burdens of producing a work on so gigantic a scale as was now proposed, so Diderot felt himself unequal to the task of arranging and supervising every department of a book that was to include the whole circle of the sciences. He was not skilled enough in mathematics, nor in physics, which were then for the most part mathematically conceived. For that province, he associated with himself as an editorial colleague one of the most conspicuous and active members of the philosophical party. . . .

Unlike nearly every other member of the encyclopaedic party, he was a pupil, not of the Jesuits, but of their rivals. The Jansenists recognised the keenness and force of their pupil, and hoped that they had discovered a new Pascal. But he was less docile than his great predecessor in their ranks. When his studies were completed, he devoted himself to geometry, for which he had a passion that nothing could extinguish. For the old monastic vow of poverty, chastity, and obedience, he adopted the substitute of poverty, truth, and liberty. When he awoke in the morning, he thought with delight of the work that had been begun the previous day and would occupy the day before him. In the necessary intervals of his meditations, he recalled the lively pleasure he felt at the play: at the play, between the acts, he thought of the still greater pleasure that was promised to him by the work of the morrow. His mathematical labours led to valuable results in the principles of equilibrium and the movement of fluids, in a new calculus, and in a new solution of the problem of the precession of the equinoxes.

These contributions to what was then the most popular of the sciences brought him fame, and fame brought him its usual distractions. D'Alembert resisted these influences steadfastly. His means were very limited, yet he could never be induced to increase them at the cost either of his social independence or of his scientific pursuits. He lived for forty years under the humble roof of the poor woman who had treated him as a son. "You will never be anything better than a philosopher," she used to cry reproachfully, "and what is a philosopher?' Tis a madman who torments himself all his life, that people may talk about him when he is dead." D'Alembert zealously adhered to his destination. . . .

Though the mathematical sciences remained the objects of his special study, D'Alembert was as free as the other men of the encyclopaedic school from the narrowness of the pure specialist. He naturally reminds us of the remarkable saying imputed to Leibnitz, that he only attributed importance to science because it enabled him to speak with authority in philosophy and religion. His correspondence with Voltaire, extending over the third quarter of the century, is the most instructive record we possess of the many-sided doings of that busy time. His series of eloges on the academicians who died between 1700 and 1772 is one of the most interesting works in the department of literary history. He paid the keenest attention to the art of writing. Translations from Tacitus, Bacon, and Addison show his industry in a useful practice. A long collection of synonyms bears witness to his fine discrimination in the use of words. And the clearness, precision, and reserved energy of his own prose mark the success of the pains that he took with style. He knew the secret. Have lofty sentiments, he said, and your manner of writing will be firm and noble. Yet he did not ignore the other side and half of the truth, which is expressed in the saying of another important writer of that day, —By taking trouble to speak with precision, one gains the habit of thinking rightly. (Condillac)

Like so many others to whom literature owes much, D'Alembert was all his life fighting against bad health. Like Voltaire and Rousseau, he was born dying, and he remained delicate and valetudinarian to the end. He had the mental infirmities belonging to his temperament. He was restless, impatient, mobile. When the young Mademoiselle Phlipon, in after years famous as wife of the virtuous Roland, was taken to a sitting of the Academy, she was curious to see the author of the Preliminary Discourse to the Encyclopaedia, but his small face and sharp thin voice made her reflect with some disappointment, that the writings of a philosopher are better to know than his mask. In everything except zeal for light and emancipation, D'Alembert was the opposite of Diderot. Where Diderot was exuberant, prodigal, and disordered, D'Alembert was a precisian. Difference of temperament, however, did not prevent their friendship from being for many years cordial and intimate. When the Encyclopaedia was planned, it was to D'Alembert, as we have said, that Diderot turned for aid in the mathematical sciences, where his own knowledge was not full, nor well grounded. They were in strong and singular agreement in their idea of the proper place and function of the man of letters. One of the most striking facts about their alliance, and one of the most important facts in the history of the Encyclo-

Jean Le Roud d'Alembert, after a pastel by Maurice Quentin de la Tour.

paedia, is that henceforth the profession of letters became definite. They did not look to patrons, nor did they bound their vision by Versailles. They were the first to assert the lawful authority of the new priesthood. They revolted deliberately and in set form against the old system of suitorship and protection. "Happy are men of letters," wrote D'Alembert,

> if they recognise at last that the surest way of making themselves respected is to live united and almost shut up among themselves; that by this union they will come without any trouble to give the law to the rest of the nation in all affairs of taste and philosophy; that the true esteem is that which is awarded by men who are themselves worthy of esteem. . . . As if the art of instructing and enlightening men were not, after the too rare art of good government, the noblest portion and gift in human reach.

This consciousness of the power and exaltation of their calling which men of letters now acquired, is much more than the superficial fact which it may at first seem to be. It marked the rise of a new teaching order, and the supersession of the old. The highest moral ideas now belonged no longer to the clergy, but to the writers; no longer to official Catholicism, but to that fertilising medley of new notions about human knowledge and human society which then went by the name of philosophy. What is striking is that the ideas sown by philosophy became eventually the source of higher life in Catholicism. If the church of the Revolution showed something we may justly admire, it was because the encyclopaedic band had involuntarily and inevitably imparted a measure of their own clear-sightedness, fortitude, moral energy, and spirit of social improvement to a church that was, when they began their work, a sore burden on the spiritual life of the nation. If the Catholicism of Chateaubriand, of Lamennais, of Montalembert, was a different thing from the Catholicism of a Dubois or a Rohan, from the corruptions of the Jesuits and the superstitions of the later Jansenists, it was the free-thinkers whom the church and mankind had to thank for the change. The most enlightened Catholic of to-day might admit that Voltaire, Diderot, Rousseau, were the true reformers of his creed. They supplied it with ideas that saved it from becoming finally a drawback to civilisation. It was no Christian prelate, but Diderot who burst the bonds of a paralysing dogma by the supreme cry, *Détruisez ces enceintes qui rétrécissent vos idées! Élargissez Dieu!*

The Encyclopaedia became a powerful engine for aiding such a transformation. Because it was this, and because it rallied all that was then best in France round the standard of light and social hope, we ought hardly to grudge time or pains to its history. For it was not merely in the field of religious ideas that the Encyclopaedists led France in a new way. They affected the national life on every side, pressing forward with enlightened principles in all the branches of material and political organisation. Their union in a great philosophical band gave an impressive significance to their work. The collection, within a single set of volumes, of a body of new truths relating to so many of the main interests of men, invested the book and its writers with an aspect of universality, of collective and organic doctrine, which the writers themselves would without doubt have disowned, and which it is easy to dissolve by tests of logic. But the popular impression that the Encyclopaedists constituted a single body with a common doctrine and a common aim was practically sound. Comtè has pointed out with admirable clearness the merit of the conception of an encyclopaedic workshop. It united the members of rival destructive schools in a constructive task. It furnished a rallyingpoint for efforts otherwise the most divergent. Their influence was precisely what it would have been if popular impressions had been literally true. Diderot and D'Alembert did their best to heighten this feeling. They missed no occasion of fixing a sentiment of co-operation and fellowship. They spoke of their dictionary as the transactions of an Academy. Each writer was answerable for his own contribution, but he was in the position of a member of some learned corporation. To every volume, until the great crisis of 1759, was prefixed a list of those who had contributed to it. If a colleague died, the public was informed of the loss the work had sustained, and his services were worthily commemorated in a formal eloge. Feuds, epigrams, and offences were not absent, but on the whole there was steadfast and generous fraternity.

Voltaire eloquently said that officers of war by land and by sea, magistrates, physicians who knew nature, men of letters whose taste purified knowledge, geometers, physicists, all united in a work that was as useful as it was laborious, without any view of interest, without even seeking fame, as many of them concealed their names; finally without any common understanding and agreement, and therefore without anything of the spirit of party. Turning over the pages on which the list of writers is inscribed, we find in one place or another nearly every name that has helped to make the literature of the time famous. Montesquieu, who died in the beginning of 1755, left behind him the unfinished fragment of an article on Taste, and it may be noticed in passing that our good-natured Diderot was the only man of letters who attended the remains of the illustrious writer to the grave. The article itself, though no more than a fragment, has all the charms of Montesquieu's style; it is serious without pedantry, graceful without levity, and is rich in observations that are precise and pointed without the vice of emphasis. Turgot, diligently solicitous for the success of every enterprise that promised to improve human happiness by adding to knowledge and spreading enlightenment, wrote some of the most valuable articles that the work contained, and his discussion of Endowments perhaps still remains the weightiest contribution to that important subject. He was one of the very few writers who refused to sign his name to his contributions. His assistance only ceased when he perceived that the scheme was being coloured by the spirit of sect he always counted the worst enemy of the spirit of truth. Rousseau, who had just won a singular reputation by his paradoxes on natural equality and the corruptions of civilisation, furnished the articles on music in the first half-dozen volumes. They were not free from mistakes, but his colleagues chivalrously defended him by the plea of careless printing or indifferent copying. The stately Buffon very early in the history of the Encyclopaedia sent them an article upon Nature, and the editors made haste to announce to their subscribers the advent of so superb a colleague. The articles on natural history, however, were left by Buffon in his usual majestic fashion to his faithful lieutenant and squire at arms, Daubenton. And even his own article seems not to have been printed. Before the eleventh volume appeared, storms had arisen, not a few of the shipmen had parted company, and Buffon may well have been one of them. Certainly the article on Nature, as it stands, can hardly be his.

In the supplementary volumes, which appeared in 1776—ten years after the completion of the original undertaking—two new labourers came into the vineyard, whose names add fresh lustre and give still more serious value to the work. One of these was the prince of the physiologists of the eighteenth century, Haller, who contributed an elaborate history of those who had been his predecessors in unfolding the intricate mechanism of the human frame, and analysing its marvels of complex function. The other was the austere and generous Condorcet. Ever loyal to good causes, and resolute against despairing of the human commonwealth, he began in the pages of the Encyclopaedia a career that was brilliant with good promise and high hopes, and ended in the grim hall of the Convention and a nobly tragic death amid the Terror.

Among the lesser stars in the encyclopaedic firmament are some whose names ought not to be wholly omitted. Forbonnais, one of the most instructive economic writers of the century, contributed articles to the early volumes that were afterwards republished in his *Elements of Commerce*. Light-hearted Marmontel wrote cheerful articles on Comedy, Eloges, Eclogues, Glory, and other matters of literature and taste. Quesnai, the eminent founder of the economic sect, dealt with two agricultural subjects, and reproduced both his theoretical paradoxes and his admirable practical maxims on the material prosperity of nations. D'Holbach, not yet author of the memorable *System of Nature*, compiled a vast number of articles on chemistry and mineralogy, chiefly and avowedly from German sources. The name of Duclos should not be passed over in the list of the foremost men who helped to raise the encyclopaedic monument. He was one of the shrewdest and most vigorous intelligences of the time. His quality was coarse, but this was only the defect of a thoroughly penetrating and masculine understanding. His articles in the Encyclopaedia (*Déclamation des anciens, Étiquette,* etc.) are not very remarkable, but the reflections on conduct which he styled *Considérations sur les moeurs de ce siècle* (1750), though hard in tone, abound in acuteness, breadth, and soundness of perception that entitle the book to the rare distinction, among the writings of moralists and social observers, of still being worth reading. Morellet wrote upon some of the subjects of theology, and his contributions are remarkable as being the chief examples in the record of the encyclopaedic body of a distinctively and deliberately historic treatment of religion. "I let people see," he wrote many years after, "that in such a collection as the Encyclopaedia we ought to treat the history and experience of the dogmas and discipline of the Christian exactly like those of the religion of Brahma or Mahomet." This principle enabled him to write the article, *Fils de Dieu* (vol. vi.), without sliding into Arian, Nestorian, Socinian, or other heretical view. We need not linger over the names of other writers, who indeed are now little more than mere shadows of names, such as La Condamine, a scientific traveller of fame and merit in his day and generation; of Du Marsais, the poverty-stricken and unlucky scholar who wrote articles on grammar; of the President De Brosses, who was unfortunate enough to be in the right in a quarrel about money with Voltaire, and who has since been better known to readers through the fury of the provoked patriarch, than through his own meritorious contributions to the early history of civilisation.

The name of one faithful worker in the building of this New Jerusalem ought not to be omitted, though his writings were *multa non multum*. The Chevalier de Jaucourt (1704-1779), as his title shows, was the younger son of a noble house. He studied at Geneva, Cambridge, and Leyden, and published in 1734 a useful account of the life and writings of Leibnitz. When the Encyclopaedia was projected, his services were at once secured, and he became its slave from the beginning of A to the end of Z. Jaucourt revelled in this drudgery. God made him for grinding articles, said Diderot. For six or seven years, he wrote one day, Jaucourt has been in the middle of half a dozen secretaries, reading, dictating, slaving, for thirteen or fourteen hours a day, and he is not tired of it even now. When he

was told that the work must positively be brought to an end, his countenance fell, and the prospect of release from such happy bondage filled his heart with desolation. "If," says Diderot in the preface to the eighth volume (1765), "we have raised a shout of joy like the sailor when he espies land after a sombre night that has kept him midway between sky and flood, it is to M. de Jaucourt that we are indebted for it."

Besides those who were known to the conductors of the Encyclopaedia, was a host of unsought volunteers. "The further we proceed," the editors announced in the preface to the sixth volume (1756), "the more are we sensible of the increase both in matter and in number of those who are good enough to second our efforts." They received many articles on the same subject. They were constantly embarrassed by an emulation which, however flattering as a testimony to their work, obliged them to make a difficult choice, or to lose a good article, or to sacrifice one of their regular contributors, or to offend some influential newcomer. Every one who had a new idea in his head, or what he thought a new idea, sent them an article upon it. Men who were priests or pastors by profession, and unbelievers in their hearts, sent them sheaves of articles in which they permitted themselves the delicious luxury of saying a little of what they thought. Women, too, pressed into the great work. Unknown ladies volunteered sprightly explanations of the technicalities of costume, from the falbala adorning the bottom of their skirts, up to that little knot of riband in the hair, that had come in to replace the old appalling edifice of ten stories high, in hierarchic succession of duchess, solitary, musketeer, crescent, firmament, tenth heaven, and mouse. The oldest contributor was Lenglet du Fresnoy, whose book on the Method of Studying History is still known to those who have examined the development of men's ideas about the relations of the present to the past. Lenglet was born in 1674. From the birth of Lenglet to the death of Morellet in 1819—what an are of the circle of western experience!

No one will ask whether the keen eye and stimulating word and helpful hand of Voltaire were wanting to an enterprise that was to awaken men to new love of tolerance, enlightenment, charity and justice. Voltaire was playing the refractory courtier at Potsdam when the first two volumes appeared. With characteristic vehemence he instantly pronounced it a work that should be the glory of France and the shame of its persecutors. Diderot and D'Alembert were raising an immortal edifice. They and their colleagues were cutting their wings for a flight to posterity. They are Atlas and Hercules bearing a world upon their shoulders. It is the greatest work in the world; it is a superb pyramid; and so forth, in every phrase of stimulating sympathy and energetic interest. Nor does his sympathy blind him to faults of execution. Voltaire's good sense and sound judgment were as much at the service of his friends in warning them of shortcomings, as in eulogising what they achieved. And he had good faith enough to complain to his friends, instead of complaining of them. Everywhere he recommends them to insist on a firm and distinct method in their contributors—etymologies, definitions, examples, reasons, clearness, brevity. "You are badly seconded," he writes; "there are bad soldiers in the army of a great general." "I am sorry to see that the writer of the article Hell declares that hell was a point in the doctrine of Moses; now by all the devils, that is not true. Why lie about it? Hell is an excellent thing, to be sure, but it is evident that Moses did not know it.' Tis this world that is hell."

D'Alembert in reply always admitted the blemishes for which the patriarch and master reproached them, but urged various pleas in extenuation. He explains that Diderot is not always the master, either to reject or to prune the articles that are offered to him. A writer who happened to be useful for many excellent articles would insist as the price of good work that they should find room for his bad work also. "No doubt we have bad articles in theology and metaphysics, but with theologians for censors, and a privilege, I defy you to make them any better. There are other articles that are less exposed to the daylight, and in them all is repaired. Time will enable people to distinguish what we have thought from what we have said." This last is a bitter and humiliating word, but before any man hastens to cast a stone, let him first make sure that his own life is free from every trace of hypocritical conformity and mendacious compliance. Condorcet seems to make the only remark that is worth making, when he says that the true shame and disgrace of these dissemblings lay not with the writers, whose only other alternative was to leave the stagnation of opinion undisturbed, but with the ecclesiastics and ministers whose tyranny made dissimulation necessary. And the veil imposed by authority did not really serve any purpose of concealment. Every reader was let into the secret of the writer's true opinion of the old mysteries by means of a piquant phrase, an adroit parallel, a significant reference, an equivocal word of dubious panegyric.

It is one of the most deplorable things in the history of literature to see a man endowed with Diderot's generous conceptions and high social aims, forced to stoop to odious economies. In reading his Prospectus, and still more directly in his article, *Encyclopédie*, we are struck by the beneficence and breadth of the great designs which inspire and support him. The Encyclopaedia, it has been said, was no peaceful storehouse in which scholars and thinkers of all kinds could survey the riches they had acquired; it was a gigantic siege-engine and armoury of weapons of attack. This is only true in a limited sense of one part of the work, and that not the most important part. Such a judgment is only possible for one who has not studied the book itself, or else who is ignorant of the social requirements of France at the time. We shall show this presently in detail. Meanwhile it is enough to make two observations. The implements which the circumstances of the time made it necessary to use as weapons of attack, were equally fitted for the acquisition in a happier season of those treasures of thought and knowledge that are the object of disinterested research. And what is still more important, we have to observe that it was the characteristic note and signal glory of the French revolutionary school to subordinate mere knowledge to the practical work of raising society up from the corruption and paralysis to which it had been brought by the double action of civil and ecclesiastical authority. The efforts of the Encyclopaedists were not disinterested

in the sense of being vague blows in the air. Their aim was not theory but practice, not literature but life. The Encyclopaedists were no doubt all men of battle, and some of them were hardly more than mere partisans. But Diderot at least had constantly in mind the great work which remained after the battle should be won. He was profoundly conscious that the mere accumulation of knowledge of the directly physical facts of the universe would take men a very short way towards reconstruction. And he struck the key-note in such admirable passages as this:—

> One consideration especially that we ought never to lose from sight is that, if we ever banish man, or the thinking and contemplative being, from above the surface of the earth, this pathetic and sublime spectacle of nature becomes no more than a scene of melancholy and silence. The universe is dumb; the darkness and silence of the night take possession of it. . . . It is the presence of man that gives its interest to the existence of other beings; and what better object can we set before ourselves in the history of these beings than to accept such a consideration? Why shall we not introduce man into our work in the same place which he holds in the universe? Why shall we not make him a common centre? Is there in infinite space any other point from which we can with greater advantage draw those immense lines that we propose to extend to all other points? What a vivid and softening reaction must result between man and the beings by whom he is surrounded! . . . Man is the single term from which we ought to set out, and to which we ought to trace all back, if we would please, interest, touch, even in the most arid reflections and the driest details. If you take away my own existence and the happiness of my fellows, of what concern to me is all the rest of nature?

In this we hear the voice of the new time, as we do in his exclamation that the perfection of an Encyclopaedia is the work of centuries; centuries had to elapse before the foundations could be laid; centuries would have to elapse before its completion: "*mais à la postérité, et* A L'ETRE QUI NE MEURT POINT!"

The succession of obstacles and embarrassments against which its intrepid conductor was compelled to fight his way was beyond description. The project was fully conceived and its details worked out between 1745 and 1748. The Encyclopaedia was announced in 1750 in a Prospectus of which Diderot was the author. At length in 1751 the first volume of the work itself was given to the public, followed by the second in January 1752. The clerical party at once discerned what tremendous fortifications, with what deadly armament, were rising up in face of their camp. The Jesuits had always been jealous of an enterprise in which they had not been invited to take a part.

Their first attack was indirect. An Abbé de Prades sustained a certain thesis in an official exercise at the Sorbonne, and Diderot was suspected, without good reason, of being its true author. An examination of its propositions was ordered. It was pronounced pernicious, dangerous, and tending to deism, chiefly on account of some too suggestive comparisons between the miraculous healings in the New Testament and those ascribed in the more ancient legend to Æsculapius. . . . The Abbé de Prades was condemned, and deprived of his licence (Jan. 27, 1752). As he was known to be a friend of Diderot, and was suspected of being the writer of articles on theology in the Encyclopaedia, the design of the Jesuit cabal in ruining De Prades was to discredit the new undertaking, and to induce the government to prohibit. Their next step was to procure a pastoral from the archbishop of Paris. This document not only condemned the heretical propositions of De Prades, but referred in sombre terms to unnamed works teeming with error and impiety. Every one understood the reference, and among its effects was an extension of the vogue and notoriety of the Encyclopaedia. The Jesuits were not allowed to retain a monopoly of persecuting zeal, and the Jansenists refused to be left behind in the race of intrigue. The bishop of Auxerre, who belonged to this party, followed his brother prelate of Paris in a more direct attack, in which he included not only the Encyclopaedia, but Montesquieu and Buffon. De Prades took to flight. . . .

Bourdaloue more than half a century before had taunted the freethinkers of his day with falseness and inconsistency in taking sides with the Jansenists, whose superstitions they notoriously held in open contempt. Circumstances had now changed. The freethinkers were becoming strong enough to represent opposition to authority on their own principles and in their own persons. Diderot's vigorous remonstrance with the bishop of Auxerre incidentally marks for us the definite rupture of philosophic sympathy for the Jansenist champions. "It is your disputatiousness," he said, "which within the last forty years has made far more unbelievers than all the productions of philosophy." As we cannot too clearly realise, it was the flagrant social incompetence of the church which brought what they called Philosophy, that is to say Liberalism, into vogue and power. Locke's Essay had been translated in 1700, but it had made no mark, and as late as 1725 the first edition of the translation remained unsold. It was the weakness and unsightly decrepitude of the ecclesiastics that opened the way for the thinkers.

The victory however was not yet. Diderot had still a dismal wilderness to traverse. He was not without secret friends even in the camp of his enemies. After his reply to Pére Berthier's attack on the Prospectus, he received an anonymous letter to the effect that if he wished to avènge himself on the Jesuits, there were both important documents and money at his command. Diderot replied that he was in no want of money, and that he had no time to spare for Jesuit documents. He trusted to reason. Neither reason nor eloquence availed against the credit at court of the ecclesiastical cabal. The sale of the second volume of the Encyclopaedia was stopped by orders that Malesherbes was reluctantly compelled to issue. A decree of the king's council (Feb. 7, 1752) suppressed both volumes, as containing maxims hostile to the royal authority and to religion. The publishers were forbidden to reprint them, and the booksellers were forbidden to deliver any copies that might still be in hand. The decree, however, contained no prohibition of the continuance of the work. . . .

A curious triumph awaited the harassed Diderot. He was compelled, under pain of a second incarceration, to hand over to the authorities all the papers, proof-sheets, and plates in his possession. The Jesuit cabal supposed that if they could obtain the materials for the future volumes, they could easily arrange and manipulate them to suit their own purposes. Their ignorance and presumption were speedily confounded. In taking Diderot's papers, they had forgotten, as Grimm says, to take his head and his genius: they had forgotten to ask him for a key to articles which, so far from understanding, they with some confusion vainly strove even to decipher. The government was obliged (May 1752) to appeal to Diderot and D'Alembert to resume a work for which their enemies had thus proved themselves incompetent. Yet, by one of the weaknesses of decaying authority, the decree of three months before was left suspended over their heads.

The third volume of the Encyclopaedia appeared in the autumn of 1753. D'Alembert prefixed an introduction, vindicating himself and his colleague with an admirable manliness, a sincerity, a gravity, a fire. "Let us remember," he concludes, "the fable of Bocalini: 'A traveller was disturbed by the importunate chirrupings of the grasshoppers; he would fain have slain them every one, but got belated and missed his way; he need only have fared peacefully on his road, and the grasshoppers would have died of themselves before the end of a week.' "

A volume was now produced each year, until the autumn of 1757 and the issue of the seventh volume. This brought the work down to Gyromancy and Gythium. Then there arose storms and divisions marking a memorable epoch alike in the history of the book, in the life of Diderot and others, and in the thought of the century. The progress of the work in popularity during the five years between 1752 and 1757 had been steady and unbroken. The original subscribers were barely two thousand. When the fourth volume appeared they were three thousand. The seventh volume found nearly a thousand more. Such prodigious success wrought the chagrin of the party of superstition to fever heat. As each annual volume came from the press and found a wider circle of readers, their malice and irritation waxed a degree more intense. They scattered malignant rumours abroad; they showered pamphlets; no imputation was too odious or too ridiculous. Diderot, D'Alembert, Voltaire, Rousseau, Buffon, were denounced as heads of a formal conspiracy, a clandestine association, a midnight band, united in a horrible community of pestilent opinions and sombre interests.

In the seventh volume an article appeared that made the ferment angrier. D'Alembert had lately been the guest of Voltaire at Ferney, whence he had made frequent visits to Geneva. In his intercourse with the ministers of that famous city he came to the conclusion that their religious opinions were really Socinian, and when he wrote the article on Geneva he stated this. He stated it in such a way as to make their heterodox opinions a credit to the Genevese pastors, because he associated disbelief in the divinity of Jesus Christ, in mysteries of faith; and in eternal punishment, with a practical life of simplicity, purity, and tolerance. Each line of this eulogy on the Socinian preachers of Geneva veiled a burning and contemptuous reproach against the spirit of the churchmen in France. We have to realise that official religion was then a strange union of Byzantine decrepitude with the energetic ferocity of the Holy Office. Within five years of this indirect plea of D'Alembert for tolerance and humanity, Calas was murdered by the orthodoxy of Toulouse Nearly ten years later (1766), we find Louis the Fifteenth, with the steam of the Parc aux Cerfs about him, rewarded by the loyal acclamations of a Parisian crowd, for descending from his carriage as a priest passed bearing the sacrament, and prostrating himself in the mud before the holy symbol. The same year the youth La Barre was first tortured, then beheaded, then burnt, for some presumed disrespect to the same holy symbol—then become the ensign of human degradation, of fanatical cruelty, of rancorous superstition. Yet I should be sorry to be unjust. It is to be said that even in these bad days when religion meant cruelty and cabal, the one or two men who boldly withstood face to face the king and the Pompadour for the vileness of their lives, were priests of the church.

D'Alembert's article hardly goes beyond what to us seems the axioms of all men of sense. We must remember the time. Even members of the philosophic party itself, like Grimm, thought the article misplaced and hardy. The Genevese ministers indignantly repudiated the compliment of Socinianism, and the eulogy of being rather less irrational than their neighbours. Voltaire read and read again with delight, and plied the writer with reiterated exhortations in every key, not to allow himself to be driven from the great work by the raging of the heathen and the vain imaginings of the people.

While the storm seemed to be at its height, an incident occurred that let loose a new flood of violent passion. Helvétius published that memorable book, in which he was thought to have told all the world its own secret. His *De l'esprit* came out in 1758. It provoked a general insurrection of public opinion. The devout and the heedless agreed in denouncing it as scandalous, licentious, impious, and pregnant with peril. The philosophic party felt that their ally had dealt a sore blow to liberty of thought and the free expression of opinion. "Philosophy," said Grimm, by philosophy meaning Liberalism,

> will long feel the effect of the rising of opinion
> which this author has caused by his book; and
> for having described too freely a morality that
> is bad and false in itself, M. Helvétius will have
> to reproach himself with all the restraints now
> sure to be imposed on the few men of lofty ge-
> nius who still are left to us, whose destiny was
> to enlighten their fellows and to spread truth
> over the earth.

At the beginning of 1759 the procureur-général laid an information before the court against Helvétius's book, against half a dozen minor publications, and finally against the Encyclopaedia. *De l'esprit* was alleged to be a mere abridgment of the Encyclopaedia, and the Encyclopaedia was denounced as being the opprobrium of the nation by its impious maxims and its hostility to morals and religion. . . .

The government, however, had no intention of finally ex-

terminating an enemy who might some day happen to be a convenient ally. They encouraged or repressed the philosophers according to the political calculations of the moment, sometimes according to the caprices of the king's mistress, or even a minister's mistress. . . .

The arbitrary attempt to arrest Diderot's courageous and enlightened undertaking, was only the customary inference from an accepted principle, that it is the business or the right of governments to guide thought and regulate its expression. The Jesuits acted on this theory, and resorted to repressive power and the secular arm whenever they could. The Jansenists repudiated the principle, but eagerly acted upon it whenever the turn of intrigue gave them the chance.

An unforeseen circumstance changed the external bearings of this critical conflict. The conception of the duties of the temporal authority in the spiritual sphere had been associated hitherto with Catholic doctrine. The decay of that doctrine was rapidly discrediting the conception allied with it. But the movement was interrupted. And it was interrupted by a man who suddenly stepped out from the ranks of the Encyclopaedists themselves. Rousseau from his solitary cottage at Montmorency (1758) fulminated the celebrated *Letter to D'Alembert on Stage Plays*. The article on Geneva in the seventh volume of the Encyclopaedia not only praised the pastors for their unbelief; it also assailed the time-honoured doctrine of the churches that the theatre is an institution from hell and an invention of devils. D'Alembert paid a compliment to his patriarch and master at Ferney, as well as shot a bolt at his ecclesiastical foes in Paris, by urging the people of Geneva to shake off irrational prejudices and straightway to set up a playhouse. Rousseau had long been brooding over certain private grievances of his own against Diderot. He took the occasion of D'Alembert's mischievous suggestion to his native Geneva, not merely to denounce the drama with all the force and eloquence at his command, but formally to declare the breach between himself and Diderot. From this moment he treated the Holbachians, so he contemptuously styled the Encyclopaedists, as enemies of the human race and disseminators of deadly poisons.

This was no mere quarrel of rival authors. It marked a fundamental divergence in thought, and proclaimed the beginning of a disastrous reaction in the very heart of the school of Illumination. Among the most conspicuous elements of the reaction were these: the subordination of reason to emotion; the displacement of industry, science, energetic and many-sided ingenuity, by dreamy indolence; and finally, what brings us back to our starting-point, the suppression of opinions deemed to be anti-social by the secular arm. The old idea was brought back in a new dress; the absolutist conception of the function of authority, associated with a theistic doctrine. Unfortunately for France, Rousseau's idea prospered, and ended by vanquishing its antagonist.

The crisis of 1758-59, then, is a date of the highest importance. It marks a collision between the old principle of Louis the Fourteenth, of the Bartholomew Massacre, of the revocation of the Edict of Nantes, and the new rationalistic principle of spiritual emancipation. The old principle was decrepit, it was no longer able to maintain itself; the hounds were furious, but their fury was toothless. Before the new principle could achieve mastery, Rousseau had made mastery impossible. Two men came into the world at this very moment, whom destiny made incarnations of the discordant principles. Danton and Robespierre were both born in 1759. Diderot seems to have had a biblical presentiment, says Michelet. "We feel that he saw beyond Rousseau something sinister, a spectre of the future. Diderot-Danton already looks in the face of Rousseau-Robespierre [Louis XV et Louis XVI]."

A more vexatious incident now befell Diderot than either the decree of the council or the schism of the heresiarch at Montmorency. D'Alembert declared his intention of abandoning the work, and urged his colleague to do the same. His letters to Voltaire show intelligibly enough how he brought himself to this resolution. "I am worn out," he says,

> with the affronts and vexations of every kind that this work draws down upon us. The hateful and even infamous satires they print against us, which are not only tolerated, but protected, authorised, applauded, nay actually commanded by the people with power in their hands; the sermons, or rather the tocsins that are rung against us at Versailles in the presence of the king, *nemine reclamante*; the new intolerable inquisition that they are bent on practising against the Encyclopaedia, by giving us new censors who are more absurd and more intractable than could be found at Goa; all these reasons, joined to some others, drive me to give up this accursed work once for all.

Voltaire for some time remonstrated against this retreat before the hated *Infâme*. At length his opinion came round to D'Alembert's reiterated assertions of the shame and baseness of men of letters subjecting themselves to the humiliating yoke of ministers, priests, and police. Voltaire wrote to Diderot, protesting that before all things it was necessary to present a firm front to the foe; it would be atrocious weakness to continue the work after D'Alembert had quitted it; it was monstrous that such a genius as Diderot should make himself the slave of booksellers and the victim of fanatics. Must this dictionary, he asked, that is a hundred times more useful than Bayle's, be fettered by the superstition which it should annihilate; must they make terms with scoundrels who keep terms with none; could the enemies of reason, the persecutors of philosophers, the assassins of our kings, still dare to lift up their voices in such a century as that? "Men are on the eve of a great revolution in the human mind, and it is you to whom they are most of all indebted for it."

More than once Voltaire entreated Diderot to finish his work in a foreign country where his hands would be free. "No," said Diderot in a reply of pathetic energy,

> to abandon the work is turning our back on the breach, and to do precisely what the villains who persecute us desire. If you knew with what joy they have learnt D'Alembert's desertion! It is not for us to wait until the government have punished the brigands to whom they have given

us up. Is it for us to complain, when they associate with us in their insults men who are so much better than ever we shall be? What ought we to do then? Do what becomes men of courage, —despise our foes, follow them up, and take advantage, as we have done, of the feebleness of our censors. If D'Alembert resumes, and we complete our work, is not that vengeance enough? . . . After all this, you will believe that I cling at any price to the Encyclopaedia. My dear master, I am over forty. I am tired out with tricks and shufflings. I cry from morning till night for rest, rest; and scarcely a day passes when I am not tempted to go and live in obscurity and die in peace in the depths of my old country. There comes a time when all ashes are mingled. Then what will it boot me to have been Voltaire or Diderot, or whether it is your three syllables or my three syllables that survive? One must work, one must be useful, one owes an account of one's gifts, etcetera, etcetera. Be useful to men! Is it quite clear that one does more than amuse them, and that there is much difference between the philosopher and the fluteplayer? They listen to one and the other with pleasure or disdain, and remain what they were. The Athenians were never wickeder than in the time of Socrates, and perhaps all they owe to his existence is a crime the more. That there is more spleen than good sense in all this, I admit—and back to the Encyclopaedia I go.

Thus for seven years the labour of conducting the vast enterprise now fell upon Diderot alone. He had not only to write articles upon the most exhausting and various kinds of subjects: he had also to distribute topics among his writers, to shape their manuscripts, to correct proof-sheets, to supervise the preparation of the engravings, to write the text explanatory of them, and all this amid constant apprehension and alarm from government and police. . . .

As his toil was drawing to a close, he suddenly received the most mortifying of all the blows that were struck at him in his adventure. After the interruption in 1759, it was resolved to bring out the ten volumes still wanting, in a single issue. Le Breton was entrusted with the business of printing them. The manuscript was set in type, Diderot corrected the proof-sheets, saw the revises, and returned each sheet duly marked with his signature for the press. At this point the nefarious operation of Le Breton began. He and his foreman took possession of the sheets, and proceeded to retrench, cut out, and suppress every passage, line, or phrase, that appeared to them to be likely to provoke clamour or the anger of the government. They thus, of their own brute authority, reduced most of the best articles to the condition of fragments, mutilated and despoiled of all that had been most valuable in them. They did not even trouble themselves to secure any appearance of order or continuity in these mangled skeletons. Their murderous work done, they sent the pages to the press, and to make the mischief beyond remedy, they committed all the original manuscripts and proof-sheets to the flames. One day, when the printing was nearly completed (1764), Diderot, having occasion to consult an article under the letter S, found it entirely spoiled. He stood confounded. An instant's thought revealed the printer's atrocity. He eagerly turned to the articles on which he and his subordinates had taken most pains, and found everywhere the same ravage and disorder. "The discovery," says Grimm, "Threw him into a state of frenzy and despair which I shall never forget." He wept tears of rage and torment in the presence of the criminal himself, and before wife and children and sympathising domestics. For weeks he could neither eat nor sleep. "For years," he cried to Le Breton,

> you have been basely cheating me. You have massacred, or got a brute beast to massacre, the work of twenty good men who have devoted to you their time, their talents, their vigils, from love of right and truth, from the simple hope of seeing their ideas given to the public, and reaping from them a little consideration richly earned, which your injustice and thanklessness have now stolen from them for ever. . . . You and your book will be trailed through the mud; you will henceforth be cited as a man who has been guilty of an act of treachery, an act of vile hardihood, to which nothing that has ever happened in this world can be compared. Then you will be able to judge your panic terror, and the cowardly counsels of those barbarous Ostrogoths and stupid Vandals who helped you in the havoc you have made.

Yet he remained undaunted to the very last. His first movement to throw up the work, and denounce Le Breton's outrage to the subscribers and the world, was controlled. His labour had lost its charm. The monument was disfigured and defaced. He never forgot the horrible chagrin, and he never forgave the ignoble author of it. But the last stone was at length laid. In 1765 the subscribers received the concluding ten volumes of letterpress. The eleven volumes of plates were not completed until 1772. The copies bore Neufchâtel on the title-page, and were distributed privately. The clergy in their assembly at once levelled a decree at the new book. The parliament quashed this, not from love of the book, but from hatred of the clergy. The government, however, ordered all who possessed the Encyclopaedia to deliver it over forthwith to the police. Eventually the copies were returned to their owners with some petty curtailments. . . .

All writers on the movement of Illumination in France in the eighteenth century, call our attention to the quick transformation that took place after the middle of the century, of a speculative or philosophical agitation into a political or social one. Readers often find some difficulty in understanding plainly how or why this metamorphosis was brought about. The metaphysical question which men were then so fond of discussing, whether matter can think, appears very far removed from the sphere of political conceptions. The psychological question whether our ideas are innate, or are solely given to us by experience through the sensations, may strike the publicist as having the least possible to do with the type of a government or the aims of a community. Yet it is really the conclusions to which men come in this region, that determine the quality of the civil sentiment and the significance of political organisation. The theological doctors who persecuted De Prades for suggestions of Locke's psychology, and for high treason against Cartesianism, were guided by a right instinct

of self-preservation. De Maistre, by far the most penetrating of the Catholic school, was never more clear-sighted than when he made a vigorous and deliberate onslaught upon Bacon the centre of his movement against revolutionary principles.

[The] immediate force of speculative literature hangs on practical opportuneness. It was not merely because Bacon and Hobbes and Locke had written certain books, that the Encyclopaedists, who took up their philosophic succession, inevitably became a powerful political party and multiplied their adherents in an increasing proportion as the years went on. From various circumstances the attack acquired a significance and a weight in France which it had never possessed in England. For one thing, physical science had in the interval taken immense strides. This both dwarfed the sovereignty of theology and theological metaphysics, and indirectly disposed men's minds for nontheological theories of moral as well as of physical phenomena. In France, again, the objects of the attack were inelastic and unyielding. Political speculation in England followed, and did not precede, political innovation and reform. In France its light played round institutions too deeply rooted in absolutism and privilege to be capable of substantial modification. . . .

"It would be a mistake," wrote that sagacious and well-informed observer, D'Argenson, so early as 1753,

> to attribute the loss of religion in France to the English philosophy, which has not gained more than a hundred philosophers or so in Paris, instead of setting it down to the hatred against the priests, which goes to the very last extreme. All minds are turning to discontent and disobedience, and everything is on the high road to a great revolution both in religion and in government. And it will be a very different thing from the rude Reformation, a medley of superstition and freedom, that came to us from Germany in the sixteenth century! As our nation and our century are enlightened in so very different a fashion, they will go whither they ought to go; they will banish every priest, all priesthood, all revelation, all mystery.

This, however, only represents the destructive side of the vast change which D'Argenson thus foresaw six-and-thirty years before its consummation. That change had also a constructive side. If one of its elements was hate, another and more important element was hope. This constructive and reforming spirit which made its way in the intelligence of the leading men in France from 1750 to 1789, was represented in the encyclopaedic confederation, and embodied in their forty folios. And, to return to our first point, it was directly and inseparably associated with the philosophy of Bacon and Locke. What is the connection between their speculations and a vehement and energetic spirit of social reform? . . .

The broad features of the speculative revolution of which the Encyclopaedia was the outcome, lie on the surface of its pages and cannot be mistaken. The transition from Descartes to Newton meant the definite substitution of observation for hypothesis. The exaltation of Bacon meant the advance from supernatural explanations to explanations from experience. The acceptance and development of the Lockian psychology meant the reference of our ideas to bodily sensations, and led men by what they thought a tolerably direct path to the identification of mind with functions of matter. We need not here discuss the philosophical truth or adequateness of these ways of considering the origin and nature of knowledge, or the composition of human character. All that now concerns us is to mark their tendency. That tendency clearly is to expel Magic as the decisive influence among us, in favour of ordered relations of cause and effect, only to be discovered by intelligent search. The universe began to be more directly conceived as a group of phenomena that are capable of rational and connected explanation. Then, the wider the area of law, the greater is man's consciousness of his power of controlling forces, and securing the results that he desires. Objective interests and their conditions acquire an increasing preponderance in his mind. On the other hand, as the limits of science expand, so do the limits of nescience become more definite. The more we know of the universal order, the more are we persuaded, however gradually and insensibly, that certain matters which men believed themselves to know outside of this phenomenal order, are in truth inaccessible by those instruments of experience and observation to which we are indebted for other knowledge. Hence, a natural inclination to devote our faculty to the forces within our control, and to withdraw it from vain industry about forces, —if they be forces, —that are beyond our control and beyond our apprehension. Thus man becomes the centre of the world to himself, nature his servant and minister, human society the field of his interests and his exertions. The sensational psychology, again, whether scientifically defensible or not, clearly tends to heighten our idea of the power of education and institutions upon character. The more vividly we realise the share of external impressions in making men what they are, the more ready we shall be to concern ourselves with external conditions and their improvement. The introduction of the positive spirit into the observation of the facts of society was not to be expected until the Cartesian philosophy, with its reliance on inexplicable intuitions and its exaggeration of the method of hypothesis, had been laid aside.

Diderot struck a key-note of difference between the old Catholic spirit and the new social spirit, between quietist superstition and energetic science, in the casual sentence in his article on alms-houses and hospitals:—*"It would be far more important to work at the prevention of misery, than to multiply places of refuge for the miserable."*

It is very easy to show that the Encyclopaedists had not established an impregnable scientific basis for their philosophy. Anybody can now see that their metaphysic and psychology were imperfectly thought out. The important thing is that their metaphysic and psychology were calculated, not-withstanding all their superficialities, to inspire an energetic social spirit, because they were pregnant with human sentiment. To represent the Encyclopaedia as the gospel of negation and denial is to omit four-fifths of its contents. Men may certainly, if they please, describe it as merely negative work, for example, to denounce such institutions as examination and punishment by torture (see

Question, Peine), but if so, what gospel of affirmation can bring better blessings? If the metaphysic of these writers had been a thousandfold more superficial than it was, what mattered that, so long as they had vision for every one of the great social improvements on which the progress and even the very life of the nation depended? It would be obviously unfair to say that reasoned interest in social improvement is incompatible with a spiritualistic doctrine, but we are at any rate justified in saying that, as a matter of fact, energetic faith in possibilities of social progress has been first reached through the philosophy of sensation and experience.

In describing the encyclopaedic movement as being, among other things, the development of political interest under the presiding influence of a humanistic philosophy, we are using the name of politics in its widest sense. The economic conditions of a country, and the administration of its laws, are far more vitally and directly related to its well-being than the form of its government. The form of government is indeed a question of the first importance, but then this is owing in a paramount degree to the influence it may have upon the other two sets of elements in the national life. Form of government is like the fashion of a man's clothes; it may fret or may comfort him, may be imposing or mean, may react upon his spirits to elate or depress them. In either case it is less intimately related to his welfare than the state of his blood and tissues. In saying, then, that the Encyclopaedists began a political work, what is meant is that they drew into the light of new ideas, groups of institutions, usages, and arrangements which affected the real well-being and happiness of France, as closely as nutrition affected the health and strength of an individual Frenchman. It was the Encyclopaedists who first stirred opinion in France against the iniquities of colonial tyranny and the abominations of the slave trade. They demonstrated the folly and wastefulness and cruelty of a fiscal system that was eating the life out of the land. They protested in season and out of season against arrangements that made the administration of justice a matter of sale and purchase. They lifted up a strong voice against the atrocious barbarities of an antiquated penal code. It was this band of writers, organised by a harassed man of letters, and not the nobles swarming round Louis the Fifteenth, nor the churchmen singing masses, who first grasped the great principle of modern society, the honour that is owed to productive industry. They were vehement for the glories of peace, and passionate against the brazen glories of war.

We are not to suppose that the Encyclopaedia was the originating organ of either new methods or new social ideas. The exalted and peculiarly modern views about peace, for instance, were plainly inspired from the writings of the Abbé de Saint-Pierre (1658-1743), —one of the most original spirits of the century, who deserves to be remembered among other good services as the inventor of the word *bienfaisance*. Again, in the mass of the political articles we feel the immense impulse that was given to sociological discussion by the *Esprit des lois*. Few questions are debated here which Montesquieu had not raised, and none are debated without reference to Montesquieu's line of argument. The change of which we are conscious in turning from the *Esprit des lois* to the Encyclopaedia is that political ideas have been grasped as instruments. Philosophy has become patriotism. The Encyclopaedists advanced with grave solicitude to the consideration of evils to which the red-heeled parasites of Versailles were insolently and incorrigibly blind.

The articles on Agriculture, for example, are admirable alike for the fullness and precision with which they expose the actual state of France; for the clearness with which they trace its deplorable inadequateness back to the true sources; and for the strong interest and sympathy in the subject, which they both exhibit and inspire. If now and again the touch is too idyllic, it was still a prodigious gain to let the country know in a definite way that of the fifty million *arpents* of cultivable land in the realm, more than one quarter lay either unbroken or abandoned. And it was a prodigious gain to arouse the attention of the general public to the causes of the forced deterioration of French agriculture, namely, the restrictions on trade in grain, the arbitrariness of the imposts, and the flight of the population to the large towns. Then the demonstration, corroborated in the pages of the Encyclopaedia by the too patriotic vaunts of contemporary English writers, of the stimulus given to agriculture by our system of free exports, contained one of the most useful lessons that the French had to learn.

Again, there are some abuses that cannot be more effectively attacked than by a mere statement of the facts in the plainest and least argumentative terms. The history of such an impost as the tax upon salt (*gabelle*), and a bold outline of the random and incongruous fashions in which it was levied, were equivalent to a formal indictment. It needed no rhetoric nor discussion to heighten the harsh injustice of the rule that "persons who have changed domicile are still taxed for a certain time in the seat of their former abode, namely farmers and labourers for one year, and all other tax-payers for two years, provided the parish to which they have removed is within the same district; and if otherwise, then farmers to pay for two years, and other persons for three years" (*taille*). Thus a man under the given circumstances would have to pay double taxes for three years, as a penalty for changing his dwelling. . . .

It is no innate factiousness, as flighty critics of French affairs sometimes imply, that has made civil equality the passion of modern France. The root of this passion is an undying memory of the curse inflicted on its citizens, morally and materially, by the fiscal inequalities of the old régime. The article on *Privilége* urges the desirableness of inquiring into the grounds of the vast multitude of fiscal exemptions, and of abolishing all that were no longer associated with the performance of real and useful service. "A bourgeois," says the writer, anticipating a cry that was so soon to ring through the land,

> a bourgeois in comfortable circumstances, and who could himself pay half of the *taille* of a whole parish, if it were imposed in its due proportion; a man without birth, education, or talents, buys a place in a local salt office, or some useless charge at court, or in the household of some prince. . . . This man proceeds to enjoy

in the public eye all the exemptions possessed by the nobility and the high magistracy. . . . From such an abuse of privileges spring two very considerable evils; the poorer part of the citizens are always burdened beyond their strength, though they are the most useful to the State, since this class is composed of those who cultivate the land, and procure a subsistence for the upper classes; the other evil is that privileges disgust persons of education and talent with the idea of entering the magistracy or other professions demanding labour and application, and lead them to prefer small posts and paltry offices.

And so forth, with a gravity and moderation that was then common in political discussion in France. It gradually disappeared by 1789, when it was found that the privileged orders even at that time in their *cahiers* steadily demanded the maintenance of every one of their most odious and iniquitous rights. When it is said, then, that the Encyclopaedists deliberately prepared the way for a political revolution, let us remember that what they really did was to shed the light of rational discussion on such practical grievances as even the most fatuous conservative in France does not now dream of bringing back.

Let us turn to two other of the most oppressive institutions that then scourged France. First the *corvée*, or feudal rule which forced every unprivileged farmer and peasant in France to furnish so many days' labour for the maintenance of the highways. Arthur Young tells us [in his *Travels in France*], and the statement is confirmed by the *Minutes* of Turgot, that this wasteful, cruel, and inefficient system was annually the ruin of many hundreds of persons, and he mentions that no less than three hundred farmers were reduced to beggary in filling up a single vale in Lorraine. Under this all-important head, the Encyclopaedia has an article that does not merely add to the knowledge of its readers by a history of the *corvées*, but proceeds to discuss, as in a pamphlet or review article, the inconveniences of the prevailing system, and presses schemes for avoiding them. Turgot had not yet shown in practice the only right substitute. The article was printed in 1754, and it was not until ten years later that this great administrator, then become intendant of the Limousin, did away in his district with compulsory personal service on the roads, and required in its place a money payment assessed on the parishes. The writer of the article in the Encyclopaedia does not anticipate this obviously rational plan, but he paints a striking picture of the thousand abuses and miserable inefficiencies of the practice of *corvées*, and his piece illustrates that vigorous discussion of social subjects which the Encyclopaedia stimulated. It is worth remarking that the writer was a sub-engineer of roads and bridges in the generality of Tours. The case is one example among others of the importance of the Encyclopaedia as a centre to which activeminded men of all kinds might bring the fruits of their thought and observation.

Next to the *corvées*, the monster grievance of the third estate was the system of enrolments for the militia. The article, *Milice*, is very short, but it goes to the root of the matter. The only son of a cultivator of moderate means, forced to quit the paternal roof at the moment when his labour might recompense his straitened parents for the expense

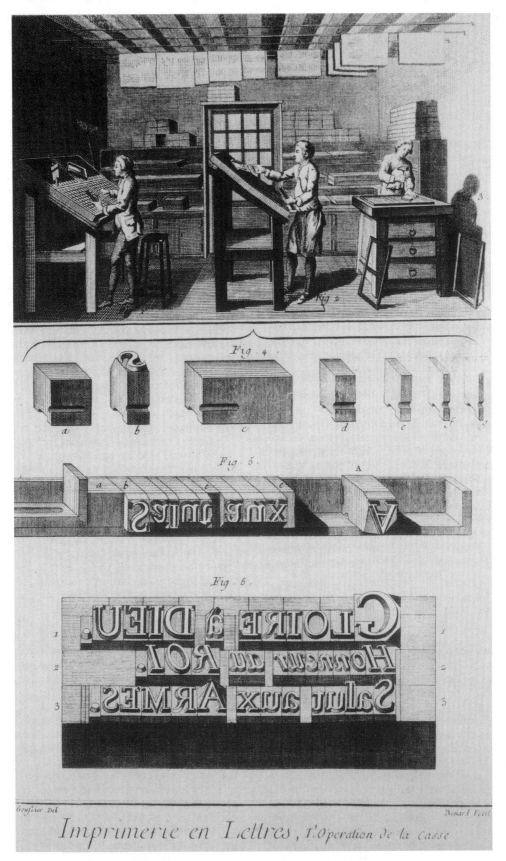

Plate from the Encyclopédie, *showing work in a print shop.*

of having brought him up, is justly described as an irreparable loss. The writer, after hinting that it would be well if such an institution were wholly dispensed with, urges that at least its object might be more effectively and more humanely reached by allowing each parish to provide its due contingent of men in its own way. This change was indeed already (1765) being carried out by Turgot in the Limousin, and with excellent results. The writer concludes with the highly civilised remark that we ought to weight whether the good of the rural districts, the culture of the land, and population, are not preferable objects to the glory of setting enormous hosts of armed men on foot, after the example of Xerxes. Alas, it is one of the discouragements of the student of history, that he often finds highly civilised remarks made one or two or twenty centuries ago, that are just as useful and just as little heeded now as they were when they were made.

The same reflection occurs to one in reading the article on Foundations. As I have already said, this carefully written and sagacious piece still remains the most masterly discussion we possess of the advantages and disadvantages of endowments. . . . Passing from *Fondation* to *Foire* in the same volume, also from the pen of Turgot, we see an almost equally striking example of the economic wisdom of the encyclopaedic school. The provincial fairs, with their privileges, exemptions, exclusions, were a conspicuous case of the mischief done by that "mania for regulating and guiding everything," which then infected commercial administration, and interrupted the natural course of trade by imbecile vexations of police. Another vicious example of the same principle is exposed in the article on *Maîtrises*. This must have convinced every reader capable of rising above "the holy laws of prejudice," how bad faith, idleness, disorder, and all the other evils of monopoly were fomented by a system of jealous trade-guilds, carrying compulsory sub-division and restriction of all kinds of skilled labour down to a degree that would have been laughable enough, if it had only been less destructive.

One of the loudest cries in 1789 was for the destruction of game and the great manorial chases or *capitaineries.* "By game," says Arthur Young, "must be understood whole droves of wild boars, and herds of deer not confined by any wall or pale, but wandering at pleasure over the whole country, to the destruction of crops, and to the peopling of the galleys by the wretched peasants who presumed to kill them, in order to save that food which was to support their helpless children." In the same place he enumerates the outrageous and incredible rules that ruined agriculture over hundreds of leagues of country, in order that the seigneurs might have sport. In most matters the seven volumes of the Encyclopaedia printed before 1757, are more reserved than the ten volumes conducted by Diderot alone after the great schism of 1759. On the subject of sport, however, the writer of the article *Chasse* enumerates all the considerations a patriotic minister could desire to see impressed on public opinion. Some of the paragraphs startle us by their directness and freedom of complaint, and even a very cool reader would still be

likely to feel some of the wrath stirred in the breast of our shrewd and sober Arthur Young a generation later (1787). . . .

This brings us to what is perhaps the most striking of all the guiding sentiments of the book. Virgil's *Georgics* have been described as a glorification of labour. The Encyclopaedia seems inspired by the same motive, the same earnest enthusiasm for all the purposes, interests, and details of productive industry. Diderot, as has been justly said, himself the son of a cutler, might well bring handicraft into honour; assuredly he had inherited from his good father's workshop sympathy and regard for skill and labour. The illustrative plates to which Diderot gave the most laborious attention for a period of almost thirty years, are not only remarkable for their copiousness, their clearness, their finish, and in all these respects they are truly admirable. But they strike us even more by the semi-poetic feeling that transforms the mere representation of a process into an animated scene of human life, stirring the sympathy and touching the imagination of the onlooker as by something dramatic. The bustle, the dexterity, the alert force of the iron foundry, the glass furnace, the gunpowder mill, the silk calendry, are as skilfully reproduced as the more tranquil toil of the dairy-woman, the embroiderer, the confectioner, the setter of types, the compounder of drugs, the chaser of metals. The drawings recall the eager and personal interest in his work, the nimble complacency, which is so charming a trait in the best French craftsman. The animation of these folios of plates is prodigious. They affect one like looking down on the world of Paris from the heights of Montmartre. To turn over volume after volume is like watching a splendid panorama of all the busy life of the time. Minute care is as striking in them as their comprehensiveness. The smallest tool, the knot in a thread, the ply in a cord, the curve of wrist or finger, each has special or proper delineation. The reader smiles at a complete and elaborate set of tailor's patterns. He shudders as he comes upon the knives, the probes, the bandages, the posture, of the wretch about to undergo the most dangerous operation in surgery. In all the chief departments of industry there are plates good enough to serve for practical specifications and working drawings. It has often been told how Diderot himself used to visit the workshops, to watch the men at their toil, to put a thousand questions, to sit down at the loom, to have the machine pulled to pieces and set together again before his eyes, to slave like any apprentice, and to do bad work, in order, as he says, to be able to instruct others how to do good work. That was no movement of empty rhetoric which made him cry out for the Encyclopaedia to become a sanctuary in which human knowledge might find shelter against time and revolutions. He actually took the pains to make it a complete storehouse of the arts, so perfect in detail that they could be at once reconstructed after a deluge in which everything had perished save a single copy of the Encyclopaedia. Such details, said D'Alembert, will perhaps seem extremely out of place to certain scholars, for whom a long dissertation on the cookery or the hairdressing of the ancients, or on the site of a ruined hamlet, or on the baptismal name of some obscure writer of the tenth century, would be vastly interesting and precious.

He suggests that details of economy and of arts and trades have as good a right to a place as the scholastic philosophy, or some system of rhetoric still in use, or the mysteries of heraldry. Yet none even of these had been passed over.

The importance given to physical science and the practical arts in the Encyclopaedia is the sign and exemplification of two elements of the great modern transition. It marks both a social and an intellectual revolution. We see in it first, the distinct association with pacific labour of honour and a kind of glory, such as had hitherto been reserved for knights and friars, for war and asceticism, for fighting and praying. It is the definite recognition of the basis of a new society. If the nobles and the churchmen could only have understood, as clearly as Diderot and D'Alembert understood, the irresistible forces that were making against the maintenance of the worn-out system, all the worst of the evils attending the great political changes of the last decade of the century would have been avoided. That the nobles and churchmen would not see this, was the fatality of the Revolution. We have a glimpse of the profound transformation of social ideas that was at work, in the five or six lines of the article, *Journalier*. "Journeyman—a workman who labours with his hands, and is paid day-wages. This description of men forms the great part of a nation; it is their lot which a good government ought to keep principally in sight. If the journeyman is miserable, the nation is miserable." And again: "The net profit of a society, if equally distributed, may be preferable to a larger profit, if it be distributed unequally, and have the effect of dividing the people into two classes, one gorged with riches, the other perishing in misery" (*Homme*).

The second element in the modern transition is only the intellectual side of the first. It is the substitution of interest in things for interest in words, of positive knowledge for verbal disputation. Few now dispute the services of the schoolmen to the intellectual development of Europe. But conditions had fully ripened, and it was time to complete the movement of Bacon and Descartes by finally placing verbal analysis, verbal definition, verbal inferences, in their right position. Form was no longer to take precedence of matter. The Encyclopaedists are never weary of contrasting their own age of practical rationalism with "the pusillanimous ages of taste." A great collection of books is described in one article (*Bibliomanie*) as a collection of material for the history of the blindness and infatuation of mankind. The gatherer of books is compared to one who should place five or six gems under a pile of common pebbles. If a man of sense buys a work in a dozen volumes, and finds that only half a dozen pages are worth reading, he does well to cut out the half-dozen pages and fling the rest into the fire. . . .

The attitude of the Encyclopaedia to religion is almost universally misrepresented in the common accounts. We are always told that the aim of its conductors was to preach dogmatic atheism. Such a statement could not be made by any one who had read the theological articles, whether the more or the less important among them. Whether Diderot had himself advanced definitely to the dogma of atheism at this time or not, it is certain that the Encyclopaedia represents only the phase of rationalistic scepticism. That the criticism was destructive of much of the fabric of popular belief, and was designed to destroy it, is undeniable, as it was inevitable. But when the excesses of '93 and '94—and all the revolutionary excesses put together are but a drop compared with the oceans of blood with which Catholicism and absolutism have made history crimson—when the crimes and confusion of the end of the century are traced by historians to the materialism and atheism of the Encyclopaedia, we can only say that such an account is a misrepresentation. The materialism and atheism are not there. The religious attack was prompted and guided by the same social feeling that inspired the economic articles. The priest was the enemy of society, the patron of indolence, the hater of knowledge, the mutineer against the civil laws, the unprofitable devourer of the national substance, the persecutor. Sacerdotalism is the object of the encyclopaedic attack. To undermine this, it was necessary first to establish the principle of toleration, because the priest claims to be recognised as the exclusive possessor of saving doctrine. Second, it was necessary to destroy the principle of miracle, because the priest professes himself in his daily rites the consecrated instrument of thaumaturgy. "Let a man," says Rosenkranz very truly [in *Diderots Leben*], "turn over hundreds of histories of church, of state, of literature, and in every one of them he will read that the Encyclopaedia spread abroad an irreligious spirit. The accusation has only a relative truth, to the extent that the Encyclopaedia assailed the belief in miracles, and the oppression of conscience supported by a priestly aristocracy."

No consistent and definite language is adhered to from beginning to end. D'Alembert's prophecy that time would disclose to people what the writers really thought, behind what fear of the censorship compelled them to say, is only partially fulfilled.

The idea of miracle is sapped not by direct arguments, but by the indirect influences of science, and the exposition of the successes of scientific method. It was here that the Encyclopaedia exerted really destructive power, and it did so in the only way in which power of that kind can be exerted either wisely or effectually.

Diderot constantly insists on the propriety, the importance, the indispensableness, of keeping the provinces of science and philosophy apart from the province of theology. This separation is much sought in our own day as a means of saving theology. Diderot designed it to save philosophy. He felt that the distinct recognition of positive thought as supreme within the widest limits then covered by it, would ultimately lead to the banishment of theological thought to a region of its own, too distant and too infertile for men to weary themselves in pursuit of it. His conception was to supplant the old ways of thinking and the old objects of intellectual interest by new ones. He trusted to the intrinsic fitness and value of the new knowledge and new views of human life, to displace the old. This marks him a constructive thinker. He replaced barren interests that had outlived their time, by all those great groups of living and fruitful interests that glow and sparkle in the volumes of the Encyclopaedia. Here was the effective damage that the Encyclopaedia inflicted on the church as the organ of a stationary faith.

Of the gross defects in the execution of the Encyclopaedia nobody was so sensible as Diderot himself. He drew up a truly formidable list of the departments where the work was badly done. But when the blunders and omissions in each subject were all counted, the value of the vast grouping of the subjects was hardly diminished. The union of all these secular acquisitions in a single colossal work invested them with something imposing. Secular knowledge was made to present a massive and sumptuous front. It was pictured before the curious eyes of that generation as a great city of glittering palaces and stately mansions; or else as an immense landscape, with mountains, plains, rocks, waters, forests, animals, and a thousand objects, glorious and beautiful in the sunlight.

Even more important than the exposition of human knowledge, was the exposition of the degrees by which it has been slowly reared. The Preliminary Discourse to the Encyclopaedia, of which by far the greater and more valuable portion was written by D'Alembert, contains a fine survey of the progress of science, thought, and letters since the revival of learning. It is a generous canonisation of the heroes of secular knowledge. It is rapid, but the contributions of Bacon, Descartes, Newton, Locke, Leibnitz, are thrown into a series that penetrates the reader's mind with the idea of ordered growth and measured progress. This excited a vivid hopefulness of interest, which insensibly but most effectually pressed the sterile propositions of dogmatic theology back into a dim and squalid background. Nor was this all. The Preliminary Discourse and the host of articles marshalled behind it, showed that the triumphs of knowledge and true opinion had all been gained on two conditions. The first of these conditions was a firm disregard of authority; the second was an abstention from the premature concoction of system. The true merit of the philosopher or the physicist is described as being to have the spirit of system, yet never to construct a system. The notion expressed in this sentence promises a union of the advantages of an organic synthesis, with the advantages of an open mind and unfettered inquiry.

On the line of argument taken in the Encyclopaedia as to Toleration we need say nothing. The Encyclopaedists were the most ardent propagators of the modern principle of tolerance. No one has to be reminded that this was something more than an abstract discussion among the doctors of social philosophy, in a country where youths were broken on the wheel for levity in face of an ecclesiastical procession, where nearly every considerable man of the century had been either banished or imprisoned for daring to use his mind, and which had been half ruined by the great proscription of Protestants, more than once renewed. The article *Tolérance* was greatly admired in its day, and it is an eloquent and earnest reproduction of the pleas of Locke. One rather curious feature in it is the reproduction of the passage from the *Social Contract*, in which Rousseau explains the right of the magistrate to banish any citizen who has not enough religion to make him do his duties, and who will not make a profession of civil faith. The writer of the article interprets this as implying that "atheists in particular, who remove from the pow-

erful the only rein, and from the weak their only hope," have no right to claim toleration. This is an unexpected stroke in a work that is vulgarly supposed to be a violent manifesto on behalf of atheism.

Diderot himself in an earlier article (*Intolérance*) had treated the subject with more trenchant energy. He does not argue his points systematically, but launches a series of maxims, as with set teeth, clenched hands, and a brow like a thundercloud. He hails the oppressors of his life, the priests and the parliaments, with a pungency that is exhilarating, and winds up with a description of the intolerant as one who forgets that a man is his fellow, and, for holding a different opinion, treats him like a ravening brute; as one who sacrifices the spirit and precepts of his religion to his pride; as the rash fool who thinks that the arch can only be upheld by his hands; as a man who is generally without religion, and to whom it comes easier to have zeal than morals. Every page of the Encyclopaedia was, in fact, a plea for toleration.

Having thus described the general character and purport of the Encyclopaedia, we have still to look at a special portion of it from a more particular point of view. We have already shown how multifarious were Diderot's labours as editor. It remains to give a short account of his labours as a contributor. Everything was on the same vast scale; his industry in writing would have been in itself most astonishing, even if it had not been accompanied by the more depressing fatigue of revising what others had written. Diderot's articles fill more than four of the large volumes of his collected works.

The confusion is immense. There is no rigorous measure and ordered proportion. We constantly pass from a serious treatise to a sally, from an elaborate history to a caprice. There are not a few pages where we know that Diderot is saying what he does not think. Some of the articles seem only to have found a place because Diderot happened to have taken an interest in their subjects at the moment. After reading Voltaire's concise account of Imagination, we are amazed to find Diderot devoting a larger space than Voltaire had needed for the subject at large, to so subordinate and remote a branch of the matter as the Power of the Imagination in Pregnant Women upon the Unborn Young. The article on Theosophs would hardly have been so disproportionately long as it is, merely for the sake of Paracelsus, Van Helmont, Poiret, and the Rosicrucians, unless Diderot had happened to be curiously and half sympathetically brooding over the mixture of inspiration and madness, of charlatanry and generous aim, of which these semimystic, semi-scientific characters were composed.

Many of Diderot's articles, again, have no rightful place in an Encyclopaedia. Genius, for instance, is dealt with in what is neither more nor less than a literary essay, vigorous, suggestive, diffuse; and containing, by the way, the curious assertion that, although there are few errors in Locke and too few truths in Shaftesbury, yet Locke is only an acute and comprehensive intelligence, while Shaftesbury is a genius of the first order.

Under the word Laborious, we have only a dozen lines of angry reproach against the despotism that makes men idle by making property uncertain. Under such words as Frivolous, Gallantry, Perfection, Importance, Politeness, Melancholy, Glorieux, the reader is amused and edified by miniature essays on manners and character, seldom ending without some pithy sentence and pointed moral.

Little bursts of grotesque sentimentalism justify the description of Diderot as the most German of all the French. Equally characteristic and more sensible is the writer's outbreak against Formalists.

> The formalist knows exactly the proper interval between receiving and returning a visit; he expects you on the exact day at the exact time; if you fail, he thinks himself neglected and takes offence. A single man of this stamp is enough to chill and embarrass a whole company. There is nothing so repugnant to simple and upright souls as formalities; as such people have within themselves the consciousness of the goodwill they bear to everybody, they neither plague themselves to be constantly displaying a sentiment that is habitual, nor to be constantly on the watch for it in others.

We have spoken in the previous section of the contempt expressed by D'Alembert for mere literary antiquarianism—a very different thing, let us remember, from scientific inquiry into the origin and classification of institutions and social organs. Diderot's article on the Germans is an excellent illustration of this wholesome predominance of the scientific spirit over the superficialities of barren erudition. The word "Allemand," says Diderot, "has a great many etymologies, but they are so forced, that it is almost as well to know none of them as to know them all. As for the origin of this famous stock, all that has been said on that matter, between Tacitus and Clovis, is simply a tissue of guesses without foundation." Of course, in this some persons will see a shameful levity; others will regard it as showing very good sense, and a right estimate of what is knowable and worth knowing, and what is neither one nor the other. In the article on Celibacy we notice the same temper. A few sentences are enough for the antiquarianism of the subject, what the Egyptians, Greeks, and Romans thought and ordained about celibacy. The substance of the article is a reproduction of the Abbé de Saint-Pierre's discussion of the advantages that would be gained for France, with her declining population, if her forty thousand curés were allowed to marry, and to bring into the world eighty thousand children. We may believe that Diderot smiled as he transcribed the Abbé's cunning suggestion that a dispensing power to relieve from the obligation of celibacy should be recognised in the Pope, and that the Roman court should receive a sum of money for every dispensation so granted.

Although, however, Diderot despised mere bookishness, his article on Libraries in one of the longest and most painstaking, furnishing a tolerably complete list of the famous collections, from the beginning of books down to the latest additions to the King's Library in the rue Vivienne. In the course of this article he quotes with seeming approval the quaint words in which old Richard of Bury, author of the *Philobiblon* (1340), praised books as the best of masters, much as the immortal defender of the poet Archias had praised them: "Hi sunt magistri qui nos instru-

unt sine virgis et ferulis, sine cholera, sine pecuniâ; si accedis non dormiunt; si inquiris non se abscondunt; non obmurmurant si oberres; cachinnos nesciunt si ignores."

In literature proper, as in philosophy, Diderot loses no opportunity of insisting on the need of being content with suspended judgment. For instance, he blames historians of opinion for the readiness with which they attribute notions found in one or two rabbis, to the whole of the Jews, or because two or three Fathers say something, set this boldly down as the sentiments of a whole century, although perhaps we have nothing else left of the century, save these two or three Fathers, and although we do not know whether their writings were applauded or were even widely known.

> It were to be wished that people should speak less affirmatively, especially on particular points and remote consequences, and that they should only attribute them directly to those in whose writings they are actually to be found. I confess that the history of the sentiments of antiquity would not seem so complete, and that it would be necessary to speak in terms of doubt much more often than is common; but by acting otherwise we expose ourselves to the danger of taking false and uncertain conjectures for ascertained and unquestionable truths. The ordinary man of letters does not readily put up with suspensive expressions, any more than common people do so.

All this is an odd digression to be found under the head of Hylopathianism, but it must always remain wholesome doctrine.

We cannot wonder at Diderot's admiration for Montaigne and for Bayle, who, with Hume, would make the great trinity of scepticism. "The work of Montaigne," said Diderot,

> is the touchstone of a good intelligence; you may be sure that any one whom the reading of Montaigne displeases, has some vice either of heart or of understanding. As for Bayle, he has had few equals in the art of reasoning, and perhaps no superior; and though he piles doubt upon doubt, he always proceeds with order; an article of his is a living polypus, which divides itself into a number of polypuses, all living, engendered one from the other.

Yet Diderot had a feeling of the necessity of advancing beyond the attitude of Bayle and Montaigne. Intellectual suspense and doubt were made difficult to him by his vehement and positive demand for emotional certainties.

He is always ready to fling away his proper subject in a burst of moralising. The article on Man, as a branch of natural history, contains a correct, if rather superficial, account of that curious animal; at length the writer comes to a table showing the probable duration of life at certain ages. "You will observe," he says, "1st, that the age of seven is that at which you may hope for a longer life; 2nd, that at twelve or thirteen you have lived a quarter of your life; at twenty-eight or twenty-nine you have lived half; at fifty more than three quarters." And then he suddenly winds up the whole performance by the exclamation: "O ye who have laboured up to fifty, who are in the enjoyment of comfort, and who still have left to you health and strength, what then are you waiting for before you take rest? How long will you go on saying *To-morrow, to-morrow?*"

There are many casual brilliancies in the way of analogy and parallel, many aptnesses of thought and phrase. The Stoics are called the Jansenists of Paganism. "For a single blade of grass to grow, it is necessary that the whole of nature should cooperate." "A man comes to Pyrrhonism by one of two opposite ways; either because he does not know enough, or because he knows too much; the latter is not the most common way." And so forth.

If we turn to the group of articles dealing with theology, it is difficult to know exactly where we are. Sometimes Diderot writes of popular superstitions with the gravity proper to a dictionary of mythology. Sometimes he sews on to the sober grey of his scepticism a purple patch of theistic declamation. The article on *Jésus Christ* is obviously a mere piece of common form, and more than one passage in his article on *Christianisme* is undoubtedly insincere. When we come to his more careful article, *Providence*, we find it impossible to extract from it a body of coherent propositions of which we could confidently say that they represented his own creed or the creed that he desired his readers to bear in mind.

It is hardly worth while to measure the more or the less of his adherence to Christianity, or even to Deism, as inferred from the Encyclopaedia. We need only turn to Diderot's private letters to find that he is in no degree nor kind an adherent, but the most hardy, contemptuous, and thoroughgoing of opponents. At the risk of shocking, I am bound to reproduce a passage from one of his letters, in which there can be no doubt that we have Diderot's true mind, as distinguished from what it was convenient to print. "The Christian religion," he says,

> is to my mind the most absurd and atrocious in its dogmas; the most unintelligible, the most metaphysical, the most intertwisted and obscure, and consequently the most subject to divisions, sects, schisms, heresies; the most mischievous for the public tranquillity, the most dangerous to sovereigns by its hierarchic order, its persecutions, its discipline; the most flat, the most dreary, the most Gothic, and the most gloomy in its ceremonies; the most puerile and unsociable in its morality, considered not in what is common to it with universal morality, but in what is peculiarly its own, and constitutes it evangelical, apostolical, and Christian morality, which is the most intolerant of all. Lutheranism, freed from some absurdities, is preferable to Catholicism; Protestantism to Lutheranism, Socinianism to Protestantism, Deism, with temples and ceremonies, to Socinianism. Since it is necessary that man, being superstitious by nature, should have a fetish, the simplest and most harmless will be the best fetish.

We need not discuss nor extend the quotation; enough has been said to relieve us from the duty of analysing or criticising articles in which Christianity is treated with all the formal respect that the secular authority insisted upon.

This formal respect is not incompatible with many veiled and secret sarcasms that were as well understood as they were sharply enjoyed by those who read between the lines. It is not surprising that these sarcasms were constantly unjust and shallow. Even those who repudiate theology and all its works, may feel a shock at the coarseness and impurity of innuendo which now and then disfigures Diderot's treatment of theological as of some other subjects. For this the attitude of the church itself was much to blame, virulent, unspiritual as it was in France in those days. Voltaire, Diderot, Holbach, would have written in a very different spirit, even while maintaining and publishing the same attacks on theological opinion, if the church of France had possessed such a school of teachers as the church of England found in the Latitudinarians in the seventeenth century, or such as she found in the nineteenth century in those who imported, partly from the poetry of Wordsworth, partly from the historic references of the Oxford Tracts, an equity, a breadth, an elevation, a pensive grace, that effectually forbid the use of those more brutal weapons of controversy that were the only weapons possible in France in the eighteenth century.

We have already said so much of the great and important group of articles on arts and trades, that important group of articles on arts and trades, that it is unnecessary to add anything further as to Diderot's particular share in them. He visited all the workshops in Paris; he sent for information and specifications to the most important seats of manufacture in the kingdom; he sometimes summoned workmen from the provinces to describe to him the paper works of Montargis, and the silk works and velvet works of Lyons. Much of Diderot's work, even on leading practical subjects, was, no doubt, the reproduction of mere book-knowledge acquired at second hand. Take, for instance, Agriculture, which was undoubtedly the most important of all subjects for France at that date, as indeed at every other date. There are a dozen pages of practical precepts, for which Diderot was probably indebted to one of the farmers at Grandval. After this he fills up the article with about twenty pages in which he gives an account of the new system of husbandry, described by our English Jethro Tull to an unbelieving public between 1731 and 1751. Tull's volume was translated into French by Duhamel, with notes and the record of experiments of his own; from this volume Diderot drew the pith of his article. Diderot's only merit in the matter—and it is hardly an inconsiderable one in a world of routine—is that he should have been at the pains to seek the newest lights, and above all that he should have urged the value of fresh experiments in agriculture. Tull was not the safest authority in the world, but it is to be remembered that the shrewd-witted Cobbett thought his ideas on husbandry worth reproducing years after Diderot had thought them worth compiling into an article.

It was not merely in the details of the practical arts that Diderot wrote from material acquired at second hand. The article on the *Zend-Avesta* is taken from the *Annual Register* for 1762. The long series of articles on the history of philosophy is in effect a reproduction of what he found in Bayle, in Deslandes, and in Brucker. There are one or two considerable exceptions. Perhaps the most important is under the heading of Spinoza. The article on *Hobbisme* contains an analysis, evidently made by the writer's own hand, of the bulk of Hobbes's propositions; it is scarcely, however, illuminated by a word of criticism. If we turn to the article on *Société*, it is true, we find Hobbes's view of the relations between the civil and temporal powers tolerably effectively combated, but even here Diderot hardly does more than arm himself with the weapons of Locke.

Of course, he honestly refers his readers to these sources of wider information. All that we can say of the articles on the history of philosophy is that the series is fairly complete; that Diderot used his matter with intelligence and the spirit of criticism, and that he often throws in luminous remarks and far-reaching suggestions of his own. This was all the purpose of his book required. To imitate the laborious literary search of Bayle or of Brucker, and to attempt an independent history of philosophy, would have been to sacrifice the Encyclopaedia as a whole to the superfluous perfection of a minor part.

I shall venture to quote an equally hardy passage from another article (*Pyrrhonienne*) which some will think a measure of Diderot's philosophical incompetency, and others will think a measure of his good sense. "We will conclude," he says,

> for our part that as all in nature is bound together, there is nothing, properly speaking, of which man has perfect, absolute, and complete knowledge, because for that he would need knowledge of all. Now as all is bound together, it inevitably happens that, from discussion to discussion, he must come to something unknown: then in starting again from this unknown point, we shall be justified in pleading against him the ignorance or the obscurity or the uncertainty of the point preceding, and of that preceding this, and so forth, up to the most evident principle. So we must admit a sort of sobriety in the use of reason. When step by step I have brought a man to some evident proposition, I shall cease to dispute. I will listen no longer to anybody who goes on to deny the existence of bodies, the rules of logic, the testimony of the senses, the difference between good and evil, true and false, etc., etc. I will turn my back on everybody who tries to lead me away from a simple question, to embark me in discussion as to the nature of matter, of the understanding, of thought, and other subjects shoreless and bottomless.

Whatever else may be said of this, we have to recognise that it is exactly characteristic of the author. But then, why have written on metaphysics at all?

The article on Spinoza is characteristic of both the good and the bad sides of Diderot's work. Half of it is merely a reproduction of Bayle's criticisms on Spinoza and his system. The other half consists of original objections propounded by Diderot with marked vigour of thrust against Spinoza, but there is no evidence that he had gone deeper into Spinoza than the first book of the *Ethics*. There is no certain sign that he had read anything else, or that he had more of that before him than the extracts furnished by Bayle. Such treatment of a serious subject hardly conforms to the modern requirements of the literary conscience, for in truth the literary conscience has now turned specialist and shrinks from the encyclopaedic. Diderot's objections are, as we have said, pushed with marked energy of speech. "However short a way," he says,

> you penetrate into the thick darkness in which Spinoza has wrapped himself up, you discover a succession of abysses into which this audacious reasoner has precipitated himself, of propositions either evidently false or evidently doubtful, of arbitrary principles substituted for natural principles and sensible truths; an abuse of terms taken for the most part in a wrong sense, a mass of deceptive equivocations, a cloud of palpable contradictions.

This system is monstrous. It is Spinoza's plausible method that has deceived people; they supposed that one who employed geometry, and proceeded by way of axioms and definitions, must be on the track of truth. They did not see that these axioms were nothing better than very vague and very uncertain propositions; that the definitions were inexact, defective, and bizarre.

I have no space to follow the reasoning by which Diderot supports this scornful estimate of the famous thinker, of whom it can never be settled whether he be pantheist, atheist, akosmist, or God-intoxicated man. He returns to the charge again and again, as if he felt a certain secret uneasiness lest for scorn so loudly expressed he had not brought forward adequate justification. And the reader feels that Diderot has scarcely hit the true line of cleavage that would have enabled him—from his own point of view—to shatter the Spinozist system. He tries various bouts of logic with Spinoza in connection with detached propositions. Thus he deals with Spinoza's third proposition, that, *in the case of things that have nothing in common with one another, one cannot be the cause of the other.* This proposition, Diderot contends, is false in all moral and occasional causes. The sound of the name of God has nothing in common with the idea of the Creator which that name produces in my mind. A misfortune that overtakes my friend has nothing in common with the grief that I feel in consequence. When I move my arm by an act of will, the movement has nothing in common in its nature with the act of my will; they are very different. I am not a triangle, yet I form the idea of one and I examine its properties. So with the fifth proposition, that *there cannot be in the universe two or more substances of the same nature or the same attributes.* If Spinoza is only talking of the essence of things or of their definition, what he says is naught; for it can only mean that there cannot be in the universe two different essences having the same essence. Who doubts it? But if Spinoza means that there cannot be an essence which is found in various single objects, in the same way as the essence of triangle is found in the triangle A and the triangle B, then he says what is manifestly untrue. It is not, however, until the last two or three pages that Diderot sets forth his dissent in its widest from. "To refute Spinoza," he says at last,

> all that is necessary is to stop him at the first

step, without taking the trouble to follow him into a mass of consequences; all that we need do is to substitute for the obscure principle which he makes the base of his system, the following: namely, *that there are several substances*—a principle that in its own way is clear to the last degree. And, in fact, what proposition can be clearer, more striking, more close to the understanding and consciousness of man? I here seek no other judge than the most just impression of the common sense that is spread among the human race. . . . Now, since common sense revolts against each of Spinoza's propositions, no less than against the first, of which they are the pretended proofs, instead of stopping to reason on each of these proofs where common sense is lost, we should be right to say to him: —Your principle is contrary to common sense; from a principle in which common sense is lost, nothing can issue in which common sense is to be found again.

The passage sounds unpleasantly like an appeal to the crowd in a matter of science, which is as the sin against the Holy Ghost in these high concerns. What Diderot meant, probably, was to charge Spinoza with inventing a conception of substance which has no relation to objective experience; and further with giving fantastic answers to questions that were in themselves never worth asking, because the answers must always involve a violent wrench of the terms of experience into the sphere transcending experience, and because, moreover, they can never be verified.

The article on Leibnitz has less original matter in it than that on Spinoza. The various speculations of that great and energetic intellect in metaphysic, logic, natural theology, natural law, are merely drawn out in a long table of succinct propositions, while the account of the life and character of Leibnitz is simply taken from the excellent eloge which had been published upon him by Fontenelle in 1716. Fontenelle's narrative is reproduced in a generous spirit of admiration and respect for a genius that was like Diderot's own in encyclopaedic variety of interest, while it was so far superior to Diderot's in concentration, in subtlety, in precision, in power of construction. If there could exist over our heads, says Diderot, a species of beings who could observe our works as we watch those of creatures at our feet, with what surprise would such beings have seen those four marvellous insects, Bayle, Descartes, Leibnitz, and Newton. And he then draws up a little calendar of the famous men out of whom we must choose the name to be placed at the very head of the human race. The list contains, besides Julian the Apostate—who was inserted, we may presume, merely by way of playful insult to the ecclesiastical enemy—Socrates, Marcus Aurelius, Trajan, Bacon, and the four great names that have just been cited. Germany derives as much honour from Leibnitz alone, he concludes with unconsidered enthusiasm, as Greece from Plato, Aristotle, and Archimedes, all put together. As we have said, however, there is no criticism, nor any other sign that Diderot had done more than survey the façade of the Leibnitzian structure admiringly from without.

The article on Liberty would be extremely remarkable, appearing where it does, and coming from a thinker of Diderot's general capacity, if only we could be sure that Diderot was sincere. As it happens, there is good reason to suppose that he was wholly insincere. It is quite as shallow, from the point of view of philosophy, as his article on the Jews or on the Bible is from the point of view of erudition. One reason for this might not be far to seek. We have repeatedly observed how paramount the social aim and the social test are in Diderot's mind over all other considerations. But this reference of all subjects of discussion to the good of society, and this measurement of conclusions by their presumed effect on society, is a method that has its own dangers. The aversion of ecclesiastics to unfettered discussion, lest it should damage institutions and beliefs deemed useful to mankind, is the leading example of this peril. Diderot, it might be said by those who should contend that he wrote what he thought, did not escape exactly the same predicament, as soon as ever he forgot that of all the things that are good for society, Truth is the best. Now, who will believe that it is Diderot, the persecuted editor of the Encyclopaedia, and the author of the manly article on Intolerance, who introduces such a passage as the following into the discussion of the everlasting controversy of Free Will and Necessity?—

> Take away Liberty, and you leave no more vice nor virtue nor merit in the world; rewards are ridiculous, and punishments unjust. The ruin of Liberty overthrows all order and all police, confounds vice and virtue, authorises every monstrous infamy, extinguishes the last spark of shame and remorse, degrades and disfigures beyond recovery the whole human race. *A doctrine of such enormity as this ought not to be examined in the schools; it ought to be punished by the magistrates.*

Of course, this was exactly what the Jesuits said about a belief in God, about revelation, and about the institutions of the church. To take away these, they said, is to throw down the bulwarks of order, and an attempt to take them away, as by encyclopaedists or others, ought to be punished by the magistrates. Diderot had for the moment clearly lost himself.

We need hardly be surprised if an article conceived in this spirit contains no serious contribution to the difficult question with which it deals. Diderot had persuaded himself that, without Free Will, all those emotional moralities in the way of sympathy and benevolence and justice which he adored, would be lowered to the level of mere mechanism. "If men are not free in what they do of good and evil, then," he cries, in what is surely a paroxysm of unreason, "good is no longer good, and evil no longer evil." As if the outward quality and effects of good and evil were not independent of the mental operations which precede human action. Murder would not cease to be an evil, simply because it had been proved that the murderer's will to do a bad deed was the result of antecedents. Acts have marks and consequences of their own, good or bad, whatever may be the state of mind of those who do them. But Diderot does not seem to divine the true issue; he writes as if Necessarians or Determinists denied the existence of volitions, and is if the question were whether volitions do exist. Nobody denies that they exist; the real question is of the conditions under which they exist. Are they determined by antecedents, or are they self-determined, spontaneous, and unconnected? Is Will independent of cause?

Diderot's argumentation is, in fact, merely a protest that man is conscious of a Will. And just as in other parts of his article Diderot by Liberty means only the existence of Will, so by Liberty he means only the healthy condition of the soul, and not its independence of causation. We need not waste words on so dire a confusion, nor on the theory that Will is sometimes dependent on cerebral antecedents and sometimes not.

Turning from the philosophical to the political or social group of articles, we find little to add to what has been said in the previous section. One of the most excellent essays in this group is that on Luxury. Diderot opens ingeniously with a list of the propositions that state the supposed evils of luxury, and under each proposition he places the most striking case that he can find in history of its falseness. He goes through the same process with the propositions asserting the gains of luxury to a society. Having thus effectually disposed of any wholesale way of dealing with the subject, he proceeds to make a number of observations on the gains and drawbacks of luxury; these are full of sense and freedom from commonplace. Such articles as *Pouvoir, Souverain, Autorité*, do little more than tell over again the old unhistoric story about a society surrendering a portion of its sovereign power to some individual or dynasty to hold in trust. It is worth remarking how little democratic were Diderot and his school in any Jacobinical, or anarchic, or even more respectable modern sense. There is in Diderot's contributions many a firm and manly plea for the self-respect of the common people, but not more than once or twice is there a syllable of the disorder which smoulders under the pages of Rousseau. Thus:—

> When the dwellers among the fields are well treated, the number of proprietors insensibly grows greater, the extreme distance and the vile dependence of poor on rich grow less; hence the people have courage, force of soul, and strength of body; they love their country, they respect the magistrates, they are attached to a prince, to an order, and to laws to which they owe their peace and well-being. And you will no longer see the son of the honourable tiller of the soil so ready to quit the noble calling of his forefathers, nor so ready to go and sully himself with the liveries and with the contempt of the man of wealth.

No one can find fault with democratic sentiment of this kind, nor with the generous commonplaces of the moralist, about virtue being the only claim to honour, and vice the only true course of shame and inferiority. The little article on Multitude seems merely inserted for the sake of buffeting unwarranted pretensions.

> Distrust the judgment of the multitude in all matters of reasoning and philosophy; there its voice is the voice of malice, folly, inhumanity, irrationality, and prejudice. Distrust it again in things that suppose much knowledge or a fine taste. The multitude is ignorant and dulled. Distrust it in morality; it is not capable of strong and

Portrait of Diderot by Michel Van Loo.

generous actions; it rather wonders at such actions than approves them; heroism is almost madness in its eyes. Distrust it in the things of sentiment; is delicacy of sentiment so common a thing that you can accord it to the multitude? In what then is the multitude right? In everything, but only at the end of a very long time, because then it has become an echo, repeating the judgment of a small number of sensible men who shape the judgment of posterity for it beforehand. If you have on your side the testimony of your conscience, and against you that of the multitude, take comfort and be assured that time does justice.

It is far from being a universal gift among men of letters and others to unite this fastidious estimation of the incapacity of the crowd in the higher provinces of the intellectual judgment, with a fervid desire that the life of the crowd should be made worthy of self-respecting men.

The same hand that wrote the defiance of the populace that has just been quoted, wrote also this short article on Misery:—

> There are few souls so firm that misery does not in the long run cast them down and degrade them. The poor common people are incredibly stupid. I know not what false dazzling prestige closes their eyes to their present wretchedness, and to the still deeper wretchedness that awaits the years of old age. Misery is the mother of great crimes. It is the sovereigns who make the

miserable, and it is they who shall answer in this world and the other for the crimes that misery has committed.

So far as the mechanism of government is concerned, Diderot writes much as Montesquieu had done. Under the head of *Représentants* he proclaims the advantages, not exactly of government by a representative assembly, but of assisting and advising the royal government by means of such an assembly. There is no thought of universal suffrage. "*It is property that makes the citizen*; every man who has possessions in the state is interested in the state, and whatever be the rank that particular conventions may assign to him, it is always as a proprietor; it is by reason of his possessions that he ought to speak, and that he acquires the right of having himself represented." Yet this very definite statement does not save him from the standing difficulty of a democratic philosophy of politics. Nor can it be reconciled in point of logic with other propositions to which Diderot commits himself in the same article. For instance, he says that "no order of citizens is capable of stipulating for all; if one order had the right, it would very soon come to stipulate only for itself; each class ought to be represented by men who know its condition and its needs; *these needs are only well known to those who actually feel them*." But then, in that case, the poorest classes are those who have most need of direct representation; they are the most numerous, their needs are sharpest, they are the classes to which war, consumption of national capital and way of expending national income, equal laws, judicial administration, and the other concerns of a legislative assembly, come most close. The problem is to reconcile the sore interests of the multitude with the ignorance and the temper imputed in Diderot's own description of them.

An interesting study might be made, if the limits of our subject permitted a digression, on the new political ideas that subsequent experience in England, France, Germany, the American Union, has added to the publicist's stock. Diderot's article on the Legislator is a curious mixture of views that political thinkers have left behind, with views that the most enlightened statesmen have taken up. There is much talk after the fashion of Jean Jacques Rousseau about the admirable legislation of Lycurgus at Lycurgus at Sparta, the philosophical government of the great empire of China, and the fine spirit of the institutions of Peru. We perceive that the same influences that made Rousseau's political sentimentalism so overwhelming, also brought even strong heads like Diderot to believe in the unbounded power of a government to mould men at its will, and to impose institutions at discretion. The idea that it is the main function of a government to make its people virtuous, is generally as strong in Diderot as it was in Rousseau, and as it became in Robespierre. He admires the emperors of China, because their edicts are as the exhortation of a father to his children. All edicts, he says, ought to instruct and to exhort as much as they command. Yet two years after the Encyclopaedia was finished (1774), when Turgot prefaced his reforming edicts by elaborate and reasoned statements of the grounds for them, it was found that his prefaces caused greater provocation than the very laws they introduced.

Apart from the common form of enthusiasm for the "sublime legislation" of countries that the writer really knew nothing about, the article on the Legislator has some points worth noticing. We have seen how Diderot made the possession of property the true note of citizenship, and of a claim to share in the government. But he did not pay property this compliment for nothing. It is, he says, the business of the legislator to do his best to make up to mankind for the loss of that equality which was one of the comforts that men surrendered when they gave up the state of nature. Hence the legislator ought to take care that no one shall reach a position of extreme opulence otherwise than by an industry enriching the state. "He must take care that the charges of society shall fall upon the rich, who enjoy the advantages of society." Even those who agree with Diderot, and are convinced of the merits of a graduated income tax, will admit that he comes to his conclusion without knowing or reflecting about either the serious arguments for it or the serious objections against it.

Not the least interesting thing in this long article is its anticipation of those ideas which in England we associate with the name of Cobden.

> All the men of all lands have become necessary to one another for the exchange of the fruits of industry and the products of the soil. Commerce is a new bond among men. Every nation has an interest in these days in the preservation by every other nation of its wealth, its industry, its banks, its luxury, its agriculture. The ruin of Leipzig, of Lisbon, and of Lima has led to bankruptcies on all the exchanges of Europe, and has affected the fortunes of many millions of persons.

In the same spirit he foresees the decline of patriotism in its older and narrower sense, and the predominance of the international over the national sentiment.

> All nations now have sufficiently just ideas of their neighbours, and consequently, they have less enthusiasm for their country than in the old days of ignorance. There is little enthusiasm where there is much light; enthusiasm is nearly always the emotion of a soul that is more passionate than it is instructed. By comparing among all nations laws with laws, talents with talents, and manners with manners, nations will find so little reason to prefer themselves to others, that if they preserve for their own country that love which is the fruit of personal interest, at least they will lose that enthusiasm which is the fruit of an exclusive self-esteem.

Yet Diderot had the perspicacity to discern the drawbacks to such a revolution in the conditions of social climate.

> Commerce, like enlightenment, lessens ferocity, but also, just as enlightenment takes away the enthusiasm of self-esteem, so perhaps commerce takes away the enthusiasm of virtue. It gradually extinguishes the spirit of magnanimous disinterestedness, and replaces it by that of hard justice. By turning men's minds rather to use than beauty, to prudence rather than to greatness, it may

be that it injures the strength, the generosity, the nobleness of manners.

All this, whether it come to much or little, is at least more true than Diderot's assurance that henceforth for any nation in Europe to make conquests must be a moral impossibility. Napoleon Bonaparte was then a child in arms. Whether his career was on the whole a fulfilment or a contradiction of Diderot's proposition, may be disputed.

And so my sketch of the book may at length end. Let me make a concluding remark. Is it not surprising that a man of Diderot's speculative boldness and power should have failed to rise from the mechanical arrangement of thought and knowledge, up to some higher and more commanding conception of the relation between himself in the eighteenth century, or ourselves in our own day, and all those vast systems of thought, method, and belief, that in various epochs and over different spaces of the globe have given men working answers to the questions their leading spirits were moved to put to themselves and to the iron universe around them? We constantly feel how near Diderot is to the point of view that would have brought light. We feel how very nearly ready he was to see the mental experiences of the race in east and west, not as superstition, degradation, grovelling error, but as aspects of intellectual effort and aspiration richly worthy of human interest and scientific consideration, and in their aim as well as in their substance all of one piece with the newest science and the last voices of religious or anti-religious development. Diderot was the one member of the party of Philosophers who was capable of grasping such a thought. If this guiding idea of the unity of the intellectual history of man, and the organic integrity of thought, had happily come into Diderot's mind, we should have had an Encyclopaedia indeed; a survey and representation of all the questions and answers of the world, such as would in itself have suggested what questions are best worth putting, and at the same time furnished its own answers.

For this the moment was not yet. An urgent social task lay before France and before Europe; it could not be postponed until the thinkers had worked out a scheme of philosophic completeness. The thinkers did not seriously make any effort after this completeness. The Encyclopaedia was the most serious attempt, and it did not wholly fail. As I replace in my shelves this mountain of volumes, "dusky and huge, enlarging on the sight," I have a presentiment that their pages will seldom again be disturbed by me or by others. They served a great purpose over a hundred years ago. They are now a memorable ruin, clothed with all the profuse associations of history. It is no Ozymandias of Egypt, king of kings, whose wrecked shape of stone and sterile memories we contemplate. We think rather of the grey and crumbling walls of an ancient stronghold, reared by the endeavour of stout hands and faithful, whence in its own day and generation a band once went forth against barbarous hordes, to strike a blow for humanity and truth.

J. B. Priestley

SOURCE: "The Enlightenment," in *Literature and Western Man,* Harper & Brothers, 1960 pp. 98-110.

[Priestley was an English playwright, novelist, and essayist whose books include Angel Pavement *(1930),* Lost Empires *(1965), and* The Image Men *(1968). In the following excerpt, he comments on the literary, philosophical, and psychological context of the Encyclopedists' great project, remarking that it is in Diderot, during a crisis, that "we seem to catch a glimpse of a sinister regress spiralling down to some eternal darkness of the spirit, infinitely removed from the bright surface of [his] rational optimism, altruism, alert social conscience, reasonable benevolence."]*

We do not know where literature begins and ends. And even when we are certain that something is literature, we cannot be equally certain that we know how far its roots go and from what it draws its nourishment. The movement known as the 'Enlightenment', which had its home in France but reached out to all Europe and indeed further still, was not primarily a literary movement. The literature it created was a by-product. The work of its mathematicians, naturalists, political theorists, cannot be considered here, unless, as with Diderot, it breaks through into literature or may be said to have had strong literary influences. But the general movement itself cannot be ignored. Too much came out of it, and we have not done with it yet. The French Revolution, of course, owed much to the *philosophes* of the Enlightenment. though they were not themselves politicians and did not concern themselves with political action. We are apt to forget, however, that something even more important to us today came out of the eighteenth century of the Enlightenment, namely, the American Revolution. If the vast American continent, the wide rich land itself, able to feed and shelter uncounted millions of immigrants, is the mother of the United States, then the father, the creative *logos*, is the characteristic thought of this movement and its era—the concepts of freedom, equality, tolerance, a refusal to believe that war is inevitable, the idea that men inspired by these concepts can progress by giant strides. The note of brisk rationalistic optimism sounded in the American Constitution might have been heard, almost any night in the mid-eighteenth century, in the *salons* of Madame Geoffrin and Mlle. de Lespinasse or round the dinner tables of Baron d'Holbach and Helvétius.

The three great figures of the movement are undoubtedly Voltaire, Diderot and Rousseau. . . . [However, Rousseau] is really the figure that bestrides the transition from this age to the next, which explains, apart from his various personal weaknesses, why Voltaire and the *philosophes* viewed him with mistrust: when they looked at him they were looking beyond their own age, into the next. (The contemporary French term, *philosophes*, is worth keeping, not only because this is how these men were known, in and out of France, but also because to call them 'philosophers' would suggest they were metaphysical rivals of a Leibniz or a Kant when in fact they were not metaphysicians at all.) Voltaire and Diderot, then, are our men. They are very different but may be seen against the same fantastic background. It is fantastic because its elements are so wildly mixed. The Paris of Voltaire's plays and tales and Diderot's Encyclopaedia is an incredible city. It represents all that is most luxurious in a highly artificial age, and yet is almost bankrupt and is surrounded by starvation and despair. Louis XV's mistress, Madame de Pompadour, encourages him to waste fortunes, often on idle entertainment, and yet is herself a cultivated woman, ready to befriend men of letters. Boucher is painting his dainty marquises, while round the corner, before a crowd of all ranks, a man is having boiling lead poured over him before being torn to pieces by wild horses. Some of the drawing-rooms and supper-tables are loud with scientific discussion and arguments between liberal deists and atheistic materialists, yet at any moment the Jesuits may strike, officers bearing a *letter de cachet* may arrive, and one of the theorists may be removed to the Bastille. The new age of reason and the fifteenth century seem to jostle each other in this city, where there is at once more progress and more reaction than in any other capital in Western Europe. A Montesquieu can be laying the foundation of modern political science, a Buffon can begin exploring and recording all natural history, a d'Alembert can produce his treatises on dynamics, a d'Holbach enlarge upon his dogma of determinism and atheism, all within a society still officially committed to a despotic monarchy and the most rigid and bigoted ecclesiastical censorship. Books may be burned by the common hangman, authors hurried away to prison, unbelievers threatened with torture; yet Louis XV, idling among his girls, is almost as ready to cancel a *lettre de cachet* as to sign one; Marmontel finds himself with a comfortably furnished room and an excellent dinner in the Bastille; the gayer gentlemen in holy orders arrange elaborate seductions and adulteries; the powdered and beribboned aristocratic ladies argue and quarrel not only about the latest poem or play but also about religion, the rise of civilisation, the origin of life; and a rich kind-hearted Madame de Geoffrin, with no pretensions to culture or science herself, can spend much of her time and most of her money entertaining and helping to support the *philosophes*, the most dangerous men in the country. One or two of them may have to leave the country at any moment, but the age is well supplied with eccentric despots ready to receive them. So Frederick the Great flatters Voltaire into staying with him, and Diderot spends months with the Empress Catherine of Russia, arguing with her at length every evening. In our time Bernard Shaw visited Stalin, but not on these easy terms. He would have done better—or much worse—in this fantastic eighteenth century.

Earlier than d'Holbach, a young man called La Mettrie, in *L'homme-machine*, had advanced the theory that man was simply an automaton, with an enthusiasm rarely found among automata. In advanced intellectual circles—though Voltaire declared himself outside them in this matter—it was generally held not merely that man should be guided by reason, to which Voltaire would have readily agreed, but that, having been produced by an entirely material universe, itself a great machine, man is a kind of little machine, with no claim to immortality and only a mere verbal one to a soul or mind. And if we believe that whatever is built too high, unbalanced or one-sided in consciousness will be compensated for in the unconscious,

which will produce the opposite in an inferior form, we might expect to discover in the intimate lives of these people, behind the be-wigged masks, a compulsive emotionalism, all the ecstasies and miseries of romantic passion, the ravages of mad infatuations. And this is what we do find, beginning with the nervous frenzies and amorous antics of Voltaire, the tearful literary taste of Diderot, and culminating in the tragically impassioned correspondence, the appalling secret life, of that smiling hostess of the *philosophes*, Julie de Lespinasse. Already the next age was being formed in these disturbed hidden depths, which even now were beginning to shape and colour the romantic image of Western Man. No wonder its prophet, Rousseau, was not much liked.

The great instrument of the Enlightenment was the *Encyclopédie*, originally begun as a publishing enterprise borrowed from England. There had been a number of earlier attempts to provide readers with works of universal knowledge, usually in dictionary form, but the *Cyclopaedia, or an Universal Dictionary of Arts and Sciences*, published in two volumes by Ephraim Chambers in 1728, was more ambitious and systematic than any earlier work because of its cross-references. The French *Encyclopédie, ou Dictionnaire raisonné des Sciences, des Arts et des Métiers*, though taking its start from the English compilation, was more ambitious still and ran to 28 volumes, between 1751 and 1765. Its early volumes were quickly suppressed, and then it began to lead an underground existence. All the philosophes contributed to it, but the man who had to do most of the work, both as editor and contributor, was Diderot. It is easy to say, strictly speaking, what Diderot was not, for he was not really a scientist, he was not technically a philosopher, he was not a novelist or dramatist of any great talent, he was not actually a man of letters of real distinction, and even his friends admitted that he was always too enthusiastic and in too much of a hurry to correct his faulty gift of expression. He could not have written the preliminary discourse to the *Encyclopédie* as well as the mathematical d'Alembert did; and he has not the easy flow of his contributor, Marmontel, whose *Moral Tales* were widely read throughout Europe for many years, and whose memoirs, written in old age, give a very pleasant, if obviously idealised, picture of a country childhood in the earlier eighteenth century. Yet Diderot emerges as the most considerable figure in his group. He seems to reach forward to our own world. A lot of things, important now, appear to date from him. His editorial labours, his central position in the group, and his tremendous zest for ideas, together seem to produce in him a profound intuitive feeling for what is germinal and of widening and deepening significance. This explains the growth of his reputation. Though he cannot be placed exactly—and is so unlike a monumental author that most of his best things were only properly published long after his death—he has a looming if indistinct importance: he is a figure not steadily illuminated but either half-lost in the blur of two centuries or suddenly and brilliantly lit by some flash of genius.

Here are some examples of the way in which he seems to reach forward to us. Though educated by the Jesuits, he early turned deist, and then became a thorough materialist (a metaphysical one, not a materialist by temperament, for thought was his passion) and atheist. And much of his thought after that seems to anticipate the dialectical materialism afterwards elaborated by Marx and Engels. Indeed, though nobody could be less like the typical Communist intellectual than Diderot, so enthusiastic, impetuous, emotional, his varied criticism has in it a suggestion of the 'socialist realism' of Soviet critics. This is particularly true of his periodical art criticism, a form of journalism he may be said to have invented. It came into existence through his friend Grimm, a German who lived in Paris and long supported himself by sending a monthly letter, giving news of literature and the arts in Paris, to private subscribers, mostly German princes. To these cultural news- letters Diderot contributed criticisms of the picture exhibitions in the Salon. Their aesthetics are dubious and they are not the kind of art criticism much appreciated now, outside 'socialist realist' circles, but such was Diderot's enthusiasm, both in praise and blame, and so apt was he in communicating his pleasure at what he thought a fine picture (he greatly admired Greuze, and very frequently attacked Boucher and Fragonard), that his art criticisms when published became extremely popular, and, years later, even Carlyle refers to them, with a few German exceptions, as "the only Pictorial Criticisms worth reading". In the theatre his own two plays are of no importance; Diderot was no dramatist; but here as elsewhere he did some pioneer work in criticism and theory, and Lessing wrote that he owed his own change of taste, towards realism, to Diderot, whose two plays and Essay on Dramatic Poetry he translated. And the best eighteenth-century discussion of acting can be found in Diderot's *Le Paradoxe sur le Comédien*, in which he argues that an actor can best move his audience not, as was thought then, when he allows himself to be gripped by an emotion but when he keeps his head and simulates the emotion. He is excellent, too, on the danger of over-emphasis, the dramatic value of silence, the necessity of establishing through constant rehearsal a balance between players. His direct experiments in fiction were not successful; he tried to follow Richardson in his novel *The Nun*, and Sterne in *Jacques the Fatalist*, which Goethe admired and which contains at least one story, that of Madame de Pommeraye's revenge on her lover, that has offered a powerful plot to later authors. But his admiration for these two novelists, his understanding of new techniques and interests in fiction, combined as they were with his interest in and knowledge of many crafts and trades, acquired through writing articles about them for the *Encyclopédie*, make us feel that he is already pointing the way to the sharply realistic fiction a hundred years ahead. And indeed, in one of his innumerable occasional pieces, his most extraordinary production, he pointed much further still, to our own century.

This piece, a long dialogue but sometimes referred to as a novel, is *Rameau's Nephew*. . . . There had never been any doubt among good judges that in its own way *Rameau's Nephew* is Diderot's masterpiece. Its form suggests his limitations as an artist; if Voltaire had been visited by these thoughts he would have found some better form in which to display them, probably that of his philosophical stories. But the dialogue, in which he dramatises himself talking to this impudent scoundrel, the nephew of

Rameau, was probably more than a convenient literary form to Diderot. It helped him to discover, to face, to express, the shadow-side of his own mind. Not all the dialogue is on this profound level. Some of it merely attacks enemies of the *Encyclopédie* like Fréron and Palissot; and the first version of the dialogue was probably written just after the production in 1760 of Palissot's comedy satirising Diderot and his friends. Some of it is concerned with the intense rivalry between the French and Italian schools of music. There is indeed much of the dialogue devoted to topical subjects, and very amusing it is. But its originality, force and phosphorescent brilliance belong elsewhere. Rameau's nephew was a real person, and Diderot was later accused of making him appear a great deal worse than he actually was. This could never have been said by anybody with the slightest appreciation of the work. Rameau's nephew here, though no doubt sharing some traits and a style of life with the real person, is essentially Diderot's creation. The dialogue wherever it is most brilliant and original is between the Diderot known to his friends and the public, the man who risked a return to the Bastille and toiled for years at the *Encyclopédie*, who devoted his life to the Enlightenment, and the other Diderot nobody knew, the *alter ego*, the Shadow, whispering and chuckling like Mephistopheles in the dark. We are seeing the shining medal reversed. Something had happened to Diderot. It may have been the impact of his love for Sophie Voland, an exceptional woman with whom he could be completely frank—a significant fact that appals his most prudish biographer, John Morley—and whose combination of masculine and feminine qualities delighted him. Whatever crisis it was, out of it came this tremendous dialogue, in which all the brilliant wit, daring and originality are given to the confessions and brazen arguments of the parasite, the shameless preyer on a society that is in its turn both predatory and without shame; in which we seem to catch a glimpse of a sinister regress spiralling down to some eternal darkness of the spirit, infinitely removed from the bright surface of Diderot's rational optimism, altruism, alert social conscience, reasonable benevolence. It is a work that does not seem to belong to this age of reason, nor to the following age of romance already beginning to take shape, nor to the one following that. It appears to leap forward two centuries, to this very time of ours, when what was lying in the dark then has come blinking and grinning into the glare of our lights, when you may take up half a dozen novels, in the movement and much admired, and find as their central character, hardly different except for a change of costume and style of dialogue and a decline in wit, no other than Rameau's nephew.

Diderot, in whom all the minds of the Enlightenment seem to meet, to share something of his enthusiasm and natural warmth of heart, lived until the high summer of 1784. In the last conversation his daughter remembered, he said: "The first step towards philosophy is incredulity." A little later, at the dining-table, his wife asked him a question, and then, when she received no reply, she looked at him and saw that he was dead. It was probably the only question Diderot had left unanswered for the last fifty years. He had tried to answer all the questions, in his attractive, impetuous fashion; and yet, when he was getting old and putting an end to a series of notes on anatomy that he had been collecting for years, he could write: "What do I perceive? Forms. And what besides? Forms. Of the substance I know nothing. We walk among shadows, ourselves shadows to ourselves and to others." By this time, the age at an end, Pope's "order'd garden" where all was light could no longer be recognised; strange weeds covered it and among them flowers, scarlet or deathly white, began to bloom mysteriously; and above it the moon was rising, to create fantastic shadows, in which reason was lost to romance.

The Times Literary Supplement

SOURCE: "Manifesto of Rationalism: The Encyclopedists' Fight against Church and State," in *The Times Literary Supplement,* No. 3490, January 16, 1969, pp. 49-50.

[*In the following excerpt, the critic discusses the principal Encyclopedists, with particular emphasis on their role in creating a new and progressive intellectual climate in France*]

The *Encyclopédistes* were not a band of brothers. They included in their ranks almost all the famous names in eighteenth-century political, social and economic thought in France. Voltaire, D'Alembert, Rousseau, Turgot, Quesnay, D'Holbach, Helvétius and Condorcet were all contributors; even Buffon allowed his name to appear in the list. That they held together long enough to produce these volumes was due to the quite extraordinary pertinacity and courage of Diderot. D'Alembert was joint editor until his withdrawal in 1759. Diderot did most of the work throughout and remained on to fight the battle by himself. He managed not to quarrel with any of these remarkable men of letters except Rousseau, who differed from the other *philosophes* in being essentially an anti-rationalist and in not belonging, like the others, to the new intellectual middle class.

Diderot was the most characteristic of all the *philosophes*—a journalist and publicist who dabbled, more or less profoundly, in all the ideas and theories that were fashionable at the moment. The unifying factor was hatred of clerical authority. The Church was supported, fiercely but spasmodically, by the Court. It was a period in which a boy could be executed, after first being condemned to death by torture, for ridiculing the Virgin Mary, but it was not a steady or uniform tyranny. The Court, the Parlement and the Jesuits, as well as many literary toadies, were all at war with the *Encyclopédistes*. These authorities quarrelled among themselves and were therefore inefficient in suppressing Diderot. He was always harassed and once imprisoned and he could never be sure whether Mme, de Pompadour would effectively come to his rescue, if only to spite the Jesuits.

Happily Malesherbes was the censor of literature or, technically, magistrate in charge of regulating the book trade. He sympathized even if he did not agree with Diderot, and he always carried out any decree of suppression with reluctance. When the two first volumes of the *Encyclopédie* were denounced by royal prerogative in 1752, the publishers were for-bidden to print them and booksellers ordered to cease distribution, but there was no prohibition against continuing publication. No sustained effort was made to suppress the project as a whole, at least until 1759 when the letter "G" was reached and D'Alembert's article on "Geneva" had raised a storm of protest.

D'Alembert's lapse—for he was usually a cautious man—was on this occasion the result of the encouragement of Voltaire, with whom he had been staying in Ferney. Voltaire had been an enthusiast about the *Encyclopédie* from the beginning: he sometimes contributed to it and always criticized its many defects. He had written to D'Alembert, for instance, in May, 1757:

> I am sorry to see that the writer of the article, Hell, declares that Hell was a point in the doctrine of Moses; now by all the devils, this is not true. Why lie about it? Hell is an excellent thing, no doubt, but it is evident that Moses did not know it. It is this world that is hell.

On this occasion he appears to have persuaded D'Alembert to run risks in writing about Geneva. The good Protestant parsons there did not like being told that Calvin "was as enlightened a theologian as a heretic can be" and that many of them were Socinians. The Jesuits in France were even more angry at being told that they were badly educated and illiterate in comparison with Genevese Protestants. The most famous row that followed the Geneva article was with Rousseau, who rushed to the defence of his puritan native city when D'Alembert expressed regret that it did not permit theatrical performances within its walls. D'Alembert refused to face the storms he had provoked and announced his retirement from the joint enterprise. Voltaire at first protested against his withdrawal and then, apparently frightened that the Court, and not merely the Jesuits, was involved, reversed his position and lectured Diderot on the folly of continuing publication.

This incident will serve to illustrate the atmosphere in which the *Encyclopédie* was produced and the complex obstacles which Diderot had to surmount. He had set out

> to gather together the knowledge scattered over the face of the earth—that our descendants, being better instructed, may become at the same time more virtuous and more happy; and that we may not die without having deserved well of the human race.

Thus Diderot's project had a far larger compass than Bayle's *Dictionnaire* or Chambers's *Cyclopedia*. He wished to show above all how far science had advanced, and how foolish as well as wicked were clerical intolerance and state absolutism. He wanted the *Encyclopédie* to be not only polemical but also useful for everyday reference. He visited most of the workshops of Paris and, unlike his colleagues, who only talked about science and philosophy, he was interested in every new invention and in the practical application of scientific theory. The volumes of plates which he added to the text illustrated existing methods and new techniques in medicine, agriculture, and manufacture.

There is no balance or proportion in the *Encyclopédie*. There are long articles on little subjects and little articles on big subjects. Much depended on what engaged Diderot's attention at the moment. He could write a valuable article amounting in length to a pamphlet on the problem of composing an *Encyclopédie*, and outraged the rulers of France by an article on "Political Authority" in which he said that "it is not the State which belongs to the Prince, but the Prince who belongs to the State". This was bold and serious at a time when Louis XV was solemnly pronouncing the doctrine of Divine Right as applied to his own person. In this, as in the other political articles such as "Representation", the *Encyclopédie* did not strive after democratic theory, but always spoke of the rule of law and the limited rights of a monarch; in fact, the *Encyclopédie* favoured the British compromise not democracy.

After such serious articles Diderot could turn his mind to dealing with the proper way to pay cad-drivers to prevent them cheating: he could write a careful piece about "Needles":, and then wander off into an examination of the role of a very minor Roman deity or into a curiously learned discussion of "Theosophy".

In dealing with economic subjects the *Encyclopédie*'s main technique was to describe, often without comment, the fantastic injustices which survived from the feudal system. Nobody, after reading the *Encyclopédie*, could easily forget how heavily the Corvée system weighed upon the peasant, or fail to be angry when they read under the heading. "Chasse" how the peasants' crops were destroyed and the land kept barren for the convenience of the hunters. The damage to trade by ancient systems of taxation was clarified by articles on "Taille" and "Gabelle" and many injustices exposed in an article on "Privilege".

The chief target was the Church. A common method was to undermine superstition by expounding the universality of law and adding, where the Church might raise objections, that though it seemed as if law was universal, the revelation of Holy Scripture had shown on this occasion that an exception was made. Sometimes Diderot would add a pious flourish which could be quoted in reply to angry ecclesiastics. He had usually to be more circumspect than Voltaire, who wrote, when the Government closed a cemetery in which hysterical miracles were taking place:

> De par le Roi, défense à Dieu
> De faire miracles en ce lieu.

But on occasion Diderot could be almost as daring as Voltaire. In a short article on "Damnation" he argued that to condemn men to an eternity of torment seemed not in accord with the justice or benevolence of God, but the authority of Holy Scripture and the decisions of the Church had put the fact of hell beyond question. "What must be the enormity of our disobedience, seeing that the disobedience of the First Man could only be wiped out by the blood of the Son of God?"

Diderot's "Toleration" closely followed John Locke's argument, and the politics and psychology of the *Encyclopédie* also spring from his close knowledge of Locke's philosophy. One may summarize the doctrines of the *Encyclopédie* by saying that there is no such thing as Original Sin, that man, having no innate ideas, is reasonable and, with right instruction, will be happy and good. The immediate

job of the philosophers was to expose the superstitions which had been fastened on to the human race. Once that is achieved, there is no reason for arbitrary government, and the solution for happiness is constitutional government.

The British compromise was accepted in philosophy as well as in politics. The essential was that the world was governed according to the discoveries of Newton. Privately Diderot, like D'Holbach, might have been called an atheist, but publicly he was as much troubled as Voltaire about what would happen to mankind if people no longer believed in God. Like Voltaire, he was anxious not to be overheard throwing doubts on the Deity in the presence of the servants. If there were no God it would be necessary to invent him. It was wise to maintain a Creator or, as the Revolution was afterwards to say, a Supreme Being, even if he had ceased to interfere with his own creation and allowed it to proceed as an eternal mechanism. Indeed, until the idea of evolution had seized men's minds, the argument that a watch proved the existence of a watchmaker seemed unanswerable.

It was not, however, the materialism of D'Holbach's *Système de la nature* that finally got Diderot into trouble. Rather it was Helvétius's *De l'esprit* (1759), which enlarged the sensational philosophy of Locke into complete utilitarianism. People suddenly saw that something new and terrifying was being said. Men were only guided by desire for pleasure and escape from pain: morality was, in the last analysis, only self-interest, which is what Mme, du Deffand meant when she said that Helvétius had betrayed everyone's secret. The salons were prepared to discuss this idea and Bentham was to develop it into a working philosophy in Britian. In the pre-Revolutionary period the *Encyclopédie* was condemned as the vehicle of this most antisocial and dangerous opinion.

Some years earlier Palissot, one of the enemies of the *Encyclopédie*, suggested that it was becoming something like a church. "At the front of certain philosophic productions one may observe a tone of authority and assurance that, until now, only the pulpit has exercised." This comment was premature, but far-sighted. Something like a new religion was being built up. The road to perfectibility was being cleared by the *Encyclopéistes*, though it was not until the French Revolution itself that the utopia to which men believed they were moving through their acceptance of liberty, equality and fraternity was envisaged.

It was the youngest of the *Encyclopédistes*, Condorcet, who most clearly saw the whole picture which men needed if they were to have an inspiring religion without any transcendental doctrine. According to the Christian story, man had been originally happy, had fallen from grace, but had heaven to hope for. The *Encyclopédistes*, in discovering the Noble Savage, had found an alternative to the Garden of Eden and, in the new psychology of the Locke, had shown the possibility of progress through education and scientific knowledge. But they did not provide an alternative to the heaven of the scriptures. What they needed was a philosophy of history, so that the individual might feel that he had a part to play in creating a happier world. Turgot, who outlined history in a series of stages leading to a happier future, nearly achieved this and Diderot himself was inspired by the idea of working for posterity. "Posterity", he said, "is for the philosopher what the Other World is for the religious." Under the shadow of the guillotine. Condorcet wrote of a wonderful future for man when he is freed from the chains of ignorance and superstition. He believed in a world of truth virtue and happiness and argued that in its contemplation a philosopher might find consolation "for the errors, crimes, injustices which still soil the earth and of which he himself is often victim. It is in the contemplation of this picture . . . that he finds his true recompense for virtue". In this asylum for the imagination, "he can forget mankind, corrupted and tormented by agreed, fear, envy. It is in this asylum that he truly lives with his fellows in a heaven which his reason has created, and which his love of humanity embellishes with the purest joys".

This was the vision of progress in terms which would satisfy a few philosophers. For the mass of mankind in the next century it meant, whether they still believed in a heaven beyond the clouds or not, that here on this earth a better future awaited us. This liberal view was generally accepted in the nineteenth century and was not essentially changed by Marx, even though he interpreted the past as a struggle of classes and envisaged utopia only after revolution. The essential was the identification of the individual with the historical process; one could be in harmony with a world movement and look forward to a happier future, at any rate for one's children or one's children's children. Though Christianity remained the accepted faith of the nineteenth century, it was this belief in a republic of heaven upon earth which inspired most of the great men of the last century. If we moan today about our loss of faith, it is not, as men often assume, so much the loss of a belief in the Christian heaven above the skies from which we suffer; it is the loss of any confidence in the future of mankind on earth. This faith in progress held the field from the French Revolution at least until the First World War and, with many, until Hiroshima. It was only implicit in the *Encyclopédie*, but it is the fact that the *philosophes* gathered together the scientific knowledge of the age, broke with past superstitions and laid the foundations for belief in progress which gives them their great historical interest and importance.

Henry Vyverberg

SOURCE: An introduction to *Human Nature, Cultural Diversity and the French Enlightenment,* Oxford University Press, Inc., 1989, pp. 3-19.

[*Vyverberg is an American historian whose books include* Historical Pessimism in the French Enlightenment *(1958),* The Living Tradition: Art, Music, and Ideas in the Western World *(1978), and* Human Nature, Cultural Diversity, and the French Enlightenment. *Below, in his introduction to the last-named work, he examines the* Encyclopedia, *remarking that although "by itself the* Encyclopedia *destroyed neither the Old Regime nor all traditional ways of thinking, it did publicize the mood and goals of the French Enlightenment, thus supplementing the work of many individual authors of that day, some of whom were never contributors to the project."*]

The European age of Enlightenment has long been considered the seedbed of the contemporary western mind, and among all eighteenth-century European thinkers the French have usually been taken as prototypes. It is not my purpose, in the study that follows, to question either of these venerable if somewhat dubious assumptions. This work does recognize, however, the crucial importance of the French philosophes in the evolution of modern western thought, whether as models to be cherished or as demons to be exorcised. Such authors as Montesquieu, Voltaire, and Diderot have left indelible marks in the pattern of modern intellectual history.

One assumption that this study does make concerning the history of the human mind has become a subject of argument in recent decades—the assumption that the contribution of first-class minds is important in the human record. Probably only a handful of scholars today would categorically maintain the opposite—that first-class minds are wholly unimportant, and that it is only the mind of the masses that deserves commemoration. The new historians of mass culture have performed invaluable services, long overdue, in recording and analyzing the vast popular substructure of human thought and feeling; and indeed their labors have only begun. Few, however, among this new breed would deny any historical significance whatsoever to "elitist" thought. The aspirations and utterances of the masses have long cried out for their own historians, but much still remains to be done with the more high-powered thinkers. The present study is based on the premise that much can still be learned from the ideas of first- and second- and third-rate published authors, and that such analyses contribute truly significantly to an understanding of the mind and the world-view of any historical period, from top to bottom.

Here the primary focus will be the philosophes of the French eighteenth century—those authors who, if not necessarily top-ranking philosophers or theorists, at least contributed most visibly to the liberal, antiauthoritarian movement in early modern thought that is known as the Enlightenment. For support or contrast there will also be occasional references to antiphilosophes and to non-French writers of the eighteenth century. The rough chronological limits, with a few obvious exceptions, will be 1748 and 1778, the dates respectively of the appearance of Montesquieu's *Spirit of Laws* and the death of Voltaire; the dates also are very close to those of the gestation and completion of the great *Encyclopedia* of Denis Diderot. Sociological and phychological observation and analysis of mass currents in the history of these three decades are cheerfully left to other chroniclers and scholars: this study is an unabashed analysis of published texts, by an unregenerate historian of ideas.

The purpose of this work is to examine, as open-mindedly as possible, several ideas that have long been considered central tenets of French Enlightenment thought. The first is the eighteenth-century concept of the uniformity of human nature. In this area the substance of modern charges has commonly been that the Enlightenment, or more specifically the French philosophes, possessed a fixed view of this uniformity, which blocked all, or virtually all, appreciation of cultural and historical diversity around the globe. The reader should realize at the outset that my investigation of these charges has been not exhaustive, but preliminary; that my intention has been not combative, but inquiring; and that the outcome of the search will be not dogmatic but, I hope, at least illuminating.

The reigning scholarly perception of Enlightenment views on human nature has involved an assertion not only of its uniformity but of a degree of abstraction that allegedly made the Enlightenment blind to empirical reality. I have attempted to bring somewhat more subtlety to this perception. This study will ask, for example, how eighteenth-century views of human nature were developed, and how fixed they were. Further, it will inquire into the possibility that theoretical views were sometimes modified by empirical observation, both of past ages and of foreign peoples in the contemporary world.

The raising of questions concerning human nature, incidentally, did not end with the eighteenth century. On the ingredients and the origins of human nature the discussion has in fact been especially lively in very recent years among sociologists, anthropologists, and psychologists. My study certainly does not pretend to find direct eighteenth-century predecessors of recent speculations: dissimilarities between the centuries are too obvious, and intensive social and biological investigation has intervened to bring much greater understanding to modern scholars than the philosophes ever could attain. For one thing, present knowledge of the vital role and specific mechanisms of heredity, though certainly incomplete and possibly mistaken, has infinitely surpassed eighteenth-century speculation, which indeed rarely involved heredity at all. The critical Enlightenment divergence of opinion, however, over the relative roles of "climate"—or physical environment in general—and "moral" factors such as education and legislation is still echoed in recent debate.

The French Enlightenment understanding, or misunderstanding, of human nature is, I believe, of genuine importance in the historical picture of the age: it throws light, first of all, on both of those concepts that were even more central to the philosophes' world-view—"nature" and "reason." The Enlightenment view of human nature, as modified if not basically shaken by a realization of the diversity of human individuals and groups, also illuminates the debate concerning the abstractness or the empirical realism of the philosophes. Most interesting of all is the relevance of Enlightened perceptions of human nature and diversity to the presumed total absorption of that age in its own standards and to its alleged inability to understand, or even want to understand, other peoples and other historical periods.

These presumptions rank high among commonly received notions about the French Enlightenment, such as its cold rationalism, its lack of originality, its tendency toward oversimplification, and its natural, inevitable culmination in the idea of progress. All these notions have been challenged by modern scholarship, with varying degrees of success. This work attempts, in its middle and final chapters, to reappraise the perception of cultural and historical insularity in the French Enlightenment. This insularity was certainly very often evident, for reasons that will be advanced at the end of this study. But did the insularity have its limits and exceptions? I suggest that it did, and that the limits and exceptions are explicable by certain other assumptions and beliefs of the age.

At the risk of sometimes straying a bit from concepts of human nature, but still in pursuit of ideas of cultural diversity, this survey attempts to summarize several specific Enlightenment views of varying peoples of the world outside western Europe. Of necessity in any cursory study this summary must be selective and suggestive rather than exhaustive and final. I have not investigated French Enlightenment views of all peoples and have not treated even my chosen samples in full detail. Certain trends, however, do become evident as we discover how the eighteenth century viewed, for example, Jews, blacks, native Americans, Asian Indians, and Chinese. Evidence of ideas of cultural diversity will be tentatively weighed against evidence of resistance to such ideas.

Finally, my investigation arrives at Enlightenment views of history, and to that historical diversity the Enlightenment has often been accused of totally failing to acknowledge. Enlightenment receptivity to historical diversities certainly was, at least, limited—but was it totally absent? Not only is some of the evidence examined in the final chapters, but the question is raised of whether any serious attempts may have been made to understand and enter the spirit of past ages, and not simply to transplant Enlightenment preoccupations and standards to historically different periods. Here again the sampling is limited—restricted, in fact, to French Enlightenment views of ancient Greece and of the Middle Ages. These were representative historical ages on which nearly all writers of the time expressed opinions, usually firm ones, over the years.

Such, then, are the major issues and a few of the pertinent questions asked in this study. Findings will prove to be mildly revisionist rather than radically revolutionary. They also, I repeat, will be tentative, since limitations are inherent both in the material studied and in the author himself. Ideally, perhaps, the material should cover every word published in the French Enlightenment, and especially every word in the massive *Encyclopedia*. What follows is the fruit, first of all, of having studied carefully the bulk of the *Encyclopedia*, and of having scanned the remainder. For the even more massive accumulation of French Enlightenment publication in general, the problem has been even more daunting. Nor, of course, can this author claim expertise, on all subjects treated in the *Encyclopedia* and by its French contemporaries.

I should also refer to the omission here of any computerized word, phrase, or subject counts—an omission that may be deplored by some readers. I can only say that I felt such methodology close to pointless in the intellectual history of an age that was so notoriously imprecise in its terminology and that dealt so cavalierly in abstractions. Tables and graphs, similarly, might have given this study a certain cachet, but I believe their utility would have been largely spurious. All in all, while recognizing the immense value elsewhere in recent scholarship of many newer historical techniques, I believe that the material of the present study is better served by the application of more standard procedures, and by the discretionary latitude of traditional scholarship.

The reader of this study deserves not only this short apologia on goals and on methodology, but also a summary of the source materials to which the methodology, has been applied. Such a summary may also serve to supply a framework of historical facts to the nonspecialist, and to give some notion of the conclusions of past scholarship on the significance of each principal source, as relevant to the subject of this study. In brief, the questions now to be addressed are these: what have been the sources used in this study, and what have other scholars seen as their relevance to the specific subjects to be examined here?

This research project was at first conceived as a study of Diderot's great *Encyclopedia* alone, and this monumental work has remained one of its prominent concerns. Soon, however, it became evident that understanding of the *Encyclopedia*'s position on human nature and cultural diversity, and on national and historical individuality, would be greatly enhanced by placing that work in its contemporary context. Other writings by such contributors as Diderot and d'Holbach would throw a more evenly distributed light on those authors, and might lead to a better understanding of the *Encyclopedia*'s position relative to that of the whole Enlightenment movement. So too, obviously, would the introduction of some of those French Enlightenment authors who either contributed rather insignificantly or not at all to Diderot's ambitious enterprise. As more and more outside writing was investigated, the *Encyclopedia* slipped farther from being the study's only focus. The inevitable comparisons that remain between the *Encyclopedia* and its Enlightenment setting have come to parallel, with only somewhat greater emphasis, comparisons among individual authors in the entire French Enlightenment panorama.

The emphasis still accorded here to the *Encyclopedia* is, however, amply justified by the prominence and symbolic status of that great enterprise in the mid-century French Enlightenment. Let us briefly recall its history and significance.

The *Encyclopedia* project had been conceived in 1745, first simply as a translation of Chambers' *Cyclopaedia*. By the next year Diderot and d'Alembert were already involved, and in 1747 Diderot became the director of the work and d'Alembert his associate, also supervising its scientific and mathematical portions. The project by then had advanced well beyond the confines of mere translation, and in 1750 Diderot published the *Prospectus* for an expanded, truly new publication. The first volume of the *Encyclopedia, or Reasoned Dictionary of the Sciences, Arts and Crafts, by a Society of Men of Letters* was published in 1751. Largely because of conservative clerical influence on the government, publication came to a halt in 1759, after seven volumes had appeared. D'Alembert resigned his position but Diderot continued for many discouraging years the collecting and editing of further material. In 1765, with tacit

consent of the authorities, the final ten volumes of text were published, together with five volumes of handsome plates. Other volumes of plates would follow, and Diderot's involvement did not wholly end until 1772. Five *Supplement* volumes under other direction would appear in 1776 and 1777, and a two-volume *Index* in 1780. By that time the original Paris edition in thirty-five volumes (some under a misleading Swiss imprint) was already being reprinted and pirated in several European cities.

Some four thousand copies of the Paris edition were issued, but it has been estimated that by the outbreak of the French Revolution perhaps twenty thousand sets of various editions were available in Europe, of which something like fifteen thousand could be found in France. All told, several times that number of readers surely had access to the work—a very sizable segment of the literate and well-to-do population. The primary audience for the *Encyclopedia*, like most of its contributors, was middle-class, although in both categories there was substantial representation of the clergy (both Catholic and Protestant) and even some members of the aristocracy.

Certainly the impressive *Encyclopedia* set was occasionally bought just for show, or consulted simply as a reference work. Given, however, the bitter and very public controversy surrounding its first decade, with conservative clerics leading the attack and liberals presenting heated rebuttals, most subscribers and readers must have been well aware of the project's reputation as a liberal organ—and other less well-informed users must have eventually discovered this nontraditional flavor on their own. A significant number of readers surely perused d'Alembert's celebrated *Preliminary Discourse* and must have taken it, as we do today, as an important manifesto of the rational and empirical, the scientific and at least implicitly progressive spirit of the Enlightenment.

Unquestionably there were parts of the *Encyclopedia* that were essentially propaganda for the ideals of the French Enlightenment; in this sense the work was indeed the "war machine" that some historians and polemicists have found to be its preeminent function. It did in fact sometimes slyly ridicule organized religion; it did suggest or broadly hint at political, economic, and social reform; it did unabashedly lobby for science and technological progress. Certain contributors were, however, quite traditionalist, and others (more than most casual students realize) were able to ignore controversial topics and implications completely. Nearly all critics have agreed that the *Encyclopedia* avoided extremes, especially in religion and politics: neither atheism nor democracy was a characteristic doctrine in its pages—or, for that matter, in the French Enlightenment as a whole. One function of the present study will be to compare the *Encyclopedia* on specific points with its age: where were the greater radicalism and the greater originality to be found—or is the comparison meaningless? Would the *Encyclopedia* always lag well behind the insights of the most fertile minds of its day—and what, if anything, happened to that fertility when insightful writers themselves turned from their personal publications to Diderot's project? Was any consistency of orientation or polemics maintained in the Encyclopedic enterprise, aside from the utilitarian urge toward the improvement of self and society? Was anticlericalism, or negative Biblical criticism, or the professed goal of religious tolerance always evident in the *Encyclopedia*? Above all, for purposes of this study, was the work ever objective and detached, and could it ever see or empathize with cultures outside its own experience and preconceptions? Such are some of the questions to which this work must turn more than once.

Despite the moderate tone of much of the *Encyclopedia*, and despite many omissions, inconsistencies, and other flaws in the completed work, the influence of the undertaking was undoubtedly extensive. Production of the work did bring together many of the best minds, and best stocked minds, of its time—among others, Montesquieu, Voltaire, Rousseau, and d'Holbach, in addition to Diderot and d'Alembert—and in most respects, even with Rousseau's eventual estrangement, the project gave them some sense of common effort and achievement. The published *Encyclopedia* made few new contributions to knowledge, but it did help organize and make evident the interconnections amid a growing and already immense variety of information, theoretical and factual. Although by itself the *Encyclopedia* destroyed neither the Old Regime nor all traditional ways of thinking, it did publicize the mood and goals of the French Enlightenment, thus supplementing the work of many individual authors of that day, some of whom were never contributors to the project.

Let us turn first to a sampling of the most important writers for the *Encyclopedia*, and to the significance that modern scholarship commonly accords their articles. Later I will summarize the accepted role of several of these same authors outside the *Encyclopedia*, and finally will comment briefly on significant contemporaries who contributed not at all to Diderot's enterprise. This introductory choice of writers is based not on any dubious ranking according to their overall importance, but simply on their relative prominence in this study. With this background information, the reader may better appraise the data that will appear later in this book.

Little need be said of Jean Lerond d'Alembert (1717-1783), Diderot's associate for many years in the editing process. His specialty was mathematics, an area in which his competence has been commonly recognized. His *Preliminary Discourse* for the *Encyclopedia*, as noted above, is accepted as a prime embodiment of the values, ideals, and program of the French Enlightenment, not as an original contribution to knowledge, nor even as a wholly reliable summation of the western tradition in intellectual history.

As for Denis Diderot (1713-1784), nobody has disputed his dogged editorial dedication and courage across the years. Much has been written on his degree of responsibility for various *Encyclopedia* articles. Except for his constant, enthusiastic promotion of utilitarian technologies, his special contributions have not, actually, received much attention. The usual assumption has seemed to be that Diderot's role as editor was invaluable, but that his own production of articles was characterized by hasty compilation, not personal insight.

The extensive offerings of Paul-Henri Thiry, baron d'Holbach (1723-1789) to the *Encyclopedia* have been widely noted, but again there has been almost no credit given him for any originality. D'Holbach is generally viewed as a publicist for science and technology and a crude denigrator of Christianity; as an Encyclopedist he appears in modern histories mainly as a work-horse, like such lesser-known authors as the abbé Claude Yvon (1714-1791) and Antoine-Gaspard Boucher d'Argis (1708-ca. 1791). For his many articles on music, Jean-Jacques Rousseau (1712-1778) also has been commonly placed among the workhorses; his celebrated article *Political Economy* is a rare exception to this categorization. The contribution of Charles de Secondat, baron de Montesquieu (1689-1755) came at the end of his life and is not usually considered original or important.

The forty-odd articles by the patriarch among philosophes, François-Marie Arouet de Voltaire (1694-1778), have been hardet to dismiss, if only because of his great prestige in his own day and his extraordinarily potent symbolism in the modern perception of the Enlightenment. His *Encyclopedia* articles have not been much esteemed, but they did receive scholarly attention just before the Second World War. Voltaire's articles were mainly in the fields of literature, language, and history; on these articles Raymond Naves concluded, first of all, that the sources were rather insubstantial, but that the main interest of the essays lay not in their scholarship but in Voltaire's own views. The articles, Naves continued, were not offhand crumbs thrown to the editors, but fairly serious studies, offered to an Encyclopedic cause for which Voltaire's admiration was genuine. The articles on literary theory were of course conditioned by Voltaire's classicism, but were capable of subtlety. Those on philosophy and history were often passionately polemical; they served such favored Voltairean causes as "pragmatic fatalism, psychological sensualism, historical pyrrhonism, rationalist deism, and scorn for the common people." Throughout, Voltaire was more concerned with the broad education of the mind than with the accumulation of mere facts.

Finally there are the voluminous contributions to the *Encyclopedia* by Louis, chevalier de Jaucourt (1704-1780), who in fact is scarcely remembered in any other context than in Diderot's great publication. Amazingly, de Jaucourt wrote over a quarter of the articles appearing in the original seventeen volumes of text, and nearly a quarter of the total text. The usual low opinion of these articles' quality has followed the estimate of the baron Grimm; this estimate, to be sure, specifically covers only the last ten volumes, prepared undercover and in relative haste. Wrote Grimm: "A great number of articles of all kinds, including the most essential, were abandoned to M. le chevalier de Jaucourt, a man of great zeal and an indefatigable worker, but a pitiless compiler who has simply put to use the best known and often the most mediocre books."

Recent attempts to rehabilitate the chevalier have stressed his zeal in the philosophic cause and have rather less enthusiastically sought to refurbish his scholarly credentials. De Jaucourt, as it now seems clear, did work rapidly and with far less meticulous concern for avoiding plagiarism than is customary today among reputable scholars. He was more than a compiler, though—at least in the sense that he frequently transformed neutral sources rather cleverly into philosophic propaganda. An aristocratic French Protestant background, and later, a very liberal, almost deistic religious faith would appear to have contributed heavily to his philosophic orientation toward reform. The subjects on which he wrote for Diderot covered an immense variety of fields, but his greatest enthusiasms were medicine (he himself had earned a doctorate in medicine but never practiced), all natural sciences, philosophy (he had written extensively on Leibniz), religious history, ethics, and ancient history. He tried to use reliable sources, although these were largely secondary, not primary. In summary, de Jaucourt has been seen as representing vigorously, if not profoundly, the humanitarian and moderate side of the Enlightenment.

Such, in brief, are the prevailing views held by historians on the contributions of several prolific writers for the *Encyclopedia*. We may now turn to the qualities and characteristics of some of the same thinkers when they were writing outside that work, as they have been seen by latter-day historians. The first three philosophes—Voltaire, Diderot, and d'Holbach—were also well enough represented in the *Encyclopedia* to afford a real basis for comparing their approaches in the two sorts of publication: independent works and *Encyclopedia* articles. The last four philosophes—Montesquieu, Rousseau, Turgot, and Grimm—are too slightly represented by important *Encyclopedia* contributions to be categorized as true Encyclopedists, or to make comparisons with outside publication meaningful.

Voltaire's position in the Enlightenment has always been regarded as central, although he has almost always been thought more a propagandist than an original thinker. Beyond this perception, modern critics have disagreed widely on his qualities and achievements. In religion, for example, most commentators have taken his proclamations of deism ("theism" was the term he most commonly used) at face value; others have found him to be either an agnostic or a crypto-atheist. Traditional historians have generally proclaimed him a genial apostle of tolerance; others have stressed his occasional or even characteristic dogmatism and have deplored his persistent anti-Semitism. Some have labeled him a partisan of enlightened despotism; others have emphasized his constitutionalism, republicanism, or even (on rare occasions) democratic sympathies. Most have highlighted his rationalism, others his empiricism, his capacity for passionate feeling, or even his "mysticism."

There has also been disagreement on Voltairean approaches to subjects more directly pertinent to the present study, although usually it has been less jarring than the disagreement on those very broad issues just mentioned. Nearly all historians and critics have pronounced Voltaire a staunch supporter of a uniform "nature" and "natural law" (both ill-defined, to be sure) and of a uniform human nature. Most have been willing to admit his acknowledgement of considerable variety in human customs, specific moral directives, and personal and "national" characteris-

tics—but the great majority have found any Voltairean acceptance of cultural diversity to be superficial, and definitely not as deeply felt as his unwavering basic belief in uniformity. It is, in fact, Voltaire's writing that is most often cited as the epitome, not only of self-righteous Enlightenment certitude in general, but also of eighteenth-century Europocentrism and an almost total inability to understand, or even to seek honestly to understand, cultures departing from the reigning values of Enlightenment France. Voltaire's guilt on these charges has been accepted almost universally; mild argument has seemed possible only on the degree of guilt.

The case of Diderot has ordinarily seemed more complex, just as his own character has usually been considered more multifaceted than Voltaire's. Scholarly differences over Diderot's religion and politics have, for example, sometimes paralleled those over Voltaire's—but Diderot's views are usually seen as evolving in a more complicated way. Elements of rationalism, empiricism, and sentiment have appeared to coexist, or to make war, in Diderot more than in Voltaire; certainly Diderot has seemed much less the "typical" cold Enlightenment rationalist than has Voltaire. Because of the rich complexity that most literate moderns have fancied to find within themselves, Diderot has commonly emerged in our day as a far more real and sympathetic presence than Voltaire, and at least for the moment, Diderot's reputation is on the upswing, while Voltaire's has tended to erode. Much of Diderot's growing stature, to be sure, has derived from his remarkably original posthumous works, known in his own day only in the narrowest circles—his "transformist," quasi-evolutionist speculations, for example, or the daring psychological insights of his novel *The Nun*, or the stunning experimentalism in literary form in *Jacques the Fatalist*.

Despite all the modern analysis of his novels, despite all the discussion of Diderot as scientific or political theorist, and despite the many studies of his materialism and religious opinions, there has not been much specific discussion of his historical and sociological insights. Remarks on his general cosmopolitanism and humanitarian tolerance commonly have not been linked to any real investigation of his position on the differentiation of peoples or cultures. Perhaps this is only to say that Diderot was seldom a historian and only occasionally a sociologist. His curiosity, however, was undoubtedly wide-ranging, and his speculation adventurous; in the words of one of his biographers, "his mind was always open to alternate possibilities." Inevitably, therefore, in his writings he strewed many tidbits of speculation on the global and historical human adventure. Perhaps in this respect the present study can help fill a gap in Diderot scholarship.

The third writer well represented both by individual publications and *Encyclopedia* articles was the baron d'Holbach. Actually, the independent works whose authorship he openly acknowledged were limited to translations of German scientific works; he is, however, known today primarily for his voluminous unsigned or pseudonymous works that vigorously expounded a materialistic, atheistic philosophy. By his contemporaries he was known as the host, for about thirty-five years, of the famous (and later over-dramatized) "Holbachian Circle." Only the hard core of this group knew that the kindly baron had mounted an extensive and violent attack on contemporary religious systems.

The members of d'Holbach's circle included Diderot, Grimm, Condillac, Raynal, and (for only a brief period) Rousseau. Rousseau would eventually inaccurately denounce the whole group as atheists; probably most members can better be described as skeptics. Among the most regular attendants at the baron's dinners and discussions was Diderot—and many instances of the influence of one man upon the other have been unearthed by modern scholarship. (It now seems unlikely, however, that Diderot contributed many actual words to d'Holbach's crucial *System of Nature*, as has often been alleged.) Both writers were atheistic materialists in pursuit of a new nonreligious basis for morality, and both looked toward empirical scienctific observation to unlock human potentialities. Both also examined the nature of social and political organization and recommended reforms; both were humanitarian and meliorist by nature. It was d'Holbach who particularly stressed the universal roles of matter and motion, and who devised elaborate schemes of educational and legislative action as the foundations, together with experimental science, for a "universal morality." D'Hobach was a far more systematic thinker than Diderot, but also rather more plodding and certainly less original than his friend.

Above all, d'Holbach has been remembered, like Voltaire, as a scourge of the Christian establishment, on grounds both of Biblical criticism and scorn for the allegedly repressive, unnatural side of the Christian moral code. For d'Holbach, "nature" was the preeminent rallying cry—a nature that was characterized by a uniform natural law throughout the universe, and that had no need for a Voltairean deist god as creator or regulator. The world, d'Holbach declared, was one, and it operated on purely naturalistic principles, in a deterministic mode. Under this system it has generally been assumed that d'Holbach must have believed in an absolutely uniform human nature, everywhere the same, with happiness and virtue as its universal objects. The historians have usually concluded that, all in all, the baron meant well, but that his world-view was much too mechanical and simplistic. Attempts to refurbish his independence of thought and to grant him some real subtlety have not received much general recognition.

I can be more brief with several Enlightenment figures who will be cited frequently in this study but whose connections with the Encylopedic enterprise were tenuous. Montesquieu is one of the two in this category who were in fact at the very heart of the French Enlightenment, even though Montesquieu himself was notable for unusual caution and moderation. His main publications are well known, at least by reputation (for he is one of the least read of the philosophes), to those even most casually acquainted with the Enlightenment: the slightly titillating, definitely scandalous *Persian Letters* (1721); the vaguely scholarly but more obviously philosophical *Considerations on the Causes of the Grandeur and Decadence of the Romans* (1734); and finally the ponderous, heavily but unevenly researched *Spirit of Laws* (1748). The latter work, in addition to an early essay or so, is the main source of our knowledge of Montesquieu's views on cultural and historical diversity. These writings have often been cited for his notions of "climatic" and "moral" determinants of individual and "national" differences; the debate continues, though, on the extent of Montesquieu's objectivity, analytic skill, and adherence to empirical fact.

On the great maverick of the French Enlightenment, Jean-Jacques Rousseau, problems of summarization and analysis are immense, from the seminal *Discourses* of mid-century, through the *Social Contract* and *Emile*, to the *Confessions* and *Reveries* of his later haunted years. The great subjects of debate concerning Rousseau have included his personality and his "romanticism"; the nature and degree of his consistency or unity of thought; the meaning of his political theory; and of course the thinker's influence in subsequent centuries. Some aspects of his thought on the nature of man and on social groups will be relevant to this book, but his historical interests were slight compared with those of Voltaire or Montesquieu.

Two other writers may be summarily noted here—Turgot and Grimm; they, too, were associated only briefly with the *Encyclopedia*, but neither one was as significant in the Enlightenment record as was Montesquieu or Rousseau. Anne-Robert-Jacques Turgot (1727-1781) enters the confines of our study long before his brief moment of glory as an economic reformer under the young Louis XVI: our concern must be with the young scholar dreaming of a comprehensive, hopeful pattern to be found in human history. In these early studies, Turgot would not only contribute to the idea of progress but would show more historical empathy than was common in his day toward the spirit and achievement of medieval culture.

Friedrich-Melchior Grimm (1723-1807), a very French author of German origin, is remembered today for two sets of facts—his connection with the rather hysterical private life of Rousseau, and his primary authorship and editorial supervision of a famous literary newsletter sent for decades, in manuscript from, to some of the more liberal or broad-minded princes of central Europe. The *Literary Correspondence* was a worthy effort to disseminate the values of the Enlightenment—but it has occurred to almost nobody to grant any personal distinction or originality to the thought of Grimm himself. That he was hardly a complete nonentity might be deduced, however, from the high esteem in which both Diderot and d'Holbach held him for many years. Grimm was a philosophical skeptic and something of a pessimist about human nature.

Encyclopedists, together with their friends and sometime collaborators, determine the major focus of this study, but are not its sole concerns. Since the spotlight here does often seek out others in the French Enlightenment period, a bit of background information is advisable at least for those who will be cited rather frequently.

Many, but by no means all, of these writers were not party to the Enlightenment, and in fact, among the many, some considered themselves its dedicated enemies. In this group would have been Father Lafitau (Joseph-François Lafitau,

1681-1746), if the philosophic movement had crystallized sufficiently by 1724, when he produced the influential *Customs and Morals of the American Savages*. For him, the orthodox implications of Christian brotherhood and human unity under God would be sorely tried by the evidence of his own and his fellow-missionaries' senses. No such dogmatic preoccupations, however, seem to have troubled another observer of exotic lands, Pierre Poivre (1719-1786), who remained unaligned with either the Christian apologists or the philosophes as he described, rather sourly, the peoples of the Pacific and Indian Ocean regions.

Much farther from the Enlightenment, though more deeply influenced by it than they would have admitted, were the editors of two great conservative literary journals of the middle and later eighteenth century, Father Berthier (Guillaume-François Berthier, 1704-1782) and Elie-Catherine Fréron (1718-1776). However, Berthier's usual moderation as editor (1745-1762) of the Jesuit *Journal of Trévoux* won him a wide spectrum of readers throughout France and Europe; the journal was consulted even by Voltaire. Berthier insisted, not surprisingly, on a position of no doctrinal compromise; he was therefore distressed by those "climate" theories of religious development that cast doubt on the unique truth of Christianity. A dedicated enemy of the Encyclopedia and of Diderot's materialism, he nevertheless was able to defend the new science and technology and its use of reason and empirical observation. Fréron's approach was similar in the *Literary Year* (*Année littéraire*), which he edited from 1754 until his death. Like Berthier's journal, the *Literary Year* enjoyed a wide middle- and upper-class circulation and had a reputation for defending the Christian faith. Fréron considered himself a true, "practical" philosophe and a defender of modern progress.

Not Encyclopedists, but closer than Berthier or Fréron to the philosophes, were Charles Duclos (1704-1772) and Charles-Louis Leclerc, comte de Buffon (1707-1788). Duclos was a novelist, historian, and moralist, famous especially for his *Considerations on the Customs and Morals of This Century*; his contemporaries commonly thought of him as a philosophe. He seems to have been an agnostic, indifferent toward religion. Buffon was an immensely celebrated and much admired literary stylist and a generalist in science, remembered today primarily as a zoologist. His great *Natural History* (1749-1788) embodied some idea of the unity of nature and most characteristically stressed the unity of the human species.

Finally there are four well-known and full-fledged non-Encyclopedic representatives of the Enlightenment who are cited on occasion in this study. Claude-Adrien Helvétius (1715-1771) was a sensationalist psychologist known for a rather mechanistic view of the human animal. Also so known was Etienne Bonnot, abbé de Condillac (1714-1780); like Helvétius he was also something of a moralist. Reflecting the generalist aspirations common in the French Enlightenment, Condillac dabbled in historical writing, and not unintelligently. His elder brother Gabriel Bonnot, abbé de Mably (1709-1785) was a more original writer; his best-remembered works are on the subjects of

government and political life, and of ethics, economics, and social organization. The celebrated life-work—the *History of the Two Indies*—of Guillaume-Thomas-François Raynal (1713-1796) appeared mainly in a later period than that emphasized in this study; Diderot was among many contributors to the ever-expanding project. In these pages Raynal will be cited mainly as author of a predecessor of Grimm's *Literary Correspondence*—the *Literary News* of 1747 to 1755.

Still other writers of the period in France are cited or referred to in this study, but with Raynal the cast of leading characters is complete. We are now in a position to proceed with our investigation of human nature and cultural diversity as reflected in the *Encyclopedia* and the writing of its French contemporaries. This investigation will confirm much that has already been suspected by historians—but it will also imply several revaluations of individual writers, and it will suggest a number of new questions and answers concerning that crucial phase of modern history, the French Enlightenment.

Daniel Brewer

SOURCE: "Ordering Knowledge," in *A New History of French Literature*, edited by Dennis Holler, Cambridge, Mass.: Harvard University Press, 1989, pp. 447-55.

[*In the excerpt below, Brewer comments on the Encyclopedists' attempt to systematize knowledge, focusing the organic connection between knowledge and power and observing that the "encyclopedists' text makes clear that the discourse of reason can oppose power only by being more powerful than what it sets itself against.*"]

As conceived in 1745 by a group of enterprising Parisian publishers, the *Encyclopédie* began as a business venture limited to bringing out a French encyclopedia modeled on Ephraim Chambers' two-volume *Cyclopaedia* (1728). But by the time the first volume of articles appeared, in 1751, the project, under the editorship of Denis Diderot and the mathematician Jean Le Rond d'Alembert, had already outstripped all original plans. When completed a quarter-century later, in 1772, this monumental work comprised seventeen folio volumes containing 71,818 articles and eleven folio volumes of 2,885 plates. Judged in terms of its innovative conception, the financial and technical means marshaled, the size of its readership (some 4,500 subscribers), and the number of its eventual collaborators (over 150 identified), the *Encyclopédie* stands as one of the greatest projects in the history of French culture and capitalism. Testifying to the Enlightenment belief in the progressive and beneficial results of rational inquiry into all sectors of human activity, the *Encyclopédie* helped crystallize the Enlightenment as an intellectual and reformist movement. Providing great impetus to the technological development of French industry, the *Encyclopédie* contributed as much to the change of ideas during the last decades of the ancien régime as to the exchange of capital. Five subsequent editions, either reprints or revisions, were printed in Switzerland and Italy before 1789; roughly half of these 25,000 copies went to readers in France.

In many respects this massive text of some 20 million

words resembles the Tower of Babel that Voltaire called it. Author of only one rather conservative, elitist article, "Gens de lettres" ("Persons of Letters"), Voltaire perhaps sensed that the *Encyclopédie* project radically expanded the definition of the intellectual and thereby promoted areas of investigation and activity with which the philosophe, for personal as well as political reasons, had little affinity. New orders of knowledge take shape in the *Encyclopédie* through the reordering of old ones, whether they involve philosophical and religious questions, economic and political theory, or scientific and technological knowledge. Yet this work was not the product of a revolutionary Third Estate or a homogeneous bourgeois class. In terms of social origins and financial means, the encyclopedists constituted a fairly heterogeneous group. Most were firmly integrated in a feudal and monarchical sociopolitical system. At the same time they were sufficiently independent from it, economically and intellectually, to imagine and promote other orders of knowledge, whether philosophical, sociopolitical, economic, or scientific.

For Diderot, the *Encyclopédie*'s goal was to encourage its readers to think freely, which for him meant resisting any authority, whether divine or human. In the area of religion the encyclopedists tirelessly denounce fanaticism in the name of religious tolerance; attack Christian doctrine, the Catholic church, and its institutions; and present other beliefs favorably. At times this assault on organized religion relies on an artful use of critical irony rivaling Voltaire's. An article presenting a harmlessly orthodox statement of Christian dogma, for instance, may end with cross-references to a virulently atheistic denunciation of theology from the pen of Baron Paul Henri Thiry d'Holbach, and to a deistic apology for religious tolerance. Forcing the reader to rethink accepted ideas, the duplicitousness and irony that infiltrate the system of cross-references are emblematic of the way in which the *Encyclopédie* incites its reader to engage in interpretation and to understand it as a conflictual process. Articles on philosophy extend the conflict, presenting the argument for a deterministic materialism that Diderot relies on to treat the question of ethics. In his additions to articles on the soul and in others written entirely by himself, such as "Nature," "Périr" ("Perish"), "Volonté" ("Free Will"), "Délicieux" ("Delightfull"), "Jouissance" ("Pleasure"), and "Chasteté" ("Chastity"), Diderot rehabilitates the passions, according the body a determinate, even autocratic, role in shaping human conduct. Yet although his individual ethics are resolutely amoral, his social ethics rest on the supreme value of virtue, which he presents as the highest form of sociability. The individual may not be free to act, but the conduct of the individual can be freely modified socially and politically. In the area of political theory, Diderot's ethics correspond to a contractual absolutism typical of 18th-century liberal thinkers. In his major entries on political authority and natural law ("Autorité politique" and "Droit naturel"), he argues that individuals assign authority to a sovereign body, not to an individual person, and in return the sovereign's function is to ensure the free play of natural laws, based above all on the notion of private property, which it is the sovereign's principal duty to protect. Reflecting the growing dissatisfaction with absolutism, as well as the parlements' struggle during the 1750s

and 1760s to win greater autonomy and power from the crown, the political theory of contractual monarchism expressed in the *Encyclopédie*, though by no means insurrectionalist, represents the political corollary of the encyclopedists' economic liberalism. Thus Louis de Jaucourt's critique of despotism in the name of natural political laws meshes with Anne-Robert-Jacques Turgot's defense of laissez-faire capitalism in the name of equally natural economic laws. Contributors of articles on economy, notably François Quesnay, call for specific reforms in accordance with such laws, including limitation of the power of guilds and monopolies, tax reforms, and increased recognition of the importance of agriculture, trade, and the merchant class.

In addition to the specific positions and programs it contains, the *Encyclopédie* establishes a particular approach to knowledge in general. Its full title, *Encyclopédie, ou dictionnaire raisonné des sciences, des arts et des métiers* (*Encyclopedia, or a Descriptive Dictionary of the Sciences, Arts, and Trades*), indicates its double objective. As an analytic or descriptive dictionary, it would contain the general principles and essential details pertaining to all branches of 18th-century science as well as to the mechanical and liberal arts. As an encyclopedia, it would display the order and interrelation of all forms of human knowledge. The encyclopedists sought not only to compile and transmit all existing knowledge but also to order it rationally, according to their understanding of how the human mind works. The *Encyclopédie* thus represents far more than a vast reference work or documentational enterprise, albeit the most massive Europe had ever produced. It also reflects the most powerful tenet of European Enlightenment, the belief in human reason as an individual and innate critical faculty, capable not simply of understanding the world but, more important, of actively organizing all forms of knowledge, thereby representing the world as understandable, that is, able to be grasped, ordered, and ultimately mastered by the rational mind.

In their venture of compiling knowledge, the encyclopedists had several predecessors, including the Académie Française's *Dictionnaire* (begun in 1638), Louis Moreri's *Grand dictionnaire historique* (1674; *Great Historical Dictionary*), and Pierre Bayle's *Dictionnaire historique et critique* (1697; *Historical and Critical Dictionary*). The Jesuits saw in the *Encyclopédie* a dangerous and secular rival to their *Dictionnaire de Trévoux* (1704-1771). Following Francis Bacon in his defense of "mechanical arts," the encyclopedists made free use of the several more technologically oriented reference works that had appeared following the *Description et perfection des arts et métiers* (1761; *Description and Perfection of the Arts and Trades*) that Jean-Baptiste Colbert, minister of Louis XIV, had called upon the Royal Academy of Sciences to produce after its foundation in 1666. Among these are Antoine Furetière's *Dictionnaire universel des arts et des sciences* (1690; *Universal Dictionary of the Arts and Sciences*), Thomas Corneille's *Dictionnaire des termes d'arts et de sciences* (1732), and Jacques Savary-Desbrulon's *Dictionnaire universel de commerce* (1723; *Universal Dictionary of Commerce*). Like its predecessors, the *Encyclopédie* of course remained inaccessible to the French working class, who could hardly have afforded a subscription to it, assuming they could read. But for the better-off educated person the encyclopedic text and illustrations presented a remarkably complete and up-to-date account of the 18th-century French "mechanical arts," now called technology, integrating them within a larger economic, historical, cultural, social, and philosophical context, in a style aimed at a relatively broad readership.

Unlike its predecessors, the *Encyclopédie* has won longevity (as the recent Pergamon complete reprint testifies), and not only as a reference work for ancien régime specialists. One of the most massive attempts of the Enlightenment to present knowledge as a product of human reason and to link the question of knowledge with that of value, the *Encyclopédie* remains a founding document and event of modern Western culture. It played a tremendous role in shaping the 18th-century educated person's way of thinking about knowledge by focusing attention on the values employed to determine how knowledge should be represented. In this way it contributed greatly to consolidating the value system called Enlightenment, which from a contemporary standpoint may well seem to be one of the most natural and essential features of modern thinking. Displaying nothing less than the rational mind at work organizing things and persons into objects of knowledge, the *Encyclopédie* promoted above all the value of instrumental reason, the capacity of the human mind to think dynamically and to bring about organized change according to specific values and criteria, change that since the Enlightenment we call progress. The *Encyclopédie* played a major role in consolidating what was to become the legacy of the Enlightenment: a belief in the progress that would result from reason's power to present a critique of existing orders of knowledge by revealing their arbitrary and motivated basis, and at the same time to promote other orders of knowledge, founded on equally arbitrary yet arguably more productive values. The extent to which we wish to continue to be heirs to the Enlightenment's legacy, which may well have already been a myth in the 18th century, will determine how we read the *Encyclopédie* today. Perhaps we can no longer take pride in finding here a liberating, enlightened, rational critique and must consider as well its enabling conditions, the structures of power on which it is founded and with which it is linked. For in a very modern fashion the questions of knowledge and power merge in the pages of the *Encyclopédie*, not always perhaps as the encyclopedists may have intended, but certainly in a way that requires us to rethink the entire encyclopedic program of ordering knowledge.

Both d'Alembert in the "Discours préliminaire" ("Preliminary Discourse") and Diderot in his article "*Encyclopédie*" make explicit the ordering process at work in the *Encyclopédie*, the epistemology or theory of knowledge from which it derives, and the critique of institutions of order—especially theological institutions, but social and political ones as well—that the encyclopedic text contains and promotes. Rejecting the idealism of any theory of knowledge that locates the origin of ideas in some divine cause, d'Alembert and Diderot advance the sensationalist argument, taken from John Locke and developed by Etienne Bonnot de Condillac. According to this more empirical,

materialist epistemology, knowledge derives not from innate ideas, as René Descartes and the proponents of Cartesianims maintained, unwilling to break the causal link between theology and epistemology, but rather from the senses. Understanding (entendement), claim Diderot and d'Alembert, comprises three faculties: memory, imagination, and, chief among them, reason. Reason's function being to combine sense data, it works with its sister faculties to produce all the various categories of human knowledge. These the encyclopedists portray schematically in the form of a "genealogical tree of knowledge," which depicts not only mental order, but encyclopedic and textual order as well. The epistemological model that describes the generation of ideas thus serves as a textual model, explaining the interrelation between every article in the *Encyclopédie*.

In their attempt to interpret their world according to the rule of reason, to represent the most valuable and useful forms of knowledge as grounded in sensory experience and mental operations, not metaphysical, idealist assumptions, the encyclopedists clearly had to take on the question of God, to say nothing of the church. Their "tree of knowledge" illustrates the approach they would take. Here the concept of the divine falls under the rubric of "la science de Dieu," a term that could mean the knowledge possessed by God, but that for the encyclopedists refers only to knowledge about God. This area of knowledge they figure as a subcategory of "general metaphysics," itself a subcategory of philosophy. Needless to say, all these areas are subcategories located under the general heading "reason." Farthest away from reason, both on the tree of knowledge and for the encyclopedists, is the category of religion, labeled "religion, hence, abusively, superstition." In the rational mind as the encyclopedists depict it, theology belongs next to black magic. The encyclopedists thus reorganize the cognitive universe, rejecting the authority of all systems and institutions that claim to deliver up any absolute order of knowledge, and setting in their place more secular, empirical, and arbitrary ones.

This rejection was immediately countered by a hostile campaign launched against the *Encyclopédie* project, notably by the Jesuits and the antiphilosophes movement. The *Encyclopédie* was placed on the church's Index of Forbidden Books, and on two occasions the crown revoked the *privilège*, or royal authorization to publish. In both cases the *privilège* was soon restored, matters of religious orthodoxy playing a smaller role in the crown's decision to provide tacit approval for the project than the question of economic benefit and national prestige for France, especially after the rumor circulated that Catherine II of Russia had offered to support the project if its editors would publish the *Encyclopédie* in Russia.

As in Voltaire's *Dictionnaire philosophique* (1764; *Philosophical Dictionary*), the church and its claims to doctrinaire authority were favorite targets in the pages of the *Encyclopédie*. To be sure, not all contributors professed the staunch atheism to be found in the articles by d'Holbach, or even the probing yet less rigid materialism of a Diderot. In fact numerous articles express Christian belief and dogma in the most orthodox terms. The real issue dividing the encyclopedists and the church involves the relation between power and the encyclopedic representation of knowledge. Diderot and d'Alembert make no claim to present absolute knowledge in the pages of the *Encyclopédie*, for such knowledge they willingly leave to God. Instead they argue that all other systems of knowledge must be necessity be arbitrary, as arbitrary in fact as the alphabetical order of articles. Given the arbitrariness of any ordering principle, the encyclopedists claim themselves justified in adopting the one they have chosen for their text. "Why should we not present man in our work," Diderot asks, "as he is situated in the universe? . . . Man is the sole term from which all must be derived and to which all must be reduced" (*Encyclopédie*, 5:641). Whether in the area of science and technology or that of philosophy and literature, in descriptions of either machines or ideas, all knowledge must be presented as an exclusively human product. More important, it must be judged in terms of its usefulness to humanity. "Man," a term that refers at times to the universal human individual and at others to the educated European male, thus serves as the supreme ordering principle for the encyclopedic representation of knowledge. By claiming not to answer questions pertaining to the ultimate nature of reality, the encyclopedists seek a more limited working knowledge of human experience, partial and provisional as they admit, but in the end more useful. The encyclopedic text sets up a relation between individual and world, thinking subject and object of knowledge, that is underlaid moreover with a particularly utilitarian epistemology.

The real utilitarianism at work in the pages of the *Encyclopédie* lies in the way this text empowers its readers by proposing a particular way in which to view and interpret the world and their place and function in it. The encyclopedic plates are emblematic in this regard. Reflecting a remarkably complete view of mid-18th-century French technology, the plates work to promote a technological understanding of the world. The cross-section drawing, a fairly new form of representation in 1751, not only shows how to construct a machine—the most celebrated example being the stocking-weaving machine and Diderot's article concerning it, "Métier à bas." It also suggests a way of representing, viewing, and understanding objects that disassembles them, slices through them like the surgeon's scalpel and the viewer's gaze in the anatomy plates, and reassembles them, not as they look, but rather according to an understanding of how they function and produce. The articles also present a similar means for knowing the world; in other words, for constructing a world that can be controlled and made to work. Although the encyclopedists were quick to criticize the reductiveness of Cartesian systematization, their text amounts to an attempt to realize Descartes's dream of a philosophical system that would guarantee technical mastery over and possession of the world. With the *Encyclopédie*, the world of the Cartesian *cogito*, a world of being, explodes into a world of having, filled with objects that must be ordered and put in place. And the order of things in the *Encyclopédie* is determined above all by the status accorded them as belongings, by their usefulness to an ordering subject. Things in the encyclopedic text are not just "out there"; they are meant to be used, and the products of their use are of

value, which is one reason for the countless tools, machines, and processes of production depicted in the plates. Nor is it by chance that Diderot invariably employs the metaphor of the voyage to describe reading the *Encyclopédie*, and that of the map to figure how it structures knowledge. Like other maps used to chart the great European voyages of discovery to Africa, the Americas, and the Orient, the *Encyclopédie*, too, holds out the tantalizing promise of power to be achieved and wealth to be had. The encyclopedists' desire to transmit intact to future generations the wealth of knowledge contained in the encyclopedic storehouse begins to resemble uncannily the cartoon in which the captain of industry announces with pride to his heir: "Someday all this will be yours."

Only later in the history of rationalism would the consequences of the Enlightenment's self-destructive potential be more acutely felt, as Enlightenment transformed itself into mythology, and a philosophy of reason into an ideology designed to rationalize power structures. For the more militant 18th-century encyclopedists, however, theirs were heady times, which they willingly characterized as revolutionary. Post-Revolutionary conservative historians and intellectuals would continue for a century to denounce the *Encyclopédie* for having helped bring down an old order. But such judgments are misconceived, the nostalgia they convey masking a fear all too easily transformed into repression. What is revolutionary about the encyclopedic text, or better yet, most powerful, is the way it works, as Diderot puts it, "to undeceive people." It prompts its reader to seek out unreason in this work, in others, and indeed in all sectors of human activity. Presenting the critical practice of Enlightenment as a way of finally dispelling the shadows, the *Encyclopédie* displays the Enlighteners' awareness of the impossibility of challenging knowledge, however incorrect, irrational, or corrupt, with anything other than knowledge. The only way to dispel the shadows is to show that tenebrous knowledge does not know enough, or does not know strongly enough. The encyclopedists' text makes clear that the discourse of reason can oppose power only by being more powerful than what it sets itself against. Hence the *Encyclopédie* presents a powerful way of coming to knowledge, showing its readers how to "undeceive" themselves by leading them to interpret a world of their own construction, one of their own representation. We must confront the risk contained in such a way of coming to knowledge: the risk of redeception and a knowledge of things, not as they are, but as we desire and will them to be. Pointing out such a risk turns the encyclopedic critique of authority upon itself, in order to question the authority of any such critique. But this apparently more modern, post-Enlightenment view may be no more than Enlightenment's blind spot, already present in the encyclopedic project. The success of later editions of the *Encyclopédie*, especially those whose more cautious and canny editors sought to avoid the confrontation between knowledge and power by concentrating on the natural sciences instead of philosophy and by criticizing Protestantism in the place of Catholicism, bears witness to the ways in which the ordering of knowledge could be shaped to fit the political, social, and ideological exigencies of monarchy, revolution, and empire. Many of the encyclopedists' values and views concerning science and technology, religion and politics, today seem totally natural. The *Encyclopédie* contributed greatly to naturalizing them, that is, to representing such value systems as if they belonged to a natural order of things. We should not forget, however, reading the *Encyclopédie* today mindful of its most critically powerful dimension, that the encyclopedists' work reveals all orders of knowledge—including their own—to be arbitrary and motivated, mediated through and through by the power deployed and channeled by discourses of order. With this realization we may reach the limits of the Enlightenment understanding of knowledge as a kind of light that dispels the shadows of ignorance. Perhaps we must attempt to understand knowledge differently in order to come to terms with a power-knowledge that sometimes produces the well-being and pleasures of technological societies, and sometimes their terror and violence.

INTELLECTUAL BACKGROUND

Lucien Lévy-Bruhl

SOURCE: "The Encyclopaedists," in his *History of Modern Philosophy in France,* 1899. Reprint by The Open Court Publishing Company, 1924, pp. 207-35.

[*Lévy-Bruhl was a seminal French philosopher, anthropologist, and social scientist known for his his investigations of primitive mentality. His books include* La mentalite primitive *(1922;* Primitive Mentality *). In the following excerpt from a reprint of a 1899 English translation of a work on modern French philosophy, he traces the background, genesis, and development of the Encyclopedists' basic ideas.*]

Voltaire was, indeed, in his tendencies, both confessed and secret, in his likes and his dislikes, in his good qualities and his defects, "the representative man" of French philosophy in the eighteenth century. . . . Around him was arrayed an army of "philosophers," full of zeal but undisciplined and sometimes unruly, whose best lieutenants were the most independent. In spite, however, of the differences in their natures, tempers, aptitudes and talents, the public feeling was not mistaken in grouping them all together under one name, from La Mettrie to Condorcet, from Condillac to Abbé Raynal. Sometimes unthinkingly, but in most cases quite consciously, they worked together on a common task. Most of them used every exertion in combating the Roman Catholic Church, and in a general way Christianity itself. They rejected its conception of the universe and of man, which appeared to them false and superstitious; they condemned the social order which the Catholic hierarchy contributed to maintain, and which they thought unjust and oppressive. Against this double tyranny all weapons were lawful. They would preserve nothing of this religion except its moral teaching, and even this they reduced to its essential elements, and held it to be human rather than specifically Christian.

In the constructive part of their work likewise, in spite of inevitable divergencies, they are quite akin to one another. Eager to lose no time in putting something in the place of that which they thought they had destroyed, they set to work with great haste, and their want of experience appears so constantly as to be almost monotonous. There is a continual recurrence of the same paradoxes, accepted without discussion, and of the same dubious formulae looked upon as axioms. Their common stock consisted of a limited number of theories, often superficial and rudimentary, concerning psychology, morals, politics and history, and of certain ideas and views which were often both profound and fruitful—building stones, as it were, intended to fit into an edifice which they were as yet unable to erect. For the *Encyclopaedia*, which they thought of as destined to be this edifice, represents a workyard rather than a building. It has no unity, save in the spirit which animates it, and in the perseverance of Diderot, who, in spite of obstacles and at the cost of untold trouble and sacrifice, finally brought it to completion.

La Mettrie, by the date of his works, somewhat precedes the main body of the philosophical army. He died in 1751, four years before Montesquieu, and before Diderot, D'Alembert and Rousseau had produced their masterpieces. Being a disciple of Boerhaave, who sought to explain the phenomena of life by the mechanism of physical and chemical phenomena, being also acquainted, though somewhat superficially, with the doctrines of Descartes and Locke, he composed, with elements derived from widely different sources, a system which he thought scientifically proven. It was a kind of materialism, based on the idea which often reappeared in the course of the century, that the diversity in the orders of phenomena is due to the more or less complex organization of matter. As this organization is not the same in animals as in plants, nor (in certain points) in man as in animals, the functions which exist in plants, animals and in man must also be different; there is no need whatever of a special principle to explain certain of these functions rather than others. In opposition to spiritualistic dualism, which sets an abyss between the substance of the soul and that of the body, La Mettrie advanced, in his *Histoire Naturelle de l'Âme*, the ancient peripatetic and scholastic conception which makes of the soul the form of the body. Like some Aristotelians of the Renaissance, he slipped his own materialism into this theory. He openly expounded it in the *Homme-Machine*. While he praised Descartes for saying that an animal is a machine, he reproached him for not having dared to say the same of man. Not that La Mettrie denied the existence of feeling or thought in animals or in man; such a paradox would seem to him absurd. He means that feeling, thought, consciousness, are all produced by the machine; the whole soul is explained by it, depends upon it, and in consequence disappears when it gets out of order or is decomposed. As a physician he quotes in support of his theory definite facts borrowed from mental physiology and pathology, and he declares that he will accept as his judges none but scientific men, acquainted with anatomy and with the philosophy of the body.

La Mettrie's reputation in the eighteenth century was very bad. In our days some have tried to rehabilitate him. No doubt a philosopher may have been a declared materialist and atheist, have written insipid defenses of physical voluptuousness, and have died from eating too freely of patties, and yet may none the less have been a sincere man and have honestly sought after truth. No doubt also La

Mettrie more than once served as a scapegoat for the philosophers who followed him and perhaps from time to time imitated him. The nearer they came to him the more fiercely they expressed their indignation against his abominable doctrines, for he, being dead, had nothing to fear either from the police or the parliament. His good name may have suffered from this maneuver. Yet if we examine his works closely, we shall conclude that he has not been seriously wronged. He does not sufficiently distinguish between what is proved and what is merely asserted; he has no absorbing concern for close reasoning and exact expression, and his language is often rash in proportion to the looseness of his demonstrations. Let us grant that he introduced French materialism in the eighteenth century, but let us acknowledge at the same time that he too often presented it under an aggressive and unacceptable form.

In 1751 appeared the *Discours Préliminaire of the Encyclopaedia*. Diderot had acted wisely in asking D'Alembert to write it, and in contenting himself with drawing up the prospectus of his great enterprise. He had already been at odds with the authorities, and had spent several months in Vincennes on account of his *Lettre sur les Aveugles*; in a word, he was looked upon as a suspicious character. D'Alembert, a great mathematician, renowned for his *Traité de Dynamique*, and a member of the Academy of Sciences, was just the man to present the *Encyclopaedia* to the public, and his name insured it against the ill-will of the enemies of philosophy.

This discourse was much admired, but we now find it rather difficult to understand this admiration. Though we do not refuse our homage to the dignity of its tone and the elevation of its thought, we are rather disappointed as we read it. This is owing to several causes. Ideas which were new in those days have now become familiar and commonplace. Several important points in D'Alembert's philosophy do not appear in the *Discours*, or are merely hinted at. Others, on the contrary, are developed which do not express his real thought; but he believed this concession to be indispensable in order to gain acceptance for the rest. "In the accursed country in which we write," he said to Voltaire, "such phrases as these are notarial style, and serve only as passports for the truths that we wish to establish. Moreover, nobody is deceived by them. . . . Time will teach men to distinguish what we have thought from what we have said." D'Alembert never would deviate from this prudent course. Accordingly we see in the works offered to the public a D'Alembert whose attitude is irreproachable and whose irony is hidden under the forms of respect. But the letters to Voltaire and to Frederick the Great show us a quite different sort of man, eager for the fray, and as much incensed against parliaments, Jesuits, Jansenists, priests in general and religion as the most determined "philosopher."

Being a fervent admirer of Bacon, D'Alembert borrowed from him his classification of sciences, with a few alterations which he himself explains. To tell the truth, the *Discours Préliminaire* contains not one but three classifications of human knowledge, from three different points of view. D'Alembert first examines "the origin and development of our ideas and sciences from the philosophical or metaphysical—i. e., psychological—point of view." Like a true disciple of Locke and Condillac, he divides all our knowledge into direct ideas and ideas derived from reflexion. Our direct knowledge is only that which has come to us through our senses; in other words, to our sensations alone do we owe our ideas. The classification here consists, therefore, in tracing our complex ideas back to simple ones—that is, to those derived from sensation.

The "encyclopaedic order of sciences," which comes next, is a logical order. It must not be confused with the order which the human mind has actually followed in the production of the sciences. In all likelihood man, spurred on by his bodily wants, must first have set out to meet the most urgent needs, and then, as he met with difficulties, have tried another way, then have retraced his steps, etc. If so, the sciences which we look upon as containing the principles of all others, and which must come first in the encyclopaedic order, were not the first to be developed. Moreover, in the historical order of the progress of the human mind, the various sciences can be viewed only in succession, one after another, whereas the encyclopaedic order consists in embracing all sciences at one glance, as if from a height one should perceive at one's feet a maze of interweaving paths. Or, again, this encyclopaedic order may be compared to a map of the world, on which we see at one glance the whole surface of the globe. And just as in preparing such a map we may choose among various systems of projection, so we may also conceive the encyclopaedic order in several different ways. None of these ways is necessarily to be adopted to the exclusion of all others, and if D'Alembert chose that of Bacon it was because, without being more defective than the others, it has the advantage of suggesting with tolerable accuracy the genealogy of human knowledge.

Lastly, a third order considered by D'Alembert is that according to which our sciences have been historically developed since the Renaissance. It differs from the order which the human mind would follow if left to its own lights. In this order, then, the sciences of erudition came first, owing to the prestige of antiquity, which after long ages of barbarism and ignorance was rising again fair and luminous before the delighted eyes of men.

Thus D'Alembert had a clear perception of the psychological genesis of our knowledge, of the logical order of the sciences, and of their historical succession. Could not these three orders have been combined to form a higher one? Comte later on attempted such a combination, but D'Alembert contented himself with a rapid criticism of each of the sciences, and a summary appreciation of the great minds who had created or developed them.

And, first of all, in the already formidable mass of our knowledge, how few branches deserve the name of sciences! History, according to D'Alembert, is in no wise entitled to it. It is only of practical interest. Why should we not, for instance, cull from it the best catechism of morals that could be given to children, by collecting into one book the really memorable deeds and words? It would be particularly useful to philosophers and to the "unfortunate class" of princes, to teach them by what they learn of men who lived in former times to know the men with whom they live. Metaphysics should be strictly limited to what is treated of in Locke's *Essay*. Nearly all the other questions it proposes to solve are either beyond solution or idle. It is the food of rash or ill-balanced minds—in one word, a vain and contentious science. D'Alembert is not allured, like Voltaire, by the hypothesis which attributes to matter, under certain conditions, the power to think. To him it appears uncalled for and dangerous. If it inclines toward materialism, we fall back into a metaphysical doctrine no more clearly proven than any other. Is it not better for us to confess that we do not know at all what substance, soul and matter are? Likewise, as regards the existence and nature of God, skepticism is the only reasonable attitude of mind. And we should be compelled to say the same of the existence of the outer world and of man's liberty, did not instinct here supplement the deficiency of reason; whether the outer world exists or not, we have such a strong inclination to believe in it that everything appears to us as if it existed; and, in the same way, everything appears to us as if we were free.

Even in the natural sciences, how limited did man's knowledge appear! Physiology had hardly yet begun to exist. Of medicine D'Alembert speaks as a man who has measured all its risks; in his eyes it is a purely empirical science. The physician who builds systems and clings to a theory is most dangerous; that one is least to be feared who has seen many patients and has learned to make an accurate diagnosis and not to dose at random. Physics is more advanced and its conquests are lasting. Here we stand on firmer ground, but progress is slow and the human mind has to guard against itself. D'Alembert insists upon the prudent advice already given by Bacon: we should distrust even the most probable explanations, so long as they have not been tested by experience, and if possible, by calculation.

Sciences in the highest sense of the word, D'Alembert called those he had been studying all his lifetime, and to which he owed the best of his glory—the mathematical sciences, which he divides into pure mathematics, mixed mathematics and physico-mathematical sciences. Certitude, properly so called, which is founded upon principles necessarily true and self-evident, does not belong equally or in the same way to all these branches of mathematics. Those which rest on physical principles, that is, on experimental truths or on physical hypotheses, have, so to speak, only an experimental or hypothetical certitude.

One might infer from this that D'Alembert looks upon pure mathematics, in opposition to physico-mathematical sciences, as being really *a priori* and independent of experience. But how could he have harmonized such a conception with the principle borrowed from Locke, according to which all our knowledge comes, either directly or indirectly, from experience? D'Alembert did not fall into this contradiction. He avoided it by means of a theory of mathematics which was consistent with his sensationalistic principles, and much clearer than the ones to which Hume and Condillac resorted. Mathematics, in his opinion, belongs to natural philosophy. "The science of dimensions in general is the remotest term to which the contemplation of the properties of matter may lead us." Experience

shows us individual beings and particular phenomena, the sun, the moon, rain and wind. By means of successive abstractions and of more and more comprehensive generalizations, we separate the qualities common to all these phenomena and beings, till at last we reach the fundamental properties of all bodies: impenetrability, extension and size. We cannot further subdivide our perceptions, and we find at this point a subject for sciences which, in virtue of the simplicity of this subject, may be made deductive. Thus, in geometry, we strip matter of nearly all its material qualities, and consider, so to speak, only its ghost. "Thus," says D'Alembert in language that foreshadows Stuart Mill, "it is merely by a process of abstraction that the geometrician considers lines as having no breadth, and surfaces as having no thickness. The truths he demonstrates about the properties of all are *purely hypothetical* truths. But they are none the less useful, considering the consequences that result from them." This empirical theory of mathematics, which stands in such direct opposition to that of Plato and Descartes, has made its appearance again in our century, and is anything but abandoned at the present day. Even such men as Helmholtz, though reared under the influence of Kant, have deemed it indispensable to accept the statement that geometry contains elements derived from experience.

As the certainty of mathematics rests on the evidence of ideas so closely related that the mind perceives the connection between them at a glance, so the certainty of morals rests on the "heart's evidence" which rules us as imperiously. D'Alembert's theory of morals is almost entirely identical with Voltaire's. The only original feature about it is the personal accent that D'Alembert gives it, especially in his letters. To him sympathy for the hapless, indignation against the "monstrous inequality of fortunes" are not mere commonplaces, hackneyed expressions of a trite sentimentality, and homage paid to the reigning fashion. They are the words of a man who has seen the poor, who has lived among them, who has witnessed their sufferings, and to whom misery is a living reality, not a theme for literary amplification. D'Alembert goes so far as to ask himself whether, when driven to despair and reduced without fault of his own to the verge of starvation, a man is morally bound to respect the surplus that another has beyond his needs.

In dignity of life and independence of character, as well as in genius, D'Alembert was among the glories of the party of philosophers. He more than once dared to contradict Voltaire. His friendship with Frederick never cost any sacrifice of his pride, and he fell out with Catherine of Russia because she rather haughtily rejected his intercession on behalf of some Frenchmen who had been taken prisoners in Poland. His two great passions were for mathematics and against "priests"; and it is characteristic of the times that the latter should have contributed no less than the former to constitute him a "philosopher."

Diderot was as adventurous, expansive and lyrical as D'Alembert was prudent, reserved and methodical. But his disorder is rich in ideas. Diderot was one of the most extraordinary mind-stirring writers that the world has ever seen. The brightness and charm of his conversation seem to have been prodigious. He was called "the philosopher." It must indeed be admitted that if we always meant by this word a man whose methodical and persevering meditation does not rest satisfied till it has found out a first principle from which it can deduce the whole world of reality, Diderot would occupy but a low place among philosophers. Not that he was incapable of reducing his ideas to a system; but the starting-point of his attempts at such a synthesis was variable, depending on a chance encounter, conversation or reading. Before his reason went deep into things, his imagination had to be stirred. But on the other hand, he was without a rival in rising from an apparently insignificant point to general ruling principles, and in discovering from that vantage ground many roads, some of which led him to new points of view; his curiosity was indefatigable, his reflection sometimes profound and always suggestive.

Unfortunately, though all this be sufficient to exercise a considerable influence upon contemporaries, it may easily fail to produce many durable works. All Diderot's writings wear an air of improvisation, due to his ready and sudden enthusiasm, and to the facility with which he could put together *ex tempore* a vast structure of ideas. It can therefore hardly be said that the *Encyclopaedia*, by compelling him to scatter his labors for twenty years upon an infinite and varied task, prevented him from bringing forth the great masterpiece which his intelligence, if concentrated, might have produced. It was rather because Diderot felt no strong desire to concentrate himself thus that he poured into the *Encyclopaedia* and into a multitude of pamphlets his wonderful gifts for quick assimilation, and uninterrupted but fragmentary production.

Diderot was at first a deist, after the manner of Voltaire, and, like him, under the influence of the English, particularly of Locke and Shaftesbury. He then thought, as did Voltaire, that modern physics had dealt materialism and skepticism a fatal blow. "The discovery of germs in itself has dispelled one of the strongest objections of atheism." But this style of philosophy soon ceased to satisfy him, and he gradually inclined to what he himself called the most attractive form of materialism—that which attributes to organic molecules desires, aversions, feeling and thought—to end at last in a sort of pantheistic naturalism.

Several paths led Diderot to this goal. First of all, he perceived that the irreducible dualism of soul and body was generally upheld for religious quite as much as for philosophical reasons; and this alone was sufficient to drive him away from it. Then, in his *Lettre sur les Aveugles* and *Sur les Sourds Muets*, he insists upon the relative character of our metaphysical conceptions. For a blind man, what becomes of the proof of the existence of God based upon final cases? Diderot attempted, as Condillac did afterward, to work out the psychological development of sensationalism. All our knowledge comes from the senses; how does it come from them? What do we owe to each of our senses? Can we analyze their data, and afterward from them reconstruct the whole? Cheselden's experiment and Molyneux's problem were known; Diderot wished to go beyond these, to carry this kind of "metaphysical anatomy" still farther, and to take in pieces, so to speak, the senses of man. He imagined the "conventional mute," and the conclusions that he drew from his psychological analysis alarmed many a Christian.

But Diderot's pantheistic tendencies seem to have been chiefly determined by the discoveries made about this time in natural science. These he followed with passionate interest, and his imagination soon swept him on to bold hypotheses concerning life and thought. "We are," he says, "on the verge of a great revolution in science." In mathematics such men as Bernoulli, Euler, D'Alembert, Lagrange, have "set the pillars of Hercules." Nobody will go further. The natural sciences, on the other hand, have only just been born; and already the little that is known about them entirely changes our view of the world. For instance, to a mathematician studying abstract mechanics a body may undoubtedly, by convention, be looked upon as inert; but if we examine the facts, the inertia of bodies is a "fearful error," contrary to all sound principles of physics and chemistry. In itself, whether we consider its particles or its mass, a body is full of activity and strength. The distinction between inorganic and living matter is therefore superficial, and strictly speaking, even false; for do we not plainly see that the same matter is alternately living and not living, according as it is assimilated or eliminated by a plant or an animal? Nature makes flesh with marble, and marble with flesh. Therefore, is it not very rash to assert that sensibility is incompatible with matter, since we do not know the essence of anything whatever, either of matter or of insensibility? But, it is said, sensibility is a simple quality, one and indivisible, and incompatible with a divisible subject. "Metaphysico-theological gibberish," answers Diderot. Experience show that life is everywhere; who knows but feeling may be everywhere, too?

One of the most serious objections raised against such a doctrine rests on the stability and permanence of living species, which seem to set an insurmountable barrier between man and other animals, between any two living species, and above all, between the realm of life and that of inorganic matter. Diderot was aware of this difficulty. He answered it by asserting the natural evolution of all the species that ever appeared on the globe. It does not follow because of the present state of the earth, and consequently of the living species and of the inanimate bodies which are to be found thereon, that this state has always been similar in the past, or is to remain similar in the future. What we mistake for the history of nature is only the history of an instant of time. Just as in the animal or vegetable kingdom an individual begins to exist, grows, matures, decays and disappears, may it not be the same with an entire species? Who knows what races of animals have preceded us? And who knows what races of animals will succeed ours? Let us then waive the apparently unanswerable question of the origin of life. If you are puzzled by the question of the egg and the owl, it is because you suppose animals to have been originally what they are now. What folly! We do not know what they have been any more than we know what they are to be.

To Diderot's eager, universal and insatiable scientific curiosity was joined a conception of science itself which might already be termed "positivism." We know little; let us be contented with what we can know. Our means of gaining knowledge reach as far as our real needs do, and where these means are denied us, knowledge is probably not very necessary for us. I might as well feel seriously grieved at not having four eyes, four feet, and two wings. We must accept the fact that we are as we are, and not aspire to a science that would be beyond our comprehension. If men were wise, they would at last give their attention to investigations that would promise to promote their comfort, and no longer deign to answer questions which are idle because they are unanswerable. For a similar reason they would cease to aim at a greater degree of precision in science than practical considerations demand. In a word, "utility is the measure of everything." Utility will a few centuries hence set limits to experimental physics, as it is on the point of doing with regard to geometry. "I will allow centuries to this study (physics), because its sphere of utility is infinitely wider than that of any other abstract science, and because it is unquestionably the basis of our real knowledge."

The same fervent love of humanity which animates and limits Diderot's idea of science, is also to be found in his polemics against the Christian religion. Of course his language varied according to circumstances. When he did not intend to publish he gave free rein to his bold tongue. In this way he wrote the *Supplément au Voyage de Bougainville, Le Neveu de Rameau* (his masterpiece), the *Entretien avec la Maréchale de. . . .* In private letters he sometimes vents his rage in invectives against that religion, "the most absurd and atrocious in its dogmas, the most unintelligible, metaphysical and intricate, and consequently the most liable to divisions, schisms and heresies, the most fatal to public peace and to sovereigns, the most insipid, the most gloomy, the most Gothic, the most puerile, the most unsociable in its morals, the most intolerant of all." In the *Encyclopaedia* he makes a show of respect. Yet significant sallies will sometimes escape him: "The Hebrews knew what Christians term the true God; as if there were any false one!"

His ethics, extremely lax as regards the union of the sexes, is unfortunately influenced by the lachrymose sentimentality of the times. The moment that virtue is mentioned Diderot gets excited. Tears come into his eyes, his heart throbs, he gasps, he must embrace his friends, and they must share his transports. This overflow of feeling seriously impairs the precision of his ideas. Diderot taught his daughter that every virtue has two rewards: the pleasure of doing good, and that of winning the good will of others; and every vice has two punishments: one in our inmost hearts, the other in the feeling of aversion which we never fail to excite in others. He wished her to have no prejudices, but to have morals and principles "common to all centuries and nations." Here we recognize ideas dear to Voltaire. Like him, also, Diderot considered that justice was rooted in the very nature of man, and not, in spite of Locke, variable according to times and places. "The maxims engraved, so to speak, on the tables of mankind are as ancient as man and preceded his laws, for which they ought to furnish the guiding principles." But Diderot, in accord here with Rousseau, added that nature has not created us wicked, and that it is bad education, bad examples and bad legislation that deprave us.

The originality of Diderot must not therefore be sought in his ethics; it lies elsewhere, in the mass of ideas set in motion by this indefatigable mind, a real precursor on many points of the present century, which has justly shown a predilection for him. He anticipates the progress of the natural sciences and the change they were to bring to the general conception of the universe, and consequently to the whole life of mankind. He was among the first to recognize the social importance of the mechanic arts, by giving them the place they were entitled to in the *Encyclopaedia*. He raised in public esteem the men who practice these arts, and thus did for the workman what the physiocrats were at the same time doing for the husbandman. At the same time his Salons were making the beginnings of art criticism, and teaching his contemporaries how to look at pictures and statues. On dramatic art and the art of the comedian he brought forward many ingenious and profound ideas—and finally he revealed in many articles of the *Encyclopaedia* a searching knowledge of the history of philosophy, then neglected and almost unknown in France.

Goethe, who greatly admired him, said that his was "the most Germanic of French heads." Indeed very few French philosophers have had as keen a sense of the great pulse of universal life and of the creative power of nature, or as sound and penetrating an insight into manifold reality. He occupies a special place, which we must almost despair of defining in a satisfactory manner. We can neither set forth his philosophical thoughts without exhibiting their shortcomings, nor yet point out these drawbacks without run-

Denis Diderot, by Jean-Baptiste Greuze.

ning the risk of being unjust to this vast, powerful and un-restrained genius.

Even as compared with lesser men than D'Alembert and Diderot, Helvetius is not the most original of the "philosophers," yet his book, *De l'Esprit*, created a wonderful sensation, both in France and abroad. This success was partly due, at least in France, to the personality of the author, who was a great financier and a kind, generous, hospitable and friendly man, who approached very near to the most esteemed type of man of the eighteenth century: the man of feeling who is virtuous and made happy by his virtue. The success was undoubtedly also due in part to a captivating style; easy to read, composed with a manifest concern for the favor of women, and weaving in short stories and anecdotes *De l'Esprit* did not repel even the most indolent reader. Lastly, its success was due to the apparent boldness of the paradoxes, which however were nothing but the fashionable opinions carried to their logical conclusions. The strange thing was that the success of Helvetius lasted for a long time, and at the end of the century it was still thought worth while to refute him.

Apart from the current doctrine of sensationalism, for which Helvetius was evidently indebted to Condillac or to some other contemporary writer, his two main paradoxes are the following: (1) That personal interest or the pursuit of happiness is the only principle, whether confessed or not, of human actions; (2) that education can do everything. The first paradox was not new. Many a moralist, not to mention La Rochefoucauld, had already shown the infinite cunning of self-love, and concluded that men, even in the actions that seem most disinterested actions, are always more or less hypocritical. But Helvetius gives his argument a quite different turn. There is no pessimism or bitterness about him; he is full of kindness. "It was not the love of paradoxes," he writes, "that led me to my conclusion, but solely a desire for men's happiness." And he flatters himself that his doctrine may contribute to it. Indeed, if it be once granted that man never seeks anything but his own interest, let law-givers so contrive that the general interest shall always agree with private interests, and all men will be good and happy. Everything, therefore, depends upon the laws. Wherever private interest is identified with public interest, virtue in each individual becomes the necessary effect of self-love and personal interest. "All the vices of a nation almost invariably originate in some defects of its legislation."

Diderot justly observed that this omnipotence attributed to the laws repeats in an exaggerated form the conception of Montesquieu, who saw an inseparable connection between morals and the system of government, and thus attributed to political laws an influence not always confirmed by experience. Furthermore, with Montesquieu the forms of government depend, in their turn, upon climate and a multitude of conditions, whereas Helvetius expressly opposes Montesquieu's theory of climates. He maintains that the action of the law-giver is supreme everywhere, and that no obstacles are insuperable if this action be properly directed. If it be objected that the pursuit of personal interest is rather a narrow basis to sustain the whole edifice of human society, he answers that as all

things come from experience, the feeling which was afterward to be called altruism is no exception to the rule. The moral instinct, the moral sense, the natural capacity for beneficence and benevolence, appealed to by the English, are not to be admitted. "The vaunted system of the morally beautiful is really nothing but the system of innate ideas, demolished by Locke, and brought forward again under a somewhat different form." No individual is born good, no individual is born wicked. Both goodness and wickedness are accidents, being the result of good or bad laws.

Thence logically follows the second paradox, according to which education alone creates differences among men. Since nothing is innate or hereditary, every human soul is at first a blank page, and all souls are identical at birth. Inequality among minds is therefore due to the various circumstances in which men have been placed, to the passions aroused by these circumstances, to the power of attention that these passions produce, in short, to a thousand causes, but above all to education. Pedagogy is to individuals what political science is to nations. Error is an evil which, like vice, may be avoided. To insure the happiness of mankind, it will only be necessary to bring the art of education to perfection. Education will make enlightened men and even "men of genius as numerous as they have hitherto been scarce." The enormity of the paradox did not prevent its making an impression upon the public. It had at least the merit of calling attention to the then quite new science of pedagogy, and of preparing the public to welcome Rousseau's *Émile*. Besides, the influence of Rousseau was already quite perceptible in Helvetius. "Everything is acquired" is, indeed, according to Locke's conception, the negation of innate ideas; but it is also, according to Rousseau's conception, the assertion that the errors, sufferings and crimes of men are their own work, and that it is for the educator and the law-giver to cure them.

Le Système de la Nature, by Baron D'Holbach, which appeared in 1770, is a less superficial and more vigorous work than the writings of Helvetius. Being a confessed materialist, D'Holbach defines man as a material being, organized so as to feel, think and be modified in certain ways peculiar to himself—that is, to the particular combinations of substances of which he is composed. The intellectual faculties may be reduced to changes produced by motion in the brain. The word "spirit" has no meaning. The savages admit the existence of "spirits" to explain effects for which they cannot account, and which seem to them marvelous. Such an idea of spirit is preserved only by ignorance and sloth. It is more useful to divines, but most harmful to the progress of society, which keeps pace with science. The immortality of the soul is a religious dogma which never was of any use except to priests, and is not even a check upon the passions if they are at all violent, as experience sufficiently proves. And as necessary laws govern all natural phenomena, intellectual and moral phenomena included, moral freedom is quite out of the question.

So far this materialism had nothing remarkable about it unless it be its perfect frankness. But on the question of the existence of God, D'Holbach subjected deism and theism to a searching criticism, obviously directed against

Voltaire's natural religion, and worthy of some notice. People make a wrong use of physics in behalf of metaphysics, says D'Holbach, and the study of nature should have nothing to do with moral or theological interests lest a new chance of errors be added to all those we already have to guard against. But even if we overlook this point, the argument based on final causes does not prove what it is thought to prove. First of all, the idea of order is relative to human canons of propriety, and if we leave these out of account, disorder is in itself no less natural and normal than order, nor illness than health; all phenomena being produced by virtue of the same laws. Then "to be surprised that the heart, the brain, the arteries, etc., of an animal should work as they do, or that a tree should bear fruit, is to be surprised that an animal or a tree should exist." What we call finality is but the total sum of the conditions required for the existence of every being. When these conditions are found combined, the living being subsists; if they cease to be so, it disappears; and this very simple proposition, which is true as regards individuals, is no less so as regards species and even suns. There is nothing in this which compels us to have recourse to a Providence, the author and maintainer of the world's order.

The divine personality, upheld by theists, is untenable. Newton, the vast genius who divined Nature and its laws, is only a child when he leaves the domain of physics; and his theology shows that he had remained in bondage to the prejudices of his childhood. What is that God, lord and sovereign of all things, who rules the universe, but an anthropomorphic conception, which was only a reminiscence of Newton's Christian education? And what is Voltaire's retributive and vengeful God but a reminiscence of precisely the same kind?

The deists' God is useless, the theists' God is full of contradictions. If we nevertheless accept him, we have no right to reject anything in the name of reason, and we are inconsistent if we refuse to go further and to submit to religious dogma. Theism is liable to as many heresies and schisms as religion, and is, from a logical point of view, even more untenable. So there will always be but a step "from theism to superstition." The least derangement in the machine, a slight ailment, some unforeseen affliction, are sufficient to disturb the humors, and nothing more is required. Natural religion is only a variety of the other kind of religion, and speedily comes back to the original type. It is fear and ignorance of causes that first suggested to man the idea of his gods. He made them rude and fierce, then civilized, like himself; and nothing but science can cause this instinctive theology to disappear.

The appearance of this book, in which the author (though under an assumed name) so boldly carried his principles to their utmost logical conclusions, created great commotion among the "philosophers." Though they did not all feel indignant, they nearly all thought it advisable to simulate indignation. Voltaire strongly protested, and this time he was sincere. Diderot, who was suspected of having had a hand in the work, kept very quiet. D'Alembert confessed that the *Système de la Nature* was a "terrible book." Frederick II, very much shocked, wrote a refutation of it. He clearly perceived the revolutionary ideas lurking in it, and

became out of humor with the Encyclopaedists, who were friends and intimates of Baron D'Holbach. As for Rousseau, he had already broken with them long before, and had not waited for this book before opening the battle against materialism and atheism, which he "held in abhorrence."

Nevertheless Rousseau had contributed to the *Encyclopaedia* in the first years of its publication; Condillac, Turgot, Quesnay had likewise written articles for it, and unfortunately other men besides, who were unworthy of such neighbors. In spite of Diderot's efforts there are strange incongruities in the *Encyclopaedia*, and we easily understand voltaire's frequent indignation at the vapid or highflown nonsense which Diderot was compelled to insert. D'Alembert, who ceased in 1757 to be associated with him in publishing the *Encyclopaedia*, though he went on contributing to it, often pleads extenuating circumstances in his Letters to Voltaire. It was he who, in his *Discours Préliminaire*, gave perhaps the best characterization of this undertaking in which the philosophical spirit of the age found its expression: "The present century," said, "which thinks itself destined to alter laws of all kinds and to secure justice . . ."

The philosophers proceeded to "alter the laws" with an eagerness, a confidence in their own reason and in their paradoxes and a power of self-delusion that were extraordinary. The government they controlled existed only in imagination, and there was no check of experience to bring them to a halt in time. The work which they did too hastily now seems to us rather poor and out of proportion to their claims; but it does not follow that this work was not necessary, or that they were wrong in undertaking it. On the contrary, their impulse on the whole was generous, and for this reason, in spite of all their failings, it proved irresistible and carried away the very men who ought to have been its natural adversaries. Hatred of falsehood, superstition, oppression, confidence in the progress of reason and science, belief in the power of education and law to overcome ignorance, error and misery, which are the sources of all our misfortunes, and lastly warm sympathy for all that is human were shed abroad from this focus to the ends of the civilized world. Events followed which left an indelible mark upon history. And though a clearsighted reaction showed the weaknesses, inconsistencies and lapses of this philosophy, it may well be believed that its virtue is not yet quite exhausted, and that by laying its foundations deeper it may yet rise again with new strength.

Émile Bréhier

SOURCE: "The Theory of Nature," in *The History of Philosophy, Vol. 5: The Eighteenth Century,* translated by Wade Baskin, The University of Chicago Press, 1967, pp. 121-4.

[*Bréhier was an eminent French philosopher and historian of philosophy whose writings include* Histoire de philosophie *(1926-32) and* La philosophie et son passe *(1940). In the following excerpt from the English translation, published in 1967, of the former work's 1930 segment entitled*

Le dix-huitième siecle (The Eighteenth Century), *he discusses the general ideas which informed the Encyclopedists' world view.*]

I *Diderot, D'Alembert, and the Encyclopedia*

In the group of philosophers known as the Encyclopedists, either because they actually participated in Diderot and D'Alembert's undertaking or because of their affinity with them, we find a spirit quite different from that of [their predecessors]. Generally speaking, they placed little stress on the philosophy of mind, for they were inclined to think that Locke had had the last word on the matter and to look with deep distrust on metaphysical subtleties. They were interested not so much in mental faculties as in nature and society. In Diderot in particular and in his materialist friends, D'Holbach, Helvétius and, previously, La Mettrie, we find an emergent conception of nature.

The history of the foundation of the *Encyclopedia* by Diderot and D'Alembert is well known. Denis Diderot, born at Langres in 1713, studied under the Jesuits at the Collège Louis-le-Grand. Interested in all the sciences and arts, he first translated Stanyan's Grecian History (1743), then James's *A Medicinal Dictionary* (1744), and finally Shaftesbury's *Inquiry concerning Virtue or Merit* (1745). In 1746 the publisher Le Breton entrusted him with the translation of Chamber's *Cyclopaedia; or an Universal Dictionary of Arts and Sciences*, published with great success in 1728. The idea of such a work was in the air, and in an oration delivered in 1737 Ramsay, the great exponent of Freemasonry, is reported to have exhorted his colleagues to "unite to shape the materials for a universal dictionary of the liberal arts and all useful sciences. Diderot enlarged the original project and brought in his friend, the mathematician D'Alembert. Jean le Rond d'Alembert, born in 1717, had already written his *Treatise on Dynamics* and was a member of the Academy of Sciences and a friend of Frederick II. Associated with them were various collaborators, men of letters, scholars, and scientists, but Diderot himself wrote a large number of articles. Imprisoned at Vincennes for six months in 1749 for writing *Philosophical Thought* (1746) and *Letter on the Blind* (1749), he published the first volume of the *Encyclopedia* (*Encyclopédie, ou Dictionnaire raisonné des arts et des métiers*) in 1751 (he had also written *The Way of the Skeptic*, published in 1830, and *On the Sufficiency of Natural Religion*, published in 1770). The first volume of the *Encyclopedia*, by a group of men of letters, was preceded by a "Preliminary Discourse," written by D'Alembert. Pious partisans, supported by the *Journal de Trévoux* and Christophe de Beaumont, Archbishop of Paris, took up as a pretext a thesis upheld at the Sorbonne by the Abbé de Prades in which they found condemnable propositions such as the origin of ideas in the senses or the defense of natural morality, and then placed the responsibility for the scandal on the *Encyclopedia* and succeeded in having it interdicted just as the second voluem was being published, early in 1752. Nevertheless, with the tacit support of Malesherbes, director of publications, and in spite of the incessant attacks by the enemies of the Philosophes, Palissot and Fréron, five new volumes of the *Encyclopedia* were published between 1753 and 1757. But 1758 was another critical year for the work: as a result of polemics occasioned by his article "Geneva," D'Alembert, with the clandestine approval of Voltaire, abandoned the work, as did Duclos and Marmontel. The *Encyclopedia*, held accountable for the materialism of Helvétius (whose book *Essays on the Mind*, published in 1758, was condemned), was again interdicted by royal decree and condemned by the pope; not until much later, in 1766, did the last ten volumes appear. Around the *Encyclopedia* was formed, chiefly from 1753 on, the society which included not only Diderot but also Rousseau, Grimm, D'Holbach, and Helvétius. Several of Diderot's philosophical works—his *Thoughts on the Interpretation of Nature* and *The Dream of D'Alembert*, both written in 1769, and *Supplement to the Voyage to Bougainville*, written in 1772, were not published until after his death. Diderot died in 1784.

"We are witnessing a great revolution in the sciences," wrote Diderot in *The Interpretation of Nature*. "Considering the penchant which intellects seem to me to have for ethics, belles-letters, natural history, and experimental physics, I would almost dare to assert that within the next hundred years there will not be three great geometers in Europe." What might be called a veritable demathematization of the philosophy of nature occurred as men turned away from the Cartesian ideal according to which every difficulty in physics should be rendered "almost identical to the ideals of mathematics."

The nature and origin of such a new mentality merits investigation. Three reasons for its emergence, all closely interconnected, stand out: (1) the manner in which Newton's mathematical science of nature was interpreted; (2) the transformation of the ideal of the mathematicians; (3) the development, for their own sake, of the life sciences.

The result of Newtonian science was to point up the contrast between the rigor of mathematical reasoning and the merely approximate character of experimental measures. It was wrong for anyone to assume that there was in the law of attraction a principle from which all natural phenomena could be deduced. This law failed to account for the electrical, chemical and biological phenomena which were receiving more and more attention. Moreover, as Diderot, Bradly, and Le Monnier observed, even in the study of the heavens the new mathematical science "did not dispense with observing the sky."

But certainly this new attitude goes beyond the brutal observation which caused Diderot to say that someone should write a *Treatise on the Aberration of Measures*. It seems, in fact, that through the idea of his science which he fashioned for himself, the geometer took the initiative in dissociating himself from physics, at least in proportion as natural science asserted its originality. D'Alembert, the theoretician of geometry, combines the traits (not incompatible by any stretch of the imagination!) of the empiricist and the logician. On the one hand, mathematics is an experimental science because of its subject matter. It is even the first of the sciences since it deals with figures, the most abstract and general characteristics of bodies: "By successive operations and abstractions, we divest matter of almost all of its properties and somehow consider only its ghost, extension" (we recall that this is the language of

Hobbes). Geometry studies matter reduced almost to nothingness, and arithmetic, still more abstract, originates when the object is to find the relation between the parts of that from which we imagine geometrical bodies to be composed. Thus, since it is no longer anything but "a kind of general metaphysics in which bodies are divested of their individual qualities," mathematics relegates to the experience of the physicist almost everything that can be discovered.

On the other hand, as a logician the mathematician seeks to deduce all truths from the smallest possible number of principles. His course, like that of philosophers in general, is the reverse of the course dictated by common sense: "The most abstract notions—those which the common man considers the most inaccessible—are often those through which the greatest light is conveyed. The smaller they are in number, the more fruitful the principles are . . . ; they must be expanded through reduction" [Discours sur L'Encyclopedie]. The mathematician's virtuosity therefore consists in dispensing with the greatest possible number of concrete notions. This is true, for example, of D'Alembert's work in dynamics, which is the complete opposite of the dynamics attempted by Leibnitz, who had reintroduced into Cartesian mechanics the notion of moving cause or force. D'Alembert requires only motion. "Solely from consideration of motion viewed in the simplest and clearest way," he deduces three principles by means of which reason can obtain results coincident with those of experience.

Thus the truths of dynamics, contrary to what Leibnitz thought, are necessary and not contingent. Mathematics, understood in this way, relinquishes the eminent place assigned to it by Descartes and becomes only one science among others. But if we adopt D'Alembert's interpretation, we see that it has something in common with the others. Like D'Alembert, almost every other mid-eighteenth century thinker relied on empiricism and deduction, trying to find in each science the fundamental fact from which all the rest could be deduced. For example, nothing bears a closer resemblance to D'Alembert's ideas on mathematics, than Condillac's theory of mind. "Anyone who examines a series of geometrical propositions deduced from each other," writes D'Alembert in his Discourse on the Encyclopedia, "will notice that all of them are merely disfigurations of the first proposition; it is distorted, gradually and successively, as the geometer passes from one consequence to the next; instead of being multiplied, however, it is simply given different forms." Is this not, mutatis mutandi, what Condillac said of sensation and the mental faculties? This is the same type of thinking that we find, in another form, in the philosophy of nature and again in social philosophy.

One of the most characteristic aspects of this type of thinking is seen in Linnaeus' discussions of the classification of living beings. Diderot voices the most general criticism of those called "methodists" in these words: "Instead of reforming their notions of beings, it seems that they take it upon themselves to model beings on their notions." Linnean classes are categories abritrarily fabricated by the mind and forced to accommodate any living being which pres-

ents the characteristics which define its class; furthermore, any other characteristics are disregarded, even though they might relate a particular being to other beings placed in a remote class. Contrary to the rule established by Locke, Linnaeus thought that he could utilize archetypal ideas of substances.

Diderot is instinctively hostile to any thought that fixes and limits beings. "There is nothing precise in nature. . . . Nothing is of the essence of a particular being. And you speak of essence, you poor philosophers." His work abounds in intuitions concerning nature conceived as a whole in which particular beings are reabsorbed. After being a deist with Shaftesbury, he arrived at a kind of naturalism of which the most vivid expression is given in *The Dream of D'Alembert*. Through Bordeu, the vitalistic doctor of the school of Montpellier, he expounds the thesis that an animal is an aggregate of animalcules which join together and become organs for the whole; the individual has no unity other than the unity of aggregation which is forever varying and being transformed, without any true death occurring and without the whole being affected. He urges us to "steer clear of the sophism of ephemerality," which supports the belief that diurnal forms endure eternally; there is a general flux which must cause the species which constitute the whole to change completely from one planet to the next and from one epoch to the next. Diderot had a presentiment of Lamarck's transformism: "Organs produce needs and needs produce organs." The transient identity of the self exists only through this whole: "Change the whole and you necessarily change me." But there is also in each being (this is the old alchemy of the Renaissance) an image of every other being: "Any animal is to some degree a man; any mineral is to some degree a plant; any plant is to some degree an animal."

To this naturalism is linked an ethic based on the return to nature. Diderot's *Supplement to the Voyage to Bougainville*, in a Tahitian fantasy, describes what human life would be like if entrusted to completely pure, primitive instincts not yet transformed by laws and religion. It contrasts at every point with the naturalism of Rousseau, who stressed the natural, spontaneous character of conscience and duty. To Diderot the return to nature is the return to instinct.

II *La Mettrie, D'Holbach, Helvétius, Maupertuis*

Apart from his scintillating style, there are only slight differences between Diderot's ideas and those of his friends, D'Holbach and Helvétius. Before them came Julien Offray de La Mettrie (1709-51), a doctor who was banished first from France (1746) and then from Holland (1748) because of his publications. He found refuge with Frederick II, who granted him a pension and appointed him court reader. He was always held in bad repute in philosophical circles. Paul Henri Thiry, Baron d'Holbach (1723-89), was born in the Palatinate and spent most of his life at Paris, where he was the friend and host of the Philosophes, whom he assembled in his hotel on the Rue Saint-Roch. He contributed to the *Encyclopedia* articles on chemistry and diverse scientific subjects and, beginning in 1766, published a great number of antireligious writings. Claude

Adrien Helvétius (1715-71) came from a family of physicians of German ancestry. His grandfather, the first of them, settled in France, where Helvétius himself became farmer general. During his lifetime he published only his *Essays on the Mind*, which was condemned; the book *On Man* did not appear until 1772.

The superficial view that La Mettrie's and D'Holbach's materialism is grounded on the sensationalist theory of knowledge was long ago refuted in Lange's *History of Materialism*. Decided sensationalists like Condillac were actually strict spiritualists, and simple chronology rules out the possibility that the first known French materialist, La Mettrie, profited from Condillac's works. Besides, that materialism had existed in England since the emergence of the seventeenth-century "mortalists" is attested by Locke's confession concerning the spirituality of the mind, by Toland's books, and by Collins' polemic.

Materialism asserts the fundamental unity of all phenomena—observable, physical, vital, moral, social, human, or animal—and posits as their common link their relation to the entity which he calls nature. "Everything that is not taken from the very bosom of nature," says La Mettrie, "everything that is not a phenomenon, a cause, or an effect—in short, everything that is not in the realm of natural science—does not concern philosophy and comes from an alien source." Here again the object is not to describe a real genesis of these phenomena but to produce the impression or intuition of their intrinsic relationship.

The thesis of the materialists is simple enough, but the intellectual circumstances under which it is upheld are more complex. Their thesis, though predicated on rigorous determinism, is different from Cartesian mechanics. In *Man a Machine*, for example, La Mettrie refers to the Cartesian thesis of animal-machines, but he thinks that each part of the body has its own structure to allow it to act and to function without the whole; and, as a doctor, he stresses the survival of organs after their separation from an organism (examples then known include the continued beating of the heart of a frog and the reproduction of the whole polyp from one of its parts); it follows, then, that every action of an organism is due to the combined actions of each part, with its own structure and force, as in the automatons then being fabricated by Vaucanson. "If only it is conceded that organized matter is endowed with a moving principle which alone differentiates it from matter which is not so endowed," he says, "and that in animals everything depends on diversity of organization, that is enough to explain the energy of substances and of man."

It is in D'Holbach's *System of Nature* that the thesis stands out most clearly. It is concentrated in an ancient Ionian concept against which Plato and Aristotle had fought persistently and which D'Holbach expresses in this way: "Motion is a mode of being which necessarily flows from the essence of matter." D'Holbach reprimands the physicists who, like Descartes, thought that bodies were inert and preferred (for instance in the case of heavy bodies) to explain their fall through an imaginary external cause of which they had no idea rather than to attribute an inner force to them, and he undertakes (in a passage that makes little sense) to deduce Newtonian gravitation from the essence of matter. By inherent motion D'Holbach means something that differs qualitatively according to the matter under consideration, for "each being can act and move only in one particular way. . . . Each being has laws of motion which are peculiar to it and acts constantly in accordance with these laws unless a stronger cause interrupts its action." D'Holbach puts primary stress on the Cartesian error of the homogeneity of matter, which he refutes by praising the Leibnitzian principle of indiscernibles as stated by Bilfinger. After positing these substances endowed with qualitatively different properties, D'Holbach concludes that each being is a composite of simple beings and that its essence consists wholly in the mingling of these beings.

Like many of his contemporaries, D'Holbach tries to apprehend the series of essences, beginning with matter. But he stresses the philosophy of nature almost solely for the purpose of showing the extent to which his thesis renders natural religion nugatory, and he effectively destroys the argument, then almost unique, used by the Philosophes to demonstrate the existence of God—the argument of final causes. Order in nature is but one rigorously necessary arrangement of its parts, founded on the essence of things; for example, the beautiful regularity of the seasons is not the effect of a divine plan but the result of gravitation.

But D'Holbach was especially concerned with applying his ideas to the moral world and showing how they should be used to construct a new morality not connected with any positive religion. Man, too, is a mixture of matter "whose arrangement is called organization and whose essence is to sense, to think, and to act." The mind of each depends on his physical sensibility, which depends in turn on his temperament. The sole law of his activity is to love pleasure and to fear pain. He is surrounded by sensible beings different from him and unequal among themselves; it is this inequality which supports society inasmuch as it causes men to have need of each other. But of course "men contribute to the well-being of other men only when they are persuaded to do so in order to procure pleasure thereby; they refuse to contribute to it when they are hurt. Those are the principles on which to ground a universal system of ethics, one common to all individuals belonging to the human species." Ethics, then, consists in willing the well-being of others, but the benefits associated with it are in no way natural consequences of the social process; on the contrary, "the powers of the earth must lend to ethics the expedient of rewards and penalties of which they are depositaries." The moral problem is a problem of legislation: the establishment of a system of sanctions in which pleasure is used to incite men to perform virtuous acts, that is, acts useful to others. It therefore implies a political reorganization in which the power of education, until now religious, is replaced by an enlightened, unprejudiced secular power which recognizes, along with the motives of human conduct, social utility.

No morality without social restraint: this notion, notwithstanding appearances, clearly separates the view of D'Holbach and his circle from the teachings of the Epicureans, who were radically isolated from society. D'Holbach, whose books are suffused with the idea of social utility, seeks to achieve the conformity associated with religion, but by surer, more rational measures. Here his views contrast starkly with those of La Mettrie, who states bluntly: "In ethics we have no choice except to resemble others, to live and almost to think as they do. What a comedy!"

Hence the relentless struggle against religion, which philosophy is supposed to replace. In this struggle D'Holbach probably used the arguments common to the philosophers of his time—the absurdity of theological quarrels, intolerance and its dangers, the fragility of traditions—but he relied mainly on the antinaturalistic character of Christianity. Religion preaches asceticism and insists that man should not desire what his nature compels him to desire; such principles "produce no effect, or simply reduce man to despair by inciting an unrelenting struggle between the passions of his heart, his vices, his habits, and the fantastic fears through which superstition has sought to crush him"; these principles are wholly arbitrary since they are grounded "on the chimercial will of a supernatural being" and not, like those of the new ethics, "on the eternal, invariable relations subsisting between human beings living in a society." Notions which are inherently as ineffective as these can be fortified only by artificial notions, such as the notion of the soul, of a future life, or of a God who rewards and punishes. Here again, then, man's conduct is motivated by pleasure, yet a purely imaginary pleasure. Who could have contrived and maintained such inventions but those who use them to lead men wherever they will—in other words, priests? That religion is the invention of priests determined to impose all kinds of ceremonies and practices in order to hold men in their power is the thesis transmitted from Toland to D'Holbach.

The doctrines expressed in Helvétius' *Essays on the Mind* (1758) is essentially the same: it is the application, in intellectual matters, of D'Holbach's ethical tenets. He attempts to solve this problem: Everything in the mind originates by means of physical sensitivity, which is identical in all men and even in many animals; but there is a great diversity of minds, which are different both in nature and worth; how can such diversity spring from a single source? This difference derives immediately from the variable capacity of the attention and its orientation or choice of particular objects; furthermore, this capacity and direction exist solely by virtue of passion, and "one becomes stupid as soon as one ceases to be impassioned." Passion itself amounts simply to pursuit of pleasure and flight from pain—that is, to physical sensibility, which therefore proves to be the source of the diversity of minds. As for the worth of a mind, it is based not on something intrinsic but only on the esteem accorded to it by other men, and this esteem is proportionate to the general interest of the members of the society to which the individual belongs; a miser may evidence as much intelligence in his schemes as the leader of a victorious army, but the latter is superior by far to the former. Depending on its nature, each kind of society—commoners, aristocrats, men of letters—confers superiority on a mind which would lose its worth by changing its setting; moreover, since each individual benefits by conforming to the interest of the society in which he lives, this society inspires passions which should

produce the minds it esteems. Hence Helvétius deduces the social role of the philosopher, who alone pursues the interests of all—those interests which are truly universal—and not the interests of a particular society: "It was the philosophers who brought societies from the state of savagery to the state of perfection which they have now reached." The "prejudices" of the savage (by this Helvétius means ceremonies such as sacrifices to ancestors or the offering of first-fruits, ceremonies which nineteenth-century sociologists viewed as symbols of the social bond) were imposed for the particular benefit of the priesthood.

No one could outdo Helvétius in deprecating the essential, intrinsic qualities of the mind. A genius is such only by virtue of his worth to society; circumstances are responsible for the reputation of statesmen; as for inventive talents, it must be remembered that no scientist or philosopher is without precursors and that, in consequence, they are merely continuers. Here we have the total reversal of Vauvenargues' theses.

The mind is so dependent on external conditions that education encounters no resistance in shaping it at will. From start to finish the treatise *On Man* (1722), which was written partly to refute Rousseau's *Émile*, purports to show the power of instruction. Helvétius is convinced that man's passions (and consequently his whole mind) are in no way dependent on nature and physiological structure but are due to the circumstances of his education; that is, they are due essentially to the system of sanctions that has been applied to them. Idolatry of education or the artificial fabrication of minds could not be pushed further, and D'Holbach himself criticized Helvétius for not having seen that there are "rebellious, volatile, or dull dispositions" which nothing can improve.

It sometimes happens that materialists try to shirk responsibility for the practical consequences of their doctrine. Helvétius, of course, assures us that ignorance (he means religious prejudice) is no guarantee of the fidelity of those who practice it, that revelation of truth is disastrous only to the speaker, that knowledge of truth is always useful, that its revelation never disturbs states. La Mettrie, on the other hand, presents materialism as a purely speculative doctrine which, though it attains truth, cannot and will not exert any influence on rules of conduct: "It is futile for the materialists to prove that man is only a machine, for the people will never believe anything of the sort. What great harm would result if they did? Laws are so strict that they could be Spinozists, and society would still have no reason to fear the destruction of its altars, which seems to be the goal of this audacious system." And later, speaking of the proof he thinks he has given of the mechanical necessity of all human acts, he says: "All these questions can be put in the same class as mathematical points, which exist only in the geometer's head"; the theory of man as a machine "is so difficult to apply in practice that it proves to be as useless as all the metaphysical truths of the highest geometry." Conduct calls for social restraint, truth for speculation; this is the sense of his reply (at the beginning of *Christianity Unveiled*, 1767) to the objection that "the people must have a religion, good or bad" and that religion "acts as a necessary restraining force on simple, uncouth minds." He says: "The common people read no more than they reason . . . ; if one of them were able to read a philosophical work, he would no longer be a scoundrel to be feared . . . ; fanatics incite revolutions . . . ; enlightened, disinterested, sensible men are friends of peace." It is obvious that indecision reigned in matters that seemed crystal clear. Here we find confusion and indications of an almost irreconcilable disagreement between speculation and practical necessities; the world, as it was revealed to reason, provided men with nothing to guide their conduct. But this introduces a problem which looms large throughout the remaining part of the history of philosophy.

These books stirred up a violent polemic. The incidents are not important in the history of doctrines; besides, they quickly fell into oblivion, and they seemed for the most part dry and dull. "We did not understand," said Goethe [*in Poetry and Truth*], referring to The System of Nature, how such a book could be dangerous. "It seemed to us so spiritless, so Cimmerian, so cadaverous that we could hardly bear the sight of it." Critics soon saw that the aim of materialistic naturalism was to replace, by a rational construction, old traditions in the form of government, religion, society, and education. "A hundred times," observed Nicolas Bergier, "philosophers have drawn up plans for politics and for government; every time they have failed because they have always made plans for men as they imagined them, that is, for men who do not exist and who will never exist."

The most profound of these critical examinations is that of Holland in his *Philosophical Reflections* (*Réflexions philosophiques sur le Système de la Nature*, 1773). Leaving aside facile declamations against atheism, he stresses the radical contrast between materialistic dogmatism and the critical movement that originated with Locke and Hume (one more proof, if such is necessary, of the independence of empiricism with respect to materialism). Whereas D'Holbach represented nature as a necessary concatenation of facts, each deriving from another to infinity, Hume observed that this causality implied only a constant connection, not a necessary one. No one has been able to validate D'Holbach's hypothesis of a geometric deduction of the laws of motion, and the very notion of an infinite series "implies a contradiction since it would have the greatest possible number of terms and no real number can be the greatest possible number." Furthermore, the sufficient reason of a real effect would be relegated to infinity, which means that it would be found nowhere. Here we see the outlines of the finite thesis of the Kantian antimony. Holland found no less intolerable the transformation of attraction into "an undefinable metaphysical being which resides in bodies and acts in places where it is not present", and this despite the anticipated protestation of Newton. Finally and most important, Holland refuses to admit that empiricism leads to egotism in ethics and to negation of the spirituality of the soul and liberty, whereas the opposite theses are linked to innate ideas. As an empiricist Hutcheson posited benevolence as a moral principle, and D'Holbach never proved that a combination of motions can produce thought. As for hostility between philosophy and religion, Holland notes that religion is one aspect of the human mind and that it progresses or declines with the mind as a whole; but it neither prevents nor produces progress. "The progress of the sciences was retarded not by religion but by the invasion of the barbarians. . . . It was not religion that caused the fall of Constantinople, a political event to which we are indebted for the renaissance of the sciences and the arts. The state of religion," he adds with profundity, "follows the revolutions of the human mind, which in turn depend on the combination of myriad circumstances totally alien to the mind."

Maupertuis (1698-1759), who was president of the Berlin Academy, remained somewhat aloof from the other materialists, devoting a part of his activity to pure science, mathematics, astronomy, and geography (he directed the expedition charged with determining the shape of the earth). A defender of Newton against Descartes, he believed that it is beyond human intelligence to fashion a system and to "follow the order and dependence of every part of the universe." On the other hand, he imitated Leibniz and used the principle of finality to justify the general laws of nature, least action, and universal attraction. It was in the work first published in Latin under the pseudonym of Dr. Baumann (*Dissertatio inauguralis metaphysica de universali naturae systemate*, 1756) that he upheld a view of materialism complaisantly expounded by Diderot in *The Interpretation of Nature* and castigated by Rousseau in his *Profession of Faith*. Thought and extension, says Maupertuis, designate not essences but properties which can, without contradiction, belong to a subject whose essence may even be unknown to us; our aversion to attributing thought to matter is traceable to our conceiving thought as a mind similar to our own; in truth (and here Leibniz' influence is again discernible) there are countless gradations of thought, from a clear intellect to the vaguest sensation. The materialism of Maupertuis is a kind of hylozoism which attributes life and sensibility to every material molecule and assumes that any superior life or thought comes from the consensus of elementary molecules. Nevertheless, according to P. Burnet, his most recent interpreter, on some points this doctrine resembles the immaterialism of Berkeley. In particular, Maupertuis does not consider extension as being substantial; like so-called secondary qualities, it is a simple representation. Such indecisiveness is characteristic of Maupertuis' thinking.

III *Buffon and the Naturalists*

It is important for us briefly to note the existence of the same spirit in the works of the naturalists, dominated by the personality of Buffon. Georges Louis Leclerc de Buffon (1707-88), superintendent of the Jardin du Roi after 1738, published his *Natural History* between 1749 and 1788. The naturalists looked upon him as a writer and philosopher rather than a scientist: "His work," said [M. Caullery in his *Histoire de la nation francaise*], "is the antithesis of that of Linnaeus." He inspired Diderot's theses against Linnaeus.

In opposition to Linnaeus' hierarchical classification he posits the notion of a series or chain. Taking species (defined as a group of animals which are physically identical and susceptible of indefinite reproduction through copulation) as the only real units, he proposes to arrange them in a single, continuous file so that each will resemble those close to it more than those remote from it. The Leibnizian axiom of qualitative continuity or the "plenum of forms" is the rule which nature has followed in her production and which the human mind must rediscover. In Buffon's words, "We must assume that whatever can exist does exist." Though he is an exponent of the fixity of living species—which he represents in *Epochs of Nature* (1779) as having been created one by one as the earth cooled and provided the requisite conditions of habitat—he believes in the unity of a living type which exhibits every possible variation and manifests itself through the continuity of species, which is simply the unity of the natural plan. The idea of the series is not linked in any way to the idea of the descent of species, which had almost disappeared in the eighteenth century; it consists rather in asserting that there is an ideal dependence in the moments of the natural or divine plan, and Daudin is justified in saying that the postulate of this theory is that the actual state of the living world has its reason "not in the determinative circumstances of the processes that have brought it to this point, but in certain relations inherent in this state itself." [H. Daudin, *Les méthodes de classification et l'Idée de série en botanique et en zoologie de Linné à Lamarck,* 1926].

The same postulate also found support at that time in Daubenton's research in comparative anatomy, which shows, between organs in different groups, relations so essential that they nullify the petty differences on which "methods" are established. It was after citing Daubenton's works, inserted into the fourth volume of Buffon's *Natural History*, that Diderot advanced the idea that there may have been a first being or "prototype of all beings," of which living species are successive metamorphoses.

Another discovery casts a new light on Leibnitz' notion of series. Leibniz, according to whom everything is in everything and is organized to infinity, could see in the ascending series of forms only a passage from confusion to distinctiveness. Charles Bonnet's discovery of living beings with a homogeneous structure—the genus *Hydra*—proved that there were living beings without heterogeneous parts; but it also meant that the series of ascending terms could no longer be defined by the intrinsic character of a continuous progression toward distinctiveness but only by reference to one term in the series—that term considered, not without an element of arbitrariness, to be the most perfect. According to Bonnet, this being is man, and its degree of resemblance to the human organization gives each animal its place in the series.

This is also the view expressed by J. B. Robinet in his *Philosophical Considerations of the Natural Gradation of the Forms of Being, or Nature's Attempts to Create Man* (1768). He was even more ambitious than Buffon, for he taught that the series in question should embrace every being in nature. Robinet (like Buffon) rediscovers the old antimechanistic ideas of the Renaissance and believes that there is no matter in the universe which is not animated; that is, capable of nutrition, reproduction, and growth. In this sense he resembles Diderot, in whom the idea of the old alchemists reappeared. The problem posed by nature is that of realizing these three functions with the greatest

possible perfection, and man is the most elegant and most complicated solution of this problem. According to Robinet, progress toward the realization of man consists in a sort of progressive liberation of activity, which is a substance and which uses matter for the purpose of displaying its effects; in minerals activity is completely enslaved to matter, with the result that all operations are made subservient to the material subject; in that case a spontaneous motion is noted in a living being and "it seems that the active power endeavors to rise above the solid, impenetrable, extended mass to which it is connected and often forced to submit." In man, matter is no longer anything except the organ of this activity, and its progression cannot be said to have reached its limit in him; a phase must be postulated in which this activity, no longer dependent on organs and converted into pure intelligence, "is completely dematerialized." The visible world, therefore, has an invisible world as its counterpart. Thus through the idea of series a type of philosophy of nature known since antiquity is reintroduced—a philosophy of nature which focuses on the living being and extends beyond matter to pure mind.

The thesis of series, however, encountered difficulties of another kind as a result of the extension of experience. The series of beings should be linear and without ramifications if all beings tend toward man, but experience leads Bonnet himself to think that "the scale of nature might not be simple but might shoot out from all sides main branches from which subordinate branches would grow." This was also the opinion of the naturalist Pallas, to whom the linear series became a ramified tree: from the zoophyte spring the two trunks—the animal and the vegetable—and from the animal trunk spring the two branches of insects and birds. Buffon adopts a slightly more complicated image, that of a web, for "nature does not take a single step which is not a step in every direction"; beginning with a given type, nature projects species which are connected to species of all other types; quadrupeds, for example, include species similar to birds, such as bats, and species similar to reptiles, such as the anteater.

Each of these images—the chain, the ramified tree, the web—seems to have a different philosophical signification. The chain is a series of forms obtained through the degradation or attenuation of a supreme type—the old Neo-Platonic image; the tree is a tendency to realize a superior type—a tendency which sometimes misses the mark and results in aberrant, unproductive formations; the web, as Buffon indicated many times, is the realization at each stage of all possible types to the extent that each stage permits their realization. But of prime importance was the common character revealed, at the crux of these divergences, in the statement of the problem. The aim of the naturalists was to establish, among the forms or types of beings under consideration, a smooth, easy connection which would enable the mind to grasp their ideal dependence. They were concerned, not with the real, effective genesis of these forms (which they attributed to nature or to God), but with their emergence from one another and their fusion.

IV   *The Dynamism of Boscovich*

Roger Joseph Boscovich, born at Ragusa in 1711, entered

Jesuit novitiate at Rome in 1725. Versed in geometry, optics, and astronomy, he was also an engineer and an archeologist; in addition, he wrote poetry. His *Philosophiae naturalis theoria redacta ad unicam legam virium in natura existentium* is the exposition of a dynamistic theory of nature which closely parallels the theories just discussed. Boscovich, like a true disciple of Locke, thinks that we know neither substances nor the active powers of things; but he makes a distinction between power and force, and, thanks to Newton, he succeeds in defining force solely through determination of motion. In fact, we can speak of forces only when at least two material points are under consideration. These two points are determined by their distance, whether they are moving toward each other or away from each other, and "it is this determination that we call force, by which we mean not a mode of action but the determination itself—regardless of its origin—which changes in magnitude as the distances change" [D. Nedelkovitch, *La philosophie naturelle et relativiste de R. J. Boscovich,* 1922].

This force is attractive when the distance between two points surpasses a determinate limit; it becomes repulsive when the distance falls short of the limit. The universe is the whole set of points which mutually attract or repel each other. Each point is a center of force, not by itself but solely in its relations to the other points which it attracts or repels just as it is attracted or repelled by them. This conception bears some resemblance to Kant's *Monadologia physica* (1746) but differs strikingly on one point: Boscovich's center of force has no heart, no spontaneity; apart from the whole to which it belongs, it is nothing. Here as in the conceptions of nature that we have just examined, the nature of each being is determined, but in an entirely different way, by circumstances relating to its place in the whole.

Radoslav A. Tsanoff

SOURCE: "The Philosophers of the French Enlightenment," in *The Great Philosophers,* Harper & Brothers, 1953, pp. 409-21.

[*Tsanof was a Bulgarian-born American philosopher whose writings include* The Nature of Evil *(1931),* Worlds to Know: A Philosophy of Cosmic Perspective *(1962), and* Civilization and Progress *(1971). In the following excerpt, he offers a concise overview of Encyclopedist thought.*]

Descartes has been called the father of systematic modern philosophy; and during the seventeenth century his influence, and with it the influence of French ideas, was a major factor in the development of outstanding thinkers like Hobbes, Spinoza, Leibniz, Locke, and Berkeley. But Cartesianism did not achieve any further original expression in France. Aside from Gassendi, Malebranche, and Pascal, for over half a century the history of French philosophy was of no consequence. The hundred years of Fontenelle's life (1657-1757) yielded some popular expositions of Cartesian cosmology and brave radical essays in the history and criticism of religious beliefs, but no work of commanding, systematic thought.

The monarchical centralization of power in France by Louis XIV was accompanied and followed by the exaltation of traditional ideas and by political and theological authoritarianism. Freedom of thought and expression were stifled. Cartesian rationalism itself, though at first opposed by surpliced minds, was adapted to orthodox and conservative demands, and it supplemented scholastic orthodoxy as a medium of acceptable reflection. Voltaire could not obtain a copyright for his book on Newton's philosophy because in it he opposed Descartes.

In contrast to this reactionary constriction of French intelligence was the situation in eighteenth-century Britain. Britain had subdued royal and theological absolutism, and expanded the range of free discussion. Newton and Locke were its leaders into new regions of understanding. Critical deism and even freethinking infidelity were evidence of the interplay of ideas in unshackled minds. To increasing numbers of French thinkers, England came to represent the reality of a social ideal that shamed their own actualities. English ideas gained both intellectual and moral prestige in France.

Enlightened Frenchmen turned especially to Locke's philosophy of experience which in their judgment expressed the moving spirit in the new unchanneled currents of free English thinking about nature, man, society, religion. Here was a philosophy without innate ideas or axiomatic first principles, without vested rights or prerogatives, that relied on the plain course of experience in theory and respected the plain needs of people in practice. It was a pliable, malleable philosophy, suitable for an age in need of radical reconstruction, such as the *ancien régime* in France. John Locke's empiricism held out the promise of a new day to forward-looking French spirits—the fathers of the Revolution, as they have been called.

Locke's own reasonable moderation and eminent respectability and piety gained response to his ideas from critical minds that were still averse to any radical excesses. His characteristically English reserve calmed any initial alarm and gave the new ideas a chance to make an impression. But the French logical drive was sure to carry them on their way. The English freethinkers, infidels, and radicals not only were read in France but were far exceeded by their followers there.

Thus the French development proceeded along its own lines and to its final outcome. Locke's disciples in France were not content to entertain his tentative speculation that God might have endowed some kinds of matter with the ability to think. They restated his conjecture as a scientific conclusion, expanded it as a materialistic account of all human nature and all existence, and leaped the whole length of the ancient Lucretian arguments to a denial of God and immortality. When Hume was in Paris, he remarked one evening to Baron Holbach, his host, that he had never met a real atheist, whereupon Holbach replied: "It may interest you to know, Monsieur, that you are dining tonight with seventeen of them." . . .

The new critical-radical ideas of the French Enlightenment were advocated on an extensive scale in the great *Encyclopedia* which appeared in more than thirty volumes during the third quarter of the eighteenth century. Its importance exceeded that of Bayle's *Dictionary*, for it was not the work of one man, but brought together the leading minds of France and gave their views cumulative weight and influence. Voltaire, Turgot, Holbach, Rousseau were among the contributors. The outstanding mind and will that organized and directed it and brought it to a conclusion was Denis Diderot (1713-1784). Closely associated with him in editing the earlier volumes was Jean le Rond d'Alembert (1717-1783). Diderot was in ill repute with the government as a radical author; he had even served a prison term at Vincennes. Therefore he wisely entrusted to d'Alembert the "Preliminary Discourse" that introduced the *Encyclopedia*. This famous mathematician, member of all the scientific academies in Europe, honored in Berlin and St. Petersburg as in Paris, knew how to combine calm reserve and dignity of manner with personal integrity in intellectual and social reform.

Beyond his special scientific work in mathematics, and the survey of its order and development in his plan for the *Encyclopedia*, d'Alembert's general philosophical views are of interest. He resisted the materialistic trend of the age and preferred no scientific commitment in metaphysics. We can advance physical science, or like Locke explore the mind's experience. But we do not know whether our minds are thinking bodies or immaterial essences. From certain specific conditions we can draw definite inferences; but skepticism seems the most reasonable position regarding ultimate principles.

Meanwhile we have to live. On what motives, by what standards? D'Alembert required convictions in morals. He did not base them on theology, which he regarded as unsettled by criticism. They must be ascertained from the conditions of the social order evident in human experience, from the proper regulation of men's conduct in their various relations with each other, and likewise of social groups and classes. Like an eighteenth-century Confucian in Europe, d'Alembert wrote the formulas and precepts of reasonable social coöperation which constitute the good life. Injustice is disproportion. The luxury of a wealthy minority is a moral stain in a society where multitudes are indigent and hungry. D'Alembert did not forget his mathematics when he passed judgment on the inequity of civilization.

Diderot had a fertile, versatile mind, and was always an aggressive protagonist. From traditional piety he turned to liberal deism and then to unbelief, resigned and derisive in turn. Since no regular profession suited his protean intelligence, he became a literary free lance. Like Carneades in ancient Rome he argued eloquently both sides of every moral question, reveling in the transitions of emphasis. His mind and thought and career expressed the characteristically unsettled but vigorously upsurging radicalism of his age.

His speculative sweep and fertility vied with his social-revolutionary ardor. The intellectual motive was primary. Diderot was not content to overcome bigotry; he wanted to confute it. Man's knowledge is limited, but he loses even his small chance of understanding if he renounces experimental inquiry and relies on dogmatic assertion. Diderot's violent scorn of the ecclesiastics was due not only to their

support of the reactionary monarchist regime, but also to their impeding man's sole path to knowledge. "Astray at night in an immense forest, I have only a small light to guide me. A stranger comes along and tells me: 'My friend, blow out your candle so as to see your way better.' This stranger is a theologian. He would replace the priestly teleology by a cosmic theory that conforms to the facts of modern science. He revived the spirit of Bruno and Lucretius. The new cosmology, he was sure, required an adequate view of the complexity of nature. The theologian should not be allowed his imagined easy victory over the materialist because of a meager conception of matter. Matter is complex and most abundant in potentialities. It is not merely so much occupied space, inert and brute; it is capable of life, of sensation, of thought. If we duly acknowledge the versatility of material existence, we shall not have to import illegitimate hypotheses of immaterial principles in order to explain any activity of human life, even the highest. Thus confident of accounting for all the complex activities in nature by a revised and expanded interpretation of matter, Diderot was still convinced that he was confirming a strict materialism.

Diderot's ethics led in two directions between which he seemed unable to choose, for each of them appealed to strong and contending motives in his personality. His first philosophical publication was a version or paraphrase of Shaftesbury's *Inquiry Concerning Virtue or Merit*. Shaftesbury's aestheticmoral naturalism appealed to Diderot's loftier aspirations. Later, however, he was led to dignify or tolerate his lower impulses as quite natural. So spiritual aspirations and sensuality, philanthropy and philandering, contended in his nature, and he made an ethics of each one. The noble ideals of the French Enlightenment were advocated by the man who wrote some of the lewdest pages in philosophical literature. Critical subtlety may overtax itself in trying to arrive at a reconciliation of Diderot's moral ideas. Were they not, like his own life and personality, expressions of the instability of an age of radical transition?

The French materialistic revision of Locke's philosophy of experience was generally opposed to Cartesian rationalism. It was a peculiar turn in the materialistic argument that derived it from Descartes' cosmology. For had not Descartes described all animals as mechanisms and also treated human physiology like a physicist? Since animals have sensations and feelings and since sense impressions are physiological processes and all our knowledge is derivable from them, the traditional view of the mind becomes superfluous. Men's thought and activity may be explained in terms of matter. So reasoned Julien Offray de La Mettrie (1709-1751) in his Man a Machine and other similar books.

During a severe illness La Mettrie observed that bodily infirmity was followed by mental and moral disturbance. It became obvious to him that thought must be a physiological process or condition, and he assembled psychological and medical evidence in support of his materialistic thesis. Our so-called rational ideas are elaborated from sensations, and sensations are reactions of our bodily organs together with which they originate, grow, and eventually decay. Different states of soul are always correlative to different bodily conditions. Man's intelligence exceeds that of animals even as his brain is relatively larger and more furrowed. All direct and comparative study of mental activity must lead us to its ultimately material source.

The conviction that mind is essentially material led La Mettrie to revise the usual ideas about matter. He followed Diderot in regarding physical nature as versatile. It moves, it lives, it can perceive and think. Whether matter has these capacities inherently or acquires them only as a result of a certain organization of bodily particles, we cannot say. The fact is simply that all sensations and all so-called intelligence are inextricably bound up with a brain and a nervous system. This does not imply that all material particles are capable of consciousness, but it should rule out any reference to immaterial reason. Human nature shares certain qualities with animals and with plants, and like these it is a part of the mechanism of nature. But neither the human nor the animal machine can be explained simply in terms of the more elementary mechanisms of inorganic bodies. Observe the complexity and variety of material existence; it will teach you its own lessons, and you will not require any transcendent rational essences to explain its natural operation.

If we realize once and for all that all mental activity is a physiological process, our ideas of human knowledge and human conduct will be transformed. We shall see ourselves for what we are, as organisms reacting for a while to their environment and then decaying and passing away. Here there can be no question of eternal truths but only of habitual and limited impressions. There can be no meaning in alleged eternal principles of right or wrong, but only in peculiar and transitory pleasures and satisfactions. Like the Epicurean atomists, La Mettrie was led to hedonism in morals, but he preferred the Cyrenaic indulgence to any critical gradation of enjoyments. His hedonism was avowedly quantitative, and in two treatises he explored the voluptuous art to make sure that he missed no delight within his reach. He did not, it is true, ignore death, but he saw no reason for considering that unpleasant subject until he had to. Having with Lucretian scorn rejected all beliefs in immortality, he was resolved to taste to the full the delights of his one life while he had it. The Stoic's serene resignation is a fine doctrine, he thought, if one keeps it for one's last breath.

Paul Heinrich Dietrich von Holbach (1723-1789) was a German baron who had settled in Paris; his dining table was the meeting place of the radical philosophers twice weekly. He listened well and had efficient secretaries at the gatherings to note every brilliant sally by Diderot or sharp criticism by Rousseau or d'Alembert. Only his intimates knew that, while his was not an original mind, he was the most systematic and thoroughgoing of them all. The troubles that Diderot and Helvétius had had with the authorities had taught him a lesson. He preferred safety to literary fame, and twitted the censors by publishing his *System of Nature* under the name of the deceased Mirabaud, a sedate former secretary of the French Academy. The secret of Holbach's authorship was kept for years.

The author of the book needed a disguise on the title page,

for inside it was most outspoken and emphatic in its negation of all the respectable verities. It was unqualified in its materialism, atheism, denial of free will and immortality, contempt for all religious doctrines, and political and social incitement to revolt. It soon became the Bible of the radicals.

Holbach began with a strictly materialistic account of human nature. He recognized only bodily processes. So-called rational thought and moral conduct are simply special reactions of the human organism under certain conditions. Our ideas and actions can be traced to elementary sense impressions and responses, all of them strictly physiological processes. These processes are causally determined in each case. The notion of human freedom or spontaneous choice is illusory. Man is never free for a moment. His actions are determined by his nature and temperament and the counterplay of motives and ideas in his being. And these are all derived from sensations, which are physiological processes. The so-called soul is thus reduced to the organic behavior of the body; its whole career begins, grows, and ends with the body. What can justify us in expecting survival and eternal life in a world where everything changes, comes into being and passes away? This is only empty arrogance on our part, and no lofty religious pronouncements can really sustain it. The Christian hope of immortality is a vain dream. Matter is eternal, but its particular combinations which constitute you and me are changing and transitory.

That Holbach's system of nature should uphold atheism was inevitable from the outset. He saw no evidence in human life or in the external world of any immaterial, spiritual principle. The second part of the *System* is devoted to an elaborate refutation of the traditional proofs of God's existence. Holbach's negative conclusions were not only emphatic but scornful. He professed no regret in exposing the hollowness of men's hopes; he considered religious beliefs harmful superstitions and emancipation from them as a boon to mankind. "Theology and its notions, far from being useful to mankind, are the real sources of evils which afflict the earth, of errors which blind it, of prejudices which make it stupid, of ignorance which makes it credulous, of vices which plague it, of governments which oppress it." These words epitomize the spirit of Holbach's work.

The practical philosophy to which Holbach turned was philanthropic hedonism. People are stirred to action by the urge for satisfaction; they seek pleasure and avoid pain. In this drive of human passions some men find gratification at the expense of their fellows; others pursue pleasure in acts which promote the general happiness. We call the first kind of individual bad, the second good. Morality is simply bodily behavior that expands social security, peace, and satisfaction.

Holbach extended his ethical conclusions to politics. The good man enjoys the good will of his neighbors and seeks to deserve it, both in his lifetime and in their grateful memory of him after he is dead. Good governments also should be concerned with the people's happiness and appeal to their approval. Despotism runs counter to the people's interests; it thrives on a superstitious belief in the divine right of kings. An enlightened nation needs only firm resolution to sweep away hateful oppression and regain its conditions of general happiness.

Robert Darnton

SOURCE: *The Business of Enlightenment: A Publishing History of the "Encyclopedie" 1775-1800*, Cambridge, Mass.: The Belknap Press of Harvard University Press, 1979, pp. 460-519.

[*Darnton is a American historian known for his contributions to the history of books and publishing. His writings include* The Business of the Enlightenment: A Publishing History of the Encyclopedie, 1775-1800, The Literary Underground of the Old Regime *(1982), and* The Great Cat Massacre and Other Episodes in French Cultural History *(1984). In the following excerpt form the first-mentioned book, he identifies the Encyclopedists' various political orientations. According to Darnton, the Encyclopedists, despite their interest in progress, never abandoned a fundamentally elitist conception of knowledge.*]

[It] has been argued that Encyclopedism led to Jacobinism, not through any philosophical conspiracy such as the one imagined by the abbé Barruel, but by a congruity of outlook. According to C. C. Gillispie ["The *Encyclopédie* and the Jacobin Philosophy of Science," in Marshall Clagett, ed., *Critical Problems in the History of Science*, 1959], Diderot's *Encyclopédie* promoted a reaction against the esoteric, mathematical sciences and in favor of a vitalistic or "romantic" version of the biological sciences, and this reaction fed a current of anti-intellectualism that rose with the Jacobins to destroy Lavoisier, the academies, and what became construed as the aristocracy of the mind. The weak point in this interpretation concerns the connection between Encyclopedism and Jacobinism. It is difficult to show how the two "isms" came together, as most of the original Encyclopedists died before 1793 and the Jacobins did not justify their attacks on academicians by citing Diderot's text. But one important point of contact may be sought in the history of the second *Encyclopédie* of the Enlightenment [the *Encyclopédie méthodique*], whose publication stretched from the early 1780s through the entire Revolution and into the nineteenth century.

Although [Charles Joseph] Panckoucke's book differed from Diderot's, it was conceived as a revision and extension of the first *Encyclopédie*, it grew out of a plan that Diderot had originally devised, and it was understood at the time to be an up-dated version of Encyclopedism. . . . [the] *Méthodique* did indeed emphasize biology, but its authors, notably Lamarck, did not treat their subject in the vitalistic or romantic spirit of Diderot and Geothe. The *Méthodique* did not neglect mathematics and physics. And its volumes on chemistry propounded the rigorous, mathematical system that had been developed by Lavoisier as opposed to the vitalism of Venel's articles in the first *Encyclopédie*. Moreover, Panckoucke's chemists were prominent Jacobins: Guyton de Morveau, who served on the Committee of Public Safety, and Fourcroy, who succeeded Marat in the Convention. Panckoucke published his most esoteric dictionaries just when the Revolution reached its hottest point—perhaps because he thought that the Jacobinism of their authors, Monge and Fourcroy, would make them seem legitimate to the revolutionary government. He would hardly have brought out the volumes on physics and chemistry at that time if he expected them to offend the Jacobins, and his most offensive dictionaries probably were the ones that had won the approval of the censors of Louis XVI, jurisprudence and history in particular. In any case, the Jacobins never accused the *Méthodique* of being undemocratic on the grounds that its science had gone beyond the reach of ordinary readers. Yet its scientific articles were more abstruse than those in the first *Encyclopédie*. In fact, the *Méthodique* expressed a general tendency for knowledge to become specialized and professionalized—to become more esoteric, not less—and instead of fighting that tendency, the Jacobins recruited the specialists to make saltpeter, cannons, and a rational system of weights and measures.

A second attempt to find connections between Encyclopedism and Jacobinism involves group biography. By following the careers of the Encyclopedists who lived long enough to experience the Terror, Frank A. Kafker has tried to discredit the tendency among some historians to portray Diderot's collaborators as radicals who created the ideological basis of Jacobinism. Kafker found that only one of the thirty-eight Encyclopedists alive in 1793 welcomed the Terror, while eight resisted it, and the rest generally withdrew into obscurity, fear, and disgust. Of course it might be unreasonable to expect much congruity between men's reactions to the Revolution and the opinions they had expressed forty years earlier in essays on the arts and sciences. But it is still more difficult to see how the reactions of thirty-eight men could indicate the way all of the original contributors might have felt had they lived into the Revolution. Not only do the thirty-eight represent an insignificant fraction of Diderot's group—and the full size of the group cannot be known, though it may have included 300 persons—but they wrote an insignificant portion of his *Encyclopédie*. Only four of them contributed extensively, and the really important contributors—the men who wrote the great bulk of the book—all died before the Terror. Like Diderot himself, they belonged to the generation that reached maturity at mid-century. But the second generation of Encyclopedists, the men of the *Méthodique*, came of age with the leaders of the Revolution. Although their work cannot be equated with that of Diderot's collaborators, it can be taken to represent a later stage of Encyclopedism, the stage in which it came into direct contact with Jacobinism. So if anything is to be learned by studying the way a group of intellectuals reacted to the Revolution, the reactions of Panckoucke's Encyclopedists would be most revealing.

Of course one cannot hope to find many revelations about the innermost thoughts of men who lived almost two centuries ago. A few sources like the memoirs of Morellet and Marmontel describe the fears, the fantasies, and even the nightmares of an Encyclopedist trapped in the Terror. But several Encyclopedists continued their work without interruption and without leaving any record of how they felt about the great events of the time. Perhaps they had little interest in what went on outside their studies. Others found their lives invaded by the Revolution, but they responded in contradictory ways. The evidence will not fit into a single picture. After trying to piece it together, one is left with an assortment of unconnected images: Guyton de Morveau mounting in a balloon to observe the enemy's position at the battle of Fleurus; Daubenton dissecting the body of a rhinoceros from the former royal menagerie before a group of deputies to the Convention; Charles, deep in his laboratory in the Tuileries as the sans-culottes storm the palace on August 10, 1792 (they spared him, because of his heroic past as a balloonist); Lalande hiding Dupont de Nemours in the Observatory on the same day and, after Thermidor, rising in the Collège de France to denounce "Jacobinical vandalism"; Fourcroy extracting copper for cannons from the bells of former monasteries; Mongez applying his mastery of numismatics to the manufacture of republican coins; Quatremère de Quincy darting in and out of prison and conspiring with monarchists from the time of the Feuillants to the uprising of Vendémiaire; and Vicq d'Azyr, so horrified at the sight of Robespierre during the Festival of the Supreme Being that (according to a rather extravagant article in a later volume of the *Méthodique*) he died from its effects.

Some cases are relatively clear. The contributors to the *Méthodique* included one émigré (Pommereul), one victim of the guillotine (Boucher d'Argis) and three men who barely escaped death after being imprisoned as counter-revolutionary suspects (Desmarets, Ginguené, and Quatremère de Quincy). None of them could be classified as a partisan of the Terror; and the classification of several other Encyclopedists is a matter of record—though the record has aroused a good deal of debate among historians—because they played a prominent part in revolutionary politics. Desmeunier was an influential Patriot in the Constituent Assembly. He then retired from politics but re-emerged, in company with Daubenton, as a Napoleonic senator. In the Legislative Assembly, P. L. Lacretelle and Quatremère de Quincy rallied to the rightwing Feuillants, while Condorcet, Broussonet, Guyton de Morveau, Garran de Coulon, and Lacuée de Cessac generally backed the Brissotins on the left. As minister of the interior during the early months of the Convention, Roland led the Girondins on the right, while Monge, as minister of the marine, generally favored the rise of the Montagnard left. The purge of the Girondins cost Roland and Condorcet their lives (both committed suicide after fleeing from Paris). But their former collaborators on the *Méthodique*, Monge, Fourcroy, and Guyton de Morveau, played a crucial role in organizing the national defense during the Terror. Because they concentrated on technical problems, they are not usually considered hardline Montagnards. But they became deeply involved in Jacobin politics, unlike Garran de Coulon, who withdrew into noncontroversial committee work. For short periods in the spring of 1793 and the winter of 1794-1795, Guyton de Morveau sat on the Committee of Public Safety. And during the Directory, more Encyclopedists took seats near the center of power—Robert, Quatremère de Quincy, Garran de Coulon, and Guyton de Morveau in the Conseil des Cinq-Cents and Fourcroy, Marmontel, and Lacuée de Cessac in the Conseil des Anciens.

Clearly the contributors to the *Encyclopédie* included many political activists and they did not act in any consistent pattern during the Revolution. Not only did they support different factions or parties, but also they almost defy classification because the boundaries between parties shifted and blurred. Some historians even argue that parties did not exist in any coherent form during the Revolution. But that interpretation raises the danger of reducing political differences, which were meaningful for the revolutionaries, to a kind of nominalism. In fact, one can divide the Encyclopedists according to their political sympathies into three general categories: opponents of the Revolution (men who expressed hostility to it from the very beginning), moderates (men who supported the constitutional monarchy and mistrusted the popular revolution), and republicans (men who favored radicalization beyond August 10, 1792, either as Girondins, radical Jacobins, or unaligned individuals). There is virtually no information on ten of the seventy-three principal contributors listed by Panckoucke in 1789. Nine others died before 1793, leaving fifty-four—a reduced but representative sample of the second-generation Encyclopedists.

Fourteen of the fifty-four did not take any clear political stand during the Revolution. Of them, seven apparently continued their careers without interruption, four suffered losses of income or employment, and three lived in obscurity. It seems likely that half of this group supported the Revolution, at least passively and at least until August 10, 1792; but that is guesswork.

Seven Encyclopedists indicated disapproval of the Revolution at an early stage, but they remained passive in their opposition—except for Pommereul, who emigrated (he had his name struck off the list of émigrés in 1798, however, and became a prefect and baron under Napoleon), and Boucher d'Argis, who denounced the October Days from his position as a magistrate in the Châtelet and was guillotined as a counterrevolutionary on July 23, 1794.

Fifteen Encyclopedists can be considered moderates. At least six of them—Thouret, Lacretelle, Peuchet, Desmeunier, Kéralio, and Quatremère de Quincy—promoted a Feuillant-type of constitutional monarchy. They accepted the destruction of the Old Regime but, like Panckoucke, favored conservative reforms. The others are difficult to classify because they accepted official positions but did not participate actively in the Revolution. Some may have been quite radical—for example, Olivier and Bruguières, whom Roland sent on a scientific expedition to the mideast. But most of them concentrated on their scientific work, with the blessing of various revolutionary governments. These included the biologists of the Muséum d'histoire naturelle: Daubenton, Lamarck, and Thouin. If they did not share the radical views of their republican colleague Fourcroy—and they probably did—they certainly benefited from the Revolution's attempts to encourage botany and agronomy.

Eighteen Encyclopedists were republicans. Of them, five (Monge, Fourcroy, Guyton de Morveau, Doublet, and Chaussier) were associated with the extreme Jacobins; five (Roland, Condorcet, Broussonet, Lacuée de Cessac, and Mongez) favored the Girondins; and the other eight (Garran de Coulon, Ginguené, Mentelle, Robert, Naigeon, Chambon, Bertoli, and de Prony) remained unaligned, although most of them probably sympathized with some shade of Girondism.

This breakdown may give a misleading impression of mathematical precision; but even allowing for indeterminate cases and errors in classification, it suggests two conclusions. First, the Encyclopedists did not act as a group but scattered all over the political spectrum. Second, they did not scatter evenly but tended to cluster in the center-left, that is in a zone bounded by the Feuillants (constitutional monarchists) on the right and the Girondins (moderate republicans) on the left. Few of them supported the Terror but fewer still backed any counterrevolutionary attempt to restore the Old Regime. On the whole, they were more radical than one might expect.

Perhaps the Encyclopedists' involvement in the Revolution can be studied more fruitfully by examining institutions rather than political factions and by concentrating on the period after Thermidor rather than on the first five years of the revolutionary decade. The Jacobin Encyclopedists had adapted chemistry to weaponry, developed military medicine, and applied mathematics to the national defense. Their success reinforced an attempt, from 1793 through the Empire, to reorganize knowledge for service to the state. Of course the Encyclopedists had served the state before 1789, as academicians, censors, professors, and administrators; and they might have been expected to defend their posts against attack from the revolutionaries. But most of them helped to tear down the old intellectual institutions and to erect new ones in their place. Lamarck, Daubenton, Thouin, and Fourcroy helped transform the old Jardin du Roi into the Muséum d'histoire naturelle. Vicq d'Azyr and Antoine Louis began to reshape the medical profession from the Comité de salubrité of the Constituent Assembly, and Fourcroy and Thouret continued their work in 1794-1795 by organizing the Ecoles de santé. Five of the original twelve professors in the Parisian Ecole, later renamed the Ecole de médecine de Paris, had written on medicine for the *Méthodique*. The first professors from the Ecole normale also included a strong contingent of Encyclopedists: Monge, Thouin, and Mentelle. Monge was the driving spirit behind the creation of the Ecole polytechnique, where he was joined by four of his collaborators on the Méthodique: Fourcroy, Guyton de Morveau, Chaussier, and de Prony. Monge, Fourcroy, and Ginguené also played a decisive part on the Comité d'instruction publique of the Convention, which reorganized the system of higher education in France by creating not only the grandes écoles of Paris, but also the series of écoles centrales in the departments, where four other Encyclopedists—Desmarets, Mentelle, Grivel, and Bonnaterre—took up professorships. And finally, almost all of the Encyclopedists who had belonged to the royal academies took seats in the Institut, which was created as a "living encyclopedia" in 1795.

The careers of the Encyclopedists show an extraordinary pattern of continuity, across regimes and over political divisions, from the old institutions to the new. The lines lead directly from the Jardin du Roi to the Muséum d'histoire

naturelle, from the Société royale de médecine to the Ecoles de santé, from the technical schools of the monarchy to the grandes écoles of the republic, and from the royal academies to the republican Institut. Thirty Encyclopedists—half the number alive in 1796—joined the Institut, and twenty-nine had belonged to the academies of Paris. The intelligentsia that had dominated French culture during the early 1780s re-emerged, stronger than ever, in the later 1790s. But the staying-power of the intellectual elite does not illustrate that overused French proverb "Plus ça change, plus c'est la même chose," because the new institutions differed significantly from the old. Although their membership remained remarkably consistent, they eliminated all vestiges of privilege, corporatism, and aristocracy. The Revolution swept away the ancient ceremonies and hierarchical distinctions, the honorary academicians and the genteel amateurs. It perpetuated an old elite but under new terms: the openness of careers to talent and the dominance of professionalism. Those conditions had existed before 1789 but in muted form, mixed up with masses for Saint Louis, panegyrics to Louis XIV, and patronage from the Gentlemen of the King's Bedchamber. In the educational system of the republic, the Encyclopedists appeared as experts: each man had a field, and each field had its place within a modernized curriculum. Similarly, the Encyclopedists of the Institut sat in "classes," grouped according to their expertise. The Revolution had not eliminated intellectual elitism but had cast it in a new form, wiping out privilege and advancing professionalization.

Although this transformation occurred abruptly and violently in the years 1793-1796, its origins went back to the Old Regime—and in part to the *Encyclopédie méthodique*. Panckoucke did not believe that his book represented an advance over Diderot's because it spoke out louder against l'infâme and in favor of social equality—in fact, it was more cautious than its predecessor on religious and political questions. But he thought that it expressed a more progressive view of knowledge; for he had divided the topography of learning into fields and had assigned an expert to each of them, with instructions to produce the most advanced work that was possible within the professional boundaries. When it came to marketing his product, Panckoucke had put together *combinaisons* of protection and privilege, a strategy that looked reactionary after 1789. If viewed from the perspective of the sociology of knowledge, however, his venture can be seen as advanced: he organized the material of the *Encyclopédie* in the same way that the Encyclopedists were organized in the Institut—according to strictly professional standards.

Personally, Panckoucke remained a conservative, more so than most of his authors and despite his radical posturing after 1792. But his *Encyclopédie* cannot be identified with any explicit ideology, either Jacobinical or counterrevolutionary, and his authors scattered into different political camps. It was not a common political faith that united the Encyclopedists and gave cohesion to their work but rather an underlying tide that swept all learning in the direction of professionalism. Encyclopedism as an "ism" remained complex and contradictory. But as a phase of intellectual development in the late eighteenth century, it expressed a tendency for knowledge to concentrate among experts and for experts to be drawn into the service of the state—a tendency that had gathered force under Louis XVI, that became crucial for the salut public in 1793-1794, and that did not disappear from history after the French Revolution.

L. Cazamian

SOURCE: "The Need for Light" and "The Encyclopédia: Diderot," in *A History of French Literature,* Oxford at the Clarendon Press, 1955, pp. 216-18; 256-51.

[*Cazamian was an eminent French historian of English literature whose books include* Criticism in the Making *(1929),* The Development of English Humor *(1930), and* A History of French Literature. *In the following excerpt from the last-named work, he discusses the Encyclopedists' struggle against ignorance, explaining that the "fight for light was no longer waged . . . against the benighted ignorance of the Middle Ages [but against] a nearer, more tangible darkness, that was felt to be willed deliberately by arbitrary systems of faith and government."*]

During the first half of the eighteenth century, the features of the transition sketched in the last chapter were strengthened and developed. The new period bears the distinctive mark of a rational tendency, so outstanding that few ages of literature can be so safely classified under one label. With most writers of the time beauty was not the primary object; it became as it were the by-product of an energy that spent itself in the eager pursuit of truth. The language, by now a relatively perfect instrument for the expression and discussion of ideas, dropped the last traces of the oratorical and synthetic spirit that still lent fervour to classical prose. It was content to be supple and clear, somewhat impoverished indeed, but offering unlimited scope to analysis and debate. Reason being in charge of the search for truth, its method was criticism and argument, and this was successful in proportion as it worked out to knowledge and clarity of understanding, to a sense of intellectual illumination. Thus the idea of light (*les lumières*) assumed a central place in the phrasing and mental perspective of the French eighteenth century; a fortune paralleled by that of the German watchword, *Aufklärung;* while the corresponding English term, 'Enlightenment', was to be used in this historical sense only at a later date, and often with a slightly pejorative shade of meaning.

The French Renaissance had experienced the thirst for light; but it was then a richer and broader impulse, guided by an ideal of humanism in which beauty and all the higher values had a place by the side of truth, and which a religious or a political strain often impregnated but did not essentially alter. By degrees, as the discipline of the classical age forced itself upon the ardour of the humanist revival, the monarchy and the orthodoxy narrowed down the limits within which critical inquiries could be safely conducted. So, when the authority of the king and the Church suffered a weakening process at the end of the era of classicism, the new intellectual urge, a distinct aftereffect of the Renaissance, assumed a far more aggressive turn. The fight for light was no longer waged, as in the six-

teenth century, against what was held to have been the benighted ignorance of the Middle Ages; it was aimed at a nearer, more tangible darkness, that was felt to be willed deliberately by arbitrary systems of faith and government. After the death of Louis XIV, an awe-inspiring personality in spite of his weaknesses and the disasters of his last years, the inferior prestige of the Regent and of Louis XV could no longer repress the increasing restiveness of French citizens, though the administrative yoke remained as stiff as ever; and the example of orderly freedom set by the English began to sow seeds of invidious comparisons in a nation heading thenceforward for its Revolution. The indulgence quietly shown in England to the profession of deism, and the toleration of religious sects, were no less suggestive object-lessons; and English influence became inextricably woven in with the fabric of eighteenth-century French thought. The *libertins*, who had been for some time silent or reticent, spoke and wrote with renewed boldness; the confession of incredulity among men of letters, or in aristocratic circles, was no longer a defiance of the law; and a tacit consensus of opinion seemed to open the way for a collective endeavour to eradicate the abuses of the past, with which the present was still all trammelled.

Since these critical activities were inseparable from the thrashing out of concrete issues, the writers in an overpowering majority took sides with the reformers, and made up groups that more or less coalesced into a party—that of the *philosophes*, a label denoting readiness to make the solution of all problems dependent solely upon reason. The grand scheme of an *Encyclopédie*, or general inventory of extant knowledge, compiled in a purely objective and scientific spirit—an enterprise in which most of the eminent minds of the mid-century met—gave the philosophical age its climax and fit symbol.

Lingering darkness was to be expelled by the light of reason. But through an apparent paradox, the temper of the century had barely found its stable unity in a mood of rationalism, when sporadic symptoms of dissonance and contradiction became clearly perceptible. Strains of sentiment had already cropped up among the writers of the Transition after 1715. They grew more abundant and stronger. Deeper than the effect of social and political changes was the inner rhythm of the mind itself, and the cyclical law that presides over the development of European thought. After a prolonged period of predominant intellectualism, the emotions were called upon to reassert themselves; and the eighteenth century became eventually the age of sentimentalism, no less than that of rationality. The opposition of the two currents remained hidden for some time beneath a partial and superficial analogy; for, just as the intelligence was attacking the obsolete, the absurd, and the false, so the emotions were rebelling against a cool or dry tone of life: there was rebellion in both; and a typical aspect of the century was a kind of humanitarian and logical eagerness, in which the demands of the head and the heart were curiously blended. But there was a lag between the tides of rationalism and of sensibility; the former was at its height when the latter was still only rising. About 1760 there was a distinct turn, and when once sentiment was in full motion the clash with rationalism became clearly unavoidable. Despite overlapping, the age of Rousseau was different from that of Voltaire. There was some superficial agreement on practical points, but the two leaders stood at opposite poles of thought; and the sentimental movement introduced new intellectual and artistic growths which have provided rich nourishment for French literature ever since. . . .

The French Enlightenment worked up to a climax, the *Encyclopédie*. An age that emphasized above all the necessity for the mind to realize the world clearly would naturally find its essential task and supreme achievement in a sum of existing knowledge. Reason had established her right as the guide of human civilization; and her guidance was to be followed in a broad and impressive, almost a solemn, manner. The motives behind the undertaking were thus chiefly intellectual. But they were also practical, for the techniques of the arts and crafts were then entering, under the stimulus of science, upon the modern era of industry, and progress would be served by a full record of their instruments and methods. There was also a social purpose: the wider diffusion of learning plainly answered the anti-feudal and reforming, though not properly democratic, trend advocated by the majority of men of letters. Last but not least, the group of the philosophes, writers who were not a formal party in the State but to some extent acted as one, originated the plan and pressed eagerly forward with it, because it offered an almost unlimited scope to their campaign for liberalizing the public mind—that is to say, for weakening the hold of the Church, and of what they held to be superstition, upon the masses. It was never in doubt, from the first, that the venture would be animated by the purely rationalist spirit, which indeed its object—the popularizing of organized knowledge—obviously demanded.

The germ of the first scheme came from England. A Paris book-seller wanted to publish a French translation of Chambers's Cyclopaedia. Diderot was given charge, and substituted the more ambitious project of a new work on a far larger scale. A prospectus was issued at the end of 1750, and the next summer saw the publication of the first volume, with a preliminary 'Discours' by d'Alémbert. The authors who agreed to contribute included the chief *philosophes*—with Diderot and d'Alembert, Voltaire, Montesquieu, Buffon, d'Holbach, Quesnay, Turgot, Marmontel; even J.- J. Rousseau figured among them as a specialist of music. The course of the venture was anything but smooth. A decree forbade the sale of the first two volumes (1752); publication continued more or less on the sly, friends and patrons in high places managing to have it tolerated; but d'Alembert withdrew, and Diderot bore the burden of management almost single-handed. In 1759 the interdiction was renewed. Diderot discovered that the publisher was bowdlerizing the manuscript. By 1768 the seventeen folio volumes were out, and thenceforth sold more openly and quietly. Five supplementary volumes appeared in 1779, and the plates occupied eleven more. Pirated editions in several neighbouring countries testified to the international success of the work.

Although many of its articles are not strictly technical, and bear on generalities of history, philosophy, and litera-

ture, the *Encyclopédie* cannot be analysed or appreciated here. It should be noted only that the best-known members of the team contributed in fact but little, and that not always of their best; Diderot wrote most of the text on the arts and crafts. Modest jobbers were responsible for much of the rest. These relied chiefly on pre-existing publications, so that a fair proportion of the whole is not really original, but compiled. Still, it is impossible to overstate the significance and influence of the *Encyclopédie*. It broke the spell of silence, and in the teeth of a powerful opposition, the centres of which were the Church, the magistracy, the Sorbonne, and the pamphleteers of the tradition party, it allowed the rising demand for free criticism in matters of faith and government to be authoritatively voiced. The tactics uniformly followed in the work are no doubt cautious; the dangerous elements are hidden away in corners, and neither on religion nor on political subjects is anything said openly that could be too provoking. But the general atmosphere and trend are quite plain, and the conservatives, from their point of view, had good reason to feel angry.

The *Discours préliminaire* (1751) of d'Alembert (1717-83) deserves special mention. It is a masterpiece, and no writing can be more fully representative of the Enlightenment. It sets forth the two major objects of the whole work: first, to survey the development of human knowledge, in the order of its growth, from the earliest stages of mental life to the last conquests of science; next, to deal with the present-day systems of learning and technique, explaining in each case general principles, likewise methods and routines. . . . The latter aim coincides with a movement that led, during the French Revolution, to the foundation of the Conservatoire des Arts et Métiers, 1794, and, later, the creation of the 'Enseignement Technique'. Approaching

Jean-Jacques Rousseau.

his task with all the vigour and clarity of a first-rate mind, d'Alembert produces in effect a survey of the origin and progress of civilization—the very theme that had, a few years before, fascinated Montesquieu in the *Esprit des lois*, and lured him away from safe ground. The new survey, far briefer, is more philosophical and orderly. Our objection is that the whole plan is logical rather than experimental; Auguste Comte's classification of the sciences, in the next century, will be made definitely on the concrete basis of modern thought. The metaphysics of the 'Discours' may be described as theistic. Its rationalist enthusiasm does not hesitate to admit that one single formula might sum up the condition of the universe. Still, new eighteenth-century tolerance of a diversity of creatures is revealed in the attention paid to the complexities of things, and to the various families of man. After the sciences the arts are reviewed, with their originality and interrelations. A glowing homage is paid to Bacon, Locke, and Newton, the fathers of the English empirical philosophy that had driven Descartes out of the field; and d'Alembert, ending his clarion call to the crusaders of knowledge, happens to make a passing allusion to J. J. Rousseau's first *Discours*, just published—the proclamation, no less ringing, of a far different gospel.

Two thinkers must be mentioned who shared the spirit of the *Encyclopédie*, whether or not they actually contributed to it. The first, Étienne Bonnot de Condillac, 1714-80, published the *Essai sur l'origine des connaissances humaines*, 1746, the *Traité des systèmes*, 1749, and the *Traité des sensations*, 1754. With a remarkable power of lucid analysis and explanation, he pushed Locke's psychology farther, showing in full detail how from the most simple sense-impressions all the faculties of the adult mind can be gradually built up. He stands for the rational endeavour of modern thought, freed from the shackles of the deductive past, and not yet aware of its own limitations. Claude Adrien Helvétius, 1715-71, the second, was no less zealous a disciple of Locke, whose doctrine he developed more particularly towards a realist system of ethics. His chief work, *De l'esprit*, 1758, was the climax of what may be called philosophical sensualism, with materialist implications. On the passive responsiveness of the young mind, he pointed out, education and the pressure of surroundings build the fabric of intellectual habits. *De l'homme*, 1772, coolly drew further consequences from those views. The same principle can be stretched to show that self-interested behaviour should be encouraged, since, serving as well the major needs of society, it must be called 'virtue'. As the first book raised a storm, Helvétius recanted perfunctorily; but the second was distinctly a relapse. The 'Utilitarians' of the next century were to refine and improve upon this somewhat over-simple scheme.

For two very different reasons Diderot stands out from the body of the 'Encyclopédistes'; he had more to do than any of them with the inception and carrying on of the work; and yet, although he was its arch-promoter and supporter, he is not closely representative of its spirit. His temper was more complex, and successive aspects of it were revealed as time passed. So he requires a place by himself; he is, like Voltaire, a central figure of the Enlightenment; but he is

none the less a herald, and even a part, of the next age, that of Rousseau.

Diderot's rationalistic side is not illustrated solely by the *Encyclopédie*. He had already committed himself (*La Promenade du sceptique; Lettre sur les aveugles*) to negative views which brought upon him the rigour of justice; he returned to the theme much later in a charming, witty dialogue, where the hard pronouncements of scepticism are softened by tolerant humanity (*Entretien d'un philosophe . . .*). The *Pensées sur l'interprétation de la Nature*, one of his most suggestive treatises, temper the criticism of unreason by stressing the all-important study of life, in words that prefigure the theory of evolution. The *Supplément au voyage de Bougainville*, the *Rêve de d'Alembert*, are bold and pregnant ventures in ethical or scientific philosophy, away from orthodox paths. *Le Neveu de Rameau*, Diderot's most original, is perhaps as well his most masterly, work; well worthy of having fascinated Goethe, who translated into German the manuscript still unpublished in French. Beyond the wonderful bravura of the style, and the lively humour of the dialogue, these spirited outpourings of a bohemian and cynic artist have a core of rich, though tentative thought; one may read in them the audacious outline of an *immoralisme* that probes fearlessly to the depths of human nature, where the roots of good and evil are inextricably interwoven. Even the *Paradoxe sur le comédien*, one of Diderot's last writings, shows his acute analysis giving itself full play over the psychological and aesthetic problem of how much an actor is to feel in the interest of his art. The intellectual rigour of the argument, and the destruction of a sentimental prejudice, are admirable. The reader only wishes that the difference were more clearly defined between the total, vital emotion which paralyses artistic freedom, and the intellectual, imaginative feeling that moves the head but, however deep, leaves the heart cold. The former is the actor's bane, no doubt; but the latter is the very condition of his efficient playing.

No less, and indeed more plentiful, are the tokens of Diderot's addiction to the new spirit that was gaining ascendancy over thought and literature: the genius of uncontrolled, complacent sensibility. The *Éloge de Richardson* is the exultant proclamation of that faith; the English writer's novels, in which the pent-up stores of Puritan energy had been transformed into emotional effusion, are extolled with all the raptures of admiring and grateful enthusiasm: they wring the reader's heart powerfully, deliciously; they teach him how to feel, and sow the seeds of all goodness and virtue. No more significant manifesto marks the passing of France from one period of her intellectual history to another. The influence of a foreign genius upon her inner life seems paramount. But deeper than the spell cast by Richardson is the spontaneous development of France herself. The needs of the heart had been wakening for a generation, under the clamorous claims and demands of the need for light; and Clarissa Harlowe, in the Abbé Prévost's rather free though very readable translation, let loose the ready flow of tears. Among the writings in which Diderot gave vent to this spirit are stories of concentrated realism and pathos that seem strangely like foreshadowings of Balzac's manner: *Les Deux Amis de Bourbonne;*

Ceci n'est pas un conte; Sur l'inconséquence du jugement public, &c.; the plays that illustrate the theory of *comédie sérieuse* or *drame bourgeois*: *Le Fils naturel, Le Père de famille*; and the dramatic study of a concrete ethical problem: *Est-il bon, est-il méchant?*, steeped in sentiment, but shrewd and suggestive. *Jacques le fataliste*, among the thousand contradictions of human nature, finds one single clue leading out of the maze: no principle, but the impulses of a good heart. The *Salons*, full of gushing delight over the sentimentalities of Greuze, and prone to take the 'subjects' of pictures too seriously, are yet penetrating no less than animated attempts in the still scarcely tried field of art criticism.

Diderot's works were all more or less hastily written. He composed under the strain of necessity, his mind often engrossed by painful cares. His style is unequal, not always formally correct, with a sprinkling of familiar words and phrases. These slight blemishes vanish when once we are under the spell of one of the most vivacious personalities in French literature. The flow of spirit, eloquence, wit, pathos, humour, sweeps us along in sheer pleasure, and in sympathy with a writer of genius who knew no meanness, being always, whether right or wrong, transparently sincere and completely human.

VIEWS ON ESTHETICS

Alfred Richard Oliver

SOURCE: *The Encyclopedists as Critics of Music,* Columbia University Press, 1947, 227 p.

[*Oliver is an American educator and scholar whose writings include* The Encyclopedists as Critics of Music *and* Charles Nodier, Pilot of Romanticism *(1964). In the following excerpt from the former work, he comments on the Encyclopedists' ideas about music, underlining their considerable influence on the development of operatic music in France*]

Before entering upon an examination of the criticism of the opera in the articles of the *Encyclopedia*, we should consider briefly the state of the opera toward the middle of the eighteenth century. Whereas in Italy the opera had gradually receded from the pure music drama of the Monteverdi type to a melodic feast in the Neapolitan school with the works of Leo, Porpora, Vinci, Scarlatti, and Pergolesi, in France the opera tended to remain faithful to the dramatic traditions of the Lulli-Quinault invention. We [know] the Encyclopedists pointed out that the principal changes wrought by Rameau consisted in altering the proportions of drama and musical *divertissements*. The ingredients of Rameau's operas are all to be found in the Lulli-Quinault type of lyrico-dramatic compositions. Thus, the *déclamation notée* of Lulli's operas, although its importance declines in Rameau's works, remains essentially unchanged. Of most significance is the fact that in both Italy and France music took the upper hand. The Italian composers sacrificed the libretto to the singer, thus making the aria or melody the mainstay of the opera, while in France Rameau sacrificed the poéme to the music, thus emphasiz-

ing the orchestra or harmony as the principal feature of operatic composition.

It was tendency of the French opera to remain fixed that drew the Encyclopedists' fire. They did not oppose the operas of Lulli and Quinault because they felt them to be inferior creations. On the whole the Encyclopedists' attitude is favorable to these compositions, which they regarded as sufficient and even wonderful for the period in which they first appeared. But the Encyclopedists knew that this early opera had served its time and that it was now, in 1750, obsolete. When they considered the sweeping changes that had obtained in Italian opera, the Encyclopedists could not help being a little impatient with the slow progress of the local opera, and particularly with the reactionary elements in Rameau's works.

Thus, the Encyclopedists razed the venerable though crumbling works of Lulli. These masterworks had cast a shadow upon upwards of sixty years of operatic composition in France. D'Alembert suggests, in the article "Echo," that one reason for the tenacity of the old opera is to be found in the tendency on the part of Frenchmen to be traditional in their artistic tastes and to like only the sort of music they already know: "In France, good music means for many people that which resembles what they have already heard." Foreigners who have not been habituated to appreciate French opera, says Cahusac in the article "Débiter," remark with surprise upon its many shortcomings.

> When foreigners arrive we take them to the opera. In vain do they keep their eyes and ears open; they neither see nor hear the marvels we seem to see and hear there. They view us askance, talk in hushed voices about us, and guess that prejudice and pride have formed our operatic taste. Actually, it is merely habit, indifference for the progress of art, or perhaps a good-natured desire to be grateful to those who put themselves out to amuse us that causes the French to cling to their opera.

The Encyclopedists were asking the French to awaken from their musical lethargy.

Just as these men were the first group of critics to look at opera from the point of view of music, they also preceded all others in setting forth an aesthetic theory of operatic composition based upon a close examination of French works. The *philosophes*, who rationalized all natural phenomena, used the penetrating tool of reason to advantage in probing the origins of the local opera. They were quick to see that the opera in France came as the result of a dramatic transformation and that therefore the principal element of the new *tragédie lyrique* was declamation. Upon this item all contributors of musical articles agree. (Cahusac, "Déclamation," "Expression"; Marmontel, "Déclamation," "Chant"; Grimm, "Motif," "Poéme lyrique"; Alembert, "Genre"; Castillon, "Musique," Supplement.) Declamation was the basis of the recitative, which was the principal prop of the opera. (Marmontel: "Déclamation"). By following the declamation of the verse in the classical tragedy, the composer created the recitative sections of his opera. He accentuated by musical notation the actor's declamation and thus arrived at a *déclamation notée*:

> Although we know that what we improperly term recitative should give an added expression to the words of an opera **text** . . . it should, nevertheless, always remain **simple** and as true to the spirit of classical declamation as possible. The composer should study the declamation of a first rank tragedian, and shape his music along the lines suggested by the actor's delivery. As it is certain that the actor adds considerably to the dramatist's lines by his delivery, so, too, the composer must heighten the expression of the verse by means of the recitative, which thus becomes a permanently scored declamation. (Cahusac, "Expression.")

D'Alembert gives an example of the precise application of this principle; that is, that recitative, or *déclamation notée*, evolved from natural or theatrical declamation.

> The composer used the ascending notes of the chromatic scale in this recitative with all the more justice since it seems natural to us. A good actor would certainly deliver the second and third verses as they are scored, that is, in ascending semi-tones. Let us note further that if this section were sung as the recitative in the Italian opera, without unduly stressing each sound but by delivering the words as though they were being read or spoken and paying attention to proper intonation, one would hardly notice the difference between this type of recitative and good theatrical declamation; that is the model of a good recitative. (Alembert, "Genre.")

The Encyclopedists saw theatrical declamation as a basis for recitative only. Recitative formed the connection between opera and drama, and musical contributors to the *Encyclopedia* felt that since French recitative had been derived from stage declamation, it had best be composed along dramatic lines. But here the influence of the drama, albeit very important, was at an end. In no case did the Encyclopedists suggest that melody is equally a product of theatrical declamation. They saw that melody was primarily a branch of music and that the type of declamation that was to be used in writing it was far different from theatrical declamation. In the article "Expression" Rousseau states flatly that theatrical declamation cannot serve as a basis for melody. Grimm, in the article "Poème lyrique," claims that the composer must find two types of declamation—one for the recitative and one for the melody.

> The composer's first task must have been to find two entirely different kinds of declamation; the first to render ordinary conversation, and the second to portray the expression of passions in all its vigor, truth, and disorder. The latter type of declamation is called the air, or aria, the former is the recitative.

Melody, or aria, the mainstay of Italian opera, was of secondary importance in France, recitative based on a *déclamation notée* having been the chief element of French opera.

When opera is considered solely as a dramatic phenomenon, as it was by the French up to the advent of the *Encyclopedia*, melody is not likely to receive very extensive treatment. Whereas with the Italians melody rapidly settled into the *da capo* aria form, which soon became the all-important feature of their opera, in France no great distinction existed between recitative and melody. Lulli preferred to use a type of melody that grew out of the same declamation as the recitative. It was a slow, measured song that may be called tuneful recitative, in the sense that although its musical qualities cannot be denied, the influence of the words does not fail to make itself felt even when such a melody is played upon an instrument. To this type of melody the French remained faithful. The *da capo* aria never became popular in France.

The French conception of melody, then, was not very clear. Since the basic distinction between opera and drama resides in the former's use of music, which largely appears in the form of melody, the French might well be concerned as to the vigor of the national opera. It was this state of affairs that led to Rousseau's denial that opera existed in France. He had become acquainted with Italian operas in Venice in 1742, and had penned his share of the articles on music in 1749. Less irritable critics tried to remedy the situation by studying the elements of melody in Italian operas. The rich melodic strains of Pergolesi, Scarlatti, Vinci, Porpora, and the rest, heard in the performances of the Bouffons' troupe in 1752, engaged the curiosity of the Encyclopedists, and soon an adequate aesthetic of melody was available in numerous *Encyclopedia* articles. Invariably, they pointed out the works in the Bouffons' repertory as an object lesson.

In subscribing to the limitation-of-nature thesis, Grimm, in the article "Poème lyrique," states that joy probably gave rise to the first imitation of nature by means of song. In attempting to enlarge the field of musical imitation, the composer learned that all passions were susceptible to musical interpretation, each passion having, as it were, a type of melody proper to its expression. This melody allied to the power of dramatic expression gave rise to the opera, which Grimm takes to be the very finest type of spectacle. Drama alone could never rise to an adequate expression of these elemental passions. Music can express an intensity of feeling entirely unknown to words and mime. A nation of people who continuously enjoyed an exalted state of being would use song as the natural vehicle of expression. Ordinary people attain to song only when deeply moved. Thus, the opera is by definition, says Grimm, tragedy which is under the constant necessity of presenting scenes of conflict, rejoicing, anger, chargrin, love, and similar profound emotions. from the point of view of the composer, the opera is plainly a vehicle for melody. Drama prepares scenes of a highly emotional character and renders the passion in question more precise. Although music is eminently fitted to express passions, it cannot do so without the aid of text. Like all universal languages, melody is vague. The poet is then brought in to supply a canvas for melodic interpretation. Thus, the opera is vastly different from straight drama. Without music, the opera is a poor play; with music, or melody, the opera is heightened drama. However, melody must be used sparingly in the opera; scenes of a deeply passionate nature must be led up to. Just as a dramatic character could not reasonably pass immediately form a scene of anger to one of joy and then to a third scene of great sorrow, the opera could never be composed of a series of uninterrupted melodies. Melody is most effective when thoroughly prepared by recitative, which disposes of the calmer moments of dramatic action. The aria, or melody, represents the high point of passion, the breaking out of all the emotion that words are powerless to express.

In the opera *Artaserse* Metastasio has Arbace explain to Mandane, in recitative, why he must leave the city and her. Torn by anguish and sorrow at parting, Mandane reveals the depth of her suffering in the aria:

> Conservati fedele:
> Pensa ch'io resto e peno;
> E qualche volta almeno
> Ricordati di me.

Grimm observes that these lines are useless without the penetrating power of music to express the emotion behind them. Melody is to be used, then, only when the office of words has been superseded. The composer can admirably express in melody an emotion that a long tirade can only beggar. The opera poet's diction should differ from that of the tragedian: he must write with an eye to melodic adaptation, preferring to use the same precise word many times rather than attempt variety. The energy and the flexibility of the music used to comment this one word will surpass the fine poetic diction of the great Racine himself.

> A significant difference exists between the dramatist's art and that of the opera poet. When, for instance, the dramatist finds it necessary to become verbose, the opera poet must become precise and use words sparingly, because the moments of passion belong entirely to the composer. No poetry would be less susceptible to musical commentary than all that sublime and harmonius eloquence with which Racine's Clytemnestra attempts to save her daughter's life. The opera poet who places his character in a similar situation can allow her only four verses:
>
> > Rendimi il mio figlio . . .
> > Ah, mi si spezza il cor:
> > Non son più madre, oh dio,
> > Non ho più figlio!
>
> But with these four short lines the composer can work more effectively to express the pathos in question than the divine Racine could ever produce with all the magic of his poetry.

The composer will insist on these four lines, says Grimm, repeating them in all possible nuances, exploiting by means of music all the phases of Clytemnestra's passion. The poète himself should be a musician, so that he may know how to dispose scenes of recitative and prepare the aria. Not great poetry is required, says Grimm, but lines that will lend themselves to musical adaptation. The fundamental distinction between opera and drama is that the one is in constant need of musical commentary. It is essentially a sketch, a canvas, that does not arrive at its fullest expression until allied to music. Whereas drama stands alone. In writing opera, the poet's style should be gov-erned by the realization that music deploys its powers of expression best upon flexible meters. For the aria the broken line is preferable. The disorder that attends all passions should be reflected in the prosody. In no case is the Alexandrian to be employed, not even for the recitative, because musical declamation abhors long, regular verses.

The double aria, or duet, must be a *double plainte*. This does not mean that the members of the duet should sing ensemble from beginning to end, and then repeat, as in the French opera. The difficulty that attends this manner of presentation is patent. The audience cannot know what the singers are saying. Moreover, the attitude towards all melody in the opera should never be one of merely singing a song. If melody is to have any dramatic effect at all, nuances of feeling should be expressed. Song is complete in itself. Operatic melody is but an integral part of a whole, and as such must derive poetically and musically from what has preceded and blend easily into what is to follow. The opera aria differs from song in that the latter repeats the same melody without catching any of the nuances of expression that a dramatic situation requires. It was precisely in exploiting these varieties of melodic expression that singers such as Caffarelli and Gabrieli made themselves tyrants of the opera in Europe.

In the article "Motif" Grimm studies at great length the need for repetition of melody, and parts of aria, in the opera. He says in this article that the effect of music is lost unless the motif is repeated. This explains the use of the *da capo* aria. In straight drama or poetry repetition is a dangerous practice, in that it serves only to weaken the effect of a good line. But the needs of music are otherwise. The composer cannot transmit to an audience the deep significance of a theme by simply stating it. The vague character of musical expression renders repetition obligatory. In order to fix the import of a given motif, the composer must constantly return to it.

> Since the aria is to be reserved for moments of passionate outburst, and since it is, so to speak, the peroration and recapitulation of the scene being represented, the repetition of the words in the aria is rendered exciting by means of the varied declamation with which the composer seeks to grasp the various accents depicting the same passion. For instance, when Merope, overwhelmed with sorrow, says she will die forlorn, she is not content to sing that line once, but will repeat every word twenty times. Now suppliant, she will beg for pity; now desperate, she will cry out with pain and sorrow; now choked with anguish, she will no longer be able to articulate her words properly, but will gasp forth broken syllables, *ah . . . mo . . . ri . . . rà . . .* During all these varied declamations she will sing only the words *disperata morirà*. Anyone who finds in this delivery nothing but monotonous repetition will never properly understand music.

Repetition of an idea in various ways is, then, the most resourceful tool of melody.

The purpose of melody in the opera is, according to Grimm, to express the high point of an emotional crisis. Since melody is the opera's mainspring, the entire opera should be a representation involving scenes of great pathos. It was in this respect that Metastasio proved to be a great operatic poet. He set the stage for the whole of eighteenth-century Italian opera. Grimm gives the poet credit for much of the success of operas by Pergolesi, Hasse, Leo, and other eighteenth-century composers who set his texts. His style, diction, and versification were perfectly suited to musical adaptation. His neat division of recitative and aria rendered the composer's task pleasant and simple. In the article "Poème lyrique" Grimm tells us that music in Italy, having from the very start taken the right direction, that is, the expression of feeling and passion, the opera poet could not fail to grasp exactly what composers sought from him. By a happy coincidence, Metastasio came into being with a host of great composers who were able to collaborate successfully with him. Between them they produced the eighteenth-century Italian melody opera of the recitative and aria type.

But if this group of men furnished Grimm with his aesthetics of melodic composition, he did not fail to see the evils that the Italian insistence on melody was bound to lead to. Overemphasis on the aria brought the singer into prominence. Soon everything else in the opera was sacrificed to this personage. Interest in the dramatic portion of the opera flagged. So long as the audience could be assured that their favorite was to sing an aria, they were content to sit eating and talking throughout the scenes of recitative. In this way the singer became tyrant, and the object of an opera was fulfilled for the audience if he had his air. To so great an extent did he abuse his prerogative that if the aria he was to sing did not suit his taste, he would substitute one that had formerly won him applause, without regard for aptness or for dramatic or musical unity. Grimm would have the producer say to the opera poet: "the opera can't be bad with a Caffarelli or a Gabrieli singing in it." Worst of all, the opera became fixed to suit the singer's wishes in the following manner. There must be three acts, lasting in all about five hours, including the ballets during the entr'actes, a change of scene in each act, making a total of six scenes; six roles, no less than five, no more than seven, including one leading actor, one leading actress, one second actor, one second actress, one king, governor, or old man; the protagonist must be in love with the leading lady, the second actor with the second actress; each sings twice in each act, except in the third, when the hastening of the opera toward a climax forbids this. There must be a duet between the leading male and female actors in the second act—it may be in the first, but never in the third. Each actor must leave the stage after singing his or her aria. The actors will sing in turn, the last singing a brilliant air which must contain some reflection or maxim or a comparison between his situation and that of the other personages. Before an actor sings his second aria, all the others must have sung one, before his third, all the others must have sung their second. The ranks of the singers must not be confused, nor their rights infringed.

Yet these excesses, that followed in the wake of the splendid operatic achievements of Metastasio, Zeno, Pergolesi, Scarlatti, and Hasse, must not obliterate the fact that good melody could be composed as these men had prescribed. Grimm recalls, in the article "Poème lyrique," that be-

cause of the Emperor Charles VI's aversion to tragic endings, Metastasio had to bring all his operas to a happy issue. Despite all these stumbling blocks, the best type of melody, and consequently the best type of opera, was that created in Italy in the eighteenth century.

Grimm's analysis of the aria and his insistence on the importance of melody in the opera were universally subscribed to by the other Encyclopedists. The theory of opera as a vehicle to express passions and feelings is re-ëchoed in the articles "Ecole," by D'Alembert, "Expression," by Cahusac, "Opéra," by Rousseau, and "Poésie lyrique," by Jaucourt. Sulzer, the German aesthetician, in the article "Aria," for the Supplement, agrees that the aria should represent an emotional crisis, and Marmontel, in the article "Air" (Supplement, 1765), repeats Grimm verbatim. The conception of the duet as dialogue is to be found again in the articles "Duo," by Marmontel (Supplement) and by Rousseau. The latter adds "In explaining what the *duo* should be, I have told you exactly the manner of using it in the Italian opera." In attempting to account for the French opera's lack of melody, as conceived in the Italian opera aria, Marmontel, in the article "Air," states that at the time of the inception of the opera in France, the aria form was unknown in Italy and that consequently neither Lulli nor Corelli were acquainted with the recitative and aria-type opera. In France, Quinault wrote verses that were poetically harmonious, but did not lend themselves to the aria type of melody. This *chant périodique*, or *période musicale*, was discovered, says Marmontel, by the Italian composer Vinci. The Italians have since abused the aria, while the French have remained faithful to the Lulli-Quinault tradition. In scoring the excesses that the use of aria led to in the Italian opera, Marmontel deplores the fact that the French so obdurately resisted the introduction of the aria form into French opera. As an opera poet, Marmontel insists that the French language is very capable of aria in the Italian manner. When once the French have learned how to compose the aria, the vaunted superiority of the Italian opera will vanish.

> The art of molding a symmetrical musical phrase is completely unknown in France to this day. . . . As a result of experiments made by me in collaboration with a well-known composer, I venture to say that our language can be very easily adapted to writing arias in the Italian style. We are just beginning to realize that our opera lacks the aria phrased in the Italian manner. When we do learn how to use this style intelligently, not only in the aria but in the duos and recitatives as well, I predict that French opera will be superior to the Italian.

Marmontel does not doubt that the Italians had found the true type of opera, aria and recitative. Nor does he question the excellence of the aria type of melody. In concluding the article "Opéra" for the Supplement, Marmontel implicitly subscribes to Grimm's dictum that Italian opera was the only opera.

> When the correct musical phrasing of the melodious aria, sketched, molded, gracefully arching in its subtle flight is at last known in France, it will thrill the ear at any time and in any place.

> Never will truncated verses, hacked lines, and mutilated songs satisfy us. The Italians are constantly telling us, and we must end by believing them, that the essence of music is song and melody is the soul of song.

Rousseau alone was more sanguine in championing Italian melody and Italian opera.

As far as Rousseau was concerned, music was melody. Since the object of music was the expression of feelings, dramatic music, or opera, specifically the Italian opera, was the highest expression of the art. Rousseau violently opposed the French basing of *chant* on a *déclamation théâtrale*, as in Lulli, and nothing was more irksome to the *philosophe* than the application of Rameau's theory of harmony, whereby melody was to be derived from harmonic progression. He almost never mentions this notion of Rameau's without stating in some form Tartini's opposite theory that harmony is derived from melody. This is to show that in the composition of melody nothing was as useless as a knowledge of harmony.

> Let us consider the Italians, our contemporaries, whose music is the best in the world, according to everybody except the French, who prefer their own. Notice the simple chords Italian composers use in their works, and what choice they exercise in their harmony. They do not judge a composition on the basis of the multiplicity of its parts. The most beautiful chords in the world will never hold our attention as completely as do the well-modulated inflections of a beautiful voice. Any disinterested judge will have to admit that melody is, after all, the soul of music. (Rousseau: "Musique.")

Melody is more stirring than harmony. In the article "Accent" Rousseau states that since music is the language of the senses, the aims of this art are far better served by melody than by harmony.

Any theory of melody based on Rousseauistic tenets involves his theory of opera and, for the most part, his general theory of music. In the article "Sonate" Rousseau tells us that music must paint; it must present images. Now this cannot be done without the aid of words. Words and music paint best in the form of melody; that is, passions and feelings are most satisfactorily expressed in melody. Since melody is the mainstay of the opera, and since situations in which human emotions are involved are most aptly introduced by the opera, Rousseau says that dramatic music, or opera, is the highest form of musical endeavor. (Rousseau: "Harmonie".)

In studying melody as the backbone of dramatic music, Rousseau says, in the article "Imitation," that the composer must awaken in the listener the same mood that is being created by the play, so that even without the stage representation, the melody alone should give rise to an emotional experience of a more-or-less definite character. The object of the words is to render this emotion precise.

> The night, slumber, solitude, silence, all belong in the domain of musical interpretation. . . .
>
> The composer does not directly represent these things, but induces in the listener's imagination

a mood similar to that suggested by night, slumber, and silence.

Thus, melody can in no way be derived from theatrical declamation: the former aims at expressing the whole thought or mood of the scene; the latter can stress only words, or fragments of thought and emotional experience.

> Melody should grasp the mood of the sentiments being represented by imitating the natural, unaffected intonation of the voice. For this reason melody can never be based on theatrical declamation which is itself already an artistic imitation of nature. The composer should first seek a sort of melody based on an interpretation of the words, always remembering to subordinate this to an interpretation of the thought. The final melody should express the general mood the singer is supposed to represent. (Rousseau: "Expression.")

Melody is derived from a mood or passion in a scene, which in turn it helps to create. Theatrical declamation can depend only upon accent and prosody, and these two tools of operatic poetry must constantly subserve the melody. Theatrical declamation, then, is to melody as the recitative is to the aria: the former must always be a means of arriving at the latter.

In breaking down the elements of accent and prosody, Rousseau arrives at some very definite conclusions regarding French and Italian opera. In the foregoing division between melody and *déclamation théâtrale*, it is evident that he is at once pointing to the Italians as having perfected the art of opera, through successful melodic composition, and condemning the French for having created a type of opera based entirely on theatrical declamation. If aria and recitative are taken as the basic features of opera, it can be observed that the French have developed the recitative only and thus might be said to have but half an opera. That far more important half, the melody, was, according to Rousseau, completely neglected by French composers. French language may in great part have determined the course of the local opera. In the article "Accent" Rousseau states that much of the musical, and therefore melodic quality of the language depends, and in a measure derives from, accent.

> The degree of accent in a language determines its musical adaptibility. If this were not true, then we should have to observe that there is no connection between song and speech and that the singing voice does not in any way imitate the accents of the spoken word. However, we know that lack of accent in a language causes melodies composed in that tongue to be on the whole monotonous and dull.

It is not difficult to see in this excerpt a criticism of the lack of accent in the French language. Rousseau dooms the German to a similar unhappy fate. Only the Italian language possesses the elements of variety of accent required for good melodic diction.

> An observable difference in the degree of imaginativeness or sensibility between two peoples introduces an immense difference in the accents of their spoken language. The German, for in-

stance, shouts in a monotone when he is angry; the irate Italian, on the other hand, changes the tone of his voice a thousand times. The latter is transported by the same passion, but what a variety of expression he uses in his accents and in his speech! We maintain that Italian melody owes its energy as well as its grace to this variety of accent in speech successfully imitated in song.

Rousseau offers accent as an index to good melodic composition to the French composer also, for later in the same article he counsels every composer to study d'Olivet's *Traité de la prosodie française*.

The dearth of melody in the French opera was due, Rousseau tells us, first, to an exaggerated preoccupation with stage declamation on the part of French composers; secondly, to the lack of variety of accent in the French language; and thirdly, to a faulty prosody. This fault was largely the result of the weak relationship between words and music in the French opera. The French, wholly taken up with the words at the expense of the music, as in the Lulli *déclamation théâtrale* type of opera, or vice versa, sacrificing the text to harmonic versatility, as in the Rameau *divertissement* variety, never sought to develop both words and music in simultaneous agreement.

> Since the prosody of the French language is not as sensitive as was the Greek, and since our composers' heads are so full of musical sounds that they cannot think of anything else, there is as little relation between words and music in French song with reference to number and measure, as there is with reference to meaning and expression. (Rousseau: "Musique.")

The variety of expression that the Italians obtained from accent and prosody, the French tried to acquire by compiling a sort of thesaurus of musically adaptable words, such as *coulez, volez, gloire, murmure, écho*, etc. Rousseau rightly maintains that this lamentable practice tended to stultify rather than to vary musical expression. The only other possible escape from monotony for the French was to use a marked measure or rhythm for characteristic themes, such as, slow for a serious and heavy motif, fast for gaiety, and so forth. And again, this method only served to hurry the sterility of composition in France.

The fundamental distinction between French and Italian operas depended, for Rousseau, upon a definition of melody and recitative. Granting that these were the most important elements of opera, Rousseau would say that the Italians wrote good recitative and excellent melody, whereas the French wrote poor melody and had enlarged and developed the recitative until it was no longer recognizable. Good melody is defined by Rousseau as that which is drawn from and reveals deep passions and feelings. As for the recitative, "it is, properly speaking, a sort of musical declamation, wherein the composer must imitate as closely as possible the voice inflections of the person declaiming." (Rousseau: "Récitatif.") In the same article Rousseau states that Italian recitative approaches more closely to declamation than does the French. The French developed so extensively the recitative to serve all purposes of opera that the original usefulness of declamation miscarried in the recitative proper, and any air that

partook of the nature of a *déclamation chantante* could not be very rich in melodic expression. Thus, Italian recitative is simple, and French recitative is complicated and ornamental. To so great an extent is this true, that in the French opera foreigners cannot tell the recitative from the air.

In the article "Vaudeville" Jaucourt quotes Rousseau as saying that French melody is not expressive enough and that therefore it is more proper for vaudeville than for opera. The passionate nature of Italian melody, on the other hand, makes it a fit vehicle for opera. In the article "Air" (Supplement) Marmontel, in studying this feature in both French and Italian operas, arrives at the conclusion that whereas the Italians sacrifice everything to melody and take many liberties with their prosody, the French are never willing to abandon a strong sense of prosody in the interest of melodic richness. Taken together, these two statements sum up admirably Rousseau's position. He saw that successful opera involved the solution of two distinct problem: the one, based on stage declamation and verse prosody, led to the creation of recitative; the other, stressing crises in emotion, involving the expression of profound passions, naturally resolved itself into the opera aria. Stated briefly, the opera presented at the same time a dramatic and a musical problem. That the French opera was stunted because of the unwillingness to abandon any of the virtues of drama for an improvement of the music and that the Italians adequately solved both problems by presenting a melodic feast with drama as a handmaid are matters of historical record.

The third major aspect of the opera was *le merveilleux*. Within the pale of this term came scenic effects, decoration, ballets, *divertissements*, and machines. The purpose of all this paraphernalia was to create an illusion of splendor and magnificence, fit atmosphere within which the doings of gods and heroes were to be unfolded. Whereas the Italians early abandoned this idea of the opera as a vast spectacular pageant in favor of straight drama with subjects drawn from classical tragedy, the French developed the portrayal of scenes from classical mythology to an unprecedented degree, continuing to lavish tremendous sums on brilliant stage sets and complicated machinery even after the Italians had established the recitative and aria type of opera. As we shall remember, in certain aspects the beginnings of opera were similar in Italy and France and the first efforts at national opera in France inevitably partook of the nature of extensive *fêtes*, so costly in their rigging and appurtenances that only the monarch could afford them. This was the type of spectacle that was developed in Italy in the sixteenth and early seventeenth centuries; it survived as an obscure spectacle after the opera had obtained a definite place. In France the *machines* of the Marquis de Sourdéac rendered these spectacles immensely popular; indeed, the pre-Quinaultian opera depended for its success almost exclusively upon this ornamental aspect. It is not difficult to understand, then, why this use of the spectacular persisted in the later opera in France. The French love of show, which has come down to our own day in the form of parade and pageant as well as romantic grand opera—great numbers of the French opera audience still go to the opera merely for the ballet—was nurtured in these early *fêtes*. Cahusac, in the article "Féerie," asserts that Quinault employed this element of spectacle sparingly and, as it were, against his will. But Rameau reinstated pageant and ballets, immortalizing himself in Cahusac's eyes by turning the opera into a vast *fête* or *divertissement*.

Apologists of the French opera were thus afforded ample material in studying the growth and function of *merveilleux* in the opera. Encyclopedist comment upon this aspect of opera included the references to La Bruyère's qualification of the opera as *enchantement* and to its classification as spectacle by Boileau. In the article "Opéra" Jaucourt actually quotes Boileau's ringing denunciation of the opera as a spectacle wherein "more attention is given to delighting the ears than to satisfying the mind." Cahusac, Jaucourt, and Marmontel agree that the backbone of French opera is and must remain *le merveilleux*. In the article "Décoration" Cahusac defines the opera as the "spectacle du merveilleux," and adds that besides beginning to cast the spell of illusion, the decoration must constantly present elements of surprise and wonder. The *merveilleux* depends for its subjects upon mythology. The creator is to develop the supernatural powers given by the Greeks to their gods. Secondly, there is the element of *féerie et magie*. This includes the giving of occult powers to inanimate objects, and rapid changes or inordinate metamorphoses. The classical example of the latter Cahusac draws from the opera *Amadis*, wherein the hero of that name worships a *magicienne*, whom he mistakes for his beloved. All this is brought about by *enchantement*, necessary to the creation of an acceptable fiction by means of "l'illusion du spectacle du merveilleux." (Cahusac: "Enchantement.")

In defining the *spectacle lyrique*, or opera, Jaucourt states, in the article "Opéra," that it is primarily the representation of an "action merveilleuse." Whereas the Italians went on to develop opera based on classical Greek tragedy, the French preferred to continue the dramatization of the Greek epic. Thus, French opera is "the dramatization of the most sublime parts of the epic." Since the actors are to represent the gods and heroes of the epic, their actions and language must be in keeping with their roles. Hence they will not act like ordinary mortals or speak the language of men. Their actions will be of a supernatural order and will thus partake of the implausible. They will not speak, but sing concerning their affairs. This rationale of song in the opera was meant to answer the many attacks upon opera for presenting impossible characters using impossible means of communication. The quarrel concerning song in the place of speech begun by classical critics St. Evremond, Boileau, Fénelon, La Bruyére, wherein they claimed that it was not "natural" to die singing, was here given a sharp rebuke by Jaucourt. Since music takes us to an ethereal, unexplored universe, says Jaucourt in effect, it is proper to have, not ordinary human beings, but fictitious creations, such as the Greeks imagined their gods to be, people it, and they would better sing rather than speak about their affairs and move about in an atmosphere of magnificence and divine pomp. Though any single element of the opera would be a violation of nature when measured by human standards, taken as a whole, the spectacle represents a fantastic world we know nothing about. We may therefore be content to witness a spectacle that in transcending human experience can only be adequately unfolded by means of the *merveilleux*. Violation of natural laws in the French opera may be considered one reason for its success as a spectacle; it provided an escape from the severe rationalizing tendency of the age.

In the article "Poème lyrique" Grimm supports Jaucourt's argument for song in the opera and goes a step farther, saying that song would be the most plausible means of expression not only of heroes and gods, but of men as well—Men, that is, who represent a higher order of the species.

> Imagine a nation of enthusiasts and zealots living in a constant state of exltation. These people, although sharing our principles and passions, would be much superior to us in subtlety, finesse, and delicate sensibilities. With more highly developed sensory organs than ours, such a community would sing rather than speak, and music would be their natural language.

Whoever hopes to enjoy the opera must similarly be more subtle, delicate, and better versed in the art of communing by song than most people. The opera goer must be an opera hero in potential. The subjects of mythology, accompanied and aided by all the supernatural attributes of modern sorcery and witchcraft, should provide the soul of the French opera; i. e., the *merveilleux visible*, just as the transformations and magic spells furnished the soul of the Greek epic. But this is as far as Grimm is willing to go. he states that this attitude towards the opera is essentially a fantastic one. The opera hall is not large enough to house these grandiose productions, nor are gods and goddesses, the traditional characters of the epic, fit subjects for opera. Moreover, the *merveilleux* is not really susceptible to theatrical representation.

Now, it was upon this very element of *merveilleux* that Marmontel, as well as Cahusac, in his *Traité de la danse*, based all his claims for the excellence of French opera. In a work entitled *Poétique française* (1763) Marmontel had set forth, in Chapter XIV, his ideas concerning this aspect of the opera. In the article "Lyrique" Marmontel defends his position against Grimm's scathing remarks, insisting that without *merveilleux* the French opera would be nonexistent. As a matter of fact, what made French opera superior to the Italian, says Marmontel in this article for the Supplement, was this very item of the *merveilleux*, which gave to song a plausibility and *raison d'être* it does not have in the Italian opera. The opera being the representation of *la nature dans l'enchantement*, it is natural to sustain this illusion by means of the *merveilleux*. Marmontel concludes his defense by stating that this discovery of Quinault's was the greatest poetic invention since Homer and Aeschylus.

But what Grimm objected to most strongly in the *merveilleux* was its complete lack of relationship to everyday life. How could the doings of Greek gods, about which the French knew little or nothing, have any interest for an eighteenth-century Parisian? What bearing could this fantastic spectacle have upon the life of reasoning, enlightened human beings? We have seen that Grimm admitted that the soul of French opera resided in the *merveilleux*. Any attack upon this aspect of the opera in France was tantamount to a proscription of French opera in general. Grimm was entirely aware of this danger, but he did not let this realization deter him from his purpose. The portion of the article "Poéme lyrique" which treats of the *merveilleux* is a sustained diatribe against French opera.

First of all, says Grimm in this article, why must an eighteenth-century French composer turn to the gods of ancient Greece for an operatic subject? If the opera did require a religious subject, it would seem natural for a people to prefer the dramatization of its own cult. The opera would then become a religious festival, as, in great part, Greek drama had become. But though it may be said that Greek drama was in a sense a religious art, Greek dramatists used the apparition of gods upon the stage with great discretion. The French, who did not exercise similar caution, found that gods tended to lose their divine character when they appeared for three hours together on an opera stage "under the beard and talent of M. Muguet." The Greek Gods are objectionable enough, but how about those ridiculous creatures of fancy, "un génie aérien, un jeu, un ris, un plasir, une heure, une constellation, and all those bizarre allegorical beings . . . is there no limit to this sort of nonsense?" Marmontel, in the article "Merveilleux," had pointed to the *épisode de la Haine*, from *Armide*, as the model of the genre termed *merveilleux*, employing as it did all the above phenomena. Grimm analyzes this scene in detail, in the manner of a wideawake critic of opera; i. e., reading a lesson from its manifold shortcomings.

What is the upshot of this lesson on the *merveilleux*? From the point of view of drama, says Grimm, this element is hopeless. These fantastical creatures do not interest us, because they can change the course of a hero's life in the twinkling of an eye, thus impairing the dramatic unity of the opera. Dramatic ineptitude led to a stunted musical growth. How could a drama devoid of all interest and truth, how could these fanciful creations lead to a rich musical development? Grimm blames the monotony of French melody on the *merveilleux*, as well as the tendency to fix musical expression, cookbook wise, in a tacitly accepted thesaurus of appropriate themes. Thus, French music could only be mediocre, for to prefer thunder and brilliance to dramatic power, says Grimm, is to prefer mediocrity to sublimity. Any composer can represent musically an earthquake, a tempest, a Sabbath, and the like, but the composer who can really portray human passions in a good dramatic situation must remain rare. The French composers failed to seize the fundamental distinction between *aria* and *recitativo* because of the *merveilleux*. They made the recitative slow and boring, basing it upon false ideas of declamation, and what there is of aria so called in the French opera can only properly by applied to the *air de danses*, wherein the *danse* or *merveilleux* element is given much more attention than the song. Haphazard *ariettes* were thrown into the local opera, but these, aside from having no connection with the dramatic and musical thought of the opera in question, waste all their efforts upon such words as *larme, murmure, voltige, enchaîne,*

and *triomphe*, terms singled out for their musical adaptability. Finally, insistence on the *merveilleux* led the decorators astray, preoccupied as they became with fairy palaces and enchanted gardens.

We have already seen that Grimm felt that the recitative and aria, or Italian type opera, was the natural vehicle for the portrayal of human emotions. He therefore scores the influence of the *merveilleux*, because it rendered everything in the opera unnatural and *invraisemblable*. Thus, it was unnatural for the French to treat Greek gods in an eighteenth-century spectacle. Transformations, magic spells, and the animation of *jeux, ris, heures, constellations*, not to mention other bizarre allegorical creations, were all beyond human experience. It was not natural to introduce dance upon any and all occasions, nor are there any examples in nature of enchanted palaces.

As may be expected, Rousseau did not withhold comment upon the *merveilleux* in the opera. Indeed, the article "Opéra" in the Supplement, borrowed from his *Dictionnaire de musique*, may be taken as an addenda or complement to Grimm's attack. Rousseau believed that the *vols* and *machines*, were indispensable adjuncts of the opera before this spectacle came of age. he points out that in Italy Apostolo Zeno was the first to introduce historical characters into the libretto and that Vinci and Pergolesi completed the break with the old fables, transforming the spectacle into a veritable concert. It was only when the element of *merveilleux* had been excised from the opera that this spectacle became worthy of being called a work of art: "When the opera was finally rid of the cloying *merveilleux*, it became at once a majestic and moving spectacle worthy of appealing to people of taste and to sensitive souls." Rousseau did not fail to track down any element of the opera that was particularly dear to the French and to proscribe it.

Thus, with the *Encyclopedia* itself opinion was divided concerning the *merveilleux*. Typically enough, those who swore by the local opera (Jaucourt) and those who saw in the opera no farther than the dances or *divertissements* (Cahusac), favored the use of *merveilleux*, whereas the inveterate enemies of French opera (Rousseau and Grimm) opposed it. However, it would seem that here again Rousseau had the last word, when he claimed that the *merveilleux* served only as a blind to the glaring defects of French opera. Marmontel, an ardent champion of French opera and of the *merveilleux*, who insisted that "music creates an atmosphere in which the *merveilleux* thrives" ("Lyrique," Supplement), and that "Song is the *merveilleux* of the spoken word" ("Opéra," Supplement), admits, in the article "Récitatif," that dances, elaborate decorations, stage effects, machines, etc., were all brought in to bolster the sinking local opera in vain. All the glittering train of the *merveilleux* could not keep the French opera alive. Failure succeeded failure.

Of the minor aspects of opera the Encyclopedists were no less meticulous critics . . . [As] far as the French opera was concerned, the *divertissement* was conceived as an integral part of the action. These episodic tableaux were composed of dances accompanied by song, and of course, scenic display. In the article "Divertissement" Cahusac is quite specific regarding the function of this element of the *merveilleux*. In general, he is dissatisfied with their use in the French opera; too often they interrupt rather than supplement the main dramatic action. The usual manner of presenting the *divertissement* was as one or several *entrées de ballet*. Cahusac finds that the ideal *divertissement* is one in which the song and dance are indispensable to the general development and progress of the spectacle: "A good ballet entrance is made up of a plot which the singing and dancing serve to develop and unfold in an agreeable manner." (Cahusac: "Divertissement.") Cahusac mentions *Thésée, Amadis*, and *Roland*, all Lulli-Quinault operas, as containing models of the genre. We have already seen that Cahusac probably saw in the opera only a vehicle for dances. Since both the *merveilleux* and its handmaid the *divertissement* depended upon dance, this critic was their stanchest champion. He initiated more propaganda for the use of dance in the opera than any other Encyclopedist. The articles "Ballet," "Coupe," "Couper," "Divertissement," "Enchantement," "Entrée," "Expression," "Fête," "Féerie," "Figurant," and "Geste" all include either a mention or a lengthy discussion of this subject. And in each of his several articles treating of the *divertissement* Cahusac warns against including the dance in the opera merely as *postiche*.

In the article "Air" Marmontel hints that the French opera was kept alive mainly because of the dances. Though French composers had not yet found the secret of composing recitative and aria, they compensated for this lack by developing *divertissements*. Thus, for him the dance took the place of the aria in the French opera. Marmontel explains, in the article "Opéra," that the dance must carry on the main action of the opera. Dance and *fêtes* can be integrated in the opera during moments of calm. In this way the suspension of opera for the purpose of introducing dances will not be so strongly felt. He agrees with Cahusac that the French have only exceptionally succeeded in making the dance a part of the opera.

In scoring the ballets and *divertissements* of the French opera as *postiches*, Grimm suggests, in the article "Poème lyrique," that Quinault unwillingly followed popular taste in this department of operatic composition. He points to the dances in *Roland* as aptly fitting into the dramatic action, arguing from this example that had Quinault had a free hand, he might have made more extensive use of the divertissement as an integral part of the action. However, as we have already seen, Lulli could not have allowed this if he meant to retain intact the fine symmetry of his operas.

Cahusac, Marmontel, and Grimm represented Encyclopedist thought concerning the use of dance in the opera. They were all in agreement that the French had not made the most of the ballet in the opera, that Quinault had done as well as he dared, and that Noverre represented the highest aims of the opera insofar, at least, as the dance was concerned. Noverre's *ballet en action*, or *poème-ballet*, was all that the Encyclopedists dreamed for the opera. As for Rousseau, he saw no place in the opera for the dance. (Rousseau: "Opéra.")

Encyclopedist comment was extended to even the minutest details of opera. Cahusac states that the music of the entr'acte should continue the illusion of the spectacle. (Cahusac: "Entr'acte.") And the gestures and facial expression of the singer should be those of the consummate actor. (Cahusac: "Geste.") Rousseau tells us, in the article "Acteur," that the French expect the singer to be a finished actor and that his pantomime should synchronize perfectly with the musical commentary. The music itself should be an actor, carrying on a constant duet with the singer, commenting on his thought and enhancing his passion by revealing the unexpressed. Quite specifically, Marmontel sees music as an answer to speech in the *récitatif obligé*. He sums up the varied role of the orchestra in the opera as follows: (1) to play chords; (2) to supplement; and (3) to answer, as in a dialogue, the voice of the singer; (4) to provide the setting for a scene through the imitation of natural sounds. (Marmontel: "Accompagnement.") Marmontel does not seem to have been aware that in Italy the orchestra had long since been an active agent in the thematic unfolding of musical material, aside from its role of sustaining the singer, in the works of Scarlatti and Pergolesi.

In concluding this section, it may be said that the Encyclopedists saw in the opera a perfectly coördinated spectacle of drama, music, dancing, singing, painting, and scenic effects. All agreed that the Italian opera was superior, but the general consensus of Encyclopedist opinion in no way supported Rousseau's statement that the French opera was hopeless and that it had no future. In summing up his wants for the opera, Cahusac holds out a distinct hope for the French opera in particular.

> The successful opera writer should be a man of many talents with an infinite capacity to learn. . . . He should know how to make use of contrasting situations, how to introduce *divertissements*, vary them, and fit them into the action; he should know how to plan quickly; he should be a man of ideas, having more than a smattering of painting, mechanics, dancing, and perspective; he should have a feeling for effect, a rare talent, to be found only in men of lively imagination and keen sensitivity. . . . Perhaps some day the French will awaken and cast off the silly prejudices that have done so much harm to the progress of the art of opera in this country. (Cahusac: "Coupe.")

Marmontel felt that perfection had already been achieved in some of the operas of Quinault, actually, insofar as the poème was concerned, and potentially, at least, regarding other elements.

> If you can imagine that in an opera, music, dance, decoration, machinery, the singers' talent both for singing and acting, could be in the same degree of excellence as the essential portions of the poems for *Atys, Thésée, Armide*, then you have an idea of the opera as I conceive it, or as Quinault himself had wished it. (Marmontel: "Opéra.")

It was in this spirit that Marmontel rewrote Quinault's libretti for the composer Piccini.

The foregoing quotations prove that the Encyclopedists were not willing to be influenced to an inordinate degree by the opinions of their principal contributor to the articles on music. They may have agreed with Rousseau when he scored French singing (Rousseau: "Chanter," "Crier," "Forcer la Voix," "Fort"; Cahusac: "Débit," "Effort") or when he pointed out faults in execution (Rousseau: "Ensemble"; Cahusac: "Exécution") and again when he ridiculed the French tendency to insist upon certain "musical" words in the *poème* (Rousseau: "Musique"; Grimm: "Poème lyrique"), but none of these critics was willing to admit that the French could not and did not have a national opera.

The upshot of Encyclopedist criticism of the opera is that these writers were the first Frenchmen to recognize the difference between literary and musical opera. But the literary orientation of French composers prevented that naïve abandonment which enabled the Italians to create true opera. The French learned too late that the dominant element on the lyric stage must be music; this explains why despite the activity of the *Encyclopedia* on behalf of musical dramaturgy, the messiah of the new French opera had to be a foreigner.

VIEWS ON WOMEN

Terry Smiley Dock

SOURCE: "Woman as a Psychological Being," in *Woman in the "Encyclopedie": A Compendium,* Studia Humanitatis, 1983, pp. 73-110.

[*In the following excerpt, Dock comments on the Encyclopedists' ideas concerning women. Focusing on their psychological analyses of the female gender, Dock discerns a peculiar blend of male suprematism, ignorance, confusion, and some objectivity.*]

For the contributors [to the *Encyclopédie*], woman's character and her physical constitution are closely related. This is evident in direct statements, in several linguistic peculiarities, and in the contributors' attitudes. Woman, because she is a woman, possesses a lively imagination, strong passions, timidity, and modesty. Desmahis believes that woman's more animated imagination is caused by the delicacy of her organs (FEMME). Lefebvre warns against trusting women's judgment because "their imagination grasps nothing weakly" (GOUVERNEUR D'UN JEUNE HOMME). The author of SABBAT, however, quotes Malebranche on the weak imaginations of women and children. In RESOLUTION, DECISION Jaucourt writes that women rarely base their decisions on anything other than imagination and feelings.

Woman's Emotions

Women, "this sex born sensitive" (TOURNOIS), are subject to and perhaps, as Jaucourt intimates, ruled by strong passions. In fact, D'Aumont simply states that it would be impossible to express how strongly women are disposed to any violent passion (ENFANS, MALADIES DES). The author of FOIBLE (Morale) claims that women are more susceptible to "foibles of the heart" because their soul is more sensitive. Henri Fouquet, doctor of medicine, states that, in general, passions in women are much more intense than

in men. He attributes this psychological phenomenon to physiological differences. Women have a uterus, one of the major centers of their sensitivity, and the layers of their mucous membranes are more pliant and more tenuous than men's. Le Roi also sees a connection between woman's body and her personality: her passions are more lively thanks to her delicate, sensitive organs (HOMME). Le Roi speaks approvingly of women's strong passions. Women's stronger inclination to self-love and pleasure-seeking is balanced, according to him, by their more deeply felt pity. The author of GROSSESSE summarizes: "Everything indicates that woman is more delicate than man, and consequently, more sensitive; that is why she is more susceptible to the strongest passions, but she does not retain them as long as man does." Desmahis suggests that if the delicacy of their organs renders women's minds less capable of attention, women perceive more quickly and can comprehend as well (FEMME). Their inability to remain attentive for long periods may account for their fickleness, attested to by Diderot in two grammatical illustrations: "Women are fickle; that is why men become inconstant" (C'EST POURQUOI, AINSI) and, in VOLAGE: "A woman who often changes the object of her affections is said to be fickle." Jaucourt mentions the female's whims in TAURESIUM.

Jaucourt pursues the topic of strong passions and claims—to women's advantage—that, during the age of chivalry, the ladies' horror of seeing blood shed gave way to "the even more powerful attachment women feel for glory" (TOURNOIS), resulting in their attending tournaments. On the other hand, his explanation of anger in COLERE is less flattering:

> Anger is caused by an atrabilious disposition; a weak, soft, sick mind; false delicacy; a hypersensitivity; self-love; the love of trifles; idle curiosity; gullibility; hurt at being scorned and insulted; which is why a woman's anger is so sharp and complete [. . . .]

The authors of PROPOSITION, Douchet and Beauzée, professors at the École royale militaire, write: "A woman hates or loves, there is no in-between."

The *Encyclopédie* offers numerous stories of women's strong passions or violence. Jaucourt recounts the duchess of Montpensier's implacable hatred of Henri III (RAILLERIE). We discover in two articles that a Roman woman attempted to get rid of her hydropic husband by serving him toads (HYDROPISIE)—"they don't say with what sauce" (CRAPAUD). According to Jaucourt, a roman lady mixed poison from a frog in her husband's wine (RUBETE). Edmé Mallet, doctor and professor of theology, mentions a singular occasion in which Roman ladies gave their husbands poisonous philters (CLOU). In CIRCONCELLIONS ou SCOTOPITES, however, he speaks of women's natural gentleness. Jaucourt recounts the massacres carried out by the women of Lemnos whose husbands had favored Thracian slave girls, attributing the atrocities to jealousy, self-love, and vengeance (LEMNOS, SICNUS, SIKINO). In one night the women slaughtered all of the men except King Thoas, whose daughter hid him. In the second massacre the children of the concubines were killed (LEMNOS). Jaucourt supplies additional examples of woman's fury in MYSTERES DES ROMAINS and PLATEE. Jaucourt does cite examples of extremes of passion which result in more positive actions. In OLYMPIQUES, JEUX and TYPEE he portrays a mother so dedicated to her son that she broke a social tabu, punishable by death, prohibiting women's presence. Jaucourt illustrates filial devotion in PIETE where he tells of the Roman daughter who kept her imprisoned mother alive by nursing her. In TEMPLE DE LA PIETE it is a daughter who did the same for her father. Jaucourt lauds a British countess for saving her husband from execution (STEWART, GREAT). The women who saved their husbands' lives by carrying them out of the captive city on their shoulders (TRIUMVIRAT) merit notice for wifely love and fidelity. Diderot recognizes one woman's finer qualities when he writes in LANGRES of Julius Sabinus, known for his revolt against Vespasian, but even better known for the beauty, courage, tenderness, fidelity and love of his wife Epponina.

The subject of tears is treated in several articles. Mallet remarks that tears cost women nothing (CONJURATION). The author of FUNERAILLES *des Arabes* informs us that although Arab men refrain from crying as a sign of their vigor, the women more than make up for it. The ancients, we are reminded, hired professional female mourners (CONVOI, DANSE DES FUNERAILLES, FUNERAILLES *des Romains*, FUNERE, PLEUREUSES, PRAEFICA, PRETRES). Finally, Jaucourt shrewdly testifies to the power of a woman's tears in TRIBUN DU PEUPLE. After several years of disputes over a certain issue, a woman's tears succeeded where the eloquence, the intrigues, and the cabals of the tribunes had failed: "So true is it that this lovable and artful sex is never stronger than when it uses its own weakness to succeed."

Timidity and Weakness

Still basing their arguments on physiology, some Encyclopedists maintain that woman is naturally timid. Desmahis, for example, claiming that although the two sexes are distinguished by inequalities, they possess nearly equal advantages, states: "Nature put on one side strength, majesty, courage, and reason; on the other, charm, beauty, guile, and sentiment" (FEMME). He suggests that woman's timidity results from her weaker physical constitution: "If it is true that timidity is born of weakness, guile of timidity, and duplicity of guile, we must conclude that truth is a highly estimable virtue in women" (FEMME). Barthès reports Mercurialis's belief that women's bodies are defended by weak, timid souls (FASCINATION). Diderot reiterates that women are a naturally weak and timid sex (ANSICO). To compensate for their natural weakness they are imperious, unduly exercising a precarious and momentary authority (IMPERIEUX). Their weakness, Desmahis believes, accounts for their vindictiveness because vengeance, the act of momentary power, is actually a proof of weakness (FEMME).

Courage

Feminine weakness figures in the Encyclopedists' discussion of courage. Courage, in Jaucourt's words, is "that male virtue which arises from the feeling of one's own strength, and which, through character or reflection, enables one to brave dangers and their consequences" (COURAGE, [Morale]). Obviously, by definition, if woman is naturally weak, she will have little courage. The author of MALE states that the male of the animal species has more courage and more strength than the female. Barthès relates Hippocrates's conviction that apparitions had caused more women than men to perish because women have less courage and strength (FASCINATION). The writer of FUSEE (Blason) refers to cowards in these uncomplimentary terms: "They deserved to be numbered among the women." M. de Pezay, a military man, distinguishes valor from the instinct of self-preservation. He ascribes to woman the latter only (VALEUR).

Two terms designate brave women: "*virago,*" a woman of extraordinary stature or courage who has martial inclinations (VIRAGO); and "*Amazone,*" a courageous, bold woman capable of great exploits (AMAZONE). The author of VIRAGO lists Semiramis, Penthesilea, and all of the ancient Amazons as deserving of this term. He emphasizes that this word is purely Latin and is used in French only to ridicule. Mallet discusses the Amazon nation in particular and notes that some authors believe that these women warriors did not kill their sons but merely deformed their legs, to prevent them from claiming one day to be their masters (AMAZONE).

Other contributors cite examples of courageous women, wives and mothers, which in some instances support Diderot's most generous, forceful, and concise appreciation of woman's ability to participate as an equal in the human condition, to meet with stoical dignity the ultimate challenge to mankind—death:

> The soul has a given capacity of energy before the greatest of terrors, that of death. Now, many women have braved death. Every being who knows how to brave death, to wait for it unconcerned, see it without paling, suffer it without complaint, has the greatest strength in adversity, can conceive the highest of ideas, is capable of the most violent enthusiasm, and there is nothing one should not expect of him, whether he speaks or acts, especially if a suitable education has added to the natural qualities what they usually receive from it. (PYTHAGORISME, OU PHILOSOPHIE DE PYTHAGORE)

Jaucourt tells in some detail the story of Arria, wife of Cecina Poetus, who, failing to save his life and perceiving that he lacked the resolution to kill himself as ordered by the emperor, took the dagger from his hand, saying "Thus, Poet," stabbed herself, tranquilly returned the dagger to him and with her last breath said, "It doesn't hurt, Poet." (COURAGE). We read in CHEVEUX, *Des cordes de cheveux* of the Carthaginian and Roman women who cut their hair to supply ropes for the war machines. Diderot comments that courageous women have made and are still making every day greater sacrifices than that. D'Holbach writes of Czarina Catherine, wife of Peter the Great, who followed her husband in a perilous expedition against the Turks. She sent a courier to the grand vizier, commander of the Ottoman army, promising him a considerable sum if he would negotiate with the czar. The vizier consented and exhorted his deputies not to miss seeing the czarina, "because he couldn't believe that a woman had had enough courage and marital love to expose herself to such a great danger" (CATHERINE, L'ORDRE DE STE). Diderot mentions "the remarkable defense" of Tortose by the city's hatchet-wielding women (HACHE, ordre de). Jaucourt refers to the women of Argos who had "the glory" of driving back the Lacedaemonians (HYBRISTIQUES). He also remarks upon the courage of the Scottish wives who went to war with their husbands (SCOTI). The author of PALARIA states that some women occasionally participated in this Roman military exercise, but he belittles them by adding that their courage and vigor were better thought of than their honesty. Diderot recites examples of people who threw themselves on a beloved's funeral pyre and notes that several women have had "that courage" (BUCHERS). In STOICISME, *ou* SECTE STOICIENNE, *ou* ZENONISME Diderot declares that women also had the "courage" to distinguish themselves as Stoics. Diderot (COPHTE ou COPTE), Jaucourt (JEUNE), Mallet (ABSTINENCE), and D'Holbach (SINTOS *ou* SINTOISME and VARTIAS) also acknowledge woman's capacity for undertaking and enduring austerities. Finally, Diderot seems to suggest that mothers possess a sort of natural courage: "A mother who saw her child in danger would run to his aid barefoot through burning coals without feeling any pain" (IMPASSIBLE, IMPASSIBILITE). Jaucourt illustrates this notion in two articles with the story of a widow who, defying the law which forbade women, on pain of being hurled from a very high rock, to attend the Olympic games (TYPEE), dressed as a gymnastics instructor in order to conduct her son Pisidore to Olympia. As her son was being declared the winner, she threw off her men's grab, jumped over the barrier, and "was recognized for what she was" (OLYMPIQUES, JEUX). In consideration of her father, her brothers, and her son who had all been crowned at the Olympics, she was pardoned.

Modesty

Inspite of the many examples of female courage, Jaucourt insists that woman's character is essentially timid and, more importantly perhaps, modest (REGGIO). In PROPRE Jaucourt says of women: "Modesty is a virtue appropriate to their sex" and in TEMPLES DE LA PUDICITE he exclaims: "Modesty is a virtue too essential to the fair sex for it not to have been exalted as a divinity." The anonymous author of GYNECONOME alludes to punishments meted out to women who misbehaved and who strayed from the limits of modesty befitting their sex. Modesty, according to Jaucourt, is a natural, wise, honest shame, a secret fear, a feeling for those things capable of effecting infamy (PUDER). Virtue, modesty, and chastity, Jaucourt continues, are often used interchangeably (VERTU).

The loss of modesty occasions a certain insensitivity. In his account of the prostitution of the Cyprian women, Ovid comments that after the women had trampled the laws of modesty underfoot, they became so callous that only a slight change would have been needed to turn them into stone (PROPETIDES). Jaucourt finds this notion ingenious. The woman imbued with modesty is above reporting attacks on her honor—which would seem to deprive

her of all recourse in the case of rape: "She prefers to be silent about those who have outraged her, when she cannot talk about it without bringing to light actions and expressions which by themselves alarm her virtue" (PUDER). Jaucourt, however, warns against the excessive modesty which prevents women at the cost of their lives from showing certain afflictions to doctors: "Modesty, of course, is only a feeling of decency which should only turn us away from vice" (COCCYX).

Modesty manifests itself primarily in the woman's face (PUDICITE) and is her best cosmetic (MODESTIE), producing a blush called "virtue's vermilion" ("*le vermillion de la vertu*") (ROUGEUR, SENS INTERNES) or "modesty's rouge" ("*le rouge de la pudeur*") (FARD). Jaucourt, we recall, bewails in ROUGE the use of

> Cette artificieuse rougeur
> Qui supplée au défaut de celle
> Que jadis causoit la pudeur.

One may also judge a woman's modesty by her clothing; historically, the more she wears or the less of her body she reveals, the more modest she is (AMICLE, HABITS DES ROMAINS, JANSENISTE, MITRE, SEIN, TUNIQUE, VETIR). However, a scantily-clad woman is more immodest than a naked woman (TROUSSER), and one contemporary sees more danger in the artful attire of women than in their total nudity (LACEDEMONE, *république de*). The author of SAC A OUVRAGE, observing that today's woman would no more go out without this item of adornment than without her fichu, wryly comments that frequently the one is as useless as the other. Examples of women clothed only in their modesty may be found in antiquity. Diderot relates Aelien's description of Phocion's wife whose garment was first of all her modesty and then whatever she could find to cover herself (CALYPTRE). Jaucourt informs us that during Lycurgus's period of legislation the young Lacedaemonian girls danced in certain solemn festivals adorned solely by their own beauty and with no veil but their modesty (GYMNOPEDIE; LACEDEMONE, *république de*). The purpose, according to Lycurgus, was to insure that the Spartan girls, by performing the same exercises as the men, would not be inferior to the men either in glory and in corporeal health or in generosity (GYMNOPEDIE) and courage (LACEDEMONE, *république de*). An "illustrious Modern" aptly observed that such practices were suitable only to Lycurgus's students, whose frugal, laborious life, pure, strict morals, and strong wills could alone render innocent a spectacle so shocking to all peoples who are merely respectable (LACEDEMONE, *république de*).

The Double Standard

In spite of their preoccupation with modesty ("*pudeur*"), the contributors obviously consider this trait desirable in women only. For example, D'Aumont exposes the double standard in FUREUR UTERINE: "In general, nowhere do mores require of them [men] the reserve, the constraint, of which modesty consists, that virtue so recommended to women in nearly every nation, even in the least civilized of them." He accepts it unquestioningly, however, on the grounds of social utility: modesty attracts men; it makes surmounting the obstacles to their desire a pleasure and consequently maintains men's propensity for women; modesty thus promotes propagation of the species.

The Encyclopedists view the double standard and one of its causes, sexual stereotyping, as part of the natural order. A linguistic reinforcement presents itself in the word "effeminate" which derives from the weak, delicate character of woman (EFFEMINE) and is an unflattering epithet for a man. Diderot remarks, however, that the implicit reproach is reciprocal; one does not at all like to encounter in a woman the external qualities of a man: "Experience has taught us to attach to each sex a tone, a bearing, movements, features peculiar to each, and we are shocked to find them out of place" (EFFEMINE). Desmahis is of the same opinion: "What is pleasant or virtuous in one sex is a defect or a deformity in the other" (FEMME). Jaucourt likewise concurs:

> Men's cap, whip, garments, all the male paraphernalia, corrupt the ladies' delicate features and render them coarse to the senses; their embellishment is being moved; the pity inspired in them by misfortune, the ready blush, that colors their face at the least gesture, the least word; here are their luster and their charm! (ZONS TEMPEREES)

Evidence of a double standard which, in a patriarchal society, is invariably a manifestation of a belief in man's superiority and an indication of male condescension, exists in several other articles. Voltaire explains, for example, that while the term "easy" is an insult for a woman, it is sometimes in society a tribute to a man (FACILE). In RETENUE we discover that circumspection in conduct and especially in speech, particularly appropriate in youth, is a virtue in both sexes. However, it is demanded more of women than of men, and more of girls than of women. Impropriety, excusable in men when it is accompanied by a mirth which raises them above common practices, is, Diderot proclaims, insufferable in women (INDECENT). A beautiful, indecent woman is a kind of monster which Diderot would compare to a ferocious lamb; it is not something one expects.

Man's Superior Attitude

Certain traits unpardonable in men are tolerated in women. Haughtiness can be forgiven a woman because men forgive these charming creatures everything (DRAPERIE; HAUTAIN). Interest in beauty contests is excusable in women, Jaucourt concedes, but it is very strange for men to want to compete in such events (TENEDOS). Affectation, which, according to Diderot (AFFECTATION, AFFETERIE), particularly offends "advocates of candor," is more easily overlooked in women than in men. Diderot scathes jargon. It compensates for true wit, common sense, judgment, reason, and knowledge in people who know their way around in society (JARGON). Diderot concludes, to the detriment of women: "One can pardon it in women: it is unworthy of a man."

More subtle and possibly more insidious are the linguistic examples of the contributors' superior attitude towards woman. She is not only classified with the defenseless young and the infirm aged (AVANTAGE, BOUCHES INUTILES, ENNEMI, LOUP, MORAVES), but relegated to the ranks of the mentally inferior where she shares the opprobrium of imbeciles (BAT, BATTOLOGIE, BUTUBATA; MELANCHOLE; MARCOSIENS), the common herd (IMAGINATION *des femmes enceintes sur le foetus*), the gullible and the superstitious (AMULETE, HERCULE, SABBAT), and the untutored (EPITHETE). The *Encyclopédie* abounds in references to "*femmelettes*" (GYMNASTIQUE MEDICINALE, HOUX, LUTIN, MEDECINS ANCIENS, OBSERVATEUR) and "*bonnes femmes*" (CEROMANTIE, CHRONIQUE, CIRE des oreilles, MILLE-FEUILLE, SAIGNEE, SCORPION, SOURIS, TAUPE, TRANSPLANTATION, URINE [maladie de l']). In fact, a cursory semantic examination seems to indicate that man, throughout the ages, has appropriated not only strength, but most positive character traits for the male sex. The ancients, for example, observing the matriarchal bees, assumed that queen bees were "king bees" simply because people had not distinguished their sex (ABEILLE). Jaucourt, we recall, speaks of courage in terms of a "male" or "manly" virtue (COURAGE). He refers to one general's stratagem for successfully quelling a mutiny as "a manly, delicate stroke" (ORCHOMENE). Zenobia, Jaucourt continues, is renowned for her "virile" beauty, her knowledge and her conquests (PALMYRE). Still another contributor speaks of "a manly genius" (ORFEVRE). The heroine is defined in terms of the hero (HEROINE) while the entry FILLE tersely advises "voyez FILS." The author of MASCULIN (Astrologie) ridicules the practice of dividing the signs of the zodiac into masculine and feminine according to their active (masculine) or passive (feminine) qualities. The author of MALE, probably Diderot, peremptorily elucidates this linguistic phenomenon: "Because the male of the animal species has more courage and strength than the female, this term was transferred to things intellectual, and people said a manly mind, a manly (virile) style, a manly thought." Jaucourt speaks of a queen who had given up the "weaknesses" of women for the "passions" of men (PUY, LE). He opposes strength and virility to the "delectations" and "nonchalance" of women (PROPORTION). In MARRIAGE *des Romains*, Jaucourt states that the nuptial chamber remained dark the first night either to protect the bride's modesty or to prevent the groom from perceiving any hidden faults his spouse might have—as though men had no concealed defects. The author of LAIT (*maladies qui dépendent du*) implies that any prerogatives women have over men are purely physical. The author of CHEVALIER ERRANT assures us that knights-errant did not merely devote themselves to a lady they respected or loved; they were originally distinguished gentlemen concerned with public safety and tranquillity. On two occasions, Jaucourt's judicious placement of "even" ("*même*") also reveals an incredulous, mildly scornful attitude. In HEROS (Mythol. & Littérat.) he tells us that the Greeks established a cult for the souls of heroes, "and even for heroines" and in GLADIATEUR he traces the decadent custom honoring consuls and magistrates by staging gladiatorial combats at their funeral ceremonies: "Gradually this custom spread to less qualified personages; finally several private individuals stipulated it in their will and in a word, there were even gladiatorial combats at women's funerals." The most striking example of the implicit conviction of man's moral superiority occurs in the summary definition of HUMILIANT: "That which wounds the pride and lowers man below the dignity befitting his nature, rank, function, pretention, his sex."

Undesirable Traits

Bearing in mind that the Encyclopedists are of the "superior" sex, we are not surprised to see that they attribute to women various less-than-admirable qualities. Articles on the mythologies and the mores of several cultures portray women as unsubmissive, untrustworthy, troublesome creatures. Lilith, Adam's first wife, vanished after her refusal to obey him (LILITH). Odin counsels against trusting the words of a female, "because their hearts were made like the turning wheel; fickleness was put in their hearts" (ISLANDE). The author of POLYTHEISME, probably Yvon, claims that a cabal of women disrupted natural law as early as the first generation when Tital, eldest son of the first of the gods, was deprived of his rightful inheritance by his sisters' intrigues. Louis informs us that Ambroise Paré wrote a special section on the artifices of women who pretend to suffer such afflictions as breast cancer in order to gain the people's compassion and thus receive more generous alms (IMPOSTURE, *en maladie*). In certain settlements of the French islands of America one man must constantly oversee the Negroes, to prevent disorder and the very frequent quarrels among the Negresses (COMMANDEUR, [Comm.]). The English used to have a cage for dunking malicious, quarrelsome women (TREBUCHET). The Moravian's community of married people does not fail to elicit objections on the grounds that the women will inevitably sow discord among the consorts (MORAVES ou FRERES UNIS). Faiguet, author of the article, retorts that women would not cause any more disorder in a well-supervised community than they do now in their private homes. Bad-tempered women are likened historically to a scourge. Artemidor's second book of dreams promises as a punishment an ugly, spiteful, ill-tempered woman (DIMACHERUS). In SORT, Jaucourt, citing Ecclesiasticus XXV: 26, deems the sinner, rather than the virtuous man, worthy of suffering the bad temper of a wicked woman. He laments: "But unfortunately fate does not always decide thus." Pliny, says Jaucourt, sought refuge in study from his wife's indisposition (ETUDE), while Henri IV professed the greatest misfortune in life to be an ugly, bad, spiteful wife (PAU). Louis notes that accoucheurs generally complain of their charges' indocility, their spitefulness, and their unwillingness to heed salutary advice (HEMORRHOIDES). In IMPURETE, IMPUR (Morale), Diderot describes pagan religions in which women were obliged to prostitute themselves once in honor of the goddess. He rather maliciously adds: "and you can judge whether the piety natural to their sex allowed them to stop there."

Loquacity

Several contributors remark upon woman's proclivity to talk. The author of PROPOSITION lists as an example of things that are ordinarily said: "All women like to talk." In PARIS, Jaucourt describes the austerity of one convent in which the nuns strictly observe, among other things, "a perpetual silence for which the fair sex was not born." Jaucourt quotes father Caussin in POINTE: "Men built the tower of Babel, and women the tower of babble." Venel slyly wonders whether the true etymology of *pica* should

not be "magpie" because of the connection between this chattering bird and women, the usual victims of the disease (PICA). In Marmontel's article on FABLE apologue we read:

Un homme avoit perdu sa femme,
Il veut avoir un perroquet.
Se console qui peut: plein de la bonne dame,
Il veut du moins chez lui remplacer son caquet.

To prevent themselves from talking, the women of one African country, the author of BURAMOS (les) ou les PAPAIS tells us, keep a mouthful of water for half a day. In three instances, we find specific expressions appropriate for garrulous females. Douchet and Beauzée state that "*piailler*" (to squall) applies to women and "*brailler*" (to bawl) to men (FREQUENTATIF). Jaucourt explains that Juvenal's allusion to a prattling woman as one who makes enough noise "to help the Moon in labor" derives from the superstitious custom of beating metal basins to make the moon reappear (ECLIPSE). According to Dumarsais, a tutor, in Paris people refer to a nagging woman as "a market-place mute," that is, a woman who makes offensive remarks to everyone (ANTI-PHRASE). Jaucourt, however, suggests that woman's speech may be profitable, effecting her happiness as well as man's (LANGUE). He writes that three of the ancients claim Homer's nepenthe consisted of nothing but the charms of Helen's conversation (NEPENTHES). Finally, in PESANTEUR, POIDS, GRAVITE, Jaucourt declares that there is nothing like the company of women and the court to free the mind of its natural sluggishness.

Some women readily accede to the notion of the virtue of silence. Madame Dacier, Jaucourt relates, asked by a foreigner to write her name and an aphorism in his album, saw the names of the most learned men in Europe and replied that she would blush to put her name among so many famous ones. At last relenting, she wrote a line of Sophocles, in Greek: "Silence is the ornament of women" (SAUMUR). Barthès relates in FEMME that Sophocles believed silence to be womankind's greatest adornment.

Curiosity

Several Encyclopedists seem to insinuate a belief in women's monopoly on curiosity. Only Desmahis sympathizes: "How would they not be curious? They are kept in the dark about everything" (FEMME). The author of MAGIE, Polier de Bottens, a Swiss pastor, calls the witches' sabbath "the realm of underground amazons" because there have always been more female than male witches, a phenomenon he attributes to women's weak mind or to their too great curiosity. Daughters of Eve, he continues, women want to go astray as she did, in order to know all. Boucher d'Argis, citing Sauval, recounts the execution in 1445 of a woman convicted of poking out the eyes of a two-year-old child. According to Sauval, all of the women of Paris, out of curiosity, wanted to see her die (*Délit d'épingle*). In MOLAIRE DENT Jaucourt relates Highmor's story about a lady who, having had a molar tooth extracted, endured a constant, serous trickle from her sinuses. So great was her curiosity about the source of the trickle, that she inserted into the cavity a quill six fingers' breadth long. She feared she had pushed it into her brain. Toussaint, a lawyer, professor, and man of letters, and Mallet report that at one time abbesses were allowed to confess the nuns. They lost that right because of their "excessive curiosity" (ABBESSE).

Woman's curiosity is perhaps surpassed only by her naïveté. Women more frequently fall victim to impostors (SECOURS) and are the last to relinquish their superstitious beliefs (CEROMANTIE, LIEGE). In MARCOSIENS, for example, we read: "Marc was a great imposter who deceived the simple, mainly women." Mallet informs us that in 1217 the bishop of Salisbury forbade placing cane rings on women's fingers to seduce them. There were girls simple-minded enough to believe the rings were true wedding bands (ANNEAU). Mallet affirms in AMULETTE that some of the remedies described in ancient tomes are still practiced today by "empirics, women, or other credulous and superstitious persons." The exposure of woman's foibles is not without humor. In NAIVETE UNE, NAIVETE LA, Jaucourt offers the famous anecdote of the woman whose husband on his deathbed counseled her to remarry: " 'Take so and so, he suits you, believe me.' 'Alas,' said the woman, 'I was thinking about it.' "

Wit and Intelligence

If many women are simple, not all are devoid of wit. Jaucourt relates that, during a storm, Queen Henrietta of England reassured her fellow nautical travellers by calmly saying that "queens did not drown" (SUBLIME). The author of SORCIERS & SORCIERES and Jaucourt in REPONSE, REPARTIE cite Voltaire's account of the reply of the unfortunate maréchale d'Ancre, burned at the stake as a witch, to the question of what spell she had used to govern the mind of Marie de Médicis—"the power of strong souls over weak minds." Jaucourt also quotes "a witty seventeenth-century lady" who was prompted by the fact that the te Deum is ceremoniously sung to thank God publicly for a land or a naval victory to say that "the *te Deum* of kings was the *de profundis* of private citizens" (TE-DEUM).

As for the intelligence of women, Dumarsais writes in CONJONCTION: "Women have as much intelligence as men." Ménuret de Chambaud and "a prudent doctor" concede that even the most ignorant people can supply good ideas and that, consequently, one should not disdain a remedy merely because it is promoted by simple women (URINE, *maladie de l'*). Several articles describe specific women distinguished by their knowledge (CATHERINE [*chevaliers de Sainte Catherine du mont Sinaï*], PYTHAGORISME, QUAKER, SAUMUR, SOUTHHAMPTON, STRATFORD ou STRETFORD) or more enlightened than most of their sex (RIDE). Jaucourt praises Corinne (TANAGRA), Heloïse (PARACLET), Marie Touchet (ORLEANS), Marguerite de France (USSON), Isabelle Andreini (PADOUE), and Madame de Caylus (VIVARAIS, LE) for their wit or erudition and their beauty. He declares that Queen Christina, of whose "manly air" he approves, found little favor at the French court because no women there could match her genius (STOCKHOLM). Finally, lest the reader despair at the dearth of examples of successful women, Diderot offers a consoling thought. He suggests in PYTHAGORISME that proportionately more women than men have made a name for themselves if one considers that very few women are trained for important positions.

Vanity

Praise of a woman's character or mind is nearly always proof that she is ugly, says Desmahis (FEMME). It seems that women themselves are more concerned with their appearance than with nearly anything else. In fact, Venel claims that an appeal to woman's vanity will cure her of a depraved appetite: it suffices to tell her that she risks marring her beauty (PICA). Watelet, a tax official, refers to women as "the sex jealous of its charms" (EXTREMITES). Jaucourt implies that women are universally vain (SENS INTERNES). Moreover, he maintains that women so crave attention that they would rather be noticed for their weaknesses than not be noticed at all (REMARQUER, OBSERVER). However, in LIGUE, *la*, Jaucourt notes that it is not for men to reveal a woman's secret shortcomings. That is more unforgivable than an outrage against her honor.

Diderot and Mallet offer additional examples which show that female vanity transcends class and time. In FICHU Diderot comments that even the most innocent peasant girl arranges her little shawl to show off her firm, round, white bosom. Mallet points out that in ancient times girls wore buskins to give themselves a more attractive figure; travelers and hunters, on the other hand, wore them as protection from mud (BRODEQUIN).

Cahusac intimates that the female's desire to enhance her beauty and to display her graces to best advantage is present from childhood (GESTE), while Le Romain notices her natural desire to preserve that beauty (TERRES des îles Antilles). Jaucourt caters to the ladies by giving them a remedy for blackheads (TANNE). However, he sermonizes the fair sex in reply to their query on the feasibility of effacing scars. One of these marks on the skin, he says, is "like the effects of slander, whose scars remain forever after the wounds are closed" (CICATRICE).

D'Holbach recognizes woman's wish to remain eternally young and beautiful in his discussion of the fountain of youth (TALC, *huile de*). The anonymous author of LICENCES *en Peinture* tells us that artists are allowed to indulge this feminine yearning by making women appear younger than they actually are. It is Desmahis and Jaucourt who realize that women associate aging and the loss of their beauty with the end of their love life. In FEMME Desmahis depicts the dilemma old age brings to the beautiful, gay woman as he traces the decline of Chloé's acceptance in society. As she grows old, she ceases to please without ceasing to love. She still wants to be seen, but no one wants to be seen with her. She is forced to try to pass either from the love of men to the love of God (becoming a devout person) or from "the temple of love" to "the sanctuary of the muses" (becoming a "pretty wit"). Very few women succeed in making the transition, writes Desmahis. We should perhaps emulate Ninon de Lenclos who, according to Jaucourt, was not so foolish as to take seriously the abbé de Chaulieu's cajoleries that love had retreated to the wrinkles of her beautiful forehead; she herself called her wrinkles the sign of the departure of love and the marks of wisdom.

Fashion

Perhaps woman's desire for attention and her desire to

please account in part for her traditional penchant for finery which, in conjunction with her love of novelty and her capriciousness, affects the world of fashion. Saint Jerome, according to Jaucourt, called the fair sex "*philocosmon, the sex fond of ornamentation,*" and claimed to know of many women of irrefutable virtue who adorned themselves simply for their own satisfaction with no intent whatsoever of pleasing any man (VERONE). The author of PARER (Gram.), on the other hand, writes: "Women, by decking themselves out, return to men the tribute men pay them." Jaucourt proposes that women will always love to be adorned and that this taste, natural in their sex, is quite excusable (VERONE). He also notes that both sexes are capable of aspiring to luxury and novelty (NOUVEAUTE). In fact, he claims in WHISK, LE, that Frenchmen and Frenchwomen exhibit a particular weakness for frivolous styles and witty, amusing games. His countrymen snatch up all new inventions except "those whose utility has been demonstrated and which concern men's happiness or life." Diderot mentions the Frenchwomen's passion for new customs in INSENSIBILITE. In a discussion of English dandies (BEAUX), he implies that an excessive concern with such minutiae as elaborate, exquisite clothing is properly restricted to women. Collot, an administrator in military supplies, describes the dolls that the Parisian tradeswomen periodically send to the courts of Germany and the North to show the current elegant coiffures, fabrics, and female dress.

The vicissitudes of fashion may be caused by women's love of novelty and by their fickleness. In MODE, the contributor remarks that styles change without reason and that the bizarre, just because it is new, is more often preferred to the most beautiful things:

> Let a monstrous animal appear among us, the women take it from the stable and put it on their heads. Every part of their apparel takes its name, and there isn't a well-dressed woman who doesn't wear three or four rhinoceroses; another time they comb all the shops for a bonnet in the style of the rabbit, zephyrs, doves, or the comet.

Most styles are short-lived (GARNITURE DE DIAMANS, DE RUBIS, D'EMERAUDES; NOUVEAUTE; PERLE); an enumeration of fashions of the last 700—800 years in France alone would fill half of the *Encyclopédie* (MODE). However, that of the "comet" lasted nearly an entire spring which is not surprising according to the author of MODE, given the general interest in comets at the time. Apparently Indian cloth patterned with snakes and imaginary monsters also enjoyed prolonged popularity, for Diderot writes in FURIE: "How can one explain or name the oddity of our women who have for a long time bedizened themselves with designs of gothic beasts such as one sees around our old churches where they serve as gutters?" The "anonymous" woman contributor, the marquise de Jaucourt, rightly views fashion as cyclic: "This great wheel of the world that brings back all events, also brings back all fashions [. . .]" (FALBALA). She comments wryly that the scholarly antiquaries would like to trace the origin of ruffles back to the flood; it is honor enough, she says, for this style to have passed from the Persians to the Romans. In her anecdote recounting the origin of flounces, the marquise de Jaucourt testifies to women's inventiveness in matters of fashion. Two gentlemen were crossing the rooms of the Palace of looking for little pieces of finery to please their female friends. "You'll find here everything that exists," said one. The other replied, "You'll even find what doesn't exist. Invent a word and all these tradeswomen will attach a substance to it." "*Falbala*" came to their minds and the flounce was created on the spot.

In any case, however bizarre or ephemeral the new vogue might be, woman's adherence to it is total, even slavish, as D'Alembert notes in ODEUR: "When scents were outlawed in court, women could not tolerate them; now that scents are in fashion, women are infatuated with them; they delight in perfuming themselves and in living with those who wear perfume."

Women intent upon following the dictates of fashion have thwarted theologians' attempts to curb what they considered rising, blatant immorality. Saint Peter and Saint Paul condemned women's attachment to finery in vain, notes Jaucourt (VETEMENT *des Chrétiens*); women adopted sumptuous apparel in preference to the simple white attire which they found too modest. Saint Clement of Alexandria, comparing Egyptian gods in their temples to women bedecked with rich clothing, states: "The exterior of these women [. . .] is magnificent but the interior is contemptible" (TEMPLES DES EGYPTIENS). He relented somewhat, however, and allowed women to wear a more handsome garment than men's on the condition that it neither offend modesty nor smack of indolence or luxury (VETEMENT *des Chrétiens*). The author of panier (Mode) informs us that the hoop skirt's first appearance scandalized the clergy who detected in it "an incentive to debauchery" because women could easily conceal their pregnancy beneath it. Diderot notes that the ecclesiastics made the same objection to women wearing loose gowns (CEINTURE). In both cases, the clergy preached a great deal and women wore what they pleased. Fashion can be legislated only by love and pleasure, the marquise de Jaucourt suggests (FALBALA).

Still another example of the clergy's vain efforts to control women and their dress is found in HENNIN. Thomas Conecte, a Breton Carmelite friar burned as a heretic in 1434, preached against the colossal headdresses of French ladies and evidently temporarily frightened them into submission. After his death, however, "like snails, the ladies appeared with bigger horns," prompting Paradin to declare: "That's what you get for being stubborn with certain stubborn people." This headdress was revived in the seventeenth century under the name fontange. The marquise de Jaucourt describes it as a multi-story edifice of lace, hair, and ribbons: "From a base of iron wire rose the duchess, the solitaire, the cabbage, the musketeer, the croissant, the firmament, the tenth heaven, and the mouse" (FONTANGE). She adds that today it is a simple bow of ribbon. Jaucourt treats the same subject in HENNIN. His enumeration shows that he had benefitted from a reading of the marquise's article. He, however, editorializes:

> The whole thing was distinguished by names so crazy, that one would need a glossary to understand what were the duchess, the solitary, the

cabbage, the musketeer, the croissant, the firmament, the tenth heaven, the mouse, etc. which were all different parts of the scaffolding.

The fontange seems to have tried Jaucourt's patience to its utmost, for he cannot restrain himself: "It was necessary [. . .] to use the skills of an able locksmith to erect the base of this comical edifice and this iron fence on which the hairdressers attached so many different pieces." Nearing the end of his tale, Jaucourt seems to sigh with relief: "At last the ridiculous pyramid suddenly collapsed at the court and in town in the beginning of 1701." He cannot, however, resist a final sally and quotes "the pretty verses" of Madame de Lassay (or rather of the abbé de Chaulieu under her name, Jaucourt says) addressed to Madame la duchesse who had asked for news:

Paris cede á la mode, & change ses parures;
Ce peuple, imitateur, ce singe de la cour,
A commencé depuis un jour,
D'humilier enfin l'orgueil de ses coëffures:
Mainte courte beauté s'en plaint, gronde & tem-
    pête,
Et pour se rallonger consultant les destins,
Apprend d'eux qu'on retrouve en haussant ses
    patins,
La taille que l'on perd en abaissant sa tête.
Voilá le changement extrême
Qui met en mouvement nos femmes de Paris;
Pour la coéffure des maris,
Elle est toujours ici la même.

The pagans and even their comic poets, Jaucourt asseverates, were no more successful than the Church fathers in wresting from the hearts of women "the taste for finery" (VETEMENT des Chrétiens), for Athenian women were mad about it and daily invented and displayed new fashions (PARIS), and Roman women, like Frenchwomen, had elaborate paraphernalia to ready them to be seen in public (TOILETTE des dames romaines). In Aristophanes, Jaucourt says, one can find a description of the women's finery complete with bizarre names capable of trying the most accomplished men of Greek letters (VETEMENT des Chrétiens). During Juvenal's time, the Roman ladies constructed on their heads several levels of ornaments and pyramids of hair such that, Juvenal says, from the front one took them for Andromaches but from behind, they looked like dwarves (HENNIN). Jaucourt points out that these ancestors of "hennins" and "fontanges" further testify to women's eternal desire to appear taller (HENNIN).

Dress is sometimes treated as a reflection or an embodiment of morals. Those women who do not cover up their bosom are considered immodest (LESBOS); whereas those who mask their faces with bands of cloth leaving only their mouths, noses, and eyes visible, like "strolling mummies," are quite reputable (SIPHANTO). Jaucourt traces a history of the decadence of Rome through the ladies' clothing. Luxury which, according to Diderot perverts many a woman (PREVERS, PERVERTIR, PERVERSION, PERVERSITE), is the villain. Luxury transformed the temple veil into a sort of coif; what had been only an ornament in ceremonies and sacrifices was enlisted into the service of vanity (MITRE). With increased luxury, women began to reveal their bosom with impunity (TUNIQUE). Under

the republic, only courtesans wore colored garments in town; ladies dressed to cover themselves (a veil hid their heads) and were accompanied by their women; men and women donned clothing which distinguished the sexes; jewelry was worn only for sacred occasions (HABITS des Romains). Under the emperors, ladies coordinated the colors of their garments with their complexions or with the current styles; women wore transparent clothing (the veil lost its shroud function) and were accompanied by eunuchs; men and women wore each other's clothes as early as Tiberius's reign; jewelry appeared in profusion such that, according to Pliny, the most modest woman dared not go out without her diamonds (HABIT des Romains). Jaucourt concludes:

> Thus the toga, the veil, the hood of rough wool were exchanged for fine linen chemises, transparent robes, very expensive silk clothes, and countless jewels. That is the history of Rome on that score and it is the history of all corrupt peoples, because they are all alike in the origin and the progress of their luxury (HABITS des Romains).

Prudery, Coquetry, and Gallantry

The Encyclopedists distinguish several types of women. Worldly women, according to Diderot (PASSIONNER, PASSIONE), are licentious and dispassionate, while sequestered, pious women, according to Jaucourt (SAGES), are virtuous and impassioned. Jaucourt points out that une femme "régulière," that is, a virtuous woman who observes the decencies, is not a devout woman. In fact, most of the women called régulières are only virtuous pagans: "They have a great deal of modesty and very little piety" (REGLE, REGULIER). A prude is a woman who affects strict morals in her speech and in her demeanor (PRUDE). The writer of PRUDE, presumably Diderot, asserts: "By 'prudish' one usually means 'silly,' 'hypocritical,' 'ugly' or 'bad.' " Jaucourt cites La Bruyére's statement that there is a false prudence which is prudery and concedes that prudery, far from hiding age or ugliness, often presupposes them (PRUDERIE).

Coquetry in a woman, Diderot tells us, is the intent to seem obliging to several men, the art of entangling them and making them hope for something she has not resolved to give them (COQUETTERIE). Desmahis refers to coquetry as "That art of pleasing, that desire to please everyone, that longing to please more than another woman does, that silence of the heart, that derangement of the mind, that never-ending lie" (FEMME). Diderot condemns the life of a coquette as "a tissue of falsehoods, a type of profession more incompatible with goodness of mind and character and true honesty than gallantry" (COQUETTERIE). Coquetry, Diderot concludes, is the most despicable flaw for which a woman can be reproached. Jaucourt agrees entirely with Diderot (COQUETTERIE, GALANTERIE, Jaucourt's article, appears in volume seventeen). The coquette is looking for diversion. She intends to deceive. She keeps several lovers dangling at once. She is motivated by vanity, flightiness and falsehood (COQUETTERIE, GALANTERIE). She is content to be thought lovable and to pass for beautiful. The gallant woman, on the other hand, according to Jaucourt, wants someone to love her and to respond to her desires. Motivated by passion, pleasure, or interest, she is involved with one lover at a time. Desmahis discusses the stages of gallantry in FEMME. He also insists that women of questionable virtue have their own ethics. In his moral biography of Chloé, he offers the following gems from Chloé's code: no matter how much interest or passion the lover of another woman in your society shows you, you cannot take him away from her; although love is not eternal, you should not start up a relationship whose end you can foresee; between a breaking off and a new liaison, there should be a six month interval; you should not leave one lover until you have his successor in sight.

The Ideal Woman

What qualities are most desirable in a woman? The contributors furnish glimpses of the ideal woman in their references to both women and wives. Desmahis, in FEMME (Morale), describes at length the happy woman. She possesses wit to make herself loved rather than feared, virtue to gain esteem rather than to scoff at others, and enough beauty to make her virtue worth something. She is faithful, mindful of propriety, pure of heart, and sound of reason. She leaves coquetry, frivolity, caprices, jealousies, all those trifling matters that make life insignificant, to the foolish women who surround her. "Happy," Desmahis concludes, "is the woman who possesses these advantages; happier still is he who possesses the heart of such a woman!"

The contributors cite several examples which promote the association of beauty and virtue. Jaucourt renders Proverbs XI: 22 thus: "The beautiful, debauched woman is like a gold ring in a sow's snout" (POURCEAU). Mallet changes the wording of the same proverb slightly: "A beautiful but foolish woman is like a ring in a swine's snout." Mallet also writes in CONCESSION: "She is beautiful, it's true, but shouldn't she show her gratitude to heaven by a virtuous use of her beauty?" In OIE, FOIE D', Jaucourt acclaims the Greek courtesans: "They captivated the wisest men by three powerful means, beauty, a cultivated mind and talent." Jaucourt repeats Henri IV's idea of the ideal wife in PAU. She would possess seven major traits: beauty, modesty, complaisance, cleverness, fertility, impressive ancestors, and lots of land. Jaucourt, who writes so admiringly and so frequently of the Lacedaemonians (CLAUDICATION; GYMNOPEDIE; HARMOSYNIENS; JEU; LACEDEMONE; MORPHO; MOURRE; PALESTRE; PARIS; PATRIE; PEINE; RUSSIE; SAMNITES, LES; SPARTE *ou* LACEDEMONE; XENELASIE) says that the Spartans desired and found in their wives courage, fidelity, and beauty (MORPHO). Diderot explains in DOMICIUS that this god was invoked at weddings to insure that the wife would be industrious in her household and complaisant for her husband. He adds that the prayer was usually considered answered when the husband was complaisant for his wife and she had had some instruction. Jaucourt reports that Xenophon, who had, however, profited from a Spartan education (LACEDEMONE, *république de*), wished the young bride to be totally innocent, never having seen or heard anything (PYTHIE). D'Holbach asserts that the wives of Icelandic warriors were worthy of being acquired at very high cost.

They urged the men on to great things and were famous for their chastity and their fidelity (ISLANDE).

The Desire to Please

Virtue (modesty), beauty, and some degree of intelligence and education would seem to be the most desirable traits in a woman. Society demands that women cultivate modesty and beauty to make themselves appealing to the opposite sex—the ultimate beneficent goal being the propagation of mankind. Woman's function would then be to please. That all of her efforts are directed to that end is implied by Diderot in IMAGINATION *des femmes enceintes sur le foetus*: "All women, for the most part, are affected by ideas, desires, [and] objects having to do with the male sex." That this is natural is intimated by the author of FOIBLE (*un penchant quelconque*): "The desire to please [belongs to] women." Jaucourt notes that in women the task for pleasing is well-developed (FARD). He also remarks that the Spartan women were as anxious to please as "ours," but that they deemed success more certain if patriotic zeal were added to their graces (PATRIE). In POUR, AFIN Jaucourt credits Girard with: "Girls of a certain age do everything they can to please, in order to get a husband." The marquise de Jaucourt, describing the current vogue of the furbelow, observes that all the women, beautiful, ugly, coquettes, or prudes have flounces down to their most intimate apparel. Even the most pious women wear them, under the guise of cleanliness. It is easier, she explains, to give up the pleasure of loving than the desire to please (FALBALA). Collot remarks that French tastes and vices as well as French money have left their imprint on Germany; the women there have taken up gallantry and the desire to please. He asserts that when the French arrived, the girls of the lowest class, good-looking in their polished shoes and red wool stockings edged in green (the height of luxury, Collot says), found, thanks to the French, ways to get white shoes, white silk stockings, fans, and pompons (OUVRIERS ETRANGERS).

Douchet and Beauzée (QUANTITE) attribute women's success in correctly speaking a language, in distinguishing the nuances of different sounds, not only to their more delicate, sensitive organs but to their habit of, and inclination for, discerning and following what pleases. They acknowledge that men also wish to please, but the desire is not so intense: "We wish to please, but without too much expense; and nothing costs the ladies, provided that they can please." Diderot speaks of the little things we think we can do to be pleasing (AFFECTATION, AFFETERIE) and, like Douchet and Beauzée, does not exclude men from wishing to please, or at least from wishing not to displease. In ECLECTISME he praises Hypatia for her beauty, virtue, and modesty, calls her "the honor of her sex and the astonishment of ours," and avers: "But we would deserve the most just reproaches from the part of mankind we most fear displeasing, if we were to pass over the name of the famous and too unfortunate Hypatia."

Education

It is Desmahis who, although he insists that women are naturally subordinate and implies that the desire to please is an inherent female trait, recognizes the importance of education in influencing the woman's character development. He proposes that the art of pleasing, the desire to please, to be agreeable to all (coquetry) is in women

> a primitive characteristic, which, born of their naturally subordinate, but unjustly servile rank, expanded and fortified by their upbringing [éducation], can be weakened only by an effort of the mind, and destroyed only by a great warmth of feeling: this characteristic has even been compared to the sacred fire which is never extinguished. (FEMME)

Desmahis summarizes:

> Women have scarcely any but mixed, intermediary or variable characters, either because education alters their nature more than ours, or because the delicacy of their constitution makes their soul a mirror that receives all objects, reflects them sharply, and does not retain a one of them. (FEMME)

Diderot is also aware that education affects character and role development. In INDOCILE, INDOCILITE he blames the tutors for their charges' intractability: "I have difficulty conceiving," he says, "that a girl who can submit to very frivolous, very painful exercises [. . .] could not have turned her patience and her talents to better things, if someone had known how to make them attractive to her."

What is the purpose of education? According to Dumarsais (EDUCATION), education is the care one takes to nourish, rear, and instruct children, and is thus concerned with bodily health, the integrity and instruction of the intellect, and morals or social conduct and qualities. Education is important to children because it enables them to be useful to society thereby finding esteem and well-being, to their families whom they must support and to whom they must bring honor, and to the State which profits from the good education of its citizens. Since no one is born already instructed and formed, all children ought to be educated, and educated with respect to their social condition. Faiguet also speaks of useful citizens and asserts that education should be an apprenticeship in what one should know and practice in social intercourse (ETUDES). However, the contributors direct their discussions primarily to male children. Dumarsais refers once to "a child of either sex" and once to "the young people of both sexes" while he speaks several times of "young men" and of "a young man" who enthusiastically becomes "your young man." Moreover, he proposes as a model of education to those charged with raising "young people" the all-male military school. In his criticism of public education (and his suggestions for changes), D'Alembert writes of "youth," "young men," "our nephews," "school-boys," and "a young man" (COLLEGE). Boucher d'Argis informs us in COLLEGE (Jurisp.), without approving or disapproving, that women and girls are not allowed in any *collége*. Faiguet alludes to youth, children, and pupils. Finally, even in CLASSE we read: "Have your young man [. . . .]" While one could not fairly suspect the sincerity of the Encyclopedists' commitment to the education of girls as well as boys, one could easily divine a paucity of educational opportunities for females.

Of what, then, did, does, and should woman's education consist? Jaucourt testifies most ardently to the vigorous education instituted by Lycurgus. Lycurgus, we are told in LACEDEMONE (*république de*), decided that women, who hither-to seemed to be made like flowers in a beautiful garden—only for ornaments of the earth and for the pleasure of the eyes—could be used for a more noble purpose. Women, depreciated and degraded in nearly every nation, could contribute to Lacedaemon's welfare by inspiring the Spartan men, sharing their laurels and becoming at last part of the legislative power. Lycurgus thus proposed to "raise the daughters of Sparta above the customs of their sex." The girls would perform the same exercises as the men (GYMNOPEDIE, LACEDEMONE *république de*, PALESTRE, SPARTE) not just to ensure their equality in strength, health, courage or generosity (LACEDEMONE *république de*, GYMNOPEDIE) but, as the unknown contributor added to Jaucourt's SPARTA, to spur on the Spartan men:

> Lycurgus [. . .] knew that one sex is happy everywhere that it is certain to find the other sex. What a lure to make the young Spartans like wrestling and exercises were these young girls supposed either to fight with them or watch them fight! What charms such a spectacle had for the eyes of the old men who presided over the exercises and who were supposed to impose chastity on them in the moments when the law dispensed of modesty!

Thus, the pure ideals of equal education and service to society which Jaucourt so admired are somewhat tarnished by the reality of an ulterior motive.

Diderot alludes to the wisdom of Socrates in matters of female education: "You must not let your wife be ignorant of what it is important for her to know, for your happiness and for hers" (SOCRATIQUE, PHILOSOPHIE). As for the Romans, Juvenal's ideas on the limits of woman's intellectual sphere and propriety of her displaying her alleged knowledge are recounted without comment by Jaucourt: "A woman who prides herself on being a wit and capable, at the beginning of a meal, of praising Virgil, judging Homer, and excusing Dido, might as well hike her tunic halfway up her legs, like a man" (TUNIQUE). Jaucourt also remarks that Roman ladies cultivated a pronunciation defect encouraged by Ovid who considered it part of a woman's education in antiquity.

We are given glimpses of female education in foreign countries. Mallet reports Chambers's figures in CHARITE (écoles de). In eighty-eight of these English schools there were 2,181 boys and 1,221 girls; 967 boys and 407 girls were apprenticed. Jaucourt informs us that in sixteenth-century Mexico the education of youth was one of the government's principal goals and that public schools had been established for both boys and girls (MEXIQUE, L'EMPIRE DU). Diderot cursorily describes the education of young African girls in CAPES. More details are given in SANDI-SIMODISINO: for four months the naked girls and their teachers, separated from the rest of humanity, learn lascivious dances and very indecent hymns. Their male counterparts receive similar instruction (SAGGONAS). In DRUSES Diderot tells us that only the women know how to read and write. The men believe themselves destined by their strength, courage, and intelligence for something more useful and more exalted than tracing figures on paper.

An idea of what women's education comprises in eighteenth-century France emerges primarily through negative observations. The author of OISIVETE (Méd.) decries the present education of youth in general and attributes various physical ailments to this education "which, manly and vigorous among the Romans and Greeks, has become languid and effeminate among us." Several Encyclopedists sympathetically note the scarcity as well as the inferiority of women's education. Le Roi laments: "One can only moan upon seeing this lovable sex deprived of the help that would make both its happiness and its glory" (HOMME). It is important to realize that Le Roi first promotes the education of women in the context of influencing the character or maintaining the morality of the nation by pleasing men. Barthès is surprised that there are so many women famous for their erudition and their works, considering that women's education has been so badly neglected in all civilized countries (FEMME). In PYTHAGORISME, *ou* PHILOSOPHIE DE PYTHAGORE, Diderot suggests that, making allowance for the small number of women raised and destined for important things, there are perhaps more women than men who have won fame. Desmahis expresses amazement that souls so uncultivated as women's can produce so many virtues and that more vices do not thrive there (FEMME).

The results of the faulty education of eighteenth-century women are numerous. Curiously enough, one of them, according to Cahusac, consists of a defective pronunciation, an excessive rolling of the uvular "r" mistakenly believed to supplement the woman's charms (GRASSEYER). The author of FOIBLE (Morale) observes: "Women are more susceptible to weaknesses of the mind, because their education is more neglected and they are left with more prejudices." Diderot attributes to an indolent upbringing a woman's habit of screaming at a pinprick (AFFECTATION). The author of VAPEURS (Méd.) cites "the imperfect education of the fair sex" among the causes for the prevalence of this ailment. Jaucourt (LOI CRIMINELLE) and Ménuret de Chambaud (SATYRIASIS) recognize education's sometimes pernicious role in increasing the woman's feeling that her modesty must be preserved at all costs. Ménuret de Chambaud points out that women suffer more violently than men from diseases caused by insatiable sexual desire because the restricted life imposed by their education offers no outlet for their more excited imaginations.

Le Roi (HOMME) having taken stock of women's qualities and beauty and judged women potential queens of the universe, surmises that men's jealousy has conspired to disfigure women's qualities. Men focus women's attention on a small circle of objects as early as childhood; "we make their duplicity necessary." Desmahis, as we have seen above, also comments upon how education has modified women's natural dispositions and he also mentions "the dissimulation which seems to be for them a necessary state" (FEMME). Le Roi maintains that women's upbringing prepares them for slavery, reduces their high-mindedness to blind arrogance, and limits their empire to

that of the bagatelle: "Fallals become magic wands in their hands, transform their adorers like so many worshippers of Circe." The image is unflattering to men as well as to women since Circe turned men into swine. Le Roi hopefully envisions an alternative somewhat along the lines of the Spartan education: women would be taught to value noble, generous qualities from childhood; they would be rewarded for courage and superior talents; they would benefit from the virtues they had inspired. Love, writes Le Roi, would compete with the other passions to make excellence blossom in all fields. The woman would still be educated with the man in mind.

In FEMME (Morale), Desmahis notes that for men who share among themselves the tasks of public life, the state for which they are destined determines their education. They are educated according to their role in life. However, women's education, he says, is all the worse because it is more general and all the more neglected because it is practical. Desmahis eloquently indicts one contemporary female education system: "Women who have renounced the world before experiencing it are charged with giving rules of conduct to girls who are to live in it." For that reason, a girl is often led before the altar where she vows to perform duties about which she knows nothing and where she unites herself forever to a man she has never seen before. The more frequent alternative is a return to her family where she receives a second education which reverses all the ideas of her first education and which, Desmahis continues, having more to do with manners than with morals, continually exchanges diamonds in the rough for rhinestones. The author of URSULINES, on the other hand, praises this religious order for one of its principal goals, the education of girls, as day students and boarders: "The zeal and success with which they discharge this duty daily justifies the usefulness of their establishment."

Casual allusions to women's education occur in several articles. In ETUDES, Faiguet declares that the fact that so many women who lack formal grammar instruction learn nonetheless to speak their language well by "the simple means of conversation and reading," is a testimony to the determination of self-taught women. In TERRES, *Mesure des*, Faiguet allows that women can perform at least one of the same intellectual tasks as men as he describes a method by which anyone, man or woman, with the slightest knowledge of multiplication, could follow and even correct the calculation of an expert. Diderot optimistically appraises the progress of education since the seventeenth century: "There is not a woman who has not had some education, who does not use with discrimination all the expressions appropriate to Painting, Sculpture, Architecture, and the Humanities (ENCYCLOPEDIE). In BIBLIOTHEQUE we learn that one of the richest libraries in France, that of Tonance Ferréol, is divided into three classes: pious books for the devout sex, books of learning for the men, and books common to both sexes. In BROCHURE, Diderot condemns these little works for ruining taste and for using time and money better devoted to more solid, instructive books. He admits, however, that this "frivolity of the century" is not detrimental to everyone, thanks to the women consumers, who pass them around and keep the producers in business. In IMAGINATION *des femmes enceintes*, Diderot warns that philosophical works intended for the instruction of the common herd and especially for the ladies must be treated differently from a treatise. In PARIS, Jaucourt lists what the Athenian women read and what their "little libraries" contained. Jaucourt explains that Montesquieu divided *De l'Esprit des lois* into so many short chapters because the majority of men ("and the women doubtlessly are included") balk at prolonged concentration on one object (LECTURE, [Litt. mod.]). In the same article, Jaucourt derides "those women" who read everything that appears but develop no original judgment.

While the author of POURPOINT slyly remarks "These lines from Molière are not unknown," and proceeds to quote from *Les Femmes savantes* on the appropriate limits of a woman's education (II, vii, 577-580), Jaucourt proclaims in SEXE, LE the importance of improving women's minds. Desmahis suggests that males and females should receive different educations (FEMME). Unfortunately, no program designed for educating women, no female equivalent of ECOLE MILITAIRE, may be found in the *Encyclopédie*. The nearest we come to a program is Jaucourt's delineations of appropriate feminine occupations, and then we know that only a certain class of women is intended, those women who had the leisure for music, dancing, and painting (SEXE, LE). In ZONES TEMPEREES Jaucourt prays that hunting may remain foreign to the fair sex: jumping hedges and reining in a high-spirited steed do not become beauty—it is indecent. He would protect beautiful ladies from the world's harsh realities, a lover's tears being the most unhappy sight. He would have their delicate bodies gracefully and simply clothed. He would again have them please men, captivate men's souls, with the ravishing, harmonious sounds from their seductive lips, with music (the lute and the lyre), with dance (the graces would develop beneath their steps), with painting (green foliage on a snowy white canvas), and with flower-gathering (to multiply the year's perfumes). In the last volume of the opus reputed to contain the advanced ideas of the Age of Enlightenment, women still seem to be ornamental objects.

Concluding Remarks

Once again, we find in the *Encyclopédie* a curious mixture of traditional and enlightened thought which, up to a point, mirrors discussion outside the *Encyclopédie*. Physiology influences psychology; there is certainly a female personality. On the other hand, whether all of the traits are inherent or acquired is debatable. The enlightened view proposes that education (unquestionably male-oriented) influences character development, that woman's weakness and inferiority may be socially induced. Paradoxically, woman, creature of passion in the Age of Reason, seems never to be stronger, as Jaucourt remarks, than when she uses her weakness against man; she shows herself fit for survival. In any case, woman is clearly different, "other." If there is awe or approval on the Encyclopedists' part, there is also condescension. Any major discussion of women is left to the minor contributors. The Encyclopedists who take note of the woeful state of female education are content to bewail this deplorable deficiency. (Outside the *Encyclopédie*, the cries are louder, the debates longer,

the programs concrete.) The Encyclopedists offer no revolutionary solutions, no radical programs; they, indeed, offer no solutions, no programs. One would not surmise from reading the *Encyclopédie* that female education was much of an issue in the eighteenth century. Rousselot writes: "Assuredly it was not religious scruples which were holding back the authors of the *Encyclopédie*, and if they said nothing about the instruction of girls, it is for other reasons." Rousselot then explains that, at a certain point in the eighteenth century, public opinion was as hostile to the education of women as it had been in Molière's time. He concludes, however, that by the end of the eighteenth century public opinion advocated the education of women. In 1766, for example, the Académie des Inscriptions et Belles-Lettres had proposed the question: "What education did the Athenians give to their children during the flourishing centuries of the Republic?"; however, in 1776, the Académie de Besançon queried: "How can the education of women contribute to making men better?" In at least this one question proposed by a provincial academy, the problem of women's education is still man-centered. The woman is not considered as an individual being in her own right. It is Condorcet who lists as his fourth and final reason why women should be educated: "Because that is just, because the two sexes have an equal right to instruction." Perhaps, though, it is Laclos who sees most clearly of all: women's education cannot be perfected because of their position in society.

FURTHER READING

Cassirer, Ernst. "The Preparation: Carlyle." In his *The Myth of the State*, pp. 232-79. Garden City, N.Y.: Doubleday, 1955.
    Discusses Thomas Carlyle's views on the Encyclopedists.

Collison, Robert. "Diderot and the Encyclopedistes." In his *Encyclopedias: Their History throughout the Ages*, pp. 114-37. London: Hafner Publishing Co., 1966.
    Comments on the genesis and development of the *Encyclopédie*, with particular emphasis on the intellectual background and publishing history.

Foucault, Michel. *The Order of Things*, translated by Alan Sheridan. London: Tavistock Publications, 1970, 387 p.
    Includes a seminal discussion of the encyclopedic discourse, with particular emphasis on the role of economic theorists in the development of eighteenth-century encyclopedism and multidisciplinary thought. This work was originally published in French in 1966 under the title *Les Mots et les choses*.

Kafker, Frank. *The Encyclopedists as Individuals: A Biographical Dictionary of the Authors of the "Encyclopédie"*. Oxford: The Voltaire Foundation, 1988, 430 p.
    Detailed bio-bibliographical articles, in alphabetical order, on the contributors to the *Encyclopédie*; includes an index of all of the contributors.

Lough, John. *The Contributors to the "Encyclopédie"*. London: Grant and Cutler, 1973, 120 p.

Provides bio-bibliographical information on the contributors; discusses their views and areas of expertise.

Marias, Julian. "The Enlightenment." In his *History of Philosophy*, translated by Stanley Appelbaum and Clarence C. Strowbridge, pp. 261-71. New York: Dover Publications, 1967.
Examines the Encyclopedists in the philosophical context of the Enlightenment.

Payne, Harry C. "Equality." In his *The Philosophes and the People*, pp. 148-71. New Haven: Yale University Press, 1976.
Argues that the Encyclopedists, although nominally in favor of equality for all, clearly rejected the practical consequences of egalitarianism. In Payne's opinion, the Encyclopedists failed to make the leap from civil to political equality.

Schargo, Nelly Noemie. *History in the "Encyclopédie"*. New York: Columbia University Press, 1947, 251 p.
Extensive and detailed analysis of the Encyclopedists' conception of history. According to Schargo, the Encyclopedists viewed history as a precise science with the potential of enhancing critical theories.

Claude-Adrien Helvétius

1715-1771

French philosopher.

INTRODUCTION

One of the philosophes, a group of intellectuals concerned with expressing the aspirations and opinions of the bourgeois class in eighteenth-century France, Helvétius is recognized as an important figure in the development of educational theory and utilitarian thought. Although he was a member of the social circle whose members produced the *Encyclopédie*, Helvétius did not contribute to the volume; instead, he produced *De l'esprit* (1758, *On the Mind*) which, upon publication, was condemned as heretical and subversive, banned by the government, and publicly burned. His assertion that the mind comprises only what it has been exposed to, making inequality between individuals explicable by the quality of their schooling alone, made him a hero to advocates of public education, but an enemy of the social establishment from which he emerged.

Biographical Information

Helvétius was born into a wealthy medical family of German and Dutch descent. His grandfather was entitled by Louis XIV and his father served as royal physician to Queen Marie Leczinska, wife of Louis XV. After completing his study at the College Louis-le-Grand at age 23, Helvétius obtained a lucrative *fermier-général* (tax collector) position through the patronage of the queen. He resigned the post in 1750 and purchased another—the office of *maître d'hôtel* to the queen. The next year Helvétius married and retired to his country estate in the Perche district where he resided for nine months of the year. During this period he became patron to several writers and philosophers and began his own writing career with the unfinished poem *Le bonheur* (*Happiness*, published posthumously). The balance of his time was spent in Paris where he established his own salon and moved in the intellectual circle of the Encyclopédists, including Denis Diderot, Paul Henri Dietrich d'Holbach, Jean-Baptiste Rousseau, Anne-Robert-Jacques Turgot, Bernard Le Bovier de Fontenelle, François-Marie Arouet Voltaire, Comte de Buffon, and Charles-Louis Montesquieu. Following the publication of *On the Mind*, Helvétius was condemned by Parliament, the Sorbonne, the Pope, and both the Jesuits and Jansenists, and forced to resign his *maître* position and return to his estate where, despite three public retractions, he remained an intellectual and social pariah until his death in 1771.

Major Works

Helvétius's primary literary contributions were his two philosophical treatises, *On the Mind* and the posthumous-

HELVÉTIUS.

ly published *De l'homme* (1772, *On Man*). Following the thought of English philosopher John Locke, Helvétius developed in *On the Mind* a doctrine of sensationalism, believing the mind to be a *tabula rasa* and recognizing its primary function as the reception of sensations created by the external world. This faculty, which he called the *sensibilité physique*, gives rise to all knowledge, ideas, judgement, and memory. He argued that there also exist passions which are to be manipulated—by rewarding virtuous action with sexual gratification, for example—in order to encourage socially beneficial acts, and that the perfectibility of man is, while possible, hindered by such institutions as Christianity and the *ancien régime*. Due to the scandal caused by *On the Mind* and his widespread censure, Helvétius resolved not to publish again in his lifetime. *On Man* appeared in the year following his death, and expanded upon the ideas first presented in *On the Mind*, attempting to clarify some of its more contentious points.

Critical Reception

Helvétius's philosophical writings have often been considered narrow and superficial. However, he has exerted a strong influence on both his contemporary Encyclopédists, especially d'Holbach and Pierre Cabanis, and upon the British Utilitarian movement. Recognizing his importance as well as his limitations, Jeremy Bentham (who founded Utilitarianism) wrote of Helvétius: "What Bacon was to the physical world, Helvétius was to the moral. The moral world therefore had its Bacon, but its Newton is still to come." Both Diderot and James Mill applied Helvétius's theories to the education of their own children, the former to his daughter and the latter to his son, John Stuart Mill. In addition, Helvétius's sensationalist doctrine made him an early hero of Karl Marx, and critics consistently cite his work as an influential forerunner to Marx's theories of materialism. While faulting his one-sided environmentalism, many modern critics have recognized Helvétius's contribution to the theory of education, appreciating his premise of individual equality and his optimistic program for improving humanity. Feminist critics have responded favorably to Helvétius's refusal to make specific *a priori* assumptions about women, but have faulted him for his advocation of women's education only as a means to benefit men, for his characterization of human motivation (specifically that of men) as reducible to sexual desire, and his call for the subjugation of women as a means to that end.

PRINCIPAL WORKS

De l'esprit [*On the Mind*]   (philosophy)   1758
De l'homme [*On Man*]   (philosophy)   1772

CRITICISM

Claude-Adrien Helvétius   (essay date 1758)

SOURCE: A preface to his *De l'esprit: or, Essays on the Mind, and its Several Faculties,* n. p., 1759, pp. iii-iv.

[*In the following preface to the 1758 French edition of* De l'esprit, *Helvétius defends the controversial arguments of his work, claiming that "I have sought only for the truth, not merely for the honor of delivering it, but because truth is useful to man."*]

The subject I propose to examine in this work is new and interesting. People have hitherto considered the mind only under some of its views: for great writers have no more than cast a rapid glance over it; and this has emboldened me to treat of the subject.

The knowledge of the mind, when we consider it in its utmost extent, is so closely connected with the knowledge of the heart, and of the passions of men, that it was impossible to write on this subject, without treating, on that part of morality at least, which is common to men of all nations, and which in all governments can have no other object in view than the public advantage.

The principles I establish on this subject are, I think, conformable to the general interest, and to experience. It is by facts that I have ascended to causes. I imagined that morality ought to be treated like all the other sciences, and founded on experiment, as well as natural philosophy. I have adhered to this idea, from the persuasion that all morality, where its principles are of use to the public, is necessarily conformable to the morals of religion, which are only the perfection of human morals. For the rest, if I am deceived, and if, contrary to my expectation, some of my principles are not conformable to the general interest, this proceeds from an error of my judgment, and not of my heart; and I declare, beforehand, that I disown them.

I desire but one favour of my reader, that is, to hear, before he condemns me; to follow the chain that unites all my ideas together; to be my judge, and not of my party. This request is not the effect of a foolish confidence, for I have too often found that to be bad at night, which I have thought to be good in the morning, to have an high opinion of my own abilities.

Perhaps I have treated of a subject above my strength: but what man knows himself so well, as not to presume too much? I cannot, however, reproach myself with not having used my utmost endeavours to merit the approbation of the public; and if I do not obtain it, I shall be more afflicted than surprised. In this case, to desire is not sufficient to obtain.

In every thing I have said, I have sought only for the truth, not merely for the honour of delivering it, but because truth is useful to man. If I have deviated from it, I shall find, even in my errors themselves, motives of consolation. "If men," as M. de Fontenelle observes, "cannot, on any subject whatsoever, arrive at what is rational, till after having, in that very subject, exhausted all imaginable folly," my errors will then be of use to my fellow-citizens: I shall have pointed out the rock by my shipwreck. "How many absurdities," adds M. de Fontenelle, should we not now utter, "if the ancients had not already said them before us, and had in a manner delivered us from them?"

I repeat then, that I shall warrant in my work nothing but the purity and rectitude of my intentions. In the meantime, however assured we may be of our intentions, the voice of envy is so favourably heard, and its frequent declamations are so adapted to seduce the minds that are equally honest and enlightened, that we cannot write in a manner without trembling. The discouragement give to men of genius from imputations frequently filled with calumny, seem already to presage the return of the ages of ignorance. It is, in every instance, only in mediocrity of talents that people find an asylum against the pursuits of the envious. Mediocrity is now become a protection, and I have probably obtained that protection in spite of myself.

Besides, I believe that it will be difficult for envy to impute to me the desire of wounding my fellow-citizens. This kind of work, in which I consider no man in particular, but men and nations in general, ought to shelter me from all suspicion of malignity. I shall even add, that in reading these discourses, it will be perceived that I love men, and desire their happiness, without hating or despising any of them in particular.

Some of my ideas will perhaps appear too bold. If the reader thinks them false, I desire him to recollect, while he condemns them, that it is only by the boldest attempts that the greatest truths can sometimes be discovered; and that the fear of advancing an error, ought not to deter us from proceeding in the search of truth. In vain would base and cowardly men prescribe it, and sometimes give it the name of odious and licentious; in vain do they repeat, that truth is often dangerous. Supposing that this is sometimes the case, to what still greater danger would that nation be exposed, which should consent to continue in ignoranece? Every nation without knowledge, when it has ceased to be fierce and savage, is degraded, and will sooner or later be subdued. It was less the valour, than the military knowledge of the Romans, that triumphed over the Gauls.

If the knowledge of such a truth, might, at such an instant, be attended with some inconveniencies; that instant being past, that very truth will again become useful to all ages and nations.

Such is the fate of human things: there is none that may not at certain moments become dangerous; but it is only on this condition that we enjoy them. Wo to him that would from this motive deprive mankind of them.

At the very moment when they forbid the knowledge of certain truths, it will no longer be permitted to mention any. A thousand men in power, who have often ill intentions, under the pretence that it is sometimes wise to to conceal the truth, would banish it entirely from the universe. Thus the enlightened part of the public, who alone know all its value, incessantly desire it: they are not afraid to expose themselves to uncertain evils to enjoy the real advantages it procures. Among the qualities of mankind, that which they esteem the most is, that elevation of soul which refuses to submit to the meanness of a lye. They know how useful it is to think and speak every thing; and that errors cease to be dangerous, when it is permitted to to contradict them. They are soon known to be errors; they sink of themselves into the abyss of forgetfulness, and truth alone swims over the vast extent of ages.

The Critical Review   (essay date 1758)

SOURCE: "Hume's Critique of Helvétius's *De l'esprit*," in *Studies on Voltaire and the Eighteenth Century, Vol. 215,* The Voltaire Foundation, 1982, pp. 223-29.

[*The following excerpt, believed to be written by English philosopher David Hume, is a reprint of an anonymously published review of* De l'Esprit *which appeared in* The Critical Review *6 (1758). In it, the* Review's *critic presents an abstract of the work, judging it "dangerous to morals and civil government."*]

It has been the constant assertion of authors ancient and modern, that science and arts must have their rise, progress, and full growth, in liberty. How just the remark is, any one who considers the instances of modern Rome, Florence, and more particularly of France, will be able to judge. In the two former, the arts were carried to the high-

est pitch, under the slavish power of priesthood and usurpation of a private family; in the latter, both science and the arts have been cultivated with the utmost care and success, under a government which pretends not to a shadow of liberty. The most virulent national prejudice cannot deny, that if Britain produces better mathematicians and philosophers (a fact which will not be universally granted) and Italy finer painters, sculptors, and musicians, yet that France is the only country on earth which at the same time affords men equally eminent in the sciences and arts. The French mathematicians, metaphysicians, moralists, and politicians, are no less agreeable for the elegance, the purity of their diction than for the clearness, the perspicuity of their judgement, and reach of thought. It would be no uncurious disquisition to trace this fact, so apparently contradictory to the observation of all ages, to its source; as for ourselves we must drop it, to give the reader an account of an author who will by no means lessen the weight of our assertion.

L'Esprit, the much-admired work before us, is, if we are rightly informed, the production of M. Helvétius, son to the celebrated physician of that name. Some little time since, he was appointed a farmer-general of the revenues in France, a lucrative employment which he surrendered as unsuitable to his turn of mind and liberal sentiments. From the freedom and fate of the *L'Esprit,* we are inclined to believe it is possible that M. Helvétius, like placement on this side the channel, chose the genteel manner of *resigning* a post he could no longer maintain without the hazard of being *turned out.* Certain it is, that he breathes a spirit of liberty, independence, and freedom, better calculated for the meridian of a British than a French constitution. This production, however, he found means to usher into the public under the sanction of an *Imprimatur;* a favour which we are told was soon retracted, and a second edition of this book published, mangled and castrated with other marks of violence, despotism, and arbitrary sway. It must be acknowledged that he has pursued his thoughts, and extended his freedom to a length dangerous to morals and civil government. Nor do we so much wonder at the fate of his performance, as that its author has escaped banishment or the Bastile; a species of criticism we have seen passed upon works of less merit and offence. He is indeed one of those men who, according to Tacitus, *Nec totam servitutem nec totam libertatem pati possunt;* yet with great reading, fine talents, knowledge of mankind, and a happy turn for observation, there seems to be an affectation of singularity, without all the powers to constitute it, which greatly diminishes the satisfaction of the reader, throws the beauties of the author into shade, and presents a sort of extravagance of opinion no way natural to him. It would swell an article to a great length were we as particular as the work, its general reputation, and its blemishes, deserve. A future number may present the reader with a more minute *Critique* upon it, while we content ourselves now with observing that M. Helvétius has made a little too free with several English writers, many of them perhaps never much known in France, and almost forgot here. But that the reader may not be entirely left in the dark, we will present him with an abstract of the contents of the *L'Esprit,* a term, which with all the pains he has taken, our author has left as equivocal and obscure as he found it. *Où l'on regarde l'esprit* (says he) *comme l'effet de la faculté de penser,* in which sense he considers it as an assemblage of ideas under various combinations, *où l'on le considère comme la faculté même de penser;* both which it cannot possibly be. His fourth discourse, which we think ought to have been placed first, since upon the precise meaning of this term, a great part of our author's ingenious reasoning depends, is wholly taken up with an examination of the various species of this principle or faculty of the mind. Here he treats *de l'Esprit fin, de l'Esprit fort; de l'Esprit de lumière, de l'Esprit étendu, de l'Esprit pénétrant; du bel Esprit; de l'Esprit du siècle; de l'Esprit juste* (which, he says, *seroit l'Esprit universel*) with many other distinctions and acceptations of this term.

The first discourse begins with an enquiry into the origin of our ideas, which he reduces to physical sensibility and memory. Here he treats largely of the errors arising from the passions, from ignorance, and the abuse and indefinite sense of words; drawing this inference from the whole, that all misapprehension and false judgement have their foundation in accidental causes which suppose not a power of *judging* distinct from that of *perceiving* to exist in the *Esprit,* or intellect. In the second discourse, which bears this general title, *de l'Esprit par rapport à la société,* our author endeavours to prove, that *Interest* alone directs man's judgement of actions and ideas, whether we regard the individuals, communities, nations, different ages, climates and countries, or the world in general; a turn of sentiment not too much to the credit of his heart, whatever honour his judicious reasoning and accurate observation may reflect on his understanding. We must observe, that M. Helvétius has here fallen into the error of many former philosophers, mistaking the consequent for the antecedent. Were the selfish principle of human nature so much superior to the social as is asserted, we must undoubtedly maintain a contemptible opinion of human nature. But this we think, with the elegant Shaftesbury, is not the case; nay quite otherwise, for we will venture to affirm, that all the other passions derive their chief influence, force and power, from the social. M. Helvétius observes, that every act of benevolence, of friendship and public spirit, is attended with a secret pleasure; from whence he concludes, that interest and self is the first spring and principle of those greatest of human virtues. But this is a fallacy arising from inaccurate distinctions. The pleasure is the effect and not the cause of the passion or sentiment. A generous, a friendly, and a public spirit feels a pleasure in relieving merit, serving a friend or a nation; because, from a spontaneous and irresistable motion, he loves them, but his love does not arise from or for the sake of the pleasure. . . .

His third Essay is a discussion of the long-agitated question, 'Whether what he terms *Esprit* is a gift of nature, or an effect of education?' Though he determines in favour of the latter, yet it is doubtful with us, whether the instance himself affords does not contradict his fine reasoning, as nature and art seem equally combined to form M. Helvétius a writer of the first rank. Upon the whole, however, we are of the opinion, that he is rather an author of great reading than of deep judgement, of lively sensations, and quick apprehension, than of reflection, less a philosopher than a fine, elegant and polite writer.

Claude-Adrien Helvétius   (essay date 1772)

SOURCE: A preface to his *A Treatise on Man; His Intellectual Faculties and His Education,* translated by W. Hooper, 1810. Reprint by Burt Franklin, 1969, pp. iii–ix.

[*In the following essay, the preface to the 1772 French edition of* De l'homme, *Helvétius discusses the work's content and defends his philosophical arguments.*]

My inducement to engage in the following work [*De l'homme*], was merely the love of mankind and of truth; from a persuasion, that to become virtuous and happy, we want only to know ourselves, and entertain just ideas of morals.

My design can scarcely be mistaken. Had I published this book in my life-time, I should, in all probability, have exposed myself to persecution, without the prospect of any personal advantage.

That I have continued to maintain the same sentiments which I advanced in my Treatise on the Understanding, is the consequence of their appearing to me the only rational principles on the subject, and of their being generally adopted, since that time, by men of the greatest learning and abilities.

Those principles are farther extended, and more accurately examined, in the present work than in the former; my reflection having suggested a number of new ideas, while I was employed in the composition. Such thoughts as are less intimately connected with the subject, are thrown into notes, at the end of each section; those only being retained in the text, which were of an explanatory nature, or served to remove objections, which could not be directly answered, without greatly encreasing the limits, and retarding the progress of the work.

The second is the most encumbered with notes, because the principles which it contains, being more particularly controvertible, require the support of a greater accumulation of proof.

It is not improper on this occasion to observe, that there are several reasons which may render a work contemptible in the opinion of the public; such as, that the author has not taken sufficient pains to merit approbation; that he is defective in abilities, or chargeable with disingenuousness. I can safely affirm, that I have nothing with which to reproach myself on the latter of those heads. It is only in prohibited publications that truth is now to be found; for in others, falsehood is discernible. The greater number of authors are in their writings, what men of the world are in their conversation: solicitous only to please, they are wholly indifferent, provided they attain their purpose, whether it be by means of falsehood or truth.

A writer who is desirous of the favour of the great, and the transitory applause of the present hour, must adopt implicitly the current principles of the time, without ever attempting to examine or question their authority; and from this source arises the want of originality, so general among literary productions. Books of intrinsic merit, and which discover real genius, are the phenomena but of very few periods in the space of many ages; and their appearance, like that of the sun in the forest, serves only to render the intervening darkness more conspicuous. They constitute an epoch in the history of the human understanding, and it is from the principles they contain, that future improvements in science derive their origin.

It would ill become me to say any thing in praise of this work; I shall, therefore, only observe, in respect to its principles, that I have advanced no sentiment which was not suggested by my own reflection, nor affirmed any proposition which I do not believe to be true.

In exposing some prejudices, I may be thought perhaps, to have conducted myself with too little reserve. I have treated them with the same ingenuous freedom, which a young man, is apt to use towards an old woman, whom he is under no inducement either to flatter or depreciate. Through the whole inquiry, truth has been my principal object; and this consideration, it is to be hoped, will stamp some value on the work. A sincere love of truth is the disposition most favourable for discovering her.

I have all along endeavoured to express my ideas with perspicuity; and have never sacrificed any sentiment to popular prepossession. If, therefore, the book be void of merit, it ought to be imputed to the fault of my judgment, and not to a depravity of heart. Few, I believe, can with justice say so much in their own favour.

To some readers this work will appear to be written with great boldness. There are periods in every country when the word *prudent* bears the same signification with *vile;* and when those productions only are esteemed for their sentiments, which are written in a style of servility.

It was once my intention to have published this book under a fictitious name, as the only means of reconciling with my own safety the desire I entertained of rendering service to my country. But, during the time I have been employed in the work, a change has happened in the circumstances and government of my fellow-citizens. The disorder, which I hoped in some measure to remedy, is become incurable: the prospect of public utility is vanished, and I defer the publication of the work, till its author be no more.

My country has at length submitted to the yoke of despotism. She will never again produce any writer of extraordinary eminence. It is the characteristic of despotic power to extinguish both genius and virtue.

The people of this country will never more signalize themselves under the appellation of French: the nation is now so much debased as to become the contempt of Europe. No fortunate crisis can henceforth ever restore her liberty. She will expire of a consumption. Conquest alone can afford a remedy proportioned to the virulence of her disease; and the efficacy even of this, chance and circumstances must determine.

In all nations there are certain periods when the citizens, undetermined what measures they ought to take, and remaining in a state of suspense between a good and bad government, are extremely desirous of instruction, and disposed to receive it. At such a time, if a work of great merit makes its appearance, the happiest effects may be produced: but the moment once past, the people, insensible to glory, are, by the form of their government, irresistibly inclined towards ignorance and baseness. Their minds are then like parched earth: the water of truth may rain upon them, but without producing fertility. Such is the state of France.

Henceforth, among the French, the estimation of learning will daily decline, with its utility; as it can only serve to shew in a stronger light the misery of despotism, without supplying the means of evading it.

Happiness, like the sciences, is said to advance progressively over the world. Its course is now directed towards the North. There great princes cherish the seeds of genius, and genius is ever accompanied with a high degree of public felicity.

Nothing can be more opposite than the state of the south and north parts of Europe at present. Clouds of thicker darkness are perpetually over-spreading the South, produced by the mists of superstition and of Asiatic despotism. The horizon of the North becomes every day more bright and effulgent. A Catherine II and a Frederick, render themselves dear to humanity. Convinced in their own minds of the value of truth, they encourage the cultivation of it in others, and afford their patronage to every effort by which it may be farther investigated. It is to such sovereigns that I dedicate this work: it is by the auspicious influence of those that the world can be enlightened.

The former brightness of the South becomes more dim, while the dawn of the North shines forth with increasing radiance. It is the North that now emits the rays which penetrate even to Austria. Every thing there hastens towards an extraordinary change. The assiduous attention bestowed by the emperor to alleviate the weight of the imposts, and improve the discipline of his army, shews plainly that he entertains a desire of becoming the darling of his subjects; that he wishes to render them happy at home, and respectable to foreign nations. The esteem for the king of Prussia, professed from his earliest years, afford a presage of his future virtues! Esteem always indicates a similarity of disposition to the object of it.

Denis Diderot   (essay date 1774)

SOURCE: "Men Aren't Quite That Reasonable," in *The Portable Age of Reason Reader,* edited by Crane Brinton, The Viking Press, 1956, pp. 263-65.

[*One of the seminal figures of eighteenth-century thought, Diderot contributed to virtually every field of inquiry. As editor of the* Encyclopédie *he achieved a synthesis of contemporary philosophical ideas and technical knowledge. In the following excerpt from Diderot's response to De l'homme, "Réfutation d'Helvétius," originally published in 1774, he argues against Helvétius's assertion that the human mind exists* tabula rasa *before coming into contact with outside influences.*]

[*Text of Helvétius*]: *On Man: "I consider intelligence, genius, and virtue as the product of teaching."*

[*Comment of Diderot*]: And of nothing but teaching?

"This idea seems to me to hold true always."

It is a false idea and can therefore never be proved true.

"My critics have granted me that education has on genius, on the character of individuals and societies, more influence than has been usually believed."

And that's all they can grant you.

"If the educational system makes us almost entirely what we are, why blame the teacher for the ignorance and stupidity of his pupils?"

I know of no philosophy of education so consoling for parents and so encouraging for teachers. This is its advantage.

But I know of none more harmful for children thus considered capable of everything; I know of none more calculated to produce a society of mediocrities, and to damage the genius who can do but one thing—though that superbly; I know of none more dangerous in its encouragement of educational administrators who, after having tried in vain to mould a class of students to a discipline for which they have no natural bent, proceed to turn them out into a world where they are no longer good for anything.

Is man born good or bad?

If you call a man good who does good, a man bad who does evil, then surely man is born neither good nor bad. I should say the same thing were the question one of being born bright or stupid.

But is man born with a natural, an organic, *bent* towards saying stupid things—and doing them—towards harming himself and his fellows, towards listening to or disregarding parental advice, towards diligence or laziness, fairmindedness or indignation, respect for law, or contempt for it? Only a person who has never actually seen two children in his life, who has never heard them cry in their cradles, can have doubts as to how to answer these questions. Man is born nothing, but every man is born with aptitudes towards a certain kind of living.

M. Helvétius, I take it you're a hunter?

Yes.

Do you see that puppy?

The one with bow legs, long, low-swung body, narrow muzzle, red-spotted paws and hide?

Yes. What is it?

He's a basset. This breed has good scent, ardour; courage; he will burrow into a fox's den at the risk of coming out with torn ears and sides.

And this other one?

He's a hound, a tireless animal. His tough hide lets him penetrate into the thorniest bushes. . . .

And this other one?

A setter. I can't tell you much about him from a look. Will he be gentle or not? Will he have a good nose or not? It's a question of breeding.

And this fourth puppy?

He looks as though he'd grow up into a fine bird dog.

These then are all dogs?

Yes.

Now, tell me. I have a fine kennel man. Can't I ask him to rear the basset so that he will be a hound, the hound so that he will be a racing greyhound, the greyhound a terrier, the terrier a poodle?

Don't try it!

Why not? They have just been born, they are nothing; fit for everything, education can make them whatever I want them to be.

You're making fun of me.

M. Helvétius, you are quite right. But what if among human beings there should be the same variety of individuals as among dogs, if each of us had his own gait, his own game?

John Morley　(essay 1886)

SOURCE: "Helvétius," in his *Diderot and the Encyclopaedists, Vol. II,* Macmillan and Co., 1886, pp. 123-54.

[*Morley was an English politician and critic who wrote extensively on eighteenth- and nineteenth-century culture, including the studies* Voltaire, Rousseau, *and* Diderot and the Encyclopædists. *In the following essay from the lattermost work,* Morley *criticizes* De l'esprit, *citing two fatal defects: that it fails to account for the historical aspect of humanity and that it reduces human motivation to "purely egoistic impulses."*]

The great attack on the Encyclopædia was made . . . in 1758, after the publication of the seventh volume. The same prosecution levelled an angrier blow at Helvétius's famous treatise, **L'Esprit.** It is not too much to say, that of all the proscribed books of the century, that excited the keenest resentment. This arose partly because it came earliest in the literature of attack. It was an audacious surprise. The censor who had allowed it to pass the ordeal of official approval was cashiered, and the author was dismissed from an honorary post in the Queen's household. The indictment described the book as "the code of the most hateful and infamous passions," as a collection into one cover of everything that impiety could imagine, calculated to engender hatred against Christianity and Catholicism. The court condemned the book to be burnt, and, as if to show that the motive was not mere discontent with Helvétius's paradoxes, the same fire consumed Voltaire's fine poem on Natural Religion. Less prejudiced authorities thought nearly as ill of the book, as the lawyers of the parliament and the doctors of the Sorbonne had thought. Rousseau pronounced it detestable, wrote notes in refutation of its principles, and was inspired by hatred of its doctrine to compose some of the most fervid pages in the Savoyard Vicar's glowing Profession of Faith. Even Diderot, though his friendly feeling for the writer and his general leaning to speculative hardihood warped his judgment so far as to make him rank **L'Esprit** along with Montesquieu's *Spirit of Laws,* and Buffon's *Natural History,* among the great books of the century, still perceived and showed that the whole fabric rested on a foundation of paradox, and that, though there might be many truths of detail in the book, very many of its general principles are false. Turgot described it as a book of philosophy without logic, literature without taste, and morality without goodness.

In the same weighty piece of criticism [reprinted in his *Œuvres,* vol. ii], which contains in two or three pages so much permanently valuable truth, Turgot proceeds:

> When people wish to attack intolerance and injustice, it is essential in the first place to rest upon just ideas, for inquisitors have an interest in being intolerant, and viziers and subviziers have an interest in maintaining all the abuses of the government. As they are the strongest, you only give them a good excuse by sounding the tocsin against them right and left. I hate despotism as much as most people; but it is not by declamations that despotism ought to be attacked. And even in despotism there are degrees; there is a multitude of abuses in despotism, in which the princes themselves have no interest; there are others which they only allow themselves to practise, because public opinion is not yet fixed as to their injustice, and their mischievous consequences. People deserve far better from a nation for attacking these abuses with clearness, with courage, and above all by interesting the sentiment of humanity, than for any amount of eloquent reproach. Where there is no insult, there is seldom any offence. . . . There is no form of government without certain drawbacks, which the governments themselves would fain have it in their power to remedy, or without abuses which they nearly all intend to repress at least at some future day. We may therefore serve them all by treating questions of the public good in a calm and solid style; not coldly, still less with extravagance, but with that interesting warmth which springs from a profound feeling for justice and love of order.

Of course it is a question whether, even in 1758, a generation before the convulsion, it was possible for the French monarchy spontaneously to work out the long list of indispensable improvements; still, at that date, Turgot might be excused for thinking that the progress which he desired might be attained without the violence to which Helvétius's diatribes so unmistakably pointed. His words, in any case, are worth quoting for their own grave and universal sense, and because they place us exactly at the point of view for regarding *L'Esprit* rightly. He seizes on its political aspect, its assault on government, and the social ordering of the time, as containing the book's real drift. In this, as in the rest of the destructive literature of the first sixty years of the century, the church was no doubt that part of the social foundations against which the assault was most direct and most vindictive, and it was the church, in the case of Helvétius's book, that first took alarm. Indeed, we may say that, from the very nature of things, in whatever direction the revolutionary host moved, they were sure to find themselves confronted by the church. It lay across the track of light at every point. Voltaire pierced

its dogma. Rousseau shamed its irreligious temper. Diderot brought into relief the vicious absoluteness of its philosophy. Then came Helvétius and Holbach, not merely with criticism, but with substitutes. Holbach brought a new dogma of the universe, matter and motion, and fortuitous shapes. Helvétius brought a theory of human character, and a new analysis of morals—interest the basis of justice, pleasure the true interpretation of interest, and character the creature of education and laws.

To press such positions as these, was to recast the whole body of opinions on which society rested. As the church was the organ of the old opinions, Helvétius's book was instantly seized by the ecclesiastical authorities in accordance with a perfectly right instinct, and was made the occasion for the first violent raid upon a wholesale scale. When, however, we look beyond the smoke of the ecclesiastical battle, and weigh *L'Esprit* itself on its own merits, we see quite plainly that Helvétius was thinking less of the theological disputes of the day than of bringing the philosophy of sensation, the philosophy of Locke and Condillac, into the political field, and of deriving from it new standards and new forces for social reconstruction. And in spite of its shallowness and paradoxes, his book did contain the one principle on which, if it had been generally accepted, the inevitable transition might have taken place without a Reign of Terror.

It was commonly said, by his enemies and by his alarmed friends, that vanity and a restless overweening desire for notoriety was the inspiring motive of Helvétius. He came from a German stock. His great-grandfather settled in Holland, where he cured his patients by cunning elixirs, by the powder of ground stag's horn, and the subtle virtues of crocodiles' teeth. His grandfather went to push his fortunes in Paris, where he persuaded the public to accept the healing properties of ipecacuanha, and Lewis XIV (1689) gave him a short patent for that drug. The medical tradition of the family was maintained in a third generation, for Helvétius's father was one of the physicians of the Queen, and on one occasion performed the doubtful service to humanity of saving the life of Lewis XV. Helvétius, who was born in 1715, turned aside from the calling of his ancestors, and by means of the favour which his father enjoyed at court, obtained a position as farmer-general. This at once made him a wealthy man, but wealth was not enough to satisfy him without fame. He made attempts in various directions, in each case following the current of popularity for the hour. Maupertuis was the hero of a day, and Helvétius accordingly applied himself to become a geometer. Voltaire's brilliant success brought poetry into fashion, and so Helvétius wrote half a dozen long cantos on Happiness. Montesquieu caught and held the ear of the town by *The Spirit of Laws* (1748), and Helvétius was acute enough to perceive that speculation upon society would be the great durable interest of his time. He at once set to work, and this time he set to work without hurry. In 1751 he threw up his place as farmer-general, and with it an income of between two or three thousand pounds a year, and he then devoted himself for the next seven years to the concoction of a work that was designed to bring him immortal glory. "Helvétius sweated a long time to write a single chapter," if we may believe one of his intimates.

He would compose and recompose a passage a score of times. More facile writers looked at him with amazement in his country-house, ruminating for whole mornings on a single page, and pacing his room for hours to kindle his ideas, or to strike out some curious form of expression. The circle of his friends in Paris amused themselves in watching his attempts to force the conversation into the channel of the question that happened to occupy him for the moment. They gave him the satisfaction of discussion, and then they drew him to express his own views. "Then," says Marmontel [in his *Mémoires,* vol. ii],

> he threw himself into the subject with warmth—as simple, as natural, as sincere as he is systematic and sophistic in his works. Nothing is less like the ingenuousness of his character and ordinary life, than the artificial and premeditated simplicity of his works. Helvétius was the very opposite in his character of what he professes to believe; he was liberal, generous, unostentatious, and benevolent.

As it happens, there is a very different picture in one of Diderot's writings ["Voyage à Bourbonne," in his *Œuvres,* vol. xvii]. While Diderot was on a journey he fell in with a lady who knew Helvétius's country.

> She told us that the philosopher at his country seat was the unhappiest of men. He is surrounded by peasants and by neighbours who hate him. They break the windows of his mansion; they ravage his property at night; they cut his trees, and break down his fences. He dares not sally out to shoot a rabbit without an escort. You will ask me why all this? It comes of an unbridled jealousy about his game. His predecessors kept the estate in order with a couple of men and a couple of guns. Helvétius has four-and-twenty, and yet he cannot guard his property. The men have a small premium for every poacher that they catch, and they resort to every possible vexation in order to multiply their sorry profit. They are, for that matter, no better than so many poachers who draw wages. The border of his woods was peopled with the unfortunate wretches who had been driven from their homes into pitiful hovels. It is these repeated acts of tyranny that have raised up against him enemies of every kind, and all the more insolent, as Madame N. said, for having found out that the good philosopher is a trifle pusillanimous. I cannot see what he has gained by such a way of managing his property; he is alone on it, he is hated, he is in a constant state of fright. Ah, how much wiser our good Madame Geoffrin, when she said of a trial that tormented her: 'Finish my case. They want my money? I have some; give them money. And what can I do better with money than buy tranquillity with it?' In Helvétius's place, I should have said: 'They kill a few hares, or a few rabbits; let them kill. The poor creatures have no shelter save my woods, let them remain there.'

On the other hand, there are well-attested stories of Helvétius's munificence. There is one remarkable testimony to his wide renown for good-nature. After the younger Pretender had been driven out of France, he had special reasons on some occasion for visiting Paris. He wrote to Helvétius that he had heard of him as a man of the greatest probity and honour in France, and that to Helvétius, therefore, he would trust himself. Helvétius did not refuse the dangerous compliment, and he concealed the prince for two years in his house. He was as benevolent where his vanity was less pleasantly flattered. More than one man of letters, including Marivaux, was indebted to him for a yearly pension, and his house was as open to the philosophic tribe as Holbach's. Morellet [in his *Mémoires inédits . . . ,* vol. i] has told us that the conversation was not so good and so consecutive as it was at the Baron's.

> The mistress of the house, drawing to her side the people who pleased her best, and not choosing the worst of the company, rather broke the party up. She was no fonder of philosophy than Madame Holbach was fond of it; but the latter, by remaining in a corner without saying a word, or else chatting in a low voice with her friends, was in nobody's way; whereas Madame Helvétius, with her beauty, her originality, and her piquant turn of nature, threw out anything like philosophic discussion. Helvétius had not the art of sustaining or animating it. He used to take one of us to a window, open some question that he had in hand, and try to draw out either some argument for his own view or some objection to it, for he was always composing his book in society. Or more frequently still, he would go out shortly after dinner to the opera or elsewhere, leaving his wife to do the honours of the house.

In spite of all this, Helvétius's social popularity became considerable. This, however, followed his attainment of celebrity, for when **L'Esprit** was published, Diderot scarcely met him twice in a year, and D'Alembert's acquaintance with him was of the slightest. And there must, we should suppose, have been some difficulty in cordially admitting even a penitent member of the abhorred class of farmers-general among the esoteric group of the philosophic opposition. There was much point in Turgot's contemptuous question, why he should be thankful to a declaimer like Helvétius, who showers vehement insults and biting sarcasms on governments in general, and then makes it his business to send to Frederick the Great a whole colony of revenue clerks. It was the stringent proceedings against his book that brought to Helvétius both vogue with the public and sympathy from the Encyclopædic circle.

To us it is interesting to know that Helvétius had a great admiration for England. Holbach . . . did not share this, and he explained his friend's enthusiasm by the assumption that what Helvétius really saw in our free land was the persecution that his book had drawn upon him in France. Horace Walpole, in one of his letters [reprinted in his collected *Correspondence,* vol. iv], announced to Sir Horace Mann that Helvétius was coming to England, bringing two Miss Helvétiuses with fifty thousand pounds a-piece, to bestow on two immaculate members of our most august and incorruptible senate, if he could find two in this virtuous age who would condescend to accept his money. "Well," he adds, in a spirit of sensible protest against these unprofitable international comparisons, "we may be dupes to French follies, but they are ten times greater fools to be the dupes of our virtues." Gibbon met Helvétius (1763), and found him a sensible man, an agreeable companion, and the worthiest creature in the world, besides the merits of having a pretty wife and a hundred thousand livres a year. Warburton was invited to dine with him at Lord Mansfield's, but he could not bring himself to countenance a professed patron of atheism, a rascal, and a scoundrel.

Let us turn to the book which had the honour of bringing all this censure upon its author. Whether vanity was or was not Helvétius's motive, the vanity of an author has never accounted for the interest of his public, and we may be sure that neither those who approved, nor those who abhorred, would have been so deeply and so universally stirred, unless they had felt that he touched great questions at the very quick. And, first, let a word be said as to the form of his book.

Grimm was certainly right in saying that a man must be without taste or sense to find either the morality or the colouring of Diderot in *L'Esprit.* It is tolerably clear that Helvétius had the example of Fontenelle before his eyes—Fontenelle, who had taught astronomical systems in the forms of elegant literature, and of whom it was said that *il nous enjôle à la vérité,* he coaxes us to the truth. *L'Esprit* is perhaps the most readable book upon morals that ever was written, for persons who do not care that what they read shall be scientifically true. Hume, who, by the way, had been invited by Helvétius to translate the book into English, wrote to Adam Smith that it was worth reading, not for its philosophy, which he did not highly value, but for its agreeable composition. Helvétius intended that it should be this, and accordingly he stuffed it with stories and anecdotes. Many of them are very poor, many are inapposite, some are not very decent, others are spoiled in telling, but still stories and anecdotes they remain, and they carry a light-minded reader more or less easily from page to page and chapter to chapter. But an ingenuous student of ethics who should take Helvétius seriously, could hardly be reconciled by lively anecdotes to what, in his particular formula, seems a most depressing doctrine. Madame Roland read the celebrated book in her romantic girlhood, and her impression [reprinted in *Œuvres de Madame Roland,* vol. i] may be taken for that of most generous natures. "Helvétius made me wretched: he annihilated the most ravishing illusions; he showed me everywhere repulsive self-interest. Yet what sagacity!" she continues.

> I persuaded myself that Helvétius painted men such as they had become in the corruption of society: I judged that it was good to feed one's self on such an author, in order to be able to frequent what is called the world, without being its dupe. But I took good care not to adopt his principles, merely in order to know man properly so-called. I felt myself capable of a generosity which he never recognises. With what delight I confronted his theories with the great traits in history, and the virtues of the heroes that history has immortalised.

We have ventured to say that *L'Esprit* contained the one principle capable of supplying such a system of thinking about society as would have taught the French of that time in what direction to look for reforms. There is probably no instance in literature of a writer coming so close to a decisive body of salutary truth, and then losing himself in the by-ways of the most repulsive paradox that a perverse ingenuity could devise. We are able to measure how grievous was this miscarriage by reflecting that the same instrument which Helvétius actually held in his hand, but did not know how to use, was taken from him by a man of genius in another country, and made to produce reforms that saved England from a convulsion. Nobody pretends that Helvétius discovered Utilitarianism. Hume's name, for instance, occurs too often in his pages for even the author himself to have dreamed that his principle of utility was a new invention of his own. It would, as Mill has said, imply ignorance of the history of philosophy and of general literature not to be aware that in all ages of philosophy and of general literature, not to be aware that in all ages of philosophy one of its schools has been utilitarian, not only from the time of Epicurus, but long before. But what is certain, and what would of itself be enough to entitle Helvétius to consideration, is that from Helvétius the idea of general utility as the foundation of morality was derived by that strong and powerful English thinker, who made utilitarianism the great reforming force of legislation and the foundation of jurisprudence. Bentham himself distinctly avowed the source of his inspiration. [In a footnote, the author quotes John Bowring, writing in a chapter from Bentham's *Deontology:* "To that book [*L'Esprit*], Mr. Bentham has often been heard to say, he stood indebted for no small portion of the zeal and ardour with which he advocated his happiness-producing theory. It was from thence he took encouragement . . . it was there he learned to persevere."]

A fatal discredit fastened upon a book which yet had in it so much of the root of the matter, from the unfortunate circumstance that Helvétius tacked the principle of utility on to the very crudest farrago to be found in the literature of psychology. What happened, then, was that Rousseau swept into the field with a hollow version of a philosophy of reform, so eloquently, loftily, and powerfully enforced as to carry all before it. The democracy of sentimentalism took the place that ought to have been filled in the literature of revolutionary preparation by the democracy of utility. Rousseau's fiction of the Sovereignty of the People was an arbitrary and intrinsically sterile rendering of the real truth in Helvétius's ill-starred book.

To establish the proper dependence of laws upon one another, says Helvétius [in *L'Esprit*],

> it is indispensable to be able to refer them all to a single principle, such as that of the *Utility of the Public,* that is to say, of the greatest number of men submitted to the same form of government: a principle of which no one realises the whole extent and fertility; a principle that contains all Morality and Legislation.

A man is just when all his actions tend to the public good.

> To be virtuous, it is necessary to unite nobleness of soul with an enlightened understanding. Whoever combines these gifts conducts himself by *the compass of public utility.* This utility is the

principle of all human virtues, and the foundation of all legislations. It ought to inspire the legislator, and to force the nations to submit to his laws.

The principle of public utility is invariable, though it is pliable in its application to all the different positions in which, in their succession, a nation may find itself.

The public interest is that of the greatest number, and this is the foundation on which the principles of sound morality ought invariably to rest.

These extracts, and extracts in the same sense might easily be multiplied, show us the basis on which Helvétius believed himself to be building. Why did Bentham raise upon it a fabric of such value to mankind, while Helvétius covered it with useless paradox? The answer is that Bentham approached the subject from the side of a practical lawyer, and proceeded to map out the motives and the actions of men in a systematic and objective classification, to which the principle of utility gave him the key. Helvétius, on the other hand, instead of working out the principle, that actions are good or bad according as they do or do not serve the public interest of the greatest number, contented himself with reiterating in as many ways as possible the proposition that self-love fixes our measure of virtue. The next thing to do, after settling utility as the standard of virtue, and defining interest as a term applied to whatever can procure us pleasures and deliver us from pains, was clearly to do what Bentham did, —to marshal pleasures and pains in logical array. Instead of this, Helvétius, starting from the proposition that "to judge is to feel," launched out into a complete theory of human character, which laboured under at least two fatal defects. First, it had no root in a contemplation of the march of collective humanity, and second, it considered only the purely egoistic impulses, to the exclusion of the opposite half of human tendencies. Apart from these radical deficiencies, Helvétius fell headlong into a fallacy which has been common enough among the assailants of the principle of utility; namely, of confounding the standard of conduct with its motive, and insisting that because utility is the test of virtue, therefore the prospect of self-gratification is the only inducement that makes men prefer virtue to vice.

L'Esprit is perhaps the most readable book upon morals that ever was written, for persons who do not care that what they read shall be scientifically true.

—John Morley

This was what Madame du Deffand called telling everybody's secret. We approve conduct in proportion as it conduces to our interest. Friendship, *esprit-de-corps*, patriotism, humanity, are names for qualities that we prize more or less highly in proportion as they come more or less close to our own happiness; and the scale of our preferences is

in the inverse ratio of the number of those who benefit by the given act. If it affects the whole of humanity or of our country, our approval is less warmly stirred than if it were an act specially devoted to our own exclusive advantage. If you want therefore to reach men, and to shape their conduct for the public good, you must affect them through their pleasures and pains.

To this position, which roused a universal indignation that amazed the author, there is no doubt a true side. It is worth remembering, for instance, that all penal legislation, in so far as deterrent and not merely vindictive, assumes in all who come whether actually or potentially within its sphere, the very doctrine that covered Helvétius with odium. And there is more to be said than this. As M. Charles Comte has expressed it [in his *Traité de Législation,* vol. i]: If the strength with which we resent injury were not in the ratio of the personal risk that we run, we should hardly have the means of self-preservation; and if the acts which injure the whole of humanity gave us pain equal to that of acts that injure us directly, we should be of all beings the most miserable, for we should be incessantly tormented by conduct that we should be powerless to turn aside. And again, if the benefits of which we are personally the object did not inspire in us a more lively gratitude than those which we spread over all mankind, we should probably experience few preferences, and extend few preferences to others, and in that case egoism would grow to its most overwhelming proportions.

This aspect of Helvétius's doctrine, however, is one of those truths which is only valid when taken in connection with a whole group of different truths, and it was exactly that way of asserting a position, in itself neither indefensible nor unmeaning, which left the position open to irresistible attack. Helvétius's errors had various roots, and may be set forth in as many ways. The most general account of it is that even if he had insisted on making Self-love the strongest ingredient in our judgment of conduct, he ought at least to have given some place to Sympathy. For, though it is possible to contend that sympathy is only an indirect kind of self-love, or a shadow cast by self-love, still it is self-love so transformed as to imply a wholly different set of convictions, and to require a different name.

L'Esprit is one of the most striking instances in literature of the importance of care in choosing the right way of presenting a theory to the world. It seems as if Helvétius had taken pains to surround his doctrine with everything that was most likely to warn men away from it. For example, he begins a chapter of cardinal importance with the proposition that personal interest is the only motive that could impel a man to generous actions. "It is as impossible for him to love good for good's sake as evil for the sake of evil." The rest of the chapter consists of illustrations of this; and what does the reader suppose that they are? The first is Brutus, of all the people in the world. He sacrificed his son for the salvation of Rome, because his passion for his country was stronger than his passion as a father; and this passion for his country, "enlightening him as to the public interest," made him see what a service his rigorous example would be to the state. The other instances of the chapter point the same moral, that true virtue consists in suppressing inducements to gratify domestic or friendly feeling, when that gratification is hostile to the common weal.

It may be true that the ultimate step in a strictly logical analysis reduces the devotion of the hero or the martyr to a deliberate preference for the course least painful to himself, because religion or patriotism or inborn magnanimity have made self-sacrifice the least painful course to him. But to call this heroic mood by the name of self-love, is to single out what is absolutely the most unimportant element in the transaction, and to insist on thrusting it under the onlooker's eye as the vital part of the matter. And it involves the most perverse kind of distortion. For the whole issue and difference between the virtuous man and the vicious man turns, not at all upon the fact that each behaves in the way that habit has made least painful to him, but upon the fact that habit has made selfishness painful to the first, and self-sacrifice painful to the second; that self-love has become in the first case transformed into an overwhelming interest in the good of others, and in the second not so. Was there ever a greater perversity than to talk of self-interest, when you mean beneficence, or than to insist that because beneficence has become bound up with a man's self-love, therefore beneficence *is* nothing but self-love in disguise? As if the fruit or the flower not only depends on a root as one of the conditions among others of its development, but is itself actually the root! Apart from the error in logic, what an error in rhetoric, to single out the formula best calculated to fill a doctrine with odious associations, and then to make that formula the most prominent feature in the exposition. Without any gain in clearness or definiteness or firmness, the reader is deliberately misled towards a form that is exactly the opposite of that which Helvétius desired him to accept.

In other ways Helvétius takes trouble to wound the generous sensibility and affront the sense of his public. Nothing can be at once more scandalously cynical and more crude than a passage intended to show that, if we examine the conduct of women of disorderly life from the political point of view, they are in some respects extremely useful to the public. That desire to please, which makes such a woman go to the draper, the milliner, and the dressmaker, draws an infinite number of workmen from indigence. The virtuous women, by giving alms to mendicants and criminals, are far less wisely advised by their religious directors than the other women by their desire to please; the latter nourish useful citizens, while the former, who at the best are useless, are often even downright enemies to the nation. All this is only a wordy transcript of Mandeville's coarse sentences about "the sensual courtier that sets no limits to his luxury, and the fickle strumpet that invents new fashions every week." We cannot wonder that all people who were capable either of generous feeling or comprehensive thinking turned aside even from truth, when it was mixed in this amalgam of destructive sophistry and cynical illustration.

We can believe how the magnanimous youth of Madame Roland and others was discouraged by pages sown with mean anecdote. Helvétius tells us, with genuine zest, of Parmenio saying to Philotas at the court of Alexander the Great—"My son, make thyself small before Alexander; contrive for him now and again the pleasure of setting thee right; and remember that it is only to thy seeming inferiority that thou wilt owe his friendship." The King of Portugal charged a certain courtier to draw up a despatch on an affair with which he had himself dealt. Comparing the two despatches, the King found the courtier's much the better of the two: the courtier makes a profound reverence, and hastens to take leave of his friends: "*It is all over with me,*" he said, "*the King has found out that I have more brains than he has.*" Only mediocrity succeeds in the world. "Sir," said a father to his son, "you are getting on in the world, and you suppose you must be a person of great merit. To lower your pride, know to what qualities you owe this success: you were born without vices, without virtues, without character; your knowledge is scanty, your intelligence is narrow. Ah, what claims you have, my son, to the goodwill of the world."

It lies beyond the limits of our task to enter into a discussion of Helvétius's transgressions in the region of speculative ethics, from any dogmatic point of view. Their nature is tolerably clear. Helvétius looked at man individually, as if each of us came into the world naked of all antecedent predispositions, and independent of the medium around us. Next, he did not see that virtue, justice, and the other great words of moral science denote qualities that are directly related to the fundamental constitution of human character. As Diderot said, he never perceived it to be possible to find in our natural requirements, in our existence, in our organisation, in our sensibility, a fixed base for the idea of what is just and unjust, virtuous and vicious. He clung to the facts that showed the thousand different shapes in which justice and injustice clothed themselves; but he closed his eyes on the nature of man, in which he would have recognised their character and origin. Again, although his book was expressly written to show that only good laws can form virtuous men, and that all the art of the legislator consists in forcing men, through the sentiment of self-love, to be just to one another, yet Helvétius does not perceive the difficulty of assuming in the moralising legislator a suppression of self-love which he will not concede to the rest of mankind. The crucial problem of political constitutions is to counteract the selfishness of a governing class. Helvétius vaulted over this difficulty by imputing to a legislator that very quality of disinterestedness whose absence in the bulk of the human race he made the fulcrum of his whole moral system.

Into this field of criticism it is not, I repeat, our present business minutely to enter. The only question for us, attempting to study the history of opinion, is what Helvétius meant by his paradoxes, and how they came into his mind. No serious writer, least of all a Frenchman in the eighteenth century, ever sets out with anything but such an intention for good, as is capable of respectable expression. And we ask ourselves what good end Helvétius proposed to himself. Of what was he thinking when he perpetrated so singular a misconstruction of his own meaning as that inversion of beneficence into self-love of which we have spoken? We can only explain it in one way. In saying that it is impossible to love good for good's sake, Helvétius was thinking of the theologians. Their doctrine that man is predisposed to love evil for evil's sake, removes conduct from the sphere of rational motive, as evinced in the ordinary course of human experience. Helvétius met this by contending that both in good and bad conduct men are influenced by their interest and not by mystic and innate predisposition either to good or to evil. He sought to bring morals and human conduct out of the region of arbitrary and superstitious assumption, into the sphere of observation. He thought he was pursuing a scientific, as opposed to a theological spirit, by placing interest at the foundation of conduct, both as matter of fact and of what ought to be the fact, instead of placing there the love of God, or the action of grace, or the authority of the Church.

We may even say that Helvétius shows a positive side, which is wanting in the more imposing names of the century. Here, for instance, is a passage which in spite of its inadequateness of expression, contains an unmistakable germ of true historical appreciation:

> However stupid we may suppose the Peoples to be, it is certain that, being enlightened by their interests, it was not without motives that they adopted the customs that we find established among some of them. The bizarre nature of these customs is connected, then, with the diversity of interests among these Peoples. In fact, if they have always understood, in a confused way, by the name of virtue the desire of public happiness; if they have in consequence given the name of good to actions that are useful to the country; and if the idea of utility has always been privately associated with the idea of virtue, then we may be sure that their most ridiculous, and even their most cruel, customs have always had for their foundation the real or seeming utility of the public good.

If we contrast this with the universal fashion among Helvétius's friends, of denouncing the greater portion of the past history of the race, we cannot but see that, crude as is the language of such a passage, it contains the all-important doctrine which Voltaire, Rousseau, and Diderot alike ignored, that the phenomena of the conduct of mankind, even in its most barbarous phases, are capable of an intelligible explanation, in terms of motive that shall be related to their intellectual forms, exactly as the motives of the most polished society are related to the intellectual forms of such a society. There are not many passages in all the scores of volumes written in France in the eighteenth century on the origin of society where there is such an approach as this to the modern view.

Helvétius's position was that of a man searching for a new basis for morals. It was hardly possible for any one in that century to look to religion for such a base, and least of all was it possible to Helvétius. "It is fanaticism," he says in an elaborately wrought passage,

> that puts arms into the hands of Christian princes; it orders Catholics to massacre heretics; it brings out upon the earth again those tortures that were invented by such monsters as Phalaris, as Busiris, as Nero; in Spain it piles and lights up the fires of the Inquisition, while the pious Spaniards leave their ports and sail across distant seas, to plant the Cross and spread desola-

tion in America. Turn your eyes to north or south, to east or west; on every side you see the consecrated knife of Religion raised against the breasts of women, of children, of old men, and the earth all smoking with the blood of victims immolated to false gods or to the Supreme Being, and presenting one vast, sickening, horrible charnel-house of intolerance. Now what virtuous man, what Christian, if his tender soul is filled with the divine unction that exhales from the maxims of the Gospel, if he is sensible of the cries of the unhappy and the outcast, and has sometimes wiped away their tears—what man could fail at such a sight to be touched with compassion for humanity, and would not use all his endeavour to found probity, not on principles so worthy of respect as those of religion, but on principles less easily abused, such as those of personal interest would be?

This, then, is the point best worth seizing in a criticism of Helvétius. The direction of morality by religion had proved a failure. Helvétius, as the organ of reaction against asceticism and against mysticism, appealed to positive experience, and to men's innate tendency to seek what is pleasurable and to avoid what is painful. The scientific imperfection of his attempt is plain; but that, at any rate, is what the attempt signified in his own mind.

The same feeling for social reform inspired the second great paradox of *L'Esprit.* This is to the effect that of all the sources of intellectual difference between one man and another, organisation is the least influential. Intellectual differences are due to diversity of circumstance and to variety in education. It is not felicity of organisation that makes a great man. There is nobody, in whom passion, interest, education, and favourable chance, could not have surmounted all the obstacles of an unpromising nature; and there is no great man who, in the absence of passion, interest, education, and certain chances, would not have been a blockhead, in spite of his happier organisation. It is only in the moral region that we ought to seek the true cause of inequality of intellect. Genius is no singular gift of nature. Genius is common; it is only the circumstances proper to develop it that are rare. The man of genius is simply the product of the circumstances in which he is placed. The inequality in intelligence (*esprit*) that we observe among men, depends on the government under which they live, on the times in which their destiny has fallen, on the education that they have received, on the strength of their desire to achieve distinction, and finally on the greatness and fecundity of the ideas which they happen to make the object of their meditations.

Here again it would be easy to show how many qualifications are needed to rectify this egregious overstatement of propositions that in themselves contain the germ of a wholesome doctrine. Diderot pointed out some of the principal causes of Helvétius's errors, summing them up thus [reprinted in his *Œuvres,* vol ii]:

> The whole of this third discourse seems to imply a false calculation, into which the author has failed to introduce all the elements that have a right to be there, and to estimate the elements that are there at their right value. He has not

seen the insurmountable barrier that separates a man destined by nature for a given function, from a man who only brings to that function industry, interest, and attention.

In a work published after his death (1774), and entitled *De l'Homme,* Helvétius re-stated at greater length, and with a variety of new illustrations, this exaggerated position. Diderot wrote an elaborate series of minute notes in refutation of it, taking each chapter point by point, and his notes are full of acute and vigorous criticism. Every reader will perceive the kind of answers to which the proposition that character is independent of organisation lies open. Yet here, as in his paradox about self-love, Helvétius was looking, and looking, moreover, in the right direction, for a rational principle of moral judgment, moral education, and moral improvement. Of the two propositions, though equally erroneous in theory, it was certainly less mischievous in practice to pronounce education and institutions to be stronger than original predisposition than to pronounce organisation to be stronger than education and institutions. It was all-important at that moment in France to draw people's attention to the influence of institutions on character; to do that was both to give one of the best reasons for a reform in French institutions, and also to point to the spirit in which such a reform should be undertaken. If Helvétius had contented himself with saying that, whatever may be the force of organisation in exceptional natures, yet in persons of average organisation these predispositions are capable of being indefinitely modified by education, by laws, and by institutions, then he would not only have said what could not be disproved, but he would have said as much as his own object required. William Godwin drew one of the most important chapters of his once famous treatise on *Political Justice* from Helvétius, but what Helvétius exaggerated into a paradox which nobody in his senses could seriously accept, Godwin expressed as a rational half-truth, without which no reformer in education or institutions could fairly think it worth while to set to work.

The reader of Benjamin Constant's *Adolphe,* that sombre little study of a miserable passion, may sometimes be reminded of Helvétius. It begins with the dry surprise of youth at the opening world, for we need time, he says, to accustom ourselves to the human race, such as affectation, vanity, cowardice, interest have made it. Then we soon learn only to be surprised at our old surprise; we find ourselves very well off in our new conditions, just as we come to breathe freely in a crowded theatre, though on entering it we were almost stifled. Yet the author of this parching sketch of the distractions of an egoism that just fell short of being complete, suddenly flashes on us the unexpected but penetrating and radiant moral, *La grande question dans la vie, c'est la douleur que l'on cause*—the great question in life is the pain that we strike into the lives of others. We are not seldom refreshed, when in the midst of Helvétius's narrowest grooves, by some similar breath from the wider air. Among the host of sayings, true, false, trivial, profound, which are scattered over the pages of Helvétius, is one subtle and far-reaching sentence, which made a strong impression upon Bentham. "*In order to love mankind,*" he writes, "*we must expect little from them.*" This

might, on the lips of a cynic, serve for a formula of that kind of misanthropy which is not more unamiable than it is unscientific. But in the mouth of Helvétius it was a plea for considerateness, for indulgence, and, above all, it was meant for an inducement to patience and sustained endeavour in all dealings with masses of men in society. "Every man," he says, "so long as his passions do not obscure his reason, will always be the more indulgent in proportion as he is enlightened." He knows that men are what they must be, that all hatred against them is unjust, that a fool produces follies just as a wild shrub produces sour berries, that to insult him is to reproach the oak for bearing acorns instead of olives. All this is as wise and humane as words can be so, and it really represents the aim and temper of Helvétius's teaching. Unfortunately for him and for his generation, his grasp was feeble and unsteady. He had not the gift of accurate thinking, and his book is in consequence that which, of all the books of the eighteenth century, unites most of wholesome truth with most of repellent error.

G. V. Plekhanov (essay date 1896)

SOURCE: "Helvétius," in his *Essays in the History of Materialism,* translated by Ralph Fox, 1934. Reprint by Howard Fertig, 1967, pp. 79-164.

[*In the following excerpt from* Beiträge zur Geschicte des Materialismus *(1896), Plekhanov examines Helvétius as a materialist, addressing both his conception of virtue and his theory of motivation.*]

Was Helvétius what may be called a materialist in the strict sense of the word? Thanks to his reputation this is very often doubted. "The reasonable and restrained Buffon, the discreet and diplomatic Grimm, the vain and superficial Helvétius," said the late [Friedrich A.] Lange [in his *Geschichte des Materialismus,* 1873] "all approach closely to materialism, although they do not give us that firm outlook and those consistent conclusions from sound ideas by which Lamettrie, for all the lightness of his expressions, was distinguished". The French echo of the German Neokantian, Jules Soury [in his "Bréviaire de l'histoire du matérialisme", 1883], repeats this opinion word for word.

We want to examine the question for ourselves.

The question as to whether there exists in man an immaterial substance to which he owes his psychic life does not enter into the sphere of Helvétius' investigations. He only touches on this question by the way and examines it with the greatest caution. On the one hand, he tries not to annoy the censor. For this reason he speaks with obvious respect of the Church which has "established our faith on this point". On the other hand, he does not like philosophical "fantasies". We should go along the path of observation, he says, halting the moment it halts us and have the courage not to know what it is still impossible to know. This sounds rather "restrained" than "vain" or "superficial". Lange would have felt this and pointed it out if it had been a question of a less "dangerous" writer. But since he is talking of Helvétius, he finds another measure and another scale. It appeared obvious to him that the "vain and superficial" author of the book *On the Spirit* could only be "vain and superficial". In all the main questions of "metaphysics" (for example in the questions of matter, space, infinity, etc.) Helvétius in fact shared the views of the English materialist John Toland. To be convinced of this it is sufficient to compare "The Letters to Serena" (1704) of the latter with the fourth chapter of the first part of the book *On the Spirit.* For Lange, Toland without any doubt was an outstanding materialist. His ideas appeared to him as clear, in so far as that is possible. As for Helvétius, he merely "approached" materialism since his superficiality prevented him from firmly holding to one main idea. "So history is written". How fatal is the influence of "superficial" persons! The "soundest" people through reading the latter become in their turn superficial!

"Does matter possess the capacity of sensation?"

> Always and from all sides it has been maintained that matter felt or did not feel and on this subject there have been very long and very vague disputes. Only very late have people arrived at the point of asking what the dispute was about and of fixing a precise idea for this word matter. If its meaning had been fixed at first, it would have been recognised that men are, so to say, the creators of matter, that matter is not a being, that in nature there are only individuals to which the name of body has been given and that it is only possible to understand by this word matter the collection of properties common to all these bodies. Once the meaning of this word had been determined in this way, it only remained to know whether space, solidity, impenetrability were the only properties common to all bodies; and whether the discovery of a force such as attraction, for example, could not make one suspect that bodies had some other unknown properties such as the faculty of sensation which, only manifesting itself in the organised bodies of animals, might however be common to all individuals. The question reduced to this point, it would have been felt that if it is strictly impossible to show that all bodies are absolutely insensible, any man who is not on this subject enlightened by revelation can only decide the question by calculating and comparing the probability of this opinion with the probability of the contrary opinion. To put an end to this dispute it was not therefore necessary to construct different systems of the world, to lose oneself in the combination of possibilities and to make those prodigious efforts of mind which have only ended and should really only have ended in more or less ingenious errors.

This long quotation [from *De l'Esprit*] shows however both the kinship of Helvétius' materialism with Toland's materialism and the character of what it was desired to call the scepticism or probabilism of Helvétius. But in his opinion it is not the materialists but the idealists of different schools who are taken up with "philosophic fantasies". He recommends them to be prudent, careful, and to take account of probabilities. This prudence, this care should show them that at the basis of their negation of the sensitivity of matter lies their imagination, that not the qualities of "bodies" but only the definition which they give of

matter, that is, exclusively the word, prevent them from uniting the concept of the body with the capacity for sensation. Scepticism is here a weapon directed solely against the adversaries of materialism. It is exactly the same where Helvétius speaks about "the existence of bodies". The capacity of matter for sensation is only a probability! Perfectly true. But what does this prove against the materialist? For in its turn, the very existence of bodies is only a probability, and, moreover, it would be stupid to deny it. In this way Helvétius developed his argument and if it proves anything, then it is first of all that he did not stand still before his sceptical doubt.

Helvétius knew, just as well as did all his contemporaries, that we know bodies only through the sensations which they excite in us. This shows once again that Lange was mistaken in declaring that "materialism obstinately accepts the world of sensual phenomena for the world of real things". But this did not prevent Helvétius from being a convinced materialist. He quotes [in *De l'Homme*] a "famous English chemist" whose opinion on the sensitivity of matter he clearly shares. [In a footnote, the critic adds that the credited source of this quote, "Treatise on the Principles of Chemistry," was, as of yet, unlocated.] Here are the words of this chemist:

> Two kinds of properties are recognised in bodies, of which some are permanent and unchangeable: such are, impenetrability, weight, mobility, etc. These qualities belong to Physics in general.

> These same bodies have other qualities the existence of which is fugitive and transient, is in turn produced and destroyed by certain combinations, analyses, or movements in the internal parts. These kinds of properties form the different branches of Natural History, of Chemistry, etc. and belong to particular branches of Physics.

> Iron for example, is a compound of Phlogiston and a certain earth. In this form of composition it is amenable to the power of attraction of loadstone. But if the iron is decomposed this property is destroyed. Loadstone has no action upon an iron soil deprived of its Phlogiston. . . .

> Now why should not organisations in the animal Kingdom also produce this singular quality which we call the faculty of feeling? Every phenomenon of medicine and history proves that this power in animals is only the result of the structure of their bodies, that this power begins with the formation of their organs, is preserved as long as they exist, and is lost at last by the dissolution of these organs.

> If the metaphysicians ask me what becomes of the animal's faculty of sensation, I shall answer them that the same thing becomes of it as becomes of the property of iron of being attracted by loadstone.

Helvétius was not only a materialist but among his contemporaries he maintained the main ideas of his materialism with the greatest "consistency". He was so "consistent" that he horrified the other materialists. Not one of them was bold enough to follow him in his daring conclusions. In this sense he did actually only stand near to people like Holbach, since these people were only able to approximate to him.

Our soul is only the capacity for sensation. Reason is only the activity of this capacity. In man everything is sensation: "Physical sensibility is consequently the principle of his needs, of his passions, of his sociability, of his ideas, of his judgements, of his wills, of his actions. . . . Man is a machine which, put into motion by physical sensibility, must do everything which it demands" [*De l'Homme*]. Thus the starting point of Helvétius is absolutely identical with the starting point of Holbach. This is the foundation upon which our "dangerous sophist" built. Let us now examine more closely what there is original in the architecture of his building.

What is virtue? In the 18th century, there was no philosopher who did not discuss this question in his own way. For Helvétius the matter was perfectly simple. Virtue consists in the knowledge of what is due from people to one another. Its premise consequently is the education of society.

> Born on a desert island, left to myself, I live without vice and without virtue. I can show neither the one nor the other. What must I understand then by these words virtuous and vicious? Actions which are useful or harmful to society. To my mind this simple and clear idea is to be preferred to any obscure and high-sounding declamation upon virtue [*De l'Homme*].

The general interest is the measure and foundation of virtue. Therefore the more harmful to society our acts are, the more vicious they are. The more advantageous to society they are, the more virtuous they are. *Salus populi suprema lex* (the good of the people is the highest law). The "virtue" of our philosopher is in the first place political virtue. The preaching of morality leads to nothing: preaching has never yet made a single hero. We must give to society an organisation able to teach its members respect for the common interest. The corruption of morals merely means the separation of public and private interest. The best preacher of morality is the legislator who has succeeded in destroying this separation.

We often meet with the statement that J. S. Mill's "Utilitarianism" as a teaching on morality greatly surpasses the ethic of the materialists of the 18th century, since the latter wished to make personal interest the foundation of morality, whilst the English philosopher placed the principle of the greatest happiness of the greatest number in the first place. The reader now sees that in this respect the merits of J. S. Mill are more than doubtful. The happiness of the greatest number is merely a very weak copy, deprived of its revolutionary colouring, of the "general interest" of the French materialists. But if this is the case then whence comes the opinion which perceives in J. S. Mill's "Utilitarianism" a happy variation upon the 18th century materialist teaching upon morality?

What is the principle of the greatest happiness of the greatest number? It is the sanction for human action. In this respect the materialists have nothing to learn from Mill's famous book. But the materialists were not satisfied with seeking for sanctions. Before them was the task of solving a scientific problem. In what way does Man, since he is only sensation, learn to value the common good? By what miracle does he forget the demands of his physical sensations and arrive at aims which have nothing in common with the latter? In the sphere and within the limits of this problem the materialists actually did take personal interest as their starting point. But to take personal interest as the starting point only means to repeat once more the argument that man is a feeling being and nothing but a feeling being. Thus personal interest for the materialists was not a moral homily but simply a scientific fact.

Holbach got round the difficulty of this problem by means of wordy terminology. "When we say that interest is the only motive of human actions we wish by this to indicate that every man works after his own fashion for his own happiness which he places in some visible or hidden object, whether real or imaginary, and towards obtaining which the whole system of his conduct is directed" ["Système de la Nature," 1781]. In other words this means that it is impossible to reduce personal interest simply to the demand of "physical sensations". But at the same time, for Holbach, as for all the materialists of the 18th century, man is only sensation. Here is a logical jump and thanks to this logical jump Holbach's "Ethics" inspire the historians of philosophy with less disgust than the ethics of Helvétius. In Lange's opinion "Holbach's ethics are serious and pure". Hettner, on his side [in "Literaturgeschichte des XVIII Jahrhunderts," 1881], sees in them something distinct from the ethics of Helvétius.

The author of the book *On the Spirit* was the only philosopher of the 18th century who dared to touch on the question of the origin of moral feelings. He was the only one who dared to deduce them from the "physical sensations" of people.

Man is sensitive to physical satisfaction and to physical suffering. He avoids the second and aims at the first. This constant and inevitable striving is called self-love. This self-love is inseparable from man. It is his chief sensation. "Of all sentiments it is the only one of its kind. To it we owe all our desires, all our passions. They can but be the application of the sentiment of self-love to this or that object" [*De l'Homme*]. . . . "If you open the book of history you will see that in every country where certain virtues were encouraged by the hope of sensual pleasures, these virtues have been the most common and have enjoyed the greatest renown" [*De l'Esprit*]. The nations which devoted themselves most of all to love were the most manly. "For in these countries women showed favour only to the brave." With the Samnites the greatest beauty was the reward for the highest military virtue. In Sparta the wise Lycurgus, convinced that "pleasure is the only general motive of man", succeeded in making love the incentive to bravery. On the principal holidays young, half-naked and beautiful Lacedaemonian girls came out to dance in the popular assemblies. In their songs they insulted the cowards and praised the brave. Only the brave might make demands upon the favours of the fair sex. The Spartans therefore tried to be brave. The passion of love inflamed the passion for glory in their hearts. But the limits of the possible were still not reached in the "wise" institutions of Lycurgus.

> Let us suppose, to prove it, that . . . after the example of the virgins consecrated to Isis or to Vesta, the most beautiful Lacedaemonians were consecrated to virtue; that, showing themselves naked in the assembly they were carried off by the warriors as the reward of their courage; and that these young heroes experienced at the same moment the double intoxication of love and of glory; however strange and alien from our morals this legislation may be it is certain that it still made the Spartans more virtuous and more brave, since the force of virtue is always in proportion to the degree of pleasure assigned to it as a reward.

Helvétius speaks of a double intoxication, of love and of glory. This must not be wrongly understood. In "the passion" of the thirst for glory everything can be reduced to physical sensation. We love glory, like wealth, for the sake of the power which it brings. But what is power? It is the means of compelling others to serve our happiness. But happiness can, in reality, be reduced to physical pleasure. Man is only sensation. All such passions as, for example, the passion for glory, power, wealth, etc., are only artificial passions which may be deduced from physical needs. In order the better to understand this truth it is always necessary to remember that our sensual pleasures and sufferings are of a double kind: real pleasures or sufferings and those which are foreseen. I experience hunger and feel a real suffering. I foresee that I shall die from hunger: I experience a suffering which is foreseen. "When a man who loves beautiful slaves and fine pictures discovers a treasure he is in transports. However, it may be objected that from this he never experiences physical pleasure. I am in agreement with this. But at this moment he obtains the means for securing the objects of his desires. The foresight of approaching pleasure is already a pleasure." It follows of itself that foresight in no wise contradicts the starting point of Helvétius. Foresight represents the consequence of recollection. If I foresee that an insufficiency of food will bring me suffering that proceeds from the fact that I had already once experienced a similar suffering. But recollection is the property of "to a certain degree producing the same effect upon our organs" as suffering or pleasure themselves cause. It is therefore obvious that "all impressions which are called inner sufferings or pleasures are in exactly the same way physical sensations and that the words inner and outer can only be applied to such impressions as are evoked by recollection or the presence of definite objects".

Foresight, that is physical sensation, compels me to mourn the death of my friend. By his conversation he banished my boredom, "that suffering of the soul which is a purely physical pain"; he would have given his life and fortune in order to save me from death or suffering, by means of all kinds of satisfactions he always strove to increase my pleasure. By the death of my friend a means of pleasure has been taken from me and this brings tears to my eyes. "Delve into the depths of the heart and in all these feelings you will only observe the development of physical satisfaction and physical pain".

However, your friend, it might be objected against Helvétius, was ready to give up his life and fortune in order to preserve you from suffering. Consequently you yourself acknowledge by this that people do exist who for the sake of achieving an ideal aim are capable of not hearing the voice of your "physical sensation".

Our philosopher gives no direct answer to this objection. But it is not hard to understand that it should not embarrass him. What, he might ask, is the motive force of heroic acts? The hope of reward. In such acts a man encounters many dangers, but the greater the danger the greater the reward. Interest (physical sensation) prompts that the game is worth the gamble. If this is how things stand with great and famous historical actions then in the self-sacrifice of a friend there is nothing of particular note.

There are people who love science, who lose their health over books and put up with all kinds of hardships in order to obtain knowledge. One might say that love of science has nothing in common with physical pleasure, but this statement would be a mistake. Why does the miser to-day renounce the most essential things? Because he wishes to increase his means of treasure for to-morrow, for the day after to-morrow, in a word, for the future. Splendid. Let us suppose that something similar takes place with the man of learning also and we shall have the solution of the puzzle.

> Does the miser desire a fine castle and the man of talent a beautiful woman? If, in order to obtain the one or the other, great wealth and a great reputation are needed, these two men will each work for the increase, the one of his treasure, the other of his renown. But during the time they have spent in acquiring this money and this renown, if they have grown old, if they have contracted habits which they cannot break without an effort of which age has made them incapable, both the miser and the man of talent will die, the one without his castle, the other without his mistress [*De l'Homme*].

All this is already enough to excite the indignation of "respectable people" throughout the world and to make it clear how and why Helvétius got his bad reputation. But it is also sufficient to show the weak side of his "analysis". Let us add one more quotation to those we have so far made.

> While recognising that our passions originally have their source in physical sensibility, one might still believe that in the actual conditions in which civilised nations exist, these passions exist independently of the causes which produce them. I am going then, by tracing the metamorphosis of physical pains and pleasures into artificial pains and pleasures, to show that in passions such as avarice, ambition, pride and friendship, the object of which appears least of all to belong to the pleasures of the senses, it is nevertheless always physical pain and pleasure which we evade or seek [*De l'Esprit*].

Thus there is no heredity. According to Darwin [in "The Origin of Man"] the intellectual and moral properties of man are variable; "And we have every ground for believing that the variations have the property of hereditary transmission". According to Helvétius man's capacities are extremely variable, but the variations are not transmitted from one generation to another, since their basis, the capacity for physical sensation, remains unchanged. Helvétius was sufficiently penetrating to perceive the phenomena of evolution. He sees that "One and the same race of animals, independently of the character and abundance of its food, becomes stronger or weaker, develops or falls back". He also notices that the same thing is applicable to oak trees. "We see small, large, straight, crooked oaks and not one of them is absolutely like the other". On what does this depend? "Perhaps on the fact that not one of them receives the same culture from the other, does not grow in the same place, is not exposed to the actions of one and the same wind and is not sown in the same soil?" This is a perfectly logical explanation. But Helvétius does not stop here.

He asks the question: "Does the difference in different substances lie in their germs or in their development?" This is not the question of an idle mind. But mark the sense of the dilemma: either in the germs, or in their development. Our philosopher does not even suspect that the history of the species may leave its traces in the structure of the germ. The history of a species? For him, as for his contemporaries, it does not exist at all. He only takes into account the individual. He is only interested in individual "nature", he only observes individual "development". We are far from being satisfied by Darwin's theory of the inheritance of moral and intellectual "characteristics". It is only the first word in evolutionary science. But we know very well that whatever results the latter may bring us to, it will be successful only through the application of the dialectical method to the study of phenomena, which are by nature dialectical in their very essence. Helvétius remains a metaphysician even when his instincts impel him to another and completely opposite point of view, to the dialectical point of view.

He recognises that he "knows nothing" as to whether the difference in beings lies exclusively in their (individual) development. Such a hypothesis seems overbold to him. And in fact there would follow from it what Lucretius, who was well known to the materialist "philosophers", considered the greatest absurdity:

> . . . Ex omnibus rebus
> Omne genus nasci posset . . .
> · · · · ·
>
> Nec fructus idem arboribus constare solerent
> Sed mutarentur: ferre omnes omnia possent.

But when the problem is limited, when it is only a question of one species, of man, then Helvétius no longer has such doubts. He declares positively and with great confidence that all "differences" in people lie in their development, and not in their embryos, not in their heredity. At our birth we all share similar qualities. Only education makes us dissimilar from one another. We shall see again below that this thought, though without solid foundation, is very fruitful in his hands. But he approaches it by a false path, and this origin of his thought can be felt every time he makes use of it and every time he tries to prove it. It shows

that Diderot was perfectly right when he said that the statements of Helvétius are much stronger than his proofs. The metaphysical method of 18th century materialism constantly avenges itself upon the boldest and most logical of its followers.

We always seek physical pleasure and avoid physical suffering. An important statement. But how is it proved? Helvétius always takes a grown man with "passions", the causes of which are extremely numerous and complicated and undoubtedly owe their origin to social environment, i. e. to the history of the species, and tries to deduce these "passions" from physical sensations. What arises independently of consciousness is represented to us as the immediate temporary fruit of this very consciousness. Habit and instinct assume the form of thought which inspires this feeling or that in man. In our essay on Holbach we explained that this mistake was characteristic of all the "philosophers" who defend a utilitarian morality. But in Helvétius this mistake assumes a scale which is really regrettable. In the picture drawn for us by Helvétius thought in the real sense of the word disappears, yielding place to a number of images which all belong without exception to "physical sensations". This sensation which is, without doubt, the actual, and very remote cause of our moral habits, is transformed into the final cause of our acts. Thus the problem is solved by a fiction. But it is perfectly obvious that it is impossible to dissolve the problem in the acid of fiction. Further, by his "analysis" Helvétius deprives our moral feelings of their specific qualities and in this way erases that very x, the unknown quantity, the meaning of which he tries to define. He wishes to prove that all our feelings may be deduced from physical sensation. To prove this he invents a man who is always pursuing corporeal pleasures, "beautiful slaves", etc. In fact this statement is stronger than its proof.

Remy De Gourmont   (essay date 1920)

SOURCE: "Helvétius and the Philosophy of Happiness," in his *Philosophic Nights in Paris,* translated by Isaac Goldberg, John W. Luce and Company, 1920, pp. 25-33.

[*De Gourmont, a French poet, novelist, critic, and essayist, was one of the founders of the influential* Mercure de France, *a journal that championed the Symbolist movement in French poetry. Included in his criticism are the* Promenades Philosophiques *and* Promenades littéraires *which were lauded at the time as "without doubt the most important critical works of our epoch." In the following essay, which originally appeared as one of the* Promenades, *De Gourmont praises Helvétius for his philosophy of happiness which contrasts with the dreariness of the "absurd German metaphysics."*]

"M. Helvétius, in his youth," says Chamfort, "was as handsome as love itself. One evening, as he was seated very peacefully before an open fire, at the side of Mlle. Gaussin, a renowned financier came and whispered into this actress's ear, loud enough for Helvétius to hear: 'Mademoiselle, would it be agreeable to you to accept six hundred louis in exchange for a few favors?' —'Monsieur,' she replied, loud enough to be heard by Helvétius, and pointing to him at the same time, 'I'll give you two hundred of them if you will kindly call on me tomorrow morning with that fellow over there'."

Helvétius was not content with being very handsome. He was also exceedingly wise, very rich, and very happy. No mortal, perhaps, received so many gifts from the gods, the rarest of which was Mme. Helvétius, one of the most charming and gifted women of the eighteenth century. Like her husband, she was very beautiful, —so beautiful that persons paused, struck with admiration, to look at her. There is, in this connection, —quoting again from Chamfort, —a very pretty anecdote:

"M. de Fontenelle, aged ninety-seven, having just uttered to Mme. Helvétius, young, beautiful and newly wed, a thousand amiable and gallant remarks, passed by her to take his place at table, without raising his eyes to her. 'You can see,' said Mme. Helvétius, 'how much stock I may take in your compliments; you pass me by without so much as looking at me.' 'Madame,' replied the old man, 'if I had looked at you, I would not have passed by'."

Happiness is often egotistical. It is even a question whether a certain egotism is not necessary to the acquirement of a certain happiness. Helvétius gave a peremptory denial to these sorry notions. Happy himself, he had but one passion: the happiness of humanity. He noticed, in his observation of mankind, that the natural desire to be happy, which each of us bears within, is opposed by a thousand prejudices, the most terrible of which are the religious prejudices, and he determined to combat them with all his strength. M. Albert Keim, who knows Helvétius better than any other man in France, has just republished certain notes written in the philosopher's hand; the first of which runs thus:

> Prejudices. They are to the mind what ministers are to monarchs. The latter prevent their rivals from approaching the king, and in the same way prejudices prevent truths from reaching the mind, for fear of losing the power they usurp over it.

One of the most widespread prejudices is that which considers it impossible to attain happiness; as that does not prevent us from desiring it, such an idea corrupts life and often renders it unbearable. Priests have believed that they could remedy this by inventing a second life, where the person who has consented to be quite unhappy in the first will find at last a sort of equivocal happiness, little calculated to tempt one of intelligence. The people, nevertheless, snap at this bait and accept, in view of future recompense, the direst tribulations of the present life. Thus a frightful slavery is perpetuated, for it is very evident that all this is nothing but a hoax and an imposition. Whoever wishes to taste happiness, if this word stands for anything more than a dream, should set about it in this life, since the other one is but a chimera, lucrative for the clergy alone. But how be happy? Through virtue? Very well, what is virtue?

"Virtue," replies Helvétius, "is only the wisdom which harmonizes passion with reason and pleasure with duty."

He assigns a large place in life to pleasures and passions;

but he does not consider them only as elements of happiness; he makes of them sources of activity. Man instinctively seeks pleasure. When he has experienced it, and later loses it, he will work with all his might to win it anew. All forms of pleasure, then, are easily reconcilable to virtue. Who knows whether pleasure taken in wise moderation is not virtue itself ? And he dares to write this maxim, which will perhaps frighten some: *One is never guilty when one is happy.* Helvétius, who was a very gentle and kind person, is often, in his writings, rashly bold. His intimate notes are violent, impassioned, even brutal. He speaks in them of love with magnificent frankness, and one readily divines that it is chiefly in the exercise of this amiable virtue that he found happiness.

I am not at all writing here a study of Helvétius, one of the most skilful demolishers of the ancient régime; I am running through a portfolio of private notes, printed at first in a few copies, and the reading of which will reveal at once an ingenious philosopher and the most spirited of poets. He is, on the subject of love, inexhaustible; he is in turn tender, subtle, passionate, raving. His delirious attacks are of a beautiful candor; the majority of his thoughts are charming and most seductive: "Each moment of pleasure is a gift of the gods."

This verse, which would be greatly admired and celebrated if it had been found in André Chenier, —does it truly come from the pen of Helvétius? This is what M. Albert Keim asks himself. That is a query to propound to the erudite spirits of *l'Intermédiaire,* who have read all the old authors; in the meantime I consider it as being highly characteristic of the philosophy and the poetry of the author of **Bonheur** (Happiness). One can imagine nothing more pagan, more gently anti-Christian. And anti-Christianism is the real basis of Helvétius' philosophy. He oversteps the bounds a trifle when he adds: "Pleasure is the sole occupation of life." The ardor of this young man is excessive. He himself will soon learn and declare that life has other employments, such, for example, as composing a philosophy.

His second motto will be: "Minerva and Venus in turn," which is wisdom itself; he will devote himself to plucking at once "the fruits of reason and the fruits of pleasure." He is forever recurring to voluptuousness, whose images pursue him: "Who takes all pleasure takes very few of them." Love to him is the most noble of passions because it is the fecund passion and mother of life. This is what makes him say: "It is not, moreover, without a certain secret melancholy," for, he avers, "The flower that one plucks is ready to wither."

Do you wish to see him in his rôle of a serious philosopher? He will say, as if he foresaw the war against science, in which, in our own days, we have seen the Veuillots and the Brunetières distinguish themselves: "There are things over which the veil of skepticism should be spread; but, in the matter of science, it would be necessary, in order to win the right of skepticism, to know all that the human mind may learn: then one might permit himself to declare that science is nothing." Like the modern positivists, like Renan, remarks M. Keim, Helvétius had the greatest confidence in science. He is forever celebrating the triumphs of human intelligence. He believes in progress, in the transformation of society by the scientific mind. Thus he launched a powerful attack against Rousseau's thesis upon the ills of civilization. Yet at times one notes in him a little discouragement, and he will confess: "Almost all philosophical views are worthless. Not that they are not excellent, but because there are too few persons who can understand them."

The number of persons who can understand Helvétius has greatly increased, and besides, it is not so difficult as he believed; all one needs is a little common sense. It is a good sign of our intellectual health that Helvétius is coming back into fashion. Tomorrow it will be d'Holbach, d'Alembert, Tracy, the master of Stendhal, —all those eighteenth-century philosophers who are so clear, so simple, so human. The absurd German metaphysics has annihilated them for sixty years, but it seems that the day of their revenge has come. The dry notion of abstract duty according to Kant has outlived its day. It is beginning to be understood that man's first duty is to be happy. Otherwise, what is the use of living?

Mordecai Grossman (essay date 1926)

SOURCE: *The Philosophy of Helvétius,* New York: Teachers College Press, 1926, 181 p.

[*In the following excerpt, Grossman presents Helvétius's sensationalist conception of human nature and explores the implications of the sensationalist doctrine for ethical theory.*]

Severe criticisms were often directed against Helvétius. Originality and depth of interest have been denied him. In most cases, this criticism was due to a misunderstanding of Helvétius' relation to his century and to a misconception of his purpose.

As an original thinker Helvétius would not rank high. Probably there is not a single important idea presented by Helvétius which was not also presented by his contemporaries. But it is precisely in this that the importance of Helvétius lies. He was the epitome of his age. His works more than those of any single writer reflect all the interests, ideas, and ideals of his time. In speaking of the *De l'Esprit,* [George S.] Brett says [in his *History of Psychology,* 1921], "The significance of the whole work lies in its character as an epitome of current tendencies . . . the tendency to make social pressure and social relations the reasons for the various characteristics of men and nations . . . the tendency to see in the adult a complex product of education." Whatever originality there is in Helvétius it is an originality of emphasis and of extremeness of statement. In his works current tendencies find their extremest expression. *De l'Esprit,* and even more so *De l'Homme,* were not intended as theoretical statement of the theory of knowledge, the nature of man. Helvétius' aim throughout was practical—to show that given certain conditions, progress is possible; to formulate the contents of progress; to point to methods best suited to bring about progress as conceived by him; to combat those forces that hinder the progress of humanity. It is only to justify his aim and the methods whereby the aim was to be realized, in order to discover whether his purpose is possible of realization and

whether methods are adequate, that Helvétius sizes up human nature, and environment, the growth resulting from the interaction of the two, the origin and forces making for growth of society and the good of which the individual is capable.

Philosophy, with Helvétius, does not start in a disinterested love for truth. Nor does it, in his view, find its consummation in the discovery of the truth. Its origin is love of happiness; its consummation is its application.

> In the study that the philosopher makes of men, his object is their happiness. This happiness is dependent on the laws under which they live and the instructions they receive. The perfection of these laws and instructions presuppose a preliminary knowledge of the human heart and the human mind with their various operations. . . . To educate, furnish their minds and render them happy we must know to what instruction and what happiness they are susceptible [*De l'Homme*].

Psychology has as its aim control of human beings, in order to bring about their happiness.

> To guide the motions of the human puppet it is necessary to know the wires by which he is moved. . . . Let philosophers, therefore, penetrate continually onward more into the abyss of the human heart, let them search out all the principles of his actions and let the minister, profiting by their discoveries, make of them according to time, place, and circumstances a happy application [*De l'Homme*].

Man's sole consideration is the sum total of human happiness. The increase of human happiness and the human control of the instruments that are capable of bringing it about are the only criteria of progress. What is happiness? How can it be brought about? These are the main questions to Helvétius. Human nature and the universe are subjects of interest only to the extent that they prove useful in the effort to answer this question.

Sensationalism seemed to Helvétius to satisfy all the demands made by his purpose. Just as sense experience has substituted valid truths about the universe for "philosophical tales" and even worse, "religious tales" that preceded it actual observation of the facts of the behavior and growth of the soul will lead in the same way to displace the idealistic and religious "romance of the soul" by the empirical "story of the soul." Such account of human nature will give us the necessary data to determine the content and methods of human happiness. Sensationalism gave a rigid criterion of evidence. Then, sensationalism as a philosophy ruled out of consideration supernatural values which, if having a claim, might conflict with that human happiness recognized as such by man. Helvétius was an extreme sensationalist and he drew extreme conclusions from his position. "Helvétius accepted and proclaimed all the results before which the prudence of his predecessors stopped," [claims Victor Cousin in his *La Philosophie Sensualiste au XVIIIe Siècle,* 1856]. Extreme sensationalism assuming that all that we are, all that we know, all that we do, is the product of sense experience coming from the environment, from without, gave promise that the realization of human happiness can be brought about by controlling the environment will produce an individual capable of moral behavior—of happiness.

[Helvétius] conceived legislation and education as the two primary methods of bringing about general happiness. Education can, also, create a moral individual, an individual who knows that it is his interest to work in the interest of the public and, because of this knowledge, behaves virtuously. Legislation, by a system of reward and punishments, can do its share to increase those actions that tend in the direction of human happiness and decrease those that tend in an opposite direction.

The aim of the present section is to present Helvétius' view of human nature, its growth, development, and action. This done, the ethical system of Helvétius, based on human nature, as conceived by him, as a foundation will be briefly formulated. This will be, in substance, a statement of the ethical implications of sensationalism. . . .

. . . . .

The fundamental principle of Helvétius' psychology is that the human mind is entirely the product of the environment and as the environment changes, the mind, too, changes. Environment is, however, but one factor, the variable and active factor, in the making of the mind. The other factor, constant and passive, is the sensitive principle, the initial self, "the soul," as Helvétius calls it. Environment reshapes this "soul." The sum total of the modifications of the soul, caused by the varying environment, is what constitutes the mind. A passive soul is turned into an active mind. The receptivity of the soul and the variability of the environment insure the possibility of an ever-changing mind. To get at the origin, nature and development, as well as the limits, of the human mind as conceived by Helvétius, it is necessary to catch a glimpse of the nature "soul."

In the *De l'Esprit* Helvétius recognizes a possible double use of the word *mind*. "We consider the mind either as the effect of the property of thinking, and in this the mind is no more than an assemblage of our thoughts, or we consider it as the very faculty of thinking." Mind in the second sense is clearly prior in time to mind in the first sense—mind as an "assemblage of thoughts." The two are logically distinct. Due to the confusion which results from the designation of two things by the same name Helvétius thinks it necessary to assign different names to them. Consequently, in *De l'Homme* he distinguishes between mind and soul. The soul is the faculty of sensitiveness. The mind is an assemblage of ideas. The soul is a condition of the mind, its cause being environment. But conceivably, and also as a matter of experience, the soul can exist without the mind. Every one, in fact, has a soul; but those who have no ideas, have no minds. A demented person has lost his mind, but, still being sensitive, he retains his "soul." The soul is a constant; the mind is variable. The idiot and the genius have the same soul; but the difference is in their minds.

The use of the word "soul" would lead one to believe that Helvétius thought of an entity separable from the body, of a sensitive principle independent from the *res extensa*.

While, as we shall see later, Helvétius had many points in common with Condillac, he did not follow him in the acceptance of an unextended sensitive principle. On this point, Helvétius follows La Mettrie's materialism rather than Condillac's parallelism. There is no sensitive principle. Sensitivity is a property of organized matter. Just as we have no need for positing a mysterious principle in order to explain the appearance of certain chemical qualities upon the union of elements into a substance, so there is no need for positing a sensitive principle when sensitiveness appears upon a certain organization of matter. "All the phenomena that relate to medicine and natural history evidently prove that this power is not more than the result of the structure of their bodies; that the power begins with the formation of their organs, lasts as long as they subsist, and is at last destroyed by the dissolution of the same organs" [*De l'Homme*].

Not unlike La Mettrie, whose influence on Helvétius was probably very profound, he denies that man is distinguished from other animals in the respect of possessing a soul. Animals, like men, have souls. Why, then, has man reached a higher plane of action than other animals? The answer given by Helvétius agrees in some respects and differs in others from that given by La Mettrie. The element of difference is very significant. Both reply that this difference between thought and action of animals is due to a difference of structure. But, whereas to La Mettrie this difference in structure was largely a difference in brain structure resulting in different degrees of "imagination" corresponding to sensitivity in Helvétius' terminology, to the latter it was a difference in the gross structure which enabled man to take better advantage of his sensitivity, which, as far as we know, is not superior to that of animals. "If Nature, instead of hands and flexible fingers, had terminated our wrists with the hoof of a horse, mankind would doubtless have been destitute of art, habitation, and defense against other animals. Wholly employed in the care of procuring food and avoiding the beasts of prey, we would have still continued wandering like fugitive flocks" [*De l'Esprit*]. Carried to its logical absurdity, as Diderot has commented, "a Doctor of the Sorbonne would become a dog if he only miraculously were given the form of a dog, and vice versa."

The reason Helvétius did not take cognizance of differences of brain structure was probably dictated by this desire to maintain the position that all men are originally equal and that they are equally capable of learning. Admitting that brain structure sets the limits to the number of ideas a person could have, to the possibility of relating them and using them, then one could always attribute differences between men to differences of brain structure, and the possibility of education of any person would thereby be greatly limited. Helvétius, therefore, denies that brain structure sets a limit to human intelligence. The reason which he assigns for this view is that "we cannot form a clear idea of greater or lesser sensibility of the nerves "[*De l'Homme*].

The soul, then, is a potential power of the organism, not an entity. What is that function of the organism that is called "soul?" Passive observation of the things that go on about it. The organism does not originally reach out for objects. Outer objects impinge on it. When they do so, the organism becomes sensitive to them, or perhaps, more exactly, to the modification they induce in our organism. Broadly speaking, the organism is sensitive to any object in two ways. A rose is brought near us. We become sensitive to its color, scent, size, shape, etc. These together are projected in the rose. When the mind is formed, each of these items is considered as a relation between the rose and other roses, or other objects. But besides these, we also experience a certain feeling of pleasure. This feeling is not projected into an external object. When we begin to think in terms of relations—this feeling is a relation between the rose and us rather than between it and some object not us. The organism, because of its having the "soul" function, thus passively receives representative feelings or sensations and affective feelings. In the last analysis, however, both are but modifications of the organism. The first kind of feeling, as we shall see, is the source of all our numerous ideas, all our sciences. The second kind of feeling—really reducible to pleasure and pain feeling—is the source of all our passions, appetites, aversions, and valuations, even our intellectual valuations.

It might be asked: How do our mental activities come about? How do we get memory, judgment, desire, seeing that our organism is originally endowed with only sensibility? Condillac . . . considered these "faculties" as transformations of sensation. Helvétius is even more extreme. Sensing in its double aspect is, in itself, remembering, judging, and desiring and all that constitutes mental activity. For what is remembering an object—for example, an oak tree, if not "having my interior organs in the same situation as when I saw the oak," which situation constitutes a sensation. As to judgment, it is not to be conceived of as the product of an act of judging that results from a distinct power or capacity for judgment. It is simply the copresence of two sensations which, necessarily involves a sensation of difference or agreement between them. A desire is clearly nothing but a judgment or a sensation that a certain object—the desired object—will give us pleasure. The soul, or the "faculty of sensation," embraces all the faculties, which really are the same faculty under different conditions, aspects of the same activity.

This first paradox of Helvétius, that all the activities of the mind are simply different aspects of the same passive power of feeling, is, in substance, identical, as has already been suggested, to the position maintained by Condillac. We shall not enter here into a discussion as to whether Helvétius borrowed his idea from Condillac, or whether, as [Albert] Keim suggests, he arrived at it independently as a result of his analysis of Locke's thought. This is of very little importance. The important point is that Helvétius has formulated this paradox in order to convince himself, as well as others, of the great possibilities open to education as an agent of progress, while Condillac accepted it from purely theoretical considerations. If you have distinct faculties, irreducible, you will be forced to admit natural limitations to education. But if these faculties are nothing but the one passive power of sensation, and if this sensation, it once being shown, is not a differentiating ele-

ment between individuals, and is "constant and plentiful," the possibilities of education become stupendous.

Given, then, this original sensitivity to objects and their mutual relations and to the pleasure and pain that accompany them, and given a universe of objects that impinge on our organism, the mind soon begins to grow like a snowball gathering snow as it rolls along.

The constituent elements of the mind are ideas and desires—ideas of the relations between objects and desires and aversions directed to and away from objects. Every impinging object leaves a trace in the organism. These traces constitute the mind. Mind is memory or, rather, the things and relations remembered. "Relations," of course, is here used in the double sense of relations between object, expressed as agreement and disagreement, and relations between object and us, expressed as pleasure and pain. Thus, all definite content of man and his nature is acquired.

It might be asked: How does the aggressive, outreaching self that deliberately increases its knowledge, that actively evaluates things and acts accordingly, take the place of the passive mind with its sensations, judgments, desires, etc.? Helvétius' theory of the generation of the passions from self-love and his account of their function, when once generated, not only gives his answer to this question, but throws light on his general conception of the nature and conduct of the individual. To a consideration of this we shall therefore direct our attention.

At birth . . . the individual is endowed only with the capacity for feeling pleasure and pain. But he does not know what pleasure and pain are until objects which, upon affecting the individual in these ways, are brought within the sphere of his consciousness. But as soon as these objects impinge on him, he learns two things, (a) to love the particular objects that are accompanied by pleasure and to hate those that give pain, and, (b) to love his pleasure and to hate his pain. "Man is animated by a principle of life which is corporeal sensibility. This sensibility is produced by a love of pleasure and hatred for pain. It is from those two sentiments, united in man and always present in his mind, that is formed what we call the passion of self-love" [*De l'Homme*]. In the strict sense, self-love is acquired, for at birth the individual has no self to love. But in germ it is present in the sensibility to pleasure or pain that the individual in the first moment of his existence possesses. It is in this sense that "self-love, a sensation necessary to the preservation of the species, is engraven by nature in a manner not to be erased" [*De l'Esprit*]. This biologically important passion of self-love manifests itself in a search for happiness, in an effort to increase the sum total of pleasure, which, in turn, manifests itself in a search of those objects that give pleasure and alleviate pain immediately, or that are of aid in the attainment of this. The memory of an experience having been pleasant or instrumental in bringing about pleasure is the deciding factor in the choice of the experience. The general name for the passion for mastery over the objects which may be of value in the quest for pleasure is love of power. The love of power is composed, however, of a number of specific passions. Some of these are strong passions—"passions the object of which is so necessary to our happiness that without the possession of it life would be insupportable" [*De l'Esprit*]. Diagramatically, the genealogy of the passions may be represented as follows: sensibility —→ self-love —→ desire for happiness —→ desire for power —→ passions.

A distinction ought to be made between natural passions, those which a person would have even if he did not live as a member of society, those which are simply the results of natural unfolding of the biological principle of desire for pleasure and aversion to pain on the one hand, and the special forms this natural self-love takes due to man being a member of organized society on the other. Food and sex desires are good representatives of passions of the first class; and pride, avarice, ambition, love of esteem, of the second.

It is due to social pressure that man acquires the social passions. Man is an animal, "sensible, weak and formed to propagate his species." Being sensible, he feels pleasure and pain; being weak, he unites with other men to pursue his pleasure, as against animals; because he propagates his species, he has to enter certain conventions with other men in order to be certain that his own rights and liberties will be respected. It is thus in his interest to form society. Society itself is the product of man's narrow self-interest. Society, once formed, shapes our self-love. Self-love takes on special forms. We begin to love money because it is of value in social intercourse. We begin to love esteem because esteem will facilitate our social power—our employing other men to satisfy our desire for pleasure.

It should be noted that, to Helvétius, neither in the case of a "natural" nor in the case of a social passion, is it a drive toward an object, but rather toward pleasure. The end of the passion is not the attainment of the object toward which it is directed, but the pleasurable effect of the attained object on the self as an agent. The intensity of a passion is proportional to the pain and pleasure involved.

Helvétius takes great pains in establishing the reduction of all passions to the passion of self-love—of desire for pleasure and repugnance to pain. "In the passions, such as avarice, ambition, pride, and friendship, which seem least to belong to the pleasures of sense, we always either seek natural pleasure or shun natural pain" [*De l'Esprit*]. Thus wealth is valued, not for its own sake, but for the pleasure it may procure. Ambition is nothing but desire of possession of the means to reward those who can give us pleasure and punish those who would pain us. "The desire of greatness is only founded on the love of pleasure and the fear of pain. . . . We do not love esteem for its own sake, but for the advantages it procures" [*De l'Esprit*]. The passion for esteem thus differs from what we conceive as the instinct for approval or of mastery. These latter are conceived tendencies directed toward external objects, tendencies to transform them. The desire for esteem, on the other hand, is the desire for objects to produce effects on us.

Even the altruistic sentiment of friendship, the love of other persons, is, Helvétius maintains, in the last analysis, nothing but love of one's own happiness—one's own pleasure. The intensity of friendship varies with the need one has for the other. Disinterested friendship is either hypocrisy or self-delusion. We relieve the unfortunate for the pleasure it will bring us. A mother loves her child only because she loves her own pleasure. Remorse is nothing more than "bodily pain to which some crime has exposed us. . . . Remorse begins where impunity ends" [*De l'Homme*].

Helvétius, of course, does not limit the determinant of all action to immediate pleasure. He takes cognizance of the fact that persons sometimes behave in a manner not resulting in immediate pleasure. In such cases the agent's actions are determined by projected pleasure. Helvétius emphasizes that projected pleasure is, in a very important respect, also immediate pleasure.

The self being originally distinct from the environment and other selves, modified by the environment, but never fusing with it, always remains distinct from it. It always remains enclosed, self-centered, spatial, excluding all other things. It may be modified, but once modified it is again enclosed. Clearly, then, such a self can act, when it acts deliberately, only for itself, for the effects of the action on itself. This gives us the clue to Helvétius' conception that man acts because of his "interest," and to his conception of the passions. . . .

It is these passions, these desires, that account for our actions, for our evaluations, for our achievement of knowledge, as well as for the errors we commit. Men act only to satisfy their desires. They evaluate a thing "good" when it is instrumental in bringing about pleasure, "bad" when bringing about pain, "right" when in agreement with them, "wrong" in disagreement, "ingenious" when profitable or interesting, "insipid" when unprofitable or uninteresting. There is general agreement about the proposition in geometry only because persons have no interest in disagreeing with it, else there would have been disagreement. Man is a closed entity. He is distinct from everyone and everything else. His pleasure and his present ideas must, therefore, be criteria of value and truth, respectively.

That the passions supply the drive for the acquisition of knowledge is Helvétius' strongest conviction. Knowledge consists of observed relations between external objects. Whereas the observation that contact with one body is accompanied by pleasure and with another by pain is immediately observed, this observation furnishing its own motive, the observation of relations between two external objects requires ulterior motivation to bring it about. "All comparison of objects with each other supposes attention, all attention trouble, and all trouble, motive for exerting it" [*De l'Homme*]. Now, the motive for this is supplied by the passions, by the love for money, for esteem, for power. We learn to know something because we think that the knowledge acquired will help us in our quest for pleasure. The mental achievement of a person therefore varies with the intensity of his passions. The man of genius is a man of strong passions, the stupid man is devoid of them.

But the passions not only cause progress of the mind. They also cause its opposites, error and stagnation. Lassitude, caused by inactivity, has to contend with idleness. It makes search and observation painful. Pride prevents the acceptance of some truths; our "interests," of others. Passions prevent us from seeing things objectively and thus getting an adequate idea of the relationship between them.

> Passions lead us to error because they fix our attention on that particular part of the object they present to us, not allowing us to view it on every side. . . . The same passions, however, which are the germ of an infinity of errors are also the sources of our knowledge. If they mislead us, they, at the same time, impart to us the strength necessary for walking. It is they alone that can rouse us from the sluggishness and torpor always ready to seize on the faculties of our souls [*De l'Esprit*].

Helvétius holds the man of passions much superior to the man of sense. Through passions we rise to the highest mental attainment and loftiest moral level. The passions are the driving forces of history. The kaleidoscopic changes in the story of humanity are due to them.

The educational applications of Helvétius' view of the nature and function of passions are clear. Strengthen the passions, but at the same time direct them in a way that will make for mental progress. . . .

Helvétius' aim is . . . to show the great powers of education and legislation, to convince people that these agents can mold moral characters, that they can make for an enormous acceleration in cultural progress. This he does by showing that originally there is no mind and no character, that both mind and character come from environment, that all differences in character and in mind are due to differences induced by different environments. Subject all "ordinarily well organized" persons to the identical environmental situation from the first moment of their lives and you will get individuals absolutely identical in mental equipment and character traits. As far as mentality and character go there are no original differences between sexes, nations, individuals, and social classes.

That the mental equipment of a person is entirely due to his environment is clear from the consideration that the mind is constituted and exhausted by the ideas of the mutual relations between the external objects and between them and us. It is quite clear that, given the same objects, the same set of ideas and the same mind would result. To the objection that individuals vary originally in the degree of their sensitivity, he replies that this would not cause a difference in minds since it is the relations between sensations rather than the intensity of the sensations themselves that form the constituent elements of the mind. " . . . Men always perceiving the same relations between the same objects, the unequal perfection of their senses has no influence on their understanding" [*De l'Homme*]. Nor can difference in capacity for remembering account for differences in understanding. Repetition and attention can compensate for lesser capacities, if capacities really differ in extent. "Between those whom I call well organized that great disproportion visible in point of memory is not so much the effect of the unequal perfection of the organs that supply it with material as an unequal attention to improve it" [*De l'Esprit*]. Furthermore, "men being com-

monly well organized are endowed with an extent of memory sufficient to raise the most lofty ideas." The degree of attention depends solely on the motive, on the "interest" to observe relationships, on the intensity of the passions. But since passions themselves are acquired and differ with differing environments, the variation in their intensity is not an original differentiating element. Self-love is equally present in all of us. The definite direction of self-love, too, is acquired. Therefore "all men organized in a common manner are susceptible, not only of passions, but of the habitual degree of passion necessary to elevate them to the highest ideas" [*De l'Esprit*]. What constitutes an ordinarily well organized person, Helvétius does not tell us. But the meaning is clear—there are no original differences between persons who are not below normal.

This being the case, "superiority of the understanding depends . . . on a certain concourse of circumstances." Even genius is a product of environment. Genius "always supposes invention." This invention, this new creation, is not *ex nihilo*. The fact of the matter is that the genius contributes but a small share of the idea or work attributed to him. Arts develop from generation to generation. The genius adds that imperceptible step which makes it perfect. In other words, much of the growth of culture attributed to genius is really due to culture itself—to the environment by which the genius is surrounded. Many inventions attributed to genius, especially those in the arts, are really due to sheer chance. But even in the case of genius proper, resulting in the discovery "of a new combination or a new relation perceived between objects," chance supplies the necessary conditions. "Conditions" is really a mild word to describe the relation of chance to genius. Chance supplies the necessary causes. "The most striking characters are sometimes the *product* of an infinity of little accidents" [*De l'Homme*]. As evidence of the validity of his position, Helvétius cites the cases of many men whose contributions to civilization were, as he sees it, determined by chance. Milton's enforced leisure resulted in his *Paradise Lost*; Vocanson's accidental observation of the regularity of the pendulum, in the invention of the clock. Clearly, Helvétius was confusing a condition with a cause, but the point is precisely this, that environmental conditions were, to him, really causes. "Genius, then, is the remote product of incidents and chances." Institutions, education, incidents, cultural characteristics, all share in the making of genius and in the determining of the prevalent type of genius. The environment performs a double function in the creation of genius. It supplies material objects, culture, from which ideas are to be drawn, and it shapes the passions to the observation of those relationships the discovery of which constitutes genius; and the second function is by no means second in importance.

The conclusion of all these considerations is that potential genius is greater than our actual genius. Almost anyone can conceivably be a genius. Anyone who is capable of understanding a proposition in geometry is equally capable of inventing a new one. There are few geniuses, because only few are placed in an environment necessary for its production.

What applies to mind applies equally to character. Man

being born without passions is also born without character. Character is the "manner of seeing and feeling." It is the product of the linking of the passions to certain objects. Individual, as well as national character, is determined by environment. When change takes place in the environment a change also takes place in character. Thus, the character of a person undergoes a change when transferred from the company of his children and slaves and "placed in the company of lions." Man is born without ideas and without passions, but is born an imitator and docile to example; consequently, it is to instruction that he owes his habit and his character.

Like individual character national character is a product of environment—of national institutions. With changes in these, national character changes. "The liberty of which the English are so proud, and that really includes many virtues, is less the reward of their courage than the gift of fortune." He denies that the superiority of northern peoples is due to the

> superiority of courage and strength which nature has given them. . . . People can not otherwise support the opinions that they have of the strength of the peoples of the north but by the history of their conquest. . . . All nations may form the same pretensions, justify them by the same reason, and believe that each is equally favored by nature" [*De l'Esprit*].

The great factors in determining national character are education and institutions. Despotism makes for docility, and lack of virtue, while free institutions make for love of liberty, virtue, and genius. National character changes "at the moment of revolutions when people pass on a sudden from liberty to slavery." The record of the Roman people is employed by Helvétius to illustrate this.

Why, then, do individuals and nations attribute their acquired mind and character traits to original nature since it is clearly the results of environment? The answer to this question is to be found in human folly. Folly, which is common to all nations and is in part produced by their vanity, makes them "regard as a gift of nature that superiority which some have over others, a superiority that is solely owing to the political institutions of the nation" [*De l'Esprit*]. It is an attempt of people to claim "to be a superior race of mankind." But this claim has no foundation in fact. Chance, culture, opportunity, institutions, are the causative factors of their superiority.

The growth of culture of a people is conditioned by the culture it already has, its institutions, laws, education, tastes, etc. The culture may be such as to discourage growth, or to encourage it. In a democratic country where genius is needed and socially valued, geniuses make for the growth of culture. In despotic countries, on the other hand, where there is no social appreciation for genius, culture is stagnant.

Likewise is the quality of culture conditioned by the same factors. It has changed with the changing interests of society. The quality of culture has no relation whatever to original racial characteristic. It is entirely determined by social factors. "The Orientals owe to their form of government that allegorical genius which forms the underlying character of their work" [*De l'Esprit*].

Man is entirely a product of his culture and he augments it, or not, according to the cultural conditions to which he is subject. When he does augment it he does so in the way determined by the present culture, in which medium he works. It is interesting to note that though an environmentalist, Helvétius denies any influence to climate. This he does in direct contradiction to Montesquieu. He says that "it is to moral causes, and not to particular temperature, that we ought to attribute the conquests of the northern peoples" [*De l'Esprit*]. The denial of the influence of climate is so frequently repeated that it is evident that he considered his view on the subject important. In this he was possibly influenced by his desire to emphasize the unlimited possibilities of control. Though environment on the whole lends itself to deliberate control, and thus can be used as a point of leverage in bringing about desirable changes, climate is a factor in it that does not readily lend itself to this. Helvétius, therefore, tried to discount its importance.

This, then, is how Helvétius conceived the origin, the growth and activity of the self. . . .

. . . . .

Helvétius' ethical teachings deserve an important place in the history of ethical thought, for their relations to the ethical thought of his time, for the boldness and breadth of his conceptions, and for the influence he exercised on subsequent ethical thinkers.

[The] period of Helvétius was characterized by an effort to free morality from arbitrary religious and metaphysical norms and to found it on the laws of human nature, to substitute utility for self-abnegation as the criterion of the moral act, and to found a science of morality by applying these principles. Helvétius has so successfully summed up the ethical thought of his day and so clearly and fully articulated the ethical implications of sensationalist philosophy, that he has aroused the opposition of most thinkers who were allied with him in spirit, such as Diderot, Voltaire, and D'Alembert. This opposition has led [Jules] Barni [in his *Les Moralistes François du XVIIIe Siecle*, 1873] to believe that Helvétius was not the "veritable expression of the eighteenth century, since he was contradicted by the greatest spirits of his time." In this statement he clearly mistakes opposition of the less extreme adherents of an idea to one who would carry the idea to its logical conclusion, for a real opposition of principles. For, after all, Diderot's morality, having as its basis, as it would appear, some moral element in original human nature, something akin to Shaftesbury's "moral sense" and Rousseau's somewhat similar view, are but mid-point between arbitrary morals and sensationalistic morals—half-way attempts, in the eyes of a sensationalist, to base morality on human nature. Helvétius realized this and he moved to the extremity of the line. The others remained midway.

Morality, thinks Helvétius, ought to become an exact science. Its method, as the method of other sciences, is to be experimental and observational. In Helvétius' own words, "Morality ought to be treated like all other sciences and founded on experiment" [Preface to *De l'Esprit*]. "The principles of morality, like those of other sciences, ought to be established on a great number of facts and observations" [*De l'Homme*]. "In France," says Keim [in his *Helvétius, Sa Vie et Sa Oeuvre,* 1907], "he (Helvétius) has made the first great effort at establishing an independent scientific rational morality."

In order to establish this moral science two things are essential, one negative and one positive. First, morality must free itself from religion and arbitrary teachings; and second, a firm basis must be found from which the newer morality can be deduced. Helvétius is equally forceful in both these ventures.

He points to the lack of correlation between faith and moral conduct. "There are in every country a great many sound believers and but few virtuous men. Why? Because religion is not virtue. All belief and all speculative opinions have not commonly any influence on the conduct and probity of a man" [*De l'Homme*]. Morality is interreligious instead of being characteristic of any particular religion. It is, therefore, in some other principle than in faith that we must seek the source of our moral conduct, which, when found, will serve as a basis for morality. Nor is this principle to be found in dogmatic maxims. The fact that we are told to do or not to do a certain thing does not give it a moral sanction. Furthermore, these maxims, dogmatic morals, are not efficient determiners of actions.

Neither moral nature nor the experience of pain and pleasure suffered by others is the origin of our socially useful actions— only self-love. This is the great paradox of Helvétius.

—Mordecai Grossman

What, then, is the source of moral valuation? Human nature. We must know how the necessary laws of mutual action of man and his environment determine his conduct. This will give us the central principle of a possible morality, a morality of which human beings are capable, as well as the means of putting it into effect. Psychology— behavioristic psychology, as Helvétius understood it—was to be the basis of this. Ethics was to be applied psychology. This psychological principle Helvétius thought he discovered in "interest"; namely, that man's actions are determined by their judgment as to the pleasure or pain resulting therefrom.

Having thus defined moral value in terms of personal interest, he had even the stronger grounds for making morality independent of religion and other forms of dogmatism. Moral value in terms of "interest" conflicted with moral value in terms of dogmatism. One had to make room for the other.

Finally, Helvétius importance in ethics is due to his great influence on subsequent ethical thought. It is sufficient to point to his influence on Bentham, whose formula "the greatest good to the greatest number" is substantially a restatement of Helvétius' "public welfare," and through him to his influence on the Mills, to realize the extent of his influence. . . .

Having pointed out the salient features of Helvétius' moral philosophy and its importance in the history of ethics, let us get a somewhat closer view of his ethical teachings. We have seen that to Helvétius, narrow sensationalist that he was, the self, empty at first and becoming equipped with ideas and passions as it became subject to an everwidening environment, remained, nevertheless, always distinct from its environment, from other human beings, as well as from inanimate objects. The self experiences only its own modifications which are accompanied by pleasure and pain feelings. It could know only these modifications. It can feel its own pain and pleasure only. These were the only two value feelings it had. Value, therefore, could be only in terms of pleasure or pain, and pleasure and pain felt by the individual. Virtue, justice, and all other moral values, are values only because they are descriptive of actions performed by us or by others which cause us immediate or remote pleasure. Vice and injustice, on the contrary, are those actions that cause us pain. Even the objective value of truth is really subjective, since in cases that make a difference, truth is defined by our interest, even if that interest is no more than having our opinion confirmed. We cannot value external things and actions. We value only the pleasurable feeling within us. "It is always ourselves we love in other."

This is the logic of Helvétius' ethics. Self-love—the desire for pleasure and for the means of attaining pleasure and the repugnance to pain—is the prime mover of our actions. Naturally, this leads to an ethical relativity. "All men tend only to their happiness. . . . It is a tendency from which no one can be diverted" [*De l'Esprit*]. The objects that bring this happiness vary with persons, with the time, with their experiences, for with the varying experiences the persons, too, vary. Helvétius' survey of the actions of mankind discloses the fact that people have always called virtuous those actions that have happened to work in the direction of their happiness. An individual calls virtue that which tends in the direction of his pleasure. Groups call virtuous those actions which bring pleasure to them as an "assemblage of individuals." The larger public calls virtuous that action which is useful to its members. When the interests of one group conflict with those of another or with those of an individual an act virtuous with regard to one will be vicious with regard to another. Stealing was virtuous in Sparta, because it was useful there, whereas to other peoples it was vicious. "The interest of the state, like all human institutions, is subject to a thousand revolutions. The same custom becomes successively useful and prejudicial to the same people" [*De l'Esprit*], and so turns from virtue to vice. Virtue is, therefore, a name having a different meaning-content from time to time, and not a certain definable and constant norm of action, as Plato thought. The view of the constancy of the content of virtue is based, according to Helvétius, "on the ingenious, but unintelligible, dreams of Plato." Public morality is, therefore, no more than useful customs changing from time to time.

Since "probity" does not correspond to any constant particular mode of action and since it is at any single time relative to person or persons to whom it is useful, Helvétius somewhat arbitrarily defines virtue as the "desire of the happiness of mankind," as the desire for "public interest." Virtue, properly speaking, is probity with regard to the public. Virtue is relative. There is virtue with regard to the individual, with regard to a small society and with regard to the larger public. When one speaks of "probity" he must, strictly speaking, specify from whose point of view it is such—individual, small groups, or large groups. However virtue in the larger sense is the "desire" of the happiness of mankind, or the desire of what is in "public interest." This broader virtue, while measured by the happiness of the large groups, yet has its claims on the individual who is a member of it.

At this point we get to the salient feature of Helvétius' thought. It is perfectly intelligible why the public, an assemblage of individuals, will call an act which brings each and all of them pleasure a virtuous act. It is also clear why that action is designated as virtuous by a particular individual who is benefited by that act. But why shall an individual, without knowing how a certain act will affect him personally, only knowing that the public will be benefited by it, consider it virtuous? What claim does it have on him? In saying that it is virtue and that it has a claim on the individual, Helvétius at first seems to contradict himself and to say that man is to do the impossible—to value what is not valuable to him. But the point is precisely this, that self-interest always drives man to socially useful actions. There is no need of supernatural sanctions. The sanction of self-interest is all sufficient.

Perhaps a comparison of Helvétius' position with those of thinkers that have influenced him will be of aid in getting the full force of this point. Locke, we have seen, considered a man actuated by pleasure and pain, but had to appeal to extraneous forces to get full moral action. Hobbes, whose conception of personality, spatial, enclosed, and excluding the personalities of others, which Helvétius seems to have accepted, was convinced that the good of society could never be an end of individual action. Force or narrow interest always determined it. La Rochefoucauld's *Maxims,* in a sense, is a precursor of Helvétius. He, too, considers self-love as the prime mover of our actions. In fact, in many cases there is a point to point correspondence between Helvétius and La Rochefoucauld. Great actions, to him as well as to Helvétius, are due to chance and passions. A few quotations from the *Maxims* will bear out the point. "We should often be ashamed of our best actions if the world saw all their motives." "We cannot love but on our own account." "What is commonly called friendship is but a partnership." "The love of justice is in most men only the fear of suffering injustice." "Pity is the sense of our own misfortunes in those of others." "Self-love is the love of self and of all things for self . . . self-love whereof the whole of our life is but one long agitation. The sea is its living image and in the flux and reflux of its continuous waves is a faithful expression of the stormy succession of its thought and its eternal motion."

Helvétius bases his ethics on the very same elements. But he makes more of them. As in Locke, pleasure and pain remain the only determinants of action. As in Hobbes, the individual remains self-enclosed. As in La Rochefoucauld, virtue is disguised self-love. But whereas to La Rochefoucauld self-love was sterile, Helvétius builds on it a satisfactory social morality, a morality that others would think only altruism could serve as its adequate foundation. He does not say with him that "men would not live long in society if they were not the mutual dupes of one another." Primary self-love leads to another self-love which shows itself not in duping but in serving others. Nor does he agree with him in that "our virtues are only disguised vices"—they are virtues. He never posits, on the other hand, a moral sense which tells what is moral, nor does he believe in original sympathy which makes us experience the pain and pleasure of others. Neither moral nature nor the experience of pain and pleasure suffered by others is the origin of our socially useful actions—only self-love. This is the great paradox of Helvétius.

That virtue is the desire for public happiness and that it is a transformation of self-love, yet always remaining self-love, are the two salient points of Helvétius' ethics. Before we attempt to show how Helvétius conceived this transformation possible and how it took place, we shall dwell on the idea of virtue as desire for public utility. In this respect the influence of classical antiquity seems to have been dominant. Whenever Helvétius wishes to exemplify "real" virtue he refers to Rome, Athens, and Sparta. The idea of virtue as subjective and as limited to a narrow circle of action in European thought took root under the influence of Christianity and because of the breakdown of the democratic institutions of antiquity. During the heyday of Athenian democracy and republican institutions in Rome, virtue was social and objective; it pertained to those actions having a broad social significance. It is only when social interests were removed from the sphere of actions of individuals that petty virtues set in and the subjective element gained in importance. This condition Helvétius protested against. Social purposes must not be severed from individual activity. Government must be democratized. This found its ethical expression in "virtue is the desire for public happiness"—democratic social ethics. If anyone wishes to be virtuous he ought to take a hand in the realization of public purposes. The virtuous man is the "good citizen."

Helvétius, in his intenseness to establish this morality, criticised severely the older petty individual subjective morality which he characterized as either prejudical or hypocritical. "I give the name," Helvétius writes [in *De l'Esprit*], "of prejudicial virtue to all those where an exact observance of them does not in the least contribute to public happiness. . . . These false virtues are in most nations more honored than true virtues and those that practice them held in greater veneration than good citizens." Past periods in history, as well as his own time, showed amply customs and morals which, far from being useful, were injurious to the public. Hypocritical moralists are "known on the one hand by coldness with which they discuss these vices big with the fall of empires, and on the other hand by their impotent invectives against private vices. It is in vain for such to say that they have the public welfare at heart" [*De l'Esprit*]. Petty censorship, self-abnegation, conformity to certain maxims, do not constitute morality. Only an intelligent examination of what really is useful to the public and abiding by it—only the union, the identification, of private and public interests, constitutes morality. Nor is he sentimental as to the choice of means. Thus, he suggests that "fine women" be offered as prizes for publicly beneficial acts, being convinced that this would increase virtue. Individuals count for nothing when the public interest is concerned. "Everything becomes lawful and even virtuous that procures public safety" [*De l'Esprit*].

Two points should be made clear. *(a)* The social utility in question is to be entirely empirical. It is to be measured by the sum total of happiness, or, better expressed, sense pleasure of the individuals concerned. It is to be the greatest pleasure to the greatest number—not the realization of an abstract social ideal. Then *(b)* the society in question was the nation. The greatest number were to be the greatest number of men subject to the same government. Helvétius was convinced that the interests of nations conflict so much that unless "nations by reciprocal laws and conventions should unite together as families composing one state and that the love of country becoming extinguished in the heart should give place to the more extended flower of universal love . . . the actions of a single person cannot contribute to the general happiness" [*De l'Esprit*].

We are coming now to the most difficult question—the possibility of bridging of the two, self-love and the desire for public happiness. Self-love and desire for social welfare would seem to be incompatible in view of Helvétius' conception of human nature. How derive virtue from individual self-love, the only spring of human action? Helvétius recognizes throughout a group of people, few, it is true, who succeeded in freeing themselves from personal interest, who work for the general happiness. How does this become possible? The answer is to be found in Helvétius' view of the plastic nature of the individual, or rather, in the influence of the environment on the self. The social environment so acts on the plastic self that the working for public good becomes an expression of its very self-love. Moral character, justice, sympathy, virtue, are not original. They are made by social pressure.

We shall permit Helvétius himself to speak on this point. "Men having sensibility for themselves and indifference with respect to others, are neither good nor bad, but ready to be either. . . . The savage has no idea of equity in his heart" [*De l'Esprit*]. He acquires it only upon living in society. As to sympathy, man

> born without ideas . . . every idea in man, even his humanity, is an acquisition. . . . When a child has been used to put himself in the place of the wretched, this habit gained, he becomes touched with their misery, as in deploring the fate of human nature in general and for himself in particular that he is concerned. . . . Nothing is more absurd than the theological philosophy of Shaftesbury. . . . The happiness of man is

not necessarily connected with the happiness of others [*De l'Homme*].

But social pressure links these inseparably together. "Natural sensibility and personal interest have been the authors of all justice" [*De l'Esprit*], because of the social environment of individuals.

But how did this social environment come to exist? "Dispersed in the woods like other voracious animals," says Helvétius in speaking about primitive men . . .

> the first men, being too weak to oppose the wild beasts and becoming instructed by danger, necessity, or fear, perceived that it was for their natural interest to enter society and to form a league against the animals, their common enemies. . . . These men, thus assembled, soon became enemies, from the desire of possessing the same thing, and took up arms mutually to ravish them from each other. At length, instructed by their common misfortunes, they perceived that their union could be of no advantage to them and that society could not exist without adding new conventions to the first by which each individual should renounce to make use of his own strength and dexterity contrary to the interests of the whole, and all in general should reciprocally guarantee the life and substance of each [*De l'Esprit*].

"Interest and want are the principles of sociability" [*De l'Homme*].

Now society once formed through the calculating interest of individuals, makes through institutions, laws, rewards, and punishments, what is in its interests pay and thus transforms egotistic self-love into social self-love. It makes unsocial action unprofitable, and thus discourages it. Through thus associating virtue with pleasure and vice with pain, virtuous character is built up. Those acts that are virtuous bring power to the agents. The desire for power fires the passions of the agents towards the act of virtue. The institutions of a country sometimes make virtuous action the only possible choice. Regulus could not but act valorously in Rome, where cowardice, even in private soldiers, was punished harshly. "Regulus did not, then, expose himself to any danger to which, not a hero, but even a sensible or prudent man would have presented himself to avoid contempt and obtain the admiration of the Romans. The action performed by Regulus was doubtless the effect of an impetuous enthusiasm, but such an enthusiasm could nowhere be kindled but in Rome" [*De l'Esprit*]. Given a social system such as the Romans had, you would duplicate the actions of a Regulus. Society, created by man's self-interest and functioning for the utility of each of its members, can, if properly organized, produce a second self-love which manifests itself in behavior which is sometimes self-sacrificial. Virtue is generated in a social situation in which actions in the direction of public welfare, even those that are painful, are more in conformity with self-interest than those that contribute to narrow self-interest. The degree of virtue practised by citizens varies with the degree to which the social situation approaches the situation necessary to produce virtue. The individual is plastic, but nothing definite to start with. There is no heredity of characteristics. Hence in each generation the de-velopment of virtue depends on the particular social situa-tion of the generation.

The individual good and the social good are, then, in such a situation, two corresponding aspects of the same thing—the moral act resulting in both. The moral action is, there-fore, not the precipitate of a struggle between the higher and the lower self, categorical imperative as against natu-ral tendencies, the individual as against the social. It pre-cipitates from a more or less immediate judgment—in many cases the judgment is so instantaneous not even to be recognized—that, aiming at the social good, is the most profitable and least painful course. "He who, to be virtu-ous, must always conquer his inclinations," says Helvé-tius, "must necessarily be a wicked man" [*De l'Esprit*]. Wickedness, in this case, is ignorance.

Whereas, as Plekhanof remarks [in his *Essays in the Histo-ry of Materialism,* 1896], J. S. Mills merely defined the moral sanction of an action as "the greatest good to the greatest number," Helvétius not only defined this sanction but has also showed how we come to respect this sanction. More than that, he has shown that in well organized socie-ties this sanction is identical with the sanction of self-love.

Helvétius was not primarily interested in this theoretical discussion of the nature and evolution of virtue. His pur-pose was to advocate moral progress. The foregoing ideas were merely intended as a theory of moral progress. The definition of virtue as the public good was to be the criteri-on of the content of moral progress. The evidence of the generation of virtue from self-love through the instrumen-tality of a social situation was intended to serve from the development of a technique of moral progress. Moral progress meant the increase of the general happiness con-stituted of the happinesses of the individuals. It was to be attained through utilization of self-love, through the wise social control and social education of self-love.

The first step necessary to bring about moral progress, in the view of Helvétius, is to realize the truth of the princi-ples which he propounded. If it becomes clear to us that the *mores* have originated in public utility, that public util-ity, real or apparent, is their sanction, we can have a criti-cal attitude toward them and a positive criterion for their reconstruction. Then we will no longer resist the breaking up of the "prejudicial" virtues resulting in social disutility. Recognition of self-love as the basis of all human action will immediately convince of the futility of religion and moral "maxims" as a method of making for the moral conduct of individuals. These are the chief causes for the retardation of moral progress. Those who hide their faces to the fact that man is actuated by self-love do not obviate the fact from making itself felt. Instead of ignoring the fact of self-love, we must utilize our knowledge of it. In not uti-lizing it for purposes of producing virtuous conduct we fa-cilitate vice. Prudishness must be destroyed. We must rec-ognize passions as the prime movers and utilize them for our ends.

The means of utilization of the passions for social pur-poses are social organization, political and economic, leg-islation and education.

Despotic government is incompatible with "virtue." Where persons are compelled to act so as to bring about the happiness of the despot there can be no striving for public happiness. Public esteem cannot be a determiner of action since it does not spell power for the individual. In republican government where general happiness is the aim of the State and where action of public utility results in public esteem which is also power, virtue is characteristic of the individuals constituting it. Great contrasts in wealth, too, undermine-virtue. Money is power. Possess-ing this form of power the very rich need no longer do any-thing that is of public utility to procure what they desire. The very poor, on the other hand, demoralized by their economic state and reduced to a position of semi-slavery, must direct their efforts to the happiness of their superiors. The ideal social organization, then, is one in which public utility is dominant as an ideal, where acting with this as an end is expected from everybody and brings rewards, and where wealth is so distributed that no one is so rich that he could dispense with public esteem and no one so poor as to be deprived from public service. To have virtu-ous individuals we must take the practical step of social and economic reorganization. This however is rather im-plied, than clearly stated, by Helvétius.

Legislation must support social organization in bringing about virtue. "The virtues and vices of a nation are always the effect of its legislation. . . . Morality is no more than a frivolous science unless blended with legislation. . . . The moralist is to indicate the laws of which the legislation insures execution by stamping them with the seal of his au-thority" [*De l'Esprit*]. The objects of legislation, thus, are to carry out those measures that the moralist, because of his knowledge of human nature, finds necessary. Laws, like customs, are to be in conformity with human nature rather than outwardly imposed. Legislation should pro-portion rewards and punishments according to the degree of utility or injury of an action. Extrinsic rewards and pun-ishments play a great rôle in the determination of the ac-tions of an individual. Helvétius makes the statement that "the whole study of the moralist consists in the use that ought to be made of these rewards and punishments and the assistance that may be drawn from them to connect the personal with the general interest" [*De l'Esprit*]. The stress, however, is not on punishment, but on positive re-wards, for while punishment may prevent vice, it does not bring virtue, whereas rewards do bring virtue. Above all, the legislator should aim at the stimulation and the social direction of passions rather than at their suppression. The man of small passions can be neither very virtuous nor very vicious. But the man of great passions can through wise legislation be made of great public utility. A law or custom useful at one time cannot be expected to remain so for eternity. Constant reconstruction of laws and cus-toms should, therefore, be the function of legislators and moralists. . . .

Helvétius was convinced of the possibility of general hap-piness. Though there can be no society in which individu-als are equally rich and powerful, one in which all are equally happy is perfectly possible. "The almost universal unhappiness of men arises from the imperfection of their laws and the too unequal partition of their riches" [*De l'Homme*]. Labor is necessary to one's happiness. Without it men suffer from ennui. Due, however, to the too unequal distribution of wealth, the very poor labor to excess and thus a necessary condition of happiness becomes the cause of misery. The very rich, on the other hand, deprived of the need to labor, become subject to ennui. Change the laws in general, those laws that balk individuals, and change them so that by continual and insensible alterations wealth is equalized, and general happiness will be transformed from a mere possibility into an actuality.

A few of the significant features of Helvétius' ethical system have not yet been fully articulated, though they have been stated implicitly. First of these is Helvétius' belief in the omnipotence of law. We have seen how Helvétius expected general virtue and general happiness to be the outcome of wise legislation. These great expectations are, of course, the logical consequences of a sensationalistic philosophy. Individuals being originally empty, but susceptible to outside influences, can be shaped through law so that a condition of general virtue and happiness results. The dependence of moral conduct on the knowledge of the good is also a very significant trait of Helvétius' ethical theory. Knowledge that morality is based on self-love, that its content is social utility, and of what is under particular circumstances instrumental in bringing about public utility, is essential to general growth of morality. To make this knowledge more widespread he suggests an ethical dictionary and the utilization of a moral catechism. This, too, connects up with the assumptions as to human nature and the inferences drawn from it as to the nature of the "good," for if the social "good" has its aspect of good to the agent, only ignorance can account for immoral conduct. The criterion of public utility calls for objective knowledge in order that it might be applied. It is also important to notice that Helvétius recognized no qualitative differences between pleasures. The only pleasure that is immoral is the one that conflicts with the pleasure of the greatest number.

Before closing we ought also to say a few words about Helvétius' views on religion, especially in its relation to morality. We have seen Locke and Voltaire attribute definite value to religion—deistic religion—in morality. Helvétius thinks religion to be either harmful or futile. We have already referred to Helvétius' denial of religious beliefs influencing moral conduct. Helvétius differentiates between sacerdotal religions with dogmas and a priesthood, and a universal religion having for its content public morality. As to the first, it is not merely futile, but definitely harmful to the cause of morality. The dogmas of religion arising from a fear of death and a desire for immortality are maintained and strengthened by the priesthood for their own interests. In search for their own interests they create conditions which are directly opposite in influence to those essential to sound morality. Utilitarian ethics is conditioned by intelligence and knowledge; the "power of the priests depends on the superstition and stupid credulity of the people" [*De l'Homme*]. Great virtues are made possible by strong passions. But the priests, who have their own interest at heart and not that of the general welfare, in order that they might have a stronger hold on people, teach that the passions are sin. Supernaturalism, other-worldliness,

and asceticism conflict with the only good possible—pleasure. As to the second type of religion, Helvétius recognizes its possibility. Its content is "morality founded on true principles." Its saints are the great benefactors of humanity. Its ethics are, of course, utilitarian. Though Helvétius speaks in laudatory terms of such religion, it appears that it would be futile, for all of its principles would be derived by an enlightened person who lives in an adequate social environment irrespective of whether it is linked with religion or not.

Karl Marx on Helvétius and French Materialism:

The difference between French and English materialism follows from the difference between the two nations. The French imparted to English materialism wit, flesh and blood, and eloquence. They gave it the temperament and grace that it lacked. They civilized it.

In Helvétius, who . . . based himself on Locke, materialism became really French. Helvétius conceived it immediately in its application to social life (Helvétius, **De l'homme, de ses facultés intellectuelles et de son éducation**). Sensuous qualities and self-love, enjoyment and correctly understood personal interests, are the bases of morality. The natural equality of human intelligence, the unity of progress of reason and progress of industry, the natural goodness of man, and the omnipotence of education are the main points in his system.

Karl Marx, in his The Holy Family, *translated by R. Dixon, in* The Karl Marx Library, Volume V: On Religion, *McGraw-Hill Book Company, 1974.*

Joseph J. Spengler   (essay date 1942)

SOURCE: "The Philosophes," in his *French Predecessors of Malthus: A Study in English-Century Wage and Population Theory,* Duke University Press, 1942, pp. 212-63.

[*In the following excerpt, American economist and sociologist Spengler examines Helvétius's theories of wage and population as they are manifest in* De l'homme.]

The Term "philosophes" is usually applied to the group of writers who, in eighteenth-century France, gave expression to the aspirations of the emerging bourgeois class. . . .

[Among the philosophes who were content to say that if superstition were destroyed and reason enthroned, man's lot could be appreciably bettered were] Helvétius and D'Holbach (1723-1789), both of whom were influenced by Locke and Hobbes. Helvétius, inspirer of Bentham's utilitarianism and formulator of the principle of the greatest happiness of the greatest number, and D'Holbach, the most uncompromising and consistent materialist among the philosophes, were alike in that they expressed the population problem in utilitarian terms and insisted that the purpose of political organization was to assure the happiness and rights of all. While neither quite had Condorcet's faith in the future, each at times declared man's lot to be susceptible of great improvement, for each looked upon human behavior as subject to the law of self-interest and, in consequence, controllable through education, custom, government, and laws founded upon utilitarian and hedonistic principles.

Helvétius, mistakenly called "the original precursor of Malthus," traced out the economic and the political consequences of continued population growth, but did not thoroughly integrate his political and economic analyses or attempt a thoroughgoing solution of the population problem. Starting with the assumption of an underpeopled island, Helvétius [in *De l'homme*] reasoned that numbers would continue to grow until all the possible agricultural employments had been filled; that thereafter the additional and usually propertyless increments of population would either have to find employment in urban nonagricultural luxury-producing industries, or emigrate, the alternatives being destruction of the excess population by war (as in Switzerland), or recourse to such practices as child exposure. When the food supply of a country no longer sufficed for the support of its inhabitants, the surplus population was obliged to establish colonies abroad, or, preferably, to engage in manufacturing and exchange fabricated goods for foodstuffs. Accordingly, even though Helvétius was not favorably disposed to luxury per se, especially when it was a result of extreme inequality and urbanization, he nonetheless opposed curbing the consumption of luxuries, because depopulation would result. For were luxury consumption restricted, those who produced luxuries and the agricultural workers who were dependent upon luxury-makers for a market for agricultural products, would be compelled to migrate to adjoining lands. Were France to suppress the production and consumption of luxuries, it would suffer the loss of about one fourth of its population, Helvétius estimated, adding that the foreign countries to which displaced luxury workers migrated would be strengthened.

Population pressure operated directly, at least in France, to depress the wages of the bulk of the population to bare subsistence, one of the effects of "the extreme multiplication of citizens" being "the indigence of the greater part of the inhabitants. . . . Competition depresses the price of the day's work; the worker preferred is he who sells his labor least dearly, that is to say, who most curtails his subsistence. Then indigence spreads, the poor sell, the rich buy, the number of possessors diminishes, and the laws become more severe from day to day." Subsistence wages were also a result of economic inequality, itself the result in part of population pressure. For when a nation had become divided into a small class of wealthy proprietors and a large class of laborers, there were more workers than work, and the workers had to be content with a wage often inadequate even to furnish subsistence. "Besides, the rich man, whose [desire for] luxury exceeds his wealth, is interested in reducing the price of a day's work, in offering to the day-laborer only the pay absolutely necessary for his subsistence. The latter is obliged by necessity to accept it." That Helvétius considered economic inequality and the resultant exploitation of labor to be more important than population pressure as a cause of the lowness of wages

may be inferred from his emphasis upon the need for more equal distribution of property, and from his observation that wages would not increase appreciably until the land was more equally divided and the number of proprietors was increased relative to that of laborers.

Population growth, on a given area, when continued long enough, resulted in a cleavage between employers and workers, between the governed and their representatives, and therefore between the public and the private interest. Both the luxury-loving wealthy and certain classes of employers preferred that there be a large number of persons "who, having no other wealth than their hands, are always ready to employ them in the service of whomever pays them"; for, "the more there are of indigents, the less he [the employer] pays for their labor." Multiplication was not necessarily advantageous to all proprietors, however. The multiplication of propertyless workers could even prove contrary to the interest of the landed proprietors; for were the ruler a tyrant and not a true representative of the landed proprietors, he might arm the propertyless workers and use them against the proprietors. Despotism, in fact, was unlikely to develop until after a country had become densely peopled. Even in the absence of despotism the interests of the ruling class tended to differ from the interests of the governed, in especial from the interests of the landed proprietors, as population became dense. For population growth made representative government necessary, and the representatives of the governed (i. e., really of the landed proprietors), having become concentrated in the capital city and intent upon furthering their own private ambitions, ceased to give expression to the interests of the agriculturalists or to that of the nation. Group and national interests needed to be kept in proper balance; otherwise, population growth, together with accompanying concentration of economic and political power, might bring about the decay of the state. For this and other reasons he at times preached the virtues of enlightened despotism.

As has been implied, Helvétius approved of luxury as a palliative for population pressure only provided that continued population growth had already brought about concentration of wealth and made necessary the maintenance of the demand for labor through luxurious consumption. Population growth did not correlate positively with luxury as such, however; for luxury usually was the product of economic inequality which was per se unfavorable to population growth. Where luxury existed commerce flourished and destroyed the lives of many; taxes were heavy, and the rural population suffered. Indigence weakened the needy and destroyed many of their children, whilst indolence enervated the wealthy. The population was not robust, and its growth was retarded.

Although Helvétius did not conceive of an optimum density of population, his discussion suggests that he desired no greater density of population than was consistent with the prevention of marked inequality and luxury. The happiness of a people, he believed, depended not so much upon the total mass of its wealth as upon the fairly equal division of wealth and income. A state was strong when its population consisted of free and independent men, or proprietors, with a "mediocre fortune"; when everyone could obtain simple but adequate and healthful nourishment. Whatever tended to produce inequality (e. g., commerce) was to be avoided, inasmuch as inequality destroyed the simple virtues, entailed poverty for the many, and resulted in infant mortality and depopulation.

While Helvétius did not specifically pose the problem, it is evident that he did not believe population pressure and its concomitants to be unavoidable; for he subscribed to no such biological determinism as Malthus was later to espouse. Men were similar in their sensibilities, passions, and potential interests; and their social and political attitudes and relationships were the product of external circumstances. It was possible, therefore, to employ education and legislation, founded upon the use of rewards and penalties, to harmonize the individual and the general interest, for the purpose of eliminating the main obstacles to the achievement of comparative equality and of the greatest happiness of the greatest number. It was possible to use taxation and other means to bring about the desired amount of economic equality, to prevent the concentration of wealth and the division of society into useless wealthy drones and starving workers. It was possible, in short, to prevent such evils as were associated with population pressure.

Radoslav A. Tsanoff   (essay date 1942)

SOURCE: "The French Enlightenment," in his *The Moral Ideals of Our Civilization*, E. P. Dutton & Co., Inc., 1942, pp. 290-305.

[*In the following excerpt, Tsanoff presents an overview of the major themes of Helvétius's philosophy, primarily concentrating on* De l'esprit.]

Scarcely any other writer on the eve of the Revolution worked out the ethical principles of French empiricism so patiently, but also so disturbingly and disagreeably as Claude Adrien Helvétius in his books **On Mind** and **On Man.** Helvétius used Lockean psychology and theory of knowledge as materials for ethical-social construction, which was his real interest. He disavowed any doctrine of first principles, and would "construct ethics like experimental physics."

Helvétius derives all ideas and the entire character and essence of mind from the data of physical sensibility, and regards all judgments of approval or disapproval as basically motivated by considerations of personal advantage and utility. He undertakes to establish the following theses: (1) Mental capacity or activity in general is not so much the result of original endowment as of experience and education. (2) Our passions are the dynamic in our lives. They quicken wit, recruit energy, incite to action. In particular, men are moved by the sense of their own interest and by the desire for pleasure and satisfaction. Sensible ethics must therefore abandon the hypocritical or at any rate misguided disdain of passion, pleasure, and selfishness, and should rather openly rely on these real springs of action. (3) A stable social order calls for a system of laws in which concern for the public interest is individually profit-

able to the citizen. The task of a wise government is thus to align social with individual advantage.

Taking up the first of these theses, mental aptitude and capacity, the direction and energy of our activity, are described as the cumulative results of our experience. Our character is the built-up system of our habits. At the very outset we should note the radical democratic animus of this doctrine. There is no inherent preëminence of worth which distinguishes some individuals or classes or nations from others. Men are made what they are by the lives they live; to change a man's character, tastes, point of view, change his environment. This doctrine, ruling out arrogant complacent noblesse and resigned lowliness, incites social upheaval and realignment. One is reminded of the words of Cassius:

> Upon what meat doth this our Caesar feed
> That he is grown so great?

The second main thesis of Helvétius contains the substance of his ethical theory. The first thing a moralist should recognize and keep in mind is that man is a creature of passions, of selfish passions, of desires for pleasure and power. Neglecting to consider the strength of a man's passions confuses our moral estimate of his acts, for virtue always depends on the strength of the passion with which one is contending in deliberation and in choice. The alleged sage may owe his wisdom to his lukewarm passions. In the contest of motives it is not the better reason but the stronger desire which prevails. Passions are in morals what motion is in physics. Avarice, pride, love, hate, envy, lust for power and pleasure, drive and direct man's will. And in all passion the inciting motive is a desire for self-gratification of some sort.

The attraction which an idea or an object has for us is in direct ratio to the advantage which it promises us, and our estimate of the acts of others is dictated by our judgment of how they affect our own interests. Below the veneer of supposedly disinterested approval or condemnation, this substance of all our preferences is disclosed. In valuing the high esteem of others, it is not mere assurance of worth that we seek, but the assured advantage which the esteem of others procures us. And the esteem of others for us is dependent on and proportionate to whatever they may consider to be their own interest in the matter. If a man consults us, he pleases us by thus avowing his inferiority and allowing us to direct his decision as we will. This is subtle flattery which we do not easily resist; and if we do come to detest a flatterer's praise, it is not because we consider it undeserved but because we may suspect it as insincere. In all our dealing with others, each one is always playing for advantage, for position, and for assurance of satisfaction, which is the spring and goal of all activity.

There is no disinterested passion; the most ardent is the most concerned. Friendship and love are born of need, which determines their intensity. Sympathy is no exception to the rule. If we alleviate the distress of others, it is because we thus relieve our own physical discomfort of seeing others suffer (on the principle on which we dislike and seek to remove anything disagreeable or disgusting), because we invite the pleasure of gratitude which gives us evidence of our own superior state and power, and because we thus secure the esteem of others which benevolence earns. Remorse and repentance similarly spring from a disturbed sense of impending punishment: we begin to fear the frustration of our schemes and so reconsider our course of action. Every passion springs from a demand craving satisfaction; the pursuit of pleasure and avoidance of pain thus color our every opinion and estimate of our own acts and of those of others.

How does the idea of virtue arise from this tissue of opinions and passions all voicing our basic selfish desires? Helvétius undertakes to point out that probity in each sphere of relations is always relative to selfish interests. Almost one third of his book *On Mind* is devoted to the establishment of this point. All actions are judged by us either as useful or harmful or indifferent, and condition respectively our approval or condemnation or utter neglegence of them. Be it the judgment of a particular individual or of a special group or society, or of an entire nation, or of the world as a whole, the esteem or disdain of acts always corresponds to the interest or stake which one feels that he has in the matter. Now, from this point of view, I may find it good policy to take account of the interests of others, but how am I to be convinced that I should have genuine respect for the social weal?

We are consistently self-engrossed, Helvétius answers, but we are all aware of the social conditions of our own satisfactions. The hostile scorn of others is a barrier to success or enjoyment, and in their own interest men cannot ignore the importance of social regard or esteem. Though each man basically seeks his own advantage, he is aware of what others expect of him; he makes concessions to that social demand of him, or rather he yields tribute to that regard for the common good which, *in others,* would redound to his own advantage. So, each one of us really demanding his own advantage, we yet agree in collectively approving what is to the general advantage of all. This yields us a definition of virtue and vice as referring respectively to acts socially useful or harmful.

Clearly, then, we have here no genuine social sense. The demand for fair play is a demand to exert our power without undue handicap, is thus a realization that our power could not prevail if handicapped, is in other words a confession of weakness. Justice and equity are prized by those who have to rely on them, but, as men value in themselves preëminence of power over preëminence of justice, so it is not the injustice and the crime of the brigand that we detest but his eventual incompetence to prevail. In craving wealth and glory men and nations really crave power, the assurance of their ability to make their desires prevail. Prevailing and resistless power, as it makes reliance on justice and fair play quite dispensable, also in practice absolves from the corresponding obligations: and not only in practice but in our moral judgments, if we are candid and not hypocritical. A strong nation violates its treaties when and because it so wishes and can do it with impunity. A nation that proclaims its loyalty to its obligations is in fact confessing itself too weak to violate them. Virtue is respected because and so long as it is useful: what each man really values in himself and respects in others is the force which insures satisfaction.

The analysis of human motivation which directs the development of Helvétius' ethics dictates likewise his theory of government and legislation. This is his third principal idea. The practical problem of government is to assure the citizen's obedience to laws and his active support of the larger policies of the state. The effective solution of this problem demands a constant realization of the natural selfishness of men. People cannot be expected consistently to obey laws and support policies which they regard as onerous and in their way. A stable social order requires laws obedience to which is to the citizen's own advantage. This is then Helvétius' political-social program: make it worth a man's while to be a loyal citizen.

This doctrine on the face of it seemed arrant petulance, but it had some unexpected and radical democratic implications. Helvétius was using hedonistic egoism as the basis for a program of social reconstruction that safeguards the rights of the common man. Crime and lawlessness thrive in a society which pampers a few to the neglect of the many. Where the masses are oppressed by tyranny and exploited by a system of laws favoring a selected class, the multitude, having no part and lot in the state, is ever in incipient revolt. Change this system, then! Remember that all men, to the limit of their power, are seeking their own satisfaction, and to that end are seeking increase of power. Distribute as evenly as possible the available goods of life and the means and opportunities of satisfaction. Square the general interest with the individual. At the same time educate men's minds so that they may see ever more clearly that it is to their own advantage to respect the social will. Fill their hearts with love of glory and desire for the esteem of others. The base and the crown of all structure of law is the regard for the people's interest.

What is in the way of moral progress in the social system thus conceived? Mean irresolute statesmanship and fanaticism. Narrow and incompetent politicians ignore the well-being of the commonalty, exploit those whom they regard as too dull and stolid to protest, and blindly tread the path to eventual disaster. Fanaticism neglects the real needs of men and women, to exalt and impose artificial virtues, relying on credulity while contending with the healthiest forces and demands of human nature. Sound and competent statesmanship, ridding itself of hallowed prejudices, should see things human as they really are. Utilize the passionate self-regard of each, to realize the welfare of all!

The publication of Helvétius' work *On Mind* aroused the liveliest interest and the most violent opposition. Substance and form alike won for it friends and enemies in abundance. The loose logic, the straggling course of the argument and its constant diversion to allow for the insertion of a tidbit *bon mot* or gossip irritated the more serious reader and aroused severe criticism; but this very overloading of the book with succulent anecdote made it a great popular success. Madame du Deffand may have asked Voltaire to save her time by selecting for her the alleged pearls in the little brochure of fourteen hundred pages, but she read the whole of it, no doubt, and expressed the current opinion that Helvétius had "betrayed the secret of the whole world." Certainly the courtiers, the idle rich of society, the perfumed ladies felt revealed in the cynical pages, but they were all surprised that precisely Helvétius should have written such a book. For he was generous to the point of eccentricity, a paragon of the social virtues. Lavishly charitable, unvindictive and forgiving even to a fault, scrupulously honest and equitable, a loyal and self-sacrificing friend, a complacent husband, despite his infidelities commanding the utmost devotion of his wife, and one of the most liberal of hosts: his own life gave the lie to his portrayal of human nature. Friedrich in Berlin expressed the wish that Helvétius had let his heart rather than his head dictate his ideas.

Serious thought in France, philosophic and theological alike, criticized the arguments of Helvétius. Voltaire, Rousseau, D'Alembert, Diderot, Turgot admired the man personally, but rejected his doctrine which maligned the generous impulses of human nature. Helvétius, sharing the empiricism of the Enlightenment and its reliance on civilization, struck a disturbing note with his blunt dismissal of its humanitarianism. But the severity of these critics was checked and indeed turned into personal championship of Helvétius by the violent storm of orthodox persecution which swept over him. Parliament condemned and burned his book; humiliating retraction was extorted from him, and even then did not earn him security; all the forces of obscurantism were ranged against him; the affair became a public scandal. Outside of France this storm had few echoes; it even caused amusement, not only in Berlin and London, but also at Rome, and in faraway Petersburg. Throughout Europe his book continued to be read, in fifty editions.

Helvétius had his revenge in his book *On Man,* deliberately written for posthumous publication. This work restated his familiar volume *On Mind,* and in our discussion of his ideas we have used both works. But the later book is even more audacious; its full candor is unleashed against the tyranny, the bigotry and veneered iniquity of king and priest.

Irving Louis Horowitz   (essay date 1954)

SOURCE: *Claude Helvétius: Philosopher of Democracy and Enlightenment,* Paine-Whitman Publishers, 1954, 204 p.

[*Horowitz is a widely-respected American sociologist and philosopher who has written extensively on social activist movements. In the following excerpt, Horowitz describes Helvétius's political philosophy and theory of progress, specifically in contrast to the thinking of other philosophes.*]

Political practice under the *ancien regime* can best be described as Machiavellianism gone mad. Had the court nobility absorbed even a bit more than Machiavelli's "directives" for ruling class conduct, they would have seen that only their extinction could cleanse French society. The rusty feudal political mechanism ran on a combination of venality, court intrigue, sexual debasement and duplicity of all sorts. It had, by the eighteenth century, even made a mockery out of medieval mores. Honor, courage and faith were notions dragged out for window-dressing purposes only. The nobility had formalized everything. Even the dressing and undressing of the king was performed

with amazing pomp and ceremony, involving literally hundreds of people. Mortals paraded about as if they were gods, while the flock paid the bill in sweat and toil. Fundamentally though, these were superficial means disguising the real basis of feudal domination, the exploitation of the peasantry. The reaction to the narrow and barbarous state of political affairs grew with each new indication that neither the first nor second estates were in a position to solve the pressing problems the French masses faced daily. . . .

[To] Voltaire, Diderot and even Holbach, social progress is basically the forward march of the bourgeoisie. To Helvétius, social progress is the political progress of all humanity. The Encyclopedists, while admiring the benefits yielded by English bourgeois constitutionalism, believed that a strong and intelligent monarch would be better able to achieve a smoother functioning middle-class state by eliminating the procrastinating tendencies of the parliamentary system of government. No *philosophe* assumed that parliamentary government was the same as democratic government. They were, if anything, far bolder in advocating civil liberties than their English counterparts. Nor should we forget that they excelled the English even in their absolute respect for and defense of the "rights" of private property against both the "greed and envy" of the masses and the "arbitrary confiscation" of property rights by an hereditary. aristocracy. Voltaire, Diderot and Holbach were democrats to be sure, but democrats who at their very best fought a two-sided battle. As long as the *ancien regime* remained in political power, the landowning nobility and their compatriots, the Roman Catholic Church, bore the brunt of their slicing attacks. But even before the Revolution of 1789, these *philosophes* held that their democratic and egalitarian goals were inaccessible to the ordinary people, who they imagined were more cattle-like than human. Helvétius was among that minority in French intellectual circles who had any understanding of the natural endowments of all men. And he devoted more than minor attention to the possibilities for peace and prosperity of a government basically operated by these troublesome *aumailles* who were men. . . .

The relation of Helvétius to his Encyclopedic associates on the question of political power is two-fold. While paralleling their concept of the enlightened monarch as the dispenser of law and order, he disagreed with their faith in the healing powers of the bourgeoisie. He developed his theory of political rule along the lines of *la thèse democratique.* But he gave it a "proof" and a "popularity" it lacked in the hands of Morelly, Mably and Argenson, namely, the utilitarian motivation of all humanity. If everyone is driven to seek his own best interests, and those interests could only be served in social intercourse, the monarch could really be enlightened only if he served the interests of every man in every class. It is this broad humanism of Helvétius that so sharply differentiates him from his colleagues. Legislation was to be in the name of all people, without class prerogative. The admissible criterion of the success of a legislative program is the amount of happiness it brings each and every person. This is the final test of political progress. The monarch will be a good instrument for political advancement only as long as he abides by the dictums of utilitarianism. The test of his success are the mass of people; not a privileged class or sect, but the measurable wealth in the hands of the producers. All rulers, all laws and all customs must demonstrate their services to present needs. What fails in this test should be discarded, without fanfare and certainly without regrets. Find out what people desire or need and frame laws aimed at securing just that. These were the elemental principles of Helvétius' juridical and political reform program. It was his deep-felt concern with the needs of the great mass of society that prompted Helvétius to scorn the rat-maze of juridical precepts and political edifices inherited from the old order. These inherited evils, which both the adherents of a bourgeois monarchy and a feudal monarchy would subtly preserve, in effect, only "preserve the errors accumulated since the origin of the human race" [cited from a letter to Montesquieu, *Ouevres Completes,* 1818]. If the world had to be made over, let it allow for the happiness of all and not just for the enjoyment of a new privileged class.

Beginning his analysis of past theories of politics, Helvétius sharply calls to task the a-priorism inherent in the views of the Platonic *Republic* and the Augustinian *City of God.* They discussed what "heaven ordained" or what "should and would" be, but they hardly took the trouble to examine what *is.* People rightfully hold such political abstractions in contempt. For they deal not with real problems and real solutions but with distant problems and impossible solutions. "If there is a method to fix public attention on the problem of an excellent legislation, it is by rendering it simple and reducing it to two propositions." These propositions Helvétius thinks are of such a useful nature that no person can fail to recognize their critical significance. "The importance of the first should be the discovery of laws proper to render men as happy as possible, and consequently to procure for them all the amusements and pleasures compatible with the public welfare. The object of the second should be the discovery of means by which a people may be made to pass insensibly from the state of misery they suffer, to the state of happiness they might enjoy" [*De l'Homme*].

To resolve the first proposition, Helvétius suggests that we should follow the example of mathematicians. "When a complicated problem in mechanics is proposed to them, what do they do? Simplify it; calculate the velocity of moving bodies without regarding their density, the resistance of fluids that surround them, their friction with other bodies, etc." In similar manner, to resolve the problem of excellent legislation, we are told not to pay any regard to the prejudices or friction caused by the contradictory interests, or to ossified mores, laws and customs. "The inquirer should act like the founder of a religious order, who in dictating his monastic laws has no regard to the habits and prejudices of his future subjects" [*De l'Homme*]. It is apparent that Helvétius did not realize that he was setting a standard no less abstract and a-priori than Plato. He too, was telling the "inquirer" to disregard the existing levels of human development and frame a perfect utilitarian theory of legislation having no relation to historical reality.

But to discover how people can pass from conditions of misery to those of happiness Helvétius offers entirely different criteria. "It is not after our own conceptions, but from a knowledge of the present laws and customs that we can determine the means of gradually changing those customs and laws, and of making a people pass by insensible degrees, from their present legislation to the best possible" [*De l'Homme*]. Thus thesis two, unlike thesis one, is based completely on laws of history. Helvétius recognizes that there is an essential difference between these two propositions. When the first, unhistorical propositions is resolved, its solution becomes general; the same for all peoples and nations. While the resolution of the second differs widely according to the form and level of social development of each people and nation. Satisfactorily overcoming the problems generated by these contradictory but equally real propositions will inevitably lead to political progress. For it provides for the universal happiness of people, which at the same time takes into account basic differences between people. Progress therefore has two elements, the transient forms any search for happiness takes, and the universal desire of all men for happiness as as end in itself.

In a series of thirty-one "questions" ["Questions on Legislation," *De l'Homme*], Helvétius puts forth the essential features of his theory of legislation and politics. The propositions are so sharply worded that there is little question he intended them not to raise doubt but to answer all doubt as to the correctness of his conception of political progress.

In order to achieve political progress it behooves us first to understand the motives which unite men in society. To this problem Helvétius devotes much time. Society is formed when men realize that the scourges of nature cannot be overcome singly, but only by individuals banded together in common struggle. Therefore, the necessities of material conditions force men to be essentially social in spite of their essentially egoistic natures. Mankind once *united against nature* becomes *divided against one another.* The result is a division of labor, an economically torn society. With the crystallization of these economic and social divisions, people are then "obligated to form conventions and give themselves laws." These laws have as their foundation "the common desire of securing their property, their lives, and their liberty, which, in an unsocial state, is exposed to the violence of the strongest" [*De l'Homme*].

Helvétius likens the stage of savagery to modern despotism. Both have in common the destruction of all bonds of social union. Despotism, like its primitive ancestor, substitutes might for right, the lash of the ruler for the law of people. He then suggests that a certain equilibrium of power among the different classes of citizens be introduced, as it was during the English revolutions of the preceding century. Once this relative harmony of social interests comes into existence during a revolution, the class and individual strife of those on the same side is minimized. After the revolution has achieved its aims, however, Helvétius noticed that there is a resurgence of the very social antagonisms that the revolution had sought to abolish. Just as prior to the revolution, so too after the revolution, a polarization of class interests re-emerges.

The despairing insight of Helvétius concerning the harmony and polarization of social and class interests, leads him to posit a political order which can finally end this cyclical path of development. His conception of the future society may best be characterized as an early form of utopian socialism, in the traditions established by Mably, Morelly and Linguet. "Have the poor really a country?" he asks.

> Does the man without property owe anything to the country where he possesses nothing? Must not the extremely indigent, being always in the pay of the rich and powerful, frequently favor their ambition? And lastly, have not the indigent too many wants to be virtuous? Could not the laws unite the interest of the majority of the inhabitants with that of their country by the subdivision of property? After the example of the Lacedemonians, whose territory being divided in thirty-nine thousand lots, was distributed among thirty-nine thousand families, who formed the nation, might not, in case of too great an increase of inhabitants, a greater or less extent of land be assigned to each family, but still in proportion to the number that compose it? [*De l'Homme*]

Little imagination is necessary to perceive that Helvétius is not posing questions, but providing fundamental answers as to necessary preconditions for achieving a harmonious, equalitarian society.

Helvétius passes on to a different phase of political progress, the development of the legal codes of a state. Pointing out that a great number of involved legal statutes are not infrequently a maze of contradictions made useless by their abstraction from real life situations, Helvétius indicates that such multiplicity of laws leads to ignorance and a failure on the part of governing classes to execute the public will. The only purpose they serve is to institutionalize the oppression of the people and to confuse them concerning what their true interests actually are.

> The multiplicity of laws, often contrary to each other, oblige nations to employ certain men and bodies of men to interpret them. May not these men or bodies of men, charged with their interpretation, insensibly change the laws and make them the instruments of their ambition? And lastly, does not experience teach us, that wherever there are many laws, there is little justice.

Therefore, in repressive governments, the laws serve directly as an instrument of oppression.

In a good society, in a rational political arrangement, one which is concerned only with the welfare of people, a small number of clear and self-evident laws are sufficient. Complicated laws which are interpreted and reinterpreted by enemies of the people's aspirations serve only to further political reaction. Where there are no private interests there will be no need for a complex legal scaffold to keep down the public will. Simple laws are sufficient to establish the simple goal of all humankind, happiness. Just as land should be divided up among all people for the purpose of doing away with conflicts between rulers and ruled, Helvétius advocates dividing up nations into small federations equal in size and political power. In this way, wars, nation-

al oppression, and territorial aggrandizement can finally be abolished.

> May not a certain number of small republics by a federative compact, more perfect than that of the Greeks, shelter themselves from the invasion of an enemy, and the tyranny of an ambitious citizen? If a country as large as France were to be divided into thirty provinces or republics, and to each of them a territory nearly equal (in size) were to be assigned, and if each of these territories were circumscribed by immutable bounds, or its possession guaranteed by the other twenty-nine republics, is it to be imagined that any one of those republics could enslave all the others, that is, that any one man could combat with advantage against twenty-nine men? [*De l'Homme*]

For the purpose of preventing an aggressor nation from commencing warfare against a nation constituted in a democratic federation, Helvétius would impose certain safeguards. On the supposition that these democratic republics

> were governed by the same laws, where each of them took care of its interior police and the election of its magistrates, and reported its conduct to a superior council; or where the superior council composed of four deputies from each republic, and principally occupied with the affairs of war and politics, should be yet charged with observing that none of those republics changed its legislation without the consent of all the others: and where, moreover, the object of the laws should be to improve minds, exalt courage, and preserve an exact discipline in their armies. On such a supposition the whole body of the republics would be sufficiently powerful to oppose efficaciously any ambitious projects of their neighbors, or of their fellow-citizens.

As long as the legislation of such a federated republic renders the greatest happiness to the greatest number of people, procuring for them all the pleasures compatible with public welfare, these republics could be sure of continued political progress. In this manner, Helvétius unfolds his grand plan for peace and prosperity. The utopianism of his plan becomes overshadowed by its profoundly *anti-war character*.

Laws are good if they equalize the material basis of human welfare, and extirpate all possibilities of special class interests and wars of aggression. It is through peace and social equality that Helvétius sees the vast possibilities open for political progress. Legislation is moral if it secures peace and equality. It is immoral if it doesn't do so. "Whenever the public welfare is not the supreme law, and the first obligation of a citizen, does there still subsist a science of good and evil; in short, is there any morality where the public good is not the measure of reward and punishment, of the esteem or contempt due to the actions of citizens?" [*De l'Homme*]. Helvétius recognizes that political progress is measured by more than the democratization and equalization of the material sources of pleasure. It is measured also in terms of the ideals and attitudes it instills in people. Therefore, the good society and the good laws provide for emotional and psychological pleasures as well as for material goods. In fact, in a quite real sense the ideas and opinions of men help mold and shape the future course of civilization. This strain in Helvétius' thought is made explicit.

> Is it enough for a government to be good, that it secures to the inhabitants their properties, lives, and liberties, makes a more equal partition of a nation's riches, and enables the people more easily to obtain by moderate labor a sufficiency for themselves and their families, if the legislation does not at the same time exalt in the minds of men the sentiment of emulation, and for this effect the state does not propose large rewards for great talents and great virtues? And might not these rewards, always consisting of certain superfluities, and which were formerly the source of so many great and noble actions, again produce the same effects? And can the rewards decreed by government be regarded as a luxury of pleasure adopted to corrupt the manners of the people? [*De l'Homme*]

The answer is obviously that they cannot. Government has to provide for the all-round security of the people. Only by so doing can political progress be ensured.

Before us we have the heart and core of Helvétius' progressive conception of development in the political-legal structure of society. Presented, as it was, in an epoch of decomposition, cynicism, and corruption of the *ancien regime,* it stood as a mighty edifice in the cause of the rights and dignity of man. The grandeur of Helvétius' conception does not alter the serious blind-spots in his views. The basic weakness in his presentation stems from an inability to conceive of the causal relationship existing between political institutions of a country and its precise economic stage of development. [G. V.] Plekhanov's description of the utopian socialist search for *the* enlightened law-giver as the "joyless chase of some happy historical accident" [in his *In Defence of Materialism,* 1947] serves equally well in delineating an essential weak-spot in Helvétius' thinking. Plekhanov himself understood this "search" as basic to Enlightenment philosophy.

> The chase of the happy accident was the constant occupation of the writers of the Enlightenment in the eighteenth century. It was just in hope of such an accident that they sought by every means, fair and foul, to enter into friendly relations with more or less enlightened 'legislators' and aristocrats of their age. Usually it is thought that once a man has said to himself that opinion governs the world, he no longer has any reason to despair of the future: *la raison finira par avoir raison.* But this is not so. When and in what way will reason triumph? The writers of the Enlightenment said that in the life of society everything depends, in the long run, on the 'legislator'. Therefore they went on their search for legislators. But the same writers knew very well that the character and views of man depend on his upbringing, and that generally speaking their upbringing did not predispose the 'legislators' to the absorption of enlightened doctrines. Therefore they could not but realize that there was lit-

tle to be hoped from the legislators. There remained only to trust to some happy accident. Imagine that you have an enormous box in which there are very many black balls and two or three white ones. You take out ball after ball. In each individual case you have incomparably fewer chances of taking out a white ball than a black. But, if you repeat the operation a sufficient number of times, you will finally take out a white ball. The same applies to the legislators. In each individual case it is incomparably more probable that the legislator will be against the philosophers: but in the end there must appear, after all, a legislator who is in agreement with the philosophers. This one will do everything that reason dictates. Thus, literally thus, did Helvétius argue. *The subjective idealist view of history* ('opinions govern the world'), *which seems to provide such a wide field for man's freedom of action, in reality represents him as the plaything of accident.* That is why this view in its essence is very *joyless.*

The impatience of Helvétius in the face of questions concerning social evolution and revolution, the nature of historical change, revealed his political philosophy to be one-sided and ultimately idealist. In his view of history he opposed God as a *deus ex machina* only to substitute a Monarch as the *deus ex machina.* However useful this notion may have been in combatting antiquated political dogmas they had serious scientific value only in so far as they attempted to explain the ideological content of politics. Like other *philosophes,* Helvétius made a remarkable effort in this direction only to end in failure. The materialist Helvétius, in his view of political growth, adopted an idealist position—that opinions rather than economic and social conditions ultimately determine the course of civilization. When materialist considerations forced their way to the surface of Helvétius' thought, they did so mechanistically and at the risk of destroying the spirit of his efforts. Social science and humanism found themselves divided in his political outlook. When he concentrated on making politics a science he lost touch with the human participants in the struggle for progress. When he concentrated on humanizing politics he lost touch with the material roots of progress. At one point, social consciousness becomes an accidental response to atomic particles whirling about in the mind, and at another, it becomes the prime mover. This is the tragi-comedy of mechanical materialism. In the first act, humanism battles cannibalism. In the second act, science battles supernaturalism. But this philosophy never finishes the play because it never finds the proper resolution and solution to the conflicts posed.

Irrespective of what Helvétius did to make materialism a vital political philosophy the attempt failed because of his attachment to cheap metaphysical slogans which made history a stage-prop to the "individual" and forgot that the individual can read only those lines written by social history, the accumulated and collective endeavors of mankind. The reproach of idealism from Plato to Hegel to the effect that materialism was inherently ossified and static, was a proper reproach to the extent that materialism operates within a physicalist vacuum. Spinoza attempted to make political science as rigid as geometry, La Mettrie compared human society to a monster-machine and Holbach thought that men like atmos responded to the requirements of Newtonian physics. Each new effort to explain scientifically the political life of man, made it that much clearer that one would first have to find that set of laws which specifically control human behavior. This was a task the Enlightenment threw at the coming nineteenth century. Hegel grappled with the task and failed. Marx grappled with it and succeeded. Why? Because he alone started with sensuous man, but man rooted in relations he is part of not voluntarily but necessarily, not haphazardly but organically. He alone was capable of linking man to his economy, science to its technology and materialism to methodology. With him that elusive third act the Enlightenment never finished is completed.

It is certainly true that the political philosophy of Helvétius was of immeasurable aid in justifying bourgeois social and state power. This is, however, hardly a unique distinction. The significant point is that in the eighteenth century he was able to write from the standpoint of all exploited humanity. He avoided the trite and typical in the political theorizing of the Enlightenment. The narrow "career open to talents" egalitarianism found no favor in Helvétius' outlook. Politics cannot civil-servants remain the exclusive preserve of an aristocratic elite or of professional civil-servants and still claim democracy as its method or goal. By considering politics as the domain of the people as a whole his achievement has to be considered a peak in the development of French democratic political thought. His approach contained an element of negating the very class which assumed the reins of government on this type of equalitarian doctrine. As soon as the French bourgeoisie became the ruling political body, it no longer required and eventually came to bitterly resent, the possible consequences of an application of Helvetian theories of social and political equality.

Helvétius neither understood nor had patience with those political academicians who were preoccupied with forms of government. In his view they were either good or evil, the standard of judgment being their social utility. This view presupposed yet another idea, which was to gain increasing prominence in the nineteenth century, namely, that the *content* of society is its material resources—natural and human—and that the *forms* of society are in such a relation to the content as to either propel or retard the growth of the material base of society. Since, in Helvétius' view, all previous forms or stages of society rested on securing an abundance for private selfish interests, a good (useful) economic and political system was a thing of the future lacking any historical precedence. Helvétius' failure to concern himself with the political forms of government may be deplored as a negation of political science, but none can deplore the reason behind this. It stems from his revolutionary attitude to problems of social progress. The prime goal of man being happiness, all political institutions must be adapted to satisfy this aim. Political progress is not the slow, gradual and haphazard adaptation of old institutions to meet new situations, but their revolutionary transformation under the guidance of a providential monarch. As against Montesquieu, Helvétius taught that veneration of ancient laws and credos is not only a naive rejec-

tion of the requirements of the present but dangerous to a scientific comprehension of politics. For him, the individual alone is capable of determining his interest at any particular moment. The integration of these various individual interests into a common political organization makes possible a democratic society. It is this very meshing of individual interests that reveals to Helvétius the necessity of an equal distribution of wealth, labor, education, and above all, political control.

The desire to frame a democratic theory of politics rests on a comprehension that men must first change their external environment if they are to bring about any profound change in their psychology. Materialism and causal determinism are the heart of Helvétius' utilitarian science of morality. But his faith in the self-corrective powers of "man" went only so far. Unfortunately, he attributed to an enlightened monarch powers of social change that are the sole property of the masses. This exaggeration in Helvétius' political theory of the role played by a princely ruler stemmed from the almost sacred belief that once enlightened the ruler would be a dispassionate dispenser of law and justice, thereby becoming the prime agent of social progress. This entire view implies that a king in relation to social institutions acts like a mechanic does in relation to a run-down machine, the separate parts of which can be reordered through purely external intervention. This is what Plekhanov in an essay on Marx [in his *Essays in the History of Materialism,* 1934] called "the transformation of a phenomenon into a fossilized thing by abstracting it from all the inner processes of life, the nature and connection of which it is impossible to understand." Helvétius was caught in a web of his own design. On one side he developed a theory of politics which expressed the advanced democratic yearnings of the masses of Frenchmen. This remained eternally straddled to a helpless metaphysical view of political progress which rested on changing society through the enlightenment of a king. In the last analysis Platonism won out; the search for the philosopher-king was on. It mattered not to Helvétius and the Encyclopedists that they were trying to prove that the impossible was the necessary, that it was in the best interests of a monarch to act judiciously towards the very subjects he exploits and must continue to exploit if he is to remain a monarch. Such a view is the antithesis and negation of a theory of politics which rests on first altering the material conditions of life if progress is to be realized.

The political philosophy of Helvétius does not escape the dilemma that ate away at the core of his materialism, the faith in the ability of an intellectual mechanic to change the world with a stroke of his pen. History conclusively proves that an enlightened despot in an era of social decay such as eighteenth century France, never brought a stitch of real democratic gain to the masses of humanity. Helvétius was snared in trying to unite historical fact and fancy; of positing a theory of endless political progress and seeing as its instrument an aristocracy that was the rock of resistance to progress of any sort. This is truly the ultimate contradiction faced but never resolved by the Enlightenment and its philosophical crystal gazers.

Ian Cumming (essay date 1955)

SOURCE: *Helvétius: His Life and Place in the History of Educational Thought,* Routledge & Kegan Paul Limited, 1955, 260 p.

[*In the following excerpt, New Zealander educational theorist Cumming discusses the four constitutive essays of* De l'esprit, *specifically addressing Helvétius's theory of education and the role it has played in the historical development of the philosophy of education.*]

Buckle, discussing [in his *History of Civilization in England*, 1869] the immense movement by which, during the latter half of the eighteenth century, the French intellect was withdrawn from the study of the internal and concentrated upon that of the external world, regarded Helvétius's ***De l' Esprit***—for fifty years the code of French morals—as 'unquestionably the ablest and most influential treatise on morals which France produced at this period.' Imagining that morality ought to be treated like all the other sciences and, like physics, founded on experiment, Helvétius proceeded from facts to causes.

In the first Essay of ***De l' Esprit***—'De l' Esprit en lui même'—Helvétius attempted to prove that natural sensibility and memory were the causes of our ideas, and that all false judgments were the effect of passions or ignorance. The human mind, he believed, was endowed with the faculties of receiving and of remembering impressions; thence came all forms of thought. He believed that all men were endowed with different degrees of fineness of sense, strength of memory and capacity for attention but that they all had sufficient of each quality to enable them to rise to the highest notions. He reduced all our faculties to the mechanical association of sense impressions. Thus he eschewed innate ideas. Man, he said, had two passive powers. The first, Physical Sensibility, was the faculty of receiving impressions caused by external objects; the second, which was the faculty of preserving the impressions caused by these objects, he called Memory. These faculties would produce only a few ideas if unassisted by external organization. Indeed, without a certain organization, such as hands and fingers instead of hoofs, sensibility and memory would be sterile and man would differ little from animals. All operations of the mind, said Helvétius, consisted in the power we had of perceiving the resemblance and difference, the agreement or disagreement, of objects among themselves. Since this power was physical sensibility, and memory was nothing more than one of its organs, then everything was reducible to feeling. If erroneous judgments were made they were the effect of our passions or our ignorance. Passions led us into error by not allowing us to view an object impartially. Yet Helvétius was careful to stress that while passions were the germ of many errors, they were also the sources of knowledge; they alone could arouse us from the torpor that was always ready to seize on the faculties of the soul. When judgments were unaffected by passions, then, he says, ignorance alone was the cause of our errors; then we imagined that the side we viewed of an object was all that could be seen in that object. On these preliminary contentions Helvétius evolved an ethical and educational system which was intended to ensure the greatest happiness of every man.

He devoted the second essay to a study of the mind in relation to society—'De l'Esprit par Rapport à la Société'. Here he attempted to prove that the same interest which influences the judgment we form of actions and so makes us regard those actions as virtuous or vicious, according to whether they are useful or not, equally influences the judgment we form of ideas; to show that interest or self-love alone dictates all our judgments he considered virtue or probity and genius in their relation to the individual, to a small society, to a nation, to different ages and different countries, and to the world itself. The continual declamations of moralists, he said, against the malignity of mankind were a proof of their knowing but little of human nature. Men were not cruel and perfidious, but they were carried away by their own interest. Interest, said Helvétius, was the only judge of probity and the understanding. Men's interest, founded on the love of pleasure and on the fear of pain or sadness, was the sole motive of their judgments and actions. And on the foundations of personal interest he based his system of morality. The declamations of the moralist would make no change in this moral spring of the universe; they should not complain of the wickedness of mankind, but of the ignorance of the legislators, who had always placed private interest in opposition to the general interest. A nation, he said, was only an assemblage of the citizens of which it was composed, and the interest of each citizen was always attached to the public interest. Thus each society was moved by two different kinds of interest; the first, and weaker, was in common with society in general, and the second, and more powerful, was absolutely peculiar to the individual. Since he reduced morality to public welfare, actions ceased to be virtuous and became vicious depending upon their use to society, and the science of morality became the science of government. According to this utilitarian standard the law and social morality together would ensure the greatest happiness of the greatest number of people.

In the third essay Helvétius discussed whether understanding ought to be considered as a natural gift, or as an effect of education. For him, education comprised an infinite number of events; each individual, he said, had for his teachers, the form of government under which he lived, his friends, his mistresses, the people about him, whatever he read, in short—chance. He enquired whether nature had endowed men with an equal mental ability or whether some were more favoured than others and he examined whether all men who were well-organized had not in themselves the natural powers of acquiring the loftiest ideas when they had sufficient motive to overcome the pain of application. To strong passions, which animated the moral world, we owed the invention and wonder of arts; consequently Helvétius considered them as the powerful urge that carried men to great actions, to defy dangers, pain, death and even heaven itself. The passions strongly fixed men's attention on the object of their desire and caused them to view it under appearances unknown to other men; this prompted heroes to plan and execute those hardy enterprises, which, till success had proved them correct, appeared ridiculous to the multitude. He felt that the passions alone could sometimes perceive the cause of effects which the ignorant attributed to chance. And the passion, which was never at a loss and always inspired in men the greatest actions and ideas, was the love of glory. Only the force of passion could counterbalance in men the effect of indolence and inertia, rescue them from the indulgence and stupidity to which they were continually gravitating, and endow them with that continuity of attention on which a superiority of talents depended. The vivacity of the passions depended on the means used by the legislator in kindling them, or in the situations in which fortune placed men. The livelier the passions, the greater were the effects produced by them. The fact that success constantly attended the people who were animated by strong passions was too little known and so men had not profited from the art of inspiring the passions. The principles of this art, said Helvétius, though as certain as those of geometry, appeared in fact to have been hitherto perceived only by great men with respect to war and politics. Helvétius believed that most men—that is, all except the very few who possessed some defect in their organization—were capable of the attention necessary to render them capable of the highest ideas. The inequalities of abilities observable in well-organized men depended on the different education received, on the circumstances in which they were placed, on the little aptitude which they had for thought, and on the dislike for application which they had contracted in their early youth and which rendered them absolutely incapable of diligence in later years. He concluded that all well-organized men had the natural power of acquiring the highest ideas, but the inequalities of intellect depended on the various circumstances in which men were placed, and on the unequal desire for instruction; the general conclusion then was that education was of the greatest importance. Helvétius added the important theme that the general superiorities of nations were the result of culture-conditions and politics. It is a fundamental thought of Helvétius that talent, virtue, the intellect and probity or integrity were all determined by the form of a country's government. He emphasized continually the strong link binding the individual and public life. The Greeks, he said, had changed because the form of their government had changed; like water which took the shape of vessels into which it was poured, the character of nations could assume all forms, and in every country the genius of the government conditioned the genius of the nation. He held that genius was common but the circumstances required to unfold it must be extraordinary. It was a case of many being called and few chosen—'il est beaucoup d'appelés et peu d'élus.' Instead of having recourse to the influence of the air and climates Helvétius established a moral determinism. He said that we ought to search into morals for the true cause of the inequality noticed in various minds. The history of the Romans, Greeks, Jews and of philosophy itself had convinced him that the transmigrations of arts, sciences, courage and virtue were to be ascribed, not to climate, but to moral causes. The obvious inequality among men depended on the government, on the greater or less happiness of the age, on their education, on their desire for improvement, and on the importance of the ideas which they were accustomed to contemplate. Circumstances produced men of genius. Thus the art of education consisted of placing young men in positions proper to the growth and development of genius and virtue. Education would include everything in our environment which influenced

our development. It was because of this wide interpretation of the word that Helvétius could say that no two men had exactly the same education. The desire of promoting the happiness of mankind led Helvétius to conclude that a good education would make society virtuous and happy; the opinion that genius and virtue were merely gifts of nature was the great obstacle to progress in the science of education in as much as it favoured idleness and negligence. After considering the effects which nature and education might have had upon us Helvétius concluded that education made men what they were—'l'éducation nous faisoit ce que nous sommes.'

In the fourth and most ingenious essay—'Des différents noms donnés à l'Esprit'—Helvétius discussed the different names which had been applied to the mind, such as genius, imagination, talent, taste, good sense and so on. The climax was reached when he turned his attention once again to education. He was tenacious in maintaining that the art of forming men was in all countries closely connected with the form of government; indeed, it seemed impossible to plan any change in public education without making similar changes in the constitution. Knowledge of the means of forming strong and robust bodies, wise minds and virtuous souls—such was the art of education as Helvétius saw it. As many before and after him have done Helvétius recommended the bodily medicinal exercises of the ancient Greeks in order to produce healthy bodies. The production of enlightened and virtuous minds depended primarily on the proper choice of objects to be placed in the memory and on the directing of strong passions towards the general welfare. Helvétius did not go into particular details of an educational reformation; he suggested general principles to follow and obvious abuses to be corrected. For example, we ought to make the best distribution of our time. Almost unawares Helvétius entered into a long passage wherein he seriously urged the rational study of the national language in preference to the absurd waste of eight or ten years in the useless study of a dead one. While Helvétius was generous enough not to confine a young man solely to studies suitable to his station in life—since genius should not be bound—yet he was convinced that the education received should have reference to the different pursuits he might follow. There were some branches of knowledge—for example, morality and the laws of the country—which should be obligatory on all citizens. But apart from that he recognized the absurdity of giving exactly the same education to different youths to the age of sixteen or seventeen and then expecting them, when in the world outside the protective school, to be equally capable of continued application. Although it was realized that the virtues, and especially the learning, of the great have influenced the happiness or unhappiness of nations Helvétius said that the administration of education was abandoned to chance. Teachers were aware of the remedies but they could do little without the assistance of the government. The production of great men by the fortuitous concourse of circumstances must become the work of the legislature and so, by leaving less to chance an excellent education would infinitely multiply the abilities and virtues of the citizens; it would be an education reduced, first, to deciding, in each of the different states where fortune had placed us, the kind of objects and ideas that ought to be placed in youthful memories, and second, to determining the means of inflaming young men with a love of glory. . . .

. . . . .

In the history of education Helvétius has been—to quote words which Disraeli used of Shelburne—one of the suppressed characters. Yet in his own country he directly influenced Condillac who brought philosophy near to sociology by urging a more detailed study of the laws of ethics, legislation and economics, the sensualist Antoine-Louis-Claude, comte Destutt de Tracy, author of the term 'ideologie', Cabanis of the society at Auteuil, Saint-Lambert, and Volney whose *Catéchisme du citoyen français* further emphasized Helvétius's idea that the happiness of the individual and the happiness of all were inseparable. His principles prompted Mirabeau, Talleyrand, Lakanal and others to form plans for a national system of education during the Revolution. It was his disciple Condorcet who said, 'Education, if taken in its whole extent, is not limited to positive instruction, to the teaching of truths of fact and number, but includes all opinions, political, moral or religious.' But Helvétius's authority was even more significant in Britain where he proved to be the immediate forerunner of the Utilitarians. As he himself was affected by Locke, Mandeville and Hartley so he in turn induced the Benthamites to introduce into morals and politics the scientific method of investigation. Bentham, said J. S. Mill, was the father of English innovation, both in doctrines and in institutions; he was 'the great "subversive", or, in the language of continental philosophers, the great "critical", thinker of his age and country.'

Although Matthew Arnold has pointed out that the most useful part of pedagogy was a study of the lives of educators, the history of education so often lapses into a series of disconnected theories propounded by men and women divorced from the world about them. Just as the *Émile* was Rousseau's personal attack against his 'milieu' and an understanding of one is impossible without a knowledge of the other, so Helvétius, too, was a man of the eighteenth century; in truth, it is doubtful if one could be named who was more the embodiment of the spirit of his times than Helvétius.

A review of the impressionable Helvétius himself illustrates both the force of environment and the turn of chance.

He inherited not only the material wealth derived from the pharmaceutical acumen of [his father] Jean-Adrien but also the spirit of investigation, the urge to put everything to the proof, which had animated his physician forebears. His legacy also included qualities which he owed as much to the female as to the male influence in his family; his handsome appearance and elegant manners were factors which contributed in no small measure to the course of his personal behaviour, particularly in his meretricious pre-marital days. Whatever piety his mother may have tried to pass on to Claude-Adrien was counteracted by the temper of the eighteenth century. In morals the age of chivalry declined into licence and the looseness of manners; in religion itself the ecclesiastical authority was weakened; and

although the century saw the Pietistic movement in the German Lutheran states, the Methodist revival in England, and also the activities of Baptists and Quakers, the scientific spirit of the times was exemplified by the vogue which Deism had in placing so much reliance on human reason. Yet, in spite of many philosophers who were opposed to Christianity, religion kept its traditional place as the basis of education. The Jansenist Rollin had projected into the eighteenth century the strong religious principles of the seventeenth. Thirty-six years after the publication of his *Traité des Études,* when the *Parlement* of Paris had to make good the loss of Jesuit teachers, the universities within its jurisdiction—Paris, Rheims, Bourges, Poitiers, Angers and Orleans—were asked to submit plans for the instruction of youth; their answers showed that, in their opinion, the supreme ends of education were religion, character and intellectual attainment. Even La Chalotais in his *Essai* outlined a plan for better religious instruction. For Guyton de Morveau, whose *Mémoire sur l'instruction publique* appeared in 1764, religion must come before anything else in education; he, too, outlined a plan of religious instruction. Rolland d'Erceville wanted an historical and reasoned explanation of Christianity to be given in each college by a teacher specially trained for that duty. And when, in 1769, the *Parlement* and University of Paris were composing a code of rules for the Collège Louis-le-Grand they made Religion the foundation of instruction for students proceeding to the Faculty of Arts. At this time Helvétius was writing **De l'Homme** in which he showed that in reality he was more orthodox than **De l'Esprit** would have us believe. He was not an irreligious man; he only opposed clerical organizations when they became intolerant.

In the days of his childhood and during his schooldays Helvétius had impressed upon him the literary splendour of France, Greece and Rome by his private tutor and by the thorough, scholastic, competitive system of the Jesuits; so earnest and stimulating was this teaching that Helvétius, with youthful enthusiasm, decided to emulate the great contemporary French writers. His way to that cherished glory and the direction which his thoughts were to take were determined by his chance reading of John Locke. At the time when the schoolboy Helvétius was receiving his introduction to the writings of Locke, Horace Walpole was at Eton, Samuel Johnson had recently left Pembroke College, John Wesley had been made a Fellow of Lincoln College, Hume was in Bristol, and Adam Smith was only a small boy in Kirkcaldy; two other children about this time who were to cause Helvétius—and many other Frenchmen—considerable annoyance were Clive and Wolfe; and the future Chatham was still in Lord Cobham's regiment and had not yet entered Parliament for Old Sarum.

Not only did Helvétius serve his apprenticeship as a financier in Caën but during that period, too, he experienced for the first time the sensualist pleasures of an opulent roué. That he dissipated his strength and substance in a selfish pursuit of voluptuousness did not make him a phenomenon; rather did it quality him to enter the libertine ranks of eighteenth-century society. Yet, while he was recording his erotic thoughts in occasionally poetic notes, he was, at the same time, reading widely on morality, legislation and education. He was assailed by the scientific Fontenelle, the questioning Bayle, the imaginative Le Sage and the more profound Montesquieu; and the worldly-minded Voltaire presented to him some of the attributes of England, not the least of which were the experimental philosophy of Bacon, and the more recent works of John Locke. His growing interest in social problems received a great impetus when he joined the 'ferme' and saw at first hand the economic state of rural France where feudalism and colbertism weighed heavily on a dejected peasantry, and where individualism was suppressed and trade restricted by exacting taxation. What he saw excited his feelings of benevolence and charity towards humanity, and the presence of Du Marsais as his companion during some of the 'tournées' impressed upon him the value of education for social advancement. His own education was enriched as he made his rather aimless way through the Parisian salons, patronizing the arts, dancing, intriguing, and trifling with deism; nevertheless he was not unaffected by the economic discussions with Quesnay in the Versailles 'entre-sol', nor, in the midst of perils which environed him could he have escaped from Diderot, D'Alembert, Duclos, Buffon, Turgot, Galiani and Holbach had he so wished—which, in truth, he did not for their conversations were helping to mould his philosophy of life. It was good fortune which brought him to Anne-Catherine de Ligniville and his marriage to her was rich in its blessings. He grew in estimation as a man of the times—husband, father, 'seigneur', officer in the Queen's household, serious in his duties yet withal a 'bon vivant' and architect, at the rue Sainte-Anne, of the 'cénacle de la libre pensée'. To use words which Marmontel applied to D'Alembert, Helvétius mingled the grave with the gay and jested in earnest.

The intellectual world in the 1750's was in such a ferment, presaging more prodigious events than could have been imagined, that no person—especially if he were responsive to what J. S. Mill called 'the attractive, or impelling influence of public opinion'—could merely assume the role of a spectator. The comedies of manners, the appearance on the stage of humble yet virile characters, the scientific discoveries in and beyond France, the publication of the *Encyclopédie,* the financial treatises opposing restriction in trade, Montesquieu's study of the laws and countries' constitutions, the internationalism of science and the arts, Rousseau's pronouncements on national education, sciences, the arts, and the origin of inequality, the materialism of La Mettrie, Mandeville's selfish morality, the maxims of La Rochefoucauld, the sensationalism of Condillac and the associationism of Gay and Hartley—only a dullard could have remained unaffected by such external influences. The untimely appearance of *De l'Esprit* was one of the tragedies in Helvétius's life in bringing him notoriety instead of fame; but it also compelled his contemporaries to take cognizance of his ideas and it won for him disciples who made history. The misfortunes which he suffered made him re-examine his first rash excursion into philosophy, so that *De l'Homme,* although more orthodox in some matters, such as religion, is more emphatic on others, such as education and legislation. In the year of *De l'Esprit* William Markham, Headmaster of Westminster School, had as one of his pupils Jeremy Bentham who had entered in 1755 at the age of seven—he left Westminster

L.M. Van Loo's 1755 portrait of Helvétius.

in its bicentenary year, 1760—and William Godwin was then only an infant of about three years. In the year that Helvétius died Robert Owen was born; and the publication of *De l'Homme* preceded the birth of James Mill by only a few months.

De l'Homme shows the influence of Helvétius's visit to England and Prussia; the British constitution, the relative freedom of the Press, the Royal Society of London and the Berlin Academy, for example, were not lost on a Frenchman coming from a country ruled by an arbitrary government, who had suffered from restrictions placed on publications, and who believed in the power of education to improve man's existence. The domestic affairs of Britain during the eighteenth century were quiet when compared either with events of the previous century or with contemporary happenings elsewhere in Europe. This comparative calm was due to the Toleration Act of 1689, the Parliamentary union of England and Scotland in 1707, the Treaty of Utrecht which ended the War of the Spanish Succession in 1713 and gave Britain Gibraltar, Minorca, Acadia, Newfoundland and Hudson Bay, the accession of the Hanoverians, and the ascendancy of the astute Robert Walpole. It was a period of elegant aristocracy tempered by a liberal amount of Latitudinarianism, of Ranelagh and White's, of Chippendale and Adam, Gainsborough, Reynolds and Romney. Addison and Steele both lived on the patronage of the nobility; Horace Walpole, Fielding, Cowper, Fanny Burney, Collins and Gray all came from homes with comfortable incomes. But it was, no less, the century of Pope, Goldsmith and Defoe who, although not sprung from peasant families were yet not of the governing classes; it was the age of the Literary Club, presided over by Dr Johnson at the Mitre or Cheshire Cheese, and of Priestley, Darwin, James Watt, Josiah Wedgwood, Matthew Boulton and the author of *Sandford and Merton,* Thomas Day. It was a century which saw an intellectual, political and humanitarian animation among the merchant class and the dissenters. Raikes, Mary Wollstonecraft, Gay and Howard exposed the degradation of the lower classes, submerged under a social tyranny, violent in their crimes against both man and beast, brutal in their abysmal ignorance. In France Helvétius had known of the inhuman punishment of Damiens and Jean Calas; he must have been aware of such refinements as the 'examenatio', the 'strappado', the branding of thieves on the left shoulder—'V' for 'Voleur' and 'G' for 'Galérien', the wheel, hanging, whipping, and the galleys which France began to abolish in 1748 in favour of 'bagnes' or land prisons. The eighteenth century in England no less than in France, then, was a century of contrasts; but Helvétius was generally satisfied with the conditions he saw there. Further, *De l'Homme* in its anticlericalism and its impregnation with a republican equality of men, indicates typical eighteenth-century masonic tendencies. Freemasonry also strengthened Helvétius's feelings of charity towards humanity, it led him to see that in brotherhood men found their happiness, and as it actively encouraged the spread of scientific investigation it inspired all members of the craft to apportion their time between labour and refreshment.

His environment was an exceedingly strong agency in the forming of Helvétius's philosophy; its importance is heightened by the fact that a person's philosophy of life must necessarily be his philosophy of education. But herein lies a difficulty if one should wish to 'classify' him as a representative of this or that school. Of the broad philosophical trends of the eighteenth century—Sensualism, Idealism, Scepticism and Mysticism—Helvétius clearly belonged to the sensualist reaction against seventeenth-century idealism. Taking its rise from Locke, the trend first appeared in England but about 1750 it entered France; it returned to England and was represented there by Priestley, Godwin, and especially Jeremy Bentham, who has been called 'the greatest representative of the sensualist political school of all Europe.' No one was more responsible for this philosophical boomerang than Helvétius. Bearing in mind that *De l'Esprit* was written both to impress and for recognition, and that it therefore contains many examples of literary and scientific overstrain, the main principles of his ethics may be Summarized:

1. The sole motive of all human actions was self-interest.

2. Even in actions which were strictly moral, egoism was the primary factor; good will was secondary.

3. The criterion of the morality of an action was its usefulness to the community.

4. Legislation and education served to bring into harmony, by means of rewards and punishments, the egoism of the individual and the good of the community.

In one of his *Addresses to the German People* Fichte said, 'The art of education will never attain complete clearness in itself without philosophy.' Yet to bring Helvétius into an order of educational philosophers which might satisfy the fastidious would be impossible. It is doubtful if there could be even an academic value in discovering among Helvétius's writings evidence that he was at times a naturalist or an idealist, a pragmatist or a materialist, a romantic naturalist or a naturalistic realist, a rational humanist or even a Catholic supernaturalist, or whether he could have been a source of inspiration for the progressives and reconstructionists and therefore not for the more conservative perennialists, traditionalists and essentialists. The confusion of titles is of modern origin and it is consoling to know, on the authority of Brubacher [in his *Modern Philosophers of Education,* 1950], that no school has worked out an entirely complete philosophy of education. It must be remembered, too, that when Helvétius wrote he did not have to decide which school to enter and thereafter to abide by a strict rule. So, if Helvétius's writings be analysed, it must be granted to him that all deviations from recently-built channels are not necessarily contradictions. Indeed more progress would be made if educationists and legislators—whom Helvétius linked inseparably—showed greater breadth of view and were willing to adopt more suggestions from their opponents' plans and so overcome that artificial and unconvincing division on points of education. Because, for instance, Helvétius believed that through education a nation's cultural heritage could be preserved from generation to generation, or because he insisted that there were definite things which a child must be compelled to learn, he was not necessarily an idealist. At the most this merely helps to illustrate Adams' point [in *Evolution of Educational Theory*] that idealism in one form or other permeates the whole of the history of philosophy. It is much easier, however, to place Helvétius among the naturalists than with the idealists. Surrounded as he was by men of science it was not unexpected that he should attempt to see morality and legislation from a scientific point of view. Naturalists have stressed the importance of environment, and more important still, they have usually been associated with the ethical code of hedonism. The selfish Epicurean doctrine that pleasure was the only ultimate good and pain the only evil was expressed later by Spencer at a time when biology and other sciences were even stronger in their demand for recognition than in the middle of the eighteenth century when Helvétius was writing. 'The ultimate standards,' said Spencer, 'by which all men judge of behaviour, are the resulting happiness or misery.' With very little about him of idealism, but more of naturalism, Helvétius's emphasis on progress, the place which he gave to interest, attention and determination in learning, his opposition to a monopoly over education being gained by one organization, his reliance on principles of utility in judging the value of any particular field of study, and his democratic—even republican—conviction that one of the most important aspects of education is active membership of a society, demonstrates proclivities which would now be termed pragmatic.

Our words 'practice' and 'practical' are both derived from the same Greek word which, in 1878, gave Peirce his term 'pragmatism'. But the method of acquiring knowledge by factual experience or systematic experiment was an approach to subjects advocated many years before either Peirce or Helvétius. Nevertheless one cannot overlook Helvétius's contribution to the notion that practice, no less than reasoning, had its place in education. Following Bacon and Fontenelle he advocated objective, exact and persistent observation as the method of acquiring knowledge, proceeding from the particular to the general, from the simple to the complex. This is a procedure which, when applied to schools, makes continual demands on the teachers. Although a feature of the project method, which also depends for its success on the competency of the teachers, it is, in its pedagogical development, enshrined in the Herbartian plan of preparation, generalization and application—authoritarian steps for the teacher to follow. It was from Helvétius, too, that Mill took the stage of 'association' in the process of reaching general truths. Like many other educational theorists, of his time, Helvétius subjected the academic, traditional routine of the schools to impersonal investigation. 'The eighteenth century,' said Victor Cousin, 'which submitted everything to examination, made of education at first a problem, then a science, then an art; hence pedagogy; the word is perhaps a little ridiculous; the thing represented is sacred.' His inquiries convinced Helvétius that our awareness of the external world and all our ideas came to us through the senses; there were no innate ideas. From his supposition that pleasure and pain had their source in bodily sensations, he concluded that physical sensibility, along with memory (the remembering of sense impressions received) and interest, was the sole cause of actions and alone produced our understandings and our talents. This was associated with his belief that since understanding was an acquisition then it was by virtue of different types of education that different understandings were created. This extreme view is usually attributed to Helvétius without just reference to his acknowledgment of the part which bodily health plays in intellectual development, of the range of mental attainments, of the varying degrees of memory, of the acuteness of the sense organs and of the personal capacity for attention. The reason for this apparent inconsistency is that Helvétius, realizing the power of education, did not wish to see it neglected or dissipated and constantly stressed the need for earnest application. Only in this way, he felt, would men reach unsuspected heights.

Helvétius encouraged the dissemination of the liberal arts and sciences that all might learn how to apportion their time and deliver their minds from the fetters of laziness and ignorance. The improvement of the understanding through moral, intellectual and cultural pursuits he denied neither to women nor to the poor. The distinguishing difference in the status of men and women provided him with an illustration of the effect of different kinds of education. The contrast between the unrefined production of an irregular education and a lady who possessed the accomplishments of knowledge and good behaviour had been noted by Defoe [in *An Essay upon Projects,* 1697] in his effort to remedy the 'inhuman custom' that hindered women being made wiser. 'I believe it might be defended,'

he said, 'if I should say that I do suppose God has given to all mankind equal gifts and capacities in that He has given them all souls equally capable, and that the whole difference in mankind proceeds either from accidental difference in the make of their bodies or from the foolish difference of education.' The poor stood in need of enlightenment that they might be raised from the subjection of sectarianism, superstition and arbitrary government and so come at last to realize the fundamental brotherhood of man. For Helvétius education had to rescue men and women from that social ignorance which prevented them from identifying the interest of all with the interest of each. When he said that men were in general more stupid than wicked he saw that they were pliable and could be moulded by instruction. And because he was certain that public education, even more than laws and government, shaped a nation's destiny, he therefore hated the protectors of ignorance as the cruelest enemies of human beings. Critics have often been content to castigate Helvétius for discovering the motive power of self-love—indeed they usually give the impression that he advocated its sole cultivation. But they just as often overlook the fact that he attacked ignorance as even more barbarous than self-love. Ignorance, he said, had caused most of the calamities that had come over the earth.

Helvétius did not enumerate particular subjects nor did he devise a curriculum with which to defeat ignorance and establish a right knowledge in the minds of men. But his attitude was clear. With faith in the perfectibility of the common man and in the use of science and reason for the benefit of all humanity, with an enthusiasm for healthy bodily exercises, and animated, too, by that wisdom, strength and beauty which proceed from an appreciation of the arts, he joined those who criticized the secondary schools for their obstinate adherence to the traditional discipline of Latin. Doubtless he knew of the English private grammar schools and dissenting academies with their encouragement of speculation and scientific investigation; and in Berlin, Hecker, a student of Francke's, had, in 1747, established his 'aekonomisch-mathematische Realschule'; moreover, schools in France were gradually introducing history, geography, science and the French language. In higher education, the obscurantist university of Paris compared unfavourably with the foundations at Halle in 1694 and at Göttingen in 1737; but even in his own France there were naval and military schools, schools of mining and engineering, the Jardin du Roi, 'sociétées de pensée' and masonic lodges, all imbued with a utilitarian spirit. Helvétius's estimation of academic studies could be expressed in the words which Locke used in his *Essay Concerning Human Understanding:* 'We shall not have much reason to complain of the narrowness of our minds, if we will but employ them about what may be of use to us.' Helvétius's pragmatic criterion of the 'useful' was used by Bentham in his *Chrestomathia* wherein he gave as advantages derivable from useful learning or intellectual instruction, the securing to the possessor of a proportionable share of general respect, security against ennui and inordinate sensuality, escape from idleness and its consequent mischievousness, and the entry into good company.

The utilitarianism of Bentham owed more to Helvétius

than simply the test of usefulness applied to intellectual studies. Helvétius relied on the fear of punishment, as well as on education, to bring about the public good. Even in the narrow sphere of the school-room he would have punished the child who did not apply himself sufficiently to his work; nevertheless, he admitted that good teaching eliminated recourse to it. He **was** convinced, however, that in the wider field of government, citizens could be made just, virtuous and useful to society if the fear of punishment and the hope of reward worked through their habitual self-love. It was from the enlightened sentiment of self-love, the constant pursuit of pleasure and avoidance of pain, that men's intellectual activities sprang; since it was the effect of corporeal sensibility and could become vicious or virtuous according to one's education, it was actually the basis of a healthy society. There was no place in Helvétius's communion for the individual who thought only of his own pursuits. A man was just only when his actions added to the public happiness, when the object of his virtue was the general welfare. According to him there were two reasons for the unjust conduct of men of strong passions; first, men had been forced to unite in society and give themselves laws and a system of morality before they had learnt its true utilitarian principles by means of observation; second, men were unfortunately subject to chance, especially in matters of birth and wealth. The solution in both cases lay in the social purpose which he gave to education. Within his polity Helvétius did not ignore the individual person; how good it was depended on the virtue of each citizen member. The greatest happiness was unattainable unless men, strong and robust in body, were possessed.

> With flame of freedom in their souls,
> And light of knowledge in their eyes.

In the case of chance, education had to help in diminishing its influence by guiding youths with instruction suited to their differing ages and to their stations in life into situations for which they would be most suitable. Helvétius's struggle against prejudice, hypocrisy and despotism and his faith in the continuity of progress had four bases—the real knowledge of men, the science of morality, legislation and education—which, if not exactly synonymous, were at least possessed of the common aim of improving man by the modification of the social structure. Universal happiness, with its good morals and habits, was contingent on education, which would increase the number of men of genius and at the same time implant good sense in all, and on the excellence of the laws. The form of a government, said Helvétius, shaped a people's character and spirit. To remedy the defect of leaving moral teaching or ethics to chance Helvétius urged the impressing of receptive minds with those rules which experience had proved to be both useful and true. By the catechizing method of teaching, the citizen would learn that his first legal and patriotic duty was to the laws and public utility.

Helvétius's views on State or public control of education were influenced by his opinion of the enlightened monarchs beyond France, the contemporary scene within his country, and his belief in the tremendous power of education. He was not interested unduly in the moral characters of the heads of European States. Their virtue did not com-

mend to him either Maria Theresa, the Emperor Joseph II, Charles III of Spain or Leopold of Tuscany in preference to the unscrupulous Peter the Great, Frederick II and Catherine II; and it is not improbable that he would have discovered agreeable qualities in that immoral patron of the arts, Charles Theodore, Elector of the Palatinate, or even in the eccentric Eberhard Ludwig of Würtemberg whose construction of Ludwigsburg was inspired by Wilhelmina von Grävenitz. Helvétius was probably unaware of their individual up-bringings or educational capabilities. According to Frederick the Great in 1752, except for the Empress Maria Theresa and Carlo Emmanuele I of Sardinia whose genius had triumphed over their bad education, all the princes of Europe were only illustrious imbeciles. History has tempered the ungenerous estimation and those enlightened monarchs of the eighteenth century are now regarded as having been at least industrious and humanitarian. Herein lay their appeal to Helvétius. Moreover, he saw that where reforms were palpably necessary a strong monarchy was the only means by which they could be effected promptly. He had no faith in the goodwill of French governmental intervention; he himself had been persecuted by it, it was notoriously inefficient and it failed to excite in its citizens feelings of probity. Because of civil intolerance, and in spite of movements for national systems of education—from 1619 in Weimar to the foundation of the Helvetic Society in Switzerland in 1760—Helvétius was afraid of the arbitrary and excessively centralized authority of the State; for this reason he thought that a democratic, public system of education in France would work best if the country were divided into a federation of thirty republics. But education could still be a powerful force in a small republic or city-state, where there was respect for individual and common interest, where there was equality of fortunes rather than class differences, and where, above all, the door was open to merit. That knowledge had power was obvious to anyone living in the second half of the eighteenth century when intolerance, persecution and superstition were attacked in books, encyclopedias and pamphlets, when men, in their optimism, applied a scientific attitude to the study of history, to the social problems of poverty, crime, punishment and health, and convinced the world that mankind was capable of progress. Helvétius's postulation that education alone caused differences amongst men was repeated over eighty years later by J. S. Mill [in *Nature, The Utility of Religion, and Theism,* 1874]. The effect of bringing people up from infancy in a certain belief and in habits founded on it was to him 'unspeakable'. Like Helvétius, he quoted the case of Greece to prove that the power of education was almost boundless; it was, he said, 'the greatest recorded victory which education has ever achieved over a whole host of natural inclinations in an entire people' and it was the only instance 'in which any teaching, other than religious, had had the unspeakable advantage of forming the basis of education; and though much may be said against the quality of some part of the teaching, very little can be said against its effectiveness.' Helvétius decided that to increase the happiness of a people through education and yet not relinquish such a vigorous agency to an omnipotent authority, the administration of education should be placed under the control of magistrates especially interested in it, the schools should be public institutions, and the teachers, like the magistrates, should be secular.

Similar reasons that made Helvétius oppose an all-powerful State prompted him also to fear an indomitable Church. He was not an irreligious man nor was he averse to a universal religion, and his opposition to the Jesuits was not based on theology. Nevertheless he was convinced that scholastic disputes confused young people and that the hierarchy of the Roman Catholic Church purposely kept its flock ignorant; these acts of an ecclesiastical organization did not conform to the general interest. Indeed the 'cahiers' of 1789 were to disclose the lamentable illiteracy of France's rural population and the paucity of primary schools. Although primary schooling generally in Europe during the eighteenth century was at a low ebb, it is yet not unlikely that Helvétius, while aware of De La Salle and also of the English Charity Schools, was attracted by the provision of education for the common people in Presbyterian Scotland and in Lutheran Prussia where the work of the Pietist Francke had led Frederick William I to make elementary schooling compulsory in 1716-1717. When Helvétius preferred the 'Oratoriens' and the 'Ignorantins' to the Jesuits it was because of their republican organization. Briefly, he objected to clerical control of education because of its continual preparation for a future life to the exclusion of more mundane instruction, its repudiation of lay teachers for the church schools, and the monopoly of education in the hands of any one powerful body.

Although he would have resisted any organization endowed with the attributes of omnipotence and omniscience he would still have ensured the progress of mankind through environmental agencies regulated by the body of magistrates. To Helvétius every external circumstance that acted on a person contributed to the formation of his character. From his chance social environment—wealth, friends and books, for instance—an individual acquired his good or bad character. Since the unequal force of individuals' passions was due to the difference in situations in which they were placed, it became the duty of the magistracy to interest itself so much in the educational influence of environment as to attempt the elimination of chance. Because of the power both of a planned and a fortuitous environment to give permanent qualities to the mind, Helvétius strongly advocated the earliest commencement of definite instruction of children in order to prevent their customary later faults.

So it was to Helvétius that the happiness of nations lay in the interest they took in education. The task which he gave to legislators and teachers together was the exciting of men's zeal for glory which he felt would produce that equal aptitude which he was sure men had for understanding. The period of a man's life when he was most susceptible to this challenging spirit of emulation, to the urge to gain rewards for any talents possessed, was, said Helvétius, that of youth. This was the time—up to the age of seventeen or eighteen—when he would have the boy receive a rigorous and wholesome education in a public boarding school at the hands of just, yet strict teachers and with companions of his own age and physical development. Youths could acquire talents in any science or art,

said Helvétius, because the strong desire for glory, or self-interest, would sustain them in their seven or eight hours daily study and it would summon up the necessary strength of attention.

D. W. Smith   (essay date 1964)

SOURCE: "The Publication of Helvétius's *De l'Esprit*," in *French Studies,* Vol. XVIII, No. 4, October, 1964, pp. 332-44.

[*English-born Canadian scholar Smith is a professor of French language and letters who has written extensively on Helvétius. In the following excerpt, he details the circumstances surrounding the original publication of* De l'esprit.]

The history of Helvétius's *De l'esprit* (1758), his first major work, is eventful, complicated and paradoxical. No book during the eighteenth century, except perhaps Rousseau's *Émile,* evoked such an outcry from the religious and civil authorities or such universal public interest. Condemned as atheistic, materialistic, sacrilegious, immoral and subversive, it enjoyed a remarkable *succès de scandale.* The work lost its *Privilege* within a fortnight of its publication. It was attacked in Church periodicals and in polemical pamphlets, in the literary *salons* and in popular songs, from bishops' pulpits and from the stage of the *Théâtre français.* Though Helvétius retracted his book three times, he was condemned by the Archbishop of Paris (Nov. 1758), the Pope (Jan. 1759), the Parlement of Paris (Feb. 1759), the Sorbonne (Apr. 1759) and by various bishops. He was dismissed from his sinecure as *maître d'hôtel* to the Queen, Marie Leszczynska, while his censor lost his regular position as *premier commis* at the Foreign Ministry. Only through the intercession of Mme de Pompadour and the Duc de Choiseul did Helvétius secure his personal safety. . . .

The circumstances which led to the publication of three 'first' editions constitute a fascinating story. After spending six years writing his work Helvétius decided to ignore good advice and publish through official channels. His friend Charles Georges Leroy, a minor Encyclopaedist, carefully selected as censor one of his acquaintances, Jean Pierre Tercier, *premier commis* at the Foreign Ministry, who censored political works in his spare time. Preoccupied with his main duties and unqualified to censor religious and ethical works, Tercier relied upon the integrity of Leroy, who, with Helvétius's connivance, proceeded to exploit him cunningly. Assured that *De l'esprit* 'ne roulait que sur la littérature', Tercier read the work only superficially. Moreover, he received the manuscript in such a haphazard fashion that he never grasped the thread of Helvétius's work. Every cut he suggested making was contested by Leroy, who collected censored pages daily. At a dinner given by Tercier on March 25th, 1758 he was enjoined not to waste time, but to trust his friends' assurances. Finally, the publisher, Laurent Durand, who had been responsible for Diderot's clandestine works, placed the proofs before him one morning and insisted that he sign every page on the spot without checking for surreptitious additions. Overworked, unqualified, ingenuous and, it would seem, half-blind, Tercier was tricked into passing the work almost *in toto,* cutting little besides a few references to Hume and Voltaire. On May 12th, 1758, a *privilège du Roi* was granted and all the neccessary preliminaries before publication had been completed.

The first impressions of the original edition, which had begun to leave the presses by the end of June, were kept by Helvétius for his personal friends. But, before the work could be put on sale to the general public, Malesherbes, *directeur de la librairie,* ordered that publication of the work be suspended indefinitely. Warned by one of his inspectors that *De l'esprit* was a dangerous work, Malesherbes decided to take no risks, especially since Helvétius was his personal friend, but to appoint forthwith a second censor and to confiscate the typeset of the work:

> Ce livre n'a jamais paru tel que M. Helvétius l'avait composé: il fut, à la vérité, livré à l'imprimeur en entier, mais le ministère, informé de ce qu'il contenait, y fit mettre des cartons, et ordonna que toutes les feuilles cartonnées seraient exactement jetées au pilon.

The second censor is shrouded in mystery. He remained anonymous and never replaced Tercier as the censor officially responsible for granting *De l'esprit* its *approbation.* Possibly he was Helvétius's friend, Père Plesse, a Jesuit priest who was later to engineer, on the Queen's behalf, the author's first two retractations. On July 2nd, 1758 he wrote to Helvétius a letter consistent with his acting as a friendly censor. His remarks on *De l'esprit* [quoted in M. Jusselin's *Helvétius et Mme de Panpadour, a propos du livre et de l'affaire "De l'esprit,"* 1913] must be quoted at some length, since they are the only evidence to support this conjecture:

> J'ai lu tout votre ouvrage. Vous y peignez l'esprit et le génie en homme qui en a toute la plénitude . . . Mais je ne saurais vous le dissimuler, une débauche d'esprit et de savoir vous a souvent emporté au delà du bien où vous tendiez. Avant que de lire votre ouvrage qu'on dévore, j'en étais prévenu. Les reproches qu'on vous fait m'étaient revenus du sein du plus grand monde, de ce monde qui, quoique peu scrupuleux, connaît cependant des règles que les plus grands auteurs doivent le plus respecter quand ils ambitionnent, en visant à l'utilité publique, la plus flatteuse universalité des suffrages . . .

> Quoique vous parliez de la religion avec respect et avec estime, il vous échappe des traits qui la blessent . . . Je ne vous parle point du fond de l'ouvrage. Sous les auspices de l'amitié la plus tendre et de la plus haute estime j'espère en disserter avec assez d'égards pour pouvoir, sans vous déplaire, m'acquitter envers le public judicieux de ce qu'il attend. Je serai toujours plus jaloux de conserver les bonnes grâces d'un ami solide que d'éviter la violence de nos ennemis passionnés. Je me flatte de vous dire le reste à Voré.

Plesse, or whoever was the second censor, re-examined the work and cut out certain sections with Helvétius's agreement. Some criticisms of the Catholic Church, made either directly or by transparent references to other religions, were omitted and occasional declarations of conformity were added to forestall any accusations of heterodoxy.

It was at this stage, it would seem, that Durand began to show his professional cunning. Anticipating that whether or not *De l'esprit* was passed by the second censor, a new edition of the work was sure to enjoy a *succès de scandale,* the publisher appears to have already set up completely new type, modelling it upon the original edition. This type—it can easily be recognized by its different typesetting and by its several new printing errors—was adapted to suit the second censor's requirements and was used to produce the second edition. The original typeset, when returned without the censored pages, would then be kept in reserve for further emergencies. Thus, when *De l'esprit* was officially published in Paris on July 27th, 1758, nobody suspected that it was, in fact, a completely new edition.

Helvétius now hoped that his book had weathered the storm. It had been passed by two censors, it had been granted a *privilège,* it was printed by the printers to the Queen and the Dauphin, and it was ostensibly anonymous, though many knew that it was written by a man of wealth, power and influence. In fact, the storm was only just beginning. Within ten days the Queen and the Dauphin complained about the book to the Chancelier who was Malesherbes's father, Lamoignon de Blancmesnil, while the Paris Parlement informed Malesherbes of its intention to examine the work. Realizing that the Jesuits would follow the Queen's lead and that the Parlement would use an outcry against *De l'esprit* to prove the inefficiency of the censorship authorities, Malesherbes ordered Durand to suspend the sale of *De l'esprit* immediately. He confiscated Durand's typeset, doubtless thinking it unique, whereas Durand had, it seems, hidden away the original typeset for just such an eventuality. Then, after a meeting with Tercier, whose enemies at Versailles were just waiting for a chance to dismiss him, he determined to forestall the Parlement's challenge to his department by annulling the work's *privilège,* thus disclaiming all responsibility for passing dangerous ideas. A formal *Arrêt du Conseil d'État du Roi* was drawn up to suppress the *privilège* and on August 10th the King signed it. Thus what seemed a mark of censure was, in fact, a clever ruse to frustrate the Parlement's intentions. As if answering a signal the religious and civil authorities moved into the attack, sustaining their assault until late 1759.

De l'esprit became the 'talk of the town.' Laharpe recalled how the book was so popular that those ladies who had the *Encyclopédie* on their shelves had *De l'esprit* on their dressing-tables. At least fourteen surreptitious editions appeared in 1758-59, some published semi-clandestinely by Durand, some elsewhere in France, some in Holland, possibly by publishers under contract to Durand.

One of Durand's surreptitious editions should strictly be called a re-issue of the original edition. Using the typeset which Malesherbes did not know he possessed, and setting up new type to replace the pages which Malesherbes had impounded in the first place, Durand secretly published a re-issue, the text of which was identical with the second edition. Helvétius may well have been a party to this edition since he sent at least one copy of it to a personal friend. Durand seems to have been successful in passing off his clandestine re-issue as the second edition, for there is no record of police measures against him. Consequently copies of the work were so abundant by 1760 that the police probably saw no further point in applying the ban on *De l'esprit.*

Ultimately, therefore, Helvétius and his publisher achieved their purpose. *De l'esprit* reached a wide public without prejudicing the author's personal safety or the publisher's financial interests. From the outset Helvétius had tried to guarantee the availability of his work. Believing that ends justified means, he and Leroy successfully tricked Tercier into granting his *approbation.* Their ruse was discovered, but how many similar tricks must have passed unnoticed in the course of the century? With an eye to his own profit Durand likewise tricked Malesherbes into believing that the original typeset was in police hands while, in fact, it was being used to produce a clandestine re-issue which was distributed among the *colporteurs.* . . . Helvétius himself was a victim of conflicting interests often only indirectly concerned with his work, yet by private intrigue he escaped the animosity of all his foes. *De l'esprit* was overwhelmed in conflicts outside itself, but Durand's unscrupulous business methods enabled him to exploit the *succès de scandale* which the work thus enjoyed.

C. Kiernan   (essay date 1968)

SOURCE: "Helvétius and a Science of Ethics," in *Studies on Voltaire and the Eighteenth Century,* Vol. LX, 1968, pp. 229-43.

[*In the following excerpt, Kiernan examines Helvétius's atheistic and egalitarian approach to ethical theory, claiming that "each attitude was defended by reference to the physical sciences."*]

Helvétius's views on science were confined to the physical sciences. Although the son of a doctor, he showed no interest in the life sciences. He relied on the achievement of Newton and of Locke. He aimed to parallel for ethics what Newton had achieved in mechanics, to extend the sensationalist psychology of Locke into ethics, and to establish ethics as a science based on laws and subject to mathematisation.

It is not generally recognised that a change occurred in Helvétius's thought between when he wrote *De l'esprit* in 1758, and *De l'homme* which was written by 1769, but not published until 1772, two years after the death of its author. The change was from a deist to an atheist position, and from that of a supporter of enlightened despotism to a more egalitarian point of view. Each attitude was defended by reference to the physical sciences. Helvétius's thought is important as exemplifying how the proponents of the physical sciences could arrive at an egalitarian position similar to, though different from that of the proponents of the life sciences.

Helvétius was indebted to the physical sciences in two major respects: as a model for other branches of knowledge; and as revealing unchanging truth. His aim was to achieve for ethics the same kind of synthesis that had been already reached in the physical sciences. If Helvétius was to arrive at an ethics to be universally true, he needed a principle to match the laws of science, a fact about human behaviour which is true for all men at all times. The belief that such a principle exists found its equivalent in the scientists' idea of an unchanging universe, in the universalism of the proponents of the physical sciences, which was strongly denied by, for example, Rousseau and Diderot. Helvétius found his answer in the principle of pleasure and pain, which he believed to be empirically demonstrable, and which was re-enforced by his sensationalist psychology, so that 'amour propre' becomes the dominant passion in men: 'La sensibilité physique a produit en nous l'amour du plaisir et la haine de la douleur'. So the human condition was seen by Helvétius to be represented by a pleasure/pain complex: 'Le plaisir et la douleur ont ensuite déposé fait éclore dans tous les coeurs le germe de l'amour de soi, dont le développement a donné naissance aux passions, d'où sont sortis tous nos vices et toutes nos vertus'.

Helvétius likened the passions in men, from which pleasure and pain derive, as analoguous to motion in the physical sciences: 'Les passions **sont**, dans le moral, ce que, dans la physique, est le mouvement'. Just as matter and motion can be used to explain the physical universe, they can also account for all man's other achievements, and even his art. Once having established the passions, and, in particular, pleasure and pain, as the dynamic forces in men, it then becomes possible to derive a utilitarian ethics: 'La vertu n'est que le désir du bonheur des hommes; et qu'ainsi la probité, que je regarde comme la vertu mise en action, n'est, chez tous les peuples et dans tous les gouvernements divers, que l'habitude des actions utiles à sa nation'.

In *De l'esprit,* while still working within the framework of Locke's sensationalist psychology, Helvétius had reached a different orientation. To Locke what mattered was the mind, which employs sensations as its raw material from which to draw inferences. This was Voltaire's position also. It works against equality, because it depends on the individual how valuable are the conclusions he draws. For Helvétius, what mattered most were the impressions from outside. Depending on what they were, the mind would always draw the appropriate conclusions. This was still an inegalitarian resolution, however, as individuals differ greatly in their capacity to experience. So their answers vary greatly in value, from that of the genius down to that of the fool. While Helvétius made a distinction between 'sensibilité physique', or the experiences from outside, and 'mémoire', or reflection on them, what mattered most was the 'sensibilité physique' of which 'mémoire' was a mere extension. The 'grande inégalité des esprits' was not due to difference in human organisation. This could not be, as men are everywhere the same. It is due, Helvétius argued, to the strength of the passions which vary greatly in men: 'La force de notre attention est alors proportionnée à la force de notre passion'. So although men are the same in all other respects, they differ in respect of the strength of their passions.

How can we account for the variation in human capacity, due to the strength of the passions, which can produce either genius or mediocrity? Helvétius's answer was chance and circumstance, which for him, when he wrote *De l'esprit,* amounted to much the same thing: 'L'homme de génie n'est donc que le produit des circonstances dans lesquelles cet homme s'est trouvé . . . l'homme de génie est en partie l'oeuvre du hasard'. The other chance factor is the government in power, which can make or break the man of genius.

There was little difference between the views of the author of *De l'esprit* and those of Voltaire. The position taken was that of a deist whose proof for the existence of god was the Voltairean argument from a first cause and from design, with particular reference to Newton and to the physical sciences. What Helvétius intended was to extend this line of thinking, to develop a science of ethics analogous to Newton's physics, an ethics which was founded on laws that could be tested empirically: 'La physique et la morale sont comme deux colonnes isolées éloignées l'une de l'autre, mais qu'un jour un même chapiteau rejoindra' [*Pensées et Reflexions,* 1818]. Another similarity with Voltaire was that the author of *De l'esprit* relied on an enlightened despot, a king, to introduce the new order.

There was only one major respect in which Helvétius's *De l'esprit* could be said to differ from Voltaire's point of view. That was in respect of the theory of knowledge. Voltaire placed more emphasis on the rôle of reflection compared with Helvétius, who relied on the passions as the way to knowledge. Even here the difference was less than would appear at first sight, as both were inegalitarian in their emphasis, one stressing variation in the human ability to reason, the other inequality in the capacity to experience.

It was no coincidence that the views expressed in *De l'esprit* resembled those of Voltaire, who prided himself on having discovered the talents of Helvétius long before the latter published anything; but not before he sent indifferent verse to Voltaire for his opinions on it: 'Mon aimable ami, qui ferez honneur à tous les arts, et que j'aime tendrement. . . . Vous êtes né poëte' (20 January 1738). Helvétius's wealthy and influential father was physician to the queen, and had introduced his son to Voltaire. Voltaire, who valued the prospect of a protégé at Court, began a correspondence which lasted, off and on, to the death of Helvétius in 1770. Voltaire sent Helvétius a copy of the *Eléments de la philosophie de Newton* when it was first published. He employed Helvétius to introduce people to Court, and even wrote to him in English on the subject: 'Our friendship is so well known, my young Apollo, that everybody resorts to me in order to obtain your benevolence'. In return, Helvétius employed Voltaire for opinions of his work, which, after correction by Helvétius, was sometimes shown to the king of Prussia.

There was a rupture in the friendship of Voltaire and Helvétius from 1741 to 1758. They ceased to correspond after Helvétius demanded the immediate return of money he had lent to Voltaire's mistress, the marquise Du Châtelet, to help her pay gambling debts. Helvétius's way of life, which resulted in his needing the money, also played its

rôle in the severance of their correspondence. Helvétius's passion for women was well known and seemed insatiable. He sought to slake it in the salon society of Paris. So ardent was his pursuit that it cut across the intellectual lines of division of the salons, leading Helvétius from one to another. Madame la duchesse de Chaulnes, who conducted a salon, was his mistress for a time. Eventually, almost inevitably, he married. It transpired that his wife, to whom he was happily married, was a habitué of the salon of madame de Graffigny, her aunt, which was a meeting place for proponents of the life sciences, notably Turgot, who detested Helvétius, and Quesnay. While Helvétius did not thereupon become an upholder of the life sciences, there seemed on the face of it a distinct possibility that he might. Worse than that, he was dealing with people who dissented from Voltaire.

The tremendous explosion occasioned by the publication of *De l'esprit* brought Voltaire and Helvétius together again. Shocked by the impact of his work, Helvétius wrote to Voltaire and quickly identified himself with his 'master': 'Dès que je le pourrai, je vous enverrai donc mon ouvrage, comme un hommage que tout auteur doit à son maître'. Voltaire was forced to concede that the views of *De l'esprit* were, in fact, remarkably similar to his own. While he disliked the furore, he would not deny the resemblance: 'Votre livre est dicté par la saine raison: partez vite, et quittez la France'. Helvétius needed an assurance that Voltaire was in substantial agreement with *De l'esprit.* This was forthcoming: 'Vous me déplaire? et pourquoy et en quoy!' In the same letter he invited Helvétius to be his guest. Thereafter he referred to Helvétius as 'mon illustre philosophe' and Helvétius continued to refer to Voltaire as 'mon illustre maître'.

Helvétius did not publish *De l'homme* during his lifetime. It would have found far less agreement from Voltaire. In it Helvétius gave evidence of having moved away from deism and inegalitarianism to atheism and democracy.

Helvétius's humanism was hammered out on the anvil of his suffering. The publication of his *De l'esprit* became an issue in the struggle between orthodoxy and its foes. The Jesuits, who were striving to suppress Diderot's popular *Encyclopédie* saw in *De l'esprit* the Achilles heel of the philosophes, as being easier to suppress than the *Encyclopédie.* Helvétius's purpose in publishing *De l'esprit* was to provide an alternative interpretation of sensational psychology to that provided by Condillac, one which relied on a use of the physical sciences, compared with that of Condillac, which employed the arguments of the life scientists. In fact, Helvétius offered an alternative to the philosophy of Diderot and his colleagues, as set out in the *Encyclopédie,* to which Helvétius made no contributions.

Where Helvétius differed from Condillac was in his theory of the mind. Condillac revived La Mettrie's nominalist sensationalism, but married it with orthodoxy in religion, and stripped it of its mechanical camouflage. He employed the first cause proof of the proponents of the life sciences, with god demonstrating his existence as the author of life: 'Voilà la création. Elle n'est, à notre égard, que l'action d'un premier principe, par laquelle les êtres, de non-existans, deviennent existans' (*Traité des animaux*).

Where Helvétius and Condillac diverged most was in the emphasis by the latter on difference in the method of operation of individual organisms. Condillac employed a statue as his model through which to demonstrate the wide range of possibilities where sense experience is in question (*Traité des sensations*). The statue was given one sense after another, and the possible results discussed in detail. Condillac's was a descriptive science which eschewed generalisation.

Condillac carried his reaction against the mechanical world view from the human to the animal realm: 'Il est impossible de concevoir que le mécanisme puisse seul régler les actions des animaux' (*Traité des animaux*). He rejected the belief of the mechanists, for example of Descartes, that animals are machines, going even further than Buffon in the re-instatement of animals to claim that they can feel, think, and judge (*Traité des animaux*). It transpired that there were in eighteenth-century France two schools of sensationalist psychology, one upheld by Condillac, the other by Helvétius; and that each was able to claim to be the true inheritor of Locke. But whereas Condillac, like Diderot, La Mettrie and Rousseau, emphasised the nominalist psychology of the proponents of the life sciences, Helvétius upheld the mathematical, generalising proclivities of the proponents of the physical sciences.

What was seen by Helvétius as a dispute in the ranks of the philosophes was taken by their foes as part of a concerted program against orthodoxy. This becomes clear when Helvétius's frantic efforts are examined. In order to avoid trouble, and to win opinion to his side, Helvétius had *De l'esprit* passed by the official censors before publication. But the book aroused the ire of the Jesuits because they were themselves employing a mechanical world view, in their case that of Descartes; but which was being sent by Helvétius in a direction away from the orthodox position. In vain Helvétius, by his three retractions, strove to avoid a debate on religion. What he saw was his book, which he had intended to win for him a claim to be the Newton of ethics, and which had been the product of long travail, being branded as a mere anti-religious tract. The result of his struggle with orthodoxy was to lose him royal favour, and to endanger his mother's position as the friend of the queen. His struggle against authority sent Helvétius's thought along the road to humanism, egalitarianism and atheism.

How was it possible to employ the rationale of the physical sciences as a defence for a democratic credo? Whereas in *De l'esprit* Helvétius emphasised difference in the strength of the passions as distinguishing men of genius from mediocre men, in *De l'homme* he argued that, while all men start equal, their minds a blank, their potential is determined not by their own passion for learning, but by what they are taught: 'L'inégalité des esprits est l'effet d'une cause connue, et cette cause est la différence de l'éducation'. The activist element of the passions, which makes men unequal, has been replaced by the emphasis on the education of passive, receptive beings. Individual initiative, which is why people are unequal, is replaced by a social concept of training in equality, so that all men end up the same.

In order clearly to establish this change of position, Helvétius reversed his emphasis on the passions, not memory, as the way to knowledge, which is the message of *De l'esprit,* to the opposite of an emphasis on the memory, not the passions, as the appropriate road to truth: 'C'est à la mémoire (dont l'existence suppose la faculté de sentir) que l'homme doit et ses idées et son esprit . . . Sans mémoire, point d'expérience, point de comparaison d'objets, point d'idées; et l'homme serait, dans sa vieillesse, ce qu'il était dans son enfance'.

Whereas in *De l'esprit* what mattered was the 'esprit', the activist element in man, now it was to be the quality of his experience, a product of reflection, which had as its outcome the 'âme', the form of the person: 'L'esprit différe donc essentiellement de l'âme en ce qu'on peut perdre l'un de son vivant, et qu'on ne perd l'autre qu'avec la vie'.

It might appear, on the face of it, as if Helvétius's position in *De l'homme* represented a return to a strictly Voltairean theory of knowledge, namely, to the emphasis on reasoning from sense experience. This is not so. The difference is in the rejection by Helvétius of the idea of variety in mental capacity. For Helvétius in *De l'homme,* given the same experience, no two minds can draw different conclusions. Clearly, this is a vastly more optimistic and egalitarian point of view than that of Voltaire: 'Tous les hommes, il est vrai, n'éprouvent pas précisément les mêmes sensations; mais tous sentent les objets dans une proportion toujours la même. Tous ont donc une égale aptitude à l'esprit'. So the most difficult discoveries, as, for example, those of Newton, when clearly stated, can be understood by everyone. Although the passions play a smaller rôle in *De l'homme* than in *De l'esprit,* Helvétius did not dismiss then altogether. Instead he strove to equalise their importance. Towards that end he proposed a redistribution of land, so that each would have an equal capacity to enjoy, thus opening the way for Marx, who carried on in this vein.

More typically, Helvétius argued for the greater importance of teaching as compared with learning in human affairs. This was seen clearly in his controversy with Rousseau on education. Whereas in *Emile* Rousseau emphasised the importance of the individual in the learning process, Helvétius, an advocate of mass instruction, emphasised the importance of the teacher, not the pupil. Here was the difference between 'irritability', the greater emphasis on the motor factor, by the proponents of the physical sciences, and 'sensitivity', the idea of inner direction as advocated by the supporters of the life sciences. This difference explains why Rousseau was concerned to refute Helvétius's *De l'esprit* in his *Emile* and why Helvétius aimed to ridicule Rousseau in his *De l'homme.*

In *De l'esprit* the rôle of chance and circumstance was accepted as generally binding and difficult to handle. So, while genius is developed through education, it cannot be guaranteed to succeed in every instance. It will never succeed if the government is not appropriate. In *De l'homme,* however, there was a far greater emphasis on education and government than in *De l'esprit,* and far more optimism about the outcome. Every man can now be a genius if the education system is geared to it.

In *De l'esprit* education is to be undertaken apart from the state. Legislation and education are considered as separate entities to be handled by different people. The function of education is to raise one, or at most a few, to the level of genius needed to legislate. No more is needed to produce an enlightened despot.

In *De l'homme,* legislation and education are integrated: the teaching of the pleasure/pain calculus is carried out by the same people who are measuring and adjusting the system. Here the function of education is to raise up everyman to the same level of genius. This becomes possible once learning is changed from an active to a passive principle. The result of this theory is to open the way to the possibility of democratising learning. The debate between the upholders of each strand of Helvétius's opinion continues, as does the conflict between the educational individualism of Rousseau and the two schemes advocated by Helvétius.

Whereas Diderot dismissed Helvétius's *De l'esprit* with contempt, he was amazed by what he read in *De l'homme.* He wrote to his mistress Sophie Volland in 1767 that: 'Helvétius . . . s'occupe à sa terre, à prouver que son valet de chiens auroit tout aussi bien fait le livre *De l'esprit* que luis'. Five years later his opinion of Helvétius had changed. Though he did not agree with *De l'homme,* he recognised its importance when he wrote of it: 'Il sera pourtant compté parmi les grands livres du siècle'. It transpired, however, that the thoughts of Helvétius and of Diderot were incompatible. This is an important fact about European culture.

Diderot defended inner against other direction. He argued for the mind as an organism with a life of its own, against Helvétius's emphasis on the mind as an extension of the senses, which responds immediately to outside stimuli. Diderot claimed that the mind can store impressions, and compare them with new stimuli, and choose between them. Helvétius believed that the mind responds more simply and directly to impulses. Diderot argued that a person can prefer a long-term to an immediate gain: 'La folie consiste à préférer l'intérêt d'un moment au bonheur de sa vie'. Helvétius claimed that this only seems to be the case, that the anticipation of pleasure is in fact an immediate stimulus. The issue depends on whether the mind is seen as a mechanism or as an organism, a computer or a polyp.

The difference between men was another point at issue between Diderot and Helvétius. Diderot rejected Helvétius's belief that education matters most. Diderot adopted the nominalist position that the constitution of the individual, his texture or composition, the life force in him, is what counts, so that men are not the same at all. It is variety in the structure of brains, and internal pressures working on the brain, which is responsible for different levels of intelligence. So drugs can change the human constitution; and monster births can be normal ones. Helvétius took only those 'communément bien organisés' into account.

Diderot was closer to Rousseau's educational individualism than to Helvétius's emphasis on general teaching. Diderot believed that individuals have different aptitudes. Like Rousseau, Diderot put the individual needs ahead of those of organised society. Helvétius reversed the emphasis, arguing that in so doing man's best interest would be served.

Both Helvétius and Diderot strove to equate virtue and happiness. They differed in how they proposed to achieve the equation. Diderot rejected the mathematisation of politics proposed by Helvétius, his felicific calculus, seeing in it the triumph of mechanism over the lives of men. His solution was, like Rousseau's, a belief in the general will, that man will, in the end, choose the good. His opposition to Helvétius's mechanical world view drove Diderot to accept, at the expense of his logic, individual self-determination.

In both *De l'esprit* and *De l'homme* Helvétius relied on a legislator to reconcile individual self-interest with the common good. He always believed it was possible to effect a reconciliation: 'Les vices et les vertus d'un peuple sont toujours un effet nécessaire de sa législation'. The method whereby this can be achieved is by a system of rewards and punishments. There was a difference in orientation, however, between *De l'esprit* and *De l'homme.* Whereas at first the emphasis was on an enlightened despot, later it was on education as the means to the end. The trend was away from the man of genius to the genius of the people. There was less need for such a man, as the emphasis was moved from individual judgment to a more scientific approach. A sort of felicific calculus, not the individual judgment of a legislator, was most needed: 'On peut calculer la peur qu'un homme doit avoir du tonnerre dans un carrosse, dans un bateau'.

Diderot believed that Helvétius had over-simplified by reducing pleasure to the physical level. He argued for moral pleasures which are different from physical ones, thus rendering the mathematical approach inappropriate. He also argued for change in the human condition, so that no final solution is possible.

Although Helvétius defended democracy by reference to the mechanical world view, it was an uneasy resolution of the position. The intellectuality needed to develop the felicific calculus would lead more readily to an enlightened despotism than to anything else. In the debate between 'the one' and 'the many', between the universalism of the proponents of the physical sciences and the nominalism of the upholders of the life sciences, it seemed more likely that democracy would develop from the position of 'the many'. Helvétius's importance is not that he squared a circle, but that he showed that there are, at least in theory, more ways than one to democracy, and that each has its strengths and weaknesses, which can be debated by each side.

An analysis of the debate between Diderot and Helvétius results in two conclusions: that the controversy between these advocates of egalitarianism and atheism arose out of their use of contrasting scientific analyses; and that the points at issue between them, which were thoroughly analysed by Diderot, were not resolved: they still stand.

Bertrand Russell on Helvétius:

Helvétius had the honour of having his book *De l'Esprit* condemned by the Sorbonne and burnt by the hangman. Bentham read him in 1769 and immediately determined to devote his life to the principles of legislation, saying: "What Bacon was to the physical world, Helvétius was to the moral. The moral world has therefore had its Bacon, but its Newton is still to come." James Mill took Helvétius as his guide in the education of his son John Stuart.

Following Locke's doctrine that the mind is a *tabula rasa,* Helvétius considered the differences between individuals entirely due to differences of education: in every individual, his talents and his virtues are the effect of his instruction. Genius, he maintains, is often due to chance: if Shakespeare had not been caught poaching, he would have been a wool merchant. His interest in legislation comes from the doctrine that the principal instructors of adolescence are the forms of government and the consequent manners and customs. Men are born ignorant, not stupid; they are made stupid by education.

In ethics, Helvétius was a utilitarian; he considered pleasure to be the good. In religion, he was a deist, and vehemently anti-clerical. In theory of knowledge, he adopted a simplified version of Locke: "Enlightened by Locke, we know that it is to the sense-organs we owe our ideas, and consequently our mind." Physical sensibility, he says, is the sole cause of our actions, our thoughts, our passions, and our sociability. He strongly disagrees with Rousseau as to the value of knowledge, which he rates very highly.

His doctrine is optimistic, since only a perfect education is needed to make men perfect. There is a suggestion that it would be easy to find a perfect education if the priests were got out of the way.

> *Bertrand Russell, in his* A History of Western Philosophy, *Simon and Schuster, 1945.*

D. W. Smith   (essay date 1971)

SOURCE: "The 'Useful Lie' in Helvétius and Diderot," in *Diderot Studies, Vol. XIV,* edited by Otis Fellows and Diana Guiragossian, Librairie Droz S. A., 1971, pp. 185-95.

[*In the following essay, Smith examines the role of the "useful lie" (i. e., one which is socially useful) in both Diderot and Helvétius, and evaluates the attempts of the two philosophers to discredit it in favor of truth.*]

> Il nous démontra clair comme un et un font deux, que rien n'était plus utile aux peuples que le mensonge, rien de plus nuisible que la vérité.
> Diderot, *Le Neveu de Rameau*

For the eighteenth-century *philosophes* the problem of the "useful lie" was neither abstract nor isolated, but was intimately involved with their reformist beliefs and programmes. In contemporary Christianity they saw a "pious fraud" initiated and perpetuated by acquisitive priests seeking to exploit the ignorance of the masses. In the *ancien régime* they saw their rulers using deceit to maintain their unjust oppression of the ruled. Naturally they thought that society could be reformed only if such fraud and deceit were exposed and eliminated. Yet conservatives—inside as well as outside the philosophic ranks—could justify deceit in religion and politics on the grounds that lies were often useful and truth often dangerous. They claimed that people were often happier to live in error than to be confronted with unwelcome truths. They thus defended falsehood under the same banners as the more radical *philosophes* defended truth—the banners of happiness and utility. With few exceptions neither conservatives nor radicals rejected the criterion of utility. Occasionally the conservatives confused the utilitarian problem with the moral: that is, they confused what I shall call the "useful lie" (the lie justified by its useful results) with the "white lie" (the lie justified by its altruistic motives), but generally the moral issues were left aside. However, the radical *philosophes,* while talking in terms of utility, tried to gain all the advantages of a moral, idealistic approach. They went only so far in a utilitarian direction, then stopped short for fear of imperilling all the reformist ideals which they held dear.

There was on more extreme utilitarian among the eighteenth-century *philosophes* than Helvétius who, with ruthless logic, pursued his sensationalist premises to their utilitarian consequences in politics, ethics, education, and aesthetics. Yet, though he made utility the criterion of all values, his idealistic ambitions prevented him from advocating the useful lie. His faith in progress, his belief in the educability of man, his political liberalism proved too important to sacrifice to pragmatism. He tried, therefore, to reach some philosophic compromise which would enable him to keep the best of both worlds. I propose to follow Helvétius's approach to the useful lie, examine the pitfalls before which he halted, and show how he managed to avoid them. Since the views of the materialistic Diderot place him in the same camp as Helvétius, they can suitably be treated at the same time.

According to Helvétius, it was man's nature passively and mechanically to seek pleasure and avoid pain. Governed exclusively by self-interest, man was physically incapable of desiring anything but his own happiness. He subordinated all values, including truth, to his own pleasure: "Si telle est la nature de chaque individu qu'il soit nécessité de s'aimer de préférence à tous, l'amour du vrai est toujours en lui subordonné à l'amour de son bonheur: il ne peut aimer dans le vrai que le moyen d'accroître sa félicité." If it were in a man's interests to lie, he would be quite unable to tell the truth. "Nul pays où quelques particuliers n'aient intérêt d'entre-mêler les ténèbres du mensonge aux lumières de la vérité" [*De l'Homme*].

The same applied to the group of individuals comprising a nation. Social utility, the greatest happiness of the greatest number, was the criterion of all social values: "Cette utilité est le principe de toutes les vertus humaines . . . C'est enfin à ce principe qu'il faut sacrifier tous ses sentiments, jusqu'au sentiment même de l'humanité" [*De l'Esprit*]. Any action which was not useful to society could not be virtuous. All moral values other than the utilitarian had to be rejected: "Qu'importe au public la probité d'un particulier? Cette probité ne lui est de presque aucune utilité" [*De l'Esprit*]. Utility was even the yardstick of truth itself: "La vérité elle-même est soumise au principe de l'utilité publique" [*De l'Esprit*]. In these circumstances even mathematical truths were not absolute for Helvétius but relative to utility:

> Tous les hommes conviennent de la vérité des propositions géométriques: serait-ce parce qu'elles sont démontrées? Non; mais parce qu'indifférentes à leur fausseté ou à leur vérité, les hommes n'ont nul intérêt de prendre le faux pour le vrai. Leur suppose-t-on cet intérêt? Alors les propositions les plus évidemment démontrées leur paraîtront problématiques. [*De l'Homme*]

Diderot similarly laid great stress on utility: "L'utile circonscrit tout." Indeed, if Diderot did write the article "Christianisme" in the *Encyclopédie,* he went so far as to make utility a guarantee of truth: "Il n'y a rien d'universellement utile qui ne soit exactement vrai. Ces deux choses marchent, pour ainsi dire, de front."

Diderot must have been well aware that, if utility is the only criterion for establishing truth and falsehood, then truths, if harmful, must be treated as falsehoods, while errors and lies, if useful, must be considered as truths. Yet only once in his work [in *Observations sur le Nakaz*] have I found him seriously entertaining the idea of a useful error: "Il faut ou qu'un peuple soit libre, *ou qu'il croie l'être.* Celui qui détruit ce préjugé national est un scélérat." Here he comes dangerously close to advocating the useful lie which elsewhere, especially in his *Pages contre un tyran,* he held in such dread. Helvétius did admit that truth could be dangerous to the teller—the author of *De l'Esprit* had good reason to be convinced of this!—but it never harmed the receiver's ultimate interests. He also admitted that known errors might have a negative usefulness—to show men what path not to take. But he, too, refused to concede the general utility of errors or lies.

For, in the eyes of the more liberal *philosophes,* the useful lie was fraught with dangerous implications. Above all, in the hands of two main groups—well-intentioned conservatives and unscrupulous rulers—it served to perpetuate and even aggravate existing abuses in both religion and politics.

Many conservatives who were prepared to admit privately the falsehood of the Christian religion none the less insisted in all sincerity that even a false religion was a better buttress of social morality than unbelief. Transcendental sanctions seemed the only answer to the problem of undetected crime. Politically, they felt that, whatever the shortcomings of a government, the ruled should not attempt to subvert it but, for their own good, should be lulled by deception into acceptance of their rulers. In the interests not so much of the government as of the governed, peace and stability were preferable to the civil strife which was traditionally considered the normal state of society. The people were happier with their illusions than with truths which could well lead to a disastrous anarchy. Essentially this was a defeatist philosophy, pessimistic and cynical, but it played a vital role in the theories of some of France's most advanced political thinkers—Montesquieu, Morelly, Rousseau, and Mably. It ran contrary, however, to some of the Enlightenment's cherished beliefs, and it implied that prejudices and false doctrines should be preserved.

But what was more pernicious in the eyes of the liberals was that this philosophy could be exploited by rulers, whether priests or tyrants, to maintain their own power, wealth and privileges. Rapacity could be passed off as benevolence. The white lie, which the well-meaning conservatives used paternalistically in the interests of the ruled, could be imperceptibly transformed into the "black lie" which furthered only the interests of the rulers. It is perhaps not surprising to find that Frederick the Great was perhaps the eighteenth century's staunchest champion of the useful lie. In his *Examen de l'essai sur les préjugés* the Machiavellian king who, ironically, had written an *Anti-Machiavel* before his accession to the throne, justified deceit and falsehood ostensibly in the interests of his people, but in the view of the adversaries of despotism he sought only to maintain his oppression. Diderot and Helvétius saw clearly that the rejection of truth led to the condonation of exploitation and social injustice.

Advocates of the useful lie usually argued in their defence that prejudice and error were inherent in the human condition, that philosophers, who in any case rarely agreed with each other, had always advanced more errors than truths, and that the truth, if ascertainable at all, was accessible only to the enlightened few. Trying to enlighten the underprivileged masses was just a waste of time.

Diderot was well aware that there was some truth in these arguments. With his fondness for questions, he asked [in his *De la Poésie dramatique*]: "L'homme est-il donc condamné à n'être d'accord ni avec ses semblables, ni avec lui-même, sur les seuls objets qu'il lui importe de connaître, la vérité, la bonté, la beauté?" But he saw no reason to resign himself to the inevitability of error or to the rejection of moral absolutes: "Vaut-il mieux errer dans les ténèbres, n'avoir aucune idée arrêtée, faire le bien par sottise, le mal sans savoir pourquoi? . . . Les lumières sont un bien dont on peut abuser sans doute. L'ignorance et la stupidité, compagnes de l'injustice, de l'erreur, et de la superstition, sont toujours des maux."

In repudiating the same arguments Helvétius felt himself on firmer ground. He claimed that, since at birth all minds were void and therefore of equal intelligence, all subsequent differences in intelligence were attributable to environment, and especially to education. Differences in physical make-up were of negligible influence. "L'éducation peut tout." Any normally constituted man could be conditioned into becoming a genius. The ruled were thus as educable as theirs rulers. The ignorance of the masses was not their inevitable condition—"l'erreur n'est . . . pas essentiellement attachée à la nature de l'esprit humain"—it was the result of exploitation by unscrupulous rulers.

Moreover, Helvétius shared the common eighteenth-century assumption that all men could recognize the truth when they saw it, provided they were not blinded by such fallacies and prejudices as religion. For truth was essentially accessible. Of the Cartesian rational conception of abstract, absolute truth, Helvétius had inherited only the notion that truth was simple, clear and irresistible. Error was correspondingly complex: "L'erreur est de mille espèces. La vérité au contraire est une et simple; sa marche est toujours uniforme et conséquente." Provided a problem was broken down into its simplest constituent parts according to the Cartesian method, its solution would present no difficulty:

> Il n'est rien que les hommes ne puissent entendre. Quelque compliquée que soit une proposition, on peut, avec le secours de l'analyse, la décomposer en un certain nombre de propositions simples; et ces propositions deviendront évidentes . . . lorsqu'un homme ne pourra les nier sans tomber en contradiction avec luimême . . . Toute vérité peut se ramener à ce terme; et, lorsqu'on l'y réduit, il n'est plus d'yeux qui se ferment à la lumière. [*De l'Esprit*]

Diderot, more scientific and realistic, could see that this was wishful thinking. Not everybody was capable of the required analysis: "Cette réduction d'une vérité éloignée à un fait simple n'est pas l'ouvrage de tout esprit." There were some truths which only a handful of men could ever understand: "Pendant longtemps il n'y eut que trois hommes en Europe qui entendissent la petite géométrie de Descartes . . . Il n'y a aucun temps où les hautes vérités deviennent communes, et les principes de mathématiques, de philosophie naturelle de Newton ne seront jamais une lecture vulgaire" [*Réfutation d'Helvétius*].

But the essential problem still remained: how was the principle of utility to be preserved without sacrificing truth, justice, and progress? Both philosophers conceded that lies could be of temporary usefulness to individuals. It was permissible for a soldier to lie to his captors about military secrets or for a doctor to lie to a dying patient about his condition. But from these examples no general principle could be erected. Ultimately lies were always harmful and truth useful, as Diderot insistently averred [in his "Pyrrhonienne ou Sceptique philosophie"]:

> Une vérité, quelle qu'elle soit, nuisible pour le moment, est nécessairement utile dans l'avenir. Un mensonge, quel qu'il soit, avantageux peut-être pour le moment, nuit nécessairement avec le temps. Penser autrement, c'est ne pas connaître le vrai caractère ni de l'un ni de l'autre.

Ultimately truth would always triumph over falsehood. "Que peut-elle [la vérité] alors en faveur de l'humanité? Tout avec le temps . . . Elle finit et finira éternellement par être la plus forte."

Helvétius expressed similar views. Though, with rigorous logic, he had subordinated truth to utility, there was, in fact, no clash between them. Absolute truth could never be ultimately harmful: "Il n'est point . . . de vérités dont la connaissance puisse être dangereuse." And absolute error could never be useful and thus be transformed into truth relative to utility: "C'est le vrai seul qu'il faut enseigner. Mais ne peut-on en aucun cas y substituer des erreurs utiles? Il n'en est point de telles" [*De l'Homme*]. Di-

derot put it more concisely: "La vérité est toujours utile et le mensonge toujours nuisible." [*Des Délits et des peines*].

The most telling argument against the useful lie was advanced by Diderot. He claimed that lies were always told in the name of truth. Liars, therefore, implicitly acknowledged the superiority of truth over falsehood: "En prêchant le mensonge, ils [de scélérats prédicateurs] font à leurs dupes l'éloge de la vérité, mais leurs dupes n'embrassent le mensonge qui leur est prêché que sous le nom de la vérité." [*Pages contre un tyran*]. Helvétius says much the same thing with less philosophical clarity but more anti-clerical venom:

> Un prédicateur prouve en chaire que le Dieu des chrétiens est un Dieu de vérité; que c'est à leur haine pour le mensonge qu'on reconnaît ses adorateurs. Est-il descendu de chaire? Il convient qu'il est très prudent de la taire; que lui-même, en louant la vérité, se garde bien de la dire. [*De l'Homme*]

Not without some wishful thinking and self-contradiction both went on to claim that lying was not really in the individual's interests, that man would always be happier if he told the truth. Though the Neveu de Rameau had warned that some men found happiness in evil, Diderot in his moralistic vein fervently declared:

> En tout genre l'homme aime la vérité, parce que la vérité est une vertu; l'homme cherche sans cesse la vérité; c'est le but de toutes ses études, de tous ses soins, de tous ses travaux; il déteste l'erreur, parce qu'il sait bien qu'en quoi que ce soit, il ne saurait se tromper sans se nuire à lui-même; son vrai bonheur est fondé sur la vérité. [*Pages contre un tyran*]

Likewise Helvétius believed that his ideal society could make it worth men's while to seek and tell the truth:

> L'homme, je le sais, n'aime point la vérité pour la vérité même. Il rapporte tout à son bonheur. Mais, s'il le place dans l'acquisition d'une estime publique et durable, il est évident, puisque cette espèce d'estime est attachée à la découverte de la vérité, qu'il est, par la nature même de sa passion, forcé de n'aimer et de ne rechercher que le vrai. [*De l'Homme*]

How could this ideal society ever be realized? Only if the truth could be revealed freely, only if lies and errors could be frankly exposed. Prejudices such as religion would be rapidly removed, if they could be submitted to scrutiny without the restrictions of censorship. Free enquiry would speedily overcome ignorance, the only obstacle to the moral progress of society. Enlightened men would automatically be virtuous: "Plus les peuples sont éclairés, plus ils sont vertueux, puissants, et heureux. C'est à l'ignorance seule qu'il faut imputer les effets contraires."

For Helvétius, then, as for Diderot, the useful lie was not a purely academic problem, it was closely concerned with all their ethical, social and political views. It could be used to perpetuate political and religious abuses and it threatened their fundamental beliefs in social justice, human progress and the educability of man. Their utilitarianism had taken them to the very brink of the useful lie, but they fought shy of taking the last logical step. They preferred to modify their utilitarianism rather than imperil their liberal values. Their distinction between temporary and ultimate utility was a clever expedient but it amounted to a compromise with traditional ideals and absolutes. Their identification of absolute and relative truth enabled them to salvage their humanism but it was really a concession to the conservatives.

Eric Voegelin   (essay date 1975)

SOURCE: "Helvétius and the Genealogy of Passions" and "Helvétius and the Heritage of Pascal," in his *From Enlightenment to Revolution,* Duke University Press, 1975, pp. 35-73.

[*German-born American historian and political philosopher Voegelin is regarded as one of the most important scholars of the twentieth century. He is best known for his five-volume masterwork* Order and History *in which he fashioned a comprehensive view of human history by exploring modern political institutions in light of premodern political forms. In the following essay, Voegelin examines the importance and role of the passions in Helvétius's philosophy and addresses the place of Helvétius's doctrine in the theoretical discussion of historical evolution and class struggle.*]

It is difficult, if not impossible, even today to achieve a balanced view of the person and work of Helvétius. There is more than one reason for this difficulty. Helvétius lived in the age of Montesquieu and Voltaire, of Hume and Rousseau. His figure, though quite respectable, does not measure up to the stature of these dominating figures of the Age of Enlightenment and as a consequence his work has never received the same careful, detailed attention as the work of his greater contemporaries. Moreover, his work is expressive of the movement of enlightenment to such a degree that its typical features were seen more clearly than its far more important and peculiarly personal ones. Helvétius belonged intimately to the circle of the *encyclopédistes* though he himself never contributed to the *Encyclopédie.* One may say of his first great work, *De l'Esprit* (1758), that it focussed in the form of a systematic treatise the political views which, in the articles of the *Encyclopédie,* appear in the form of a wide spectrum of divergent opinions of several authors. This relation of the *Esprit* to the *Encyclopédie* was strongly sensed at the time when the treatise appeared. The *Parlement de Paris,* in 1759, when it ordered the burning of the *Esprit,* ordered at the same time an inquiry into the orthodoxy of the *Encyclopédie.* As a consequence, the permission for the publication of the *Encyclopédie,* of which seven volumes had appeared between 1751 and 1757, was withdrawn and publication could be resumed only in 1765. Quite as much as by a too close association with the *Encyclopédie,* the personal achievement of Helvétius has been obscured by its being related too closely to the evolution of English utilitarianism. What is perhaps best known today about Helvétius is his dependence upon Locke and his influence on Bentham. One may say, indeed, that Helvétius did what Locke failed to do, that is to apply the principles of the *Essay concerning Human Understanding* to the problems of politics, and there is no doubt that certain formulations of the *Esprit* suggested the principle of the greatest happiness of the greatest number both to Beccaria and Bentham. This historical function of Helvétius as the transmittor from Locke to Bentham should by no means be slighted; nevertheless, there was more substance to the French thinker than can be absorbed by this view. It was this substance that Nietzsche had in mind when he described the work of Helvétius as "the last great event in morals."

The heritage of Locke

There does exist, indeed, a relation between Helvétius's method and the ideas of Locke's *Essay.* Helvétius insists on the point with pride. Nevertheless, the relationship does not have the simple form of an adoption of certain ideas of Locke. Locke's *Essay* had appeared in 1690; sixty-five years later, at the time when Helvétius was writing his *Esprit,* conventional assumptions had developed concerning what Locke's ideas were, and these assumptions moved sometimes at a considerable distance from the original meaning of Locke's *Essay.* This latitude of interpretation was inevitably caused by the fact that Locke's theory of morals itself was an agglomeration of assumptions, hardly consistent with each other. The attack on innate ideas in the field of morals resulted in the assumption that a desire for happiness and an aversion to misery are the fundamental appetites determining human conduct. "Good and evil are nothing but pleasure and pain, or that which occasions or procures pleasure or pain to us." For every moral rule offered to us we have to demand proof of its reasonableness, and the appeal lies ultimately to this principle. This crude formula, if taken seriously, could lead to interesting results; some of them can be seen in Mandeville's *Fable of the Bees* (1723). Locke himself would not have accepted this malicious and delightful play with virtues and vices. To him right and wrong were beyond doubt and morality was "capable of demonstration as well as mathematics." But where do we find the operating rules for this mathematics of morality? Bentham's later answer was the principle of the greatest happiness of the greatest number. For Locke, the ultimate standard is the "law of God," extending the pleasure-pain principle into the beyond, for virtuous or sinful conduct will procure for man "happiness or misery from the hands of the Almighty." But how can we be assured of this "only true touchstone of moral rectitude"? Through revelation? This assumption would lead, as it did, into the movement of theological utilitarianism, and ultimately to the positions of [Abraham] Tucker and [William] Paley. Again, however, Locke would not approve. He was convinced that the Gospel was a true code of morality, but he was equally convinced that the discovery of this code did not require a revelation. How then could the true code be found? At this point, Locke's argument petered out inconclusively, and the field remained wide open for the reconstruction of a philosophy of morals. The net result of Locke's speculation, thus, is not a new philosophy of morals but a thorough devastation on which nobody could build anything. The assertion that the position of a moralist is influenced by Locke can be received, therefore, only with caution.

What Helvétius owes to Locke can best be gathered from his formulation of what he considered Locke's theory: "Our ideas," says Helvétius, "come to us from the senses; and from this principle, as from mine, one may conclude that the *esprit* in us is nothing but an acquisition." The *esprit* is an assemblage of ideas, directly or indirectly derived from sense impressions. The nature of man is basically a physical sensibility (*sensibilité physique*). "The physical sensibility is man himself, and the principle of all that he is." All differences between men are due to the differences of the educational process to which the *sensibilité physique* (which is neutrally receptive at birth) is submitted in the course of life. This radical formulation of Helvétius's position, however, is rather to be found in the later *De l'Homme* (published post-humously in 1772) than in the earlier *De l'Esprit.* The principle seems to have crystallized more clearly with the years and Helvétius admits: "In man all is physical sensation. Perhaps I have not developed this truth sufficiently in my book *De l'Esprit.*" We see emerging an image of man of impressive simplicity. The content of the mind is a transformation of sense impressions and a complicated structure is conceived as reducible to one explanatory principle, to physical sensibility. And this sensibility is not a faculty of man, but is man himself. Obviously, this is not Locke's conception of the mind, for Locke recognizes two sources of experience—sensation and reflection. The sentence: *"Nil est in intellectu, quod non fuerit in sensu,"* is not applicable to his conception unless at least we qualify the word *sensu* by the adjectives *interno et externo.* The experiences given to the internal sense of reflection—such as perceiving, thinking, doubting, believing, knowing, willing—constitute for Locke a class of experiences independent of sense impressions. The elimination of reflection and the systematic reduction of the internal experiences to sense impressions which we find in Helvétius is rather the conception of the mind that was developed by Condillac in his *Traité des Sensations* (1754). To Condillac rather than to Locke is due the attempt to interpret the structure of the mind genetically and to explain the internal experiences as *sensations transformées.*

About the motives of this radical genetic conception there is no doubt: a science of morals should be constructed "like experimental physics." Into the moral universe, as into the physical, God has injected no more than one principle. Everything else is "necessary development." The principle of matter is force and submission to the laws of motion; out of initial chaos, after many miscarriages, the elements arrange themselves in the balanced, ordered universe that we see today. The principle of man is his physical sensibility, submissive to the laws of pleasure and pain; after initial confusion and many errors, the thoughts and actions of man will achieve the order and balance of happiness in the moral world. The analogy of physics dominates the construction. This desire for fashionable construction is stronger than all critical thought. The reader may have wondered by what miracle we have achieved the transition from a sensualist theory of knowledge to a theory of morals. It was achieved quite simply, through the formula that man is under the direction of pleasure and pain: "the one and the other guard and direct his thoughts, his actions." The "thoughts" (*pensées*) generously include cognitive

functions as well as value judgments and emotions. Or, in another formulation: "Man is animated by a principle of life. This principle is his physical sensibility. What does this sensibility produce in him? a sentiment of love for pleasure, and of hatred for pain" [*De l'Homme*]. It seems almost unbelievable that such cavalier pieces of verbiage should be the foundation of a system of morals in emulation of physics. But, as a matter of fact, that is all there is.

This uncritical construction, again, is not Lockean. It is an ingredient that has entered the style of speculation in the course of the two generations after the publication of the *Essay.* Locke [in his *Essay*] was quite explicit on the point that we have no experience of a causal connection between sense impressions and the feelings of pleasure and pain.

> What certainty of knowledge can anyone have, that some perceptions, such as, *v. g.* pleasure and pain, should not be in some bodies themselves, after a certain manner modified and moved, as well as that they should be in an immaterial substance, upon the motions of the parts of body? Body, as far as we can conceive, being able only to strike and affect body; and motion, according to the utmost reach of our Ideas, being able to produce nothing but motion; so that when we allow it to produce pleasure or pain, or the *Idea* of a colour, or sound, we are fain to quit our reason, go beyond our *Ideas,* and attribute it wholly to the good pleasure of our Maker.

The ontic realms of mind and matter are carefully kept apart and any attempt to reduce the phenomena of the one to phenomena of the other is rejected. And the same holds true when Locke introduces the ideas of pleasure and pain. They are classified as "simple" ideas, irreducible to others, and they may arise either from sensation or reflection. Pleasure and pain can, but need not be, the accompaniment of "bare" sensations or reflections. They can neither be described nor defined, but are accessible to knowledge only through immediate experience. Pleasure, pain and the passions are for Locke an irreducible complex of ideas. In the face of such discrepancies between the actual theories of Locke and the theories of Helvétius which claim Lockean ancestry we have to say that, by the time of the *Esprit,* Locke had become a venerable symbol, lending a certain authority to any attempt at founding a philosophy of morals on the operations of pleasure, pain and passions.

In Helvétius this relationship with Locke is already strongly overlaid by physicism. Its meaning can be seen perhaps more clearly in the earlier reference of Vauvenargues (1715-47) to Locke. In his *Introduction à la connaissance de l'esprit humain* (1746), Vauvenargues quotes Locke almost verbatim to the effect that all our passions turn on pleasure and pain. Moreover, he still preserves the Lockean distinction between sensation and reflection. Pleasure and pain as induced by sensation are immediate and undefinable; the passions, which originate in reflection, are explicable because they are rooted in the experiences of perfection and imperfection of existence. The shift away from Locke is much slighter than in Helvétius, and the motive of the shift is revealed more clearly. Locke's undefinable pleasures and pains do not originate as sense impressions only. "By pleasure and pain, I must be understood to mean of body or mind as they are commonly distinguished; though in truth they be only different constitutions of the mind, sometimes occasioned by disorder in the body, sometimes by thoughts of the mind" [*Essay*]. The simple, undefinable pleasures and pains, thus, may arise originally from operations of the mind, such as "of rational conversation with a friend, or of well directed study in the search and discovery of truth." And even those which are "occasioned" by sensation belong to the "constitution of the mind." And because they belong to the "constitution of the mind" and not of the body they can produce further experiences of the mind, which Locke calls "internal sensations." These "internal sensations" are the passions; they result when simple pleasures and pains are submitted to consideration by reflection. Here we can lay a finger on the point where Locke himself ceases to be a sensualist and treats the "constitution of the mind" as an autonomous unit, independent of the cognitive functions of the sensations. The sensualist epistemology has no bearing on the internal dimensions of human existence in which are placed the dynamic relations between pleasures, pains, passions, good and evil. In spite of the terminology of sensations which seems to anchor the world of morals firmly in experiences of the external world, the actual analysis throws us back into an atmosphere of internal balances and tensions. We do not know of any good and evil in itself, but only call good and evil that which we associate with pleasures and pains. But there is somehow an objective good and evil which has the peculiar character of causing in us pleasure and pain. Is there, after all, a prestabilized harmony between objective good and evil and subjective pleasure and pain? Locke's *Essay,* as we have seen, does not offer an answer to the question; Locke never elaborated a philosophy of human existence, although he came near the problem through his concept of the "constitution of the mind." This question, left open by Locke, is the question which occupies the French *moralistes* of the eighteenth century. When Vauvenargues takes up the Lockean categories of sensation and reflection, he narrows the meaning of sensation to the meaning of an impression that comes through the senses—and then discards it as uninteresting; and he makes reflection the organ by which we penetrate the structure of human existence. From "the experience of our being" we derive the ideas of "grandeur, pleasure, power"; from the experience of "the imperfection of our being" we derive the ideas of "smallness, subjection, misery"—"*voilà toutes nos passions.*" Pleasure and pain are no longer irreducible, simple ideas; they refer to something more fundamental in the constitution of the mind: beyond pleasure and pain (and, incidentally, beyond good and evil) lies the experience of being, with its precarious balance of power and subjection, of perfection and imperfection, of existence under the threat of annihilation. The shift away from Locke reveals its meaning as the attempt to penetrate beyond pleasure and pain to the foundations of being and to rebuild a philosophy of morals within the framework of a philosophy of existence. The preoccupation with a genetic construction of the moral universe reveals its meaning as the attempt to find the existential foundation of morals

at a time when the traditional Christian and humanistic foundations had broken down.

The new philosophy of existence

The Lockeanism of Helvétius, thus, is a somewhat confused pattern of symbols with convergent meanings. From Locke directly stems the aversion against innate moral ideas, and consequently the necessity to search for a new basis of morals. When the immediate spiritual experiences have dried up, and when the tradition of faith and morals has lost its hold, the refoundation of morals is dominated by the symbol of an inversion of direction. The orientation toward a transcendental reality is inverted and a new foundation is sought in the direction of the somatic basis of existence. What specific symbols are used for this purpose is not so very important; it is anybody's choice whether he wishes to interpret Helvétius as a materialist because of his insistence on the *sensibilité physique* as the essence of man, or as a sensualist because the subjective sense impressions are declared to be the basis on which the structure of the mind is erected, or perhaps as a hedonist because the pleasures of the senses play an important directive role in developing standards of conduct. All these symbols are present in the work of Helvétius but none of them is decisive for the concrete analysis of passions. They have an influence on the ideas of Helvétius only as disturbing factors inasmuch as the concessions to these symbols frequently deflect the main line of the argument. The concessions to the symbol of happiness as a good in itself vitiate the otherwise quite admirable analysis of the operations of passions. Setting aside the disturbing and deflecting effects, the various symbols have the common purpose of directing the analysis toward the fundamental experiences of existence and of developing the phenomena of the moral world as transformations of elemental forces. To this isolation of the fundamental forces and the analysis of passions we shall now turn.

Inertia and ennui

The constituent forces of existence, as they are given to our experience, are on the one hand the forces which make for inertness, on the other hand the forces which counteract inertness and drive man into action. The force which makes for passivity or inertness Helvétius calls *paresse;* we shall use for it the English term *inertia.* Inertness or passivity is natural to man; attention fatigues and man gravitates toward a state of inertness like a body toward its center. And man would remain in this state of inertia unless he were pushed out of it by the counteraction of other forces, forces which Helvétius calls [in *De l'Esprit*] ennui and passion. Ennui is defined as the uneasiness (*inquiétude*) which befalls us when we do not have an active awareness of our existence through pleasure. The ennui is a minor but constant pain (*douleur*). The stronger pleasures of life are necessarily separated by intervals, and we experience the desire to fill these intervals by minor sensations. By a constant stream of new impressions we wish "to be made aware of every moment of our existence." This desire to be agitated, and the uneasiness produced by the absence of impressions, contain, in part, "the principle of the inconstancy and perfectibility of the human mind." This principle compels the mind to agitate itself in all directions and it is the source of the gradual perfection of the arts and sciences and ultimately of the *"décadence du gout."* The uneasiness of the ennui, however, is normally no more than the continuous undertone of existence. It will drive a man into activities that will procure minor pleasures, but it is not the strong passion which produces a Lycurgus, a Homer or Milton, a Caesar or Cromwell. At best it may produce a military figure like Charles XII. Nevertheless, its importance should not be underrated. Whether the ennui is the driving force of action is determined in the concrete situation to a considerable extent by the general state of society and the form of government. In times when the great passions are chained by custom or a form of government that is unfavorable to their display, as for instance despotism, the ennui has the field for itself alone and under certain social conditions it may become the *"mobile universel."* The atmosphere of the French court of the eighteenth century is for Helvétius the great example of the situation in which ennui combined with feeble ambition are sufficient to explain the conduct of most men. Outside such special situations, the combined operation of ennui and inertia is responsible for a wide-spread state of mind with vast social consequences. For in submission to these two forces, man wants to be agitated to escape the ennui, but not too much so as not to be fatigued: "for that reason we want to know everything without the pains of penetrating it." Men are inclined to accept as true a traditional body of belief because an independent examination would be too much trouble; hence arguments which might disturb the belief are readily rejected as insufficient. Helvétius, when speaking of accepted belief, has his eye specifically on Christianity. But his remarks on the subject are of general importance as an approach to a class of much neglected phenomena which constitute the ground-texture of all social life: the phenomena of conservative belief, credulity, semi-education, enlightened stupidity, resistance to knowledge, cleverly preserved ignorance, for which our awareness has been sharpened by contemporary events.

The role of the passions

From inertia and ennui alone, however, there would never arise the moral universe as embodied in history and society. A stronger force is needed to drive man into the more fatiguing actions and this force is supplied by the passions. The passions are to the moral world what movement is to the physical; they create and annihilate, conserve and animate and without them, there would be general death. Not all types of passion will supply such moving force equally; for the great effects there are needed the passions which Helvétius calls the *passions fortes*. A *passion forte* "is a passion of which the object is so necessary to our happiness that life becomes unbearable without its possession." Only passions of this strength can produce the great actions and induce men to brave danger, pain and even death, and to defy heaven. The great passions are *"le germe productif de l'esprit"*; they entertain the perpetual fermentation of ideas and carry man through the hardships of physical and intellectual adventure. Great passion makes the great man. Great passion is the source of that active intelligence which enables a man to distinguish between the extraordinary and the impossible. The absence of great passion, on the other hand, characterizes the sensible man (*l'homme sensible*), that is the mediocrity. On the man of passion depends the advancement of the human mind. The sensible man follows the beaten path, and he will do good not to leave it because he would get lost. He is the man in whom inertia dominates; he does not possess the activeness of soul which opens new perspectives and sows in the present the seeds of the future. Only the man of passion is capable of bearing the fatigue of continued meditation which enables him to see the concatenation of causes and effects stretching into the future. "It is the eagle-eye of passion which penetrates the dark abyss of the future: indifference is born blind and stupid." In social practice this differentiation of human types has the consequence that the *'génie élevé,"* which discovers in the little good of the present the greater evil of the future, is treated as a public enemy. In this treatment of the genius virtue seems to punish vice while mediocrity sneers at the spirit.

The genealogy of passions

Not all the passions are of the same type and between the several types there exists a genetical order; one passion is directly rooted in the structure of existence, all others are transformations of this fundamental passion. This relation between the several passions permits Helvétius to develop [most fully in *De l'Homme*] the idea of a *Généalogie des Passions*. We are already acquainted with the lowermost ranks of this genealogy of passions. They are the principle of physical sensibility and the sentiments of love of pleasure and hatred of pain engendered by this principle. We have now to follow the genealogy beyond these first two ranks. From the operation of the love of pleasure and the hatred of pain arises the *amour de soi*. The *amour de soi* engenders the desire for happiness, the desire for happiness the desire for power, and the desire for power gives rise to the "factitious" passions of envy, avarice and ambition, "which all are, under different names, the love of power in disguise and applied to diverse means of obtaining it."

The genealogy of passions is Helvétius's most fruitful systematic idea and, at the same time, his most disappointing in execution. We already had occasion to reflect on the flimsiness of the idea of physical sensibility as the essence of man; almost no elaboration is to be found in the work of Helvétius beyond the bare statement of the proposition. We now have to say the same with regard to the further ranks of the genealogy. The cause of this unsatisfactory thinness of the construction is clear: Helvétius tried to combine a genetic construction which we may call materialistic or sensualistic with a genetic construction that relies on the existential experiences of inertia, ennui and passion, and the rungs of the two ladders simply do not coincide. The "genealogy" which we have just presented reveals the dilemma. Helvétius wants to interpret the gamut of passions as a series of variations of one fundamental passion, that is of the passion which he calls the *desir du pouvoir*. Assuming that the idea could be carried out successfully in the concrete analysis, this attempt would fit into the set of his primary assumptions concerning inertia, ennui and passion. The *desir du pouvoir* would be in this triad of concepts the basic passion which unfolds, in certain social situations and under the pressure of biographical circumstances, into the several "factitious" passions. It would be the elemental force which overcomes inertia and assuages the uneasiness of ennui by creating through action an acute awareness of existence. This course, of interpreting the will to power as the elemental force of existence in expansive action, was later taken by Nietzsche. With Helvétius this interpretation is thwarted by the attempt to fit the sense impressions and the pleasure-pain mechanism into the analysis of passion. Hence we find in the *généalogie* the desire of happiness engendering the *desir du pouvoir*. The passion for power loses thereby its function as the elemental force and becomes an instrument for procuring happiness. This perversion of the fleeting accompaniment of action into its purpose would bring Helvétius face to face with the necessity of explaining what kind of pleasure is procured by incurring death—for we remember his definition of the *passion forte* as the passion which braves danger and makes man risk his life. Passion in existence is not a matter of life only, it is a matter of life and death. An exploration of this problem would have compelled Helvétius to revise his genealogy of passions. He escapes this necessity simply by not exploring it.

The 'amour de soi'

The strangest item in the *généalogie*, however, is the rank of the *amour de soi*. Again the *amour de soi* is placed in an instrumental position with regard to pleasure and pain. The *amour de soi* as a permanent sentiment is the guarantee that pleasures are procured and pains are avoided; we may say that the ego is integrated when the *amour de soi* is developed as the permanent control which steers the ego in the direction of pleasure and thereby keeps it in existence. This *amour de soi* is the Augustinian *amor sui*. In Christian psychology the *amor sui* is the passion of existence which prevents man from realizing his creaturely finiteness. The *amor sui* has to be broken by the *amor Dei* which directs man towards his divine origin and fulfillment, but this breaking of the *amor sui* is not entirely within the power of man; it requires assistance by the grace of God, and whether it really is broken is the mystery of Christian existence inaccessible to empirical diagnosis. Helvétius has the concept of the *amor sui* but not of the *amor Dei,* and this isolation of the *amor sui* profoundly changes its meaning as well as its systematic function. When the *amor sui* is used as a category of immanent existence, without regard to its Christian implications, it is difficult to see how it can be distinguished from the *desir du pouvoir* as the fundamental passion of existence. At best the term would emphasize the fact that human existence has as one of its important forming elements the ego, and that the *desir du pouvoir* operates in the form of actions of the ego. In the *généalogie,* however, Helvétius separates the *amour de soi* completely from the passions. Why this strange construction? By its very strangeness the construction gives us at last the key to the understanding of a group of concepts which otherwise might appear as an undigested agglomeration of traditional elements. The *amor sui* is not set by Helvétius into opposition to the *amor Dei,* but it retains from the Christian context a sector of its meaning, that is: its negative value accent. The *amour de soi* which steers man toward his personal happiness is not of

itself conducive to virtue; the moral good can be realized only by actions which go beyond the procurement of personal pleasure and have for their aim, incidental to personal pleasure, the achievement of a general interest. This moral qualification of the *amour de soi* introduces a new dimension into the construction, beyond the pleasure-pain psychology and beyond the analysis of existential experiences. In a strict analysis of existence, beyond good and evil, neither the *amour de soi* nor the *desir du pouvoir* should have moral accents; in a strict psychology of the pleasure-pain mechanism, the love of pleasure and the hatred of pain should substitute for all moral considerations. Now we are faced by standards of good and evil, and the whole *généalogie des passions* is moved thereby into the function of an instrument which can be used for the achievement of good or of evil, which may be put to the service of virtue or vice. The curious interlocking of concepts which alternately belong to the pleasure-pain-happiness group or the inertia-ennui-passion group makes sense if it is understood as a manageable means-end concatenation which can be bent to ulterior purposes by a legislator or educator who is in possession of the absolute standards of value. We are not surprised, therefore, to find that Helvétius considers the structure of existence as an acquired structure, with the exception of the *sensibilité physique* and the pleasure-pain mechanism. Even the *amour de soi* is an "acquisition." "One learns to love oneself; to be human or inhuman, virtuous or vicious. Moral man is altogether education and imitation."

The peculiarities of Helvétius's *généalogie* thus find their explanation in the instrumentalization of existence. The *amour de soi* can be developed, tempered or deflected through the conditioning of attitudes by educational rewards of pleasure and punishments of pain. The desire for happiness can be influenced with regard to the morality of its content by the previous formation of the ego. The *desir du pouvoir* will be determined in its direction by the type of happiness which it has to serve, and the factitious passions can be developed in the direction of antisocial vices, or of virtues serving the general interest, in accordance with the rewards or punishments held out by the structure of society in which they operate. The most significant detail in this process of instrumentalization is the transformation of the *amor sui* from a fundamental passion of existence into an acquired character. If we remember the Augustinian origin of the concept, we might say that in the Christian context the breaking of the *amor sui* is the combined work of human effort and the grace of God, while in the context of Helvétius the educator takes the place of God: where the grace of God has failed, the educator may achieve results by a judicious application of the psychology of conditioned reflexes. With the implications of this divinization of the educational process we shall have to deal later on in more detail.

For the present, let us consider briefly the influence which the instrumentalization of the structure of existence has on the analysis of power. The fundamental passion, from which all other passions derive, is the desire for power. In the concrete analysis the desire for power is represented by the desire to find oneself in a position of command, if possible in the role of a despot. The desire to be a despot is rooted in the love of pleasure and consequently in the nature of man. Everybody wants to be happy, and hence everybody wants to have the power to command other people to contribute to his happiness. The rule over people can either be a rule according to law or a rule by arbitrary will. In the first case, the power to command is limited and in order to exploit the position of command most effectively for the production of happiness, the ruler will have to study the laws and find the legal means for achieving his purposes. Such study is fatiguing and inertia makes itself felt as the counterforce to action. In order to satisfy his inertia, everyone will strive, if possible, for absolute power, which will avoid the fatigue of studying the law and put men slavishly at his will. *"Voilà par quel motif chacun veut être despote"* [*De l'Esprit*]. Since everybody is a despot by desire, if not in fact, social power is held in high esteem. "One hates the powerful, one does not despise him. . . . Whatever we may say: one does not really despise what one does not dare to despise face to face. . . . The respect paid to virtue is transitory, the respect paid to force is eternal" [*De l'Homme*]. This state of things is most propitious from the point of view of the educator and legislator. If virtue were a part of the organization of the individual, or a consequence of divine grace, there would be no honest men except those who are organized honestly by nature, or predestined to be virtuous by heaven. Good or bad laws in this case, or forms of government, would not influence anybody. If, however, virtue can be made the effect of the desire for power, the legislator can confer the prizes of esteem, wealth and power on virtuous conduct. Thus "under a good legislation only the fools would be vicious." That all men are inspired by the love of power is the most precious gift of heaven. What does it matter whether men are born virtuous, if only they are born with a passion which makes them virtuous if skilfully managed?

The flaw in this analysis of power as the fundamental passion is obvious: the desire for power, as presented by Helvétius, is not fundamental at all, nor is it much of a passion; it is no more than the attempt to procure happiness, understood in a hedonistic sense, through command over services and commodities. This was the flaw in Helvétius's psychology of passions against which Nietzsche directed his criticism: the idea of an Alexander or Caesar striving for power in order to be happy is preposterous beyond discussion. Helvétius, however, was no fool, and the flaw in his analysis requires explanation. That Helvétius had a keen understanding of the psychology of passions is beyond doubt to the reader of the extended, brilliant discussions of various passions in the *Esprit.* Behind this flaw in the analysis there is a definite will to see the phenomenon of power in a certain light; we have indicated this problem when we introduced the concept of instrumentalization into our interpretation. Now we have to explore a bit farther the motives as they become apparent from Helvétius's analysis.

There is one element in the motivation of Helvétius which is typical for the period of Enlightenment, as well as for theorists of the nineteenth century who were inspired by the pattern of enlightened theory: it is the substitution of a correct empirical observation for the *natura rerum.* Empirically we find, indeed, hedonists who strive for a posi-

tion of power in order to enjoy the concomitant material benefits, and we also find among those who hold a position of power by circumstance, without striving for it, men whose relation to their position is purely hedonistic. The French court of the eighteenth century could supply Helvétius with ample material in support of his analysis. The elevation of the empirically correct observation into a general theory of power, however, belongs to the same class of phenomena as the Voltairean identification of ecclesiastical abuses of the time with the essence of the Church, or the Marxian identification of the misuse of religion as an opium for the people with the essence of religion. . . . [In] Helvétius, another aspect of the problem becomes visible: the willingness to mistake the abuse for the essence in order to continue the abuse, with the best of surface intentions, for a different purpose.

The great temptation in recognizing the abusive instrumentalization of passion as the meaning of passion lies in the possibility for the analyst who makes the mistake to misuse the instrument for his own purposes. In Helvétius's analysis of power we can discern the origin of phenomena which pervade modern politics and are still increasing in importance, the origin of the artificiality of modern politics as engendered through propaganda, education, reeducation, and enforced political myth, as well as through the general treatment of human beings as functional units in private enterprise and public planning. The actual decadence of Western society which occupied the thinkers of the eighteenth century has become the model of social and political practice. The disorder which expresses itself empirically in spiritual obscurantism and the instrumentalization of the life of passion is accepted as the nature of man by the analyst—for others. In Helvétius's analysis we meet a classical instance of the destruction of the integral human person by positing as normal the disorder of the person while denying to man the remedial powers which might restore the order. The possibility of spiritual regeneration of the person, the existence of man in communion with God, the possibility of the *renovatio evangelica* in the Christian sense, are denied. The function of regeneration is transferred to the analyst in the role of the organizing legislator who will create externally the social situation which in its turn will induce the external conformance of conduct to moral standards by a play on the psychological mechanism of disordered man. It is the dream of escape from the mystery of iniquity that has been expressed by T. S. Eliot in the verses:

> They constantly try to escape
> From the darkness outside and within
> By dreaming of systems so perfect that no one
> will need to be good.

Helvétius has dreamt the dream with radical perfection: in most instances the thinker of this type is satisfied with a Pelagian assumption about the goodness of man, but Helvétius conceives man as a morally neutral force, neither good nor bad. Man is emptied of moral substance, and the forces of good and evil are transferred in their entirety to the analyst-legislator.

Salvation as a social process

The attitude of Helvétius is an early instance of political

attitudes which unfold more completely in the nineteenth and twentieth centuries. As always in the early cases, the spiritual processes which lead to the new attitude are more clearly visible than in the later period when the structure of sentiments has settled into conventional patterns. Today we take it more or less for granted that our society is swarming with leaders, left and right, who supply substance to the human automaton. The enormity of the attitude can no longer be sensed so sharply as in the case of Helvétius where it appeared in direct conflict with a living tradition. What happens is, in brief, that the analyst-legislator arrogates to himself the possession of the substance of good in society while denying it to the rest of mankind. Mankind is split into the mass of pleasure-pain mechanisms and the One who will manipulate the mechanisms for the good of society. The nature of man, by a kind of division of labor, is distributed among masses and leaders so that only society as a whole is integral man. Moreover the operations of the legislator on the members of society substitute, as we have seen, for grace and predestination. Society has become a totally closed universe with an immanent process of salvation.

The insight into the spiritual process that occurs in Helvétius will shed some light on the significance of genetic, sensualist psychology, as well as on the complex of philosophical assumptions attached to it, for the political evolution of Western society. The tenacity of faith in this complex of ideas is certainly not caused by its merits as an adequate interpretation of man and society. The inadequacy of a pleasure-pain psychology, the poverty of utilitarian ethics, the impossibility of explaining moral phenomena by the pursuit of happiness, the uselessness of the greatest happiness of the greatest number as a principle of social ethics— all these have been demonstrated over and over again in a voluminous literature. Nevertheless, even today this complex of ideas holds a fascination for a not inconsiderable number of persons. This fascination will be more intelligible if we see the complex of sensualism and utilitarianism not as number of verifiable propositions but as the dogma of a religion of socially immanent salvation. Enlightened utilitarianism is but the first in a series of totalitarian, sectarian movements to be followed later by Positivism, Communism and National Socialism.

. . . . .

[Helvétius's] fundamental thesis for practical politics is the moral neutrality of man; men are neither good nor bad, they follow their interest. "The cries of the moralists will not change this motive force (*ressort*) of the moral universe. One should not complain of the badness of man but of the ignorance of legislators who have always put private interest into opposition to the general interest" [*De l'Esprit*]. The excellence of laws is the condition of virtuous conduct. And when are the laws good? When they are consistent among themselves, and they are consistent only when they are animated by a single, simple principle, as for instance by the principle of public usefulness (*utilité public*), that is of usefulness "to the greatest number of men under one governmental organization." This principle contains in nucleus "all morals and legislation." These propositions have their practical importance because man

by nature is made to be virtuous. This virtuousness "by nature" is not a contradiction to the earlier assumption of moral neutrality since "by nature" means that massive force is on the side of justice. The principle of the greatest number is not to be understood as a mathematics of happiness in the sense that the majority should be happy rather than the minority. Rather, it involves the recognition that "the greatest number" is a political force. "If we consider that the power essentially resides in the greatest number, and that justice consists in the practice of actions useful to the greatest number, then it is evident that justice, by nature, is always equipped with the necessary power to suppress vice and to compel men to be virtuous" [*De l'Esprit*]. If justice is in harmony with power, why then is justice not realized in the concrete society of the day? Because the mass of the people is held in ignorance with regard to this truth by the ruling minority, that is by Church and Court. The critique of contemporary society given by Helvétius is extensive but cautious in the decisive formulations. He takes pains to avoid a direct attack on King and Church, and rather concentrates on the obviously abusive part of the minority whom he calls the *"fanatiques"* and the *"demi-politiques,"* the religious fanatics who indulge in persecutions and the parasitical hangers-on who prevent the enlightenment of the people. The next question would have to be: how did the minority which opposes the interest of the people ever gain its ascendancy? The answer to this question can only be furnished by a theory of the historical evolution of society.

The historical evolution of society

Helvétius's theory of social evolution is of considerable importance in the history of political ideas as well as for the understanding of certain systematic issues in later theories of politics. As far as the history of ideas is concerned, Helvétius has seen clearly for the first time that a philosophy of social justice has to rely on the historical evolution of economic institutions as its basis, if and when the insight into spiritual values is lost. As far as the systematic issue is concerned, we find in Helvétius the problem of the happiness of the greatest number still connected with the concrete issues of social revolution. In the later development of systematic ethics the greatest-happiness principle lost this connection with the concrete issue that had given it meaning and it was advanced and criticized as an abstract principle of morality. With Helvétius, the greatest number whose happiness is supposed to be the standard of social justice is not a mathematical maximum but quite concretely the "people," that is the middle class, the peasants and the workers. And the smaller number whose happiness may be neglected is not a group of idiosyncratic individuals on the fringe of mass normality, but quite concretely the ruling class of France. In its origins, with Helvétius, the greatest-happiness principle is clearly related to the differentiation of economic classes and to the problem of class struggle. English utilitarianism and Marxism are both off-shoots from the original position of Helvétius, the one stressing the middle class as the greatest number whose happiness has to be secured, the other the proletariat.

In *De l'Esprit* and *De l'Homme,* Helvétius has formulated

his theory of social evolution more than once. We have to distinguish two main variants of the theory. In one of the accounts, the emphasis lies on the issue of nationalism or internationalism: should the greatest number be the majority within a nation or the majority of mankind? In a second account, the emphasis lies on the issue of the class struggle: who specifically are the greatest number and wherein does their happiness consist? We shall deal first with the account that emphasizes the issue of nationalism or internationalism.

The question of social evolution arises with the problem why justice should be defined in terms of the general interest. The physical sensibility and the pleasure-pain mechanism are the only principles admissible in the interpretation of man; we have to ask, therefore, how the general interest can be explained as a transformation of individual interest. As long as this question is not answered, the demand addressed to the legislator that he should, by his laws, produce conformance between private and public interest, hangs in the air, and we may ask legitimately why there should be a conformance of this kind. The theory of social evolution has the purpose of showing that genetically the general interest is an outgrowth of private interest; the state of predominant private interest is a primitive social state and evolution toward the general interest marks the advancement of the social state. The phases of this evolution are the following: (1) we have to assume an initial stage of isolated families who provide for their necessities of life; (2) population increase produces neighborhood relations in which rivalries for food and women will result in quarrels and combat; (3) life in perpetual fear will induce agreements and the creation of magistrates for their enforcement; (4) up to this point the development has taken place under the economic conditions of forest life, and of a hunting and fishing civilization; further increase of population and scarcity of food supplies will compel the transition to cattle-raising and nomadism; (5) the same factors will produce in due course agriculture and the development of landed property; (6) the necessities of a barter economy will result in the creation of money, and with this invention the primary equality is broken; society is on its path toward stratification into the rich and the poor; (7) since wealth procures pleasure, the desire to belong to the economic upper class produces the factitious passions and, generally, the texture of sentiment which characterizes civilized society. Society has become a body of men who are bound together by their economic interdependence; the destruction of this body would result in misery for all, hence its preservation is everybody's private interest. Under these circumstances, a differentiation of interests that would result in cleavages in the social body along class lines has to be avoided; the pursuit of the "general interest" means therefore the creation of social attitudes, in the concrete society of the eighteenth century, that will forestall a revolutionary disintegration of the nation, with the inevitably ensuing misery for all.

The "general interest" thus is the stable balance of the private interests of the members of a society. This stable balance can be created only by law and its effective enforcement. If the magistrates are not equipped with the necessary powers of enforcement, the greatest number of men

will violate the law, and in this case it would be violated justly by the single individual in pursuit of his private interest. A law that is not enforced is useless, and with its uselessness it loses its validity. The questions of the greatest number and the general interest are closely bound up with the existence of an organized body politic and the economic interdependence of its members. The insight into this connection determines Helvétius's analysis of the question whether the principle of the greatest number and their general interest can be extended beyond the national state into international relations. This question cannot be answered by a simple yes or no. The international community is no more a fit object for wishful thinking than is the national community; both are stages in the scale of evolution. The principle of the general interest is applicable to the national state because the national state exists historically. Whether it is applicable to the international community of mankind depends on whether this community exists. As a matter of fact, it exists only in a very rudimentary form, as evidenced by the fact that acts of violence in international relations are not considered dishonorable in the same degree as violent acts within the national body politic. The nations have hardly reached in their relations the stage of conventions; they have not even guaranteed each other their possessions as have the individuals within the state. And they have not done it because, hitherto, they had no pressing interest to do it; they are able to coexist without a legal order and a machinery of enforcement. The Church and the kings permit slave trade and the same Christian who condemns a disturbance of family life at home gives his blessings to the merchant who breaks up native families and purchases their members in exchange for Western products. These facts indicate that in public opinion the relations between peoples are still governed by nothing but force and cunning. Even when, in single instances, the stage of conventions is reached, the treaties have the character of a truce for they are always concluded with the tacit understanding of the *clausula rebus sic stantibus.* The actual state of brigandage among nations will not cease until the majority of them will have entered into general conventions and until a federal league is concluded between them, with powers of enforcement, following such plans as those of Henri IV and the Abbé de Saint-Pierre. Only when the international community exists in fact, and that means as an organized body with enforcement of its order, can speculation concerning the greatest number and their interest be extended beyond the national scene [*De l'Esprit*].

The class struggle

In his late work, **De l'Homme,** Helvétius has given the second account of evolution, which emphasizes the problems of class struggle. The outline of phases, on the whole, is the same as in the **Esprit.** The new elements are introduced into the analysis at the stage where society has increased to the size of a nation on a considerable territory, when economic interdependence is highly developed through division of labor, and when the differentiation of social strata is expressing itself in the growth of towns and particularly of a capital city which overshadows the rest of the country by its splendor; in brief: the situation in France. At this stage, the single member of the community has ceased to be an active citizen, and he can participate in politics only through "representatives"; the economic man separates from the political man; politics becomes a differentiated social function and with it enters the possibility of abuse. For the people are now divided into economic classes and it is not possible that the interests of the various classes should always be in harmony. Nothing, for instance, is more contrary to the national interest than a great number of men without property. They are so many secret enemies whom a despot might arm at his discretion against the property owners. The business community, on the other hand, has an interest in great numbers of poor people; the needier they are, the less a businessman will have to pay in wages. The interest of the business community thus is opposed to the public interest, and a business community (*un corps de négocians*) is frequently a power in trading nations because it is the great employer. When a people thus is composed of a plurality of peoples with conflicting interests, there will be no uniform national interest on which all are ready to agree. The ruling "representatives" can play off the various groups against each other, and in the general confusion they will increase their power and wealth until it equals the power and wealth of the nation. The country is split into the rulers and the ruled; the people have lost their power over the "representatives" and can hardly hold their own against them. For wealth has a tendency to accumulate in an ever smaller number of hands of the ruling class, and the number of independent proprietors, the mainstay of liberty, will decrease. The end is an economic despotism of a small minority which rules the people for its private interest. This evolution has been the cause of the fall of many empires in history.

What can the legislator do to prevent a similar misfortune in the concrete case under discussion? Helvétius suggests a number of measures for a solution of the problem, such as abolition of inheritance for great fortunes and redistribution of accumulated wealth on the death of the owner, or a progressive land-tax which for land holdings over a certain acreage will be higher than the profit. These measures, however, do not have the purpose of equalizing wealth—economic inequality cannot and should not be abolished, only excess accumulation should be prevented in order to preserve the political stability of the nation [*De l'Homme*].

The Jesuit Order

. . . In his capacity as the presumptive legislator, Helvétius is strongly disturbed by the existence of a group of men who have organized themselves effectively for the operations of bending men to their will. The previously described differentiation of society into economic classes with conflicting interests is a grave danger to the general interest. This danger, however, pales before the danger presented by a particular interest group which has organized itself as what we would call today "a state within the state," and which uses its efficient organization for the purpose of establishing itself as a ruling class against the general interest. This efficient organization is the Jesuit Order. Helvétius is deeply interested in the means by which the Jesuit Order achieves its success. This "master-

piece of politics" combines the advantages of monarchical and republican government. It depends equally on secrecy and promptitude of execution, and on an ardent love for the grandeur of the Order. At the head of the organization is an enlightened despot, who at the same time is an elective officer. This chief is carefully chosen from a number of prospective, well-trained candidates. He is under the same rules as the rank and file, has made the same vows, has renounced, like his brethren, all dignities and all bonds of love and friendship. He has no other interest than the grandeur and power of the Order and in his subjects he has the perfect instrument of execution. His independence from temporal powers is secured through his residence at Rome. From his cell, "like the spider from the center of its web," he instructs his sons in all Europe, and there he receives from them the intelligence of what is going on in the capitals of the world. His peculiar power and the terror which he inspires is not due to his principles (which are, on the whole, not different from those of the Church), but to the perfection of his governmental organization. The members of the Order are chosen with equal care among fanatics. In the monastic environment, surrounded by other fanatics, the sentiments of the recruits are formed in the proper direction. Enthusiasm, as Shaftesbury said, is a communicable disease. Among all religious Orders that of the Jesuits is "at the same time the most powerful, the most enlightened and the most enthusiastic." No other Order could exert a similar fascination over the imagination of a fanatic. The *esprit de corps* gives each member a feeling of security and, consequently, full freedom of the mind to concentrate on the task at hand [*De l'Homme*].

Helvétius hates the Jesuit Order. He analyzes its organization because it is the most dangerous enemy to the general interest and he rejoices in its fall. Nevertheless, throughout these chapters on the Jesuits there is an undertone of admiration and envy. "The true crime of the Jesuits was the excellence of their government. Its excellence was altogether destructive to public happiness." Still: excellence was the crime. And could such excellence not be used some day for virtuous purposes? "We must admit that the Jesuits have been the most cruel scourge of the nations; but without them we would never have gained a full insight into the power which a body of laws inspired by one purpose can have over men." "No legislation has ever realized with so little means so perfectly the great object of power and wealth." Regrettably, no people has a legislation of comparable excellence; and in order to create it "one would have to found a new empire like Romulus." Unfortunately, the legislator is rarely in this situation; "and in any other situation it is perhaps impossible to give an excellent legislation" [*De l'Homme*]. Helvétius ends on a melancholy note. His dream of excellence could not be dreamed into history in the eighteenth century. Still, he had the right instinct: the political cadre has become the great instrument for making the greatest number as happy as only the leaders of such cadres can make them.

Conclusion

The historian of ideas has to do more than to report the doctrines advanced by a thinker or to give an account of a few great systems. He has to explore the growth of sentiments which crystallize into ideas, and he has to show the connection between ideas and the matrix of sentiments in which they are rooted. The idea has to be studied, not as a concept, but as a symbol which draws its life from sentiments; the idea grows and dies with the sentiments which engender its formulation and, with the great thinkers, its integration into a system of thought approximating the asymptote of rationality. Only insofar as the idea is understood as the approximately rational expression of the life of sentiments can we understand it as a historical entity. For the interpretation of ideas in this process of historical growth, the minor thinkers sometimes may be more important than the great ones in whose systems the motivation of ideas through sentiment is covered by the exigencies of immanent logical consistency. Helvétius was a thinker whose awareness of systematic exigencies was strong enough to make him face the major problems raised by his approach to politics, but his desire to elaborate a system of politics was not so strong that it abolished the essentially aphoristic style of his work. Aphoristic style means, as was later clarified by Nietzsche who used it deliberately, that the author preserves in the presentation of his ideas the connection with the experiences and sentiments which produce the ideas. This aphoristic character of the work of Helvétius makes it unusually valuable for the historian of ideas because here he will find ideas, which in themselves are elaborated more clearly and consistently in later systems, at the point where they begin to separate as symbols from the matrix of sentiments and where the motives which animate their creation are still visible.

Jean H. Bloch   (essay date 1979)

SOURCE: "Rousseau and Helvétius on Innate and Acquired Traits: The Final Stages of the Rousseau-Helvétius Controversy," in *Journal of the History of Ideas,* Vol. XL, No. 1, January-March, 1979, pp. 21-41.

[*In the following essay, Bloch presents Helvétius's delineation of innate and acquired traits as developed in his critique of Rousseau's* Emile.]

The controversy between Rousseau and Helvétius, concerned mainly with questions of epistemology and what we might term early psychology, takes us beyond the confines of French literature during the Enlightenment into the history of philosophy, psychology, and education. The earlier stages of the controversy, and especially Rousseau's reactions to Helvétius's *De l'Esprit* of 1758, have been studied at length by Keim [*Helvétius, sa vie et son oeuvre*], Schinz and Masson [in *Revue d'Historie littéraire de la France,* 17 and 18, respectively], and more recently by D. W. Smith in his excellent book on the *affaire* of *De l'Esprit,* viz., *Helvétius: A Study in Persecution* (1965). There is, however, no detailed analysis of the later stages of the controversy, namely, Helvétius's attempt in *De l'Homme* (completed in 1769 but published only posthumously in 1772) to strengthen the position he had taken in his earlier work through criticisms of important passages of *Emile* and of the letter on education in *La Nouvelle Héloïse*. These criticisms, important as the only full response by eighteenth-century pedagogical writers to the psychological theories of *Emile,* are also of considerable

interest in the wider context of the history of ideas. It seems therefore apposite to take a close look at the final stages of the controversy and to assess the importance of Helvétius's criticism of *Emile.*

Rousseau's philosophical position in *Emile* is an attempted synthesis of Cartesian dualism and the sensationalist theory of knowledge. We know that the idea of reconciling conflicting philosophies was present early in Rousseau's thought. In the *Confessions* he describes how he first read Locke, Malebranche, Leibniz, Descartes, and others, and, finding them almost everywhere at odds, decided to try to reconcile them. He gave up the attempt as beyond his powers at the time of his studies at *Les Charmettes;* nevertheless, his work abounds in syntheses of apparently incompatible elements: in *Emile* these are notably art and nature, particularly in respect of child care, and natural and social man. The attempted synthesis of Cartesianism and sensationalism may therefore be simply characteristic of Rousseau.

There are, however, specific historical reasons for this particular synthesis in *Emile.* Rousseau had accepted the sensationalist psychology of Condillac's *Essai sur l'origine des connaissances humaines* and composed his treatise on education in line with its assumptions. His definition of ideas as a kind of mixed or complex sensation is very close to what we find in Condillac and Buffon. Moreover, the whole of Books I to III of *Emile* is based on the idea that since the senses are the first organs to develop in the child they must be exercised first, and that it is through the senses that the intelligence can develop. When, however, Rousseau read in *De l'Esprit* that "to judge is to feel," he realized that the sensationalism which he had accepted in Condillac could lead to the materialism and atheism to which he was radically opposed. He therefore interpolated passages in the "Profession de Foi du Vicaire Savoyard" of Book IV of *Emile* which would serve to refute the reductive tendencies of extreme sensationalism and reestablish the freedom of the will and the activity of human judgment. He now stressed not only an active judgment, but also an active creative force, the will, which enables man to control his actions and combat the lowering influences of sense and passion. Rousseau here was quite close to Malebranche who, while maintaining the traditional dualism of body and mind, had also acknowledged a kind of natural judgment which was merely a juxtaposition of sensations. Malebranche was careful to distinguish these from "free" judgments, which in his terminology were judgments dependent on free will. To feel pain in one's hand would be a natural judgment, but to *believe* that one feels pain in one's hand would be to confirm the natural judgment by an act of the will.

Rousseau could, by staying close to Malebranche, have rendered the arguments of the "Profession de Foi" compatible with the sensationalist premises of Books I to III. Since he posits in *Emile* a system of gradually developing faculties in the child and insists on the very different natures of juvenile and adult reason, he could simply have focussed on "natural" or sensitive judgments in the preadolescent period and introduced "free" intellectual judgments at adolescence. Thus he would have been consistent with the distinction he makes between the purely physical sensitivity of the child and the emergence of the second principle, *sentiment,* at adolescence, together with the awakening of conscience and the implied connection with the divine. But Rousseau failed to do this, leaving the term *jugement* in Books I to III to suggest a kind of natural judgment based on sensation, while in the "Profession de Foi" *jugement* is to be understood quite differently, in the Cartesian sense of an active principle in man, opposed to passive sensation and associated with free will. This uneasy synthesis was, inevitably, unacceptable to dualists and sensationalists alike, and it was this in part which gave material to Helvétius for his refutation of Rousseau in *De l'Homme.* Moreover, although Rousseau had been largely at pains to refute the reduction of the thinking faculty to sensation, Helvétius also felt that in *Emile* and the *Nouvelle Héloïse* Rousseau was directly attacking a position he had taken in *De l'Esprit* on the question of acquired or innate characteristics. In the letter on education in *La Nouvelle Héloïse* and by means of the characters of Wolmar and Saint-Preux, Rousseau contrasted his own notion of innate characteristics with Helvétius's emphasis on acquired ones. Helvétius regarded this letter as an attack and wished to defend himself. In his second major work, therefore, he attempted both to refute Rousseau and to justify his own position on this and related topics.

Though Helvétius offers positive alternative proposals to Rousseau's theories, he attempts primarily (like other contemporary critics of *Emile*) to refute Rousseau by producing evidence of his illogicality and inconsistency. He discusses seven or eight points in all: the question of the inequality of individual minds; whether vice and virtue are innate and, consequently, whether man has an innate moral sense; the relationship between private and public good and human self-interest; attention as a motivating principle in man; natural goodness and compassion and their relevance to the problem posed by cruelty; also the value of education and the degree of judgment of which a child is capable; the value of ignorance. Many of these are interrelated and can be grouped together for the purposes of our analysis. Indeed, helvétius himself focusses in the first instance on two main issues, which he associates: the importance of the sensory organs for the inequality of minds and the innateness of character and virtue. To him these are the main differences between his philosophy and Rousseau's and the chief source of Rousseau's errors.

Helvétius's reading of *Emile* shows him that Rousseau believes that the inequality of individual minds is the result of the greater or lesser perfection of the sensory organs. Indeed, on this particular point, Rousseau is much more of a materialist than Helvétius. In the early books of *Emile* he insists that the training of the senses is vital to the subsequent development of the mind. Working from sensationalist premises Rousseau accepts the notion that, since our ideas come from sensation, the better the training of the organs which produce our sensations the better our ideas will be. He therefore subjects the young Emile to an intensive program of sense perfection.

Although Helvétius goes much further than Rousseau in believing that "sense" and "mind" are one and the same,

he nevertheless holds, as Malebranche had, that the perfection of the mind is independent of the perfection of the senses. He is able to do this because he believes that all normally endowed human beings possess sufficient sensitivity to form all possible ideas and he reiterates this belief in both *De l'Esprit* and *De l'Homme.* For him, the inequality of individual minds stems from an unequal capacity for attention, which is itself stimulated by the strength of the passions. This stimulation constitutes Helvétius's second principle, "self-interest" (*intérêt*), which renders everyone equally capable of the same degree of attention. Any inequality between individuals in this respect is therefore not the result of physiological differences, but of differences in the education they receive, which affect the degree to which they are stimulated.

When Helvétius criticizes Rousseau, however, he concentrates solely on Rousseau's definition of the mind in Books I to III, to the exclusion of his attempt in Book IV to unite an education based on the senses with a belief in the combination of material and immaterial substances of the human soul. Rousseau in fact nowhere says that the intelligence is always entirely dependent on the development of the senses, though he certainly implies it in Books I to III, since at this early stage in life Rousseau's second principle, *sentiment,* which directs the adult to discriminate between ideas, is still dormant. Moreover, the method of education suggested by Rousseau in *Emile,* based on the senses and carried out by means of concrete examples, implies that his pupil could only benefit from an intensive preparatory sensory and physical education. Helvétius is, however, over-emphasizing Rousseau's insistence on this sort of education and stresses the sensationalist aspects of Rousseau's system at the expense of its Cartesian elements. Helvétius and Rousseau are basically at odds on this question in an unexpected way. Here the dualist goes further than the materialist on his own ground. Diderot, a true materialist, was later to rally to Rousseau's side on the question of the influence of the physical organs on the capacities of the mind. He in fact shifts the exphasis of the problem from the perfection of the senses to the detrimental effect of bodily illness or indisposition on the intellectual faculties. In his refutation of Helvétius's *De l'Homme* he argues that the state of the body directly affects our mental capacities. If we sleep or digest food badly, then we think badly. In either case the fundamental question remains the same: does physiology affect sensation and hence the mind, or is it exclusively environmental factors which produce intellectual differences?

The second major issue on which helvétius finds himself at odds with Rousseau is that of acquired versus innate characteristics. Helvétius himself emphasizes the importance of knowing whether our vices and virtues are innate, but at bottom this question is part of a wider discussion of nature versus environment. Helvétius finds Rousseau self-contradictory in this matter. What he first offers to illustrate the contradiction is a paraphrased version of part of the letter on education in the *Nouvelle Héloïse* in which Rousseau reveals an obvious determination to regard individual temperamental differences and intellectual potential as innate and fundamentally unchangeable: if a man is stupid you will not make him talented. Helvétius extends this view in his interpretation of Rousseau, to a general assumption that our talents, vices, virtues, and characters depend on our natural organization. This interpretation Helvétius contrasts with another of Rousseau's statements which appears to be saying the opposite, i. e., that at least certain characteristics are not innate, but acquired. The quotation, taken from the *Nouvelle Héloïse,* enquires how vice could exist in a child before he has had any experience of it, and very obviously reflects Rousseau's belief in the natural goodness of man. Helvétius as a thorough-going environmentalist accepts the second proposition, viz., that virtues are acquired.

In *La Nouvelle Héloïse* Rosseau's position on this question is, indeed, ambiguous. [According to Masson], Wolmar opposes Saint-Preux (who . . . takes up some of Helvétius's points), on the question of innate or acquired characteristics. Wolmar argues that it is impossible to change an individual's natural dispositions, which must be allowed to develop freely. Consequently, education must be individualistic and not universalistic, as Rousseau believes Helvétius to have suggested. The educator can suppress undesirable characteristics, but he cannot create new ones; human beings cannot be educated according to a common model. But Wolmar and Saint-Preux are of course only characters in a novel, and although they are made to grapple with some of the problems with which Rousseau was concerned, they do not necessarily represent his point of view. *Emile* is a surer guide for establishing Rousseau's opinions, and the basic principle of uniqueness of character (*tempérament*) is followed throughout *Emile.* One of Rousseau's main points is that the tutor should study and know the particular potentialities of the child ("le génie particulier de l'enfant") before trying to educate him in one direction rather than another. It is this proposition much more than any question of self-contradiction that Helvétius is attacking. He simply does not accept the idea of individual innate characteristics, including that of intellectual potential. For Helvétius, everything in man is acquired and can be changed by education. Like Rousseau, Diderot in his *Réfutation* supports the idea that characteristics are innate. The differences between them and Helvétius were to become much more pronounced in the arguments over nature and nurture (*tempérament* and *milieu*) in the nineteenth and twentieth centuries, and have not been fully resolved even today.

Helvétius, however, turns away from the central issue here, by specifically including good and bad qualities ("nos vices, nos vertus") in the category of innate characteristics. This is, in fact, Helvétius's interpretation of what Rousseau is saying in *La Nouvelle Héloïse,* since the final sentence of his "quotation": "nos talens, nos vices, nos vertus et par conséquent nos caractères ne dépendent-ils pas entièrement de notre organisation?" does not appear in Rousseau's text. Rousseau does refer to a headstrong temperament, "un emporté" which might be taken to imply a bad characteristic in the individual, but he does not specifically include the question of good and evil in that passage. Nor is the question of a child's violent temper, "vôtre enfant discole" (which Rousseau discusses in *Emile* and explains as meaning "difficile à vivre"), to be identified with innate viciousness. There he is simply talk-

ing about that violence which he thinks results from a disproportion between the child's desires and his actual physical strength, and not an original propensity to violence in the child. However, the issue is confused in *La Nouvelle Héloïse* by Julie's reference to children who are of a good natural disposition ("bien nés"), which lets the reader suppose there are others who are not, and thus could be used to justify Helvétius's interpretation and criticism of contradiction in Rousseau. Here again, however, we come to the question whether we should identify, as Helvétius does, the characters of the *Nouvelle Héloïse* with Rousseau's opinion. Julie is a Christian, and presumably a Calvinist, and would therefore accept notions of original sin and divine grace which Rousseau himself did not hold. When she speaks of children as "bien nés" we cannot assume that Rousseau would do the same. And, indeed, it is Wolmar, not Julie, who accepts the notion of "bonté naturelle," and who on this point is closest to Rousseau's own position. In *Emile* Rousseau is in fact careful to distinguish between what are for him two separate issues; on the one hand, the existence of innate temperamental factors, on the other, the question of good and evil. As we have said, Rousseau adheres to the notion of innate individual temperament throughout *Emile,* while at the same time he bases his educational treatise on the dictum of man's natural goodness. In *Emile* Rousseau entirely excludes the possibility of the child's possessing an innate tendency towards evil. Interestingly enough, Helvétius and Rousseau are quite close on this point, but by mistakenly associating vice and virtue with the question of innate characteristics, Helvétius has widened the gap between himself and Rousseau and shifted the emphasis of their disagreement. It is in fact on the question of innate and acquired characteristics that they stand radically opposed.

The question of innate vice and virtue opens up the way for a discussion of whether we have an innate moral sense or conscience. On this point Helvétius again accuses Rousseau of being self-contradictory. He quotes two passages in which Rousseau clearly shows that he believes conscience to be innate, then quotes a third passage to show that Rousseau, at other moments, upholds the completely opposite view, e. g., when referring to the poor. Rousseau, according to Helvétius, denies conscience to the poor, maintaining that they can only think of how to feed themselves and cannot hear the "inner voice of virtue." Much depends here on the meaning of "conscience." A Protestant conscience in the manner of the Savoyard Vicar associated with the divine, an immortal and infallible judge of right and wrong, is indeed incompatible with Rousseau's psychology and is part of the Vicar's metaphysics. For the most part, however, "conscience" or the *voix intérieure* is to be understood in *Emile* in conjunction with the instinct for self-preservation (*amour de soi*). Because, according to Rousseau, man is not naturally wicked, the infant's instincts will be good (*droits*), but, because man's only innate principle is that of self-preservation, they will be self-regarding. Rousseau's psychology suggests that "conscience" only awakens with the feelings aroused at the age of puberty. There is therefore a long period in early life in which conscience is dormant and appears non-existent, when the individual acts entirely according to *amour de soi*. There are also conditions in which this dormant but nevertheless innate principle can be completely stifled and, again, appear to be non-existent. Such is the case of the young man (usually assumed to be Rousseau) who consults the Savoyard Vicar. His bad luck in life has stifled his feeling of good and evil, but the accent is quite clearly on "stifled" and does not imply that conscience never had existed or never could exist in the young man. It is then that Rousseau makes a generalization which is quoted only in part by Helvétius and which lends itself to misinterpretation: that there is a level of degradation which removes life from the soul, and renders the man who is only concerned with surviving deaf to the voice of conscience. The person in this situation has been forced back, in Rousseau's terms, to the situation of the natural man or the child, for whom conscience simply means self-preservation.

Helvétius's fourth quotation is concerned with the lower classes and is intended to show that Rousseau believes they have no sense of what is *"honnête"* "Le peuple a peu d'idées, de ce qui est beau et honnête." But it is clear that Rousseau did not mean to say that some people do not possess an innate but latent sense of justice and that, consequently, conscience is either not innate in principle but acquired (which would, indeed, as Helvétius maintains, be a contradiction of his statements elsewhere), or is granted only to a privileged few. Rousseau simply means that the peasant is held at a sub-social level in which conscience cannot develop. He in fact goes on to say in the same passage that the distinction between the social classes in this respect is the result of social injustice, not innate inequalities. Furthermore, still in the same passage, he divides men into his own classes of those who think and those who do not, and attributes the difference not to innate inequalities but to inequality of education, a point which Helvétius mentions in another context. Once again, Rousseau and Helvétius are closer than Helvétius's comments suggest.

Helvétius's final quotation on this point, however, which states that before the age of reason man commits good or evil acts without knowing it "qu'avant l'âge de raison l'homme fait le bien et le mal sans le connoître," presents a greater problem. At first sight it looks like a direct contradiction of Rousseau's statements elsewhere. It in fact hinges on the question whether Rousseau can logically argue that conscience is an innate principle if he accepts a stage in which it is ineffectual and apparently non-existent.

In *Emile*, Rousseau supposes that from birth until about fifteen the child is asexual, amoral, asocial. Time and again he states that before the age of reason, i. e., for him about fifteen, one can have no idea of moral and social relationships. If the child has no notion of moral relationships, then he has no notion of right and wrong, except as agreed by a simple form of contract, as in the case of Emile's garden and his arrangement with the gardener. Consequently, he can have no conscience in the normal sense. What he does have is a basic desire for his own well-being (*amour de soi*), which, as we have seen, is good in itself, since it is entirely restricted to the individual who, at this stage, has no social relationships. Later, with the emotion-

al development of the adolescent, this principle combines with a natural capacity for compassion, and prompts the individual to seek the good of his fellowmen as well as his own. Since man is prone to error, however, by virtue of his free will, this same principle can degenerate into selfish self-interest (*amour-propre* in its narrower sense) and prompt the individual to commit evil. The adolescent's developing intellectual faculties, however, allow him to understand the difference between good and evil, and his free will, guided by reason, enables him to choose the good and attain rational and not merely instinctive virtue. For Rousseau, however, knowledge of right and wrong is not, as it is for Helvétius, entirely based on an intellectual understanding of morality gained from environmental experience, any more than morality itself is merely an established code of behavior based on men's social relationships. It is, rather, the manifestation of God's will, communicated to man by the voice of conscience, which in Rousseau's terms is an appreciation based on *sentiment,* of "suitability" or "unsuitability". It is this *inner sentiment,* which desires the good, but it develops in conjunction with the rational faculties, and it is only when our understanding shows us the good that the inner sentiment, or conscience, prompts us to desire it. Consequently, for Rousseau, man has no innate *knowledge* of right and wrong; like Locke he is entirely opposed to the notion of innate *ideas* and Helvétius realizes this fact, but man does have an innate capacity to desire what is right once his understanding provides him with this knowledge. Rousseau argues that during the "arational" period of childhood man has no conscience since he has no knowledge of morality; but with the advent of the moral judgment and the development of social relationships, conscience, a latent but innate faculty, can develop and guide man towards the good, which is now no longer an individual "good," relevant only to *amour de soi,* but a moral good, affecting the whole species. Rousseau thus distinguishes between the innate principle of self-preservation and the inner sentiment of conscience only insofar as *amour de soi* and its attributes are manifest from birth, whereas principles related to the species as a whole become manifest only at adolescence. At bottom conscience is *amour de soi* and is therefore innate. Man is *capable* of conscience from the start, though it will not develop until later. For Rousseau *amour de soi* is capable of becoming virtue. That is part of his notion of the "perfectibility" of man, which he discusses in the second *Discours.*

Consequently, the quotations chosen by Helvétius on the subject of conscience do not effectively prove inconsistency on Rousseau's part, provided we take the whole of Rousseau's system into account and delve below his apparent meaning. Helvétius's final point on this subject, that all men would be good if, as Rousseau suggests, they had an innate sense of what is just, completely ignores Rousseau's insistence on man's capacity for error, and hence, evil, and his more emotional conviction that, once corruption has made its entry, the voice of conscience is extremely difficult to hear. It also, of course, ignores the thesis of the second *Discours,* central to Rousseau's thought, that man's corruption results from the emergence of the social state. Helvétius presumably avoids such points out of a desire to refute his opponent on purely logical grounds. This makes little difference, however, to the main point of Helvétius's criticism, which is to establish his own belief in the acquired nature of conscience in opposition to Rousseau's conviction that conscience is innate in principle. For Helvétius, conscience is entirely dependent on the development of reason, and the result of merely knowing what is right and wrong. The young can therefore be given a moral catechism which will lead them to virtue. We find here a conflict not only between the nativist and the environmentalist, but also between the religious man and the atheist. Knowing Rousseau we can expect the belief in conscience at some point. Helvétius stands firm in his belief that morality is learned.

With Rousseau the notion of conscience is inevitably linked to the question of the natural goodness of man. So far we have simply accepted that Rousseau posits this link and although Helvétius brings up the subject of natural goodness only at a later point, it would be well to discuss it here. Basing his arguments on various passages of *La Nouvelle Héloïse* and *Emile,* Helvétius sees Rousseau as a decided advocate of natural goodness, which he as an environmentalist does not accept. Once again, however, Rousseau appears to be surprisingly contradictory on a point he so obviously wants to enforce.

That Rousseau believes in the non-wickedness of man is clear from his statements both in *Emile* and elsewhere. The opening sentence of *Emile* stresses the goodness of creation, and its subsequent degeneration in the hands of man, but as the second *Discours* had tried to prove, degeneration was not because man is naturally wicked, but rather in consequence of a combination of fortuitous circumstances. In *La Nouvelle Héloïse* Rousseau applies the principle of natural goodness to the young child, and the whole of the educational system of *Emile* is based on the idea that evil is not an innate characteristic but is acquired through environmental influences. Does Helvétius's quotation from Rousseau, therefore, to the effect that one never feels compassion for others except with regard to those things one might suffer oneself, constitute the serious contradiction he maintains?

Our earlier analysis of Rousseau's notion of *amour de soi* helps to explain the apparent discrepancy. According to Rousseau, commiseration with those with whom we can identify is merely a product of *amour de soi* and, therefore, good in itself. Hence, our sensitivity, which is the origin of our self-love, is also the natural origin of the extension of our self-love to pity. It is because of this progression, and not because of self-interest (*amour-propre* in Rousseau's vocabulary) that he believes that we can only feel pity for those with whom our sensitivity identifies us. Helvétius, who spends a good deal of time here refuting the Shaftesburyists rather than Rousseau on compassion and the moral sense, believes that compassion is the natural derivative of *amour de soi,* but in his case *amour de soi* means self-interest. His further criticisms on this point are based on the belief that no positive results can come of telling people in their present state of corruption that they are naturally good, which is hardly an effective refutation of Rousseau's system, since Rousseau, even more radically than the rest of his generation accepts the corruption of

modern man and vehemently criticizes it, while stressing nonetheless his belief in man's hypothetical natural goodness.

Although Helvétius says in *De l'Homme* that man is born neither good nor evil he nevertheless extends his criticism of the belief in natural goodness to an attempt to prove that man, if not naturally evil, is naturally cruel. He seems to ignore the fact that Rousseau also raises the question of cruelty in the young child and answers it very differently. For rousseau, cruelty before the age of fifteen cannot be defined as evil, since, as we have seen, at this stage the child has no knowledge of right and wrong. Moreover, since compassion is a relatively late development, which occurs only in conjunction with the birth of the imagination and other emotions, the child cannot, according to Rousseau, extend his experience of suffering and physical pain to a creature other than himself. Consequently, his cruelty is not the result of an evil intention, but of the discrepancy between his desires and physical strength. Make him strong and he will not be cruel.

What is the entire German philosophy, starting from Kant, with all its French, English, and Italian offshoots and by-products? A semi-theological attack upon Helvétius, a rejection of the slowly and laboriously acquired views and signposts of the right road, which in the end he collected and expressed so well. To this day Helvétius is the best-abused of all good moralists and good men in Germany.

—*Friedrich Nietzsche, in his* Human, All-Too-Human, *translated by Paul V. Cohn, 1964.*

Helvétius, however, follows in the Hobbesian tradition to which Rousseau is consciously opposed. Helvétius sees strength as the cause of injustice in adult and child alike. Moreover, the child's cruelty to insects, for example, proves that he has no natural feeling of compassion. Helvétius clearly does not accept Rousseau's theory of developing faculties, in which compassion is a late development, any more than he accepts the similarly late development of conscience and the early incapacity to commit evil. Helvétius wrongly equates the notion of a moral sense leading to compassion with the notion of innate ideas and consequently opposes it. For him goodness and humanity, like ideas, are entirely the result of education. Again the two men stand radically opposed.

One of the main aspects of Helvétius's psychology and one of his greatest points of difference from Rousseau is the second principle of his psychological theory, *intérêt*. We have seen *intérêt* in action when we talk about conscience and natural goodness, but it comes particularly to the fore in Helvétius's discussion of public and private good. Helvétius takes Rousseau to task for suggesting that one of the "proofs" of conscience is that without it the individual could not sacrifice his own interests for the achievement of the public good. Helvétius criticizes this statement on two counts: first, he believes that by achieving the public good the individual *is* satisfying his own interests in that he receives honor and public esteem, and secondly, he feels once again that Rousseau is contradicting statements he has made elsewhere.

The first part of the problem revolves around Rousseau's insistence in *Emile* that public and private good are not identical. Since the individual is first conscious only of his own needs and desires and does not contract any social relationships until the period of adolescence, his innate principle of self-love (*amour de soi*) can only prompt him to seek his own good. Such self-love can only be good, since it does not involve any consideration of social morality. However, when the adolescent enters society, and forms moral relationships, he becomes a fraction of a total society and, consequently, must subordinate his interests to the common good. Here, Rousseau inevitably encounters difficulties by refusing to identify private and public good (except in the ideal state of the *Contrat Social*) yet attempting to reconcile the two. Emile is to be educated first as "natural" man, for himself alone; then, on reaching maturity, he is expected to take his place in society. But although his study of history and morality, first through books, then through travels, has prepared him for his future role as citizen, he is told at the same time to retain the "natural" and individualistic attitudes he acquired as a child. The synthesis is, again, an uneasy one. In his comments Helvétius shows that he either fails to understand or simply does not wish to understand Rousseau's distinction between the individual's desire for his own well-being and his decision to sacrifice it for the public good. Helvétius himself bases all human actions on self-interest, since anything which achieves public good is in fact only an incidental result of an attempt to achieve individual good. Moreover, Helvétius fails to accept, or possibly even to understand, Rousseau's notions of *amour de soi* and *amour-propre* which Helvétius associates with his own principle, *intérêt,* and thus is led to his second concern, viz., Rousseau's contradictions.

Throughout *Emile* Rousseau carefully distinguishes between the desired development from indifferent self-love (*amour de soi*) to virtue (*vertu*) which identifies the individual good with the common good, and the possible degeneration of self-love into self-interest (*amour-propre*). When Rousseau declares, therefore, that without some inner conviction of the general good and its desirability (*conscience*), a man cannot be expected to sacrifice his own self-love (*amour de soi*) for the interests of the community, he does not mean, as Helvétius maintains he does, that without conscience man could only act out of *amour-propre* and would therefore never sacrifice himself for the public good. Helvétius's criticism seems to be based on a misunderstanding of Rousseau's arguments. Consequently, his accusation of subsequent contradictions is merely an extension of his original misinterpretation.

For Helvétius, the term *intérêt* means, in the first instance,

the active aspect of sensation in the formation of ideas, and as such is a parallel to Rousseau's second principle, *sentiment. Intérêt,* however, in Helvétius's terms is a personal interest which directs the mind towards those objects which are of interest to the individual and is based on a pain-pleasure psychology. Since *intérêt* provides the sole motivating principle in human beings, it follows that we always act out of self-interest regardless of others, or alternatively that we are prompted by a kind of self-esteem to seek the general good, whatever disadvantages it may hold for us immediately, in an attempt to gain public esteem. Why, Helvétius argues, cannot Rousseau accept this second kind of self-interest (Rousseau's *amour-propre*) as a principle of motivation throughout *Emile?* The whole problem arises out of Helvétius's failure to understand or accept Rousseau's distinction between *amour de soi* and *amour-propre.* And, indeed, for every other writer of the period they were synonymous. *Amour-propre,* however, had been used as the basis of an "aristocratic" morality which Rousseau could not accept. He attempts, therefore, a radical distinction between the two terms, though it is true that the differences are not always entirely clear. When Rousseau says, for example, that the pupil must be prompted by an immediate and conscious interest to fulfill his promise—"un intérêt présent et sensible à remplir son engagement"—he is dealing at this stage uniquely with the notion of self-love, which during the pre-adolescent period prompts the pupil to see external objects merely in their physical relationship to himself and without any moral, and hence social, connotations. Rousseau's method here is to make the child fulfill his promise by forcing him to understand its importance through concrete, physical repercussions, which will affect his immediate interest ("l'intérêt présent et sensible"), not his moral self-interest, which would imply a notion of moral relationships and the motivating principle of vanity, which Emile does not possess. The same remarks can be applied to Helvétius's other quotations on this point. Once again either Rousseau has failed to define his terms clearly enough, or Helvétius, holding different assumptions, has again been unwilling to find harmony beneath surface contradictions. In either case the result is a transformation of Rousseau's original meaning. What is interesting, however, is that although they are diametrically opposed on the question of human motivation, the psychologies of the two men are in some ways very close. Rousseau builds on sensation as a base, following this with his second principle, *sentiment;* while Helvétius, also starting from sensation, follows it with *intérêt,* in a way that is close to Hobbes's sensation plus desire or attention leading to selective perception. What is important here, in the context of the development of eighteenth-century French thought, is Rousseau's rejection of *intérêt* in favor of *sentiment.*

For Helvétius self-interest involves the principles of attention and application. Attention is only possible if it is in the pupil's interest to be attentive. Helvétius would even go so far as to punish the child in an attempt to make him attentive through fear of future punishment. Rousseau holds a very different position. Although he allows self-love (or "indifferent self-interest"), as a motivating principle in the child, he cannot accept arbitrary punishment. To avoid this, and to support his view that *amour-propre* ("interested self-interest") is not behind all human action, he maintains that natural curiosity is a satisfactory motivating force. Rousseau is here in line with thinkers who, like Hume, see curiosity as a natural cause of learning, and despite differences elsewhere, Rousseau is actually quite close to Hobbes, who also saw curiosity as the basis of our capacity to reason deductively. Rousseau's theory is that the child's developing strength will bring him, around the age of ten or twelve, to a period when, his needs adequately satisfied by an excess of physical strength, his superfluous strength will automatically turn to curiosity about the world around him. Helvétius finds Rousseau again self-contradictory on this point, at one moment allowing self-interest and at the next maintaining that natural curiosity is sufficient. Again Rousseau's distinction between *amour de soi* and *amour-propre* is the chief stumbling block, but the fact that Rousseau only suggests *amour de soi* as a motivating force for the period prior to the intellectual age (i. e., before twelve) also causes confusion. After twelve, curiosity can develop through an excess of physical strength and *amour de soi* gives way to curiosity as a motivating principle. There is, therefore, no real illogicality about Rousseau's arguments but a basic opposition between the thinkers: Rousseau's theory of developing strength leading to intellectual curiosity versus Helvétius's theory of attention based on self-interest. In wider terms it is the opposition of the Shaftesbury-Hume tradition to the Hobbesian.

Helvétius's further comments on *Emile* and *La Nouvelle Héloïse* are concerned with the purpose and usefulness of education, and involve us in social and moral issues. They are, however, still closely linked to the central psychological debate, particularly insofar as they are concerned with the extent to which the child can be said to judge.

It is well known that Rousseau's anxiety to save the child from an unsuitable, and therefore worthless, education, prompts him to put forward some rather extreme statements. Like many of Rousseau's critics in the early years Helvétius picks *inter alia* on one of these: the idea that, if the child did not know his right hand from his left at the age of twelve, provided he was healthy and strong, his understanding would nonetheless immediately respond to his first lessons. He opposes that idea with a theory of his own: that without long years of training, the child would not acquire the necessary degree of attention with which to succeed in later life. This takes us back to the earlier arguments on the principles of motivation. It also highlights the basic opposition of the two thinkers. Helvétius simply cannot accept Rousseau's system of "negative" yet "progressive" education, in which the child is left to develop physically until the exercise of his senses prompts him to intellectual activity, and in which the methods used to educate him develop and change according to his physical and intellectual capacities. Since Helvétius equates sensation and judgment, he believes the child can judge at an early age. His unwillingness to accept the fundamentals of Rousseau's theory of man and the system of education based on it pushes him once again to look for contradictions in Rousseau's statements, this time on the question of what Rousseau terms a premature education.

One of Rousseau's main concerns in his program of education is that, during the period from birth to about twelve, the child should learn nothing he cannot properly understand. Since, according to Rousseau's suppositions, the child does not have any notion of moral and social relationships, any education he receives must be entirely concerned with the physical relationships between himself and the world around. Moreover, the period from birth to twelve constitutes the most dangerous times in a child's existence. It is then that the seeds of vice and error are sown and cannot be destroyed, since the powers of moral judgment and conscience are as yet undeveloped. It is, therefore, useless to educate children in the traditional manner, which wrongly supposes that they are in full possession of adult reason and its attributes. The only solution is to "waste" time until the child is ready for abstract reasoning and moral considerations. By avoiding a premature education (this is the point Helvétius seizes upon) and, instead, allowing the child's faculties to develop freely and naturally by teaching him only what he is able to understand, one will create an educational wonder and, at the same time, preserve the child from error and vice.

Rousseau's plea against orthodox education is, therefore, to a large extent the result of logical reasoning within his system. Confusion arises, as Helvétius aptly points out, from Rousseau's inability to define properly what he means by lack of reasoning power or judgment in the young child. There is an apparent contradiction between statements in which he argues, for example, that children simply retain visual images of matters like geometrical demonstrations and do not properly understand them and other statements in which he maintains that children reason perfectly well on everything concerning their immediate, sensitive experience. Indeed, as Helvétius knows, Rousseau himself is aware of the apparent contradictions in what he says about reasoning. The problem arises because Rousseau attempts with insufficient clarity, and in too absolute a manner, to distinguish between the young child's obvious inability to reason in an abstract manner, and his capacity to deduce information from concrete material which he has been taught to handle. In *Emile* he insists on training the child's judgment through the exercise of his senses, at the same time declaring that the child cannot judge. It is because of Rousseau's inability to define his terms that Helvétius thinks he can refute Rousseau's theory by observation. He argues that we know that children can judge distances, size, texture, etc., and master most of their native language and learn to express themselves in it by the age of twelve. Such is in fact exactly the sort of education Rousseau's system is supposed to achieve in the first two books of *Emile,* as we can see from the summary of Emile's prowess at the end of the first stage in his education. He is skillful and strong, he can judge and reason within the limits of his physical experience, he can judge distances, invent games, etc. Rousseau does not, then, as some of his contemporaries would have us believe, and as Helvétius himself realizes, proscribe all education until the age of twelve, nor does he think the child totally incapable of judgment. He merely condemns book-learning and similar methods which teach the child what he is not ready to understand, stressing the importance of giving the child an education which corresponds to his abilities.

Helvétius now uses his contention, that observation demonstrates the child's abilities before the age of twelve, to show that the mind exercises itself as the body grows stronger. He opposes what he maintains to be Rousseau's contention, that the body gets stronger before the mind begins to work. Helvétius is misrepresenting Rousseau's view here. Although he emphasizes the primacy of sensation in the development of the mind and believes physical exercise will aid intellectual development, the whole of Rousseau's method of education is based on the idea of the corresponding development of the physical and mental. As Emile's body is exercised, so his mind is exercised too. Helvétius has simply taken Rousseau's insistence on first training the senses and extended it to the whole of his educational psychology. Helvétius and Rousseau are in fact basically in agreement on this point, despite Helvétius's assertions to the contrary.

Rousseau does, however, tend to see the development of intellectual or human reason ("la raison intellectuelle ou humaine") as a more or less automatic development which occurs at a certain stage in the individual's physical development: intellectual curiosity develops at about twelve and "adult reason" (which includes the moral judgment) at about fifteen, when it coincides with the development of the passions, imagination, and the desire for human relationships. On the other hand, Rousseau makes it quite clear that sensory experience is vital to intellectual reasoning, maintaining that a human being born with adult stature would be an imbecile. What he seems to be saying, particularly in extreme statements which claim that if a child is kept in a state of complete ignorance till twelve, the child's reason would develop with the first instruction received, is that simple sense experience of the physical world is sufficient to allow the child's intellect to develop of its own accord at twelve. Instruction before twelve is therefore unnecessary. Helvétius, on the other hand, is merely concerned with the degree, and not the type of judgment of which the child is capable. He accepts judgment in the normal sense of intellectual activity and, believing that the young learn more quickly than adults, would take advantage of this from an early age. He has no place for Rousseau's subtle distinctions.

Rousseau's condemnation of an unsuitable, premature education is part of the material Helvétius draws on for the general question, whether education is useful or not. He asserts that Rousseau constantly affirms and then denies that education is useful. Unfortunately, however, Helvétius chooses as an illustration a passage which appears to condemn most education as inappropriate and damaging, but which, once it is replaced in its context, does not refer to education in general but only to education in a limited sense. Rousseau in fact prefaces his condemnation with the question: what can come of a *uniform* education which disregards individual characteristics. This takes us back to our earlier discussion of *tempérament*. It also shows that Rousseau's belief in the detrimental effects of education in fact only serves to condemn that very education which he thought Helvétius sought to recommend. Indeed, although Helvétius insists that intellectual inequalities are the result of environmental variants and might therefore be controlled, and although he maintains that all men are

capable of the same intellectual achievement, even he does not insist on complete uniformity in education. In *De l'Esprit* he asserts that he would not give an identical education to three men, one of whom was to become a small public employee and the other two to hold high office in the army or government. In this case it seems that Rousseau has also misread Helvétius. What interests us here, however, is that throughout *Emile,* whenever Rousseau condemns education, it is always either a uniform education or the traditional education of his time that he has in mind. As for education in general, he stresses its importance right from the start. Everything we do not have at birth and which we need as adults is given us by education. The two men are in fact united, despite themselves, in the faith they place in the importance of education. They stand opposed only in the type of education they would give to the young child.

Helvétius, however, like many of his contemporaries, wishes to paint Rousseau as an advocate of universal ignorance, and to do so he draws the conclusion he desires from Rousseau's apparently contradictory statements. However, to illustrate his point, Helvétius unfortunately chooses once again a passage—that children cannot obtain knowledge from books, because the knowledge is not in them—which, when correctly placed in context, clearly does not prove the point he wishes to make "ce n'est point des livres que les enfants doivent tirer leurs connaissances; les connaissances ne s'y trouvent pas." This does not mean that knowledge is completely worthless, but merely that the method whereby knowledge is culled from books without reference to observation and concrete facts leads to error and hence, according to Rousseau, to vice. We must suppose that Helvétius's criticism is prompted less by such a statement, which he must certainly have understood, than by the reputation Rousseau had already gained for himself by condemning the arts and sciences in the first *Discours,* the main thesis of which Helvétius critically discusses in some detail in *De l'Homme.* By his radical and somewhat ambiguous statements, however, Rousseau certainly lays himself open to abuse from his critics.

It is, of course, true that like many of his predecessors in pedagogical theory (the Abbé de Saint-Pierre and Rollin, for example) Rousseau prefers virtue to knowledge, which explains such remarks as that it is unnecessary to be knowledgeable and essential to be wise and good "peum'importe, dit Julie . . . que mon fils soit savant: il me suffit qu'il soit sage et bon." Helvétius, on the other hand, is obliged to object, since he believes that virtue is actually based on knowledge. If we *know* what is right, then we can follow it. Consequently Helvétius either fails to notice, or refuses to allow, that Rousseau's remark is merely a relative statement, not an absolute condemnation of knowledge.

Rousseau's real plea in favor of ignorance, however, is based on the Cartesian belief that error comes from Judgment. If we never needed to judge, we would never be wrong. Hence, the more men know, the more occasion they have to judge and the more prone they are to error. The only solution, therefore, is ignorance. It is because of this tendency to err through judgment that Rousseau believes there are more errors in the Paris Academy of Science than in a whole tribe of Hurons, since the Hurons have little knowledge to submit to their judgment. That problem is central to the argument of the first *Discours*. Helvétius counters with arguments concerning cruelty caused by ignorance, but he fails to draw attention to Rousseau's concluding remark. Total ignorance, Rousseau argues, is now impossible. Since man has lost his primitive independence and innocence and is forced to live in a state of dependence where he needs to know how to choose and judge, he must, therefore be suitably educated. The purpose of education will be to teach him to judge well, and *Emile* will show how this can be achieved.

It should be apparent from our analysis that few of Helvétius's allegations of contradiction on Rousseau's part in fact constitute the serious criticism of the logically and coherence of Rousseau's ideas that Helvétius intended. There are instances of misunderstanding, misquotation, and even misrepresentation on Helvétius's part, all designed to show that Rousseau's inconsistencies render his philosophical system unacceptable. On the other hand, it is obvious that Rousseau's failure to define his terms clearly and to systematize and coordinate the various ideas basic to his theory of human nature, and subsequently to his system of education, gives rise to a certain amount of ambiguity. It is not surprising that his dialectics should not always be understood. In the final analysis, however, it must be said that Helvétius based his criticisms on very shaky foundations. Most of the apparent inconsistencies he stressed can be reconciled when replaced in the context of *Emile*.

In their different ways, both these thinkers were making positive contributions. Rousseau's historical influence on educational theory needs no discussion here, and though he harks back to the epistemology of traditional dualism, which may have been thought of as retrograde by Helvétius, Rousseau was nevertheless giving his support to the tradition of introspection in psychology, and, as D. W. Smith points out, was making it possible for sensationalism to be refuted later. Helvétius, for his part, by denying essential differences among individuals was giving valuable support to the environmentalists and anticipating later social and educational reforms.

Moreover, despite the many issues over which they clash, Rousseau and Helvétius stand united, albeit unconsciously, on a central point. Whereas many of their predecessors and contemporaries propose a reformed public education without questioning its practicability in the unreformed society of eighteenth-century France, Rousseau and Helvétius both express independently the need for concurrent reform in politics and education. It seems a pity that they should have found so much in philosophy, psychology, and ethics on which to differ. United on the political and educational front they might have offered a viable alternative to the society of their times.

Elizabeth J. Gardner   (essay date 1979)

SOURCE: "The Philosophes and Women: Sensationalism and Sentiment" in *Women and Society in Eighteenth-Century France,* edited by Eva Jacobs and others, The Athlone Press, 1979, pp. 19-27.

[In the following excerpt, Gardner describes how the doctrine of sensationalism shaped Helvétius's attitude toward women.]

Feminism was not a cause espoused by the *philosophes,* with the obvious exception of Condorcet, who is anyway not always included in their ranks. It is not sufficient, however, merely to claim that women were naturally included in the general programme of amelioration these thinkers envisaged. For the views of the *philosophes* on women must be considered within their own terms of reference; and while it would be anachronistic to labour any supposedly anti-feminist remarks culled from their disparate writings, it is of interest to examine the various theoretical conclusions which writers like Helvétius, Diderot, D'Holbach and Condorcet drew from a common premise—sensationalism. We can then see how this doctrine was applied to one half of the human race.

The works of Helvétius provide a starting point . . . , since in his rigid expression of sensationalism we find some of the logically egalitarian implications of this theory applied to the subject of women, although not in a systematic or coherent fashion.

All men, Helvétius claims, are equal, at least in potential, at birth, and therefore subsequent inequality is the result of differences in education and environment. If women do not achieve eminence in the Arts and Sciences it is because they are hampered even more than their male counterparts by the type of education they receive and their lifestyle. Thus when accounting for the relatively small number of great minds in Paris, Helvétius automatically disqualifies women: 'Or, de ces huit cent mille âmes, si d'abord l'on en supprime la moitié, c'est-à-dire les femmes, dont l'éducation et la vie s'opposent au progrès qu'elles pourraient faire dans les sciences et les arts . . .'

Helvétius side-steps the question of educational reform in *De l'esprit,* arguing that since the possibility of reform is so remote, lengthy proposals would be superfluous. He returns to the theme of women's education and its ills in *De l'homme.* However, if Helvétius strikes a more constructive note on the subject of male education, little mention is made of the female of the species when he draws up plans for public education and professional training. There is, Helvétius states, a basic incompatibility between what is taught to the child or adolescent and what is expected of him or her in the world. This dichotomy is particularly blatant in the education girls receive in convents: 'C'est dans les maisons religieuses et destinées à l'instruction des jeunes filles que ces contradictions sont les plus frappantes.' For instance, girls are taught to be truthful but they are not allowed to express their opinion if their parents' choice of husband does not please them. They order these things differently in Turkey where at least women receive training appropriate to their future submissive role. Helvétius insists on the primacy of education. Intelligence is not proportionate to the degree of refinement of the senses. Women, for instance, have a more acute sense of touch but are not thereby more intelligent than, say, Voltaire. By the same token the intellectual inferiority of women cannot be related to specifically female characteristics. Helvétius leaves us in no doubt whatsoever about this:

> L'organisation des deux sexes est sans doute très-différente à certains égards: mais cette différence doit-elle être regardée comme la cause de l'infériorité de l'esprit des femmes? Non: la preuve du contraire, c'est que nulle femme n'étant organisée comme un homme, nulle en conséquence ne devroit avoir autant d'esprit. Or les Saphos, les Hyppathies, les Elizabeths, les Catherines II, etc. ne le cedent point aux hommes en génie. Si les femmes leur sont en général inférieures, c'est qu'en général elles reçoivent encore une plus mauvaise éducation.

The optimism prevalent in such aspects of Helvétius's thinking on women was far from being commonplace at the time, as Diderot's comments constantly show. In his notes on *De l'homme* Diderot offers a much narrower interpretation of the facts. He seems to suggest that exceptions do not affect the norm, otherwise one swallow would make a summer. Similarly, 'Le petit nombre de femmes de génie fait exception et non pas règle', and moreover, as he churlishly asserts, the standards expected of women are lower than those expected of men; like the rich they are surrounded by flatterers. He is equally sceptical about the role of education as a universal panacea. Helvétius, Diderot states, had claimed that 'les femmes sont susceptibles de la même éducation que les hommes'; Diderot's contention is far less radical: 'Dites: on pourrait les élever mieux qu'on ne fait'.

Although Helvétius, unlike Diderot, makes no distinction between male and female potential, he fails to implement his theory of the absolute equality of the sexes when he rhapsodises on the role women would play in an ideal society. Reforms in education, changes in marriage laws and sexual mores seem to be inspired chiefly with the benefit of men in mind. Not only does woman fail to emerge as an independent entity—and we should not be too harsh on Helvétius for this—but the only means of acquiring status allowed to her is to submit her one source of power, sex, to the control of the state. Helvétius is obviously less concerned with being consistent with his own theories than with seizing every available opportunity of attacking the Church's views on sex and morals. Women's education should be improved, he argues, because of the deleterious influence they have on men. Women are a distraction and prevent some men from fulfilling themselves intellectually. If sex were demystified, the power women exercise over their lovers through the cult that is demanded of the latter would be lessened and men could indulge their pleasure and be free to pursue intellectual matters as well.

Helvétius reiterates this point in *De l'homme* where he advocates a more matter-of-fact approach to sex, particularly for busy men: 'Il faut donc des coquettes aux oisifs, et de jolies filles aux occupés;' and again: 'La chasse des dames comme celle du gibier, doit être différente selon le temps qu'on veut y mettre.'

Since men are motivated chiefly by a desire for sexual grat-

ification, the solution to the problem that women pose for men would be, in Helvétius's view, to put women at the disposal of the state. Helvétius wistfully speculates that the Spartans would have been even more heroic if their goal had been sexual favours rather than mere glory. Woman's lot too would have been enhanced:

> Tout concourait, dans cette législation, à métamorphoser les hommes en héros; mais, pour l'établir, il fallait que Lycurgue, convaincu que le plaisir est le moteur unique et universel des hommes, eût senti que les femmes, qui partout ailleurs semblaient, comme les fleurs d'un beau jardin, n'être faites que pour l'ornement de la terre et le plaisir des yeux, pouvaient être employées à un plus noble usage; que ce sexe, avili et dégradé chez presque tous les peuples du monde, pouvait entrer en communauté de gloire avec les hommes, partager avec eux les lauriers qu'il leur faisait cueillir, et devenir enfin un des plus puissants ressorts de la législation.

This is pure sophistry: being a tool of the state is scarcely an active role. Woman, however venerable, however revered, is still an object, as Helvétius makes abundantly clear in *De l'homme*: 'Qu'une belle esclave, une concubine devienne chez un peuple le prix, ou des talens, ou de la vertu . . . les moeurs de ce peuple n'en seront pas plus corrompues.' In *De l'homme,* Section II, Chapter IX, an unrepentant Helvétius answers his critics, expanding the theory he had tentatively expounded in *De l'esprit.* He implicitly rejects the theoretical equality he accorded to women. Ideally women would be owned communally and would be taught to favour only those men who had distinguished themselves intellectually, physically or morally. How could this be implemented, one wonders? Helvétius is hazy about details; 'exiger', for example, is suitably vague but leaves plenty of scope for a fertile imagination:

> Supposons . . . un pays où les femmes soient en commun . . . Tout ce que l'on pourroit encore exiger d'elles, c'est qu'elles conçussent tant de vénération pour leur beauté et leurs faveurs, qu'elles crussent n'en devoir fair part qu'aux hommes déjà distingués par leur génie, leur courage ou leur probité. Leurs faveurs par ce moyen deviendroient un encouragement aux talens et aux vertus.

In addition, what would be the lot of those women who, although desirous of implementing the state's policy, found that they were undesirable?

It would, however, be unwise to make too much of Helvétius's fantasies. He was similarly naive about the condition of peasants. He paints a somewhat rosy picture of their marital bliss and harmony, which he attributes to the fact that they are mutually dependent on each other for their livelihood and also so busy that they do not see each other very much! In contrast, the boredom of the rich leads to infidelity. Condorcet, for instance, found his own experience proof enough against Helvétius's theories: 'Il ne me fera pas croire que, si je résous des problèmes, c'est dans l'espérance que les belles dames me rechercheront; car je n'ai pas vu jusqu'ici qu'elles raffolassent des géomètres. Helvétius's muddled and inconsistent statements on the subject of women should be seen not as a conscious attempt to debase woman herself: they stem rather from his desire to relate all activity to his system of interest and male sexuality. They should not obscure his great merit, which lies in the fact that like true feminists he makes no *a priori* assumptions about women. This is particularly refreshing in view of the very different conclusions his contemporaries Diderot and D'Holbach infer from a sensationalist framework.

Seamus Deane   (essay date 1988)

SOURCE: "Godwin, Helvétius, and Holbach: Crime and Punishment," in his *The French Revolution and Enlightenment in England,* Cambridge, Mass.: Harvard University Press, 1988, pp. 72-94.

[*Deane is an Ulster-born poet and scholar whose career has been centered around Anglo-Irish culture and the political crisis in Northern Ireland. In the following excerpt, taken from a work discussing French influence on the Enlightenment in Great Britain, Deane addresses Helvétius's themes of self-love and power, and how the two, in unison, may be abused under his philosophical system.*]

It might be well to begin a consideration of Claude-Adrien Helvétius with a quotation from [William Godwin's] *Political Justice* which should remind us of the differences between [the two]. Godwin's consistent interest in the motives for action—an important consideration in his novels—gives his writing an emphasis which Helvétius, in his constant preoccupation with the consequences of action, avoids:

> If self-love be the only principle of action, there can be no such thing as virtue. Benevolent intention is essential to virtue. Virtue, where it exists in any eminence, is a species of conduct, modelled upon a true estimate of the different reasons inviting us to preference. He that makes a false estimate, and prefers a trivial and a partial good to an impartial and comprehensive one, is vicious. Virtue requires a certain disposition and view of the mind, and does not belong to the good which may accidentally and unintentionally result from our proceeding.

Against that, on the subject of virtue, Helvétius [in his *De l'esprit*] declares: "The virtuous man is by no means he who sacrifices his pleasures, habits, and strongest feelings in the public interest, for such a man is impossible. Rather it is he whose strongest desire is so much in conformity with the general interest that he is almost always obliged to be virtuous."

The utilitarianism of Helvétius, with its emphasis on the consequences of action and on self-love as its only source, leads inevitably to the notion that man in order to be happy must live in a rationally controlled environment. After all, the environment determines the degree of coincidence possible between self-love and public interest. To Helvétius it seemed obvious that the influence of the Catholic Church in France severely reduced the possibility of such coincidence, not only by its system of laws and punishments but also by its various attacks on the (to him) le-

gitimate selfishness of the individual. Education was all-powerful, and therefore control over it had to be absolute. The totalitarian implications of this are clear now, but Helvétius would have defended his system on the grounds that the philosopher-king, or Legislator, who would lead the people from ignorance to enlightenment would do so in their own best interest, since he would be acting rationally in accord with the nature of things. Nevertheless, his whole emphasis is on the formulation of a legislative system based entirely on his redaction of the epistemology of Locke and Condillac. The essence of his whole system is that every area of human life is controlled by necessary forces, that knowledge reveals their workings to man, who then adapts himself to these known surroundings in a manner calculated to give him the greatest possible pleasure and the least possible pain. This type of thinking produced many books which were in fact blueprints for a new society, such as *De l'esprit* and *Political Justice,* in which the prejudices of the past and the accumulations of history were regarded with a uniform hostility. It is typical of Helvétius that he should use the simile of a religious order to illustrate his conception of what the new legislator would need initially to do: "Therefore, the first step in the formulation of an excellent legal system, is to pay no attention to the hostility of prejudiced views, nor to the friction of competing personal interests, nor to already established customs, laws, or usages. One must look upon oneself as the founder of a religious order who, in dictating his monastic rule, has no regard whatsoever for the conventions and prejudices of his future subjects." [From *De l'homme*]

Although the Godwinian concepts of virtue with its altruistic bias and of Mind with its spontaneous and, from a political point of view, anarchic capacity to create relationships free from the interference of laws or systems are both far removed from this philosophy, there are on other levels many points of contact. They share a belief in the unimportance of heredity, in the identification of vice with error, and in the pernicious effect of vested interests in the state. More important, though, Helvétius sketched out a genealogy of the passions which led him directly to confront the problem of self-love in its severest form; that is, when self-love takes the shape of the desire to dominate others. If self-love is conceived of as nothing more than a rather petty selfishness, it is a politically manageable problem, given the possibility of creating a controlled environment which would actually help to promote that selfishness toward consequences which were never part of its intentions. But Helvétius, looking for a Newtonian coherence in the moral as in the physical world, announces that "the passions are in the moral world what movement is in the physical universe. It creates, destroys, conserves, and animates all; without movement, all is bead. So too, the passions inform the moral universe."

It follows that the intensity of moral compulsion is in proportion to the extent to which the self-love of the agent is involved. Legislation could indeed stimulate human progress by recognizing this fact. All this holds, though, only as long as Helvétius can keep his epistemology and his political philosophy anchored in the conviction that happiness is identical with pleasure. He does, however, describe other and more complex passions, and these are not so readily referred to a physical basis. There is for Helvétius a natural and automatic desire for physical pleasure; but passion in becoming more complicated becomes less natural and, one would think, less dependent for its satisfaction on anything which could be called physical. He sketches the stages of a psychological development which, deriving from our physical nature, passes from love of pleasure and fear of pain to a condition of self-love in which the wish for happiness is born. This in turn leads to a longing for power so that happiness may be achieved. This wish for power is the agent of all the dangerous and artificial passions which derive from "natural" self-love. Power has close connections with reputation, and reputation is itself closely related to self-esteem, since the public and the private image of a man often supplement each other. Helvétius at this point completely evades the serious questions which his description of the power drive involves by asserting that true greatness consists in its pursuit, since to attain power is to forsake the esteem of tiny cliques in society for the sake of gaining the esteem of the whole social world. To seek fame is to seek self-respect, and to despise fame is a sign of failure. Still a problem remains. If power can be so justified as a legitimate human impulse, them how can its abuse be punished? It is possible that a man in power could commit a crime against society which would remain secret. His reputation would be untarnished, yet it would not correspond to his worth. Helvétius can give no answer to this problem, since he makes worth and reputation *necessarily* coincident. It is no complete answer to say that wickedness is caused by the laws and mores of a society.

FURTHER READING

Creighton, Douglas George. "Man and Mind in Diderot and Helvétius." *PMLA* LXXI, No. 4 (September 1956): 705-24.
 Compares the philosophies of Helvétius and Diderot principally through an examination of the latter's *Réfutation suivie de l'ouvage d'Helvétius intitulé l'homme.*

Ladd, Everett C., Jr. "Helvétius and D'Holbach, 'La moralisation de la politique'." *Journal of the History of Ideas* XXIII, No. 2 (1962): 221-38.
 Discusses the parallels in the political thought of Helvétius and d'Holbach.

Lough, J. "Helvétius and D'Holbach." *The Modern Language Review* XXXIII, No. 3 (July 1938): 360-84.
 Attempts to demonstrate "how far [Helvétius and d'Holbach] agree on certain fundamental questions."

McConnell, Allen. "Helvétius' Russian Pupils." *Journal of the History of Ideas* XXIV, No. 1 (January 1963): 373-86.
 Describes Helvétius's influence, specifically of his *On Mind*, on the thought and works of Russian writer Aleksandr Radischev.

Meckier, Jerome. "A Neglected Huxley 'Preface': His Earliest Synopsis of *Brave New World*." *Twentieth-Century Literature: A Scholarly and Critical Journal* 25, No. 1 (Spring 1979): 1-20.
 Asserts that in *Brave New World* Huxley parodies and repudiates Helvétius's philosophy of pleasure-driven environmentalism, a doctrine which he had initially addressed in his preface to J. H. Burns's *A Vision of Education*.

Rogister, J. M. J. "Louis-Adrien Lepaige and the Attack on *On Mind* and the *Encyclopédie* in 1759." *The English Historical Review* XCII, No. 364 (July 1977): 522-39.
 Examines the attack on *De l'esprit* and the *Encyclopédie* mounted by the fundamentalist Jansenists, who were led by Lepaige.

Smith, D. W. *Helvétius: A Study in Persecution*. Oxford: Clarendon Press, 1965, 248 p.
 Seminal study which details the publication of *De l'esprit* and the subsequent persecution of its author by his religious, philosophical, and political contemporaries.

Topazio, Virgil W. "Diderot's Supposed Contribution to Helvétius' Works." *Philological Quarterly* XXXIII, No. 111 (July 1954): 313-29.
 Attempts to disprove allegations that Diderot was a major contributor to the works of Helvétius by examining the former's published critiques of the latter as well as other circumstantial evidence.

Wickwar, William H. "Helvétius and Holbach." In *The Social & Political Ideas of Some Great French Thinkers of the Age of Reason*, edited by F. J. C. Hearnshaw, pp. 195-216. London: George G. Harrap & Co., 1930.
 Discusses Helvétius and d'Holbach as they related to and emerged from the intellectual circle of the Encyclopédists.

Anne-Robert-Jacques Turgot

1727-1781

French economist, philosopher, and statesman.

INTRODUCTION

Turgot was an influential economist and philosopher as well as a government official dedicated to the improvement of his society. In the opinion of many critics, he laid the basis for a theory of progress that dominated the philosophy of history in the nineteenth and early twentieth centuries. In addition, his writings on economics are recognized as original contributions to our understanding of the free market. A man with broad intellectual interests, he investigated almost every field of study, writing articles for the *Encyclopedia* and translating works from seven languages. As the chief administrative officer of the district of Limoges, and later as Louis XVI's minister of finance, Turgot worked to reform and rationalize public services and the system of taxation.

Biographical Information

Turgot was born the third son of a comfortable bourgeois family, and, like many younger children of his class, he was destined for religious life. A precocious student, he began attending lectures in theology at the Seminary of Saint-Sulpice in 1743 when he was sixteen years old. In 1749 Turgot entered the Sorbonne, where he was to study for a master's degree; six months after admission, he was elected prior, a position that required him to preside over student assemblies and to deliver discourses in Latin on religious subjects. The strength of his vocation to the priesthood, however, soon began to weaken, and after his father's death in 1750, he left the Sorbonne, having written earlier to his friends, ". . . I cannot condemn myself to wear a mask throughout my life." Once in the secular world, he accepted a number of government posts including the Master of Requests (a position similar to a judge on a court of appeals), which gave him the leisure to participate in the rich intellectual life of eighteenth-century Paris. He became an acquaintance of François-Marie Arouet Voltaire and contributed to the *Encyclopedia* until authorization for its publication was withdrawn by the government. Drawn to economics since his student days, Turgot became associated with its leading theoreticians in France, François Quesnay and Vincent de Gournay. In 1761, Turgot received the opportunity to put his economic theories in practice when he was appointed chief administrative officer (*intendant*) for Limoges, a poor district area in central France. Once in office, he undertook a methodical investigation of its wealth and property in order to make equitable revisions of the tax assessments, and he adjusted tax burdens to match more accurately the ability of the citizens to pay. Until his administration, peasants were required to undertake road building and road repair as

part of their feudal dues. Turgot freed them from this obligation and instead used tax money to subsidize highway maintenance. According to some historians, the thoroughfares of Limoges became the best in France. During a famine, Turgot asked the prosperous landlords to keep their hired laborers and support them to the next harvest, and he established unemployment offices to help people find work. In 1774, the first year of Louis XVI's reign, Turgot entered his government and soon became *contrôleur général*, or the minister of finance, trade, and public works. He used his authority to implement a series of innovations including the abolition of internal tariffs on grain. In 1776, he attempted his most daring reforms, the so-called six edicts. By these measures, not only did he commute the road building and maintenance service throughout France, but he also placed the burden for its funding on the nobility, who had hitherto been tax exempt. In an effort to foster free enterprise, Turgot's edicts also abolished the guilds—institutions that exercised trade and manufacturing monopolies. These measures, along with his desire to keep public expenditures at a minimum, alienated the privileged classes and eventually the king. Turgot was dismissed on 12 May 1776, and his legislation was revoked. He never again entered public service and he died in Paris in 1781.

Major Works

Turgot's first major writings were two Latin lectures that he gave as prior of the Sorbonne in 1750, and they are among his most important since in them he delineates his philosophy of history. In the first, *Les Avantages que l'établissement du christianisme a procurés au genre humain* (1750; *The Advantages that the Establishment of Christianity Has Conferred upon the Human Race*), he describes the role of religion as a civilizing force, and in the second, *Tableau philosophique des progrès successifs de l'esprit humain* (1750; *A Philosophic Review of the Successive Advances of the Human Mind*), he argues that we have progressed materially and morally over the centuries through our ability to accumulate and store knowledge. His most important economic writing, "Réflexions sur la formation et la distribution des richesses" (1766; "Reflections on the Formation and Distribution of Wealth"), is an outline of political economy prepared for two Chinese students about to return to home. Turgot also wrote five articles for the *Encyclopedia*: "Étymologie" (1756; "Etymology"), "Existence" (1756), "Expansibilité" (1756; "Expansibility") and "Foires et Marchés" (1757; "Fairs and Markets"), and "Fondation" (1757; "Endowments").

Critical Reception

In the opinion of Robert Flint, Turgot rendered a great service to the philosophy of history by demonstrating that history is no mere aggregate of random facts, "but an organic whole with an internal plan realized by internal forces." According to Turgot, the gradual improvement in material culture and the growth in understanding shapes human experience and gives history meaning. In the view of many scholars, he provided the model for the theories of progress that were developed by Condorcet and Auguste Comte. Even in our less optimistic age, Eric Voegelin, who finds the theory of progress flawed and somewhat naive, has praised the subtlety with which Turgot makes his arguments. In the opinion of most critics, Turgot's economic thought was heavily influenced by the physiocrats, who emphasized free trade and land as a source of wealth. Yet, Werner Stark has maintained that Turgot understood the importance of labor, and that he presented a labor theory that links his thought with that of John Locke and Karl Marx. Victor Cousin has declared Turgot's article "Existence" for the *Encyclopedia* an important contribution to philosophical literature of the eighteenth century. Many scholars consider Turgot to have combined the intellectual curiosity and breath of knowledge typical of major Enlightenment figures with a profundity that would be unique in any age.

PRINCIPAL WORKS

Les Avantages que l'établissement du christianisme a procurés au genre humain [*The Advantages that the Establishment of Christianity Has Conferred upon the Human Race*] (lecture) 1750

Sur l'histoire universelle [*Notes on Universal History*] (philosophy) 1750

Tableau philosophique des progrès successifs de l'esprit humain [*A Philosophical Review of the Successive Advances of the Human Mind*] (lecture) 1750

Lettres sur la tolérance [*Letters on Tolerance*] (letters) 1754

"Étymologie" ["Etymology"] (linguistics) 1756

"Existence" (philosophy) 1756

"Expansibilité" ["Expansibility"] (philosophy) 1756

"Foires et Marchés" ["Fairs and Markets"] (economics) 1757

"Fondation" ["Endowments"] (economics) 1757

Éloge de Gournay [*Elegy to Gournay*] (economics) 1759

"Réflexions sur la formation et la distribution des richesses" ["Reflections on the Formation and the Distribution of Wealth"] (economics) 1766

The Life and Writings of Turgot, Comptroller General of France, 1774-6 (economics, essays, letters, philosophy) 1895

Œuvres de Turgot et documents le concernant. 5 vols. [*Works of Turgot and Documents Concerning Him*] (economics, essays, letters, philosophy) 1913-23

CRITICISM

Anne-Robert-Jacques Turgot　(lecture date 1750)

SOURCE: *Turgot on Progress, Sociology and Economics,* edited and translated by Ronald L. Meek, Cambridge at the University Press, 1973, pp. 41-59.

[*In the following essay, which was originally given as a lecture at the Sorbonne in 1750, Turgot outlines his theory of progress.*]

The phenomena of nature, governed as they are by constant laws, are confined within a circle of revolutions which are always the same. All things perish, and all things spring up again; and in these successive acts of generation through which plants and animals reproduce themselves time does no more than restore continually the counterpart of what it has caused to disappear.

The succession of mankind, on the other hand, affords from age to age an ever-changing spectacle. Reason, the passions, and liberty ceaselessly give rise to new events: all the ages are bound up with one another by a succession of causes and effects which link the present state of the world with all those that have preceded it. The arbitrary signs of speech and writing, by providing men with the means of securing the possession of their ideas and communicating them to others, have made of all the individual stores of knowledge a common treasure-house which one generation transmits to another, an inheritance which is always being enlarged by the discoveries of each age. Thus the human race, considered over the period since its origin, appears to the eye of a philosopher as one vast whole, which itself, like each individual, has its infancy and its advancement.

We see the establishment of societies, and the formation of nations which in turn dominate other nations or become subject to them. Empires rise and fall; laws and forms of government succeed one another; the arts and the sciences are in turn discovered and perfected, in turn retarded and accelerated in their progress; and they are passed on from country to country. Self-interest, ambition, and vainglory continually change the world scene and inundate the earth with blood; yet in the midst of their ravages manners are softened, the human mind becomes more enlightened, and separate nations are brought closer to one another. Finally commercial and political ties unite all parts of the globe, and the whole human race, through alternate periods of rest and unrest, of weal and woe, goes on advancing, although at a slow pace, towards greater perfection.

In the time placed at my disposal I could not hope to portray for you the whole of so vast a panorama. I shall try merely to indicate the main lines of the progress of the human mind; and this discourse will be wholly taken up with some reflections on the origin and growth of the arts and sciences and the revolutions which have taken place in them, considered in their relation to the succession of historical events.

Holy Writ, after having enlightened us about the creation of the universe, the origin of man, and the birth of the first arts, before long puts before us a picture of the human race concentrated again in a single family as the result of a universal flood. Scarcely had it begun to make good its losses when the miraculous confusion of tongues forced men to separate from one another. The urgent need to procure subsistence for themselves in barren deserts, which provided nothing but wild beasts, obliged them to move apart from one another in all directions and hastened their diffusion through the whole world. Soon the original traditions were forgotten; and the nations, separated as they were by vast distances and still more by the diversity of languages, strangers to one another, were almost all plunged into the same barbarism in which we still see the Americans.

But natural resources and the fertile seeds of the sciences are to be found wherever there are men. The most exalted mental attainments are only and can only be a development or combination of the original ideas based on sensation, just as the building at whose great height we gaze in wonder necessarily has its foundation in the earth upon which we tread. The same senses, the same organs, and the spectacle of the same universe, have everywhere given men the same ideas, just as the same needs and inclinations have everywhere taught them the same arts.

Now a faint light begins occasionally to penetrate the darkness which has covered all the nations, and step by step it spreads. The inhabitants of Chaldea, closest to the source of the original traditions, the Egyptians, and the Chinese apparently lead the rest of the peoples. Others follow them at a distance, and progress leads to further progress. The inequality of nations increases; in one place the arts begin to emerge, while in another they advance at a

rapid rate towards perfection. In some nations they are brought to a standstill in the midst of their mediocrity, while in others the original darkness is not yet dissipated at all. Thus the present state of the world, marked as it is by these infinite variations in inequality, spreads out before us at one and the same time all the gradations from barbarism to refinement, thereby revealing to us at a single glance, as it were, the records and remains of all the steps taken by the human mind, a reflection of all the stages through which it has passed, and the history of all the ages.

But is not nature everywhere the same?—and if she leads all men to the same truths, if even their errors are alike, how is it that they do not all move forward at the same rate along the road which is marked out for them? It is true that the human mind everywhere contains the potential for the same progress, but nature, distributing her gifts unequally, has given to certain minds an abundance of talents which she has refused to others. Circumstances either develop these talents or allow them to become buried in obscurity; and it is from the infinite variety of these circumstances that there springs the inequality in the progress of nations.

Barbarism makes all men equal; and in early times all those who are born with genius are faced with virtually the same obstacles and the same resources. Societies are established and expanded, however; national hatreds and ambition—or rather greed, the only ambition of barbarous peoples—cause war and devastation to increase; and conquests and revolutions mix up peoples, languages, and customs in a thousand different ways. Chains of mountains, great rivers and seas confine the dealings of peoples with one another, and consequently their intermingling, within fixed boundaries. This results in the formation of common languages which become a tie binding several nations together, so that all the nations of the world become divided as it were into a number of different classes. Tillage increases the permanence of settlements. It is able to feed more men than are employed in it, and thus imposes upon those whom it leaves idle the necessity of making themselves either useful or formidable to the cultivators. Hence towns, trade, the useful arts and accomplishments, the division of occupations, the differences in education, and the increased inequality in the conditions of life. Hence that leisure, by means of which genius, relieved of the burden of providing for primary necessities, emerges from the narrow sphere within which these necessities confine it and bends all its strength to the cultivation of the arts. Hence that more rapid and vigorous rate of advance of the human mind which carries along with it all parts of society and which in turn derives additional momentum from their perfection. The passions develop alongside genius; ambition gathers strength; politics lends it ever-widening perspectives; victories have more lasting results and create empires whose laws, customs, and government, influencing men's genius in different ways, become a kind of common education for the nations, producing between one nation and another the same sort of difference which education produces between one man and another.

United, divided, the one raised up on the other's ruins, empires rapidly succeed one another. The revolutions which they undergo cause them to run the whole gamut of possible states, and unite and disunite all the elements of the body politic. Like the ebb and flow of the tide, power passes from one nation to another, and, within the same nation, from the princes to the multitude and from the multitude to the princes. As the balance shifts, everything gradually gets nearer and nearer to an equilibrium, and in the course of time takes on a more settled and peaceful aspect. Ambition, when it forms great states from the remains of a host of small ones, itself sets limits to its own ravages. Wars no longer devastate anything but the frontiers of empires; the towns and the countryside begin to breathe the air of peace; the bonds of society unite a greater number of men; ideas come to be transmitted more promptly and more widely; and the advancement of arts, sciences, and manners progresses more rapidly. Like a storm which has agitated the waves of the sea, the evil which is inseparable from revolutions disappears: the good remains, and humanity perfects itself. Amidst this complex of different events, sometimes favourable, sometimes adverse, which because they act in opposite ways must in the long run nullify one another, genius ceaselessly asserts its influence. Nature, while distributing genius to only a few individuals, has nevertheless spread it out almost equally over the whole mass, and with time its effects become appreciable.

Genius, whose course is at first slow, unmarked, and buried in the general oblivion into which time precipitates human affairs, emerges from obscurity with them by means of the invention of writing. Priceless invention!— which seemed to give wings to those peoples who first possessed it, enabling them to outdistance other nations. Incomparable invention!—which rescues from the power of death the memory of great men and models of virtue, unites places and times, arrests fugitive thoughts and guarantees them a lasting existence, by means of which the creations, opinions, experiences, and discoveries of all ages are accumulated, to serve as a foundation and foothold for posterity in raising itself ever higher!

But what a spectacle the succession of men's opinions presents! I seek there for the progress of the human mind, and I find virtually nothing but the history of its errors. Why is its course, which is so sure from the very first steps in the field of mathematical studies, so unsteady in everything else, and so apt to go astray? Let us try to discover the reasons. In mathematics, the mind deduces one from another a chain of propositions, the truth of which consists only in their mutual dependence. It is not the same with the other sciences, where it is no longer from the intercomparison of ideas that truth is born, but from their conformity with a sequence of real facts. To discover and verify truth, it is no longer a question of establishing a small number of simple principles and then merely allowing the mind to be borne along by the current of their consequences. One must start from nature as it is, and from that infinite variety of effects which so many causes, counterbalanced one by the other, have combined to produce. Notions are no longer assemblages of ideas which the mind forms of its own accord and of whose range it has exact knowledge. Ideas emerge and are assembled in our minds almost without our knowing it; we are beset by the

images of objects right from the cradle. Little by little we learn to distinguish between them, less by reference to what they are in themselves than by reference to their relation to our habits and needs. The signs of language impress themselves on the mind while it is still undeveloped. At first, through habit and imitation, they become attached to particular objects, but later they succeed in calling up more general notions. This chaotic blend of ideas and expressions grows and becomes more complex all the time; and when man starts to seek for truth he find himself in the midst of a labyrinth which he has entered blindfold. Should we be surprised at his errors?

Spectator of the universe, his senses show him the effects but leave him ignorant of the causes. And to examine effects in an endeavour to find their unknown cause is like trying to guess an enigma: we think of one or more possible key words and try them in turn until one is found which fulfils all the conditions.

The natural philosopher erects hypotheses, follows them through to their consequences, and brings them to bear upon the enigma of nature. He tries them out, so to speak, on the facts, just as one verifies a seal by applying it to its impression. Suppositions which are arrived at on the basis of a small number of poorly understood facts yield to suppositions which are less absurd, although no more true. Time, research, and chance result in the accumulation of observations, and unveil the hidden connections which link a number of phenomena together.

Ever restless, incapable of finding tranquillity elsewhere than in the truth, ever stimulated by the image of that truth which it believes to be within its grasp but which flies before it, the curiosity of man leads to a multiplication of the number of questions and debates, and obliges him to analyse ideas and facts in a manner which grows ever more exact and more profound. Mathematical truths, becoming from day to day more numerous and hence more fruitful, point the way to the development of hypotheses which are more far-reaching and more precise, and indicate new experiments which, in their turn, present new problems for mathematics to resolve. Thus the need perfects the tool; thus mathematics is sustained by natural philosophy, upon which it sheds its light; thus everything is bound together; thus, in spite of the diversity in their development, all the sciences render mutual aid to one another; thus, by feeling his way, by multiplying systems and draining them, as it were, of their errors, man at last attains to the understanding of a great number of truths.

What ridiculous opinions marked our first steps! How absurd were the causes which our fathers thought up to make sense of what they saw! What sad monuments they are to the weakness of the human mind! The senses constitute the unique source of our ideas: the whole power of our mental faculties is restricted to combining the ideas which they have received from the senses: hardly even can they form combinations of ideas of which the senses do not provide them with a model. Hence that almost irresistible tendency to judge of what one does not know by what one knows; hence those delusive analogies to which the first men in their immaturity abandoned themselves with so little thought; hence the monstrous aberrations of idolatry.

Men, oblivious of the original traditions, when affected by sensible phenomena, imagined that all effects which were independent of their own action were produced by beings similar to them, but invisible and more powerful, whom they substituted for the Divinity. When they were contemplating nature, it was as if they fixed their gaze on the surface of a deep sea instead of on the sea-bed hidden by the waters, and saw there only their own reflection. All objects of nature had their gods, which, being created after the model of man, shared his attributes and vices. Throughout the world, superstition sanctified the caprices of the imagination; and the only true God, the only God worthy of adoration, was known only in one corner of the earth, by the people whom he had expressly chosen.

In this slow progression of opinions and errors, pursuing one another, I fancy that I see those first leaves, those sheaths which nature has given to the newly-growing stems of plants, issuing before them from the earth, and withering one by one as other sheaths come into existence, until at last the stem itself makes its appearance and is crowned with flowers and fruit—a symbol of late-emerging truth!

Woe betide those nations, then, in which the sciences, as the result of a blind zeal for them, are confined within the limits of existing knowledge in an attempt to stabilise them. It is for this reason that the regions which were the first to become enlightened are not those where the sciences have made the greatest progress. The respect for the new-born philosophy which the glamour of its novelty inspires in men tends to perpetuate the first opinions: the sectarian spirit comes to be attached to it. Such a spirit is natural for the first philosophers, because arrogance feeds on ignorance, because the less one knows the less one doubts, and because the less one has discovered the less one sees what remains to be discovered. In Egypt, and long after in the Indes, superstition, which made the dogmas of the ancient philosophy the patrimony of the priestly families, who by consecrating them enchained them and incorporated them in the dogmas of a false religion; in great Asia, political despotism, the result of the establishment of great empires during the centuries of barbarism; the civic despotism born of slavery and of the plurality of wives which is a consequence of it; the want of vigour on the part of princes; the prostration of their subjects; in China, the very care which the Emperors took to regulate research and to tie up the sciences with the political constitution of the state, held them back forever in mediocrity: these trunks which since their origin had been too productive of branches soon ceased to grow higher.

With the passing of time new peoples came into being. In the course of the unequal progress of nations, the civilised peoples, surrounded by barbarians, now conquering, now conquered, intermingled with them. Whether the latter received from the former their arts and their laws together with servitude, or whether as conquerors they yielded to the natural empire of reason and culture over brute force, the bounds of barbarism steadily retreated.

The Phoenicians, inhabitants of a barren coast, had made themselves the agents of exchanges between peoples. Their ships, spread out over the whole Mediterranean, began to reveal nation to nation.

Astronomy, navigation, and geography were perfected, one by means of the other. The coasts of Greece and Asia Minor came to be filled with Phoenician colonies. Colonies are like fruits which cling to the tree only until they have reached their maturity: once they had become self-sufficient they did what Carthage was to do later, and what America will one day do.

Out of the intermingling of these colonies, each independent of the others, with the ancient peoples of Greece and with the remnants of all the swarms of barbarians who had successively ravaged her, there arose the Greek nation, or rather that family of nations comprised of a large number of small peoples who were prevented from aggrandising themselves at one another's expense by the fact that they were all equally weak and by the nature of the terrain, which was broken up by mountains and sea, and who were intermingled, divided, and reunited in a thousand different ways by their associations, their public and private interests, their civil and national wars, their migrations, the reciprocal duties of colonies and metropolises, one language, customs, a common religion, trade, public games, and the Amphictyonic league. In the course of these revolutions, and by means of these manifold interminglings, there was formed that rich, expressive, and sonorous language, the language of all the arts.

Poetry, which is no more than the art of painting with words, and the perfection of which depends so greatly on the genius of the languages which it employs, assumed in Greece a grandeur which it had never previously known. It was no longer, as it had been with the first men, a succession of barbarous words chained to the beat of a rustic song and to the steps of a dance as uncouth as the riotous joy which it expressed. It had decked itself out in a harmony which was all its own. The ear, ever more difficult to please, had laid down stricter rules; and if the burden of these had become heavier, the new expressions, turns of phrase, and felicitous boldnesses of style, which had increased in proportion, lent greater strength to bear it.

Good taste had finally succeeded in outlawing those involved figures and elephantine metaphors which we object to in Oriental poetry.

In those countries of Asia where societies arrived earlier at a stable state, and where writers appeared earlier, languages became stabilised at a point nearer to their first origin, and as a result were marked by that high-flown style which is characteristic of a language in its first imperfect stage. Languages are the measure of men's ideas: thus in early times there were names only for the objects which were most familiar to the senses; and to express these imperfect ideas it was necessary to have recourse to metaphors. A word which is coined signifies nothing, so that one must try, by putting together the signs of the ideas which are nearest akin, to set the mind on the track of what one wishes to communicate to it. The imagination attempts to grasp the thread of a certain analogy which binds together our senses with their different objects. An imperfect or farfetched analogy gives birth to those clumsy and abundant metaphors which necessity, more ingenious than fastidious, employs, which good taste disavows, of which the first languages are full, and of which even now etymologists find vestiges in the most cultivated.

Languages, which are necessarily used by all men, and thus often by men of genius, are always perfected over time, when they are not immobilised by written works which become a permanent standard by which to judge of their purity. The habitual use of the spoken word leads continually to new combinations of ideas, calls attention to new relationships between them and to new shades of meaning, and makes felt the need for new expressions. Moreover, through the migrations of peoples, languages blend with one another like rivers and are enriched by the coming together of several languages.

Thus the Greek language, formed by the intermingling of a greater number of languages, and stabilised later than those of Asia, unites together harmony, richness, and variety. Homer consummated its triumph, poured into it the treasures of his genius, and lifted it to the greatest heights by the harmonious character of his poetry, the charm of his expression, and the splendour of his images.

Following on this, liberty, **which** as the result of a revolution natural to small states **came** to be established in all cities on the ruins of the government of a single man, gave a new stimulus to the genius of the Greeks. The different forms of government into which the opposing passions of the powerful and the people turn by turn precipitated them, taught the legislators to compare and to weigh up all the different elements in society, and to find the proper equilibrium between their forces; while at the same time the combined quarrels and interests of so many ambitious, weak, and jealous neighbouring republics taught the states to fear one another, to keep constant watch on one another, and to counterbalance successes with leagues, and led at the same time to the perfecting of politics and the art of war.

It was only after several centuries that philosophers appeared in Greece—or rather it was only then that the study of philosophy became the business of particular thinkers and appeared sufficiently extensive in its scope to occupy them fully. Until then, the poets had been at the same time the only philosophers and the only historians. When men are ignorant it is easy to know everything. But ideas were not yet by any means clear enough. A sufficiently large number of facts was not available; the time of truth had not by any means arrived, and the systems of the Greek philosophers could not yet be anything but adroit. Their metaphysics, shaky on the most important truths and often superstitious or blasphemous, was scarcely more than a collection of poetic fables or a tissue of unintelligible words; and their natural philosophy itself was nothing but shallow metaphysics.

Morality, although still imperfect, was less affected by the infancy of reason. The recurring needs which constantly call men into society and force them to bow to its laws; that instinct, that feeling for the good and the honourable which Providence has graven on all our hearts, which comes before reason, and which often seduces it in spite

of itself, leads the philosophers of all ages to the same fundamental principles of the science of behaviour. Socrates guided his fellow-citizens along the path of virtue; Plato sowed this path with flowers; the charm of his eloquence beautified even his errors. Aristotle, the most wide-ranging, profound, and truly philosophical mind of all antiquity, was the first to carry the torch of exact analysis into the sphere of philosophy and the arts. Unveiling the principles of certitude and the springs of feeling, he subjected the development of reason and even the fire of genius to constant rules.

Happy centuries, in which all the fine arts spread their light on every side, and in which the passion of a noble emulation was swiftly transmitted from one city to another! Painting, sculpture, architecture, poetry, and history grew up everywhere at the same time, as we see in the expanse of a forest a thousand different trees springing up, growing, and being crowned together.

Athens, governed by the decrees of a multitude whose tumultuous waves the orators calmed or agitated at their pleasure; Athens, where Pericles had taught the leaders how to buy the state at the expense of the state itself, and how to dissipate its treasures in order to exempt themselves from giving an account of them; Athens, where the art of governing the people was the art of amusing them, the art of feasting their ears, their eyes, and their curiosity always greedy for novelties, with festivities, pleasures, and constant spectacles, Athens owed to the very vices of its government which made it succumb to Lacedaemon that eloquence, that taste, that magnificence, and that splendour in all the arts which have made it the model of nations.

While the Athenians, the Spartans, and the Thebans are in turn arrogating to themselves superiority over the other cities, the Macedonian power, unnoticed, like a river which overflows its banks, slowly extends into Greece under Philip, and violently inundates Asia under Alexander. This host of regions and states, from which the conquests of the Assyrians, the Medes, and the Persians, in successively swallowing one another up, had formed this great body, the product of so many conquerors and so many centuries, breaks up with a crash on the death of the conqueror of Darius. Wars between his generals establish new kingdoms; Syria and Egypt become a part of Greece, and receive the language, the customs, and the sciences of their conquerors.

Commerce and the arts render Alexandria the rival of Athens. Astronomy and the mathematical sciences are carried there to an even higher level than they have ever been before. Above all we see flourishing there that erudition with which until then the Greeks had been little acquainted—that kind of study which is concerned less with things than with books, which consists less in producing and discovering than in assembling together, comparing, and evaluating what has been produced and what has been discovered; which does not move forward at all, but which turns its gaze backwards in order to survey the road which has been taken. The studies which demand the most genius are not always those which imply the greatest progress in the mass of mankind. There are minds to whom nature has given a memory which is capable of assembling together a large number of pieces of knowledge, a power of exact reasoning which is capable of comparing them and arranging them in a manner which puts them in their full light, but to whom at the same time she has denied that fire of genius which invents and which opens up new roads for itself. Created to unite past discoveries under one point of view, to clarify and even to perfect them, if they are not torches which shine with their own light, they are diamonds which brilliantly reflect a borrowed light, but which total darkness would confound with the meanest stones.

The known world, if I may put it like that, the commercial world, the political world, had expanded as a result of the conquests of Alexander. The dissensions of his successors began to present a vaster spectacle, and, amid these clashes and these oscillations of the great powers, the little cities of Greece, situated in the midst of them, often the arena of their struggles and a prey to the ravages of all the parties, were no longer conscious of anything but their weakness. Eloquence was no longer the mainspring of politics: henceforth, degraded in the obscurity of the schools by childish declamations, it lost its brilliance along with its power.

But for several centuries already, Rome, in Italy as if in a world apart, had been advancing by a continual succession of triumphs towards the conquest of the world. Victorious over Carthage, she appeared suddenly in the midst of the nations. Peoples trembled and were brought into subjection: the Romans, conquerors of Greece, became aware of a new empire, that of intellect and learning. Their austere uncouthness was tamed. Athens found disciples, and soon rivals, among her conquerors. Cicero displayed, at the Capitol and on the rostrum, an eloquence derived from the lessons of the Greeks, of which its enslaved masters no longer knew anything but the rules. The Latin language, softened and enriched, brought Africa, Spain, and Gaul under orderly government. The boundaries of the civilised world were identical with those of the Roman power, and two rival languages, Greek and Latin, shared it between them.

The laws of Rome, created to govern one city, sank under the burden of the whole world: Roman liberty was extinguished in waves of blood. Octavius alone finally gathered in the fruit of the civil strife. Cruel usurper, temperate prince, he gave tranquillity to the earth. His enlightened protection stimulated all the arts. Italy had a Homer, less productive than the first, but wiser, more equable, just as harmonious, and perhaps more perfect. Sublimity, reason, and the graces united to create Horace. Taste was perfected in every sphere.

Knowledge of nature and of truth is as infinite as they are: the arts, whose aim is to please us, are as limited as we are. Time constantly brings to light new discoveries in the sciences; but poetry, painting, and music have a fixed limit which the genius of languages, the imitation of nature, and the limited sensibility of our organs determine, which they attain by slow steps and which they cannot surpass. The great men of the Augustan age reached it, and are still our models.

From this time until the fall of the Empire, we see nothing but a general decadence in which everything is plunged. Do men raise themselves up, then, only to fall? A thousand causes combine to deprave taste more and more: tyranny, which degrades minds below all things which are great; blind luxury, which, born of vanity, and judging works of art less as objects of taste than as symbols of opulence, is as opposed to their perfection as a civilised love of magnificence is favourable to it; enthusiasm for new things among those who, not having enough genius to invent them, only too often have enough wit to spoil the old; the imitation of the vices of great men and even the misplaced imitation of their beauties. Writers proliferate in the provinces and corrupt the language: I know not what remnants of the old Greek philosophy, mixed up with oriental superstitions, confounded with a host of empty allegories and magical spells, take possession of men's minds and smother the healthy natural philosophy which was beginning to spring up in the writings of Seneca and Pliny the Elder.

Soon the Empire, abandoned to the caprices of an insolent militia, becomes the prey of a host of tyrants, who, in the process of seizing it from one another, bring desolation and havoc to the provinces. Military discipline is destroyed, the northern barbarians penetrate on every side, peoples fall upon peoples, the cities become deserted, the fields are left uncultivated, and the western Empire, weakened by the transference of all its power to Constantinople, ruined everywhere by so many repeated ravages, at last suddenly collapses, and the Burgundians, Goths, and Franks are left to quarrel over its far-flung ruins and to found kingdoms in the different countries of Europe.

Could it be, in this sanctuary, that I should pass over in silence that new light which, while the Empire was proceeding towards its ruin, had spread out over the world—a light a thousand times more precious than those of letters and philosophy? Holy religion, could it be that I should forget you? Could I forget the perfecting of manners, the dissipation at last of the darkness of idolatry, and the enlightenment of men on the subject of the Divinity! Amid the almost total ruin of letters, you alone still created writers who were animated by the desire to instruct the faithful or to repel the attacks of the enemies of the faith; and when Europe fell prey to the barbarians, you alone tamed their ferocity; you alone have perpetuated the knowledge of the discarded Latin tongue; you alone have transmitted to us across so many centuries the minds, so to speak, of so many great men which had been entrusted to that language; and the conservation of the treasure of human knowledge, which was about to be dissipated, is one of your benefactions.

But the wounds of the human race were too deep; centuries were necessary to heal them. If Rome had been conquered by one people alone, their leader would have become a Roman, and his nation would have been absorbed in the Empire together with its language. We would have seen what the history of the world presents to us more than once: the spectacle of a civilised people invaded by barbarians, communicating to them its manners, its language, and its knowledge, and forcing them to make one people with it. Cicero and Virgil would have sustained the Latin language, just as Homer, Plato, and Demosthenes had defended theirs against the Roman power. But too many peoples, and too many ravages, succeeded one another; too many layers of barbarism were added one after the other before the first had time to disappear and yield to the force of the Roman sciences. Too many conquerors, too single-mindedly devoted to war, were for several centuries too much occupied with their quarrels. The genius of the Romans was extinguished and their language was lost, confounded with the Germanic languages.

It is a consequence of the intermingling of two languages that a new one is formed from them which is different from each; but a long time passes before they can be combined in a really intimate manner. Memory, wavering between the two, decides at random between the expressions of one and the other. Analogy, that is, the art of forming conjugations and declensions, of expressing the relationships between objects, and of arranging the expressions in discourse, has no longer any fixed rules. Ideas are associated in a confused manner; there is no longer any harmony or clarity in the language. Pour two liquids into the same vessel: you will see them become turbid and cloudy, and not recover the transparency they had when they were separate until time has rendered their mixture more intimate and more homogeneous. Thus, until a long succession of centuries has succeeded in giving the new language a uniform quality of its own, poetry, eloquence, and taste disappear almost completely. Thus new languages grew up in Europe, and in the chaos of their first formation ignorance and vulgarity ruled everywhere.

Unhappy empire of the Caesars, must new misfortunes be visited even upon those remnants which have escaped from thy wreck! Must it be that barbarism destroys at once all the refuges of the arts! And thou too, Greece, thine honours are then eclipsed! Finally the north seems to become exhausted, and new storms gather in the south against the only provinces which are not yet groaning under a foreign yoke!

The standard of a false prophet unites the wandering shepherds in the Arabian deserts; in less than a century Syria, Persia, Egypt, and Africa are covered by a raging torrent which ravages the whole territory from the Indian frontiers to the Atlantic Ocean and the Pyrenees. The Greek empire, confined within narrow boundaries, devastated in the south by the Saracens and then by the Turks, and in the north by the Bulgarians, laid waste internally by factions and by the instability of its throne, falls into a state of weakness and lethargy, and the cultivation of letters and arts ceases to occupy a debased, slack, and indolent populace.

In vain does Charlemagne in the west try to revive a few sparks of a fire which is buried under the ashes; their glow is as evanescent as it is feeble. Soon the quarrels of his grandsons disturb his empire; the north once again raises and sends forth new destroyers; the Normans and the Hungarians once again cover Europe with new ruins and a new darkness. Amid the general weakness, a new form of government puts the finishing touch to the ruin: the annihilated royal power gives way to that host of small sovereignties, subordinate one to another, among which the feudal laws maintain I know not what false semblance of order in the midst of the very anarchy which they perpetuate.

The kings without any authority, the nobles without any constraint, the peoples enslaved, the countryside covered with fortresses and ceaselessly ravaged, wars kindled between city and city, village and village, penetrating, so to speak, the whole mass of the kingdoms; all commerce and all communications cut off; the towns inhabited by poor artisans enjoying no leisure; the only wealth and the only leisure which some men still enjoy lost in the idleness of a nobility scattered here and there in their castles who do nothing but engage in battles which are useless to the fatherland; the grossest ignorance extending over all nations and all occupations! An unhappy picture—but one which was only too true of Europe for several centuries!

But nevertheless, from the midst of this barbarism, perfected arts and sciences will one day rise again. Amid all the ignorance, progress is imperceptibly taking place and preparing for the brilliant achievements of later centuries; beneath this soil the feeble roots of a far-off harvest are already developing. The towns among all civilised peoples constitute by their very nature the centres of trade and the backbone of society. They continued to exist; and if the spirit of feudal government, born of the ancient customs of Germany, combined with a number of accidental circumstances, had abased them, this was a contradiction in the constitution of states which was bound to disappear in the long run. Soon we see the towns revive again under the protection of the princes; and the latter, in holding out their hands to the oppressed peoples, reduce the power of their vassals and little by little re-establish their own.

Latin and theology were already being studied in the universities, together with the Aristotelian dialectic. For a long time the Mussulman Arabs had been teaching themselves Greek philosophy, and their learning was spreading to the west. Mathematics had been extended as a result of their work. More independent than the other sciences of the perfection of taste and perhaps even of precision of intellect, one cannot study mathematics without being led to the truth. Always certain, always pure, its truths were emerging, encompassed about by the errors of judicial astrology. The chimerical search for the philosopher's stone, by encouraging the Arab philosophers to separate and to recombine all the elements of bodies, had led to the blossoming under their hands of the vast science of chemistry, and had spread it to all places where men were capable of being imposed upon by their greedy desires. Finally, on all sides, the mechanical arts were coming to be perfected by virtue of the simple fact that time was passing, because even in the decline of the sciences and taste the needs of life preserve them, and because, consequently, among that host of artisans who successively cultivate them it is impossible not to meet every now and then with one of those men of genius who are blended with the rest of mankind as gold is blended with the clay in a mine.

As a result, what a host of inventions unknown to the ancients and standing to the credit of these barbarous ages! Our art of musical notation, our bills of exchange, our paper, window glass, plate glass, windmills, clocks, spectacles, gunpowder, the magnetic needle, and the perfection of navigation and commerce. The arts are nothing but the utilisation of nature, and the practice of the arts is a succession of physical experiments which progressively unveil nature. Facts were accumulating in the darkness of the times of ignorance, and the sciences, whose progress although hidden was no less real, were bound to reappear one day augmented by this new wealth, like those rivers which after disappearing from our view for some time in a subterranean passage, reappear further on swollen by all the waters which have seeped through the earth.

Different series of events take place in different countries of the world, and all of them, as if by so many separate paths, at length come together to contribute to the same end, to raise up once again the ruins of the human spirit. Thus, in the night, we see the stars rise one after the other; they move forward, each in its own orbit; they seem in their common revolution to bear along with them the whole celestial sphere, and to bring in for us the day which follows them. Germany, Denmark, Sweden, and Poland through the efforts of Charlemagne and the Othos, and Russia through trade with the Greek empire, cease to be uncultivated forests. Christianity, in bringing together these scattered savages, in settling them in towns, is going to dry up forever the source of those inundations which have so often been fatal to the sciences. Europe is still barbarous; but the knowledge brought by her to even more barbarous peoples represents for them immense progress. Little by little the customs introduced by Germany into the south of Europe disappear. The nations, amid the quarrels of the nobles and the princes, begin to fashion for themselves the principles of a more stable government, and to acquire, in accordance with the different circumstances in which they find themselves, the particular character which distinguishes them. The wars against the Mussulmans in Palestine, by giving a common interest to all Christian states, teach them to know one another and to unite with one another, and sow the seeds of that modern political state of affairs in which so many nations seem to comprise nothing but one vast republic. Already we see the royal authority reviving again in France; the power of the people establishing itself in England; the Italian towns constituting themselves into republics and presenting the likeness of ancient Greece; the little monarchies of Spain driving the Moors before them and little by little joining up again into one whole. Soon the seas, which have hitherto separated the nations, come to be the link between them through the invention of the compass. The Portuguese in the east and the Spaniards in the west discover new worlds: at last the world as a whole is known.

Already the intermingling of the barbarous languages with Latin has during the course of the centuries produced new languages, of which the Italian, less removed from their common source and less mixed with foreign languages, takes precedence in the elegance of its style and the beauties of its poetry. The Ottomans, spreading through Asia and Europe with the swiftness of a violent wind, end by overthrowing the empire of Constantinople, and disseminate in the west the feeble sparks of those sciences which Greece still preserved.

What new art is suddenly born, as if to wing to every corner of the earth the writings and glory of the great men who are to come? How slow in every sphere is even the least progress! For two thousand years medals have presented to all eyes characters impressed upon bronze—and then, after so many centuries, some obscure individual realises that they can be impressed upon paper. At once the treasures of antiquity, rescued from the dust, pass into all hands, penetrate to every part of the world, bear light to the talents which were being wasted in ignorance, and summon genius from the depths of its retreats.

The time has come. Issue forth, Europe, from the darkness which covered thee! Immortal names of the Medici, of Leo X, of Francis I, be consecrated for ever! May the patrons of the arts share the glory of those who cultivate them! I salute thee, O Italy!—happy land, for the second time the homeland of letters and of taste, the spring from which their waters have spread to fertilise our territories. Our own France still only beholds thy progress from afar. Her language, still tainted by remnants of barbarism, cannot follow it. Soon fatal discords will rend the whole of Europe; audacious men have shaken the foundations of the faith and those of the empires; do the flowered stems of the fine arts grow when they are watered with blood? A day will come, and it is not far off, when they will beautify all the countries of Europe.

Time, spread your swift wings! Century of Louis, century of great men, century of reason, hasten! Already, even amidst the turmoil of heresy, the long-disturbed fortunes of states have ended by settling down, as if as the result of a final shock. Already the unremitting study of antiquity has brought men's minds back again to the point where its progress was arrested; already that host of facts, experiments, instruments, and ingenious exercises which the practice of the arts has accumulated over so many centuries, has been rescued from obscurity through printing; already the productions of the two worlds, brought together before our eyes as the result of a far-flung commerce, have become the foundation of a natural philosophy hitherto unknown, and freed at last from alien speculations; already on every hand attentive eyes are fixed upon nature: the remotest chances, turned to profit, give birth to discoveries. The son of an artisan in Zealand brings together for amusement two convex glasses in a tube; the boundaries of our senses are made to recede, and in Italy the eyes of Galileo have discovered a new firmament. Already Kepler, seeking in the stars for the numbers of Pythagoras, has discovered those two famous laws of the movements of the planets which one day in the hands of Newton will become the key to the universe. Already Bacon has traced out for posterity the road which it must follow.

Who is the mortal who dares to reject the learning of all the ages, and even those notions which he has believed to be the most certain? He seems to wish to extinguish the torch of the sciences in order to relight it all on his own at the pure fire of reason. Does he wish to imitate those peoples of antiquity among whom it was a crime to light at other fires that which was made to burn on the altars of the Gods? Great Descartes, if it was not always given to you to find the truth, at least you have destroyed the tyranny of error.

France, whom Spain and England have already outstripped in the glory of poetry; France, whose genius finishes forming itself only when the philosophical spirit begins to spread, will owe perhaps to this very backwardness the exactitude, the method, and the austere taste of her writers. Rarefied and affected thoughts, and the ponderous display of an ostentatious erudition, still corrupt our literature: a strange difference between our progress in taste and that of the ancients! The real advancement of the human mind reveals itself even in its aberrations; the caprices of Gothic architecture are never found among those who possess nothing but wooden huts. The acquisition of knowledge among the first men and the formation of taste kept pace, as it were, with one another. Hence a crude severity and an exaggerated simplicity were their prerogative. Guided by instinct and imagination, they seized little by little upon those relations between men and the objects of nature which are the sole foundations of the beautiful. In later times, when, in spite of the imperfection of taste, the number of ideas and perceptions was increased, when the study of models and rules had caused nature and feeling to become lost from men's view, it was necessary for them through reflection to take themselves back to where the first men had been led by blind instinct. And who is not aware that it is here that the supreme effort of reason lies?

At last all the shadows are dispelled: and what a light shines out on all sides! What a host of great men in every sphere! What a perfection of human reason! One man, Newton, has subjected the infinite to the calculus, has revealed the properties of light which in illuminating everything seemed to conceal itself, and has put into his balance the stars, the earth, and all the forces of nature. And this man has found a rival. Leibniz encompasses within his vast intellect all the objects of the human mind. The different sciences, confined at first to a small number of simple notions common to all, can no longer, when as a result of their progress they have become more extensive and more difficult, be envisaged otherwise than separately; but greater progress once again unites them, because there is discovered that mutual dependence of all truths which in linking them together illuminates each through the other; because, if each day adds to the vast extent of the sciences, each day also makes them easier, because methods are multiplied with discoveries, because the scaffolding rises with the building.

O Louis, what majesty surrounds thee! What splendour thy beneficent hand has spread over all the arts! Thine happy people has become the centre of refinement! Rivals of Sophocles, of Menander, and of Horace, gather around his throne! Arise, learned academies, and unite your efforts for the glory of his reign! What a multitude of public monuments, of works of genius, of arts newly invented, and of old arts perfected! Who could possibly picture them? Open your eyes and see! Century of Louis the Great, may your light beautify the precious reign of his successor! May it last for ever, may it extend over the whole world! May men continually make new steps along the road of truth! Rather still, may they continually become better and happier!

In the midst of these vicissitudes of opinions, of sciences, of arts, and of everything which is human, rejoice, gentlemen, in the pleasure of seeing that religion to which you have consecrated your hearts and your talents, always true to herself, always pure, always complete, standing perpetuated in the Church, and preserving all the features of the seal which the Divinity has stamped upon it. You will be her ministers, and you will be worthy of her. The Faculty expects from you her glory, the Church of France her illumination, Religion her defenders. Genius, learning, and piety are united to give ground for their hopes.

Eleanor C. Lodge   (essay date 1931)

SOURCE: "Turgot and His Ministry," *Sully, Colbert, and Turgot: A Chapter in French Economic History,* 1931. Reprint by Kennikat Press, 1970, pp. 227-52.

[*In the excerpt below, Lodge argues that Turgot exercised his ministry for Louis XVI with competence and foresight.*]

Perhaps the first mistake of the new reign [of Louis XVI] was the summons of Monsieur de Maurepas to act as a more or less unofficial first minister; as a matter of fact Louis himself had wished to choose Machault for the position, but he was overruled by his two old aunts who acted to some extent as the evil geniuses of the young man. Maurepas did much to encourage Louis in his fatal indecision and lack of self-confidence; but at first his advice seemed to be good. In the place of the old Minister for Foreign Affairs, the Duc d'Aiguillon, the able Comte de Vergennes was appointed; and Turgot was made Comptroller-General instead of the unscrupulous though clever Abbé Terray. Turgot joined the ministry first as head of Naval Affairs (July 1774), but that was only intended as an interim position, and a month later he was given the office which practically meant the control of finance, the interior, public works and trade. The greatest hopes were felt in such an appointment; but a contemporary (Abbé Galliani) prophesied the coming disaster: "He will have too little time to carry out his system; he will punish a few rascals but he will find others everywhere; he will retire or be dismissed; he will break his neck over the free exportation of corn." Turgot himself fully realized the responsibility of his appointment and the difficulties that lay ahead of him. His first interview with the King was encouraging. Both men were impressed by the sincerity and good feeling of the other. Unfortunately Louis was unable to maintain the steadfast support of the minister which he promised at first wholeheartedly and without misgiving. On August 24th, 1774, Turgot drew up a letter to the King, in which he promised him "his respectful gratitude and devotion," and proceeded to lay down the principles on which he intended to conduct his ministry. His three main decisions were: No bankruptcy; no increase of taxation; no loans. To carry out these principles the strictest economy would be necessary, and all heads of departments would have to consult the Minister of Finance before sanctioning any new expenditure. The minister realized that the King's own generosity and the solicitations to which he was certain to be subjected constituted one very great danger to this campaign of economy, and he writes: "It is necessary, Sire, to arm yourself against your kindheartedness by your own increased sense of the same virtue; to consider whence comes to you this money which you are able to distribute amongst your courtiers, and to compare the misery of those from whom it has to be exacted with the situation of the class of persons who push their claims on your liberality." The letter goes on to say that though improvements in cultivation and the suppression of abuses should render the country better able to contribute to national expenditure, the writer fully appreciated the difficulty of the task before him, and that he could only face it on the faith of the royal promises:

> I foresee that I shall be alone in fighting against abuses of every kind, against the power of those who oppose themselves to all reform, and who are such powerful instruments in the hands of interested parties for perpetuating the disorder. I shall have to struggle even against the natural goodness and generosity of your Majesty, and of the persons who are most dear to you. I shall be feared, hated even, by nearly all the Court, by all who solicit favours. They will impute to me all the refusals; they will describe me as a hard man because I shall have advised your Majesty that you ought not to enrich even those you love at the expense of your people's subsistence. And this people, for whom I shall sacrifice myself, are so easily deceived that perhaps I shall encounter their hatred by the very measures I take to defend them against exactions. I shall be calumniated, having perhaps appearances against me, in order to deprive me of your Majesty's confidence. I shall not regret losing a place which I never solicited. I am ready to resign it to your Majesty as soon as I can no longer hope to be useful in it.

Turgot foresaw too truly the certain unpopularity of a minister whose main principle was economy; and though the King had the best of intentions, it was very hard for him to keep others up to the mark, and Marie-Antoinette frankly thought the whole thing rather nonsense. There is rather a pathetic story of Louis feeling that his wife's coiffures were unnecessarily expensive and exaggerated, and trying to induce her to wear instead a diamond aigrette which he gave her. "I had it when I was Dauphin," he said, "so that I can give it you quite safely." But perhaps still all would have been well but for one big mistake on the part of the King—the recall of the old Parliament of Paris. The first indignation at the exile was over, and the *Parlement Maupeou* was fairly well established and would soon have been accepted without comment; but the King was urged to do justice to an injured body, and though the Comptroller-General was against it Maurepas advocated it and public opinion generally was in favour of the measure. And so the fatal mistake was made. The privileged members returned more hostile to reform than before, and though Louis did at first back up his minister against them, he was not the man to continue a prolonged struggle against determined opposition and the hostility of his own family in addition. And yet at first things went not too badly. In July 1775 Malesherbes, a great friend of Turgot's, was called to the ministry and reform was in the ascendant.

The first step taken by the new Comptroller-General was the freeing of the corn trade. In 1763 an edict had been issued allowing all places to buy corn and flour freely throughout the kingdom. This permission had been suspended by Terray, and Turgot now restored it (September 13th, 1774) together with the clause that the King might also permit export when circumstances were favourable. In reissuing this edict Turgot initiated the excellent policy of prefacing his acts with a preamble explaining their purpose and justification; one sentence runs: "C'est par le commerce seul et par le commerce libre que l'inégalite des récoltes peut être corrigée." Further reforms followed, all excellent measures, but calculated to increase the number of Turgot's enemies. He refused himself, and abolished for the future, the gift which former Comptroller-General had accepted from the *fermiers-généraux,* and decreed that the money should be spent in Paris to provide wool and yarn to set the poor on work; but he was not content to forego only his own *pots de vin.* Other gifts of a similar nature which had been given by financiers to influential persons at Court were likewise abolished, and the influential persons were none too pleased. In his first year of office he got rid of the restored *droit d'aubaine* which had made it difficult for foreigners to do work in the country; he reformed some of the abuses of the octrois, which, paid by country people, were constantly avoided by the more wealthy shop-keepers; and early next year he made an end throughout the country of the *contrainte solidaire.* His measures of economy, coupled as they were with the sweeping away of sinecures and monopolies, and the reform of various Government contracts, were all tending to improve the finances of the country, when a serious reverse was experienced from what was known as the *Guerre des farines.* Unfortunately the harvest of 1774 was exceptionally bad, the price of corn rose considerably, and the Government as usual was credited with the responsibility. Many people felt doubtful about the wisdom of freedom of trade in corn, and their doubts were increased by a pamphlet published by Necker, who was beginning to make his name as a financier of repute. There is a good deal of mystery about this Corn War, and it is possible that some of Turgot's more important enemies were influential in backing up the risings. The riots were senseless as well as dangerous, for the rioters raided bakers' shops and threw into the river sacks of flour, apparently as a protest against scarcity. Fairly soon the risings were put down, and the minister remained unshaken in his policy, but the happy prospects of 1774 were clouded over by the events of 1775, and people began to be suspicious of the wisdom of the new Comptroller-General. The number of the minister's enemies began to swell; the financiers, monopolists, parliamentarians and to some extent the nobles dreaded his reforms; to these were added the clergy who looked on him as a free-thinker. Turgot and Malesherbes were both in favour of toleration, and the King was only too anxious to avoid any persecution of those who were not orthodox Catholics. Trouble arose over the coronation oath, in which he had to swear to extirpate heretics. Turgot urged him to drop the objectionable words altogether, and to allow free exercise of all forms of worship in the country.

Poor Louis was in great difficulty, and finally—rather characteristically—retained the words, but mumbled them so that they could not be heard, and certainly he did all he could to render this part of his coronation oath a dead letter for the future. It was not, however, till the publication of his famous "Six Edicts" in 1776 that the minister's difficulties became really over-whelming. Of these six edicts only two were of vital importance, and it was over these two that the main struggle began. The first was for the conversion of the Government *corvée* into a money contribution, to be spread amongst all classes who were benefited by the roads, and the second was for the abolition of the *maîtrises* and *jurandes,* a complete revolution in the whole organization of trade throughout the kingdom.

In the case of the *corvées* Turgot desired to extend to the whole kingdom the reform he had already carried out to some extent in Limousin. His proposal was to get money for the roads by a tax on all landed proprietors; this it was impossible to do except by a law of the Government; in his own generality it had still been the *taillables* who had been also *corvéables.* The opposition to this edict came from the supporters of privilege, and was voiced by Miromesnil, the Keeper of the Seals, who prepared an elaborate report to prove that it was dangerous to place any burden on the nobility: "Deprive the nobility of its distinction and you destroy the national character; and the nation ceasing to be martial, will soon become the prey of stronger neighbouring nations." The argument was hard to maintain, and the Comptroller-General had little difficulty in answering the objections. He showed how the privilege of nobility dated from the time when they were obliged to render military service at their own expense, whereas the army was now paid by the State; that now, the nobles might fight or no as they wished, whilst the peasants were forced to serve in the militia; and he adds:

> Another reason operates to render privilege most unjust and at the same time less respectable. It is that by means of the facility existing to acquire nobility by a payment in money, there is no rich man that does not speedily become noble, so that the body of nobles comprehends the body of the rich, and the cause of the privileged is no longer the cause of distinguished families against the *roturiers,* but the cause of the rich against the poor.

The King had no hesitation in agreeing with the argument of Turgot rather than that of Miromesnil; and this edict was signed by him in Council on January 6th, 1776.

The next decree proposed was still more epoch making. Turgot's whole economic outlook was based on the need for freedom; freedom for all to adopt what industry they wished, freedom for each industry to carry on work as it wished, freedom to buy and sell so as best to meet the requirements of supply and demand. The whole guild system he felt to be arbitrary and out of date, a hindrance to work and trade in every way: "des codes obscurs rédigés par l'avidité, adoptés sans examen dans les temps d'ignorance, et auxquels il n'a manqué pour être l'objet de indignation publique, que d'être connus." His proposal was to abolish the trade corporations in Paris first, and,

as soon as arrangements could be made, throughout the whole kingdom. The chief provisions of the edict were as follows:

> 1. Any man to be free to enter any trade.
>
> 2. Associations and corporations of all kinds to be suppressed, both of those of patrons and those of workmen.
>
> 3. All privileges, statutes and regulations of the said corporations to be abolished.
>
> 4. Visits of *gardes jurés* (guild inspectors) to cease.
>
> 5. In every quarter a syndic and two assistants to be elected by the merchants and artisans (for the first year the Lieutenant-General to nominate) to watch over and report on all matters of trade and industry.
>
> 6. The names of patrons and workmen to be registered with the Lieutenant-General.

The clauses were headed by a long explanatory preamble showing clearly the unfairness of the system of monopoly, the delay and expense caused by the elaborate regulations which had to be observed, and the tyranny exercised over trade and industrial work, and over a large body of the people. The preamble began by asserting

> the right to work is the property of every man the most sacred and most imprescribable of all . . . we wish, therefore, to abolish the arbitrary institutions which prevent the poor from living by their work . . . which extinguish emulation and industry . . . which deprive the State of the valuable knowledge foreigners can bring, which discourage invention . . . which force artisans to pay for the faculty of working and which waste money by endless disputes over privileges, . . . which give power to their members to league together and for the rich to force their wishes on the poor . . . and which as a result force up unnaturally the price of commodities and the subsistence of the people . . . we shall not be kept from this act of justice by fear lest a crowd of artisans take up work of which they are ignorant and deluge the country with badly done work. Where liberty has existed it has not produced these disastrous results.

This edict also was approved by the King, and received his signature on February 5th, 1776. At once it aroused a storm of opposition. The patrons were of course against it as a body; a swarm of pamphlets appeared prophesying disaster to the whole industry of the country and the most terrible friction between masters and workmen. Some urged that it would certainly result in bad work, others that all subordination would be destroyed, that the greed of gain would pervade every workshop, and that all commerce would languish. The Parliament of Paris refused to register both the two main edicts; and gave as the reason that "to destroy necessary distinctions will soon bring disorder, the result of absolute equality, and will overturn the whole civil society, hitherto kept in harmony by preeminence and distinction." Louis still remained firm, and wrote sadly: "The more I think of it, dear Turgot, the more I repeat to myself that there are only you and myself who really love the people." The only way to obtain the registration of the edicts was to hold a *Lit de Justice,* and the Parliament of Paris was summoned to Versailes for the purpose, the King attended in state, and the Six Edicts became law. Voltaire wrote admiringly: "un lit de bienfaisance, le premier lit dans lequel on a fait coucher le peuple depuis la fondation de la monarchie."

The edicts had been passed, but it was not easy to get them carried out. Provincial Parliaments joined their protests to those of Paris, Turgot's enemies became more and more clamorous, and Louis was distracted. Maurepas, who had once supported the minister, was obviously jealous of him, and began insidiously to awake distrust in the mind of the King, and to weaken their mutual affection. Once when Turgot was ill and unable to come to see his royal master, Louis without hesitation sprang up with the words: "All right, I'll go to him," but Maurepas hurriedly interfered and prevented the simple act of kindness, so consistent with the King's good nature, and which might have cemented the old friendship. The Queen, who was anxious for money to shower on her friends the Polignacs, was by now alienated from the man whom she had at first tried to appreciate, and there was a serious dispute over the Comte de Guines, ambassador in England, who had to be recalled on account of grave diplomatic indiscretion. Marie Antoinette unfortunately took up his cause, and though he lost his post, the King, on his wife's urgent request, gave him a duchy and cleared him of all blame. Little by little things were getting to an impossible position, and all sorts of accidental circumstances came to accentuate the misfortunes of the country, which were of course ascribed without hesitation to the minister. Bread was very high in price, which disturbed the country, where those with property were already grumbling at the charges for the corvée now levied upon them; and in the towns various riots of workmen and abandonment of work were put down to the relaxation of guild rules. Things seemed to be really going badly; Abbé Terray, the former Comptroller-General, who had a pretty wit, remarked that "pendant mon ministère j'ai fait le mal bien, et Monsieur Turgot fait le bien on ne peut plus mal."

The continued unpopularity of the minister and the new measures frightened the King, and some very odious attacks were made on Turgot; one especially violent pamphlet, rumoured to be the work of the King's eldest brother, the Comte de Provence, declared that he was ruining the monarchy. The worst blow came when his friend Malesherbes resigned, leaving him to bear the brunt of all the opprobrium, and when against his repeated entreaties a very inferior person called Amelot was put in his place. It has even been suspected that the King was finally influenced by a forged letter, purporting to be from the minister, and casting aspersions on Marie Antoinette. Whether or no this was the case, Turgot himself realized that he no longer possessed Louis' confidence, and that without it his work was hopeless and he was bound to go. He did not think, however, that his fall would come quite so soon, and he tried to stay in office long enough to get a few administrative details completed. His worst trouble was the refusal of the King to see him, and he finally wrote him

a long letter in which he lamented his lack of trust, and criticised the conduct of Maurepas. After alluding to the deep pain he felt at the King's long-continued silence and neglect of his requests, he continued:

> I owe to Monsieur de Maurepas the place which your Majesty has entrusted to me. I shall never forget this, I shall never fail in the respect due to him; but I owe a thousand times more to the State and to your Majesty, and I cannot without guilt sacrifice their interest. It costs me much pain to have to say to you that Monsieur de Maurepas if he proposes to you Monsieur Amelot, is really culpable; or, at least, that his pliancy in the hands of others would be as fatal to your Majesty as a wilful crime. . . . You, Sire, have been sometimes believed to be weak, but I have seen you in trying circumstances show real courage. . . . Never forget, Sire, that it was weakness which brought Charles I to the block. It was weakness which made Charles IX cruel.

Louis again did not reply, and on May 12th, 1776, Turgot received the definite dismissal from his office, by the hands of the old minister, Bertin. The Court party had succeeded and were triumphant. The reformers felt that their best hopes were over. Voltaire wrote: "Ah, mon Dieu, what sad news I hear! I am overwhelmed in despair"; and later: "I see only death before me since Turgot is out of place. I cannot conceive how he could have been dismissed. . . . I am really dead since Turgot has been deprived of power."

The minister himself accepted his dismissal with dignity. He wrote once more to the King, and his only word of reproach was to express grief that the King has not himself notified his intentions, but had allowed the order to resign to be sent through a colleague:

> I trusted that you would graciously have informed me of your intentions: I will not hide from you that the form in which you at last notified them to me has caused me very acute pain. Your Majesty will not misapprehend the nature of this impression if you have been conscious of the truth and depth of the attachment I held to you. . . . My whole desire, Sire, is that I have been mistaken and have warned you of imaginary dangers. I hope that time will never justify me, and that your reign may be as happy and as peaceful, both for you and for your people, as it deserves to be.

Turgot wasted no time in idle regrets. The last few years of his life he devoted to science and literature. He studied, he wrote, he became Vice-Director of the *Académie des Incriptions,* he corresponded with Condorcet on stars and telescopes, with Adam Smith, Richard Price, and Benjamin Franklin on economic questions. In 1781 he died of an attack of gout at the age of fifty-four. All his life he had been a martyr to gout and never a very strong man. Once when reproved for over-haste in his measures, he replied that he had no time to waste, all his family died at fifty, and there was so much to do.

It is hard to estimate Turgot's work. At first he seemed to have failed. He fell in May 1776. On August 11th the *cor-*

vées were re-established, on August 19th the guilds, in September the corn trade was once more restricted. But, nevertheless, the old system had been shaken; the new guilds were in some ways less oppressive than the old; even when laws were still severe the interpretation of them became more and more lenient. The fact is that by degrees the old system was bound to break down of itself. Not only was the trend of thought against it, not only were Inspectors determined to turn a blind eye to many delinquencies; there was always a certain amount of work in the country which was bound to be free, and over which no manner of restrictions had the least control. This was especially the case in rural industries, and these were growing extensively at the close of the century. It was no good trying to reduce the work of the peasants to exact rule and to subject these home workers to the same restrictions which were enforced on town workers. The peasants could not read and would not listen, and the inspection of every cottage and every loom throughout the kingdom was clearly impossible. The guild system was weakened by criticism, shaken by Turgot, and practically destroyed by village industry.

But this was only one of Turgot's measures. How ought his work to be judged as a whole? Were his views right? Was his fall fatal to the old monarchy? Could he have averted the Revolution, or did his ministry actually hasten it? There will always be differences of opinion as to the merits of his theories and as to the results of what he was able to achieve. To some he was mistaken in the speed of his reforms, if not in the reforms themselves, because he weakened the only prop which kept up the old monarchy, namely, the nobles; they think that, strong royalist as he was, he ought to have realized that the aristocracy was necessary to support the Throne, and that privilege was the life-blood of the aristocracy. Others feel that even though reform was necessary, it was a reform for which only part of France was ready, and that great tact and patience were essential if the change was to be accomplished without dangerous friction. Others think that he was too much of a theorist, and that he lacked real practical insight. Malesherbes' own judgment on himself and Turgot leans to this view: "Monsieur Turgot and myself," he wrote, "were passionate for good, but we only knew men from books, were lacking in business training, and were foolish in allowing the King to be directed by Monsieur de Maurepas . . . without wishing it, by our very own ideas we contributed to the Revolution." Perhaps to some extent this judgment is true, though Turgot can scarcely be said to have lacked any business training after his long and successful administration in Limoges; but that he hastened the Revolution may possibly be true. Sorel passes this judgment upon him: "He showed to all," writes the historian, "the need for reform; and he showed the powerlessness of the monarchy to effect it."

Turgot can indeed be ranked rather amongst the benevolent despots than amongst the more democratic reformers; he was very certain of what was right, and he had either too little regard for public opinion, or else too much belief in the commonsense of mankind, for he always explained to the public the why and wherefore of what he was doing. A sincere and devoted royalist he felt that what France needed above all else was unity of government under a supreme sovereign whose interests were those of the nation. He feared the tyranny of the people and realized only too clearly their ignorance and selfishness. "La tyrannie d'un peuple," he writes, "est de toutes les tyrannies la plus cruelle et la plus intolerable. . . . Une multitude ne calcule rein, n'a jamais de remords et se décerne à elle-même la gloire, lorsqu'elle mérite le plus de honte." To accomplish unity he believed in the reform of law for the whole country and in the destruction of the old local variations. In economic life he believed in the breaking down of all barriers and restrictions, freedom of trade, and unlimited competition. His last great scheme, which he had no time even to initiate, was the carrying out of a complete administrative revolution; the establishment of elective assemblies in each parish, arrondissement, district and province, headed by a real National Assembly in the centre. The people, he felt, were not yet ready to bring forward schemes of their own; but he did not neglect their progress, for a system of national education was part of his complete plan for the country. As it was he did much to improve agricultural and technical education; and in the higher sphere he founded a chair of Law and a chair of French Literature in the *Collège de France,* and helped on the School of Medicine in Paris.

The central idea of Turgot's economic policy was his belief in the right of all to work, and to work freely without restrictions or hindrances. He was a strong supporter of individual property in land, based on the cultivation of it. The real claim to the soil was gained, he felt, by the labour of improving it. He was a physiocrat, since to him the main source of wealth was the land, but this not in the narrowest sense, but as meaning all that could be produced from the land both above and below. He saw the great importance of capital both for industry and agriculture, and thus he realized that for the real improvement of the land large farms and rich farmers could do the most. He was, as has been already said, a determined free trader and a believer in the new ideas of *laissez-faire.*

Most of Turgot's schemes materialized in time. The administrative revolution of 1787 introduced a mutilated form of his scheme of local government; the work of the National Assembly was really carrying out his theory in the creation of one uniform tax on land; the abolition of all feudal privileges (1789) and of the *jurandes* and *maîtrises* (1791) was merely a rather more extensive renewal of Turgot's measures. Monsieur Léon Say, a biographer of Turgot, ascribes to his work in 1776 the saving in France of the enfranchisement of work, threatened repeatedly by the Convention, the Empire, the Restoration, and the Revolution of 1848. He considers that even if he failed in the eighteenth century he founded the political economy of the nineteenth, and stamped on it the main characteristic which distinguished it. He writes: "Thanks to the freedom of work the nineteenth century has been the age of industry on a large scale, the age of the application to the development of work and of riches, of the great scientific, geographical, and economic discoveries. By causing the principles of the freedom of work to penetrate deeply into the conscience of France and of Europe, Turgot has opened the way to the conquest of the world by the civilization of the West, and it is the nineteenth century which has accomplished that conquest."

In telling the story of Turgot's life perhaps some idea has been given of his personality, for with him his work was so very much a part of himself that it is hard to think of one without the other. All his interests were bound up with science, education, and things of the mind, but he had time also for friendships, and his friends were all the more important to him because he never married and had no family ties. A description has been left of him by Dupont de Nemours, himself an economist of note, who has written on his life and works.

> He was tall and well-proportioned; his face was beautiful. Owing to his dislike of self-assertion, he did not hold his head pretentiously high. His eyes were of a clear brown, and expressed perfectly the blending of firmness and character. His forehead was dome-shaped, lofty, noble, and serene; his features well pronounced. . . . He had a peculiar smile difficult to describe, which by persons who did not know him was thought to express disdain, although it was really the effect of shyness and of the habit of embarrassment formed in youth, from which he had never been entirely able to free himself. He blushed with a too great facility, and at every kind of emotion, either of impatience or of sensibility. His hair was brown, abundant, and very fine, he retained it completely to the last; clad as magistrate, his locks scattered on his shoulders with a natural and negligent grace, he formed a striking picture.

He goes on to speak of his friends, both men and women, who loved him dearly, and adds: "He was never carried away by the fashionable gallantry of the time." Others less friendly make more of Turgot's stiffness and awkwardness, and think he would have done better could he have been a little more tactful and conciliatory and an abler speaker in his own interests. This may be, but, nevertheless, the honesty and single-mindedness of the man is obvious throughout, and undoubtedly his virtues were part of his charm. Louis was won by him completely in the first interview, and a man's friends are generally a better judge than his enemies. One very pleasant trait in Turgot's character which has been preserved is his kindness to his servants, whom he insisted on being lodged as comfortably as he was himself. This in itself tends to prove that the minister was very far from being merely a theorist.

To complete the picture of this great man it may be worth while giving a few of his ideas on subjects other than economies as set forth in his writings. On education he was a forerunner of Rousseau, and some time before *Emile* was written he was advocating a freer and more liberal education, a greater knowledge of nature, and far more development of the body. "Do not say to your son, be virtuous," he writes, "but make him find pleasure in being so. Develop in his heart the germ of the sentiments which Nature has put there. We often need more barriers against our education than against Nature. Give the child the opportunity of being true, liberal, compassionate, rely upon the heart of man, let the precious seeds of virtue expand in the air that surrounds them. Do not smother them under a

load of straw-mattings and wooden frames." And again: "We wish our child to be serious, we make it a virtue in him not to run about; we fear every instant that he is going to fall. What happens? We weary and vex him, and we enfeeble him. We have forgotten that above all it is a part of education to form the body."

The question of his religious views and his desire for toleration have already been touched on; he was a keen advocate of the sweeping away of all barriers from the freedom of thought and the freedom of worship. He was in favour of marriage being a matter to be settled by the individuals themselves, not by their parents, and considered that all marriages should be based on the love of husband and wife. He writes: "I know that even marriages of inclination are not always happy; but because in choosing we are sometimes deceived, it is concluded that we must never choose. The consequence drawn is amusing . . . but I fear it will take a long time to correct society on this matter." As early as 1750, when still a student at the Sorbonne, the future minister gave a discourse in which he urged well-timed reform in order to avert revolution. His words could have been spoken at the end of his life as well as at the beginning. "Unhappy are those nations in which false principles of government have actuated their legislations. . . . Almost all have neglected to keep open the door for the improvements of which all the works of man have need, or have neglected to make the means for those easy. . . . The only remedy for abuses that remains—revolution—is one sadder than the abuses themselves."

An excerpt from a letter to Dr. Price, dated 22 March 1778:

How happens it that you are about the first among your men of letters to set forth just notions of freedom, and to expose the fallacy of that notion, harped upon by almost all republican writers, 'that freedom consists in being subjected to laws alone,' as if a man were free who is oppressed by an unjust law?

This would not be true, even supposing all laws to be the work of the assembled nation; for, after all, the individual has also his rights, of which the nation can deprive him only by violence and by an illegitimate use of the general power. Although you have had regard for this truth and have expressed yourself upon it, perhaps it deserves of you a more extended development considering the scant attention it has received even from the most zealous followers of Freedom.

Anne-Robert-Jacques Turgot, quoted in Turgot, *by Léon Say, translated by Melville B. Anderson, A. C. McClurg and Company, 1888.*

Charles A. Ellwood (essay date 1938)

SOURCE: "Turgot," *The Story of Social Philosophy,* 1938. Reprint by Books for Libraries Press, 1971, pp. 162-75.

[*An internationally known sociologist and educator, Ellwood has had many of his publications translated into foreign languages, including Japanese and Chinese. In this excerpt, he discusses Turgot's social philosophy and his use of the scientific method.*]

It is difficult to say with any certainty what scientific methods Turgot employed in reaching his conclusions. But it is certain that he had a clearer conception of the correct method in the field of the social sciences than any of his precursors. He contrasts the method of the mathematical sciences with the methods of the concrete natural sciences. He tells us:

> The mind, in mathematics, deduces one from another a chain of propositions whose truth consists only in their mutual dependence. The case is not the same for the other sciences, where it is no longer the comparison of ideas with one another whence springs truth, but their conformity with a train of real facts. To discover it and show it, it suffices no longer to establish a small number of simple principles whence the mind has only to allow itself to be led on by the thread of deduction. It is necessary to start from nature as she is.

Thus the physicist forms hypotheses by aid of the imagination "in the light of a few badly known facts." These he tests by all the facts he can discover. "He tries them, so to speak, on the facts, as a seal is verified by being replaced on its impression in the wax." In this way, "Time, research, and chance accumulate observations and unveil the hidden bonds that connect phenomena."

Such passages show that Turgot understood clearly that the method of the concrete sciences was "hypothesis-testing." Indeed, he says that the sciences advance "by dint of groping, of multiplying systems, and of exhausting, so to speak, errors." Thus scientific truth is reached over the ruins of false hypotheses.

But Turgot tells us that "all the sciences lend one another mutual aid," and that therefore mathematics can be of some use in all the concrete sciences, even though these must be built upon the facts of experience. As a good follower of Locke, he holds that all the facts of experience come to us through the senses. "The senses are the sole source of ideas," he tells us; "the whole power of imagination is limited to the combining of the ideas it has received from them."

But in social philosophy, the facts of experience are the history of the race. Therefore history contains the facts by which the social philosopher must test his hypotheses. Hence Turgot appears in social philosophy as preeminently an advocate of the historical method. But it is the examination of the successive phases of the human mind, or the history of thought in various lines, that he emphasizes.

Nevertheless, Turgot was fully conscious of other factors in the historical process. He speaks especially of the effects of economic and geographical conditions, of human passions, of wars, and of the intermingling of peoples. In his mature life he was much influenced, as we have seen, by the physiocratic school of economists, but he did not attempt to reconcile his general social philosophy with their overemphasis upon physical nature. While he was not entirely free from their errors, it is worthy of note that he did not subscribe to their doctrine that self-interest is "the born servant of the general interest," nor to their other doctrine that free competition is "the mainspring of human perfectibility."

Turgot warns particularly against that scientific and philosophical complacency which "would restrict the limits of existing knowledge and fix these limits once for all." This sectarian spirit in philosophy and science is one of the main reasons why nations that are pioneers in philosophy and science frequently fail to advance, for it is a pride "fed on ignorance," and shuts the door to new inquiries. "The less the knowledge," Turgot tells us in one of his brilliant aphorisms, "the less the doubt."

We are forced to conclude, then, that while Turgot recognized the need of a complex method in social philosophy, his own method seems to have been mainly the exercise of scientific imagination and insight. For without extensive research and without extensive critical analysis, he seems to have achieved a well-balanced view of human affairs and a remarkable insight into human history.

. . . . .

Doctrine of social development. It is difficult to analyze Turgot's social philosophy under conventional rubrics. His main thinking centered about the problem of social progress, but this was to be solved, according to his method, by the study of the processes of history. Turgot has no doubt that the accumulation of knowledge and the developing intelligence of man, unceasingly correcting errors and unveiling truth, has been the main factor in social development. But he does not deny "the infinite variety of circumstances" that has quickened the pace of social and cultural evolution in some nations and slowed it down in others.

At the very outset of his second discourse, Turgot points to language as the chief instrument used by man for the accumulation and diffusion of knowledge and ideas, and hence for the building of civilization. He says, "The arbitrary signs of speech and writing, by giving men the means wherewith to make sure of the possession of their ideas and to communicate them to others, have formed from individual stores of knowledge a common treasure, that one generation transmits to another, like unto a heritage continually augmented by the discoveries of each age"; and thus "all the ages of mankind are enchained one with another." Well might John Morley see in these lines "the germs of a new and most fruitful philosophy of society," for we have here an anticipation of the cultural theory of human society.

"Invention of every sort, material and nonmaterial, springing from the accumulation and diffusion of knowledge, is the ladder on which man climbs." But inventions that enable man better to conserve and diffuse knowledge are of peculiar importance. Hence Turgot's apostrophe to the invention of writing, as marking a great turning point in the history of mankind: "Precious invention! which seemed to give the peoples that first possessed it wings to outstrip the other nations! Inestimable invention! which snatches from the power of death the memory of great men and examples of valor and integrity, unites times and places, fixes the fugitive thought and assures it lasting existence, whereby the products, the opinions, the experiences, the discoveries accumulated through all the ages serve as groundwork and as stairs on which posterity may rise ever higher." Almost of equal importance for the development of civilization was the invention of the art of printing.

But the unequal distribution of talent among mankind may also have had much to do with the unequal social development of peoples. "Nature, not impartial in the bestowal of her gifts, has given to certain minds a fullness of talent that she has refused to others; circumstances develop these talents or leave them buried in obscurity; and from the infinite variety of such circumstances springs the inequality that marks the progress of nations." The circumstances that Turgot particularly mentions as tending to bury the talent of peoples are wars, conquests, revolutions, geographic isolation, and inequalities of economic conditions and of education.

Hence the historical process in any given nation, as well as in mankind as a whole, is never a straight line. Social decay is almost as much in evidence as social progress. Progress is through errors, mistakes, and difficulties. It is not without interruption. If Turgot had used the language of our time, he would have said that it was "a trial-and-error process." He fully recognizes, then, periods of reaction and of decadence; but men learn from their mistakes and even from their calamities. Experience and the knowledge that it brings will accumulate again, and after a time progress will be resumed. Just as in the progress of science, so in all other fields of human endeavor, man learns from his mistakes. It is this possibility of learning through experience which assures social progress in the long run. Thus it is not too much to say, as many have said, that Turgot made progress "organic in human history." He believed apparently that man cannot escape from learning through experience, and that therefore history, as so many eighteenth-century thinkers asserted, is a process of the education of the race. While we must not expect uniform social progress, it is a necessary development of human history. If one group fails to progress, some other group will profit by the mistakes made by the first group and carry human achievements to a still higher level.

It is clear that Turgot considered the learning process to be back of all human progress. He does not use such a phrase, but he frequently speaks of man's learning. Men live, he says, by the aid of past experience. The history of every nation is therefore a process of self-development, and explanation of progress is to be found in the nature of the human mind, in its capacity to learn from experience. The processes of history are processes of testing out adjustments. This testing necessarily proceeds through what we call fumbling and success. It is a process of trial and error, as we have just said, but the movement is inevitably toward a higher degree of perfection of both knowl-

edge and practical adjustments, even though it is not without interruption.

This progress away from ignorance and error to the attainment of true knowledge is particularly illustrated by Turgot in his famous theory of the three states of man's intellectual conceptions, which anticipated Comte's law of the three states. This is found in Turgot's notes on a *Plan for Two Discourses on Universal History.* Though often quoted, it is worth quoting again:

> Before the relation between physical facts was known, there was nothing more natural than to suppose that they were produced by intelligent beings, invisible and like ourselves; for what else would they have resembled? Everything that happened without man's having had a part in it had its god, to the worship of whom fear or hope soon gave rise; and this worship was later developed in the light of the regard paid to powerful men; for gods were only men more powerful or less perfect; according as they were the work of an age more or less enlightened as to the true perfection of mankind.
>
> When philosophers had recognized the absurdity of these fables, without having, however, acquired true light upon natural history, they imagined they could explain the cause of phenomena by means of abstract expressions, such as essences or faculties, expressions which yet explained nothing, and in regard to which men reasoned as if they had been beings, new divinities substituted for the old. These analogies were followed out, and faculties were multiplied to account for each effect.
>
> It was only later, when the mechanical action of bodies upon one another was observed, that from this mechanical relation were drawn other hypotheses that mathematicians could develop and experience verify.

Whether the above quotation applies only to the physical sciences, as some think, or whether it applies to all man's knowledge, anticipating Comte's classification of all man's conceptions into a theological, a metaphysical, and a positive or scientific stage, is of no great importance. The important thing is to see that Turgot emphasized progress away from ignorance and error, even though one error sometimes led into another. It is equally important to observe that, according to Turgot, the process is fundamentally an intellectual one. It depends upon the development of man's knowledge of his world and of himself. The active agent in all this progress is therefore the development of intelligence in man, not so much, however, in the individual, as in that accumulated experience that we call "social culture."

Doctrine of social order. Turgot's theories of social organization and social order were rather vague. In a general way he accepted the physiocrats' "system of natural liberty." Like practically all eighteenth-century social thinkers, the concepts of natural right and the law of nature dominated his mind. While he held that men are by nature intellectually unequal and are thus naturally fitted for division of labor, yet they should, he thought, find by free competition the place for which they are fitted. He was opposed, therefore, to all social institutions, such as slavery, that interfere with the natural liberty of individuals. He also favored freedom of trade and commerce and the minimum interference by government in industrial and business enterprises.

Perhaps this general attitude was inconsistent with his belief that constitutional monarchy was the best form of government for France. Perhaps it was also inconsistent with his exaltation of the family as the fundamental institution in society and his condemnation of polygyny in all of its forms. But it was consistent with his belief that justice and morality are not merely social conventions, and that a wise social order would seek to maximize and maintain justice between individuals and classes. Injustice between classes he thought to be the root of revolution. Hence he said, "Well-timed reform may avert revolution."

We have already noted Turgot's very modern ideas regarding the part that religion may play in human society. He was perhaps over-optimistic in making mutual tolerance the sufficient basis for a reunited church that would teach and exemplify "the Christianity of Christ"; but religious tolerance is certainly one of the bases necessary for church unity.

It is hardly necessary to say in conclusion that Turgot represented eighteenth-century optimism at its very best. Perhaps a little breath of such scientific optimism is the thing most needed in the social philosophy of the present time. Turgot was not one of those who believed that "the only lesson of history is that the lessons of history are never learned." Probably he would acknowledge that some stupid ages might fail in learning them, but that sooner or later mankind must learn from its own experience. He would surely come near to agreeing with Pascal that "the whole series of human generations during the course of the ages should be regarded as one man, ever living and ever learning," though he would emphasize that the learning has proceeded with many interruptions and at times with great signs of forgetfulness.

It is also hardly necessary to point out that Turgot's social philosophy is in fundamental conflict with all crude theories of environmental determinism by natural conditions. It is in conflict, for example, with Montesquieu's exaltation of natural conditions and natural law. It is equally in conflict with the economic determinism of Karl Marx, which would reduce the intellectual conceptions of man to rationalizations of his economic condition. In brief, it is in conflict with every social philosophy that would make nature more important in historical development than the active, learning mind of man, even though this mind is so subject to errors and aberrations.

Finally, we must agree, I think, with Professor McQuilkin De Grange [Turgot, **"On the Progress of the Human Mind,"** translated by McQuilkin De Grange, 1929] that "seldom has there been born into the world a greater potential sociologist than Turgot." It is much to be regretted, therefore, that the chief energies of his life were spent upon the practical problems of statesmanship, in an effort to save his country from disaster. Again, all historically

minded social thinkers would agree that "in the work of this youth has been found clear anticipation of the thought and perhaps of the fundamental principles on which Auguste Comte was later to erect the science to which he gave the name 'sociology.'"

Joseph J. Spengler (essay date 1942)

SOURCE: "The Nonphysiocratic Economists," *French Predecessors of Malthus: A Study of Eighteenth-Century Wage and Population Theory,* Duke University Press, 1942, pp. 264-322.

[*An economist and educator, Spengler has written many books on demography and economic theory, including* Francois Quesnay et La Physiocratie *(1958) and* Essays in Economic Thought *(1960). In the following excerpt, he discusses Turgot's economic theories and their relationship to those of Thomas Malthus.*]

Turgot (1727-1781), intendant at Limoges and for a time (1774-1776) controller-general, treated population problems in connection with his analyses of wage formation. An advocate of economic liberalism, Turgot believed that if artificial restrictions upon competition were removed, the economic condition of the working masses and of the nation as a whole would improve more than under any alternative system.

Turgot's wage theory was shaped in large measure by his acceptance of the proposition that population growth is governed primarily by the supply of subsistence. For, although he developed a marginal productivity theory with respect to the application of "advances" to land, he found in the conditions governing the long-run supply of labor the main ultimate determinants of the wage level. Wages, he concluded [in *Reflections on the Formation and Distribution of Riches*], while subject to the varying influences of supply and demand, were set primarily by the worker's requirements for "livelihood."

> The mere Workman, who has only his arms and his industry, has nothing except in so far as he succeeds in selling his toil to others. He sells it more or less dear; but this price, more or less high as it may be, does not depend upon himself alone: it results from the agreement which he makes with him who pays [for] his labour. The latter pays him as little as he can; as he has the choice among a great number of Workmen, he prefers the one who works cheapest. The Workmen are therefore obliged to lower the price, in competition with one another. In every kind of work it cannot fail to happen, and as a matter of fact it does happen, that the wages of the workman are limited to what is necessary to procure him his subsistence.

Turgot here seems merely to have accepted the prevalent subsistence theory of wages, for, as Cannan indicates [in *A Review of Economic Theory*, 1930], Turgot's purpose in this portion of his *Reflections* was to show that agricultural workers could produce more than their subsistence.

Cultivators of land, as distinguished from owners and proprietors, fared no better than the laborers; they received "as small a part of the produce" as was necessary to secure their services. "In a word, the Cultivator and the Artisan receive, neither of them, more than the recompense of their labour." Turgot noted that, because of temporary variation from one occupation to another in the ratio of the supply of labor to the demand for it, wages at times were higher in some occupations than in others; but he believed that such differences tended to disappear under conditions of competition. It is almost inferable that Turgot believed that under equilibrium conditions the members of each occupational class would tend to receive little, if any, more than enough money to purchase the ordinary means of existence. He indicated that only the landowners received, in consequence of their title to the net product of the land, an income that might include "a considerable superfluity."

From Turgot's various comments one gets an imprecise conception of his notion of a subsistence wage. First, the wage rate per hour needed to be high enough to enable a workman to earn the necessary minimum means of existence within a physiologically reasonable number of hours a day. For while "no man works as much as he could," workmen normally relaxed little if any more than was physiologically necessary. Second, the minimum money wage that was necessary to induce workmen to continue to work needed to suffice for the support of the workman and his family at a level of life slightly above the bare subsistence level.

> If a workman cannot live by his labour, he becomes a mendicant or leaves the country. That is not all: it is necessary that the workman obtain a certain profit, to provide for accidents, to bring up his family. In a nation where trade and industry are free and vigorous, competition fixes this profit at the lowest possible rate. . . . That kind of superfluity out of which retrenchment can, strictly speaking, be made, is nevertheless a necessary element in the usual subsistence of the workmen and their families.

Actually competition was never "keen enough" in industrial occupations "to prevent at any time a man who was more expert, more active, and, above all, more economical than others in his personal consumption, from gaining a little more than was necessary for the subsistence of himself and his family and from saving this surplus to create therewith a little store." Third, although, as we show below, Turgot at times assumed the necessary standard of life or "livelihood" to be subject to secular expansion, he noted also the downward pressure exerted by growth in numbers upon such expansionist tendencies. Conditions of "supply and demand," he observed, often pushed "the current price" of labor above its "fundamental price" (i.e., "what his subsistence costs the workman"). Yet, since "wants" remained "always the same," and a suprafundamental wage level served to attract immigrants and to stimulate natural increase, the competition of the resultant growing supply of labor tended to depress the market price of labor back to the "fundamental" level. He reasoned, therefore, as did a number of his contemporaries, that taxes on consumption goods used by wage earners usually fell upon the landed proprietors, the only recipi-

ents of "net produce," inasmuch as the "current price" of labor usually approximated its "fundamental price." For, given this condition and given a tax which increased the monetary cost of that which the workman and his family normally consumed, the number of workmen would continue to diminish (through emigration and presumably through death or morbidity) until the reduction in their number had elevated the money wage by the amount of the tax; the number of workers would remain intact only on condition that the money wage were increased by the amount of the tax.

It is implicit in what has been said that Turgot assumed the supply of subsistence to be the main determinant of population growth. Population increases when wages and the level of comfort rise. If, on the contrary, the supply of subsistence diminishes, numbers decline. If each man consumes 3 *setiers* of grain, or the equivalent thereof, and production declines by x *setiers*, population will decline by x/3 men. Given a deficiency of subsistence and an infra-subsistence wage level, death, sickness, and emigration serve to reduce numbers, affecting first the laboring classes and eventually (assuming land to yield no net product) the noncultivating proprietors. Given comfort and abundance, natural increase and immigration swell the population.

That population growth, in Turgot's opinion, was conditioned in some degree by living standards, is evident in his occasional references to this relationship. Men "fear . . . the bonds of marriage [and] the cares and cost of children," he wrote in 1751, adding that dominance of marriage by ambition and economic interests was inimical to family survival and to the morality of customs. In 1770 he indicated that while the line of causation ran from increases in the level of comfort to increases in population to increases in the price of provisions to extensions of cultivation to declines in the price of provisions, the secular recurrence of this chain of events was accompanied by a secular rise in the level of comfort. "It is by these alternative and slight undulations in prices that the entire nation advances by degrees to a higher point [the level of] cultivation, of comfort, of population that it is able to enjoy, given the extent of its territory." Presumably, judging from his early (about 1750) discourses on "progress," and from his emphasis upon the progressive and perfectible character of the human mind, Turgot anticipated a secular improvement in the human lot. He did not integrate his treatment of the cumulative character of culture with his discussion of population, however, as did Condorcet, his disciple.

Turgot virtually ignored the influence of the power and tastes of proprietors upon wage levels and population trends. He did not in general subscribe to a "force" theory of wages, presumably because he supposed that wages usually were fixed by forces of supply and demand beyond individual control; and that when the profits of the proprietors and cultivators (whose expenditures constituted the "unique fonds des salaires de toutes les autres classes de la société") increased, employment and wages also increased. He recognized, however, that workers tended to be exploited when employers arranged not to compete effectively for labor; therefore, he sought the suppression of all French regulations and institutions which limited the opportunities open to workers and curbed the competition of employers for the services of labor.

Turgot at times came close to being a Malthusian. Although he believed everyone to possess the right to work, to security, and to succor, he condemned indiscriminate charity, because it diverted resources from productive uses, destroyed wealth, increased the number of idle, multiplied disorder, and burdened the industrious. He advocated, as an administrator, sought, the suppression of mendicancy and the employment of all idle able-bodied persons, whether men, women, or children.

> To enable a large number of men to live gratuitously is to subsidize idleness and all the disorders which are its consequences. [Charity which renders the ne'er-do-well's condition preferable to that of the honest workman] diminishes for the State the sum of labour and of the productions of the earth, a large part of which is thus left necessarily uncultivated. Hence frequent scarcities, the increase of misery, and depopulation.

Yet he was not essentially Malthusian in his philosophy. He at times subscribed to a kind of wages-fund doctrine, and noted that wages tend to increase in consequence of capital accumulation. But he did not advocate the limitation of population growth; nor did he specifically condemn luxury as a check to progress in numbers and wages, perhaps because "the fall in the rate of interest proves that, in general, economy has prevailed over luxury in Europe."

In his discussion of the capacity of given areas of land to yield subsistence and thereby support population, Turgot pointed out that such capacity is definitely limited, the limit being fixed by the skill of the population using the land and by the operation of the laws of diminishing returns at the extensive and the intensive margins. He added, however, that the population of France had by no means approached the supportable limit. "The fertility of the soil is limited," he wrote in 1768. "A determined extent of land is able to support a certain number of men, and when it [number] is not there, it is the fault of the administration," he wrote in 1755. Land varied in fertility, the best tending to be occupied first, he observed in 1766, thus implying that an increase in numbers resulted in diminishing returns at the extensive margin. In 1768, in a commentary embodying what is probably the first explicit formulation of the laws of increasing and diminishing returns at the intensive margin, Turgot indicated that successive increments of "advances," or of cultivation, would be accompanied up to a certain point by increasingly larger increments of yield per marginal increment of input; that "past this point, if the advances be still increased, the produce will increase, but less, and always less and less until the fecundity of the earth being exhausted, and art unable to add anything further, an addition to the advances will add nothing whatever to the produce." In another commentary made in the same year (1768) Turgot indicated that cultivation had not yet become so intense that further advances would produce little or no additional profits.

As the fertility of the soil is limited, there is without doubt a point at which the augmentation of advances would not augment production in the same proportion as the augmentation of expenses, but until now this limit is far from being attained, and experience proves that where advances are most heavy, that is to say, where cultivators are most wealthy, there is not only the greatest total production, but there are the greatest net products.

Despite his grasp of the laws of returns, Turgot did not effectively integrate his treatment of these laws with his discussion of wage and population theory.

Turgot devoted very little attention to the relation between the foreign trade of a country, and its capacity to support population. He noted that Holland could support part of its population through international trade, but implied that a nation derived its support principally from its own agriculture. Freedom of trade in grain, he wrote fifteen years later (1770), would not injure France, inasmuch as production proportioned itself to habitual consumption and habitual exportation; moreover, by augmenting the demand for grain, it would increase the "somme des travaux," diminish unemployment if it existed, and tend to increase the wages and comfort of the working population. He not only opposed mercantilistic colonial policy, but also predicted its doom. Mother countries, he wrote in 1776, "will be forced to abandon all empire over their colonies, to leave them entire freedom of commerce with all nations, to content themselves in partaking along with the others this liberty, and in maintaining with their colonies the ties of friendship and fraternity." In one place, however, he suggested that, however well administered a state was, it could free itself completely of poor and needy persons only if it had colonies to people.

Bury on Turgot's theory of progress:

[While] Turgot might have subscribed to Voltaire's assertion that history is largely "un ramas de crimes, de folies, et de malheurs," his view of the significance of man's sufferings is different and almost approaches the facile optimism of Pope—"whatever is, is right." He regards all the race's actual experiences as the indispensable mechanism of Progress, and does not regret its mistakes and calamities. Many changes and revolutions, he observes, may seem to have had most mischievous effects; yet every change has brought some advantage, for it has been a new experience and therefore has been instructive. Man advances by committing errors. The history of science shows (as Fontenelle had pointed out) that truth is reached over the ruins of false hypotheses.

J. B. Bury, The Idea of Progress: An Inquiry into Its Origin and Growth, *Macmillan and Company, 1920.*

Charles Frankel   (essay date 1948)

SOURCE: "The Reign of Reason and Truth," *The Faith*

of Reason: The Idea of Progress in the French Enlightenment, 1948. Reprint by Octagon Books, 1969, pp. 101-27.

[*A scholar and educator, Frankel served as Assistant Secretary of State for Educational and Cultural Affairs from 1965 to 1967. In the following excerpt, he emphasizes the role of providence in Turgot's theory of progress.*]

The idea that science operated within a cultural context, and that it was a factor in freeing other institutions from prejudice, encrusted tradition, and ignorance, became a guiding principle for the understanding of history in the work of Voltaire and D'Alembert. Their histories gave impetus to the belief in social progress. Society would improve insofar as it was permeated by the methods and results of science. Since "science" sometimes meant one thing, however, and sometimes another, the idea of social progress had varying connotations. The growth of science in comprehensiveness and reliability might be explained in terms of its method as, for example, in Pascal and Fontenelle, or it might be explained in terms of larger metaphysical conceptions. If the latter were used, the continuous and cumulative growth of human reason became a condition for the growth of science rather than a consequence of its establishment. This made a very great difference. Men and nations would grow wiser as they grew older even if they possessed no method for learning from experience. The belief in progress could be held as a necessary inference from the laws of nature.

The figure of Turgot is perhaps outstanding in this respect. Turgot's belief in the ubiquity of law, making for the continuous growth of reason through history, was indeed so strong that he seems somewhat separate from the rest of the *philosophes.* The principle of the ubiquity of reason imparted to Turgot's speculations on progress a much greater emphasis on the reasonableness of what had happened, and much less emphasis upon the curious lapses from reason that, for example, strew the pages of Voltaire's histories. Like Voltaire and the *philosophes,* Turgot found "sects" pernicious, but he was apparently more sensitive than others to the fact that the Encyclopedists themselves might be, or become, a sect, and he consequently laid great stress on the processes of cross-fertilization that enriched seemingly opposed doctrines. In July of 1750, Turgot delivered a discourse at the Sorbonne, ***On the Advantages that the Establishment of Christianity Has Brought for the Human Race.*** His argument was that Christianity had been one of the most important factors that had made for progress. It had saved antiquity from superstition, had preserved the sciences through ages that would otherwise have been completely dark, and had presented to the minds of men the emancipating conception of a law transcending individual human interests and prejudices.

> In order to bring back rights and justice a principle was necessary which could lift men out of themselves and of all that surrounds them, which could make them envisage every nation and every condition with an equitable view. . . . That is what religion has done. . . . Could one hope for this from any other principle than religion? What else could have been able to combat and vanquish the alliance of interest and prejudice? The Christian religion alone has suc-

ceeded. It alone has brought to light the rights of humanity.

Turgot's theory of progress placed emphasis upon the continuity between past and present, rather than upon purging the present of the vestiges of its unenlightened ancestry. His fundamental principle was that human communication is the basis of progress, that language is the essential medium for the preservation and transmission of the historically accumulated intellectual wealth to which every generation makes its own contribution. It is, consequently, the arts of communication like writing and printing which are of critical importance.

> All the ages are linked by a series of causes and effects which bind the present situation of the world to all those that have preceded. The multifarious signs of language and writing, in giving men the means of assuring themselves of the possession of their ideas, and of communicating them to others, have turned every individual discovery into a common treasure, which one generation transmits to another, so as to grant a constantly augmented heritage to each century; and the human species considered from its origin appears to the eyes of a philosopher as an immense whole, which has, like every individual, its childhood and its progress.

Turgot found continuity everywhere, and wherever he found continuity he inferred progress. More clearly than anyone else among the *philosophes* who came before Condorcet, Turgot formulated the conception of necessary and inevitable progress. Universal history was ultimately a study in the progress of mankind. Turgot's conception approached the philosophy of history of St. Augustine or Bossuet in finding every historic event to be meaningful as part of the unitary, all-embracing movement of the human race towards its goal. There were not several human histories, nor several lines of continuity, nor various possible outcomes; there was only one history with one meaning and outcome possible for it.

> Universal history embraces the consideration of the successive stages in the progress of the human species, and the specific causes that have contributed to it; the formation and mixing of nations; the origins, the revolutions of governments; the progress of languages, of physics, of morals, of manners, of the sciences and arts; the revolutions which have made Empires succeed Empires, nations follow on nations, religions on religions; the human species, always the same through these upheavals, and constantly advancing towards its perfection.

There was thus a kind of cosmic Toryism about Turgot's philosophy of progress. Nothing in history was wasted, nothing did not turn out in the end to have promoted human happiness. Every event was continuous with every other, and progress followed automatically from the communication of ideas. Every human experience became part of the historic tradition with which men work, and was therefore automatically instructive. "No mutation has taken place which has not brought some advantage; because none has been made without producing some experience, and without extending or improving or preparing instruction." indeed, not only truth and reason, but error and passion as well, have been factors in progress. "The real advancement of the human mind is revealed even in its aberrations."

Turgot went farther than the position that error had in fact turned out to be the precursor and sufficient condition for the discovery of truth. For Turgot, who applied the idea of the necessary Order of Nature to history and time, it was an essential condition as well. Not only did everything have a place in nature but no two things could exchange places, and this was true for the dimension of time as well as for space. This temporalizing of the conception of the harmonious and economical Order of Nature resulted in Turgot's theory of progress, and led, for example, to the conclusion that at certain stages in history reason would have been an obstacle to progress because it would have retarded communication. "The passions multiplied ideas, extended knowledge, perfected minds in the absence of reason, whose day had not yet come, and which would have been less powerful if it had reigned earlier. . . . Reason and justice, better understood, would have fixed everything, as has nearly happened in China."

Turgot developed this conception that progress moves through necessary stages into two laws of social development. The first was a principle of historic acceleration: every progressive step causes an acceleration in the rate of progress; and since every historic event was progressive in function, the principle implies that the tempo of historic change necessarily increases steadily. The second was that intellectual development must go through three necessary stages: (1) the explanation of events in terms of spiritual powers; (2) the explanation of events in terms of essences and powers; (3) the mechanistic explanation of events. No stage can be eliminated, nor can the necessary order of succession be changed. Turgot stated these laws only in passing, but they have had a significant influence. In the next century Auguste Comte took up Turgot's observation and developed systematically the positivist conception of the three stages of progress—the theological, the metaphysical, and the positive.

Turgot was aware of the gap that existed between his *a priori* affirmation of progress and the evidence found when the actual record of human history was appraised. "But what a spectacle is presented by the succession of the opinions of men! I seek there for the progress of the human mind, and I see almost nothing but the history of its errors." His attempt to resolve the paradox was ingenious. Turgot fell back upon Condillac's empiricist account of the development of ideas. . . . [In] Condillac's theory the progress of empirical knowledge rested upon chance, that is, upon the uncontrolled presentation of new sensations. Turgot employed this notion to explain the origin (and necessity) of error. The slower advance of the empirical sciences as compared with mathematics was due to the fact that the empirical sciences depended upon chance experience. The conceptions contained in the empirical sciences "are not collections of ideas that the mind forms of its own accord, and whose extent it knows precisely. The ideas are born and combine in our soul almost without our knowing. . . ."

Turgot's appeal to chance is illustrative of the disproportionately large part that accident or chance tend to play in a philosophy of history that holds all events to have but one meaning. All events in general are explained in terms of the *a priori* assumptions of continuity and necessity—that everything that is partakes of what has been, and that what is could not have come about in any other way. But when the *specific* question is asked, "Why this particular error at this particular time?" Turgot must appeal to chance. That we sometimes "learn by trial and error" in the sense that certain errors have preceded truthful discoveries is one thing; but it is a very different thing to assert that those particular errors had to be made in order to discover the truth, or that all errors ultimately issue in discovery. In *general,* Turgot argued, it is "reason" that makes this take place; but, in any *particular* case, it is chance. He gave no details of the manner in which errors were converted into truths, asserting that we learn continuously from error apart from any specific method for learning from experience. Turgot's ingenuity lay in his attempt to exploit the Cartesian separation of history from philosophy for the purpose of explaining the ubiquity of error in a world that was entirely progressive. But his generalization that all errors were instructive removed him from the more experimental tradition of Pascal, who emphasized the specific method of experimental science as the condition for the cumulative efficiency of inquiry. In experimental science larger, more general systems are developed from the smaller systems that have already been incorporated into the structure of science. In this process these smaller systems are corrected as they are enlarged, and consequently, if one wishes to stretch the term, one may, looking at them retrospectively, call them "errors," and speak of the progress of truth "over the ruins of 'false' opinions." But to speak of the usefulness of smaller systems, which have been incorporated into the structure of science, in the pursuit of truth is very different from speaking of the general "necessity" of errors that have not been part of the history of organized experimental inquiry. Was the opinion, for example, that the earth was flat a necessary prerequisite to the discovery that it is round?

Turgot's philosophy restated Fontenelle's observation that the history of science was marked by the progress of truth over the ruins of inadequate opinions. But Turgot went on to convert this empirical observation into a universal and necessary principle, affirming that every error was necessary for truth. In the last analysis, his philosophy of history contained the difficulties of any monistic theory which sees all events necessarily converging upon a single goal. There is a teleology in his theory, no less real because it is suppressed than the teleology of St. Augustine. The lines of continuity which we explore when we move back in time carry us out in many directions; to urge, as did Turgot, that they all necessarily converge suggests not only that they were all evaluated from one point of view, but that Turgot had an antecedent certainty that history has a single goal. Further, under what conditions might we test Turgot's hypothesis? An empirical test of the proposition that all events are progressive must permit of the possibility of a negative instance. But it is precisely the point of Turgot's theory to rule out such a possibility. Everything may be interpreted as progressive in the light of his *a priori* assurance concerning communication and continuity.

A monistic philosophy of history, as Turgot's illustrates, makes it difficult to make moral distinctions, and implicitly disparages the creative role of human will or intelligence in history. In the last analysis, Turgot had only two alternatives. On the basis of his monistic assumption that all human experience was continuous and cumulative, he could assert that we *must* learn from error, that progress was necessary: but the consequence of this alternative would be to make it impossible to apply a standard of progress to any specific case, because, since everything is defined *a priori* as progressive, it is impossible to distinguish between particular progressive and nonprogressive events. The second alternative was simply to depend on chance. For if progress depended on no specific condition such as the presence of a peculiar method, what guaranteed its continuation? What, apart from a *fortuitous chance,* or a providential concurrence of events, could guarantee that we should continue to learn from our errors?

Universal history was thus a grand unit, a course of events that took on significance in the light of a single, all-embracing goal towards which it moved inexorably. The coming together of Progress and Providence in the work of Turgot is so striking that one might hold him to be a rebel against the dominant empiricism, the growing naturalism, and the struggling secularism of his age. It would be wrong to imagine, however, that Turgot did not share the *philosophes'* excitement at the development of science, or that, because he held that Christianity was a "progressive force," he did not share the worldly values of his contemporaries. Turgot's philosophy marks a stage in the secularization of the idea of Providence. He held Christianity to be progressive because it had promoted and preserved science, and because it was an indispensable agent in the making of good citizens. Turgot's measures of progress, as they emerge at the end of his ***Second Discourse,*** are the degree to which the sciences are progressively unified, the extent to which they mark the quality of public enlightenment, and the degree to which their methods are made more efficient. These are Encyclopedic ideals.

Furthermore, Turgot attributed to the analytic method the same power as did his contemporaries—the power of undermining authority and its intellectual ally, the *esprit de système;* and his specific evaluations of particular historical events (such as despotism) were anything but the complacent reactions of a cosmic Tory. Turgot's view took on a critical, rather than apologetic, direction in his sporadic emphasis on the crucial significance of analysis as a continuous and critical refinement of grosser modes of communication. It was this idea of analysis as a working factor within and upon a culture that was seized upon by Condorcet. What obscured its significance in Turgot's philosophy was his disposition to hold that progress would take place in any case—a position that made the specific function of a cumulative and critical method seem relatively unimportant.

R. Grimsley (essay date 1952)

SOURCE: "Turgot's Article 'Existence' in the *Encyclopédie*," *The French Mind: Studies in Honour of Gustave Rudler,* Will Moore, Rhoda Sutherland, Enid Starkie, eds., Oxford at the Clarendon Press, 1952, pp. 126-51.

[*A native of England, Grimsley was a professor of French who wrote numerous books and articles on literature and philosophy. In this essay, he analyzes Turgot's "Existence," his article for the Encyclopédie, as a response to the epistemological problems that he confronted.*]

Turgot the political economist and social philosopher has tended to obscure the contributor to the *Encyclopédie*. His own insistence upon anonymity and his withdrawal from the enterprise after its official condemnation in 1759 are further reasons which help to explain this neglect. This paper is concerned with only one of his articles, the long one on **"Existence,"** published anonymously in 1756 in the sixth volume of the *Encyclopédie*. My purpose, moreover, is not to relate it to Turgot's general thought, but to give some account of it as the attempt of an eighteenth-century thinker to grapple with a specific philosophical problem. This effort is made more interesting by the fact that Turgot officially adhered to no 'school', though he was sympathetic to the progressive thought of his day.

After a brief verbal clarification of the meaning of the word 'existence', the article begins by indicating the main problems that are to be discussed. From the very first, insists Turgot, it is essential to distinguish between two important aspects of the question. There is, first of all, the task of psychological analysis or, as Turgot puts it, of deciding exactly 'what most men have in their minds when they use the word "existence" '. Once this has been established, it will be necessary to trace the history of the notion of 'existence' from its rudimentary origins to its most developed and abstract expression. This involves a further step, that of marking off 'existence' from 'subordinate notions' with which it is apt to be confused. The first part of the article follows these three divisions, namely, (i) the meaning of the everyday notion of existence in men's minds, (ii) its psychological history, (iii) the separation of 'existence' from 'subordinate notions' and its final definition. There still remains a second fundamental aspect of the question. Even when we have moved from an empirical starting-point, through a more rigorous psychological analysis, towards a philosophical definition, we are faced by what is perhaps a more genuinely philosophical question, namely, that of establishing proofs of the objectivity of the external world, or, as the article puts it, of examining 'the way we pass from the mere inner, passive impression of our sensations to the judgements we make about the actual existence of objects'.

Turgot insists that the best way of dealing with the first part of the problem is to begin with the Cartesian *cogito*. Now, although Descartes intended to provide a sure basis for all knowledge, the elementary truth contained in the *cogito, ergo sum* itself presupposed 'two very abstract notions the development of which was very difficult', namely, 'thought' and 'existence'. No such certainty as Descartes strove to establish can really be admitted until more is known about the actual thought-processes that make possible the postulation of the *cogito*. In other words, it is essential to understand 'the generation of ideas', that is, the psychological history of even the most abstract concepts. In Turgot's opinion, a sound starting-point for any attempt to find a correct answer to this problem has fortunately been provided by John Locke, who shows how all our ideas depend ultimately upon sense-experience. To understand an abstract concept we must see how it develops from 'sensations'. In this general position Turgot does not of course differ from many contemporary French thinkers. Already in 1746 Condillac's *Essai sur l'origine des connaissances humaines* had tried to show how the most abstract thinking is rooted in sense-experience, and these views had been further developed in the *Traité des systèmes* (1749) and the *Traité des sensations* (1754), this latter work having even attempted to show how belief in the external world emerges naturally from our sensations. In 1751 d'Alembert's 'Discours préliminaire' to the *Encyclopédie* had sought to account for the growth and interrelation of various branches of modern knowledge by tracing 'the generation of our ideas' in Locke's sense. The method of psychological analysis used by Turgot in his article was thus following well-established precedents.

Turgot explicitly ignores problems of the more remote psychological origin of concepts. He does not discuss, for example, the transformation of 'sensations' into 'ideas'. After indicating a point of difference between his own views and those of Condillac—whereas Condillac thinks that 'experience' is sufficient to draw out the notion of 'extension' from the interrelations of the sensations themselves, Turgot holds that sensations cannot by themselves account for such a notion—he is content to suppose that man 'must have known how to see before he learnt to reason and speak' and it is 'at this certain period of his existence that I begin to consider him'.

In order to reconstitute the more primitive types of experience we must temporarily suspend those reflective habits and processes which are the acquisition of later mental development. This means, in fact, that it is necessary to try and return to the level of 'pure sensation'. What is the effect of this reduction? 'On stripping him (man) of all that he has since acquired through the progress of his reflections, I see him, at whatever moment I take him, or rather I see myself, assailed by a crowd of sensations and images which are brought to me by each of the senses, and the combination of which presents me with a world of distinct objects.' The word 'objects' is apparently being used here as a purely descriptive term, the purpose of which is to indicate that our early psychic experience does in fact involve sensations having certain definite characteristics. As yet there is no question of discussing their ontological status. These 'primary sensations' are spread out before us, says Turgot, rather like the colours on a painter's canvas. We soon see that many of them are distinct from others and that they are at greater or lesser distances from one another, so that they appear as 'a certain number of contiguous points' forming an extended figure. We express this experience by saying that the sensations are to be located in some kind of three-dimensional space 'the different points of which they determine'. It is true that some

sensations like those of hearing and smell at first seem to resist such a description, but these too are eventually considered as being either near to or far from the sense-organs with which they are associated. This primary sense-experience may be said to consist of a 'crowd of sensations of colour, resistance, sound, &c., which are at various distances from one another and spread out in an indeterminate space like so many points, the conjunction and combination of which form a solid figure (in the geometrical sense), to which all our senses at once supply varied and indefinitely multiplied images'. If certain 'collections of points' are called 'objects' or 'individuals', this means simply that there are some 'masses of co-ordinated sensations' which have a more consistent pattern than others.

In addition to sensations relating directly to objects scattered in space, there is a second important group which is never present except in 'sensations of a certain type'. Such sensations are remarkable for their 'penetrating' power and for the fact that they are confined entirely 'within our body', so that 'though contained within very narrow limits when compared with the vast space in which the others are to be found', they 'attract our attention more than all the rest taken together'. This inner experience, which Turgot calls *tact intérieur* or *sixième sens,* is revealed through pain, hunger, thirst, the 'emotion accompanying every passion', in short, through 'this multitude of confused sensations which never abandon us and which, for this reason, some metaphysicians have called "the sense of our body's co-existence" '. This group is distinguished by two important characteristics, firstly, by its 'continual presence' (for without these sensations all the rest would disappear), and secondly, by 'the peculiar nature' of these sensations which become particularly intense in pleasure and pain and are 'never related to any other point in space'. We identify these sensations with an object 'which I later learn to call my *self* ' and, although this object is only one among the vast number constituting 'the great picture which forms the universe of ideas', the persistence and intensity of the sensations cause us to treat it as 'the centre of the whole universe' and as 'our own peculiar being'. Thus 'although the sensations which depict for us the moon and the stars are no more distinct from us than those which relate to our body, we look upon them as alien to us and we limit the feeling of the self to this little space which is circumscribed by pleasure and pain'.

It is through the interaction of these two groups of sensations that man arrives at an awareness of 'external' objects. The continual presence and the special intensity of one group cause us to separate it from those 'objects' which come and go and have varying relations with one another. Consequently, we come to look upon this less intimate and less persistent group as 'outside us', and in this way we come to an awareness of 'external' objects. (Whether or not the attribution of externality to such objects can be proved philosophically is of course another question, with which Turgot is not at the moment concerned.) Since, however, the perception of objects 'outside us' is accompanied by an awareness of the 'self ', we attribute the same degree of reality to each group of sensations, the external 'object' being as certainly present as the 'self '.

At this point Turgot recognizes that he still is far from the notion of 'existence' or even of 'presence' in the fullest sense, since we shall see that all objects are not immediately present to the self. However, the establishment of a distinction between the two groups has an important consequence. The first reaction of the 'self' is to seek those objects which bring pleasure and shun those which suggest pain. We are soon compelled to admit that the limits of our sensations are not those of the universe, since these basic reactions, though to some extent voluntary, can procure only a limited degree of satisfaction. The realization that there are definite obstacles to the satisfaction of our desires and that many painful sensations are unavoidable forces us to play the part of 'a pilot steering his craft on a sea strewn with rocks and covered with hostile vessels'. We are thus made aware of one aspect of man's place in nature as a creature who is 'encompassed, pressed, thwarted and jostled by every object'.

Further consideration of the metaphor of the pilot, which is not used, says the article, simply 'as an ornament', brings us to another point. Just as the pilot has to reckon with hidden reefs as well as with those he sees, so must we take into account not only immediate sensations but others which relate to objects that are not actually present. Sleep or the mere closing of our eyes is enough to assure us that 'objects are not annihilated simply because they have disappeared' and that the 'limits of our freedom are not those of the universe'. 'Whence is born a new order of things and a new intellectual world as vast as the world of sense-experience was limited'. This remarkable widening of our mental horizon is due mainly to the activity of our imagination and memory which enable us to think of objects when they are not immediately present. The anticipations and calculations of the imagination are, moreover, verified by 'experience', with the result that both absent and present objects are fully integrated into the 'general system of our desires, fears, motives and actions, and man, like the pilot, avoids and seeks objects which escape all his senses'.

We have now established between supposedly external objects and the consciousness of the self a relation which is no longer 'a mere simultaneous perception', since such objects are often 'not perceived at all', but a 'connexity which links together the changes of every object and our own sensations as the causes and effects of one another'. This means that we can clearly distinguish in thought between 'sensations' and 'objects', since, on the one hand, we are aware of 'present objects, that is, those contained within the limits of immediate sensation, and linked to self-consciousness through a simultaneous perception', and, on the other hand, 'absent objects, that is, those indicated solely through their effects, or through the memory of past sensations which we no longer see but which act on what we see through some chain of cause and effect; which we should see if they were placed in a suitable position and at a suitable distance, and which other beings like ourselves perhaps do see at this very moment'. The constant relation of this new type of sensations and the consciousness of the self means that absent objects are held to possess the same degree of reality as those which are present.

We have now reached a stage where we can point to at least three groups of sensations: those relating to the self, those immediate sensations relating to a 'perceived' world, and those which, though deemed to be related to a 'perceived' world because they too are 'spread out in space', are not directly present. A consideration of the last two groups has also caused us to separate the idea of 'sensation' and that of 'object'. Moreover, in the whole of this development, self-consciousness has played a particularly important role. In spite of this progress, it is important to make a reservation, for 'neither the mere sensation of present objects, nor the imagination's depiction of absent objects, nor the mere relation of distance and reciprocal action, common to both, are precisely what the mind would like to denote by the noun "existence"; it is upon the very basis of these relations, a basis which is assumed to be common to the self, the perceived object, and the merely distant object, that the noun "existence" and our own affirmation really fall when we say that a thing exists'. Although we suppose that the different groups of sensations and objects have a 'common basis', an essential reservation must be made, for 'this common basis is not and cannot be immediately known', as it is indicated only through 'the different relations which presuppose it'. In other words, we first of all abstract a certain 'idea' from the consciousness of those sensations which relate immediately to ourselves and then 'we convey, so to speak, this self-consciousness to external objects, by a kind of vague assimilation, which is immediately belied by a separation from all that characterizes the self, but which is nevertheless sufficient to become the basis of an abstraction or common sign, and to be the object of our judgements'.

In a sense, therefore, we can say that the concept of existence is the same whether it is attached to the 'objects' of sensations or imaginatively extended to 'objects' which are not immediately present, for it is always contained—in its origins at least—within 'the consciousness of the more or less generalized self'. Turgot thinks that his point can be supported by reference to the psychology of children who 'lend feeling to all they see' and of primitive man who is 'inclined to extend intelligence and sensibility to the whole of nature'. These tendencies are to be explained by the simple process of conferring upon objects seen outside us what we 'immediately experience concerning ourselves'. Later distinctions, such as that established between, say, animate and inanimate objects, are due to the abstraction of intelligence and feeling from the general concept which corresponds to the total experience. This constitutes a repetition of what we have already seen to be operative at a lower level: at first we did not clearly distinguish our own sensations from those relating to objects other than ourselves and, even when the distinction had been made, we still clung to the idea of a common basis for the self and the 'world'. This experience was further widened by the action of the memory and the imagination which compelled us to realize that the world could not be limited to immediate sensation but must include 'the relation of distance and activity generalized by the imagination and conveyed from objects of immediate sensation to other supposed objects'. The result of this process is that the notion of existence is freed from dependence on sensation, which no longer remains important in its own right but only as the 'sign of a presence, i. e. of a particular case comprised within the general concept of existence'.

The importance of distinguishing the notion of existence from subordinate notions includes a consideration not only of 'presence' but of various 'illusions of the senses' and 'vagaries' of the imagination. The difficulty of such 'illusions' is that they usually have the same sensory features as the supposedly 'real' world. Experience alone can help us to separate the two orders and attribute 'existence' to one of them only. Through experience we notice that there are certain 'pictures' which appear with a relative fixity of order and pattern, whereas other impressions are 'absolutely transient' and have 'no permanent effect' and 'no power to inspire fear or desire or serve as motives for our behaviour'. Ultimately the test of the 'reality' of any particular group of sensations will be the possibility or impossibility of establishing a relation between the sense-experience and the 'permanent self-consciousness, which supposes a basis outside the self'. In this way we distinguish 'existing' objects from 'merely apparent' objects, between 'reality' and 'illusion'. The basic principle remains the way in which the sensations accord with the 'general system of already known beings'. This rule is also enough to put us on our guard against cases where the 'vivacity of the images and the lack of points of comparison would have made error inevitable', as in dreams and delirium, as well as in cases of optical illusions.

If we take into account the attitude and experience of the ordinary man (and it is with him that the whole inquiry began) we shall find that he is not disturbed by the subtle distinctions established by 'modern philosophers' between 'sensations' and the 'objects they represent' or by the knowledge that 'sensations are only modifications of our soul' (an allusion to Condillac), for he is content to solve the problem of 'existence' and 'illusion' solely by reference to 'practical' consequences. 'Experience alone' is sufficient to direct 'even the least philosophical man' towards the 'real order of things' and, when no practical inconvenience results from so doing, he readily identifies 'sensations' and 'objects'. Confusion is sometimes produced by this attitude, but, generally speaking, since we find that 'our fears, desires and movement' are always directed upon the 'movement and distance' of objects, the mind thereby learns to make a complete separation of 'sensation' and 'existence', as well as of 'presence' and 'existence'.

This widening of the concept of existence through the differentiation of 'existence' and various 'subordinate notions' is further facilitated by the development of the time-sense. The temporal aspect of the world is brought to our attention by the 'destruction, death and annihilation' of sensory objects. The continual disappearance of certain groups of sensations and the appearance and reappearance of others means that 'we see beings succeed one another like our thoughts'. Turgot is not here interested in discussing the problem of time in itself, but he wants to emphasize that, through the memory, we are able to assign to objects a fixed place in duration as well as in extension. Memory and imagination, which we have already seen to be so important in freeing us from dependence upon immediate sensation, enable us to go beyond mere sensation in a tem-

poral as well as a spatial sense. This means also that the role of our self-consciousness, which had hitherto been so important, gradually loses its significance as our experience of 'objects' is extended in space and time. In fact, what finally happens is that 'we are compelled to detach the notion of existence from all relationship with ourselves'. 'We are compelled to lose sight of ourselves and, in order to attribute "existence" to objects, to consider nothing but their connexion with the total system of beings, the existence of which is, as a matter of fact, known to us only through their relation to our own existence, but which is none the less independent of it, and which will none the less exist when we exist no longer.' The function of our existence in relation to objects consists chiefly in determining their temporal aspect. While we ourselves are one of the 'terms' to which the whole 'chain of present relations' is connected, those objects 'exist'. We say that they 'have existed' when, in order to establish their connexion with the present system, it is necessary to go back from their effects to their causes. On the other hand, we say that they 'will exist' if we have to go from causes to effects—whence the idea of existence as 'past', 'present', or 'future', according to its relation to 'different points of duration'.

Whatever the temporal aspect of objects, their existence cannot be 'certified' unless it establishes some relationship, whether directly through sensation or indirectly through cause and effect, with our self-consciousness. Now although this may be necessary for us to be able to say that a particular object exists, we cannot thereby deny the existence of objects which have not been certified in this way. This becomes clearer still when we realize that the establishment of cause and effect involves consideration of many objects 'with which we are acquainted only for a very small part of their duration and which may never even come to our knowledge'. There arises in this way an area of 'uncertainty' which gives way to the idea of possibility. Although possibility does not exclude existence, 'it does not necessarily contain it'. 'A possible thing which exists is an actual thing; thus every actual thing is existent (and every existing thing is actual), although *existence* and *actualité* are not two perfectly synonymous terms, because that of *existence* is absolute, while that of *actualité* is correlative of possibility.'

So far our inquiry has been concerned with developing the notion of existence as it is to be found in the 'minds of most men' and the way in which it has been formed by 'a series of more and more general abstractions'. But, insists Turgot, 'we have not yet followed it to that point of abstraction and generality to which philosophy has brought it'. We have indeed seen how the *sentiment du moi* which is the 'source of the notion of existence' has been transferred by 'abstraction' to sensations and objects which are 'outside us'. The feeling of the self is thus generalized in such a way that it is conveyed from mere objects of sensation to 'all those effects which indicate any relation of distance and activity with ourselves'. This is usually sufficient for the 'ordinary uses of life'. 'Philosophy alone needs to take some further steps, although it has only to follow the same road.' This final step was, moreover, already suggested by Turgot's emphasis upon the necessity of extending the notion of existence from its immediate connexion with ourselves and objects to the 'connexion with the system of which we form part'. There still remains an indirect relation between objects and ourselves, but we are not an essential part of the 'general system which has certainly existed before us and will continue to exist when we are gone'. Since, moreover, the relation of this system with ourselves is not a necessary condition of its existence, why should we not suppose that 'other entirely similar systems may exist in the vast realm of space, isolated from one another, without any reciprocal action' and having as their sole relationship the fact that they exist in the same space. Though we do not 'conceive of them', who has given us the right to deny their existence and establish our own ideas as 'the limit of the universe'? It is this last question which leads Turgot to the final stage of his analysis. By what right, he asks, do we make sensation the criterion of existence? By what right, for example, do we suppose that the type of sensation 'which gives us evidence of our own bodies' is a surer guide for fixing their position in space than the 'sensation which gives us evidence of the stars and which, necessarily distorted by aberration, makes us always see them where they are not'? 'Now if it is possible for the self, the consciousness of which is the sole source of the notion of existence, not to exist, how should this notion necessarily contain a relationship of distance (*rapport de distance*) with us?' In other words, the very fact of our being able to raise these questions is a sufficient reason for completely separating the notion of existence from all dependence on ourselves. 'Then the notion of existence will be as abstract as possible, and will have no other sign than the word "existence" itself; this word will not correspond to any idea in the senses or the imagination, unless it be the consciousness of the self, but generalized and separated from all that characterizes not only the self, but even all the objects to which it may have been conveyed by abstraction.'

> I know (concludes Turgot) that this generalization contains a real contradiction, but every abstraction is in the same position, and that is why the generality of abstractions is never anywhere except in signs (and not in things): the notion of existence being made up of no other particular idea than that of self-consciousness itself, which is necessarily a simple idea, being moreover applicable to all beings without exception, this word cannot, strictly speaking, be defined and it is enough to show by what steps it has been possible to form the notion indicated by it.

Turgot then turns to his final problem in a section entitled 'proofs of the existence of external objects'. He puts the well-known difficulty of sensationalist theories in his first paragraph. Since such phenomena as the reflection and refraction of light, optical illusions, and dreams show that we may experience sensations without there being any corresponding object, why should we not suppose that all our sensations exist without 'objects'? This difficulty becomes all the greater when we recall that all these supposed objects are never given directly but always through the medium of our sensations.

He points out that for ordinary men the problem does not arise, since they assume from the very outset that they are in immediate contact with objects, mistakes being attri-

buted not to 'false judgement' (as they ought to be) but to a belief that 'false and deceptive images' have taken the place of the 'object'. The 'common experience of life' shows such a marked correspondence between the 'order of sensations' and the 'order of things' that such an error 'becomes, so to speak, natural and involuntary'. 'We must not therefore be surprised that most men cannot imagine that there is any need to prove the existence of objects.' It is only philosophers who have realized that 'their judgements and sensations light upon two very different orders of things and that they have felt the whole difficulty of setting their judgement upon a solid basis'.

One way out of the difficulty is that of the 'immaterialists', who have denied the existence of objects altogether, and Turgot mentions in this connexion the 'Indian philosophers' and especially 'the famous bishop of Cloyne, Dr. Berkeley, who is known by a large number of works, all of which are full of wit and odd ideas, and who by his dialogues of Hylas and Philonous has recently drawn the attention of metaphysicians to this forgotten system'. 'Most people have found it quicker to despise him than to answer him, and that was indeed easier.'

Although Turgot reserves a detailed reply to Berkeley for a later article (on 'Immatérialisme', which he never wrote), he here contents himself with pointing out how necessary it is to refute him and with calling attention to 'the only type of proofs' capable of demonstrating the existence not merely of objects but of 'all that is not contained within immediate sensation'. He devotes a long paragraph to an enumeration of the difficulties inherent in any assumption that we have direct knowledge of objects. He argues that, since sensation is the result of a complex series of events starting from the supposed object and terminating in our minds, the idea of any immediate knowledge of objects may at once be eliminated. We cannot rely even on the activity of our sense-organs and nerve-impulses, since they may be stimulated when no object is present. Moreover, what reason is there to suppose that the 'stimulation of our organs is the only possible cause of our sensations'? To attempt to attribute greater certainty to those sensations which relate directly to the body is equally mistaken, for why should we suppose that pleasure and pain are safer indications of the presence of a 'body' than the testimony of, say, the sense which attributes colour to physical objects? Finally Turgot rejects the arguments of those who see in our natural 'inclination' to believe in the existence of objects evidence of their actual existence, since such an inclination may be due simply to a mistaken habit. He concludes that 'no sensation can immediately and by itself assure us of the existence of any object'.

There is, in Turgot's opinion, only one way to escape 'from this kind of prison in which nature holds us shut up and isolated in the midst of all things'. We must rely on the 'induction which extricates itself from effects in order to go back to causes'. Thus 'evidence'—'the source of all historical certainty'—and the 'monuments' confirming this evidence are merely 'phenomena' which are explained by the supposition of a 'historical fact'. In physics, such phenomena as the movement of mercury through air-pressure, the path of the heavenly bodies, the daily movement of the earth 'and its yearly motion around the sun', and the 'gravitation of bodies' are 'so many facts which are proved only by the exact concordance of the supposition made about them with observed phenomena'. Now, although our sensations are not and cannot be 'substances existing outside us' and although 'present sensations are not and cannot be past sensations', they still remain facts demanding explanation. 'If we go back from these facts to their causes, we are forced to admit a system of intelligent and corporal beings existing outside us, and a series of sensations preceding immediate sensation and linked to the previous state of the system of existing beings; these two things, the existence of external beings and our past experience, will rest upon the sole type of proofs to which they are susceptible, for, since present sensation is the only immediate certain things, everything that is not this sensation can acquire no other certainty than that which goes back from the effect to its cause.'

We can go back from effect to cause in two ways: we may say either that any given effect is the necessary result of a single cause; or else this effect may be produced by several causes. In the first case, there is a direct correlation between the certainty of the cause and its effect. It is on this principle that we base the reasoning of a statement like 'something exists, therefore it has existed from all eternity'. The metaphysical proofs of God's existence have a similar foundation. Scientific problems make use of the same principle, as we see from a consideration of 'recognized hypotheses' concerning 'the known laws of nature'. 'It is thus that, given the laws for the fall of heavy bodies, the speed which a falling body acquires is a conclusive indication of the height from which it has fallen.'

The other method, which involves 'going back from known effects to an unknown cause', has to treat nature like a 'riddle' which must be solved by intelligent guessing. In this case we have 'to imagine successively one or several hypotheses, follow them in their consequences, compare them with the circumstances of the phenomenon, and try them out on the facts', just as we verify a seal by 'applying it to its imprint'. 'Such', concludes our author, 'are the bases of the art of deciphering, of the criticism of facts, and of physics; and since neither external objects nor past facts have with present sensation any connexion the necessity of which may be proved, they are the only possible bases for any certainty about the existence of external objects and of our past existence.'

Although a detailed examination of the sources of the article **"Existence"** does not fall within the scope of this paper, it may be useful to indicate in conclusion some of its main philosophical trends. A lack of complete consistency between these different tendencies is explained not only by the character of eighteenth-century thought as a whole, with its combination of empiricist and rationalist influences, but also by the fact that Turgot was a comparatively young philosopher when he wrote the article (he was barely twenty-nine in the year of its publication) and that, far from committing himself to a particular doctrine, he deliberately tried to assimilate what he thought was best in different schools of thought.

Turgot's early reference to Descartes suggests a general starting-point and method rather than an adherence to specific Cartesian doctrines. It was, moreover, an attitude readily acceptable to eighteenth-century empiricists who substituted, as has frequently been pointed out, *sentio* for cogito and rejected 'innate ideas' in favour of 'sensations'. Both rationalists and empiricists linked up the problem of real being with that of our own being, although a totally different emphasis was naturally given to the problem by thinkers who accepted the necessity of a *cogito*-analysis but rejected the metaphysical conclusions to which Descartes himself thought it inevitably led. The great importance assigned by Turgot to self-consciousness as the basis of the wider notion of existence perhaps gives a Cartesian flavour to much of his article, but a closer examination reveals that for him consciousness is characterized by sensation rather than thought. There is no mention of a cleavage between mind and matter, and the only dualism admitted by his psychological analysis is the one existing between two groups of sensations, those of inner and outer experience. This, moreover, involves only a difference of intensity and not of quality or substance. It would appear that, in Turgot's view, the wider notion of 'existence' is capable of clarification only on the assumption that there is a certain identity of being between the nature of consciousness and that of the 'world'. Cartesian dualism, therefore, seems to be explicitly rejected. In a more general sense, however, Turgot's final appeal to the causal principle implies that he assigned definite limits to a strict sensationalism. His acceptance of causation as a principle that is not capable of immediate empirical observation suggests the attitude of a thinker who did not doubt the power of reason to bridge any apparent gap between the conclusions of philosophical analysis and those of common sense. Although Turgot's use of causation is not in itself Cartesian, as I shall try to show, it is a principle that is developed without difficulty in an atmosphere still permeated by the general spirit of Cartesian rationalism.

Once the necessity of starting with the *cogito* has been admitted Turgot hastens to rectify the inadequacy of the Cartesian analysis by examining the notion of 'existence' in the light of Locke's empiricism. An early insistence on the need for basing a thorough psychological analysis on sensations and not on 'innate ideas' or *a priori* metaphysical concepts clearly shows, as Turgot explicitly acknowledges, the presence of Locke's influence. Indeed, without Locke the whole article could never have been written. However, the more rigorously 'sensationalist' character of Turgot's analysis, which allows, for example, little place to Locke's 'ideas of reflection' in shaping the early development of the notion of existence, reminds us of Condillac, the one short reference to whom (and that to note a divergence of views) probably does not represent the true extent of Turgot's debt. Since the *Traité des Sensations* was published at the time when Turgot must have been actually writing or at least meditating his article (1754), some preoccupation with Condillac's views was quite natural. Moreover, as Condillac's work was partly intended as a stricter and more systematic application of Locke's principles than Locke himself had been able to give, it is not always easy or (for my immediate purpose) necessary to separate the two influences. In many respects Turgot's article appears to be an attempt to apply Condillac's method of psychological analysis to the development of a particular 'notion'.

Several considerations, however, seem to indicate that it is Condillac's method rather than his doctrines which exerted an influence on Turgot's thought. Whereas, for example, Condillac was especially interested in the development of the human 'faculties' and the way they produce 'ideas', Turgot is mainly concerned with elucidating the meaning of a 'notion'. He agrees that the method of psychological analysis is the only way of dealing with this problem, but concludes that in itself such a method cannot overcome the strictly philosophical difficulty, namely, that of establishing the objective validity of the 'notion' examined. Even at the more elementary psychological level Turgot seems to be aware of certain difficulties in the sensationalist position. He refuses to follow Condillac in attributing the notion of 'extension' entirely to the activity of sensations. His discussion of the problem of the external world reveals an even more fundamental disagreement. Condillac had insisted that the sense of touch was primarily responsible for a valid belief in the external world and that this sense, during the course of psychological development, 'taught' the other senses to make judgements about external objects. It was, therefore, unnecessary to go beyond the content of our inner consciousness in order to justify belief in the external world. Now although, at the phenomenalist level, Turgot shows how the belief in an external world emerges from the interplay of the sensations, he refuses to accept this fact as a proof of objective validity. That is why he makes use of a non-sensationalist principle (causality) to free us from imprisonment by immediate sense-experience. This new development implies therefore, that in Turgot's eyes Condillac's position has not overcome the dangers of idealism.

Turgot felt far more acutely than Condillac the force of Berkeley's criticism of Locke's representationalism. One probable explanation of this is that Turgot had been preoccupied by the problem of Berkeley's 'Dialogues' as early as 1750, whereas Condillac was made aware of certain difficulties in his own position only after Diderot's *Lettre sur les Aveugles* (1749) had drawn his attention to the dangers of idealism and urged him to undertake a refutation of Berkeley. Having already laid down the basic principles of his philosophy, Condillac did not think that this new difficulty demanded a radical modification of his principles, but only adaptation and refinement. Turgot, on the other hand, had taken far more seriously the difficulties of a sensationalism which can help us to clarify the meaning of a 'notion' by showing us how we acquire it, of what 'ideas' it is compounded, and even how it is extended to the 'world' around us, but which nevertheless still fails to prove the objective validity of the 'notion' with which it deals. To say that the world exists is not to say simply that man experiences sensations of a certain kind, for 'sensations', however vivid, give no proof of the reality of the 'object' to which they refer.

A very similar difficulty is implied in Turgot's admission that to interpret genuine abstractions solely on the basis of descriptive psychological analysis involves a 'real contradiction'. Since Turgot follows contemporary thought in

thinking that perception must always be of particulars, he is confronted by the problem of remaining within the sphere of empirical inquiry and yet accounting for abstractions. His solution consists, as we have seen, in attributing the reality of abstractions to 'signs' and not to 'things'. All that can be done with an abstract 'notion' is to show from what simple 'ideas' it is evolved. Turgot examines, for example, how existence develops from the 'simple idea' of self-consciousness as revealed through sensations and then admits that no exact definition is possible. This no doubt explains why the notion of a 'more or less generalized self' is rather vague and unsatisfactory, for what precise meaning can be attached to an idea which is 'simple' and yet so 'generalized' that it is no longer to be explained in terms of psychological data relating to either inner or outer sense?

Turgot tries to remedy the deficiencies of psychological analysis by using the principle of causality. He holds that causality is involved in all forms of knowledge which go beyond immediate sensation; it is involved not only in particular beliefs like that in the external world, but in the conclusions of psychology, history, science, and metaphysics. The proof of God's existence which argues back from the existence of something now to the existence of something from all eternity is not different in kind from a physical law like that of gravitation. In each case there is an inductive process which goes back from empirical phenomena to another 'fact' necessarily presupposed by them, though not directly observable. Both 'God' and the 'force of attraction' are 'facts'—not abstract *a priori* principles—the reality of which must be assumed in order for us to be able to account for phenomena which can be related in no other way. In every case a 'cause' must be carefully related to its empirical 'effects', even when the complexity of those effects makes it necessary to use 'guessing' and 'conjecturing'. This use of causality, the exact nature of which is not defined, suggests that Turgot was here trying to adopt and extend to all branches of knowledge the Newtonian method of scientific reasoning. That he was interested in scientific problems is clear from the long article on **"Expansibilité"** as well as an earlier (1748) Newton-inspired criticism of Buffon. Since, moreover, one of his teachers at the Collège de Bourgogne, the abbé Sigorgne, had been a keen supporter of Newton's views, it is not surprising that meditation upon scientific problems should have led Turgot to find in Newtonian science a principle that could be given far more extended use than a mere application to problems of physics.

The article **"Existence"** shows, therefore, a certain complexity of philosophical influences—Descartes, Locke, Condillac, Berkeley, and Newton. To these names ought probably to be added that of d'Alembert, who developed (though more elaborately) a form of 'scientific positivism' which in many ways resembles Turgot's approach, and who may have exerted some direct personal influence. This, however, is a question that would need more detailed examination than is possible here. It will perhaps be sufficient for my immediate purpose to indicate the general pattern of the main tendencies already examined. The influence of Locke and Condillac had been strong enough to make Turgot develop the Cartesian starting-point in a firmly empiricist sense. Acquaintance with Berkeley's 'Dialogues', however, revealed considerable difficulties in the empiricist position, especially in the problem of establishing proof of the external world. Turgot overcame the dilemma by making general use of the principle of causality as used in Newtonian science. He thus escaped Hume's difficulty—the impossibility of proving the existence of causation on strictly empirical grounds. Although Dilthey [*Sitzungsberichte der Berliner Akademie*] was justified in seeing Hume, Turgot, and d'Alembert as three precursors of positivism, neither Turgot nor d'Alembert experienced any uneasiness on this fundamental point, for both of them thought that the causal principle could be easily contained within the framework of empiricism.

The general pressure of his eighteenth-century background was, of course, too great for Turgot to have discussed his subject in any 'existentialist' sense. Curiously enough, however, Turgot's initial criticism of Descartes' cogito is the same as that made in our own day by Professor Karl Jaspers [*Descartes und die Philosophie,* 1937]. For both philosophers the Cartesian position fails to take into account the full meaning of 'existence'. Turgot tries to fill this lacuna by a psychological analysis which is concerned mainly with sensations. Professor Jaspers, on the other hand, says that Descartes was not a radical doubter, but a thinker whose doubt reflected a predetermined certainty that excluded the deeper aspects of human existence in favour of an impersonal 'scientific' or 'metaphysical' principle. Professor Jaspers would probably condemn the 'sensationalist' method for the same reason, because, in spite of its avowed intention to be more 'real' than its predecessors, it did not probe the deeper level of personal existence. The 'existentialist' inadequacy of the article **"Existence"** would be explained by the optimism of the eighteenth-century thinker who, with his faith in nature, reason, and humanity, had no occasion to experience the 'anguish' of our own age. Since man was separated from happiness only by his ignorance and stupidity, there seemed no reason why, in Turgot's words, 'the very foundations of philosophy' should not be uncovered by means of the intellectual tools which were at the disposal of every 'enlightened' thinker.

Frank E. Manuel   (essay date 1962)

SOURCE: "Turgot, Baron de l'Aulne: The Future of Mind," *The Prophets of Paris,* Cambridge Mass.: Harvard University Press, 1962, pp. 11-15.

[*A historian with a specialty in European intellectual history of the eighteenth and nineteenth centuries, Manuel includes among his many publications,* The Age of Reason *(1951) and* The Eighteenth Century Confronts the Gods *(1959). In the following excerpt, he describes the mechanics of Turgot's theory of progress.*]

Turgot's philosophy of progress is firmly rooted in the current sensationalist theory of knowledge. The capacity of man to receive new impressions from the outside world, to combine them, and to reflect upon them was an ultimate assurance of the inevitable and indefinite advancement of the human mind. Sheer accumulation of experi-

ence in time was the underlying process of the education of mankind, as it was for the child. In the primordial stages of historical development the motives of human beings are nakedly passionate and they partake of almost no reflective elements. Men are goaded into action by their pains and their pleasures, their lusts and their necessities, their hunger, their thirst for power and conquest. Only in the latter days of Enlightenment have rational forces begun to assume direction of world history.

This recognition of the predominance of the passionate rather than the rational element in the history of mankind raised for Turgot a problem common to most exponents of temporal teleologies: how could a being who to the ordinary observer has acted primarily, if not solely, out of passion, whose conduits open to the external world are mere sensation, ever achieve a transcendent destiny called Reason? Turgot's man, though created by God, is bound by the laws of the Locke-Condillac epistemology, and within this framework he must accomplish his historic mission—become a civilized moral being living up to the standards of eighteenth-century Christian Stoicism; exert ever greater control over nature through technology; acquire and preserve beyond the possibilities of destruction an increasing body of knowledge about himself and about the physical world; achieve and sustain a measure of artistic creativity.

In most of their writings the *philosophes,* and Turgot among them, prided themselves on their emancipation from the *esprit de système* which they associated with scholasticism and the secular philosophical system-builders of the seventeenth century. They were confident of the purity of their empirical method; they looked only at the facts. But often enough the categorical denial of innate ideas or a priori axioms was only a preparatory device which preceded a dogmatic affirmation of innate sentiments or principles of behavior. Western thought has experienced its greatest difficulties in driving out the demon of the absolute; if he was exorcised from the mind he sought refuge in feelings. Thus Rousseau, for example, in his *Discourse on Inequality,* invented the tragic "instinct" of perfectibility to explain man's unfortunate emergence from the lowest stage of the state of nature. Turgot posited a similar principle, which, though he shunned the word rendered odious by Locke, was virtually "innate." There is for Turgot a basic drive in human nature to innovate, to create novelty, to bring into being new combinations of sensations. And once this novelty-making impulse has been assumed, rock-bottom has been reached. One either accepts or rejects it.

Simultaneously Turgot identified in civilized society a hostile negating principle which, through the operation of institutions, had always sought to stall man in the rut of sameness, in a routine, in a state of treadmill repetitiveness. World history turned into a war eternal between these polar principles. In depicting the struggle, Turgot was of course no indifferent bystander, for the battle between the spirit of novelty and the spirit of routine, between the desire for movement and the tendency toward quiescence, was the underlying conflict of human destiny, a new philosophical version of the religious war between good and evil.

This idea of innovation remained the basic new concept in Turgot's view of the historical world. Traditional society had accepted a changeless state of being as the greatest good. In the most ancient documents of Near Eastern civilization the plea to the gods for an enduring order was the prayer behind the quest for peace. When Messianism with its foretelling of a great transformation appeared in Judaic and Christian history its promise of a radical metamorphosis had invariably been considered a dangerous disruptive agent by the rulers of society. With an acute sense of self-preservation institutionalized religions have always fought the millenarians. Change of the earthly order and a prediction of the change were equally disturbing. Was not the proclamation of the Jubilee of 1300 an attempt to smother under an official garment the strange stadial prognostications of the followers of Joachim of Flora? Even in war and in conquest traditionalist societies invariably aimed at establishing a stable, enduring, even immutable order. Turgot may have considered himself a devoted servant of the French monarchy, but no principle was more inimical to its preservation than his absolute commitment to eternal change and perfectibility.

By raising the spirit of novelty to the level of a major passion of human nature, Turgot established a fundamental distinction between the physical and the moral sciences, one which was increasingly emphasized as the eighteenth century passed its halfway mark. In this Socratic age, along with deep respect for the new physics there were real misgivings about man's complete immersion in the universe of the natural philosophers. The eighteenth-century moralist, though fascinated by the Newtonian world-machine, a model he longed to imitate, was not without hidden doubts about its applicability to the social sciences. The facile analogy between the movement of the spheres obeying the law of gravity and a harmony in human relationships that would reflect the natural order, a frequent correspondence, was not always convincing. A number of major eighteenth-century thinkers, though committed to the principle of the existence of moral scientific laws, dwelt upon the differences as well as the similarities between the two orders of nature and of man. Vico's *Scienza Nuova* was a deliberate attack upon preoccupation with the laws of matter, the lesser element, to the neglect and abandonment of the laws of men and nations which had their own peculiar character. Vico had made a great show of contrasting the loftier, nobler truths of his new science of history and human experience with the more limited certainty of the mathematical world of the Cartesians—a paradox to the average intellectual of the age. Rousseau, following up his earlier attack on the arts and sciences, had shouted a challenge in his *Second Discourse:* "It is of Man that I shall speak"—and he meant that he was again dealing with human problems, not the laws of nature and the achievements of technology, even though in the next breath he rendered obeisance to the Newtonian image. By contrast, Montesquieu's great masterpiece of mid-century Enlightenment was still written in the shadow of the old subservience to Newtonian physics, and his model was basically mechanistic; the good polity was subject to techni-

cal breakdown because of a failure to operate in accordance with its true character, and the genius legislator by fathoming the spirit of a nation's laws could effect a restoration, set the machine working once more so that it might continue its orderly revolutions. "Ed io anche son pittore," Montesquieu had affirmed without modesty before the unveiling of his fundamental law of climate, the equivalent of universal gravity in physics. Turgot drew upon Montesquieu for factual information, but he abjured the slavish patterning of the science of man after the science of physics. Though far from emancipated from mechanical imagery, he introduced another dimension: if the physical order expressed its innermost being in the principle of recurrence, the human order had a unique principle all its own, an antithetic principle—Progress. While Turgot rarely used organismic similes, he was already affirming the intrinsically different nature of the world of men, in which the repetitive movements were far outstripped by the novelties.

The order of men was an endless innovation. But the new was not a mere fortuitous alignment and realignment of elements in the Epicurean manner. In human events real, lasting, and enduring novelty was being created. The new configuration brought about by each successive age was not merely a replacement of one set of forms by another, nor was it only a rectification of an old structure. There was a process of eternal transmission, an ever-growing accumulation, an increasing inheritance, a sort of vast worldly repository of intellectual merit. The variations brought forth in history were additive, and the piling up of new experience was the law of mankind. Civilized man was distinguished from the savage and from the child precisely because he had recorded more diverse and complex combinations—the language of Locke's epistemology.

The constancy of the physical order had so ravished men's minds in the eighteenth century that the apparently accidental and chaotic human order had begun to appear inferior. Turgot's idea of progress, by sharply distinguishing the human order and discovering in it a relative superiority, re-established its faltering status. In this discovery there was an admixture of Christian apology and humanism. Mankind was vindicated, was restored to a central position in a separate historical world, and was granted a quality which no other part of the natural order could pretend to possess. Man was also rescued from the Epicurean view of the world, which had many somber attractions for the eighteenth-century philosophical historian. While Turgot's historical universe could not boast the obvious constancy of physical nature where events repeated themselves, it was blessed with a more sublime rule of constancy, the extraordinary law of steady perfectibility. Sameness and repetition, the very attributes which men contemplated with admiration in nature, were evil if they long endured in the world of men. Constant inconstancy, eternal change and progress, were the true distinctions of mankind.

The opening periods of the *Tableau philosophique des progrès successifs de l'esprit humain,* the second Sorbonique, contrasted the rival virtues of the two orders: "The phenomena of nature, subject to constant laws, are enclosed in a circle of revolutions which are always the same. Everything is reborn, everything perishes, and through successive generations in which vegetation and animal life reproduce themselves time merely restores at each instant the image which it has caused to disappear.

"The succession of men, however, presents a changing spectacle from century to century. Reason, the passions, liberty, produce new events without end. All ages are linked to each other by a series of causes and effects which binds the present state of the world with all those which have preceded it. The conventional signs of language and writing, affording men the means of assuring the possession of their ideas and of communicating them to others, have fashioned of all detailed forms of knowledge a common treasury, which one generation transmits to another like a legacy that is ever being augmented with the discoveries of each century, and thus the human race, considered from its beginnings, appears to the eyes of a philosopher to be one immense whole which, like every individual, has its infancy and its progress."

Turgot's conception of the progressive accumulation of knowledge through time, particularly in the physical sciences, was hardly an unheralded novelty by the mid-eighteenth century. Roger Bacon probably had at least an inkling of the idea. Francis Bacon's *Novum Organum* and Bernard Fontenelle's *Digression sur les anciens et les modernes*, written incident to the famous literary "quarrel," have been recognized as respect-worthy antecedents. Passages in Descartes and particularly Pascal's *Fragment de préface sur le traité du vide* were forerunners insofar as they conceived of the accretion of scientific truth through the mere performance and recording of new experiments over the centuries. Turgot's theory rested upon a far broader concept. In contrast to Pascal's severe restriction of the idea to the physical sciences, accompanied by tortured doubts about the meaning of this progress to man's moral and religious nature, Turgot extended progress to virtually the whole realm of being and implanted it as the central shaft of a system of worldly morality.

Turgot's theory mirrored a profound revolution in man's attitude toward change which in the eighteenth century imposed itself with ever greater force in western European society and was soon to conquer the world. He had a pervasive psychological horror of the static, his friends have reported, and in public office he was always impatient of any curbs on his zeal reform and rearrange whatever ancient practices came within his jurisdiction. In a playful couplet Voltaire said that Turgot did not quite know what he wanted but he was sure it would be something different. In violent rebellion against traditionalist society, as chief minister of Louis XVI he spearheaded its disruption with new ways of thought and new methods of action. He seemed to revel in its break-up. Turgot had an almost twentieth-century sense of the rapid flux of events, a succession of changes so fast that it was almost impossible to grasp the meaning of a stable structure. In the "Plan d'un ouvrage sur la géographie politique" he expressed this feeling in a brilliant *aperçu*. "Before we have learned that things are in a given situation they have already been altered several times. Thus we always become aware of

events when it is too late, and politics has to foresee the present, so to speak."

In the plan of the second discourse at the Sorbonne, *movement* was described as the primordial force which dispelled chaos. Only through movement had men acquired ideas of distinctiveness and of unity. If an innate sense of movement were not an aspect of human nature, men would have contented themselves with mere sensation and they would never have established differences. If they did not synthesize new combinations of feelings to yield novel reflections, they would have gone on perceiving the same things without change forever throughout history. Fortunately movement had always thrust objects into fresh relationships. Wars, migrations, catastrophes, had made discoveries possible by allowing for unprecedented confluences of events. If man were not submitted to such violent stimuli, Turgot saw him lapsing into a state of somnolence and barren decay followed by death. In Vico's doctrine the energizing drive had to be roused by necessity. Surely Turgot's early man—and perhaps man in all ages—has to be provoked and excited to produce new ideas, to assimilate new juxtapositions of phenomena. Any mutation—and he used the world—was desirable, even if it should temporarily lead men astray, because something was to be learned from any occurrence. It was preferable to allow men to wander into dangerous pathways and break their legs rather than to limit experience and to promote the false belief that perfection had already been attained. Error was more salutary than imitation, he declared with an almost romantic defiance, anticipating Schiller's defense of a similar paradox. Turgot sanctioned the free exercise of caprice as long as it did not harm other persons. In a fragment on morals written when he was a young man he attacked the "sheeplike conformity" which society calls "good sense." His belief in the right to error expressed itself in an absolute intellectual openness. "He tolerated equally," wrote Condorcet, "both pyrrhonism and the staunchest belief in opinions opposed to his own." [Condorcet, *Vie de Turgot*, 1786]. Since mere repetition added nothing to the total acquisitions of mankind, *to progress*, in one of its nuclear definitions, came to mean simply to innovate, to make the new, without an implied judgment of worth and excellence, and in this crude form the idea has often been adopted in Western society.

Turgot's disrespect for the dead weight of the past was dramatically set forth in his *Encyclopédie* article on Foundations. If all the graves that had ever been dug had been preserved, it would be necessary in order to cultivate the soil to overturn "these sterile monuments and to stir the ashes of the dead to nourish the living." He was prepared to violate the wishes of ancestors if their endowments, their ancient wills, usurped the needs of their descendants and barred them from access to the tremendous hoards of wealth controlled by monasteries. If past generations impeded the free enjoyment of liberty, the wills of the ancestors should be annulled. The past had to be overcome, brushed aside, lest it gain a stranglehold on the unborn. Living meant an eternal breaking out of old forms, an emancipation, a liberation. When Turgot tried to refashion the traditionalist monarchy of France he was acting out his own philosophy of history. In the edict of 1776 suppressing the jurandes he proclaimed the "right to work" as the possession of every man, an "inalienable right" of humanity—familiar language that year, but his words should not be interpreted with the socialist overtones of 1848. Work was eulogized as the creative act of man cleansed of the stigma of original sin; and even though rooted in necessity it was the key instrument of liberty. Since any activity was potentially productive of innovation, it contained the germ of progress. To shackle work with the restrictions of the feudal system, with prohibitions and tariffs, was to smother the possibilities of change. Limitations on the movement of grain among the provinces, on the free circulation of ideas, on the mobility of labor, on the accessibility of knowledge, were kindred antiprogressive regulations. Whatever was fixed, set, hardened, a religious dogma or an economic restriction, literally anything that might block new combinations of ideas, was a source of evil, deadly. Turgot's prognostication of the independence of the American colonies was the expression of a libertarian desire of the philosopher of progress, even though his analysis preserved the form of a cold diplomatic state paper. Turgot favored all freedom from tutelage, any independence, because these political acts of liberty were conditions precedent to creative innovation. The very term liberty lost its medieval connotation of a privilege and became the right to bring into being what had not existed before. Turgot knew that the present and the future were locked in a sequence of relationships with the past, but there are few thinkers who have respected its survival less.

The archenemy of progress, the sickly tendency toward repetition and sameness, had historically sunk whole societies in a rut where they languished and died. "It is not error which is opposed to the progress of truth; it is not wars and revolutions which retard the progress of governments; it is softness, stubbornness, routine, and everything which leads to inaction." The spirit of routine tended to become the controlling force in any intellectual elite which managed to seize power before it was permeated with a full consciousness of the morality of progress. Turgot's favorite illustration was the mandarin class and his evidence the well-nourished eighteenth-century debate on the character of the despotism of China. Here was a classic example of a society in which rational scientific progress had so far outstripped the spirit of liberty and moral progress that the rulers created a monopoly for themselves, froze education, and insisted upon mere traditional reiteration. Though the scientific level the Chinese mandarins had attained was high, their whole intellectual world became desiccated because it was static. Sects of every kind, philosophical as well as religious, faced the debilitating influence of the spirit of routine when they enjoyed power for long. Turgot was so wary of this pernicious proclivity of sects to stereotype their ideas that he even abandoned the *philosophes* on the *Encyclopédie,* repelled by their dogmatism. Only with great reluctance did he concede to his friend Condorcet, the Permanent Secretary of the Academy of Sciences, that academies might conceivably serve a useful purpose during a brief transitional period. In the bright future of mankind he saw no more need for these learned assemblies than for other corporate bodies tainted with the stigmas of feudalism. The *esprit de corps* was in

itself a stultifying evil. A few common projects of direct benefit to the participants he was willing to tolerate, though not without misgivings. His historical appreciation of the sects and ancient priesthoods of Babylon and Egypt was barbed with an antagonism which derived from his hostility toward the theologians who had trained him. The definition of a priesthood as a conspiracy to withhold religious truth in order to maintain uncontested sway over the people was common enough in eighteenth-century Europe. Turgot added the further reflection that in time these intellectual monopolists lost the capacity to understand their own traditional learning; and whatever scientific treasure they had amassed soon either evaporated or was destroyed by a superior force. The accumulation of scientific knowledge required absolute freedom of inquiry—a Turgot conception which became a cornerstone of liberalism in modern times, a highly controversial contention that has often proved itself to be an article of the new faith rather than a historical proposition that is universally applicable. Hume, Turgot's friend, doubted it when the idea was first propounded.

Turgot was openly dissatisfied with the great Montesquieu's typology of polities based on climate or geography. He posed a fundamental dichotomy between those societies which featured a maximum of mobility in all branches of human activity and those which were hostile to movement. Montesquieu had betrayed a strong preference for a political configuration in a state of balance, perhaps with tension in the atmosphere, but with equilibrium maintained. Turgot extolled every manifestation of expansiveness and condemned every form of self-containment as deadening. A precondition of progress was that a society be wide open to the spirit of change, that it welcome energy and action. Progress required a climate in which novelty was passionately sought after, not only tolerated. Turgot's philosophy of history set the tone for the Revolution.

GENIUS THE DYNAMIC AGENT

In Turgot the idea of progress had not yet become completely dehumanized. There was a unique being, the Genius, who played a crucial role as its dynamic agent. There were continually new encounters, new contingencies, unprecedented relationships in the world, but most of them passed unperceived, leaving no lasting imprint on a human mind, and they were gone forever. A living intermediary was necessary for the consummation of the progressive act; a human being had to experience the sensations, make the proper combinations, and after reflection create a new truth. The genius was that receptive mediator who grasped novelty, who was unbound by previous modes of perception, and who dared to articulate what he saw. History functioned through genius—the new Logos—and if unfavorable circumstances prevented him from exercising his superb talents on the novel play of events, progress was temporarily arrested. Turgot, unlike Montesquieu, was in search of a human moral force, rather than a physical force such as the challenge of the environment, to spark the movement of world history. In his theory of genius and its relation to the dynamics of progress Turgot discovered a uniform single principle that was operative everywhere which could account for diversity in the tempo and character of progress in time and place without abandoning the whole mechanism to Epicurean chance.

Though Turgot recognized only minor differences in the natural physical equipment of men, he did establish a "real inequality" in the character of their souls, and though he confessed to his inability to define the causes of genius, he was convinced of its qualitative superiority. His appreciation of genius was in the romantic spirit of one segment of eighteenth-century thought and has its parallel in Diderot, though Turgot introduced none of the psychological complexities which were raised by *Le Neveu de Rameau.* Turgot's genius was a more old-fashioned respectable figure, one who could still be admitted into Fontenelle's academic society. But Turgot created the type in the philosophy of history and he grew in stature until he ultimately became Hegel's daemonic world-historical hero-monster, the embodiment of Spirit at a crucial *Moment.*

Turgot still dealt with his genius as a mechanical principle, since the most important thing about him was the mathematical frequency of his appearance in the world. The problem of the relative number of geniuses emerging in various historical periods had been debated in the course of the late-seventeenth-century quarrel between the ancients and the moderns. In their zeal to prove that it was possible for contemporary literature to be as great as the creations of the classical world, the moderns had steadfastly maintained that nature was equally prolific of genius in all times and in all places. For evidence of this constancy in the fertility of nature they used homely analogies. Since trees were obviously no thicker in antiquity than in modern times, why should genius then have been more plentiful or more sublime? The eighteenth century tended to regard an increase in the population of a society as an absolute good. For Turgot, who believed in a fixed ratio of genius births to ordinary natalities at any historic moment, the modern increase in the number of inhabitants was especially felicitous, for it presaged a greater yield of geniuses. "Genius is spread among mankind like gold in a mine. The more ore you take out the more metal you will get."

Turgot introduced a new twist into the old conception of genius. To be sure, the extraordinary man was a natural phenomenon which appeared at more or less equal intervals throughout history, the same natural potential being present in an identical amount, but the crux of the problem of genius lay elsewhere. Circumstances in the world of political reality and in the accidental world of the natural genius either fostered his development or crushed him. Therefore the first task which Turgot posed for humanity was to actualize genius more frequently and to minimize the instances when a born genius was lost to mankind and to progress. If under favorable conditions in a given society many potential geniuses were trained to their full capacity, progress was assured. If only a few were suitably perfected, at best the age might become an epoch of conservation. And should genius be generally suffocated by external conditions, a temporary decline might set in. Thus the preservation of the genius and the maximization of his talents became the central function of the good soci-

ety, for he held the power of the keys of progress. A whole moral system was involved in this rather simple idea. Those forces which stifled genius were evil and those which fostered it, allowed it to attain fruition, were good. During the long historic past the central role of genius had not been recognized, with the result that mankind had benefited from only a small proportion of the geniuses whom nature had proffered to civilization. This waste of genius in the world economy of knowledge had retarded progress.

All of the utopian projects for the subsidization of genius drafted by Condorcet and Saint-Simon at the turn of the century were direct outgrowths of Turgot's stress upon the critical role of genius in the historic process. The rather fanciful and complicated mechanical schemes they devised were specific responses to the problem of how to salvage more geniuses and how to increase their productivity, since both of these heirs to the Turgot conception were convinced that genius set the pace of development for progress. The rate of the fulfillment of genius established the over-all rate of progress in an absolute sense.

LANGUAGE THE VESSEL

One factor above all others determined whether the perceptions of genius were destined to become part of the main stream of universal progress or whether they were fated to be forgotten in the darkness of time: the ready accessibility of an appropriate vessel for the containment of ideas, an orderly language. If for reasons related to the political life of nations—wars, conquests, turmoils—no proper language was fashioned, novelty would have sprouted in vain. Normally in the great civilizations the genius had available adequate symbols for the preservation of his thoughts and their transmission to posterity. In the future language was destined to become an even superior instrument; it would be stripped of its rhetoric, cleansed of its ambiguities, so that the only means of communication for true knowledge would be the mathematical symbol, verifiable, unchanging, eternal. The ideal of Descartes's clear and distinct ideas, terminological economy, would become a reality.

In the past one of the unfortunate consequences of the conquest of a decadent higher civilization by vigorous barbarians had been the linguistic confusion which followed the disaster. A long period of time elapsed before the vanquished merged their different forms of speech, and during the interval language, the only receptacle for the storing of scientific progress then available, was lacking. Geniuses continued to perceive new phenomena, but since they were deprived of a stable body of rational linguistic symbols their observations were stillborn. During the barbarian invasions of western Europe the Latin language, which previously had diffused works of speculative science, was adulterated by admixture with primitive tongues. The Babel of languages resulted in a protracted period of intellectual sterility during which it was impossible for a creative genius to express himself because there was no settled linguistic medium for scientific thought. Turgot compared this historical situation to the pouring of two different liquids into a bottle; a passage of time was required before their fusion could be effected, before the murky color was dissipated and a new homogeneous fluid appeared. The Middle Ages were that long interval during which favorable linguistic conditions were created for the Renaissance emergence of genius. In the Byzantine Empire a stultification like that in the medieval West had occurred, but there at least the speculative science which the ancients had accumulated could be preserved intact, for in this isolated society continuity of language with the source of knowledge in Greece had never been severed.

Language was not only a means of communication for new ideas, it was also a repository for the history of progress. In an article on Languages which Turgot had projected for the *Encyclopédie* but which, like so many of his plans, never came to fruition, he intended to show that throughout the ages language was an index of the stadial development of nations, since words were invented only when there were ideas demanding utterance. The mere existence of certain words was witness to a complex civilization. Should two nations "unequally advanced in their progress" intermingle, the more highly civilized people, even if defeated, would predominantly color the new language fusion because they alone possessed words corresponding to the more complicated ideas of a rich social fabric. Thus even when a decadent civilization succumbed before young barbarians its idea structure would survive. Language recorded the triumph of real progress in science even amid the ruins of once glorious empires. This conception of the history of language and literature as the embodiment of the successive stages of human development had of course been more copiously presented in the axioms of Vico's *Scienza Nuova,* but there is no evidence of any direct influence. In his *Réflexions sur les langues,* a youthful polemic against Maupertuis written about 1751, Turgot proposed historical semantic studies as the clue to mythology and to the illumination of prehistoric traditions.

> The study of language, if well done, would perhaps be the best of logics. In analyzing, in comparing the words of which they are fashioned, in tracing from the beginning the different meanings which they acquired, in following the thread of ideas, we will see through which stages, through which metamorphoses men passed. . . . This kind of experimental metaphysics would be at one and the same time the history of the human mind and the history of the progress of its thoughts, always fitted to the needs which gave birth to them. Languages are at once their expression and their measure.

Like so many of Turgot's insights, the formula is so laconic, so apparently casual, that it would pass unnoticed were we not already sensitized to the ideas by parallel themes in other eighteenth-century thinkers.

The primitive language structure of each nation was developed independently but along similar lines, because the sensations from which speech derived were the same. While Turgot was not as militantly antidiffusionist as Vico, he had broken completely with the traditional theory of language. By mid-century there was already widespread disbelief in the orthodox notion that language was born a complete and perfect rational instrument, a fully developed means of communication which Adam already possessed in the Garden of Eden. Though still utilizing subterfuges necessitated by censorship, the weight of opinion tended to establish a hypothetical historical pattern for the growth of language, from the first emotive grunts of man in the state of nature, through a period of sentence structure, to the highest form of expression in a mathematical formula. This ideal history of the origins and development of language had roots in Locke, was repeated in Condillac, in Adam Smith, in Monboddo, in the *Encyclopédie,* in Rousseau, in Hume, and could count even respectable English bishops among its adherents. Language had become the record of the human intelligence as it passed from a stage in which man, like a child or a savage, could only record the concrete to the highest levels of abstraction, those mathematical symbols in which neither human feelings nor concrete objects obtruded. Along the way men had resorted to images, similes, poetic metaphors, admixtures of ideas and sensations. There were transitional stages during which both language and thought lacked the precision and the conciseness of the French spoken in Mlle. de L'Espinasse's salon; but even the most philosophical language was vastly inferior to a theorem as a method of rational discourse.

In all of these stadial views of human development, whether the mirror of mankind was the history of language, of writing, of religion, of civilization, of perception itself, there was one recurrent theme: the record revealed a steady rationalization of man at the expense of his emotional and imaginative faculties, a constant movement toward greater abstraction. Like Vico, Turgot's fragments also recognized a stage of human consciousness which was so primitive that man could only give voice to his ideas in myth, in metaphor, in pictorial images. And for Turgot, as for Hume, there is a manifest superiority in the abstract attitude over the concrete. Turgot was ultimately led by his worship of reason to prefer the purest mathematical abstraction over all other forms of knowledge and to look upon the metaphors and images in which the ancients communicated their ideas as a sort of baby-talk, expressive perhaps, but a form which had to be outgrown. Eighteenth-century French thinkers like Turgot were conscious of the death of the poetic spirit in their society, and they did not regret it.

In his theory of language Turgot was skirting along the borders of one of the commonest and yet most controversial conceptions in modern philosophies of history, the idea that there has been an evolvement of human modes of perception, that the differences between the primitive and the civilized are qualitative, and that they could be defined as different mentalities. Thinkers from a wide variety of disciplines seemed to be groping in this general direction throughout the eighteenth and early nineteenth centuries until the idea culminated in Comte's law of the three states, a source from which it was diffused throughout modern psychology and anthropology—though by no means without challenge. It has often been pointed out that a number of passages in Turgot already contain this positivist law in embryo. knowledge had once been exclusively theological, then it turned metaphysical, and finally it was becoming positive. By the theological stage Turgot—writing in the tradition of Fontenelle and paralleling the works of his friends Hume and de Brosses on the natural history of primitive religion—meant the propensity of men to project intelligent divine power into all manner of objects and forces in nature. The metaphysical described a stage when knowledge was thought of and expressed in terms of essences. The final, third stage was one in which men recognized the real objective nature of things and were beginning to formulate their relationships in mathematical terms. Language had recorded this growth of human modes of perception, and in their normal development all peoples would have to pass from one stage to another. In a general historico-philosophical sense Turgot conceived of progress as the ascent of mankind from one state of perception to another, each leap accompanied by the introduction of new signs and symbols.

This aspect of Turgot's theory of progress can be interpreted as an extension to the historical process of Condillac's epistemology as presented in the *Essai sur l'origine des connaissances humaines.* Those conditions which Condillac found necessary for the original acquisition of abstract thought in an individual were discovered to be the motive drives in the progress of the species throughout time. The stimulating effects of intricate and numerous social communications, the existence of a language whose symbols were clear and distinct rather than blurred, a sense of the fragility and susceptibility to error of even the greatest intellects, the importance of chance, are all ideas he drew directly from Condillac. What Turgot did was to translate the investigation from an abstract inquiry into how human knowledge should be acquired under the direction of a philosophical tutor by an ideal pupil to the vast canvas of the history of mankind, and thus to fill in with empirical detail that ancient analogy between phylogeny and ontogeny. Mankind did in fact amass its knowledge in precisely the same way as every newborn child. Its mistakes have been numerous but it has learned from experience, and in the future it may be able to minimize error by perfecting its geniuses, the men who have special talents for the manipulation of symbols and the combination of ideas. Condillac's "operations of the soul and the causes of its progressions" was transmuted by Turgot into the operations of the human mind or mankind and its progressions.

ETHNOLOGY THE RECORD

Universal progress has left a record of its movement from one stage to another that is far more complete and circumstantial than written historical documents and even language; this is the living record of ethnology, the actual existence of aboriginal tribes and nations dispersed over the face of the globe, each on a different level of culture. The travel literature and the missionary reports on primitive, barbaric, semibarbaric, and heathen civilized societies had come to constitute an indisputable body of data, there for any scholar to examine and for any intrepid explorer to verify, proving without recourse to conjecture that there had in fact been a stadial development of mankind. Contemporary barbaric societies were vestiges of previous stages; primarily because of their isolation, they had become frozen at a given moment in time or they were developing more slowly. "In the over-all progress of the human

mind, all nations start from the same point, proceed to the same goal, follow more or less the same path, but at a very uneven pace," Turgot wrote in the article **"Etymologie"** in the sixth volume of the *Encyclopédie.*

The idea that savage societies were exemplars of what the more advanced civilizations had once been was by the mid-eighteenth century no longer startling, but not until the writings of Turgot and de Brosses [*Du culte des dicux fétiches,* 1760] in the 1750's did this momentous hypothesis become the springboard for grandiose conceptions of stadial progress. For Turgot the ethnographic record contained the whole from one primitive society to another the philosopher could—if he wisely chose appropriate examples—establish the true historical series from the most barbaric through the most enlightened. Turgot defined the quintessential nature of the series as it advanced from one stage to another in terms of a history of changing capacities of perception, or at least different ways of confronting the external world, transformations in the human mind which were by no means accidental but were clearly ranged in an order of being from the less to the more perfect. The societies which exemplified the stadial development were a historical roster of excellences in which the primitive savage was the inferior and the civilized Frenchman the most recent expression of the superior.

Political geography, as Turgot outlined the discipline in one of his unfinished sketches, became the description of world areas in the light of his one central theme: how proximate was each society, barbaric or civil, to the bellwether nation leading the movement of progress. Or was a people perhaps veering in the opposite direction, toward decadence, and eliminating itself from world history? When Turgot propounded his conception of progress he never implied that all nations were progressing regularly in a straight line and at an even tempo. He was neither so simple nor so obtuse as to envisage simultaneous unchecked development, though this has sometimes been inferred in crude distillations of his theory. On the contrary, in the spirit of Vico and Montesquieu and Gibbon, he was acutely conscious of the phenomenon of grandeur and decadence, of growth, maturity, fall, and decline. What he intended to demonstrate from the record of world historical geography was that some society was always carrying the torch of progress forward; when it was about to be extinguished in one area the sacred fire was seized by another. As one haven of science crumbled there was always another polity which inherited the discoveries and, after an interval necessary for assimilation, advanced still further. "Thus it has happened that in alternating periods of agitation and calm, of good and evil, the total mass of the human species has moved ceaselessly toward its perfection." Turgot was not precise in his definition of the societal unit in which progress was incorporated; most often he drew examples from large areas like the Greek world, the Roman Empire, Christendom, or China, though sometimes he used an individual dynastic state or even an American tribe. This vagueness in the establishment of the unit of discourse makes it difficult to relate the cyclical patterns of individual societies with the world development of progress which, *mutatis mutandis,* assumes a role analogous to Hegel's World Spirit triumphing amid the tragic death of cultures. The linking of individual instances of growth and decay with the central thread of world development has been the rock on which the most magnificent constructs of philosophical history have foundered, and Turgot was often hard put to document the transmissions, particularly from Rome to medieval Europe, though he managed to squeak through with a felicitous use of metaphor.

Political geography endowed with a time dimension became universal history. At most a few names had to be added, the key inventive geniuses and the towering political figures. History, almost entirely divested of its heroic qualities, became a record of the relations of societies to one another spatially and temporally. The images with which Turgot tried to communicate these relationships remained predominantly spatial. There was distance in time as there was distance in space, and each people, nation, and tribe could be located in time on some rung of the ladder of progress with the same precision that it could be fixed in space on a world map.

The **"Plan d'un ouvrage sur la géographie politique"** was an outline of history demonstrating in schematic form how from a diversity of peoples on different levels of civilization one enlightened world with a uniform culture would inevitably result. The whole process was depicted in a set of geometric images. In the beginning there were numerous isolated units; with time, in any world area, the nation which had surpassed others in progress became the center of a group of political satellites. The same process was repeated in various parts of the globe which had no contact with one another. Ultimately the independent constellations extended their circles until they collided and established relations through war and commerce. In the end of the days the major political areas would coalesce, and one world whose boundaries were coterminous with the physical world would be created. Turgot extolled this ideal of one political world not only because it would unite men but because it would provide an opportunity for the maximum interpenetration of diverse perceptions among the greatest number of human beings, the necessary prerequisite for accelerated progress. The uniformity and insipidity of one world was an idea remote from his imagination.

ANATOMY OF THE FOUR PROGRESSIONS

Progress naturally divided itself into four subsidiary progressions, and Turgot anatomized them, established their mutual relationships, and derived from them a law of unequal development. These types of progress were identified with distinct areas of human creative activity: speculative science, technology, moral behavior, and artistic expression. The "inequality of the progressions" was a central thesis, for he had discovered in each progression a different pattern of growth, and when referring to them as a group he constantly used the term in the plural, *les progrès,* a form which Condorcet retained in the *Esquisse.* Thus there was uneven development of progressions *within* a society as there was among various geographic entities throughout the world, a law which accounted for the extraordinary diversity of human experience despite the identity of mankind's underlying historic destiny. What

conditions, asked Turgot the philosophical historian, had in the past furthered one or more progressions, and what had been the negative elements destructive of progress or blocking its path? Since progress is the integrating concept which bestows meaning upon the history of man, since it is virtually the sole historical subject, this experience of the progressions in the past will enlighten mankind about its future prospect. The diagnosis of the progressions is preliminary to a prognosis.

Of all the progressions, the technological had been the hardiest growth of man's genius, the least evanescent, for mechanical capacities were common, shared by a vast number of human beings, and it would be impossible to destroy totally the productive techniques of artisans even during periods when the political framework of society was shattered. Because the body of men who practiced mechanical arts was large, the chance of novelty was greater than in other forms of progress, for the incidence of genius was the same in all fields. Since artisans dealt with elementary needs of life, were plentiful and yet indispensable, the mechanical arts were perfected by the "mere fact that time passed." Once a new device had been invented and accepted by the artisans it was hard to envisage its abandonment, because the advantages of the innovation were so manifest to utilitarian common sense. Since the preservation and transmission of technology were not dependent upon language, it could even survive a barbarian conquest. No tyrannical power had a special interest in interfering with the artisan's processes of cloth manufacture. As a consequence, technological discoveries had accumulated throughout history at a relatively even tempo; and during long epochs progress in the mechanical arts had continued without interruption even while science and artistic creativity had suffered a total eclipse. Turgot appreciated the technical progress achieved in medieval Europe, a rare insight for an eighteenth-century *philosophe,* and he was one of the first to suggest that the regeneration of speculative science in the Renaissance had been facilitated by an antecedent succession of mechanical inventions during the Middle Ages: the introduction of maritime instruments, the magnifying glass, and, most important of all, the art of printing, which diffused scientific knowledge over a wide area, made the discoveries of the ancient Greeks generally available and stimulated potential geniuses by making them aware of the achievements of their predecessors. Up to the eighteenth century, science owed more to technology than technology to science, a relationship which Turgot was prepared to see reversed by the imminent revolutionary explosion of speculative science. Whatever the past interdependence of science and technology, for the future the scientists were the unchallenged vanguard of the battalions of progress.

The fine arts was one area of creativity where Turgot modified his theory of limitless infinite progress. In the literary quarrel of the ancients and the moderns he still found for the giants of antiquity. Aesthetic achievement was the tenderest plant of human genius, sensitive to political contingencies. Good taste, which had to prevail in a society before genius in the fine arts could be honored, was fragile and delicate, and it could be easily corrupted by decree throughout a whole civilization if a capricious ruling prince were imbued with bizarre or fantastic notions of the beautiful. Of all forms of human expression, art was the most vulnerable to the influence of a hostile environment. Turgot clung to the neoclassic idea that the Augustan age had reached the artistic zenith, a level that might perhaps be equaled again under proper guidance but could never be surpassed. Knowledge of the fine arts, unlike knowledge in the mechanical arts and in speculative science, was not cumulative; hence the very concept of progress was not, strictly speaking, applicable in this sphere. Atrociously bad taste could predominate in the same age when mechanical arts were accomplishing marvels of engineering. The Gothic cathedral which Turgot, in conformity with the prevailing judgment of the eighteenth century, considered a monstrosity, was a superb expression of man's ingenuity in the mechanical arts. Men still had not learned how these structures had been raised by the medieval artisans, but there was no doubt about their hideousness.

Turgot had no conception of the high seriousness of art. While discovery in mechanical arts and speculative science was part of an infinite movement, the fine arts aimed only to please. Once the philosophical canon of the pleasurable had been established on the basis of a knowledge of human psychology—which **was** uniform—a specific art object either obeyed and conformed to the rules or violated them. While other branches of human endeavor were infinitely expansible, progress in the arts of poetry, painting, and music was bound by intrinsic natural limitations. Since our artistic sensibilities were restricted by the nature and sensitivity of our organs, once perfection had been attained in the Augustan age later generations were reduced to mere imitation of these models. At most there might conceivably be an improvement in the technical media of artistic production, never progress in art itself. Turgot the poetaster and translator of Vergil and Horace was unable to extol the creations of eighteenth-century France above those of the Romans, and he expressed a measure of contempt for those who deluded themselves that they were perfecting the arts when they were only rendering the artistic object more complex. "The knowledge of nature and of truth is as infinite as they are," he wrote in the second Sorbonique. "The arts whose purpose it is to please are as limited as we are. Time continually brings forth new discoveries in science, but poetry, painting, music, have a fixed limit which the genius of language, the imitation of nature, and the sensibilities of our organs determine. . . ."

By contrast moral behavior was clearly subject to improvement, though what he meant by the moral implied a set of fixed criteria, ideals common to the wise philosophers of his age, universally accepted by Hume and Montesquieu, Beccaria, Lessing, and Kant. The moral was a combination of Stoic virtues and rules of general conduct with a measure of utility, the whole suffused with Christian love and charity. Future moral progress signified the end of war, cruelty, and crime, and the extension of virtues throughout all strata of European society and among all the nations of the world. It entailed the general practice of tolerance and leniency and obedience to reason, acceptance of law out of rational conviction rather than any dread of worldly punishment or superstitious fear of tor-

ments in Hell. If men acted solely on grounds of utility and reason, if they extended free inquiry and assimilated its scientific findings into the practical sphere of everyday action, then they were progressing. To the degree that man became mild, gentle, loving, tranquil, his moral behavior was improving.

Turgot never fell in with the rabid anticlericalism of some of his Encyclopedist friends, even after he had left the Church. He retained a profound respect for the moral virtues of Christianity, which he considered a further purification and not a corruption of natural religion. Under the canopy of the medieval church the bestial nature of the northern barbarians had been tamed and in time they had been transformed into polite, reasonable, well-behaved, compassionate members of society. Christianity had abolished slavery, prohibited infanticide, established asylums for the sick and the weak, preached brotherhood and love. The church had been one of the great civilizing and moralizing forces in the history of mankind. His friend and loyal disciple Condorcet, alive to bloody religious persecutions, inquisitions, massacres, and crusades, was unable to stomach this summation of the historical evidence.

About the future moral progress of mankind, however, Condorcet and Turgot were in agreement. The reduction of morals to a science of observation would inevitably lead to the wider prevalence of those ways of conduct which every *philosophe* appreciated and whose essence was an extension of altruism, "contributing to the happiness of others."

THE DEMONSTRATION OF INEVITABILITY

Turgot's doctrine supported itself on two central arguments: an empirical proof that progress had in fact occurred in the past from the dark primitive stage of humanity's origins through the enlightened present; and a demonstration that since retrogression was no longer possible future progress was inevitable. The past history of progress had been proved by ethnology. The prediction of its future was based upon an evaluation of the increasing momentum of progress, its accelerating tempo; upon an estimate of the global diffusion of enlightenment; and finally upon the observation that all knowledge was actually in the process of becoming encased in mathematical symbols which granted it certitude. Historical reflections in the grand manner of a Bossuet illustrated these bold and novel ideas in the Sorbonne discourses, refuting both pessimist Christian theologians and antihistorical *philosophes* who tended to regard the past as a meaningless parade of crimes and cruel accidents. Hitherto, Turgot conceded, progress had been consistently waylaid by two enemies: either barbarian invasions overwhelmed societies that had attained a high level of civilization and temporarily stifled the progress of science; or advanced societies became corroded by an equally vicious internal disease in their own bodies politic, that spirit of routine, the rut, which was always for him the very incarnation of evil. In the future, however, these two dread enemies of progress would be powerless, since the eighteenth-century reality of a unified world civilization had rendered it impossible for mankind as a whole ever again to suffer stagnation or catastrophic relapse. Knowledge of science was now so widely diffused among societies throughout the world that even the irruption of a barbarian horde intent upon devastation, even suppression by an obscurantist tyrant, could not wholly extinguish the light of progress. In the past the isolation of political societies had rendered them peculiarly susceptible to internal putrescence, but henceforward if a nation tended to fall into a stagnant state, either it would be forcibly awakened, shaken out of its torpor by commercial stimuli from abroad, or it would be conquered by a more vigorous nation which would ultimately inherit its progress. To the extent that war had kept humanity alert and constantly aroused it had not been an unmitigated evil. In the future this terrible remedy might not be necessary, but it was always available to assure humanity's forward movement.

Turgot tended to evaluate progress in two dimensions. One was intensive, vertical so to speak, the accretion of units of scientific truth in time; the other was extensive, horizontal, and entailed the gradual sowing of these scientific truths throughout the world until ultimately no area would remain barren. During his retirement Turgot toyed with inventions of cheap processes for the reproduction of writing, in order to multiply communications and extend progress among those elements in society which were still beyond its pale. The extension of the communications network became a crucial practical measure for the acceleration of the progressive process and was in harmony with the other elements in his theory. Increase communications and an ever greater number and variety of new idea combinations are transmitted to an ever larger number of human beings. Among those exposed to the new configurations would be a new quota of geniuses who would grasp the meaning of novel contingencies, formalize them, and make them a part of the accumulating body of world knowledge. To learn truth and to spread it was the essential social mission of man bequeathed by Turgot to his disciple Condorcet. "To know the truth in order to make the social order conform to it, that is the sole source of public happiness. It is therefore useful, even necessary, to extend the limits of knowledge. . . ." To gather new peoples under the protection of science was from the beginning a vital element in the idea of progress. When no spot on earth was excluded from the illumination of science, then and only then was it safe from an attack by the forces of evil and ignorance, free of the threat of submersion by waves of darkness from beyond the pale of the civilized world. Only thereafter would intensive scientific progress be accelerated indefinitely, without setback or impediment. Europe's mission to civilize the world was for Turgot, as it was later for Condorcet and Saint-Simon, a necessary requirement for its own development. No region of the globe, however enlightened, could enjoy perfect tranquillity as long as savages lurked on the rim of civility. Since temporarily at least barbarians throttled a more advanced culture when they took possession, the mere existence of an uncivilized penumbra endangered civilization. The function of enlightenment was to draw the whole of the world into the orbit of civilization as an absolute insurance against retrogression. Turgot's rational belief in the inevitability of future progress was bolstered by his confidence that eighteenth-century Europeans were in manifest control of the savage world and had only to disseminate

their teachings to eradicate the last remnants of the historic dread of barbarian invasions which hung over them. Intensive and extensive progress were thus interrelated; they fortified each other and were dependent upon each other.

Turgot's optimism derived from the realization that the growth of science had by now gathered so great a momentum that interruption of the process had been rendered impossible. *Vires acquirit eundo.* In the early stages of history the plant of civilization could be trampled down by outsiders, the horde, or it could be shriveled from within by sloth, luxury, an absence of challenge. But the strength and the speed of movement achieved in modern times made every progression easier and every backward lapse more improbable. An accelerating wheel became the image of progress.

Finally, the richest source of confidence for the believer in the inevitability of progress lay in the special mathematical character of all forms of scientific knowledge in recent ages. Mathematics, of which Turgot had only an amateur's smattering, was for him the loftiest expression of human thought, at the summit of intellectuality. In mathematics and only in mathematics did Turgot feel an absolute sense of security about the survival of acquired knowledge. Throughout his life he had toyed with fantasies about devoting himself to science, and he was always wistfully contrasting the turbulent, ungrateful, political world in which, alas, he had expended his energies as an administrator with the peaceful, finite, enduring world of science from which the rhetoric and the prejudice that governed the politics of men had been expunged. On August 24, 1761, he had written to Voltaire: "I have the misfortune to be an Intendant. I say misfortune because in this century of quarrels there is no happiness but in living philosophically among one's studies and one's friends." Science to Turgot connoted the mathematical world, the realm of the purest of the sciences, the ideal form of knowledge. Here was certainty for this uneasy intellectual.

The progress of speculative science was now solidly safeguarded by the new symbolic forms which knowledge had assumed since the Renaissance. Once mathematics had become the universal language of science, intellectual progress was emancipated from the historical vicissitudes to which the ordinary spoken vernaculars were subject. Mathematical language would soon set up an impregnable barrier against retrogression. To reduce all knowledge to mathematical symbols would become the highest achievement of mankind. For the moment only the social sciences seemed to be standing apart; but their mathematization was the inevitable next stage of intellectual progress. In the formula no room was left for the vague, for the exaggeration of enthusiasts, for superstition—the great vices of mankind. The mathematization of the study of man would become a double security against antiprogressive forces, for moral knowledge would find itself protected by the armor of numbers and equations, and moral problems would be removed from the disputes of the marketplace where they always provoked destructive violence. In his last years Turgot, wracked with the pains of illness, drew consolation from the vision of humanity on the threshold of this wondrous transmutation of knowledge, a leap comparable in his mind to the passage of human speech from a myth-ridden, metaphoric, poetic language to the relatively rational style of the contemporary European world. As long as mankind relied upon language and rhetoric to express its truths, knowledge would inevitably become polluted with chimeras of the imagination, with personal prejudice. Even civilized languages, rational instruments of communication though they were, had never succeeded in freeing themselves from their primitive origins and remained encumbered with similes and images which obfuscated rational thought. There was always something suspect about an idea that was not mathematized because it was subject to passion, to political influences, to the weaknesses of the imaginative faculty. In the past scientific knowledge had been acquired rather haphazardly, and as a consequence of unpropitious external circumstances it had been stagnant for long periods at a time. Only since the regeneration of the sciences through mathematics had a long succession of geniuses been steadfastly adding to this body of knowledge and at the same time extending the dominion of science over new peoples who had once been victims of superstitious belief or obscure theological reasoning. In technical terms the new vista opening before Turgot was the imminent application of the calculus of probabilities to human behavior, thus the invasion of a whole moral world from which mathematics had previously been excluded.

Turgot is in a long tradition of French thinkers ranging from Descartes through Paul Valéry who have sought refuge in mathematics as an ultimate haven. When all other arguments in support of the inevitability of future progress were momentarily weakened by the spectacle of the real world with its oppressive stupidity and irrationality, the triumph of the mathematical spirit was a last resort. As long as the knowledge of abstract relationships in the mathematical world was growing there was progress. The final consolation lay in the existence of the equation. Princes might prove weak and false, but nothing could assail one's confidence in a theorem.

As a result of the manifold demonstrations of inevitability the burden of proof was shifted to the shoulders of the antiprogressists. Wherefrom was the antiscientific destructive storm to blow if enlightenment became universal? To impede the natural impetus of scientific progress a countervailing force equally potent was required. Since there was no such power on the historical horizon, progress would be "indefinite" or without limit, like an infinite progression in mathematics.

PROGRESS A THEODICY

The progressists have sometimes been read and interpreted as if they were continually mouthing optimist shibboleths. Turgot, whose half-smile sometimes disturbed contemporaries, was not immune to moments of disenchantment and even despair. Declarations of war by the philosophical monarchs of the Enlightenment evoked from him a cry of horror. "Poor humans!" he exclaimed in a letter of March 19, 1778, reporting to his friend Dupont de Nemours the imminent outbreak of hostilities in Germany and in Turkey. He sighed when he contemplated the enduring stupidity of his race. Few of the eighteenth-century

philosophes were naive or blissfully unconscious of contradictions in their own optimist posture. Turgot was gnawed by a deep sense of the persistence of tragedy in the human condition. In a letter to Condorcet in 1772, four years before the failure of his attempt to rescue the monarchy from collapse, Turgot revealed his feeling of futility about administrative reforms and confided a secret conviction that men would probably never overcome the evils which they inflicted upon themselves, that physical ills and moral grief would always be with us. Progress would therefore have to limit itself to the eradication of "artificial evils" generated by ignorance. Turgot's optimism was rarely without qualms. His economic theory had led him to rather gloomy conclusions about any possible improvement of the lot of the ordinary worker, who was bound by a law which limited him to a subsistence level of wages—an antecedent of Marx's iron law. Turgot's version of the idea of progress did not involve any utopian total elimination of evil, error, or misery from an empirical view of human experience. The Turgot who at the height of his powers was rejected by the King and ousted by a palace cabal was not the simplistic unquestioning believer in progress which some of the popularizers of his ideas have made him out to be; and neither was Condorcet, who after overthrowing the king found himself condemned to the guillotine in absentia; and neither was Saint-Simon, the perennial failure who cried out with anguish at the sight of the terrible harvest of death during the Napoleonic wars; and neither was Comte, who saw the Europe of 1848 bathed in a bloody fratricidal class war. None of these men were starry-eyed fools repeating stereotyped formulas about progress and the betterment of mankind. They all saw progress as an overcoming of contrary forces in organized society, in physical nature, in man himself. They were wrestling with the problem of evil which reappeared in a new mask in each generation, its most recent embodiment the forces of antiprogress. The war of good and evil, of Christ and anti-Christ, became the war of progressive history and antihistory. Process, movement, social dynamics, did not lose their Christian moral overtones. The doctrine of progress was born in the bosom of Christianity, and Saint-Simon and Comte even tried to retain the epithet "religious" as a key descriptive word for their new progressist systems. Turgot was aware of the overwhelming potency of the deadening forces of tradition and routine, Condorcet of the power of tyranny, sect, and lust for dominion, Saint-Simon and Comte of the divisive forces of anarchy which endangered the cohesion of the social fabric. The evil passions and even the dissolving demons of madness were not unknown to the philosophers of progress.

In the last analysis their systems were fervent attempts to solve the theodicy problem and to give meaning to historical experience once the sanctions of future rewards and punishments were removed. If Providence was a source of goodness, why the long chronicle of wars and devastations, the spectacle of crimes and barbarities perpetrated throughout the ages? The answer is common to most eighteenth-century philosophers of history—in this respect Turgot's concept is only one offshoot of a general theme. Without the impetus of the aggressive, evil passions, without the ambitions of individuals, the "leading strings" of nature, there would have been no progress in the early stages of history and man would have been doomed to peace and mediocrity. "The ambitious ones themselves in forming the great nations have contributed to the views of Providence, to the progress of enlightenment, and consequently to the increase of the happiness of the human species, a thing which did not at all interest them. Their passions, their very rages, have led them without their knowing where they were going. I seem to see an immense army all of whose movements are directed by a great genius. At the sight of the military signals, at the tumultuous noise of the trumpets and the drums, the squadrons move forward, the horses themselves are driven by a fire which has no purpose. Each section makes its way over obstacles without knowing what may result. Only the chief sees the effect of so many related steps. Thus the passions multiplied ideas, extended knowledge, perfected minds, in default of the reason whose day had not yet dawned and which would have been less potent if it had reigned earlier.

> Reason, which is justice itself, would never have carried away what belonged to another, would have forever banished war and usurpation, would have left men divided into a mob of nations, isolated from one another, speaking different languages.
>
> Limited, as a result, in their ideas, incapable of progress in any branch of knowledge, of science, of art, of civility, which is born of the meeting of geniuses assembled from different provinces, the human species would have forever remained in a state of mediocrity. Reason and justice, had they been hearkened to, would have fixed everything—approximately the way it happened in China.

The attainment of the providential (or nature's) purpose of progress required the free play of the passions. This did not mean that individual acts of wickedness were willed by God, pleaded the former theologian Turgot. Since men committed these acts, they had to bear the moral responsibility. Progress merely utilized the opportunities created by the self-willed men who broke the moral law. And they thereby unwittingly achieved a divine purpose. The idea of progress thus comes to the rescue of the religious man who might otherwise have begun to question divine guidance of the world of men steeped in evil. Vice is enlisted in the service of Progress, and Progress in turn becomes a part of Christian apologetics.

An individual immoral deed, inspired by personal lust, can generate historical forces which lead to the perfection and humanization of the species. This theodicy, which explains the emergence of objective good for mankind from subjective evil intent, was one of the most persistent motifs in eighteenth- and early nineteenth-century philosophies of history. With variations it can be found in Vico, Herder, Kant, and Hegel as well as among the progressists of the French school. Inevitably the philosophical historians were forced into a divorcement of the will of individual morality from the unfolding of a rational purpose in history. Turgot was the first of the French group to resort to this justification of God's way in time, the equivalent of what Vico had called a civil theology. Even in its later de-

velopment the secular idea of progress was never completely divested of the theological robes in which it had made its first appearance at the Sorboniques. Whatever the balance of good and evil in the world may be at any specific moment, the historic ledger always shows a credit in favor of the good. Ever since his youth Turgot, who had read Leibniz, had been profoundly disturbed by the question of the origin and purpose of evil in a world that was created by a God who was perfect good. His article on Manichaeism for the *Encyclopédie* had wrestled with this, "the hardest and thorniest problem which presents itself to the mind." The idea of progress provided the solution. "He saw in physical Evil, in moral Evil," Condorcet reported, "only a necessary consequence of the existence of sensitive beings capable of reason but limited. The perfectibility with which a few species, and in particular the human species, are endowed is a slow but infallible remedy to these evils." And it was this insight into progress which, to the obvious annoyance of his anticlerical friend, sustained Turgot in the belief in a beneficent, providential design. "The universe viewed in its totality, in the whole range of the progressions, is a most glorious spectacle, witness to the wisdom which presides over it."

Validation of the passions, however, was usually limited by Turgot to the past. Once enlightenment had spread over the world this stimulus to progress was no longer necessary, since full-grown Reason should be able to care for its own and humanity's future development. The evil passions which were useful in the infancy of the species were superfluous in man's mature rational age. Turgot recognized the complexity of the individual drives which had motivated the great discoveries of the past, and he refrained from emphasizing exclusively either love of knowledge or a quest for glory. A human desire for fame, he realized, had hitherto limited researches which required many generations to achieve fruition, but he was hopeful that in the future society, with the equalization of wealth and a diminution of the importance of political action, more men of talent would devote themselves to the pursuit of reason without the excitation of the passions. With time, Turgot hoped, reason would occupy more and more space in the finite area of the spirit, casting out the disorderly passions and limiting severely the scope of the imagination. Emotion was thus progressively blotted out until in the end of the days there was only reason. The impoverishment of the spirit under the hegemony of pure reason did not trouble the eighteenth-century philosophe, because as he saw the world about him, the prejudice, the superstition, the ignorance, the fanaticism, he felt that mankind had only begun to fight the battle of rationality. The prospect of an undernourishment of the passions and the imaginative faculties for the sake of reason did not yet appear real to men of Turgot's generation. He was acutely aware of how young was the reign of reason—only the mathematical sciences had pursued appropriate analytic methods before the end of the seventeenth century—if measured against the background of historic time. When Turgot contemplated the irrationality of the world, he derived consolation from the simple historical realization that the mathematical perception of the universe was so relatively recent an acquisition of the human spirit that its influence upon laws and morals had not as yet had an opportunity to make itself felt.

At the close of the biography of his friend, Condorcet presented an Isaiah-like vision of the end of the days as it had been unfolded to him in Turgot's conversation. Most of the elements in this progressist heaven he later repeated in the last part of the tenth epoch of his own *Esquisse,* the form in which the ideas penetrated into European thought.

> He [Turgot] hoped that day would come when men, disabused of the fantastic project of opposing nation to nation, power to power, passion to passion, vice to vice, would occupy themselves with hearkening to what reason would dictate for the happiness of humanity. Why should politics, based like all the other sciences on observation and reason, not be perfected in the measure that one brings to observations more subtlety and exactitude, to reasoning more precision, profundity, and good judgment? Shall we dare to fix what point could be attained in this field by minds fortified by a better education, exercised at an early age in the combination of the most varied and extensive ideas, accustomed to manipulate more general and easier methods? Let us beware of despairing of the human kind. Let us dare to envisage, in the immensity of the centuries which will follow us, a happiness and an enlightenment about which we cannot today even form a vague and indefinite idea. Let us count on that perfectibility with which nature has endowed us, on the power of genius from which long experience has taught us to expect prodigies, and let us console ourselves for the fact that we shall not witness those happier times with the pleasure of foretelling them, of enjoying them in advance, and perhaps with the even sweeter satisfaction of having accelerated that all-too-distant epoch by a few moments.

In the correspondence of his last years Turgot recorded the progress of the American Revolution, the Gordon riots, the outbreak of the war with Turkey, and the ravages of the mutual passion which consumed his friends Madame Helvétius and Benjamin Franklin (who was then seventy-three). He watched these events with tender sympathy for the victims of war and civil strife and emotional excess. These were moral ills of which men had not yet been cured, and perhaps the pains were yet destined to endure for some time, like the gout with which both Turgot and the sage from Philadelphia were afflicted. Turgot's disgrace provoked no misanthropic outburst. If he was outraged at his betrayal by the King, there is no report of his indignation. The slightly skeptical smile continued to hover about the lips; it is preserved in Ducreux's pastel in the Château de Lantheuil. Not so his faithful lieutenant Condorcet. In a letter to Voltaire he gave vent to his anger with a vehemence which Turgot would never have permitted himself:

> I have not written to you, my dear illustrious master, since the fatal event which has robbed all honest men of hope and courage. I waited for my wrath to cool down somewhat and for grief alone to remain. This event has changed all of

nature for me. I no longer take the same pleasure in looking at the beautiful countryside where he would have spread happiness. The spectacle of the gaiety of the people makes my heart ache. They dance as if they had lost nothing. The wolves from which you delivered the country of Gex are going to invade the rest of France, and two years of abstinence have transformed their thirst for the blood of the people into a fury. Would you believe they dared demand that no writing against them be allowed and that this vile progeny of lackeys, bitches, and pimps of the past century be respected? They want to muzzle us out of fear lest the cries which our pain tears from us trouble their peace. This is where we have fallen, my dear illustrious master, and from what a lofty pinnacle! . . .

The day of the *philosophes* was drawing to a close, and the men of action were about to take over. If the conspiracy of the privileged ones ousted the last hope of France there were other means of bringing about the triumph of reason. Condorcet recovered from his dejection, girded himself for war, and flung himself into the revolutionary battle. In his turn he suffered the fate of the philosopher engaged— as had his master.

Turgot remembered at a salon:

The gathering was a large one, and among those present was a tall, well-proportioned, impressive young lawyer, a *maître des requêtes.* Mme Du Hausset had forgotten his title, but she remembered him as being the son of Michel-Étienne Turgot, the late *Prévôt des marchands* in the city of Paris. The general conversation ran upon administrative problems, and Mme Du Hausset paid little attention. But later there began a discussion upon the love of the French nation for their king. The young Turgot ventured an opinion. To his mind the love of the monarchy was really something more than a blind and superstitious veneration for a man and an office. And, strange as it may seem, his argument, which was generally appreciated for its subtlety, was the somewhat crude assertion that the adoration of the monarch derived from a memory of the great material benefits of kingly rule. He went on to explain himself more fully: France, Europe, even humanity at large owed their liberty to a king of France (whose name Mme Du Hausset could not remember). This king had established communes in the cities of his realm, had given a multitude of men a civil existence, and had freed them from the bonds of feudal authority. But in doing this he had been following his own self-interest; he had wanted the support of the towns against over-mighty feudal subjects; he had needed money to govern his kingdom; and he had therefore compelled the burgesses to pay for their rights. But whatever the motive, the outcome was laudable. Out of self-interest accrued a good to humanity.

Douglas DaKin, Turgot and the Ancien Régime in France, *Octagon Books, 1980.*

Ronald L. Meek   (essay date 1973)

SOURCE: An introduction, in *Turgot on Progress, Sociology and Economics*, edited and translated by Ronald L. Meek, Cambridge at the University Press, 1973, pp. 1-33.

[*Meek was an educator and author who included among his many publications* The Economics of Physiocracy: Essays and Translations *(1962) and* Social Science and the Ignoble Savage *(1973). In the following excerpt, Meek delineates the ideas found in three of Turgot's principal works,* A Philosophic Review of the Successive Advances of the Human Mind *(1750),* On Universal History *(1750), and* Reflections on the Formation and the Distribution of Wealth *(1770).*]

THE 'PHILOSOPHICAL REVIEW' AND
'ON UNIVERSAL HISTORY'

Turgot's notes . . . on **The Causes of the Progress and Decline of the Sciences and the Arts,** were probably written in 1748, at any rate if we are to judge from a marginal note referring to a prize to be offered early in 1749 by the Academy of Soissons for a discourse on this subject. It is clear from these fragmentary but quite extensive notes that many of the view which Turgot was later to express in the **Philosophical Review** and **On Universal History** were already formed before he entered the Sorbonne: the notes obviously constituted part of the raw material upon which he drew when he was writing these two pieces. A number of the more picturesque analogies used in the latter are to be found already in the notes; there are distinct traces of the 'materialist' approach which he was later to employ much more extensively; the critique of Montesquieu's theory of the influence of climate which appears in **On Universal History** is present in the notes in embryo; and there, too, is the famous prophecy about the coming revolt of the American colonies. But three major unifying constituents of the later works are still lacking. First, although there is a passing reference to Locke's notion that 'all our ideas come to us from the senses', there is no indication of the important role which this notion was later to play in Turgot's thinking. Second, although the notes contain several references to different arts and sciences being 'perfected', no general doctrine of perfectibility is explicitly stated. And third, there is no indication of the stadial theory of socio-economic development which was to become part of the framework of **On Universal History.**

In a critique which Turgot wrote in March 1750 of a book on the origin of languages by Maupertuis, however, the sensationalist theory of Locke pervades the whole, and, even more important, the outlines of a stadial theory of the development of early society are fairly clearly delineated. 'Thence arose the different languages', Turgot writes, 'according to whether the people were hunters, shepherds, or husbandmen . . . The hunter would have few words, very vivid, not closely linked together, and progress would be slow; the shepherd, with his peaceful life, would construct a gentler and more refined language; the husbandman, one that was colder and more coherent.' The general idea implied here—that early society proceeds naturally and successively through the hunting, pastoral, and agricultural stages, each with its own 'superstructure' of languages,

laws, customs, etc.—was destined to be of great importance, not only for Turgot's own work, but also for the emergence and development of social science as a whole in the eighteenth century.

It is possible that the inspiration for this seminal idea came to Turgot from Montesquieu. At the end of Book I of *L'Esprit des Lois,* Montesquieu says that the laws ought to be related to (*inter alia*) 'the principal occupation of the natives, whether husbandmen, huntsmen, or shepherds', and in Book XVIII ('Of Laws in the Relation they Bear to the Nature of the Soil') we find the following statement:

> The laws have a very great relation to the manner in which the several nations procure their subsistence. There should be a code of laws of a much larger extent for a nation attached to trade and navigation than for people who are content with cultivating the earth. There should be a much greater for the latter than for those who subsist by their flocks and herds. There must be a still greater for these than for such as live by hunting.

These statements, and some of the rather haphazard comments which follow, may well have seized Turgot's imagination. But it must be emphasised that the clarity with which Turgot expressed the idea, the way in which he refined and developed it, and the uses to which he put it, mark him and not Montesquieu out as the one who really deserves the name of innovator.

On 3 July 1750, in his capacity as *prieur,* Turgot gave the first of his two discourses at the Sorbonne, under the title **The Advantages which the Establishment of Christianity has Procured for the Human Race.** This rather over-eloquent piece is usually compared unfavourably with his second discourse of II December 1750—the famous **Philosophical Review of the Successive Advances of the Human Mind** which is translated below. But the 3 July discourse is rather more significant than it is usually made out to be. In it, Turgot sets out to show how the doctrines of Christianity have helped to temper human passions, to perfect governments, and to make men better and happier. He begins by considering the effects of the Christian religion on men considered in themselves, concentrating here on such matters as the preservation of classical literature by the monks, the abolition of cruel customs such as the exposure of children, and, generally, the way in which Christianity has improved morals and manners and made men more humane. He then goes on, in the second and more interesting part of the discourse, 'to examine the progress of the art of government, and to show how Christianity has contributed to it'. After a diatribe against great legislators, whose laws have a tendency to 'acquire a fatal immutability', he goes on to say this:

> More happy are the nations whose laws have not been established by such great geniuses; they are at any rate perfected, although slowly and through a thousand detours, without principles, without perspectives, without a fixed plan; chance and circumstances have often led to wiser laws than have the researches and efforts of the human mind; an abuse which had been ob-

served would give rise to a law; the abuse of that law would give rise to a second which modified it: by passing successively from one excess to the opposite excess, men little by little drew nearer to the happy medium.

The important thing here, of course, is that it is not Christianity—nor, apparently, even the Deity—which produces 'these slow and successive advances'. They occur, as it were, of themselves, and the role of Christianity is confined to eradicating injustices from the laws, spreading the idea that men—and nations—are brothers, and moderating the potentially despotic behaviour of monarchs.

In the discourse of 11 December 1750 these 'slow and successive advances' become in effect the main theme, and the part played by Christianity in the historical process of attaining perfection is summarised in a single paragraph. And by the time one reaches this paragraph, with its question 'Holy religion, could it be that I should forget you?', one feels strongly not only that it could, but also that it almost was. Perhaps this is unfair to Turgot: it could be argued that the two discourses are in fact all of a piece—both are about progress and perfection, but the first deals with their sacred and the second with their secular aspects. There is an interesting parallel here with Bossuet's *Discours sur l'Histoire Universelle,* by which Turgot was greatly (if perversely) influenced: in that book, a sacred history (mainly of the Jews) is followed by a completely separate secular history entitled 'The Empires'. Possibly what appears at first sight to be a conflict between Turgot's 3 July and 11 December discourses is merely another example of this kind of conscious and disciplined compartmentalisation. But it is rather more probable, I think, that the conflict was, at least in part, a real one, reflecting a mental struggle which was going on in his mind in the months immediately before he announced that he was abandoning his ecclesiastical career.

'The whole human race, through alternate periods of rest and unrest, of weal and woe, goes on advancing, although at a slow pace, towards greater perfection.' This is the main theme of Turgot's 11 December discourse, in which the idea of progress which we particularly associate with the second half of the eighteenth century was put forward for the first time. The oratorical flights are sometimes tiresome, and the ritualistic passages at the end sound rather strangely in modern ears, but for all that the new message is clear enough. The keynote is sounded in the first two paragraphs. The 'succession of mankind', says Turgot, 'affords from age to age an ever-changing spectacle . . . All the ages are bound up with one another by a succession of causes and effects . . . Thus the human race, considered over the period since its origin, appears to the eye of a philosopher as one vast whole, which itself, like each individual, has its infancy and its advancement.' And this advancement', as the next paragraph makes clear, is 'towards greater perfection.

The aim of the discourse, then, is to illustrate this idea by indicating 'the main lines of the progress of the human mind', with particular reference to the development of the arts and sciences. The aim is, of course, over-ambitious, and it is often difficult to discern these 'main lines' beneath the wealth of detail and apostrophes. The unifying theme, however, is the Lockean notion that 'the senses constitute the unique source of our ideas', and the associated notion that 'the need perfects the tool'. Turgot's argument seems to be that since all men have the same organs and senses, the spectacle of the same universe has always given them the same ideas; and since their needs and inclinations are broadly the same, they have always originated and perfected the same arts, and have proceeded through roughly the same stages of development from barbarism to refinement. But 'they do not all move forward at the same rate along the road which is marked out for them'. Turgot argues that 'circumstances' either encourage or discourage development, and it is the infinite variety of these 'circumstances' which brings about the manifest inequality in the progress of nations.

Given his general aim and this conceptual framework, then, Turgot is obliged to deal with two main questions—first, what exactly are these 'circumstances' which either increase or decrease the rate of progress; and second, why exactly is it that the general long-run tendency is in fact towards 'greater perfection' rather than towards, say, the reverse? Turgot does not clearly distinguish between these two questions, and his answer to the second and more important one is by no means fully worked out. The elements of his answer to it, however, may with a little effort be disentangled from the rest. First, the general process of the growth and development of societies is a *natural* process, comparable to the process of growth of the individual from infancy to adulthood, or that of the plant from seed to flower. Second, the main (although by no means the only) reasons why societies tend in the long run to develop towards 'greater perfection' are to be sought in the *economic* sphere. In the discourse, Turgot emphasises in this connection (a) the crucial importance of the emergence in the agricultural stage of development of a *social surplus,* which not only makes possible the development of 'towns, trade, the useful arts and accomplishments, the division of occupations', etc., but also facilitates the creation of a leisured class which 'bends all its strength to the cultivation of the arts'; (b) the way in which the development of commerce is associated with the perfection of 'astronomy, navigation, and geography'; (c) the important role of the towns—'the centres of trade and the backbone of society'—in preventing the decline of the arts and sciences in periods of barbarism; and (d) the way in which the 'mechanical arts' are preserved in times of general decline by the 'needs of life', and are developed in the long run merely by virtue of the fact that time passes. To describe Turgot's argument in these terms is not, I think, to misrepresent it, although one is bound to look at it to some extent with the hindsight afforded by one's knowledge of his later work in this field.

All these ideas were clarified and developed further in **On Universal History,** which, together with its companion work **On Political Geography,** was written by Turgot according to Du Pont 'while he was at the Sorbonne, or shortly after he left it'. Du Pont tells us that Turgot was planning a succession of three works, of which the first would have been Universal History, the second Political Geography, and the third a treatise on the Science of Government. ***On Political Geography*** is interesting not only as further evidence of the extraordinary breadth and novelty of the young Turgot's interests and ideas, but also because it contains an important development of the 'three stages' theory. Turgot's notes consist essentially of a description of five 'political maps of the world', the first of which would contain details of (*inter alia*) the following:

> The successive changes in the manner of life of men, and the order in which they have followed one another: peoples who are shepherds, hunters, husband-men.

> The causes which have been able to keep certain peoples for longer periods in the state of hunters, then shepherds. The differences which result from these three states, in relation to the number of men, to the movements of nations, to the greater or lesser degree of ease in surmounting the barriers by which nature has, so to speak, assigned to different societies their portion of the terrestrial globe, to communications, to the greater or lesser degree of ease with which peoples are intermingled.

And the second 'political map of the world', similarly, would contain details of:

> The first formation of governments among peoples who are savages, hunters, shepherds, husbandmen. The variations relative to these three manners of life.

The 'three stages' theory which is expressed so clearly here by Turgot was, as I have already said, of great importance in the subsequent development of social science in the eighteenth century. Not only did it enable a plausible explanation of *differences* between societies to be given; but it also facilitated the formulation of a general theory of the *development* of society from lower to higher levels.

In ***On Universal History,*** Turgot makes a much more extensive use of the 'three stages' theory than in any of his earlier works. After a short introduction in which he describes the aim of 'universal history' as he understands it, he proceeds in the first of the two 'discourses' of which the work consists to consider the state of mankind immediately after the Flood. In the beginning, when men could devote themselves to nothing but obtaining their subsistence, they were primarily hunters, in much the same situation as the savages of America. But in countries where certain animals like oxen, sheep, and horses were to be found, 'the pastoral way of life' was introduced, resulting in an increase in wealth and a greater understanding of 'the idea of property'. Eventually, in fertile countries, pastoral peoples moved on to the state of agriculture, and as a result of the surplus which agriculture was able to generate there arose 'towns, trade, and all the useful arts and accomplishments', a leisured class, and so on. Within this conceptual framework, Turgot sets an account of wars and conquests among early peoples, the ways in which different nations were led to intermingle, and the overall effects of this intermingling.

Immediately after this section there is an important passage in which Turgot comes very close to the idea, later to be used so effectively by the members of the Scottish Historical School, that the development of society is essentially a kind of unintended by-product of the conflict of human wills and actions which are often directed towards quite different ends. The passions of ambitious men, says Turgot, 'have led them on their way without their being aware of where they were going . . . They were, so to speak, the leading-strings with which nature and its Author guided the human race in its infancy . . . It is only through upheavals and ravages that nations have been extended, and that order and government have in the long run been perfected'.

> I seem to see [Turgot says] a huge army, every movement of which is directed by some mighty genius. When the military signals are given, when the trumpets sound tumultuously and the drums beat, whole squadrons of cavalry move off, the very horses are filled with a passion which has no aim, and each part of the army makes its way through the obstacles without knowing what may result from it: the leader alone sees the combined effect of all these different movements. Thus the passions have led to the multiplication of ideas, the extension of knowledge, and the perfection of the mind, in the absence of that reason whose day had not yet come and which would have been less powerful if its reign had arrived earlier.

One feels very strongly here that when Turgot speaks of the way in which, through this kind of mechanism, 'nature and its Author' guided the human race, it is nature rather than its Author to which he is mainly referring—that he is, in fact, feeling his way towards the idea that social development is due to the unfolding of certain immanent laws of history rather than to the conscious intervention of the Deity. This is a point on which I shall have something more to say later.

In the remaining part of the first 'discourse', Turgot is concerned in the main with the development of different forms of government—as related in particular to the size and geographical situation of the nation concerned—and with the formation and conflicts of empires. These sections, although they contain many stimulating insights, are perhaps not as well organised as the earlier ones. A number of interesting themes are developed, however, notably the association of the 'spirit of equality' with the 'spirit of commerce', and the idea that knowledge and reason almost always, in one way or another, prevail over force. And towards the end, when Turgot comes on to the subject of slavery, the 'three stages' idea is brought in once again as a conceptual framework.

In the second 'discourse', Turgot is concerned mainly with progress in the arts and sciences. He begins with a fairly detailed account of the sensationalist psychology which, as we have already seen, was one of his great unifying themes, and, closely linked with this, a sketch of his theory of language. He then propounds a kind of 'law of uneven development' of the human mind comparable to the similar law relating to human society which he has in effect put forward in the first 'discourse', the basic idea here being that genius is spread evenly throughout all peoples, but that 'the chances of education and of events' either develop it or leave it buried in obscurity. The inequality in the development of knowledge which results from this is closely associated—both as cause and as effect—with that inequality in the general development of the nations concerned, which Montesquieu tries mistakenly to account for in terms of differences in climate.

In the wide-ranging accounts of the development of music, dance, poetry, history, metaphysics, physics, mathematics, logic, the arts of taste, and eloquence which follow this introduction, a number of the themes which Turgot has used before—including the 'three stages' theory—reappear yet again. The most pervasive theme, perhaps, is the simple idea that the arts and sciences come to man not from heaven but from earth—from his sensations, from his psychological and economic needs, from experiences 'which are common to and within the reach of all men', and that they change as these sensations, needs, and experiences change. This theme is prominent in Turgot's account of the way in which the needs of tillage and navigation developed astronomy; the primitive origins of music, dance, and poetry; the reason why the fables of all peoples resemble one another; the origins of design, sculpture, and painting; the origin of mathematics; the 'god-making' activities of early peoples; the reason why the English have not been able to produce any great painters; the connection between trade and taste; the reasons for the continuation of the mechanical arts when letters and taste have fallen; the necessity for the cultivation and perfection of the mechanical arts in order that 'real physics and the higher philosophy' could arise; and in a dozen other places as well. Turgot is not consistent in his use of this theme, and it appears side by side with a number of others, but it would be absurd to pretend that it does not exist or that it is not important.

The final point I want to make about **On Universal History** is that in it Turgot goes some way towards clarifying his views about the state of perfection towards which society is advancing in the Age of Reason. In the *Philosophical Review* the general picture we get is one of an infinite advance on all fronts, of everlasting progress in every sphere, and we are apt to pass over the following significant paragraph:

> Knowledge of nature and of truth is as infinite as they are: the arts, whose aim is to please us, are as limited as we are. Time constantly brings to light new discoveries in the sciences; but poetry, painting, and music have a fixed limit which the genius of languages, the imitation of nature, and the limited sensibility of our organs determine, which they attain by slow steps and which they cannot surpass. The great men of the Augustan age reached it, and are still our models.

In **On Universal History** this idea is repeated and expanded a little. In particular, Turgot describes in a very interesting way the manner in which poetry, although it has already reached perfection in certain basic respects, will continue to change and progress in certain other respects as time goes on.

On Universal History finishes in midstream, just at the point where Turgot is embarking upon an interesting dis-

cussion of the way in which progress in the sciences depends upon 'inventions and technical processes'; and the great plan of a geographical-cum-sociological-cum-political treatise was never achieved. Turgot became a civil servant and statesman, and his intellectual interests turned more and more in the direction of economics. Echoes of his early perfectibilist views, and, more particularly, of the theory of history with which they were associated, are however to be found scattered among some of his later works on language and literature, in some of his letters to friends, and in his economic work—notably, as we shall see, in the **Reflections.** Turgot gradually became known, at any rate among a small circle, as a pioneer perfectibilist, and the verbal tradition was handed on by men like Du Pont and, more importantly, Condorcet. In his *Life of Turgot*, which appeared in 1786, Condorcet described Turgot's view concerning the unbounded perfectibility of the human understanding and the limitless progress of the sciences as 'one of the great principles of his philosophy', which he 'never once abandoned'. And when, a few years later, in the shadow of the guillotine, Condorcet came to write his own great work on the advances of the human mind [Esquisse d'un Tableau Historique des Progrès de l'Esprit Humain], he gave Turgot his full due, placing him together with Price and Priestley as 'the first and most illustrious apostles' of the doctrine of the limitless perfectibility of the human species—that new doctrine which, in Condorcet's words, was to give 'the final blow to the already tottering structure of prejudice'. Bliss was it indeed, in that dawn, to be alive.

THE 'REFLECTIONS'

> I have done a lot of scribbling since I saw you last [wrote Turgot to Du Pont on 9 December 1766] . . . I have drawn up some **Questions** for the two Chinese about whom I have spoken to you, and, in order to make their object and meaning clear, I have prefaced them with a kind of analytical sketch of the work of society and of the distribution of wealth. I have not put any algebra at all in it, and there is nothing of the **Tableau Économique** but the metaphysical part; moreover, I have left on one side a large number of questions which would have to be dealt with in order to make the work complete, but I have dealt pretty thoroughly with what concerns the formation and course of capitals, interest on money, etc.; it is a kind of groundwork.

The 'two Chinese' mentioned by Turgot, according to Du Pont, were MM. Ko and Yang, two clever young men who, after having been brought up in France by the Jesuits, were being sent back to Canton with a pension from the Crown so that they could carry on a correspondence about Chinese literature and science. Turgot gave them books, valuable instruments, the **Questions** referred to, and the **Reflections** (presumably in manuscript form). But the departure of MM. Ko and Yang, who were thus unknowingly immortalised, was of course only the occasion and not the cause of the production of the **Reflections.** Even though Turgot himself described the work in a letter to Du Pont some years later as having had 'no other object than to render intelligible the questions I put to the Chinese about their country', there is no need to take this too literally: Turgot was adept at finding pegs on which to hang important works, and if Ko and Yang had not conveniently presented themselves he would no doubt have found some other occasion for summarising the great system of economic theory at which he had arrived by the end of 1766.

This system cannot be fully understood, I believe, without an appreciation of the way in which its leading propositions were connected with Turgot's historical and sociological theories. But let us leave this on one side for the time being, and consider briefly the development of Turgot's main *economic* ideas up to 1766.

Among the 'works to be written' in the extraordinary list mentioned above was a 'Treatise on circulation; interest, banking, Law's system, credit, exchange, and commerce'; and among Turgot's papers there is a manuscript, apparently written about 1753-4, entitled **Plan of a Work on Commerce, the Circulation and Interest of Money, the Wealth of States,** which was presumably intended as a first step in the realisation of this part of his programme. This document is interesting partly because of the absence from it of any peculiarly 'Physiocratic' principles, and partly because of the presence in it of (*a*) a very clear statement of the way in which supply and demand determine the equilibrium price of a commodity, which can be regarded as a first sketch of the rather more developed treatment of this subject in the **Reflections;** (*b*) a clear statement in favour of free competition and against the regulation of prices; and (*c*) a fairly clear statement, remarkable enough for its time, to the effect that free competition would establish a price for all commodities which was sufficient to cover not only the vendor's subsistence and paid-out costs, but also 'the interest on the advances which their trade requires'. Even if the 'vendors' referred to in the latter statement are assumed to be merchants (in the narrow sense) rather than producers, the statement when read in its context may be regarded as the germ of the *general* theory of returns to capital which was later to be used with such striking effect in the **Reflections.**

In 1759, when the celebrated Vincent de Gournay died and Marmontel asked Turgot (who had known Gournay well and been greatly influenced by him) to provide some notes about him for an obituary, Turgot wrote an **Éloge** which purported to summarise Gournay's economic beliefs. Whether the summary was a wholly accurate one so far as Gournay's views were concerned is rather doubtful, but there is very little doubt that it represented Turgot's own views at the time. The work is note-worthy for an elaborate and uncompromising statement of the *laissez-faire* principle, and for a number of passages which indicate that Quesnay's influence, as well as that of Gournay, was already becoming important. Near the beginning of the piece, Turgot ascribes to Gournay the view that 'a worker who manufactures a piece of material adds real wealth to the total wealth of the State'; and a few pages further on he similarly ascribes to him the view that 'the only real wealth which the State possesses is the annual product of its land *and of the industry of its inhabitants*', and that the sum of the revenues produced annually in the State consists of 'the net revenue of each piece of land *and*

the net product of the industry of each individual'. These non-Physiocratic (or perhaps deliberately anti-Physiocratic) statements, however, are followed shortly afterwards by three distinct bows in the Physiocratic direction: a favourable reference to Quesnay's article Corn; a statement that it is 'agriculture and commerce, *or rather agriculture animated by commerce'* which is the source of the revenue accruing to the State; and, more important, a rather implausible ascription to Gournay of the view that 'all taxes, of whatever kind, are always in the last analysis paid by the proprietor of land'. The latter statement, and the advocacy of a single tax on land rent which accompanies it, would seem at first sight to be logically incompatible with the views ascribed to Gournay earlier in the piece—and this was indeed a real problem, with which Turgot was later to wrestle in the **Reflections.** Even more important, however, is a statement in the **Éloge** to the effect that a high rate of interest 'excludes the nation from all branches of commerce of which the product is not one or two per cent above the current rate of interest'—a statement which was to reappear in a generalised and more accurate form in the **Reflections,** and which suggests that by 1759 Turgot had already advanced a considerable way towards his general theory of the returns to capital.

Between 1759 and 1766, the date of the writing of the **Reflections,** the main intellectual influence on Turgot was of course that of Physiocracy. He would almost certainly have seen a copy of the 'third edition' of the *Tableau Économique* when Quesnay distributed it privately in 1759; and the period from 1759 to 1766 was precisely that in which almost all of the most important economic works of Quesnay and Mirabeau were published. The basic economic idea of the Physiocrats, upon which a great deal of the remainder of their system depended, was their doctrine of the exclusive 'productivity' of agriculture. It was only agriculture, they claimed, which was inherently capable of yielding a disposable surplus over necessary cost—the famous 'net product', which according to them crystallised out into land rent. Manufacture and commerce, they argued, were *not* 'productive' *in this sense*—i. e., they were not inherently capable of yielding a disposable surplus over necessary cost. Turgot was evidently very impressed by this doctrine, although his own interpretation of it, and the uses to which he put it, were appreciably different from Quesnay's.

But the feature of Quesnay's work which obviously impressed Turgot more than anything else was its emphasis on the necessity of *capital* in agriculture. 'M. Quesnay', wrote Turgot in his **Plan of a Mémoire on Taxes,** 'has dealt with the mechanism of cultivation, wholly based on very large *original advances* and demanding *annually other advances* which are equally necessary. And in the same document, Turgot gave Quesnay the credit for having been the first to lay down clearly the true distinction between *gross product* and *net product,* and 'to exclude from the *net product* the profits of the cultivator, which are the inducement, the unique and indispensable cause of cultivation'. It is very significant that Turgot should have singled out the latter point, because it was precisely on this that Quesnay was *not* clear. What was now required, Turgot came to believe, was (*a*) a generalisation of Quesnay's concept of 'advances', and its use as the basis for an explanation of the economic 'mechanism' *as a whole*—i. e., not simply for an explanation of the 'mechanism of cultivation'; and (*b*) a clarification and development of the idea that the profit of the entrepreneur who makes the 'advances' is part of the absolutely necessary expenses of production. Both these themes begin to appear in Turgot's work from about 1763 onwards. By 1766 he is talking clearly about the existence and crucial importance of an entrepreneurial class—that 'precious species of men' who turn their capitals to account not only in agriculture but also 'in every other kind of commerce'. What still appears to be missing is a clear recognition that 'commerce' in this connection includes not only 'commerce' in the strict sense—i. e. buying and selling—but also manufacturing. Turgot is still talking about enterprises 'in agriculture and commerce': it is not until the **Reflections** that he begins to talk clearly and consistently about 'agricultural, manufacturing, and commercial enterprises'.

In this respect, an important influence on Turgot on the eve of his composition of the **Reflections** may possibly have been that of Hume, most of whose economic essays (with which Turgot was of course quite familiar) had been published as early as 1752, and who was himself in Paris from October 1763 to January 1766. In the latter half of 1766, Turgot corresponded with Hume on the question of the incidence of taxation, and in particular on the question of the validity or otherwise of the proposition that all taxes are ultimately paid by the landowners. In one of Hume's letters to Turgot, [*The Letters of David Hume*, 1932] which was apparently written in late September 1766, he made the following point:

> I beg you also to consider, that, besides the Proprietors of Land and the labouring Poor, there is in every civilized Community a very large and a very opulent Body who employ their Stocks in Commerce and who enjoy a great Revenue from their giving Labour to the poorer sort. I am perswaded that in France and England the Revenue of this kind is much greater than that which arises from Land: For besides Merchants, properly speaking, I comprehend in this Class all Shop-Keepers and Master-Tradesmen of every Species. Now it is very just, that these should pay for the Support of the Community, which can only be where Taxes are lay'd on Consumptions. There seems to me no Pretence for saying that this order of Men are necessitated to throw their Taxes on the Proprietors of Land, since their Profits and Income can surely bear Retrenchment.

Hume's explicit division of that 'very opulent Body who employ their Stocks in Commerce' into 'Merchants, properly speaking' on the one hand and 'all Shop-Keepers and Master-Tradesmen of every Species' on the other was quite remarkable for its time, and may well have helped to supply Turgot with an essential constituent of his system.

We do not know why Turgot kept the **Reflections** by him for three years before sending it to Du Pont for publication, or whether the work was changed and developed in any way during those three years. So far as the first question is concerned, it is possible that Turgot was waiting to see how *Éphémérides* would progress under Du Pont's editorship; but it seems rather more likely that he was hoping that he might find time to 'make something passable' of a piece which, however much thought may have gone into the making of its basic propositions, was no doubt written down hastily and with perhaps a little more than passing reference to the occasion of the departure of MM. Ko and Yang. On the second question, it would seem unlikely that any really substantial changes were made in the work during the period concerned. The significant thing here is that during those three years Turgot's ideas on a number of the subjects treated in the **Reflections** underwent a certain amount of development. In his notes on the mémoires which Graslin and Saint-Péravy submitted in 1767 for a prize offered by the Royal Agricultural Society of Limoges, for example, Turgot not only put forward his famous statement of the law of diminishing returns, but also appreciably clarified his analysis of the nature of entrepreneurial profit—an analysis carried to a still higher stage in his letters of October-December 1770 to Terray on the corn trade. Yet there is no real trace of any of these developments in the **Reflections.**

Turning now to the **Reflections** itself, one of the most interesting things about it is the way in which the staggeringly 'modern' theory of capital in which it culminates, and the basic 'Physiocratic' theory of production of which it makes use, are both set within the context of a broad historical and sociological analysis, deriving from Turgot's early works of the Sorbonne period. Turgot's intellectual development in this respect mirrored that of his great contemporary Adam Smith and anticipated that of Marx: all three began with some kind of 'materialist' theory of history, and then went on to develop from this a system of economics which in one way or another embodied or made use of its basic propositions. It is perfectly possible, of course, if one wishes, to abstract Turgot's theory of capital from its context and present it purely as an anticipation of the best nineteenth-century analytical work in this field—which it indeed was. But by doing this alone, one tends to underestimate the brilliance of Turgot's achievement, and cuts oneself off from any hope of understanding the way in which the 'modern' and 'Physiocratic' parts of his analysis were related to one another.

Turgot's main aim in the **Reflections** was to investigate the way in which the economic 'machine' operated in a society where there were three main classes or 'orders' of economic agents—landowners, wage-earners, *and capitalist entrepreneurs*. His very postulation of an entrepreneurial society of this kind was a highly remarkable achievement, given the time and place in which he was working: Turgot evidently possessed to the full that peculiar feature of genius which sometimes allows it not only to observe what *is* typical, but also to discern and analyse what is *becoming* typical. But even more remarkable was the way in which he appreciated, whether consciously or unconsciously, that one could arrive at an understanding in depth of such a society by beginning with an analysis of the working of the 'machine' *in the type of society which historically preceded it,* and then asking oneself what alterations in its working were brought about when a new class of capitalist entrepreneurs entered upon the historic scene. This is a methodological device which was later to be used very effectively by Smith, Ricardo, and Marx; the only real difference between their approach and Turgot's—and it is indeed a significant difference—is that whereas the preceding state of society which they postulated was one in which there were neither landlords nor capitalists, so that the labourer owned what Smith called 'the whole produce of his labour', that which Turgot postulated was one in which landlords—although not of course capitalists—*did* exist.

What Turgot did, in effect, was to accept the view—already adumbrated by Quesnay and Mirabeau in their *Philosophie Rurale* and later to be developed by the Scottish Historical School—that after the hunting, pastoral, and agricultural stages society proceeded to a fourth stage—the so-called 'commercial' stage; to assume that in this fourth stage a capitalist or entrepreneurial form of organisation was paramount; and to analyse this form of society by examining the way in which it arose from and impinged upon the 'agricultural' stage and altered the basic relations which were characteristic of it.

Turgot's starting-point in the **Reflections,** then, is a society which has already proceeded through the hunting and pastoral stages to the *agricultural stage.* This society is characterised (*a*) by the social division of labour and the mutual exchange of the products of the different kinds of labour; (*b*) by a basic social division between the class of cultivators, which is 'productive' in the sense that the fertility of the soil enables it to produce a surplus over subsistence, and the class of artisans, which is 'stipendiary' in the sense that it is in effect supported by this surplus; (*c*) by the eventual emergence of a 'disposable' class of private landowners, to whom the surplus or 'net product' of the land accrues in the form of 'revenue'; and (*d*) by the existence of various different arrangements which the landowners may make with the cultivators in order to get their land cultivated and to ensure that they receive the 'net product'. These arrangements, which are dealt with in more or less the order in which they actually appeared on the historic scene, culminate in 'tenant-farming, or the letting-out of Land'. The importance of the latter kind of arrangement, as the sequel shows, is that the farmers to whom the land is leased are *capitalist entrepreneurs,* who make all the 'advances' involved in cultivation and pay the landowners the 'net product' in the form of an annual rent.

Having at last—one quarter of the way through the book—introduced the concept of *capital,* Turgot proceeds immediately to the subject of 'capitals in general, and of the revenue of money', thereby making the vital transition from the agricultural society which was his historical (and analytical) starting-point to the specifically *capitalist or entrepreneurial* society which it was his main concern to examine. He begins with what may appear at first sight to be a digression on the use of gold and silver in commerce and the general principles according to which the prices of exchangeable commodities are determined in a competitive market. A 'digression' of this kind, however, overlong though it may perhaps be, was essential in order to set the stage for much of what was to follow. *Capitals* are then reintroduced, and the historical process of their accumulation—at first in the form of various items of 'movable wealth' and then in the form of money—is briefly discussed.

The ordering of the sections which immediately follow leaves something to be desired: it is not always easy, as Turgot found at this point, to make history and analysis run hand in hand. But the main lines of his argument are clear enough. 'Advances' in the form of movable wealth are necessary in every occupation. They are necessary, first, in *agriculture,* where they have historically taken various different forms, and where the demands of large-scale cultivation lead to the separation of the broad class of cultivators into ordinary wage-earners and 'Entrepreneurs or Capitalists who make all the advances', the latter necessarily receiving, over and above the return of their capital, their 'wages', and compensation for their various costs, 'a profit equal to the revenue they could acquire with their capital without any labour'. They are necessary, second, in *manufacture and industry,* where large-scale production leads similarly to the separation of the industrial stipendiary class into 'ordinary Workmen' and 'capitalist Entrepreneurs', each of the latter necessarily receiving, over and above the return of his capital, his 'wages', and compensation for his various costs, 'a profit sufficient to compensate him for what his money would have been worth to him if he had employed it in the acquisition of an estate'. And they are necessary, finally, in commerce, in respect of which a similar analysis leads to similar conclusions. This picture of a society in which, behind the veil of money, we see the whole of agriculture, industry, and commerce depending upon the continual advance and return of capitals owned by a great entrepreneurial class, was extraordinarily advanced for its time.

In a society of this kind, Turgot explains, capital may be invested not only in agricultural, industrial, and commercial enterprises, but also in the purchase of *land,* the revenue from which will then in effect constitute the return on the capital so invested. Or, alternatively, the capital may simply be lent out to a borrower in return for interest on it at an agreed rate. This loan transaction, in essence, is one in which the *use of money* is bought and sold; and the price of this use of money is determined, like the prices of all other commodities, 'by the haggling which takes place between the seller and buyer, by the balance of supply and demand', and not, as a number of earlier economists had believed, by the quantity of money. The receipt of interest is morally justifiable, in spite of the contrary view expressed by certain theologians; and the level of the rate of interest ought never to be fixed by law. Turgot's theory of interest, with its clear recognition that 'the rate of interest is relative to the quantity of values accumulated and put into reserve in order to create capitals', represents a considerable advance over Hume's theory; and there is some substance in Schumpeter's claim [*History of Economic Analysis,* 1954] that it was 'not only by far the greatest performance in the field of interest theory the eighteenth century produced but it clearly foreshadowed much of the best thought of the last decades of the nineteenth.'

After a 'recapitulation of the five different methods of employing capitals', Turgot goes on to explain the way in which the returns to capital in these different employments are, as he puts it, 'mutually limited by one another'. The basic idea lying behind the four sections which follow would seem to be that if there were no differences in the trouble and risk involved in the different uses of capital, an equilibrium situation would be reached in which the rates of return on capital were equal in all these uses. Since there are in fact marked differences in the trouble and risk involved, however, the equilibrium situation actually reached is characterised not by an equality but by an inequality of returns—capital invested in land bringing in the least, capital lent out at interest bringing in a little more, and capital invested in agricultural, manufacturing, and commercial enterprises bringing in the most, so that equilibrium is perfectly compatible with inequality of returns and indeed necessarily produces it. It follows, according to Turgot, that the rate of interest is the 'thermometer' of the extent to which production will be carried: if interest were at five per cent, for example, no agricultural, manufacturing, or commercial enterprises which were incapable of yielding a net return higher than this would in fact be undertaken—once again a very 'modern' proposition.

After two sections dealing with certain problems of social accounting, Turgot proceeds to his final task—to ask what essential difference, if any, was made to the basic relations characteristic of the simple 'agricultural' society with which he had started by the impingement upon it of the new class of capitalist entrepreneurs. The coming of the new class had certainly resulted in the division of the productive class and the stipendiary class into capitalists and labourers: but did this necessarily mean that the basic relations previously existing between the productive class as a whole and the stipendiary class as a whole, and between these two classes and the disposable class, now no longer existed? The way in which Turgot himself formulated the question was simply this: 'Let us now see how what we have just said about the different methods of employing capitals squares with what we previously laid down about the division of all the members of Society into three classes—the productive class, or that of agriculturists, the industrial or commercial class, and the disposable class, or that of proprietors'.

In the agricultural society, it will be remembered, the product of the labour of the (undifferentiated) productive class had been sufficient not only to provide its own wages, but also to provide a net product, or revenue, which accrued in one form or another to the proprietors of the land. This revenue alone was 'disposable', in the sense that it did not have to be earmarked for use in the reproduction of the annual product at the same level in the following year; and the class of proprietors which received it was itself also 'disposable', in the sense that its members were not 'earmarked' for any particular kind of work. And it was the expenditure of this revenue by the proprietors, together with the expenditure of the cultivators, which was conceived to generate the incomes of the third social class, which for this reason was called the stipendiary class.

How, then, is this picture altered when capitals and capitalist entrepreneurs are introduced? At first sight the alterations would seem to be very radical indeed. For, in the first place, if agriculture, manufacture, and commerce are to be maintained, the entrepreneurs in these occupations must now receive a return which is sufficient not only to secure for them their subsistence, the refund of their capital, and compensation for their paid-out costs, but also to provide a net 'profit' sufficiently high to prevent them from transferring their capital out of the particular sector concerned and either investing it in the purchase of land or lending it out at interest. Turgot's discussions of this 'profit' are somewhat vague: there are hardly two places in which he describes it in exactly the same way, and one is never really clear what precisely it is supposed to be a reward *for,* or indeed whether it can be said to be a 'reward' at all. But whatever it actually is, and wherever it actually comes from, there is no doubt that its level will be sufficiently high to enable its recipients to live at well above the subsistence level; and the question therefore arises as to whether this part of the entrepreneur's income is in fact 'disposable', so that in the entrepreneurial society the rent of land is no longer the *only* 'disposable' (and taxable) form of income. And, in the second place, the interest on money placed on loan, and the recipient of this interest, would both also appear at first sight to be 'disposable', thereby raising a rather similar problem.

The problem of the entrepreneurs' 'profit', Turgot believed, was fairly easy to deal with. If we define a 'disposable' income as one whose receipt is not absolutely necessary in order to ensure that an enterprise carries on its operations next year at the same level (at least) as it is carrying them on this year, then the 'profit' of the entrepreneur is definitely *not* 'disposable', since if it is not received the enterprise will not be carried on at all. What Turgot was doing here, in effect, was to argue that in an entrepreneurial society the 'absolutely necessary' receipts must be taken to include not only compensation for paid-out and subsistence costs (which was all that they normally included in a simple agricultural society), but also a risk and 'special ability' premium, and compensation for the *opportunity cost* involved in employing one's capital in the enterprise concerned rather than investing it in the purchase of land or lending it out at interest.

The problem of interest was more difficult, because the recipient of interest, unlike the entrepreneur, is indeed clearly 'disposable' so far as his person is concerned; and at first sight it would appear that the interest itself is also 'disposable', since 'the entrepreneur and the enterprise can do without it'. The way in which Turgot gets over this is simple enough, in essence, although his argument becomes rather tortuous at this point. What he does, in effect, is to put a further gloss on the concept of 'absolutely necessary' receipts. If the operations of enterprises over the economy as a whole are to be maintained at their existing level, then it is not only 'absolutely necessary' that each entrepreneur should receive a sufficient amount of 'profit' to prevent him from closing down his enterprise and becoming a landowner or money-lender, but it is also 'absolutely necessary' that the class of money-lenders should receive a rate of interest which is not artificially reduced below its market level (e. g. by taxing it). For, says Turgot, if this interest is 'encroached upon', the rate charged on advances to all enterprises will increase, thereby causing the operations of the enterprises themselves to be reduced. Thus the interest received by money-lending capitalists is very different from the revenue received by landowners, and the latter is revealed as being still the only *truly* 'disposable' (and therefore taxable) form of income in the entrepreneurial society. It also still remains true that the wages and profits of the industrial and commercial classes are 'paid either by the proprietor out of his revenue, or by the agents of the productive class out of the part which is earmarked for their needs', so that the adjective 'stipendiary' still correctly describes them; and there is even a sense—although a somewhat rarefied one—in which capitals themselves 'come from the land'.

How far does all this make Turgot a Physiocrat? He certainly used a great deal of the Physiocrats' economic terminology—although he clearly objected to the use of the unnecessarily inflammatory adjective 'sterile' to describe the industrial and commercial classes. He accepted Quesnay's crucial concept of 'advances'—although he generalised and developed it out of all recognition. He accepted the Physiocrats' basic class stratification—although not really as much more than a kind of historical and logical starting-point. He accepted, in a sense, the quite basic Physiocratic doctrine that land rent was the only 'disposable' (and taxable) income—although the arguments which enabled him to reach this conclusion for an entrepreneurial (as distinct from an agricultural) society owed relatively little to Physiocratic inspiration, and were in some respects anti-Physiocratic. Finally, he accepted the Physiocratic idea that the incomes of the industrial and commercial classes were 'paid' by agriculture—although he put a distinctive gloss of his own on this idea too. To describe him as a Physiocrat, then, would be as wrong as to describe him as a non-Physiocrat, or for that matter as anything else. 'I may be wrong,' wrote Turgot to Du Pont in 1770, 'but everyone wants to be himself, and not another . . . All your additions tend to make me out to be an economist, something which I do not want to be any more than an encyclopedist. So although he himself was prepared to say that he was a disciple of Quesnay *and* *Gournay,* he would probably have preferred not to be regarded as anyone's disciple. 'Would you care to join my following?' asked the Comte de Guiche. 'No sir', answered Cyrano de Bergerac, 'I do not follow.'

SOCIOLOGY, ECONOMICS, AND PROGRESS

Turgot's **On Universal History,** as we have seen, stopped short at the point where he had begun enlarging upon the role of the 'mechanical arts' in the development of society, and the great work on geography, sociology, and politics which he had projected was never in fact achieved. What emerged instead was the theory of an entrepreneurial economy which he sketched out in the **"Reflections."** In this respect, as I have already said, Turgot's intellectual development was very similar to that of Smith and Marx: all three thinkers began by working out the elements of a universal 'sociological' system, embodying a theory of history which laid emphasis on economic causes, and then developed *from* these 'sociological' systems the great systems of economic theory by which we mainly know them today.

The basic concept which united the 'sociological' and 'economic' systems, in the case of all three thinkers, was the revolutionary idea that the historical processes of social development, and the manner in which any particular society (or economy) operated, were not arbitrary, but were in an important sense 'subject to law'. What had happened in history, and what was happening in contemporary society, reflected the working of certain law-governed, almost mechanistic processes, which operated independently of the wills of individual men, and which it was the task of the social scientist to analyse and explain. In Turgot's sociology, we see the beginnings of this idea in, for example, his account of the way in which the evil passions of ambitious princes promoted progress; in his theory that the mathematical frequency of the appearance of geniuses was constant; and in a number of his biological and mechanical analogies. In his economics, we see the idea again in a rather different form: the concept of the economy as a kind of great 'machine', always tending of itself to bring about a situation of 'equilibrium', becomes quite central. It emerges very clearly, for example, in a letter which Turgot wrote to Hume on 25 March 1767, where he speaks of 'a kind of equilibrium' which establishes itself between certain economic quantities; of the way in which, if one of the 'weights' is changed, 'it is impossible that there should not result from this in the whole of the machine a movement which tends to re-establish the old equilibrium'; and of the way in which 'in every complicated machine, there are frictions which delay the results most infallibly demonstrated by theory'.

It remained true, of course, that society and its history were made by human beings; but the important point was that they were not, in general, made consciously, but emerged as what I have called above a kind of unintended by-product of the conflict of human wills and actions which were often directed towards quite different ends. There is already an inkling of this in a passage in *L'Esprit des Lois,* where Montesquieu, talking about the principle of monarchy, says:

> It is with this kind of government as with the system of the universe, in which there is a power that constantly repels all bodies from the centre, and a power of gravitation that attracts them to it. Honor sets all the parts of the body politic in motion, and by its very action connects them; thus each individual advances the public good, while he only thinks of promoting his own interest.

And there is much more than an inkling of it, as we have seen, in Turgot's analogy of the army 'directed by some mighty genius'.

The fact that men in their social and economic life were 'subject to law' did not of course mean, in Turgot's view, that free will was an illusion. Nor did it mean that the heavens were empty. Providence still existed, and still in a sense worked through men, but it did so in a much more remote and roundabout way than most of the ecclesiastical practitioners of 'universal history' had thought. Bossuet, for example, in his celebrated *Discourse on Universal History,* had argued that God controlled human affairs in part directly, by influencing great men on strategic occasions, and in part indirectly, by bringing it about that all the parts of the whole depended upon one another, and by 'preparing the effects in the most distant causes'. Even though this account left the 'particular causes' of historical events as a worth-while subject of study, Turgot felt that it still gave far too much weight to the influence of Providence. The most that it could be assumed that the latter had done was to create a law-governed universe in which the complex interplay of cause and effect was likely to produce a long-run—but often very slow and unsteady—tendency towards perfection. It was only in this rather attenuated sense, then, that the world could be said to be 'the most glorious witness to the wisdom which presides over it'. And the purpose of social science was simply to analyse the processes whereby history, as it were, made itself and the economy ran itself. If the results of this analysis turned out to justify the ways of God to man, then that was all to the good, but it was not the primary object of the exercise.

Up to a point, then, it is true to say that Turgot's theory of history was put forward as an alternative to the 'Providential' theories of men like Bossuet. And it is also no doubt true that Turgot, like all of us on such occasions, was influenced more than he knew by the very doctrines which he was combating. The parallels between Turgot's and Bossuet's work are certainly quite striking. Bossuet had talked in terms of a succession of religious 'epochs'; Turgot talked in terms of a succession of socio-economic 'stages'. Bossuet had emphasised the way in which God worked through individual law-givers and conquerors, so that although they made history they did not make it as they wished; Turgot emphasised the way in which certain historical laws and necessities worked through them, with much the same kind of result. Bossuet had proclaimed that 'all the great empires which we have seen on earth have led in different ways towards the good of religion and the glory of God'; Turgot proclaimed that through all its vicissitudes mankind in the long run advances towards greater perfection.

But there is no need to go all the way with Professor Baillie [*The Belief in Progress,* 1950], who has described the eighteenth-century doctrine of progress as 'essentially a redisposition of the Christian ideas which it seeks to replace'. There is no doubt that Turgot's version of the doctrine of progress was influenced in an important way by these 'Christian ideas', but there were other important influences as well. One, obviously, was the spectacular progress of the sciences in the seventeenth and eighteenth centuries, which led many others besides Turgot to conclude that no bounds could be put to their further development. Another, perhaps equally important, was the stimulus afforded by the succession of studies of the Indian tribes of North America which had appeared earlier in the century. If, as everyone soon came to appreciate, 'our ancestors and the Pelasgians who preceded the Greeks were like the savages of America', then it was fairly obvious that something

which most people would want to call 'progress' had been taking place since the time of the Pelasgians.

If we want to regard Turgot as the unconscious vehicle of some kind of *zeitgeist,* surely we would be on safer ground looking in his work for 'bourgeois' rather than for 'Christian' currents. Professor Pollard [*The Ideal of Progress,* 1968] has gone so far as to say that Turgot 'personifies the French bourgeoisie in the full flower of its hope'; and it is certainly true that if we look at his life's work as a whole—not only his sociology and his economic theory, but also his practical work as an administrator—it appears more of a piece when looked at from this viewpoint than from any other. Even if one is not prepared to see anything distinctively 'bourgeois' in his respect for English rights and liberties, his worship of science, his faith in reason, and his immense optimism about the future of mankind, one can surely not deny the aptness of the label when applied, say, to his numerous statements to the effect that 'the State has the greatest interest in conserving the mass of capitals', and above all, to the theoretical system of the **Reflections.**

There is no doubt that the system of the **Reflections** is basically 'capitalist', and that the particular form of 'capitalism' which it envisages and analyses is by no means a primitive one. This can be brought home if one contrasts Turgot's system with Cantillon's, which was certainly the most advanced prior to Turgot's and from which Turgot may well have learned a great deal. Chapter XIII of Part One of Cantillon's *Essay on the Nature of Commerce in General,* indeed, reads at first sight rather like a concise summary of the **Reflections.** The very heading of the chapter—'The circulation and exchange of produce and commodities, as well as their production, are carried on in Europe by Entrepreneurs, and at a risk'—is reminiscent enough; and the content of the chapter, with its distinction between entrepreneurs and hired people, its emphasis on the way in which all entrepreneurs bear risks, and its association (in certain cases) of entrepreneurship with capital, is even more so. When one looks into it, however, the differences between Cantillon's and Turgot's accounts are seen to be rather more striking than the resemblances. With Cantillon, the 'entrepreneurs' include those who are 'Entrepreneurs of their own labour without any capital'—chimney sweeps, water carriers, and even beggars and robbers; with Turgot, all entrepreneurs are assumed to be employers of labour, and independent workmen and artisans do not enter the picture at all. With Cantillon, although the fact that an entrepreneur may set himself up with a capital to conduct his enterprise is quite often mentioned, it is not particularly emphasised; with Turgot, the large capitals or 'advances' assumed to be employed by entrepreneurs are constantly emphasised and play a crucial role in the working of the system as a whole. With Cantillon, finally, the 'profit' of the entrepreneur seems to be regarded as a kind of superior but unfixed wage; with Turgot, there is a much sharper differentiation between the profit of the entrepreneur and the wage of the hired workman. Clearly Cantillon is analysing a society where the capitalist entrepreneur is just beginning to separate himself out from the ranks of the independent workmen; Turgot on the other hand is analysing a society where it is assumed that this process has been completed and that the capitalist system has consolidated itself in all fields of economic activity.

Now the interesting and important thing about all this is that in contemporary France, and even in contemporary England, a capitalist system of this kind was very far from having in fact emerged: at most, it was in the process of emerging. And Turgot, of course, was well aware of this: having spent thirteen years of his life working in the backward but not untypical provinces of Limousin and Angoumois he could hardly have been under any illusions about it. In Turgot's France, capitalism had some hold in agriculture, but only in certain areas; it had very little hold in 'manufacture', which was quite largely carried on by independent workmen; and competition was seriously restricted in almost every field of activity. Yet in the *Reflections* we have a clear picture of an economy in which capitalism embraces all spheres of production; in which the 'industrious' classes are divided sharply into entrepreneurs and wage-earners; in which free competition is universal and there appears to be no monopoly whatsoever; in which even landownership seems to be little more than just another form of investment of capital; and in which there is no possibility of a 'general glut of commodities' because savings are transformed immediately into investment.

This marked gap between the model and contemporary reality would not have appeared in any way mysterious to Turgot's readers, assuming that the latter were by this time familiar with the writings of the Physiocrats. Quesnay, in order to draw attention in a striking way to the backwardness of the contemporary economy, had adopted the device of beginning with an analytical model for the economy in what he called 'a state of prosperity'. This model was in part descriptive, in the sense that it contained certain elements which were already evident on the surface of contemporary reality; in part predictive, in the sense that it embodied the assumption that certain current trends had continued and intensified; and in part a kind of ideal, in the sense that it was assumed to represent a highly desirable state of affairs towards the attainment of which government policies should properly be directed. Turgot's model of an entrepreneurial society in the *Reflections* was of precisely the same general type, and would have been clearly recognised as such by the majority of his readers, at any rate in France. They would also have recognised the essential difference between Quesnay's model and Turgot's—that in the former capitalism was assumed to be paramount only in agriculture, whereas in the latter it was assumed to be paramount in every field of economic activity. And they would not have been misled by the absence in the *Reflections* of any elaborate panegyrics in praise of the postulated system into believing that the model was intended to be merely descriptive and predictive, and not in addition an ideal to which Turgot felt it was quite practicable and eminently desirable that society should endeavour to attain. As such, they would almost certainly have regarded it as part and parcel of Turgot's general doctrine of progress.

But before we ourselves accept it as such, and as yet another reflection of the views of 'the French bourgeoisie in the full flower of its hope', there are two qualifications which

must be made. In the first place, we do not get any clear picture in the *Reflections* of an economy which is capable of continuous and indefinite advance: rather, we get a picture of an economy which, in some respects at any rate, has reached a kind of ceiling—even if a very high one— and which is subject to certain important constraints on further development. For example, 'the wage of the Workman is limited to what is necessary in order to enable him to procure his subsistence', and there is no suggestion that he can ever expect any more than this. There appears to be no guarantee that the rate of interest fixed by the market will be low enough to enable a nation to carry its industry and agriculture to the full extent of its potential. There is no built-in specification about technological progress, and the main emphasis in the model is more on its static than on its dynamic aspects. And if we incorporate into the model, as we probably should, the law of diminishing returns in agriculture which Turgot formulated in 1767, it becomes even more evident that his optimism and hope were tempered by a fairly healthy sense of realism.

In the second place, although Turgot's 'capitalism' was relatively advanced as compared with Cantillon's, it was still relatively backward as compared with Adam Smith's. Smith's capitalists, generally speaking, are not themselves 'industrious': they use their capital to employ labour, and receive, over and above the return of their paid-out costs and interest on their capital at the normal rate, a *net* income, profit, which is as it were exuded by the capital-labour relationship, and which bears a regular proportion not to the effort, if any, which they expend but to the value of the capital they have invested. Turgot's capitalists, on the other hand, are definitely 'industrious', and the 'profit' which they receive from their enterprises is not clearly differentiated from the wages of their labour or the interest on their capital. Nor is this 'profit' exuded by the capital-labour relationship: basically, it is simply a risk and 'special ability' premium plus compensation for an opportunity cost whose level is determined by the general demand-and-supply situation. Smith's capitalists, again, are an independent class, standing on their own, whose income is as it were original rather than derived. Turgot's industrial and commercial capitalists, on the other hand, are still a 'stipendiary' class, and their incomes are 'paid either by the proprietor out of his revenue, or by the agents of the productive class' . . . Clearly Turgot was unable completely to transcend the limitations of the 'agricultural' framework within which the analysis in the first part of the *Reflections* was set. The flower of the French bourgeoisie's hope was still rooted—even if only loosely—in feudal soil.

Eric Voegelin   (essay date 1975)

SOURCE: "Positivism and Its Antecedents," and "The Conflict Between Progress and Political Existence After Turgot," *From Enlightenment to Revolution*, edited by John H. Hallowell, Duke University Press, 1975, pp. 74-109, 110-35.

[*One of the twentieth century's leading political philoso-*

phers, Voegelin is best known for his Order and History *(1956-87), a multi-volume study of the problem of order in human existence. In the following excerpt, he dissects Turgot's categories of history and their relationship to political philosophy.*]

The historism of Turgot

The movement of Positivism has absorbed a highly diversified aggregate of sentiments and ideas. . . . A . . . strain [of] importance is to be found in the historism of Turgot. The principal sources for Turgot's ideas are the two ***Discourses*** which he delivered at the opening and closing sessions of the Sorbonne in 1750, when he was 23 years of age. To these have to be added his fragments of the ***Discourses on Universal History*** of the same period; and, perhaps the richest in ideas, the project of a ***Political Geography.*** The theory of knowledge which Turgot implied in these works he set forth in a formal manner in the article ***Existence*** in the *Encyclopédie.* [All of these pieces, as well as the reprint of ***Existence,*** are to be found in ***Oeuvres de Turgot,*** ed. Daire and Dussard 1844]

Let us begin with that idea of Turgot's which has become the centerpiece of Comte's philosophy of history under the title of the law of the three stages. Turgot was concerned about the different rate of progress in the various sciences, particularly of mathematics and physics. The development of mathematics begins earlier and its advancement is more rapid than that of physics. What is the cause of this difference? In search of an explanation Turgot goes back to Locke's theory of knowledge, in the radicalized, monistic form which it had assumed in France. All knowledge starts with sensation; all ideas are derived reflectively from sensation. Mathematics and physics have different rates of progress because in mathematics, reason has to operate with ideas only, while in physics the symbols of science refer to events in the external world. In physics we search for the causes of events which impress themselves on our senses. We try to ascend from effects to causes, from the senses to bodies, from the present to the past, from visible to invisible bodies, from the world to the Divinity. In this search we do not combine and compare ideas as in mathematics, we try to ascertain the structure of corporeal existence. Errors are inevitable and corrections are slow. Among the various sources of error, one is of specific relevance because it determines a style of hypothesis which stands at the beginning of our interpretation of the external world, and can only slowly be overcome in the history of science; that is the penchant for analogical thinking. In searching for the causes of effects, the first hypothesis which offers itself is the assumption of intelligent, invisible beings, similar to ourselves, who cause the events which impress us. Everything that happens and that cannot be attributed to a human agency must be due to a god who is conceived analogically to man. For this first phase of interpretation Turgot himself has not coined a term; it has been termed successively the fetishistic, or animistic phase of thinking but closest to Turgot's meaning would be the term anthropomorphic. The second phase of interpretation is characterized by a critical, philosophical attitude. The anthropomorphic interpretation of natural forces is abandoned in favor of "abstract expres-

sions," such as essences or faculties, "expressions which explain nothing and about which one speculated as if they were beings, new divinities substituted for the old ones." Only in a last phase were the mechanical interactions of bodies properly observed and interpreted in such a manner that they could be expressed in mathematical terms and verified by experience.

Definition of progress

First of all, the sequence developed by Turgot is not a general law of history but definitely a series of phases through which our interpretation of the external world passes. The question whether there are three or more phases is quite irrelevant; the crucial point is that the mathematized science of the external world disengages itself historically from a context of anthropomorphical symbols which in themselves may be at various stages of rationalization. The critical purification of science from anthropomorphisms is the problem. Turgot designates this process of purification as progress. This designation is valuable in various respects: (1) it attributes to the term progress a clear meaning, (2) it fixes the empirical core of the idea of progress and (3) by this fixation it enables us to distinguish the political, evocative meanings of progress from this by no means unimportant but politically not very exciting core. In particular, the clearness of Turgot gives us a precise criterion for the political misuse of the idea. This misuse can assume two main forms: (1) when the idea of purification from anthropomorphisms is transferred indiscriminately as a criterion of value from the realm of mathematical physics to other spheres of intellectual and spiritual expression, and (2) when the evolution of mathematical physics, however valuable and progressive in itself, is uncritically used as the criterion of the value or progress of a civilization.

The political, evocative amplification of the idea is not absent from the work of Turgot, but the amplification of the sequence is carefully distinguished from its basic meaning. The distinction must be a grave problem for a conscientious thinker because, taken in itself, the emergence of mathematized science has no connection with the problem of meaning in history. What are the considerations which would induce a thinker to make this specific process a symbol for historical meaning? The title of the fragments: ***Discours sur l'Histoire Universelle,*** contains the key to Turgot's considerations, for the title resumes consciously the problem of Bossuet's *Discours.* Turgot grapples with the problem of meaning in history after the Christian meaning is lost. In this respect he is the rival of Voltaire, though he far surpasses Voltaire in his penetrating, theoretical analysis of the problem. He knows that encyclopaedic completeness is no substitute for the universality of the Christian drama of fall and redemption and the profoundness of his historical knowledge does not permit him to relegate the whole history of mankind into some prehistoric abyss and to let meaning begin with the Renaissance. The thinker who tries to find meaning in human history from an intramundane position must, in the first place, establish that there is such a thing as mankind at all, that the succession of human generations in time has a discernible structure which possibly could lend itself to a construction of meaning. Turgot thinks that he can see such a structure by which the succession of men in time is integrated into a whole that can be called mankind. In nonhuman nature he finds the cycles of growth and decay as the fundamental structure. The successive generations of vegetables and animals reproduce the same state over and over again and there is no structure overlapping the single generations. In the succession of human generations we do not see repetition but infinite variety by virtue of the operations of reason, the passions and freedom. This infinite variety, furthermore, is not a discontinuous variety but is held together in time by the chain of cause and effect which links every present generation to all past ones. And, finally, the chain is not a simple continuum, for the intellectual and spiritual life of previous generations is preserved through language and script in the life of the later generations. A *"trésor commun"* accumulates that is transmitted from one generation to the next and passed on, with new increments, as a heritage which grows from century to century. The unity of mankind, thus, is constituted through three principles: (1) the historic individuality of every man, the substance out of which the whole can be built; (2) continuity through the chain of cause and effect linking the generations and (3) accumulation of substance through the collective memory in language and script.

The masse totale *as the Carrier of Meaning*

The continuously accumulating substance is mankind itself and this mankind is conceived as a carrier of meaning. But does this process of accumulation have a meaning as a whole? The meaning of the whole, however, is inaccessible to the intraworldly thinker because he is living in the finite present and the whole, extending into an infinite future, is unknown to him. The meaning of the whole is an unsolvable problem from the intraworldly perspective. Hence Turgot can do no more than search for finite lines of meaning which may have become visible in the known history of the arts and sciences, of morals and politics. Such lines of meaning can be found in great numbers—lines of growth, of decay and of recuperation. But are there any lines which run through the whole body of known history up to the present? Are there lines of growth, not of decay? Turgot thinks that he can discern such lines and he names them as the softening of the mores, the enlightenment of the mind, and the intensified commerce between formerly isolated nations to the point of global intercourse. These lines do not run an even course through history. They suffer frequent interruptions and not all men participate equally in this meaningful increase of human substance. But in spite of all retardations of the process, in spite of interruptions, and in spite of the distribution of the process over a multitude of civilizations and nations who do not all move at the same speed, while some do not move at all—in spite of all this *"la masse totale"* of mankind marches towards an ever increasing perfection.

The considerations of Turgot offer the rare opportunity to watch a progressive philosophy of history *in statu nascendi.* We are not faced yet by a final dogma, as in Comte, and we can trace the motives and the means of construc-

tion. The decisive instruments in the construction are the lines of meaning which run through the whole process of known history and the idea of the *masse totale.* The process of history in its full broadness has no meaning, not even a finite one; that much Turgot admits. The lacunae in time through the interruptions in positive growth of substance, and the restriction of the growth to a tiny trickle of men as its bearers while the vast majority participate in progress only at a respectful distance, reduce the field of actual progress to a comparatively small area in the total flux of human history. One has to look very hard indeed in order to find in this rather turgid flux *"le fil des progrès"* at all. And if we have found such a "thread," of which the critical purification of physics is an instance, what have we gained? Of what concern can it be to a man, who lives and dies in his finite present, whether mankind has progressed in the past or will progress in the future, if he himself leads a miserable life in an unenlightened, isolated community where the mores are restrictive? Turgot's answer is the *masse totale.* The triumphant brutality of the answer is unsurpassable. History has no meaning for man. What does it matter? It has meaning for the *masse totale.*

The loss of the Christian meaning of history

This answer is heavily fraught with implications. Let us first see what has happened to the problem of meaning in history. In the Christian philosophy of history, as it was still represented by Bossuet, the problem of meaning is solved by means of the dichotomy between sacred and profane history. Profane history has no autonomous meaning and the problem of meaning is concentrated in sacred history. Sacred history has meaning insofar as it is a spiritual drama, beginning with the creation of man and ending with the second coming of Christ. The drama is known from the first to the last act and for this reason it is a true line of universal meaning. The drama of salvation has a meaning of human relevance because involved in it is the spiritual destiny of every single human being. Precisely because it has this bearing on every single human destiny, because it is not the drama of a *masse totale,* we see certain thorny questions of doctrine arise in the history of Christianity, such as: what happens to men who lived before Christ, what happens to those who lived after Christ but have never heard of him, what happens to those who have heard of him but resist the Evangel, what happens to those who are called but not elected? The sacred line of meaning which runs through history is inseparable from the meaning which it has for the individual person. Without meaning for man, understood as the concrete person, there is no meaning in history. Turgot transposes the Christian dichotomy of sacred and profane history into the context of intramundane thought through his dichotomy of the "thread of progress" and the vast ballast of historical ups and downs which have no meaning in themselves. However, he cannot extract from the "sacred" thread of progress a meaning for the spiritual destiny of the concrete person. At this point, therefore, the evocative amplifications have to be introduced. Since the finite lines of meaning, which can be found in the civilizational process, can have no meaning for man as a spiritual person, man and his concrete problems have to be brushed aside. Since concrete man cannot be the subject for whom history has a meaning, the subject has to be changed—man is replaced by the *masse totale*. The *masse totale*, however, has no concrete existence, nor is the *masse* given to human experience. It is the evocation of a carrier of meaning, of a new divinity, into which a man who has lost his openness towards transcendental Being has projected his desire for salvation. The masse totale is not a reality in the experimental sense, rather it is the tentative evocation of a new worldly divinity. In Comte we shall see the new god finally enthroned as the *Grand-Etre,* together with a clergy and a rite.

The loss of the Christian idea of man

Let us now consider what happened to man through the creation of the *masse totale.* The reader will have noticed that in the preceding paragraph we did not speak simply of man, but several times used the term "concrete man." The necessity for such usage, in order to make clear the intended sense of the word "man," illustrates best the terminological difficulties which have been created through the Positivist dogmatism and its uncritical acceptance. It ought to be a matter-of-course that the term "man," when used in a philosophical or political discourse, should denote the "concrete man," that is the concrete human person in the fullness of his dimensions, including the intellectual and spiritual. Unfortunately, this is no longer a matter-of-course. The thinkers of the eighteenth century have mutilated the idea of man beyond recognition. In the case of d'Alembert, for instance, . . . man was deprived of his *bios theoretikos* and reduced in essence to the utilitarian level of a *homo faber.* In Voltaire . . . the fierce attack on the life of the spirit and its elimination from the "true" idea of man. Diderot has spoken of the "useless contemplator." Bentham has excluded from his political speculation the "ascetic" type as a repulsive abnormality which ought to be neglected by the philosopher. Turgot, in his capacity as Prior of the Sorbonne, delivered a discourse on the ominous subject of the "profits" which mankind has derived from the establishment of Christianity, and the editor candidly notes that the *Discours* originally contained an opening paragraph in which the author disagreed with those who believe that Christianity is "useful" only for the other life. This reduction of man and his life to the level of utilitarian existence is the symptom of the critical breakdown of Western civilization through the atrophy of the intellectual and spiritual substance of man. In the progressive, Positivist movement since the middle of the eighteenth century, as well as with the followers of the movement, the term man no longer designates the mature man of the humanist and Christian tradition, but only the crippled, utilitarian fragment.

The loss of the Christian idea of mankind

A crippled man, however, does not cease to be a man. Spiritual obscurantists, or antihumanistic utilitarians, are not animals; they continue to function as humans. Still, they can no longer solve human problems rationally, or on the basis of the spiritual experiences the possession of which characterizes mature man. Hence there appear the curious transpositions of the problems of mature Western civilization to the new level of utilitarian immaturity. There arises the necessity of substituting for transcenden-

tal reality an intraworldly evocation which is supposed to fulfill the functions of transcendental reality for the immature type of man. As a consequence, not only the idea of man but also the idea of mankind has changed its meaning. The Christian idea of mankind is the idea of a community whose substance consists of the Spirit in which the members participate; the *homonoia* of the members, their like-mindedness through the Spirit that has become flesh in all and each of them, welds them into a universal community of mankind. This bond of the spirit is timeless. The Spirit is not more present today than it was yesterday and it will not be more present tomorrow than it is today. Only because the Spirit is transcendentally out of time can it be universally present in time, living in each man equally, irrespective of the age or place in which the man lives. Only because the source of the community is out of time is mankind a universal community within historical time. Turgot's evocation of the *masse totale* transposes the Christian idea of mankind into the utilitarian key. Man is no longer a spiritual center but a mere link in the chain of generations. The spirit which welds the plurality of men into the unity of mankind is no longer a transcendental reality to be experienced by every individual soul but has become a thread of meaning to be touched at one point by a man if he is fortunate but beyond the reach of the vast majority of mankind. And the eternal presence of the Spirit to every soul that willingly opens itself is transposed into a precarious, fleeting meaning which can be ascertained only with some difficulty by scholars who know a good deal about the problems of mathematized science. At first sight, this whole transposition looks so much like an infantile insult to the dignity of man that the mass appeal, which the idea undoubtedly has to this day, is hardly intelligible.

The appeal to utilitarian immaturity

Let us consider therefore, finally, the conditions under which this idea of man can appeal to men. Obviously it can have no appeal to a mature humanist and Christian, and whenever Positivist ideas spread in a socially menacing form, the clash with the traditions of Western high-civilization is inevitable. With equal obviousness the mass appeal exists. In quest of its conditions we have only to summarize various remarks which we had to make incidental to the previous analysis. The idea of being in substance a member of a *masse totale* can only appeal to a man who has not much substance of his own. His personality must be sufficiently underdeveloped, that is to say it must be deficient in spiritual organization and balance to such a degree, that the anxiety of existence cannot be controlled and absorbed by the normal processes of the mature, meditative life. As a consequence he will be plagued by insecurities, frustrations, fears, aggressiveness, paranoic obsessions and uncontrollable hatreds. The great escape for the man who cannot extricate himself from this state through the personal solution has always been, and will always be, to submerge himself in a collective personality which he either will find ready at hand in his environment, or which he can evoke for the occasion. Tribalism is the answer to immaturity because it permits man to remain immature with the sanction of his group.

A man who is not much of a person can still be quite a useful individual. Hence a tribe of immature utilitarians can be a highly efficient and very powerful community and at the same time a very dangerous one if its insecurities, its provincialism, its xenophobia and paranoia turn, for one reason or another, aggressively towards others. The tribes which emerge in the crisis of a civilization can display a considerable political effectiveness while they last. Immaturity is no argument against political power. The political effectiveness and survival value of a tribalist movement not only add to its appeal but make it possible as a form of political existence, of appreciable duration, for the masses of men who, in increasing numbers, are set free for reorganization in new political forms in an age where the institutions of a high civilization begin to break down, as they did in the eighteenth century. The conditions for a successful tribalist evocation are present: there is given he type of man which exists at all times in large numbers; there is given the situation of a civilizational breakdown in which masses of this type are ready to respond to a new appeal (the internal proletariat, to use Toynbee's term); and, finally, there is given an idea which has the twin merit (1) of being close enough to the tradition (because it is a transposition of traditional ideas) to deceive the not so discerning, and (2) of supplying a collective personality to those who want to paddle through life with that minimum of effort that goes by the respectable name of usefulness.

The tribalism of mankind

We have surveyed the general conditions which make a tribalist idea attractive to the members of a community and which offer a certain guarantee of durable political existence. We have not yet, however, exhausted the particular charms of a tribalism of mankind. Tribalism as such exhales a bad odor in a civilization which is still permeated by traditions of Christian universalism. The various tribalist movements which have sprung up in the period of the crisis have run into conflicts with Western tradition. But not all of them have developed conflicts of the same severity. The differences in the violence of tension are caused by the different contents of the tribal evocations in the several totalitarian movements. A combination of nationalism with racialism, of the type in which the National Socialist movement indulged, is apt to arouse considerable tensions, as it actually did, because the vast majority of mankind cannot acquire membership in the *masse totale*. The universalist aspiration, combined with the restrictive content of the idea, must result in the extinction of the evocation when the tribe that was constituted by the idea meets defeat in an armed clash. The Communist tribal evocation is in a much more favorable position. The tribe also is restricted in principle, but it is restricted to "toilers." And toilers exist in great number in every society on earth. Moreover, non-toilers can be converted into toilers by the simple device of taking away their possessions. The universal aspirations of the Communist idea can be implemented "in the flesh" through changes in the economic structure of society and through the application of the great clyster which purges the *masse totale* of unassimilable elements by their liquidation. The end of Western civilization through diarrhoea is so much wider in its appeal than the end through gas-chambers and incinerators because the number of those who are made happy by the

process can be envisaged at some date to be coextensive with the number of those who survive. The progressive, Positivist evocation, finally, is obviously in the most favorable position because it can use the symbol "man" for the designation of membership in the *masse totale*. The difficulty of distinguishing between tribalism and universalism, which is serious even in the case of the Communist idea, is practically unsurmountable for a progressive intellectual (who himself belongs to the *masse*) when the tribe is coextensive with mankind at any given point of time.

The appeal of the *masse* for the common man, in the progressive version of Turgot, lies in the possibility of obtaining the benefits of mankind without incurring its obligations. All he has to do is to make himself useful to the extent of earning a living; for the rest, he can feel himself on top of the historical world by identifying himself with the progress of the *masse*. This is the appeal for the ordinary member of the movement. For the leaders, the idea holds . . . added appeal . . . The thinkers who evoke the idea, and the group of men who represent progress actively, are the measure of meaning in history. The *masse totale* is in progress as a whole because select individuals and groups are actively in progress. If intramundane mankind as a whole is the new *realissimum,* its standard-bearers are the god-men. The *masse totale* holds great temptation for the active elements since they can place themselves at a comfortable rank in the hierarchy. Turgot does not go to the extreme of Comte, that is of making himself the Messiah and the Pope rolled into one; nevertheless, the clerical pride cannot be overlooked. The mass of mankind certainly does not progress at an even speed. Some groups are leading, some are lagging behind, still others are in the most primitive stages of barbarism. "The present state of the universe contains at the same time on earth all the shades of barbarism and civilization; at one glance we can see all the monuments and traces of all the steps of the human mind, at one glance the picture of all the grades through which it has passed, at one glance the history of all the ages." By no means do Turgot and the French nation hold the most insignificant place in the simultaneous picture of the chronological stages. As a matter of fact, they are the authoritative present and consequently the summit of the hierarchy. Bacon and Galilei, Kepler and Descartes, Newton and Leibniz receive their due as the bearers of the torch, but the climax is France. The second **Discours en Sorbonne** closes with the apotheosis of the King and the praise: "Thy happy people has become the center of civilization (*politesse*)". The idea of the *masse totale* blends with nationalism. What might be the innocuous pastime of an exultant intellectual becomes a political force because it gains, on the international scene, the momentum of a powerful state if it can capture the nation to the degree that the national mass identifies itself with the leadership of mankind. In its outline we see the idea of mankind dominated by a chosen people which embodies the progressive essence of humanity. In historical actuality that would mean a totalitarian organization of mankind in which the dominating power would beat down in the name of mankind and freedom everybody who does not conform to its standards.

Profane history versus sacred history

There is evil in Turgot as in every totalitarian but in him it is not yet more than a spark. Turgot was much too deeply imbued with the spirit of Bossuet to fall naively into the radicalism of a new salvation. The "thread of progress," that is the new sacred history, is certainly his dominating idea, and the *masse totale* is his obsession. However, this aspect of Turgot's historicism is balanced by a wideness of the historical horizon, as well as by a surprising penetration of historical forms, which is peculiarly his own. A good deal of this historical openness has become the precious heritage of Comte but most of it was lost to the later development of progressivism, and it was not only lost to progressivism. We must say quite generally that, setting aside such landmarks as Hegel, Burckhardt, Spengler and Toynbee, there is not much in the average occupation with problems of politics and history that can equal in breadth of conception or flair for problems the work of Turgot. This richness of Turgot's historical perspective is due to the momentum, not yet exhausted, of Bossuet's treatment of profane history.

We have hitherto neglected the profane section of the Christian philosophy of history. We have dealt only with the particular line of meaning which assumed for Turgot the function of sacred history, and we have not yet dealt with the problem that such a finite line of meaning could be found at all and that its discovery did not create a sensation. It did not create a sensation because the traditional profane history abounded in finite lines of meaning. The problem for Turgot was not to discover such a line for the first time; rather, his problem was to discover a line that would cut across the plurality of lines already known in such a manner that history could be interpreted as a meaningful whole from its beginnings to the present. We have insisted repeatedly that the meaning of history as a whole is inaccessible from the intramundane position but from this inaccessibility it does not follow that history does not have a finite structure of meaning, that is, that it does not have a recognizable meaningful articulation into the finite histories of civilizations and peoples. This finite meaning, since it is not a universal meaning, cannot touch the whole of human existence, but it touches very strongly the finite existence in community, as well as the civilizational values of which the community is the carrier. The understanding of this finite meaning, the insight into the order which prevails in it (if such an order should be discoverable empirically), is a human concern because it enables man to orient himself in his own historical situation and by virtue of this positive orientation to gain also the proper distance to the realm of civilizational values, that is: the Christian *contemptus mundi.*

The structure of history, however, can become a human concern in this sense only if it is understood as the structure of profane history, as a realm of finite meaning. As soon as any part of the profane structure is hypostatized into a process of universal meaning, the finite structure is falsified and orientation becomes impossible. This consequence of an intramundane construction of sacred history is rarely appreciated in its full importance. Once a strand of history is isolated and endowed with a sacred meaning, the tendency is irresistible to neglect all other structural elements of history as irrelevant. The "sacred history" be-

comes a restrictive principle of selection for historical materials. Within the Positivist movement we have to observe, therefore, a characteristic swelling and sinking of historical understanding. With Turgot, at the beginning of the movement, the view of history is still surprisingly full and well balanced, on the whole. The "thread of progress" is singled out from a historical manifold which for its greater part is not progressive at all. With Comte the construction has already become rigid—the wealth of materials is still considerable but the materials fit with a suspicious willingness into the sweeping course of progress. With the later Positivists the construction degenerates into a progressivism so thoroughly selective that selection becomes indistinguishable from ignorance. A movement which originates as a reinterpretation of history ends in the dogmatic destruction of history. Moreover, the tendency towards the destruction of contemplative history is not confined to the Positivist movement. In the course of the nineteenth century it prevails generally where ever history is written with a view to legitimate an authoritative present. The Whiggist misconstruction of English constitutional history is a match for the nationalist misconstructions of German history. The nonsense written about the medieval emperors who betrayed the German national interest through their hankering after Rome is the counterpart to the nonsense written about the Magna Carta. And the nationalist and progressive misconstructions are even surpassed by the nightmare of Marxist and National Socialist historical writing. Towards the end of the nineteenth century, this writing of selective history with a view to support a contemporary political interest was even theorized through a logic of historiography chiefly through the efforts of German methodologists. In this movement, the writing of history was considered to be a selection of materials in orientation towards a "value" (*Wertauswahl*) and correspondingly it was considered to be the function of the historian to impose meaning on history (*Sinngebung*). The immanent logic of this attitude could hardly lead to any other conclusion than the postulate that history has to be rewritten in every generation to suit the new political developments.

The resulting anarchy of liberal and racist, of progressive and Marxist history, and, in addition, of as many nationalist histories as there were nations, spelled the end of history as a science. Or, rather, it would have spelled the end unless remedial forces had been at work which tended towards a restoration of contemplative history. The awareness of this problem had never died completely. Ranke held fast to the principle that all periods of history are equal in their immediacy to God, and Burckhardt knew that all civilization is not worth the death of a single human being. In the twentieth century the restorative tendencies became strongly visible, particularly through their first great summary in Toynbee's *Study of History.* Nevertheless, there is not yet much cause to rejoice. The restorative movement is a comparatively think trickle of little effectiveness. In areas in which an intramundane political religion has become institutionalized as the state church, as for instance in the Soviet Union, history as a contemplative science cannot live in the person of even a single individual because the body-killing governmental terror would be immediately used against it. In a society like the

American the chances of development are slim in the face of the soul-killing social pressure of the progressive creed, and whether the remnants of the European national societies can resist the advancing civilizational destruction is a question which only the future can answer. Still, the restorative movement exists for the time being and the problem of a science of profane history has been reopened. As a consequence of this curious course of historical science, we have returned today to approximately the point where Turgot began to depart from the classical treatment of profane history. To be sure, our knowledge of historical facts has increased greatly in the two centuries which have passed, but the categories of interpretation have not changed decisively. A few reflections on Turgot's principles of historiography have, therefore, the double function (1) of showing the state of the problem at the time when profane history begins to separate from its traditional, Christian context, and (2) of showing in what respects the problem has changed in the present.

Turgot's categories of history

Let us survey first the basic stock of categories employed by Turgot in the classification of historico-political phenomena. This stock of categories is drawn from a number of sources which are still clearly distinguishable in the analyses. The principal ones are: (1) the Christian tradition, (2) the Graeco-Roman tradition, (3) the events of the migration period, (4) some knowledge of the origin of government through the conquest of sedentary tribes by nomadic tribes, (5) speculation about the stagnation of Far Eastern civilizations, (6) the complex of problems which arises through the assumption of a "thread of progress." A few examples will illustrate these sources.

From the tradition of Augustine-Orosius stems the general view of the ups and downs in history, that is of the rise and fall of empire, of the succession of laws and forms of government and of the retardations and accelerations of the arts and sciences. The *metathesis,* the transfer of empire from one people to the next, in such a manner that the great periods of history are characterized by the succession of imperial peoples, is the first category determining the structure of history. In his use of the *metathesis* Turgot emphasizes the cultural domination which accompanies political domination more strongly than does the tradition, but his use of the category does not go, on the whole, beyond the practice that had been established by Machiavelli's idea of a wandering of the *virtù* from one leading nation to another. It is the pattern of history which we still find in Hegel. In one decisive point, however, Turgot's use of the *metathesis* differs from that of Orosius or Hegel: for him the rise and fall of empire is not the exhaustive structural principle of profane history. History is not organized as a strict sequence of no more than four empires like the Orosian, nor as a strict sequence of "worlds" like the Hegelian. The category of empire is no longer the focus as it was under the impression of the world-filling importance of the Roman Empire, and the category of the civilization (Chinese, Hellenic, Roman, Western) which determines the Hegelian speculation is not yet developed. The rise and fall of the political units is an open movement with an average of progress running through the ups and

downs. Moreover, other structural features overlap with the structure of dominating peoples.

One of these overlapping features is the rhythm of political form within any of the nations which in succession may characterize one of the great historical epochs. This category of the internal rhythm stems from the Graeco-Roman tradition, though it is possible that the history of the Italian city-state has had some influence on its formation. The problem of internal rhythm is formulated on one occasion in such a manner that obviously the history of the Hellenic polis from the primordial kingship to Alexander, or of Rome from the first kings to the principate, is the model. On this occasion Turgot speaks of "the flux and reflux of power" from the prince to the multitude and back from the multitude to the prince, with the result of a more stable situation because in the course of flux and reflux the smaller political units are replaced by an empire which enforces peace within its borders. On another occasion Turgot analyses the internal rhythm specifically for the case of the city-state. The sequence of governmental forms begins with kingship. This form is unstable because abuse of power in the small confines of a town will be easily detected and resented and, in due course, will engender a revolution. The resulting aristocratic republic again will be unstable and tend towards democracy because the tyranny of a republican oligarchy is even more unbearable than that of a king, and it is more unbearable because the abuse of power through a group will always assume the disguise of virtue and thus add insult to injury. The explanation of causes differs from the Platonic discussion of the same typical sequence but the sequence itself, from kingship to democracy, and to a final despotic monarchy, is substantially the same.

The combination of the *metathesis* with the internal rhythm alone would result in a picture of the structure of history both richer in content and empirically more adequate than the later progressivist constructions, for this combination permits the assumption of a thread of progress running through the sequence of the larger historical units (empires or civilizations), while it does not neglect the rhythms of growth and decay within the units. Turgot's combination makes a theory of progress compatible with a theory of civilizational cycles. A civilization may decay, and still mankind may advance. Turgot, at least, would not run into the emotional impasse of contemporary intellectuals who howl with anxiety that civilization is at stake when our particular Western civilization will have reached the end of its course. But he adds further factors to the combination which build the periods of decay into a theory of historical dynamics. We have seen that the flux and reflux of power from the prince to the multitude and back to the prince does not produce a neutral sequence of governmental forms, but that in the course of the process the smaller units are absorbed into a larger imperial unit which enforces peace. The process is a rather bloody one, but from the struggle of the smaller units emerges the peaceful order of the larger unit—a progress for Turgot, though it would not be considered one, for instance, by Burckhardt. The violent upheaval (*les bouleversements*) becomes in Turgot's speculation the vehicle of progress. No advance is possible without decadence and destruction. The forests of America are the model of the historical process: trees grow and fall in the virgin forest and their decay fertilizes the soil for new growth. In the same manner, on the surface of the earth, governments succeed each other and empires rise on the ruins of empires. Only through bloody revolution has despotism learned to moderate and liberty to regulate itself. "And thus, by alternatives of agitation and calm, of good and evil, the *masse totale* of mankind is marching steadily towards perfection." Here again the *masse totale* makes its ominous appearance—as if it were a satisfaction to the victims of an upheaval (for instance to those who were cremated in Auschwitz) to be the fertilizer for the progress of mankind. But the progressivisit is happy because "no upheaval has ever occurred which has not produced some advantage." Nevertheless, we must stress the importance of the "upheaval" as an empirical category for the interpretation of political history. While the upheaval does not result in progress, it certainly results in the destruction of old political forms and the growth of new ones. And the dynamics of disintegration and growth are a problem in contemplative history quite independent of the question of whether a line of meaning runs through the succession of political forms.

With regard to this problem, Turgot has laid foundations which can be improved upon in detail but hardly in the essentials. Under the title of *mélange des nations* he has classified the processes in which existing communities break up and new ones are formed. The classic instance of such formation is the growth of the Western nations from the *mélange* of the original settlers and the Germanic conquerors. Both elements of the symbiosis lose their former identity and a new political entity, the nation, emerges from the mixture. These processes are noticed and remembered only when they occur on the level of civilized groups with written records. The principle, though, has to be applied generally to the dynamics of communal growth. Hence Turgot extrapolates the process from the migration case into more primitive social relations and develops the theory that differences of economy are the first incentive towards the *mélange*. Nomadic and agricultural tribes are differentiated by their ability to move: sedentary populations are by nature not conquerors; nomadic tribes are ready to move, and compelled to move if pasture is exhausted, and are inclined to descend on agricultural communities for plunder. Hence the permanent tensions between these two types in which the nomads have the role of aggressors and conquerors. The agricultural economy, on the other hand, creates more wealth and gives rise to towns with their technological and commercial civilization, so that the war potential of agricultural communities is comparatively high if they are pressed on the path of defense and defensive expansion. From the clashes result conquests with subsequent symbiosis of the warring elements, amalgamation of larger populations on larger territories, diffusion of culture and the incorporation of slaves and lower-class populations. In brief: Turgot outlines a complex of problems which later was elaborated in Gobineau's theory of Western civilization as the symbiosis of sedentary with conquering populations, in Franz Oppenheimer's theory of the origin of the state through conquest and, more recently, in Toynbee's comprehensive analysis of "upheaval" through the internal and external proletariat.

The enlargement of the historical horizon beyond the Mediterranean area to the Far East has introduced into the speculation on progress a problem for which Turgot does not find a quite satisfactory solution. Still, he recognized it and did not evade it. Even under the assumption of the *masse totale* as the subject of progress, the overall picture is somewhat marred by the fact that the great Asiatic civilizations, in particular the Chinese, do not seem to participate in what we fondly consider our progress. The Asiatic "stagnation," which is the form of existence for a vast part of mankind, does not fit easily into a picture of progressing mankind and at least requires some explanation. Turgot suggests that in China, India and Egypt the earliness of civilizational achievement is the very cause of stagnation. The respect which the nascent philosophies commanded tended to perpetuate the first opinions. "Pride is nourished by ignorance; the less one knows, the less one doubts; the less one has discovered, the less one sees what remains to be discovered." As a further retarding factor he considers the governmental regulation of studies, particularly in China, and the integration of an early, comparatively high state of science, into the political institutions—which inevitably makes for mediocrity. We may agree with Turgot's excellent common sense suggestions and still not be quite satisfied with the explanation. Nevertheless we have to acknowledge Turgot's merit in having tackled a problem which even today we have not penetrated sufficiently. This is not the occasion to offer our own solution; may we only suggest that the first step towards a solution of the very real problem of differences in civilizational structure between East and West lies in the recognition that the "stagnation" of the East is quite as unfounded an idea as the "progress," of the West. If we drop the category of Western "progress," the category of Eastern "stagnation" will disappear automatically.

Systematically of the greatest interest are, finally, those categories of Turgot which support the assumption of progress itself. That progress seems to be possible only in the *masse totale* but not uniformly throughout mankind is, after all, disquieting. Could this inequality of progress perhaps be caused by inequalities between the various communities or between single individuals? Turgot rejects inequality between communities or races, but admits inequalities between individuals. The *esprit humain* is uniformly endowed with the possibilities of progress throughout mankind, but nature has given an abundance of talent to some which it has refused to others. Circumstances develop talents or leave them in obscurity and from the infinite variety of circumstances derive the differences of progress in the several societies. This principle implies that primitive conditions put approximately the same type of obstacles in the way of everybody. "A state of barbarism equalizes all men." Only when the first steps of progress in the face of the general obstacles have been taken and when the changes wrought in the environment by these first steps have created circumstances more favorable to the unfolding of talents can differences of progress appear as the result of a more accelerated or more retarded accumulation of such steps.

Again we have to praise Turgot's rare honesty in facing a problem and his skill in offering a methodologically clean solution. Inequality at some point has to be assumed in order to explain the panorama of civilizational inequality which lies before our eyes. Since a clear relation between natural factors and civilizational differences cannot be found, the source of inequality must lie in man himself even if we reduce this inequality to small initial differences between men and explain major civilizational differences as the result of retarded or accelerated accumulation. We are driven back to inequalities between men—a formidable problem metaphysically as well as empirically. "Genius is distributed among mankind approximately like gold in a mine. The more mineral you take out, the more metal you have gained. The more men you take, the more great men you will take." What then makes the great man? First, natural differences may be a factor in human quality: a lucky arrangement of the cells in the brain, strength or delicacy of the senses or of memory, or differences of blood pressure. Beyond these natural factors, which are too rough-hewn to be used in explanation of the nuances of human differences, lie the strength and character of the soul. And the souls "have a real inequality the causes of which will always be unknown to us, and can never be the object of our reasoning."

This is the finest early exposition of the problem of human inequality in civilizational action. If we make the implications explicit, we would have to render them in the following manner: (1) human civilization is not uniform throughout mankind but shows empirically various degrees of differentiation in the several communities, (2) the natural environment is a factor in the differentiation but the factor does not suffice to explain exhaustively the actual differences, (3) the explanation through inequalities between human groups is inadmissible because the human groups are not constants—*mélange* is the principle of historical dynamics, (4) the source of the differences must lie ultimately in inequalities between single human individuals, (5) this source must not be sought in a radical inequality between men which would touch the equality of spiritual substance in the Christian sense, (6) it may be found in part in physiological inequalities—a slightly higher reaction speed, as we would say today, may affect the course of a human life and be the cause of differences between mediocrity and brilliance, (7) all this still leaves an irreducible residuum which Turgot characterizes as "talents" or "strength and character" of the soul. The recognition of this last factor, however insufficiently described, is the methodological masterpiece. It does not abolish the spiritual equality of men but it recognizes as an irreducible factor the stratum in the nature of man which is characterized by such functions as imagination, sensitiveness for minute differences of value, loyalty to work, intellectual energy, ability to concentrate and to give form to an idea, the ability to have "good ideas" and to grasp them when they come. In the possession of this stratum, of course, all men are equal, but it is a stratum which has a considerable amplitude of degrees and in this amplitude is room for such differences as dullness and brilliance, mediocrity and greatness.

Turgot's dilemma

In recognizing this irreducible stratum as the source of civilizational differentiation, Turgot has gone almost to the limit of invalidating his metaphysics of progress in history. The assumption of superior talents which at all times are distributed among mankind in approximately the same proportions and which, therefore, constitute the perpetual ferment of progress excludes from progress man himself. However much civilization progresses, man does not progress. The social environment may change in such a manner that it favors the unfolding and effectiveness of talents, but the talents do not change. "If Racine had been born among the Hurons in Canada, or in the Europe of the eleventh century, he would never have unfolded his genius." But, though he could unfold it in the seventeenth century, his peculiar gifts at the later point did not differ from those which he would have had at the earlier point. The nature of man remains constant, including its amplitude of higher and lower endowment. Thus the locus of progress is the objective structure of civilization with its works of art and science, its technology, its mores, its organizational knowledge in economics and politics. The problem of man is the same, whether he is placed in the civilization of an African native tribe or in that of a modern Western nation. A higher degree of differentiation in the objective structure does not mean that the men who are born into it have a superior ability for grappling with its problems. On the contrary, the differentiation may become so complicated that the "talents" in the society are no longer sufficient to penetrate it and to develop it further. A crisis of this kind is apt to issue in a social upheaval in the course of which the great "simplifiers" (to use Burckhardt's term) destroy the complicated civilizational structure and make room for a fresh and simpler start. The possibility that the complications of the civilizational structure might outrun the human ability to deal with it does not seem to have occurred to Turgot although in the eighteenth century it was a concern of such thinkers as Rousseau and Ferguson.

. . . . .

Turgot presses his analysis far enough to make it clear that the central problem of history and politics is always man in society. On the other hand, he makes the objective content of civilization the center of his philosophy of history. Both problems must concern the theorist of politics but Turgot did not achieve their integration into a system. The emphasis on civilizational content to the neglect of the existence of man in society is characteristic of progressivism in all its variants. The emphasis on political existence to the neglect of civilizational content has become characteristic of various countermovements to progressivism.

Let us restate the problem. The "thread of progress" is concerned with the meaningful differentiation of a civilizational content, especially with the rationalization of our view of the external world. Assuming the description of the thread to be empirically correct, nothing would follow from the existence of the thread for the healthy state of a concrete society at any period of history. A highly developed system of mathematical physics means nothing to people who do not understand it and for societies who can master it and translate it into technology it may become a factor contributing to social disintegration. The problems of a concrete political society can be strongly affected by the "thread of progress," favorably as well as unfavorably, but their course has, nevertheless, a high degree of autonomy. In the more extreme variants of progressivism (which command mass appeal in our time) this autonomy of the course of a political society is so strongly neglected that the historical process assumes the character of an automation which can be depended upon to deliver ever further installments of progress. When the concrete societies follow their own course and disturb the dream of automatic progress, the reaction is indignant surprise, expressed, for instance, in the formula: it is outrageous that such things should happen in the twentieth century—for the twentieth century is, of course, better than the nineteenth as the nineteenth is better than the eighteenth. Back of this attitude lies the identification of the "thread of progress" with the state of the concrete society. That this identification is inadmissible did not remain hidden from the more discerning thinkers, not even from the progressivists. Saint-Simon and Comte understood well that the progress of science and industry is no substitute for the order of society. To prevent the disintegration of Western society, a danger which was felt to be imminent, it would be necessary to devise new institutions with an authority equivalent to the authority of the decaying institutions. This was the purpose they wanted to serve with their idea of a new *pouvoir spirituel*. The internal coherence of society through leadership and hierarchy thus became the absorbing problem even within the Positivist movement itself. Later political events increased the awareness of the problem, and after 1848 we have to observe an intensive occupation with the questions of political existence, resulting in such expositions as Mosca's and Pareto's theory of the ruling class and of the circulation of elites, and, in our time, in Toynbee's broad survey of the functions of a "creative minority" in the course of a civilization.

The analyses of Mosca, Pareto and Toynbee are the principal instances of a theoretical penetration of the problem that was neglected by Turgot. At the same time, however, the question received increasing attention on the part of political activists who sensed the decay both of the old institutions and of the minorities supporting them, and experienced the call to supply a new elite, and therewith a new coherence, to society. Helvétius had cast envious looks on the Jesuit Order as the model of a new elite. Saint-Simon and Comte attempted to create a new hierarchy and after 1815 this creation of new elites becomes a permanent occupation among political intellectuals. There is a continuum of elitarian formations running from the political clubs of the eighteenth century, through the clubs of the French Revolution, the conspiratorial organizations of Italy, the progressivist, nationalist, and internationalist groupings of the nineteenth century, to the twentieth-century organizations of elites in the Communist, Fascist and National Socialist movements. In appraising the meaning of this continuum, however, we have to beware of the temptation to project into the beginnings the meaning which ultimately emerged and to avoid labeling these formations indiscriminately as Fascist. In spite of the close relations between certain ideas of Blanqui and Rousseau, or of Mussolini and Mazzini, or of Hitler and

Fichte, or of Lenin and the French philosophers of Enlightenment, it will be advisable to use a neutral term for designating this phenomenon and as such a neutral term we shall use "the short-circuit evocation of elites." By this term we mean to say that the persons engaged in the evocation of elites are agreed in the insight that the traditional "creative minorities" (Toynbee) can no longer cope adequately with the complications of an industrialized Western society, that they have become (to use Toynbee's term again) "dominant" minorities devoid of competence and authority, that the Western societies depend for their continued existence and internal cohesion on the formation of new creative minorities and that, moreover, in their judgment concerning the traditional social structure of Western society and its survival value, the political activists are all pessimists. By characterizing the attempts at creating new elites through the adjective "short-circuit," we mean to say that, on the basis of an analysis which in itself is fundamentally correct, the political activists rush into the formation of elites with a blissful ignorance concerning the difficulties of the enterprise. This ignorance, of course, has degrees. Bakunin, for instance, was acutely aware that the formation of a new elite without a profound spiritual renovation was senseless. Marx, at least in his younger years, knew quite well that a change of economic order without a change of heart was no remedy for the evils of the capitalist system, and even Lenin was aware of this point, though he assumed naively that one could start on a communist order of society organizationally and that the spiritual reform would take care of itself in the course of time. Nevertheless, the political activists, on the whole, did not sense clearly that a renovation of society through a new elite would have to rest on deeper foundations than any of them were able to lay. The readiness to embark on the task of forming a new elite, without properly gauging its magnitude, is what we designate by the "short-circuit" character of the attempts.

Emphasis on political existence

The cross pattern of civilizational progress and of the autonomous course of political society in history, of theoretical penetration of the problem and of political action for its practical solution, has resulted in a curious interlocking of ideas. Today unfortunately this relationship is rather obscured by interpretations in partisan terminology. Let us try to clarify the main outlines of these relations.

Turgot's analysis has led to the point where the conflict between an emphasis on progress and the autonomous problems of political existence became clearly visible. One course to be taken in this situation would have been to drop the emphasis on progress and to cope with the problem of political existence. This was the course taken by the contemplative critics of Western civilization who discerned the disintegration of society behind the facade of progress. The short-circuit evocations by political activists, on the other hand, are characterized by the attempt to solve the problem of political existence and at the same time not to surrender the amenities of progress. It is still too little realized that the great elitarian movements of Communism, Fascism and National Socialism have a factor in common which, moreover, they share with the variants of progressivism: that is their adoration of science, of the industrial system and of the values of technology. However widely they may differ with regard to the solutions which they offer for the problem of political existence, they all agree that the industrial system has to be developed to the limits of its potentialities as the basis of the welfare of the people. This is the factor through which the modern political mass movements are the heirs of the progressivism and positivism of Saint-Simon and Comte.

In other respects, however, there persists a hysterical enmity between the various activist movements. The optimism of the progressivist creed is in conflict with the civilizational pessimism which lies at the basis of the elitarian movements. From this conflict stems the hatred of progressivists, not only against the elitarian activists, but against the thinkers who inquire into the problems of political existence. Every political scientist or historian who recognizes that there exist such problems as the cohesion of society through a ruling class or creative minority, or who considers the question that a society may be in full decline in spite of the advancement of science, or who indulges in the supreme insolence of recognizing that Communist Russia owes its coherence to an elitarian ruling class just as much as did National Socialist Germany, becomes the target of calumniations as "Fascist"—whether he be Pareto, or Mosca, or Nietzsche, or Spengler. In such judgments we reach the point where selectiveness in historical interpretation shades off into plain ignorance: when progressivists fly into indignation at the mere mention of the name of Spengler. They simply do not know that Spengler has not discovered the decline of the West, but that the topic has been under continuous discussion for the last two centuries. On the other hand, we have to observe the political activists who claim eagerly that their courses of action are justified by the critics of Western civilization. When the critics are still alive, such claims may lead to tensions and disappointments for the activists, such as the National Socialists experienced with Stefan George, Ernst Juenger and Oswald Spengler. When they are dead, the game is easier: Renan could not defend himself against the title of prefascista bestowed on him by Mussolini, and Nietzsche is defenseless against National Socialists in search of ancestry.

Emphasis on progress

In the face of Turgot's dilemma, one course that was open, as we said, was to drop the emphasis on progress and to concentrate the inquiry on the problems of political existence. There is, however, another course open: to take Turgot's "thread of progress" seriously and to explore its meaning without hypostatizing it into a total meaning of human history or making it the dogma of a religion of the Comtean type. At first sight this seems to be a quite sober suggestion. The dissolution of the anthropomorphic interpretation of the external world, and the substitution of a rational view, is a historical process which can be observed empirically. It would be a finite line of meaning among others and, divested of the progressive emphasis, reveals itself as a line of meaning of some importance, at least for Western civilization if not for the history of mankind. Unfortunately, a closer inspection does not render such a

comparatively innocuous result. Turgot's "thread of progress" is not as simple a sequence of phases as it seems to be in his *Discours* and neither does the sequence of phases in the Comtean version have the simplicity which it seems to have before analysis.

Let us turn to Turgot's text in order to establish precisely the problem involved in the "thread of progress." The first phase of our interpretation of the external world, the anthropomorphic phase, is characterized by Turgot in the following terms: "before one knew the interrelation of physical effects, there was nothing more natural than to suppose that they were produced by intelligent beings, invisible and similar to us." We can omit the second, transitional phase as irrelevant to our problem. In the third phase "the mechanical interactions of bodies were observed" and only then "hypotheses were evolved which could be formulated by mathematicians [*Discours sur l'histoire universelle, Oeuvres de Turgot,* 2]." Comte's formulation of the law of the three phases is more polished, but does not add anything to the substance of Turgot's idea. Nevertheless, it will be good to have the text before us: "In whatever way we study the general development of the human intellect, whether according to the rational method or empirically, we discover, despite all seeming irregularities, a fundamental Law to which its progress is necessarily and invariably subjected. The content of this Law is that the intellectual system of man, considered in all its aspects, had to assume successively three distinct characters: the theological, the metaphysical and, finally, the positive or scientific (physique) character. Thus man began by conceiving phenomena of every kind as due to the direct and continuous influence of supernatural agents; he next regarded them as products of various abstract forces, inherent in the bodies, but distinct and heterogeneous; and, finally, he restricts himself to viewing them as subject to a certain number of invariable natural laws which are nothing but the expression in general terms of relations observed in their development." [*Considérations philosophiques sur les sciences et les savants* (November, 1825)]

In spite of slight variants between the texts of Turgot and Comte, there can be no doubt about the intention of the theory. The *esprit humain,* or human intellect, is the subject for which a certain necessary evolution is predicated. The title "progress" given to this evolution implies a positive evaluation but it adds nothing to the content of the law itself, and the human intellect is not defined in any other terms but those of the characteristic phases through which it passes. Hence we must concentrate the analysis on the description of the phases themselves. When, however, we try to trace the identity of the intellectual functions through the three phases, we discover that the functions which are supposed to assume three successive characteristics are not identical in the three phases. Since the functions are not identical, or, since there is no identical subject of which successive characteristics could be asserted, there are no three phases—progressive or otherwise. The evolution described by Turgot and Comte is not an evolution of the human intellect in general at all, but rather the evolution of a very specific problem that is well known to us, that is, the problem of phenomenalism. The transition from the anthropomorphic to the positive phase does not mark a progress in our understanding of the external world; it is the transition from speculation on substance to the science of phenomena. In the anthropomorphic phase the knowledge of phenomena is still embedded in the knowledge of substances; in the positive phase the knowledge of phenomena is differentiated into the critical system of mathematized science. This development in itself certainly is an advance of our knowledge of phenomena, but it is not a progress of the human intellect. On the contrary, insofar as the knowledge of the universe is now restricted to the knowledge of phenomena, the knowledge of substance is lost. As far as the development of the integral functions of the intellect and spirit is concerned, the transition is distinctly a retrogression. This was the problem of Giordano Bruno in his attack on a science of the "accidences of the accidents," it was the issue in the debate between Kepler and Fludd, and in the Kantian distinction between noumena and phenomena; it is the problem to which Schelling gave the solution of the *Potenzenlehre* and the philosophy of the unconscious.

Hence a serious occupation with Turgot's and Comte's idea of progress can lead nowhere but to a dissolution into its component parts. On the one hand, we can isolate the advances of our knowledge of phenomena, and this results in the flourishing discipline of the history of science. On the other hand, we can isolate the speculation on the substance of the universe. This isolation, in the wake of Schelling, results in the philosophy of history. This latter development deserves our attention because it forms an increasingly important strand in the fabric of modern political ideas. In spite of its confusion, the law of the three stages touches upon a very serious problem in the philosophy of history. The construction of Turgot-Comte was defective because in the concept of the third stage the problem of substance was not shown in a further phase of development, but was simply excluded from consideration. If we do not exclude it, but conscientiously continue the line of thought initiated in the description of the first phase, the question will arise: what becomes of the problem of substance once it has passed beyond the stage of anthropomorphic symbolism? We know the answer given by Schelling in his philosophy of the theogonic process and in the new roles assigned to the protodialectic experiences and their dialectical elaboration. But we also know Schelling's ultimate dissatisfaction with a type of philosophical speculation that is a poor substitute for the forceful imagery of mythology, a dissatisfaction that leads him to expound the necessity for a new myth of nature. When it comes to the symbolization of substances, the myth is a more adequate mode of expression than a critical concept which can only clarify our experience but cannot incarnate the substance itself. Through the critical disintegration of the myth, both pagan and Christian, a universe of symbols has been destroyed, the *koine* in which communities of men could express the identity of the ground in themselves with the ground in the universe. The weakening and destruction of the myth is at the same time the weakening and destruction of the sacramental bond between men who hold it in common. The answer to this destruction of the myth, to the dedivinization (*Entgötterung*) of the world, is again

twofold, as it was to the problem of political existence—it is either contemplative or activist.

The contemplative response to the disintegration of the myth is contained in Schelling's *Philosophie der Mythologie und der Offenbarung*. The spiritual process in which the symbols of myth and dogma are created is recovered from the unconscious through *anamesis* (recollection), and the symbols actually created in the course of human history are interpreted as meaningful phases of the theogonic process, manifesting itself in history on rising levels of spiritual consciousness. In this contemplative attitude the myth of the past need not be abandoned as the aberration of an undeveloped intellect but can be understood as a necessary step in the expression of spiritual reality. It can be superseded historically but not invalidated in its own place by subsequent fuller and more differentiated symbolic expressions. This was the method already employed in principle by St. Paul when he interpreted the Natural, the Hebrew and the New Laws as successive phases of divine revelation. Schelling draws into the orbit of his interpretation a vast historical material, including the pagan myth, Oriental symbolisms, and the Catholic and Protestant Churches, and the further enlargement of this orbit, particularly through the inclusion of primitive symbolisms and of the Oriental civilizations, is the principal problem for a philosophic history of the spirit after Schelling. Of more recent attempts in this direction I mention only Bergson's *Deux sources de la morale et de la religion,* written strongly under the influence of Schelling. Bergson's treatise has become of special interest because Toynbee, in his *Study of History,* has drawn considerably on Bergson's principles for his own construction of historical evolution.

The activist response, as we have seen, begins in the Positivist movement itself through the religious foundations of Saint-Simon and Comte. The speculation on substance, which was eliminated from the third of the Three Phases, is reintroduced in the integral system of Comte in the form of an evocation of a new *pouvoir spirituel*. The foundation of Comte, as well as the later activist attempts to solve the spiritual problem through the foundation of political religions, are incidental to the previously surveyed attempts at solving the problem of political elites and they share with them their "short-circuit" character. This question of the spiritual "short-circuit" forms part of the general problem of the pneumapathology of the crisis.

In this context we shall touch only on the political tensions which develop between the "short-circuit" political religions and the new philosophy of the spirit in history and politics which is represented by Schelling. The political fronts determined by this issue differ somewhat from the fronts determined by the issue of political existence. Concerning this latter issue, the progressive activist (with the exceptions stated above) will not be inclined to recognize the problem of the creative minority and he will even condemn the mere contemplative occupation with it because of its pessimistic implications. The activist of the Fascist or National Socialist type will be in sympathy with the thinkers who recognize the problem—though the sympathy will not always be reciprocal. Besides the various types of activists will be at odds with each other. Concerning the spiritual issue, the political front follows a much simpler line: the "short-circuit" activists are all agreed on the intramundane character of the new divinities—whether it be the progressives' tribalist idea of mankind, or the nation, or the race, or the proletariat; moreover, they are all agreed that under no circumstance can the "inner return" (in Schelling's sense) to the sources of spirituality be tolerated. As a consequence the spiritualist is faced implacably by the united front of liberal progressives, Fascists, Communists and National Socialists. With regard to their antispiritualism, the great activist movements are again in harmony, in the same manner as they are with regard to their insistence on preserving the amenities of industrialism however widely they may differ in their elitarian solutions.

The *Géographie Politique*

We have analysed Turgot's categories of profane history as well as the thread of progress which marks the sacred line of meaning, but we have not yet seen how these various conceptual instruments are applied to the concrete historical materials in the building of an integrated view of world history. Such a view Turgot has unfolded in his fragments concerning a *Géographie Politique* rather than in his better known *Discours.* We have indicated previously that these fragments are particularly rich in ideas. For our purpose we have to select only one or two leading ideas which have a direct bearing on the problems of Positivist history and politics.

The title of the fragments, with its amalgamation of geography and politics, indicates the basic idea which Turgot employs in his construction of history. We have touched on this idea before, when we dealt with Turgot's criteria of progress. The line of progress from anthropomorphism to science is only one of the strands in the "thread of progress" running through history, namely the line which Turgot called the enlightenment of the mind. The other two lines were the softening of the mores and the intensified commerce between formerly isolated nations to the point of global intercourse. This problem of global intercourse, drawing all mankind into the actual unit of enlightenment, is now coming to the fore in the construction of a positive philosophy of history. The magnitude of the problem may easily escape the modern reader and that is probably the reason why this part of Turgot's speculation has received scant attention. Today we have become so thoroughly accustomed to such terms as world economy, world government, global politics and global warfare that the awareness of the formidable metaphysical problem involved in this terminology is all but dead. Again the work of Turgot has its extraordinary importance because here we can catch the problem *in statu nascendi.* It is a problem which had to emerge, like the "sacred" line of enlightenment, at the juncture when the Christian philosophy of history was disintegrating and the Christian problems had to be transposed into the secular key. The problem of geography in politics, down to its modern crystallization in geopolitics, can become intelligible only when it is understood as the secular variation on a Christian theme that was transmitted to Turgot by Bossuet. It is the problem of the function which the earth has in the existence of man in society.

In the Christian view of the world, the earth is the symbol of the substance from which we come and to which we return bodily. In birth and death it binds and frees the soul, and the brief interval of earthly life is passed in the mysteriously ordained tension between the two duties of keeping soul and body together physically and of preserving the integrity of the soul against the spiritual temptations of the earth. In the Christian hierarchy of existence, the earth is, furthermore, in its morphological features as well as in the realms of being which it carries, the gift of God to man as the field of his sustenance and of his civilizational achievement. In the eighteenth century, with the atrophy of Christianity and the growth of the intramundane ideas of man and mankind, this problem of the earth does not disappear but assumes a corresponding intramundane form. The substitution of the thread of progress for the drama of salvation is paralleled by the substitution of political geography for the Christian mystery of the physical creation as the scene of the pneumatic drama. The tribe of mankind now has the globe for its habitat, the globe understood as a physical object among others of which we wish to give a description as it would be given "by an observer from the moon with good telescopes"—*rien que la terre.* The intramundane progress of the *masse totale* means the increase of knowledge concerning this habitat and its increased technological exploitation. The abysmal mystery of creation has become the phenomenal mastery of a spherical surface and its resources. The history of mankind would have to proceed, therefore, from "the nations isolated by their ignorance in the middle of other nations," to the contemporary situation of general commerce between all men. The dogma of progress is supplemented by the correlations of ignorance and isolation, of enlightenment and global intercourse.

In spite of the concentrated form of the fragments, there is again clearly discernible Turgot's oscillation between a contemplative history in the tradition of Bossuet's profane history and the intramundane meaning of the whole which corresponds to the Christian sacred history. The oscillation expresses itself through a variety of suggestions for the organization of the subject matter and in some hesitation concerning the course which should be taken ultimately. Well within the range of contemplative history is a first series of suggestions concerning the topics to be included, such as: (1) the morphological features of the earth in their relation to the distribution of peoples, the geographical facilities for, and obstacles to, the formation of larger political units; (2) the natural resources of the various nations and the effect of their distribution on commercial relations; (3) the facilities of communication (rivers, oceans), their effect on the friendly or hostile relations between peoples, and on the type of commerce that can be carried on; (4) geography in its relation to the national character, its genius, courage and industry. The last point stems from the tradition of the Ptolemaic theory of climates and from Bodin. Turgot qualifies it cautiously by the suggestion that we separate the "moral causes" from the physical and inquire whether and how the physical causes have a part in this question at all.

Climatic conditions, natural resources and means of communication are factors which have to be taken into account in history and politics as empirical sciences. Physical factors of this type have their effects on the technological possibilities, the wealth and the historical course of political societies, but not much can follow from them for those central problems of a philosophy of history that are concerned with the human factor. The difficulties of Turgot begin when he tries to go beyond the analysis of physical factors and their effects and to construct the whole of human history as a function of the geographical factors. For he attempts, indeed, to establish a *géographie politique* as an independent science. This science will consist of two parts: of a theoretical *géographie politique* and of a positive or historical *géographie politique.* The theoretical part is supposed to deal with the relations of the art of government to physical geography. But a misgiving arises: "Since the earth is the theatre of all human actions, this part would include practically the whole art of government; in order not to include it in this part totally, one would often have to do violence to the systematic development of ideas." After this admission, Turgot quite rightly asks himself why a treatise on government should be disguised under the strange name of political geography. "Would it not be better to present the part under the name of the whole than the whole under the name of the part, however important the part may be?" We have to agree with Turgot: why, indeed, should one resort to this strange device? It is the same question that we would have to ask with regard to the later development of geopolitics. But Turgot does not answer his question explicitly. We can only assume that the subsequent development of the positive political geography is supposed to explain his insistence on the strange course.

The positive political geography is subdivided into two parts: the present and the past. By the present Turgot means *"l'état actuel du monde politique,"* that is, the manifold of national forces under their physical, moral, and political aspects. A national force has to be expressed in terms of population, the wealth of a state, the character of its inhabitants, the ease or difficulty of aggrandizement arising from the nature of the government. In the relations between nations we have to observe the national commerce, the respective pretensions, the true or false national interests, the policies which the nations pursue at the moment and their direction towards further progress or towards decadence. The political unit in the field, thus, is a national force on a given territory and the political problem is the potential of aggrandizement. At this point, Turgot reveals the function of his *géographie politique* as a source of advice to governments concerning the question of aggrandizement. This does not mean, however, that Turgot favored a policy of national aggrandizement. On the contrary, his standard of right policy was the coincidence of territorial expanse with *"un corps de nation."* Acquisition of provinces beyond the national territory he considered "unnatural." His "natural order" is the balance of national powers, and his criticism is directed against the principles of public law which rely on succession treaties for the establishment of order. In clarifying this point, he uses as his conceptual instrument the distinction between state (*état*) and power (*puissance*).

Charles V had a power but not a state, and Spain remained a power until Philip V. "The King of Prussia is a power; the King of France has a state." A power becomes a state when it reduces itself to the limits which nature has assigned to it. Political geography has drawn the limits of the state, public law forms the powers; but in the long run political geography is stronger than public law, "because always in the long run nature is stronger than the laws." Political geography, thus, is a normative science which establishes the natural law that the long-range order of Europe is the division into national territorial states of the French type. At least one of the reasons for the overemphasis on the geographical aspects of politics is Turgot's interest in the territorial reorganization of Europe according to the national principle. The political principle determining the "present" *ought* to be the organization of the nation, and the nation covers a delimited area on the surface of the globe. Principles of politics which disregard the territorial settlement of the nation, that is principles which lead to the formation of a *puissance* without regard to territorial limitations, should be abolished. The standard example for the disregard of the national principle is the attempt of Spain and Austria to maintain the possession of the Low Lands. The political acumen of Turgot shows itself more clearly in the prediction (in 1750) of the inevitability of American independence. And he is acutely aware, as we have seen, of the peculiar Prussian problem as a *puissance* which has not yet become a state—leaving open the question whether the state of the Prussian *puissance* has to be achieved by reduction, like the Spanish, or by further expansion. The political front of Turgot is turned against the past with its distribution of power according to the dynastic principle; his "present" is dominated by the idea of the nation as determining the territorial division. But in principle his argument opens the way for any collectivist idea which may supersede the nation as the unit which occupies a territory.

The absorbing interest in the geography of the "present" induces Turgot's fascinating construction of the "past" as a series of "presents" leading up to the actual present. This construction is perhaps the most convincing document for the devastating consequences of the assumption of an "authoritative present." Turgot is aware, of course, that a geography as the *tableau du présent* is a somewhat ephemeral affair because tomorrow the present is past and the new present would require a new political geography. But he is not to be deterred. "All that is past has been a present; history, which is a recital of the past, should consequently be a sequence of the *tableaux* of world-history at each moment." Human existence in society has two dimensions: space and time. Geography is the present tense is the spatial dimension: historical chronology is the temporal dimension. Geography and chronology place men at their distances in a system of ordinates: "The one expresses the ordinate of space, the other the ordinate of time." Both together determine the "situation." *"Voilà l'histoire universelle."* "Each moment has its peculiar political geography; and this title is especially appropriate to the description of the actual present in which terminate of necessity the various courses of events." In this conception we see the metaphysics of "current events" fully developed. The historicity of existence is abolished—all events are "current" in space-time, history is a film of such events which are current in their place and the substantially eternal presence before God is replaced by the phenomenally current present before the photographer or "observer." Not even the fine nuance is missing in the formulation of Turgot that the actual present is a little more present than the presents which are already relegated to the limbo of the past.

Religion and political geography

The ***Esquisse d'un plan de géographie politique*** itself we shall not analyse. We shall extract from it only one idea: that of the impact of religions on the problems of political geography. Religions, in the opinion of Turgot, have not always had a bearing on political geography. In the age of polytheism the gods and their cults were compatible with each other; the gods were different, the religion was the same. There may have been an occasional war for religious reasons, like the sacred wars of the Phoenicians, but such wars were intended to take revenge for a particular injury done to a sacred place. "The peoples fought for their gods like our knights for their ladies." Political problems make themselves felt only with the rise of exclusive religions. If an exclusive religion was confined to one people, like the Hebrew, the political consequences were still not great since they would consist mainly in separation. Only when the object of religions becomes truth, "as in some philosophical sects," and when, in addition, the truth did not remain sectarian but was propagated with the intention to embrace all men and nations, do the political problems begin. To claim possession of truth is "a sort of injury to the rest of mankind" and the attempt at conversion cuts politically across the national organization. Such religions are Christianity and Islam.

The problem presented by the rise of the universal religions is in itself well observed. The consensus of the faithful as a new type of community in politics has become the topic of one of the more convincing chapters in Spengler's *Decline of the West,* under the title of the Magian nations, and the function of the universal church as the "chrysalis" of a new civilization has been clarified by Toynbee. The rise of the universal religions in the epoch between two "generations" (Toynbee) of civilizations is, indeed, one of the great morphological features of world history. Though he recognizes its importance, Turgot regards it with clear disfavor as a disturbance of the clean geographical affairs of history. The religions *should* not exert an influence in political geography because they disturb the territorial political order. If several religions with equal universal claims find adherents in the same nation, the stronger will suppress the weaker and wars for the freedom of conscience will result. The persecuted subjects of one prince will form alliances with neighboring princes who are their coreligionists and under such conditions a nation cannot live in peace on its territory. The solution for such evils is unconditional tolerance on the part of the state, including the freedom of worship. "Only then will religions cease to be a factor in political geography; if for no other reason, because a state governed by the principle of tolerance will be wealthier and more populated than any other." The principle of the universal Church must be abandoned, just

as the dynastic principle, because it interferes with the existence of the organized nation. What Christianity has given to the world should not be belittled, but the best it has given was "to inspire and propagate natural religion." The characteristics of this essence of true Christianity are "sweetness and charity" which permit the nation to live in peace, without mutual persecutions of its citizens [*Lettres sur la tolérance,*]. And what will the nation do when it lives in peace? The future is full of promise. Hitherto we have lived on the globe like savages, exploiting the fertility of the soil. This was possible because there was enough fertile soil for the comparatively small number of men. In the future, however, mankind will increase, and the increased mankind will have to use its ingenuity on lands which have been hitherto uncultivated. There is no reason to despair of this future; the technology of soil improvement and the technical means of artificial water-supply are well developed. Mankind faces a rich and meaningful existence through artificial fertilizers and irrigation projects.

The three strands in the thread of progress, that is (1) the enlightenment of the mind, (2) the intensification of global intercourse, and (3) the softening of the mores, thus, are intertwined in the authoritative knot of the present. In spite of the nearness to Bossuet, in spite of Turgot's conscientiousness, and in spite of the impasses and honest hesitations, the intramundane sentiment predominates and the anti-Christian dogmatism outweighs the contemplative elements. Still, Turgot is so close to the Christian tradition that the lines of derivation through which the Positivist creed is connected with Western high civilization become visible in every detail. The creed is fully developed as an intellectual position but it has not yet acquired the characteristics of a conscious religious movement. Nevertheless, just as d'Alembert's radical progressivism, the variant of Turgot represents a definite phase in Positivism which has its historical importance independent of the Comtean additions. In Turgot's speculation, the creed of enlightenment, despiritualized morality and technology has entered into the momentous combination with nationalism. The national state of the Western type is supposed to be, and to remain, the vessel of progressive civilization. This particular evocative aggregate of ideas has profoundly influenced the course of Western political history insofar as it has become one of the great obstacles in adjusting political forms to the necessities of an industrialized society. Toynbee has given a thorough analysis of the problem which arises when democracy and industrialism, both of which require larger political units for their functioning, have to function within the unsuitable framework of the European national state. The amalgamation of the Positivist aggregate of ideas with nationalism has an aggravating, parallel effect on the resistance of national political units against their blending into larger communities.

FURTHER READING

Condorcet, Marie Jean Antoine Nicolas Caritat de. *Vie de Monsieur Turgot*. London, 1786, 322 p.
    First biography of Turgot, available only in French.

Dakin, Douglas. *Turgot and the* Ancien Régime *in France.* 1939. Reprint. New York: Octagon Books, 1965, 361 p.

Places the life and work of Turgot in the context of his times by providing a lengthy historical background.

Flint, Robert. "Turgot." In his *The Philosophy of History in France and Germany*, pp. 109-15. 1874. Reprint. Geneva: Slatkine, 1971.

Compares Turgot's philosophy of history with that of Montesquieu and Comte.

Groenewegen, P. D. "A Re-Interpretation of Turgot's Theory of Capital and Interest." *Economic Journal* 81, No. 322 (June 1971): 327-40.

Notes Turgot's contribution to the theory of saving-investment analysis.

Kaplan, Steven Laurence. "Social Classification and Representation in the Corporate World of Eighteenth-Century France: Turgot's 'Carnival.'" In his *Work in France: Representations, Meaning, Organization, and Practice*, edited by Steven Laurence Kaplan and Cynthia J. Koepp, pp. 176-228. Ithaca, N. Y.: Cornell University Press, 1986.

Studies the response to Turgot's edict abolishing the guilds and claims that it hastened the revolution by eroding the class structure of the Old Regime.

Löwith, Karl. "Progress versus Providence." In his *Meaning in History*, pp. 60-103. Chicago: University of Chicago Press, Phoenix Books, 1949.

Appreciates the complex nature of Turgot's understanding of the historical process.

Lundberg, I. C. *Turgot's Unknown Translator: The "Réflexions" and Adam Smith.* The Hague: Martinus Nijhoff, 1964, 122 p.

Suggests that Adam Smith may have been the translator of the first English edition of the *Refections on the Formation and the Distribution of Wealth*, which was published in 1793.

Morley, John. "Turgot." In his *Biographical Studies*, pp. 1-92. 1923. Reprint. Freeport, N. Y.: Books for Libraries Press, 1969.

Gives a full account of Turgot's early years and a good summary of his economic and philosophical thought.

Orton, William Aylott. "France and Individualism." In his *The Liberal Tradition: A Study of the Social and Spiritual Conditions of Freedom*, pp. 136-58. New Haven, Conn.: Yale University Press, 1945.

Describes Turgot as a proponent of laissez-faire economics and emphasizes his contribution to the secular origins of individualism.

Payne, Harry. "The Philosophes and Popular Ritual: Turgot, Voltaire, Rousseau." In *Studies in Eighteenth-Century Culture*, edited by O. M. Brack Jr., Vol. 14, pp. 307-16. Madison: University of Wisconsin Press, 1985.

Notes the disdain that Turgot and other philosophes expressed toward local religious festivals, believing them to conflict with the demands of economic productivity and social order.

Salmon, J. H. M. "Turgot and Condorcet: Progress, Reform and Revolution." *History Today* XXVII, No. 5 (May 1977): 288-96.

Surveys briefly the life and thought of Turgot with emphasis on his theory of progress.

Say, Léon. *Turgot.* Translated by Melville B. Anderson. Chicago: A. C. McClurg and Co., 1888, 231 p.

A biography that calls Turgot the founder of French political economy.

Smyth, William. "Louis XVI, Turgot, Necker." In his *The Lessons of History: Lectures on Modern History and the French and American Revolutions*, abridged and edited by Wallace Brockway, pp. 270-82. 1840-60. Reprint. New York: Simon and Schuster, 1955.

Chronicles Turgot's role as Louis XVI's finance minister from the perspective of a nineteenth-century liberal.

White, Andrew Dickson. "Turgot." In his *Seven Great Statesmen in the Warfare of Humanity with Unreason*, pp. 165-238. New York: The Century Co., 1910.

Surveys Turgot's life and emphasizes his role as an administrator who worked to reform the French economic and social system.

Literature Criticism from 1400 to 1800

Cumulative Indexes

How to Use This Index

The main references

> **Calvino, Italo**
> 1923-1985.....CLC **5, 8, 11, 22, 33, 39,**
> **73; SSC 3**

list all author entries in the following Gale Literary Criticism series:

BLC = *Black Literature Criticism*
CLC = *Contemporary Literary Criticism*
CLR = *Children's Literature Review*
CMLC = *Classical and Medieval Literature Criticism*
DA = *DISCovering Authors*
DC = *Drama Criticism*
HLC = *Hispanic Literature Criticism*
LC = *Literature Criticism from 1400 to 1800*
NCLC = *Nineteenth-Century Literature Criticism*
PC = *Poetry Criticism*
SSC = *Short Story Criticism*
TCLC = *Twentieth-Century Literary Criticism*
WLC = *World Literature Criticism, 1500 to the Present*

The cross-references

> See also CANR 23; CA 85-88;
> obituary CA 116

list all author entries in the following Gale biographical and literary sources:

AAYA = *Authors & Artists for Young Adults*
AITN = *Authors in the News*
BEST = *Bestsellers*
BW = *Black Writers*
CA = *Contemporary Authors*
CAAS = *Contemporary Authors Autobiography Series*
CABS = *Contemporary Authors Bibliographical Series*
CANR = *Contemporary Authors New Revision Series*
CAP = *Contemporary Authors Permanent Series*
CDALB = *Concise Dictionary of American Literary Biography*
CDBLB = *Concise Dictionary of British Literary Biography*
DLB = *Dictionary of Literary Biography*
DLBD = *Dictionary of Literary Biography Documentary Series*
DLBY = *Dictionary of Literary Biography Yearbook*
HW = *Hispanic Writers*
JRDA = *Junior DISCovering Authors*
MAICYA = *Major Authors and Illustrators for Children and Young Adults*
MTCW = *Major 20th-Century Writers*
SAAS = *Something about the Author Autobiography Series*
SATA = *Something about the Author*
YABC = *Yesterday's Authors of Books for Children*

Literary Criticism Series
Cumulative Author Index

A.
See Arnold, Matthew

A. E. . . . . **TCLC 3, 10**
See also Russell, George William
See also DLB 19

A. M.
See Megged, Aharon

A. R. P-C
See Galsworthy, John

Abasiyanik, Sait Faik 1906-1954
See Sait Faik
See also CA 123

Abbey, Edward 1927-1989 . . . . . . **CLC 36, 59**
See also CA 45-48; 128; CANR 2, 41

Abbott, Lee K(ittredge) 1947- . . . . . . **CLC 48**
See also CA 124; DLB 130

Abe, Kobo 1924-1993 . . . . . **CLC 8, 22, 53, 81**
See also CA 65-68; 140; CANR 24; MTCW

Abelard, Peter c. 1079-c. 1142 . . . **CMLC 11**
See also DLB 115

Abell, Kjeld 1901-1961 . . . . **CLC 15**
See also CA 111

Abish, Walter 1931- . . . . **CLC 22**
See also CA 101; CANR 37; DLB 130

Abrahams, Peter (Henry) 1919- . . . . . **CLC 4**
See also BW 1; CA 57-60; CANR 26;
DLB 117; MTCW

Abrams, M(eyer) H(oward) 1912- . . . **CLC 24**
See also CA 57-60; CANR 13, 33; DLB 67

Abse, Dannie 1923- . . . . **CLC 7, 29**
See also CA 53-56; CAAS 1; CANR 4;
DLB 27

Achebe, (Albert) Chinua(lumogu)
1930- . . . . . **CLC 1, 3, 5, 7, 11, 26, 51, 75;
BLC; DA; WLC**
See also BW 2; CA 1-4R; CANR 6, 26;
CLR 20; DLB 117; MAICYA; MTCW;
SATA 38, 40

Acker, Kathy 1948- . . . . **CLC 45**
See also CA 117; 122

Ackroyd, Peter 1949- . . . . **CLC 34, 52**
See also CA 123; 127

Acorn, Milton 1923- . . . . **CLC 15**
See also CA 103; DLB 53

Adamov, Arthur 1908-1970 . . . . . . **CLC 4, 25**
See also CA 17-18; 25-28R; CAP 2; MTCW

Adams, Alice (Boyd) 1926- . . . **CLC 6, 13, 46**
See also CA 81-84; CANR 26; DLBY 86;
MTCW

Adams, Andy 1859-1935 . . . . **TCLC 56**
See also YABC 1

Adams, Douglas (Noel) 1952- . . . **CLC 27, 60**
See also AAYA 4; BEST 89:3; CA 106;
CANR 34; DLBY 83; JRDA

Adams, Francis 1862-1893 . . . . **NCLC 33**

Adams, Henry (Brooks)
1838-1918 . . . . **TCLC 4, 52; DA**
See also CA 104; 133; DLB 12, 47

Adams, Richard (George)
1920- . . . . **CLC 4, 5, 18**
See also AITN 1, 2; CA 49-52; CANR 3,
35; CLR 20; JRDA; MAICYA; MTCW;
SATA 7, 69

Adamson, Joy(-Friederike Victoria)
1910-1980 . . . . **CLC 17**
See also CA 69-72; 93-96; CANR 22;
MTCW; SATA 11, 22

Adcock, Fleur 1934- . . . . **CLC 41**
See also CA 25-28R; CANR 11, 34;
DLB 40

Addams, Charles (Samuel)
1912-1988 . . . . **CLC 30**
See also CA 61-64; 126; CANR 12

Addison, Joseph 1672-1719 . . . . **LC 18**
See also CDBLB 1660-1789; DLB 101

Adler, C(arole) S(chwerdtfeger)
1932- . . . . **CLC 35**
See also AAYA 4; CA 89-92; CANR 19,
40; JRDA; MAICYA; SAAS 15;
SATA 26, 63

Adler, Renata 1938- . . . . **CLC 8, 31**
See also CA 49-52; CANR 5, 22; MTCW

Ady, Endre 1877-1919 . . . . **TCLC 11**
See also CA 107

Aeschylus
525B.C.-456B.C. . . . . **CMLC 11; DA**

Afton, Effie
See Harper, Frances Ellen Watkins

Agapida, Fray Antonio
See Irving, Washington

Agee, James (Rufus)
1909-1955 . . . . **TCLC 1, 19**
See also AITN 1; CA 108;
CDALB 1941-1968; DLB 2, 26

Aghill, Gordon
See Silverberg, Robert

Agnon, S(hmuel) Y(osef Halevi)
1888-1970 . . . . **CLC 4, 8, 14**
See also CA 17-18; 25-28R; CAP 2; MTCW

Aherne, Owen
See Cassill, R(onald) V(erlin)

Ai 1947- . . . . **CLC 4, 14, 69**
See also CA 85-88; CAAS 13; DLB 120

Aickman, Robert (Fordyce)
1914-1981 . . . . **CLC 57**
See also CA 5-8R; CANR 3

Aiken, Conrad (Potter)
1889-1973 . . . **CLC 1, 3, 5, 10, 52; SSC 9**
See also CA 5-8R; 45-48; CANR 4;
CDALB 1929-1941; DLB 9, 45, 102;
MTCW; SATA 3, 30

Aiken, Joan (Delano) 1924- . . . . **CLC 35**
See also AAYA 1; CA 9-12R; CANR 4, 23,
34; CLR 1, 19; JRDA; MAICYA;
MTCW; SAAS 1; SATA 2, 30, 73

Ainsworth, William Harrison
1805-1882 . . . . **NCLC 13**
See also DLB 21; SATA 24

Aitmatov, Chingiz (Torekulovich)
1928- . . . . **CLC 71**
See also CA 103; CANR 38; MTCW;
SATA 56

Akers, Floyd
See Baum, L(yman) Frank

Akhmadulina, Bella Akhatovna
1937- . . . . **CLC 53**
See also CA 65-68

Akhmatova, Anna
1888-1966 . . . . **CLC 11, 25, 64; PC 2**
See also CA 19-20; 25-28R; CANR 35;
CAP 1; MTCW

Aksakov, Sergei Timofeyvich
1791-1859 . . . . **NCLC 2**

Aksenov, Vassily . . . . **CLC 22**
See also Aksyonov, Vassily (Pavlovich)

Aksyonov, Vassily (Pavlovich)
1932- . . . . **CLC 37**
See also Aksenov, Vassily
See also CA 53-56; CANR 12

Akutagawa Ryunosuke
1892-1927 . . . . **TCLC 16**
See also CA 117

Alain 1868-1951 . . . . **TCLC 41**

Alain-Fournier . . . . **TCLC 6**
See also Fournier, Henri Alban
See also DLB 65

Alarcon, Pedro Antonio de
1833-1891 . . . . **NCLC 1**

Alas (y Urena), Leopoldo (Enrique Garcia)
1852-1901 . . . . **TCLC 29**
See also CA 113; 131; HW

Albee, Edward (Franklin III)
1928- . . . . . . **CLC 1, 2, 3, 5, 9, 11, 13, 25,
53; DA; WLC**
See also AITN 1; CA 5-8R; CABS 3;
CANR 8; CDALB 1941-1968; DLB 7;
MTCW

Alberti, Rafael 1902- . . . . **CLC 7**
See also CA 85-88; DLB 108

Alcala-Galiano, Juan Valera y
See Valera y Alcala-Galiano, Juan

Alcott, Amos Bronson 1799-1888 . . **NCLC 1**
See also DLB 1

Alcott, Louisa May
1832-1888 . . . . **NCLC 6; DA; WLC**
See also CDALB 1865-1917; CLR 1;
DLB 1, 42, 79; JRDA; MAICYA;
YABC 1

Aldanov, M. A.
See Aldanov, Mark (Alexandrovich)

Aldanov, Mark (Alexandrovich)
1886(?)-1957 . . . . **TCLC 23**
See also CA 118

Aldington, Richard 1892-1962 . . . . . . **CLC 49**
See also CA 85-88; CANR 45; DLB 20, 36, 100

Aldiss, Brian W(ilson)
1925- . . . . **CLC 5, 14, 40**
See also CA 5-8R; CAAS 2; CANR 5, 28; DLB 14; MTCW; SATA 34

Alegria, Claribel 1924- . . . . **CLC 75**
See also CA 131; CAAS 15; HW

Alegria, Fernando 1918- . . . . **CLC 57**
See also CA 9-12R; CANR 5, 32; HW

Aleichem, Sholom . . . . **TCLC 1, 35**
See also Rabinovitch, Sholem

Aleixandre, Vicente 1898-1984 . . . **CLC 9, 36**
See also CA 85-88; 114; CANR 26; DLB 108; HW; MTCW

Alepoudelis, Odysseus
See Elytis, Odysseus

Aleshkovsky, Joseph 1929-
See Aleshkovsky, Yuz
See also CA 121; 128

Aleshkovsky, Yuz . . . . **CLC 44**
See also Aleshkovsky, Joseph

Alexander, Lloyd (Chudley) 1924- . . **CLC 35**
See also AAYA 1; CA 1-4R; CANR 1, 24, 38; CLR 1, 5; DLB 52; JRDA; MAICYA; MTCW; SATA 3, 49

Alfau, Felipe 1902- . . . . **CLC 66**
See also CA 137

Alger, Horatio, Jr. 1832-1899 . . . . . **NCLC 8**
See also DLB 42; SATA 16

Algren, Nelson 1909-1981 . . . . **CLC 4, 10, 33**
See also CA 13-16R; 103; CANR 20; CDALB 1941-1968; DLB 9; DLBY 81, 82; MTCW

Ali, Ahmed 1910- . . . . **CLC 69**
See also CA 25-28R; CANR 15, 34

Alighieri, Dante 1265-1321 . . . . **CMLC 3**

Allan, John B.
See Westlake, Donald E(dwin)

Allen, Edward 1948- . . . . **CLC 59**

Allen, Paula Gunn 1939- . . . . **CLC 84**
See also CA 112; 143; NNAL

Allen, Roland
See Ayckbourn, Alan

Allen, Sarah A.
See Hopkins, Pauline Elizabeth

Allen, Woody 1935- . . . . **CLC 16, 52**
See also AAYA 10; CA 33-36R; CANR 27, 38; DLB 44; MTCW

Allende, Isabel 1942- . . . . **CLC 39, 57; HLC**
See also CA 125; 130; HW; MTCW

Alleyn, Ellen
See Rossetti, Christina (Georgina)

Allingham, Margery (Louise)
1904-1966 . . . . **CLC 19**
See also CA 5-8R; 25-28R; CANR 4; DLB 77; MTCW

Allingham, William 1824-1889 . . . **NCLC 25**
See also DLB 35

Allison, Dorothy E. 1949- . . . . **CLC 78**
See also CA 140

Allston, Washington 1779-1843 . . . . **NCLC 2**
See also DLB 1

Almedingen, E. M. . . . . **CLC 12**
See also Almedingen, Martha Edith von
See also SATA 3

Almedingen, Martha Edith von 1898-1971
See Almedingen, E. M.
See also CA 1-4R; CANR 1

Almqvist, Carl Jonas Love
1793-1866 . . . . **NCLC 42**

Alonso, Damaso 1898-1990 . . . . **CLC 14**
See also CA 110; 131; 130; DLB 108; HW

Alov
See Gogol, Nikolai (Vasilyevich)

Alta 1942- . . . . **CLC 19**
See also CA 57-60

Alter, Robert B(ernard) 1935- . . . . . . **CLC 34**
See also CA 49-52; CANR 1

Alther, Lisa 1944- . . . . **CLC 7, 41**
See also CA 65-68; CANR 12, 30; MTCW

Altman, Robert 1925- . . . . **CLC 16**
See also CA 73-76; CANR 43

Alvarez, A(lfred) 1929- . . . . **CLC 5, 13**
See also CA 1-4R; CANR 3, 33; DLB 14, 40

Alvarez, Alejandro Rodriguez 1903-1965
See Casona, Alejandro
See also CA 131; 93-96; HW

Amado, Jorge 1912- . . . . . **CLC 13, 40; HLC**
See also CA 77-80; CANR 35; DLB 113; MTCW

Ambler, Eric 1909- . . . . **CLC 4, 6, 9**
See also CA 9-12R; CANR 7, 38; DLB 77; MTCW

Amichai, Yehuda 1924- . . . . . . **CLC 9, 22, 57**
See also CA 85-88; MTCW

Amiel, Henri Frederic 1821-1881 . . **NCLC 4**

Amis, Kingsley (William)
1922- . . **CLC 1, 2, 3, 5, 8, 13, 40, 44; DA**
See also AITN 2; CA 9-12R; CANR 8, 28; CDBLB 1945-1960; DLB 15, 27, 100, 139; MTCW

Amis, Martin (Louis)
1949- . . . . **CLC 4, 9, 38, 62**
See also BEST 90:3; CA 65-68; CANR 8, 27; DLB 14

Ammons, A(rchie) R(andolph)
1926- . . . . **CLC 2, 3, 5, 8, 9, 25, 57**
See also AITN 1; CA 9-12R; CANR 6, 36; DLB 5; MTCW

Amo, Tauraatua i
See Adams, Henry (Brooks)

Anand, Mulk Raj 1905- . . . . **CLC 23**
See also CA 65-68; CANR 32; MTCW

Anatol
See Schnitzler, Arthur

Anaya, Rudolfo A(lfonso)
1937- . . . . **CLC 23; HLC**
See also CA 45-48; CAAS 4; CANR 1, 32; DLB 82; HW 1; MTCW

Andersen, Hans Christian
1805-1875 . . **NCLC 7; DA; SSC 6; WLC**
See also CLR 6; MAICYA; YABC 1

Anderson, C. Farley
See Mencken, H(enry) L(ouis); Nathan, George Jean

Anderson, Jessica (Margaret) Queale
. . . . **CLC 37**
See also CA 9-12R; CANR 4

Anderson, Jon (Victor) 1940- . . . . . . **CLC 9**
See also CA 25-28R; CANR 20

Anderson, Lindsay (Gordon)
1923- . . . . **CLC 20**
See also CA 125; 128

Anderson, Maxwell 1888-1959 . . . . . **TCLC 2**
See also CA 105; DLB 7

Anderson, Poul (William) 1926- . . . . **CLC 15**
See also AAYA 5; CA 1-4R; CAAS 2; CANR 2, 15, 34; DLB 8; MTCW; SATA 39

Anderson, Robert (Woodruff)
1917- . . . . **CLC 23**
See also AITN 1; CA 21-24R; CANR 32; DLB 7

Anderson, Sherwood
1876-1941 . . . . **TCLC 1, 10, 24; DA; SSC 1; WLC**
See also CA 104; 121; CDALB 1917-1929; DLB 4, 9, 86; DLBD 1; MTCW

Andouard
See Giraudoux, (Hippolyte) Jean

Andrade, Carlos Drummond de . . . . . . **CLC 18**
See also Drummond de Andrade, Carlos

Andrade, Mario de 1893-1945 . . . . . **TCLC 43**

Andreas-Salome, Lou 1861-1937 . . . **TCLC 56**
See also DLB 66

Andrewes, Lancelot 1555-1626 . . . . **LC 5**

Andrews, Cicily Fairfield
See West, Rebecca

Andrews, Elton V.
See Pohl, Frederik

Andreyev, Leonid (Nikolaevich)
1871-1919 . . . . **TCLC 3**
See also CA 104

Andric, Ivo 1892-1975 . . . . **CLC 8**
See also CA 81-84; 57-60; CANR 43; MTCW

Angelique, Pierre
See Bataille, Georges

Angell, Roger 1920- . . . . **CLC 26**
See also CA 57-60; CANR 13, 44

Angelou, Maya
1928- . . . . **CLC 12, 35, 64, 77; BLC; DA**
See also AAYA 7; BW 2; CA 65-68; CANR 19, 42; DLB 38; MTCW; SATA 49

Annensky, Innokenty Fyodorovich
1856-1909 . . . . **TCLC 14**
See also CA 110

Anon, Charles Robert
See Pessoa, Fernando (Antonio Nogueira)

Anouilh, Jean (Marie Lucien Pierre)
1910-1987 . . . . . . **CLC 1, 3, 8, 13, 40, 50**
See also CA 17-20R; 123; CANR 32; MTCW

Anthony, Florence
See Ai

Anthony, John
See Ciardi, John (Anthony)

Anthony, Peter
See Shaffer, Anthony (Joshua); Shaffer, Peter (Levin)

Anthony, Piers 1934- .... **CLC 35**
See also AAYA 11; CA 21-24R; CANR 28; DLB 8; MTCW

Antoine, Marc
See Proust, (Valentin-Louis-George-Eugene-) Marcel

Antoninus, Brother
See Everson, William (Oliver)

Antonioni, Michelangelo 1912- ..... **CLC 20**
See also CA 73-76; CANR 45

Antschel, Paul 1920-1970...... **CLC 10, 19**
See also Celan, Paul
See also CA 85-88; CANR 33; MTCW

Anwar, Chairil 1922-1949 .... **TCLC 22**
See also CA 121

Apollinaire, Guillaume .. **TCLC 3, 8, 51; PC 7**
See also Kostrowitzki, Wilhelm Apollinaris de

Appelfeld, Aharon 1932- .... **CLC 23, 47**
See also CA 112; 133

Apple, Max (Isaac) 1941-........ **CLC 9, 33**
See also CA 81-84; CANR 19; DLB 130

Appleman, Philip (Dean) 1926- ..... **CLC 51**
See also CA 13-16R; CAAS 18; CANR 6, 29

Appleton, Lawrence
See Lovecraft, H(oward) P(hillips)

Apteryx
See Eliot, T(homas) S(tearns)

Apuleius, (Lucius Madaurensis)
125(?)-175(?) .... **CMLC 1**

Aquin, Hubert 1929-1977......... **CLC 15**
See also CA 105; DLB 53

Aragon, Louis 1897-1982....... **CLC 3, 22**
See also CA 69-72; 108; CANR 28; DLB 72; MTCW

Arany, Janos 1817-1882........ **NCLC 34**

Arbuthnot, John 1667-1735 .... **LC 1**
See also DLB 101

Archer, Herbert Winslow
See Mencken, H(enry) L(ouis)

Archer, Jeffrey (Howard) 1940- .... **CLC 28**
See also BEST 89:3; CA 77-80; CANR 22

Archer, Jules 1915- .... **CLC 12**
See also CA 9-12R; CANR 6; SAAS 5; SATA 4

Archer, Lee
See Ellison, Harlan

Arden, John 1930- .... **CLC 6, 13, 15**
See also CA 13-16R; CAAS 4; CANR 31; DLB 13; MTCW

Arenas, Reinaldo
1943-1990 .... **CLC 41; HLC**
See also CA 124; 128; 133; HW

Arendt, Hannah 1906-1975 .... **CLC 66**
See also CA 17-20R; 61-64; CANR 26; MTCW

Aretino, Pietro 1492-1556 .... **LC 12**

Arghezi, Tudor. .... **CLC 80**
See also Theodorescu, Ion N.

Arguedas, Jose Maria
1911-1969 .... **CLC 10, 18**
See also CA 89-92; DLB 113; HW

Argueta, Manlio 1936-........... **CLC 31**
See also CA 131; HW

Ariosto, Ludovico 1474-1533........ **LC 6**

Aristides
See Epstein, Joseph

Aristophanes
450B.C.-385B.C.... **CMLC 4; DA; DC 2**

Arlt, Roberto (Godofredo Christophersen)
1900-1942 .... **TCLC 29; HLC**
See also CA 123; 131; HW

Armah, Ayi Kwei 1939- .... **CLC 5, 33; BLC**
See also BW 1; CA 61-64; CANR 21; DLB 117; MTCW

Armatrading, Joan 1950-.......... **CLC 17**
See also CA 114

Arnette, Robert
See Silverberg, Robert

Arnim, Achim von (Ludwig Joachim von Arnim) 1781-1831 .... **NCLC 5**
See also DLB 90

Arnim, Bettina von 1785-1859.... **NCLC 38**
See also DLB 90

Arnold, Matthew
1822-1888 ..... **NCLC 6, 29; DA; PC 5; WLC**
See also CDBLB 1832-1890; DLB 32, 57

Arnold, Thomas 1795-1842 ...... **NCLC 18**
See also DLB 55

Arnow, Harriette (Louisa) Simpson
1908-1986 .... **CLC 2, 7, 18**
See also CA 9-12R; 118; CANR 14; DLB 6; MTCW; SATA 42, 47

Arp, Hans
See Arp, Jean

Arp, Jean 1887-1966.............. **CLC 5**
See also CA 81-84; 25-28R; CANR 42

Arrabal
See Arrabal, Fernando

Arrabal, Fernando 1932-... **CLC 2, 9, 18, 58**
See also CA 9-12R; CANR 15

Arrick, Fran. .... **CLC 30**

Artaud, Antonin 1896-1948 ..... **TCLC 3, 36**
See also CA 104

Arthur, Ruth M(abel) 1905-1979.... **CLC 12**
See also CA 9-12R; 85-88; CANR 4; SATA 7, 26

Artsybashev, Mikhail (Petrovich)
1878-1927 .... **TCLC 31**

Arundel, Honor (Morfydd)
1919-1973 .... **CLC 17**
See also CA 21-22; 41-44R; CAP 2; SATA 4, 24

Asch, Sholem 1880-1957 .... **TCLC 3**
See also CA 105

Ash, Shalom
See Asch, Sholem

Ashbery, John (Lawrence)
1927- ...... **CLC 2, 3, 4, 6, 9, 13, 15, 25, 41, 77**
See also CA 5-8R; CANR 9, 37; DLB 5; DLBY 81; MTCW

Ashdown, Clifford
See Freeman, R(ichard) Austin

Ashe, Gordon
See Creasey, John

Ashton-Warner, Sylvia (Constance)
1908-1984 .... **CLC 19**
See also CA 69-72; 112; CANR 29; MTCW

Asimov, Isaac
1920-1992 ...... **CLC 1, 3, 9, 19, 26, 76**
See also BEST 90:2; CA 1-4R; 137; CANR 2, 19, 36; CLR 12; DLB 8; DLBY 92; JRDA; MAICYA; MTCW; SATA 1, 26, 74

Astley, Thea (Beatrice May)
1925- .... **CLC 41**
See also CA 65-68; CANR 11, 43

Aston, James
See White, T(erence) H(anbury)

Asturias, Miguel Angel
1899-1974 .... **CLC 3, 8, 13; HLC**
See also CA 25-28; 49-52; CANR 32; CAP 2; DLB 113; HW; MTCW

Atares, Carlos Saura
See Saura (Atares), Carlos

Atheling, William
See Pound, Ezra (Weston Loomis)

Atheling, William, Jr.
See Blish, James (Benjamin)

Atherton, Gertrude (Franklin Horn)
1857-1948 .... **TCLC 2**
See also CA 104; DLB 9, 78

Atherton, Lucius
See Masters, Edgar Lee

Atkins, Jack
See Harris, Mark

Atticus
See Fleming, Ian (Lancaster)

Atwood, Margaret (Eleanor)
1939- ..... **CLC 2, 3, 4, 8, 13, 15, 25, 44, 84; DA; PC 8; SSC 2; WLC**
See also AAYA 12; BEST 89:2; CA 49-52; CANR 3, 24, 33; DLB 53; MTCW; SATA 50

Aubigny, Pierre d'
See Mencken, H(enry) L(ouis)

Aubin, Penelope 1685-1731(?)........ **LC 9**
See also DLB 39

Auchincloss, Louis (Stanton)
1917- .... **CLC 4, 6, 9, 18, 45**
See also CA 1-4R; CANR 6, 29; DLB 2; DLBY 80; MTCW

Auden, W(ystan) H(ugh)
1907-1973 ...... **CLC 1, 2, 3, 4, 6, 9, 11, 14, 43; DA; PC 1; WLC**
See also CA 9-12R; 45-48; CANR 5; CDBLB 1914-1945; DLB 10, 20; MTCW

Audiberti, Jacques 1900-1965 ...... **CLC 38**
See also CA 25-28R

Auel, Jean M(arie) 1936-......... **CLC 31**
See also AAYA 7; BEST 90:4; CA 103;
CANR 21

Auerbach, Erich 1892-1957 .... **TCLC 43**
See also CA 118

Augier, Emile 1820-1889 .... **NCLC 31**

August, John
See De Voto, Bernard (Augustine)

Augustine, St. 354-430 .... **CMLC 6**

Aurelius
See Bourne, Randolph S(illiman)

Austen, Jane
1775-1817 .... **NCLC 1, 13, 19, 33; DA;
WLC**
See also CDBLB 1789-1832; DLB 116

Auster, Paul 1947-............... **CLC 47**
See also CA 69-72; CANR 23

Austin, Frank
See Faust, Frederick (Schiller)

Austin, Mary (Hunter)
1868-1934 .... **TCLC 25**
See also CA 109; DLB 9, 78

Autran Dourado, Waldomiro
See Dourado, (Waldomiro Freitas) Autran

Averroes 1126-1198 .... **CMLC 7**
See also DLB 115

Avison, Margaret 1918-.......... **CLC 2, 4**
See also CA 17-20R; DLB 53; MTCW

Axton, David
See Koontz, Dean R(ay)

Ayckbourn, Alan
1939-............ **CLC 5, 8, 18, 33, 74**
See also CA 21-24R; CANR 31; DLB 13;
MTCW

Aydy, Catherine
See Tennant, Emma (Christina)

Ayme, Marcel (Andre) 1902-1967... **CLC 11**
See also CA 89-92; CLR 25; DLB 72

Ayrton, Michael 1921-1975........ **CLC 7**
See also CA 5-8R; 61-64; CANR 9, 21

Azorin........................ **CLC 11**
See also Martinez Ruiz, Jose

Azuela, Mariano
1873-1952 .... **TCLC 3; HLC**
See also CA 104; 131; HW; MTCW

Baastad, Babbis Friis
See Friis-Baastad, Babbis Ellinor

Bab
See Gilbert, W(illiam) S(chwenck)

Babbis, Eleanor
See Friis-Baastad, Babbis Ellinor

Babel, Isaak (Emmanuilovich)
1894-1941(?) ...... **TCLC 2, 13; SSC 16**
See also CA 104

Babits, Mihaly 1883-1941 .... **TCLC 14**
See also CA 114

Babur 1483-1530.................. **LC 18**

Bacchelli, Riccardo 1891-1985 ..... **CLC 19**
See also CA 29-32R; 117

Bach, Richard (David) 1936-....... **CLC 14**
See also AITN 1; BEST 89:2; CA 9-12R;
CANR 18; MTCW; SATA 13

Bachman, Richard
See King, Stephen (Edwin)

Bachmann, Ingeborg 1926-1973..... **CLC 69**
See also CA 93-96; 45-48; DLB 85

Bacon, Francis 1561-1626 .... **LC 18**
See also CDBLB Before 1660

Bacovia, George................. **TCLC 24**
See also Vasiliu, Gheorghe

Badanes, Jerome 1937-............ **CLC 59**

Bagehot, Walter 1826-1877 ...... **NCLC 10**
See also DLB 55

Bagnold, Enid 1889-1981 .... **CLC 25**
See also CA 5-8R; 103; CANR 5, 40;
DLB 13; MAICYA; SATA 1, 25

Bagrjana, Elisaveta
See Belcheva, Elisaveta

Bagryana, Elisaveta
See Belcheva, Elisaveta

Bailey, Paul 1937- .... **CLC 45**
See also CA 21-24R; CANR 16; DLB 14

Baillie, Joanna 1762-1851 .... **NCLC 2**
See also DLB 93

Bainbridge, Beryl (Margaret)
1933-.... **CLC 4, 5, 8, 10, 14, 18, 22, 62**
See also CA 21-24R; CANR 24; DLB 14;
MTCW

Baker, Elliott 1922-.............. **CLC 8**
See also CA 45-48; CANR 2

Baker, Nicholson 1957-........... **CLC 61**
See also CA 135

Baker, Ray Stannard 1870-1946 ... **TCLC 47**
See also CA 118

Baker, Russell (Wayne) 1925-...... **CLC 31**
See also BEST 89:4; CA 57-60; CANR 11,
41; MTCW

Bakhtin, M.
See Bakhtin, Mikhail Mikhailovich

Bakhtin, M. M.
See Bakhtin, Mikhail Mikhailovich

Bakhtin, Mikhail
See Bakhtin, Mikhail Mikhailovich

Bakhtin, Mikhail Mikhailovich
1895-1975 .... **CLC 83**
See also CA 128; 113

Bakshi, Ralph 1938(?)-............ **CLC 26**
See also CA 112; 138

Bakunin, Mikhail (Alexandrovich)
1814-1876 .... **NCLC 25**

Baldwin, James (Arthur)
1924-1987 ...... **CLC 1, 2, 3, 4, 5, 8, 13,
15, 17, 42, 50, 67; BLC; DA; DC 1;
SSC 10; WLC**
See also AAYA 4; BW 1; CA 1-4R; 124;
CABS 1; CANR 3, 24;
CDALB 1941-1968; DLB 2, 7, 33;
DLBY 87; MTCW; SATA 9, 54

Ballard, J(ames) G(raham)
1930- .... **CLC 3, 6, 14, 36; SSC 1**
See also AAYA 3; CA 5-8R; CANR 15, 39;
DLB 14; MTCW

Balmont, Konstantin (Dmitriyevich)
1867-1943 .... **TCLC 11**
See also CA 109

Balzac, Honore de
1799-1850 .... **NCLC 5, 35; DA; SSC 5;
WLC**
See also DLB 119

Bambara, Toni Cade
1939- .... **CLC 19; BLC; DA**
See also AAYA 5; BW 2; CA 29-32R;
CANR 24; DLB 38; MTCW

Bamdad, A.
See Shamlu, Ahmad

Banat, D. R.
See Bradbury, Ray (Douglas)

Bancroft, Laura
See Baum, L(yman) Frank

Banim, John 1798-1842 .... **NCLC 13**
See also DLB 116

Banim, Michael 1796-1874 ...... **NCLC 13**

Banks, Iain
See Banks, Iain M(enzies)

Banks, Iain M(enzies) 1954-....... **CLC 34**
See also CA 123; 128

Banks, Lynne Reid .... **CLC 23**
See also Reid Banks, Lynne
See also AAYA 6

Banks, Russell 1940- .... **CLC 37, 72**
See also CA 65-68; CAAS 15; CANR 19;
DLB 130

Banville, John 1945-.............. **CLC 46**
See also CA 117; 128; DLB 14

Banville, Theodore (Faullain) de
1832-1891 .... **NCLC 9**

Baraka, Amiri
1934- .... **CLC 1, 2, 3, 5, 10, 14, 33;
BLC; DA; PC 4**
See also Jones, LeRoi
See also BW 2; CA 21-24R; CABS 3;
CANR 27, 38; CDALB 1941-1968;
DLB 5, 7, 16, 38; DLBD 8; MTCW

Barbellion, W. N. P............... **TCLC 24**
See also Cummings, Bruce F(rederick)

Barbera, Jack (Vincent) 1945-...... **CLC 44**
See also CA 110; CANR 45

Barbey d'Aurevilly, Jules Amedee
1808-1889 .... **NCLC 1**
See also DLB 119

Barbusse, Henri 1873-1935 .... **TCLC 5**
See also CA 105; DLB 65

Barclay, Bill
See Moorcock, Michael (John)

Barclay, William Ewert
See Moorcock, Michael (John)

Barea, Arturo 1897-1957 .... **TCLC 14**
See also CA 111

Barfoot, Joan 1946-.............. **CLC 18**
See also CA 105

Baring, Maurice 1874-1945....... **TCLC 8**
See also CA 105; DLB 34

Barker, Clive 1952- .... **CLC 52**
See also AAYA 10; BEST 90:3; CA 121;
129; MTCW

Barker, George Granville
1913-1991 .... **CLC 8, 48**
See also CA 9-12R; 135; CANR 7, 38;
DLB 20; MTCW

Barker, Harley Granville
See Granville-Barker, Harley
See also DLB 10

Barker, Howard 1946- . . . . CLC 37
See also CA 102; DLB 13

Barker, Pat 1943- . . . . CLC 32
See also CA 117; 122

Barlow, Joel 1754-1812 . . . . NCLC 23
See also DLB 37

Barnard, Mary (Ethel) 1909- . . . . CLC 48
See also CA 21-22; CAP 2

Barnes, Djuna
1892-1982 . . . CLC 3, 4, 8, 11, 29; SSC 3
See also CA 9-12R; 107; CANR 16; DLB 4,
9, 45; MTCW

Barnes, Julian 1946- . . . . CLC 42
See also CA 102; CANR 19; DLBY 93

Barnes, Peter 1931- . . . . CLC 5, 56
See also CA 65-68; CAAS 12; CANR 33,
34; DLB 13; MTCW

Baroja (y Nessi), Pio
1872-1956 . . . . TCLC 8; HLC
See also CA 104

Baron, David
See Pinter, Harold

Baron Corvo
See Rolfe, Frederick (William Serafino
Austin Lewis Mary)

Barondess, Sue K(aufman)
1926-1977 . . . . CLC 8
See also Kaufman, Sue
See also CA 1-4R; 69-72; CANR 1

Baron de Teive
See Pessoa, Fernando (Antonio Nogueira)

Barres, Maurice 1862-1923 . . . . TCLC 47
See also DLB 123

Barreto, Afonso Henrique de Lima
See Lima Barreto, Afonso Henrique de

Barrett, (Roger) Syd 1946- . . . . CLC 35
See also Pink Floyd

Barrett, William (Christopher)
1913-1992 . . . . CLC 27
See also CA 13-16R; 139; CANR 11

Barrie, J(ames) M(atthew)
1860-1937 . . . . TCLC 2
See also CA 104; 136; CDBLB 1890-1914;
CLR 16; DLB 10, 141; MAICYA;
YABC 1

Barrington, Michael
See Moorcock, Michael (John)

Barrol, Grady
See Bograd, Larry

Barry, Mike
See Malzberg, Barry N(athaniel)

Barry, Philip 1896-1949 . . . . TCLC 11
See also CA 109; DLB 7

Bart, Andre Schwarz
See Schwarz-Bart, Andre

Barth, John (Simmons)
1930- . . . . . . CLC 1, 2, 3, 5, 7, 9, 10, 14,
27, 51; SSC 10
See also AITN 1, 2; CA 1-4R; CABS 1;
CANR 5, 23; DLB 2; MTCW

Barthelme, Donald
1931-1989 . . . . . . CLC 1, 2, 3, 5, 6, 8, 13,
23, 46, 59; SSC 2
See also CA 21-24R; 129; CANR 20;
DLB 2; DLBY 80, 89; MTCW; SATA 7,
62

Barthelme, Frederick 1943- . . . . CLC 36
See also CA 114; 122; DLBY 85

Barthes, Roland (Gerard)
1915-1980 . . . . CLC 24, 83
See also CA 130; 97-100; MTCW

Barzun, Jacques (Martin) 1907- . . . . CLC 51
See also CA 61-64; CANR 22

Bashevis, Isaac
See Singer, Isaac Bashevis

Bashkirtseff, Marie 1859-1884 . . . NCLC 27

Basho
See Matsuo Basho

Bass, Kingsley B., Jr.
See Bullins, Ed

Bass, Rick 1958- . . . . CLC 79
See also CA 126

Bassani, Giorgio 1916- . . . . CLC 9
See also CA 65-68; CANR 33; DLB 128;
MTCW

Bastos, Augusto (Antonio) Roa
See Roa Bastos, Augusto (Antonio)

Bataille, Georges 1897-1962 . . . . CLC 29
See also CA 101; 89-92

Bates, H(erbert) E(rnest)
1905-1974 . . . . CLC 46; SSC 10
See also CA 93-96; 45-48; CANR 34;
MTCW

Bauchart
See Camus, Albert

Baudelaire, Charles
1821-1867 . . . . . NCLC 6, 29; DA; PC 1;
WLC

Baudrillard, Jean 1929- . . . . CLC 60

Baum, L(yman) Frank 1856-1919 . . . TCLC 7
See also CA 108; 133; CLR 15; DLB 22;
JRDA; MAICYA; MTCW; SATA 18

Baum, Louis F.
See Baum, L(yman) Frank

Baumbach, Jonathan 1933- . . . . . . CLC 6, 23
See also CA 13-16R; CAAS 5; CANR 12;
DLBY 80; MTCW

Bausch, Richard (Carl) 1945- . . . . . . CLC 51
See also CA 101; CAAS 14; CANR 43;
DLB 130

Baxter, Charles 1947- . . . . CLC 45, 78
See also CA 57-60; CANR 40; DLB 130

Baxter, George Owen
See Faust, Frederick (Schiller)

Baxter, James K(eir) 1926-1972 . . . . CLC 14
See also CA 77-80

Baxter, John
See Hunt, E(verette) Howard, Jr.

Bayer, Sylvia
See Glassco, John

Beagle, Peter S(oyer) 1939- . . . . CLC 7
See also CA 9-12R; CANR 4; DLBY 80;
SATA 60

Bean, Normal
See Burroughs, Edgar Rice

Beard, Charles A(ustin)
1874-1948 . . . . TCLC 15
See also CA 115; DLB 17; SATA 18

Beardsley, Aubrey 1872-1898 . . . . . NCLC 6

Beattie, Ann
1947- . . . . CLC 8, 13, 18, 40, 63; SSC 11
See also BEST 90:2; CA 81-84; DLBY 82;
MTCW

Beattie, James 1735-1803 . . . . NCLC 25
See also DLB 109

Beauchamp, Kathleen Mansfield 1888-1923
See Mansfield, Katherine
See also CA 104; 134; DA

Beaumarchais, Pierre-Augustin Caron de
1732-1799 . . . . DC 4

**Beauvoir, Simone (Lucie Ernestine Marie
Bertrand) de**
1908-1986 . . . . CLC 1, 2, 4, 8, 14, 31, 44,
50, 71; DA; WLC
See also CA 9-12R; 118; CANR 28;
DLB 72; DLBY 86; MTCW

Becker, Jurek 1937- . . . . CLC 7, 19
See also CA 85-88; DLB 75

Becker, Walter 1950- . . . . CLC 26

Beckett, Samuel (Barclay)
1906-1989 . . . . . . CLC 1, 2, 3, 4, 6, 9, 10,
11, 14, 18, 29, 57, 59, 83; DA; SSC 16;
WLC
See also CA 5-8R; 130; CANR 33;
CDBLB 1945-1960; DLB 13, 15;
DLBY 90; MTCW

Beckford, William 1760-1844 . . . . NCLC 16
See also DLB 39

Beckman, Gunnel 1910- . . . . CLC 26
See also CA 33-36R; CANR 15; CLR 25;
MAICYA; SAAS 9; SATA 6

Becque, Henri 1837-1899 . . . . NCLC 3

Beddoes, Thomas Lovell
1803-1849 . . . . NCLC 3
See also DLB 96

Bedford, Donald F.
See Fearing, Kenneth (Flexner)

Beecher, Catharine Esther
1800-1878 . . . . NCLC 30
See also DLB 1

Beecher, John 1904-1980 . . . . CLC 6
See also AITN 1; CA 5-8R; 105; CANR 8

Beer, Johann 1655-1700 . . . . LC 5

Beer, Patricia 1924- . . . . CLC 58
See also CA 61-64; CANR 13; DLB 40

Beerbohm, Henry Maximilian
1872-1956 . . . . TCLC 1, 24
See also CA 104; DLB 34, 100

Begiebing, Robert J(ohn) 1946- . . . . . CLC 70
See also CA 122; CANR 40

Behan, Brendan
1923-1964 . . . . CLC 1, 8, 11, 15, 79
See also CA 73-76; CANR 33;
CDBLB 1945-1960; DLB 13; MTCW

Behn, Aphra
1640(?)-1689 . . . . LC 1; DA; DC 4; WLC
See also DLB 39, 80, 131

Boell, Heinrich (Theodor) 1917-1985
See Boll, Heinrich (Theodor)
See also CA 21-24R; 116; CANR 24; DA;
DLB 69; DLBY 85; MTCW

Boerne, Alfred
See Doeblin, Alfred

Bogan, Louise 1897-1970..... **CLC 4, 39, 46**
See also CA 73-76; 25-28R; CANR 33;
DLB 45; MTCW

Bogarde, Dirk .... **CLC 19**
See also Van Den Bogarde, Derek Jules
Gaspard Ulric Niven
See also DLB 14

Bogosian, Eric 1953- .... **CLC 45**
See also CA 138

Bograd, Larry 1953-............. **CLC 35**
See also CA 93-96; SATA 33

Boiardo, Matteo Maria 1441-1494 .... **LC 6**

Boileau-Despreaux, Nicolas
1636-1711 .... **LC 3**

Boland, Eavan (Aisling) 1944-... **CLC 40, 67**
See also CA 143; DLB 40

Boll, Heinrich (Theodor)
1917-1985 .... **CLC 2, 3, 6, 9, 11, 15, 27,
39, 72; WLC**
See also Boell, Heinrich (Theodor)
See also DLB 69; DLBY 85

Bolt, Lee
See Faust, Frederick (Schiller)

Bolt, Robert (Oxton) 1924-........ **CLC 14**
See also CA 17-20R; CANR 35; DLB 13;
MTCW

Bombet, Louis-Alexandre-Cesar
See Stendhal

Bomkauf
See Kaufman, Bob (Garnell)

Bonaventura.................... **NCLC 35**
See also DLB 90

Bond, Edward 1934-....... **CLC 4, 6, 13, 23**
See also CA 25-28R; CANR 38; DLB 13;
MTCW

Bonham, Frank 1914-1989........ **CLC 12**
See also AAYA 1; CA 9-12R; CANR 4, 36;
JRDA; MAICYA; SAAS 3; SATA 1, 49,
62

Bonnefoy, Yves 1923-........ **CLC 9, 15, 58**
See also CA 85-88; CANR 33; MTCW

Bontemps, Arna(ud Wendell)
1902-1973 .... **CLC 1, 18; BLC**
See also BW 1; CA 1-4R; 41-44R; CANR 4,
35; CLR 6; DLB 48, 51; JRDA;
MAICYA; MTCW; SATA 2, 24, 44

Booth, Martin 1944-............. **CLC 13**
See also CA 93-96; CAAS 2

Booth, Philip 1925-............. **CLC 23**
See also CA 5-8R; CANR 5; DLBY 82

Booth, Wayne C(layson) 1921- ..... **CLC 24**
See also CA 1-4R; CAAS 5; CANR 3, 43;
DLB 67

Borchert, Wolfgang 1921-1947 ..... **TCLC 5**
See also CA 104; DLB 69, 124

Borel, Petrus 1809-1859........ **NCLC 41**

Borges, Jorge Luis
1899-1986 ... **CLC 1, 2, 3, 4, 6, 8, 9, 10,
13, 19, 44, 48, 83; DA; HLC; SSC 4;
WLC**
See also CA 21-24R; CANR 19, 33;
DLB 113; DLBY 86; HW; MTCW

Borowski, Tadeusz 1922-1951...... **TCLC 9**
See also CA 106

Borrow, George (Henry)
1803-1881 .... **NCLC 9**
See also DLB 21, 55

Bosman, Herman Charles
1905-1951 .... **TCLC 49**

Bosschere, Jean de 1878(?)-1953... **TCLC 19**
See also CA 115

Boswell, James
1740-1795 .... **LC 4; DA; WLC**
See also CDBLB 1660-1789; DLB 104, 142

Bottoms, David 1949-............ **CLC 53**
See also CA 105; CANR 22; DLB 120;
DLBY 83

Boucicault, Dion 1820-1890...... **NCLC 41**

Boucolon, Maryse 1937-
See Conde, Maryse
See also CA 110; CANR 30

Bourget, Paul (Charles Joseph)
1852-1935 .... **TCLC 12**
See also CA 107; DLB 123

Bourjaily, Vance (Nye) 1922- .... **CLC 8, 62**
See also CA 1-4R; CAAS 1; CANR 2;
DLB 2, 143

Bourne, Randolph S(illiman)
1886-1918 .... **TCLC 16**
See also CA 117; DLB 63

Bova, Ben(jamin William) 1932-.... **CLC 45**
See also CA 5-8R; CAAS 18; CANR 11;
CLR 3; DLBY 81; MAICYA; MTCW;
SATA 6, 68

Bowen, Elizabeth (Dorothea Cole)
1899-1973 ...... **CLC 1, 3, 6, 11, 15, 22;
SSC 3**
See also CA 17-18; 41-44R; CANR 35;
CAP 2; CDBLB 1945-1960; DLB 15;
MTCW

Bowering, George 1935-........ **CLC 15, 47**
See also CA 21-24R; CAAS 16; CANR 10;
DLB 53

Bowering, Marilyn R(uthe) 1949-... **CLC 32**
See also CA 101

Bowers, Edgar 1924- .... **CLC 9**
See also CA 5-8R; CANR 24; DLB 5

Bowie, David .... **CLC 17**
See also Jones, David Robert

Bowles, Jane (Sydney)
1917-1973 .... **CLC 3, 68**
See also CA 19-20; 41-44R; CAP 2

Bowles, Paul (Frederick)
1910- .... **CLC 1, 2, 19, 53; SSC 3**
See also CA 1-4R; CAAS 1; CANR 1, 19;
DLB 5, 6; MTCW

Box, Edgar
See Vidal, Gore

Boyd, Nancy
See Millay, Edna St. Vincent

Boyd, William 1952-........ **CLC 28, 53, 70**
See also CA 114; 120

Boyle, Kay
1902-1992 ..... **CLC 1, 5, 19, 58; SSC 5**
See also CA 13-16R; 140; CAAS 1;
CANR 29; DLB 4, 9, 48, 86; DLBY 93;
MTCW

Boyle, Mark
See Kienzle, William X(avier)

Boyle, Patrick 1905-1982......... **CLC 19**
See also CA 127

Boyle, T. C.
See Boyle, T(homas) Coraghessan

Boyle, T(homas) Coraghessan
1948- .... **CLC 36, 55; SSC 16**
See also BEST 90:4; CA 120; CANR 44;
DLBY 86

Boz
See Dickens, Charles (John Huffam)

Brackenridge, Hugh Henry
1748-1816 .... **NCLC 7**
See also DLB 11, 37

Bradbury, Edward P.
See Moorcock, Michael (John)

Bradbury, Malcolm (Stanley)
1932- .... **CLC 32, 61**
See also CA 1-4R; CANR 1, 33; DLB 14;
MTCW

Bradbury, Ray (Douglas)
1920- ... **CLC 1, 3, 10, 15, 42; DA; WLC**
See also AITN 1, 2; CA 1-4R; CANR 2, 30;
CDALB 1968-1988; DLB 2, 8; MTCW;
SATA 11, 64

Bradford, Gamaliel 1863-1932..... **TCLC 36**
See also DLB 17

Bradley, David (Henry, Jr.)
1950- .... **CLC 23; BLC**
See also BW 1; CA 104; CANR 26; DLB 33

Bradley, John Ed(mund, Jr.)
1958- .... **CLC 55**
See also CA 139

Bradley, Marion Zimmer 1930-..... **CLC 30**
See also AAYA 9; CA 57-60; CAAS 10;
CANR 7, 31; DLB 8; MTCW

Bradstreet, Anne
1612(?)-1672 .... **LC 4; DA; PC 10**
See also CDALB 1640-1865; DLB 24

Bragg, Melvyn 1939-............. **CLC 10**
See also BEST 89:3; CA 57-60; CANR 10;
DLB 14

Braine, John (Gerard)
1922-1986 .... **CLC 1, 3, 41**
See also CA 1-4R; 120; CANR 1, 33;
CDBLB 1945-1960; DLB 15; DLBY 86;
MTCW

Brammer, William 1930(?)-1978 .... **CLC 31**
See also CA 77-80

Brancati, Vitaliano 1907-1954..... **TCLC 12**
See also CA 109

Brancato, Robin F(idler) 1936-..... **CLC 35**
See also AAYA 9; CA 69-72; CANR 11,
45; CLR 32; JRDA; SAAS 9; SATA 23

Brand, Max
See Faust, Frederick (Schiller)

Brand, Millen 1906-1980 . . . . **CLC 7**
See also CA 21-24R; 97-100

Branden, Barbara . . . . **CLC 44**

Brandes, Georg (Morris Cohen)
1842-1927 . . . . **TCLC 10**
See also CA 105

Brandys, Kazimierz 1916- . . . . **CLC 62**

Branley, Franklyn M(ansfield)
1915- . . . . **CLC 21**
See also CA 33-36R; CANR 14, 39;
CLR 13; MAICYA; SAAS 16; SATA 4,
68

Brathwaite, Edward (Kamau)
1930- . . . . **CLC 11**
See also BW 2; CA 25-28R; CANR 11, 26;
DLB 125

Brautigan, Richard (Gary)
1935-1984 . . . . **CLC 1, 3, 5, 9, 12, 34, 42**
See also CA 53-56; 113; CANR 34; DLB 2,
5; DLBY 80, 84; MTCW; SATA 56

Braverman, Kate 1950- . . . . **CLC 67**
See also CA 89-92

Brecht, Bertolt
1898-1956 . . . . . . **TCLC 1, 6, 13, 35; DA;
DC 3; WLC**
See also CA 104; 133; DLB 56, 124; MTCW

Brecht, Eugen Berthold Friedrich
See Brecht, Bertolt

Bremer, Fredrika 1801-1865 . . . . . **NCLC 11**

Brennan, Christopher John
1870-1932 . . . . **TCLC 17**
See also CA 117

Brennan, Maeve 1917- . . . . **CLC 5**
See also CA 81-84

Brentano, Clemens (Maria)
1778-1842 . . . . **NCLC 1**

Brent of Bin Bin
See Franklin, (Stella Maraia Sarah) Miles

Brenton, Howard 1942- . . . . **CLC 31**
See also CA 69-72; CANR 33; DLB 13;
MTCW

Breslin, James 1930-
See Breslin, Jimmy
See also CA 73-76; CANR 31; MTCW

Breslin, Jimmy . . . . **CLC 4, 43**
See also Breslin, James
See also AITN 1

Bresson, Robert 1907- . . . . **CLC 16**
See also CA 110

Breton, Andre 1896-1966 . . . **CLC 2, 9, 15, 54**
See also CA 19-20; 25-28R; CANR 40;
CAP 2; DLB 65; MTCW

Breytenbach, Breyten 1939(?)- . . **CLC 23, 37**
See also CA 113; 129

Bridgers, Sue Ellen 1942- . . . . **CLC 26**
See also AAYA 8; CA 65-68; CANR 11,
36; CLR 18; DLB 52; JRDA; MAICYA;
SAAS 1; SATA 22

Bridges, Robert (Seymour)
1844-1930 . . . . **TCLC 1**
See also CA 104; CDBLB 1890-1914;
DLB 19, 98

Bridie, James . . . . **TCLC 3**
See also Mavor, Osborne Henry
See also DLB 10

Brin, David 1950- . . . . **CLC 34**
See also CA 102; CANR 24; SATA 65

Brink, Andre (Philippus)
1935- . . . . **CLC 18, 36**
See also CA 104; CANR 39; MTCW

Brinsmead, H(esba) F(ay) 1922- . . . . **CLC 21**
See also CA 21-24R; CANR 10; MAICYA;
SAAS 5; SATA 18, 78

Brittain, Vera (Mary)
1893(?)-1970 . . . . **CLC 23**
See also CA 13-16; 25-28R; CAP 1; MTCW

Broch, Hermann 1886-1951 . . . . . . **TCLC 20**
See also CA 117; DLB 85, 124

Brock, Rose
See Hansen, Joseph

Brodkey, Harold 1930- . . . . **CLC 56**
See also CA 111; DLB 130

Brodsky, Iosif Alexandrovich 1940-
See Brodsky, Joseph
See also AITN 1; CA 41-44R; CANR 37;
MTCW

Brodsky, Joseph . . **CLC 4, 6, 13, 36, 50; PC 9**
See also Brodsky, Iosif Alexandrovich

Brodsky, Michael Mark 1948- . . . . . **CLC 19**
See also CA 102; CANR 18, 41

Bromell, Henry 1947- . . . . **CLC 5**
See also CA 53-56; CANR 9

Bromfield, Louis (Brucker)
1896-1956 . . . . **TCLC 11**
See also CA 107; DLB 4, 9, 86

Broner, E(sther) M(asserman)
1930- . . . . **CLC 19**
See also CA 17-20R; CANR 8, 25; DLB 28

Bronk, William 1918- . . . . **CLC 10**
See also CA 89-92; CANR 23

Bronstein, Lev Davidovich
See Trotsky, Leon

Bronte, Anne 1820-1849 . . . . **NCLC 4**
See also DLB 21

Bronte, Charlotte
1816-1855 . . . **NCLC 3, 8, 33; DA; WLC**
See also CDBLB 1832-1890; DLB 21

Bronte, (Jane) Emily
1818-1848 . . . . **NCLC 16, 35; DA; PC 8;
WLC**
See also CDBLB 1832-1890; DLB 21, 32

Brooke, Frances 1724-1789 . . . . **LC 6**
See also DLB 39, 99

Brooke, Henry 1703(?)-1783 . . . . **LC 1**
See also DLB 39

Brooke, Rupert (Chawner)
1887-1915 . . . . . . **TCLC 2, 7; DA; WLC**
See also CA 104; 132; CDBLB 1914-1945;
DLB 19; MTCW

Brooke-Haven, P.
See Wodehouse, P(elham) G(renville)

Brooke-Rose, Christine 1926- . . . . . . **CLC 40**
See also CA 13-16R; DLB 14

Brookner, Anita 1928- . . . . . . **CLC 32, 34, 51**
See also CA 114; 120; CANR 37; DLBY 87;
MTCW

Brooks, Cleanth 1906- . . . . **CLC 24**
See also CA 17-20R; CANR 33, 35;
DLB 63; MTCW

Brooks, George
See Baum, L(yman) Frank

Brooks, Gwendolyn
1917- . . . . . . **CLC 1, 2, 4, 5, 15, 49; BLC;
DA; PC 7; WLC**
See also AITN 1; BW 2; CA 1-4R;
CANR 1, 27; CDALB 1941-1968;
CLR 27; DLB 5, 76; MTCW; SATA 6

Brooks, Mel . . . . **CLC 12**
See also Kaminsky, Melvin
See also DLB 26

Brooks, Peter 1938- . . . . **CLC 34**
See also CA 45-48; CANR 1

Brooks, Van Wyck 1886-1963 . . . . . . **CLC 29**
See also CA 1-4R; CANR 6; DLB 45, 63,
103

Brophy, Brigid (Antonia)
1929- . . . . **CLC 6, 11, 29**
See also CA 5-8R; CAAS 4; CANR 25;
DLB 14; MTCW

Brosman, Catharine Savage 1934- . . . . **CLC 9**
See also CA 61-64; CANR 21

Brother Antoninus
See Everson, William (Oliver)

Broughton, T(homas) Alan 1936- . . . **CLC 19**
See also CA 45-48; CANR 2, 23

Broumas, Olga 1949- . . . . **CLC 10, 73**
See also CA 85-88; CANR 20

Brown, Charles Brockden
1771-1810 . . . . **NCLC 22**
See also CDALB 1640-1865; DLB 37, 59,
73

Brown, Christy 1932-1981 . . . . **CLC 63**
See also CA 105; 104; DLB 14

Brown, Claude 1937- . . . . **CLC 30; BLC**
See also AAYA 7; BW 1; CA 73-76

Brown, Dee (Alexander) 1908- . . **CLC 18, 47**
See also CA 13-16R; CAAS 6; CANR 11,
45; DLBY 80; MTCW; SATA 5

Brown, George
See Wertmueller, Lina

Brown, George Douglas
1869-1902 . . . . **TCLC 28**

Brown, George Mackay 1921- . . . . **CLC 5, 48**
See also CA 21-24R; CAAS 6; CANR 12,
37; DLB 14, 27, 139; MTCW; SATA 35

Brown, (William) Larry 1951- . . . . . **CLC 73**
See also CA 130; 134

Brown, Moses
See Barrett, William (Christopher)

Brown, Rita Mae 1944- . . . . . **CLC 18, 43, 79**
See also CA 45-48; CANR 2, 11, 35;
MTCW

Brown, Roderick (Langmere) Haig-
See Haig-Brown, Roderick (Langmere)

Brown, Rosellen 1939- . . . . **CLC 32**
See also CA 77-80; CAAS 10; CANR 14, 44

Brown, Sterling Allen
1901-1989 . . . . **CLC 1, 23, 59; BLC**
See also BW 1; CA 85-88; 127; CANR 26;
DLB 48, 51, 63; MTCW

Brown, Will
See Ainsworth, William Harrison

Brown, William Wells
1813-1884 . . . . **NCLC 2; BLC; DC 1**
See also DLB 3, 50

Browne, (Clyde) Jackson 1948(?)-. . . **CLC 21**
See also CA 120

Browning, Elizabeth Barrett
1806-1861 . . . . . **NCLC 1, 16; DA; PC 6; WLC**
See also CDBLB 1832-1890; DLB 32

Browning, Robert
1812-1889 . . . . **NCLC 19; DA; PC 2**
See also CDBLB 1832-1890; DLB 32;
YABC 1

Browning, Tod 1882-1962 . . . . **CLC 16**
See also CA 141; 117

Bruccoli, Matthew J(oseph) 1931- . . **CLC 34**
See also CA 9-12R; CANR 7; DLB 103

Bruce, Lenny . . . . **CLC 21**
See also Schneider, Leonard Alfred

Bruin, John
See Brutus, Dennis

Brulard, Henri
See Stendhal

Brulls, Christian
See Simenon, Georges (Jacques Christian)

Brunner, John (Kilian Houston)
1934- . . . . **CLC 8, 10**
See also CA 1-4R; CAAS 8; CANR 2, 37;
MTCW

Brutus, Dennis 1924- . . . . **CLC 43; BLC**
See also BW 2; CA 49-52; CAAS 14;
CANR 2, 27, 42; DLB 117

Bryan, C(ourtlandt) D(ixon) B(arnes)
1936- . . . . **CLC 29**
See also CA 73-76; CANR 13

Bryan, Michael
See Moore, Brian

Bryant, William Cullen
1794-1878 . . . . **NCLC 6, 46; DA**
See also CDALB 1640-1865; DLB 3, 43, 59

Bryusov, Valery Yakovlevich
1873-1924 . . . . **TCLC 10**
See also CA 107

Buchan, John 1875-1940 . . . . **TCLC 41**
See also CA 108; DLB 34, 70; YABC 2

Buchanan, George 1506-1582 . . . . **LC 4**

Buchheim, Lothar-Guenther 1918- . . . **CLC 6**
See also CA 85-88

Buchner, (Karl) Georg
1813-1837 . . . . **NCLC 26**

Buchwald, Art(hur) 1925-. . . . . **CLC 33**
See also AITN 1; CA 5-8R; CANR 21;
MTCW; SATA 10

Buck, Pearl S(ydenstricker)
1892-1973 . . . . **CLC 7, 11, 18; DA**
See also AITN 1; CA 1-4R; 41-44R;
CANR 1, 34; DLB 9, 102; MTCW;
SATA 1, 25

Buckler, Ernest 1908-1984. . . . . **CLC 13**
See also CA 11-12; 114; CAP 1; DLB 68;
SATA 47

Buckley, Vincent (Thomas)
1925-1988 . . . . **CLC 57**
See also CA 101

Buckley, William F(rank), Jr.
1925- . . . . **CLC 7, 18, 37**
See also AITN 1; CA 1-4R; CANR 1, 24;
DLB 137; DLBY 80; MTCW

Buechner, (Carl) Frederick
1926- . . . . **CLC 2, 4, 6, 9**
See also CA 13-16R; CANR 11, 39;
DLBY 80; MTCW

Buell, John (Edward) 1927-. . . . . **CLC 10**
See also CA 1-4R; DLB 53

Buero Vallejo, Antonio 1916- . . **CLC 15, 46**
See also CA 106; CANR 24; HW; MTCW

Bufalino, Gesualdo 1920(?)-. . . . . . . **CLC 74**

Bugayev, Boris Nikolayevich 1880-1934
See Bely, Andrey
See also CA 104

Bukowski, Charles
1920-1994 . . . . **CLC 2, 5, 9, 41, 82**
See also CA 17-20R; 144; CANR 40;
DLB 5, 130; MTCW

Bulgakov, Mikhail (Afanas'evich)
1891-1940 . . . . **TCLC 2, 16**
See also CA 105

Bulgya, Alexander Alexandrovich
1901-1956 . . . . **TCLC 53**
See also Fadeyev, Alexander
See also CA 117

Bullins, Ed 1935- . . . . **CLC 1, 5, 7; BLC**
See also BW 2; CA 49-52; CAAS 16;
CANR 24; DLB 7, 38; MTCW

Bulwer-Lytton, Edward (George Earle Lytton)
1803-1873 . . . . **NCLC 1, 45**
See also DLB 21

Bunin, Ivan Alexeyevich
1870-1953 . . . . **TCLC 6; SSC 5**
See also CA 104

Bunting, Basil 1900-1985. . . . **CLC 10, 39, 47**
See also CA 53-56; 115; CANR 7; DLB 20

Bunuel, Luis 1900-1983 . . **CLC 16, 80; HLC**
See also CA 101; 110; CANR 32; HW

Bunyan, John 1628-1688 . . **LC 4; DA; WLC**
See also CDBLB 1660-1789; DLB 39

Burford, Eleanor
See Hibbert, Eleanor Alice Burford

Burgess, Anthony
. **CLC 1, 2, 4, 5, 8, 10, 13, 15, 22, 40, 62, 81**
See also Wilson, John (Anthony) Burgess
See also AITN 1; CDBLB 1960 to Present;
DLB 14

Burke, Edmund
1729(?)-1797 . . . . **LC 7; DA; WLC**
See also DLB 104

Burke, Kenneth (Duva)
1897-1993 . . . . **CLC 2, 24**
See also CA 5-8R; 143; CANR 39; DLB 45,
63; MTCW

Burke, Leda
See Garnett, David

Burke, Ralph
See Silverberg, Robert

Burney, Fanny 1752-1840 . . . . **NCLC 12**
See also DLB 39

Burns, Robert
1759-1796 . . . . . . **LC 3; DA; PC 6; WLC**
See also CDBLB 1789-1832; DLB 109

Burns, Tex
See L'Amour, Louis (Dearborn)

Burnshaw, Stanley 1906-. . . . . **CLC 3, 13, 44**
See also CA 9-12R; DLB 48

Burr, Anne 1937-. . . . . **CLC 6**
See also CA 25-28R

Burroughs, Edgar Rice
1875-1950 . . . . **TCLC 2, 32**
See also AAYA 11; CA 104; 132; DLB 8;
MTCW; SATA 41

Burroughs, William S(eward)
1914- . . . . **CLC 1, 2, 5, 15, 22, 42, 75; DA; WLC**
See also AITN 2; CA 9-12R; CANR 20;
DLB 2, 8, 16; DLBY 81; MTCW

Burton, Richard F. 1821-1890. . . . **NCLC 42**
See also DLB 55

Busch, Frederick 1941- . . . **CLC 7, 10, 18, 47**
See also CA 33-36R; CAAS 1; CANR 45;
DLB 6

Bush, Ronald 1946- . . . . **CLC 34**
See also CA 136

Bustos, F(rancisco)
See Borges, Jorge Luis

Bustos Domecq, H(onorio)
See Bioy Casares, Adolfo; Borges, Jorge
Luis

Butler, Octavia E(stelle) 1947- . . . . . **CLC 38**
See also BW 2; CA 73-76; CANR 12, 24,
38; DLB 33; MTCW

Butler, Robert Olen (Jr.) 1945-. . . . . **CLC 81**
See also CA 112

Butler, Samuel 1612-1680 . . . . **LC 16**
See also DLB 101, 126

Butler, Samuel
1835-1902 . . . . . . **TCLC 1, 33; DA; WLC**
See also CA 104; CDBLB 1890-1914;
DLB 18, 57

Butler, Walter C.
See Faust, Frederick (Schiller)

Butor, Michel (Marie Francois)
1926- . . . . **CLC 1, 3, 8, 11, 15**
See also CA 9-12R; CANR 33; DLB 83;
MTCW

Buzo, Alexander (John) 1944-. . . . . . **CLC 61**
See also CA 97-100; CANR 17, 39

Buzzati, Dino 1906-1972 . . . . **CLC 36**
See also CA 33-36R

Byars, Betsy (Cromer) 1928-. . . . . . . **CLC 35**
See also CA 33-36R; CANR 18, 36; CLR 1,
16; DLB 52; JRDA; MAICYA; MTCW;
SAAS 1; SATA 4, 46

Byatt, A(ntonia) S(usan Drabble)
1936- . . . . **CLC 19, 65**
See also CA 13-16R; CANR 13, 33;
DLB 14; MTCW

Byrne, David 1952-. . . . . **CLC 26**
See also CA 127

Byrne, John Keyes 1926-. . . . . **CLC 19**
See also Leonard, Hugh
See also CA 102

Chaucer, Daniel
See Ford, Ford Madox

Chaucer, Geoffrey
1340(?)-1400 . . . . **LC 17; DA**
See also CDBLB Before 1660

Chaviaras, Strates 1935-
See Haviaras, Stratis
See also CA 105

Chayefsky, Paddy . . . . **CLC 23**
See also Chayefsky, Sidney
See also DLB 7, 44; DLBY 81

Chayefsky, Sidney 1923-1981
See Chayefsky, Paddy
See also CA 9-12R; 104; CANR 18

Chedid, Andree 1920- . . . . **CLC 47**

Cheever, John
1912-1982 . . . . . . **CLC 3, 7, 8, 11, 15, 25,**
64; DA; SSC 1; WLC
See also CA 5-8R; 106; CABS 1; CANR 5,
27; CDALB 1941-1968; DLB 2, 102;
DLBY 80, 82; MTCW

Cheever, Susan 1943- . . . . **CLC 18, 48**
See also CA 103; CANR 27; DLBY 82

Chekhonte, Antosha
See Chekhov, Anton (Pavlovich)

Chekhov, Anton (Pavlovich)
1860-1904 . . . . . **TCLC 3, 10, 31, 55; DA;**
SSC 2; WLC
See also CA 104; 124

Chernyshevsky, Nikolay Gavrilovich
1828-1889 . . . . **NCLC 1**

Cherry, Carolyn Janice 1942-
See Cherryh, C. J.
See also CA 65-68; CANR 10

Cherryh, C. J. . . . . **CLC 35**
See also Cherry, Carolyn Janice
See also DLBY 80

Chesnutt, Charles W(addell)
1858-1932 . . . . **TCLC 5, 39; BLC; SSC 7**
See also BW 1; CA 106; 125; DLB 12, 50,
78; MTCW

Chester, Alfred 1929(?)-1971 . . . . **CLC 49**
See also CA 33-36R; DLB 130

Chesterton, G(ilbert) K(eith)
1874-1936 . . . . **TCLC 1, 6; SSC 1**
See also CA 104; 132; CDBLB 1914-1945;
DLB 10, 19, 34, 70, 98; MTCW;
SATA 27

Chiang Pin-chin 1904-1986
See Ding Ling
See also CA 118

Ch'ien Chung-shu 1910- . . . . **CLC 22**
See also CA 130; MTCW

Child, L. Maria
See Child, Lydia Maria

Child, Lydia Maria 1802-1880 . . . . **NCLC 6**
See also DLB 1, 74; SATA 67

Child, Mrs.
See Child, Lydia Maria

Child, Philip 1898-1978 . . . . **CLC 19, 68**
See also CA 13-14; CAP 1; SATA 47

Childress, Alice
1920- . . . . **CLC 12, 15; BLC; DC 4**
See also AAYA 8; BW 2; CA 45-48;
CANR 3, 27; CLR 14; DLB 7, 38; JRDA;
MAICYA; MTCW; SATA 7, 48

Chislett, (Margaret) Anne 1943- . . . . **CLC 34**

Chitty, Thomas Willes 1926- . . . . **CLC 11**
See also Hinde, Thomas
See also CA 5-8R

Chomette, Rene Lucien 1898-1981 . . **CLC 20**
See also Clair, Rene
See also CA 103

Chopin, Kate . . . . . . **TCLC 5, 14; DA; SSC 8**
See also Chopin, Katherine
See also CDALB 1865-1917; DLB 12, 78

Chopin, Katherine 1851-1904
See Chopin, Kate
See also CA 104; 122

Chretien de Troyes
c. 12th cent. - . . . . **CMLC 10**

Christie
See Ichikawa, Kon

Christie, Agatha (Mary Clarissa)
1890-1976 . . . . . . **CLC 1, 6, 8, 12, 39, 48**
See also AAYA 9; AITN 1, 2; CA 17-20R;
61-64; CANR 10, 37; CDBLB 1914-1945;
DLB 13, 77; MTCW; SATA 36

Christie, (Ann) Philippa
See Pearce, Philippa
See also CA 5-8R; CANR 4

Christine de Pizan 1365(?)-1431(?) . . . . **LC 9**

Chubb, Elmer
See Masters, Edgar Lee

Chulkov, Mikhail Dmitrievich
1743-1792 . . . . **LC 2**

Churchill, Caryl 1938- . . . . **CLC 31, 55**
See also CA 102; CANR 22; DLB 13;
MTCW

Churchill, Charles 1731-1764 . . . . **LC 3**
See also DLB 109

Chute, Carolyn 1947- . . . . **CLC 39**
See also CA 123

Ciardi, John (Anthony)
1916-1986 . . . . **CLC 10, 40, 44**
See also CA 5-8R; 118; CAAS 2; CANR 5,
33; CLR 19; DLB 5; DLBY 86;
MAICYA; MTCW; SATA 1, 46, 65

Cicero, Marcus Tullius
106B.C.-43B.C. . . . . **CMLC 3**

Cimino, Michael 1943- . . . . **CLC 16**
See also CA 105

Cioran, E(mil) M. 1911- . . . . **CLC 64**
See also CA 25-28R

Cisneros, Sandra 1954- . . . . . **CLC 69; HLC**
See also AAYA 9; CA 131; DLB 122; HW

Clair, Rene . . . . **CLC 20**
See also Chomette, Rene Lucien

Clampitt, Amy 1920- . . . . **CLC 32**
See also CA 110; CANR 29; DLB 105

Clancy, Thomas L., Jr. 1947-
See Clancy, Tom
See also CA 125; 131; MTCW

Clancy, Tom . . . . **CLC 45**
See also Clancy, Thomas L., Jr.
See also AAYA 9; BEST 89:1, 90:1

Clare, John 1793-1864 . . . . **NCLC 9**
See also DLB 55, 96

Clarin
See Alas (y Urena), Leopoldo (Enrique
Garcia)

Clark, Al C.
See Goines, Donald

Clark, (Robert) Brian 1932- . . . . **CLC 29**
See also CA 41-44R

Clark, Curt
See Westlake, Donald E(dwin)

Clark, Eleanor 1913- . . . . **CLC 5, 19**
See also CA 9-12R; CANR 41; DLB 6

Clark, J. P.
See Clark, John Pepper
See also DLB 117

Clark, John Pepper 1935- . . . . **CLC 38; BLC**
See also Clark, J. P.
See also BW 1; CA 65-68; CANR 16

Clark, M. R.
See Clark, Mavis Thorpe

Clark, Mavis Thorpe 1909- . . . . **CLC 12**
See also CA 57-60; CANR 8, 37; CLR 30;
MAICYA; SAAS 5; SATA 8, 74

Clark, Walter Van Tilburg
1909-1971 . . . . **CLC 28**
See also CA 9-12R; 33-36R; DLB 9;
SATA 8

Clarke, Arthur C(harles)
1917- . . . . . . **CLC 1, 4, 13, 18, 35; SSC 3**
See also AAYA 4; CA 1-4R; CANR 2, 28;
JRDA; MAICYA; MTCW; SATA 13, 70

Clarke, Austin 1896-1974 . . . . **CLC 6, 9**
See also CA 29-32; 49-52; CAP 2; DLB 10,
20

Clarke, Austin C(hesterfield)
1934- . . . . **CLC 8, 53; BLC**
See also BW 1; CA 25-28R; CAAS 16;
CANR 14, 32; DLB 53, 125

Clarke, Gillian 1937- . . . . **CLC 61**
See also CA 106; DLB 40

Clarke, Marcus (Andrew Hislop)
1846-1881 . . . . **NCLC 19**

Clarke, Shirley 1925- . . . . **CLC 16**

Clash, The . . . . **CLC 30**
See also Headon, (Nicky) Topper; Jones,
Mick; Simonon, Paul; Strummer, Joe

Claudel, Paul (Louis Charles Marie)
1868-1955 . . . . **TCLC 2, 10**
See also CA 104

Clavell, James (duMaresq)
1925- . . . . **CLC 6, 25**
See also CA 25-28R; CANR 26; MTCW

Cleaver, (Leroy) Eldridge
1935- . . . . **CLC 30; BLC**
See also BW 1; CA 21-24R; CANR 16

Cleese, John (Marwood) 1939- . . . . . **CLC 21**
See also Monty Python
See also CA 112; 116; CANR 35; MTCW

Cleishbotham, Jebediah
See Scott, Walter

Day Lewis, C(ecil)
1904-1972 . . . . **CLC 1, 6, 10**
See also Blake, Nicholas
See also CA 13-16; 33-36R; CANR 34;
CAP 1; DLB 15, 20; MTCW

Dazai, Osamu . . . . **TCLC 11**
See also Tsushima, Shuji

de Andrade, Carlos Drummond
See Drummond de Andrade, Carlos

Deane, Norman
See Creasey, John

de Beauvoir, Simone (Lucie Ernestine Marie Bertrand)
See Beauvoir, Simone (Lucie Ernestine
Marie Bertrand) de

de Brissac, Malcolm
See Dickinson, Peter (Malcolm)

de Chardin, Pierre Teilhard
See Teilhard de Chardin, (Marie Joseph)
Pierre

Dee, John 1527-1608 . . . . **LC 20**

Deer, Sandra 1940- . . . . **CLC 45**

De Ferrari, Gabriella . . . . **CLC 65**

Defoe, Daniel
1660(?)-1731 . . . . **LC 1; DA; WLC**
See also CDBLB 1660-1789; DLB 39, 95,
101; JRDA; MAICYA; SATA 22

de Gourmont, Remy
See Gourmont, Remy de

de Hartog, Jan 1914- . . . . **CLC 19**
See also CA 1-4R; CANR 1

de Hostos, E. M.
See Hostos (y Bonilla), Eugenio Maria de

de Hostos, Eugenio M.
See Hostos (y Bonilla), Eugenio Maria de

Deighton, Len . . . . **CLC 4, 7, 22, 46**
See also Deighton, Leonard Cyril
See also AAYA 6; BEST 89:2;
CDBLB 1960 to Present; DLB 87

Deighton, Leonard Cyril 1929-
See Deighton, Len
See also CA 9-12R; CANR 19, 33; MTCW

Dekker, Thomas 1572(?)-1632 . . . . . . **LC 22**
See also CDBLB Before 1660; DLB 62

de la Mare, Walter (John)
1873-1956 . . **TCLC 4, 53; SSC 14; WLC**
See also CDBLB 1914-1945; CLR 23;
DLB 19; SATA 16

Delaney, Franey
See O'Hara, John (Henry)

Delaney, Shelagh 1939- . . . . **CLC 29**
See also CA 17-20R; CANR 30;
CDBLB 1960 to Present; DLB 13;
MTCW

Delany, Mary (Granville Pendarves)
1700-1788 . . . . **LC 12**

Delany, Samuel R(ay, Jr.)
1942- . . . . **CLC 8, 14, 38; BLC**
See also BW 2; CA 81-84; CANR 27, 43;
DLB 8, 33; MTCW

De La Ramee, (Marie) Louise 1839-1908
See Ouida
See also SATA 20

de la Roche, Mazo 1879-1961 . . . . . . **CLC 14**
See also CA 85-88; CANR 30; DLB 68;
SATA 64

Delbanco, Nicholas (Franklin)
1942- . . . . **CLC 6, 13**
See also CA 17-20R; CAAS 2; CANR 29;
DLB 6

del Castillo, Michel 1933- . . . . **CLC 38**
See also CA 109

Deledda, Grazia (Cosima)
1875(?)-1936 . . . . **TCLC 23**
See also CA 123

Delibes, Miguel . . . . **CLC 8, 18**
See also Delibes Setien, Miguel

Delibes Setien, Miguel 1920-
See Delibes, Miguel
See also CA 45-48; CANR 1, 32; HW;
MTCW

DeLillo, Don
1936- . . . . . **CLC 8, 10, 13, 27, 39, 54, 76**
See also BEST 89:1; CA 81-84; CANR 21;
DLB 6; MTCW

de Lisser, H. G.
See De Lisser, Herbert George
See also DLB 117

De Lisser, Herbert George
1878-1944 . . . . **TCLC 12**
See also de Lisser, H. G.
See also BW 2; CA 109

Deloria, Vine (Victor), Jr. 1933- . . . . **CLC 21**
See also CA 53-56; CANR 5, 20; MTCW;
SATA 21

Del Vecchio, John M(ichael)
1947- . . . . **CLC 29**
See also CA 110; DLBD 9

de Man, Paul (Adolph Michel)
1919-1983 . . . . **CLC 55**
See also CA 128; 111; DLB 67; MTCW

De Marinis, Rick 1934- . . . . **CLC 54**
See also CA 57-60; CANR 9, 25

Demby, William 1922- . . . . **CLC 53; BLC**
See also BW 1; CA 81-84; DLB 33

Demijohn, Thom
See Disch, Thomas M(ichael)

de Montherlant, Henry (Milon)
See Montherlant, Henry (Milon) de

Demosthenes 384B.C.-322B.C. . . . **CMLC 13**

de Natale, Francine
See Malzberg, Barry N(athaniel)

Denby, Edwin (Orr) 1903-1983 . . . . . **CLC 48**
See also CA 138; 110

Denis, Julio
See Cortazar, Julio

Denmark, Harrison
See Zelazny, Roger (Joseph)

Dennis, John 1658-1734 . . . . **LC 11**
See also DLB 101

Dennis, Nigel (Forbes) 1912-1989 . . . . **CLC 8**
See also CA 25-28R; 129; DLB 13, 15;
MTCW

De Palma, Brian (Russell) 1940- . . . . **CLC 20**
See also CA 109

De Quincey, Thomas 1785-1859 . . . **NCLC 4**
See also CDBLB 1789-1832; DLB 110; 144

Deren, Eleanora 1908(?)-1961
See Deren, Maya
See also CA 111

Deren, Maya . . . . **CLC 16**
See also Deren, Eleanora

Derleth, August (William)
1909-1971 . . . . **CLC 31**
See also CA 1-4R; 29-32R; CANR 4;
DLB 9; SATA 5

Der Nister . . . . **TCLC 56**

de Routisie, Albert
See Aragon, Louis

Derrida, Jacques 1930- . . . . **CLC 24**
See also CA 124; 127

Derry Down Derry
See Lear, Edward

Dersonnes, Jacques
See Simenon, Georges (Jacques Christian)

Desai, Anita 1937- . . . . **CLC 19, 37**
See also CA 81-84; CANR 33; MTCW;
SATA 63

de Saint-Luc, Jean
See Glassco, John

de Saint Roman, Arnaud
See Aragon, Louis

Descartes, Rene 1596-1650 . . . . **LC 20**

De Sica, Vittorio 1901(?)-1974 . . . . . **CLC 20**
See also CA 117

Desnos, Robert 1900-1945 . . . . **TCLC 22**
See also CA 121

Destouches, Louis-Ferdinand
1894-1961 . . . . **CLC 9, 15**
See also Celine, Louis-Ferdinand
See also CA 85-88; CANR 28; MTCW

Deutsch, Babette 1895-1982 . . . . **CLC 18**
See also CA 1-4R; 108; CANR 4; DLB 45;
SATA 1, 33

Devenant, William 1606-1649 . . . . **LC 13**

Devkota, Laxmiprasad
1909-1959 . . . . **TCLC 23**
See also CA 123

De Voto, Bernard (Augustine)
1897-1955 . . . . **TCLC 29**
See also CA 113; DLB 9

De Vries, Peter
1910-1993 . . . . **CLC 1, 2, 3, 7, 10, 28, 46**
See also CA 17-20R; 142; CANR 41;
DLB 6; DLBY 82; MTCW

Dexter, Martin
See Faust, Frederick (Schiller)

Dexter, Pete 1943- . . . . **CLC 34, 55**
See also BEST 89:2; CA 127; 131; MTCW

Diamano, Silmang
See Senghor, Leopold Sedar

Diamond, Neil 1941- . . . . **CLC 30**
See also CA 108

di Bassetto, Corno
See Shaw, George Bernard

Dick, Philip K(indred)
1928-1982 . . . . **CLC 10, 30, 72**
See also CA 49-52; 106; CANR 2, 16;
DLB 8; MTCW

Dickens, Charles (John Huffam)
1812-1870 . . . . . NCLC 3, 8, 18, 26; DA;
WLC
See also CDBLB 1832-1890; DLB 21, 55,
70; JRDA; MAICYA; SATA 15

Dickey, James (Lafayette)
1923- . . . . CLC 1, 2, 4, 7, 10, 15, 47
See also AITN 1, 2; CA 9-12R; CABS 2;
CANR 10; CDALB 1968-1988; DLB 5;
DLBD 7; DLBY 82, 93; MTCW

Dickey, William 1928- . . . . CLC 3, 28
See also CA 9-12R; CANR 24; DLB 5

Dickinson, Charles 1951- . . . . CLC 49
See also CA 128

Dickinson, Emily (Elizabeth)
1830-1886 . . NCLC 21; DA; PC 1; WLC
See also CDALB 1865-1917; DLB 1;
SATA 29

Dickinson, Peter (Malcolm)
1927- . . . . CLC 12, 35
See also AAYA 9; CA 41-44R; CANR 31;
CLR 29; DLB 87; JRDA; MAICYA;
SATA 5, 62

Dickson, Carr
See Carr, John Dickson

Dickson, Carter
See Carr, John Dickson

Diderot, Denis 1713-1784 . . . . LC 26

Didion, Joan 1934- . . . . . CLC 1, 3, 8, 14, 32
See also AITN 1; CA 5-8R; CANR 14;
CDALB 1968-1988; DLB 2; DLBY 81,
86; MTCW

Dietrich, Robert
See Hunt, E(verette) Howard, Jr.

Dillard, Annie 1945- . . . . CLC 9, 60
See also AAYA 6; CA 49-52; CANR 3, 43;
DLBY 80; MTCW; SATA 10

Dillard, R(ichard) H(enry) W(ilde)
1937- . . . . CLC 5
See also CA 21-24R; CAAS 7; CANR 10;
DLB 5

Dillon, Eilis 1920- . . . . CLC 17
See also CA 9-12R; CAAS 3; CANR 4, 38;
CLR 26; MAICYA; SATA 2, 74

Dimont, Penelope
See Mortimer, Penelope (Ruth)

Dinesen, Isak . . . . CLC 10, 29; SSC 7
See also Blixen, Karen (Christentze
Dinesen)

Ding Ling . . . . CLC 68
See also Chiang Pin-chin

Disch, Thomas M(ichael) 1940- . . . CLC 7, 36
See also CA 21-24R; CAAS 4; CANR 17,
36; CLR 18; DLB 8; MAICYA; MTCW;
SAAS 15; SATA 54

Disch, Tom
See Disch, Thomas M(ichael)

d'Isly, Georges
See Simenon, Georges (Jacques Christian)

Disraeli, Benjamin 1804-1881 . . NCLC 2, 39
See also DLB 21, 55

Ditcum, Steve
See Crumb, R(obert)

Dixon, Paige
See Corcoran, Barbara

Dixon, Stephen 1936- . . . . . CLC 52; SSC 16
See also CA 89-92; CANR 17, 40; DLB 130

Dobell, Sydney Thompson
1824-1874 . . . . NCLC 43
See also DLB 32

Doblin, Alfred . . . . TCLC 13
See also Doeblin, Alfred

Dobrolyubov, Nikolai Alexandrovich
1836-1861 . . . . NCLC 5

Dobyns, Stephen 1941- . . . . CLC 37
See also CA 45-48; CANR 2, 18

Doctorow, E(dgar) L(aurence)
1931- . . . . . CLC 6, 11, 15, 18, 37, 44, 65
See also AITN 2; BEST 89:3; CA 45-48;
CANR 2, 33; CDALB 1968-1988; DLB 2,
28; DLBY 80; MTCW

Dodgson, Charles Lutwidge 1832-1898
See Carroll, Lewis
See also CLR 2; DA; MAICYA; YABC 2

Dodson, Owen (Vincent)
1914-1983 . . . . CLC 79; BLC
See also BW 1; CA 65-68; 110; CANR 24;
DLB 76

Doeblin, Alfred 1878-1957 . . . . TCLC 13
See also Doblin, Alfred
See also CA 110; 141; DLB 66

Doerr, Harriet 1910- . . . . CLC 34
See also CA 117; 122

Domecq, H(onorio) Bustos
See Bioy Casares, Adolfo; Borges, Jorge
Luis

Domini, Rey
See Lorde, Audre (Geraldine)

Dominique
See Proust, (Valentin-Louis-George-Eugene-)
Marcel

Don, A
See Stephen, Leslie

Donaldson, Stephen R. 1947- . . . . . . CLC 46
See also CA 89-92; CANR 13

Donleavy, J(ames) P(atrick)
1926- . . . . CLC 1, 4, 6, 10, 45
See also AITN 2; CA 9-12R; CANR 24;
DLB 6; MTCW

Donne, John
1572-1631 . . . . LC 10, 24; DA; PC 1
See also CDBLB Before 1660; DLB 121

Donnell, David 1939(?)- . . . . CLC 34

Donoso (Yanez), Jose
1924- . . . . CLC 4, 8, 11, 32; HLC
See also CA 81-84; CANR 32; DLB 113;
HW; MTCW

Donovan, John 1928-1992 . . . . CLC 35
See also CA 97-100; 137; CLR 3;
MAICYA; SATA 29

Don Roberto
See Cunninghame Graham, R(obert)
B(ontine)

Doolittle, Hilda
1886-1961 . . . . . CLC 3, 8, 14, 31, 34, 73;
DA; PC 5; WLC
See also H. D.
See also CA 97-100; CANR 35; DLB 4, 45;
MTCW

Dorfman, Ariel 1942- . . . . CLC 48, 77; HLC
See also CA 124; 130; HW

Dorn, Edward (Merton) 1929- . . . CLC 10, 18
See also CA 93-96; CANR 42; DLB 5

Dorsan, Luc
See Simenon, Georges (Jacques Christian)

Dorsange, Jean
See Simenon, Georges (Jacques Christian)

Dos Passos, John (Roderigo)
1896-1970 . . . . . . CLC 1, 4, 8, 11, 15, 25,
34, 82; DA; WLC
See also CA 1-4R; 29-32R; CANR 3;
CDALB 1929-1941; DLB 4, 9; DLBD 1;
MTCW

Dossage, Jean
See Simenon, Georges (Jacques Christian)

Dostoevsky, Fedor Mikhailovich
1821-1881 . . . . . . NCLC 2, 7, 21, 33, 43;
DA; SSC 2; WLC

Doughty, Charles M(ontagu)
1843-1926 . . . . TCLC 27
See also CA 115; DLB 19, 57

Douglas, Ellen
See Haxton, Josephine Ayres

Douglas, Gavin 1475(?)-1522 . . . . LC 20

Douglas, Keith 1920-1944 . . . . TCLC 40
See also DLB 27

Douglas, Leonard
See Bradbury, Ray (Douglas)

Douglas, Michael
See Crichton, (John) Michael

Douglass, Frederick
1817(?)-1895 . . . . . . NCLC 7; BLC; DA;
WLC
See also CDALB 1640-1865; DLB 1, 43, 50,
79; SATA 29

Dourado, (Waldomiro Freitas) Autran
1926- . . . . CLC 23, 60
See also CA 25-28R; CANR 34

Dourado, Waldomiro Autran
See Dourado, (Waldomiro Freitas) Autran

Dove, Rita (Frances)
1952- . . . . CLC 50, 81; PC 6
See also BW 2; CA 109; CAAS 19;
CANR 27, 42; DLB 120

Dowell, Coleman 1925-1985 . . . . CLC 60
See also CA 25-28R; 117; CANR 10;
DLB 130

Dowson, Ernest Christopher
1867-1900 . . . . TCLC 4
See also CA 105; DLB 19, 135

Doyle, A. Conan
See Doyle, Arthur Conan

Doyle, Arthur Conan
1859-1930 . . . . TCLC 7; DA; SSC 12;
WLC
See also CA 104; 122; CDBLB 1890-1914;
DLB 18, 70; MTCW; SATA 24

Doyle, Conan 1859-1930
See Doyle, Arthur Conan

Doyle, John
See Graves, Robert (von Ranke)

Doyle, Roddy 1958(?)- . . . . CLC 81
See also CA 143

Doyle, Sir A. Conan
See Doyle, Arthur Conan

Doyle, Sir Arthur Conan
See Doyle, Arthur Conan

Dr. A
See Asimov, Isaac; Silverstein, Alvin

Drabble, Margaret
1939- ...... **CLC 2, 3, 5, 8, 10, 22, 53**
See also CA 13-16R; CANR 18, 35;
CDBLB 1960 to Present; DLB 14;
MTCW; SATA 48

Drapier, M. B.
See Swift, Jonathan

Drayham, James
See Mencken, H(enry) L(ouis)

Drayton, Michael 1563-1631 .... **LC 8**

Dreadstone, Carl
See Campbell, (John) Ramsey

Dreiser, Theodore (Herman Albert)
1871-1945 ...... **TCLC 10, 18, 35; DA;
WLC**
See also CA 106; 132; CDALB 1865-1917;
DLB 9, 12, 102, 137; DLBD 1; MTCW

Drexler, Rosalyn 1926- .... **CLC 2, 6**
See also CA 81-84

Dreyer, Carl Theodor 1889-1968.... **CLC 16**
See also CA 116

Drieu la Rochelle, Pierre(-Eugene)
1893-1945 .... **TCLC 21**
See also CA 117; DLB 72

Drop Shot
See Cable, George Washington

Droste-Hulshoff, Annette Freiin von
1797-1848 .... **NCLC 3**
See also DLB 133

Drummond, Walter
See Silverberg, Robert

Drummond, William Henry
1854-1907 .... **TCLC 25**
See also DLB 92

Drummond de Andrade, Carlos
1902-1987 .... **CLC 18**
See also Andrade, Carlos Drummond de
See also CA 132; 123

Drury, Allen (Stuart) 1918- .... **CLC 37**
See also CA 57-60; CANR 18

Dryden, John
1631-1700 ... **LC 3, 21; DA; DC 3; WLC**
See also CDBLB 1660-1789; DLB 80, 101,
131

Duberman, Martin 1930- .... **CLC 8**
See also CA 1-4R; CANR 2

Dubie, Norman (Evans) 1945- ...... **CLC 36**
See also CA 69-72; CANR 12; DLB 120

Du Bois, W(illiam) E(dward) B(urghardt)
1868-1963 ...... **CLC 1, 2, 13, 64; BLC;
DA; WLC**
See also BW 1; CA 85-88; CANR 34;
CDALB 1865-1917; DLB 47, 50, 91;
MTCW; SATA 42

Dubus, Andre 1936- ... **CLC 13, 36; SSC 15**
See also CA 21-24R; CANR 17; DLB 130

Duca Minimo
See D'Annunzio, Gabriele

Ducharme, Rejean 1941- .... **CLC 74**
See also DLB 60

Duclos, Charles Pinot 1704-1772 ..... **LC 1**

Dudek, Louis 1918- .... **CLC 11, 19**
See also CA 45-48; CAAS 14; CANR 1;
DLB 88

Duerrenmatt, Friedrich
.... **CLC 1, 4, 8, 11, 15, 43**
See also Duerrenmatt, Friedrich
See also DLB 69, 124

Duerrenmatt, Friedrich
1921-1990 ...... **CLC 1, 4, 8, 11, 15, 43**
See also Duerrenmatt, Friedrich
See also CA 17-20R; CANR 33; DLB 69,
124; MTCW

Duffy, Bruce (?)- .... **CLC 50**

Duffy, Maureen 1933- .... **CLC 37**
See also CA 25-28R; CANR 33; DLB 14;
MTCW

Dugan, Alan 1923- .... **CLC 2, 6**
See also CA 81-84; DLB 5

du Gard, Roger Martin
See Martin du Gard, Roger

Duhamel, Georges 1884-1966 .... **CLC 8**
See also CA 81-84; 25-28R; CANR 35;
DLB 65; MTCW

Dujardin, Edouard (Emile Louis)
1861-1949 .... **TCLC 13**
See also CA 109; DLB 123

Dumas, Alexandre (Davy de la Pailleterie)
1802-1870 .... **NCLC 11; DA; WLC**
See also DLB 119; SATA 18

Dumas, Alexandre
1824-1895 .... **NCLC 9; DC 1**

Dumas, Claudine
See Malzberg, Barry N(athaniel)

Dumas, Henry L. 1934-1968 ..... **CLC 6, 62**
See also BW 1; CA 85-88; DLB 41

du Maurier, Daphne
1907-1989 .... **CLC 6, 11, 59**
See also CA 5-8R; 128; CANR 6; MTCW;
SATA 27, 60

Dunbar, Paul Laurence
1872-1906 ...... **TCLC 2, 12; BLC; DA;
PC 5; SSC 8; WLC**
See also BW 1; CA 104; 124;
CDALB 1865-1917; DLB 50, 54, 78;
SATA 34

Dunbar, William 1460(?)-1530(?) .... **LC 20**

Duncan, Lois 1934- .... **CLC 26**
See also AAYA 4; CA 1-4R; CANR 2, 23,
36; CLR 29; JRDA; MAICYA; SAAS 2;
SATA 1, 36, 75

Duncan, Robert (Edward)
1919-1988 .... **CLC 1, 2, 4, 7, 15, 41, 55;
PC 2**
See also CA 9-12R; 124; CANR 28; DLB 5,
16; MTCW

Dunlap, William 1766-1839 .... **NCLC 2**
See also DLB 30, 37, 59

Dunn, Douglas (Eaglesham)
1942- .... **CLC 6, 40**
See also CA 45-48; CANR 2, 33; DLB 40;
MTCW

Dunn, Katherine (Karen) 1945- ..... **CLC 71**
See also CA 33-36R

Dunn, Stephen 1939- .... **CLC 36**
See also CA 33-36R; CANR 12; DLB 105

Dunne, Finley Peter 1867-1936.... **TCLC 28**
See also CA 108; DLB 11, 23

Dunne, John Gregory 1932-........ **CLC 28**
See also CA 25-28R; CANR 14; DLBY 80

Dunsany, Edward John Moreton Drax
Plunkett 1878-1957
See Dunsany, Lord
See also CA 104; DLB 10

Dunsany, Lord. .... **TCLC 2**
See also Dunsany, Edward John Moreton
Drax Plunkett
See also DLB 77

du Perry, Jean
See Simenon, Georges (Jacques Christian)

Durang, Christopher (Ferdinand)
1949- .... **CLC 27, 38**
See also CA 105

Duras, Marguerite
1914- ...... **CLC 3, 6, 11, 20, 34, 40, 68**
See also CA 25-28R; DLB 83; MTCW

Durban, (Rosa) Pam 1947-........ **CLC 39**
See also CA 123

Durcan, Paul 1944-............ **CLC 43, 70**
See also CA 134

Durkheim, Emile 1858-1917 ...... **TCLC 55**

Durrell, Lawrence (George)
1912-1990 .... **CLC 1, 4, 6, 8, 13, 27, 41**
See also CA 9-12R; 132; CANR 40;
CDBLB 1945-1960; DLB 15, 27;
DLBY 90; MTCW

Dutt, Toru 1856-1877........... **NCLC 29**

Dwight, Timothy 1752-1817...... **NCLC 13**
See also DLB 37

Dworkin, Andrea 1946- .... **CLC 43**
See also CA 77-80; CANR 16, 39; MTCW

Dwyer, Deanna
See Koontz, Dean R(ay)

Dwyer, K. R.
See Koontz, Dean R(ay)

Dylan, Bob 1941-...... **CLC 3, 4, 6, 12, 77**
See also CA 41-44R; DLB 16

Eagleton, Terence (Francis) 1943-
See Eagleton, Terry
See also CA 57-60; CANR 7, 23; MTCW

Eagleton, Terry .... **CLC 63**
See also Eagleton, Terence (Francis)

Early, Jack
See Scoppettone, Sandra

East, Michael
See West, Morris L(anglo)

Eastaway, Edward
See Thomas, (Philip) Edward

Eastlake, William (Derry) 1917-..... **CLC 8**
See also CA 5-8R; CAAS 1; CANR 5;
DLB 6

Eastman, Charles A(lexander)
1858-1939 .... **TCLC 55**
See also YABC 1

Engel, Marian 1933-1985 . . . . **CLC 36**
See also CA 25-28R; CANR 12; DLB 53

Engelhardt, Frederick
See Hubbard, L(afayette) Ron(ald)

Enright, D(ennis) J(oseph)
1920- . . . . **CLC 4, 8, 31**
See also CA 1-4R; CANR 1, 42; DLB 27;
SATA 25

Enzensberger, Hans Magnus
1929- . . . . **CLC 43**
See also CA 116; 119

Ephron, Nora 1941- . . . . **CLC 17, 31**
See also AITN 2; CA 65-68; CANR 12, 39

Epsilon
See Betjeman, John

Epstein, Daniel Mark 1948- . . . . **CLC 7**
See also CA 49-52; CANR 2

Epstein, Jacob 1956- . . . . **CLC 19**
See also CA 114

Epstein, Joseph 1937- . . . . **CLC 39**
See also CA 112; 119

Epstein, Leslie 1938- . . . . **CLC 27**
See also CA 73-76; CAAS 12; CANR 23

Equiano, Olaudah
1745(?)-1797 . . . . **LC 16; BLC**
See also DLB 37, 50

Erasmus, Desiderius 1469(?)-1536. . . . **LC 16**

Erdman, Paul E(mil) 1932- . . . . **CLC 25**
See also AITN 1; CA 61-64; CANR 13, 43

Erdrich, Louise 1954- . . . . **CLC 39, 54**
See also AAYA 10; BEST 89:1; CA 114;
CANR 41; MTCW

Erenburg, Ilya (Grigoryevich)
See Ehrenburg, Ilya (Grigoryevich)

Erickson, Stephen Michael 1950-
See Erickson, Steve
See also CA 129

Erickson, Steve . . . . **CLC 64**
See also Erickson, Stephen Michael

Ericson, Walter
See Fast, Howard (Melvin)

Eriksson, Buntel
See Bergman, (Ernst) Ingmar

Eschenbach, Wolfram von
See Wolfram von Eschenbach

Eseki, Bruno
See Mphahlele, Ezekiel

Esenin, Sergei (Alexandrovich)
1895-1925 . . . . **TCLC 4**
See also CA 104

Eshleman, Clayton 1935- . . . . **CLC 7**
See also CA 33-36R; CAAS 6; DLB 5

Espriella, Don Manuel Alvarez
See Southey, Robert

Espriu, Salvador 1913-1985 . . . . **CLC 9**
See also CA 115; DLB 134

Espronceda, Jose de 1808-1842 . . . **NCLC 39**

Esse, James
See Stephens, James

Esterbrook, Tom
See Hubbard, L(afayette) Ron(ald)

Estleman, Loren D. 1952- . . . . **CLC 48**
See also CA 85-88; CANR 27; MTCW

Eugenides, Jeffrey 1960(?)- . . . . **CLC 81**
See also CA 144

Euripides c. 485B.C.-406B.C. . . . . **DC 4**
See also DA

Evan, Evin
See Faust, Frederick (Schiller)

Evans, Evan
See Faust, Frederick (Schiller)

Evans, Marian
See Eliot, George

Evans, Mary Ann
See Eliot, George

Evarts, Esther
See Benson, Sally

Everett, Percival L. 1956- . . . . **CLC 57**
See also BW 2; CA 129

Everson, R(onald) G(ilmour)
1903- . . . . **CLC 27**
See also CA 17-20R; DLB 88

Everson, William (Oliver)
1912- . . . . **CLC 1, 5, 14**
See also CA 9-12R; CANR 20; DLB 5, 16;
MTCW

Evtushenko, Evgenii Aleksandrovich
See Yevtushenko, Yevgeny (Alexandrovich)

Ewart, Gavin (Buchanan)
1916- . . . . **CLC 13, 46**
See also CA 89-92; CANR 17; DLB 40;
MTCW

Ewers, Hanns Heinz 1871-1943 . . . **TCLC 12**
See also CA 109

Ewing, Frederick R.
See Sturgeon, Theodore (Hamilton)

Exley, Frederick (Earl)
1929-1992 . . . . **CLC 6, 11**
See also AITN 2; CA 81-84; 138; DLB 143;
DLBY 81

Eynhardt, Guillermo
See Quiroga, Horacio (Sylvestre)

Ezekiel, Nissim 1924- . . . . **CLC 61**
See also CA 61-64

Ezekiel, Tish O'Dowd 1943- . . . . **CLC 34**
See also CA 129

Fadeyev, A.
See Bulgya, Alexander Alexandrovich

Fadeyev, Alexander . . . . **TCLC 53**
See also Bulgya, Alexander Alexandrovich

Fagen, Donald 1948- . . . . **CLC 26**

Fainzilberg, Ilya Arnoldovich 1897-1937
See Ilf, Ilya
See also CA 120

Fair, Ronald L. 1932- . . . . **CLC 18**
See also BW 1; CA 69-72; CANR 25;
DLB 33

Fairbairns, Zoe (Ann) 1948- . . . . **CLC 32**
See also CA 103; CANR 21

Falco, Gian
See Papini, Giovanni

Falconer, James
See Kirkup, James

Falconer, Kenneth
See Kornbluth, C(yril) M.

Falkland, Samuel
See Heijermans, Herman

Fallaci, Oriana 1930- . . . . **CLC 11**
See also CA 77-80; CANR 15; MTCW

Faludy, George 1913- . . . . **CLC 42**
See also CA 21-24R

Faludy, Gyoergy
See Faludy, George

Fanon, Frantz 1925-1961 . . . . . **CLC 74; BLC**
See also BW 1; CA 116; 89-92

Fanshawe, Ann . . . . **LC 11**

Fante, John (Thomas) 1911-1983 . . . **CLC 60**
See also CA 69-72; 109; CANR 23;
DLB 130; DLBY 83

Farah, Nuruddin 1945- . . . . **CLC 53; BLC**
See also BW 2; CA 106; DLB 125

Fargue, Leon-Paul 1876(?)-1947 . . . **TCLC 11**
See also CA 109

Farigoule, Louis
See Romains, Jules

Farina, Richard 1936(?)-1966 . . . . **CLC 9**
See also CA 81-84; 25-28R

Farley, Walter (Lorimer)
1915-1989 . . . . **CLC 17**
See also CA 17-20R; CANR 8, 29; DLB 22;
JRDA; MAICYA; SATA 2, 43

Farmer, Philip Jose 1918- . . . . **CLC 1, 19**
See also CA 1-4R; CANR 4, 35; DLB 8;
MTCW

Farquhar, George 1677-1707 . . . . **LC 21**
See also DLB 84

Farrell, J(ames) G(ordon)
1935-1979 . . . . **CLC 6**
See also CA 73-76; 89-92; CANR 36;
DLB 14; MTCW

Farrell, James T(homas)
1904-1979 . . . . **CLC 1, 4, 8, 11, 66**
See also CA 5-8R; 89-92; CANR 9; DLB 4,
9, 86; DLBD 2; MTCW

Farren, Richard J.
See Betjeman, John

Farren, Richard M.
See Betjeman, John

Fassbinder, Rainer Werner
1946-1982 . . . . **CLC 20**
See also CA 93-96; 106; CANR 31

Fast, Howard (Melvin) 1914- . . . . . . **CLC 23**
See also CA 1-4R; CAAS 18; CANR 1, 33;
DLB 9; SATA 7

Faulcon, Robert
See Holdstock, Robert P.

Faulkner, William (Cuthbert)
1897-1962 . . . . . **CLC 1, 3, 6, 8, 9, 11, 14,
18, 28, 52, 68; DA; SSC 1; WLC**
See also AAYA 7; CA 81-84; CANR 33;
CDALB 1929-1941; DLB 9, 11, 44, 102;
DLBD 2; DLBY 86; MTCW

Fauset, Jessie Redmon
1884(?)-1961 . . . . **CLC 19, 54; BLC**
See also BW 1; CA 109; DLB 51

Faust, Frederick (Schiller)
1892-1944(?) . . . . **TCLC 49**
See also CA 108

Ford, Elbur
See Hibbert, Eleanor Alice Burford

Ford, Ford Madox
1873-1939 . . . . **TCLC 1, 15, 39**
See also CA 104; 132; CDBLB 1914-1945;
DLB 34, 98; MTCW

Ford, John 1895-1973. . . . . **CLC 16**
See also CA 45-48

Ford, Richard 1944- . . . . **CLC 46**
See also CA 69-72; CANR 11

Ford, Webster
See Masters, Edgar Lee

Foreman, Richard 1937-. . . . . **CLC 50**
See also CA 65-68; CANR 32

Forester, C(ecil) S(cott)
1899-1966 . . . . **CLC 35**
See also CA 73-76; 25-28R; SATA 13

Forez
See Mauriac, Francois (Charles)

Forman, James Douglas 1932-. . . . . . **CLC 21**
See also CA 9-12R; CANR 4, 19, 42;
JRDA; MAICYA; SATA 8, 70

Fornes, Maria Irene 1930-. . . . . . **CLC 39, 61**
See also CA 25-28R; CANR 28; DLB 7;
HW; MTCW

Forrest, Leon 1937- . . . . **CLC 4**
See also BW 2; CA 89-92; CAAS 7;
CANR 25; DLB 33

Forster, E(dward) M(organ)
1879-1970 . . . . . **CLC 1, 2, 3, 4, 9, 10, 13,**
15, 22, 45, 77; DA; WLC
See also AAYA 2; CA 13-14; 25-28R;
CANR 45; CAP 1; CDBLB 1914-1945;
DLB 34, 98; DLBD 10; MTCW;
SATA 57

Forster, John 1812-1876 . . . . **NCLC 11**
See also DLB 144

Forsyth, Frederick 1938-. . . . . . **CLC 2, 5, 36**
See also BEST 89:4; CA 85-88; CANR 38;
DLB 87; MTCW

Forten, Charlotte L. . . . . **TCLC 16; BLC**
See also Grimke, Charlotte L(ottie) Forten
See also DLB 50

Foscolo, Ugo 1778-1827. . . . . **NCLC 8**

Fosse, Bob . . . . **CLC 20**
See also Fosse, Robert Louis

Fosse, Robert Louis 1927-1987
See Fosse, Bob
See also CA 110; 123

Foster, Stephen Collins
1826-1864 . . . . **NCLC 26**

Foucault, Michel
1926-1984 . . . . **CLC 31, 34, 69**
See also CA 105; 113; CANR 34; MTCW

Fouque, Friedrich (Heinrich Karl) de la Motte
1777-1843 . . . . **NCLC 2**
See also DLB 90

Fournier, Henri Alban 1886-1914
See Alain-Fournier
See also CA 104

Fournier, Pierre 1916- . . . . **CLC 11**
See also Gascar, Pierre
See also CA 89-92; CANR 16, 40

Fowles, John
1926- . . . . **CLC 1, 2, 3, 4, 6, 9, 10, 15, 33**
See also CA 5-8R; CANR 25; CDBLB 1960
to Present; DLB 14, 139; MTCW;
SATA 22

Fox, Paula 1923-. . . . . **CLC 2, 8**
See also AAYA 3; CA 73-76; CANR 20,
36; CLR 1; DLB 52; JRDA; MAICYA;
MTCW; SATA 17, 60

Fox, William Price (Jr.) 1926- . . . . . **CLC 22**
See also CA 17-20R; CAAS 19; CANR 11;
DLB 2; DLBY 81

Foxe, John 1516(?)-1587 . . . . **LC 14**

Frame, Janet . . . . **CLC 2, 3, 6, 22, 66**
See also Clutha, Janet Paterson Frame

France, Anatole . . . . **TCLC 9**
See also Thibault, Jacques Anatole Francois
See also DLB 123

Francis, Claude 19(?)- . . . . **CLC 50**

Francis, Dick 1920- . . . . **CLC 2, 22, 42**
See also AAYA 5; BEST 89:3; CA 5-8R;
CANR 9, 42; CDBLB 1960 to Present;
DLB 87; MTCW

Francis, Robert (Churchill)
1901-1987 . . . . **CLC 15**
See also CA 1-4R; 123; CANR 1

Frank, Anne(lies Marie)
1929-1945 . . . . **TCLC 17; DA; WLC**
See also AAYA 12; CA 113; 133; MTCW;
SATA 42

Frank, Elizabeth 1945-. . . . . **CLC 39**
See also CA 121; 126

Franklin, Benjamin
See Hasek, Jaroslav (Matej Frantisek)

Franklin, Benjamin 1706-1790. . . **LC 25; DA**
See also CDALB 1640-1865; DLB 24, 43,
73

Franklin, (Stella Maraia Sarah) Miles
1879-1954 . . . . **TCLC 7**
See also CA 104

Fraser, (Lady) Antonia (Pakenham)
1932- . . . . **CLC 32**
See also CA 85-88; CANR 44; MTCW;
SATA 32

Fraser, George MacDonald 1925-. . . . **CLC 7**
See also CA 45-48; CANR 2

Fraser, Sylvia 1935-. . . . . **CLC 64**
See also CA 45-48; CANR 1, 16

Frayn, Michael 1933-. . . . . . . **CLC 3, 7, 31, 47**
See also CA 5-8R; CANR 30; DLB 13, 14;
MTCW

Fraze, Candida (Merrill) 1945-. . . . . **CLC 50**
See also CA 126

Frazer, J(ames) G(eorge)
1854-1941 . . . . **TCLC 32**
See also CA 118

Frazer, Robert Caine
See Creasey, John

Frazer, Sir James George
See Frazer, J(ames) G(eorge)

Frazier, Ian 1951-. . . . . **CLC 46**
See also CA 130

Frederic, Harold 1856-1898. . . . . . **NCLC 10**
See also DLB 12, 23

Frederick, John
See Faust, Frederick (Schiller)

Frederick the Great 1712-1786 . . . . . . **LC 14**

Fredro, Aleksander 1793-1876. . . . . **NCLC 8**

Freeling, Nicolas 1927- . . . . **CLC 38**
See also CA 49-52; CAAS 12; CANR 1, 17;
DLB 87

Freeman, Douglas Southall
1886-1953 . . . . **TCLC 11**
See also CA 109; DLB 17

Freeman, Judith 1946-. . . . . **CLC 55**

Freeman, Mary Eleanor Wilkins
1852-1930 . . . . **TCLC 9; SSC 1**
See also CA 106; DLB 12, 78

Freeman, R(ichard) Austin
1862-1943 . . . . **TCLC 21**
See also CA 113; DLB 70

French, Marilyn 1929-. . . . . . **CLC 10, 18, 60**
See also CA 69-72; CANR 3, 31; MTCW

French, Paul
See Asimov, Isaac

Freneau, Philip Morin 1752-1832. . **NCLC 1**
See also DLB 37, 43

Freud, Sigmund 1856-1939 . . . . **TCLC 52**
See also CA 115; 133; MTCW

Friedan, Betty (Naomi) 1921-. . . . . . **CLC 74**
See also CA 65-68; CANR 18, 45; MTCW

Friedman, B(ernard) H(arper)
1926- . . . . **CLC 7**
See also CA 1-4R; CANR 3

Friedman, Bruce Jay 1930-. . . . **CLC 3, 5, 56**
See also CA 9-12R; CANR 25; DLB 2, 28

Friel, Brian 1929-. . . . . **CLC 5, 42, 59**
See also CA 21-24R; CANR 33; DLB 13;
MTCW

Friis-Baastad, Babbis Ellinor
1921-1970 . . . . **CLC 12**
See also CA 17-20R; 134; SATA 7

Frisch, Max (Rudolf)
1911-1991 . . . . . **CLC 3, 9, 14, 18, 32, 44**
See also CA 85-88; 134; CANR 32;
DLB 69, 124; MTCW

Fromentin, Eugene (Samuel Auguste)
1820-1876 . . . . **NCLC 10**
See also DLB 123

Frost, Frederick
See Faust, Frederick (Schiller)

Frost, Robert (Lee)
1874-1963 . . . . **CLC 1, 3, 4, 9, 10, 13, 15,**
26, 34, 44; DA; PC 1; WLC
See also CA 89-92; CANR 33;
CDALB 1917-1929; DLB 54; DLBD 7;
MTCW; SATA 14

Froude, James Anthony
1818-1894 . . . . **NCLC 43**
See also DLB 18, 57, 144

Froy, Herald
See Waterhouse, Keith (Spencer)

Fry, Christopher 1907-. . . . . . . **CLC 2, 10, 14**
See also CA 17-20R; CANR 9, 30; DLB 13;
MTCW; SATA 66

Gelbart, Larry (Simon) 1923- ... **CLC 21, 61**
See also CA 73-76; CANR 45

Gelber, Jack 1932-........**CLC 1, 6, 14, 79**
See also CA 1-4R; CANR 2; DLB 7

Gellhorn, Martha (Ellis) 1908-.. **CLC 14, 60**
See also CA 77-80; CANR 44; DLBY 82

Genet, Jean
1910-1986 ... **CLC 1, 2, 5, 10, 14, 44, 46**
See also CA 13-16R; CANR 18; DLB 72;
DLBY 86; MTCW

Gent, Peter 1942-................**CLC 29**
See also AITN 1; CA 89-92; DLBY 82

Gentlewoman in New England, A
See Bradstreet, Anne

Gentlewoman in Those Parts, A
See Bradstreet, Anne

George, Jean Craighead 1919-......**CLC 35**
See also AAYA 8; CA 5-8R; CANR 25;
CLR 1; DLB 52; JRDA; MAICYA;
SATA 2, 68

George, Stefan (Anton)
1868-1933 ....**TCLC 2, 14**
See also CA 104

Georges, Georges Martin
See Simenon, Georges (Jacques Christian)

Gerhardi, William Alexander
See Gerhardie, William Alexander

Gerhardie, William Alexander
1895-1977 ....**CLC 5**
See also CA 25-28R; 73-76; CANR 18;
DLB 36

Gerstler, Amy 1956-..............**CLC 70**

Gertler, T. ....**CLC 34**
See also CA 116; 121

Ghalib 1797-1869 ....**NCLC 39**

Ghelderode, Michel de
1898-1962 ....**CLC 6, 11**
See also CA 85-88; CANR 40

Ghiselin, Brewster 1903-........**CLC 23**
See also CA 13-16R; CAAS 10; CANR 13

Ghose, Zulfikar 1935-.............**CLC 42**
See also CA 65-68

Ghosh, Amitav 1956- ....**CLC 44**

Giacosa, Giuseppe 1847-1906 ......**TCLC 7**
See also CA 104

Gibb, Lee
See Waterhouse, Keith (Spencer)

Gibbon, Lewis Grassic ....**TCLC 4**
See also Mitchell, James Leslie

Gibbons, Kaye 1960- ....**CLC 50**

Gibran, Kahlil
1883-1931 ....**TCLC 1, 9; PC 9**
See also CA 104

Gibson, William 1914-........**CLC 23; DA**
See also CA 9-12R; CANR 9, 42; DLB 7;
SATA 66

Gibson, William (Ford) 1948-... **CLC 39, 63**
See also AAYA 12; CA 126; 133

Gide, Andre (Paul Guillaume)
1869-1951 ....**TCLC 5, 12, 36; DA;**
SSC 13; WLC
See also CA 104; 124; DLB 65; MTCW

Gifford, Barry (Colby) 1946-.......**CLC 34**
See also CA 65-68; CANR 9, 30, 40

Gilbert, W(illiam) S(chwenck)
1836-1911 ....**TCLC 3**
See also CA 104; SATA 36

Gilbreth, Frank B., Jr. 1911-.......**CLC 17**
See also CA 9-12R; SATA 2

Gilchrist, Ellen 1935-.. **CLC 34, 48; SSC 14**
See also CA 113; 116; CANR 41; DLB 130;
MTCW

Giles, Molly 1942-................**CLC 39**
See also CA 126

Gill, Patrick
See Creasey, John

Gilliam, Terry (Vance) 1940-.......**CLC 21**
See also Monty Python
See also CA 108; 113; CANR 35

Gillian, Jerry
See Gilliam, Terry (Vance)

Gilliatt, Penelope (Ann Douglass)
1932-1993 ....**CLC 2, 10, 13, 53**
See also AITN 2; CA 13-16R; 141; DLB 14

Gilman, Charlotte (Anna) Perkins (Stetson)
1860-1935 ....**TCLC 9, 37; SSC 13**
See also CA 106

Gilmour, David 1949-.............**CLC 35**
See also Pink Floyd
See also CA 138

Gilpin, William 1724-1804.......**NCLC 30**

Gilray, J. D.
See Mencken, H(enry) L(ouis)

Gilroy, Frank D(aniel) 1925-........**CLC 2**
See also CA 81-84; CANR 32; DLB 7

Ginsberg, Allen
1926- ......**CLC 1, 2, 3, 4, 6, 13, 36, 69;**
DA; PC 4; WLC 3
See also AITN 1; CA 1-4R; CANR 2, 41;
CDALB 1941-1968; DLB 5, 16; MTCW

Ginzburg, Natalia
1916-1991 ....**CLC 5, 11, 54, 70**
See also CA 85-88; 135; CANR 33; MTCW

Giono, Jean 1895-1970..........**CLC 4, 11**
See also CA 45-48; 29-32R; CANR 2, 35;
DLB 72; MTCW

Giovanni, Nikki
1943- ......**CLC 2, 4, 19, 64; BLC; DA**
See also AITN 1; BW 2; CA 29-32R;
CAAS 6; CANR 18, 41; CLR 6; DLB 5,
41; MAICYA; MTCW; SATA 24

Giovene, Andrea 1904-.............**CLC 7**
See also CA 85-88

Gippius, Zinaida (Nikolayevna) 1869-1945
See Hippius, Zinaida
See also CA 106

Giraudoux, (Hippolyte) Jean
1882-1944 ....**TCLC 2, 7**
See also CA 104; DLB 65

Gironella, Jose Maria 1917- ....**CLC 11**
See also CA 101

Gissing, George (Robert)
1857-1903 ....**TCLC 3, 24, 47**
See also CA 105; DLB 18, 135

Giurlani, Aldo
See Palazzeschi, Aldo

Gladkov, Fyodor (Vasilyevich)
1883-1958 ....**TCLC 27**

Glanville, Brian (Lester) 1931-......**CLC 6**
See also CA 5-8R; CAAS 9; CANR 3;
DLB 15, 139; SATA 42

Glasgow, Ellen (Anderson Gholson)
1873(?)-1945 ....**TCLC 2, 7**
See also CA 104; DLB 9, 12

Glaspell, Susan (Keating)
1882(?)-1948 ....**TCLC 55**
See also CA 110; DLB 7, 9, 78; YABC 2

Glassco, John 1909-1981 ....**CLC 9**
See also CA 13-16R; 102; CANR 15;
DLB 68

Glasscock, Amnesia
See Steinbeck, John (Ernst)

Glasser, Ronald J. 1940(?)-........**CLC 37**

Glassman, Joyce
See Johnson, Joyce

Glendinning, Victoria 1937-........**CLC 50**
See also CA 120; 127

Glissant, Edouard 1928-........**CLC 10, 68**

Gloag, Julian 1930- ....**CLC 40**
See also AITN 1; CA 65-68; CANR 10

Glowacki, Aleksander 1845-1912
See Prus, Boleslaw

Gluck, Louise (Elisabeth)
1943- ....**CLC 7, 22, 44, 81**
See also Glueck, Louise
See also CA 33-36R; CANR 40; DLB 5

Glueck, Louise.................**CLC 7, 22**
See also Gluck, Louise (Elisabeth)
See also DLB 5

Gobineau, Joseph Arthur (Comte) de
1816-1882 ....**NCLC 17**
See also DLB 123

Godard, Jean-Luc 1930-...........**CLC 20**
See also CA 93-96

Godden, (Margaret) Rumer 1907-... **CLC 53**
See also AAYA 6; CA 5-8R; CANR 4, 27,
36; CLR 20; MAICYA; SAAS 12;
SATA 3, 36

Godoy Alcayaga, Lucila 1889-1957
See Mistral, Gabriela
See also BW 2; CA 104; 131; HW; MTCW

Godwin, Gail (Kathleen)
1937- ....**CLC 5, 8, 22, 31, 69**
See also CA 29-32R; CANR 15, 43; DLB 6;
MTCW

Godwin, William 1756-1836......**NCLC 14**
See also CDBLB 1789-1832; DLB 39, 104,
142

Goethe, Johann Wolfgang von
1749-1832 ....**NCLC 4, 22, 34; DA;**
PC 5; WLC 3
See also DLB 94

Gogarty, Oliver St. John
1878-1957 ....**TCLC 15**
See also CA 109; DLB 15, 19

Gogol, Nikolai (Vasilyevich)
1809-1852 ....**NCLC 5, 15, 31; DA;**
DC 1; SSC 4; WLC

Goines, Donald
1937(?)-1974 . . . . **CLC 80; BLC**
See also AITN 1; BW 1; CA 124; 114;
DLB 33

Gold, Herbert 1924- . . . . **CLC 4, 7, 14, 42**
See also CA 9-12R; CANR 17, 45; DLB 2;
DLBY 81

Goldbarth, Albert 1948- . . . . **CLC 5, 38**
See also CA 53-56; CANR 6, 40; DLB 120

Goldberg, Anatol 1910-1982 . . . . **CLC 34**
See also CA 131; 117

Goldemberg, Isaac 1945- . . . . **CLC 52**
See also CA 69-72; CAAS 12; CANR 11,
32; HW

Golding, William (Gerald)
1911-1993 . . . . **CLC 1, 2, 3, 8, 10, 17, 27,
58, 81; DA; WLC**
See also AAYA 5; CA 5-8R; 141;
CANR 13, 33; CDBLB 1945-1960;
DLB 15, 100; MTCW

Goldman, Emma 1869-1940 . . . . . . **TCLC 13**
See also CA 110

Goldman, Francisco 1955- . . . . **CLC 76**

Goldman, William (W.) 1931- . . . . **CLC 1, 48**
See also CA 9-12R; CANR 29; DLB 44

Goldmann, Lucien 1913-1970 . . . . . . **CLC 24**
See also CA 25-28; CAP 2

Goldoni, Carlo 1707-1793 . . . . **LC 4**

Goldsberry, Steven 1949- . . . . **CLC 34**
See also CA 131

Goldsmith, Oliver
1728-1774 . . . . **LC 2; DA; WLC**
See also CDBLB 1660-1789; DLB 39, 89,
104, 109, 142; SATA 26

Goldsmith, Peter
See Priestley, J(ohn) B(oynton)

Gombrowicz, Witold
1904-1969 . . . . **CLC 4, 7, 11, 49**
See also CA 19-20; 25-28R; CAP 2

Gomez de la Serna, Ramon
1888-1963 . . . . **CLC 9**
See also CA 116; HW

Goncharov, Ivan Alexandrovich
1812-1891 . . . . **NCLC 1**

Goncourt, Edmond (Louis Antoine Huot) de
1822-1896 . . . . **NCLC 7**
See also DLB 123

Goncourt, Jules (Alfred Huot) de
1830-1870 . . . . **NCLC 7**
See also DLB 123

Gontier, Fernande 19(?)- . . . . **CLC 50**

Goodman, Paul 1911-1972 . . . . **CLC 1, 2, 4, 7**
See also CA 19-20; 37-40R; CANR 34;
CAP 2; DLB 130; MTCW

Gordimer, Nadine
1923- . . . . **CLC 3, 5, 7, 10, 18, 33, 51, 70;
DA**
See also CA 5-8R; CANR 3, 28; MTCW

Gordon, Adam Lindsay
1833-1870 . . . . **NCLC 21**

Gordon, Caroline
1895-1981 . . . **CLC 6, 13, 29, 83; SSC 15**
See also CA 11-12; 103; CANR 36; CAP 1;
DLB 4, 9, 102; DLBY 81; MTCW

Gordon, Charles William 1860-1937
See Connor, Ralph
See also CA 109

Gordon, Mary (Catherine)
1949- . . . . **CLC 13, 22**
See also CA 102; CANR 44; DLB 6;
DLBY 81; MTCW

Gordon, Sol 1923- . . . . **CLC 26**
See also CA 53-56; CANR 4; SATA 11

Gordone, Charles 1925- . . . . **CLC 1, 4**
See also BW 1; CA 93-96; DLB 7; MTCW

Gorenko, Anna Andreevna
See Akhmatova, Anna

Gorky, Maxim . . . . **TCLC 8; WLC**
See also Peshkov, Alexei Maximovich

Goryan, Sirak
See Saroyan, William

Gosse, Edmund (William)
1849-1928 . . . . **TCLC 28**
See also CA 117; DLB 57, 144

Gotlieb, Phyllis Fay (Bloom)
1926- . . . . **CLC 18**
See also CA 13-16R; CANR 7; DLB 88

Gottesman, S. D.
See Kornbluth, C(yril) M.; Pohl, Frederik

Gottfried von Strassburg
fl. c. 1210- . . . . **CMLC 10**
See also DLB 138

Gould, Lois . . . . **CLC 4, 10**
See also CA 77-80; CANR 29; MTCW

Gourmont, Remy de 1858-1915 . . . . **TCLC 17**
See also CA 109

Govier, Katherine 1948- . . . . **CLC 51**
See also CA 101; CANR 18, 40

Goyen, (Charles) William
1915-1983 . . . . **CLC 5, 8, 14, 40**
See also AITN 2; CA 5-8R; 110; CANR 6;
DLB 2; DLBY 83

Goytisolo, Juan
1931- . . . . **CLC 5, 10, 23; HLC**
See also CA 85-88; CANR 32; HW; MTCW

Gozzano, Guido 1883-1916 . . . . **PC 10**
See also DLB 114

Gozzi, (Conte) Carlo 1720-1806 . . **NCLC 23**

Grabbe, Christian Dietrich
1801-1836 . . . . **NCLC 2**
See also DLB 133

Grace, Patricia 1937- . . . . **CLC 56**

Gracian y Morales, Baltasar
1601-1658 . . . . **LC 15**

Gracq, Julien . . . . **CLC 11, 48**
See also Poirier, Louis
See also DLB 83

Grade, Chaim 1910-1982 . . . . **CLC 10**
See also CA 93-96; 107

Graduate of Oxford, A
See Ruskin, John

Graham, John
See Phillips, David Graham

Graham, Jorie 1951- . . . . **CLC 48**
See also CA 111; DLB 120

Graham, R(obert) B(ontine) Cunninghame
See Cunninghame Graham, R(obert)
B(ontine)
See also DLB 98, 135

Graham, Robert
See Haldeman, Joe (William)

Graham, Tom
See Lewis, (Harry) Sinclair

Graham, W(illiam) S(ydney)
1918-1986 . . . . **CLC 29**
See also CA 73-76; 118; DLB 20

Graham, Winston (Mawdsley)
1910- . . . . **CLC 23**
See also CA 49-52; CANR 2, 22, 45;
DLB 77

Grant, Skeeter
See Spiegelman, Art

Granville-Barker, Harley
1877-1946 . . . . **TCLC 2**
See also Barker, Harley Granville
See also CA 104

Grass, Guenter (Wilhelm)
1927- . . . . . **CLC 1, 2, 4, 6, 11, 15, 22, 32,
49; DA; WLC**
See also CA 13-16R; CANR 20; DLB 75,
124; MTCW

Gratton, Thomas
See Hulme, T(homas) E(rnest)

Grau, Shirley Ann
1929- . . . . **CLC 4, 9; SSC 15**
See also CA 89-92; CANR 22; DLB 2;
MTCW

Gravel, Fern
See Hall, James Norman

Graver, Elizabeth 1964- . . . . **CLC 70**
See also CA 135

Graves, Richard Perceval 1945- . . . . **CLC 44**
See also CA 65-68; CANR 9, 26

Graves, Robert (von Ranke)
1895-1985 . . . . . . **CLC 1, 2, 6, 11, 39, 44,
45; PC 6**
See also CA 5-8R; 117; CANR 5, 36;
CDBLB 1914-1945; DLB 20, 100;
DLBY 85; MTCW; SATA 45

Gray, Alasdair 1934- . . . . **CLC 41**
See also CA 126; MTCW

Gray, Amlin 1946- . . . . **CLC 29**
See also CA 138

Gray, Francine du Plessix 1930- . . . . **CLC 22**
See also BEST 90:3; CA 61-64; CAAS 2;
CANR 11, 33; MTCW

Gray, John (Henry) 1866-1934 . . . . **TCLC 19**
See also CA 119

Gray, Simon (James Holliday)
1936- . . . . **CLC 9, 14, 36**
See also AITN 1; CA 21-24R; CAAS 3;
CANR 32; DLB 13; MTCW

Gray, Spalding 1941- . . . . **CLC 49**
See also CA 128

Gray, Thomas
1716-1771 . . . . . . **LC 4; DA; PC 2; WLC**
See also CDBLB 1660-1789; DLB 109

Grayson, David
See Baker, Ray Stannard

Grayson, Richard (A.) 1951- .... **CLC 38**
See also CA 85-88; CANR 14, 31

Greeley, Andrew M(oran) 1928- .... **CLC 28**
See also CA 5-8R; CAAS 7; CANR 7, 43;
MTCW

Green, Brian
See Card, Orson Scott

Green, Hannah .... **CLC 3**
See also CA 73-76

Green, Hannah
See Greenberg, Joanne (Goldenberg)

Green, Henry.................... **CLC 2, 13**
See also Yorke, Henry Vincent
See also DLB 15

Green, Julian (Hartridge) 1900-
See Green, Julien
See also CA 21-24R; CANR 33; DLB 4, 72;
MTCW

Green, Julien .... **CLC 3, 11, 77**
See also Green, Julian (Hartridge)

Green, Paul (Eliot) 1894-1981..... **CLC 25**
See also AITN 1; CA 5-8R; 103; CANR 3;
DLB 7, 9; DLBY 81

Greenberg, Ivan 1908-1973
See Rahv, Philip
See also CA 85-88

Greenberg, Joanne (Goldenberg)
1932- .... **CLC 7, 30**
See also AAYA 12; CA 5-8R; CANR 14,
32; SATA 25

Greenberg, Richard 1959(?)- .... **CLC 57**
See also CA 138

Greene, Bette 1934- .... **CLC 30**
See also AAYA 7; CA 53-56; CANR 4;
CLR 2; JRDA; MAICYA; SAAS 16;
SATA 8

Greene, Gael .... **CLC 8**
See also CA 13-16R; CANR 10

Greene, Graham
1904-1991 .... **CLC 1, 3, 6, 9, 14, 18, 27,
37, 70, 72; DA; WLC**
See also AITN 2; CA 13-16R; 133;
CANR 35; CDBLB 1945-1960; DLB 13,
15, 77, 100; DLBY 91; MTCW; SATA 20

Greer, Richard
See Silverberg, Robert

Greer, Richard
See Silverberg, Robert

Gregor, Arthur 1923- .... **CLC 9**
See also CA 25-28R; CAAS 10; CANR 11;
SATA 36

Gregor, Lee
See Pohl, Frederik

Gregory, Isabella Augusta (Persse)
1852-1932 .... **TCLC 1**
See also CA 104; DLB 10

Gregory, J. Dennis
See Williams, John A(lfred)

Grendon, Stephen
See Derleth, August (William)

Grenville, Kate 1950- .... **CLC 61**
See also CA 118

Grenville, Pelham
See Wodehouse, P(elham) G(renville)

Greve, Felix Paul (Berthold Friedrich)
1879-1948
See Grove, Frederick Philip
See also CA 104; 141

Grey, Zane 1872-1939 .... **TCLC 6**
See also CA 104; 132; DLB 9; MTCW

Grieg, (Johan) Nordahl (Brun)
1902-1943 .... **TCLC 10**
See also CA 107

Grieve, C(hristopher) M(urray)
1892-1978 .... **CLC 11, 19**
See also MacDiarmid, Hugh
See also CA 5-8R; 85-88; CANR 33;
MTCW

Griffin, Gerald 1803-1840 .... **NCLC 7**

Griffin, John Howard 1920-1980.... **CLC 68**
See also AITN 1; CA 1-4R; 101; CANR 2

Griffin, Peter .... **CLC 39**

Griffiths, Trevor 1935- .... **CLC 13, 52**
See also CA 97-100; CANR 45; DLB 13

Grigson, Geoffrey (Edward Harvey)
1905-1985 .... **CLC 7, 39**
See also CA 25-28R; 118; CANR 20, 33;
DLB 27; MTCW

Grillparzer, Franz 1791-1872...... **NCLC 1**
See also DLB 133

Grimble, Reverend Charles James
See Eliot, T(homas) S(tearns)

Grimke, Charlotte L(ottie) Forten
1837(?)-1914
See Forten, Charlotte L.
See also BW 1; CA 117; 124

Grimm, Jacob Ludwig Karl
1785-1863 .... **NCLC 3**
See also DLB 90; MAICYA; SATA 22

Grimm, Wilhelm Karl 1786-1859 .. **NCLC 3**
See also DLB 90; MAICYA; SATA 22

Grimmelshausen, Johann Jakob Christoffel
von 1621-1676 .... **LC 6**

Grindel, Eugene 1895-1952
See Eluard, Paul
See also CA 104

Grisham, John 1955(?)- .... **CLC 84**
See also CA 138

Grossman, David 1954- .... **CLC 67**
See also CA 138

Grossman, Vasily (Semenovich)
1905-1964 .... **CLC 41**
See also CA 124; 130; MTCW

Grove, Frederick Philip .... **TCLC 4**
See also Greve, Felix Paul (Berthold
Friedrich)
See also DLB 92

Grubb
See Crumb, R(obert)

Grumbach, Doris (Isaac)
1918- .... **CLC 13, 22, 64**
See also CA 5-8R; CAAS 2; CANR 9, 42

Grundtvig, Nicolai Frederik Severin
1783-1872 .... **NCLC 1**

Grunge
See Crumb, R(obert)

Grunwald, Lisa 1959- .... **CLC 44**
See also CA 120

Guare, John 1938- .... **CLC 8, 14, 29, 67**
See also CA 73-76; CANR 21; DLB 7;
MTCW

Gudjonsson, Halldor Kiljan 1902-
See Laxness, Halldor
See also CA 103

Guenter, Erich
See Eich, Guenter

Guest, Barbara 1920-............. **CLC 34**
See also CA 25-28R; CANR 11, 44; DLB 5

Guest, Judith (Ann) 1936-....... **CLC 8, 30**
See also AAYA 7; CA 77-80; CANR 15;
MTCW

Guild, Nicholas M. 1944-......... **CLC 33**
See also CA 93-96

Guillemin, Jacques
See Sartre, Jean-Paul

Guillen, Jorge 1893-1984 .... **CLC 11**
See also CA 89-92; 112; DLB 108; HW

Guillen (y Batista), Nicolas (Cristobal)
1902-1989 ..... **CLC 48, 79; BLC; HLC**
See also BW 2; CA 116; 125; 129; HW

Guillevic, (Eugene) 1907-.......... **CLC 33**
See also CA 93-96

Guillois
See Desnos, Robert

Guiney, Louise Imogen
1861-1920 .... **TCLC 41**
See also DLB 54

Guiraldes, Ricardo (Guillermo)
1886-1927 .... **TCLC 39**
See also CA 131; HW; MTCW

Gunn, Bill .... **CLC 5**
See also Gunn, William Harrison
See also DLB 38

Gunn, Thom(son William)
1929- .... **CLC 3, 6, 18, 32, 81**
See also CA 17-20R; CANR 9, 33;
CDBLB 1960 to Present; DLB 27;
MTCW

Gunn, William Harrison 1934(?)-1989
See Gunn, Bill
See also AITN 1; BW 1; CA 13-16R; 128;
CANR 12, 25

Gunnars, Kristjana 1948-......... **CLC 69**
See also CA 113; DLB 60

Gurganus, Allan 1947-............ **CLC 70**
See also BEST 90:1; CA 135

Gurney, A(lbert) R(amsdell), Jr.
1930- .... **CLC 32, 50, 54**
See also CA 77-80; CANR 32

Gurney, Ivor (Bertie) 1890-1937... **TCLC 33**

Gurney, Peter
See Gurney, A(lbert) R(amsdell), Jr.

Guro, Elena .... **TCLC 56**

Gustafson, Ralph (Barker) 1909-.... **CLC 36**
See also CA 21-24R; CANR 8, 45; DLB 88

Gut, Gom
See Simenon, Georges (Jacques Christian)

Guthrie, A(lfred) B(ertram), Jr.
1901-1991 .... **CLC 23**
See also CA 57-60; 134; CANR 24; DLB 6;
SATA 62; SATA-Obit 67

Guthrie, Isobel
See Grieve, C(hristopher) M(urray)

Guthrie, Woodrow Wilson 1912-1967
See Guthrie, Woody
See also CA 113; 93-96

Guthrie, Woody .... **CLC 35**
See also Guthrie, Woodrow Wilson

Guy, Rosa (Cuthbert) 1928- .... **CLC 26**
See also AAYA 4; BW 2; CA 17-20R;
CANR 14, 34; CLR 13; DLB 33; JRDA;
MAICYA; SATA 14, 62

Gwendolyn
See Bennett, (Enoch) Arnold

H. D. .... **CLC 3, 8, 14, 31, 34, 73; PC 5**
See also Doolittle, Hilda

Haavikko, Paavo Juhani
1931- .... **CLC 18, 34**
See also CA 106

Habbema, Koos
See Heijermans, Herman

Hacker, Marilyn 1942- .... **CLC 5, 9, 23, 72**
See also CA 77-80; DLB 120

Haggard, H(enry) Rider
1856-1925 .... **TCLC 11**
See also CA 108; DLB 70; SATA 16

Haig, Fenil
See Ford, Ford Madox

Haig-Brown, Roderick (Langmere)
1908-1976 .... **CLC 21**
See also CA 5-8R; 69-72; CANR 4, 38;
CLR 31; DLB 88; MAICYA; SATA 12

Hailey, Arthur 1920- .... **CLC 5**
See also AITN 2; BEST 90:3; CA 1-4R;
CANR 2, 36; DLB 88; DLBY 82; MTCW

Hailey, Elizabeth Forsythe 1938- ... **CLC 40**
See also CA 93-96; CAAS 1; CANR 15

Haines, John (Meade) 1924- .... **CLC 58**
See also CA 17-20R; CANR 13, 34; DLB 5

Haldeman, Joe (William) 1943- ..... **CLC 61**
See also CA 53-56; CANR 6; DLB 8

Haley, Alex(ander Murray Palmer)
1921-1992 .... **CLC 8, 12, 76; BLC; DA**
See also BW 2; CA 77-80; 136; DLB 38;
MTCW

Haliburton, Thomas Chandler
1796-1865 .... **NCLC 15**
See also DLB 11, 99

Hall, Donald (Andrew, Jr.)
1928- .... **CLC 1, 13, 37, 59**
See also CA 5-8R; CAAS 7; CANR 2, 44;
DLB 5; SATA 23

Hall, Frederic Sauser
See Sauser-Hall, Frederic

Hall, James
See Kuttner, Henry

Hall, James Norman 1887-1951 ... **TCLC 23**
See also CA 123; SATA 21

Hall, (Marguerite) Radclyffe
1886(?)-1943 .... **TCLC 12**
See also CA 110

Hall, Rodney 1935- .... **CLC 51**
See also CA 109

Halliday, Michael
See Creasey, John

Halpern, Daniel 1945- .... **CLC 14**
See also CA 33-36R

Hamburger, Michael (Peter Leopold)
1924- .... **CLC 5, 14**
See also CA 5-8R; CAAS 4; CANR 2;
DLB 27

Hamill, Pete 1935- .... **CLC 10**
See also CA 25-28R; CANR 18

Hamilton, Clive
See Lewis, C(live) S(taples)

Hamilton, Edmond 1904-1977 ...... **CLC 1**
See also CA 1-4R; CANR 3; DLB 8

Hamilton, Eugene (Jacob) Lee
See Lee-Hamilton, Eugene (Jacob)

Hamilton, Franklin
See Silverberg, Robert

Hamilton, Gail
See Corcoran, Barbara

Hamilton, Mollie
See Kaye, M(ary) M(argaret)

Hamilton, (Anthony Walter) Patrick
1904-1962 .... **CLC 51**
See also CA 113; DLB 10

Hamilton, Virginia 1936- .... **CLC 26**
See also AAYA 2; BW 2; CA 25-28R;
CANR 20, 37; CLR 1, 11; DLB 33, 52;
JRDA; MAICYA; MTCW; SATA 4, 56

Hammett, (Samuel) Dashiell
1894-1961 .... **CLC 3, 5, 10, 19, 47**
See also AITN 1; CA 81-84; CANR 42;
CDALB 1929-1941; DLBD 6; MTCW

Hammon, Jupiter
1711(?)-1800(?) .... **NCLC 5; BLC**
See also DLB 31, 50

Hammond, Keith
See Kuttner, Henry

Hamner, Earl (Henry), Jr. 1923- ... **CLC 12**
See also AITN 2; CA 73-76; DLB 6

Hampton, Christopher (James)
1946- .... **CLC 4**
See also CA 25-28R; DLB 13; MTCW

Hamsun, Knut .... **TCLC 2, 14, 49**
See also Pedersen, Knut

Handke, Peter 1942- .. **CLC 5, 8, 10, 15, 38**
See also CA 77-80; CANR 33; DLB 85,
124; MTCW

Hanley, James 1901-1985 ... **CLC 3, 5, 8, 13**
See also CA 73-76; 117; CANR 36; MTCW

Hannah, Barry 1942- .... **CLC 23, 38**
See also CA 108; 110; CANR 43; DLB 6;
MTCW

Hannon, Ezra
See Hunter, Evan

Hansberry, Lorraine (Vivian)
1930-1965 ...... **CLC 17, 62; BLC; DA; DC 2**
See also BW 1; CA 109; 25-28R; CABS 3;
CDALB 1941-1968; DLB 7, 38; MTCW

Hansen, Joseph 1923- .... **CLC 38**
See also CA 29-32R; CAAS 17; CANR 16,
44

Hansen, Martin A. 1909-1955 ..... **TCLC 32**

Hanson, Kenneth O(stlin) 1922- .... **CLC 13**
See also CA 53-56; CANR 7

Hardwick, Elizabeth 1916- .... **CLC 13**
See also CA 5-8R; CANR 3, 32; DLB 6;
MTCW

Hardy, Thomas
1840-1928 ..... **TCLC 4, 10, 18, 32, 48,
53; DA; PC 8; SSC 2; WLC**
See also CA 104; 123; CDBLB 1890-1914;
DLB 18, 19, 135; MTCW

Hare, David 1947- .... **CLC 29, 58**
See also CA 97-100; CANR 39; DLB 13;
MTCW

Harford, Henry
See Hudson, W(illiam) H(enry)

Hargrave, Leonie
See Disch, Thomas M(ichael)

Harjo, Joy 1951- .... **CLC 83**
See also CA 114; CANR 35; DLB 120

Harlan, Louis R(udolph) 1922- ..... **CLC 34**
See also CA 21-24R; CANR 25

Harling, Robert 1951(?)- .... **CLC 53**

Harmon, William (Ruth) 1938- ..... **CLC 38**
See also CA 33-36R; CANR 14, 32, 35;
SATA 65

Harper, F. E. W.
See Harper, Frances Ellen Watkins

Harper, Frances E. W.
See Harper, Frances Ellen Watkins

Harper, Frances E. Watkins
See Harper, Frances Ellen Watkins

Harper, Frances Ellen
See Harper, Frances Ellen Watkins

Harper, Frances Ellen Watkins
1825-1911 .... **TCLC 14; BLC**
See also BW 1; CA 111; 125; DLB 50

Harper, Michael S(teven) 1938- .. **CLC 7, 22**
See also BW 1; CA 33-36R; CANR 24;
DLB 41

Harper, Mrs. F. E. W.
See Harper, Frances Ellen Watkins

Harris, Christie (Lucy) Irwin
1907- .... **CLC 12**
See also CA 5-8R; CANR 6; DLB 88;
JRDA; MAICYA; SAAS 10; SATA 6, 74

Harris, Frank 1856(?)-1931 ...... **TCLC 24**
See also CA 109

Harris, George Washington
1814-1869 .... **NCLC 23**
See also DLB 3, 11

Harris, Joel Chandler 1848-1908 ... **TCLC 2**
See also CA 104; 137; DLB 11, 23, 42, 78,
91; MAICYA; YABC 1

Harris, John (Wyndham Parkes Lucas)
Beynon 1903-1969 .... **CLC 19**
See also CA 102; 89-92

Harris, MacDonald
See Heiney, Donald (William)

Harris, Mark 1922- .... **CLC 19**
See also CA 5-8R; CAAS 3; CANR 2;
DLB 2; DLBY 80

Harris, (Theodore) Wilson 1921- .... **CLC 25**
See also BW 2; CA 65-68; CAAS 16;
CANR 11, 27; DLB 117; MTCW

Harrison, Elizabeth Cavanna 1909-
See Cavanna, Betty
See also CA 9-12R; CANR 6, 27

Harrison, Harry (Max) 1925-...... **CLC 42**
See also CA 1-4R; CANR 5, 21; DLB 8;
SATA 4

Harrison, James (Thomas)
1937-............... **CLC 6, 14, 33, 66**
See also CA 13-16R; CANR 8; DLBY 82

Harrison, Kathryn 1961-.......... **CLC 70**
See also CA 144

Harrison, Tony 1937-............. **CLC 43**
See also CA 65-68; CANR 44; DLB 40;
MTCW

Harriss, Will(ard Irvin) 1922-...... **CLC 34**
See also CA 111

Harson, Sley
See Ellison, Harlan

Hart, Ellis
See Ellison, Harlan

Hart, Josephine 1942(?)-.......... **CLC 70**
See also CA 138

Hart, Moss 1904-1961............. **CLC 66**
See also CA 109; 89-92; DLB 7

Harte, (Francis) Bret(t)
1836(?)-1902 .... **TCLC 1, 25; DA;
SSC 8; WLC**
See also CA 104; 140; CDALB 1865-1917;
DLB 12, 64, 74, 79; SATA 26

Hartley, L(eslie) P(oles)
1895-1972 .... **CLC 2, 22**
See also CA 45-48; 37-40R; CANR 33;
DLB 15, 139; MTCW

Hartman, Geoffrey H. 1929-....... **CLC 27**
See also CA 117; 125; DLB 67

Haruf, Kent 19(?)- .... **CLC 34**

Harwood, Ronald 1934-.......... **CLC 32**
See also CA 1-4R; CANR 4; DLB 13

Hasek, Jaroslav (Matej Frantisek)
1883-1923 .... **TCLC 4**
See also CA 104; 129; MTCW

Hass, Robert 1941-............ **CLC 18, 39**
See also CA 111; CANR 30; DLB 105

Hastings, Hudson
See Kuttner, Henry

Hastings, Selina................. **CLC 44**

Hatteras, Amelia
See Mencken, H(enry) L(ouis)

Hatteras, Owen................. **TCLC 18**
See also Mencken, H(enry) L(ouis); Nathan,
George Jean

Hauptmann, Gerhart (Johann Robert)
1862-1946 .... **TCLC 4**
See also CA 104; DLB 66, 118

Havel, Vaclav 1936-........ **CLC 25, 58, 65**
See also CA 104; CANR 36; MTCW

Haviaras, Stratis................. **CLC 33**
See also Chaviaras, Strates

Hawes, Stephen 1475(?)-1523(?) ..... **LC 17**

Hawkes, John (Clendennin Burne, Jr.)
1925- ...... **CLC 1, 2, 3, 4, 7, 9, 14, 15,
27, 49**
See also CA 1-4R; CANR 2; DLB 2, 7;
DLBY 80; MTCW

Hawking, S. W.
See Hawking, Stephen W(illiam)

Hawking, Stephen W(illiam)
1942-...................... **CLC 63**
See also BEST 89:1; CA 126; 129

Hawthorne, Julian 1846-1934 ..... **TCLC 25**

Hawthorne, Nathaniel
1804-1864 ...... **NCLC 39; DA; SSC 3;
WLC**
See also CDALB 1640-1865; DLB 1, 74;
YABC 2

Haxton, Josephine Ayres 1921- .... **CLC 73**
See also CA 115; CANR 41

Hayaseca y Eizaguirre, Jorge
See Echegaray (y Eizaguirre), Jose (Maria
Waldo)

Hayashi Fumiko 1904-1951....... **TCLC 27**

Haycraft, Anna
See Ellis, Alice Thomas
See also CA 122

Hayden, Robert E(arl)
1913-1980 ...... **CLC 5, 9, 14, 37; BLC;
DA; PC 6**
See also BW 1; CA 69-72; 97-100; CABS 2;
CANR 24; CDALB 1941-1968; DLB 5,
76; MTCW; SATA 19, 26

Hayford, J(oseph) E(phraim) Casely
See Casely-Hayford, J(oseph) E(phraim)

Hayman, Ronald 1932-............ **CLC 44**
See also CA 25-28R; CANR 18

Haywood, Eliza (Fowler)
1693(?)-1756 .... **LC 1**

Hazlitt, William 1778-1830...... **NCLC 29**
See also DLB 110

Hazzard, Shirley 1931- .... **CLC 18**
See also CA 9-12R; CANR 4; DLBY 82;
MTCW

Head, Bessie 1937-1986... **CLC 25, 67; BLC**
See also BW 2; CA 29-32R; 119; CANR 25;
DLB 117; MTCW

Headon, (Nicky) Topper 1956(?)- ... **CLC 30**
See also Clash, The

Heaney, Seamus (Justin)
1939- .... **CLC 5, 7, 14, 25, 37, 74**
See also CA 85-88; CANR 25;
CDBLB 1960 to Present; DLB 40;
MTCW

Hearn, (Patricio) Lafcadio (Tessima Carlos)
1850-1904 .... **TCLC 9**
See also CA 105; DLB 12, 78

Hearne, Vicki 1946-.............. **CLC 56**
See also CA 139

Hearon, Shelby 1931-............. **CLC 63**
See also AITN 2; CA 25-28R; CANR 18

Heat-Moon, William Least......... **CLC 29**
See also Trogdon, William (Lewis)
See also AAYA 9

Hebbel, Friedrich 1813-1863..... **NCLC 43**
See also DLB 129

Hebert, Anne 1916- .... **CLC 4, 13, 29**
See also CA 85-88; DLB 68; MTCW

Hecht, Anthony (Evan)
1923- .... **CLC 8, 13, 19**
See also CA 9-12R; CANR 6; DLB 5

Hecht, Ben 1894-1964 .... **CLC 8**
See also CA 85-88; DLB 7, 9, 25, 26, 28, 86

Hedayat, Sadeq 1903-1951....... **TCLC 21**
See also CA 120

Hegel, Georg Wilhelm Friedrich
1770-1831 .... **NCLC 46**
See also DLB 90

Heidegger, Martin 1889-1976 ...... **CLC 24**
See also CA 81-84; 65-68; CANR 34;
MTCW

Heidenstam, (Carl Gustaf) Verner von
1859-1940 .... **TCLC 5**
See also CA 104

Heifner, Jack 1946-.............. **CLC 11**
See also CA 105

Heijermans, Herman 1864-1924 ... **TCLC 24**
See also CA 123

Heilbrun, Carolyn G(old) 1926-..... **CLC 25**
See also CA 45-48; CANR 1, 28

Heine, Heinrich 1797-1856 .... **NCLC 4**
See also DLB 90

Heinemann, Larry (Curtiss) 1944- .. **CLC 50**
See also CA 110; CANR 31; DLBD 9

Heiney, Donald (William)
1921-1993 .... **CLC 9**
See also CA 1-4R; 142; CANR 3

Heinlein, Robert A(nson)
1907-1988 ...... **CLC 1, 3, 8, 14, 26, 55**
See also CA 1-4R; 125; CANR 1, 20;
DLB 8; JRDA; MAICYA; MTCW;
SATA 9, 56, 69

Helforth, John
See Doolittle, Hilda

Hellenhofferu, Vojtech Kapristian z
See Hasek, Jaroslav (Matej Frantisek)

Heller, Joseph
1923- .... **CLC 1, 3, 5, 8, 11, 36, 63; DA;
WLC**
See also AITN 1; CA 5-8R; CABS 1;
CANR 8, 42; DLB 2, 28; DLBY 80;
MTCW

Hellman, Lillian (Florence)
1906-1984 ...... **CLC 2, 4, 8, 14, 18, 34,
44, 52; DC 1**
See also AITN 1, 2; CA 13-16R; 112;
CANR 33; DLB 7; DLBY 84; MTCW

Helprin, Mark 1947- ..... **CLC 7, 10, 22, 32**
See also CA 81-84; DLBY 85; MTCW

Helvetius, Claude-Adrien
1715-1771 .... **LC 26**

Helyar, Jane Penelope Josephine 1933-
See Poole, Josephine
See also CA 21-24R; CANR 10, 26

Hemans, Felicia 1793-1835 ...... **NCLC 29**
See also DLB 96

Hemingway, Ernest (Miller)
1899-1961 .... **CLC 1, 3, 6, 8, 10, 13, 19,
30, 34, 39, 41, 44, 50, 61, 80; DA; SSC 1;
WLC**
See also CA 77-80; CANR 34;
CDALB 1917-1929; DLB 4, 9, 102;
DLBD 1; DLBY 81, 87; MTCW

Hempel, Amy 1951-.............. **CLC 39**
See also CA 118; 137

Isaacs, Susan 1943- . . . . **CLC 32**
See also BEST 89:1; CA 89-92; CANR 20,
41; MTCW

Isherwood, Christopher (William Bradshaw)
1904-1986 . . . . **CLC 1, 9, 11, 14, 44**
See also CA 13-16R; 117; CANR 35;
DLB 15; DLBY 86; MTCW

Ishiguro, Kazuo 1954- . . . . . . **CLC 27, 56, 59**
See also BEST 90:2; CA 120; MTCW

Ishikawa Takuboku
1886(?)-1912 . . . . **TCLC 15; PC 10**
See also CA 113

Iskander, Fazil 1929- . . . . **CLC 47**
See also CA 102

Ivan IV 1530-1584 . . . . **LC 17**

Ivanov, Vyacheslav Ivanovich
1866-1949 . . . . **TCLC 33**
See also CA 122

Ivask, Ivar Vidrik 1927-1992 . . . . . . **CLC 14**
See also CA 37-40R; 139; CANR 24

Jackson, Daniel
See Wingrove, David (John)

Jackson, Jesse 1908-1983 . . . . **CLC 12**
See also BW 1; CA 25-28R; 109; CANR 27;
CLR 28; MAICYA; SATA 2, 29, 48

Jackson, Laura (Riding) 1901-1991
See Riding, Laura
See also CA 65-68; 135; CANR 28; DLB 48

Jackson, Sam
See Trumbo, Dalton

Jackson, Sara
See Wingrove, David (John)

Jackson, Shirley
1919-1965 . . . . . **CLC 11, 60; DA; SSC 9;
WLC**
See also AAYA 9; CA 1-4R; 25-28R;
CANR 4; CDALB 1941-1968; DLB 6;
SATA 2

Jacob, (Cyprien-)Max 1876-1944 . . . **TCLC 6**
See also CA 104

Jacobs, Jim 1942- . . . . **CLC 12**
See also CA 97-100

Jacobs, W(illiam) W(ymark)
1863-1943 . . . . **TCLC 22**
See also CA 121; DLB 135

Jacobsen, Jens Peter 1847-1885 . . **NCLC 34**

Jacobsen, Josephine 1908- . . . . **CLC 48**
See also CA 33-36R; CAAS 18; CANR 23

Jacobson, Dan 1929- . . . . **CLC 4, 14**
See also CA 1-4R; CANR 2, 25; DLB 14;
MTCW

Jacqueline
See Carpentier (y Valmont), Alejo

Jagger, Mick 1944- . . . . **CLC 17**

Jakes, John (William) 1932- . . . . **CLC 29**
See also BEST 89:4; CA 57-60; CANR 10,
43; DLBY 83; MTCW; SATA 62

James, Andrew
See Kirkup, James

James, C(yril) L(ionel) R(obert)
1901-1989 . . . . **CLC 33**
See also BW 2; CA 117; 125; 128; DLB 125;
MTCW

James, Daniel (Lewis) 1911-1988
See Santiago, Danny
See also CA 125

James, Dynely
See Mayne, William (James Carter)

James, Henry
1843-1916 . . . . . . **TCLC 2, 11, 24, 40, 47;
DA; SSC 8; WLC**
See also CA 104; 132; CDALB 1865-1917;
DLB 12, 71, 74; MTCW

James, M. R.
See James, Montague (Rhodes)

James, Montague (Rhodes)
1862-1936 . . . . **TCLC 6; SSC 16**
See also CA 104

James, P. D. . . . . **CLC 18, 46**
See also White, Phyllis Dorothy James
See also BEST 90:2; CDBLB 1960 to
Present; DLB 87

James, Philip
See Moorcock, Michael (John)

James, William 1842-1910 . . . . . **TCLC 15, 32**
See also CA 109

James I 1394-1437 . . . . **LC 20**

Jameson, Anna 1794-1860 . . . . **NCLC 43**
See also DLB 99

Jami, Nur al-Din 'Abd al-Rahman
1414-1492 . . . . **LC 9**

Jandl, Ernst 1925- . . . . **CLC 34**

Janowitz, Tama 1957- . . . . **CLC 43**
See also CA 106

Jarrell, Randall
1914-1965 . . . . **CLC 1, 2, 6, 9, 13, 49**
See also CA 5-8R; 25-28R; CABS 2;
CANR 6, 34; CDALB 1941-1968; CLR 6;
DLB 48, 52; MAICYA; MTCW; SATA 7

Jarry, Alfred 1873-1907 . . . . **TCLC 2, 14**
See also CA 104

Jarvis, E. K.
See Bloch, Robert (Albert); Ellison, Harlan;
Silverberg, Robert

Jeake, Samuel, Jr.
See Aiken, Conrad (Potter)

Jean Paul 1763-1825 . . . . **NCLC 7**

Jeffers, (John) Robinson
1887-1962 . . . . **CLC 2, 3, 11, 15, 54; DA;
WLC**
See also CA 85-88; CANR 35;
CDALB 1917-1929; DLB 45; MTCW

Jefferson, Janet
See Mencken, H(enry) L(ouis)

Jefferson, Thomas 1743-1826 . . . . **NCLC 11**
See also CDALB 1640-1865; DLB 31

Jeffrey, Francis 1773-1850 . . . . **NCLC 33**
See also DLB 107

Jelakowitch, Ivan
See Heijermans, Herman

Jellicoe, (Patricia) Ann 1927- . . . . . . **CLC 27**
See also CA 85-88; DLB 13

Jen, Gish . . . . **CLC 70**
See also Jen, Lillian

Jen, Lillian 1956(?)-
See Jen, Gish
See also CA 135

Jenkins, (John) Robin 1912- . . . . **CLC 52**
See also CA 1-4R; CANR 1; DLB 14

Jennings, Elizabeth (Joan)
1926- . . . . **CLC 5, 14**
See also CA 61-64; CAAS 5; CANR 8, 39;
DLB 27; MTCW; SATA 66

Jennings, Waylon 1937- . . . . **CLC 21**

Jensen, Johannes V. 1873-1950 . . . . **TCLC 41**

Jensen, Laura (Linnea) 1948- . . . . . . **CLC 37**
See also CA 103

Jerome, Jerome K(lapka)
1859-1927 . . . . **TCLC 23**
See also CA 119; DLB 10, 34, 135

Jerrold, Douglas William
1803-1857 . . . . **NCLC 2**

Jewett, (Theodora) Sarah Orne
1849-1909 . . . . **TCLC 1, 22; SSC 6**
See also CA 108; 127; DLB 12, 74;
SATA 15

Jewsbury, Geraldine (Endsor)
1812-1880 . . . . **NCLC 22**
See also DLB 21

Jhabvala, Ruth Prawer
1927- . . . . **CLC 4, 8, 29**
See also CA 1-4R; CANR 2, 29; DLB 139;
MTCW

Jiles, Paulette 1943- . . . . **CLC 13, 58**
See also CA 101

Jimenez (Mantecon), Juan Ramon
1881-1958 . . . . **TCLC 4; HLC; PC 7**
See also CA 104; 131; DLB 134; HW;
MTCW

Jimenez, Juan Ramon 1881-1958
See Jimenez (Mantecon), Juan Ramon

Jimenez, Ramon
See Jimenez (Mantecon), Juan Ramon

Jimenez Mantecon, Juan
See Jimenez (Mantecon), Juan Ramon

Joel, Billy . . . . **CLC 26**
See also Joel, William Martin

Joel, William Martin 1949-
See Joel, Billy
See also CA 108

John of the Cross, St. 1542-1591 . . . . **LC 18**

Johnson, B(ryan) S(tanley William)
1933-1973 . . . . **CLC 6, 9**
See also CA 9-12R; 53-56; CANR 9;
DLB 14, 40

Johnson, Benj. F. of Boo
See Riley, James Whitcomb

Johnson, Benjamin F. of Boo
See Riley, James Whitcomb

Johnson, Charles (Richard)
1948- . . . . **CLC 7, 51, 65; BLC**
See also BW 2; CA 116; CAAS 18;
CANR 42; DLB 33

Johnson, Denis 1949- . . . . **CLC 52**
See also CA 117; 121; DLB 120

Johnson, Diane 1934- . . . . **CLC 5, 13, 48**
See also CA 41-44R; CANR 17, 40;
DLBY 80; MTCW

Johnson, Eyvind (Olof Verner)
1900-1976 . . . . **CLC 14**
See also CA 73-76; 69-72; CANR 34

King, Martin Luther, Jr.
        1929-1968 . . . . **CLC 83; BLC; DA**
    See also BW 2; CA 25-28; CANR 27, 44;
    CAP 2; MTCW; SATA 14

King, Stephen (Edwin)
        1947- . . . . **CLC 12, 26, 37, 61**
    See also AAYA 1; BEST 90:1; CA 61-64;
    CANR 1, 30; DLB 143; DLBY 80;
    JRDA; MTCW; SATA 9, 55

King, Steve
    See King, Stephen (Edwin)

Kingman, Lee . . . . **CLC 17**
    See also Natti, (Mary) Lee
    See also SAAS 3; SATA 1, 67

Kingsley, Charles 1819-1875 . . . . . **NCLC 35**
    See also DLB 21, 32; YABC 2

Kingsley, Sidney 1906- . . . . **CLC 44**
    See also CA 85-88; DLB 7

Kingsolver, Barbara 1955- . . . . . . **CLC 55, 81**
    See also CA 129; 134

Kingston, Maxine (Ting Ting) Hong
        1940- . . . . **CLC 12, 19, 58**
    See also AAYA 8; CA 69-72; CANR 13,
    38; DLBY 80; MTCW; SATA 53

Kinnell, Galway
        1927- . . . . **CLC 1, 2, 3, 5, 13, 29**
    See also CA 9-12R; CANR 10, 34; DLB 5;
    DLBY 87; MTCW

Kinsella, Thomas 1928- . . . . **CLC 4, 19**
    See also CA 17-20R; CANR 15; DLB 27;
    MTCW

Kinsella, W(illiam) P(atrick)
        1935- . . . . **CLC 27, 43**
    See also AAYA 7; CA 97-100; CAAS 7;
    CANR 21, 35; MTCW

Kipling, (Joseph) Rudyard
        1865-1936 . . . . . . **TCLC 8, 17; DA; PC 3;**
                                                    SSC 5; WLC
    See also CA 105; 120; CANR 33;
    CDBLB 1890-1914; DLB 19, 34, 141;
    MAICYA; MTCW; YABC 2

Kirkup, James 1918- . . . . **CLC 1**
    See also CA 1-4R; CAAS 4; CANR 2;
    DLB 27; SATA 12

Kirkwood, James 1930(?)-1989 . . . . . . **CLC 9**
    See also AITN 2; CA 1-4R; 128; CANR 6,
    40

Kis, Danilo 1935-1989 . . . . **CLC 57**
    See also CA 109; 118; 129; MTCW

Kivi, Aleksis 1834-1872 . . . . **NCLC 30**

Kizer, Carolyn (Ashley)
        1925- . . . . **CLC 15, 39, 80**
    See also CA 65-68; CAAS 5; CANR 24;
    DLB 5

Klabund 1890-1928 . . . . **TCLC 44**
    See also DLB 66

Klappert, Peter 1942- . . . . **CLC 57**
    See also CA 33-36R; DLB 5

Klein, A(braham) M(oses)
        1909-1972 . . . . **CLC 19**
    See also CA 101; 37-40R; DLB 68

Klein, Norma 1938-1989 . . . . **CLC 30**
    See also AAYA 2; CA 41-44R; 128;
    CANR 15, 37; CLR 2, 19; JRDA;
    MAICYA; SAAS 1; SATA 7, 57

Klein, T(heodore) E(ibon) D(onald)
        1947- . . . . **CLC 34**
    See also CA 119; CANR 44

Kleist, Heinrich von
        1777-1811 . . . . **NCLC 2, 37**
    See also DLB 90

Klima, Ivan 1931- . . . . **CLC 56**
    See also CA 25-28R; CANR 17

Klimentov, Andrei Platonovich 1899-1951
    See Platonov, Andrei
    See also CA 108

Klinger, Friedrich Maximilian von
        1752-1831 . . . . **NCLC 1**
    See also DLB 94

Klopstock, Friedrich Gottlieb
        1724-1803 . . . . **NCLC 11**
    See also DLB 97

Knebel, Fletcher 1911-1993 . . . . **CLC 14**
    See also AITN 1; CA 1-4R; 140; CAAS 3;
    CANR 1, 36; SATA 36; SATA-Obit 75

Knickerbocker, Diedrich
    See Irving, Washington

Knight, Etheridge
        1931-1991 . . . . **CLC 40; BLC**
    See also BW 1; CA 21-24R; 133; CANR 23;
    DLB 41

Knight, Sarah Kemble 1666-1727 . . . . . **LC 7**
    See also DLB 24

Knister, Raymond 1899-1932 . . . . . **TCLC 56**
    See also DLB 68

Knowles, John
        1926- . . . . **CLC 1, 4, 10, 26; DA**
    See also AAYA 10; CA 17-20R; CANR 40;
    CDALB 1968-1988; DLB 6; MTCW;
    SATA 8

Knox, Calvin M.
    See Silverberg, Robert

Knye, Cassandra
    See Disch, Thomas M(ichael)

Koch, C(hristopher) J(ohn) 1932- . . . **CLC 42**
    See also CA 127

Koch, Christopher
    See Koch, C(hristopher) J(ohn)

Koch, Kenneth 1925- . . . . **CLC 5, 8, 44**
    See also CA 1-4R; CANR 6, 36; DLB 5;
    SATA 65

Kochanowski, Jan 1530-1584 . . . . **LC 10**

Kock, Charles Paul de
        1794-1871 . . . . **NCLC 16**

Koda Shigeyuki 1867-1947
    See Rohan, Koda
    See also CA 121

Koestler, Arthur
        1905-1983 . . . . **CLC 1, 3, 6, 8, 15, 33**
    See also CA 1-4R; 109; CANR 1, 33;
    CDBLB 1945-1960; DLBY 83; MTCW

Kogawa, Joy Nozomi 1935- . . . . **CLC 78**
    See also CA 101; CANR 19

Kohout, Pavel 1928- . . . . **CLC 13**
    See also CA 45-48; CANR 3

Koizumi, Yakumo
    See Hearn, (Patricio) Lafcadio (Tessima
    Carlos)

Kolmar, Gertrud 1894-1943 . . . . . . **TCLC 40**

Konrad, George
    See Konrad, Gyoergy

Konrad, Gyoergy 1933- . . . . . . **CLC 4, 10, 73**
    See also CA 85-88

Konwicki, Tadeusz 1926- . . . . . **CLC 8, 28, 54**
    See also CA 101; CAAS 9; CANR 39;
    MTCW

Koontz, Dean R(ay) 1945- . . . . **CLC 78**
    See also AAYA 9; BEST 89:3, 90:2;
    CA 108; CANR 19, 36; MTCW

Kopit, Arthur (Lee) 1937- . . . . **CLC 1, 18, 33**
    See also AITN 1; CA 81-84; CABS 3;
    DLB 7; MTCW

Kops, Bernard 1926- . . . . **CLC 4**
    See also CA 5-8R; DLB 13

Kornbluth, C(yril) M. 1923-1958 . . . . **TCLC 8**
    See also CA 105; DLB 8

Korolenko, V. G.
    See Korolenko, Vladimir Galaktionovich

Korolenko, Vladimir
    See Korolenko, Vladimir Galaktionovich

Korolenko, Vladimir G.
    See Korolenko, Vladimir Galaktionovich

Korolenko, Vladimir Galaktionovich
        1853-1921 . . . . **TCLC 22**
    See also CA 121

Kosinski, Jerzy (Nikodem)
        1933-1991 . . . . **CLC 1, 2, 3, 6, 10, 15, 53,**
                                                                                70
    See also CA 17-20R; 134; CANR 9; DLB 2;
    DLBY 82; MTCW

Kostelanetz, Richard (Cory) 1940- . . **CLC 28**
    See also CA 13-16R; CAAS 8; CANR 38

Kostrowitzki, Wilhelm Apollinaris de
        1880-1918
    See Apollinaire, Guillaume
    See also CA 104

Kotlowitz, Robert 1924- . . . . **CLC 4**
    See also CA 33-36R; CANR 36

Kotzebue, August (Friedrich Ferdinand) von
        1761-1819 . . . . **NCLC 25**
    See also DLB 94

Kotzwinkle, William 1938- . . . **CLC 5, 14, 35**
    See also CA 45-48; CANR 3, 44; CLR 6;
    MAICYA; SATA 24, 70

Kozol, Jonathan 1936- . . . . **CLC 17**
    See also CA 61-64; CANR 16, 45

Kozoll, Michael 1940(?)- . . . . **CLC 35**

Kramer, Kathryn 19(?)- . . . . **CLC 34**

Kramer, Larry 1935- . . . . **CLC 42**
    See also CA 124; 126

Krasicki, Ignacy 1735-1801 . . . . **NCLC 8**

Krasinski, Zygmunt 1812-1859 . . . . **NCLC 4**

Kraus, Karl 1874-1936 . . . . **TCLC 5**
    See also CA 104; DLB 118

Kreve (Mickevicius), Vincas
        1882-1954 . . . . **TCLC 27**

Kristeva, Julia 1941- . . . . **CLC 77**

Kristofferson, Kris 1936- . . . . **CLC 26**
    See also CA 104

Krizanc, John 1956- . . . . **CLC 57**

Krleza, Miroslav 1893-1981 . . . . **CLC 8**
    See also CA 97-100; 105

Larsen, Eric 1941- . . . . **CLC 55**
See also CA 132

Larsen, Nella 1891-1964 . . . . . **CLC 37; BLC**
See also BW 1; CA 125; DLB 51

Larson, Charles R(aymond) 1938- . . . **CLC 31**
See also CA 53-56; CANR 4

Latham, Jean Lee 1902- . . . . **CLC 12**
See also AITN 1; CA 5-8R; CANR 7;
MAICYA; SATA 2, 68

Latham, Mavis
See Clark, Mavis Thorpe

Lathen, Emma . . . . **CLC 2**
See also Hennissart, Martha; Latsis, Mary
J(ane)

Lathrop, Francis
See Leiber, Fritz (Reuter, Jr.)

Latsis, Mary J(ane)
See Lathen, Emma
See also CA 85-88

Lattimore, Richmond (Alexander)
1906-1984 . . . . **CLC 3**
See also CA 1-4R; 112; CANR 1

Laughlin, James 1914- . . . . **CLC 49**
See also CA 21-24R; CANR 9; DLB 48

Laurence, (Jean) Margaret (Wemyss)
1926-1987 . . **CLC 3, 6, 13, 50, 62; SSC 7**
See also CA 5-8R; 121; CANR 33; DLB 53;
MTCW; SATA 50

Laurent, Antoine 1952- . . . . **CLC 50**

Lauscher, Hermann
See Hesse, Hermann

Lautreamont, Comte de
1846-1870 . . . . **NCLC 12; SSC 14**

Laverty, Donald
See Blish, James (Benjamin)

Lavin, Mary 1912- . . . . . . **CLC 4, 18; SSC 4**
See also CA 9-12R; CANR 33; DLB 15;
MTCW

Lavond, Paul Dennis
See Kornbluth, C(yril) M.; Pohl, Frederik

Lawler, Raymond Evenor 1922- . . . . **CLC 58**
See also CA 103

Lawrence, D(avid) H(erbert Richards)
1885-1930 . . . . **TCLC 2, 9, 16, 33, 48;
DA; SSC 4; WLC**
See also CA 104; 121; CDBLB 1914-1945;
DLB 10, 19, 36, 98; MTCW

Lawrence, T(homas) E(dward)
1888-1935 . . . . **TCLC 18**
See also Dale, Colin
See also CA 115

Lawrence of Arabia
See Lawrence, T(homas) E(dward)

Lawson, Henry (Archibald Hertzberg)
1867-1922 . . . . **TCLC 27**
See also CA 120

Lawton, Dennis
See Faust, Frederick (Schiller)

Laxness, Halldor . . . . **CLC 25**
See also Gudjonsson, Halldor Kiljan

Layamon fl. c. 1200- . . . . **CMLC 10**

Laye, Camara 1928-1980 . . . **CLC 4, 38; BLC**
See also BW 1; CA 85-88; 97-100;
CANR 25; MTCW

Layton, Irving (Peter) 1912- . . . . . **CLC 2, 15**
See also CA 1-4R; CANR 2, 33, 43;
DLB 88; MTCW

Lazarus, Emma 1849-1887 . . . . **NCLC 8**

Lazarus, Felix
See Cable, George Washington

Lazarus, Henry
See Slavitt, David R(ytman)

Lea, Joan
See Neufeld, John (Arthur)

Leacock, Stephen (Butler)
1869-1944 . . . . **TCLC 2**
See also CA 104; 141; DLB 92

Lear, Edward 1812-1888 . . . . **NCLC 3**
See also CLR 1; DLB 32; MAICYA;
SATA 18

Lear, Norman (Milton) 1922- . . . . . . **CLC 12**
See also CA 73-76

Leavis, F(rank) R(aymond)
1895-1978 . . . . **CLC 24**
See also CA 21-24R; 77-80; CANR 44;
MTCW

Leavitt, David 1961- . . . . **CLC 34**
See also CA 116; 122; DLB 130

Leblanc, Maurice (Marie Emile)
1864-1941 . . . . **TCLC 49**
See also CA 110

Lebowitz, Fran(ces Ann)
1951(?)- . . . . **CLC 11, 36**
See also CA 81-84; CANR 14; MTCW

Lebrecht, Peter
See Tieck, (Johann) Ludwig

le Carre, John . . . . **CLC 3, 5, 9, 15, 28**
See also Cornwell, David (John Moore)
See also BEST 89:4; CDBLB 1960 to
Present; DLB 87

Le Clezio, J(ean) M(arie) G(ustave)
1940- . . . . **CLC 31**
See also CA 116; 128; DLB 83

Leconte de Lisle, Charles-Marie-Rene
1818-1894 . . . . **NCLC 29**

Le Coq, Monsieur
See Simenon, Georges (Jacques Christian)

Leduc, Violette 1907-1972 . . . . **CLC 22**
See also CA 13-14; 33-36R; CAP 1

Ledwidge, Francis 1887(?)-1917 . . . **TCLC 23**
See also CA 123; DLB 20

Lee, Andrea 1953- . . . . **CLC 36; BLC**
See also BW 1; CA 125

Lee, Andrew
See Auchincloss, Louis (Stanton)

Lee, Don L. . . . . **CLC 2**
See also Madhubuti, Haki R.

Lee, George W(ashington)
1894-1976 . . . . **CLC 52; BLC**
See also BW 1; CA 125; DLB 51

Lee, (Nelle) Harper
1926- . . . . **CLC 12, 60; DA; WLC**
See also CA 13-16R; CDALB 1941-1968;
DLB 6; MTCW; SATA 11

Lee, Julian
See Latham, Jean Lee

Lee, Larry
See Lee, Lawrence

Lee, Lawrence 1941-1990 . . . . **CLC 34**
See also CA 131; CANR 43

Lee, Manfred B(ennington)
1905-1971 . . . . **CLC 11**
See also Queen, Ellery
See also CA 1-4R; 29-32R; CANR 2;
DLB 137

Lee, Stan 1922- . . . . **CLC 17**
See also AAYA 5; CA 108; 111

Lee, Tanith 1947- . . . . **CLC 46**
See also CA 37-40R; SATA 8

Lee, Vernon . . . . **TCLC 5**
See also Paget, Violet
See also DLB 57

Lee, William
See Burroughs, William S(eward)

Lee, Willy
See Burroughs, William S(eward)

Lee-Hamilton, Eugene (Jacob)
1845-1907 . . . . **TCLC 22**
See also CA 117

Leet, Judith 1935- . . . . **CLC 11**

Le Fanu, Joseph Sheridan
1814-1873 . . . . **NCLC 9; SSC 14**
See also DLB 21, 70

Leffland, Ella 1931- . . . . **CLC 19**
See also CA 29-32R; CANR 35; DLBY 84;
SATA 65

Leger, Alexis
See Leger, (Marie-Rene Auguste) Alexis
Saint-Leger

Leger, (Marie-Rene Auguste) Alexis
Saint-Leger 1887-1975 . . . . **CLC 11**
See also Perse, St.-John
See also CA 13-16R; 61-64; CANR 43;
MTCW

Leger, Saintleger
See Leger, (Marie-Rene Auguste) Alexis
Saint-Leger

Le Guin, Ursula K(roeber)
1929- . . . . . **CLC 8, 13, 22, 45, 71; SSC 12**
See also AAYA 9; AITN 1; CA 21-24R;
CANR 9, 32; CDALB 1968-1988; CLR 3,
28; DLB 8, 52; JRDA; MAICYA;
MTCW; SATA 4, 52

Lehmann, Rosamond (Nina)
1901-1990 . . . . **CLC 5**
See also CA 77-80; 131; CANR 8; DLB 15

Leiber, Fritz (Reuter, Jr.)
1910-1992 . . . . **CLC 25**
See also CA 45-48; 139; CANR 2, 40;
DLB 8; MTCW; SATA 45;
SATA-Obit 73

Leimbach, Martha 1963-
See Leimbach, Marti
See also CA 130

Leimbach, Marti . . . . **CLC 65**
See also Leimbach, Martha

Leino, Eino . . . . **TCLC 24**
See also Loennbohm, Armas Eino Leopold

Leiris, Michel (Julien) 1901-1990 . . . **CLC 61**
See also CA 119; 128; 132

Leithauser, Brad 1953- . . . . **CLC 27**
See also CA 107; CANR 27; DLB 120

Lukacs, Gyorgy (Szegeny von) 1885-1971
See Lukacs, George
See also CA 101; 29-32R

Luke, Peter (Ambrose Cyprian)
1919- .... **CLC 38**
See also CA 81-84; DLB 13

Lunar, Dennis
See Mungo, Raymond

Lurie, Alison 1926- .... **CLC 4, 5, 18, 39**
See also CA 1-4R; CANR 2, 17; DLB 2;
MTCW; SATA 46

Lustig, Arnost 1926- .... **CLC 56**
See also AAYA 3; CA 69-72; SATA 56

Luther, Martin 1483-1546 .... **LC 9**

Luzi, Mario 1914- .... **CLC 13**
See also CA 61-64; CANR 9; DLB 128

Lynch, B. Suarez
See Bioy Casares, Adolfo; Borges, Jorge
Luis

Lynch, David (K.) 1946- .... **CLC 66**
See also CA 124; 129

Lynch, James
See Andreyev, Leonid (Nikolaevich)

Lynch Davis, B.
See Bioy Casares, Adolfo; Borges, Jorge
Luis

Lyndsay, Sir David 1490-1555 ...... **LC 20**

Lynn, Kenneth S(chuyler) 1923- .... **CLC 50**
See also CA 1-4R; CANR 3, 27

Lynx
See West, Rebecca

Lyons, Marcus
See Blish, James (Benjamin)

Lyre, Pinchbeck
See Sassoon, Siegfried (Lorraine)

Lytle, Andrew (Nelson) 1902- ...... **CLC 22**
See also CA 9-12R; DLB 6

Lyttelton, George 1709-1773 .... **LC 10**

Maas, Peter 1929- .... **CLC 29**
See also CA 93-96

Macaulay, Rose 1881-1958 ..... **TCLC 7, 44**
See also CA 104; DLB 36

Macaulay, Thomas Babington
1800-1859 .... **NCLC 42**
See also CDBLB 1832-1890; DLB 32, 55

MacBeth, George (Mann)
1932-1992 .... **CLC 2, 5, 9**
See also CA 25-28R; 136; DLB 40; MTCW;
SATA 4; SATA-Obit 70

MacCaig, Norman (Alexander)
1910- .... **CLC 36**
See also CA 9-12R; CANR 3, 34; DLB 27

MacCarthy, (Sir Charles Otto) Desmond
1877-1952 .... **TCLC 36**

MacDiarmid, Hugh
.... **CLC 2, 4, 11, 19, 63; PC 9**
See also Grieve, C(hristopher) M(urray)
See also CDBLB 1945-1960; DLB 20

MacDonald, Anson
See Heinlein, Robert A(nson)

Macdonald, Cynthia 1928- ...... **CLC 13, 19**
See also CA 49-52; CANR 4, 44; DLB 105

MacDonald, George 1824-1905 ..... **TCLC 9**
See also CA 106; 137; DLB 18; MAICYA;
SATA 33

Macdonald, John
See Millar, Kenneth

MacDonald, John D(ann)
1916-1986 .... **CLC 3, 27, 44**
See also CA 1-4R; 121; CANR 1, 19;
DLB 8; DLBY 86; MTCW

Macdonald, John Ross
See Millar, Kenneth

Macdonald, Ross ..... **CLC 1, 2, 3, 14, 34, 41**
See also Millar, Kenneth
See also DLBD 6

MacDougal, John
See Blish, James (Benjamin)

MacEwen, Gwendolyn (Margaret)
1941-1987 .... **CLC 13, 55**
See also CA 9-12R; 124; CANR 7, 22;
DLB 53; SATA 50, 55

Macha, Karen Hynek
1810-1846 .... **NCLC 46**

Machado (y Ruiz), Antonio
1875-1939 .... **TCLC 3**
See also CA 104; DLB 108

Machado de Assis, Joaquim Maria
1839-1908 .... **TCLC 10; BLC**
See also CA 107

Machen, Arthur .... **TCLC 4**
See also Jones, Arthur Llewellyn
See also DLB 36

Machiavelli, Niccolo 1469-1527 .. **LC 8; DA**

MacInnes, Colin 1914-1976 ...... **CLC 4, 23**
See also CA 69-72; 65-68; CANR 21;
DLB 14; MTCW

MacInnes, Helen (Clark)
1907-1985 .... **CLC 27, 39**
See also CA 1-4R; 117; CANR 1, 28;
DLB 87; MTCW; SATA 22, 44

Mackay, Mary 1855-1924
See Corelli, Marie
See also CA 118

Mackenzie, Compton (Edward Montague)
1883-1972 .... **CLC 18**
See also CA 21-22; 37-40R; CAP 2;
DLB 34, 100

Mackenzie, Henry 1745-1831 .... **NCLC 41**
See also DLB 39

Mackintosh, Elizabeth 1896(?)-1952
See Tey, Josephine
See also CA 110

MacLaren, James
See Grieve, C(hristopher) M(urray)

Mac Laverty, Bernard 1942- .... **CLC 31**
See also CA 116; 118; CANR 43

MacLean, Alistair (Stuart)
1922-1987 .... **CLC 3, 13, 50, 63**
See also CA 57-60; 121; CANR 28; MTCW;
SATA 23, 50

Maclean, Norman (Fitzroy)
1902-1990 .... **CLC 78; SSC 13**
See also CA 102; 132

MacLeish, Archibald
1892-1982 .... **CLC 3, 8, 14, 68**
See also CA 9-12R; 106; CANR 33; DLB 4,
7, 45; DLBY 82; MTCW

MacLennan, (John) Hugh
1907-1990 .... **CLC 2, 14**
See also CA 5-8R; 142; CANR 33; DLB 68;
MTCW

MacLeod, Alistair 1936- .... **CLC 56**
See also CA 123; DLB 60

MacNeice, (Frederick) Louis
1907-1963 .... **CLC 1, 4, 10, 53**
See also CA 85-88; DLB 10, 20; MTCW

MacNeill, Dand
See Fraser, George MacDonald

Macpherson, (Jean) Jay 1931- ...... **CLC 14**
See also CA 5-8R; DLB 53

MacShane, Frank 1927- .... **CLC 39**
See also CA 9-12R; CANR 3, 33; DLB 111

Macumber, Mari
See Sandoz, Mari(e Susette)

Madach, Imre 1823-1864 .... **NCLC 19**

Madden, (Jerry) David 1933- .... **CLC 5, 15**
See also CA 1-4R; CAAS 3; CANR 4, 45;
DLB 6; MTCW

Maddern, Al(an)
See Ellison, Harlan

Madhubuti, Haki R.
1942- .... **CLC 6, 73; BLC; PC 5**
See also Lee, Don L.
See also BW 2; CA 73-76; CANR 24;
DLB 5, 41; DLBD 8

Madow, Pauline (Reichberg) .... **CLC 1**
See also CA 9-12R

Maepenn, Hugh
See Kuttner, Henry

Maepenn, K. H.
See Kuttner, Henry

Maeterlinck, Maurice 1862-1949 ... **TCLC 3**
See also CA 104; 136; SATA 66

Maginn, William 1794-1842 ...... **NCLC 8**
See also DLB 110

Mahapatra, Jayanta 1928- .... **CLC 33**
See also CA 73-76; CAAS 9; CANR 15, 33

Mahfouz, Naguib (Abdel Aziz Al-Sabilgi)
1911(?)-
See Mahfuz, Najib
See also BEST 89:2; CA 128; MTCW

Mahfuz, Najib .... **CLC 52, 55**
See also Mahfouz, Naguib (Abdel Aziz
Al-Sabilgi)
See also DLBY 88

Mahon, Derek 1941- .... **CLC 27**
See also CA 113; 128; DLB 40

Mailer, Norman
1923- ...... **CLC 1, 2, 3, 4, 5, 8, 11, 14,
28, 39, 74; DA**
See also AITN 2; CA 9-12R; CABS 1;
CANR 28; CDALB 1968-1988; DLB 2,
16, 28; DLBD 3; DLBY 80, 83; MTCW

Maillet, Antonine 1929- .... **CLC 54**
See also CA 115; 120; DLB 60

Mais, Roger 1905-1955 .... **TCLC 8**
See also BW 1; CA 105; 124; DLB 125;
MTCW

Martin, Richard
  See Creasey, John

Martin, Steve 1945- .... **CLC 30**
  See also CA 97-100; CANR 30; MTCW

Martin, Violet Florence
  1862-1915 .... **TCLC 51**

Martin, Webber
  See Silverberg, Robert

Martindale, Patrick Victor
  See White, Patrick (Victor Martindale)

Martin du Gard, Roger
  1881-1958 .... **TCLC 24**
  See also CA 118; DLB 65

Martineau, Harriet 1802-1876.... **NCLC 26**
  See also DLB 21, 55; YABC 2

Martines, Julia
  See O'Faolain, Julia

Martinez, Jacinto Benavente y
  See Benavente (y Martinez), Jacinto

Martinez Ruiz, Jose 1873-1967
  See Azorin; Ruiz, Jose Martinez
  See also CA 93-96; HW

Martinez Sierra, Gregorio
  1881-1947 .... **TCLC 6**
  See also CA 115

Martinez Sierra, Maria (de la O'LeJarraga)
  1874-1974 .... **TCLC 6**
  See also CA 115

Martinsen, Martin
  See Follett, Ken(neth Martin)

Martinson, Harry (Edmund)
  1904-1978 .... **CLC 14**
  See also CA 77-80; CANR 34

Marut, Ret
  See Traven, B.

Marut, Robert
  See Traven, B.

Marvell, Andrew
  1621-1678 ..... **LC 4; DA; PC 10; WLC**
  See also CDBLB 1660-1789; DLB 131

Marx, Karl (Heinrich)
  1818-1883 .... **NCLC 17**
  See also DLB 129

Masaoka Shiki.................. **TCLC 18**
  See also Masaoka Tsunenori

Masaoka Tsunenori 1867-1902
  See Masaoka Shiki
  See also CA 117

Masefield, John (Edward)
  1878-1967 .... **CLC 11, 47**
  See also CA 19-20; 25-28R; CANR 33;
  CAP 2; CDBLB 1890-1914; DLB 10;
  MTCW; SATA 19

Maso, Carole 19(?)- .... **CLC 44**

Mason, Bobbie Ann
  1940- .... **CLC 28, 43, 82; SSC 4**
  See also AAYA 5; CA 53-56; CANR 11,
  31; DLBY 87; MTCW

Mason, Ernst
  See Pohl, Frederik

Mason, Lee W.
  See Malzberg, Barry N(athaniel)

Mason, Nick 1945- .... **CLC 35**
  See also Pink Floyd

Mason, Tally
  See Derleth, August (William)

Mass, William
  See Gibson, William

Masters, Edgar Lee
  1868-1950 ...... **TCLC 2, 25; DA; PC 1**
  See also CA 104; 133; CDALB 1865-1917;
  DLB 54; MTCW

Masters, Hilary 1928- .... **CLC 48**
  See also CA 25-28R; CANR 13

Mastrosimone, William 19(?)- ...... **CLC 36**

Mathe, Albert
  See Camus, Albert

Matheson, Richard Burton 1926- ... **CLC 37**
  See also CA 97-100; DLB 8, 44

Mathews, Harry 1930- .... **CLC 6, 52**
  See also CA 21-24R; CAAS 6; CANR 18,
  40

Mathews, John Joseph 1894-1979... **CLC 84**
  See also CA 19-20; 142; CANR 45; CAP 2

Mathias, Roland (Glyn) 1915- ...... **CLC 45**
  See also CA 97-100; CANR 19, 41; DLB 27

Matsuo Basho 1644-1694........... **PC 3**

Mattheson, Rodney
  See Creasey, John

Matthews, Greg 1949- .... **CLC 45**
  See also CA 135

Matthews, William 1942-.......... **CLC 40**
  See also CA 29-32R; CAAS 18; CANR 12;
  DLB 5

Matthias, John (Edward) 1941-...... **CLC 9**
  See also CA 33-36R

Matthiessen, Peter
  1927- .... **CLC 5, 7, 11, 32, 64**
  See also AAYA 6; BEST 90:4; CA 9-12R;
  CANR 21; DLB 6; MTCW; SATA 27

Maturin, Charles Robert
  1780(?)-1824 .... **NCLC 6**

Matute (Ausejo), Ana Maria
  1925- .... **CLC 11**
  See also CA 89-92; MTCW

Maugham, W. S.
  See Maugham, W(illiam) Somerset

Maugham, W(illiam) Somerset
  1874-1965 ...... **CLC 1, 11, 15, 67; DA;
  SSC 8; WLC**
  See also CA 5-8R; 25-28R; CANR 40;
  CDBLB 1914-1945; DLB 10, 36, 77, 100;
  MTCW; SATA 54

Maugham, William Somerset
  See Maugham, W(illiam) Somerset

Maupassant, (Henri Rene Albert) Guy de
  1850-1893 .... **NCLC 1, 42; DA; SSC 1;
  WLC**
  See also DLB 123

Maurhut, Richard
  See Traven, B.

Mauriac, Claude 1914-............ **CLC 9**
  See also CA 89-92; DLB 83

Mauriac, Francois (Charles)
  1885-1970 .... **CLC 4, 9, 56**
  See also CA 25-28; CAP 2; DLB 65;
  MTCW

Mavor, Osborne Henry 1888-1951
  See Bridie, James
  See also CA 104

Maxwell, William (Keepers, Jr.)
  1908- .... **CLC 19**
  See also CA 93-96; DLBY 80

May, Elaine 1932- .... **CLC 16**
  See also CA 124; 142; DLB 44

Mayakovski, Vladimir (Vladimirovich)
  1893-1930 .... **TCLC 4, 18**
  See also CA 104

Mayhew, Henry 1812-1887 ...... **NCLC 31**
  See also DLB 18, 55

Maynard, Joyce 1953-............ **CLC 23**
  See also CA 111; 129

Mayne, William (James Carter)
  1928- .... **CLC 12**
  See also CA 9-12R; CANR 37; CLR 25;
  JRDA; MAICYA; SAAS 11; SATA 6, 68

Mayo, Jim
  See L'Amour, Louis (Dearborn)

Maysles, Albert 1926- .... **CLC 16**
  See also CA 29-32R

Maysles, David 1932-............ **CLC 16**

Mazer, Norma Fox 1931- .... **CLC 26**
  See also AAYA 5; CA 69-72; CANR 12,
  32; CLR 23; JRDA; MAICYA; SAAS 1;
  SATA 24, 67

Mazzini, Guiseppe 1805-1872 .... **NCLC 34**

McAuley, James Phillip
  1917-1976 .... **CLC 45**
  See also CA 97-100

McBain, Ed
  See Hunter, Evan

McBrien, William Augustine
  1930- .... **CLC 44**
  See also CA 107

McCaffrey, Anne (Inez) 1926-...... **CLC 17**
  See also AAYA 6; AITN 2; BEST 89:2;
  CA 25-28R; CANR 15, 35; DLB 8;
  JRDA; MAICYA; MTCW; SAAS 11;
  SATA 8, 70

McCann, Arthur
  See Campbell, John W(ood, Jr.)

McCann, Edson
  See Pohl, Frederik

McCarthy, Charles, Jr. 1933-
  See McCarthy, Cormac
  See also CANR 42

McCarthy, Cormac 1933-........ **CLC 4, 57**
  See also McCarthy, Charles, Jr.
  See also DLB 6, 143

McCarthy, Mary (Therese)
  1912-1989 ... **CLC 1, 3, 5, 14, 24, 39, 59**
  See also CA 5-8R; 129; CANR 16; DLB 2;
  DLBY 81; MTCW

McCartney, (James) Paul
  1942- .... **CLC 12, 35**

McCauley, Stephen (D.) 1955- ..... **CLC 50**
  See also CA 141

McClure, Michael (Thomas)
  1932- .... **CLC 6, 10**
  See also CA 21-24R; CANR 17; DLB 16

McCorkle, Jill (Collins) 1958-...... **CLC 51**
See also CA 121; DLBY 87

McCourt, James 1941-............ **CLC 5**
See also CA 57-60

McCoy, Horace (Stanley)
1897-1955 .... **TCLC 28**
See also CA 108; DLB 9

McCrae, John 1872-1918........ **TCLC 12**
See also CA 109; DLB 92

McCreigh, James
See Pohl, Frederik

McCullers, (Lula) Carson (Smith)
1917-1967 .... **CLC 1, 4, 10, 12, 48; DA;**
SSC 9; WLC
See also CA 5-8R; 25-28R; CABS 1, 3;
CANR 18; CDALB 1941-1968; DLB 2, 7;
MTCW; SATA 27

McCulloch, John Tyler
See Burroughs, Edgar Rice

McCullough, Colleen 1938(?)-...... **CLC 27**
See also CA 81-84; CANR 17; MTCW

McElroy, Joseph 1930- .... **CLC 5, 47**
See also CA 17-20R

McEwan, Ian (Russell) 1948- ... **CLC 13, 66**
See also BEST 90:4; CA 61-64; CANR 14,
41; DLB 14; MTCW

McFadden, David 1940-.......... **CLC 48**
See also CA 104; DLB 60

McFarland, Dennis 1950- .... **CLC 65**

McGahern, John 1934-........ **CLC 5, 9, 48**
See also CA 17-20R; CANR 29; DLB 14;
MTCW

McGinley, Patrick (Anthony)
1937- .... **CLC 41**
See also CA 120; 127

McGinley, Phyllis 1905-1978 ...... **CLC 14**
See also CA 9-12R; 77-80; CANR 19;
DLB 11, 48; SATA 2, 24, 44

McGinniss, Joe 1942-............ **CLC 32**
See also AITN 2; BEST 89:2; CA 25-28R;
CANR 26

McGivern, Maureen Daly
See Daly, Maureen

McGrath, Patrick 1950-.......... **CLC 55**
See also CA 136

McGrath, Thomas (Matthew)
1916-1990 .... **CLC 28, 59**
See also CA 9-12R; 132; CANR 6, 33;
MTCW; SATA 41; SATA-Obit 66

McGuane, Thomas (Francis III)
1939- .... **CLC 3, 7, 18, 45**
See also AITN 2; CA 49-52; CANR 5, 24;
DLB 2; DLBY 80; MTCW

McGuckian, Medbh 1950-........ **CLC 48**
See also CA 143; DLB 40

McHale, Tom 1942(?)-1982....... **CLC 3, 5**
See also AITN 1; CA 77-80; 106

McIlvanney, William 1936-........ **CLC 42**
See also CA 25-28R; DLB 14

McIlwraith, Maureen Mollie Hunter
See Hunter, Mollie
See also SATA 2

McInerney, Jay 1955-............ **CLC 34**
See also CA 116; 123

McIntyre, Vonda N(eel) 1948- ..... **CLC 18**
See also CA 81-84; CANR 17, 34; MTCW

McKay, Claude ..... **TCLC 7, 41; BLC; PC 2**
See also McKay, Festus Claudius
See also DLB 4, 45, 51, 117

McKay, Festus Claudius 1889-1948
See McKay, Claude
See also BW 1; CA 104; 124; DA; MTCW;
WLC

McKuen, Rod 1933-............ **CLC 1, 3**
See also AITN 1; CA 41-44R; CANR 40

McLoughlin, R. B.
See Mencken, H(enry) L(ouis)

McLuhan, (Herbert) Marshall
1911-1980 .... **CLC 37, 83**
See also CA 9-12R; 102; CANR 12, 34;
DLB 88; MTCW

McMillan, Terry (L.) 1951-..... **CLC 50, 61**
See also BW 2; CA 140

McMurtry, Larry (Jeff)
1936- .... **CLC 2, 3, 7, 11, 27, 44**
See also AITN 2; BEST 89:2; CA 5-8R;
CANR 19, 43; CDALB 1968-1988;
DLB 2, 143; DLBY 80, 87; MTCW

McNally, T. M. 1961- .... **CLC 82**

McNally, Terrence 1939-...... **CLC 4, 7, 41**
See also CA 45-48; CANR 2; DLB 7

McNamer, Deirdre 1950-......... **CLC 70**

McNeile, Herman Cyril 1888-1937
See Sapper
See also DLB 77

McPhee, John (Angus) 1931- ...... **CLC 36**
See also BEST 90:1; CA 65-68; CANR 20;
MTCW

McPherson, James Alan
1943- .... **CLC 19, 77**
See also BW 1; CA 25-28R; CAAS 17;
CANR 24; DLB 38; MTCW

McPherson, William (Alexander)
1933- .... **CLC 34**
See also CA 69-72; CANR 28

McSweeney, Kerry .... **CLC 34**

Mead, Margaret 1901-1978....... **CLC 37**
See also AITN 1; CA 1-4R; 81-84;
CANR 4; MTCW; SATA 20

Meaker, Marijane (Agnes) 1927-
See Kerr, M. E.
See also CA 107; CANR 37; JRDA;
MAICYA; MTCW; SATA 20, 61

Medoff, Mark (Howard) 1940- ... **CLC 6, 23**
See also AITN 1; CA 53-56; CANR 5;
DLB 7

Medvedev, P. N.
See Bakhtin, Mikhail Mikhailovich

Meged, Aharon
See Megged, Aharon

Meged, Aron
See Megged, Aharon

Megged, Aharon 1920-............ **CLC 9**
See also CA 49-52; CAAS 13; CANR 1

Mehta, Ved (Parkash) 1934-...... **CLC 37**
See also CA 1-4R; CANR 2, 23; MTCW

Melanter
See Blackmore, R(ichard) D(oddridge)

Melikow, Loris
See Hofmannsthal, Hugo von

Melmoth, Sebastian
See Wilde, Oscar (Fingal O'Flahertie Wills)

Meltzer, Milton 1915-............ **CLC 26**
See also AAYA 8; CA 13-16R; CANR 38;
CLR 13; DLB 61; JRDA; MAICYA;
SAAS 1; SATA 1, 50

Melville, Herman
1819-1891 .... **NCLC 3, 12, 29, 45; DA;**
SSC 1; WLC
See also CDALB 1640-1865; DLB 3, 74;
SATA 59

Menander
c. 342B.C.-c. 292B.C.... **CMLC 9; DC 3**

Mencken, H(enry) L(ouis)
1880-1956 .... **TCLC 13**
See also CA 105; 125; CDALB 1917-1929;
DLB 11, 29, 63, 137; MTCW

Mercer, David 1928-1980.......... **CLC 5**
See also CA 9-12R; 102; CANR 23;
DLB 13; MTCW

Merchant, Paul
See Ellison, Harlan

Meredith, George 1828-1909... **TCLC 17, 43**
See also CA 117; CDBLB 1832-1890;
DLB 18, 35, 57

Meredith, William (Morris)
1919- .... **CLC 4, 13, 22, 55**
See also CA 9-12R; CAAS 14; CANR 6, 40;
DLB 5

Merezhkovsky, Dmitry Sergeyevich
1865-1941 .... **TCLC 29**

Merimee, Prosper
1803-1870 .... **NCLC 6; SSC 7**
See also DLB 119

Merkin, Daphne 1954-............ **CLC 44**
See also CA 123

Merlin, Arthur
See Blish, James (Benjamin)

Merrill, James (Ingram)
1926- .... **CLC 2, 3, 6, 8, 13, 18, 34**
See also CA 13-16R; CANR 10; DLB 5;
DLBY 85; MTCW

Merriman, Alex
See Silverberg, Robert

Merritt, E. B.
See Waddington, Miriam

Merton, Thomas
1915-1968 .. **CLC 1, 3, 11, 34, 83; PC 10**
See also CA 5-8R; 25-28R; CANR 22;
DLB 48; DLBY 81; MTCW

Merwin, W(illiam) S(tanley)
1927- ...... **CLC 1, 2, 3, 5, 8, 13, 18, 45**
See also CA 13-16R; CANR 15; DLB 5;
MTCW

Metcalf, John 1938-.............. **CLC 37**
See also CA 113; DLB 60

Metcalf, Suzanne
See Baum, L(yman) Frank

Mew, Charlotte (Mary)
1870-1928 .... **TCLC 8**
See also CA 105; DLB 19, 135

Mewshaw, Michael 1943-.......... **CLC 9**
See also CA 53-56; CANR 7; DLBY 80

Montesquieu, Charles-Louis de Secondat
  1689-1755 . . . . LC 7

Montgomery, (Robert) Bruce 1921-1978
  See Crispin, Edmund
  See also CA 104

Montgomery, L(ucy) M(aud)
  1874-1942 . . . . TCLC 51
  See also AAYA 12; CA 108; 137; CLR 8;
  DLB 92; JRDA; MAICYA; YABC 1

Montgomery, Marion H., Jr. 1925- . . CLC 7
  See also AITN 1; CA 1-4R; CANR 3;
  DLB 6

Montgomery, Max
  See Davenport, Guy (Mattison, Jr.)

Montherlant, Henry (Milon) de
  1896-1972 . . . . CLC 8, 19
  See also CA 85-88; 37-40R; DLB 72;
  MTCW

Monty Python . . . . CLC 21
  See also Chapman, Graham; Cleese, John
  (Marwood); Gilliam, Terry (Vance); Idle,
  Eric; Jones, Terence Graham Parry; Palin,
  Michael (Edward)
  See also AAYA 7

Moodie, Susanna (Strickland)
  1803-1885 . . . . NCLC 14
  See also DLB 99

Mooney, Edward 1951- . . . . CLC 25
  See also CA 130

Mooney, Ted
  See Mooney, Edward

Moorcock, Michael (John)
  1939- . . . . CLC 5, 27, 58
  See also CA 45-48; CAAS 5; CANR 2, 17,
  38; DLB 14; MTCW

Moore, Brian
  1921- . . . . CLC 1, 3, 5, 7, 8, 19, 32
  See also CA 1-4R; CANR 1, 25, 42; MTCW

Moore, Edward
  See Muir, Edwin

Moore, George Augustus
  1852-1933 . . . . TCLC 7
  See also CA 104; DLB 10, 18, 57, 135

Moore, Lorrie . . . . CLC 39, 45, 68
  See also Moore, Marie Lorena

Moore, Marianne (Craig)
  1887-1972 . . . . CLC 1, 2, 4, 8, 10, 13, 19,
                                47; DA; PC 4
  See also CA 1-4R; 33-36R; CANR 3;
  CDALB 1929-1941; DLB 45; DLBD 7;
  MTCW; SATA 20

Moore, Marie Lorena 1957-
  See Moore, Lorrie
  See also CA 116; CANR 39

Moore, Thomas 1779-1852 . . . . NCLC 6
  See also DLB 96, 144

Morand, Paul 1888-1976 . . . . CLC 41
  See also CA 69-72; DLB 65

Morante, Elsa 1918-1985 . . . . CLC 8, 47
  See also CA 85-88; 117; CANR 35; MTCW

Moravia, Alberto . . . . . . CLC 2, 7, 11, 27, 46
  See also Pincherle, Alberto

More, Hannah 1745-1833 . . . . NCLC 27
  See also DLB 107, 109, 116

More, Henry 1614-1687 . . . . LC 9
  See also DLB 126

More, Sir Thomas 1478-1535 . . . . LC 10

Moreas, Jean . . . . TCLC 18
  See also Papadiamantopoulos, Johannes

Morgan, Berry 1919- . . . . CLC 6
  See also CA 49-52; DLB 6

Morgan, Claire
  See Highsmith, (Mary) Patricia

Morgan, Edwin (George) 1920- . . . . . CLC 31
  See also CA 5-8R; CANR 3, 43; DLB 27

Morgan, (George) Frederick
  1922- . . . . CLC 23
  See also CA 17-20R; CANR 21

Morgan, Harriet
  See Mencken, H(enry) L(ouis)

Morgan, Jane
  See Cooper, James Fenimore

Morgan, Janet 1945- . . . . CLC 39
  See also CA 65-68

Morgan, Lady 1776(?)-1859 . . . . . NCLC 29
  See also DLB 116

Morgan, Robin 1941- . . . . CLC 2
  See also CA 69-72; CANR 29; MTCW

Morgan, Scott
  See Kuttner, Henry

Morgan, Seth 1949(?)-1990 . . . . CLC 65
  See also CA 132

Morgenstern, Christian
  1871-1914 . . . . TCLC 8
  See also CA 105

Morgenstern, S.
  See Goldman, William (W.)

Moricz, Zsigmond 1879-1942 . . . . . TCLC 33

Morike, Eduard (Friedrich)
  1804-1875 . . . . NCLC 10
  See also DLB 133

Mori Ogai . . . . TCLC 14
  See also Mori Rintaro

Mori Rintaro 1862-1922
  See Mori Ogai
  See also CA 110

Moritz, Karl Philipp 1756-1793 . . . . . . LC 2
  See also DLB 94

Morland, Peter Henry
  See Faust, Frederick (Schiller)

Morren, Theophil
  See Hofmannsthal, Hugo von

Morris, Bill 1952- . . . . CLC 76

Morris, Julian
  See West, Morris L(anglo)

Morris, Steveland Judkins 1950(?)-
  See Wonder, Stevie
  See also CA 111

Morris, William 1834-1896 . . . . NCLC 4
  See also CDBLB 1832-1890; DLB 18, 35, 57

Morris, Wright 1910- . . . CLC 1, 3, 7, 18, 37
  See also CA 9-12R; CANR 21; DLB 2;
  DLBY 81; MTCW

Morrison, Chloe Anthony Wofford
  See Morrison, Toni

Morrison, James Douglas 1943-1971
  See Morrison, Jim
  See also CA 73-76; CANR 40

Morrison, Jim . . . . CLC 17
  See also Morrison, James Douglas

Morrison, Toni
  1931- . . CLC 4, 10, 22, 55, 81; BLC; DA
  See also AAYA 1; BW 2; CA 29-32R;
  CANR 27, 42; CDALB 1968-1988;
  DLB 6, 33, 143; DLBY 81; MTCW;
  SATA 57

Morrison, Van 1945- . . . . CLC 21
  See also CA 116

Mortimer, John (Clifford)
  1923- . . . . CLC 28, 43
  See also CA 13-16R; CANR 21;
  CDBLB 1960 to Present; DLB 13;
  MTCW

Mortimer, Penelope (Ruth) 1918- . . . . CLC 5
  See also CA 57-60; CANR 45

Morton, Anthony
  See Creasey, John

Mosher, Howard Frank 1943- . . . . . . CLC 62
  See also CA 139

Mosley, Nicholas 1923- . . . . CLC 43, 70
  See also CA 69-72; CANR 41; DLB 14

Moss, Howard
  1922-1987 . . . . CLC 7, 14, 45, 50
  See also CA 1-4R; 123; CANR 1, 44;
  DLB 5

Mossgiel, Rab
  See Burns, Robert

Motion, Andrew 1952- . . . . CLC 47
  See also DLB 40

Motley, Willard (Francis)
  1909-1965 . . . . CLC 18
  See also BW 1; CA 117; 106; DLB 76, 143

Motoori, Norinaga 1730-1801 . . . . NCLC 45

Mott, Michael (Charles Alston)
  1930- . . . . CLC 15, 34
  See also CA 5-8R; CAAS 7; CANR 7, 29

Mowat, Farley (McGill) 1921- . . . . . CLC 26
  See also AAYA 1; CA 1-4R; CANR 4, 24,
  42; CLR 20; DLB 68; JRDA; MAICYA;
  MTCW; SATA 3, 55

Moyers, Bill 1934- . . . . CLC 74
  See also AITN 2; CA 61-64; CANR 31

Mphahlele, Es'kia
  See Mphahlele, Ezekiel
  See also DLB 125

Mphahlele, Ezekiel 1919- . . . . CLC 25; BLC
  See also Mphahlele, Es'kia
  See also BW 2; CA 81-84; CANR 26

Mqhayi, S(amuel) E(dward) K(rune Loliwe)
  1875-1945 . . . . TCLC 25; BLC

Mr. Martin
  See Burroughs, William S(eward)

Mrozek, Slawomir 1930- . . . . CLC 3, 13
  See also CA 13-16R; CAAS 10; CANR 29;
  MTCW

Mrs. Belloc-Lowndes
  See Lowndes, Marie Adelaide (Belloc)

Mtwa, Percy (?)- . . . . CLC 47

Mueller, Lisel 1924-.......... **CLC 13, 51**
See also CA 93-96; DLB 105

Muir, Edwin 1887-1959 .... **TCLC 2**
See also CA 104; DLB 20, 100

Muir, John 1838-1914 .... **TCLC 28**

Mujica Lainez, Manuel
1910-1984 .... **CLC 31**
See also Lainez, Manuel Mujica
See also CA 81-84; 112; CANR 32; HW

Mukherjee, Bharati 1940-......... **CLC 53**
See also BEST 89:2; CA 107; CANR 45;
DLB 60; MTCW

Muldoon, Paul 1951-.......... **CLC 32, 72**
See also CA 113; 129; DLB 40

Mulisch, Harry 1927-............. **CLC 42**
See also CA 9-12R; CANR 6, 26

Mull, Martin 1943-.............. **CLC 17**
See also CA 105

Mulock, Dinah Maria
See Craik, Dinah Maria (Mulock)

Munford, Robert 1737(?)-1783 .... **LC 5**
See also DLB 31

Mungo, Raymond 1946-.......... **CLC 72**
See also CA 49-52; CANR 2

Munro, Alice
1931-........ **CLC 6, 10, 19, 50; SSC 3**
See also AITN 2; CA 33-36R; CANR 33;
DLB 53; MTCW; SATA 29

Munro, H(ector) H(ugh) 1870-1916
See Saki
See also CA 104; 130; CDBLB 1890-1914;
DA; DLB 34; MTCW; WLC

Murasaki, Lady.................. **CMLC 1**

Murdoch, (Jean) Iris
1919-...... **CLC 1, 2, 3, 4, 6, 8, 11, 15,
22, 31, 51**
See also CA 13-16R; CANR 8, 43;
CDBLB 1960 to Present; DLB 14;
MTCW

Murnau, Friedrich Wilhelm
See Plumpe, Friedrich Wilhelm

Murphy, Richard 1927-.......... **CLC 41**
See also CA 29-32R; DLB 40

Murphy, Sylvia 1937-............. **CLC 34**
See also CA 121

Murphy, Thomas (Bernard) 1935-... **CLC 51**
See also CA 101

Murray, Albert L. 1916- .... **CLC 73**
See also BW 2; CA 49-52; CANR 26;
DLB 38

Murray, Les(lie) A(llan) 1938- ..... **CLC 40**
See also CA 21-24R; CANR 11, 27

Murry, J. Middleton
See Murry, John Middleton

Murry, John Middleton
1889-1957 .... **TCLC 16**
See also CA 118

Musgrave, Susan 1951- .... **CLC 13, 54**
See also CA 69-72; CANR 45

Musil, Robert (Edler von)
1880-1942 .... **TCLC 12**
See also CA 109; DLB 81, 124

Musset, (Louis Charles) Alfred de
1810-1857 .... **NCLC 7**

My Brother's Brother
See Chekhov, Anton (Pavlovich)

Myers, Walter Dean 1937- ... **CLC 35; BLC**
See also AAYA 4; BW 2; CA 33-36R;
CANR 20, 42; CLR 4, 16; DLB 33;
JRDA; MAICYA; SAAS 2; SATA 27, 41,
71

Myers, Walter M.
See Myers, Walter Dean

Myles, Symon
See Follett, Ken(neth Martin)

Nabokov, Vladimir (Vladimirovich)
1899-1977 ..... **CLC 1, 2, 3, 6, 8, 11, 15,
23, 44, 46, 64; DA; SSC 11; WLC**
See also CA 5-8R; 69-72; CANR 20;
CDALB 1941-1968; DLB 2; DLBD 3;
DLBY 80, 91; MTCW

Nagai Kafu..................... **TCLC 51**
See also Nagai Sokichi

Nagai Sokichi 1879-1959
See Nagai Kafu
See also CA 117

Nagy, Laszlo 1925-1978............ **CLC 7**
See also CA 129; 112

Naipaul, Shiva(dhar Srinivasa)
1945-1985 .... **CLC 32, 39**
See also CA 110; 112; 116; CANR 33;
DLBY 85; MTCW

Naipaul, V(idiadhar) S(urajprasad)
1932-.......... **CLC 4, 7, 9, 13, 18, 37**
See also CA 1-4R; CANR 1, 33;
CDBLB 1960 to Present; DLB 125;
DLBY 85; MTCW

Nakos, Lilika 1899(?)-............ **CLC 29**

Narayan, R(asipuram) K(rishnaswami)
1906-.................. **CLC 7, 28, 47**
See also CA 81-84; CANR 33; MTCW;
SATA 62

Nash, (Frediric) Ogden 1902-1971 .. **CLC 23**
See also CA 13-14; 29-32R; CANR 34;
CAP 1; DLB 11; MAICYA; MTCW;
SATA 2, 46

Nathan, Daniel
See Dannay, Frederic

Nathan, George Jean 1882-1958 ... **TCLC 18**
See also Hatteras, Owen
See also CA 114; DLB 137

Natsume, Kinnosuke 1867-1916
See Natsume, Soseki
See also CA 104

Natsume, Soseki .... **TCLC 2, 10**
See also Natsume, Kinnosuke

Natti, (Mary) Lee 1919-
See Kingman, Lee
See also CA 5-8R; CANR 2

Naylor, Gloria
1950-.......... **CLC 28, 52; BLC; DA**
See also AAYA 6; BW 2; CA 107;
CANR 27; MTCW

Neihardt, John Gneisenau
1881-1973 .... **CLC 32**
See also CA 13-14; CAP 1; DLB 9, 54

Nekrasov, Nikolai Alekseevich
1821-1878 .... **NCLC 11**

Nelligan, Emile 1879-1941....... **TCLC 14**
See also CA 114; DLB 92

Nelson, Willie 1933-.............. **CLC 17**
See also CA 107

Nemerov, Howard (Stanley)
1920-1991.............**CLC 2, 6, 9, 36**
See also CA 1-4R; 134; CABS 2; CANR 1,
27; DLB 6; DLBY 83; MTCW

Neruda, Pablo
1904-1973 ..... **CLC 1, 2, 5, 7, 9, 28, 62;
DA; HLC; PC 4; WLC**
See also CA 19-20; 45-48; CAP 2; HW;
MTCW

Nerval, Gerard de 1808-1855...... **NCLC 1**

Nervo, (Jose) Amado (Ruiz de)
1870-1919 .... **TCLC 11**
See also CA 109; 131; HW

Nessi, Pio Baroja y
See Baroja (y Nessi), Pio

Nestroy, Johann 1801-1862...... **NCLC 42**
See also DLB 133

Neufeld, John (Arthur) 1938-...... **CLC 17**
See also AAYA 11; CA 25-28R; CANR 11,
37; MAICYA; SAAS 3; SATA 6

Neville, Emily Cheney 1919-....... **CLC 12**
See also CA 5-8R; CANR 3, 37; JRDA;
MAICYA; SAAS 2; SATA 1

Newbound, Bernard Slade 1930-
See Slade, Bernard
See also CA 81-84

Newby, P(ercy) H(oward)
1918-.................... **CLC 2, 13**
See also CA 5-8R; CANR 32; DLB 15;
MTCW

Newlove, Donald 1928- .... **CLC 6**
See also CA 29-32R; CANR 25

Newlove, John (Herbert) 1938-..... **CLC 14**
See also CA 21-24R; CANR 9, 25

Newman, Charles 1938-.......... **CLC 2, 8**
See also CA 21-24R

Newman, Edwin (Harold) 1919- .... **CLC 14**
See also AITN 1; CA 69-72; CANR 5

Newman, John Henry
1801-1890 .... **NCLC 38**
See also DLB 18, 32, 55

Newton, Suzanne 1936- .... **CLC 35**
See also CA 41-44R; CANR 14; JRDA;
SATA 5, 77

Nexo, Martin Andersen
1869-1954 .... **TCLC 43**

Nezval, Vitezslav 1900-1958 ...... **TCLC 44**
See also CA 123

Ng, Fae Myenne 1957(?)-......... **CLC 81**

Ngema, Mbongeni 1955- .... **CLC 57**
See also BW 2; CA 143

Ngugi, James T(hiong'o)........ **CLC 3, 7, 13**
See also Ngugi wa Thiong'o

Ngugi wa Thiong'o 1938-..... **CLC 36; BLC**
See also Ngugi, James T(hiong'o)
See also BW 2; CA 81-84; CANR 27;
DLB 125; MTCW

Nichol, B(arrie) P(hillip)
1944-1988 .... **CLC 18**
See also CA 53-56; DLB 53; SATA 66

Nichols, John (Treadwell) 1940- .... **CLC 38**
See also CA 9-12R; CAAS 2; CANR 6;
DLBY 82

Nichols, Leigh
See Koontz, Dean R(ay)

Nichols, Peter (Richard)
1927- .... **CLC 5, 36, 65**
See also CA 104; CANR 33; DLB 13;
MTCW

Nicolas, F. R. E.
See Freeling, Nicolas

Niedecker, Lorine 1903-1970.... **CLC 10, 42**
See also CA 25-28; CAP 2; DLB 48

Nietzsche, Friedrich (Wilhelm)
1844-1900 .... **TCLC 10, 18, 55**
See also CA 107; 121; DLB 129

Nievo, Ippolito 1831-1861 .... **NCLC 22**

Nightingale, Anne Redmon 1943-
See Redmon, Anne
See also CA 103

Nik.T.O.
See Annensky, Innokenty Fyodorovich

Nin, Anais
1903-1977 ...... **CLC 1, 4, 8, 11, 14, 60;**
                                              SSC 10
See also AITN 2; CA 13-16R; 69-72;
CANR 22; DLB 2, 4; MTCW

Nissenson, Hugh 1933-.......... **CLC 4, 9**
See also CA 17-20R; CANR 27; DLB 28

Niven, Larry .... **CLC 8**
See also Niven, Laurence Van Cott
See also DLB 8

Niven, Laurence Van Cott 1938-
See Niven, Larry
See also CA 21-24R; CAAS 12; CANR 14,
44; MTCW

Nixon, Agnes Eckhardt 1927-...... **CLC 21**
See also CA 110

Nizan, Paul 1905-1940.......... **TCLC 40**
See also DLB 72

Nkosi, Lewis 1936-......... **CLC 45; BLC**
See also BW 1; CA 65-68; CANR 27

Nodier, (Jean) Charles (Emmanuel)
1780-1844 .... **NCLC 19**
See also DLB 119

Nolan, Christopher 1965-......... **CLC 58**
See also CA 111

Norden, Charles
See Durrell, Lawrence (George)

Nordhoff, Charles (Bernard)
1887-1947 .... **TCLC 23**
See also CA 108; DLB 9; SATA 23

Norfolk, Lawrence 1963-......... **CLC 76**
See also CA 144

Norman, Marsha 1947- .... **CLC 28**
See also CA 105; CABS 3; CANR 41;
DLBY 84

Norris, Benjamin Franklin, Jr.
1870-1902 .... **TCLC 24**
See also Norris, Frank
See also CA 110

Norris, Frank
See Norris, Benjamin Franklin, Jr.
See also CDALB 1865-1917; DLB 12, 71

Norris, Leslie 1921- .... **CLC 14**
See also CA 11-12; CANR 14; CAP 1;
DLB 27

North, Andrew
See Norton, Andre

North, Anthony
See Koontz, Dean R(ay)

North, Captain George
See Stevenson, Robert Louis (Balfour)

North, Milou
See Erdrich, Louise

Northrup, B. A.
See Hubbard, L(afayette) Ron(ald)

North Staffs
See Hulme, T(homas) E(rnest)

Norton, Alice Mary
See Norton, Andre
See also MAICYA; SATA 1, 43

Norton, Andre 1912- .... **CLC 12**
See also Norton, Alice Mary
See also CA 1-4R; CANR 2, 31; DLB 8, 52;
JRDA; MTCW

Norway, Nevil Shute 1899-1960
See Shute, Nevil
See also CA 102; 93-96

Norwid, Cyprian Kamil
1821-1883 .... **NCLC 17**

Nosille, Nabrah
See Ellison, Harlan

Nossack, Hans Erich 1901-1978 ..... **CLC 6**
See also CA 93-96; 85-88; DLB 69

Nosu, Chuji
See Ozu, Yasujiro

Notenburg, Eleanora (Genrikhovna) von
1877-1913
See Guro, Elena

Nova, Craig 1945-.............. **CLC 7, 31**
See also CA 45-48; CANR 2

Novak, Joseph
See Kosinski, Jerzy (Nikodem)

Novalis 1772-1801 .... **NCLC 13**
See also DLB 90

Nowlan, Alden (Albert) 1933-1983 .. **CLC 15**
See also CA 9-12R; CANR 5; DLB 53

Noyes, Alfred 1880-1958 .... **TCLC 7**
See also CA 104; DLB 20

Nunn, Kem 19(?)- .... **CLC 34**

Nye, Robert 1939-............. **CLC 13, 42**
See also CA 33-36R; CANR 29; DLB 14;
MTCW; SATA 6

Nyro, Laura 1947- .... **CLC 17**

Oates, Joyce Carol
1938- ......**CLC 1, 2, 3, 6, 9, 11, 15, 19,**
                              33, 52; DA; SSC 6; WLC
See also AITN 1; BEST 89:2; CA 5-8R;
CANR 25, 45; CDALB 1968-1988;
DLB 2, 5, 130; DLBY 81; MTCW

O'Brien, E. G.
See Clarke, Arthur C(harles)

O'Brien, Edna
1936- ... **CLC 3, 5, 8, 13, 36, 65; SSC 10**
See also CA 1-4R; CANR 6, 41;
CDBLB 1960 to Present; DLB 14;
MTCW

O'Brien, Fitz-James 1828-1862... **NCLC 21**
See also DLB 74

O'Brien, Flann........ **CLC 1, 4, 5, 7, 10, 47**
See also O Nuallain, Brian

O'Brien, Richard 1942-.......... **CLC 17**
See also CA 124

O'Brien, Tim 1946-.......... **CLC 7, 19, 40**
See also CA 85-88; CANR 40; DLBD 9;
DLBY 80

Obstfelder, Sigbjoern 1866-1900... **TCLC 23**
See also CA 123

O'Casey, Sean
1880-1964 .... **CLC 1, 5, 9, 11, 15**
See also CA 89-92; CDBLB 1914-1945;
DLB 10; MTCW

O'Cathasaigh, Sean
See O'Casey, Sean

Ochs, Phil 1940-1976............. **CLC 17**
See also CA 65-68

O'Connor, Edwin (Greene)
1918-1968 .... **CLC 14**
See also CA 93-96; 25-28R

O'Connor, (Mary) Flannery
1925-1964 .... **CLC 1, 2, 3, 6, 10, 13, 15,**
                         21, 66; DA; SSC 1; WLC
See also AAYA 7; CA 1-4R; CANR 3, 41;
CDALB 1941-1968; DLB 2; DLBY 80;
MTCW

O'Connor, Frank.......... **CLC 23; SSC 5**
See also O'Donovan, Michael John

O'Dell, Scott 1898-1989.......... **CLC 30**
See also AAYA 3; CA 61-64; 129;
CANR 12, 30; CLR 1, 16; DLB 52;
JRDA; MAICYA; SATA 12, 60

Odets, Clifford 1906-1963 .... **CLC 2, 28**
See also CA 85-88; DLB 7, 26; MTCW

O'Doherty, Brian 1934-........... **CLC 76**
See also CA 105

O'Donnell, K. M.
See Malzberg, Barry N(athaniel)

O'Donnell, Lawrence
See Kuttner, Henry

O'Donovan, Michael John
1903-1966 .... **CLC 14**
See also O'Connor, Frank
See also CA 93-96

Oe, Kenzaburo 1935-.......... **CLC 10, 36**
See also CA 97-100; CANR 36; MTCW

O'Faolain, Julia 1932-........ **CLC 6, 19, 47**
See also CA 81-84; CAAS 2; CANR 12;
DLB 14; MTCW

O'Faolain, Sean
1900-1991 .... **CLC 1, 7, 14, 32, 70;**
                                              SSC 13
See also CA 61-64; 134; CANR 12;
DLB 15; MTCW

O'Flaherty, Liam
1896-1984 .... **CLC 5, 34; SSC 6**
See also CA 101; 113; CANR 35; DLB 36;
DLBY 84; MTCW

Ogilvy, Gavin
See Barrie, J(ames) M(atthew)

O'Grady, Standish James
1846-1928 .... **TCLC 5**
See also CA 104

O'Grady, Timothy 1951- .... **CLC 59**
See also CA 138

O'Hara, Frank
1926-1966 .... **CLC 2, 5, 13, 78**
See also CA 9-12R; 25-28R; CANR 33;
DLB 5, 16; MTCW

O'Hara, John (Henry)
1905-1970 ...... **CLC 1, 2, 3, 6, 11, 42;
SSC 15**
See also CA 5-8R; 25-28R; CANR 31;
CDALB 1929-1941; DLB 9, 86; DLBD 2;
MTCW

O Hehir, Diana 1922- .... **CLC 41**
See also CA 93-96

Okigbo, Christopher (Ifenayichukwu)
1932-1967 ..... **CLC 25, 84; BLC; PC 7**
See also BW 1; CA 77-80; DLB 125;
MTCW

Olds, Sharon 1942-............ **CLC 32, 39**
See also CA 101; CANR 18, 41; DLB 120

Oldstyle, Jonathan
See Irving, Washington

Olesha, Yuri (Karlovich)
1899-1960 .... **CLC 8**
See also CA 85-88

Oliphant, Margaret (Oliphant Wilson)
1828-1897 .... **NCLC 11**
See also DLB 18

Oliver, Mary 1935-........... **CLC 19, 34**
See also CA 21-24R; CANR 9, 43; DLB 5

Olivier, Laurence (Kerr)
1907-1989 .... **CLC 20**
See also CA 111; 129

Olsen, Tillie
1913- .... **CLC 4, 13; DA; SSC 11**
See also CA 1-4R; CANR 1, 43; DLB 28;
DLBY 80; MTCW

Olson, Charles (John)
1910-1970 ..... **CLC 1, 2, 5, 6, 9, 11, 29**
See also CA 13-16; 25-28R; CABS 2;
CANR 35; CAP 1; DLB 5, 16; MTCW

Olson, Toby 1937- .... **CLC 28**
See also CA 65-68; CANR 9, 31

Olyesha, Yuri
See Olesha, Yuri (Karlovich)

Ondaatje, (Philip) Michael
1943- .... **CLC 14, 29, 51, 76**
See also CA 77-80; CANR 42; DLB 60

Oneal, Elizabeth 1934-
See Oneal, Zibby
See also CA 106; CANR 28; MAICYA;
SATA 30

Oneal, Zibby .... **CLC 30**
See also Oneal, Elizabeth
See also AAYA 5; CLR 13; JRDA

O'Neill, Eugene (Gladstone)
1888-1953 ..... **TCLC 1, 6, 27, 49; DA;
WLC**
See also AITN 1; CA 110; 132;
CDALB 1929-1941; DLB 7; MTCW

Onetti, Juan Carlos 1909- .... **CLC 7, 10**
See also CA 85-88; CANR 32; DLB 113;
HW; MTCW

O Nuallain, Brian 1911-1966
See O'Brien, Flann
See also CA 21-22; 25-28R; CAP 2

Oppen, George 1908-1984 .... **CLC 7, 13, 34**
See also CA 13-16R; 113; CANR 8; DLB 5

Oppenheim, E(dward) Phillips
1866-1946 .... **TCLC 45**
See also CA 111; DLB 70

Orlovitz, Gil 1918-1973 .... **CLC 22**
See also CA 77-80; 45-48; DLB 2, 5

Orris
See Ingelow, Jean

Ortega y Gasset, Jose
1883-1955 .... **TCLC 9; HLC**
See also CA 106; 130; HW; MTCW

Ortiz, Simon J(oseph) 1941- .... **CLC 45**
See also CA 134; DLB 120

Orton, Joe .... **CLC 4, 13, 43; DC 3**
See also Orton, John Kingsley
See also CDBLB 1960 to Present; DLB 13

Orton, John Kingsley 1933-1967
See Orton, Joe
See also CA 85-88; CANR 35; MTCW

Orwell, George
.... **TCLC 2, 6, 15, 31, 51; WLC**
See also Blair, Eric (Arthur)
See also CDBLB 1945-1960; DLB 15, 98

Osborne, David
See Silverberg, Robert

Osborne, George
See Silverberg, Robert

Osborne, John (James)
1929- .... **CLC 1, 2, 5, 11, 45; DA; WLC**
See also CA 13-16R; CANR 21;
CDBLB 1945-1960; DLB 13; MTCW

Osborne, Lawrence 1958- .... **CLC 50**

Oshima, Nagisa 1932- .... **CLC 20**
See also CA 116; 121

Oskison, John Milton
1874-1947 .... **TCLC 35**
See also CA 144

Ossoli, Sarah Margaret (Fuller marchesa d')
1810-1850
See Fuller, Margaret
See also SATA 25

Ostrovsky, Alexander
1823-1886 .... **NCLC 30**

Otero, Blas de 1916-1979.......... **CLC 11**
See also CA 89-92; DLB 134

Otto, Whitney 1955-............. **CLC 70**
See also CA 140

Ouida .... **TCLC 43**
See also De La Ramee, (Marie) Louise
See also DLB 18

Ousmane, Sembene 1923- .... **CLC 66; BLC**
See also BW 1; CA 117; 125; MTCW

Ovid 43B.C.-18th cent. (?)... **CMLC 7; PC 2**

Owen, Hugh
See Faust, Frederick (Schiller)

Owen, Wilfred (Edward Salter)
1893-1918 ...... **TCLC 5, 27; DA; WLC**
See also CA 104; 141; CDBLB 1914-1945;
DLB 20

Owens, Rochelle 1936-............ **CLC 8**
See also CA 17-20R; CAAS 2; CANR 39

Oz, Amos 1939- ... **CLC 5, 8, 11, 27, 33, 54**
See also CA 53-56; CANR 27; MTCW

Ozick, Cynthia
1928- .... **CLC 3, 7, 28, 62; SSC 15**
See also BEST 90:1; CA 17-20R; CANR 23;
DLB 28; DLBY 82; MTCW

Ozu, Yasujiro 1903-1963 .... **CLC 16**
See also CA 112

Pacheco, C.
See Pessoa, Fernando (Antonio Nogueira)

Pa Chin
See Li Fei-kan

Pack, Robert 1929-.............. **CLC 13**
See also CA 1-4R; CANR 3, 44; DLB 5

Padgett, Lewis
See Kuttner, Henry

Padilla (Lorenzo), Heberto 1932-... **CLC 38**
See also AITN 1; CA 123; 131; HW

Page, Jimmy 1944-............... **CLC 12**

Page, Louise 1955-.............. **CLC 40**
See also CA 140

Page, P(atricia) K(athleen)
1916- .... **CLC 7, 18**
See also CA 53-56; CANR 4, 22; DLB 68;
MTCW

Paget, Violet 1856-1935
See Lee, Vernon
See also CA 104

Paget-Lowe, Henry
See Lovecraft, H(oward) P(hillips)

Paglia, Camille (Anna) 1947-...... **CLC 68**
See also CA 140

Paige, Richard
See Koontz, Dean R(ay)

Pakenham, Antonia
See Fraser, (Lady) Antonia (Pakenham)

Palamas, Kostes 1859-1943 .... **TCLC 5**
See also CA 105

Palazzeschi, Aldo 1885-1974....... **CLC 11**
See also CA 89-92; 53-56; DLB 114

Paley, Grace 1922-.... **CLC 4, 6, 37; SSC 8**
See also CA 25-28R; CANR 13; DLB 28;
MTCW

Palin, Michael (Edward) 1943-..... **CLC 21**
See also Monty Python
See also CA 107; CANR 35; SATA 67

Palliser, Charles 1947-........... **CLC 65**
See also CA 136

Palma, Ricardo 1833-1919........ **TCLC 29**

Pancake, Breece Dexter 1952-1979
See Pancake, Breece D'J
See also CA 123; 109

Pancake, Breece D'J.............. **CLC 29**
See also Pancake, Breece Dexter
See also DLB 130

Panko, Rudy
See Gogol, Nikolai (Vasilyevich)

Papadiamantis, Alexandros
1851-1911 .... **TCLC 29**

Papadiamantopoulos, Johannes 1856-1910
See Moreas, Jean
See also CA 117

Papini, Giovanni 1881-1956....... **TCLC 22**
See also CA 121

Paracelsus 1493-1541 .... **LC 14**

Parasol, Peter
See Stevens, Wallace

Parfenie, Maria
See Codrescu, Andrei

Parini, Jay (Lee) 1948- .... **CLC 54**
See also CA 97-100; CAAS 16; CANR 32

Park, Jordan
See Kornbluth, C(yril) M.; Pohl, Frederik

Parker, Bert
See Ellison, Harlan

Parker, Dorothy (Rothschild)
1893-1967 .... **CLC 15, 68; SSC 2**
See also CA 19-20; 25-28R; CAP 2;
DLB 11, 45, 86; MTCW

Parker, Robert B(rown) 1932-...... **CLC 27**
See also BEST 89:4; CA 49-52; CANR 1,
26; MTCW

Parkes, Lucas
See Harris, John (Wyndham Parkes Lucas)
Beynon

Parkin, Frank 1940-............. **CLC 43**

Parkman, Francis, Jr.
1823-1893 .... **NCLC 12**
See also DLB 1, 30

Parks, Gordon (Alexander Buchanan)
1912- .... **CLC 1, 16; BLC**
See also AITN 2; BW 2; CA 41-44R;
CANR 26; DLB 33; SATA 8

Parnell, Thomas 1679-1718 .... **LC 3**
See also DLB 94

Parra, Nicanor 1914- .... **CLC 2; HLC**
See also CA 85-88; CANR 32; HW; MTCW

Parrish, Mary Frances
See Fisher, M(ary) F(rances) K(ennedy)

Parson
See Coleridge, Samuel Taylor

Parson Lot
See Kingsley, Charles

Partridge, Anthony
See Oppenheim, E(dward) Phillips

Pascoli, Giovanni 1855-1912 ...... **TCLC 45**

Pasolini, Pier Paolo
1922-1975 .... **CLC 20, 37**
See also CA 93-96; 61-64; DLB 128;
MTCW

Pasquini
See Silone, Ignazio

Pastan, Linda (Olenik) 1932- ...... **CLC 27**
See also CA 61-64; CANR 18, 40; DLB 5

Pasternak, Boris (Leonidovich)
1890-1960 ..... **CLC 7, 10, 18, 63; DA;**
PC 6; WLC
See also CA 127; 116; MTCW

Patchen, Kenneth 1911-1972 ... **CLC 1, 2, 18**
See also CA 1-4R; 33-36R; CANR 3, 35;
DLB 16, 48; MTCW

Pater, Walter (Horatio)
1839-1894 .... **NCLC 7**
See also CDBLB 1832-1890; DLB 57

Paterson, A(ndrew) B(arton)
1864-1941 .... **TCLC 32**

Paterson, Katherine (Womeldorf)
1932- .... **CLC 12, 30**
See also AAYA 1; CA 21-24R; CANR 28;
CLR 7; DLB 52; JRDA; MAICYA;
MTCW; SATA 13, 53

Patmore, Coventry Kersey Dighton
1823-1896 .... **NCLC 9**
See also DLB 35, 98

Paton, Alan (Stewart)
1903-1988 ...... **CLC 4, 10, 25, 55; DA;**
WLC
See also CA 13-16; 125; CANR 22; CAP 1;
MTCW; SATA 11, 56

Paton Walsh, Gillian 1937-
See Walsh, Jill Paton
See also CANR 38; JRDA; MAICYA;
SAAS 3; SATA 4, 72

Paulding, James Kirke 1778-1860.. **NCLC 2**
See also DLB 3, 59, 74

Paulin, Thomas Neilson 1949-
See Paulin, Tom
See also CA 123; 128

Paulin, Tom .... **CLC 37**
See also Paulin, Thomas Neilson
See also DLB 40

Paustovsky, Konstantin (Georgievich)
1892-1968 .... **CLC 40**
See also CA 93-96; 25-28R

Pavese, Cesare 1908-1950 .... **TCLC 3**
See also CA 104; DLB 128

Pavic, Milorad 1929- .... **CLC 60**
See also CA 136

Payne, Alan
See Jakes, John (William)

Paz, Gil
See Lugones, Leopoldo

Paz, Octavio
1914- .... **CLC 3, 4, 6, 10, 19, 51, 65;**
DA; HLC; PC 1; WLC
See also CA 73-76; CANR 32; DLBY 90;
HW; MTCW

Peacock, Molly 1947-............. **CLC 60**
See also CA 103; DLB 120

Peacock, Thomas Love
1785-1866 .... **NCLC 22**
See also DLB 96, 116

Peake, Mervyn 1911-1968 ...... **CLC 7, 54**
See also CA 5-8R; 25-28R; CANR 3;
DLB 15; MTCW; SATA 23

Pearce, Philippa .... **CLC 21**
See also Christie, (Ann) Philippa
See also CLR 9; MAICYA; SATA 1, 67

Pearl, Eric
See Elman, Richard

Pearson, T(homas) R(eid) 1956- .... **CLC 39**
See also CA 120; 130

Peck, Dale 1968(?)- .... **CLC 81**

Peck, John 1941- .... **CLC 3**
See also CA 49-52; CANR 3

Peck, Richard (Wayne) 1934- ...... **CLC 21**
See also AAYA 1; CA 85-88; CANR 19,
38; JRDA; MAICYA; SAAS 2; SATA 18,
55

Peck, Robert Newton 1928-.... **CLC 17; DA**
See also AAYA 3; CA 81-84; CANR 31;
JRDA; MAICYA; SAAS 1; SATA 21, 62

Peckinpah, (David) Sam(uel)
1925-1984 .... **CLC 20**
See also CA 109; 114

Pedersen, Knut 1859-1952
See Hamsun, Knut
See also CA 104; 119; MTCW

Peeslake, Gaffer
See Durrell, Lawrence (George)

Peguy, Charles Pierre
1873-1914 .... **TCLC 10**
See also CA 107

Pena, Ramon del Valle y
See Valle-Inclan, Ramon (Maria) del

Pendennis, Arthur Esquir
See Thackeray, William Makepeace

Penn, William 1644-1718.......... **LC 25**
See also DLB 24

Pepys, Samuel
1633-1703 .... **LC 11; DA; WLC**
See also CDBLB 1660-1789; DLB 101

Percy, Walker
1916-1990 .... **CLC 2, 3, 6, 8, 14, 18, 47,**
65
See also CA 1-4R; 131; CANR 1, 23;
DLB 2; DLBY 80, 90; MTCW

Perec, Georges 1936-1982 .... **CLC 56**
See also CA 141; DLB 83

Pereda (y Sanchez de Porrua), Jose Maria de
1833-1906 .... **TCLC 16**
See also CA 117

Pereda y Porrua, Jose Maria de
See Pereda (y Sanchez de Porrua), Jose
Maria de

Peregoy, George Weems
See Mencken, H(enry) L(ouis)

Perelman, S(idney) J(oseph)
1904-1979 ... **CLC 3, 5, 9, 15, 23, 44, 49**
See also AITN 1, 2; CA 73-76; 89-92;
CANR 18; DLB 11, 44; MTCW

Peret, Benjamin 1899-1959 .... **TCLC 20**
See also CA 117

Peretz, Isaac Loeb 1851(?)-1915... **TCLC 16**
See also CA 109

Peretz, Yitzhok Leibush
See Peretz, Isaac Loeb

Perez Galdos, Benito 1843-1920 ... **TCLC 27**
See also CA 125; HW

Perrault, Charles 1628-1703 .... **LC 2**
See also MAICYA; SATA 25

Perry, Brighton
See Sherwood, Robert E(mmet)

Perse, St.-John .... **CLC 4, 11, 46**
See also Leger, (Marie-Rene Auguste) Alexis
Saint-Leger

Peseenz, Tulio F.
See Lopez y Fuentes, Gregorio

Pesetsky, Bette 1932-............. **CLC 28**
See also CA 133; DLB 130

Peshkov, Alexei Maximovich 1868-1936
See Gorky, Maxim
See also CA 105; 141; DA

Quiller-Couch, Arthur Thomas
1863-1944 .... **TCLC 53**
See also CA 118; DLB 135

Quin, Ann (Marie) 1936-1973 .... **CLC 6**
See also CA 9-12R; 45-48; DLB 14

Quinn, Martin
See Smith, Martin Cruz

Quinn, Simon
See Smith, Martin Cruz

Quiroga, Horacio (Sylvestre)
1878-1937 .... **TCLC 20; HLC**
See also CA 117; 131; HW; MTCW

Quoirez, Francoise 1935- .... **CLC 9**
See also Sagan, Francoise
See also CA 49-52; CANR 6, 39; MTCW

Raabe, Wilhelm 1831-1910 .... **TCLC 45**
See also DLB 129

Rabe, David (William) 1940-... **CLC 4, 8, 33**
See also CA 85-88; CABS 3; DLB 7

Rabelais, Francois
1483-1553 .... **LC 5; DA; WLC**

Rabinovitch, Sholem 1859-1916
See Aleichem, Sholom
See also CA 104

Radcliffe, Ann (Ward) 1764-1823 .. **NCLC 6**
See also DLB 39

Radiguet, Raymond 1903-1923 .... **TCLC 29**
See also DLB 65

Radnoti, Miklos 1909-1944 .... **TCLC 16**
See also CA 118

Rado, James 1939- .... **CLC 17**
See also CA 105

Radvanyi, Netty 1900-1983
See Seghers, Anna
See also CA 85-88; 110

Rae, Ben
See Griffiths, Trevor

Raeburn, John (Hay) 1941-........ **CLC 34**
See also CA 57-60

Ragni, Gerome 1942-1991 .... **CLC 17**
See also CA 105; 134

Rahv, Philip 1908-1973 .... **CLC 24**
See also Greenberg, Ivan
See also DLB 137

Raine, Craig 1944- .... **CLC 32**
See also CA 108; CANR 29; DLB 40

Raine, Kathleen (Jessie) 1908- ... **CLC 7, 45**
See also CA 85-88; DLB 20; MTCW

Rainis, Janis 1865-1929 .... **TCLC 29**

Rakosi, Carl .... **CLC 47**
See also Rawley, Callman
See also CAAS 5

Raleigh, Richard
See Lovecraft, H(oward) P(hillips)

Rallentando, H. P.
See Sayers, Dorothy L(eigh)

Ramal, Walter
See de la Mare, Walter (John)

Ramon, Juan
See Jimenez (Mantecon), Juan Ramon

Ramos, Graciliano 1892-1953 ..... **TCLC 32**

Rampersad, Arnold 1941-......... **CLC 44**
See also BW 2; CA 127; 133; DLB 111

Rampling, Anne
See Rice, Anne

Ramuz, Charles-Ferdinand
1878-1947 .... **TCLC 33**

Rand, Ayn
1905-1982 ..... **CLC 3, 30, 44, 79; DA; WLC**
See also AAYA 10; CA 13-16R; 105; CANR 27; MTCW

Randall, Dudley (Felker)
1914- .... **CLC 1; BLC**
See also BW 1; CA 25-28R; CANR 23; DLB 41

Randall, Robert
See Silverberg, Robert

Ranger, Ken
See Creasey, John

Ransom, John Crowe
1888-1974 .... **CLC 2, 4, 5, 11, 24**
See also CA 5-8R; 49-52; CANR 6, 34; DLB 45, 63; MTCW

Rao, Raja 1909- .... **CLC 25, 56**
See also CA 73-76; MTCW

Raphael, Frederic (Michael)
1931- .... **CLC 2, 14**
See also CA 1-4R; CANR 1; DLB 14

Ratcliffe, James P.
See Mencken, H(enry) L(ouis)

Rathbone, Julian 1935- .... **CLC 41**
See also CA 101; CANR 34

Rattigan, Terence (Mervyn)
1911-1977 .... **CLC 7**
See also CA 85-88; 73-76; CDBLB 1945-1960; DLB 13; MTCW

Ratushinskaya, Irina 1954-........ **CLC 54**
See also CA 129

Raven, Simon (Arthur Noel)
1927- .... **CLC 14**
See also CA 81-84

Rawley, Callman 1903-
See Rakosi, Carl
See also CA 21-24R; CANR 12, 32

Rawlings, Marjorie Kinnan
1896-1953 .... **TCLC 4**
See also CA 104; 137; DLB 9, 22, 102; JRDA; MAICYA; YABC 1

Ray, Satyajit 1921-1992........ **CLC 16, 76**
See also CA 114; 137

Read, Herbert Edward 1893-1968.... **CLC 4**
See also CA 85-88; 25-28R; DLB 20

Read, Piers Paul 1941- ...... **CLC 4, 10, 25**
See also CA 21-24R; CANR 38; DLB 14; SATA 21

Reade, Charles 1814-1884 .... **NCLC 2**
See also DLB 21

Reade, Hamish
See Gray, Simon (James Holliday)

Reading, Peter 1946- .... **CLC 47**
See also CA 103; DLB 40

Reaney, James 1926- .... **CLC 13**
See also CA 41-44R; CAAS 15; CANR 42; DLB 68; SATA 43

Rebreanu, Liviu 1885-1944 .... **TCLC 28**

Rechy, John (Francisco)
1934- .... **CLC 1, 7, 14, 18; HLC**
See also CA 5-8R; CAAS 4; CANR 6, 32; DLB 122; DLBY 82; HW

Redcam, Tom 1870-1933 .... **TCLC 25**

Reddin, Keith .... **CLC 67**

Redgrove, Peter (William)
1932- .... **CLC 6, 41**
See also CA 1-4R; CANR 3, 39; DLB 40

Redmon, Anne .... **CLC 22**
See also Nightingale, Anne Redmon
See also DLBY 86

Reed, Eliot
See Ambler, Eric

Reed, Ishmael
1938- ... **CLC 2, 3, 5, 6, 13, 32, 60; BLC**
See also BW 2; CA 21-24R; CANR 25; DLB 2, 5, 33; DLBD 8; MTCW

Reed, John (Silas) 1887-1920 ...... **TCLC 9**
See also CA 106

Reed, Lou .... **CLC 21**
See also Firbank, Louis

Reeve, Clara 1729-1807 .... **NCLC 19**
See also DLB 39

Reid, Christopher (John) 1949-..... **CLC 33**
See also CA 140; DLB 40

Reid, Desmond
See Moorcock, Michael (John)

Reid Banks, Lynne 1929-
See Banks, Lynne Reid
See also CA 1-4R; CANR 6, 22, 38; CLR 24; JRDA; MAICYA; SATA 22, 75

Reilly, William K.
See Creasey, John

Reiner, Max
See Caldwell, (Janet Miriam) Taylor (Holland)

Reis, Ricardo
See Pessoa, Fernando (Antonio Nogueira)

Remarque, Erich Maria
1898-1970 .... **CLC 21; DA**
See also CA 77-80; 29-32R; DLB 56; MTCW

Remizov, A.
See Remizov, Aleksei (Mikhailovich)

Remizov, A. M.
See Remizov, Aleksei (Mikhailovich)

Remizov, Aleksei (Mikhailovich)
1877-1957 .... **TCLC 27**
See also CA 125; 133

Renan, Joseph Ernest
1823-1892 .... **NCLC 26**

Renard, Jules 1864-1910 .... **TCLC 17**
See also CA 117

Renault, Mary .... **CLC 3, 11, 17**
See also Challans, Mary
See also DLBY 83

Rendell, Ruth (Barbara) 1930- .. **CLC 28, 48**
See also Vine, Barbara
See also CA 109; CANR 32; DLB 87; MTCW

Renoir, Jean 1894-1979 .... **CLC 20**
See also CA 129; 85-88

Resnais, Alain 1922-.............. **CLC 16**

Robinson, William, Jr. 1940-
See Robinson, Smokey
See also CA 116

Robison, Mary 1949- . . . . **CLC 42**
See also CA 113; 116; DLB 130

Rod, Edouard 1857-1910 . . . . **TCLC 52**

Roddenberry, Eugene Wesley 1921-1991
See Roddenberry, Gene
See also CA 110; 135; CANR 37; SATA 45

Roddenberry, Gene . . . . **CLC 17**
See also Roddenberry, Eugene Wesley
See also AAYA 5; SATA-Obit 69

Rodgers, Mary 1931- . . . . **CLC 12**
See also CA 49-52; CANR 8; CLR 20;
JRDA; MAICYA; SATA 8

Rodgers, W(illiam) R(obert)
1909-1969 . . . . **CLC 7**
See also CA 85-88; DLB 20

Rodman, Eric
See Silverberg, Robert

Rodman, Howard 1920(?)-1985 . . . . . **CLC 65**
See also CA 118

Rodman, Maia
See Wojciechowska, Maia (Teresa)

Rodriguez, Claudio 1934- . . . . **CLC 10**
See also DLB 134

Roelvaag, O(le) E(dvart)
1876-1931 . . . . **TCLC 17**
See also CA 117; DLB 9

Roethke, Theodore (Huebner)
1908-1963 . . . . . . **CLC 1, 3, 8, 11, 19, 46**
See also CA 81-84; CABS 2;
CDALB 1941-1968; DLB 5; MTCW

Rogers, Thomas Hunton 1927- . . . . . **CLC 57**
See also CA 89-92

Rogers, Will(iam Penn Adair)
1879-1935 . . . . **TCLC 8**
See also CA 105; 144; DLB 11

Rogin, Gilbert 1929- . . . . **CLC 18**
See also CA 65-68; CANR 15

Rohan, Koda . . . . **TCLC 22**
See also Koda Shigeyuki

Rohmer, Eric . . . . **CLC 16**
See also Scherer, Jean-Marie Maurice

Rohmer, Sax . . . . **TCLC 28**
See also Ward, Arthur Henry Sarsfield
See also DLB 70

Roiphe, Anne (Richardson)
1935- . . . . **CLC 3, 9**
See also CA 89-92; CANR 45; DLBY 80

Rojas, Fernando de 1465-1541 . . . . . **LC 23**

**Rolfe, Frederick (William Serafino Austin
Lewis Mary)** 1860-1913 . . . . . . **TCLC 12**
See also CA 107; DLB 34

Rolland, Romain 1866-1944 . . . . . . **TCLC 23**
See also CA 118; DLB 65

Rolvaag, O(le) E(dvart)
See Roelvaag, O(le) E(dvart)

Romain Arnaud, Saint
See Aragon, Louis

Romains, Jules 1885-1972 . . . . **CLC 7**
See also CA 85-88; CANR 34; DLB 65;
MTCW

Romero, Jose Ruben 1890-1952 . . . **TCLC 14**
See also CA 114; 131; HW

Ronsard, Pierre de 1524-1585 . . . . **LC 6**

Rooke, Leon 1934- . . . . **CLC 25, 34**
See also CA 25-28R; CANR 23

Roper, William 1498-1578 . . . . **LC 10**

Roquelaure, A. N.
See Rice, Anne

Rosa, Joao Guimaraes 1908-1967 . . . **CLC 23**
See also CA 89-92; DLB 113

Rosen, Richard (Dean) 1949- . . . . . . **CLC 39**
See also CA 77-80

Rosenberg, Isaac 1890-1918 . . . . . . **TCLC 12**
See also CA 107; DLB 20

Rosenblatt, Joe . . . . **CLC 15**
See also Rosenblatt, Joseph

Rosenblatt, Joseph 1933-
See Rosenblatt, Joe
See also CA 89-92

Rosenfeld, Samuel 1896-1963
See Tzara, Tristan
See also CA 89-92

Rosenthal, M(acha) L(ouis) 1917- . . . **CLC 28**
See also CA 1-4R; CAAS 6; CANR 4;
DLB 5; SATA 59

Ross, Barnaby
See Dannay, Frederic

Ross, Bernard L.
See Follett, Ken(neth Martin)

Ross, J. H.
See Lawrence, T(homas) E(dward)

Ross, Martin
See Martin, Violet Florence
See also DLB 135

Ross, (James) Sinclair 1908- . . . . **CLC 13**
See also CA 73-76; DLB 88

Rossetti, Christina (Georgina)
1830-1894 . . . **NCLC 2; DA; PC 7; WLC**
See also DLB 35; MAICYA; SATA 20

Rossetti, Dante Gabriel
1828-1882 . . . . **NCLC 4; DA; WLC**
See also CDBLB 1832-1890; DLB 35

Rossner, Judith (Perelman)
1935- . . . . **CLC 6, 9, 29**
See also AITN 2; BEST 90:3; CA 17-20R;
CANR 18; DLB 6; MTCW

Rostand, Edmond (Eugene Alexis)
1868-1918 . . . . **TCLC 6, 37; DA**
See also CA 104; 126; MTCW

Roth, Henry 1906- . . . . **CLC 2, 6, 11**
See also CA 11-12; CANR 38; CAP 1;
DLB 28; MTCW

Roth, Joseph 1894-1939 . . . . **TCLC 33**
See also DLB 85

Roth, Philip (Milton)
1933- . . . . . . **CLC 1, 2, 3, 4, 6, 9, 15, 22,
31, 47, 66; DA; WLC**
See also BEST 90:3; CA 1-4R; CANR 1, 22,
36; CDALB 1968-1988; DLB 2, 28;
DLBY 82; MTCW

Rothenberg, Jerome 1931- . . . . **CLC 6, 57**
See also CA 45-48; CANR 1; DLB 5

Roumain, Jacques (Jean Baptiste)
1907-1944 . . . . **TCLC 19; BLC**
See also BW 1; CA 117; 125

Rourke, Constance (Mayfield)
1885-1941 . . . . **TCLC 12**
See also CA 107; YABC 1

Rousseau, Jean-Baptiste 1671-1741 . . . **LC 9**

Rousseau, Jean-Jacques
1712-1778 . . . . **LC 14; DA; WLC**

Roussel, Raymond 1877-1933 . . . . . **TCLC 20**
See also CA 117

Rovit, Earl (Herbert) 1927- . . . . **CLC 7**
See also CA 5-8R; CANR 12

Rowe, Nicholas 1674-1718 . . . . **LC 8**
See also DLB 84

Rowley, Ames Dorrance
See Lovecraft, H(oward) P(hillips)

Rowson, Susanna Haswell
1762(?)-1824 . . . . **NCLC 5**
See also DLB 37

Roy, Gabrielle 1909-1983 . . . . **CLC 10, 14**
See also CA 53-56; 110; CANR 5; DLB 68;
MTCW

Rozewicz, Tadeusz 1921- . . . . **CLC 9, 23**
See also CA 108; CANR 36; MTCW

Ruark, Gibbons 1941- . . . . **CLC 3**
See also CA 33-36R; CANR 14, 31;
DLB 120

Rubens, Bernice (Ruth) 1923- . . . **CLC 19, 31**
See also CA 25-28R; CANR 33; DLB 14;
MTCW

Rudkin, (James) David 1936- . . . . . . **CLC 14**
See also CA 89-92; DLB 13

Rudnik, Raphael 1933- . . . . **CLC 7**
See also CA 29-32R

Ruffian, M.
See Hasek, Jaroslav (Matej Frantisek)

Ruiz, Jose Martinez . . . . **CLC 11**
See also Martinez Ruiz, Jose

Rukeyser, Muriel
1913-1980 . . . . **CLC 6, 10, 15, 27**
See also CA 5-8R; 93-96; CANR 26;
DLB 48; MTCW; SATA 22

Rule, Jane (Vance) 1931- . . . . **CLC 27**
See also CA 25-28R; CAAS 18; CANR 12;
DLB 60

Rulfo, Juan 1918-1986 . . . . **CLC 8, 80; HLC**
See also CA 85-88; 118; CANR 26;
DLB 113; HW; MTCW

Runeberg, Johan 1804-1877 . . . . . . **NCLC 41**

Runyon, (Alfred) Damon
1884(?)-1946 . . . . **TCLC 10**
See also CA 107; DLB 11, 86

Rush, Norman 1933- . . . . **CLC 44**
See also CA 121; 126

Rushdie, (Ahmed) Salman
1947- . . . . **CLC 23, 31, 55**
See also BEST 89:3; CA 108; 111;
CANR 33; MTCW

Rushforth, Peter (Scott) 1945- . . . . . **CLC 19**
See also CA 101

Ruskin, John 1819-1900 . . . . **TCLC 20**
See also CA 114; 129; CDBLB 1832-1890;
DLB 55; SATA 24

Secundus, H. Scriblerus
See Fielding, Henry

Sedges, John
See Buck, Pearl S(ydenstricker)

Sedgwick, Catharine Maria
1789-1867 . . . . NCLC 19
See also DLB 1, 74

Seelye, John 1931- . . . . CLC 7

Seferiades, Giorgos Stylianou 1900-1971
See Seferis, George
See also CA 5-8R; 33-36R; CANR 5, 36;
MTCW

Seferis, George . . . . CLC 5, 11
See also Seferiades, Giorgos Stylianou

Segal, Erich (Wolf) 1937- . . . . CLC 3, 10
See also BEST 89:1; CA 25-28R; CANR 20,
36; DLBY 86; MTCW

Seger, Bob 1945- . . . . CLC 35

Seghers, Anna . . . . CLC 7
See also Radvanyi, Netty
See also DLB 69

Seidel, Frederick (Lewis) 1936- . . . . . CLC 18
See also CA 13-16R; CANR 8; DLBY 84

Seifert, Jaroslav 1901-1986 . . . . . CLC 34, 44
See also CA 127; MTCW

Sei Shonagon c. 966-1017(?) . . . . . . CMLC 6

Selby, Hubert, Jr. 1928- . . . . . CLC 1, 2, 4, 8
See also CA 13-16R; CANR 33; DLB 2

Selzer, Richard 1928- . . . . CLC 74
See also CA 65-68; CANR 14

Sembene, Ousmane
See Ousmane, Sembene

Senancour, Etienne Pivert de
1770-1846 . . . . NCLC 16
See also DLB 119

Sender, Ramon (Jose)
1902-1982 . . . . CLC 8; HLC
See also CA 5-8R; 105; CANR 8; HW;
MTCW

Seneca, Lucius Annaeus
4B.C.-65. . . . . CMLC 6

Senghor, Leopold Sedar
1906- . . . . CLC 54; BLC
See also BW 2; CA 116; 125; MTCW

Serling, (Edward) Rod(man)
1924-1975 . . . . CLC 30
See also AITN 1; CA 65-68; 57-60; DLB 26

Serna, Ramon Gomez de la
See Gomez de la Serna, Ramon

Serpieres
See Guillevic, (Eugene)

Service, Robert
See Service, Robert W(illiam)
See also DLB 92

Service, Robert W(illiam)
1874(?)-1958 . . . . . . TCLC 15; DA; WLC
See also Service, Robert
See also CA 115; 140; SATA 20

Seth, Vikram 1952- . . . . CLC 43
See also CA 121; 127; DLB 120

Seton, Cynthia Propper
1926-1982 . . . . CLC 27
See also CA 5-8R; 108; CANR 7

Seton, Ernest (Evan) Thompson
1860-1946 . . . . TCLC 31
See also CA 109; DLB 92; JRDA; SATA 18

Seton-Thompson, Ernest
See Seton, Ernest (Evan) Thompson

Settle, Mary Lee 1918- . . . . CLC 19, 61
See also CA 89-92; CAAS 1; CANR 44;
DLB 6

Seuphor, Michel
See Arp, Jean

Sevigne, Marie (de Rabutin-Chantal) Marquise
de 1626-1696 . . . . LC 11

Sexton, Anne (Harvey)
1928-1974 . . . . CLC 2, 4, 6, 8, 10, 15, 53;
DA; PC 2; WLC
See also CA 1-4R; 53-56; CABS 2;
CANR 3, 36; CDALB 1941-1968; DLB 5;
MTCW; SATA 10

Shaara, Michael (Joseph Jr.)
1929-1988 . . . . CLC 15
See also AITN 1; CA 102; DLBY 83

Shackleton, C. C.
See Aldiss, Brian W(ilson)

Shacochis, Bob . . . . CLC 39
See also Shacochis, Robert G.

Shacochis, Robert G. 1951-
See Shacochis, Bob
See also CA 119; 124

Shaffer, Anthony (Joshua) 1926- . . . . CLC 19
See also CA 110; 116; DLB 13

Shaffer, Peter (Levin)
1926- . . . . CLC 5, 14, 18, 37, 60
See also CA 25-28R; CANR 25;
CDBLB 1960 to Present; DLB 13;
MTCW

Shakey, Bernard
See Young, Neil

Shalamov, Varlam (Tikhonovich)
1907(?)-1982 . . . . CLC 18
See also CA 129; 105

Shamlu, Ahmad 1925- . . . . CLC 10

Shammas, Anton 1951- . . . . CLC 55

Shange, Ntozake
1948- . . . . CLC 8, 25, 38, 74; BLC; DC 3
See also AAYA 9; BW 2; CA 85-88;
CABS 3; CANR 27; DLB 38; MTCW

Shanley, John Patrick 1950- . . . . CLC 75
See also CA 128; 133

Shapcott, Thomas William 1935- . . . CLC 38
See also CA 69-72

Shapiro, Jane . . . . CLC 76

Shapiro, Karl (Jay) 1913- . . CLC 4, 8, 15, 53
See also CA 1-4R; CAAS 6; CANR 1, 36;
DLB 48; MTCW

Sharp, William 1855-1905 . . . . TCLC 39

Sharpe, Thomas Ridley 1928-
See Sharpe, Tom
See also CA 114; 122

Sharpe, Tom. CLC 36
See also Sharpe, Thomas Ridley
See also DLB 14

Shaw, Bernard. . . . . TCLC 45
See also Shaw, George Bernard
See also BW 1

Shaw, G. Bernard
See Shaw, George Bernard

Shaw, George Bernard
1856-1950 . . . . TCLC 3, 9, 21; DA; WLC
See also Shaw, Bernard
See also CA 104; 128; CDBLB 1914-1945;
DLB 10, 57; MTCW

Shaw, Henry Wheeler
1818-1885 . . . . NCLC 15
See also DLB 11

Shaw, Irwin 1913-1984 . . . . . . CLC 7, 23, 34
See also AITN 1; CA 13-16R; 112;
CANR 21; CDALB 1941-1968; DLB 6,
102; DLBY 84; MTCW

Shaw, Robert 1927-1978 . . . . CLC 5
See also AITN 1; CA 1-4R; 81-84;
CANR 4; DLB 13, 14

Shaw, T. E.
See Lawrence, T(homas) E(dward)

Shawn, Wallace 1943- . . . . CLC 41
See also CA 112

Sheed, Wilfrid (John Joseph)
1930- . . . . CLC 2, 4, 10, 53
See also CA 65-68; CANR 30; DLB 6;
MTCW

Sheldon, Alice Hastings Bradley
1915(?)-1987
See Tiptree, James, Jr.
See also CA 108; 122; CANR 34; MTCW

Sheldon, John
See Bloch, Robert (Albert)

Shelley, Mary Wollstonecraft (Godwin)
1797-1851 . . . . NCLC 14; DA; WLC
See also CDBLB 1789-1832; DLB 110, 116;
SATA 29

Shelley, Percy Bysshe
1792-1822 . . . . NCLC 18; DA; WLC
See also CDBLB 1789-1832; DLB 96, 110

Shepard, Jim 1956- . . . . CLC 36
See also CA 137

Shepard, Lucius 1947- . . . . CLC 34
See also CA 128; 141

Shepard, Sam
1943- . . . . CLC 4, 6, 17, 34, 41, 44
See also AAYA 1; CA 69-72; CABS 3;
CANR 22; DLB 7; MTCW

Shepherd, Michael
See Ludlum, Robert

Sherburne, Zoa (Morin) 1912- . . . . . CLC 30
See also CA 1-4R; CANR 3, 37; MAICYA;
SAAS 18; SATA 3

Sheridan, Frances 1724-1766 . . . . LC 7
See also DLB 39, 84

Sheridan, Richard Brinsley
1751-1816 . . . NCLC 5; DA; DC 1; WLC
See also CDBLB 1660-1789; DLB 89

Sherman, Jonathan Marc. . . . . CLC 55

Sherman, Martin 1941(?)- . . . . CLC 19
See also CA 116; 123

Sherwin, Judith Johnson 1936- . . . CLC 7, 15
See also CA 25-28R; CANR 34

Sherwood, Frances 1940- . . . . CLC 81

Sherwood, Robert E(mmet)
1896-1955 . . . . TCLC 3
See also CA 104; DLB 7, 26

Shestov, Lev   1866-1938 . . . . **TCLC 56**

Shiel, M(atthew) P(hipps)
  1865-1947 . . . . **TCLC 8**
  See also CA 106

Shiga, Naoya   1883-1971 . . . . **CLC 33**
  See also CA 101; 33-36R

Shimazaki Haruki   1872-1943
  See Shimazaki Toson
  See also CA 105; 134

Shimazaki Toson . . . . **TCLC 5**
  See also Shimazaki Haruki

Sholokhov, Mikhail (Aleksandrovich)
  1905-1984 . . . . **CLC 7, 15**
  See also CA 101; 112; MTCW; SATA 36

Shone, Patric
  See Hanley, James

Shreve, Susan Richards   1939- . . . . . . **CLC 23**
  See also CA 49-52; CAAS 5; CANR 5, 38;
    MAICYA; SATA 41, 46

Shue, Larry   1946-1985 . . . . **CLC 52**
  See also CA 117

Shu-Jen, Chou   1881-1936
  See Hsun, Lu
  See also CA 104

Shulman, Alix Kates   1932- . . . . . . **CLC 2, 10**
  See also CA 29-32R; CANR 43; SATA 7

Shuster, Joe   1914- . . . . **CLC 21**

Shute, Nevil . . . . **CLC 30**
  See also Norway, Nevil Shute

Shuttle, Penelope (Diane)   1947- . . . . . **CLC 7**
  See also CA 93-96; CANR 39; DLB 14, 40

Sidney, Mary   1561-1621 . . . . **LC 19**

Sidney, Sir Philip   1554-1586 . . . . **LC 19; DA**
  See also CDBLB Before 1660

Siegel, Jerome   1914- . . . . **CLC 21**
  See also CA 116

Siegel, Jerry
  See Siegel, Jerome

Sienkiewicz, Henryk (Adam Alexander Pius)
  1846-1916 . . . . **TCLC 3**
  See also CA 104; 134

Sierra, Gregorio Martinez
  See Martinez Sierra, Gregorio

Sierra, Maria (de la O'LeJarraga) Martinez
  See Martinez Sierra, Maria (de la
    O'LeJarraga)

Sigal, Clancy   1926- . . . . **CLC 7**
  See also CA 1-4R

Sigourney, Lydia Howard (Huntley)
  1791-1865 . . . . **NCLC 21**
  See also DLB 1, 42, 73

Siguenza y Gongora, Carlos de
  1645-1700 . . . . **LC 8**

Sigurjonsson, Johann   1880-1919 . . . **TCLC 27**

Sikelianos, Angelos   1884-1951 . . . . **TCLC 39**

Silkin, Jon   1930- . . . . **CLC 2, 6, 43**
  See also CA 5-8R; CAAS 5; DLB 27

Silko, Leslie (Marmon)
  1948- . . . . **CLC 23, 74; DA**
  See also CA 115; 122; CANR 45; DLB 143

Sillanpaa, Frans Eemil   1888-1964 . . . **CLC 19**
  See also CA 129; 93-96; MTCW

Sillitoe, Alan
  1928- . . . . **CLC 1, 3, 6, 10, 19, 57**
  See also AITN 1; CA 9-12R; CAAS 2;
    CANR 8, 26; CDBLB 1960 to Present;
    DLB 14, 139; MTCW; SATA 61

Silone, Ignazio   1900-1978 . . . . **CLC 4**
  See also CA 25-28; 81-84; CANR 34;
    CAP 2; MTCW

Silver, Joan Micklin   1935- . . . . **CLC 20**
  See also CA 114; 121

Silver, Nicholas
  See Faust, Frederick (Schiller)

Silverberg, Robert   1935- . . . . **CLC 7**
  See also CA 1-4R; CAAS 3; CANR 1, 20,
    36; DLB 8; MAICYA; MTCW; SATA 13

Silverstein, Alvin   1933- . . . . **CLC 17**
  See also CA 49-52; CANR 2; CLR 25;
    JRDA; MAICYA; SATA 8, 69

Silverstein, Virginia B(arbara Opshelor)
  1937- . . . . **CLC 17**
  See also CA 49-52; CANR 2; CLR 25;
    JRDA; MAICYA; SATA 8, 69

Sim, Georges
  See Simenon, Georges (Jacques Christian)

Simak, Clifford D(onald)
  1904-1988 . . . . **CLC 1, 55**
  See also CA 1-4R; 125; CANR 1, 35;
    DLB 8; MTCW; SATA 56

Simenon, Georges (Jacques Christian)
  1903-1989 . . . . **CLC 1, 2, 3, 8, 18, 47**
  See also CA 85-88; 129; CANR 35;
    DLB 72; DLBY 89; MTCW

Simic, Charles   1938- . . . **CLC 6, 9, 22, 49, 68**
  See also CA 29-32R; CAAS 4; CANR 12,
    33; DLB 105

Simmons, Charles (Paul)   1924- . . . . . **CLC 57**
  See also CA 89-92

Simmons, Dan   1948- . . . . **CLC 44**
  See also CA 138

Simmons, James (Stewart Alexander)
  1933- . . . . **CLC 43**
  See also CA 105; DLB 40

Simms, William Gilmore
  1806-1870 . . . . **NCLC 3**
  See also DLB 3, 30, 59, 73

Simon, Carly   1945- . . . . **CLC 26**
  See also CA 105

Simon, Claude   1913- . . . . . . **CLC 4, 9, 15, 39**
  See also CA 89-92; CANR 33; DLB 83;
    MTCW

Simon, (Marvin) Neil
  1927- . . . . **CLC 6, 11, 31, 39, 70**
  See also AITN 1; CA 21-24R; CANR 26;
    DLB 7; MTCW

Simon, Paul   1942(?)- . . . . **CLC 17**
  See also CA 116

Simonon, Paul   1956(?)- . . . . **CLC 30**
  See also Clash, The

Simpson, Harriette
  See Arnow, Harriette (Louisa) Simpson

Simpson, Louis (Aston Marantz)
  1923- . . . . **CLC 4, 7, 9, 32**
  See also CA 1-4R; CAAS 4; CANR 1;
    DLB 5; MTCW

Simpson, Mona (Elizabeth)   1957- . . . **CLC 44**
  See also CA 122; 135

Simpson, N(orman) F(rederick)
  1919- . . . . **CLC 29**
  See also CA 13-16R; DLB 13

Sinclair, Andrew (Annandale)
  1935- . . . . **CLC 2, 14**
  See also CA 9-12R; CAAS 5; CANR 14, 38;
    DLB 14; MTCW

Sinclair, Emil
  See Hesse, Hermann

Sinclair, Iain   1943- . . . . **CLC 76**
  See also CA 132

Sinclair, Iain MacGregor
  See Sinclair, Iain

Sinclair, Mary Amelia St. Clair   1865(?)-1946
  See Sinclair, May
  See also CA 104

Sinclair, May . . . . **TCLC 3, 11**
  See also Sinclair, Mary Amelia St. Clair
  See also DLB 36, 135

Sinclair, Upton (Beall)
  1878-1968 . . . . . . **CLC 1, 11, 15, 63; DA;**
                                              WLC
  See also CA 5-8R; 25-28R; CANR 7;
    CDALB 1929-1941; DLB 9; MTCW;
    SATA 9

Singer, Isaac
  See Singer, Isaac Bashevis

Singer, Isaac Bashevis
  1904-1991 . . . . **CLC 1, 3, 6, 9, 11, 15, 23,**
                            38, 69; DA; SSC 3; WLC
  See also AITN 1, 2; CA 1-4R; 134;
    CANR 1, 39; CDALB 1941-1968; CLR 1;
    DLB 6, 28, 52; DLBY 91; JRDA;
    MAICYA; MTCW; SATA 3, 27;
    SATA-Obit 68

Singer, Israel Joshua   1893-1944 . . . **TCLC 33**

Singh, Khushwant   1915- . . . . **CLC 11**
  See also CA 9-12R; CAAS 9; CANR 6

Sinjohn, John
  See Galsworthy, John

Sinyavsky, Andrei (Donatevich)
  1925- . . . . **CLC 8**
  See also CA 85-88

Sirin, V.
  See Nabokov, Vladimir (Vladimirovich)

Sissman, L(ouis) E(dward)
  1928-1976 . . . . **CLC 9, 18**
  See also CA 21-24R; 65-68; CANR 13;
    DLB 5

Sisson, C(harles) H(ubert)   1914- . . . . . **CLC 8**
  See also CA 1-4R; CAAS 3; CANR 3;
    DLB 27

Sitwell, Dame Edith
  1887-1964 . . . . **CLC 2, 9, 67; PC 3**
  See also CA 9-12R; CANR 35;
    CDBLB 1945-1960; DLB 20; MTCW

Sjoewall, Maj   1935- . . . . **CLC 7**
  See also CA 65-68

Sjowall, Maj
  See Sjoewall, Maj

Skelton, Robin   1925- . . . . **CLC 13**
  See also AITN 2; CA 5-8R; CAAS 5;
    CANR 28; DLB 27, 53

Theroux, Paul (Edward)
1941- . . . . **CLC 5, 8, 11, 15, 28, 46**
See also BEST 89:4; CA 33-36R; CANR 20,
45; DLB 2; MTCW; SATA 44

Thesen, Sharon 1946- . . . . **CLC 56**

Thevenin, Denis
See Duhamel, Georges

Thibault, Jacques Anatole Francois
1844-1924
See France, Anatole
See also CA 106; 127; MTCW

Thiele, Colin (Milton) 1920- . . . . **CLC 17**
See also CA 29-32R; CANR 12, 28;
CLR 27; MAICYA; SAAS 2; SATA 14,
72

Thomas, Audrey (Callahan)
1935- . . . . **CLC 7, 13, 37**
See also AITN 2; CA 21-24R; CAAS 19;
CANR 36; DLB 60; MTCW

Thomas, D(onald) M(ichael)
1935- . . . . **CLC 13, 22, 31**
See also CA 61-64; CAAS 11; CANR 17,
45; CDBLB 1960 to Present; DLB 40;
MTCW

Thomas, Dylan (Marlais)
1914-1953 . . . **TCLC 1, 8, 45; DA; PC 2;
SSC 3; WLC**
See also CA 104; 120; CDBLB 1945-1960;
DLB 13, 20, 139; MTCW; SATA 60

Thomas, (Philip) Edward
1878-1917 . . . . **TCLC 10**
See also CA 106; DLB 19

Thomas, Joyce Carol 1938- . . . . **CLC 35**
See also AAYA 12; BW 2; CA 113; 116;
CLR 19; DLB 33; JRDA; MAICYA;
MTCW; SAAS 7; SATA 40, 78

Thomas, Lewis 1913-1993 . . . . **CLC 35**
See also CA 85-88; 143; CANR 38; MTCW

Thomas, Paul
See Mann, (Paul) Thomas

Thomas, Piri 1928- . . . . **CLC 17**
See also CA 73-76; HW

Thomas, R(onald) S(tuart)
1913- . . . . **CLC 6, 13, 48**
See also CA 89-92; CAAS 4; CANR 30;
CDBLB 1960 to Present; DLB 27;
MTCW

Thomas, Ross (Elmore) 1926- . . . . . . **CLC 39**
See also CA 33-36R; CANR 22

Thompson, Francis Clegg
See Mencken, H(enry) L(ouis)

Thompson, Francis Joseph
1859-1907 . . . . **TCLC 4**
See also CA 104; CDBLB 1890-1914;
DLB 19

Thompson, Hunter S(tockton)
1939- . . . . **CLC 9, 17, 40**
See also BEST 89:1; CA 17-20R; CANR 23;
MTCW

Thompson, James Myers
See Thompson, Jim (Myers)

Thompson, Jim (Myers)
1906-1977(?) . . . . **CLC 69**
See also CA 140

Thompson, Judith . . . . **CLC 39**

Thomson, James 1700-1748 . . . . **LC 16**

Thomson, James 1834-1882 . . . . . . **NCLC 18**

Thoreau, Henry David
1817-1862 . . . . . . **NCLC 7, 21; DA; WLC**
See also CDALB 1640-1865; DLB 1

Thornton, Hall
See Silverberg, Robert

Thurber, James (Grover)
1894-1961 . . . **CLC 5, 11, 25; DA; SSC 1**
See also CA 73-76; CANR 17, 39;
CDALB 1929-1941; DLB 4, 11, 22, 102;
MAICYA; MTCW; SATA 13

Thurman, Wallace (Henry)
1902-1934 . . . . **TCLC 6; BLC**
See also BW 1; CA 104; 124; DLB 51

Ticheburn, Cheviot
See Ainsworth, William Harrison

Tieck, (Johann) Ludwig
1773-1853 . . . . **NCLC 5, 46**
See also DLB 90

Tiger, Derry
See Ellison, Harlan

Tilghman, Christopher 1948(?)- . . . . . **CLC 65**

Tillinghast, Richard (Williford)
1940- . . . . **CLC 29**
See also CA 29-32R; CANR 26

Timrod, Henry 1828-1867 . . . . **NCLC 25**
See also DLB 3

Tindall, Gillian 1938- . . . . **CLC 7**
See also CA 21-24R; CANR 11

Tiptree, James, Jr. . . . . **CLC 48, 50**
See also Sheldon, Alice Hastings Bradley
See also DLB 8

Titmarsh, Michael Angelo
See Thackeray, William Makepeace

**Tocqueville, Alexis (Charles Henri Maurice
Clerel Comte)** 1805-1859 . . . . . **NCLC 7**

Tolkien, J(ohn) R(onald) R(euel)
1892-1973 . . . . . . **CLC 1, 2, 3, 8, 12, 38;
DA; WLC**
See also AAYA 10; AITN 1; CA 17-18;
45-48; CANR 36; CAP 2;
CDBLB 1914-1945; DLB 15; JRDA;
MAICYA; MTCW; SATA 2, 24, 32

Toller, Ernst 1893-1939 . . . . **TCLC 10**
See also CA 107; DLB 124

Tolson, M. B.
See Tolson, Melvin B(eaunorus)

Tolson, Melvin B(eaunorus)
1898(?)-1966 . . . . **CLC 36; BLC**
See also BW 1; CA 124; 89-92; DLB 48, 76

Tolstoi, Aleksei Nikolaevich
See Tolstoy, Alexey Nikolaevich

Tolstoy, Alexey Nikolaevich
1882-1945 . . . . **TCLC 18**
See also CA 107

Tolstoy, Count Leo
See Tolstoy, Leo (Nikolaevich)

Tolstoy, Leo (Nikolaevich)
1828-1910 . . . . . . **TCLC 4, 11, 17, 28, 44;
DA; SSC 9; WLC**
See also CA 104; 123; SATA 26

Tomasi di Lampedusa, Giuseppe 1896-1957
See Lampedusa, Giuseppe (Tomasi) di
See also CA 111

Tomlin, Lily . . . . **CLC 17**
See also Tomlin, Mary Jean

Tomlin, Mary Jean 1939(?)-
See Tomlin, Lily
See also CA 117

Tomlinson, (Alfred) Charles
1927- . . . . **CLC 2, 4, 6, 13, 45**
See also CA 5-8R; CANR 33; DLB 40

Tonson, Jacob
See Bennett, (Enoch) Arnold

Toole, John Kennedy
1937-1969 . . . . **CLC 19, 64**
See also CA 104; DLBY 81

Toomer, Jean
1894-1967 . . . . . . **CLC 1, 4, 13, 22; BLC;
PC 7; SSC 1**
See also BW 1; CA 85-88;
CDALB 1917-1929; DLB 45, 51; MTCW

Torley, Luke
See Blish, James (Benjamin)

Tornimparte, Alessandra
See Ginzburg, Natalia

Torre, Raoul della
See Mencken, H(enry) L(ouis)

Torrey, E(dwin) Fuller 1937- . . . . **CLC 34**
See also CA 119

Torsvan, Ben Traven
See Traven, B.

Torsvan, Benno Traven
See Traven, B.

Torsvan, Berick Traven
See Traven, B.

Torsvan, Berwick Traven
See Traven, B.

Torsvan, Bruno Traven
See Traven, B.

Torsvan, Traven
See Traven, B.

Tournier, Michel (Edouard)
1924- . . . . **CLC 6, 23, 36**
See also CA 49-52; CANR 3, 36; DLB 83;
MTCW; SATA 23

Tournimparte, Alessandra
See Ginzburg, Natalia

Towers, Ivar
See Kornbluth, C(yril) M.

Townsend, Sue 1946- . . . . **CLC 61**
See also CA 119; 127; MTCW; SATA 48,
55

Townshend, Peter (Dennis Blandford)
1945- . . . . **CLC 17, 42**
See also CA 107

Tozzi, Federigo 1883-1920 . . . . **TCLC 31**

Traill, Catharine Parr
1802-1899 . . . . **NCLC 31**
See also DLB 99

Trakl, Georg 1887-1914 . . . . **TCLC 5**
See also CA 104

Transtroemer, Tomas (Goesta)
1931- . . . . **CLC 52, 65**
See also CA 117; 129; CAAS 17

Vonnegut, Kurt, Jr.
1922- . . . . . . **CLC 1, 2, 3, 4, 5, 8, 12, 22, 40, 60; DA; SSC 8; WLC**
See also AAYA 6; AITN 1; BEST 90:4; CA 1-4R; CANR 1, 25; CDALB 1968-1988; DLB 2, 8; DLBD 3; DLBY 80; MTCW

Von Rachen, Kurt
See Hubbard, L(afayette) Ron(ald)

von Rezzori (d'Arezzo), Gregor
See Rezzori (d'Arezzo), Gregor von

von Sternberg, Josef
See Sternberg, Josef von

Vorster, Gordon 1924- . . . . **CLC 34**
See also CA 133

Vosce, Trudie
See Ozick, Cynthia

Voznesensky, Andrei (Andreievich)
1933- . . . . **CLC 1, 15, 57**
See also CA 89-92; CANR 37; MTCW

Waddington, Miriam 1917- . . . . **CLC 28**
See also CA 21-24R; CANR 12, 30; DLB 68

Wagman, Fredrica 1937- . . . . **CLC 7**
See also CA 97-100

Wagner, Richard 1813-1883. . . . . . **NCLC 9**
See also DLB 129

Wagner-Martin, Linda 1936- . . . . **CLC 50**

Wagoner, David (Russell)
1926- . . . . **CLC 3, 5, 15**
See also CA 1-4R; CAAS 3; CANR 2; DLB 5; SATA 14

Wah, Fred(erick James) 1939- . . . . . **CLC 44**
See also CA 107; 141; DLB 60

Wahloo, Per 1926-1975 . . . . **CLC 7**
See also CA 61-64

Wahloo, Peter
See Wahloo, Per

Wain, John (Barrington)
1925- . . . . **CLC 2, 11, 15, 46**
See also CA 5-8R; CAAS 4; CANR 23; CDBLB 1960 to Present; DLB 15, 27, 139; MTCW

Wajda, Andrzej 1926- . . . . **CLC 16**
See also CA 102

Wakefield, Dan 1932- . . . . **CLC 7**
See also CA 21-24R; CAAS 7

Wakoski, Diane
1937- . . . . **CLC 2, 4, 7, 9, 11, 40**
See also CA 13-16R; CAAS 1; CANR 9; DLB 5

Wakoski-Sherbell, Diane
See Wakoski, Diane

Walcott, Derek (Alton)
1930- . . . . **CLC 2, 4, 9, 14, 25, 42, 67, 76; BLC**
See also BW 2; CA 89-92; CANR 26; DLB 117; DLBY 81; MTCW

Waldman, Anne 1945- . . . . **CLC 7**
See also CA 37-40R; CAAS 17; CANR 34; DLB 16

Waldo, E. Hunter
See Sturgeon, Theodore (Hamilton)

Waldo, Edward Hamilton
See Sturgeon, Theodore (Hamilton)

Walker, Alice (Malsenior)
1944- . . . . **CLC 5, 6, 9, 19, 27, 46, 58; BLC; DA; SSC 5**
See also AAYA 3; BEST 89:4; BW 2; CA 37-40R; CANR 9, 27; CDALB 1968-1988; DLB 6, 33, 143; MTCW; SATA 31

Walker, David Harry 1911-1992. . . . **CLC 14**
See also CA 1-4R; 137; CANR 1; SATA 8; SATA-Obit 71

Walker, Edward Joseph 1934-
See Walker, Ted
See also CA 21-24R; CANR 12, 28

Walker, George F. 1947- . . . . **CLC 44, 61**
See also CA 103; CANR 21, 43; DLB 60

Walker, Joseph A. 1935- . . . . **CLC 19**
See also BW 1; CA 89-92; CANR 26; DLB 38

Walker, Margaret (Abigail)
1915- . . . . **CLC 1, 6; BLC**
See also BW 2; CA 73-76; CANR 26; DLB 76; MTCW

Walker, Ted. . . . . **CLC 13**
See also Walker, Edward Joseph
See also DLB 40

Wallace, David Foster 1962- . . . . **CLC 50**
See also CA 132

Wallace, Dexter
See Masters, Edgar Lee

Wallace, Irving 1916-1990 . . . . . . **CLC 7, 13**
See also AITN 1; CA 1-4R; 132; CAAS 1; CANR 1, 27; MTCW

Wallant, Edward Lewis
1926-1962 . . . . **CLC 5, 10**
See also CA 1-4R; CANR 22; DLB 2, 28, 143; MTCW

Walpole, Horace 1717-1797. . . . . **LC 2**
See also DLB 39, 104

Walpole, Hugh (Seymour)
1884-1941 . . . . **TCLC 5**
See also CA 104; DLB 34

Walser, Martin 1927- . . . . **CLC 27**
See also CA 57-60; CANR 8; DLB 75, 124

Walser, Robert 1878-1956 . . . . **TCLC 18**
See also CA 118; DLB 66

Walsh, Jill Paton . . . . **CLC 35**
See also Paton Walsh, Gillian
See also AAYA 11; CLR 2; SAAS 3

Walter, Villiam Christian
See Andersen, Hans Christian

Wambaugh, Joseph (Aloysius, Jr.)
1937- . . . . **CLC 3, 18**
See also AITN 1; BEST 89:3; CA 33-36R; CANR 42; DLB 6; DLBY 83; MTCW

Ward, Arthur Henry Sarsfield 1883-1959
See Rohmer, Sax
See also CA 108

Ward, Douglas Turner 1930- . . . . **CLC 19**
See also BW 1; CA 81-84; CANR 27; DLB 7, 38

Ward, Mary Augusta
See Ward, Mrs. Humphry

Ward, Mrs. Humphry
1851-1920 . . . . **TCLC 55**
See also DLB 18

Ward, Peter
See Faust, Frederick (Schiller)

Warhol, Andy 1928(?)-1987. . . . . **CLC 20**
See also AAYA 12; BEST 89:4; CA 89-92; 121; CANR 34

Warner, Francis (Robert le Plastrier)
1937- . . . . **CLC 14**
See also CA 53-56; CANR 11

Warner, Marina 1946- . . . . **CLC 59**
See also CA 65-68; CANR 21

Warner, Rex (Ernest) 1905-1986. . . . **CLC 45**
See also CA 89-92; 119; DLB 15

Warner, Susan (Bogert)
1819-1885 . . . . **NCLC 31**
See also DLB 3, 42

Warner, Sylvia (Constance) Ashton
See Ashton-Warner, Sylvia (Constance)

Warner, Sylvia Townsend
1893-1978 . . . . **CLC 7, 19**
See also CA 61-64; 77-80; CANR 16; DLB 34, 139; MTCW

Warren, Mercy Otis 1728-1814. . . **NCLC 13**
See also DLB 31

Warren, Robert Penn
1905-1989 . . . . **CLC 1, 4, 6, 8, 10, 13, 18, 39, 53, 59; DA; SSC 4; WLC**
See also AITN 1; CA 13-16R; 129; CANR 10; CDALB 1968-1988; DLB 2, 48; DLBY 80, 89; MTCW; SATA 46, 63

Warshofsky, Isaac
See Singer, Isaac Bashevis

Warton, Thomas 1728-1790. . . . . **LC 15**
See also DLB 104, 109

Waruk, Kona
See Harris, (Theodore) Wilson

Warung, Price 1855-1911. . . . . **TCLC 45**

Warwick, Jarvis
See Garner, Hugh

Washington, Alex
See Harris, Mark

Washington, Booker T(aliaferro)
1856-1915 . . . . **TCLC 10; BLC**
See also BW 1; CA 114; 125; SATA 28

Washington, George 1732-1799. . . . . . **LC 25**
See also DLB 31

Wassermann, (Karl) Jakob
1873-1934 . . . . **TCLC 6**
See also CA 104; DLB 66

Wasserstein, Wendy
1950- . . . . **CLC 32, 59; DC 4**
See also CA 121; 129; CABS 3

Waterhouse, Keith (Spencer)
1929- . . . . **CLC 47**
See also CA 5-8R; CANR 38; DLB 13, 15; MTCW

Waters, Roger 1944- . . . . **CLC 35**
See also Pink Floyd

Watkins, Frances Ellen
See Harper, Frances Ellen Watkins

Watkins, Gerrold
See Malzberg, Barry N(athaniel)

Watkins, Paul 1964- . . . . **CLC 55**
See also CA 132

Wyss, Johann David Von
1743-1818 .... **NCLC 10**
See also JRDA; MAICYA; SATA 27, 29

Yakumo Koizumi
See Hearn, (Patricio) Lafcadio (Tessima Carlos)

Yanez, Jose Donoso
See Donoso (Yanez), Jose

Yanovsky, Basile S.
See Yanovsky, V(assily) S(emenovich)

Yanovsky, V(assily) S(emenovich)
1906-1989 .... **CLC 2, 18**
See also CA 97-100; 129

Yates, Richard 1926-1992 ..... **CLC 7, 8, 23**
See also CA 5-8R; 139; CANR 10, 43;
DLB 2; DLBY 81, 92

Yeats, W. B.
See Yeats, William Butler

Yeats, William Butler
1865-1939 ..... **TCLC 1, 11, 18, 31; DA;**
WLC
See also CA 104; 127; CANR 45;
CDBLB 1890-1914; DLB 10, 19, 98;
MTCW

Yehoshua, A(braham) B.
1936- .... **CLC 13, 31**
See also CA 33-36R; CANR 43

Yep, Laurence Michael 1948- ...... **CLC 35**
See also AAYA 5; CA 49-52; CANR 1;
CLR 3, 17; DLB 52; JRDA; MAICYA;
SATA 7, 69

Yerby, Frank G(arvin)
1916-1991 .... **CLC 1, 7, 22; BLC**
See also BW 1; CA 9-12R; 136; CANR 16;
DLB 76; MTCW

Yesenin, Sergei Alexandrovich
See Esenin, Sergei (Alexandrovich)

Yevtushenko, Yevgeny (Alexandrovich)
1933- .... **CLC 1, 3, 13, 26, 51**
See also CA 81-84; CANR 33; MTCW

Yezierska, Anzia 1885(?)-1970 ..... **CLC 46**
See also CA 126; 89-92; DLB 28; MTCW

Yglesias, Helen 1915-.......... **CLC 7, 22**
See also CA 37-40R; CANR 15; MTCW

Yokomitsu Riichi 1898-1947 ...... **TCLC 47**

Yonge, Charlotte (Mary)
1823-1901 .... **TCLC 48**
See also CA 109; DLB 18; SATA 17

York, Jeremy
See Creasey, John

York, Simon
See Heinlein, Robert A(nson)

Yorke, Henry Vincent 1905-1974 ... **CLC 13**
See also Green, Henry
See also CA 85-88; 49-52

Yoshimoto, Banana .... **CLC 84**
See also Yoshimoto, Mahoko

Yoshimoto, Mahoko 1964-
See Yoshimoto, Banana
See also CA 144

Young, Al(bert James)
1939- .... **CLC 19; BLC**
See also BW 2; CA 29-32R; CANR 26;
DLB 33

Young, Andrew (John) 1885-1971 .... **CLC 5**
See also CA 5-8R; CANR 7, 29

Young, Collier
See Bloch, Robert (Albert)

Young, Edward 1683-1765 .... **LC 3**
See also DLB 95

Young, Marguerite 1909-......... **CLC 82**
See also CA 13-16; CAP 1

Young, Neil 1945-............... **CLC 17**
See also CA 110

Yourcenar, Marguerite
1903-1987 .... **CLC 19, 38, 50**
See also CA 69-72; CANR 23; DLB 72;
DLBY 88; MTCW

Yurick, Sol 1925-................ **CLC 6**
See also CA 13-16R; CANR 25

Zabolotskii, Nikolai Alekseevich
1903-1958 .... **TCLC 52**
See also CA 116

Zamiatin, Yevgenii
See Zamyatin, Evgeny Ivanovich

Zamyatin, Evgeny Ivanovich
1884-1937 .... **TCLC 8, 37**
See also CA 105

Zangwill, Israel 1864-1926....... **TCLC 16**
See also CA 109; DLB 10, 135

Zappa, Francis Vincent, Jr. 1940-1993
See Zappa, Frank
See also CA 108; 143

Zappa, Frank.................... **CLC 17**
See also Zappa, Francis Vincent, Jr.

Zaturenska, Marya 1902-1982.... **CLC 6, 11**
See also CA 13-16R; 105; CANR 22

Zelazny, Roger (Joseph) 1937- ..... **CLC 21**
See also AAYA 7; CA 21-24R; CANR 26;
DLB 8; MTCW; SATA 39, 57

Zhdanov, Andrei A(lexandrovich)
1896-1948 .... **TCLC 18**
See also CA 117

Zhukovsky, Vasily 1783-1852 .... **NCLC 35**

Ziegenhagen, Eric .... **CLC 55**

Zimmer, Jill Schary
See Robinson, Jill

Zimmerman, Robert
See Dylan, Bob

Zindel, Paul 1936- .... **CLC 6, 26; DA**
See also AAYA 2; CA 73-76; CANR 31;
CLR 3; DLB 7, 52; JRDA; MAICYA;
MTCW; SATA 16, 58

Zinov'Ev, A. A.
See Zinoviev, Alexander (Aleksandrovich)

Zinoviev, Alexander (Aleksandrovich)
1922- .... **CLC 19**
See also CA 116; 133; CAAS 10

Zoilus
See Lovecraft, H(oward) P(hillips)

Zola, Emile (Edouard Charles Antoine)
1840-1902 ...... **TCLC 1, 6, 21, 41; DA;**
WLC
See also CA 104; 138; DLB 123

Zoline, Pamela 1941-............. **CLC 62**

Zorrilla y Moral, Jose 1817-1893 .. **NCLC 6**

Zoshchenko, Mikhail (Mikhailovich)
1895-1958 .... **TCLC 15; SSC 15**
See also CA 115

Zuckmayer, Carl 1896-1977....... **CLC 18**
See also CA 69-72; DLB 56, 124

Zuk, Georges
See Skelton, Robin

Zukofsky, Louis
1904-1978 .... **CLC 1, 2, 4, 7, 11, 18**
See also CA 9-12R; 77-80; CANR 39;
DLB 5; MTCW

Zweig, Paul 1935-1984......... **CLC 34, 42**
See also CA 85-88; 113

Zweig, Stefan 1881-1942 .... **TCLC 17**
See also CA 112; DLB 81, 118

Literary Criticism Series
Cumulative Topic Index

This index lists all topic entries in the Gale Literary Criticism Series *Classical and Medieval Literature Criticism, Contemporary Literary Criticism, Literature Criticism from 1400 to 1800, Nineteenth-Century Literature Criticism,* and *Twentieth-Century Literary Criticism.*

Topic Index

LC Cumulative Nationality Index

LC Cumulative Title Index

Title Index

Title Index

Title Index

Title Index

Title Index

Title Index

Title Index

Title Index

Title Index

Title Index

Title Index

ISBN 0-8103-8464-7